Annotated Instructor's Edition

SOCIOLOGY

A Down-to-Earth Approach

James M. Henslin

Southern Illinois University, Edwardsville

Instructor's Section and Annotations Prepared by

Diana Kendall

Austin Community College

Allyn and Bacon

Boston   London   Toronto   Sydney   Tokyo   Singapore

Editor in Chief–Social Sciences: Susan Badger
Senior Editor: Karen Hanson
Series Editorial Assistant: Marnie Greenhut
Editorial-Production Service: Susan McNally
Text Designer: Glenna Collett
Cover Administrator: Linda Dickinson
Composition Buyer: Linda Cox
Manufacturing Buyer: Megan Cochran

Copyright © 1993 by Allyn & Bacon
A Division of Simon and Schuster, Inc.
160 Gould Street
Needham Heights, Massachusetts 02194

ISBN 0-205-14718-6
Printed in the United States of America

92-41575
CIP

10 9 8 7 6 5 4 3 2 1   97 96 95 94 93 92

Annotated Instructor's Edition

Contents

Instructor's Section   *IS-i*
  Introduction to Henslin's Sociology   *IS-xiii*
  Instructor's Preface   *IS-xxiii*
  Acknowledgments   *IS-xxvi*
  Instructor's Section Table of Contents   *IS-xxix*
Annotated Text Section   *i*

PART I   THE SOCIOLOGICAL PERSPECTIVE

1   The Sociological Perspective   1

The Sociological Perspective   2
  Seeing the Broader Social Context
Sociology and the Other Sciences   4
  The Natural Sciences ■ The Social Sciences
The Goals of Science   5
  ▪ *Down-to-Earth Sociology:* An Updated Version of the Old
  Elephant Story   6
The Development of Sociology   7
  ▪ *Down-to-Earth Sociology:* Enjoying a Sociological Quiz:
  Sociological Findings versus Common Sense   7
  Auguste Comte ■ Herbert Spencer ■ Karl Marx ■ Emile
  Durkheim ■ Max Weber
The Role of Values in Social Research   12
***Verstehen* and Social Facts**   13
  Weber and *Verstehen* ■ Durkheim and Social Facts ■
  How Social Facts and *Verstehen* Fit Together
Sociology in North America   15
Theoretical Perspectives in Sociology   16
  Symbolic Interactionism ■ Functional Analysis ■ Conflict
  Theory ■ Levels of Analysis: Macro and Micro ■ Putting
  the Theoretical Perspectives Together
Applied and Clinical Sociology   25
  ▪ *Perspectives:* Sociology in a World of Turmoil   26
Summary   27
Suggested Readings   28

2   Culture   30

What Is Culture?   32
  Culture and Taken-for-Granted Orientations to Life ■
  Practicing Cultural Relativism

Components of Culture   35
  ▪ *Down-to-Earth Sociology:* Communicating across Cultural
  Boundaries   36
  The Symbolic Basis of Culture ■ Language
  ▪ *Perspectives:* Miami—Language and a Changing City   39
  Gestures ■ Values, Norms, and Sanctions ■ Folkways
  and Mores
Subcultures and Countercultures   41
Values in American Society   42
  ▪ *Perspectives:* Why Do Native Americans Like
  Westerns?   44
  Value Clusters ■ Value Contradictions and Social
  Change ■ Emergent Values ■ Reactions to Changes in
  Core Values ■ Values as Blinders ■ "Ideal" versus "Real"
  Culture
Cultural Universals   47
  ▪ *Thinking Critically about Social Controversy:* Are We
  Prisoners of Our Genes?   48
Animals and Culture   49
  Do Animals Have Language?
Cultural Diffusion and Cultural Leveling   53
Summary   54
Suggested Readings   55

3   Socialization   56

What is Human Nature?   58
  Feral Children ■ Isolated Children
  ▪ *Down-to-Earth Sociology:* Heredity or Environment? The
  Case of Oskar and Jack, Identical Twins   59
  Institutionalized Children ■ Deprived Animals ■ Bringing
  It All Together

The Social Development of the Self, Mind, and Emotions *63*
    Cooley and the Looking-Glass Self ■ Mead and Role Taking ■ Piaget and the Development of Thinking ■ Freud and the Subconscious ■ The Sequential Development of Emotions ■ Socialization into Emotions ■ The Self and Emotions as Social Constraints on Behavior
Socialization into Gender *70*
    Gender, the Family, and Sex-Linked Behaviors ■ Gender Images in the Mass Media
Agents of Socialization *73*
    Perspectives: Manhood in the Making *74*
    The Family ■ Religion ■ The School ■ Peer Groups
    Perspectives: Caught Between Two Worlds *77*
    The Mass Media ■ The Workplace
Resocialization *79*
    Involuntary Resocialization: Total Institutions ■ Voluntary Resocialization
Socialization Through the Life Course *80*
    The Life Course ■ Distinctive Life-Course Patterns
Are We Prisoners of Socialization? *84*
Summary *85*
Suggested Readings *85*

4   Social Structure and Social Interaction: Macrosociology and Microsociology *86*

Levels of Sociological Analysis *88*
    Macrosociology and Microsociology
Social Structure: The Macrosociological Perspective *89*
    Down-to-Earth Sociology: College Football as Social Structure *90*
    Culture ■ Social Class ■ Social Status ■ Roles ■ Groups
Social Institutions *95*
    Changes in Social Structure ■ What Holds Society Together?

The Microsociological Perspective: Social Interaction in Everyday Life *99*
    Perspectives: The Amish—*Gemeinschaft* Communities in a *Gesellschaft* Society *100*
    Symbolic Interaction ■ Dramaturgy: The Presentation of Self in Everyday Life ■ Ethnomethodology: Discovering Background Assumptions ■ The Social Construction of Reality
The Need for Both Microsociology and Macrosociology *109*
Summary *110*
Suggested Readings *111*

5   How Sociologists Do Research *112*

What is a Valid Sociological Topic? *114*
Common Sense and the Need for Sociological Research *114*
A Research Model *115*
    Selecting a Topic ■ Defining the Problem ■ Reviewing the Literature ■ Formulating a Hypothesis ■ Choosing a Research Method ■ Collecting the Data ■ Analyzing the Results ■ Sharing the Results
Six Research Methods *119*
    Surveys
    Down-to-Earth Sociology: Loading the Dice *121*
    Secondary Analysis ■ Documents ■ Participant Observation (Fieldwork) ■ Experiments ■ Unobtrusive Measures
    Down-to-Earth Sociology: The Hawthorne Experiments *128*
    Deciding Which Method to Use
    Thinking Critically about Social Controversy: Counting the Homeless *129*
Ethics in Sociological Research *131*
    The Brajuha Research ■ The Humphreys Research
How Research and Theory Work Together *133*
    A Final Word: When the Ideal Meets the Real
Summary *136*
Suggested Readings *136*

PART II   SOCIAL GROUPS AND SOCIAL CONTROL

6   Social Groups: Societies to Social Networks *138*
Social Groups and Societies *140*
The Transformation of Societies *141*
    Hunting and Gathering Societies ■ Pastoral and Horticultural Societies ■ Agricultural Societies ■ Industrial Societies ■ Postindustrial Societies

    Perspectives: A Tribal Mountain People Meets Postindustrial Society *147*
Groups within Society *149*
    Primary Groups ■ Secondary Groups ■ In-Groups and Out-Groups ■ Reference Groups ■ Social Networks
Group Dynamics *154*
    Group Size ■ Leadership

■ *Down-to-Earth Sociology:* How Group Size Affects Willingness to Help Strangers   *157*
Conformity to Peer Pressure: The Asch Experiment ■ Obedience to Authority: The Milgram Experiment ■ Groupthink and Decision Making ■ Preventing Groupthink
Summary   *162*
Suggested Readings   *163*

7   Bureaucracy and Formal Organizations   *164*
The Rationalization of Society   *166*
The Contribution of Max Weber ■ Marx on Rationalism
Formal Organizations and Bureaucracy   *168*
Formal Organizations ■ The Essential Characteristics of Bureaucracies ■ "Ideal" versus "Real" Bureaucracy ■ Dysfunctions of Bureaucracies
Voluntary Associations   *175*
The Functions of Voluntary Associations ■ The Problem of Oligarchy
Careers in Bureaucracies   *178*
The Corporate Culture: Consequences of Hidden Values
■ *Down-to-Earth Sociology:* Maneuvering the Hidden Culture—Women Surviving in the Male-Dominated Business World   *179*
Humanizing the Corporate Culture
■ *Perspectives:* Managing Diversity in the Workplace   *181*
Quality Circles ■ Employee Stock Ownership ■ Small Work Groups
■ *Down-to-Earth Sociology:* Self-Management Teams   *183*
Developing an Alternative: The Cooperative   *184*
The Japanese Corporate Model   *184*
■ *Perspectives:* Bottom-Up Decision Making in Japanese Corporations   *186*
■ *Down-to-Earth Sociology:* Home on the Range—Japanese-Style   *187*

Summary   *188*
Suggested Readings   *188*

8   Deviance and Social Control   *190*
Gaining a Sociological Perspective of Deviance   *192*
The Relativity of Deviance
■ *Perspectives:* Deviance in Cross-Cultural Perspective   *193*
Social Control ■ How Norms Make Social Life Possible ■ Comparing Biological, Psychological, and Sociological Explanations
The Symbolic Interactionist Perspective   *197*
Differential Association Theory
■ *Perspectives:* When Cultures Clash—Problems in Defining Deviance   *198*
Control Theory ■ Labeling Theory
The Functionalist Perspective   *200*
How Deviance Is Functional for Society ■ Strain Theory: How Social Values Produce Crime ■ Illegitimate Opportunity Theory: Explaining Social Class and Crime
The Conflict Perspective   *204*
Class, Crime, and the Criminal Justice System
Reactions to Deviants   *205*
Sanctions ■ Labeling: The Saints and the Roughnecks ■ The Trouble with Official Statistics ■ Degradation Ceremonies ■ Imprisonment
Reactions by Deviants   *210*
Primary, Secondary, and Tertiary Deviance ■ Neutralizing Deviance ■ Embracing Deviance
The Medicalization of Deviance: Mental Illness   *213*
Neither Mental nor Illness? ■ The Homeless Mentally Ill
The Need for a More Humane Approach   *215*
■ *Down-to-Earth Sociology:* Taking Back Children from the Night   *215*
Summary   *216*
Suggested Readings   *217*

■■■■■■■■■■■■■■■■■■■■■■ **PART III   SOCIAL INEQUALITY** ■■■■■■■■■■■■■■■■■■■■■■

9   Stratification in Global Perspective   *218*
What Is Social Stratification?   *220*
Systems of Social Stratification   *221*
Slavery ■ Caste: India and South Africa ■ Class
■ *Perspectives:* Social Stratification among Polish Jews   *226*
Clan and Class as Parallel Forms of Social Stratification
Gender and Social Stratification   *227*
What Determines Social Class   *228*
Karl Marx: The Means of Production ■ Max Weber: Power, Property, and Prestige

Why Is Social Stratification Universal?   *230*
The Functionalist View of Davis and Moore: Motivating Qualified People ■ Tumin: A Critical Response ■ Mosca: A Forerunner of the Conflict View ■ The Conflict View: Class Conflict and Competition for Scarce Resources ■ Toward a Synthesis
Comparative Social Stratification   *233*
Social Stratification in Great Britain ■ Social Stratification in the Former Soviet Union
Maintaining National Stratification   *235*
Why Not Total Exploitation?

Global Stratification: The Three Worlds   *237*
The First World ■ The Second World ■ The Third
World ■ Imperfections in the Model
How the World's Nations Became Stratified   *240*
Imperialism and Colonialism ■ World System Theory ■
Dependency Theory ■ Culture of Poverty ■ Evaluating
the Theories
Maintaining Global Stratification   *242*
Neocolonialism ■ Multinational Corporations
Perspectives: The Patriotic Prostitute   *243*
Summary   *244*
Suggested Readings   *245*

**10   Social Class in American
Society   246**

What is Social Class?   *248*
Measures of Social Class
Dimensions of Social Class   *249*
Wealth ■ Power ■ Prestige ■ Status Inconsistency
Social Class in Industrial Society   *258*
Updating Marx: Wright's Model ■ Updating Weber:
Gilbert's and Kahl's Model ■ Social Class in the Automobile
Industry ■ Life Chances ■ Physical and Mental Health ■
Below the Ladder: The Homeless
Consequences of Social Class   *265*
Family Life ■ Values and Attitudes ■ Political
Involvement ■ Religion ■ Education ■ The Criminal
Justice System
Social Mobility   *267*
Intergenerational, Structural, and Exchange Mobility ■
Social Mobility in the United States ■ Costs of Social
Mobility
Thinking Critically about Social Controversy: Upward Mobility
for American Workers—A Vanishing Dream?   *269*
Where is Horatio Alger?
Poverty in the United States   *271*
Drawing the Line: What Is Poverty? ■ Who Are the
Poor? ■ Children in Poverty: A New Social Condition?
Thinking Critically about Social Controversy: Children in
Poverty   *273*
Short-Term and Long-Term Poverty ■ Individual versus
Structural Explanations of Poverty
Summary   *276*
Suggested Readings   *276*

11   Inequalities of Gender   278

Why Are Males and Females Different?   *280*
Biology or Culture? The Continuing Controversy
Thinking Critically about Social Controversy: Biology versus
Culture   *282*
An Emerging Position in Sociology? ■ The Question of
Superiority

Women as a Minority Group   *285*
Cross-Cultural Gender Inequality: Sex-Typing of Work ■
Cross-Cultural Gender Inequality: Prestige of Work ■ The
Genesis of Female Minority Status
Gender Inequality in American Society   *289*
Fighting Back: The Rise of Feminism ■ Gender Inequality
in Education: Creating Sex-Linked Aspirations
Down-to-Earth Sociology: Making the Invisible Visible—The
Deadly Effects of Sexism   *291*
Gender Inequality in Everyday Life
Gender Inequality in the Workplace   *294*
Women in the Work Force ■ Discrimination in Hiring ■
The Pay Gap
Perspectives: Sexual Harassment in Japan   *298*
The "Mommy" Track ■ Sexual Harassment
Down-to-Earth Sociology: Women on Wall Street—From
Subtle Put-Downs to Crude Sexual Harassment   *301*
**Gender Inequality and Violence: The Case of
Murder**   *302*
**Why Don't Women Take Over Politics and
Transform American Life?**   *303*
Changes in Gender Relations   *305*
Glimpsing the Future—With Hope   *305*
Summary   *306*
Suggested Readings   *307*

**12   Inequalities of Race and
Ethnicity   308**

**Basic Concepts in Race and Ethnic
Relations**   *310*
Race: Myth and Reality ■ Ethnic Groups ■ Minority
Groups
Prejudice and Discrimination   *313*
Perspective: Clashing Cultures   *313*
When Prejudice and Discrimination Don't Match ■ The
Extent of Prejudice
Theories of Prejudice   *316*
Thinking Critically about Social Controversy: Racism on
College Campuses   *316*
Psychological Perspectives ■ Sociological Perspectives:
Functionalism, Conflict, and Symbolic Interaction
Individual and Institutional Discrimination   *320*
Patterns of Intergroup Relations   *322*
Genocide ■ Population Transfer ■ Internal
Colonialism ■ Segregation ■ Assimilation ■ Pluralism
**Race and Ethnic Relations in the United
States**   *325*
The Dominance of White Anglo-Saxon Protestants ■ White
Ethnics ■ African Americans ■ Hispanic Americans
(Latinos)
Down to Earth Sociology: The Illegal Travel Guide   *331*
Perspectives: The Browning of America   *332*
Asian Americans ■ Native Americans

■ *Thinking Critically about Social Controversy:* Whose History?   337
Principles for Improving Ethnic Relations   339
Summary   339
Suggested Readings   340

13   Inequalities of Age

Social Factors in Aging   344
Aging among Abkhasians ■ Aging in Industrialized Nations
■ *Down-to-Earth Sociology:* Applying Life Expectancy Figures   347
The Symbolic Interactionist Perspective   348
Self, Society, and Aging ■ The Relativity of Aging: Cross-Cultural Comparisons ■ Ageism in American Society ■ The Mass Media: Purveyor of Symbol and Status
The Functionalist Perspective   354
Disengagement Theory ■ Activity Theory

The Conflict Perspective   356
Social Security Legislation ■ Rival Interest Groups
■ *Down-to-Earth Sociology:* Changing Sentiment about the Elderly   357
■ *Thinking Critically about Social Controversy:* Social Security—Fraud of the Century?   358
Fighting Back: The Gray Panthers
Problems of Dependency   360
Nursing Homes
■ *Down-to-Earth Sociology:* Pacification—Turning People into Patients   362
Elder Abuse ■ The Question of Poverty
The Sociology of Death and Dying   365
Effects of Industrialization ■ Death as a Process ■ Suicide and the Elderly ■ Hospices
Summary   368
Suggested Readings   368

PART IV   SOCIAL INSTITUTIONS

14   The Economy: Money and Work   370

The Transformation of Economic Systems   372
Hunting and Gathering Economies: Subsistence ■ Pastoral and Horticultural Economies: The Creation of Surplus ■ Agricultural Economies: The Growth of Trade ■ Industrial Economies: The Birth of the Machine ■ Postindustrial Economies: The Information Age
The Transformation of the Medium of Exchange   376
Earliest Mediums of Exchange ■ Medium of Exchange in Agricultural Economies ■ Medium of Exchange in Industrial Economies ■ Medium of Exchange in Postindustrial Economies
World Economic Systems   378
Capitalism ■ Socialism ■ Ideologies of Capitalism and Socialism ■ Criticisms of Capitalism and Socialism
■ *Down-to-Earth Sociology:* Selling the American Dream—The Creation of Constant Discontent   381
The Systems in Conflict and Competition ■ The Future: Convergence?
The Inner Circle of Capitalism   384
Corporate Capitalism ■ Interlocking Directorates ■ Multinational Corporations
Work in American Society   387
Three Economic Sectors ■ Women and Work ■ The Underground Economy ■ Patterns of Work and Leisure
Applying Sociological Theories   392
The Funtionalist Perspective ■ The Conflict Perspective ■ The Symbolic Interaction Perspective
■ *Perspectives:* Who is Unemployed?   395
The Future of the U.S. Economy   397

Summary   398
Suggested Readings   399

15   Politics: Power and Authority   400

Micropolitics and Macropolitics   402
Power, Authority, and Coercion   402
Authority and Legitimate Violence ■ Traditional Authority ■ Rational-Legal Authority ■ Charismatic Authority ■ Authority as Ideal Type ■ The Transfer of Authority
Types of Government   409
Monarchies: The Rise of the State ■ Democracies: Citizenship as a Revolutionary Idea ■ Dictatorships and Oligarchies: The Seizure of Power
The American Political System   411
Political Parties and Elections ■ Democratic Systems in Europe ■ Voting Patterns
■ *Perspectives:* Immigrants—Ethnicity and Class as the Path to Political Participation   416
The Depression as a Transforming Event ■ Lobbyists and Special-Interest Groups ■ PACs and the Cost of Elections
Who Rules America?   419
The Functionalist Perspective: Pluralism ■ The Conflict Perspective: Power Elite and Ruling Class ■ Which View Is Right?
War: A Means to Implement Political Objectives   422
Is War Universal? ■ Why Do Nations Go to War? ■ How Common Is War? ■ Costs of War ■ War and Dehumanization

INSTRUCTOR'S SECTION

Perspectives: Nations versus States—Implications of a New
    World Order   425
A Coming World Order?   426
Summary   426
Suggested Readings   427

16   The Family: Our Introduction to Society

Marriage and Family in Cross-Cultural Perspective   430
    Defining Family ■ Variations across Cultures ■ Common Cultural Themes
Marriage and Family in Theoretical Perspective   434
    The Functionalist Perspective: Functions and Dysfunctions ■ The Conflict Perspective: Gender, Conflict, and Power
    Thinking Critically About Social Controversy: The Second Shift—Strains and Strategies   437
    The Symbolic Interactionist Perspective: Marital Communication
The Family Life Cycle   440
    The Ideological Context: Love and Courtship
    Perspectives: East Is East and West Is West—Love and Arranged Marriages in India   441
    Marriage
    Down-to-Earth Sociology: Why Do People Become Jealous? A Sociological Interpretation   442
    Childbirth ■ Child Rearing ■ The Family in Later Life
Diversity in American Families   446
    African-American Families ■ Hispanic-American Families (Latinos) ■ Asian-American Families ■ One-Parent Families
    Perspectives: Peering beneath the Facade—Problems in the Korean-American Family   450
    Families without Children ■ Blended Families ■ Homosexual Families
Trends in American Families   451
    Postponing Marriage ■ Cohabitation ■ Child Care
Divorce and Remarriage   455
    Problems in Measuring Divorce ■ Children of Divorce ■ The Ex-Spouses ■ Remarriage
Two Sides of Family Life   458
    Abuse: Battering, Marital Rape, and Incest ■ Families That Work
The Future of Marriage and Family   461
Summary   462
Suggested Readings   462

17   Education: Transferring Knowledge and Skills   464

Today's Credential Society   466
The Development of Modern Education   467

Education in Cross-Cultural Perspective   468
    Great Britain ■ Japan ■ The Former Soviet Union
Education in the United States   471
    The Beginning of Universal Education
The Functionalist Perspective: Providing Social Benefits   472
    Teaching Knowledge and Skills ■ Cultural Transmission of Values ■ Social Integration ■ Gatekeeping ■ Promoting Personal Change ■ Promoting Social Change ■ Replacing Family Functions ■ Other Functions
The Conflict Perspective: Maintaining Social Inequality   477
    The Hidden Curriculum ■ Stacking the Deck: Unequal Funding
    Down-to-Earth Sociology: Kindergarten as Boot Camp   478
    Discrimination by IQ: Tilting the Tests ■ The Correspondence Principle ■ The Bottom Line: Reproducing the Social Class Structure
    Thinking Critically about Social Controversy: The "Cooling-Out" Function of Higher Education   483
The Symbolic Interactionist Perspective: Teacher Expectations and the Self-Fulfilling Prophecy   484
    The Rist Research ■ The Rosenthal/Jacobson Experiment ■ How Do Teacher Expectations Work?
How Can We Improve Schools?   487
    The Coleman Report ■ Compensatory Education ■ Busing ■ The National Report Card: Falling Test Scores ■ The Rutter Report
    Down-to-Earth Sociology: Positive Peer Pressure and the Problem of Drugs   491
    Thinking Critically about Social Controversy: Improving America's Schools   491
Summary   493
Suggested Readings   493

18   Religion: Establishing Meaning   494

What Is Religion?   496
The Functionalist Perspective   497
    Functions of Religion ■ Functional Equivalents of Religion ■ Dysfunctions of Religion
The Symbolic Interactionist Perspective   499
    Religious Symbols ■ Rituals ■ Beliefs ■ Religious Experience ■ Community
The Conflict Perspective   502
    Opium of the People ■ A Reflection of Social Inequalities ■ A Legitimation of Social Inequalities
Religion and the Spirit of Capitalism   504
The World's Major Religions   505
    Judaism ■ Christianity ■ Islam ■ Hinduism ■ Buddhism ■ Confucianism

Types of Religious Organizations   *510*
Cult ■ Sect ■ Church
■ *Down-to-Earth Sociology:* Mass Shortage   *513*
Ecclesia ■ Variations in Patterns ■ A Closer Look at Cults and Sects
■ *Perspectives:* Religion and Culture in India   *514*
Secularization   *515*
The Secularization of Religion
■ *Down-to-Earth Sociology:* Bikers and Bibles   *517*
The Secularization of Culture ■ *518*
The Main Characteristics of Religion in the United States   *520*
Diversity ■ Pluralism and Freedom ■ Competition ■ Commitment ■ Privacy ■ Toleration ■ Fundamentalist Revived ■ The Electronic Church ■ Characteristics of Members
The Future of Religion   *523*
Summary   *524*
Suggested Readings   *525*

19 Medicine: Health and Illness   *526*

The Sociological Perspective of Health and Illness   *528*
Defining Health ■ The Cultural Relativity of Health ■ The Sick Role

Historical Patterns of Health   *532*
Physical Health ■ Mental Health
Medicine in the United States   *534*
The Professionalization of Medicine ■ The Monopoly of Medicine
■ *Thinking Critically about Social Controversy:* Midwives and Physicians: The Expanding Boundaries of a Profession   *536*
■ *Thinking Critically about Social Controversy:* In the Care of Strangers—The Hospital in American Society   *536*
Mental Illness and Social Inequality
Issues in Health and Health Care   *539*
Medical Care as a Commodity ■ Malpractice Suits and Defensive Medicine ■ Inequality in Distribution ■ Depersonalization: The Cash Machine ■ Sexism in Medicine
■ *Down-to-Earth Sociology:* The Doctor Nurse Game   *543*
Medicalization of Society ■ Controversy about Death
■ *Thinking Critically about Social Controversy:* The Legalization of Euthanasia   *545*
Health Insurance
Threats to Health   *546*
Disease ■ Drugs ■ Disabling Environments
The Search for Alternatives   *552*
Treatment or Prevention? ■ Holistic Medicine
■ *Perspectives:* Health Care in Other Countries   *553*
Summary   *556*
Suggested Readings   *556*

PART V   SOCIAL CHANGE

20 Population and Urbanization   *558*

Population   *560*
The Specter of Overpopulation   *560*
Thomas Malthus: Sounding the Alarm ■ The New Malthusians ■ The Anti-Malthusians ■ Who Is Correct? ■ Why Are There Famines?
Population Growth   *565*
Why the Poor Nations Have So Many Children ■ Implications of Different Rates of Growth ■ Estimating Population Growth: The Three Demographic Variables ■ Industrialization and the Demographic Equation ■ Problems in Forecasting Population Growth
■ *Perspectives:* Where the United States Population Is Headed   *572*
Urbanization   *574*
The City in History   *574*
Models of Urban Growth   *576*
The Concentric-Zone Model ■ The Sector Model ■ The Multiple-Nuclei Model ■ Critique of the Models
Experiencing the City   *578*
Alienation

■ *Perspectives:* Urbanization in the Third World   *579*
Community ■ Types of Urban Dwellers ■ Urban Sentiment
■ *Down-to-Earth Sociology:* Giving Access Information—The Contrasting Perspectives of Males and Females   *583*
Insiders' and Outsiders' Views: Implications for Urban Planners ■ Urban Networks ■ Urban Overload ■ Diffusion of Responsibility
The Changing City   *585*
Urban Politics: The Transition to Minority Leadership ■ Suburbanization ■ Trends in Suburbs and Cities
Summary   *588*
Suggested Readings   *589*

21 Collective Behavior and Social Movements   *590*

Collective Behavior   *592*
Early Explanations: The Transformation of the Individual   *593*
Charles Mackay: The "Herd Mentality" ■ Gustave LeBon:

How the Crowd Transforms the Individual ■ Robert Park: Social Unrest and Circular Reaction ■ Herbert Blumer: The Acting Crowd ■ Comparing LeBon and Blumer

The Contemporary View: The Rationality of the Crowd   *595*

Critique of LeBon and Blumer: More Than a Creature of the Crowd ■ Ralph Turner and Lewis Killian: Emergent Norms ■ Richard Berk: Minimax Strategy ■ Can Collective Behavior Really Be So Rational? ■ The Anatomy of a Lynching

Other Forms of Collective Behavior   *599*

Riots ■ Panics ■ Rumors ■ Fads and Fashions ■ Urban Legends

Social Movements   *605*

Understanding Social Movements: The Case of the Nazis   *605*

Why Social Movements Exist ■ Dehumanization: Why Normal People Do Evil Things ■ Propaganda and Advertising: Manufacturing and Selling Ideas

Breadth, Types, and Tactics of Social Movements   *609*

Breadth of Social Movements

Down-to-Earth Sociology: "Tricks of the Trade"—The Fine Art of Propaganda   *610*

New Social Movements ■ Types of Social Movements ■ Tactics of Social Movements ■ The Life Course of Social Movements

Thinking Critically about Social Controversy: Which Side of the Barricades? Abortion as a Social Movement   *614*

Why People Join Social Movements   *616*

Deprivation Theory ■ Mass Society Theory

The Success and Failure of Social Movements   *617*

Resource Mobilization

Summary   *618*

Suggested Readings   *619*

22   Social Change, Technology, and the Environment   *620*

Social Change: A Review   *622*

The Four Social Revolutions ■ From *Gemeinschaft* to *Gesellschaft* ■ The Transformation of Society through Capitalism ■ Effects of Industrialization on the Third World ■ Globalization and Dependency ■ Shifts in International Stratification ■ Changes in the Social Institutions of the United States

Theories of Social Change   *624*

Evolutionary Theories ■ Cyclical Theories ■ Conflict Theory ■ Modernization

Social Change and Technology   *628*

Ogburn's Processes of Cultural Innovation ■ Types of Technology ■ How Technology Transforms Society ■ An Extended Example: Effects of the Automobile ■ An Extended Example: Effects of the Computer ■ Concerns about Computers ■ Telecommunications and Global Social Change

Social Change and the Natural Environment   *640*

Environmental Degradation in the Past

Perspectives: Lost Tribes, Lost Knowledge   *644*

The Environmental Problem Today ■ Environmental Problems in the Second World ■ Environmental Problems in the Third World ■ The Environmental Movement

Thinking Critically about Social Controversy: Ecosabotage   *644*

Environmental Sociology ■ The Goal of Harmony between Technology and the Environment

Summary   *646*

Suggested Readings   *647*

Boxes

■ DOWN-TO-EARTH SOCIOLOGY

An Updated Version of the Old Elephant Story *6*
Enjoying a Sociological Quiz: Sociological Findings versus
    Common Sense *7*
Communicating across Cultural Boundaries *36*
Heredity or Environment? The Case of Oskar and Jack,
    Identical Twins *59*
College Football as Social Structure *90*
Loading the Dice *121*
The Hawthorne Experiments *128*
How Group Size Affects Willingness to Help
    Strangers *157*
Maneuvering the Hidden Culture: Women Surviving in the
    Male-Dominated Business World *179*
Self-Management Teams *183*
Home on the Range—Japanese-Style *187*
Taking Back Children from the Night *215*
Making the Invisible Visible—The Deadly Effects of
    Sexism *291*
The Illegal Travel Guide *331*
Applying Life Expectancy Figures *347*
Changing Sentiment about the Elderly *357*
Pacification—Turning People into Patients *362*
Selling the American Dream—The Creation of Constant
    Discontent *381*
Why Do People Become Jealous? A Sociological
    Interpretation *442*
Kindergarten as Boot Camp *478*
Positive Peer Pressure and the Problem of Drugs *491*
Mass Shortage *513*
Bikers and Bibles *517*
Midwives and Physicians—The Expanding Boundaries
    of a Profession *536*

■ PERSPECTIVES

Sociology in a World of Turmoil *26*
Miami—Language and a Changing City *39*
Why Do Native Americans Like Westerns? *44*
Manhood in the Making *74*
Caught between Two Worlds *77*
The Amish—*Gemeinschaft* Communities in a *Gesellschaft*
    Society *100*
A Tribal Mountain People Meets Postindustrial
    Society *147*

Managing Diversity in the Workplace *181*
Bottom-Up Decision Making in Japanese
    Corporations *186*
Deviance in Cross-Cultural Perspective *192*
When Cultures Clash—Problems in Defining
    Deviance *198*
Social Stratification among Polish Jews *226*
The Patriotic Prostitute *243*
Sexual Harassment in Japan *298*
Clashing Cultures *313*
The Browning of America *332*
Who Is Unemployed? *395*
Immigrants—Ethnicity and Class as the Paths to Political
    Participation *416*
Nations versus States—Implications of a New World
    Order *425*
East Is East and West Is West—Love and Arranged
    Marriages in India *441*
Peering beneath the Facade—Problems in the
    Korean-American Family *450*
Religion and Culture in India *514*
Health Care in Other Countries *553*
Where the United States Population Is Headed *572*
Urbanization in the Third World *579*
Lost Tribes, Lost Knowledge *644*

■ THINKING CRITICALLY ABOUT SOCIAL CONTROVERSY

Are We Prisoners of Our Genes? *48*
Counting the Homeless *129*
Upward Mobility for American Workers—A Vanishing
    Dream? *269*
Children in Poverty *273*
Biology versus Culture *282*
Racism on College Campuses *316*
Social Security—Fraud of the Century? *358*
The Second Shift—Strains and Strategies *437*
The "Cooling-Out" Function of Higher Education *483*
Improving America's Schools *491*
In Care of Strangers—The Hospital in American
    Society *536*
The Legalization of Euthanasia *545*
Which Side of the Barricades? Abortion as a Social
    Movement *614*
Ecosabotage *644*

Sociology: A Down-to-Earth Approach
by James Henslin

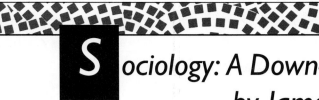

- A "down-to-earth" approach that makes sociological concepts accessible to your students.

- Exemplary coverage of diversity in the United States and around the world.

- Written in an engaging, articulate, personal style that students will enjoy.

- Challenging pedagogy encourages students to think critically.

- An extensive support package, including CNN videos and the "Breaking the Ice" reader written especially to accompany this text and enhance your presentations.

- A comprehensive Annotated Instructor's Edition (AIE) that helps you to give a thorough, coordinated presentation.

The Development of Sociology   7

Just how did sociology begin? Has it always been around? Or is it relatively new?

In some ways it is difficult to answer these questions. By the time Jesus Christ was born, the Greeks and Romans had already developed intricate systems of philosophy about human behavior. Even preliterate peoples made observations about their tribal lives and were most likely aware, for example, which classes of people were more privileged and powerful. They also analyzed *why* life was as it was, but in doing so they often depended on magic, superstition, or explanations based on the positions of the stars.

Simple assertions of truth—or observations mixed with magic or superstition or the stars—are not adequate. *All science requires the development of theories that can be proved or disproved by systematic research.*

This fact simplifies the question of the origin of sociology, for measured by this standard sociology is clearly a recent discipline. It emerged about the middle of the nineteenth century when European social observers began to use scientific methods to test their ideas. Three factors combined to lead to the development of sociology.

The first was social upheaval in Europe. By the middle of the nineteenth century, Europe found itself experiencing the effects of the Industrial Revolution. This change from agriculture to factory production brought violent changes to people's lives. Masses of people, forced off the land, moved to the cities in search of work. There they were met with anonymity, crowding, filth, and poverty. Their ties to the land, to the generations that had lived there before them, and to their way of life were abruptly broken. The city greeted them with horrible working conditions: low pay, long, exhausting hours, dangerous work, bad ventilation, and much noise. To survive, families had to permit their children to work in these same conditions, some of them even chained to factory machines to make certain they did not run away.

No area of people's lives was left untouched, not even their personal relationships.

DOWN-TO-EARTH SOCIOLOGY

Enjoying a Sociology Quiz—Sociological Findings versus Common Sense

Some findings of sociology support commonsense understandings of social life, while others contradict them. Can you tell the difference? If you want to enjoy this quiz fully, before turning the page to check your answers complete *all* the questions.

1. True/False The earnings of American women have just about caught up with those of American men.

2. True/False People on city streets at night are less helpful and friendly than people on city streets during the day.

3. True/False When faced with natural disasters such as floods and earthquakes, people panic and social organization disintegrates.

4. True/False Revolutions are more likely to occur when conditions are consistently bad than when they are improving rapidly.

5. True/False Most people on welfare are lazy and looking for a handout. They could work if they wanted to.

6. True/False Most American Roman Catholics oppose birth control.

7. True/False Compared with men, women touch each other more while they are conversing.

8. True/False Compared with women, men maintain more eye contact while they are conversing.

9. True/False Because of the rapid rise in the divorce rate in the United States, American children are much more likely to live in a single-parent household now than they were a century ago.

10. True/False The first statement *is* true, but what about the second? Each year the federal government computes an official poverty line, used to determine who is eligible for welfare and food stamps. Most welfare families live in poverty for at least five years.

11. True/False The more available alcohol is (as measured by the number of places to purchase alcohol per one hundred people), the more alcohol-related injuries and fatalities occur on American highways.

12. True/False Couples who live together before marriage usually report higher satisfaction with their marriages than couples who do not live together before marriage.

Henslin shows students what sociological principles really mean!

In Jamie's case, there may be an underlying organic cause to her behavior, such as a chemical imbalance. Other homeless people, however, may have no psychiatric history, yet exhibit strange behaviors, for *just being on the streets can cause mental illness*—or whatever we want to label socially inappropriate behaviors that we find difficult to classify.

Place yourself in the situation of the homeless. Suppose that you had no money, no place to sleep, no bathroom, did not know *if* you were going to eat, much less where, had no friends or anyone you could trust, and lived in constant fear of rape and violence. Wouldn't that be enough to drive you "over the edge"? Maybe, maybe not. But it is certainly enough for some people.

All of these conditions bring severe consequences, but consider just the problems involved in not having a place to bathe. (Shelters are often so dangerous that the homeless prefer to take their chances sleeping in public settings.) You will try at first to wash in the toilets of gas stations, bars, the bus station, or a shopping center. But you are dirty, and people stare when you enter, and they call the management when they see you wash your feet in the sink. You are thrown out, and told in no uncertain terms to never come back. So you get dirtier and dirtier. Eventually you come to think of being dirty as a fact of life. Soon, maybe, you don't even care. No longer do the stares bother you—at least not as much.

No one will talk to you, and you withdraw more and more into yourself. You begin to build a fantasy life. You talk openly to yourself. People stare, but so what? They stare anyway. Besides, they are no longer important to you. Perhaps, like a small child, you begin to imagine that you can control vehicles by pointing at them. Eventually you become convinced of it.

The point is that *homelessness and mental illness are reciprocal:* Just as "mental illness" can cause homelessness, so the trials of being homeless, of living on cold, hostile streets, can lead to unusual and unacceptable thinking and behaviors.

THE NEED FOR A MORE HUMANE APPROACH

As Durkheim (1893, 1958:68) pointed out, deviance is inevitable—even in a group of saints.

DOWN-TO-EARTH SOCIOLOGY

Taking Back Children from the Night

Lois Lee is a sociologist who isn't afraid to take a stand— or to apply her sociological training to social problems. Lee did her master's thesis on the pimp-prostitute relationship, her doctoral dissertation on the social world of the prostitute. After receiving her Ph.D. from United States International University in 1981, Lee began to work with adult prostitutes. They told her, "You know, it's too late for you to help us, Lois. You've got to do something about these kids. We made a choice to be out here . . . a conscious decision. But these kids don't stand a chance."

Lee began by taking those teenagers who were prostituting themselves, into her home, where she lives with her husband and baby son. In three years, she brought back 250. Lee then founded "Children of the Night," which reaches the kids by means of "a twenty-four-hour hotline, a street outreach program, a walk-in crisis center, crisis intervention for medical or life-threatening situations, family counseling, job placement, and foster home

or group placement." By [...]
tution and petty crime, Le[...]
Night has helped over five[...]
prostitutes get off the stre[...]

Lee's work has broug[...]
a presidential award. She[...]
ogy, especially to the sens[...]
tween groups that her dis[...]
that her sociological train[...]
and move safely through[...]
relate positively to police[...]
retaining a critical perspe[...]
play in which situation."

As Lee remarked du[...]
what the street rules are, [...]
I know what the con game[...]
that game correctly. . . . It's[...]
people call me a social w[...]

Source: Based on Buff 1987.

Distinguished author James M. Henslin has crafted this text in answer to a pressing need — the need to bring sociological concepts down to earth for students. The aim of the text is not merely to list sociological concepts, but actually to show students these concepts at work, to help them understand how the study of sociology relates to real life — to their lives.

A framework of relevant, real-world examples

Using relevant, real-world and personal examples, Henslin helps students to see the links between sociology and situations that occur every day in the world around them. Through this trademark "down-to-earth" approach, Henslin provides students with a familiar framework from which they can view sociological ideas. He puts theory into context so that concepts that might otherwise seem abstract are grounded in relevant examples from everyday life. Students begin to see what these ideas really mean when put into practice.

232   9 ■ Social Stratification in Global Perspective

applicants. If money were the main motivator, why would
college, then average another six or seven years pursuin
slightly more than someone who works in the post office?
offers more than monetary rewards: high prestige (most pe
up to people in this position), autonomy (college teachers h
in their activities), rewarding social interaction (much of th
people), security (when given tenure, college teachers have
the opportunity to travel (professors work short days, enj
during the school year, and have the entire summer off).

Fourth, if social stratification is so functional, it ought t
In actual fact, however, social stratification is *dysfunctional* t
individuals who could have made invaluable contributions to
born in a slum and had to drop out of school, taking a mer
family; or had they not been born female and assigned "wor
they could not maximize their mental abilities (Huber 1988)

> Expanding this "down-to-earth" approach to include people of diverse backgrounds, Henslin asks students to take a look at the world from a perspective other than their own. Through the use of regularly occurring examples, students are encouraged to see how sociological ideas affect people of different races, classes, and genders.

Mosca: A Forerunner of the Conflict View

In 1896 Italian sociologist Gaetano Mosca wrote an influenti
Class. In it, he argued that every society will be stratified
reasons.

1. A society cannot exist unless it is organized. This means that there must be politics of some sort in order to coordinate people's actions and get society's work done.
2. Political organization always results in inequalities of power, for it requires that some people take leadership positions, while others follow.
3. It is human nature to be self-centered. Therefore, persons in positions of power will use their positions to bring greater rewards for themselves.

There is no way around these facts of life, said Mosca. Social stratification is inevitable, and every society will stratify itself along lines of power. Because the ruling class is well organized and enjoys easy communication among its relatively few members, it is extremely difficult for the majority they govern to resist (Marger 1987). Mosca's argument is a forerunner of explanations developed by conflict theorists.

The Conflict View: Class Conflict and Competition for Scarce Resources

Conflict theorists such as G. William Domhoff (1967, 1983, 1991), C. Wright Mills (1956), and Irving Louis Horowitz (1966) stress that conflict, not function, is the basis of social stratification. In short, every society has only limited resources to go around, and in every society groups struggle with one another for those resources. Whenever a group gains power, it uses that power to extract what it can from the groups beneath it. The dominant group takes control of the social institutions, using them to keep other groups weak and to preserve for itself the best resources. Class conflict, then, is the key to understanding social stratification, for society is far from being a harmonious system that benevolently distributes greater resources to society's supposedly more qualified members.

All ruling classes—whether slave masters or modern elites—develop an ideology to justify people's relative positions. This ideology not only helps prevent the ruling class from feeling guilty about possessing wealth in the midst of deprivation, but also affirms its position in power by seducing the oppressed into **false consciousness.** For example, the ideology encourages the oppressed to believe that their welfare depends on keeping society stable—so they support laws against their own interests and even sacrifice their children as soldiers in wars designed to support the entrenchment of the bourgeoisie.

Marx predicted that the workers would revolt. The day will come, he claimed,

Nelson Mandela, leader of the African National Congress (ANC), has spent his life fighting the white government of South Africa and the system of apartheid it developed to keep blacks from control of the country's resources.

> As the world seems to grow smaller day by day, having a global outlook becomes more and more important. Henslin realizes this and extends text coverage of diversity beyond the borders of the United States. Global issues are examined throughout; especially in the chapters on social institutions — the economy, the family, religion and politics. This global theme is expanded in other chapters including the final chapter on the environment, technology and social change, and in "Perspectives" boxes throughout.

Inequalities of Gender

than the average female college graduate. Could *you* use an extra half million

The gender penalty persists both in low-skilled jobs and in the professions. Female rs in corporate settings make $40,000 less per year than do male lawyers (Hagan . In colleges and universities, female Ph.D.'s earn about 23 percent less than Ph.D.'s—and that holds true regardless of their field of work, their experience, ature of their jobs, or the quality of their training (Andersen 1988). A survey of 25 largest corporations in the United States showed that the average chief execu- fficer receives an annual salary of $1 million. These CEOs also earned another 000 from stock options. *Not one of these 325 CEOs is a female.* (*The Wall Street al,* April 18, 1990)

elice Schwartz, president of Catalyst, a nonprofit research organization that fo- on women's issues in the workplace, surveyed female executives in the largest d States corporations (Lopez 1992). She found that women face a "glass ceiling" glass walls." The "glass ceiling" prevents women from advancing to top executive ons, while it lets men pass through. Thus in companies where about half of the ssional employees are women, women hold fewer than 5 percent of the senior gement positions. The "glass walls" are obstacles that keep women from moving lly into core positions in marketing, production, and sales from which senior tives are tapped. Stereotyped as being better at providing "support," women are d into such positions as public relations and human resources—which do not de the experience needed for jobs in top management.

n the upper ranks, the pay gap is maintained through an "old boys'" network. is, a network of acquaintances brings access to jobs, promotions, and opportuni- Excluded from this network, female professionals find themselves at a disadvan- when it comes to professional opportunities (Andersen 1988). To combat this disadvantage, some female professionals are developing alternative networks to help

P E R S P E C T I V E S
Cultural Diversity Around the World

Sexual Harassment in Japan

The public relations department had come up with an eye-catcher: Each month, the cover of the company's magazine would show a woman taking off one more piece of clothing. The men were pleased, looking forward to each new issue.

Six months later, with the cover girl poised to take off her tank top in the next edition, the objections of women employees had grown too loud to ignore. "We told them it was a lousy idea," said Junko Takashima, assistant director of the company's women's affairs division. The firm, Rengo, dropped the striptease act.

The Japanese men didn't get the point. "What's all the fuss about?" they wondered. "Beauty is beauty. We're just admiring the ladies. It's a wish, or maybe a hope. It's nothing serious. It just adds a little spice to boring days at the office."

"It's degrading to us, and it must stop," responded female workers, who, encouraged by the American feminist movement, have broken their long tradition of passive silence.

The Japanese have no word of their own to describe this situation, so they have borrowed the English phrase "sexual harassment." They are now struggling to apply it to their own culture. In Japan a pat on the bottom has long been taken for granted as a boss's way of getting his secretary's attention. But now the men no longer know how a woman will react.

Differing cultural expectations have led to problems when Japanese executives—always male—have been sent to overseas factories. A managing director of Honda learned this the hard way. During business meetings he repeatedly put his hand on the knee of an American employee. When she threatened to sue, he was transferred back to Japan.

The Japanese expectation that everyone will work together harmoniously does not make it easy for female employees. A woman who complains is viewed as violating corporate harmony. But women are speaking out, and discovering how to apply the Western concept "sexual harassment."

Source: Based on Graven 1990.

Women as a Minority (

The Question of Superiority

Let's consider a thorny question that people have debated through the ages: W
sex is superior? Since men have dominated societies, it is they who have come up
the "official" answers. It is not surprising, therefore, that they have identified
own sex as superior. Looking at the matter more objectively, however, we find
this is not an easy question to answer. In fact, there can be no answer unless we
rephrase the question to ask *in what ways*. It seems that males and females are
superior—but in different ways.

On the one hand, males are biologically superior to the extent that they
stronger and larger. This difference is considerable, for the average female is
two-thirds as strong as the average male (Gallese 1980). On the other hand, fer
are biologically superior in the sense that they outlive males. The average life e
tancy of American females is about seventy-eight, while for males it is only a
seventy. Although about 105 male babies are born for every 100 female babies i
United States, by the time those children reach the age of thirty-five there are as
females as males. At age seventy-five, for every male almost two females have
vived (*Statistical Abstract* 1991:Table 13).

Females are intellectually superior to the extent that they generally begin to s
sooner than boys, to use sentences earlier, to score higher in tests of verbal flue
and to do better in grammar and spelling. But boys are intellectually superior t
extent that they do better on spatial tasks and score higher on math (Bardwick
Lengermann and Wallace 1985; Goleman 1987). Why such differences exist is a m
of debate among social scientists, a debate that, of course, takes us back to the pro
discussed above, that of social learning versus inherited abilities (Holden 1987).

With neither sex biologically or socially superior, then, how is it that aroun
world males dominate human societies?

Henslin's inviting writing style puts students at ease, helping them to feel more comfortable with the subject matter. His concerned "down-to-earth" approach to this intriguing material makes them want to keep reading, while challenging in-text features get them thinking! He builds students interest by offering concrete examples of the principles he discusses. Rather than burying terms in jargon and abstract theories, he clearly describes important terms and concepts in language students can understand — helping students to quickly grasp these complex topics.

WOMEN AS A MINORITY GROUP

As noted, gender discrimination pervades every society, touching almost every aspect of social life. Consequently, even though women outnumber men, sociologists have found it useful to refer to women as a **minority group,** one that is discriminated against on the basis of physical characteristics. Sociologist Helen Hacker (1951), who was the first to apply this concept to women, noted that women are discriminated against economically, in education, in politics, and in everyday life. While some of the particulars of gender discrimination in our society have changed since Hacker's observation—women are no longer barred from jury duty, for example—gender inequality still exists in the areas she identified: jobs, education, politics, and everyday life.

Cross-Cultural Gender Inequality: Sex-Typing of Work

Before looking at gender inequality in American society, let's consider a brief overview of gender inequality around the world. Anthropologist George Murdock (1937), who surveyed 324 premodern societies around the world, found that in all of them activities are **sex-typed;** in other words, every society associates activities with one sex or the other. He also found that activities considered "female" in one society may be "male" activities in another society, and vice versa. In some groups, for example, taking care of cattle is women's work, while other groups assign this task to men.

Metalworking was the exception, being men's work in all the societies examined. Three other pursuits—making weapons, pursuing sea mammals, and hunting—were almost universally the domain of men, but in a few societies women were allowed to participate. Although Murdock found no particular work that was universally assigned to women, he did find that making clothing, cooking, carrying water, and grinding grain

minority group: a group that is discriminated against on the basis of its members' physical characteristics

sex-typed: the association of behaviors with one sex or the other

Carefully constructed in-text pedagogy challenges students to think for themselves!

48 2 ■ Culture

of doing any of them. Humans have no biological imperative that results in one particular form of behavior throughout the world. As indicated in the Thinking Critically section below, a few sociologists do take the position that genes significantly influence human behavior, although almost all sociologists disagree with this view.

THINKING CRITICALLY ABOUT SOCIAL CONTROVERSY

Are We Prisoners of Our Genes? Sociobiology

A controversial view of human behavior called **sociobiology** provides a sharp contrast to the view presented in this chapter. Instead of looking at human behavior as shaped by culture, sociobiology stresses natural selection as responsible for humans' particular biological characteristics, which shape human behavior.

According to Charles Darwin (1859), natural selection is based on four principles. First, reproduction occurs within a natural environment. Second, the genes of a species, the basic units of life that contain the individual's traits, are passed on to offspring. These genes have a degree of random variability; that is, different characteristics are distributed among the members of a species. Third, because the members of a species possess different characteristics, some members have a better chance of surviving in the natural environment than do others—and of passing their particular genetic traits to the next generation. Fourth, over thousands of generations, those genetic traits that aid survival in the natural environment tend to become common in a species, while those that do not tend to disappear.

Natural selection is used to explain the physical characteristics of plants and animals. It is also used to explain the behavior of animals: Over countless generations instincts emerged. Edward O. Wilson (1975), an insect specialist, claims that the principles of natural selection that led to human physical characteristics also led to human behavior as well. Human behavior, he said [...] cats, dogs, rats, bees, or mosquitoes—it has b[...] evolutionary principles.

Wilson deliberately set out to create a stor[...] claims that religion, competition and cooperation, [...] envy and altruism—all can be explained throug[...] that because human behavior can be explained i[...] new discipline of sociobiology will eventually abso[...] and psychology.

Obviously, most sociologists find Wilson's p[...] is it a direct attack on their discipline, it bypass[...] focus on: humans designing their own cultures, [...] life. Sociologists do not deny that genetic princip[...] not in the sense that it takes a highly developed [...] abstract thought could not exist if we did not hav[...]

But sociologists find the claim that human be[...] to be quite another matter (Lewontin et al. 198[...] have a cerebral cortex, and instincts control thei[...] deer, elephants, and so on. But humans are far f[...] Humans have abstract thought. They communica[...] ples that underlie what they do. They decide [...] develop reasons and purposes and goals. They c[...]

In short, sociologists stress that we are no[...] precisely why around the world we have develo[...] ways of life.

sociobiology: a framework of thought that views human behavior as the result of natural selection and considers biological characteristics to be the fundamental cause of human behavior

Cultural universals are those values, norms, rites, customs, or other cultural traits which are found in all societies. One such cultural universal is marriage.

"Thinking critically about social controversy"

This boxed feature asks students to consider current social situations and come up with constructive suggestions for positive change. Students are prompted to consider questions such as, "Why do these social situations exist?" "What perpetuates them," and "What can be done to turn negative situations into positive ones?"

Controversial, thought-provoking issues get them thinking!

The text's friendly, conversational tone, along with special boxed features and other in-text pedagogy compliment and expand upon the text material, challenging students to think for themselves and draw their own conclusions.

Prejudice and Discrimination 313

PREJUDICE AND DISCRIMINATION

Although virtually all Americans are familiar with prejudice and discrimination, the United States certainly has no monopoly on these negative features of social life. On the contrary, they appear to characterize every society, regardless of size. The Perspectives box below recounts the prejudice and discrimination now rampant in Europe. In Northern Ireland, Protestants discriminate against Roman Catholics; in Israel, Ashkenazi Jews, primarily of European descent, discriminate against Sephardi Jews from Asian and African backgrounds; and in Japan, the Japanese discriminate against just about anyone who isn't Japanese, especially the Koreans and Ainu who live there (Spivak 1980; Fields 1986). In some places the elderly discriminate against the

PERSPECTIVES
Cultural Diversity Around the World

Clashing Cultures

"Africans and Italians don't mix," shouts Michele Corti, who has organized a protest against new housing for Arabs and Africans in Milan, Italy. "Milan is becoming the Bronx of Italy," he says.

Western European countries that once sent their huddled masses to the United States are now fending off the tired and poor from the Third World. When the economy of western Europe boomed, accompanied by plummeting birthrates (see Chapters 14 and 20), a need was created for immigrant labor. Workers from the Third World answered that need.

The result has been clashing cultures, accompanied by prejudice and discrimination—some of it mild, some violent, all of it ugly.

Heiko Baumert of Berlin, who sports tattoos of swastikas and storm troopers on his arms, says, "If you mix races in Germany, it never works." The young man next to him, with shaved head and black, steel-toed boots, adds, "We want to wake up Germans and pressure the state to kick the foreigners out."

"Foreigners Out" declare the graffiti on a nearby nightclub. The young men, numbering about three hundred, who have battled Africans in an adjoining block, say, "It is demagoguery to ignore the achievements of the Nazis."

In France, where immigrants from North Africa make up 8 percent of the population, the National Front was dismissed as a racist fringe group just a few years ago. The party's slogan, "Let's Make France for the French," has hit a national nerve. Jean-Marie Le Pen, the head of the party, says, "If integration between Islamic immigrants and the French were possible, it would have happened already. We must make these people go back to their homes." Bruno Megret, the chief strategist of the National Front, adds, "France must be made racially pure. Racial integration corrupts. There is a worldwide cosmopolitan conspiracy that seeks to abolish national identity and infect the world with the AIDS virus." In 1992, the National Front carried 14 percent of votes nationwide.

Italy is home to a million immigrants, and thousands more are arriving weekly. In the city of Florence, residents have thrown bottles and set guard dogs on North Africans. "There is a long tradition in Italy of regarding anyone from outside your own village with suspicion," explains Roberto Formigoni, a vice president of the European Parliament.

The slowing economies of Europe have made the situation even more tense. In Austria, the birthplace of Hitler, the right-wing Freedom party has scored big gains on an anti-immigration platform.

And the immigrants? They are caught between two worlds. For many, their native country has become as foreign as their adopted land. With this upsurge in racism, however, their desire for a better life—which drew them from their homelands—is now tinged with fear. As Phung Tien, a thirty-year-old factory worker from Vietnam, who is living in Germany, succinctly expresses the matter, "I don't want to go home, but I don't want to die either."

Source: Based on Horwitz and Forman 1990; Forman and Carrington 1991; Gumbel 1992; Shlaes 1992.

In an earlier publication (Henslin 1975), I updated Williams's analysis by adding the following three values.

13. *Education*   Americans are expected to go as far in school as their abilities and finances allow. Over the years, the definition of an "adequate" education has changed sharply, and today the expectation of a college education is held as an appropriate goal for almost all Americans. Some even view people who have an opportunity for higher education and who do not take it as doing something "wrong," not merely making a bad choice, but somehow involved in an immoral act.

14. *Religiosity*   There is a feeling that "every true American ought to be religious." This does not mean that everyone is expected to join a church or synagogue, but that everyone ought to acknowledge a belief in a Supreme Being and follow some set of matching precepts. This value is so pervasive that Americans stamp "In [God We Trust]" on their money and declare in their national pledge of allegiance [that they are] one nation under God." We shall examine this value in Chapter 18.

[15. *Love and monogamy*]   Americans feel that the only proper basis for mar[riage is roman]tic love. Songs, literature, mass media, and "folk beliefs" all stress [this and] sometimes include the theme that "love conquers all." Similarly, [Americans feel that t]he only proper form of marriage is that of one man to one woman [monogamy] predominates in American society. When the Mormons challenged [this in th]e 1800s, they were driven out of several states. They finally settled [in what was the]n a wilderness, but even there the federal government would not

---

Chapter Outlines
Chapter Vignettes

Cultural Diversity in the U.S.

This special perspectives box helps students appreciate the diversity among subcultures in U.S. society. In keeping with the text content, these boxes focus on various diverse groups taking into account race, class, and gender considerations.

Global Diversity

This special perspectives box shows students how other societies experience social life. It widens their frame of reference and opens their eyes to the sociological considerations of other cultures.

"Down-to-earth sociology"

Found throughout the text, these crucial boxed features give examples of everyday situations. They support theories advanced in the text, and show students how these theories really do apply to their lives.

PERSPECTIVES
[Cultural Di]versity in U.S. Society

identified with the cowboys, however, were quite different, for each projected a different fantasy onto the story. While Anglos saw the movie as an accurate portrayal of the Old West and a justification of their own status in the social system, Native Americans saw it as embodying a free, natural way of life. In fact, Native Americans said that they were the "real cowboys." By this, they referred to their idealization of freedom and being "one's own [own] man."

Shively concludes

In westerns, Indians are different from the [rest] of the core myths of [westerns, they] express their real ide[ntity and their] ality on the one han[d and] about the land, auto[nomy] a cultural vehicle (th[e western] glos, but it is one in [which the] set of meanings that [they find] which they can read [into the] life they value, or a [...]

In other words, va[lues are at] issue. If a Native Ame[rican and a] Native Americans wit[nessing the] movie industry proje[cts, Native] Americans would ide[ntify, as] says Shively, Native [Americans as] "honorary Indians," fo[r their ideals] of bravery, autonomy, [...]

---

prime example is the United Fruit Company, which for decades controlled national and local politics in the Central American nations, running them as a fiefdom for the company's own profit while the United States marines waited in the wings in case the company's interests needed to be backed up. Most commonly, however, multinational

multinational corporations: companies that operate across many national boundaries

---

PERSPECTIVES
Cultural Diversity Around the World

The Patriotic Prostitute

Holidays with the most beautiful women of the world. An exclusive tour by Life Travel . . . You fly to Bangkok and then go to Pattaya . . . Slim, sunburnt and sweet, they . . . are masters in the art of making love by nature, an art we European people do not know . . . In Pattaya costs of living and loving are low (from a Swiss pamphlet)

A new wrinkle in the history of prostitution is the "patriotic prostitute." These are young women who are encouraged by their governments to prostitute themselves to help the country's economy. Patriotic prostitution is one of the seediest aspects of global stratification. Some Third World nations encourage prostitution to help pay their national debts. A consequence is that [per]haps 10 percent of all Thai women be[tween the] ages of fifteen and thirty have be[come pro]stitutes [...] [o]ne reports [...]—plus

heroic patriotism." With such an official blessing, "sex tourism" has become big business. Travel agencies in Germany openly advertise "trips to Thailand with erotic pleasures included in the price." Japan Air Lines hands out brochures that advertise the "charming attractions" of Kisaeng girls, advising men to fly JAL for a "night spent with a consummate Kisaeng girl dressed in a gorgeous Korean blouse and skirt."

What the enticing advertising fails to mention is the misery underlying Third World prostitution. Many of the prostitutes are held in bondage. Some are forced to work for pimps to pay family debts. Some are kept under lock and key to keep them from escaping. The advertisements also fail to mention the incidence of AIDS among Third World prostitutes. Somewhere between 25 percent and 50 percent of Nairobi's ten thousand prostitutes appear to be infected.

Women's groups pro[test interna]tional [...]

DOWN-TO-EARTH SOCIOLOGY

An Updated Version of the Old Elephant Story

It is said that in the recent past five wise men and women, all blindfolded, were led to an elephant. Each was asked to explain what they "saw." The first, a psychologist, feeling the top of the head, said, "This is the only thing that counts. All feeling and thinking takes place inside here. To understand this beast, we need study only this."

The second, an anthropologist, tenderly touching the trunk and the tusks, said, "This is really primitive. I feel very comfortable here. Concentrate on these."

The third, a political scientist, feeling the gigantic ears, said, "This is the power center. What goes in here controls the entire beast. Concentrate your studies here."

The fourth, an economist, feeling the mouth, said, "This is what counts. What goes in here is distributed throughout the body. Concentrate your studies on this."

Then came the sociologist (of course!), who, feeling [the] entire body, said, "You can't understand the beast [by concen]trating on only one part. Each is but part of [the whole. Th]e head, th[e trunk an]d tusks, the ears, the

mouth—all are important. And so are the parts of the beast that you haven't even mentioned. We must remove our blindfolds so we can see the larger picture. We have to see how everything works together to form the entire animal."

Pausing for emphasis, the sociologist added, "And we also need to understand how this creature interacts with similar creatures. How does their life in groups influence their behaviors?"

I wish I could conclude this fable by saying that the psychologist, the anthropologist, the political scientist, and the economist, dazzled upon hearing the wisdom of the sociologist, amidst gasps of wonderment threw away their blindfolds and, joining together, began to examine the larger picture. But, alas and alack! Upon hearing this sage advice, each stubbornly bound their blindfolds even tighter to concentrate all the more on the single part. And if you listened very, very carefully you could even hear them saying, "The top of the head is mine—stay away from it." "Don't touch the tusks." "Take your hand off the ears." "Stay away from the mouth—that's my area."

CNN *VIDEOS II*
Designed specifically for this text, these exciting videos bring current sociological issues into the classroom. Over 120 minutes of fascinating footage devoted to issues and events directly related to text content.

Video Disc
This convenient resource includes videos, teaching transparencies and much more, all combined into video disc format.

Computerized Instructor's Manual
In addition to the Instructor's Section found in the AIE, an alternate version is available, featuring teaching notes, lectures lead ins, debate topics, discussion questions and video and transparency references. All this in an easy-to-use computerized format, that puts this valuable teaching tool literally at your fingertips. Available for IBM and Apple Computers.

Printed and Computerized Test Banks

Study Guide Plus: Language and Multicultural Enrichment
This study guide is specially written to accomodate the non-native speaker.

Ourselves & Others: The Washington Post Sociology Companion
Featuring 96 articles on multicultural and crosscultural issues, this reader is a valuable resource for widening scope of study and enriching course content.

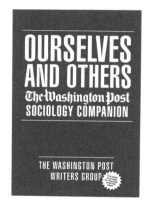

Breaking the Ice: A Guide to Understanding People from Other Cultures
by Daisy Kabagarama

Transparencies
Numerous color transparencies and transparency masters serve as an indispensible visual aid.

The Allyn & Bacon Sociology Video Library

All information is accurate as of date of printing. Subject to change without notice.

And to help put all this together...

The Annotated Instructor's Edition

helps you make the best possible use of this complete and coordinated teaching package.

This all-in-one resource combines the student text and the Instructor's Manual into one comprehensive and east to use volume.

In-text annotations help you pinpoint the right time to use supplementary materials and also suggest ideas for appraoching text content. With the Instructor's Section bound into the front, complete notes and other references are only a few pages away.

The AIE features:
- Class Discussion Questions
- Learning Objectives
- Key People
- Projects
- Essays
- Speaker Suggestions

The AIE is a valuable supplement to the text material that will prove it's worth again and again. Rather than merely reiterating the text, the annotations often suggest items that go further, take a different approach, or add a different perspective to the text content. It is a truly comprehensive volume that will aid you in pulling together all available resources to help you prepare a thoroughly coordinated presentation.

---

330 12 ■ Inequalities of Race and Ethnicity

L. Obj. 10: Compare and contrast the experiences of Hispanics (Latinos), Asian Americans, and Native Americans in the United States.

CDQ 14: What kind of changes do you think will occur, if any, as a result of the "Browning of America?"

TR#22: Country of Origin of Hispanic-American Population in the United States

TR#19M: Geographic Distribution of the Hispanic-American Population

Chicanos: Hispanic Americans whose country of origin is Mexico

Hispanic Americans (Latinos)

Numbers, Origins, and Location. The second-largest ethnic group in the United States is the *Hispanic Americans*, or Latinos, people of Spanish origin. In addition to the fourteen to twenty million **Chicanos** (those whose country of origin is Mexico), this minority includes about two million Puerto Ricans, a million Cuban Americans, and about three million people from Central or South America, primarily Venezuela and Colombia. While most Chicanos live in the southwestern states, most Puerto Ricans live in New York City and Cuban Americans are concentrated in the Miami area.

Officially tallied at twenty-one million (see Figure 12.5), the actual number of people of Hispanic origin living in the United States is considerably higher and could reach twenty-five or twenty-seven million. No one knows for certain because, although the vast majority of Latinos are legal residents, large numbers have entered the country illegally. Such individuals, not surprisingly, avoid contact with both public officials and census forms. Each year more than one million persons are apprehended at the border or at points inland and deported to Mexico (Armstrong 1986), but perhaps as many as two or three million manage to enter the United States. Most migrate for temporary work and then return to their homes and families. (The Down-to-Earth Sociology box on page 331 explores this vast subterranean immigration.) Their immigration has been so extensive that although 85 percent of Chicanos in 1960 were born in the United States, today a majority of all Hispanic Americans are immigrants or the children of immigrants (Chavez 1990).

To gain an understanding of these numbers, note that roughly as many people of Hispanic origin live in the United States as there are Canadians in Canada. To midwesterners, such a comparison often comes as a surprise, for members of this minority are virtually absent from vast stretches of Middle America. Hispanic Americans, however, are bringing seismic changes to some areas of the country. As shown in Figure 12.6, three out of four are concentrated in just four states: California, Texas, New York, and Florida (Vega 1990). Florida's Dade County is nearly half Hispanic, while Los Angeles, New York City, and Houston are about one-quarter Hispanic. In the largest state, California, Hispanic Americans are expected to *outnumber* Anglos before the end of the century (Engardio 1988). And by the year 2015 their population is expected to top forty million, making this nation's largest minority group (Corchado 1989). For changes in the ethnic composition of the United States, see the Perspectives box on page 332.

---

294 11 ■ Inequalities of Gender

saying, "Can't hack it, little girls?" (Eisenhart 1975). In the Marines, the worst insult to male recruits is to compare their performance to a woman's (Gilham 1989).

The same phenomenon occurs in male sports. Sociologist Douglas Foley (1990) notes that football coaches insult boys who don't play well by saying that they are "wearing skirts," and sociologists Jean Stockard and Miriam Johnson (1980), who observed boys playing basketball, heard boys who missed a basket called a "woman."

This name-calling is sociologically significant. As Stockard and Johnson (1980:12) point out, such insults embody the generalized devaluation of women in American society. As they noted, "There is no comparable phenomenon among women, for young girls do not insult each other by calling each other 'man.'"

K.P.: Jean Stockard and Miriam Johnson

Project 4

CNN: Glass Ceiling

L. Obj. 7: Explain how gender discrimination occurs in the workplace, including hiring practice, the pay gap, the "mommy track," and sexual harassment.

CDQ 13: Why is gender discrimination most visible in the workplace? Can you give examples?

FIGURE 11.1 Women's and men's proportion of the American labor force. Note: Pre-1940 figures include women fourteen and over; figures for 1940 and after are for women sixteen and over. (*Source:* 1969 *Handbook on Women Workers,* 1969:10; *Manpower Report to the President,* 1971:203, 205; Mills and Palumbo, 1980:6, 45; *Statistical Abstract of the United States,* 1991:Table 636.)

Gender Inequality in Conversation. As you may have noticed, gender inequality also shows up in everyday talk. Because men are more likely to interrupt a conversation and to control changes in topics, sociologists have noted that talk between a man and a woman is often more like talk between an employer and an employee than between social equals (Hall 1984; West and Garcia 1988; Smith-Lovin and Brody 1989; Tannen 1990). Even in college, male students interrupt their instructors more often than do female students, especially if the instructor is female (Brooks 1982). In short, conversations between men and women mirror their relative positions of power in society.

Derogatory terms and conversation represent only the tip of the iceberg, however, for as we have seen, underlying these aspects of everyday life is a structural inequality based on gender that runs throughout society. Let's examine that structural feature in the workplace.

GENDER INEQUALITY IN THE WORKPLACE

In many ways, gender discrimination is most visible in the workplace, where most Americans spend a huge portion of their lives. Here, some will be the victims of gender inequality, others its beneficiaries.

Women in the Work Force

In all industrialized nations, huge numbers of women enter the world of paid employment. Figure 11.1 documents this trend for the United States. Each decade since 1890

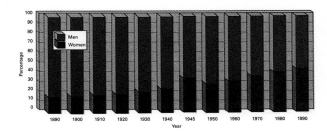

Blue annotations appear only in the margins of the AIE.
They do not appear in the Student text.

Instructor's Preface

Sociology is like a huge jigsaw puzzle. Only very gradually, and with a lot of hard work, do the intricate pieces start to fit together. As they do so, our perspective changes as we shift our eyes from the many small, disjointed pieces onto the whole that is being formed. Although this analogy may be lacking, it indicates a fascinating process of sociological discovery. Of all the endeavors we could have entered, we chose sociology because of the broadening perspective it offers, especially the ways in which it joins together the "pieces" of society and the challenges it poses to "ordinary" thinking. Sharing the sociological perspective is our privilege as we engage in that enterprise called teaching sociology.

Over the years, I have found the introductory course to be especially enjoyable to teach. Even after many years of teaching, it remains a pleasure to see students' faces light up as they begin to perceive the world in a different way, as disparate pieces of their world begin to fit together, and as they gain different ideas of how their social experiences have shaped them—even their innermost desires. This is precisely what this text is designed to do—to stimulate the sociological imagination so students can better perceive how the "pieces" of society fit together, and what that means for their own lives.

THE ORGANIZATION OF THIS TEXT

The text is laid out in five parts. Part I focuses on the sociological perspective. After introducing the sociological perspective in the first chapter, I then contrast macrosociology and microsociology, present an overview of culture, examine socialization, and then look at how sociologists do research. You may find the placement of the chapter on sociological research somewhat unusual, as it is typically the second chapter of introductory texts. In my own teaching experience, however, I have found it preferable to first allow students to "get their feet wet" in sociology, and only after having introduced the inherently interesting materials on culture and socialization to provide a survey of research methods. Of course, you may prefer to teach these materials in a different order.

Part II, which focuses on groups and social control, provides students with an understanding of how significantly social groups influence our lives. It first provides an overview of groups—from society, which encompasses us, to the smaller networks in which we are immersed. After examining bureaucracy and formal organizations, it turns to the issue of how groups exert social control on those who violate their norms.

Part III examines how social inequality is the hallmark of society and how those inequalities affect students' own lives. Because social stratification is so significant, there are two chapters on this topic. The first, with a global focus, presents an overview of the principles of stratification. The second, with an emphasis on variations in social class, focuses on stratification in American society. After establishing this broader context, it then examines gender, the most global of the social inequalities. Part III concludes with an analysis of inequalities of race/ethnicity and age.

Social institutions are the topic of Part IV. This overview of six major social institutions makes students more aware of the encompassing power of social institutions in our lives. It begins by examining the economy and politics, which have become such overarching social institutions in contemporary society. These chapters are followed by analyses of the family, education, religion, and medicine.

Part V, which concludes the book, focuses on social change. Here students will gain insight into why their world is changing so rapidly, as well as catch a glimpse of what is yet to come. This concluding part opens by examining effects of population and urbanization, then collective behavior and social movements. The book closes with a chapter on the environment, technology, and social change, an exploration into the "cutting edge" of the changes that engulf us all.

THEMES AND FEATURES

Two central themes, Diversity and Down-to-Earth Sociology, inform *Sociology: A Down-to-Earth Approach.* The first theme explores subgroups that make up the United States, as well the cultures of peoples worldwide. The second theme, Down-to-Earth Sociology, examines sociological processes that underlie commonly-held assumptions and phenomena of everyday life in search of underlying sociological processes.

Diversity in the United States and Around the World

Today any attempt to explain society in the United States must take into consideration its diverse populations. In addition to a focus on diversity throughout the text, special "Perspectives" boxes highlight key issues of multicultural diversity in American society ("Cultural Diversity in U.S. Society") and introduce students to cultures around the world ("Society in Cross-Cultural Perspective").

Cultural Diversity in U.S. Society.   Each year over one million persons from around the world legally immigrate to the United States. The number of illegal entrants, though undocumented, also represents large numbers. Currently, almost one American in four defines him or herself as Hispanic or Nonwhite. If current trends in immigration and birth persist, by the year 2000 the population of Asian Americans will increase by 22 percent, that of Hispanic Americans by 21 percent, and that of African Americans by 12 percent. During this same period non-Hispanic whites are expected to increase by a mere 2 percent. In some places, such as California and New York, the future has already arrived. In New York, for example, 40 percent of all primary and secondary students belong to an ethnic minority, while in California that figure stands at 51 percent.

A sociology textbook that does not acknowledge and explore the many implications of this fundamental demographic shift simply cannot adequately introduce the realities of life in a multicultural society. Thus, Perspectives boxes entitled "Cultural Diversity in U.S. Society" explore issues such as conflict over the primacy of English versus Spanish in Miami and other cities (chapter 2); a Hispanic American's belated reaction to his school socialization (chapter 3); problems in defining deviance among newly-arrived immigrants from vastly dissimilar cultures (chapter 8); the immigrant's path to political participation (chapter 15); and problems in the Korean-American family (chapter 16) (see page IS-xi for a complete listing of features).

These featured sections, as well as in-text discussion, allow students to apply the sociological imagination to present-day society and to connect key sociological concepts, such as culture, socialization, deviance, race, gender, and social class, to their own and others' experiences—and to their understanding of the social structure of U.S. society.

Society in Cross-Cultural Perspective.   In the new global economy, the interdependent fate of nations affects students' lives in many crucial areas, from influencing the kinds of skills and knowledge they need, types of work available to them, and costs of the goods and services they consume, to whether their country is at war or peace. In addition to a strong emphasis on global issues in individual chapters—including a separate chapter on "Stratification in Global Perspective," extensive coverage in the six institutions chapters, and a global focus in the final chapter on Social Change, Technology and the Environment—the "Society in Cross-Cultural Perspective" feature address issues such as ethnic conflict among nations and states (chapter 15); health care in other countries (chapter 19); urbanization in the Third World (chapter 20); and the threats posed to the world's remaining preliterate tribes and the consequences, including the loss of important kinds of knowledge, this poses to developed nations (see page IS-xi for a complete listing of features).

The focus on global diversity is further reinforced through a special collection of CNN videos, a multi- and cross-cultural reader containing nearly 100 articles from the Washington Post, and a supplement titled *Breaking the Ice: A Guide to Understanding People from Other Cultures,* all of which are described below.

Down-to-Earth Sociology

Text chapters also contain Down-to-Earth Sociology features, which explore the sociological implications of everyday events. Making use of the central insights provided by the major perspectives—including the symbolic interactionist contribution that we use symbols to create social life; the functionalist insight that people's actions have both manifest and latent consequences; and the conflict insight that groups compete for scarce resources, the Down-to-Earth feature illustrates how these processes occur in such areas as college football as social structure (chapter 4); women surviving in the male-dominated business world (chapter 7); a sociological explanation of jealousy (chapter 16); and kindergarten as boot camp (chapter 17) (see page IS-xi for a complete listing of Down-to-Earth features).

A "Down-to-Earth" Writing Style.   The Down-to-Earth theme is reinforced throughout the text by a friendly, accessible writing style. As long years of teaching have shown me, all too often textbooks are written to appeal to the adopters of texts rather than to the students who must learn from them. Thus, a central concern in writing *Sociology: A Down-to-Earth Approach* has been to expose students to the concepts covered in an introductory course in a manner that facilitates understanding—and excitement. During the course of writing other texts, I have often been told that my explanations and writing style were "down-to-earth," or accessible and inviting to students—so much so that we have used the phrase in the title of this text. The term is also highlighted in my introductory reader *Down to Earth Sociology,* 7/e (Free Press 1993).

This down-to-earth quality is seen in the introductory vignettes, some of which are based on my personal sociological investigations, which invite the student into each chapter. It is also manifested by the absence of unnecessary jargon, concise explanations, the use of clear and simple (but not reductive) language, and by the many student-relevant examples used to illustrate key concepts. In addition, "In Sum" sections appear at several points throughout each chapter, summarizing the major points made in each section.

Thinking Critically about Social Controversy

Integrated directly within the body of many chapters, the reader will also find "Thinking Critically about Social Controversy" sections. These address pressing and often controversial social issues, such as racism on campus, abortion as a social movement, children in poverty, downward social mobility, and the "second shift." These features contrast several points of view or theoretical interpretations about an area of social controversy and, after presenting these multiple perspectives, ask the student to evaluate the issue for him- or herself. In "Whose History," for instance (chapter 12), the controversy over multiculturalism in textbooks is presented, along with the many unresolved questions it has brought in its wake. These sections make excellent points of departure for class discussion.

IN-TEXT LEARNING AIDS

Sociology: A Down-to-Earth Approach includes a number of pedagogical aids to help students learn, including:

Marginal Key Terms.   Key terms are boldfaced in the text and defined in the margins. These terms provide students with a working definition of the most important sociological concepts as they are introduced and applied.

"In Sum" Sections.   Summarizing paragraphs labeled "In Sum" appear at several points within each chapter, reviewing the important concepts of the preceeding discussion. These sections help students intermittently review important points before proceeding to new material.

Chapter Summaries.   Numbered chapter summaries review, highlight, and reinforce the most important concepts and issues discussed in each chapter.

Recommended Readings.   Each chapter concludes with a list of recommended readings, which are useful for student papers. Relevant sociological journals are also listed.

Comprehensive Glossary.   A comprehensive glossary found at the end of the book brings together all important concepts and terms introduced throughout the text into a single, accessible format.

ACKNOWLEDGMENTS

Although writing this text engulfed my life for longer than I care to recall, it represents the contributions of many people. First, I owe a debt of gratitude to the fine reviewers whose perceptive comments have improved its presentation. I was pleased with the efforts they put into the reviewing process, and I have done my best to accommodate their suggestions. I wish to thank:

Sandra L. Albrecht
The University of Kansas

Kenneth Ambrose
Marshall University

Karren Baird-Olsen
Kansas State University

Linda Barbera-Stein
The University of Illinois

John K. Cochran
The University of Oklahoma

John Darling
University of Pittsburgh—Johnstown

Nanette J. Davis
Portland State University

Lynda Dodgen
North Harris Community College

Obi N. I. Ebbe
State University of New York—
        Brockport

David O. Friedrichs
University of Scranton

Norman Goodman
State University of New York—Stony
        Brook

Donald W. Hastings
The University of Tennessee—
    Knoxville

Charles E. Hurst
The College of Wooster

Mark Kassop
Bergen Community College

Alice Abel Kemp
University of New Orleans

Diana Kendall
Austin Community College

Gary Kiger
Utah State University

Abraham Levine
El Camino Community College

Ron Matson
Wichita State University

Armand L. Mauss
Washington State University

Robert Meyer
Arkansas State University

W. Lawrence Neuman
University of Wisconsin—Whitewater

Laura O'Toole
University of Delaware

Phil Piket
Joliet Junior College

Adrian Rapp
North Harris Community College

Walt Shirley
Sinclair Community College

Marc Silver
Hofstra University

Susan Sprecher
Illinois State University

Larry Weiss
University of Alaska

Douglas White
Henry Ford Community College

Stephen R. Wilson
Temple University

Stuart Wright
Lamar University

Second, I also am indebted to the capable staff of Allyn & Bacon—especially to Karen Hanson, who gave such positive feedback to the early manuscript; to Susan Badger, who initiated the project; to Deborah Fogel, for thorough copyediting; to Susan McNally for coordinating the project; and to those fine people in the art and production departments.

Finally, I cannot adequately express my appreciation to Hannah Rubenstein. If I were to compile a list of characteristics I desired in a development editor, it would include intelligence and dedication, of course. Those I received in abundance. By themselves, that would have been adequate. The surprise was the remarkable insight, and the humor under pressure—all wrapped up in a tireless worker who insisted on perfection. It was my privilege, Hannah.

It is with this goal—of making the introductory course in sociology an enjoyable, challenging, and eye-opening experience—that I have written this book. It is my privilege that you have selected *Sociology: A Down-to-Earth Approach* to use in your teaching. I will also count it a privilege if you will share your teaching experiences, including any suggestions for improving the text. I am not averse to receiving criticisms, for they allow me to see matters in a different light and to improve my efforts.

I wish you the very best in your teaching, and it is my sincere hope that this text contributes to that success. I look forward to hearing from you.

James M. Henslin
Department of Sociology
Southern Illinois University
Edwardsville, Illinois 62026

About the Author

James M. Henslin, who was born in Minnesota, graduated from high school and junior college in California and from college in Indiana. He earned his Master's and doctorate in sociology at Washington University in St. Louis, Missouri. His primary interests in sociology are the sociology of everyday life, deviance, social psychology, and the homeless. Among his more than a dozen books is *Down to Earth Sociology* (Free Press), now in its seventh edition, a book of readings that reflects these sociological interests. He has also published widely in sociology journals, including *Social Problems* and *American Journal of Sociology*.

While a graduate student, James Henslin taught at the University of Missouri at St. Louis. After completing his doctorate, he joined the faculty at Southern Illinois University, Edwardsville, where he is Professor of Sociology. He requests the introductory course, teaching it several times each year. He says, "I've always found the introductory course enjoyable to teach. I love to see students' faces light up when they first glimpse the sociological perspective and begin to see how society has become an essential part of how they view the world."

Henslin enjoys spending time with his family, reading, and fishing. His two favorite activities are writing and traveling. He especially enjoys living in other cultures, for this brings him face to face with behaviors that he cannot take for granted, experiences that "make sociological principles come alive."

Instructor's Section Contents

1 The Sociological Perspective *IS-1*

Summary *IS-1*
Outline *IS-1*
Learning Objectives *IS-2*
Key Terms *IS-3*
Key People *IS-3*
Class Discussion Questions *IS-3*
Projects *IS-4*
Transparencies *IS-4*
Videos/Movies *IS-4*
Speaker Suggestions *IS-5*
Pop Quiz Questions *IS-5*
Essay Questions *IS-5*

2 Culture *IS-6*

Summary *IS-6*
Outline *IS-6*
Learning Objectives *IS-7*
Key Terms *IS-8*
Key People *IS-8*
Class Discussion Questions *IS-8*
Projects *IS-8*
Transparencies *IS-9*
Videos/Movies *IS-9*
Speaker Suggestions *IS-9*
Pop Quiz Questions *IS-10*
Essay Questions *IS-10*

3 Socialization *IS-11*

Summary *IS-11*
Outline *IS-11*
Learning Objectives *IS-13*
Key Terms *IS-13*
Key People *IS-13*
Class Discussion Questions *IS-13*
Projects *IS-14*
Transparencies *IS-14*
Videos/Movies *IS-15*
Speaker Suggestions *IS-15*
Pop Quiz Questions *IS-15*
Essay Questions *IS-15*

4 Social Structure and Social Interaction: Macrosociology and Microsociology *IS-16*

Summary *IS-16*
Outline *IS-16*
Learning Objectives *IS-17*
Key Terms *IS-18*
Key People *IS-18*
Class Discussion Questions *IS-18*
Projects *IS-18*
Transparencies *IS-19*
Videos/Movies *IS-19*
Speaker Suggestions *IS-19*
Pop Quiz Questions *IS-19*
Essay Questions *IS-20*

5 How Sociologists Do Research *IS-21*

Summary *IS-21*
Outline *IS-21*
Learning Objectives *IS-22*
Key Terms *IS-23*
Key People *IS-23*
Class Discussion Questions *IS-23*
Projects *IS-23*
Transparencies *IS-24*
Videos/Movies *IS-24*
Speaker Suggestions *IS-25*
Pop Quiz Questions *IS-25*
Essay Questions *IS-25*

6 Social Groups: Societies to Social Networks *IS-26*

Summary *IS-26*
Outline *IS-26*
Learning Objectives *IS-27*
Key Terms *IS-28*
Key People *IS-28*
Class Discussion Questions *IS-28*
Projects *IS-29*
Transparencies *IS-29*
Videos/Movies *IS-29*

INSTRUCTOR'S SECTION

Speaker Suggestions   *IS-30*
Pop Quiz Questions   *IS-30*
Essay Questions   *IS-30*

7   Bureaucracies and Formal Organizations   IS-31

Summary   *IS-31*
Outline   *IS-31*
Learning Objectives   *IS-32*
Key Terms   *IS-33*
Key People   *IS-33*
Class Discussion Questions   *IS-33*
Projects   *IS-33*
Transparencies   *IS-34*
Videos/Movies   *IS-34*
Speaker Suggestions   *IS-34*
Pop Quiz Questions   *IS-35*
Essay Questions   *IS-35*

8   Deviance and Social Control   IS-36

Summary   *IS-36*
Outline   *IS-36*
Learning Objectives   *IS-38*
Key Terms   *IS-38*
Key People   *IS-39*
Class Discussion Questions   *IS-39*
Projects   *IS-39*
Transparencies   *IS-40*
Videos/Movies   *IS-40*
Speaker Suggestions   *IS-41*
Pop Quiz Questions   *IS-41*
Essay Questions   *IS-41*

9   Stratification in Global Perspective   IS-42

Summary   *IS-42*
Outline   *IS-42*
Learning Objectives   *IS-44*
Key Terms   *IS-44*
Key People   *IS-45*
Class Discussion Questions   *IS-45*
Projects   *IS-45*
Transparencies   *IS-46*
Videos/Movies   *IS-46*
Speaker Suggestions   *IS-47*
Pop Quiz Questions   *IS-47*
Essay Questions   *IS-47*

10   Social Class in American Society   IS-48

Summary   *IS-48*
Outline   *IS-48*
Learning Objectives   *IS-50*
Key Terms   *IS-50*
Key People   *IS-51*
Class Discussion Questions   *IS-51*
Projects   *IS-51*
Transparencies   *IS-52*
Videos/Movies   *IS-52*
Speaker Suggestions   *IS-53*
Pop Quiz Questions   *IS-53*
Essay Questions   *IS-53*

11   Inequalities of Gender   IS-54

Summary   *IS-54*
Outline   *IS-54*
Learning Objectives   *IS-56*
Key Terms   *IS-56*
Key People   *IS-56*
Class Discussion Questions   *IS-56*
Projects   *IS-57*
Transparencies   *IS-57*
Videos/Movies   *IS-58*
Speaker Suggestions   *IS-58*
Pop Quiz Questions   *IS-59*
Essay Questions   *IS-59*

12   Inequalities of Race and Ethnicity   IS-60

Summary   *IS-60*
Outline   *IS-60*
Learning Objectives   *IS-62*
Key Terms   *IS-62*
Key People   *IS-62*
Class Discussion Questions   *IS-62*
Projects   *IS-63*
Transparencies   *IS-63*
Videos/Movies   *IS-63*
Speaker Suggestions   *IS-65*
Pop Quiz Questions   *IS-65*
Essay Questions   *IS-65*

13   Inequalities of Age   IS-66

Summary   *IS-66*
Outline   *IS-66*
Learning Objectives   *IS-68*
Key Terms   *IS-68*

Key People   *IS-68*
Class Discussion Questions   *IS-68*
Projects   *IS-69*
Transparencies   *IS-69*
Videos/Movies   *IS-69*

Speaker Suggestions   *IS-70*
Pop Quiz Questions   *IS-70*
Essay Questions   *IS-70*

14 The Economy: Money and Work   *IS-71*

Summary   *IS-71*
Outline   *IS-71*
Learning Objectives   *IS-73*
Key Terms   *IS-73*
Key People   *IS-74*
Class Discussion Questions   *IS-74*
Projects   *IS-74*
Transparencies   *IS-75*
Videos/Movies   *IS-75*

Speaker Suggestions   *IS-75*
Pop Quiz Questions   *IS-76*
Essay Questions   *IS-76*

15 Politics: Power and Authority   *IS-77*

Summary   *IS-77*
Outline   *IS-77*
Learning Objectives   *IS-79*
Key Terms   *IS-79*
Key People   *IS-80*
Class Discussion Questions   *IS-80*
Projects   *IS-80*
Transparencies   *IS-80*
Videos/Movies   *IS-81*

Speaker Suggestions   *IS-81*
Pop Quiz Questions   *IS-81*
Essay Questions   *IS-82*

16 The Family: Our Introduction to Society   *IS-83*

Summary   *IS-83*
Outline   *IS-83*
Learning Objectives   *IS-86*
Key Terms   *IS-86*
Key People   *IS-86*
Class Discussion Questions   *IS-86*
Projects   *IS-87*
Transparencies   *IS-87*

Videos/Movies   *IS-87*
Speaker Suggestions   *IS-88*
Pop Quiz Questions   *IS-89*
Essay Questions   *IS-89*

17 Education: Transferring Knowledge and Skills   *IS-90*

Summary   *IS-90*
Outline   *IS-90*
Learning Objectives   *IS-92*
Key Terms   *IS-92*
Key People   *IS-92*
Class Discussion Questions   *IS-93*
Projects   *IS-93*
Transparencies   *IS-93*
Videos/Movies   *IS-93*
Speaker Suggestions   *IS-94*
Pop Quiz Questions   *IS-94*
Essay Questions   *IS-95*

18 Religion: Establishing Meaning   *IS-96*

Summary   *IS-96*
Outline   *IS-96*
Learning Objectives   *IS-98*
Key Terms   *IS-99*
Key People   *IS-99*
Class Discussion Questions   *IS-99*
Projects   *IS-99*
Transparencies   *IS-100*
Videos/Movies   *IS-100*
Speaker Suggestions   *IS-101*
Pop Quiz Questions   *IS-101*
Essay Questions   *IS-101*

19 Medicine: Health and Illness   *IS-102*

Summary   *IS-102*
Outline   *IS-102*
Learning Objectives   *IS-105*
Key Terms   *IS-105*
Key People   *IS-105*
Class Discussion Questions   *IS-105*
Projects   *IS-106*
Transparencies   *IS-106*
Videos/Movies   *IS-107*
Speaker Suggestions   *IS-108*
Pop Quiz Questions   *IS-108*
Essay Questions   *IS-108*

INSTRUCTOR'S SECTION

20 Population and Urbanization *IS-109*

Summary   *IS-109*
Outline   *IS-109*
Learning Objectives   *IS-111*
Key Terms   *IS-112*
Key People   *IS-112*
Class Discussion Questions   *IS-112*
Projects   *IS-112*
Transparencies   *IS-113*
Videos/Movies   *IS-113*
Speaker Suggestions   *IS-114*
Pop Quiz Questions   *IS-114*
Essay Questions   *IS-114*

21 Collective Behavior and Social Movements *IS-115*

Summary   *IS-115*
Outline   *IS-115*
Learning Objectives   *IS-118*
Key Terms   *IS-118*
Key People   *IS-119*

Class Discussion Questions   *IS-119*
Projects   *IS-119*
Transparencies   *IS-119*
Videos/Movies   *IS-119*
Speaker Suggestions   *IS-120*
Pop Quiz Questions   *IS-120*
Essay Questions   *IS-120*

22 Social Change, Technology and the Environment *IS-121*

Summary   *IS-121*
Outline   *IS-121*
Learning Objectives   *IS-123*
Key Terms   *IS-124*
Key People   *IS-124*
Class Discussion Questions   *IS-124*
Projects   *IS-124*
Transparencies   *IS-124*
Videos/Movies   *IS-125*
Speaker Suggestions   *IS-126*
Pop Quiz Questions   *IS-126*
Essay Questions   *IS-126*

CHAPTER

1

The Sociological Perspective

CHAPTER SUMMARY

Sociology offers a perspective—a view of the world—which stresses that people's social experiences underlie their behavior. Sociology is the scientific study of society and human behavior and, as such, is one of the social sciences, which study human behavior, as contrasted with the natural sciences, which focus on nature. Although it is difficult to state precisely when it began, sociology emerged during the upheavals of the Industrial Revolution. Early sociologists were Auguste Comte, Herbert Spencer, Karl Marx, Emile Durkheim, and Max Weber. Sociologists agree on the ideal of objectivity, but disagree concerning the proper purposes and uses of sociology. Because no one theory encompasses all of reality, sociologists use three primary theoretical frameworks: (1) *symbolic interactionism*—which concentrates on the meanings that underlie people's lives—usually focuses on the micro level; (2) *functional analysis*—which stresses that society is made up of various parts which, when working properly, contribute to the stability of society—focuses on the macro level; and (3) *conflict theory*—which stresses inequalities and sees the basis of social life as a competitive struggle to gain control over scarce resources—also focuses on the macro level. The current direction in sociology is toward more applied sociology, which is the application of sociology to solve problems in a variety of settings—from the workplace to the family—in society.

CHAPTER OUTLINE

I. The Sociological Perspective
   A. Importance of perspective: It provides a different way of looking at life, and provides an understanding of why people are the way they are.
   B. Seeing the broader social context looks at (1) social location—culture, social class, gender, religion, age, and education—of people; (2) the relationship of one group to another; and (3) external influences (people's experiences) which are internalized and become part of one's thinking and motivations. An example would be a hypothetical newborn child taken away from American parents and placed with the Yanomamo tribe.
II. Sociology and the Other Sciences
   A. Sociology and the "scientific study of society and human behavior." Science is the systematic methods used to obtain knowledge and the knowledge obtained by those methods; it can be divided into the natural sciences and the social sciences.
   B. Natural sciences attempt to comprehend, explain, and predict events in our natural environment.
   C. Social sciences attempt to objectively understand the social world, and include the following:
      1. political science (focuses on politics or government);
      2. economics (analyzes the production, distribution, and allocation of material goods and services of a society);
      3. anthropology (primarily focuses on preliterate peoples and attempts to understand culture);
      4. psychology (concentrates on processes that occur within the individual); and
      5. sociology (looks at all social institutions, focuses on industrialized societies, and looks at external factors which influence people).
   D. Goals of science: (1) explain why something happens; (2) generalize—go beyond individual cases to make statements applying to a broader area, based on patterns, etc.; and (3) predict—specify what will happen in the future.
III. The Development of Sociology
   A. Sociology developed in the mid-19th century as a result of three factors:
      1. social upheaval in Europe resulting from the Industrial Revolution;
      2. imperialism (conquering other nations exposed people to differing cultures); and
      3. the success of the natural sciences created a desire for answers about the social world as well.
   B. Contributions of early sociologists

1. Auguste Comte coined the term "sociology" and suggested the use of positivism (applying the scientific approach to the social world) but did not utilize this approach himself.
2. Herbert Spencer viewed societies as evolutionary; he coined the term "survival of the fittest;" became known for social Darwinism.
3. Karl Marx, founder of the conflict perspective, believed that class conflict (struggle between proletariat and bourgeoisie) was the key to human history.
4. Emile Durkheim studied social factors underlying suicide; found people with low levels of social integration (weak social ties) are most likely to commit suicide. He coined the term anomie to refer to lack of social integration; stated that industrial societies encourage anomie by their division of labor (into occupational specialties); and found that altruistic suicide may occur when people have very strong social bonds.
5. Max Weber defined the role of religion as a central force in social change.

IV. The Role of Values in Social Research
A. Value free sociology (i.e., that a sociologist's personal values and/or biases should not influence social research) was advocated by Weber.
B. Objectivity (total neutrality) should be a hallmark of sociological research, according to Weber. Although it is a proper goal, no one can escape values entirely. Replication (repeating a study to see if same results produced) is one means to avoid the value distortions.
C. Proper purposes and uses of sociology are important.

V. *Verstehen* and Social Facts
A. Weber and *Verstehen* ("to grasp by insight"): To understand behavior, look at the subjective meanings that people attach to their own behavior. Example is studies of the homeless in which understanding of people's behavior can be gained by applying *Verstehen*.
B. Durkheim and Social Facts: Social facts are patterns of behavior that characterize a group; the patterns of behavior reflect underlying conditions of society.

VI. Sociology in North America
A. The first U.S. sociology department was at the University of Chicago. Albion Small founded that department and the *American Journal of Sociology*. Other early University of Chicago sociologists included Robert E. Park, Ernest Burgess, and George Herbert Mead.
B. W. E. B. Du Bois conducted research on race relations in the United States; he subsequently helped found the NAACP.

C. Other sociologists making outstanding contributions include:
1. Talcott Parsons who demonstrated with models how the parts of society harmoniously work together.
2. Robert K. Merton who stressed that sociologists need to develop middle-range theories (explanations of behavior that go beyond the particular observation or research but avoid sweeping generalizations that attempt to account for everything).
3. C. Wright Mills who urged sociologists to get back to social reform.
D. The Present: American sociology is not dominated by one theoretical orientation, and relatively few sociologists are social activists. Sociologists are employed in teaching, government, the private sector (management and planning positions), and in other fields.

VII. Theoretical Perspectives in Sociology
A. Theory is defined as a statement about how some parts of the world fit together and how they work; how two or more facts relate to each other.
B. The three major theoretical perspectives in sociology are:
1. Symbolic interactionism, which asserts that society is composed of symbols people use to establish meaning, develop a world view, and communicate.
2. Functional analysis, which asserts that society is composed of various parts, each with a function which contributes to society's equilibrium.
3. Conflict theory, which asserts that society is composed of groups competing for scarce resources.
C. Levels of Analysis: Macro and Micro. The macro level examines large-scale patterns of society, while the micro level examines small-scale patterns of society.
D. Putting the theoretical perspectives together: Each provides a different (often sharply contrasting) picture of the world. Sociologists use all three because no one theory or level of analysis encompasses all of reality.

VIII. Applied and Clinical Sociology
A. There are three phases of sociology: The first was concerned with making the world a better place; the second sought to establish sociology as a respected field of knowledge; while the current phase seeks to merge sociological knowledge and practical work.
B. "Pure" sociology makes discoveries about life in human groups, while applied sociology tries to use sociology to solve problems. Evaluative applied sociologists recommend changes, while clinical sociologists become directly involved in bringing about social change through work in various social settings.

LEARNING OBJECTIVES

After reading and studying Chapter 1, the student should be able to:

1. Explain the importance of the sociological perspective in understanding human behavior.

2. Define sociology and compare it with the other social sciences.
3. Discuss how and why sociology emerged as a science in the middle of the 19th century in Europe.

4. Identify and explain the theoretical perspectives of Auguste Comte, Herbert Spencer, Karl Marx, Emile Durkheim, and Max Weber.
5. State the key issues in the sociological debate about the proper role of values in sociology.
6. Explain what Max Weber meant by *Verstehen* and Emile Durkheim meant by social facts.
7. Trace the development of sociology in the United States from its origins at the University of Chicago to its present-day perspectives.
8. Explain the major differences in the three major theoretical perspectives: symbolic interactionism, functional analysis, and conflict theory.
9. Compare micro-level and macro-level analyses and state which level of analysis is utilized by each of the major theoretical perspectives.
10. Describe the three phases of sociology and note the differences in pure, applied, and clinical sociology.

KEY TERMS

anomie
applied sociology
authority
bourgeoisie
class conflict
clinical sociology
common sense
conflict theory
division of labor
functional analysis
generalization
macro level analysis

micro level analysis
middle-range theories
natural sciences
nonverbal interaction
objectivity
patterns
positivism
proleteriat
pure or basic sociology
science
social integration
social interaction

social location
social sciences
social facts
sociological perspective
sociology
subjective meanings
symbolic interactionism
theory
values
value free
Verstehen

KEY PEOPLE

Auguste Comte
Karl Marx
Max Weber
W. E. B. Du Bois
C. Wright Mills

Herbert Spencer
Emile Durkheim
Albion Small
Robert K. Merton

CLASS DISCUSSION QUESTIONS

1. What do you think you may learn from looking at your own world in a different light? How can the sociological perspective be useful for you?
2. What types of subjects might interest political scientists? Economists? Anthropologists? Psychologists? Sociologists?
3. What does the updated version of the old elephant story tell you about the relationship between the social sciences?
4. What commonsense notions did you learn as you were growing up? Would sociologists argue with them?
5. Why do you think the timing was "ripe" in Europe for sociology to develop? Do you think the timing is "ripe" in the United States today for a resurgence of interest in sociology?
6. What do we know about suicide today that confirms some of Durkheim's assumptions of over 100 years ago? In what ways has our knowledge of suicide grown beyond that of Durkheim's day?
7. Can religion bring about social change? Did the teachings of religious leaders such as Dr. Martin Luther King, Jr. lead to social change in the United States?
8. Do you think it is possible for a researcher's preconceived ideas or personal values to interfere with his or her research on capital punishment? Abortion? Euthanasia (mercy killing)?
9. How can *Verstehen* help us to understand why homeless men in a shelter might be silent while college students often are noisy and sometimes boisterous?
10. Do you know why more Americans are born on Tuesday than any other day of the week? How can a combination of social facts and *Verstehen* be useful in explaining this phenomenon?
11. Why were some early American sociologists more interested in social reform or activism than others? Do you think sociologists today are more interested in academic pursuits or social reform?
12. Do you behave differently around relatives than around your closest friends? How would symbolic interactionists interpret your behaviors?
13. How do we learn that "true love" is emotionally satisfying and that it will keep us constantly "turned on"?
14. Have you decided how you wish to divide up family responsibilities with a marriage partner?
15. Do you think divorce should be readily available in a society?

16. Can you think of *any* good reason for your school to double the amount of tuition you currently are paying?
17. Using functional analysis, what do you think accounts for the divorce rate in the United States today?
18. Is the assumption of conflict theory that women have always been assigned the role of taking care of the personal needs of men still valid today? Why or why not?

19. How do you think that micro- and macro-level analyses can contribute to our knowledge of homelessness?
20. Does the sociology department at your school offer applied sociology courses? Would you be interested in taking such courses?

PROJECTS

1. Write a term paper or do an oral report on issues pertaining to the homeless. Read one or more of the following books: (a) Blau, Joel. *The Visible Poor: Homeless in the United States.* NY: Oxford University Press, 1992. (b) Burt, Martha R. *Over the Edge: The Growth of Homelessness in the 1980s.* Washington, DC: The Urban Institute Press, 1992. (c) Golden, Stephanie. *The Women Outside: Meanings and Myths of Homelessness.* Berkeley: University of California Press, 1992. (d) Rossi, Peter H. *Down and Out in America: The Origins of Homelessness.* Chicago: University of Chicago Press, 1989. (e) Snider, Noah. *When There's No Place Like Home: An Autobiography of the Homeless.* Nashville: Thomas Nelson, 1991.
2. Look at the problems of homelessness from the perspective of political scientists, economists, anthropologists, psychologists, and sociologists. Discuss in class or present as a paper.
3. In class, complete and discuss "Enjoying a Sociological Quiz: Sociological Findings versus Common Sense." For an outside project, have individuals not enrolled in a sociology class an-

swer the questions and compare their responses to those of your class.
4. Present a paper or oral discussion on the problems of using common sense to generalize about human behavior. Find examples in the media of "bad" generalizations (e.g., tabloid newspapers and talk shows on television).
5. Draw a timeline placing the lives and works of Comte, Spencer, Marx, Durkheim, and Weber on it, and note the relationship of their lives to the changes in Europe which led to the development of sociology. Write a paper on your findings.
6. Read current articles and books on suicide (e.g., Colt, George Howe. *The Enigma of Suicide.* NY: Summit Books, 1991). Discuss with the class or use your readings as a basis for a paper.
7. Analyze marriage and divorce in the United States. Talk to married, single, divorced, and widowed persons about their views of marriage and divorce. Using your informal survey, write your conclusions based on one of the three major theoretical perspectives.

TRANSPARENCIES

1. (TR#1) Major Theoretical Perspectives in Society

TRANSPARENCY MASTERS

1. (TR#1M) American Marriage, American Divorce
2. (TR#2M) Percentage of a Country's Births to Unmarried Mothers

VIDEOS/MOVIES

Homelessness
Children of Poverty. Profiles some of America's children of poverty, showing the toll taken on children and their mothers by the problems of finding shelter and enough food to survive, trying to prevent kids from becoming victims or perpetrators of crime, and trying to nurture self-esteem in poor children. 26 min. Available from A&B Video Library or from FHS.
Life Stinks. 1991. (Color). Starring Mel Brooks. A money-hungry developer bets he can survive on the streets of Los Angeles for one month without any money. (Rated PG-13). 95 min. Available at video rental stores.
Temporary Dwellings. 1992. Describes a tent city run by the homeless in Seattle. 28 min. Available from FML.

Shelter. 1987. Examines the causes of homelessness through interviews and portraits of the homeless; shows conflicting views of policy makers, government officials, and social providers about what should be done and who should pay. 55 min. Available from FML.

Suicide
Dying to be Heard . . . Is Anybody Listening? Offers specific advice on how to recognize teens in danger of committing suicide and successful intervention. Talks to teens who have attempted suicide about their reasons for trying and about their lives after treatment; profiles a Texas community that

banded together to stop a rash of teen suicides, showing how they turned tragedy into triumph. 25 min. Available from A&B Video Library or FHS.

Elderly Suicide. Suicide is an increasingly common choice as the perceived alternative to chronic disease and pain, waning mental and physical powers, economic stress, and fear of helplessness and total dependence, but leaves family members with high levels of guilt. 28 min. Available from A&B Video Library or FHS.

Marriage/Divorce

Family and Survival. Less than 5% of American households fit the profile of the traditional nuclear family. Broken homes, battered wives, estranged children, and corporate nomads are commonplace today. 52 min. Available from A&B Video Library or from FHS.

Kramer vs. Kramer. 1979. (Color). Fictional representation of divorce and custody in the 1980s. (Rated PG) 130 min. Available at video rental stores.

The War of the Roses. 1989. (Color) Saga of a marriage that goes sour, and two people who become irrational in the process of getting a divorce. Danny DeVito, Michael Douglas, Kathleen Turner. (Rated R) 116 min. Available at video rental stores.

SPEAKER SUGGESTIONS

1. A case worker from a shelter for the homeless—such as the Salvation Army—in your area to talk with students about the realities of life on the streets and, if possible, to share information about the number and types of homeless persons in your city.

2. A colleague who is working on an interesting research project or application to talk briefly about what she/he is doing and whether a specific theoretical perspective is being employed.

3. A marriage or family researcher or therapist to talk about the dynamics of divorce.

POP QUIZ QUESTIONS

True-False

F 1. Sociologists believe that people do what they do because of some sort of internal mechanism, such as instincts.

T 2. Economics is one of the social sciences.

T 3. Sociologists primarily focus on industrialized societies.

F 4. The discipline of sociology started at the University of Chicago.

T 5. Auguste Comte coined the term sociology.

F 6. Emile Durkheim is considered to be the founder of conflict theory.

T 7. Durkheim believed that the division of labor found in industrial societies contributed to anomie.

T 8. Objectivity is a goal of sociology.

F 9. There are five major theories within the discipline of sociology.

F 10. Most clinical sociologists work in medical settings.

ESSAY QUESTIONS

1. Compare and contrast sociology with the other social sciences.

2. Outline the major contributions of the following theorists to the field of sociology: Auguste Comte, Herbert Spencer, Karl Marx, Emile Durkheim, and Max Weber.

3. Discuss the ongoing debate among sociologists over the role of values in social research.

4. Explain the high rate of divorce in the United States from the perspectives of symbolic interactionism, functional analysis, and conflict theory.

5. Differentiate between pure, applied, and clinical sociology.

CHAPTER

2

Culture

CHAPTER SUMMARY

This chapter introduces students to key sociological concepts pertaining to culture. First, it explains what culture is and notes that all human groups have material and nonmaterial culture. Then it compares ideal culture with real culture. All people perceive and evaluate the world through the lens of their own culture. Ethnocentrism is compared with cultural relativism. Components of culture include symbols, language, gestures, values, norms and sanctions, folkways and mores; however, language is the essence of culture, for it allows us to move beyond the present. According to the Sapir-Whorf hypothesis, language not only expresses our thinking and perceptions but actually shapes them. American society is composed of a dominant culture and many subcultures. It also contains a number of countercultures which subscribe to values that set members in opposition to the dominant culture. Core values in American society identified by Robin Williams emphasize personal achievement and success, hard work, and moral orientation. Even though all human groups have certain cultural universals, the specific customs differ from one group to another. To the extent that some animals teach their young certain behavior, animals also have culture; however, no animals have language in the sociological sense of the term.

CHAPTER OUTLINE

I. What Is Culture?
   A. Culture can be defined as the language, beliefs, values, norms, behaviors, and material objects passed from one generation to the next. Material culture consists of jewelry, art, buildings, weapons, etc. Nonmaterial culture consists of beliefs, values, assumptions, and common patterns of behavior (language, gestures, etc.).
   B. Culture provides a taken-for-granted orientation to life. We assume that our own culture is normal or natural, when in fact it is learned. Culture provides the lens through which we evaluate things; it provides a behavioral imperative (what to do) and a moral imperative (defines what we think is right and wrong). Culture shock is the result of coming into contact with a radically different culture which challenges our basic assumptions. Ethnocentrism is using our own culture to judge that of others (it is functional when it creates in-group solidarity; dysfunctional if it leads to harmful discrimination)
   C. Cultural relativism consists of trying to appreciate other groups' ways of life in context, without judging them superior/inferior to our own.
II. Components of Culture
   A. The symbolic basis of culture. Sociologists sometimes refer to nonmaterial culture as symbolic culture, since symbols are used to communicate. A symbol is something to which people attach meaning and then use it to communicate; it includes language, gestures, values, norms, sanctions, folkways, and mores.
   B. Language is a system of symbols (words) that can be put together in an infinite number of ways to communicate abstract thought. It is important because: (1) it is the primary means of communication between people; (2) it allows human experience to pass on to the next generation, which builds on it; (3) it provides a social or shared past; (4) it provides a social or shared future (e.g., the ability to plan future events); (5) it allows shared perspectives or understandings; (6) it allows complex, shared, goal-directed behavior; and (7) it expands connections beyond immediate, face-to-face groups. The Sapir-Whorf hypothesis states that language shapes reality; an example is that of Eskimos having many words for snow, thus differentiating various types of snow.
   C. Gestures are another form of symbols, but may mean one thing in one society and something else in another.
   D. Values, Norms, and Sanctions. Values are standards defining good/bad, beautiful/ugly, etc.; norms are expectations, or rules of behavior; and sanctions are posi-

tive (e.g., a reward, even a smile) or negative (e.g., a fine, a frown) reactions to how people follow norms.

   E. Folkways and Mores. Folkways are norms that are not strictly enforced; mores are norms that are believed essential to core values, and enforced. What is a folkway and what is a more may vary by who is doing it, and where. For example, a man walking down street with upper half of body uncovered is violating a folkway, whereas a woman doing same thing violates mores. Taboos are norms so strongly ingrained that even the thought of them is greeted with revulsion.

III. Subcultures and Countercultures

   A. Subcultures are groups whose values/behaviors are so distinct that they set their members off from the general culture. Society contains thousands of subcultures, both broad and narrow. Occupations are a rich source of subcultures: cabdrivers, artists, pool hustlers, police, prostitutes, thieves, etc., all are subcultures— each is a world within the larger culture, with a distinct view of life, but remains compatible with the dominant culture.

   B. Countercultures are groups whose values set their members in opposition to the dominant culture.

IV. Values in American Society

   A. Sociologist Robin Williams identified the following core values:

     1. achievement and success
     2. individualism
     3. activity and work
     4. efficiency/practicality
     5. science and rationality
     6. progress
     7. material comfort
     8. equality of opportunity
     9. freedom
     10. democracy
     11. humanitarianism
     12. group superiority
     13. education

     14. religiosity
     15. romantic love/monogamy

   B. Values are not independent; value clusters come together to form a larger whole.

   C. Value contradictions exist where values conflict with each other; as society changes, some values are modified (a process known as social change).

   D. Values are dynamic, changing over time; examples of emergent values in the United States are:

     16. leisure (including expectancy of retirement benefits)
     17. physical fitness
     18. self-fulfillment
     19. concern for the environment

   E. Core values do not change without meeting strong resistance.

   F. Values and supporting beliefs may blind people to social problems.

   G. Ideal culture is the ideal values and norms of a people, while

   H. Real culture is the norms and values that people actually follow.

V. Cultural Universals

George Murdock concluded that all human groups have certain cultural universals (courtship, cooking, family, funerals, games, etc.); however, specific customs differ from one group to another.

VI. Animals and Culture

Most animal behavior is controlled by instincts, not culture; however, Jane Goodall discovered that chimpanzees make and use a form of simple tool, evidencing animal culture (learned, shared behavior among animals). By way of example, mating behavior of some animals is learned, rather than pure instinct (e.g., young gorillas raised in captivity mating after watching movie of two adult gorillas mating).

VII. Cultural Diffusion and Cultural Leveling

   A. Cultural diffusion: groups "borrow" culture from one another as a result of contact.

   B. Cultural leveling: The process in which cultures become similar to one another.

LEARNING OBJECTIVES

After reading and studying Chapter 2, the student should be able to:

1. Define culture and explain its material and nonmaterial components.
2. Differentiate between ethnocentrism and cultural relativism.
3. Discuss the symbolic components of culture, including language and gestures.
4. Define the following terms: values, norms, sanctions, folkways, mores and taboos.
5. Compare and contrast dominant culture, subcultures, and countercultures.

6. List the core values in American society as identified by Robin Williams.
7. Explain what is meant by value clusters and value contradictions.
8. Discuss the emergent values in American society and analyze why core values do not change without meeting strong resistance.
9. Define cultural universals and state whether, in actuality, they exist or not.
10. Answer the question, "Do animals have culture?"

KEY TERMS

animal culture
counterculture
cultural diffusion
cultural leveling
cultural relativism
cultural universal
culture
culture shock
ethnocentrism
folkways
gestures

ideal culture
language
material culture
mores
negative sanctions
nonmaterial culture
norms
pluralistic society
positive sanctions
real culture
sanction

Sapir-Whorf hypothesis
sociobiology
subculture
subculture
symbol
symbolic gesture
taboo
tool
value contradictions
value clusters
values

KEY PEOPLE

Edward Sapir
Robin Williams
Jane Goodall

Benjamin Whorf
George Murdock

CLASS DISCUSSION QUESTIONS

1. When we travel to another country, why is it important for us to be aware of the culture in that society?
2. Why are we more comfortable with the customs we learn during childhood, and uncomfortable when our basic assumptions about life are challenged?
3. Do you think that fan or spectator behavior at sports events and patriotic gatherings is an example of ethnocentrism? Why?
4. What would your life be if you had not learned a language? How would you communicate with others if you were hearing impaired?
5. Why do you think language has become a political and a social issue in the United States and Canada?
6. How do gestures help you to communicate your emotions to other people? Give specific examples.
7. Do you think there are any universal gestures? If so, give examples.
8. How do your family and friends use positive and negative sanctions to get you to do what they want?
9. What are the folkways in a fast-food restaurant? What about in an expensive, "white tablecloth" restaurant with tuxedoed waitpersons?
10. How do the values, norms, and sanctions of your fraternity, sorority, or other social club differ from those of the general culture?
11. What do you consider to be an "adequate" education? Is this the same for everyone?
12. Why do some college graduates ask about "retirement benefits" when they apply for their first job? Do you plan to ask this question?
13. Do you think that values can be blinders? If yes, give examples.
14. Are humans programmed by their genes to behave in certain ways? Why or why not?
15. Have you had a pet with which you could communicate? Do social scientists think that animals have language?
16. Can you think of examples of cultural diffusion in the United States? What about types of food? Music? Arts and crafts? Clothing?

PROJECTS

1. Assume that you have arrived for the first time in the United States and that you are going to analyze American culture as an "outsider" might. You may wish to include some of the following in your research: language, values and morality, war, money, friendship, love, use of space, and so forth. If you are an international student, give your first impressions of the United States.
2. Write a paper or give an oral presentation on what a knowledge of the hearing impaired can teach us about the importance of language.
3. Watch entertainment shows, news programs, and advertisements on television with the sound turned off. Take notes and report to the class on the nonverbal communication patterns you observe.
4. Explore these questions: "What values do you think are changing in the United States today? Can you think of emergent values besides those listed in the text?" For a semester project, analyze the ways in which advertisements use American values to sell products and services.
5. Read a number of business-oriented publications, such as *Fortune* and *Forbes,* and analyze the "virtues" which are extolled for getting ahead. Look at biographical data for highly successful individuals—such as the late Sam Walton (founder of WalMart Stores), Ross Perot, or other corporate "ty-

coons." How are their successes used to reinforce the importance of society's core values? According to the "ideal" culture, is success available to everyone? How does this compare with the "real" culture? Present your findings to the class.

6. Go to nearby museums—including those at your own university—to look at the cultural artifacts of societies and to write a paper on the insights you receive about culture, cultural diffusion, and other concepts in this chapter.

Instructors may wish to get additional ideas for projects regarding culture from *Breaking the Ice: A Guide to Understanding People from Other Cultures* by Daisy Akiiki Kabagarama-Muhwezi from Allyn and Bacon.

VIDEOS/MOVIES

Culture

The Five Pillars of Islam. (Color) The world of Islam is shared by some 800 million people of all colors, economic levels and social strata. The five pillars—essential principles—on which Islam rests are discussed, described and put into historical context, as well as the conflict between traditional teaching and the effects of industrialization. 30 min. Available from FHS.

Islam Today. (Color) Oil is the impetus that brought Islam into the late 20th century. The conflicts between traditional values and modern life styles, between vast wealth and indigenous poverty, between the civilization once believed eternally monolithic and the thousands of voices, each demanding satisfaction on a different level—these are the seismic fracture points of the Islamic scene today. 30 min. Available from A&B Video Library and FHS.

Not Without My Daughter. 1991. (Color) An American woman, played by Sally Field, accompanies her Iranian-born husband on a visit to his homeland. Once there, he decides to stay, and she learns that in Iran she has no rights as a wife or a woman. She tries to flee the country with her daughter. (Based on real-life story of Betty Mahmoody.) (Rated PG-13). 114 min. Available at video rental stores.

CNN Video II. *Effects of Losing and Regaining a Culture Among Native-American Women.* Native American women suffer from the breakdown of their group social structure and culture; tape illustrates how they seek to build group cohesiveness through emphasis on native cultural traditions. Available from A&B Video Library.

CNN Video II. *Culture Classes.* As part of a nationwide trend, freshmen at the University of California, Berkeley are required to take at least one class stressing cultural diversity in American studies. The trend to expand traditional American studies is spreading across the nation. Critics say that requiring students to take such cultural diversity courses is a response to social pressure and has no place in higher education. Available from A&B Video Library.

Language

CNN Video II. *Changing U.S. Population and Bilingual Education.* Tape discusses changing U.S. composition and the problems of integrating newest Americans into the greater U.S.

culture. (86 different languages in Los Angeles alone). Available from A&B Video Library.

Language Says It All: Communicating with the Hearing-Impaired Child. 1987. This Academy Award nominated film explores the difficulties of bringing up a hearing-impaired child in a hearing family. Parents candidly express their first shocked reactions on learning their child was deaf. One mother reveals how at first she stopped singing, smiling and talking to her new baby, as she had done so naturally with her other children. 23 min. Available from FML.

The Children Who Learned to Listen. 1990. This film is a follow-up on deaf adults who, as profoundly deaf children, were taught to speak by stimulation of residual hearing. They are now outgoing, well adjusted, and accomplished because they are integrated into society and can communicate with hearing people. 47 min. Available from FML.

Wall Street. 1987. (Color) Starring Michael Douglas, this is a modern-day morality tale about a Wall Street high roller who sells out his values in return for being admitted to that high-powered world. Deals with core values. (Rated R—some adult scenes). 124 min. Available at video rental stores.

Animals: Culture and Language?

Animals: How Smart Are They? Are humans endowed with a unique form of intelligence that separates us from the rest of the animal world, or do animals actually "think" more than we suppose? This program explores some of the research projects under way to answer these questions. 26 min. Available from A&B Video Library and FHS.

Gorillas in the Mist. 1988. (Color) Sigourney Weaver plays Dian Fossey, who journeyed to Africa in 1967 to document the vanishing breed of mountain gorillas for *National Geographic,* learned to communicate with the gorillas, and saw the devastating effect of global capitalism on this endangered species. (PG-13) 129 min. Available at video rental stores.

The Family of Chimps. Based on ethologist Dr. Frans de Waal's book *Chimpanzee Politics* (his unique study at the Amhen Zoo in Holland) this video shows how the largest group of chimpanzees in captivity created a society of its own in what constitutes an almost human community. 55 min. Available from FML.

SPEAKER SUGGESTIONS

1. A person from a different culture or a person who has traveled extensively in other countries to relate his or her experiences in various cultures.

2. A curator from a museum with collection of artifacts from other cultures.

3. A specialist who works with hearing-impaired children to pro-

vide additional insight into the role language plays in human behavior.
4. An anthropologist or ethologist who has worked in primate labs or conducted field research with chimps or gorillas to discuss the extent to which animals have language and culture.

POP QUIZ QUESTIONS

True-False

T 1. Culture is learned by individuals in a given society; it is not "natural."
T 2. Although the particulars of culture differ from one group of people to another, culture itself is universal.
F 3. Ethnocentrism is always dysfunctional in societies.
F 4. According to sociologists, nonmaterial culture and symbolic culture are different components of culture.
T 5. The Sapir-Whorf hypothesis states that thinking and perception are shaped by language.
F 6. Gestures convey somewhat universal meanings to people regardless of their cultural background.

F 7. To sociologists, subcultures and countercultures are virtually identical.
T 8. Values are not independent units; value clusters come together to form a larger whole.
T 9. Core values in a society do not change without meeting strong resistance.
F 10. Cultural universals have existed across societies throughout history.

ESSAY QUESTIONS

1. Define the concept of culture and explain why it "becomes the lens through which we perceive and evaluate what is going on around us."
2. Discuss the importance of language in the development of an ongoing continuity in human culture.
3. Differentiate between subcultures and countercultures. Give several examples of each.
4. Explain why personal achievement, success, hard work, individualism and other core values are so important to many Americans.
5. Outline the key points in the debate regarding whether or not animals have culture in the same sense that members of the human species do. State your own opinion and give reasons why you believe the way you do.
6. Define cultural leveling and explain why there almost is no "other side of the world" today.

CHAPTER

3

Socialization

CHAPTER SUMMARY

Scientists have attempted to determine how many of people's characteristics come from heredity and how many from the social environment. Sociologists have observed feral, isolated, and institutionalized children to help answer this question. These studies have concluded that language and intimate interaction are essential to the development of human characteristics. Research findings of Charles H. Cooley and George H. Mead are discussed to demonstrate that the self is socially constructed. Jean Piaget's four stages in the development of the ability to reason, and Sigmund Freud's components of the personality are presented and discussed. Gender socialization is a primary means of controlling human behavior, and a society's ideals of sex-linked behaviors are reinforced by its social institutions. The main agents of socialization—family, religion, school, peer groups, the mass media, and the workplace are analyzed in terms of the influence of each in socializing people to become full-fledged members of society. Resocialization can occur on either a voluntary or involuntary basis. Involuntary resocialization typically takes place in total institutions. Socialization itself occurs throughout the life course. Although socialization lays down the basic self and establishes other frameworks in which we live, humans are not robots but rational beings who consider options and make choices.

CHAPTER OUTLINE

I. What Is Human Nature?
  A. Feral children: abandoned by parents at early age, raised by animals, they allegedly act like wild animals but, in actuality, probably were raised by their parents as infants, but then abandoned because of mental retardation.
  B. Isolated children show what humans might be like if secluded from society at an early age. Isabelle (isolated in a room with her deaf-mute mother until age six) appeared severely retarded—she had been unable to develop into an intelligent human; subsequent interaction with others at a fairly early age allowed her to reach normal intellectual levels.
  C. Institutionalized children—such as those in orphanages—show that "human" traits (intelligence, cooperative behavior, etc.) result from early close relations.
  D. Studies of monkeys show that the longer and more severe the isolation, the more difficult adjustment becomes.
  E. Babies do not "naturally" develop into human adults—human interaction is necessary to acquire the normal human traits.
II. The Social Development of the Self, Mind, and Emotions
  A. Charles H. Cooley coined the term looking glass self to describe the process whereby human development is created by interaction with others. The process (which is lifelong) contains three steps:
    1. we imagine how we look to others;
    2. we interpret others' reactions (how they evaluate us); and
    3. we develop a self-concept, even if it is erroneous.
  B. George H. Mead referred to how others think of us as the generalized other. He found three stages in the development of the self:
    1. children initially only mimic the gestures/words of others;
    2. at about age three, they play the roles of specific people;
    3. in the first years of school, they become involved in organized (team) games, learning the role of each position.
  Mead distinguished between "I" and "me" in developing the self: the "I" component is a subjective, active, creative part of the social self (e.g., "I shoved him"); and the "me" component is objective, made up of attitudes from interactions with others (e.g., "He shoved me").
  C. Jean Piaget studied children's "cognitive development" and defined four stages they go through in learning:
    1. sensorimotor stage (understanding is limited to di-

rect contact with the environment: touching, listening, etc.);
2. preoperational stage (developing ability to use symbols);
3. concrete operational stage (reasoning abilities become more developed, understand numbers, causation, etc.); and
4. formal operational stage (beginning of abstract thinking). Some people never reach the fourth stage, perhaps because biology may set limits on a particular person and/or social experiences may help some people develop the capacity for abstract thought, while limiting others.
D. Sigmund Freud believed that personality consists of three elements:
1. the id (inherited drives for self-gratification);
2. the ego (balances between the needs of the id and the demands of society; and
3. the superego (social conscience internalized from social groups).
Sociologists object to his view that inborn and unconscious motivations are the primary reasons for human behavior.
E. Development of human emotions parallels the growth in reasoning skills, in the same orderly sequence.
F. Emotions depend on socialization, and vary depending on many factors (e.g., Americans shake hands to express pleasure in meeting someone, while Japanese bow, and Arabs kiss).
G. Most socialization is intended to turn us into conforming members of society.

III. Socialization into Gender
A. Society expects different behaviors from people because they are male or female, and it nudges boys and girls in separate directions: parents begin the process and schools continue it, sorting males and females for various activities and giving them different aspirations.
B. Mass media reinforce society's expectations of gender in many ways: children's books have few females in central roles; women on television are depicted the same way—and dominated by men; commercials rarely use women's voices as the voice-over; music perpetuates stereotypes about sex roles; and newspaper reports are more likely to feature men than women and to depict them in stereotypical roles.

IV. Agents of Socialization
A. Experiences within the family have a life-long impact on us.
1. Working-class parents focus on a child's outward conformity (i.e., be neat and clean, and follow the rules); and
2. Middle-class parents show greater concern for the motivations for their children's behavior.
The type of job held by a parent is a factor: The more closely supervised the job, the more likely the parent is to insist on outward conformity in the child.
B. Religion plays a major role in the socialization of most Americans, even in families that are not "religious."
C. Schools serve manifest (intended) functions for society (e.g., teaching skills and values thought to be appropriate), but also have latent (unintended) functions that

help socialization: Schools place children outside the control of friends/relatives and expose them to new values/ways of looking at the world; and teach that the same rules apply to all and that there are consequences for their actions. Schools also have a hidden curriculum: Values not explicitly taught but an inherent part of school activities.
D. Peer groups—persons of roughly the same age, linked by common interests—are a powerful socializing force because they provide guidelines, form norms regarding values and standards, and enforce values by threat of expulsion.
E. The mass media shapes attitudes, values, and other basic orientations to life: TV has a tremendous impact on the American public because (on the average) adults watch 15 hours of television weekly, and schoolchildren spend more time watching TV than they do in school or interacting with their parents.
F. The workplace is a major agent of socialization for adults: Wilbert Moore divided career socialization into four phases—career choice, anticipatory socialization, conditioning and commitment, and continuing commitment.

V. Resocialization refers to learning new norms, values, attitudes and behaviors, voluntarily or involuntarily.
A. Involuntary resocialization: Erving Goffman coined the term total institution to refer to a place (e.g., boot camps, prisons) where people are cut off from the rest of society and under total control. As part of the process, a degradation ceremony (e.g., fingerprinting, shaving the head, banning personal items, wearing a uniform, etc.) strips away a person's former identity. Involuntary resocialization is extremely effective (isolates the individual from outside influences/information; suppresses previous roles, statuses, norms; replaces them with new rules and values).
B. Voluntary resocialization is learning something contrary to prior experiences, such as may be involved in taking a new job.

VI. Socialization through the Life Course
A. Socialization occurs throughout life.
1. Children formerly were considered miniature adults, but today, children are tender and "innocent," to be guided and developed, and provided with care, comfort, and protecting.
2. Adolescence is a recent social invention, resulting from economic changes which left youth outside the labor force while simultaneously demanding higher levels of education (it is a time of inner turmoil in which youths develop their own standards to claim an identity).
3. Early adulthood (18–29) is now another period during which postadolescents continue to postpone adult responsibilities through extended education.
4. In middle adulthood (30–39), people are much surer of themselves and their goals in life than before, while later adulthood (40–65) results in trying to evaluate the past and come to terms with what lies ahead.
5. "Old age" may result in social devaluation (being

viewed as one who once was worthwhile, but now only offers useless advice).
   B. Alice Rossi asserts that this does not account for the effect of society on our lives—our own experiences must be considered.

VII. Are We Prisoners of Socialization?
   No—each person has a self, which is dynamic, making choices. Each of us is actively involved even in the social construction of the self—we are not doomed to keep our orientations if we do not like them.

LEARNING OBJECTIVES

After reading and studying Chapter 3, the student should be able to:

1. Discuss major studies of feral, isolated, and institutionalized children, stating what they demonstrate about the importance of early contact with other humans for the social development of children.
2. Define socialization.
3. Explain and distinguish between the theories of social development by Charles H. Cooley, George H. Mead, Jean Piaget, and Sigmund Freud.
4. Analyze the relationship between socialization into emotions and social control in society.

5. Describe ways in which gender socialization channels human behavior.
6. Identify the major ways in which cultural stereotypes of the sexes are perpetuated in the mass media.
7. List and describe the influence of each agent of socialization on individuals.
8. Define the term resocialization and give examples of involuntary and voluntary resocialization.
9. Discuss socialization through the life course by summarizing each of the stages. Note the major criticisms of this perspective.
10. Explain why human beings are not prisoners of socialization.

KEY TERMS

degradation ceremony
ego
feral children
gender socialization
generalized other
id
latent functions
looking-glass self
manifest functions

mass media
object permanence
operational
peer group
personal identity kit
resocialization
role
role performance
self

significant other
social devaluation
social environment
social inequality
socialization
superego
taking the role of the other
total institution

KEY PEOPLE

Harry and Margaret Harlow
George Herbert Mead
Sigmund Freud
Alice Rossi

Charles Horton Cooley
Jean Piaget
Erving Goffman

CLASS DISCUSSION QUESTIONS

1. Why do you think it is necessary for infants to be around adult human beings in order to become "human" themselves?
2. Do you think it would be unethical for sociologists to place children in isolation or in institutions to study their development? Why or why not?
3. Can you make a comparison between monkeys and human infants raised in isolation?
4. Is it possible to define yourself apart from the other people in your life? Do you have a totally unique identity that is not tied to others?
5. What were your favorite childhood games? When did you

first become aware that games have rules and other players to deal with?
6. Why do you think it was important for Piaget to add rigorous observation and testing of children to the informal observations and theorizing of Cooley and Mead?
7. Why do most sociologists react negatively to most of Freud's analysis? Can you think of some experts who may still rely on Freudian analysis today?
8. Do you think all people feel the same emotions? Does socialization have anything to do with emotions?
9. Are you free to do whatever you want? Why or why not?

10. How did your family instruct you in what it means to be a girl or boy?
11. What examples can you give of gender stereotyping in the media?
12. How does television serve as an agent of gender socialization?
13. Do you agree with the finding that middle-class parents do not focus on teaching obedience, neatness, and cleanliness to their children as much as working-class parents do? Why or why not?
14. What did you learn in school in addition to academics—such as history, English, or calculus? Were some of the things you learned part of the hidden curriculum?
15. What influence does your peer group have on your choice in clothes? Music? Entertainment? Can you think of other areas?
16. What television programs and movies have you seen recently that you would not want your own children to see? Why?
17. In what way is your college education a part of your career socialization?
18. Do you think that prisons should have a severe resocialization process? Why or why not?
19. Have you, in essence, agreed to participate in voluntary resocialization as a result of your enrollment in college?
20. Is childhood defined in the same way in all societies? If you were given the choice, would you choose to grow up in the society in which you were raised?
21. Why is adolescence a difficult period of transition for some of us?
22. Why do you think some people in later adulthood focus more on the time they have left to live rather than the time since their birth?
23. Can you give examples of positive and negative stereotypes about older adults? Do you think these will change in the future?
24. Will human beings become robots because of socialization?

PROJECTS

1. Read several sources on feral or isolated children. List traits that we take for granted as being "human" (e.g., high intelligence, cooperative behavior, and friendliness). Prove that these are socially created, not inherited behaviors. Find current cases of extreme neglect and abuse reported in the media and compare these with the earlier studies of feral or isolated children. Present your findings in a paper or oral presentation.
2. Conduct a participant observation study to determine the ways in which adults, and especially students, still use others as their "looking glass self" (e.g., clothing styles, jokes, behavior, attitudes, etc.). Present your observations to the class and explain your findings in sociological language.
3. Keep a diary or personal journal describing your activities and make notations about how your emotions vary in different situations.
4. Collect ads from magazines/newspapers, or take notes on television ads depicting men's and/or women's roles. Analyze the pictures for overt and subtle messages about what constitutes "appropriate" behavior for women or men. Be sure to look at ads for alcoholic beverages, cigarettes, cosmetics, perfumes, men's colognes, clothing, and cars. Do a visual presentation for the class, presenting your observations and conclusions in a systematic manner.
5. Do a content analysis of the catalogues, course schedules, and handbooks at your school to determine its manifest functions. Compare these manifest functions with those of other colleges and universities. How are they similar? How are they different? What latent functions does your institution have? Record your findings on a chart to be shown to the class and discussed.
6. Analyze the impact of agents of socialization on children. You may wish to choose the family, religion, schools, peer groups, or mass media. For example, you could look at children's books, toys, or games. In your written analysis, include the following: What were your favorite childhood books, toys, or games? When did you first become aware that games have rules and other players to deal with?
7. Read one or more of the following books and write a term paper on issues pertaining to socialization by television: (a) Ball-Rokeach, Sandra, et al. *The Great American Values Test: Influencing Behavior and Belief Through Television.* NY: Free Press, 1984. (b) Leibert, Robert, and Joyce Sprafkin. *The Early Window: Effects of Television on Children and Youth,* 3rd ed. NY: Pergamon, 1988. (c) Lichter, S. Robert, et al. *Watching America.* New York: Prentice-Hall, 1991. (d) Parenti, Michael. *Inventing the News: The Politics of the Mass Media.* NY: St. Martin's, 1986. (e) Wilson, Clint C., II, and Felix Gutierrez. *Minorities and Media.* Beverly Hills: Sage, 1985.

TRANSPARENCIES

1. (TR#2) Theories of Human Development

TRANSPARENCY MASTERS

1. (TR#3M) Socialization Values

VIDEOS/MOVIES

Human Nature/Socialization

Nature and Nurture. This program from the critically acclaimed "Human Animal" series looks at identical twins separated at birth and finds that biology is not everything: a supportive environment helps to produce well-adjusted adults while a hostile home can produce the contrary. 52 min. Available from A&B Video Library and FHS.

The End of the Line, Orphan Trains. (1991) This program tells about homeless youths from eastern cities who were resettled during the Depression with families on farms in the Midwest as an alternative to institutionalization. Although the orphan trains and traumatic lineups for selection by families seem barbaric by today's standards, the children were saved from almshouses, and when we meet them as adults, we see that their lives were reshaped by the journey because they have grown into healthy, productive individuals. 47 min. Available from FML.

Socialization

CNN Video II. *Kids, TV, Sexism.* Tape explores sexism in children's television. Studies show children pick up on stereotypes by age of 3 or 4. Market research reveals that both boys and girls believe that "boys are better" and prefer to watch programs in which boys take the lead. Some progress is being made, as in the *Beetlejuice* cartoons, which feature girls in leading roles. Critics claim that too little is being done to present a balanced picture of both genders. Available from A&B Video Library.

Shock Waves: Television in America. 1984. Television may be unsurpassed as a communications tool, but what is it communicating? What is the role of TV in our society? Does nightly exposure to violence affect the children watching it? How does the world portrayed on TV differ from the real world? 32 min. Available from A&B Video Library.

Resocialization: Total Institutions

One Flew Over the Cuckoo's Nest. 1975. (Color), starring Jack Nicholson as a feisty misfit who enters a mental institution and inspires his fellow patients to assert themselves. Won five Oscars. (R). 133 min. Available at video rental stores.

Crazy People. 1990. (Color), starring Dudley Moore as a stressed-out advertising executive who is placed in a mental institution because he creates a series of brutally honest advertisements. Moore's character inspires the other patients to believe that they do not need to be in the institution. (R). 90 min. Available at video rental stores.

SPEAKER SUGGESTIONS

1. A person who has worked with feral or autistic children to discuss the importance of socialization in the development of "human" behavior.
2. A colleague who specializes in gender-related research, especially regarding the family or mass media.
3. A therapist who has worked in a total institution in your area, such as a prison, mental hospital, or in-patient chemical-dependency treatment center.

POP QUIZ QUESTIONS

True-False

F 1. The case of Isabelle shows that children can talk even if they have been deprived of human contact.

T 2. Most social scientists today dismiss the significance of feral children, taking the position that children cannot be raised by animals.

T 3. To develop into adults with the characteristics that we take for granted as "human," children need to be surrounded by people who care for them.

F 4. George Herbert Mead coined the term looking-glass self.

T 5. Jean Piaget discovered that children pass through four stages in the development of thinking.

T 6. According to Sigmund Freud, when the id gets out of hand, individuals follow their desires for pleasure and break society's norms.

T 7. Gender serves as a primary basis for social inequality.

F 8. The manifest function of formal education is difficult to identify.

F 9. Resocialization is always an involuntary process which takes place in total institutions.

T 10. The self is never a finished product, and people continue to be in the process of becoming.

ESSAY QUESTIONS

1. State the major issues in the heredity-environment debate. Discuss the importance of human interaction in the development of human adults.
2. Compare and contrast the major theories of social development.
3. Identify the major agents of socialization in contemporary societies. Briefly describe the role of each in the socialization process.
4. Explain the difference in socialization and resocialization. Differentiate between involuntary and voluntary resocialization and give examples of each.
5. Discuss how socialization takes place throughout the life course and state the major criticism of the life-course perspective.

CHAPTER

4

Social Structure and Social Interaction

CHAPTER SUMMARY

Macrosociology investigates the large-scale features of social structure, while microsociology focuses on social interaction. Functional and conflict theorists tend to use a macrosociological approach; symbolic interactionists are more likely to use a microsociological approach. The individual's location in the social structure affects his or her perceptions, attitudes, and behaviors. Culture, social class, social status, roles, groups, and institutions are the major components of the social structure. Functionalists view social institutions as established ways of meeting universal group needs; however, conflict theorists see social institutions as the primary means by which the elite maintains its privileged position. Over time, social structure undergoes changes— sometimes very dramatic—as illustrated by Durkheim's concepts of mechanical and organic solidarity, and Tönnies' constructs of *Gemeinschaft* and *Gesellschaft* at the macro-level of society. In contrast to functionalist and conflict theorists, who as macrosociologists focus on the "big picture," symbolic interactionists tend to be microsociologists who look at social interaction in everyday life. They examine how people look at things and how that, in turn, affects their behavior. The contributions of Erving Goffman's dramaturgical analysis and of ethnomethodologists are discussed. Both macrosociology and microsociology are needed to understand human behavior because we must grasp both social structure and social interaction.

CHAPTER OUTLINE

I. Levels of Sociological Analysis
   A. Macrosociology focuses on large-scale features of social structure; investigates effects of large-scale forces on societies; and is utilized by functionalists and conflict theorists.
   B. Microsociology places emphasis on social interaction— symbolc interaction is an example. Exchange theory looks at human behavior in terms of rewards/costs.

II. Social Structure: The Macrosociological Perspective
   A. Social structure can be defined as the patterned relationships between people that persist over time. Personal feelings/desires tend to be overridden by the social structure; the individual behaviors/attitudes are determined by location in social structure. Major components of social structure are culture, social class, social status, roles, groups, and institutions.
   B. Culture refers to a group's language, beliefs, values, behaviors, and gestures; it includes material objects used by a group; and it determines what kind of people we will become.
   C. Social class in U.S. society generally is based on income, education, and occupational prestige.
   D. Social status refers to positions an individual occupies. A status set is all statuses/positions an individual occupies. Ascribed statuses are positions an individual either inherits at birth or receives involuntarily later in life; achieved statuses are positions earned, accomplished, or that involve at least some effort/activity on the individual's part. Status symbols are signs that identify a status; a master status cuts across other statuses an individual occupies. Status inconsistency is a contradiction or mismatch between statuses.
   E. Roles are behaviors, obligations, and privileges attached to a status. The individual occupies a status, but plays a role; roles are essential to culture: they lay out what is expected of people.
   F. A group is people who regularly and consciously interact with one another and typically share similar values, norms, and expectations. Involuntary associations (e.g., one's family, or sexual, ethnic, and racial group) are groups to which one is assigned, while voluntary associations are groups which people choose to join.
   G. Social institutions are standard ways of meeting society's basic needs. The family, religion, law, politics, economics, education, science, medicine, and the military are examples; these institutions establish the context in which people live. Functional and conflict perspectives on social institutions:

1. Functionalist view: social institutions are established ways of meeting universal group needs;
2. To conflict theorists, social institutions are the primary means by which the elite maintains its privileged position.

H. Changes in social structure occur due to changes in culture, shifts in social classes/racial and ethnic groups, globalization, etc.

I. What holds society together? Social cohesion (the degree to which members of a society feel united by shared values and other social bonds). Emile Durkheim used (1) mechanical solidarity (the collective consciousness people have due to performing the same or similar tasks) and organic solidarity (the collective consciousness based on the interdependence resulting from division of labor) to explain what holds society together.

J. Ferdinand Tönnies analyzed how *Gemeinschaft* (a society in which life is intimate, each knows the other, and shares a sense of togetherness) was being replaced by *Gesellschaft* (society dominated by impersonal relationships, individual accomplishments, self-interest).

III. The Microsociological Perspective: Social Interaction in Everyday Life

A. Emphasizes face-to-face social interaction (what people do when they are in the presence of one another).

B. Symbolic interactionists examine symbols people use to define their worlds, how they look at things, and how that affects their behavior. Stereotypes are first impressions shaped by assumptions based on another's sex, race, age, and physical appearance; they affect ideas about and conduct toward the person, and tend to bring out the behavior that fits the stereotype. The term personal space is used to define people's "boundaries." The amount preferred varies from one culture to another. Edward Hall found Americans use four distance zones:
1. intimate distance (18 inches);
2. Personal distance (up to 4 feet) for friends, etc.;

3. social distance (4 to 12 feet) for impersonal or formal relationships such as job interviews; and
4. public distance (beyond 12 feet) for speakers, etc.

C. Dramaturgy—the approach pioneered by Erving Goffman for analyzing social life. According to Goffman, socialization prepares people for learning to perform on the stage of everyday life. Role performance is the emphasis/interpretation an individual gives a role, the person's "style." Role conflict occurs when expectations attached to one role are incompatible (and conflict) with those of another role. Role strain refers to conflicts someone feels within a role. Impression management is a person's efforts to manage the impressions others have of her or him. Three sign vehicles used to communicate information about the self to others are:
1. social setting (where action unfolds);
2. appearance when playing the role; and
3. manner (attitudes demonstrated in playing the role).

D. Ethnomethodology studies how people make sense of everyday life; it tries to uncover people's background assumptions which form the basic core of one's reality. Background assumptions are deeply embedded in understandings concerning world view. Harold Garfinkel founded this approach.

E. Social construction of reality refers to what people define as real because of their background. Symbolic interactionists believe people define their own reality, then live within those definitions. The (W. I.) Thomas theorem: "If people define situations as real, they are real in their consequences." Sociologists Peter Berger and Thomas Luckmann note that members of a society agree on definitions of what is going on and then cooperate to maintain those definitions.

IV. The Need for Both Microsociology and Macrosociology
To understand human behavior, it is necessary to grasp both social structure (macrosociology) and social interaction (microsociology)

LEARNING OBJECTIVES

After reading and studying Chapter 4, the student should be able to:

1. Differentiate between macrosociology and microsociology.
2. Indicate which levels of analysis are most likely to be used by functionalists, conflict theorists, and symbolic interactionists.
3. Discuss social structure and explain why one's location in this structure affects that person's perceptions, attitudes, and behaviors.
4. Define the following concepts: culture, social class, social status, roles, groups, and social institutions.
5. Compare and contrast functionalists' and conflict theorists' views regarding social institutions.
6. Use Durkheim's concepts of mechanical and organic solidar-

ity and Tönnies' typologies of *Gemeinschaft* and *Gesellschaft* to explain what holds societies together.
7. State the key assumptions of the symbolic interaction perspective regarding social life.
8. Explain how stereotypes influence an individual's expectations and behavior.
9. Name the sociologist who originated the dramaturgical perspective and outline the key components of this view of everyday life.
10. State the major assumptions of ethnomethodology and of the social construction of reality.
11. Indicate why both macrosociology and microsociology are necessary for a full understanding of social life.

KEY TERMS

achieved statuses
appearance
ascribed statuses
back stage
background assumptions
division of labor
dramaturgy
embarrassment
ethnomethodology
face-saving behavior
front stage
functional requisites
Gemeinschaft
Gessellschaft
group
impression management

involuntary membership (involuntary
    association)
macrosociology
manner
master status
mechanical solidarity
microsociology
organic solidarity
props
role
role conflict
role performance
role strain
scenery
sign-vehicles
social class

social cohesion
social construction of reality
social institutions
social interaction
social setting
social structure
status
status inconsistency
status set
status symbols
status inconsistency
studied nonobservance
tact
teamwork
Thomas theorem
voluntary memberships (voluntary
    association)

KEY PEOPLE

Emile Durkheim
Edward Hall
Harold Garfinkel
Peter Berger

Ferdinand Tönnies
Erving Goffman
W. I. Thomas
Thomas Luckmann

CLASS DISCUSSION QUESTIONS

1. Why do you think that most people avoid street people? How might sociologists analyze street people?
2. If people know that you are in college, what does that tell them about you?
3. Do you feel uncomfortable if you enter a crowded classroom and find that someone has already placed their books or coat on the chair in which you usually sit? Why or why not?
4. In what ways are our ideas, attitudes, and behaviors dependent on the social class to which we belong?
5. What do you think of when you hear the word "status?" What do sociologists mean when they use this term?
6. Why do some people wear wedding rings? What are some reasons for not wearing a ring?
7. What is your master status?
8. Why are our roles a sort of fence that keeps us doing what society wants us to do?
9. What are the rules of some of the groups to which you belong that must be followed or you will no longer be in "good standing"?
10. Why are social institutions so important in everyone's life?
11. How do societies manage to stay together in spite of the presence of many competing groups and extensive social change?

12. How do our first impressions about a person affect our ideas about the person? How we will act toward the person? The way that person subsequently will act toward us?
13. What are your "front stages" on which you are expected to perform? What are your "back stages" where you can let your hair down?
14. Does everyone experience role conflict at one time or another? What about role strain?
15. Why is showing ourselves as adept role players a chief requirement for receiving positive recognition from others?
16. Why would we be shocked and surprised if a physician gave us a haircut? (Except as preparation for brain surgery, of course!)
17. Is reality something "out there" that hits us in the face?
18. Do you believe that germs pose a threat to your well-being because you know for a fact that germs are real or because you were taught that they were real?
19. If you were a sociologist conducting a study on juvenile offenses, would you use microsociology, macrosociology, or both? Why?

PROJECTS

1. Create a chart which shows: (a) all groups and organizations—including family and friendship groups—to which you belong; (b) your status(es) in each group; (c) whether each status is ascribed or achieved; and (d) what, if any, status

symbol goes with each status. Then analyze your roles in regard to the various statuses you occupy. Present a written analysis of your observations. Compare your chart and conclusions with other class members to determine similarities and differences in your perceptions.

2. Analyze personal space or your own "personal bubble." Keep a record of situations in which you feel uncomfortable because a person or other people are "too close" for comfort. Examples: (1) You are in an elevator alone; one person gets on. How close are you willing for that individual to stand to you? Do you have any objection to the person looking right at you for the duration of the elevator ride? (2) You are on an almost full elevator; you are standing near the doors, and an additional person gets on. How close are you willing for that additional person to stand to you? (3) You are sitting in an almost empty movie theater, and a person sits down right beside you. Will you stay there or will you move? (4) You are sitting in a packed movie theater, and a person sits down

right beside you. Will you stay there or will you move? Think of hypothetical situations of your own and find real situations in your everyday life to present to the class.

3. Select a situation in which you will act as if you do not understand the basic rules of social life. Examples: washing clothes (without soap) in the apartment complex swimming pool; bargaining with a grocery store clerk about prices; or doing something "out of character" around someone who knows you well. Observe—and later record—the reactions of other people. DO NOT DO ANYTHING ILLEGAL OR DANGEROUS! Stop the activity before you have created a problem, gotten in trouble, or lost a friend! Report your findings to the class.

4. Analyze your daily activities by using Goffman's dramaturgical approach. Take notes as you act out your various roles, on front stages and back stages, etc. Using dramaturgical language, write a report about your activities.

TRANSPARENCIES

1. (TR#3) Self-Fulfilling Stereotypes
2. (TR#4) Role Strain and Role Conflict

VIDEOS/MOVIES

College Football as Social Structure
Knute Rockne, All American. 1940 (New colorized version) Biography of famed Notre Dame football coach, with Ronald Reagan as his star player. 96 min. Available at video rental stores.

The Amish People
CNN Video II. *The Amish People.* A description of the Amish in Lancaster, PA. Available from A&B Video Library.

The Amish: Not to Be Modern. 1985. Looks at the Amish over four seasons, capturing the day-to-day life of a people who have preserved rural traditions. 57 min. Available from FML.

Amish Riddle. 1992. Video on the Amish in Pennsylvania who have gently modified their rules so they are able to prosper in commercial enterprises. While they shun modern conveniences, they are permitted to incorporate them into their business endeavors (e.g., use of telephones for business but not for social calls). 50 min. Available from FML.

SPEAKER SUGGESTIONS

1. A colleague who has been conducting cross-cultural research to talk about ways in which social class, social status, ascribed and achieved statuses, status symbols, master statuses, roles, groups, and social institutions are experienced in other cultures.
2. A symbolic interactionist to talk about how research is conducted at the microsociological level.

3. A cartoonist who draws satirical or political cartoons for your university or local newspaper to discuss the use of exaggerated physical and character traits (stereotypes) to help encapsulate ideas easily for viewers.

POP QUIZ QUESTIONS

True-False
T 1. Sociologists who use the macrosociological approach analyze such things as social class and how groups are related to one another.
F 2. Microsociology places emphasis on social interaction.
F 3. People in a specific society learn similar behaviors and attitudes regardless of their location in the social structure.

F 4. When sociologists use the term "status," they are referring to prestige.
F 5. Ascribed statuses are voluntary and are earned or accomplished by the individual.
T 6. A person occupies a status, but she or he plays a role.
T 7. The family into which a person is born is an involuntary membership group.

F   8. Most people are aware of how profoundly their lives are affected by social structure.

F   9. Conflict theorists believe that social institutions exist because they perform vital functions for society.

F 10. The dramaturgical perspective was developed by Emile Durkheim.

ESSAY QUESTIONS

1. Explain why social structure and social interaction are of interest to sociologists. Not why both microsociology and macrosociology are important in understanding human behavior.

2. Using college football as an example, demonstrate how sociologists might study this sport from the standpoint of its social structure.

3. Discuss how one's location in the social structure affects her or his perceptions, attitudes, and behaviors.

4. Compare the functionalists' and conflict theorists' views on social institutions.

5. Outline the major findings of symbolic interactionists regarding the following: (1) the importance of stereotypes in everyday life; and (2) how people use physical space.

6. Explain what is meant by "the social construction of reality" and not how the dramaturgical and ethnomethodological approaches attempt to learn about a person's realities.

CHAPTER

5

How Sociologists Do Research

CHAPTER SUMMARY

Sociologists conduct research about almost every area of human behavior. Sociological research is needed because common sense is highly limited and its insights often incorrect. Eight basic steps are included in scientific research: (1) selecting a topic, (2) defining the problem, (3) reviewing the literature, (4) formulating a hypothesis, (5) choosing a research method, (6) collecting the data, (7) analyzing the results, and (8) sharing the results. Sociologists use six research methods (or research designs) for gathering data: surveys, documents, secondary analysis, participant observation, experiments, and unobtrusive measures. The choice of the research method depends on the research questions to be answered, the researcher's access to potential subjects, the resources available, the researcher's training, and ethical considerations. Research and theory must work together because research without theory is of little value, and if theory is unconnected to research, it is unlikely to represent the way life really is. Real-life situations often force sociologists to conduct research in less than ideal circumstances, but even research conducted in an imperfect world stimulates the sociological theorizing by which sociology combines data and theory.

CHAPTER OUTLINE

I. What Is a Valid Sociological Topic?
   A. Just about every area of human behavior—date rape is an example.
   B. The behavior being researched may be routine or unusual, respectable or reprehensible, free or forced.
II. Common Sense and the Need for Sociological Research
   A. Common sense cannot be relied on as a source of knowledge, as it is highly limited, and its insights often are incorrect.
   B. Commonsense notions about rape are an example.
III. A Research Model
   A. Selecting a topic includes the following factors: (1) sociological curiosity; (2) interest in a particular topic; (3) research funding from governmental or private sources; and (4) pressing social issues.
   B. Defining the problem—specifying what the researcher wants to learn.
   C. Reviewing the literature.
   D. Formulating a hypothesis. A hypothesis is a statement of the expected relationship between variables according to predictions from a theory. Hypotheses need operational definitions—precise ways in which variables in a hypothesis are measured.
   E. Choosing a research method.
   F. Collecting the data. The researcher must be concerned with validity (the extent to which operational definitions measure what was intended), which is a persistent problem for researchers. Reliability (consistency of results) also is important.
   G. Analyzing the results is accomplished by statistical tests, content analysis—examining the content of something (e.g., magazine article, television program) to identify its theme—and other approaches.
   H. Sharing the results involves writing a report and possibly publishing the results. Replication—repetition of research to test its findings—is possible by others in the scientific community.
IV. Six Research Methods
   A. Surveys (collecting data by having people answer questions)
      1. Determine a population—the target group to be studied—based on money and time available.
      2. Select a sample (individuals from the target population who are intended to represent the larger population to be studied). Best is a random sample (everyone in the target population has the same chance of being included in the study). A stratified random sample consists of specific subgroups of the target population in which everyone in the subgroup has an equal chance of being included in the study.
      3. Respondents—people who respond to a survey—must express their own ideas so that findings will not be biased.
      4. Two basic techniques for administering question-

naires are self-administered questionnaires (filled out by respondents) and interviews (direct questioning of respondents). Interview bias is the effect that interviewers have on respondents that lead to biased answers Interviews may be structured (closed-ended questions) or unstructured (open-ended questions which people answer in their own words).

5. Rapport—trust between researchers and subjects—is vital.

B. Secondary analysis (analysis of data already collected by other researchers) is used when resources are limited and/or existing data is an excellent source of information.

C. Documents may be obtained from many sources, including books, newspapers, police reports, and records kept by organizations.

D. In participant observation, the researcher participates in a research setting while observing what is happening in that setting. Personal characteristics (e.g., gender, age, race, personality, even height and weight) of the researcher are important here. Generalizability—the extent to which findings from one sample can be generalized or applied to other populations—is a problem in participant observation studies.

E. Experiments are used to identify causal relationships, find out what is the cause and what is the effect. They involve independent variables (factors that cause a change in something) and dependent variables (factors that are changed). A spurious correlation is the correlation of two variables actually caused by a third variable. Experiments require two groups: (1) the experimental group—subjects exposed to the independent variable; and (2) the control group—subjects not exposed to the independent variable.

F. Unobtrusive research measures consist of observing the social behavior of people who do not know they are being studied.

G. Deciding which method to use involves four primary factors: (1) resources—time and money available; (2) access to subjects; (3) purpose of the research; and (4) the researcher's background or training—those trained in the use of quantitative techniques (emphasis on precise measurement, use of statistics and numbers) are likely to use surveys, while those trained in the use of qualitative techniques (emphasis on describing and interpreting people's behavior) lean toward participant observation.

V. Ethics in Sociological Research

A. Ethics is of fundamental concern to sociologists.

B. A commitment to protecting subjects from harm and to researchers not misrepresenting themselves is necessary. A positive example: the Brajuha research (researcher refused to turn notes from participant observation over to law officers). A more questionable situation was the Humphreys research on homosexuals. It focused on social interaction in "tearooms" (restrooms in a park where some male homosexuals met for sex) and potentially jeopardized the identity of respondents by "snooping" into their personal lives.

VI. How Research and Theory Work Together

A. Research without theory is of little value: it becomes a collection of meaningless "facts." Theory unconnected to research is abstract and empty. Sociologists therefore combine them: theory is used to interpret data (i.e., functionalism, symbolic interaction, and conflict theory provide frameworks for interpreting research findings). Theory helps to generate research, while research helps to generate theory.

B. Social researchers must operate under less than ideal circumstances because of real-life situations. The dilemma is whether to study or not to study, if under less than ideal conditions. Sociology needs more imaginative (sometimes daring) research. Research takes people beyond common sense and allows them to penetrate surface realities so they can better understand social life.

LEARNING OBJECTIVES

After reading and studying Chapter 5, the student should be able to:

1. Describe how sociologists go about selecting a topic for their research.
2. Explain why common sense is an inadequate source of knowledge about human behavior.
3. Identify the eight steps in a research model.
4. Define the following terms: hypothesis, operational definition, validity, reliability, content analysis, and replication.
5. List and describe each of the six research methods, noting the major advantages and disadvantages of each.
6. State the meaning of these terms: population, sample, random sample, stratified random sample, self-administered questionnaires, interview, structured interview, experimental group, control group, independent variable and dependent variable.
7. Enumerate the four primary factors involved in a researcher's choice of research method.
8. Differentiate between quantitative techniques and qualitative techniques.
9. Describe the major ethical issues involved in sociological research; briefly demonstrate these issues by use of the Brajuha research and the Humphreys research as examples.
10. Discuss how research and theory work together. Note reasons why most research must be conducted under less than ideal circumstances.

KEY TERMS

closed-ended questions	interview	replication
coding	interview bias	research method
content analysis	open-ended questions	respondents
control group	operational definitions	sample
correlation	participant observation	secondary analysis
dependent variable	population	self-administered questionnaires
documents	qualitative techniques	social psychology
experiment	quantitative techniques	spurious correlation
experimental group	questionnaires	stratified random sample
generalizability	random sample	structured interviews
hypothesis	rapport	survey
independent variable	reliability	unobtrusive measures

KEY PEOPLE

Mario Brajuha

C. Wright Mills

Diana Scully and Joseph Marolla

Laud Humphreys

Peter Berger

Elton Mayo

CLASS DISCUSSION QUESTIONS

1. Do you think some aspects of human behavior—such as date rape—should be off-limits for sociological research? Why or why not?
2. What are some of the commonsense notions about rape that have been proven untrue?
3. Do you think it is possible that sociologists might have a problem with objectivity if their research is funded by a governmental agency, such as the Department of Defense, or by a private source, such as a multinational corporation? Are there ways they could circumvent such a problem?
4. Why is an operational definition for rape not as simple to determine as it might seem?
5. If you were investigating rape on your college campus, would you have an adequate sample if you surveyed the other students enrolled in your introductory sociology class? Why or why not?
6. Is there a problem with asking research subjects, "What do you think should be done to rapists?" and listing only castration and execution as possible options? Why or why not?
7. If you were to walk up to female strangers on the street and ask if they had ever been raped, what type of response would you most likely receive? Why is rapport essential for good research?

8. Why do most researchers prefer to gather their own data rather than relying on data collected by other researchers?
9. Can you think of reasons why a rape crisis center might be unwilling to cooperate with a researcher who wanted to talk with rape victims at the center?
10. Do you think a male researcher could conduct participant observation research at a rape crisis intervention center? Why or why not?
11. Do you think that pornography creates attitudes that favor rape?
12. Why is it necessary to have a control group as well as an experimental group when conducting experiments?
13. Do you think Mario Brajuha should have turned over his participant observation field notes when detectives asked him to do so?
14. How would you feel if you learned that a researcher was conducting observations in a restroom you frequently use? Was Humphreys' research ethical?
15. Why do you think sociologists often end up conducting research under less than ideal conditions?

PROJECTS

1. Set up a hypothetical research model for a relatively straight-forward sociological problem. Here is a way to think through the steps hypothetically:
   a. Select a topic: What is a social problem you would like to know more about?
   b. Define the problem: What exactly do you want to learn about this topic?
   c. Review the literature: What sources would you use if you were actually going to conduct this research? (Give specific names of professional journals and other references.)
   d. Formulate a hypothesis: Can you predict a relationship between or among the variables you have chosen? (If there is a change in one variable, how will the other variable(s) be affected?)

e. Choose a research method: Which of the following methods would be best for gathering the data you need: surveys, secondary analysis, documents, participant observation, experiments, or unobtrusive measures? Why?

f. Collect the data: How would you go about gathering the information needed for your study? How would you assure the validity and reliability of your data?

g. Analyze the results: Would statistical tests be useful in your analysis? Content analysis? Other means of analysis?

h. Share the results: How would you go about sharing the results with social scientists? Would you get the results published? Present your papers at professional meetings? Other options?

Present your hypothetical model in small group or class discussion for feedback.

2. Read "Down-to-Earth Sociology—Loading the Dice" in the text. Find examples of "bad" research in the media. Look for findings based on a very small number of respondents or for studies which draw conclusions based on questionable assumptions. (Hint: Read women's or men's magazines, watch "experts" on television talk shows such as *Oprah, Donahue, Geraldo,* or *Sally Jessie Raphael,* or find ads which rely on "research" to sell products or services.) Present your examples and criticisms in an oral or written report. Relate the problems you found to general issues facing sociologists conducting research. (For example, a widely-reported study about the sex lives of the elderly concluded that those who drank coffee had "better" and more active sex lives than those who did not because of their higher intake of caffeine. However, retractions of the study's findings were published because the researchers failed to determine whether the elderly were drinking regular or decaffeinated coffee!)

3. Develop "pro" or "con" arguments on the following statement: "The research methods of Laud Humphreys in his study, *Tearoom Trade,* were ethical." Participate in a class discussion or debate using the arguments you have written. How would you handle ethical problems in "sensitive research"? Are there some topics that are virtually impossible to research without invading people's privacy? For a term project, read Humphreys' book to gain more insight about his work and then read some of the criticisms subsequently written about his methods.

4. For a semester project, read some of the following and write a report on issues involved in social science research: (a) Babbie, Earl R. *The Practice of Social Research.* 5th ed. Belmont, CA: Wadsworth, 1989. (b) Hoover, Kenneth R. *The Elements of Social Scientific Thinking.* 5th ed. NY: St. Martin, 1992. (c) Jaffe, A. J. *Misused Statistics: Straight Talk for Twisted Numbers.* NY: Marcel Dekker, 1987. (d) Reynolds, Paul D. *Ethics and Social Science Research.* Englewood Cliffs, NJ: Prentice Hall, 1982.

TRANSPARENCIES

1. (TR#5) The Research Model

TRANSPARENCY MASTERS

1. (TR#4M) Terms Commonly Used in Sociological Research

VIDEOS/MOVIES

Rape

CNN Video II. *Attitudes toward Rape: A Nationwide Survey of Males.* Conference of New York Academy of Sciences report on a nationwide survey asking men if they would rape a woman if no one would know and if they knew they would not be punished. Thirty percent said there was at least some likelihood that they would. The researchers then "softened" the question by replacing "rape" with "force." This time, 50% of the respondents said there was some likelihood that they would force a woman to have sex if there were no repercussions. Critics say that just because men fantasize about such things, it does not mean that the percentages reflected in the survey are an accurate reflection of the numbers of men who would actually rape women. Available from A&B Video Library.

Date Rape. In this specially adapted Phil Donahue program, two victims of date rape are joined by the director of the Rape Treatment Center in Santa Monica, CA and Chicago psychiatrist Helen Morrison in discussions about the growing number of these rapes, the psychological trauma involved, and the social and legal difficulties this crime presents. 28 min. Available from A&B Video Library or FHS.

Rape and Marriage: The Rideout Case. 1980. (Color). A made-for-television movie about the landmark 1978 Oregon marital rape case in which a woman brought a rape charge against her husband. Average movie but demonstrates complexity of the issue. 96 min. Available at some video rental stores.

Rape: Face to Face. 1985. Examines the causes and consequences of rape, including the emotional confrontation between rapists and victims of rape (though not by these particular men). The documentary provides an understanding of the thought processes and behavior patterns of violent sex offenders. 55 min. Available from FML.

Rapists: Can They Be Stopped? 1989. Focuses on participants in a program in Oregon State Hospital aimed at rehabilitating sex offenders. Shows various methods of rehabilitation. Included is an audio tape of an actual police recording of a phone call from a woman about to be attacked which is used in the therapy process to break through the detachment of the rapist. Very few graduates of this program have become repeat offenders. 55 min. Available from FML.

SPEAKER SUGGESTIONS

1. Social science reference librarian from your library to explain the various sources of data, including professional sociological journals, available in the library. For smaller classes, plan a field trip to the library.
2. A nonacademic statistician or researcher to explain how data is gathered and used in his or her field (e.g., political, environmental, health care).
3. A specialist in ethics from your department or from the schools of business, law, or medicine to discuss the ethical and legal issues in conducting research with human subjects.
4. A colleague who has conducted research on rape or other violent criminal conduct to talk about her or his methods and conclusions.

POP QUIZ QUESTIONS

True-False

T   1. Sociologists research just about every area of human behavior, including styles in home decorations for Christmas.
F   2. The first step involved in scientific research is defining the problem.
F   3. A hypothesis and an operational definition are the same thing.
F   4. Reliability refers to the extent to which operational definitions measure what they are intended to measure.
T   5. Replication is the repetition of research in order to test its findings.

T   6. The two major techniques of surveys are questionnaires and interviews.
F   7. Sociologists frequently use experiments for conducting research.
T   8. Experiments must have both an experimental group and a control group.
F   9. Researchers who have been trained in qualitative techniques tend to emphasize precise measurement, numbers, and statistics.
T 10. Ethical issues in sociological research are of constant concern to sociologists.

ESSAY QUESTIONS

1. Outline the steps in setting up a research model. Select a topic of interest to you and briefly explain how you might go about conducting the research. (Note you are not expected to be a professional sociologist, but rather should demonstrate your basic knowledge of the steps in the model.)
2. Compare the survey method of research with participant observation. Explain what the researcher may gain and/or lose by using each of the methods.
3. Discuss the use of secondary analysis and documents in social science research and give examples of topics in which this type of data might be the most useful.
4. Use the Hawthorne Experiments to demonstrate some of the major problems inherent in experimental research involving human subjects.
5. Analyze the major ethical problems faced by sociologists, using the research by Brajuha and by Humphreys as examples.
6. Describe how research and theory work together and explain why social science research often is conducted under less than ideal conditions.

CHAPTER

6

Societies to Social Networks

CHAPTER SUMMARY

Groups are the essence of life in society. An essential feature of a group is that its members have something in common and that they believe what they have in common makes a difference. Society is the largest and most complex group that sociologists study. Five types of societies have existed: (1) hunting and gathering, (2) pastoral and horticultural, (3) agricultural, (4) industrial, and (5) postindustrial. The nature and extent of social inequality in each type of society is analyzed. Dramatic transformations have occurred within all social institutions in society, and this transformation has continued into the current postindustrial society, which is based on information, services, and high technology. Within society, the following types of groups exist: primary groups, secondary groups, in-groups and out-groups, reference groups, and social networks. Group dynamics concerns the ways in which individuals affect groups and the ways in which groups affect individuals. Group size is a significant aspect of group dynamics. Leaders can be either instrumental or expressive. Three main leadership styles are: authoritarian, democratic, and laissez-faire. The Asch experiment demonstrates the influence of peer groups over their members, while the Milgram experiment shows how powerfully people are influenced by authority. Groupthink—which occurs when political leaders become isolated—poses a serious threat to society's well-being.

CHAPTER OUTLINE

I. Social Groups and Societies
   A. Groups are the essence of life in society—they stand between the individual and the larger society and help prevent anomie. An essential element of a social group is that its members have something in common which they believe makes a difference.
   B. Society (people who share a culture and a territory) is the largest, most complex group that sociologists study.
II. The Transformation of Societies
   A. The first societies were hunting and gathering societies. Their survival depended on hunting animals and gathering plants; the groups were small and nomadic, moving when food ran out. They had few social divisions, being based primarily on the family, and they did not accumulate things—no one became wealthier or a ruler.
   B. Then, pastoral and horticultural societies developed. The domestication of plants and animals was the first social revolution, producing food surpluses that allowed for increased population size and some specialized division of labor. Increased trade (interaction between groups) developed, and people began to accumulate objects they considered valuable. Leaders accumulated more possessions than other people did and passed advantages on to descendants; inequality resulted.
   C. The second social revolution produced agricultural societies, which developed with the invention of the plow 5,000–6,000 years ago. A larger food surplus resulted, allowing people to engage in other activities—the "dawn of culture." Cities developed, and an elite gained control of the surplus. The "state" emerged when the elite surrounded itself with guards to protect possessions, and began to levy taxes. Social inequalities became more complex; females became subjugated to males.
   D. The third social revolution (the industrial revolution) began in 1765, when the steam engine first was used to run machinery. Harnessing power resulted in a shift from agriculture to manufacturing as basis of power, wealth, and prestige. The population increased greatly, as did social inequality: those who first utilized the new technology accumulated great wealth, controlling the means of production and dictating working conditions. Initially denied the right to unionize or strike, American workers later won their demands for better living conditions. Social institutions were transformed greatly—ascribed statuses gave way to achieved statuses; while traditional family functions were eroded:
      1. economic production moved outside the home;
      2. responsibility for the socialization of children was transferred to the schools;
      3. care of the sick was taken over by hospitals, and care of the aged passed to nursing homes; and

4. home recreation yielded to organized sports, electronic entertainment, and mass media.

E. Postindustrial societies are moving away from production and manufacturing to service industries, whose basic component is providing or applying information. The computer chip is the primary technological change involved in this information revolution.

III. Groups within Society

A. Sociologists distinguish aggregates (collections of people with similar characteristics) from groups.

B. Primary groups and secondary groups

1. Primary groups is the name Charles H. Cooley coined for groups characterized by face-to-face association and cooperation. These groups become part of each member's identity and the lens through which a member views life; they are essential to an individual's psychological well-being, providing feelings of self-esteem, but can be dysfunctional (e.g., a family that quarrels).

2. Secondary groups are larger, relatively temporary, more anonymous, formal, and impersonal, usually based on some interest or activity. Their members interact on the basis of specific roles. In industrial societies, they have multiplied and become essential, but tend to break down into primary groups within the larger group.

C. In-groups are those groups toward which individuals feel loyalty; out-groups are those toward which they feel antagonisms. Robert K. Merton noted a double standard: the in-group's behavior is seen as a virtue, while the same conduct by out-group members is seen as a vice.

D. Reference groups are used as a standard of evaluation, even when we don't belong. They exert great influence over behavior (people change clothing, hair style, speech, etc., to match the group's expectations). Having conflicting reference groups can produce intense internal conflict.

E. Social networks consist of people linked by various social ties; they provide members with valuable information and provide socioemotional support and self-esteem. However, they tend to perpetuate social inequality: Most jobs are secured through social networks, and the "old boy" network tends to keep the best positions available to men only, rather than women. "Networking" is the conscious use or even cultivation of contacts who will be helpful.

IV. Group Dynamics

A. Group dynamics is the term for how individuals affect groups and groups affect individuals. Group size is significant on its dynamics. A small group is one small enough for everyone to interact directly. Georg Simmel

noted the significance of group size: a dyad contains two members and is the most fragile of human groups; a triad contains three persons. A triad is stronger than a dyad, but still extremely unstable (e.g., bonds between two members seem stronger; the third person feels hurt and excluded). As more members are added to a group, intensity decreases and stability increases (more linkages between more people), and a more formal structure is established. Larger groups tend to break into smaller groups (e.g., guests at a party break into smaller groups to talk).

B. A leader is defined as someone who influences the behavior of others. There are two types of group leaders: instrumental (task-oriented) leaders, who try to keep the group moving toward its goals; and expressive (socioemotional) leaders, who help with the group's morale, minimizing the friction instrumental leaders produce. There are three types of leadership styles:

1. authoritarian—give orders and frequently do not explain why they praise or condemn a person's work;

2. democratic—try to gain a consensus; and

3. laissez-faire—passive, allowing almost total freedom. Ronald Lippitt and Ralph White discovered that leadership styles produced different results.

C. The Asch experiment: Solomon Asch held cards up in front of small groups, asking which sets of cards matched; each person responded aloud, one at a time. Peer pressure resulted in people giving incorrect answers much of the time, even when they knew answers were wrong.

D. The Milgram experiment: Stanley Milgram conducted 18 experiments in which a "teacher" was instructed to administer an electric shock to a "learner" for each wrong answer to certain questions, and to increase the voltage of the shock after each wrong answer. In fact, the "learner" was playing a role, intentionally giving wrong answers but only pretending to receive the shock. Since an "authority" figure continually said the experiment had to go on, most of the "teachers" continued to administer the "shocks" even when they appeared to produce extreme pain. The scientific community was disturbed by Milgram's findings and his methods; ethics codes were adopted as a result.

E. Groupthink is the term coined by Irving Janis to refer to a group of people who think alike and to whom any suggestion of alternatives becomes a sign of disloyalty. U.S. history provides examples: presidents and their inner circles have committed themselves to a single course of action even when objective evidence showed the course to be wrong. Groupthink can be prevented only by insuring that leaders are exposed to persons with views conflicting with those of the inner circle.

LEARNING OBJECTIVES

After reading and studying Chapter 6, the student should be able to:

1. Explain why groups are so important to individuals and to societies.

2. Trace the transformation of societies through the five stages of development, and note the degree of social inequality present in each stage.

3. Describe the characteristics of postindustrial society, and

indicate some of the major changes occurring in such societies.

4. Define each of the following: primary groups, secondary groups, in-groups, out-groups, reference groups, and social networks.
5. Explain what is meant by group dynamics, and indicate how group size affects interaction.
6. Describe the two types of leaders in groups, and the three basic styles of leadership.
7. State the reasons why researchers have concluded that democratic leaders are more effective than authoritarian ones.
8. Demonstrate the importance of peer pressure to conformity by analyzing the Asch experiment.
9. Explain the following about the Milgram experiment: purpose of study, how it was conducted, conclusions reached, and why the methodology was questioned.
10. Discuss groupthink, and explain how it can be dangerous for a society.

KEY TERMS

aggregate
agricultural revolution
agricultural society
anomie
authoritarian leader
coalition
cultural diffusion
cultural lag
democratic leader
domestication revolution
dyad
expressive leader
group

group dynamics
groupthink
horticultural society
hunting and gathering society
industrial revolution
industrial society
information revolution
in-groups
instrumental leader
laissez-faire leader
leader
leadership styles
networking

out-groups
pastoral society
postindustrial society
primary group
reference group
secondary group
shaman
small group
social networks
society
triad

KEY PEOPLE

William F. Ogburn
Robert K. Merton
Solomon Asch
Irving Janis

Charles H. Cooley
Georg Simmel
Stanley Milgram

CLASS DISCUSSION QUESTIONS

1. What would your life be like if you were not a member of any group?
2. Do you think you would like to live in a society in which age and gender were virtually the only bases for group membership? Why or why not?
3. Why do you think the male hunters have more prestige in hunting and gathering societies even though the women gatherers contribute more food to the group?
4. Why are hunting and gathering societies the most egalitarian of all types of societies?
5. What types of advances had to occur before permanent settlements could develop?
6. What was the "first social revolution"?
7. Why do you think discoveries related to animal husbandry and plant cultivation were fundamental to the development of human societies?
8. When did the second social revolution occur and what were its characteristics?
9. What factors contributed to the growth of social inequality in agricultural societies?
10. Why do you think females became subjugated to males during the agricultural period?
11. What factors in Britain contributed to the development of industrial society?
12. In what ways do you think "change feeds change"?
13. How has technology changed your life from that of your parents and grandparents? What about computers? Telephone answering machines? Car phones?
14. Why did social inequality become even more pronounced during the first stage of industrialization?
15. Do you agree that the type of society in which you live is fundamental to the type of person you will become? Why or why not?
16. Do you think your career will be in information, services, and/or high technology? Will your career be characteristic of those found in postindustrial societies?
17. What changes do you think will occur in American society as a result of the information revolution?
18. How do primary group relationships become fused into the individual's identity? Can you think of examples in your own life?
19. Do you think all primary groups function positively? Why or why not?
20. Why do secondary groups tend to break down into primary

groups? Can you give examples from your own membership groups?

21. In what ways are sports teams examples of in-groups and out-groups?

22. How do reference groups exert influence over people's behavior? What do you do if you have two reference groups that clearly conflict with each other?

23. What kinds of valuable information do you get from social networks at school? If you are employed, from social networks at work?

24. How are your communications different when you are talking with one other person than when you are talking with two other people?

25. Why do some couples experience difficulties adjusting to the birth of their first child? Can you think of ways to prevent this problem?

26. Do you think that it is difficult for one person to be both an instrumental and an expressive leader?

27. Do you prefer an authoritarian, democratic, or laissez-faire leadership style when you are the group leader? How about when you are a follower?

28. Are some leaders simply "born?" Why or why not?

29. How influential do you think groups are in people's lives? Does the Asch experiment correspond with your thoughts?

30. How would you have reacted if you had been a student in Dr. Stanley Milgram's class when he conducted his experiments on obedience to authority?

31. Do you feel that groupthink has disturbing implications for individuals and for societies? Why or why not?

PROJECTS

1. As a small group or class project, develop a chart to trace the transformation of societies through the five stages of development. Focus on the varying degree of social inequality present in each stage and the reasons for these inequalities. When you present your results to the class, indicate whether or not you think these inequalities were inevitable.

2. Brainstorm about the future of the United States. Describe this country in the year 2020 in regard to the types of technology available, advances which have occurred in science and medicine, and other "sociology of the future" issues. Present your forecast to the class. For a term project, do more extensive research on the social consequences of technological surveillance, advanced robotic devices, genetic splicing, etc.

3. Make a chart with the following words across the top: Primary Groups/Secondary Groups/In-Groups/Out-Groups/Reference Groups/Social Networks. Personalize the chart by listing all of your groups and networks on the sheet. Put a plus (+) by the groups you believe will become more important in your future and a minus (−) by the ones you believe will become less important. Write a brief summary about the groups in your life and predict how some of these relationships will change in the future. No one but the professor will see this unless you choose to share it with someone.

4. Suggestion to instructor: To demonstrate the three basic leadership styles, divide your class into three groups. Give all three groups the same problem to solve, and appoint a leader for each—one "authoritarian," another "democratic," and the third "laissez-faire." After each group has tried to solve the problem, have the class observe the three types of leadership in action and determine which they think works best. Suggested problems to "solve" include: How can our college or university reduce sexual and racial discrimination on campus? Is there a "better" way to deal with student parking? What can we do about students who cheat on examinations? Can we get a student appointed to the governing board of our university?

5. Suggestion to instructor: Conduct an experiment along the lines of Dr. Asch's with your class. Discuss students' perceptions about the experiment.

6. Think of groupthink experiences in your own lives. Be sure to include pressure to do things you would not do under "normal" circumstances. For example, if you joined a fraternity, sorority, or other social group, were you instructed to do things you typically would not do? (If you want to make the question less personal, focus it on "other people." For example, "Why do you think practices of hazing still occur in some fraternities and sororities even though such practices are both illegal and in violation of college policy?")

TRANSPARENCIES

1. (TR#6) The Social Transformation of Society
2. (TR#7) The Multiplying Effects of Group Size on Relationships

VIDEOS/MOVIES

The Transformation of Societies

Blue Collar and Buddha. 1989. Documents the dilemma of a community of Laotian refugees torn between preserving their cultural identity and adapting to their new life in Rockford, Illinois. They face rising tensions with their working-class neighbors who resent their economic gains and view their Buddhism with hostility. Although this video looks at race/ethnic/social class relationships, it also shows the problems experienced by people who move from a society at one stage of development to one at another stage. Likewise, it demonstrates the impact of groupthink, as the people of Rockford—many of whom are unemployed—voice their hatred for the newcomers and terrorize the Laotians when they build a Buddhist temple on a small farm outside of town. 57 min. Available from FML.

Group Dynamics

Dead Poets Society. 1989. (Color) Starring Robin Williams as a charismatic English teacher in a staid New England prep school, this movie demonstrates the powerful influence one individual in a leadership role can have on others, especially when they are impressionable students. 128 min. Available at video rental stores.

Captive Minds; Hypnosis and Beyond. 1985. Illustrates how cults hold on to their disciples, how the Marines command such loyalty, and why Jesuit priests submit to a lifetime of strict authority because of long-term conditioning. Recruits are isolated in unfamiliar environments and after a period of isolation, exhaustion, and fright, a strong leader demands their loyalty. Although this film takes a psychological perspective, it demonstrates the power of the group and of leaders over their followers. 55 min. Available from FML.

Obedience and Independence. 1975. Reviews basic research findings and concepts in the area of conformity. The studies of Asch, Sherif, Milgram, and Kelman are included. 23 min. Available from Harper and Row.

SPEAKER SUGGESTIONS

1. A social scientist who recently has traveled or lived in the former Soviet Union to discuss the ways people in those states have adapted to changes in their society.
2. A colleague in computer science or engineering to talk about what lies "beyond the postindustrial society" or to explore the implications of the information explosion.
3. Invite someone who conducts group dynamics or leadership seminars to talk to the class about their techniques. (Caveat: Discourage them from turning this presentation into a "sales pitch" for their seminar or course.)
4. A psychologist conducting research on conformity, peer pressure, groupthink, or other appropriate social psychological topics.

POP QUIZ QUESTIONS

True-False

T   1. Society is the largest and most complex group that sociologists study.
F   2. The simplest societies are called pastoral and horticultural societies.
T   3. Social inequality developed in agricultural societies.
T   4. Cultural lag occurs when changes in nonmaterial culture occur more slowly than changes in material culture.
T   5. The basic component of the postindustrial society is information.
F   6. Emile Durkheim coined the term "primary group."

F   7. Primary groups are more temporary than secondary groups.
T   8. A primary characteristic of social networks is that they supply their members with valuable information.
F   9. A person must be a member of a reference group in order to use it as a standard to evaluate himself or herself.
T 10. One of the most disturbing implications of the Asch and Milgram experiments is the power of groupthink.

ESSAY QUESTIONS

1. Discuss the growth of social inequality as societies were transformed through various economic and social revolutions.
2. Explain how small groups help prevent anomie in larger impersonal societies.
3. Differentiate between primary and secondary groups, and explain how the experiences of individuals are different in each.
4. Distinguish between dyad and triad, and discuss ways in which group size affects the individuals involved in the group.

5. Identify and distinguish between different types of leaders in societies.
6. Demonstrate the influence of peer groups over their members, using the Asch experiment.
7. Describe the criticisms which arose as a result of Milgram's experiment. Indicate the purpose of his study, how it was conducted, and his findings.

CHAPTER

7

Bureaucracy and Formal Organizations

CHAPTER SUMMARY

A major transition has occurred in the way people think—from tradition-based protection of time-honored ways to rationality, a concern with efficiency and practical results. Max Weber traced the rationalization of society to Protestantism, while Marx attributed it to capitalism. As a result of the emphasis on rationality, formal organizations—secondary groups designed to achieve explicit objectives—have proliferated. Their most common form is a bureaucracy which Weber characterized as having a hierarchy of authority, a division of labor, written rules, written communications, and impersonality. Weber's characteristics of bureaucracy are an "ideal type" which may not accurately describe any actual organization. In Weber's view, the impersonality of bureaucracies tends to produce alienation among workers. The concept of alienation is explored from the standpoints of Weber and Marx. Other dysfunctions of bureaucracies are trained incapacity, goal conflict, goal displacement, engorgement and incompetence. In the United States voluntary associations—groups made up of volunteers who organize on the basis of some mutual interest—also have proliferated. Oligarchy—the tendency of formal organizations to be dominated by a small, self-perpetuating elite—is a problem in voluntary associations. Corporate culture affects its members, and greater emphasis is now being placed on humanizing work settings. Finally, Chapter 7 compares the Japanese and American corporate models.

CHAPTER OUTLINE

I. The Rationalization of Society
   A. Rationality (acceptance of rules, efficiency, and practical results) is a characteristic of industrial societies.
   B. According to Max Weber, the traditional wisdom presumed that the past was the best guide for the present; however, this stood in the way of industrialization. Weber's *The Protestant Ethic and the Spirit of Capitalism* asserts that people wanted to show they were among the chosen of God; success in life was the sign of God's approval, but spending money on oneself was sinful; thus, capitalism allowed the investment of excess money, and the profits from those investments showed more approval from God.
   C. According to Karl Marx, rationalization resulted from capitalism. Capitalism caused people to change their way of thinking: the new form of production did in traditional relationships; since capitalism was efficient, people changed their ideas; rationality thus resulted from economics, not from Protestantism.
II. Formal Organizations and Bureaucracy
   A. Formal organizations (secondary groups designed to achieve explicit objectives) proliferated as industrialization occurred.
   B. The essential characteristics of bureaucracies are: (1) an hierarchy with assignments flowing down, accountability upward; (2) division of labor; (3) written rules; (4) written communications and records; and (5) impersonality.
   C. Weber's characteristics of bureaucracy are "ideal" types—a composite of characteristics based on many specific examples. Actual ("real") bureaucracy often differs from its ideal image.
   D. Dysfunctions of bureaucracies:
      1. Bureaucratic alienation (feeling powerless/normless; cut off from product of own labor) leaves individual needs unfulfilled. Workers want to feel respected and worthwhile; to resist alienation, they form primary groups within the larger organization. Alienated bureaucrats feel trapped in the job, do not take initiative, do nothing that is not strictly required, and use rules to justify doing as little as possible.
      2. Trained incapacity (thinking in terms of own activity and unit and failing to grasp larger goals) impedes organizational goals.
      3. Goal conflict occurs when the goals of a unit conflict with those of the organization.
      4. Goal displacement occurs when an organization adopts new goals after the original goals have been achieved.

5. Bureaucratic engorgement is the tendency of an organization to keep on growing. Parkinson's law: Work expands to fill the time available for its completion. The importance of bureaucrats depends on size of budget, staff, office, etc.; thus, growth seems desirable.

6. Bureaucratic incompetence—the Peter Principle asserts that each employee is promoted to his or her level of incompetence; in fact, bureaucracies do have difficulty dealing with exceptional cases.

7. The "bottom line" is easier to compute in a bureaucracy whose goal is to produce profit; it is more difficult in other organizations. Some organizations solve the "bottom line" problem by issuing annual reports that may inflate their accomplishments.

III. Voluntary Associations

A. Groups of volunteers are organized on the basis of mutual interest. They have one or more of the following functions:

1. to advance the particular interests they represent;

2. to offer people an identity (and sense of purpose in life);

3. to govern and maintain social order;

4. to mediate between the government and the individual;

5. to train people in organizational skills and help them climb the occupational ladder;

6. to help disadvantaged groups; and

7. to challenge society's definitions of "normal" and socially acceptable.

B. The problem of oligarchy: Robert Michels' "iron law of oligarchy" refers to the tendency of self-perpetuating elites to dominate formal organizations. For example, Elaine Fox and George Arquitte found that the leaders of certain VFW posts maintained ongoing control while making it look like a democratic process was occurring.

IV. Careers in Bureaucracies

A. Rosabeth Moss Kanter's research demonstrates that the corporate elite not only stay in power but also have better access to information, networking, and "fast tracks." Females and minorities do not match the hidden values of the corporate culture and thus may experience "showcasing" (being put in highly visible positions with little power) and/or "slow-track" jobs that are seldom seen by management, thus resulting in few promotions. Morale and style of leadership are influenced by the level a person has achieved in an organization.

B. Humanizing the corporate culture includes organizing the work place in such a way that it develops rather than impedes human potential. Characteristics of more humane bureaucracies include availability of opportunities on the basis of ability and contributions rather than personal characteristics, a more equal distribution of power, and less rigid rules and more open decision-making.

C. Modifying Bureaucracy

1. A quality circle is a small group of workers and a manager who meet regularly to try to improve the quality of the work setting and the product.

2. Employee stock ownership does not mean that working conditions and employee-management relations are friction-free—profitability still is the key.

3. Small work groups establish primary relationships among their members; the workers' identities become tied up with their group, and the group's success becomes the individual's success.

4. Conflict theorists point out that the basic relationship between workers and owners is confrontational regardless of how the work organization is structured.

V. Developing an Alternative: Collectives are organizations owned by members who collectively make decisions, determine goals, evaluate resources, set salaries, and assign work tasks. Since the 1970s, about 5,000 cooperatives have been established—their economic results have been mixed, as some are more profitable than private organizations, some less.

VI. The Japanese Corporate Model

A. William Ouchi lists five differences between the Japanese and U.S. models:

1. Hiring and promotion—the Japanese model uses a team approach; starting workers get same salary; rotate through the company. U.S. employees are hired on a competitive basis.

2. Lifetime security—the Japanese model takes this for granted, while in the United States, workers must look out for themselves.

3. Almost total involvement—work is like a marriage in Japan. In the United States, workers are only expected to perform their jobs.

4. Training—in Japan, workers move between jobs within the company; in the United States, employees are expected to do one job well, then get promoted.

5. Decision-making—in Japan, there is much deliberation among those to be affected by a decision; in the United States, few people actually make the decision.

B. Both systems depend on the cultural base of which they are a part; thus, it would be difficult to transplant one system to another culture.

LEARNING OBJECTIVES

After reading and studying Chapter 7, the student should be able to:

1. Explain what is meant by the "rationalization of society," and differentiate between the views of Max Weber and Karl Marx on this process.

2. State the definition of formal organizations, and list the essential characteristics of bureaucracies.

3. Describe the difference in "ideal" versus "real" bureaucracy.

4. Discuss the major dysfunctions of bureaucracies, and give examples of each type of problem.

5. Indicate the functions of voluntary associations, and explain how the problem of oligarchy occurs in such organizations.
6. Identify the consequences of hidden values in the corporate culture, especially noting their impact on women and minority participants.
7. Evaluate the major approaches to humanizing the corporate culture.

8. Explain how quality circles, employee stock ownership, and small work groups have been used to modify bureaucratic organizational structure.
9. Describe the role of cooperatives, or collectives, in providing an alternative to bureaucracy.
10. Compare and contrast the Japanese and United States corporate organizational models.

KEY TERMS

alienation
bureaucracy
bureaucratic engorgement
capitalism
corporate culture
formal organization

goal conflict
goal displacement
humanizing a work setting
ideal type
the iron law of oligarchy
Peter Principle

rationality
rationalization of society
traditional orientation
trained incapacity
voluntary association

KEY PEOPLE

Max Weber
Robert Michels
William Ouchi

Karl Marx
Rosabeth Moss Kanter

CLASS DISCUSSION QUESTIONS

1. What does "rationality" mean to a sociologist? What does "rationality" mean to you in everyday usage?
2. Why do you think a traditional orientation in society would stand in the way of industrialization?
3. Why did Max Weber believe that religion could be a force for social change in societies? Do you think this idea is still valid today?
4. How did worldly success become transformed into a spiritual value for the Calvinists? Do we view worldly success in the same way now?
5. Can you state in your own words the way in which Karl Marx's views on the development of capitalism differed from those of Max Weber?
6. Why do you think formal organizations are necessary in contemporary societies?
7. Does this college/university have all of the essential characteristics of bureaucracy? Can you give specific examples?
8. Do you agree that real bureaucracies differ from their ideal image? If so, how?
9. Have you encountered some of the dysfunctions of bureaucracies?
10. Why do some workers experience bureaucratic alienation? Do you think there is anything organizations can do to keep this from happening? If so, what?
11. How does trained incapacity impede the goals of an organization? Have you ever encountered this problem?

12. Why do bureaucracies have an almost irresistible tendency to keep on growing? Can you give examples from your own experience?
13. What is the Peter Principle? Do you agree with it? Why or why not?
14. Why are Americans so involved in voluntary associations? Are you involved in them?
15. Do you think that voluntary associations meet people's basic needs? Why do these organizations typically have a high turnover rate?
16. Why do the majority of members allow the iron law of oligarchy to occur in an organization?
17. In what ways will bureaucracy affect your career?
18. Do you agree with Rosabeth Moss Kanter's assessment of who gets ahead in a large corporation? Why or why not?
19. What attempts have been made to humanize the corporate culture? Do you think they have been successful?
20. Do you think conflict theorists are correct in their assumption that the basic relationship between workers and owners is confrontational regardless of how the work organization is structured?
21. What factors contributed to the huge economic success of Japan since World War II?
22. Do you believe the Japanese corporate model could be transplanted to the United States? Why or why not?

PROJECTS

1. Keep a log of all of your interactions or "encounters" with bureaucracy for several days. List the bureaucracy; state the nature of your business or your goal (i.e., why you are dealing with them in the first place); describe the outcome; and indicate whether or not you are satisfied with the end result. Have students discuss their log and conclusions as a class,

or in small groups. Encourage them to explore the following:

a. What characteristics of bureaucracy were helpful in getting done what you wanted to accomplish in this organization?

b. What characteristics made it more difficult for you to achieve your goal?

c. Could the organization change some of its rules or policies to make it easier for you to accomplish what you want to do?

2. As a class project or term paper, develop an organizational structure which would minimize alienation, trained incapacity, engorgement, and incompetence. Note the types of resources you would need to make this possible. State the strengths and weaknesses of the structure you have created.

3. Conduct research on a voluntary association which interests you. Find out about its purpose, goals, organizational structure, membership requirements, and so forth. If it is possible to do so, attend one or more of the organization's meetings. Analyze how effective you think the group is in meeting its organizational objectives. Do you think an oligarchy has taken control of this group? Present your findings in a paper or oral presentation to the class.

4. In a small group or class discussion, or as an individual project, develop "pro" and "con" arguments for the following statements:

a. Lifetime employment would create higher levels of job satisfaction and commitment among U.S. workers.

b. U.S. workers would prefer pay raises and promotions based on their cohort group's work efforts, not on their individual efforts.

c. Consensus decision-making (a bottom-up approach) would work better than the current approach found in most U.S. companies.

5. Read one or more of the following books to use as a foundation for a term paper or class presentation: (a) Clegg, Stewart R. *Modern Organizations; Organizational Studies in the Postmodern World.* Newbury Park, CA: Sage, 1990. (b) Lincoln, James R. and Arne L. Kalleberg. *Culture, Control, and Commitment: A Study of Work Organization and Work Attitudes in the United States and Japan.* New York: Cambridge, 1990. See also Suggested Readings at the end of Chapter 7 in the text.

TRANSPARENCY MASTERS

1. (TR#5M) The Bureaucratic Structure of a University

VIDEOS/MOVIES

The Corporate Culture: Consequences of Hidden Values

CNN Video II. *Glass Ceiling.* A year-long study by the U.S. Department of Labor of nine randomly chosen corporations showed that progress of women stalls at low levels of management; that progress of minorities stalls lower still. The study indicates that the progress of women and minorities is being affected by more than qualifications or career choices. Available from A&B Video Library.

Baby Boom. 1987. (Color) Starring Diane Keaton as a highly successful business executive who "inherits" a baby. The movie juxtaposes her life as an executive with her decision to move to the country with the baby. (PG) 103 min. Available at video rental stores.

Big Business. 1988. (Color) Starring Bette Midler and Lily Tomlin. Two sets of twins are mismatched and separated at birth. Years later the girls from a small town come to New York City to take on the large corporation that is going to take over their little town. The corporation is run by their long-lost identical twins. The small-town twins run head-on into the greed and bureaucracy of the corporation. (PG) 97 min. Available at video rental stores.

The Secret of My Success. 1987. (Color) Starring Michael J. Fox as a bright, ambitious young man from a small town who hustles his way into the corporate world of New York City. (PG-13) 110 min. Available at video rental stores.

Working Girl. 1988. (Color) Starring Harrison Ford, Mike Nichols, Sigourney Weaver, and Melanie Griffith. A secretary tries to make it to the top of the corporate ladder with an innovative idea. Along the way, her female boss tries to steal the idea from her, and she runs into all types of bureaucratic problems. The film shows bureaucratic alienation and other organizational problems. (R—explicit scenes). 113 min. Available at video rental stores.

SPEAKER SUGGESTIONS

1. A human relations specialist or personnel manager to discuss the importance of a good organizational structure to create efficiency.

2. A community volunteer—such as the President of the local Junior League, Scouts, Rotary, NAACP, etc.—to talk about the role that volunteers play in meeting human needs in your city.

3. A sociologist (or lawyer) who has conducted research (or litigation) pertaining to the ways in which hidden values of the corporate culture may have a negative and differential impact on women and minorities.

4. A benefits expert or a colleague from the business school to present innovative methods for enhancing worker participation and productivity.

POP QUIZ QUESTIONS

True-False

T 1. The process of industrialization requires rationality and the willingness to change.

F 2. Karl Marx wrote *The Protestant Ethic and the Spirit of Capitalism.*

F 3. Max Weber believed that the rationalization of society occurred as a result of the development of capitalism.

T 4. Some formal organizations existed prior to industrialization.

T 5. Max Weber analyzed the essential characteristics of bureaucracy.

T 6. In bureaucracies, it is the office that is important, not the individual who holds the office.

F 7. It is virtually impossible for workers to overcome bureaucratic alienation.

T 8. Churches, political parties, and unions are examples of voluntary associations.

F 9. The iron law of oligarchy does not apply to organizations strongly committed to democratic principles.

F 10. According to Kanter's research, organizational environments have the same impact on all participants, whether they are white males, women, or minorities.

ESSAY QUESTIONS

1. Explain how formal organizations and bureaucracies developed in modern, industrial society.

2. Discuss ways in which the realities of bureaucracy are different from the ideal characteristics as stated by Max Weber.

3. Analyze reasons why voluntary associations have become so important in American society. Be sure to include the functions which such associations fulfill.

4. Describe some of the problems faced by those who have careers in bureaucracies, and note what some employees and organizations have done to lessen these problems.

5. Differentiate between the Japanese and American corporate models. Explain why it would be difficult to transplant these models from one nation to another.

C H A P T E R

8

Deviance and Social Control

CHAPTER SUMMARY

Deviance, which refers to violations of social norms, is relative; what people consider deviant varies from one culture to another and from group to group within a society. To explain deviance, biologists and psychologists look for reasons within people, such as genetic predispositions or personality disorders. Symbolic interactionists use differential association and control theory to analyze the extent to which group membership influences people's behaviors and views of the world. Functionalists state that deviance is functional, using strain theory and illegitimate opportunity structures to argue that widespread socialization into norms of material success accounts for much of the crime committed by the poor. Conflict theorists argue that the group in power imposes its definitions on other groups—the ruling class directs the criminal justice system against the working class, which commits highly visible property crimes, while it diverts its own criminal activities out of the criminal justice system. Reactions to deviance include negative sanctions, labeling, degradation ceremonies, and imprisonment. People not only react to the deviant behavior of others; they also react to their own violation of the norms. Primary, secondary, and tertiary deviance refer to stages in people's reactions to their own disapproved behaviors. Many people succeed in neutralizing the norms of society and are able to commit deviant acts while thinking of themselves as conformists. Although most people resist being labeled deviant, there are those who embrace deviance. Society may deal with deviance by medicalizing it and calling it mental illness. With deviance inevitable, the larger issues are how to protect people from deviant behaviors that are harmful to their welfare, to tolerate those that are not, and to develop systems of fairer treatment for deviants.

CHAPTER OUTLINE

I. Gaining a Sociological Perspective of Deviance
   A. Deviance is the violation of rules/norms, regardless of seriousness. According to Howard S. Becker, it is not the act itself that makes an action deviant, but rather how society reacts to it. Erving Goffman used "stigma" to refer to attributes that discredit one's claim to a "normal" identity; a stigma (e.g., physical deformities, skin color) defines a person's master status, superseding all other statuses the person occupies.
   B. Social control is the formal and informal means of enforcing norms in society. To functionalists, norms result from balancing tensions between individuals and groups within a society—reaching an equilibrium. To conflict theorists, the purpose of social control is to maintain power for an elite group, primarily consisting of wealthy, white males who work behind the scenes to control government.
   C. Norms make social life possible by making behavior predictable; social chaos would exist without norms.
   D. Comparing Biological, Psychological, and Sociological Explanations
      1. Psychologists and sociobiologists explain deviance by looking within individuals; sociologists look outside the individual.
      2. Biological explanations focus on genetic factors such as intelligence, "XXY" theory (an extra Y chromosome in men leads to crime), or body type (squarish, muscular persons more likely to commit street crimes); however, none of these has held up.
      3. Psychological explanations focus on personality disorders (e.g., "bad toilet training," "suffocating mothers," etc.).
      4. Sociological explanations search outside the individual: crime is a violation of norms written into law, and each society has its own laws against certain types of behavior, but social influences—such a subcultural group memberships or social class—may "recruit" some people to break norms.
II. The Symbolic Interactionist Perspective
   A. Differential association is Edwin Sutherland's term to indicate that those who associate with groups oriented

toward deviant activities learn an "excess of definitions" of deviance and, thus, are more likely to engage in deviant activities.

1. Although norms separating most groups vary only slightly from dominant society, some groups teach members to violate norms (e.g., families involved in crime may set their children on a lawbreaking path; some neighborhoods tend to encourage deviant behavior).
2. Symbolic interactionists stress that people are not mere pawns, because individuals help produce their own orientation to life and their choice of association helps to shape the self.

B. Control Theory
1. Two control systems are at work: Inner controls are one's capacity to withstand "pushes" and "pulls" (temptations) toward deviance, and include internalized morality, integrity, fear of punishment, and desire to be good, while outer controls involve groups (e.g., family, friends, the police) that influence a person to stay away from crime.
2. Travis Hirschi noted that bonding to society affects inner controls; bonds are based on attachments, commitments, involvements, and beliefs.
3. Control theory is a functional theory (when outer controls operate, person conforms to social norms), but since symbols and meanings are central, it has been adopted by symbolic interactionists.

C. Labeling theory: Labels people are given affect their own and others' perceptions of them, thus channeling their behavior either into deviance or into conformity.

III. The Functionalist Perspective
A. Emile Durkheim stated that deviance, including crime, is functional, for it contributes to social order, performing three functions: it clarifies moral boundaries (a group's ideas about how people should act and think) and affirms norms; it promotes social unity; and it promotes social change (if boundary violations gain enough support, they become new, acceptable behaviors).
B. Strain theory is the term coined by Robert Merton for the strain resulting from socializing people to desire a goal but denying many the means to reach it.
1. Merton used "anomie" (Durkheim's term) to refer to the strain people experience when they are blocked in their attempts to achieve those goals. He identified five types of responses to anomie: conformity (using lawful means to seek goals society sets); innovation (using illegitimate means to achieve them); ritualism (giving up on achieving cultural goals but clinging to conventional rules of conduct); retreatism (rejecting cultural goals, dropping out); and rebellion (seeking to replace society's goals).
2. Merton's theory has held up under examination—anomie is highest among lower social classes, which have less access to the institutionalized means to success.
C. Illegitimate Opportunity Theory

1. Social classes have distinct styles of crime due to different levels of access to institutionalized means.
2. Illegitimate opportunity structures are opportunities for remunerative crime woven into the texture of life. They may result when legitimate structures fail and thereby draw the poor into certain crimes in unequal numbers.
3. White-collar crimes result from an illegitimate opportunity structure among higher classes which makes white-collar crime functional. Such crime exist in greater numbers than commonly perceived, and can be very costly—may total about $200 billion a year. They can involve physical harm and sometimes death (concealing information that silicone breast implants might leak, for example).

IV. The Conflict Perspective
A. The criminal justice system (police, courts, and prisons) does not operate impartially because most prisoners come from the marginal working class (most desperate members of the working class, having few skills, often unemployed), which commits street crimes, which threaten the social order, and are severely punished.
B. Criminal justice system does not focus on the capitalist class and the harm it does to the masses—law is an instrument of repression, designed to maintain the powerful.

V. Reactions to Deviants
A. Sanctions are either negative (punishments ranging from frowns and gossip to imprisonment, exile, and capital punishment) or positive (rewards for desired behavior, ranging from smiles to awards).
B. Labeling
1. William J. Chambliss's study of the Saints and the Roughnecks provides an excellent illustration of labeling theory—labels given to people affect how others perceive them and how they perceive themselves, thus channeling their behavior.
2. Even though the Saints—who were from respectable middle-class families—committed more crimes, they were seen as headed for success, while the Roughnecks—who were from working-class families and hung around street corners—were seen as headed for trouble and treated as "troublemakers."
C. Official Crime Statistics—caution is needed in interpreting them because authorities may react differently toward some groups: (1) statistics are produced within a context and for a purpose; (2) who gets arrested for what is affected by social class; and (3) police discretion in whom to arrest may reflect police biases.
D. Degradation Ceremonies—individual is called before a group and denounced; when pronounced guilty, steps are taken to strip the individual of his/her identity as a group member.
E. Imprisonment—which follows the degradation ceremony (public trial/pronouncement that the person is unfit to live among law-abiding people)—is an increasingly popular reaction to crime but fails to teach in-

mates to stay away from crime. The recidivism rate in the United States runs 85–90%, and those given probation do no better. The high recidivism rate may result from not agreeing on purpose of imprisonment, which may be retribution, deterrence, rehabilitation, or incapacitation (removing offenders from circulation).

VI. Reactions by Deviants
   A. Primary, Secondary, and Tertiary Deviance:
      1. primary deviance: fleeting acts not absorbed into self-concept
      2. secondary deviance: deviant acts absorbed into self-concept
      3. tertiary deviance: deviant behavior is relabeled as nondeviant
   B. Neutralizing Deviance—Gresham Sykes and David Matza coined the term techniques of neutralization to describe the five forms of rationalization they found in a group of delinquents:
      1. denial of responsibility ("I didn't do it");
      2. denial of injury ("Who really got hurt?");
      3. denial of a victim ("She deserved it");
      4. condemnation of the condemners ("Who are *you* to talk?"); and
      5. appeal to higher loyalty ("I had to help my friends").
   C. Embracing Deviance: Most people resist being labeled deviant, but some revel in a deviant identity (e.g.,

motorcycle gangs may pride themselves on getting into trouble, laughing at death, etc.).

VII. The Medicalization of Deviance: Mental Illness
   A. Medicalization of deviance is the view of deviance as a symptom of some underlying illness that needs to be treated. But Thomas Szasz argues that mental illness is simply problem behaviors. Some forms of "mental" illnesses have organic causes (e.g., depression caused by a chemical imbalance in the brain); others are responses to trouble coping with problems. Some sociologists find Szasz's analysis refreshing because it indicates that mental illness does not underlie bizarre behaviors.
   B. The Homeless Mentally Ill: Deinstitutionalization (release of mental patients into the community) occurred during the 1960s when counseling and other outpatient services were supposed to enable former patients to adjust to outside life; however, the network of outpatient services was not set up, and patients were released into the streets anyway. Homelessness and mental illness are reciprocal: they can cause each other.

VIII. The Need for a More Humane Approach
   With deviance inevitable, one measure of a society is how it treats its deviants—a more humane approach is needed.

LEARNING OBJECTIVES

After reading and studying Chapter 8, the student should be able to:

1. Explain why deviance is difficult to define.
2. Compare and contrast biological, psychological, and sociological explanations of deviance.
3. State the key components of the symbolic interaction perspective on deviance, and briefly explain differential association theory, control theory, and labeling theory.
4. Discuss the major reasons why functionalists view deviance as functional for society.
5. Describe Merton's strain theory, and list and briefly explain the five types of responses to anomie.
6. Identify the relationship between social class and crime by

using the illegitimate opportunity theory and perspectives on white-collar crime.
7. Explain the conflict view of the relationship between class, crime, and the criminal justice system.
8. Describe the reactions to deviants, and state why official statistics may not accurately reflect the nature and extent of crime in America.
9. Distinguish between primary, secondary, and tertiary deviance. Give examples of each.
10. Summarize these reactions by deviants: neutralizing deviance and embracing deviance.
11. Explain what is meant by the medicalization of deviance. Give the major arguments that could be presented "for" and "against" the medicalization of deviance.

KEY TERMS

anomie
capitalist class
control theory
crime
criminal justice system
cultural goals
degradation ceremonies
deinstitutionalization
deterrence
deviance
deviants
differential association
genetic predisposition

halfway houses
illegitimate opportunity structures
incapacitation
institutionalized means
labeling theory
marginal working class
medicalization of deviance
negative sanctions
official deviance
personality disorders
pluralistic theory of social control
police discretion
positive sanctions

primary deviance
recidivism rate
rehabilitation
retribution
secondary deviance
social control
social order
stigma
strain theory
street crime
techniques of neutralization
tertiary deviance
white-collar crime
working class

KEY PEOPLE

Howard Becker	Erving Goffman
Edwin Sutherland	Walter Reckless
Travis Hirschi	Emile Durkheim
Robert Merton	Richard Cloward and Lloyd Ohlin
William Chambliss	Harold Garfinkel
Gresham Sykes and David Matza	Thomas Szasz

CLASS DISCUSSION QUESTIONS

1. What does the word "deviance" mean to you? Do sociologists use this term in the same way?
2. Do you agree that a college student who cheats on an exam is, in some ways, similar to a mugger on a dark street?
3. Why do you think it is more difficult to maintain social control in industrialized societies such as the United States?
4. Do you agree with the conflict view that the group that holds power must always fend off groups that desire to replace it? If so, give examples.
5. According to conflict theorists, what group controls American society? Do you agree? Why or why not?
6. What would life be like if you could never predict what others were going to do?
7. What are some recent examples of biological explanations for deviant behavior? Do you think they are valid? (e.g., PMS, high testosterone levels, etc.)
8. Do you think that an individual's childhood experiences inevitably cause that person to behave in a certain way? Why or why not?
9. How are sociological explanations of deviance different in focus from psychological ones?
10. Do you agree that teenage gangs are an example of differential association theory? Why or why not?
11. How can the concept of "honor" propel a person to deviance? Can you give examples?
12. What are some of the "pushes" and "pulls" a student experiences when he or she is thinking about cheating on an exam? What types of controls work against these forces?
13. Do you agree that acts are deviant only because people label them as such? Why or why not?
14. Can you give examples of social values which generate crime in the United States?
15. Is it possible for anyone who wants to gain an education or acquire a good job to do so in the United States? Why or why not?

16. Why do you think most people take legally and socially acceptable actions to get ahead even if there might be a "shortcut" outside the law?
17. Have you ever engaged in ritualism? For example, have you suffered "burnout" as a student but continued to attend classes?
18. Do you think television shows and movies have glamorized illegitimate opportunity structures? Can you give examples?
19. Why are white-collar crimes available only to people of respectable and high social status?
20. What types of crimes are most costly? Can you explain why it is difficult to answer this question?
21. Why do you think the media typically consider white-collar crime to be less newsworthy than street crime?
22. Do you think the American legal system provides equal justice for all? Why or why not?
23. Is it possible for the powerful to bypass the courts altogether? Why or why not?
24. What types of sanctions do you think are most effective? Why?
25. Why are we more likely to believe that a statement is true if we are presented with statistics to "prove" it?
26. Do you think degradation ceremonies can have a long-term harmful impact on the persons subjected to such activities?
27. What do you think contributes to the high rate of recidivism in the United States?
28. Why can't Americans make up their minds about the basic purpose of imprisonment?
29. Is there such a thing as "mental illness?" If we embraced Szasz's idea, what kinds of changes would have to be made in society?
30. Can you give examples of problems which may have been brought on by deinstitutionalization?
31. What do you think would be a more humane approach to dealing with deviance in the United States?

PROJECTS

1. In small group or class discussion, select one type of deviance and develop a chart showing how this deviance would be explained by biological, psychological, and sociological theories. Under sociological theories, be sure to include the major theories of the symbolic interaction, functionalist, and conflict perspectives.
2. Collect magazine articles, newspaper clippings, etc., to document the nature, extent, and penalties typically imposed on street crime and on white collar or elite deviance. Current examples of elite deviance include insider trading on Wall Street, savings and loan scandals, waste and fraud in defense spending, environmental pollution by corporations, etc. Present your findings to the class in scrapbook form or on overhead transparencies.
3. From the *Uniform Crime Reports* obtain a statistical picture of one of the index crimes (e.g., homicide, robbery, larceny, theft, arson) for your city over a five year period; these statistics are an index of crimes known to police. Interview

law enforcement officials in the area corresponding to the *UCR* to find the most recent statistics on what portion of these crimes have been cleared by arrest. Compare these data with the national figures on crimes cleared by arrest for cities of approximately the same size. Determine whether "official statistics" were an accurate representation of all crimes committed. Report your findings in oral or written form.

4. For a small group discussion, outline the good points and bad points about each of the following reasons for imprisoning people: retribution, deterrence, rehabilitation, and incapacitation. For a term project, find data to support your assertions about the effectiveness (or lack thereof) of the various approaches.

5. See one or more movies that involve deviant behavior (e.g., *Pretty Woman, Fatal Attraction, The Silence of the Lambs, Barbarians at the Gate,* and many others!). Analyze the following: What deviant behavior was portrayed? Were the "deviants" portrayed in a positive or negative light? How did the "deviants" perceive themselves (e.g., at what stage— primary, secondary, or tertiary—were they)? What happened to the "deviants" at the end (i.e., did they live happily ever after or were they "punished")? Write a paper describing how you conducted your research and giving your conclusions.

TRANSPARENCIES

1. (TR#8) Growth in the American Prison Population
2. (TR#9) Characteristics of American Prisoners
3. (TR#10) Classification of Norms

TRANSPARENCY MASTERS

1. (TR#6M) Merton's Typology of Individual Adaptation to Anomie
2. (TR#7M) Delinquent Acts
3. (TR#8M) Crime Clock

VIDEOS/MOVIES

Comparing Biological, Psychological, and Sociological Explanations

Crime and Human Nature. Are criminality and antisocial aggressive behavior due to nature or nurture? Can adult criminal behavior be predicted in the antisocial behavior of children, weak attachments to family, and fatalism about the future? Phil Donahue is joined by anthropologist Ashley Montagu and other experts in addressing these questions. 28 min. Available from A&B Video Library and FHS.

The Violent Mind. Changes in the anatomy and chemistry of the brain can cause violent behavior. Recent research suggests that even the acts of a serial killer may have a biological or genetic basis. If science can show a biological or environmental cause for any antisocial act, when are humans "guilty" of committing a crime? Available from A&B Video Library.

White Collar Crime

CNN Video II. *Crime Costs.* A 1991 Urban Institute study of the cost of crime in U.S. calculates that violent crime costs $130 billion a year, or 3% of GNP. Cost of white collar crime (such as embezzlement, tax evasion, and insider trading) is put at $200 billion yearly. The Mafia alone grosses $50 billion a year in illegal gambling, prostitution, drugs, and other activities. According to this study, at $300 billion a year, the cost of crime in the United States is greater than the national defense budget. Available from A&B Video Library.

Reactions to Deviants

Boot Camp for Troubled Teens. Describes a "tough-love" boot camp where parents who have come to the end of their rope are sending their kids. Whether the camp actually turns the kids around, or is a brutally false answer to parents' prayers is argued on this specially adapted Phil Donahue program. 28 min. Available from A&B Video Library and FHS.

Exploring Alternatives to Prison and Probation. 1992. Looks at a range of innovative solutions being tried around the country in terms of alternative sentencing programs—including paying restitution to victims and house arrest programs with electronic surveillance monitoring. 22 min. Available from FML.

Prostitution

Pretty Woman. 1990 (Color) Starring Richard Gere and Julia Roberts. A wealthy, cold-blooded businessman accidentally meets a prostitute working Hollywood Blvd. in Los Angeles. He hires her to be his companion and ultimately ends up marrying her. (R) 117 min. Available at video rental stores.

Sweet Charity. 1969. (Color) Starring Shirley McLaine as a "heart-of-gold" prostitute who falls in love with a naive young man who does not know about her work. (G) 133 min. Available at video rental stores.

We're Here Now: Prostitution. (1984) Focuses on the myths and realities of prostitution as related by seven women formerly "in the life." They talk about their personal histories and the violence they experienced on the streets. 35 min. Available from FML.

The Homeless Mentally Ill
Back Wards to Back Streets: The Deinstitutionalization of Mental Patients. 1987. Follows some of the mental patients who were deinstitutionalized as a result of a Supreme Court decree.

When community-based support did not come through, they ended up in the back streets all over America. 55 min. Available from FML.

Ironweed. 1987. (Color) Starring Jack Nicholson and Meryl Streep. Shows problems of alcoholism and mental illness among the homeless. (R) 144 min. Available at video rental stores.

SPEAKER SUGGESTIONS

1. A criminologist to discuss current issues in his or her field.
2. A police officer who investigates robberies, burglaries, drug dealing, and other street crimes.
3. A representative of a "deviant" or dissident group to talk about the impact of labeling on individuals and groups.
4. A jail or prison official to discuss problems in the criminal justice system.
5. A mental health specialist to describe some of the problems brought on by deinstitutionalization.

POP QUIZ QUESTIONS

True-False

F   1. It is the act itself that makes something deviant.

F   2. When sociologists use the term "deviant," it means that they agree that an act is bad, just as others judge it negatively.

T   3. Functionalists stress the pluralistic theory of social control.

T   4. Psychologists and sociobiologists explain deviance by looking for answers within individuals, while sociologists look for answers in factors outside the individual.

T   5. Differential association theory focuses on the effects of group membership, while control theory emphasizes how people balance pressures to conform and to deviate.

F   6. Robert Merton's strain theory is based on the conflict perspective.

F   7. White-collar crime refers to crime—such as stealing money from a coworker—that individuals in bureaucratic agencies commit.

T   8. According to conflict theorists, most of the prisoners in the United States come from the ranks of the marginal working class.

F   9. Official crime statistics are a good reflection of the nature and extent of crime committed in the United States.

T   10. Some researchers have found that the recidivism rate in the United States runs as high as 85–90%.

ESSAY QUESTIONS

1. Discuss the sociological perspective of deviance and explain how it is different from psychological and sociobiological explanations.
2. Distinguish between the following symbolic interactionist theories of deviance: differential association theory, control theory, and labeling theory.
3. Explain why functionalists state that deviance is functional for society. Use strain theory and illegitimate opportunity theory to explain the relationship between social values, social class, and crime.
4. Contrast functionalist and conflict theories on the causes of crime in society.
5. Discuss society's reactions to deviants and the reactions by deviants toward society and toward their own behavior.
6. Summarize the controversy over the medicalization of deviance. Explain the process of deinstitutionalization and how this may have failed many people in the 1960s.

9

Social Stratification in Global Perspective

CHAPTER SUMMARY

Social stratification is a system in which people are divided into layers according to their relative power, property, and prestige. Four major systems of social stratification include: (1) slavery—owning other people; (2) caste—lifelong status determined by birth; (3) class—based on possession of money or material possessions—begins as an ascribed status but may have some degree of individual social mobility through individual achievement; and (4) clan—status depends on lineage. Class systems are characteristic of industrialized societies, but class and clan systems may coexist as parallel forms of social stratification in partly industrialized societies. Gender discrimination cuts across all forms of social stratification. Early sociologists disagreed about the meaning of social class in industrialized nations. Karl Marx argued that a person's relationship to the means of production

was the only factor determining social class. Max Weber argued that three elements—property, prestige, and power—dictate an individual's standing in society. Functional and conflict views regarding the universality of stratification are noted, along with Gerhard Lenski's suggested synthesis of the perspectives. Nations, as well as people within a nation, are stratified into groups based on relative power, prestige, and property. The most common model divides nations into three groups: First, Second, and Third Worlds. Four theories explaining the origins of global stratification are imperialism and colonialism, world system theory, dependency theory, and a culture of poverty. The maintenance of international stratification through neocolonialism and multinational corporations is discussed.

CHAPTER OUTLINE

I. What Is Social Stratification?
   Social stratification is the division of nations or people according to relative power, property, and prestige.

II. Systems of Social Stratification
   A. Slavery: Form of social stratification where some people own others. Initially it was not based on race, but on punishment for violation of the law, defeat in battle, or debt. It could be temporary or permanent; slaves usually owned no property and had no power. It the New World, indentured service (contractual sale of own services for a specified time) was the first form of slavery. Due to a shortage of indentured servants, colonists tried to enslave Native Americans; when that failed, they imported Africans as slaves.
   B. Caste systems: Status determined by birth is lifelong; boundaries are enforced by endogamy (marriage within one's own group) and teaching that contact with inferior castes contaminates the superior caste. In India, it is based on religion; there are four main castes, which are divided into thousands of subcastes; the lowest caste is considered to be "untouchables." South Africa's apartheid is based on racial separation: four racial castes dictate where people live, work, etc.

   Apartheid and India's caste system are finally breaking down because of industrialization and urbanization.
   C. Class systems are a form of social stratification based on material possessions. Social class position generally is based on ascribed status, but the system allows social mobility based on achieved status.
   D. Industrialized societies tend to have class systems, but class and clan systems may coexist in partly industrialized societies. In a clan system, an individual's status depends on lineage, which is determined by birth, but interclan marriage is permitted. Arab nations have parallel class and clan social stratification.
   E. Gender and Social Stratification: Every society is stratified according to gender, although the type may vary from society to society or within the same society. Gender always is part of the distinctions in each layer.

III. What Determines Social Class?
   A. Marx: Class depends on ownership of the means of production—the bourgeoisie (capitalists) own the means of production; the proletariat (workers) sells its labor to capitalists. Class consciousness is the basis of

the unity of workers—the workers would revolt, take control of the means of production, and usher in a classless society.

B. Weber: Property, prestige, and power determine social class. Property is an essential element, but some people (e.g., heads of corporations) control the means of production without owning it. Prestige may be derived from ownership of property, but also from other factors such as athletic skills. Power is the ability to control others, even over objection.

IV. Why Is Social Stratification Universal?

A. Functionalist View (Davis and Moore): Stratification is inevitable because:
1. some positions are more important than others;
2. important positions must be filled by qualified people; and
3. society must offer them greater rewards.

B. Tumin: A Critical Response. How does one measure the importance of a position? If stratification worked as described, society would be a meritocracy (all positions awarded on basis of merit). Money/fringe benefits are not the only reasons people take jobs.

C. According to Gaetano Mosca, every society gets stratified by power because it must be organized by politics to get the work done; in politics, some people take leadership positions; the persons in positions of power use them to gain rewards. The ruling class is well organized; difficult for majority it governs to resist.

D. The Conflict View
1. Conflict, not function, is the basis of social stratification. Every society has limited resources, and in every society groups struggle with one another for those resources. When a group gains power, it uses that power to extract what it can from the groups beneath it.
2. C. Wright Mills, Ralf Dahrendorf, and Randall Collins argue that conflict between capitalists and workers is only one of the conflicts—groups within the same class compete for scarce resources, thus, conflict is between many groups (e.g., young vs. old; women vs. men).

E. Gerhard Lenski's synthesis: Functionalists are right when societies do not accumulate wealth; conflict theory is right when societies have a surplus (where humans struggle to control the surpluses).

V. Why Is Social Stratification Universal?
The elite can exploit workers in the first stages of industrialization, but industrialization is characterized by the growth of a middle class: skilled and educated workers are needed for technical jobs; with skills, workers are able to command greater resources. The elite buys off the lower classes rather than struggle with them.

VI. Comparative Social Stratification
A. In Great Britain, slightly over half the population is working class; slightly less than half is middle class; and 1% is upper class, owning 43% of nation's private capital.

B. In the former Soviet Union, "ideal" (classless) communism was never realized. Communist party member-

ship was the basis of stratification. Members had greater access to resources than nonmembers and higher levels in the party received more privileges.

VII. Maintaining National Stratification
It is maintained by controlling social institutions, including law and order. Control of ideas and information is more effective than use of brute force. Social networks of elites perpetuate social inequality.

VIII. Global Stratification
A. The First World is the heavily industrialized nations (U.S., Canada, Great Britain, France, Germany, Switzerland, Japan, Australia, New Zealand), which are capitalistic, although variations exist in economic systems. Its poor live better/longer than Third World average citizens.

B. The Second World is the more or less industrialized nations (former Soviet Union, Poland, Czechoslovakia, Hungary). Its people have considerably lower income and a poorer standard of living. A higher proportion of people live on farms with limited access to electricity, indoor plumbing, and other material goods.

C. The Third World is nations with little industrialization—such as Greece, Portugal, Mexico, Indonesia, and Ethiopia. Most people live on farms or in villages with low standards of living. It is characterized by high birth rates and rapidly growing populations (placing even greater burdens on limited facilities).

D. Imperfections in the Model: Not all nations fit the categories well (e.g., the oil-rich nations in the Middle East have become wealthy by providing oil but have not industrialized).

IX. How the World's Nations Became Stratified
A. Imperialism and Colonialism
1. Imperialism was practiced by European powers over the centuries: Industrialized nations needed consumers elsewhere; thus, conquests expanded markets, gained access to raw materials. Nations that industrialized first got ahead of the rest of the world and became the most powerful.
2. Colonialism occurred when industrialized nations made colonies of weaker nations and exploited their labor/natural resources. European nations tended to focus on Africa, while the United States concentrated on Central and South America. Some corporations were involved in this domination. Western imperialism and colonization shaped the Third World.

B. World System Theory (espoused by Immanuel Wallerstein)
1. Countries are politically and economically tied together. There are four groups of interconnected nations:
a. core nations, where capitalism first developed;
b. semi-periphery (Mediterranean area), highly dependent on trade with core nations;
c. periphery (eastern Europe), mainly limited to selling cash crops to core nations, has limited economic development;
d. external area (most of Africa/Asia) left out of

growth of capitalism, has few economic ties to core nations.

2. Capitalist dominance results from relentless expansion—even external area nations are drawn into commercial web. Globalization has occurred at such a rate that virtually no nation is able to live in isolation.

C. Dependency theory attributes lack of economic development in Third World to dominance of world economy by industrialized nations. It asserts that First World nations turned other nations into their plantations and mines, taking whatever they needed; as a result, many Third World nations began to specialize in a single cash crop.

D. Culture of poverty: A culture that perpetuates poverty. John Kenneth Galbraith argued that cultures (traditional values/religious beliefs) inhibit Third World development.

E. Evaluating the theories: Most sociologists find imperialism/world system/dependency theory explanations preferable to the culture of poverty theory, but each theory only partially explains global stratification.

X. Maintaining Global Stratification

A. Neocolonialism: The First World controls the Third World without force because it controls markets, sets prices, etc., according to Michael Harrington. The First World moves hazardous industries to the Third World. It sells weapons and manufactured goods to the Third World, preventing it from developing its own industrial capacity.

B. Multinational corporations contribute to exploitation of Third World: Some exploit Third World nations directly by controlling national and local politics, running them as a fiefdom. First World nations are primary beneficiaries of profits made in Third World nations. Michael Lipton states that multinational corporations work closely with an urban power elite of the Third World. In some situations, multinational corporations may bring prosperity to Third World nations because new factors provide salaries and opportunities which otherwise would not exist for workers in those countries.

LEARNING OBJECTIVES

After reading and studying Chapter 9, the student should be able to:

1. Define social stratification and briefly discuss the four major systems of social stratification.
2. Describe the characteristics of slavery, and note the uses of slavery in the New World.
3. Distinguish between caste and class systems. Give examples of each.
4. State the relationship between gender and social stratification.
5. Identify the basic assumptions of Karl Marx regarding what determines one's social class.
6. Explain why Max Weber was critical of Marx's perspective, and summarize Weber's views regarding social class position.
7. State the basic assumptions of functionalists like Davis and Moore, and present Tumin's criticisms of this viewpoint.

8. Discuss Mosca's perspective on the universality of social stratification and explain why he is considered to be a forerunner of the conflict view.
9. Compare Marx's early conflict-oriented perspective with that of later conflict theorists such as G. William Domhoff, C. Wright Mills, and Irving Louis Horowitz.
10. Explain why elites are not able to totally exploit other people in a given society.
11. Compare and contrast social stratification in Great Britain, the former Soviet Union, and the United States.
12. Describe the major characteristics of First World, Second World, and Third World nations, and name at least three countries which fit in each category.
13. Outline the major theories of how the world's nations became stratified.
14. Explain how global stratification has been maintained.

KEY TERMS

ablution	culture of poverty	lumpenproletariat
apartheid	dependency theory	meritocracy
bourgeoisie	divine right of kings	multinational corporation
capitalist world economy	endogamy	neocolonialism
caste	false consciousness	proletariat
clan	globalization	slavery
class	ideology	social mobility
class consciousness	imperialism	social stratification
colonization	indentured service	world system

KEY PEOPLE

Karl Marx
Kingsley Davis and Wilbert Moore
Gaetano Mosca
Immanuel Wallerstein
Michael Harrington

Max Weber
Melvin Tumin
Gerhard Lenski
John Kenneth Galbraith
Michael Lipton

CLASS DISCUSSION QUESTIONS

1. How does social class help to explain why you are in college and how many children you plan to have?
2. Why do you think slavery has been common throughout world history? Who benefits from a system of slavery?
3. Why were women some of the first slaves?
4. Why do you think a person would "sell" themselves into indentured service? Can you think of any circumstances in which you would be willing to do the same?
5. What type of ideology is necessary to justify the existence of slavery?
6. What do you think has contributed to the caste system lasting for almost three thousand years in India?
7. Why do the caste systems in India and South Africa appear to be breaking down?
8. Would you rather be born into a caste or class system? Why?
9. Do you believe that social mobility still exists in the United States? Why or why not?
10. Can you think of any society in which women are at the top of the system of social stratification? In what ways does gender discrimination cut across all systems of social stratification?
11. Do you agree with Marx that social class depends on a single factor—the means of production? Why or why not?
12. Do you think that Marx's notion of a classless society is possible? Why or why not?
13. Are property (wealth), prestige, and power central ingredients of the American class structure? Why or why not?
14. Can you give examples of how property can bring prestige and how prestige can bring property?
15. Do you think politicians should use their positions to gain property?
16. What types of positions do functionalists think should be most highly rewarded in society? Do you agree?
17. Can you explain how the Davis-Moore thesis could be used to justify social inequality?
18. What arguments can you give to justify paying a surgeon more than a garbage collector? How about paying a garbage collector more than a surgeon?
19. Do you agree with Tumin's idea that money and fringe benefits are not the only reasons people take jobs? Why or why not?
20. Why is it necessary for all ruling classes to develop an ideology to justify people's relative positions? Can you think of examples?
21. Is admission to law school or medical school largely based on competition within the same class? Why or why not?
22. Do you agree with the conflict perspective that the elite buys off the lower classes? If yes, what are some examples?
23. Why do you think most Americans are likely to claim they are middle class? Why are the British more class-conscious?
24. If you had lived in the former Soviet Union, where would you have wanted to be in their system of stratification? Why?
25. How do you think those at the top of American society are able to maintain their positions? Will they always be able to do so?
26. Do the poor in First World nations live better and longer lives than the average citizens of Third World nations?
27. Do you think the governments of First World nations have any responsibility to help Second and Third World nations?
28. Did the United States gain its powerful position at the expense of other nations?
29. Can you explain why most sociologists agree with imperialism, world systems, or dependency theories more than with theories based on a culture of poverty?
30. Are you surprised to learn that of the one hundred largest economic units in the world, fifty are nations and the other fifty are multinational corporations? Why or why not?

PROJECTS

1. For small group discussions or a semester project, design a system of social stratification for the United States or on a global basis in which power, property, and prestige would be distributed in the most equitable manner possible. You do not know where you will be living in the structure after you have devised it!
2. For a class presentation or term paper, read additional sources on issues pertaining to gender and social stratification. Some recent ones pertaining to global stratification include: (a) Sekaran, Uma, and Frederick T. L. Leong (eds.) *Womanpower: Managing in Times of Demographic Turbulence.* Newbury Park: Sage, 1991. (b) Sivard, Ruth. *Women: A World Survey.* NY: Carnegie Corp., 1985. (c) Tinker, Irene (ed.) *Persistent Inequalities: Women and World Development.* NY: Oxford, 1990.
3. Prepare for a series of class debates or discussions by preparing "pro" and "con" responses to these statements:
   a. Inequality is inevitable.

    b. There will always be poor people.

    c. The United States has not contributed in any way to poverty in other countries.

4. During the semester maintain a file of current articles about events occurring in the former Soviet Union. Write an update at the end of the semester on how recent changes in the economic and political structures have affected social stratification there.

5. Read one or more of the following books and write a term paper on issues pertaining to global stratification: (a) Chase-Dunn, Christopher. *Global Formation: Structures of the World Economy*. London: Basil Blackwell, 1989. (b) McCord, William, and Arline McCord. *Paths to Progress: Bread and Freedom in Developing Societies*. NY: W.W. Norton, 1986 (c) Rostow, W. W. *Rich Countries and Poor Countries: Reflections on the Past, Lessons for the Future*. Boulder: Westview, 1987. See also Suggested Readings at the end of Chapter 9.

6. Acquire annual reports of multinational corporations. Analyze the section of each report which discusses the global activities of that particular corporation. Relate this information to the discussion on maintaining global stratification. Here are some additional sources which may help you do your analysis: (a) Barnet, Richard J. and Ronald E. Muller. *Global Reach: The Power of the Multinational Corporation*. NY: Simon & Schuster, 1974. (b) Moskowitz, Milton. *The Global Marketplace*. NY: Macmillan, 1987. (c) Reich, Robert B. *The World of Nations: Preparing Ourselves for 21st Century Capitalism*. NY: Knopf, 1991. (d) Sampson, Anthony. *Black and Gold: Tycoons, Revolutionaries, and Apartheid*. NY: Pantheon, 1987. (An extraordinary account of the complicity of multinational corporations in repression and racial conflict in South Africa.)

TRANSPARENCIES

1. (TR#11) The Percentage of a Country's Total Income Going to the Poorest 20% of the Population for Selected Countries
2. (TR#12) Differing Explanations of Social Stratification
3. (TR#13) Income Inequality around the World

TRANSPARENCY MASTERS

1. (TR#9M) India's Caste System

VIDEOS/MOVIES

Systems of Social Stratification: Caste

Caste at Birth. 1991. There are 150 million "untouchables" in India who live a segregated life. They cannot own land or get an education and are condemned to the most menial jobs. While the government has tried to improve the condition of the untouchables, these attempts have been met by strong resistance from upper caste Hindus who profit from this source of cheap labor. 52 min. Available from FML.

Gandhi. 1982. (Color) An account of the life of Mohandas K. Gandhi, a lawyer who became India's leader and a worldwide symbol of peace and understanding. He fought against the caste system in India. 100 min. Available at video rental stores.

The Color Purple. 1985. (Color) A black woman's life and hard times in the South, spanning some forty years, based on Alice Walker's Pulitzer Prize–winning book. (PG-13) 152 min. Available at video rental stores.

Gender and Social Stratification

Maids and Madams. 1986. Shot in South Africa under the system of apartheid, this video shows the complex relationship between black household workers and white employers. This domestic situation is a microcosm of the racial issues which have divided the country. Over a million black women live in domestic bondage where they are underpaid and overworked. 52 min. Available from FML.

Colonialism

The Paths of Colonialism. Documents colonialism from the birth of empire in the 16th century, the burgeoning British Empire, including the Far East and South Africa, the efforts and successes of the French in North Africa—all in support of the mother country's search for raw materials for its industries and markets for its manufactured products. The program ends with the last of the large-scale colonial adventures: Mussolini's subjugation of Ethiopia in 1935. 17 min. Available from FHS.

Dependency Theory

CNN Video II. *Poverty*. Officials of the World Bank are worried that aid from Industrialized nations to developing nations is stagnating. In 1988, the developed nations provided developing countries with $51 billion dollars worth of aid. One-fourth of the world's inhabitants struggle to survive on less than $400 a year, according to the report, and 1 billion live in poverty. The World Bank report foresees that the cessation of the Cold War and resulting freer trade may not help developing nations in the short run because they chiefly export commodities, and an end to trade barriers might cause raw material prices to fall. Available from A&B Video Library.

The Debt Crisis—New Perspectives. 1990. Untangles the complexities of the debt crisis, the most urgent economic problem in the world today. Most developing countries, having borrowed heavily in the 70s, are unable to service their debt. This in turn has hurt industrial nations as potentially large export markets have faded away. The general threat of political unrest in many Latin American countries has increased the urgency of finding a solution. 55 min. Available from FML.

SPEAKER SUGGESTIONS

1. A researcher studying global stratification or caste systems.
2. A gender specialist conducting research on Third World women.
3. An expert on the former Soviet Union, Poland, Czechoslovakia, or other Second World countries.
4. An economist conducting research on development in First World and Third World countries.
5. A business expert knowledgeable about the inner workings of multinational corporations.

POP QUIZ QUESTIONS

True-False

T 1. Social class helps explain why a student is in college and how many children she or he plans to have.
F 2. Social stratification does not exist in all societies.
F 3. Throughout history, all slavery has been based on racism.
F 4. India no longer has a caste system of social stratification.
T 5. The United States has practiced a racial caste system.
T 6. Gender discrimination cuts across all systems of social stratification.

F 7. Karl Marx argued that property, prestige, and power were the major determinates of social class in capitalist societies.
T 8. Functionalists beieve that social inequality is functional for society.
F 9. First World and Second World nations are quite similar in their level of industrialization and standard of living.
T 10. World system theorists argue that capitalism's relentless expansion has resulted in a capitalist world economy dominated by the core nations.

ESSAY QUESTIONS

1. Analyze the major ways in which the lives of individuals are different in systems of slavery, caste, class, and clan and class.
2. State Karl Marx's assertion about social class position, and explain why Max Weber was very critical of Marx's viewpoint.
3. Distinguish between the functionalist and conflict views regarding the necessity of social stratification in societies. State Tumin's criticisms of the functionalist viewpoint.
4. Discuss global stratification, and indicate the characteristics of First, Second, and Third World nations.
5. Compare the following theories regarding global stratification: imperialism and colonialism, world system theory, dependency theory, and culture of poverty theory.
6. Discuss the role of multinational corporations in maintaining global stratification.

CHAPTER

10

Social Class in American Society

CHAPTER SUMMARY

Sociologists do not agree on how many social classes there are. Karl Marx argued that there are only two classes: the capitalists who own the means of production and the workers who sell their labor. Max Weber believed that wealth (property and income), power, and prestige all are dimensions of social class. If people have a mixture of high and low marks in the three dimensions, they are considered to be status inconsistent. The chapter presents Eric Wright's update of Marx's theory, and Gilbert and Kahl's model which updates the Weberian perspectives. Consequences of social class in terms of life chances, physical and mental health, family life, values and attitudes, political involvement, religion, education, and the criminal justice system are discussed. The various types of social mobility (including intergenerational, structural, and exchange mobility) are compared, and the costs of mobility are analyzed. The chapter concludes with an assessment of poverty in the United States, noting who the poor are and why children are more likely to live in poverty than are adults. Finally, short- and long-term poverty are compared, and individual versus structural explanations of poverty are presented.

CHAPTER OUTLINE

I. What Is Social Class?
   A. A social class is a large group of people who rank close to each other in wealth, power, and prestige.
   B. Three ways of measuring social class are: subjective method (ask people what their own social class is, but most people give the wrong answer); reputational method (ask people what class others belong to—W. Lloyd Warner pioneered this method, which is useful only in smaller cities, where people know each other's reputations); and objective method (researcher ranks people according to wealth, power, and prestige; most sociologists use this method).
II. Dimensions of Social Class
   A. Wealth consists of property and income (which are not always the same—a person may own much property yet have little income, or vice versa). Ownership of property is not distributed evenly: 10% of the U.S. population owns 68% of the property. Likewise, income is acquired disproportionately: the top 20% of Americans get 45% of the income; the bottom 20% receive less than 5%. The 1960s "war on poverty" initially increased the income of the poorest sector, but economic policies of the 1980s reversed this trend.
   B. Power follows money (1/3 of U.S. Senators are millionaires) and is concentrated in the hands of a few ("power elite") who share same ideologies and reinforce each other's world view.

C. Prestige is respect given to various occupations/accomplishments. Occupations are the primary source of prestige—those with high prestige pay more, require more education, entail more abstract thought, and offer greater autonomy. To make prestige valuable, the elite has made rules to emphasize higher status. Status symbols are ways of displaying prestige.
   D. Status inconsistency describes the situations of people with mixed high and low marks in dimensions of wealth, power, and prestige. Most people are status consistent (same rank, all three dimensions). Status inconsistent people want others to act toward them on the basis of their highest status, but judge others on lowest status. A janitor who earns more than residents of apartment house where the janitor carries out trash is an example. Gerhard Lenski asserted that status-inconsistent people are more likely to approve of political action aimed against higher status groups.
III. Social Class in Industrial Society
   A. How many classes exist in industrial society is a matter of debate, but there are two main models, one that builds on Marx and the other on Weber.
   B. Sociologist Eric Wright realized that not everyone falls into Marx's two classes (capitalists and workers), which were based on one's relationship to the means of production. Executives, managers, and supervisors would fall into Marx's category of "workers" (not owning the

means of production), but act more like capitalists. Wright therefore identified four classes:

1. capitalists, who own their enterprises and employ others;
2. petty bourgeoise, who own small businesses;
3. managers, who sell their labor but have authority over others; and
4. workers, who simply sell their labor to others.

C. Sociologists Dennis Gilbert and Joseph Kahl developed a model based on Weber to describe class structure in the United States and other capitalist countries. It divides people into these classes:

1. The capitalist class (1% of the population; annual income at least $500,000) is investors, heirs, and a few executives. Members attended prestigious universities, and can be divided into "old" money and "new" money (people whose wealth has been in the family longer have greater prestige).
2. The upper-middle class (14% of the population; annual income at least $50,000) is professionals/upper managers—attended college or university and frequently have postgraduate degrees.
3. The lower-middle class (35% of the population; annual income about $30,000) is semi-professionals, lower managers, craftsmen and foremen. Most have at least a high school education.
4. The working class (30% of the population; annual income $15,000 to $25,000) is factory workers and low-paid white collar workers. Most have high school educations and concentrate on achieving seniority and avoiding layoffs.
5. The working poor (17% of the population; annual income less than $15,000) is relatively unskilled blue-collar and white-collar workers, and those with temporary and seasonal jobs. They probably did not do well in school, are constantly in debt, and live from paycheck to paycheck.
6. The underclass (3% of the population) is concentrated in the inner cities and has little connection with the job market (the homeless are part of this class, but their condition is so bad that they occupy an unofficial rung below it).

IV. Consequences of Social Class

A. The lower a person's social class, the more likely that person is to die at an earlier age. Infants born to the poor are 50% more likely to die during the first year of life. The poor are more likely to be killed by accident, fire, or homicide.

B. Since medical care is expensive, the higher classes receive better medical care, despite government aid to the poor, who are less able to afford balanced, nutritional meals. Mental health is also worse for the lower classes.

C. Marriages are more likely to fail in the lower social classes; the children of the poor thus are more likely to live in broken homes. In general, the higher their social class, the more rewarding people find their family life. Childrearing varies by class, as parents anticipate that their children will work at similar types of jobs. Lower

class families teach children to defer to authority, as is required in their jobs. Higher class families encourage freedom, creativity, and self-expression, as is found in their jobs.

D. Higher social classes place stronger emphasis on family tradition (ancestors, history, sense of unity/purpose), "breeding" (selecting a correct mate), and being "cultured."

E. People in lower social classes are more likely to vote Democratic, and those in higher classes to vote Republican, as the parties are seen as promoting different class interests. People in higher classes are more likely to be conservative on economic issues (lower taxes, etc.) and more liberal on social issues (individual rights, etc.). Political participation is not equal: the higher classes are more likely to vote and get involved in politics than those in lower social classes.

F. Religious denominations tend to follow class lines. Episcopalians draw heavily from the middle and upper classes, Methodists from the middle class, and Baptists from the lower classes.

G. Education levels increase in proportion to social standing. The American educational system is based on middle-class values, and children from lower classes are likely to find themselves uncomfortable in school, where they do less well and tend to drop out during their high school years. The capitalist class bypasses public schools in favor of exclusive private schools, where its children are trained to take a commanding role in society.

H. The criminal justice system is not blind to class: members of lower classes are more likely to be on probation, parole, or in jail, and more crimes occur in lower class neighborhoods.

V. Social Mobility

A. Intergenerational mobility is the change (up or down) that family members make in social class from one generation to the next, as a result of individual effort or individual failure. Sociologists are more interested in structural mobility—social changes that affect large numbers of people (e.g., to upgrade vast numbers of blue-collar jobs to white-collar positions affects millions of people). Exchange mobility is movement of people up and down the social class system, where, on balance, the system remains the same (the term refers to general, overall movement of large numbers of people that leaves the class system basically untouched).

B. Studies of social mobility in the United States have focused on men, since large numbers of women in the work force is a relatively new phenomenon. Compared with their fathers: one-half of all men have moved up in social class; one-third have stayed in the same place; and one-sixth have moved down.

C. Although structural change has pushed the majority of U.S. workers into positions slightly ahead of their parents, a national economic decline could result in fewer good jobs, lower incomes, and shrinking opportunities. Since 1979, almost 3 million of the 21 million U.S. manufacturing jobs have disappeared, taking with them the dreams of upward mobility of millions of Americans. Family income has flattened despite the increase in two-incomes families.

D. Since many parents work long hours in order to earn the money necessary for their children to obtain the education necessary to rise above the parents' social class, the parents are gone much of the day, resulting in the parents and children in effect living in different worlds and not feeling close to each other.

E. Although there are abundant examples of people from humble origins climbing far up the social ladder, the widely-held belief that most Americans (including minorities and the working poor) have an average or better chance of getting ahead (the Horatio Alger myth) obviously is a statistical impossibility. Functionalists would stress that this belief is functional for society: it encourages people to compete for higher positions, while placing the blame for failure squarely on the individual.

VI. Poverty in the United States

A. The U.S. government classifies the poverty line as being families whose incomes are less than three times a low-cost food budget. Any modification of this measure instantly adds or subtracts millions of people, and thus has significant consequences.

B. Who are the poor? Race is a major factor. Although 2 out of 3 poor people are white, racial minorities are much more likely to be poor: 10% of whites, 26% of Hispanics, and 31% of African-Americans live in poverty. Old age, on the other hand, is not. The percentage of poor people over age 65 is practically the same as the percentage of persons below that age. The sex of the person who heads a U.S. family is the greatest predictor of whether a family is poor: most poor families are headed by women—35% of single-parent families headed by females are below the poverty line. The major causes of the feminization of poverty are divorce, births to unwed mothers, and the lower wages paid to women.

C. Children are more likely to live in poverty than are adults. This holds true regardless of race, but poverty is much greater among minority children: more than 1 out of 3 Hispanic-American children and more than 2 out of 5 African-American children are poor.

D. Michael Harrington and Oscar Lewis suggested in the 1960s that the poor get trapped in a "culture of poverty" due to having values and behaviors "fundamentally different" from other Americans. Patricia Ruggles subsequently determined that half the poor are short-term poor (moving out of poverty within a few years), while the long-term poor live in poverty for at least 8 years. Contrary to popular belief, most children of the poor do not grow up to be poor.

E. Sociologists do not believe that people are poor because of things such as laziness or lack of intelligence. Rather, sociologists look to such factors as inequalities in education, lack of access to learning job skills, and racial, ethnic, age, and gender discrimination. Economics is yet another factor: American society no longer has jobs—other than marginal ones that pay poverty incomes—for unskilled workers.

LEARNING OBJECTIVES

After reading and studying Chapter 10, the student should be able to:

1. Define social class and explain why sociologists do not agree on how many social classes there are.
2. Compare the three ways of measuring social class.
3. Outline and explain the dimensions of social class.
4. Explain Eric Wright's updated model of Marx's class theory.
5. Discuss Gilbert and Kahl's updated model of Weber's perspective.
6. Examine the consequences of social class on life chances, physical and mental health, family life, values and attitudes, political involvement, religion, education, and the criminal justice system.
7. Distinguish between the different types of social mobility and note some of the costs of such mobility.
8. State the major characteristics of the poor in the United States. Indicate how the poverty line is drawn.
9. Contrast short and long-term poverty.
10. Assess individual versus structural explanations of poverty.

KEY TERMS

contradictory class location
culture of poverty
deferred gratification
downward social mobility
exchange mobility
feminization of poverty
intergenerational mobility

life chances
objective method
petty bourgeoisie
poverty line
prestige
reputational method
social class

status
status inconsistency
structural mobility
subjective method
underclass
upward social mobility
wealth

KEY PEOPLE

W. Lloyd Warner
G. William Domhoff
Gary Marx
Dennis Gilbert and Joseph Kahl
Jonathan Cobb

C. Wright Mills
Gerhard Lenski
Eric Wright
Richard Sennett

CLASS DISCUSSION QUESTIONS

1. Do you think most Americans are conscious of social class? Why or why not?
2. Why do you think nine out of ten Americans identify themselves as middle class? Do you believe their assessment is correct?
3. Can you explain why most sociologists use the objective method to determine social class?
4. In your opinion, is it possible for a professional to have an annual income of over $150,000 a year and still have very little wealth?
5. Do you think property is pretty evenly distributed among the middle and upper classes in the United States? Why or why not?
6. Can you explain why U.S. income divisions have changed very little over the past 45 years?
7. Do you believe that the tasks performed by chief executive officers of the nation's largest corporations merit them being paid over $1 million a year each? Why or why not?
8. Do you agree that "power tends to follow money?" Can you give examples?
9. Are firefighters really less important to society (and thus should earn less) than professional football players? What about if your house is on fire?
10. How does making other people wait demonstrate a person's prestige? When you have a doctor's appointment, do you wait for your doctor or does your doctor wait for you?
11. Can you explain how an African-American woman doctor might experience status inconsistency in an elite, private hospital?
12. Why do you think it has been necessary for sociologists to update Marx's and Weber's ideas on social class?
13. Do you think there is really any difference in "old" and "new" money in the United States? Why or why not?
14. Why do parents and teachers push children to prepare themselves for upper-middle-class jobs? Can everyone in the United States have such a job?
15. Why is the stress level so high among the working poor? Is this problem increasing in the 1990s?
16. Do you think people are homeless because of their own personal habits or because of societal problems?
17. Why is money the single most significant factor in determining life chances?
18. Why do you think people higher up the social class ladder tend to have better physical and mental health than those in the lower classes?
19. Do you believe the government should intervene in the economy to make citizens financially secure? How do members of the working class feel about this?
20. Why might the wealthy see designer labels as cheap and showy?
21. Why do you think people in the lower classes are more likely to vote Democrat and those in the higher classes Republican?
22. Can you give examples of how social class affects one's religion and education?
23. Do you think everyone strives for upward social mobility? Why or why not?
24. How much movement do you think there is on the American social class ladder?
25. What are some of the costs of social mobility? Can you give examples from your own experiences?
26. Do you agree that the Horatio Alger belief helps to stabilize society? Why or why not?
27. Why do you think that poverty in the United States is a major public policy issue?
28. What has contributed to the feminization of poverty in the United States? Can you give examples?
29. Do you think a person living in poverty can plan far ahead? Why or why not?
30. Why do you think people tend not to see the effects of social class on their own lives?

PROJECTS

1. Find listings of the world's billionaires in *Forbes* or *Fortune* magazines. Determine from the articles the names of some of the billionaires, the amounts of wealth, and the sources of their wealth. Using the Dimensions of Social Class in the text, analyze what you have read about the billionaires. Write an analysis or present your findings to the class.
2. Analyze how power, prestige and wealth are depicted in movies and television programs. Movies about excessive wealth and greed in the 1980s are a starting point. Focus on class differentials in terms of lifestyle, life chances, self-esteem, and other factors which are subtly, or not so subtly, present in the media depictions. Present your findings in small group discussions, for a class project, or as a term paper.
3. Create your own system for allocating wealth, power, and prestige to occupations in the United States. What positions do you think should be paid the most? The least? Which

INSTRUCTOR'S SECTION

should have the most power and/or prestige? The least? As a term project, you may wish to analyze these allocations in the United States as compared with other countries.

4. For a small group project or a term paper, gather additional information about life chances across social class lines for your city, county, and state. Secure data from census surveys; the local health, fire, and sheriff's departments; and other services of the city/county/state in which you reside. These may include information on life expectancy, physical and mental health, family life, political involvement, etc. Compare the data you gathered with the Consequences of Social Class section of your text. In your summary and conclusions, indicate whether your data confirm the statements made in the text.

5. Read the section in your text entitled "Thinking Critically about Social Controversy: Children in Poverty," then seek out additional sources such as the following: (a) Kotlowitz, Alex. *There Are No Children Here*. NY: Doubleday, 1991, and (b) Kozol, Jonathan. *Rachael and Her Children: Homeless Families in America*. NY: Fawcett Columbine, 1988. In small group discussion, an oral presentation to the class, or a term paper, explain what you have learned about this important issue and why it is an alarming problem in the United States.

6. Interview people of various ages, socioeconomic statuses, and occupations to determine their response to the questions, "If the wealth were redistributed in the United States so that everyone had the same amount, what do you think would happen to the money over the next five years? Would the money stay were it was redistributed? Might large sums of the money be back in the hands of the people who currently possess the most? Why or why not?" Write a summary of your research and findings.

TRANSPARENCIES

1. (TR#10) Percentages of Households with at Least One of Its Primary Family Members 18–24 Years Old, in College, by Family, Income, Race, Origin

2. (TR#15) The Concentration of U.S. Wealth
3. (TR#16) The American Social Class Ladder

TRANSPARENCY MASTERS

1. (TR#10M) Distribution of Wealth of Americans
2. (TR#11M) How the Pay Gap Grew in the Eighties
3. (TR#12M) The Percentage of the Nation's Income Received

by Each Fifth and the Top Five Percent of America's Families Since World War II

4. (TR#13M) Different Grocery Lists
5. (TR#14M) Percentage below the Poverty Line

VIDEOS/MOVIES

Social Mobility

CNN Video II. *Separate and Unequal*. Report on the different social classes among African-Americans. Contrary to stereotypes, they are not found only in one class; there are two distinct classes including middle class and lower class. In 1991, one in seven black families made $50,000. By contrast, in 1967 the figure was one in seventeen. Black middle class rose largely through affirmative action programs in government and business. The greatest surge in income has been for black women. The report illustrates the widening gap between black middle and lower classes. Available from A&B Video Library.

Who Are the Poor?

CNN Video II. *New Poor*. Report on the new poor. Increasingly, welfare recipients come from all social classes. Single mothers, couples with children, and older people are interviewed. Available from A&B Video Library.

CNN Video II. *Child Poverty*. Children's Defense Fund study on children and poverty in the United States. As of 1991, there were 12 million poor children—one in five live in poverty. Most are white and live in rural areas. Most have two parents, one of whom works. Available from A&B Video Library.

Children of Poverty. This program profiles some of America's children of poverty, and shows the toll taken on the children and their mothers by the problem of finding shelter and enough food to survive. 26 min. Available from A&B Video Library and FHS.

Family in Crisis. Adapted Phil Donahue program that centers on the plight of poor children growing up in single parent households. Experts examine the problems facing children growing up without fathers and the seemingly irreversible cycle of poverty that especially affects minority families. 28 min. Available from A&B Video Library and FHS.

Workfare, Welfare: What's Fair? Conservatives claim that welfare exacerbates poverty, while liberals say welfare grants are so small that families can't find their way out of poverty. This program focuses on a workfare program, designed to get people off welfare rolls and into jobs. 26 min. Available from A&B Video Library and FHS.

Movies Dealing with Social Class in the United States
OLD MONEY: *The Philadelphia Story* or in musical form as *High Society; Reversal of Fortune; Arthur; Beaches*

NEW MONEY: *Troop Beverly Hills; Down and Out in Beverly Hills; The Bonfire of the Vanities; Trading Places; Barbarians at the Gate*

WORKING CLASS: *Moonstruck; Thelma and Louise; Steel Magnolias; Norma Rae; Stanley and Iris; Roger and Me; Frankie and Johnny*

THE UNDERCLASS: *Grapes of Wrath; Ironweed; Life Stinks*

SPEAKER SUGGESTIONS

1. A social scientist conducting research on social class.
2. A physician from a public, "charity" hospital or clinic in your city to talk about the problems of indigent patients and of hospitals which provide medical services for them.
3. A psychiatrist who treats patients from diverse social classes to discuss the relationship between mental health/illness and social class.
4. A public defender to speak on social class and the criminal justice system.
5. A supervisor from a welfare agency to discuss eligibility requirements and procedures for getting welfare benefits in your city.

POP QUIZ QUESTIONS

True-False

T   1. Sociologists have no clear-cut, accepted definition of social class.
F   2. Sociologists use the subjective method almost exclusively in determining social class position of people.
T   3. The poorest twenty percent of people in the United States now receive the same share of the national income as they did in 1945.
T   4. C. Wright Mills coined the term "power elite" to refer to those who make the big decisions in American society.
T   5. Occupational prestige rankings remain remarkably consistent across countries and over time.

F   6. College professors do not tend to experience status inconsistency.
F   7. Eric Wright's revision of Marx's theory no longer maintained the primary distinction between employer and worker.
F   8. Social class position has a greater impact on the individual's mental health than on his or her physical health.
T   9. Most Americans believe that they have an average or better than average chance of getting ahead.
T 10. Sociologists examine poverty in terms of the structural features of society that create poverty.

ESSAY QUESTIONS

1. Explain the major dimensions of social class and note how Gilbert and Kahl's model updates the original Weberian dimensions.
2. Discuss status inconsistency and give specific examples of occupations in which such inconsistency is most likely to occur.
3. Compare and contrast Wright's four classes with Gilbert and Kahl's six class categories.
4. Describe the consequences of social class on life chances, physical and mental health, family life, values and attitudes, political involvement, religion, education, and the criminal justice system.
5. Discuss intergenerational, structural, and exchange mobility and analyze the extent to which each occurs in the United States.
6. Identify the major problems researchers experience in trying to use the U.S. government poverty line in their research. List the characteristics of those who are most likely to be among the poor in the United States.
7. Distinguish between the following: short- and long-term poverty, and individual versus structural explanations of poverty.

CHAPTER

11

Inequalities of Gender

CHAPTER SUMMARY

Sex refers to biological distinctions between males and females; gender refers to what a society considers to be proper behaviors and attitudes for its males and females. Gender inequality refers to men's and women's unequal access to a society's power, property, and prestige. Each society establishes a structure that, on the basis of gender, permits or limits access to privileges. Women are defined as a minority group because they experience gender inequality in all areas of life. In the workplace women's problems include discrimination in hiring and in pay, the

"mommy" track, and sexual harassment. Traditional gender patterns still exist in regard to violent behavior, especially murder patterns. American women have the numerical capacity to take over politics and transform society, but the higher the office, the fewer the women. Changing images of gender in American society indicate greater equality. It is possible that a new concept of the human personality—one that allows males and females to pursue their individual interests unfettered by gender—might occur.

CHAPTER OUTLINE

I. Why Are Males and Females Different?
   A. Gender stratification refers to men's and women's unequal access to power, prestige, and property.
   B. Sex is biological characteristics distinguishing males and females—primary (organs related to reproduction) and secondary (physical distinctions not related to reproduction).
   C. Gender is a social characteristic which varies from one society to another, referring to what the group considers proper for males and females. The sociological significance of gender is that it serves as a primary sorting device by which society controls its members and thus is a structural feature of society.
   D. Some sociologists argue that biological factors (two X chromosomes in females, one X and one Y in males) result in differences in male (more aggressive and domineering) and female (more comforting and nurturing) conduct. The dominant sociological position is that gender differences result from sex being used to mark people.
   E. Symbolic interactionists stress that society interprets the physical differences: males and females take the relative positions that society assigns to them.
   F. Alice Rossi suggested that women are better prepared biologically for "mothering" than are men: natural biological predispositions are overlaid with culture. The case of two identical twins, one of whom underwent a sex-change operation during infancy and was brought up as a girl, is given as an example.

   G. Males are stronger and larger than females, but females outlive males. Females generally begin to speak sooner, use sentences earlier, score higher in tests of verbal fluency, grammar and spelling; males do better on spatial tasks and in math. Why such differences exist is a matter of debate among social scientists.
II. Women as a Minority Group
   A. Since gender discrimination pervades most aspects of social life, women are referred to as a minority even though they outnumber men.
   B. George Murdock, who surveyed 324 premodern societies, found activities to be sex-typed in all of them, although activities considered female in one society may be male in another. There is nothing about anatomy that requires this.
   C. Universally, greater prestige is given male activities regardless of what they are. If caring for cattle is men's work, it carries high prestige; if it is women's work, it has less prestige.
   D. The genesis of female minority status. Although the origin of patriarchy (male dominance) is unknown, two theories have emerged, both assuming patriarchy to result from universal conditions:
      1. As a result of carrying a child, giving birth, etc., women in early human history were limited in movement and activities for much of their lives. Thus, they assumed tasks associated with the home and child care; men took over tasks requiring greater speed and longer absences, such as hunting

animals, enabling them to contact other tribes, trade with those other groups, and wage war. They gained prestige by returning home with prisoners of war or with large animals to feed the tribe.

2. Marvin Harris argued that in prehistoric times, each group was threatened with annihilation by other groups, and each had to recruit members to fight enemies in dangerous, hand-to-hand combat. Men (bigger and stronger) were coaxed into this bravery to promises of rewards; females were the reward. Thus, men were trained for combat; women were conditioned from birth to acquiesce in male demands. The "drudge work" was assigned to women, since men preferred to avoid those tasks.

III. Gender Inequality in American Society

A. A society's institutions maintain its customary forms of gender inequality. Men (reluctant to abandon their privileged positions) use various cultural devices to keep women subservient.

B. Women in the United States did not have the right to vote, hold property, testify in court, or serve on a jury until this century; a woman's pay was handed over to her father or husband. Males did not willingly surrender their privileges; rather, in the United States and Europe women's rights resulted from a prolonged and bitter struggle. While women enjoy more rights today, gender inequality still exists. Women continue to press for more rights and a greater share of society's power through lawsuits, lobbying, and the mass media. From the conflict perspective, gender discrimination will end only when men yield their power, which is unlikely to be voluntary.

C. Schools sort students by sex; expecting males and females to be different, teachers still nurture the differences, perpetuating gender inequalities by steering boys into some occupations, girls into others. Sports contribute to this—boys play football, girls join the drill team. At college 92% of home economics degrees are awarded to females; 86% of engineering degrees are awarded to males.

D. Women's capacities, interests, attitudes, and contributions are devalued—not taken as seriously as those of men. Masculinity (representing strength, success) is valued higher; femininity is seen as failure, weakness.

IV. Gender Inequality in the Workplace

A. Males outnumber females in the U.S. work force by ten to eight. In 1900, only 1 in 5 females was employed outside the home; today at least half of all females over age 16 are so employed.

B. The law states that family obligations cannot be a factor in hiring, transfer, or promotion, and forbids employers from even inquiring about a prospective employee's family status. Fearing that a child's needs may interfere with a woman's ability to do her job, many employers nonetheless discriminate against mothers.

C. Women in the work force are more likely to be excluded from the inner circle, and average only 69% of men's wages.

1. Half this pay gap results from women choosing lower-paying jobs (e.g., grade school teaching).

But starting salaries for females are 11% lower than those of males even in the same field. At all educational levels women earn less than men. Over his career, the average male college graduate will earn about $630,000 more than his female peer.

2. In upper ranks, the gap is preserved through an "old boys'" network (acquaintances who bring access to jobs, promotions, opportunities). To combat this, some female professionals develop alternative networks to help their own careers.

3. "Glass ceiling" describes an invisible barrier that women face in the work force. Even in companies where over half the professional employees are women, only 5% of senior management is female. "Glass walls" prevent women from moving laterally into core positions from which senior executives are chosen.

D. Since most wives spend more time and take greater responsibility in caring for the children, some corporations offer women a choice of two parallel career paths: the "fast track" (may require 60 or 70 hours of work per week, unexpected out-of-town meetings, etc.); or the "mommy track" (stresses both career and family). The latter encourages women to be satisfied with lower aspirations and fewer promotions, and critics suggest: (1) it is intended to perpetuate or increase the executive pay gap; and (2) a better way is for husbands to share responsibility at home and for firms to provide day care.

E. Until 1976, women did not draw a connection between unwanted sexual advances on the job and their subordinate positions at work.

1. As women began to discuss the problem, they named it and came to see unwanted sexual advances by men in powerful positions as a structural problem. The change resulted from reinterpreting women's experiences—giving them a name.

2. Sexual harassment may be a single encounter or a series of incidents; it may be a condition to being hired, retained, or promoted. It is not exclusively a female problem.

3. Judge Clarence Thomas' confirmation hearings focused attention on this problem.

V. Gender Inequality and Violence: The Case of Murder

A. Some theorists claim males have a greater predisposition to kill, but most sociologists disagree. Females who kill are more likely to kill an intimate at home (usually a male partner) in a domestic dispute; males are more likely to kill strangers and acquaintances in public places (e.g., bars).

B. Despite women spending more time in the work force, murder continues to follow gender roles.

VI. Why Don't Women Take Over Politics and Transform American Life?

A. Women are underrepresented in political office, especially in higher office. Two reasons are given: (1) women find the roles of mother and politician incompatible; and (2) due to marginality (belonging to two groups with incompatible values, not feeling accepted in either), they may be uncomfortable in politics.

B. Also, males seldom incorporate women into the centers of decision making or present them as viable candidates.

C. Trends in the 1990s indicate that women will participate in political life in far greater numbers than in the past.

VII. Changes in Gender Relations

A. Symbols of masculinity and femininity change over time, and there is evidence of growing respect for the abilities of women.

B. Without doubt, the historical trend is toward greater equality between the sexes, and the barriers are being reduced.

VIII. Glimpsing the Future—With Hope

A. The vast increase in the number of employed women will gradually force changes in gender images and gender relations.

B. As women play a fuller role in the decision-making processes, further structural obstacles to women's participation in society will give way.

LEARNING OBJECTIVES

After reading and studying Chapter 11, the student should be able to:

1. Define gender stratification and differentiate between sex and gender.

2. Discuss the continuing controversy regarding biological and cultural factors which come into play in creating gender differences in societies.

3. Explain why women are considered to be a minority group and summarize the theories of how this minority status occurred.

4. Describe the major factors which led to the rise of feminism in the United States and note how successful this movement has been up to this point in time.

5. Discuss ways in which educational systems may perpetuate gender inequality.

6. Describe the general devaluation of things feminine in American society.

7. Explain how gender discrimination occurs in the workplace, including hiring practice, the pay gap, the "mommy track," and sexual harassment.

8. Distinguish between female and male patterns of violence, especially in the case of murder.

9. Explain why women historically have not taken over politics and transformed American life.

10. Describe what the future looks like in terms of gender relations in the United States.

KEY TERMS

gender
gender stratification
labor force participation rate
marginality

matriarchy
minority group
patriarchy

sex
sex-typed
sexual harassment

KEY PEOPLE

Alice Rossi
George Murdock
Carol Whitehurst
Jean Stockard and Miriam Johnson
Felice Schwartz
Marcia M. Lee

Helen Hacker
Marvin Harris
Samuel Stouffer
Rex Fuller and Richard Schoenberger
Nancy Jurik and Russ Winn
Janet Giele

CLASS DISCUSSION QUESTIONS

1. Which do you think is most significant in explaining why males and females act the way they do—biology or culture? Why?

2. Can you explain why gender is the primary division between people in every society? Is this true in the United States?

3. If it was impossible to tell whether your own newborn child was a male or female, how would you deal with the situation?

4. Why is it difficult to answer the question, "Which sex is superior?" What have you been socialized to believe?

5. Why do you think sociologists refer to women as a minority group?

6. Can you give examples of sex-typed work in the United States today?

7. Do you think that childbirth limits women's abilities to achieve on the level of men today? Why or why not?

8. Do you believe that women should be involved in warfare? What about on the front lines of combat duty?

9. Why have some men resisted changes in women's and men's roles in American society?

10. Can you give examples of how today's schools still use sex to sort students into different activities?

11. Why do you think it is true that the further one climbs the

educational ladder, the more the educational experience itself becomes a masculine endeavor?

12. Do you agree that women's capacities, interests, attitudes, and contributions are not taken as seriously as those of men? Why or why not?

13. Why is gender discrimination most visible in the workplace? Can you give examples?

14. Do you think the pay gap between men and women can be explained by the fact that women tend to choose lower-paying jobs than men? Why or why not?

15. Is the "mommy track" a good idea for women who want to get ahead at work and also have a family? Why or why not?

16. Do you think sexual harassment is an individual problem or a societal problem?

17. Can problems of sexual harassment be solved? What would you suggest be done?

18. In what ways do the differences between male and female killers reflect their different experiences in the social world?

19. Do you think a woman will be elected President of the United States during the next ten years? Twenty years?

20. What changes—if any—have you seen in the participation levels of women in politics in the past ten years?

21. Do you predict that there will be greater equality between the sexes in the future? Why or why not?

PROJECTS

1. Read recent articles or books on the ongoing argument about the biological and cultural aspects of gender differentiation. Analyze the arguments presented in the Thinking Critically section of your text on whether biology or culture is the answer to the biology versus culture argument. Add your resources to these arguments and present this information to the class or in a written paper.

2. Conduct research on primary (early) gender socialization in American society by interviewing older individuals, members of your peer group, and individuals who are younger than you are to determine how they learned to be "male" or "female." You may wish to do a cross-cultural analysis, if you have the opportunity to interview people from diverse backgrounds. Ask the people you interview to recall their toys, books, clothes, and other material items of culture which send gender messages. Then ask them to discuss the behavioral norms and acceptable types of work for women and for men that were transmitted to them by significant others. Compare your findings with those of other members of your discussion group or class.

3. Analyze your college in terms of gender inequalities. Determine the majors which have a vast majority of male students and those with predominantly female students. Find out how much your institution spends for female sports as compared with male athletics. In your classes, watch for situations in which the professor and/or other students give more or less attention to students that may be attributable to gender. If your university has graduate and/or professional schools, gather information about enrollment and graduation by sex. Prepare a report on how you conducted your research, state your sources, present your findings, and draw some conclusions from your data and observations.

4. Find current issues regarding gender inequality in the workplace in the media and supplement the information in your text about discrimination in hiring, the pay gap, the "mommy track," the "glass ceiling," or sexual harassment. Periodicals such as *Working Woman, Time, Newsweek, U.S. News and World Report, Fortune,* and *Forbes* frequently have articles about these problems. Summarize your research for the class or in a term paper.

5. Interview women who are involved in politics to learn what types of obstacles they believe they had to overcome to be elected and what problems they have had while in office. Compare these with the problems often experienced by male officeholders to determine the commonalities and differences in their experiences. Commonalities might include the fact that both men and women in state legislatures or on school boards often work long hours, which takes them away from their families and friends, while at the same time they make little or no money for their efforts. Differences might include the fact that women are more likely to have problems raising adequate money to fund a campaign, are more likely to have family and child care problems to deal with, and may experience discrimination or harassment to which men typically are not subjected.

6. Do cross-cultural research on gender issues. Look for commonalities and differences in the treatment of women across cultures on some specific issue(s). In your oral presentation or paper, determine the extent to which you think things will be the same or will change in the future.

TRANSPARENCIES

1. (TR#17) American Women in Political Office, 1990
2. (TR#18) Women's and Men's Proportion of the American Labor Force
3. (TR#19) Gender Allocation in Selected Technological Activities in 224 Societies

TRANSPARENCY MASTERS

1. (TR#15M) What Proportion of American Women Work for Wages?
2. (TR#16M) Male and Female Murderers: Their Characteristics and Victims

VIDEOS/MOVIES

Why are Males and Females Different?

Sex Hormones and Sexual Destiny. This program visits a laboratory where research has demonstrated that hormone levels have a measurable effect on "masculine" and "feminine" behavior and that the structures of male and female brains differ. It also discusses the effect of right-brain and left-brain communication and the influence of environment on male and female behavior. 26 min. Available from A&B Video Library and FHS.

The Sexual Brain. This program shows some startling effects of hormone injections on brain structure and raises provocative questions about the sexual and reproductive roots of structural differences between males and females. 28 min. Available from A&B Video Library and FHS.

Women as a Minority Group

CNN Video II. *Women's Rights in Kenya: A Case of Cultural Lag.* A Kenyan woman goes to court for the right to bury her husband and retain property. She claims she is "detribalized" but the system remains in cultural lag. Available from A&B Video Library.

Women in the Military. In this *60 Minutes* segment, women are seen to be succeeding at all those tasks that servicemen have always considered particularly macho. Now, permitted for the first time into situations that would put them into the equivalent of the front line, women in the military respond as they are supposed to—professionally. 14 min. Available from A&B Video Library and FHS.

Gender Inequality in American Society

She's Nobody's Baby: A History of American Women in the 20th Century. 1982. Narrated by Marlo Thomas and Alan Alda, this award-winning documentary goes back to the turn of the century to show how women redefined their role and shaped the nation's history. 36 min. Available from A&B Video Library.

CNN Video II. *Girl's Education.* A "landmark" American Association of University Women study claims that girls are receiving an unequal education beginning as early as kindergarten. According to the report, girls are the objects of sexual harassment from boys at a very young age, and math and science teachers exhibit gender bias toward female students, among

other findings. Critics of the report argue that the study misses the mark. They say that 55% of females go into higher education. Available from A&B Video Library.

CNN Video II. *Glass Ceiling.* (See description in AIE Chapter 7.)

Problems of Working Women. Examines the pressures facing working women with small children: salaries too low to pay for proper child care, and inadequate or unavailable child care facilities, inadequate or absent household help. 24 min. Available from A&B and FHS.

CNN Video II. *Baby Boom.* Working mothers profiled. Today's mothers remain at home in less than one in ten families. By the year 2000, 85% of women aged 25–54 will be in the workforce. A flexible work schedule has benefits, both for the corporation and for parents. *Working Mother Magazine* rates companies on their working mother and parent policies. Available from A&B Video Library.

Women, Work, and Babies: Can America Cope? 1985. Featuring Jane Pauley, this video examines issues resulting from the dramatic increase in the number of working mothers over the last two decades. Includes redefining traditional mother-father roles, corporate responsibility toward employees becoming parents, the absence of government support for the single parent, and the effects of day care on children and parents. 49 min. Available from Films Incorporated, Wilmette, Illinois.

Baby Boom. (Movie—see description in AIE Chapter 7.)

Sexual Harassment from 9 to 5. This program looks at the legal and the human side of sexual harassment in the workplace, portraying women whose lives were deeply affected by this highly aggressive and largely hidden form of discrimination. Available from A&B Video Library and FHS.

9 to 5. 1980. (Color) Starring Jane Fonda, Lily Tomlin, Dolly Parton, and Dabney Coleman, this movie looks at three secretaries who have to contend with a sexist boss—and inadvertently find their chance for revenge. Although this is a comedy, it demonstrates some of the problems experienced by women in male-dominated work environments. 110 min. Available at video rental stores.

Woman and Man. Phil Donahue speaks with men and women in many walks of life and finds the role differences between women and men beginning to fade. 52 min. Available from A&B Video Library and FHS.

SPEAKER SUGGESTIONS

1. A specialist in gender roles.
2. An affirmative action officer to discuss guidelines, policies, and procedures at your institution.
3. An economist who has studied the pay gap between women and men.
4. A lawyer who has represented clients in sexual discrimination or sexual harassment lawsuits to discuss current legal thinking on these problems.

5. A representative of the National Organization of Women (NOW), EMILY's List (an organization set up to help raise funds for women running for public office), or other advocacy groups in your city to talk about their perspective. If you decide to have someone speak on a controversial issue—such as abortion—you may wish to have speakers from both sides talk to your class. Have them come on separate days if the issue is very emotionally charged!

POP QUIZ QUESTIONS

True-False

T 1. Gender is a social, not a biological characteristic.

F 2. Sociologists do not consider women to be a minority group.

T 3. Universally, greater prestige is given to male activities than female ones, according to cross-cultural researchers.

F 4. Throughout American history, women have had most of the same rights as men.

T 5. The further one climbs the educational ladder, the more the educational experience itself becomes a masculine endeavor.

T 6. In all industrialized nations, huge numbers of women enter the world of paid employment.

T 7. The pay gap between men and women is the best indicator of gender discrimination in the work world.

F 8. Since the 1920s, sexual harassment has been known as a social and legal problem in the United States.

T 9. Around the world, without exception, males kill at a rate several times that of females.

F 10. Male and female politicians are equally likely to experience marginality.

ESSAY QUESTIONS

1. Discuss some of the major ways in which males and females are different and explain why these differences result in gender stratification in all societies.

2. Explain why women are considered to be a minority group even though they are in the numerical majority in the United States. Note the ways in which life in a society is different for members of a minority group than for dominant group members.

3. Describe the rise of feminism in the United States and compare the functional and conflict perspectives regarding the possible elimination of gender discrimination.

4. Explain how educational institutions may perpetuate gender inequality at all educational levels.

5. Describe the methods used by some employers to discriminate against mothers seeking employment.

6. Analyze the ways in which gender relations have changed in the United States. Discuss ways in which they have remained the same. Specify what the future may look like concerning gender roles.

CHAPTER

12

Inequalities of Race and Ethnicity

CHAPTER SUMMARY

Race is a complex and often misunderstood concept. In one sense, race—inherited physical characteristics that distinguish one group from another—is a reality. However, race is a myth in the sense of one race being superior to another and of there being pure races. The chapter differentiates between race and ethnicity and defines a minority group as one singled out for unequal treatment and that regards itself as the object of collective discrimination. The relationship between prejudice and discrimination is noted. Psychological and sociological theories (including functionalist, conflict, and symbolic interactionist per-

spectives) are analyzed. Dominant groups typically practice one of five policies toward minority groups: genocide, population transfer, internal colonialism, segregation, assimilation, or pluralism. White Anglo-Saxon Protestants have dominated American society since colonial times. Among minority groups in the United States, African Americans are the largest group, Hispanic Americans are the second largest, Asian Americans are the fastest growing group, and Native Americans are the worst off. Four principles for improving ethnic relations are discussed.

CHAPTER OUTLINE

I. Basic Concepts in Race and Ethnic Relations
   A. Ethnicity refers to cultural characteristics that distinguish a people. It often is confused with race (which is biological), due to the cultural differences people see and the way they define race. Race is a reality in the sense that humans come in different colors and shapes; however, two myths regarding race are that one race is superior to another, and that a pure race exists.
   B. Minority groups are people singled out for unequal treatment and who regard themselves as objects of collective discrimination. They are not necessarily in the numerical minority.
   C. A group becomes a minority through expansion of political boundaries or moving (or being moved) into a territory. The dominant group attributes its privileged position to its superiority, not to discrimination.
   E. Shared characteristics of minorities worldwide: (1) membership is ascribed—involuntarily, through birth; (2) the physical or cultural traits that distinguish them are held in low esteem by the dominant group; (3) they are unequally treated by the dominant group; (4) they tend to marry within their own group; and (5) they tend to feel strong group solidarity.
II. Prejudice and Discrimination
   A. Discrimination is unfair treatment directed toward someone. When based on race, it is known as racism.

It also can be based on features such as age, sex, sexual preference, religion, or politics.
   B. Prejudice is an attitude which may result in discrimination, but prejudice and discrimination do not always match. Robert Merton found that: (1) all-weather bigots are prejudiced and discriminate; (2) fair-weather bigots are prejudiced but do not discriminate; (3) fair-weather liberals believe in equal treatment but discriminate except when kept in line; and (4) all-weather liberals neither are prejudiced nor discriminate. People who are prejudiced against one group are likely to be prejudiced against others.
III. Theories of Prejudice
   A. Psychological Perspectives
      1. According to John Dollard, prejudice results from frustration: people unable to strike out at the real source of their frustration find scapegoats to unfairly blame.
      2. According to Theodor Adorno, highly prejudiced people are usually intolerant, insecure, and submissive to superiors.
   B. Sociological Perspectives
      1. To functionalists, the social environment can be deliberately arranged to generate either positive or negative feelings about people. Prejudice is functional in that it creates in-group solidarity. Function-

alists do not justify what they discover but simply identify functions and dysfunctions of human action.

2. To conflict theorists, the ruling class systematically pits group against group, benefiting by splitting workers along racial/ethnic lines, weakening solidarity among the workers, who do not unite to demand higher wages and better conditions.

3. To symbolic interactionists, the labels people learn color their perception. Labels are an essential ingredient of prejudice, leading people to see certain things and be blind to others. Racial and ethnic labels are especially powerful because they are shorthand for emotionally laden stereotypes.

IV. Individual and Institutional Discrimination

A. To sociologists, individual discrimination (negative treatment of one person by another) is too limited a perspective because it focuses only on one individual treating another badly.

B. Institutional discrimination (negative treatment of a minority group that is built into a society's institutions) focuses on human behavior at the group level.

V. Patterns of Intergroup Relations

A. Genocide in the actual or attempted systematic annihilation of a race or ethnic group that is labeled as less than fully human.

B. Population transfer is involuntary movement of a minority group. Indirect transfer involves making life so unbearable that members of a minority then leave; direct transfer involves forced expulsion.

C. Internal colonialism is a society's policy of exploiting a minority, using social institutions to deny it access to full benefits.

D. Segregation (keeping groups apart) accompanies internal colonialism.

E. Assimilation is the process by which a minority is absorbed into the mainstream. It can be forced (dominant group prohibits minority from using own religion, language, customs) or permissive (minority allowed to adopt dominant group's patterns in own way/at own speed).

F. Pluralism permits or encourages ethnic variation.

VI. Race and Ethnic Relations in the United States

A. White Anglo-Saxon Protestants (WASPs) established the basic social institutions in the United States when they settled the original colonies. Subsequent immigrants faced Anglo-conformity—the expectation that they would speak English and adopt other Anglo-Saxon ways of life.

B. White ethnics are white immigrants to the United States whose culture differs from that of WASPs, including the Irish, Germans, Poles, Jews, and Italians. They were discriminated against by WASPs (who felt that something was wrong with people with different customs), placing great pressure on immigrants to blend into the mainstream culture.

C. African Americans face a legacy of racism.

1. In 1955, civil disobedience tactics advocated by Dr. Martin Luther King, Jr., to protest laws believed to be unjust began to be used. Eventually, the 1964 Civil Rights Act (banning discrimination in public facilities) and 1965 Voting Rights Act (banning literacy tests) led to rising expectations, yet the lives of the poor changed little until the Civil Rights Act of 1968. Since then, African Americans have made political and economic progress, but integrated public schools remain elusive.

3. William Wilson stated that the African American community today is divided into two groups: (1) those who have moved up the class ladder, live in good housing, have well-paid jobs, and send their children to good schools; and (2) those who still live in poverty, face violent crime and dead-end jobs, attend terrible schools, and live in hopelessness and despair.

4. According to Wilson, these groups are so different that they have little in common; social class (not race) is the major determinant of quality of life. This analysis fails to take into account the effect of discrimination.

D. Hispanic Americans are the second largest ethnic group in the United States, and include Chicanos, Puerto Ricans, Cuban Americans, and people from Central or South America. While most are legal residents, large numbers have entered the United States illegally and avoid contact with public officials. Concentrated in four states (California, Texas, New York, and Florida), they are causing major demographic shifts.

1. The Spanish language distinguishes them from other minorities: perhaps half are unable to speak English without difficulty. This is a major obstacle to getting well-paid jobs.

2. Divisions prevent political unity: national origin and social class are highly significant. They find strong divisions between themselves and African Americans in addition to experiencing discrimination by Anglos.

E. Asian Americans have long faced discrimination in the United States.

1. Chinese Americans frequently were victims of vigilante groups and anti-Chinese legislation, leading to "Chinatowns"—enclaves which helped provide protection and allowed Chinese culture to flourish. After the attack on Pearl Harbor in World War II, Japanese Americans became the most hated ethnic group in the United States, with many being imprisoned in "relocation camps."

2. The three largest groups (Chinese, Filipinos, and Japanese) have their own cultures, histories, and unique problems.

F. Native Americans (although their early relations with European settlers had been peaceful) stood in the way of expansion and many were slaughtered. Government policy shifted to population transfer, with Native Americans confined to reservations. Today, they are an invisible minority—almost half live in three states; most other Americans are hardly aware of them. They have the highest rates of poverty, unemployment, suicide, and alcoholism of any U.S. minority.

VII. Principles for Improving Ethnic Relations
   A. Since it is impossible to pass laws against prejudice, it is necessary to outlaw discrimination.
   B. Gordon Allport proposed four guidelines to decrease prejudice: groups should possess equal status; should seek common goals; should feel the need to pull together; and authority, law, and custom should support interaction between the groups.

LEARNING OBJECTIVES

After reading and studying Chapter 12, the student should be able to:

1. Distinguish between the concepts of race and ethnicity, and explain how race can be both a reality and a myth.
2. Define the term "minority groups" and identify five characteristics shared by minority groups worldwide.
3. Differentiate between prejudice and discrimination and discuss reasons why prejudice and discrimination do not always match.
4. Compare psychological and sociological perspectives on prejudice. Indicate why sociologists believe psychological explanations are inadequate.
5. Outline the functionalist, conflict, and symbolic interactionist perspectives on prejudice.
6. Compare and contrast individual and institutional discrimination. Give examples of each type.
7. List and describe the six patterns of intergroup relations.
8. Discuss the differences in experiences of White Anglo-Saxon Protestants (WASPs) and those of white ethnics in the United States.
9. Outline the history of the African American experience in the United States. Discuss the role of leaders such as Dr. Martin Luther King, Jr. in creating social change.
10. Compare and contrast the experiences of Hispanics (Latinos), Asian Americans, and Native Americans in the United States.
11. State the major principles for improving ethnic relations.

KEY TERMS

Anglo-conformity
assimilation
authoritarian personality
Chicanos
civil disobedience
compartmentalize
discrimination
dominant group

ethnic (and ethnicity)
genocide
individual discrimination
institutional discrimination
minority group
Pan-Indianism
pluralism
population transfer

prejudice
race
racism
reserve labor force
rising expectations
scapegoat
segregation
selective perception

KEY PEOPLE

Louis Wirth
Robert Merton
Theodor Adorno
Dr. Martin Luther King, Jr.
Cesar Chavez

Charles Wagley and Marvin Harris
John Dollar
Muzafer and Carolyn Sherif
William Wilson
Gordon Allport

CLASS DISCUSSION QUESTIONS

1. Can you explain why race is in some ways a myth?
2. Why do you think people often confuse race and ethnicity?
3. Do you consider yourself to be a member of a minority group? Why or why not?
4. What examples can you give of situations where prejudice leads to discrimination?
5. Why do you think people who are prejudiced against one racial or ethnic group tend to be prejudiced against other groups as well?
6. Why are people more likely to look for scapegoats in tough economic times? Can you think of examples?
7. What do you believe is likely to happen when two groups are pitted against each other in an "I-win-you-lose" situation? What can we learn from the Sherif experiment?
8. Do you feel that racial and ethnic groups in the United States can make gains only at one another's expense? Does the system have to be set up this way?
9. Can you give examples of how we learn prejudices in interaction with others? Is there such a thing as a "harmless" joke?
10. Are individuals always aware that they are discriminating against other people? Are individuals who are being discriminated against always aware that this is occurring?
11. Why do you think that an African-American baby has twice the chance of dying in infancy as a white baby does?

12. Do patterns of genocide still exist today? If yes, can you give examples?
13. Do you agree with the idea that social class rather than race is the most significant factor in determining the life chances of African-Americans in the United States today? Why or why not?
14. What kind of changes do you think will occur, if any, as a result of the "Browning of America?"

15. Why do you think Japanese-Americans have been held up as the model for success to other race and ethnic groups in the United States?
16. Can you think of negative images of Native Americans in movies you have seen? What about positive images?
17. Do you believe that ethnic relations can be improved by passing laws against prejudice? What about laws against discrimination?

PROJECTS

1. Collect comic strips, political cartoons, jokes, advertisements, and other types of print media which have minority group members in them. Analyze physical appearance, attitudes, behaviors, and expectations which are depicted. Create a scrapbook of examples—both positive and negative—and write a summary of your findings.
2. Keep a record of electronic media—television programs and shows, and movies—to determine how minority group members are depicted. In what ways have these depictions improved in recent years? What types of stereotypes have remained largely unchanged? At the conclusion, present a completed log and summary of findings.
3. Do an analysis of institutional discrimination based on the video *Racism on U.S. Campuses* and other resources about the ongoing problems of racism built into institutions. (e.g., Feagin, Joe R. and Clairece Booher Feagin. *Discrimination*

American Style: Institutional Racism and Sexism, 2nd pt., Malabar, FL: Kreiger. 1986). If your institution is involved in controversy regarding such discrimination, you may wish to find out more about the issues on your campus and give a report in small group discussion or to the class.
4. Engage in "crystal ball" gazing to determine what will occur in American society in regard to race and ethnic relations in the future. You may wish to look at such things as population trends, immigration laws, and changing patterns of culture—such as language, food, music, and types of entertainment. You may want to look at additional sources such as: Hacker, Andrew. *Two Nations: Black and White, Separate, Hostile, Unequal.* NY: Charles Scribner's Sons, 1992, to see some of the negative predictions being made by some experts such as this political scientist.

TRANSPARENCIES

1. (TR#20) Race and Health
2. (TR#21) Patterns of Intergroup Relations: A Continuum

3. (TR#22) Country of Origin of Hispanic-American Population in the United States

TRANSPARENCY MASTERS

1. (TR#7M) The Relationship between Attitudes and Actions
2. (TR#18M) Percentage of White Americans Who Believe That Different Races Should Live in Segregated Housing by Education

3. (TR#19M) Geographic Distribution of the Hispanic-American Population
4. (TR#20M) Racial and Ethnic Groups in the United States
5. (TR#21M) Varying Explanations of Inequality by Race, Class, and Gender

VIDEOS/MOVIES

Prejudice and Discrimination

Racism in America. Examines resurgence of racially motivated violence; reasons people vent anger against minorities; social and economic implications of racist acts; how a community successfully responded to racial problems. 26 min. Available from A&B Video Library and FHS.

CNN Video II. *Hate Crimes.* Reports on hate crimes in the United States, which are sharply on the rise. In response to this increase, the U.S. government is now attempting to track all such crimes. Available from A&B Video Library.

Do the Right Thing. 1989 (Color) Spike Lee's controversial motion picture about an outbreak of hostilities on a sweltering

summer day at a white-owned pizza parlor in the black community of Bedford-Stuyvesant in Brooklyn. (G) 120 min. Available at video rental stores.

Boyz N the Hood. 1991 (Color) A sober look at life in the black section of South Central Los Angeles (site of 1992 riot following the verdict in the Rodney King trial). A divorced father strives to raise his son with values—and steer him away from the ignorance and aimlessness that have led to senseless violence in the neighborhood. 107 min. Available at video rental stores.

Guess Who's Coming to Dinner. 1967 (Color) Starring Spencer Tracy, Katharine Hepburn, and Sidney Poitier, this movie classic shows the family turmoil which erupts when a young white woman brings her black fiancé home to meet her parents. (Unrated) Available at video rental stores.

Crisis at Central High. 1981. (Color) Starring Joanne Woodward, this made-for-television movie is a dramatic recreation of events surrounding the 1957 integration of Central High School in Little Rock, Arkansas. (Unrated) 125 min. Available at some video rental stores.

CNN Video II. *Racism on U.S. Campuses.* Illustrates rift between African-Americans and Jews, and the general problem of racism and prejudice on campuses today. Available from A&B Video Library.

Patterns of Intergroup Relations

Nazi Hunter: The Beate Klarsfeld Story. 1986 (Color) Made-for-TV movie starring Farrah Fawcett, Tom Conti, and Geraldine Page depicts the life of Beate Klarsfeld, a real-life German housewife whose unrelenting campaign to bring Nazi war criminals to justice helped snare Klaus Barbie. (Unrated) 100 min. Available at some video rental stores.

The Diary of Anne Frank. 1959 (BW–156 min.) or 1980 (Color–100 min.) Deals with Jewish refugees hiding in Amsterdam in WWII. Shows the impact of Nazi horrors on the lives of individuals. (Unrated). Available at some video rental stores.

Dances with Wolves. 1990 (Color) starring Kevin Costner, this popular movie shows an idealistic young Civil War soldier who makes friends with a Sioux Indian tribe and, eventually, becomes one of them. (PG–13) 181 min. Available at video rental stores.

Gone with the Wind. 1939 (Color) Starring Clark Gable and Vivien Leigh, this movie classic tells of the Civil War and (unintentionally) shows the level of racism and prejudice which has continued to permeate society. (Unrated) 222 min. Available at video rental stores.

Black Like Me. 1944 (B/W) Strong drama based on the actual story of a reporter who took drugs that allowed him to pass for black so he could experience racial prejudice in the South. (Unrated) 107 min. Available at some video rental stores.

The Color Purple. 1985. See description in AIE, Chapter 9.

Individual and Institutional Discrimination

CNN Video II. *Banks/Blacks.* A study conducted by the *Atlanta Journal Constitution* reports that blacks are turned down for loans twice as often as whites with similar incomes. The study canvassed every S&L in the country and covered one trillion dollars worth of loans to ten million applicants. Critics say that credit rating and debt burden were ignored in the study. 2.20 min. Available from A&B Video Library.

N.Y. Law. 1991. A group of minority law students from England spend the summer as interns in New York where they meet East Harlem community lawyers who protect people's apartments against the "hired guns" of property developers. A black judge makes biting pronouncements on white justice. 52 min. Available from FML.

Race and Ethnic Relations in the United States

The Next Minority: White Americans. All indications point to whites becoming the new American minority. Possible sociological and political consequences of such a scenario are ex-

plored in this specially adapted Phil Donahue program. 28 min. Available from A&B Video Library and FHS.

CNN Video II. *Separate and Unequal.* See complete listing in AIE Chapter 10.

Black on Black Violence. An American Black male has a 1 in 29 chance of being murdered; for white men, the odds are one in 186. Some inner-city residents and experts, including Harvard psychiatrist Dr. Alvin Poussaint, discuss Black on Black violence. 26 min. Available from A&B Video Library and FHS.

CNN Video II. *Black Men, Mean Streets.* This CNN Special Report describes young black men in American society as being at risk because the social fabric that binds black families and provides role models has disintegrated. Vignettes present the problems, myths, realities, and the young men who have broken the cycle to achieve success. Available from A&B Video Library.

Luis Valdez and El Teatro Campesino. (Color) Valdez is the founder of this theatrical group that has given voice to the struggles of Chicano farm workers. He picked fruit as a child, and in this program he describes how he overcame the handicaps of migrant life to become a playwright and director. 26 min. Available from FHS.

The English-Speaking Amendment. (Color) The growing presence of non-English speakers in contemporary America has helped spark a movement mandating English as the national language of the United States. In this specially adapted Phil Donahue program, the focus is on Miami, center of Cuban immigration. 28 min. Available from FHS.

The Golden Cage: A Story of California's Farmworkers. 1991. The plight of migrant farmworkers has not changed much since the Depression. Only their nationality is different. This video chronicles the experiences of Mexican farmworkers in California and shows them toiling under the blazing sun for little more than the minimum wage (and sometimes less) while they are exposed daily to hazardous pesticides. The video uses historical footage, interviews, newspaper clippings and photos to document the history of the United Farmworkers Union from the sixties to its current decline. 29 min. Available from FML.

The Asianization of America. Asians are the nation's fastest growing racial group—a fact with enormous significance for our culture and the economy. This program examines Asians' successes in academia and to what extent they can or want to blend into the American melting pot. 26 min. Available from A&B Video Library and FHS.

My Mother Thought She Was Audrey Hepburn. 1992. This video is a personal statement about growing up Asian-American in a white society. Suzanne was brought up "not to be Chinese" by a mother who was proud to dress like Audrey Hepburn or Jackie Kennedy, thinking she had attained the American dream if she modeled herself after them. Her daughter had to overcome "Chinese self-hatred" to accept her ethnic heritage. 20 min. Available from FML.

Who Killed Vincent Chin? 1990. This Academy-Award nominated film is a powerful statement about racism in working-class America. Vincent Chin was at his bachelor party in a Detroit bar when an argument broke out between him and a Chrysler Motors foreman, who shouted ethnic insults. A fight broke out and Chin was bludgeoned to death with a baseball bat. The foreman was let off with a suspended sentence; outrage broke out in the Asian-American community. 82 min. Available from FML.

Writing History: The Privilege of the Victor
CNN Video II. *Hispanic History.* A teacher in an all-Hispanic Los Angeles grade school laments the dearth of history on Hispanics contained in history texts, points out that one 1,000 page text contains just 1½ pages on Hispanics. In response, the teacher wrote his own textbook. Some believe that moving too far away from the so-called "European approach" to history could serve to separate Americans, not unite them, but the Hispanic teacher disagrees. Available from A&B Video Library.

SPEAKER SUGGESTIONS

1. Individuals who are willing to discuss situations in which they have experienced prejudice and discrimination (e.g., a survivor of the Nazi Holocaust, a descendant of a Native American tribe who has lived on a reservation, an African-American who has been involved in civil rights litigation).
2. The official responsible at your college or university for increasing enrollment and retention of minority students or for recruiting minority faculty members.
3. The Director of African-American, Hispanic-American, Asian-American, or Native-American Studies at your school to discuss current research and teaching taking place in his or her department.

POP QUIZ QUESTIONS

True-False
F 1. According to your text, the idea of race is a myth.
F 2. Racial and ethnic groups are based on the same types of characteristics.
T 3. The term "minority group" does not necessarily mean that a minority group is a numerical minority in a given society.
F 4. Prejudice and discrimination always occur together.
F 5. Sociologists agree that people with authoritarian personalities are the most likely to discriminate against minority group members.
T 6. Functionalists do not justify prejudice in society but, rather, identify the functions and dysfunctions of such human actions.
T 7. Conflict theorists focus on the role of the capitalist class in exploiting racial and ethnic inequalities.
F 8. Sociologists tend to examine individual discrimination more than institutional discrimination in their research.
T 9. Whenever genocide is proposed or practiced, the targeted group is labeled as less than fully human.
T 10. Both ethnic discrimination and a disadvantaged social status contribute to the conditions experienced by African Americans in the United States.

ESSAY QUESTIONS

1. Distinguish between the concepts of race and ethnicity, and analyze the role that prejudice and discrimination have played in keeping such distinctions alive in the United States.
2. Compare and contrast functionalist, conflict, and symbolic interactionist perspectives on prejudice and discrimination.
3. Outline and briefly describe the six patterns of intergroup relations. Indicate which is most compatible with functionalist views and which is most compatible with the views of the conflict perspective.
4. Describe the experiences of each of these groups when they first entered the United States: White Anglo-Saxon Protestants, white ethnics, African Americans, Hispanic Americans, and Asian Americans.
5. Explain why it is incorrect to think of racial and ethnic minorities as "all alike" in terms of their experiences with dominant group members.
6. Analyze William Wilson's assertion that class (not race) now is the most important factor in determining the life chances of African Americans.

CHAPTER

13

Inequalities of Age

CHAPTER SUMMARY

Social factors are important in determining the outlook and behaviors of the elderly in any society. In industrialized nations, the life expectancy is increasing largely because certain diseases have been controlled. Sex and race or ethnicity have profound effects on life expectancy. The symbolic interaction perspective focuses on such issues as what makes a person old, what it means to grow old, negative stereotypes of the elderly, and the effects of the mass media. The functional perspective analyzes the withdrawal of the elderly from positions of responsibility. Disengagement theory and activity theory are two functional theories arising from research in this area. Conflict theorists study the competition for scarce resources by rival interest groups (e.g., how different age cohorts may be on a collision course regarding Social Security, Medicare, and Medicaid). Problems of dependency for the elderly include inadequate nursing homes, elder abuse, and poverty. Industrialization has changed the individual's experience with death. The process of dying involves denial, anger, negotiation, depression, and acceptance. Age cohorts have quite stable rates of suicide with the suicide rate of the elderly being the highest of all age groups. Hospices are intended to provde dignity in death, to reduce the emotional and physical burden on relatives, to reduce costs, and to make people comfortable during the living-dying interval.

CHAPTER OUTLINE

I. Social Factors in Aging
   A. In Abkhasia (a remote agricultural region in the former Soviet Union) the people commonly live to be 100, or even older. They give three reasons for their longevity: sexual abstinence other than through marriage; work (from childhood to the end of life); and diet and eating customs. Researchers suggest that the fact that they remain active, valued, contributing members of the society, and never are isolated from family and community is quite important.
   B. In the United States, life expectancy is increasing, from less than 50 years in 1900 to more than 70 years today; to a large extent, this is because certain diseases have been controlled. The graying of America refers to this trend—today, almost 13% of the population has achieved age 65. All industrialized nations are encountering this trend, which places a greater burden on the young to pay the benefits that the elderly need.
II. The Symbolic Interactionist Perspective
   A. Self, Society, and Aging
      1. Culturally sanctioned definitions of age may label a person as being "old" before that person is willing to accept that label. The person is accustomed to what he or she sees in the mirror; thus, changes in that image occur slowly. But seeing someone else after a long time may result in feeling that the other person is much older than before.
      2. Biology changes how a person lookes and feels; the person adopts the role of "old" (acts the way old people are thought to act) upon developing those symptoms. Personal history (example: an injury that limits mobility) or biography (example: becoming a grandmother at an early age) may affect self-concept regarding age. Culturally determined gender roles play a part. In the United States, a man's sexual value is determined on the basis of personality, intelligence, and earning power, while a woman's value is determined on the basis of appearance. When a particular society defines a person as "old," the person is likely to feel "old."
      3. The Relativity of Aging: The Tiwi tribe is a gerontocracy (a society run by the elderly) where older men are so entrenched in power that they control all of the wealth and all of the women. To grow old in traditional Eskimo society meant death—society was so precarious that a person no longer able to pull his or her own weight was expected to simply go off and die so that the younger population could live.
      4. Ageism in American Society: Robert N. Butler coined the term ageism to refer to prejudice, discrimination, and hostility directed at people because of their age. In the United States today, old age conjures up images of ugliness, weakness, uselessness, dependence, and crankiness. Negative ste-

reotypes of old age in the United States today (where previously the elderly were respected) may have arisen in either of two ways: (1) a loss of prestige has occurred as more people reach old age, while new techniques and machinery result in older people knowing less about things now considered important; (2) death is now associated with old age, although it was common at any age prior to the 1800s.

5. The mass media communicate messages about the aged, not only reflecting their devalued status, but also reinterpreting and refining it. On TV, the elderly are likely to be stereotyped in unflattering terms; the message is that they are past their prime and of little consequence. As a result, Americans try to deny that they are growing old; the media then exploit denial to sell things asserted to avoid even the appearance of age.

III. The Functionalist Perspective
  A. Functionalists examine age from the standpoint of how those persons who are retiring and those who will replace them in the work force make mutual adjustments. There are two theories.
  B. Disengagement Theory: Elaine Cumming and William Henry developed this theory to explain how society prevents disruption by having the elderly vacate positions. Death and incompetence would not vacate enough positions—thus, the elderly are rewarded in some way for giving up positions sooner than that.
  C. Activity Theory: This theory examines people's reactions to exchanging one set of roles for another. It is a functionalist theory because it examines how disengagement is functional or dysfunctional. Older people who maintain a high level of activity tend to be more satisfied with life than those who do not. Thus, the more that people find new (post-disengagement) activities satisfying, the more they are pleased with life itself.

IV. The Conflict Perspective
  A. Conflict theorists examine social life as a struggle between groups for scarce resources. Social Security legislation is an example of that struggle. In the 1920s–30s, two-thirds of all citizens over 65 had no savings and could not support themselves. Robert C. Townsend enrolled one-third of all Americans over 65 in clubs that sought a national sales tax to finance a monthly pension to all Americans over age 65. To avoid the plan without appearing to be opposed to old-age pensions, Social Security was enacted by Congress. Conflict theorists state that Social Security was not a result of generosity, but rather of competition among interest groups.
  B. Rival Interest Groups: Since equilibrium is only a temporary balancing of social forces, some form of continuing conflict between the younger and the older appears inevitable. The huge costs of Social Security have become a national concern. As America grays, the dependency ratio (number of workers compared with number of recipients) now is 5 working-age Americans paying to support each person over 65; by the year 2000 it will be 3 to 1. To protect their gains, older Americans organized the American Association of Retired Persons, with over 28 million members. Meanwhile, other groups are organizing to fight the elderly for these resources.

C. The Gray Panthers was organized in the 1960s to encourage persons of all ages to work for the welfare of both the elderly and the young. On the micro level, the goal is to develop positive self concepts; on the macro level, the goal is to challenge all institutions that oppress the poor, whether young or old.

V. Problems of Dependency
  A. The elderly are not as isolated as stereotypes would lead us to believe. Actually, 75% of persons over 65 see one of their children at least weekly; 33% see a sibling at least once a week; and 80% have a living brother or sister. Most older males live with their wives, although most wives outlive their husbands.
  B. Yet about 3.6% of Americans over age 65 are in nursing homes at any one time, and perhaps 20% of Americans spend at least some time in a nursing home. Those who do are likely to be quite ill, or over 80, or never to have married and thus have no family to take care of them. The cost is high (about $25,000 per year) and residents tend to be depressed, unhappy, and intellectually ineffective; when sedated or restrained, they suffer a loss of dignity.
  C. About 3 or 4% of elderly Americans are physically, verbally, emotionally, or financially abused each year. Most abusers are members of the elderly person's family. Some researchers say the abuse occurs when an individual feels obligated to take care of a person who is highly dependent and demanding. Others conclude that the abuser is dependent on the elderly person, either financially or emotionally.
  D. A major fear of the elderly is poverty—that their money may not last as long as their life does. Although in the 1960s and 1970s the poverty rate of the elderly was greater than that of the general population, this no longer is true. As a result of governmental programs, the elderly now are less likely to be poor than is the average American. This has raised the concern that improvement in the financial condition of the elderly has been at the expense of the young.

VI. The Sociology of Death and Dying
  A. In preindustrial societies, the sick were cared for at home and died at home. With the coming of modern medicine, dying has been transformed into an event to be managed by professionals, and most people never have personally seen anyone die. A consequence is that the process of dying has become strange to most people; we hide from the fact of death—we even construct a language of avoidance—a person is "gone" or "at peace now," rather than dead.
  B. Elisabeth Kübler-Ross identified the stages through which a person passes when told that she or he has an incurable disease: denial ("the doctor made a mistake"); anger; negotiation (trying to make a bargain with God or fate); depression (grieving that there is nothing that can be done to prolong life); and acceptance (getting affairs in order).
  C. Of all age groups, Americans over 65 are most likely to commit suicide. Suicide peaks between ages 75 and 84, when it is more than double the rate for teenagers. The reasons include a sense of hopelessness, failing health, deaths of spouse and friends, pain, and loneliness.

D. Elderly persons want to die with dignity in the comforting presence of friends and relatives. Hospitals are awkward places to die—surrounded by strangers in hospital garb, etc. Hospices have emerged as a solution to these problems, providing greater dignity and comfort at less cost.

LEARNING OBJECTIVES

After reading and studying Chapter 13, the student should be able to:

1. Analyze the social factors in aging and discuss the factors involved in the "graying" of industrialized nations.
2. Discuss the major conclusions drawn by symbolic interactionists regarding aging.
3. Demonstrate by using cross-cultural comparisons that societies vary widely on their perceptions of what makes a person old, what it means to grow old, and how the elderly are viewed.
4. Describe some of the negative stereotypes about the elderly and discuss ways in which the mass media perpetuate these ideas.
5. Summarize the functional perspective on aging and explain disengagement theory and activity theory.
6. Explain why conflict theorists see social life as a struggle between groups for scarce resources and note how this impacts different age cohorts.
7. State some of the problems of dependency, especially in regard to nursing homes, elder abuse, and poverty.
8. Examine the effects of industrialization on the process of death and dying.
9. Outline the five stages that people go through when they are told they have an incurable disease.
10. Give reasons for the high rate of suicide among the elderly.
11. Explain the functions of hospices in modern societies.

KEY TERMS

activity theory	dependency ratio	graying of America
age cohort	disengagement theory	hospice
ageism	gerontocracy	

KEY PEOPLE

Robert Butler	Erdman Palmore
David Fischer	Elaine Cumming
William Henry	Margaret Kuhn
Ethel Shanas	Elisabeth Kübler-Ross

CLASS DISCUSSION QUESTIONS

1. Have you seen or heard recent news reports on the factors that contribute to longevity in the United States? What about diet? Work patterns? Leisure? A sense of belonging?
2. Are you surprised to learn that at the beginning of the twentieth century the average American would not live to age fifty? Why or why not?
3. Can you explain what is meant by the statement that "age is relative"? Do you agree?
4. Why do you think some individuals feel "old" at an earlier age than other people?
5. Do you agree that there is a difference in the social aspects of "gender aging"? If so, give examples.
6. Why do you think prejudice, discrimination, and hostility are directed against people because of their age?
7. How does a fear of growing old, especially as depicted in the mass media, promote sales of "anti-aging" products? Have you bought products which claim to help you keep your "youthful" appearance?
8. Why do you think society encourages the elderly to hand over their positions voluntarily to younger people?
9. Do you believe all elderly people are happiest when they are very active? Why or why not?
10. Did programs such as Social Security come into being as a result of the generosity of Congress and U.S. taxpayers?
11. Do you agree that Social Security may be part of a national con game in which American workers are the victims? Why or why not?
12. Under what circumstances do you think it might be necessary to place one of your loved ones in a nursing home? How would you feel about doing this?
13. Why do you think abuse of the elderly is difficult to study?
14. Are the fears of the elderly that they will end up living in poverty realistic? Why or why not?
15. Why do you think many people today have never personally seen anyone die?
16. Can you explain why the elderly have a high suicide rate?

PROJECTS

1. Develop a paper or oral report on cross-cultural perspectives on growing older. Compare traditional and modern youth cultures in their perspectives on the elderly. The relationship between changes in the status of the elderly and modifications in the economic, educational, familial, political, and religious institutions could be outlined. Variations in the roles and statuses of the elderly in diverse cultures could be contrasted.
2. Analyze media stereotypes of the elderly—such as television programs and commercials, cartoons, movies, greeting cards—and present examples and findings in a paper or oral presentation.
3. Analyze the Social Security system to learn how it originally was created, what types of changes have been made, and what the future implications are for young people who contribute today and want to retire in the future. You may wish to explore the issue brought up in the section on "The Browning of America" in Chapter 12 that in the future white retirees largely will be supported by minority-group workers.
4. Study the lobbying efforts of groups advocating the rights of the elderly (e.g., Gray Panthers of the American Association of Retired Persons). Identify the issues around which older Americans have organized and their successes and failures in having these issues addressed and resolved. Include a discussion of the conflicts which can arise over the priorities of the old and of the young.
5. Conduct research on nursing homes in your area or state. Have there been any recent charges of nursing home fraud or abuse? How do ethical nursing home owners and administrators attempt to provide facilities meeting the needs of their residents?

TRANSPARENCIES

1. (TR#23) The Elderly in Cross-Cultural Perspective
2. (TR#24) The Graying of America
3. (TR#25) Health Care Costs for the Elderly and Disabled
4. (TR#26) Sources of Income for Elderly Persons

TRANSPARENCY MASTERS

1. (TR#22M) Costs of Social Security
2. (TR#23M) Differences in Age at Marriage
3. (TR#24M) Where Do America's Elderly Live?
4. (TR#25M) Percentage below the Poverty Line
5. (TR#26M) Myths about Aging
6. (TR#27M) Number of Elderly for 1950–2020
7. (TR#28M) The Growth of the Population 65 Years and Over, 1900–2020

VIDEOS/MOVIES

Aging in Industrialized Nations

How to Live Past 100. Is there a secret for living past the age of 100? This program examines the lives of some centenarians in seeking clues to longevity and to determine the reasons for the increasing number of centenarians in America today. 19 min. Available from A&B Video Library and FHS.

Aging in Japan. Provides a record of a society in flux, in which traditional mechanisms for looking after older people are breaking down. Japanese senior citizens created the economic miracle of modern Japan, only to find that the happy retirement they expected has been replaced by isolation. 45 min. Available from A&B Video Library and FHS.

Problems of Dependency

Parenting Our Parents. As the population of senior citizens grows, more middle-aged people find themselves staggering under the double burden of growing kids and chronically ill or disabled parents. The forecast is for a society of the old caring for the very old. This program examines some ways of coping with the stress of caring for aging parents and suggests personal and political remedies. 26 min. Available from A&B Video Library and FHS.

Ageless America. The focus of this program: caring for the elderly; why women live longer than men; the prospect of aging for a new generation of the middle-aged with fewer children and many more single women; the "sandwich generation" of adults with responsibility for aging parents and young children; and the process and problems of aging itself. 52 min. Available from A&B Video Library and FHS.

On Golden Pond. 1981 (Color) Starring Katharine Hepburn, Henry Fonda, and Jane Fonda, this movie shows a retired professor who is angry at being 80 years old and scared of losing his faculties. (PG) 109 min. Available at video rental stores.

Driving Miss Daisy. 1989 (Color) Starring Morgan Freeman, Jessica Tandy, and Dan Aykroyd. A black man who's hired as chauffeur for an old Southern woman (who is rather difficult to deal with) winds up being her most faithful companion. Examines not only age- but also race-related issues. 99 min. Available at video rental stores.

Nursing Homes

CNN Video II. *Nursing Home Care.* Abuse and neglect in nursing homes explored. Witnesses at a Congressional hearing recount nursing home abuse, including tranquilization with drugs and immobilization with physical restraints. According to one advocacy group for the elderly, in California 70% of nursing home residents are either physically or chemically restrained. Available from A&B Video Library.

Can't Afford to Grow Old. 1990. Narrated and hosted by Walter

Cronkite, this video focuses on families eager to keep their elderly relatives at home, having exhausted their physical and financial resources. Every year, up to one million Americans are forced into poverty by the cost of long-term care, and only then do they qualify for Medicaid, the state and federal health insurance program for the very poor. Analyzes the impact of the aging of America on our strained health-care system; debates whether the government or the private sector should ultimately pay for long-term care. 55 min. Available from FML.

No Place Like Home: Long Term Care for the Elderly. 1987. Providing home care rather than institutionalized care is often less costly to the public and more desirable for the older person. Experts estimate that one-third of the population now living in nursing homes would not need to be there if alternative services were more widely available. Shows several alternatives to institutionalizing the elderly. 55 min. Available from FML.

Elder Abuse

CNN Video II. *Elderly Abuse.* Explores problems of elder abuse. Several victims profiled, including woman who was hit by daughter-in-law; another who was put in the basement by her

sisters to whom she had paid substantial rent. According to report, 5 million Americans are being physically, emotionally, or economically abused. Most abuse takes place at the hands of relatives. Many victims do nothing because they fear being sent to nursing homes. Available from A&B Video Library.

A House Divided: Elderly Abuse. 1990. Through four portraits, this video sheds light on the hidden tragedy of elder abuse. The video portrays the emotional complexity of family relationships that can lead to abuse of the elderly and shows the isolation and helplessness of the victims as well as the need for understanding and support by those who work with the elderly. 35 min. Available for FML.

Suicide and the Elderly

CNN Video II. *Senior Suicide.* Problem of senior suicide explored. Seniors comprise 12% of U.S. population but 25% of all suicides. Available from A&B Video Library.

Elderly Suicide. Suicide is an increasingly common choice as the perceived alternative to chronic disease and pain, waning mental and physical powers, economic stress, and fear of helplessness and total dependence. In its wake, it leaves family members with guilt. 28 min. Available from A&B Video Library and FHS.

SPEAKER SUGGESTIONS

1. A physician or gerontologist to talk about the process of aging and its social and psychological consequences on individuals and on their families.
2. A Social Security administrator to discuss rules and regulations governing Social Security.
3. A spokesperson for the Gray Panthers or the AARP to discuss current elder issues in your city or state.
4. A person from Meals on Wheels or other home-visitation programs which focus on the elderly.
5. A staff member or volunteer with a hospice in your area to discuss goals and treatment philosophies of these organizations.

POP-QUIZ QUESTIONS

True-False

T   1. At the beginning of the twentieth century, the average American would not live to age 50.

T   2. Culturally sanctioned definitions of age often force the label of "old" on people sooner than they are ready to accept it.

F   3. Gerontocracy is a society run by its younger members but operating for the benefit of the elderly.

F   4. The elderly have always been seen as problematic in American society.

F   5. Television tends to convey positive messages about the elderly.

T   6. The label "old" often is applied differently to females and males.

F   7. Disengagement theory is based on the conflict perspective.

T   8. Social Security benefits are an example of the struggle between the young and old in the United States.

F   9. Most of the elderly in the Unites States tend to be quite isolated.

T 10. America's elderly are less likely to be poor than is the average American.

ESSAY QUESTIONS

1. Discuss some of the social factors involved in aging. Use cross-cultural comparisons to demonstrate the lack of universality of the aging process.
2. From the symbolic interaction perspective, describe how culturally sanctioned definitions of age may impact the individual.
3. Explain what is meant by the term "ageism" and describe how negative stereotypes of old age developed in modern society.
4. Analyze the functionalist and conflict perspectives on age inequalities.
5. Describe some of the major problems of dependency, including inadequate nursing homes, elder abuse, and poverty.
6. Explain why the process of dying has become strange to most people. Why have hospices emerged as a solution to some of the problems?

14

The Economy: Money and Work

CHAPTER SUMMARY

The United States has entered a postindustrial economy: most people work in the tertiary sector. Increasing global interconnections will force more changes in society, just as past societies made changes when moving from the preindustrial (primary) sector to the industrial (secondary) sector. Convergence theory indicates that the world's two economic systems, capitalism and socialism, are merging. Corporations are fundamental to modern capitalism; interlocking directorates and multinational corporations changed the way economies operate. Functionalists state that work is a fundamental source of social solidarity and that economic cycles are due to patterns of production, consumption, and credit, leading to excesses that must be wrung out of the economy. Conflict theorists see economic cycles as the result of the endless pursuit of profit by capitalists at the expense of workers. Symbolic interactionists analyze such things as factors that distinguish professions from jobs and the aspects that lead to work satisfaction. A quiet revolution has occurred due to the dramatic increase in the number of married women who work for pay. The availability of leisure decreased as the economy changed from preindustrial to industrial. Today, some people have a fair amount of leisure time while others find they have little, due to "double duty." The American economy has made a Great U-Turn, and the future depends on both domestic and international events.

CHAPTER OUTLINE

I. The Transformation of Economic Systems
   A. Market is the means by which we establish values for the exchange of goods and services. Earliest societies had subsistence economies—little trade with other groups, a high degree of social equality.
   B. In pastoral/horticultural economies, people created more dependable food supplies; a surplus allowed groups to grow in size, settle in a single place, develop a specialized division of labor, and trade with other groups—which fostered social inequality. Agricultural economies brought even greater surpluses, magnifying prior trends.
   C. The surplus (and greater inequality) grew in industrial societies. Emphasis changed from production of goods to consumption (Thorstein Veblen coined the term conspicuous consumption).
   D. According to Daniel Bell, postindustrial economies have six traits: extensive trade among nations; a large surplus of goods; a service sector employing the majority of workers; a wide variety and amount of goods available to the average person; an information explosion; and a global village with instantaneous, worldwide communications. Although the postindustrial economy has brought a greater availability of goods, it has not resulted in social equality.

II. The Transformation of the Medium of Exchange
   A. A medium of exchange is the means by which people value and exchange goods and services. One of the earliest mediums of exchange was barter—the direct exchange of one item for another.
   B. In agricultural economies, people came to use gold and silver coins. Deposit receipts which transferred ownership of a specified number of ounces of gold (or bushels of wheat, etc.) on deposit somewhere also were used. Toward the end of this period, the receipts became formalized into currency (paper money). Currency and deposit receipts represented stored value, and no more could be issued than the amount of gold or silver the currency represented.
   C. In industrial economies, bartering largely disappeared and gold was replaced by paper currency. The gold standard (a dollar represents a specified amount of gold) kept the number of dollars that could be issued to a specific limit. When "fiat money" came into existence, the currency no longer could be exchanged for gold or silver.
      1. Even without a gold standard, the amount of paper money that can be issued is limited: prices increase if a government issues currency at a rate higher than the growth of its gross national product. Issu-

ing more produces inflation: each unit of currency will purchase fewer goods and services.

2. Checking accounts and credit cards have become common in industrial economies, largely replacing currency.

D. In postindustrial economies paper money is being replaced by checks, credit cards, and debit cards. Spending eventually becomes an electronic transfer of numbers residing in computer memory banks.

III. World Economic Systems

A. Capitalism has three essential features: private ownership of the means of prodution; pursuit of profit; and market competition.

1. Pure (laissez faire) capitalism exists only when market forces are able to operate without interference from the government, and in the United States there are many restraints. The United States today has welfare (or state) capitalism—private citizens own the means of production and pursue profits, but do so within a vast system of laws designed to protect the public welfare.

2. Market restraints today include laws and regulations that limit the capacity a person may produce.

B. Socialism also has three essential features: public ownership of the means of production; central planning; and distribution of goods without a profit motive.

1. Under socialism, the government owns the means of production, and a central committee determines what the country needs instead of allowing supply and demand to control. Socialism is designed to eliminate competition, produce goods for the general welfare, and distribute them according to people's needs, not their ability to pay.

2. Socialism does not exist in pure form, since socialist nations found it necessary to offer higher salaries for some jobs in order to entice people to take greater responsibilities.

3. Some nations (e.g., Sweden and Denmark) have adopted democratic or welfare socialism: both the state and individuals engage in production and distribution, although the state owns certain industries (steel, mining, forestry, telephones, television stations, and airlines) while retail stores, farms, and most service industries remain in private hands.

C. Ideology: Capitalists believe that market forces should determine both products and prices, and that it is good for people to strive for profits; socialists believe that profit is immoral and represents excess value extracted from workers. The primary criticism of capitalism is that it leads to social inequality (a top layer of wealthy, powerful people, and a bottom layer of people who are unemployed or underemployed—people who must work at menial jobs in spite of their training and abilities or who can find only part-time work). Socialism has been criticized for not respecting individual rights, and for not being capable of producing much wealth (thus the greater equality of socialism actually amounts to almost everyone having an equal chance of being poor).

D. In recent years, fundamental changes have taken place in the former Soviet Union, China, and other nations, which have resulted in varying degrees of movement away from socialism. Sweden (which has provided citizens with "cradle-to-grave" security) has embarked on privatization (selling state-run industries) to generate funds to reduce its foreign debt and build more railroads and highways. At this point in history, capitalism speaks with a louder voice than does socialism.

E. Factors that may make nations grow more similar to one another include: (1) industrialization, resulting in comparable divisions of labor, emphasis on higher education, and extensive urbanization; and (2) both capitalist and socialist systems adopting features of the other (convergence theory), which may result in the emergence of a hybrid or mixed economy in the future.

IV. The Inner Circle of Capitalism

A. The corporation (joint ownership of a business enterprise, whose liabilities are separate from those of its owners) has changed the face of capitalism. Corporate capitalism refers to the domination of the economic system by giant corporations. One of the most significant aspects of large corporations is the separation of ownership and management, producing ownership of wealth without appreciable control, and control of wealth without appreciable ownership. A stockholders' revolt (stockholders of a corporation refuse to rubber stamp decisions made by the management) is likely to occur if the profits do not meet expectations.

B. Oligopolies—several large companies that dominate a single industry—dictate pricing, set the quality of their products, and protect the market. Often they use their wealth and connections for political purposes (e.g., favorable legislation giving them special tax breaks or protecting their industry from imports).

C. Interlocking directorates occur when individuals sit on the boards of several companies, concentrating power/minimizing competition.

D. Corporations outgrew national boundaries, resulting in multinational corporations. Americans (accustomed to owning property in other nations) question ownership of U.S. property by foreigners.

V. Work in American Society

A. Sociologists divide economic life into primary (extracting natural resources), secondary (turning raw materials into goods), and tertiary (service-oriented) sectors. In postindustrial societies, most of the labor force works in the tertiary sector.

B. A sharp increase in the number of women working outside the home has occurred in America. Since 1960, the proportion of married women in the labor force has almost doubled. For the first time, the number of married women who work is greater than the number who do not.

C. The underground (informal) economy is exchange of goods and services not reported to the government, including income from work done "on the side" and from illegal activities (e.g., drug dealing). Estimates place the underground economy at 10 to 20% of the regular economy, which means it may total between $500 billion and $1 trillion.

D. Different societies have had differing amounts of leisure (time not taken up by work or required activities such as eating/sleeping); early societies had much time for leisure. Industrialization brought changes: bosses and machines now control people's time. It is not the activity itself that makes something leisure, but rather its purpose (e.g., driving a car for pleasure or driving it to work).

VI. Applying Sociological Theories

A The functionalist perspective states that work is functional for society because important tasks are accomplished. It binds people together, according to Durkheim's principles of mechanical (unity from being involved in similar occupations or activities) and organic solidarity (interdependence resulting from mutual need that each fulfill his or her job). Economic booms occur when owners are confident about the future, hire more workers, increase production, etc.—money flows freely through the economy, and with easy credit and high consumption, expansion continues. Busts occur when booms overexpand. The recession wrings out excesses from the economy.

B. The conflict perspective states that oppression, exploitation, and anomie are essential in a capitalist economy. Workers are exploited by capitalists and eventually are ground down and discarded when no longer needed. Economic cycles are caused by greed, power, and ex-

ploitation: when profits decrease, workers are laid off until again needed. Capitalists maintain a reserve labor force—unemployed people they can hire for temporary work, and then fire at will during the next economic downturn. Recessions help capitalists by reducing excess inventory and depressing wages—workers are afraid to ask for higher pay when unemployment is high.

C. One example of the symbolic interaction perspective is research concerning what distinguishes a job from a profession. Sociologists identify five characteristics of professions: (1) rigorous education including graduate school and an admission examination; (2) the education is theoretical, not practical or "how to do it"; (3) self-regulation by the profession; (4) authority over clients based on specialized education/theoretical understanding; and (5) service to society. Work satisfaction also is of interest to symbolic interactionists.

VII. The Future of the U.S. Economy: The Great U-Turn of American society has occurred—workers now make less than they did in 1970 (adjusted for inflation), and people are getting farther behind. This decline in earnings and standard of living resulted from a profit squeeze felt by U.S. corporations due to a surge in imports and decline in exports, increasing use of temporary and part-time workers, and the fact that most new jobs have been in the lower-paying service industries.

LEARNING OBJECTIVES

After reading and studying Chapter 14, the student should be able to:

1. Trace the transformation of the economic systems through each of the historical stages and state the degree to which social inequality existed in each of the economies.
2. State the three essential features of capitalism and explain why "pure" capitalism does not exist.
3. Describe the three essential components of socialism and give reasons why "pure" socialism does not exist.
4. State the major criticisms of capitalism and socialism. Explain why some theorists believe the two systems are converging.
5. Define corporate capitalism, oligopolies, interlocking directorates, and multinational corporations. Note the ways in

which each of these has fundamentally altered the face of capitalism.
6. Distinguish among the three economic sectors and describe the signs which mark a society's movement into the post-industrial stage.
7. Trace the development of the "quiet revolution" in the United States.
8. Contrast the functional and conflict perspectives on economic life.
9. Give examples of the types of research conducted by symbolic interactionists regarding the economy.
10. Discuss the "Great U-Turn" and analyze the possibilities for improvement in the U.S. economy.

KEY TERMS

barter
capitalism
conspicuous consumption
convergence theory
corporate capitalism
corporation
credit card
currency
debit card
democratic socialism
deposit receipts

divest
economic cycle
economy
flat money
gold standard
gross national product
inflation
interlocking directorates
laissez faire capitalism
leisure
market

market competition
market forces
market restraints
mechanical solidarity
medium of exchange
money
monopoly
oligopoly
organic solidarity
primary sector

INSTRUCTOR'S SECTION

private ownership of the means of
    production
privatization
profession
profit

quiet revolution (the)
reserve labor force
secondary sector
socialism
stockholders' revolt

stored value
subsistence economy
tertiary sector
underemployment
underground economy

KEY PEOPLE

Thorstein Veblen
Maxine Baca Zinn and Stanley Eitzen
Bennett Harrison and Barry Bluestone

Daniel Bell
Peter Drucker

CLASS DISCUSSION QUESTIONS

1. How do you think people's lives today are affected by the American economy?
2. What examples of conspicuous consumption can you give?
3. Do you watch network or cable television newscasts? If yes, how are these broadcasts examples of the "global village?"
4. Why do you think the postindustrial economy has not resulted in social equality?
5. What medium of exchange do you most often use? Why?
6. Can you think of any kind of business you could set up in the United States today in which you would not have to comply with rules and regulations?
7. Why do most people think that the U.S. economic system is capitalistic if, in reality, it is far from "pure" capitalism?
8. How do you think an economic system which distributes resources according to a person's need, instead of financial ability to pay, would work in the United States?
9. Can you think of examples of underemployment in your city? Do you know of anyone with a Masters or Ph.D. degree working in a fast food restaurant?
10. Do you agree that at this point in history, capitalism is speaking with a louder voice than socialism? Why or why not?
11. How influential do you think major corporations are in American economic and political decision-making? In the global economy?
12. Can you foresee any problems occurring as a result of the same person sitting on the boards of directors of a number of companies?

13. Why do you think there has been an outcry among some Americans about "foreign ownership" of large amounts of property in cities such as New York and Houston?
14. If a person asked you for career advice and indicated that he or she wanted to be sure they had a job, what types of work would you be most likely to recommend? What would you not recommend?
15. What factors do you believe may contribute to women's satisfaction with work outside the home? With men's work-related satisfaction?
16. Do you know of examples of the underground economy in your hometown? Where you attend school?
17. What leisure activities do you enjoy? Is leisure the same for everyone? Why or why not?
18. Do economic cycles have any impact on you personally? Why or why not?
19. If people are willing to work harder and for lower wages if they think someone else is waiting to get their jobs, what impact do you think this has on unions?
20. Are you planning to enter a profession? What are its essential characteristics?
21. If you are currently employed, what do you find most satisfying about your work? Least satisfying?
22. Do you believe Americans will be able to straighten out the "Great U-Turn?" Why or why not?

PROJECTS

1. Conduct informal research on conspicuous consumption in the United States. Make notes on current advertising and on your personal observations about clothing, cars, beverages, and other lifestyle items to gain insight into why people buy certain products. You may wish to read some of the following: (a) Veblen, Thorstein. *The Theory of the Leisure Class.* NY: Penguin Books, 1980 (orig. 1899); (b) Brooks, John. *Showing Off in America: From Conspicuous Consumption to Parody Display.* Boston: Little, Brown, 1981; (c) Fussell, Paul. *Class: A Guide Through the American Status System.* NY: Summit Books, 1983; (d) Fairchild, John. *Chic Savages: The New Rich, The Old Rich, and the World They Inhabit.* NY: Simon and Schuster, 1989; (e) Sheehy, Sandy. *Texas Big*

Rich. NY: William Morrow, 1990; and (f) Packard, Vance. *The Ultra Rich: How Much Is Too Much.* Boston: Little, Brown, 1989. Present your findings and conclusions to the class or in a research paper.
2. Keep a journal of media presentations about political and economic changes taking place in the former Soviet Union. Analyze whether you think the U.S. media are biased or unbiased in their reporting of these happenings. Assess the extent of change you think has occurred during this semester, and present your journal and conclusions at the end of the semester.
3. Keep a record of how you spend your leisure time. Ask several people—perhaps your parents or other relatives as well

as friends—to keep a similar diary for several weeks. Compare how you spent your leisure time with how others spent theirs. Present your report as a chart indicating the types and amount of time spent in various activities. Determine whether the ages of the individuals involved are related to how much leisure time they have and how they spend it.

4. Learn more about the professions and the requirements they

place on their members by contacting state or national associations involved in licensing and regulating physicians, attorneys, accountants, architects, real estate brokers, or other fields of interest to you. Determine the extent to which their materials discuss the following: rigorous education, self-regulation, authority over clients, and service to society. Present your findings to the class.

TRANSPARENCIES

1. (TR#27) Percentage of American Households below Poverty Line
2. (TR#28) Declining Value of the Dollar

3. (TR#29) Percentage of Americans in Three Types of Work
4. (TR#30) Percentage of Married Women in the U.S. Labor Force, by Race

TRANSPARENCY MASTERS

1. (TR#29M) Average Hourly Earnings of U.S. Workers in Current Dollars
2. (TR#30M) Occupations with the Highest Concentration by Race/Ethnicity/Gender

3. (TR#31M) What Jobs Will Be Expanding Most: 1982–1995

VIDEOS/MOVIES

Industrial Economies: The Birth of the Machine
The Factory and Marketplace Revolution. 1986. Describes the origins of the Industrial Revolution and the resulting growth of urbanization, the creation of the factory system and an industrial working class, and the exploitation of the planet. 52 min. Available from Churchill Films.

World Economic Systems
Bill Moyers: A World of Ideas (#21)—An Interview with Peter Berger. 1988. Peter Berger, a professor of sociology and religion, compares capitalism in America and East Asia, commenting on the social, philosophical, religious, and political factors that have influenced the development of capitalist economies in each area. Discusses the relationship of capitalism to democracy. 29 min. Available from PBS Video.

Kitchen Talk, USSR. 1992. Although changes have occurred in the former Soviet Union since this video was filmed, it offers rare insights into the lives of people in this rapidly changing area of the world. Traveling with a small camera and one assistant, Heather MacDonald found her way into the kitchens of ordinary Soviet people, who spoke to her candidly about their worsening economic conditions. 58 min. Available from FML.

CNN Video II. *South China Part 1.* In a province 1,000 miles from Beijing an oasis of capitalism flourishes, the result of an experiment instituted a decade earlier by the Central Commu-

nist government, which wanted to test market reforms. Capitalism took off with a vengeance. One expert comments that China as a whole, even while remaining the last bastion of hard-core communism, has much more of a market economy in place than do the Eastern European countries just now digging their way out of communism. Available from A&B Video Library.

Multinational Corporations
CNN Video II. *The Maquiladoras and the Job Controversy.* Discusses the controversy over whether Mexican workers in maquiladoras are exploited or not. U.S. union officials claim jobs are lost to U.S. citizens; opposing side claims that for every job created in a maquiladora, 3 jobs are created in the United States. Available from A&B Video Library.

The Future of the United States Economy
Crisis in the Work Force: Help Wanted. 1992. The American work force is not competing in the world market nearly as well as it once did, and this is a virtual time bomb to the U.S. economy. Some of the reasons this is happening are addressed. Filmed in factories and public high schools around the country, it shows attempts by workers, employers, and schools to upgrade their level of performance. 22 min. Available from FML.

SPEAKER SUGGESTIONS

1. An anthropologist who has studied nations in the various stages of economic development.
2. An expert on finance to discuss the possibilities of a "moneyless" society.

3. A colleague who has conducted work satisfaction studies.
4. An economist to give a forecast about the U.S. economy in the 21st century.

POP QUIZ QUESTIONS

True-False

F   1. The majority of workers in postindustrial societies are employed in factory settings.

T   2. Paper money becomes less common as postindustrial societies advance.

T   3. The United States does not have true capitalism.

F   4. Private ownership of the means of production is discouraged in the United States today.

F   5. It would be impossible for socialism and capitalism to converge in the future.

F   6. An oligopoly occurs when a person sits on the board of directors of several companies at the same time.

T   7. The decline in blue-collar jobs is a characteristic of post-industrial societies.

F   8. Women who are divorced, widowed, or separated are the most likely to be in the work force.

T   9. Functional theorists believe that economic cycles function to improve the efficiency of the economy.

F 10. The symbolic interaction perspective argues that capitalists exploit workers.

ESSAY QUESTIONS

1. Discuss the nature and extent of social inequality present in capitalist and socialist economies and state the essential components of each system.

2. Distinguish between welfare capitalism and laissez faire capitalism. List reasons why the United States is far from laissez faire capitalism.

3. Describe the inner circle of capitalism. Indicate how corporate capitalism and multinational corporations have changed the economic structure of the United States.

4. Analyze these trends regarding work in American society: the increasing number of women working in paid employment, the growth of the underground economy, and the changing patterns of leisure.

5. Compare and contrast functional and conflict perspectives on the following: the importance of work in society and the degree to which economic cycles are functional or harmful to workers and to society.

C H A P T E R
15

Politics: Power and Authority

CHAPTER SUMMARY

Politics is power (the ability to carry out one's will despite resistance) and the prerogatives that come with it. The state claims a monopoly on the use of violence, and the ultimate foundation of any political order is violence. Three types of authority—traditional, rational-legal, and charismatic—were identified by Max Weber as ideal type constructs. The orderly transfer of authority at the death, resignation, or incapacitation of a leader is critical for social stability. Four forms of government are monarchies, democracies, dictatorships, and oligarchies. Although democracies are fairly new in world history, the concept of democracy and citizenship is now transforming global politics. In the United States—with its winner-takes-all electoral system—political parties must appeal to the center, and minority parties make little headway. In contrast, many democracies in Europe have a system of proportional representation which encourages the formation of minority, off-center political parties. Voting patterns in America consistently demonstrate that whites, the elderly, the rich, the employed, and the highly educated are most likely to vote. The more people feel they have a stake in the political system, the more likely they are to vote. Special interest groups, with their lobbyists and PACs, play a significant role in American politics. Functionalists and conflict theorists have very different views on who rules America. War is a common means to implement political objectives; however, dehumanization of the enemy is the particularly high cost of war. An international world order may be in the process of emerging.

CHAPTER OUTLINE

I. Micropolitics and Macropolitics
   A. Power is the ability to carry out one's will despite resistance. Symbolic interactionists use micropolitics to refer to exercise of power in everyday life (e.g., employees' attempts to impress the boss). Macropolitics is the exercise of power over a broad group.
   B. Authority (as used by Weber) is legitimate power that people accept as right, while coercion is power that people do not accept as just.
II. Power, Authority, and Coercion
   A. Authority and Legitimate Violence
      1. The state is the source of legitimate force in society; the more a government appears legitimate, the more stable it is. Violence is the ultimate foundation of political order; revolution (armed resistance to overthrow a government) is a rejection of a government's claim to rule.
      2. Three sources of authority were identified by Max Weber:
         a. Traditional authority (based on custom) is prevalent in preliterate groups, where custom sets relationships. When society changes, traditional authority is undermined, but does not die, even in postindustrial societies.
         b. Rational-legal authority (based on written rules —also called bureaucratic authority) derives from the position an individual holds, not from the person. Everyone (no matter how high the office) is subject to the rules.
         c. Charismatic authority (based on an individual's personal following) may pose a threat—this type of leader works outside the established political system.
      3. Weber's three types of authority are ideal types representing composite characteristics found in leaders in real life. In rare instances, traditional and rational-legal leaders possess charismatic traits, but most authority is one type or another.
      4. Orderly transfer of authority upon death, resignation, or incapacity of a leader is critical for stability. Succession is more of a problem with charismatic authority than with traditional or rational-legal authority. Routinization of charisma is used by Weber to refer to the transfer of authority from a charismatic leader to either traditional or rational-legal authority.
III. Types of Government
   A. A monarchy is a government headed by a king or queen. As cities developed, each city-state (an independent city whose power radiated outward, bringing adjacent

areas under its rule) had its own monarchy. As city-states warred with one another, the victors would extend their rule, eventually over an entire region.

B. A democracy is a government whose authority derives from the people. Direct democracy (eligible voters meet to discuss issues and make decisions) emerged about 2,000 years ago in Athens. Representative democracy (voters elect representatives to govern and make decisions on their behalf) emerged as the United States became more populous. Today, citizenship (citizens have basic rights) is taken for granted in the United States, although it is new to the human scene. Universal citizenship (everyone having the same basic rights) came into practice very slowly and only through fierce struggle.

C. Dictatorship is government where power is seized and held by an individual/small clique. The result is known as an oligarchy (power held by a small group of individual) Examples include the frequent coups in Central and South America. Totalitarianism is almost total control of a people by the government; in such regimes, the names of those who rule change, but the techniques of control remain the same—individual rights simply disappear.

IV. The American Political System
A. The Democratic and Republican parties emerged to compete with one another by the Civil War. Since each appeals to a broad membership, it is difficult to distinguish conservative Democrats from liberal Republicans; however, it is easy to discern the extremes. The two parties represent different slices of the center.

B. Fundamental distinctions between U.S. and European democracies:
1. U.S. elections are based on a winner-takes-all electoral system; most European countries use proportional representation (legislative seats divided according to the proportion of votes each political party received).
2. U.S. winner-takes-all system discourages minority parties; the proportional representation system encourages them. The United States has centrist parties, representing the center of political opinion. Noncentrist parties (representing marginal ideas) develop in European systems with proportional representation.
3. As a result of proportional representation, European minority parties can gain access to the media (and power) beyond their numbers. Coalition governments (a country's largest party aligns itself with one or more smaller parties to get required votes to make national decisions) may occur. In some countries that call themselves "democratic," closed elections (only a single candidate is allowed to run) are held (e.g., the former Soviet Union until recently).

C. Voting Patterns
1. American voting patterns are consistent: The percentage of people who vote increases with age; whites are more likely to vote than African-Americans, while Hispanic-Americans are consid-

ably less likely to vote than either; those with higher levels of education are more likely to vote, as are people with higher levels of income. About the same proportion of males and females vote in presidential elections.
2. The more that people feel they have a stake in the system, the more likely they are to vote. Those who have been rewarded by the system feel more socially integrated and perceive that elections directly affect their lives and the society in which they live. People who gain less from the system in terms of education, income, and jobs are more likely to be alienated.
3. Voter apathy is indifference/inaction to the political process. As a result of apathy, two out of five eligible American voters do not vote for president; less than half of the nation's eligible voters vote for members of Congress.

D. The Depression as a Transforming Event
1. Until the administration of Franklin D. Roosevelt in 1932, the country's ruling philosophy was that government should play as small a part as possible in people's lives. Government was not to run the economy but rather to run schools, take care of garbage, sewers, and streets, etc. During the depression of the 1930s, public opinion was transformed and government became much more involved in the economy.
2. Roosevelt believed it was the government's job to oversee the country's economy, and things have never been the same again. Although each political party has different versions of the philosophy, both support payments to unemployed workers, the elderly, and the poor.

E. Special-interest groups are people who think alike on a particular issue and can be mobilized for political action. Lobbyists (paid to influence legislation on behalf of their clients) are employed by special interest groups and have become a major force in politics. Political action committees (PACs) solicit and spend funds to influence legislation and bypass laws intended to limit the amount any individual, corporation, or group can give a candidate. PACs have become a powerful influence, bankrolling lobbyists and legislators, and PACs with the most clout gain the ear of Congress.

F. The cost of elections contributes to the importance of lobbyists and PACs in Washington and state capitols. An average candidate for the Senate will spend $3.5 million on the campaign. Once a candidate is elected, she/he owes people who helped with financing the campaign—and wants to get reelected.

V. Who Rules America?
A. The Functionalist Perspective: Pluralism is the diffusion of power among interest groups, preventing any one from gaining control of the government. Functionalists believe it helps keep the government from turning against its citizens. A balancing act must occur between having no government (which would lead to anarchy, a state in which disorder and violence reign) and having a government which turns against its citizens. The

United States has a system of checks and balances in which separation of powers among the three branches of government ensures that each is able to nullify the actions of the other two, thus preventing the domination of any single branch.

B. According to the conflict perspective as stated by C. Wright Mills, the power elite (heads of leading corporations, powerful generals and admirals in the armed forces, and certain elite politicians) rule America. Lobbyists and even Congress are not at the center of decision making; rather, the power elite makes the decisions that direct the country and shake the world. The corporate heads are the most powerful, as all three view capitalism as essential to the welfare of the country; thus, business interests come first.

C. According to the conflict perspective as stated by William Dumhoff, the ruling class (the wealthiest and most powerful individuals in the country) run the United States. Its members control America's top corporations and foundations; presidential cabinet members and top ambassadors to the most powerful countries are chosen from this group, which promotes the view that positions come through merit and that everyone has a chance of becoming rich.

VI. War: A Means to Implement Political Objectives

A. In some instances, the state uses violence to protect citizens from individuals and groups, at other times it turns violence against its own people or against other nations. War (armed conflict between nations or politically distinct groups) often is part of national policy.

B. Nicholas Timasheff identified three essential conditions of war: a cultural tradition of war; an antagonistic situation in which two or more states confront incompatible objectives; and a "fuel" that heats the antagonistic situation to the boiling point, so that people move from thinking about war to actually engaging in it.

C. Although people long for peace, war is glorified in the history of countries and monuments are erected to military leaders. Since 1850, the United States has intervened militarily around the world more than 150 times, an average of more than once a year.

D. War has an effect on morality. Exposure to brutality and killing often causes dehumanization (reducing people to objects that do not deserve to be treated as humans).

VII. A Coming World Order? The historical trend has been for states to grow larger and larger, and national boundaries and national patriotism are deeply entrenched. There is a possiblity that global and economic unity could come about. Some speculate that a push by a powerful group of capitalists who profit from global free trade might facilitate this occurrence. Also, totalitarianism could occur and the world's resources and people could come under the control of a dictatorship or oligarchy.

LEARNING OBJECTIVES

After reading and studying Chapter 15, the student should be able to:

1. Define the following terms: micropolitics, macropolitics, power, authority, coercion, state, and revolution.
2. Describe the three sources of authority identified by Max Weber. Indicate why these are "ideal types."
3. Differentiate between monarchies, democracies, and dictatorships and oligarchies.
4. Explain how the American political system is structured and compare American democracy with democratic systems found in Europe.
5. Describe American voting patterns and identify those most and least likely to vote in elections.
6. Analyze the ways in which special-interest groups influence the political process.
7. Distinguish between the functionalist and conflict perspectives on who rules America.
8. Compare and contrast the power elite perspective of C. Wright Mills with William Domhoff's ruling class theory.
9. Discuss the major uses of war in societies. Analyze the costs and dehumanizing aspects of war.
10. Explain why some theorists believe that there is a possibility that global and economic unity could come about. Note the main strengths and limitations of this viewpoint.

KEY TERMS

anarchy
authority
centrist party
charismatic authority
checks and balances
citizenship
city-state
coalition government
coercion
dehumanization
democracy
dictatorship

direct democracy
lobbyists
macropolitics
micropolitics
monarchy
noncentrist party
oligarchy
pluralism
political action committee (PAC)
power
power elite
proportional representation

rational-legal authority
representative democracy
revolution
routinization of charisma
special-interest group
state
totalitarianism
traditional authority
universal citizenship
voter apathy
war

INSTRUCTOR'S SECTION

KEY PEOPLE

Max Weber
C. Wright Mills
Nicholas S. Timasheff
Tamotsu Shibutani

Peter Berger
William Domhoff
Pitirim Sorokin

CLASS DISCUSSION QUESTIONS

1. From groups in which you participate, can you give examples to support the statement that "every group is political?"
2. Do you agree that violence is the ultimate foundation of any political order? Why or why not?
3. How stable do you think the U.S. government is? Is it true that the more a government is seen as legitimate, the more stable it is?
4. Do you believe that traditional authority eventually dies out in a society? Why or why not?
5. Does the President of your college or university have authority based on his or her reputation and personal characteristics? Why or why not?
6. Who would you consider to be a charismatic leader today?
7. Why do you think that the line of succession to the U.S. Presidency is so clearly spelled out in the 25th Amendment to the U.S. Constitution?
8. Do you believe that most U.S. citizens take the idea of citizenship for granted? Why or why not?
9. Why do people around the world find the ideas of citizenship and of representative democracy appealing?
10. Do you think the Republican and Democratic parties actually are different from one another? If yes, in what ways?
11. Why do you think the percentage of people who vote increases with age? Wouldn't younger people have more to gain?
12. Do you vote regularly? Why do so few people vote in the United States?
13. What are some of the special-interest groups in your city or state? Are you currently a member of any special-interest group?
14. Why are elections so costly in the United States? Do you think they have to be?
15. Do you agree with the functionalist or the conflict perspective on who rules America? Why?
16. Under what circumstances do you think the United States should engage in war? When should the United States not engage in war?
17. Do you think that war inevitably causes dehumanization?
18. Do you foresee a world order developing in the future?

PROJECTS

1. Conduct research on the platforms of the major political parties. Find out how each stands on key issues and what each suggests for social policy changes (e.g., welfare reform, gun control, or environmental concerns). In what ways are the two parties similar? In what ways different? Analyze them as if you were reading or hearing them for the first time to determine what your reaction would be. Compare your thoughts with those of other students in small group or class discussions.
2. Collect literature from special-interest groups or political action committees (PACs). Determine whose interest you think they actually are trying to serve. If possible, find out how much money is contributed to political candidates by the special-interest groups or PACs you study. Write a summary based on the literature and information you have acquired.
3. Seek out data regarding defense contracts held by firms in your community, state, or by your college or university. Such projects and dollar amounts are public information. Determine what impact downsizing the military, including these defense contracts, may have on your community, state, or academic institution. Find out how dependent your school is on such contracts. Present your findings in class or in written form.

TRANSPARENCIES

1. (TR#31) How Americans Identify with Political Parties
2. (TR#32) Percentage of Americans Who Vote for President
3. (TR#33) Definitions of Behavior as Practiced by the State and Private Citizens

TRANSPARENCY MASTERS

1. (TR#32M) Power in American Society: The Model Prepared by C. Wright Mills
2. (TR#33M) Domhoff's View of the Structure of Power
3. (TR#34M) Veto-Groups Model
4. (TR#35M) Social Status and Party Affiliation

VIDEOS/MOVIES

The American Political System
Advise and Consent
All the President's Men
The Candidate
Power
Available at video rental stores.

PACs and the Costs of Elections
CNN Video II. *Lobbying/Money.* PACs are a major source of campaign money. Available from A&B Video Library.

War: A Means to Implement Political Objectives
Women in the Military. In this *60 Minutes* segment, women are seen as succeeding at all those tasks that servicemen have always considered particularly macho. Now, permitted for the first time into situations that would put them into the equivalent of the front line, women in the military respond as they are supposed to—professionally. 14 min. Available from FHS.

War and Dehumanization
Disobeying Orders: G.I. Resistance to the Vietnam War. 1990. This documentary focuses on the anti-war movement within the armed forces. Oral history interviews with Vietnam veterans including a navy nurse are interwoven with archival photos, film footage, and popular music of the 1960s. Some G.I.'s took very courageous stands, risking court martial and jail, because of their resistance to the war, and some were pro-

testing what they considered to be the military's racial discrimination. 29 min. Available from FHS.

The Killing Fields. 1984. (Color) Based on the memoirs of a *New York Times* reporter who remained in Cambodia after the American evacuation. A frighteningly realistic depiction of life in a war-torn country. (R) 141 min. Available at video rental stores.

Platoon. 1986. (Color) A penetrating first-person account of life on the front line by a young soldier in the Vietnam War. (R) 120 min. Available at video rental stores.

Vietnam Vets: Dissidents For Peace. 1989. Documents Vietnam veterans protesting U.S. involvement in Central America because of the realities of war they had experienced. The group wanted to counteract the media's glorification of combat. 29 min. Available from FML.

A Coming World Order
CNN *Internal Conflicts within and among Developing Nations.* Internal conflicts in developing nations are proliferating worldwide. Explores the effects of devolution and the rise of nationalism. Available from A&B Video Library.

Burden on the Land. 1992. When the colonial powers left Africa, the political vacuum was filled by authoritarian regimes whose armies continued to keep them in power. Frequent tribal wars keep countless people refugees, fleeing from one nation to another. The vast number of refugees have depleted the host countries of resources. This documentary explores the conflicts and interrelated issues of politics, health, environment and culture. 52 min. Available from FML.

SPEAKER SUGGESTIONS

1. A political scientist to talk about current issues in U.S. or other political systems.
2. A Democratic or Republican party chairman or other official to talk about the positions of that party on certain policy issues.

3. A military recruiter and/or peace activist to talk about war-related topics.

POP QUIZ QUESTIONS

True-False
T 1. Micropolitics refers to the exercise of power in everyday life.
F 2. Groups that are not political do not tend to have power struggles.
T 3. Violence is the ultimate foundation of any political order.
T 4. Traditional authority never totally dies out in industrial and postindustrial societies.
F 5. When the United States was founded, the idea of universal citizenship was readily accepted by everyone.
T 6. The United States has a winner-takes-all electoral system.

F 7. People are more likely to vote if they feel that the political system needs changing.
T 8. Functionalists say that pluralism prevents any one group from gaining control of the government and using it to oppress the people.
F 9. According to conflict theorists, lobbyists have the real power in the political process.
F 10. The fact that all groups have a word for war demonstrates that war is universal.

ESSAY QUESTIONS

1. Differentiate between legitimate and illegitimate power and explain why the state is the source of legitimate force in society.
2. Describe Weber's three sources of authority and note which type is most likely to be found in bureaucratic organizations.
3. Distinguish between direct and representative democracies, and identify the type found in the United States. Explain why citizenship is taken for granted in the United States, although it is quite new to the human scene.
4. Describe the seizure of power by dictatorships and oligarchies.
5. Compare the democratic system in the United States with democratic systems in Europe.
6. Outline the trends in American voting and explain why these patterns are very consistent.
7. Summarize the functionalist and conflict perspectives on how power is distributed in the United States. State which of the theories you think is correct and justify your answer.

CHAPTER

16

The Family

CHAPTER SUMMARY

Marriage and family patterns vary remarkably across cultures, but four universal themes in marriage are mate selection, descent, inheritance, and authority. Both functionalists and conflict theorists examine the macro level. According to the functional perspective, the family is universal because it serves six essential functions: economic production, socialization of children, care of the sick and aged, recreation, sexual control, and reproduction; erosion of these functions is the reason for the high American divorce rate. Conversely, conflict theorists focus on how changing economic conditions affect families, especially gender relations. A dramatic increase in the number of married women in the labor force has created power struggles—especially over housework—within the family. In their micro-level analyses, symbolic interactionists focus on the meanings that people give their marital relationships, particularly in regard to communica-

tion between the partners. The family life cycle is analyzed in terms of love and courtship, marriage, childbirth, child rearing, and the family in later life. Family diversity in American culture includes racial and ethnic differences, one-parent families, childless families, blended families, and homosexual families. Trends in American families include postponement of marriage, cohabitation, dual-career families, and greater use of child care. Various studies have focused on problems in measuring divorce, children of divorce, ex-spouses, and remarriage. Violence and abuse—including battering, marital rape, and incest—are the "dark side" of family life. Researchers have identified variables that help marriages last and be happy. There is reason for optimism about the future of marriage and family in the United States.

CHAPTER OUTLINE

I. Marriage and Family in Cross-Cultural Perspective
   A. The term family is difficult to define, as there are many types. A broad definition is a group that considers itself related by blood, marriage, or adoption, and lives together. A family is classified as a nuclear family (husband, wife, and children) or an extended family (a nuclear family plus other relatives who live together). The family of orientation is the family in which a person grows up, while the family of procreation is the family formed when a couple's first child is born. A person who is married but has not had a child is part of a couple, not a family. Marriage is a group's approved mating arrangements, usually marked by a ritual.
   B. Looking at marriage and family from a cross-cultural perspective reveals many variations. Worldwide, most brides and grooms are fairly close in age, but in some groups the age gap is huge. Most groups consider sexual fidelity within marriage important; however, wives tend to be held to higher standards than husbands. Among some tribal groups, the father bears no responsibility for his children; responsibility goes to the wife's eldest brother because life revolves around

the brother-sister relationship instead of around husband-wife relations.
   C. Common Cultural Themes
      1. Each group establishes norms to govern who can and cannot marry. Endogamy is the practice of marrying within one's own group, while exogamy is the practice of marrying outside of one's own group. Some norms of mate selection are written into law, others are informal.
      2. Three major patterns of descent (tracing kinship over generations) are: (a) bilateral (descent traced on both the mother's and the father's side); (b) patrilineal (descent traced only on the father's side); and (c) matrilineal (descent traced only on the mother's side).
      3. Descent is regulated in all societies in order to provide an orderly way of passing property, etc., to the next generation. In a bilateral system, property passes to males and females; in a patrilineal system, property passes only to males; in a matrilineal system, property passes only to females.
      4. Patriarchy is a social system in which men dominate

women, and runs through all societies. No historical records exist of a true matriarchy—a social system in which women dominate men.

II. Marriage and Family in Theoretical Perspective
   A. The Functionalist Perspective
      1. The family is universal because it serves functions essential to the well-being of society: economic production, socialization of children, care of the sick and aged, recreation, sexual control, and reproduction.
      2. The incest taboo (rules specifying which people are too closely related to have sex or marry) helps the family avoid role confusion and forces people to look outside the family for marriage partners.
      3. Industrialization has made the family more fragile by weakening its functions and removing reasons for a family to struggle together against hardship, leading to higher rates of divorce.
      4. The nuclear family has few people it can depend on for material and emotional support; thus, the members of a nuclear family are vulnerable to "emotional overload." The relative isolation of the nuclear family makes it easier for the "dark side" of families (incest and other types of abuse) to emerge.
   B. The Conflict Perspective
      1. Industrialization forced families to change. Similarly, changes taking place in today's postindustrial society also will change families.
      2. Industrialization placed husbands and wives in such different domains of life that it changed their character. Men focused on advancement and competition as a result of being pushed into the marketplace and separated from the home. Women became guardians of the family and home; their ideal qualities became generosity, sensitivity to others' needs, and self-sacrifice. Thus "Cult of True Womanhood" had the effect of controlling women, underlining the authority of the male as head of family.
      3. The large number of wives entering the labor force today is having a profound impact on family roles. Wives are expected to juggle career and family at the same time that traditional expectations of male and female roles continue to dominate many aspects of the family.
      4. A shuffling of power has occurred as a result of more married women working for pay. If the husband is the family's sole breadwinner, he makes most of the family's major decisions; if the wife works for wages, she has increased power. This may result in an ongoing struggle between the two, especially in terms of housework. Arlie Hochschild described a second shift many wives experience: after a full workday, they put in time doing housework, creating deep discontent among wives.
   C. The Symbolic Interactionist Perspective
      1. Symbolic interactionists focus on meanings people give their marital relationships. New couples merge their worlds (the feminine and the masculine) by conversation in which they share ideas and feelings and, over time, see things from increasingly closer perspectives. Even conversation that brings husbands and wives together leaves a huge gulf, however.
      2. Because husbands and wives hold down different corners of the marriage, they actually perceive the marriage differently.

III. The Family Life Cycle
   A. Romantic love provides the ideological context in which Americans seek mates and form families. Romantic love has two components: (1) emotional, a feeling of sexual attraction; and (2) cognitive, the feeling we describe as being "in love."
   B. The social channels of love and marriage in the United States include age, education, social class, race, and religion. Interracial marriage is an exception to these social patterns.
   C. Homogamy is the tendency of people with similar characteristics to marry one another, usually resulting from propinquity (spatial nearness). People living near one another tend to marry.
   D. Marital satisfaction usually decreases with the birth of a child, according to Martin Whyte. Lillian Rubin found that social class influences how couples adjust to children. Working-class couples are more likely to have a baby nine months after marriage and have major interpersonal and financial problems; middle-class parents are more prepared because of more resources, postponement of the birth of the first child, and more time to adjust to one another.
   E. According to Melvin Kohn, parents socialize children into the norms of their respective work worlds. Working-class parents want their children to conform to behavioral expectations. Middle-class parents are more concerned that their children develop curiosity, self-expression, and self-control. Birth order is significant in child rearing: first-borns tend to be disciplined more than children who follow but also receive more attention; when the next child arrives, the first-born competes to maintain attention.
   F. The empty nest is a married couple's domestic situation after the last child has left home. According to Lillian Rubin, this syndrome is largely a myth because women's satisfaction generally increases when the last child leaves home. For many older people, giving up work provides an opportunity to do things for which they never previously had time; for others, retirement poses a threat because their sense of self-concept is intricately tied into their jobs.

IV. Diversity in American Families
   A. As with other groups, the family life of African Americans differs with social class. The upper class is concerned with maintaining family lineage and preserving positions of privilege and wealth; middle-class families focus on achievement and respectability; African-American families in poverty face the problems that poverty brings. Marriage squeeze (fewer unmarried

males than unmarried females) exists among African Americans; women thus are more likely to marry men with less education, or who are unemployed or divorced.

B. The Spanish language, Roman Catholic religion, strong family ties, and machismo (emphasis on male strength and dominance) distinguish Hispanic-American families. As a result, the husband-father plays a stronger role than in white or African-American families, and the wife-mother deals with family and child-related decisions. These families tend to be more extended than African-American or white families, and the sexual double standard is more likely to prevail.

C. Bob Suzuki points out that Chinese-American and Japanese-American families have adopted the nuclear family pattern of the United States, but have retained Confucian values that provide a distinct framework to family life—humanism, collectivity, self-discipline, hierarchy, wisdom of the elderly, moderation, and obligation. Immigrants find that their old and new cultures clash.

D. One-parent families are more likely to be formed by the poor and be headed by a female. Unwed motherhood has risen sharply. Children of one-parent families are more likely to drop out of school, become delinquent, be poor as adults, divorce, and have children outside marriage, creating an intergenerational cycle of poverty.

E. Some families are childless by choice, others due to infertility. Charlene Miall found that infertile couples often feel stigmatized; they often avoid the topic of children and select friends on the basis of attitudes toward childlessness. Childless and child-free marriages are becoming more common: In 1988, 20% of American women in their 30s did not have children, compared with 13% in 1976. The highest rate of voluntary childlessness is among Asian Americans and whites, the lowest among Hispanic Americans.

F. A blended family is one whose members were once part of other families (two divorced persons marry, bringing children into a new family unit). They are increasing in number and often experience complicated family relationships.

G. Although marriage between homosexuals is illegal in the United States, many homosexual couples live in monogamous relationships that they refer to as marriage. Facing the stigma of a disapproved lifestyle, they also have the usual problems of heterosexual marriages: housework, money, careers, problems with relatives, and sexual adjustment.

V. Trends in American Families
   A. The average age of American brides is the oldest it has been since records first were kept. Many young people postpone marriage, but not cohabitation; if cohabitation were counted as marriage, rates of family formation and age at first marriage would show little change.
   B. Cohabitation is living together as an unmarried couple, and has increased more than five-fold in two decades.

About half the couples who marry have cohabited; however, this rate is lower in the United States than in Canada and most European countries. Commitment is the essential difference between cohabitation and marriage: marriage assumes permanence; cohabiting assumes remaining together "as long as it works out."

C. Several patterns have emerged in child care: a father is more likely to take care of the children if the wife works part-time; children whose mothers work full-time are more likely to be cared for by nonrelatives. About 23,000 children under age 5 whose mothers work full-time ("latchkey children") take care of themselves, perhaps with neighbors looking in on them occasionally.

VI. Divorce and Remarriage
   A. Although the divorce rate is reported at 50%, with rare exceptions those who divorce do not come from the group who married that year. The United States has the highest divorce rate in the industrialized world. Variables contributing to marital success include college education (chances of marriage working out are higher for graduates). Women with five or more years of college are the exception, perhaps due to an unwillingness to sacrifice career ambitions. Over one million children each year are in families affected by divorce.
   B. Women are more likely to feel divorce gives them a new chance at life. Divorce does not always mean the end of a relationship; some continued contact with ex-spouses occurs due to the children. Divorce likely spells economic hardship for women, especially mothers of small children; in the first post-divorce year, the standard of living for women with dependent children drops 50%.
   C. About 80% of divorced persons remarry, with an average lapse between divorce and remarriage of only three years.

VII. Two Sides of Family Life
   A. Abuse: Battering, Marital Rape, and Incest
      1. Battering: Although wives are about as likely to attack their husbands as husbands are to attack their wives, it is generally the husband who lands the last and most damaging blow.
      2. Marital Rape: Nonbattering rape is where a husband forces his wife to have sex, with no intent to hurt her physically. Battering rape adds the element of the husband intentionally inflicting physical pain to retaliate for some supposed wrongdoing on the wife's part.
      3. Incest is sexual relations between relatives, such as brothers and sisters or parents and children. It is most likely to occur in families that are socially isolated, and is more common than it previously was thought to be.
   B. What makes marriage last? Social class makes a considerable difference; other variables include age, residence, education, and religion.

VIII. The Future of Marriage and Family
   A. Martin Whyte concluded that there is reason for optimism about the state of marriage in the United States.

The vast proportion of Americans will continue to marry; many of those who divorce will remarry and "try again."

B. It is likely that cohabitation will increase, as will the age at first marriage, and the number of women joining the work force, with a resulting shift in marital power toward a more egalitarian norm.

LEARNING OBJECTIVES

After reading and studying Chapter 16, the student should be able to:

1. Explain why it is difficult to define the term "family."
2. Discuss the functionalist, conflict, and symbolic interaction perspectives regarding marriage and family.
3. Outline the major developments in each stage of the family life cycle.
4. State the unique problems experienced by African-American, Hispanic-American, and Asian-American families.
5. Identify the major concerns of one-parent families, families without children, blended families, and homosexual families.
6. Describe the current trends affecting marriage and family life in the United States.
7. State why it is difficult to measure divorce accurately. Note some of the adjustment problems of children of divorce and of ex-spouses.
8. Explain the statement that "family life can be very rewarding or very brutal" and give examples of abuse within the family setting.
9. List some of the characteristics which tend to be present in marriages that work. Explain why happy and unhappy couples approach problems differently.
10. Summarize research findings regarding the future of marriage and family in the United States.

KEY TERMS

bilateral (system of descent)
blended family
cohabitation
descent
empty nest
endogamy
erotic property
exogamy
extended family

family
family of orientation
family of procreation
homogamy
incest
incest taboo
machismo
marriage
matriarchy

matrilineal (system of descent)
nuclear family
patriarchy
patrilineal
polyandry
polygyny
property
propinquity

KEY PEOPLE

Arlie Hochschild
Jessie Bernard
Lenore Weitzman
Diana Russell

Peter Berger and Hansfried Kellner
Lillian Rubin
Murray Straus, Susan Steinmetz, and
   Richard Gelles
Jeanette and Robert Lauer

CLASS DISCUSSION QUESTIONS

1. Do you think children are the real victims of divorce? Why or why not?
2. Are there some elements which are essential to marriage and family in all human groups?
3. Why do you think marriage is a group's approved mating arrangement?
4. Do all societies use marriage and family to establish patterns of mate selection, descent, inheritance, and authority? Why or why not?
5. Why is it considered necessary for individuals to look outside their own family for marriage partners?
6. Do you tend to agree with the functionalist or the conflict perspective on the family? Why?
7. What is meant by the "second shift?" Do you think most two-paycheck families have worked out an equitable division of household work?
8. Can you explain why symbolic interactionists believe every marriage contains two separate marriages?
9. Do you think all societies share the American infatuation with romantic love? How is this notion promoted in the United States?
10. Why do most individuals in the United States marry others

who are similar in age, education, social class, race, and religion to themselves? How do people react when a person marries someone with very different characteristics from his or her own?

11. Why does marital satisfaction decrease for some people with the birth of a child? Is this the way we are taught that it will be?

12. What examples can you give of gender styles your parents exhibited when they were rearing you or your siblings?

13. Do you think most parents experience the empty nest? Why or why not?

14. Is there such a thing as the American family? Why or why not?

15. In what ways are the experiences of African-American, Hispanic-American, and Asian-American families similar? In what ways are they different?

16. Do you think that marriages between homosexuals will be legalized in the United States during the next decade? Why or why not?

17. Why have Americans become more tolerant of cohabitation?

18. What are some of the unique problems of latchkey children? Were you a latchkey child when you were growing up?

19. If you want to know your own chances of marital success, what variables should you consider?

20. In your opinion, are people who get a divorce unhappy with the institution of marriage or with their current marriage partner? What do remarriage statistics reveal about this?

21. Can you explain why some sociologists refer to the family as "the cradle of violence?"

22. Is making a marriage last the same thing as having a happy marriage? Why or why not?

23. What do you predict will be the future of marriage and family in the United States? How will this affect your own decisions?

PROJECTS

1. Develop what might be called a "prenuptial agreement" in which you indicate both your expectations and your obligations for a marriage. For example, how would financial decisions, household tasks, childrearing responsibilities, etc., be handled? Wait until a week after you have written the agreement and write a critique of it. Present the agreement, critique, and your conclusions in a paper.

2. Watch serialized television shows which involve family relations. Make notes on the types of families presented, their interaction patterns, and what messages are being conveyed by the show. (For example, a *Murphy Brown* episode in which Murphy Brown, an unmarried professional woman, gave birth to a child was criticized by the Vice President of the United States because he thought the show undermined family values.) Create a chart showing the programs you watch, who the main characters are, what their relationships are like, and your comments which relate the shows to this chapter. Present your findings in small group or class discussion.

3. Obtain data for your city, county, or state regarding rates of marriage and divorce. Compare this data with national statistics to determine whether the rates are higher, lower, or about the same as in your area.

4. Obtain data on family abuse and violence from city, county, state, or national sources. Create a visual presentation to give to the class.

TRANSPARENCIES

1. (TR#34) Who Does the Housework?
2. (TR#35) Percentage of U.S. Households Headed by Males, Females, and Married Couples
3. (TR#36) Divorce Rates in Selected Countries

TRANSPARENCY MASTERS

1. (TR#36M) Percentage of Children under 5 by Employed Mothers, in Organized Care Facilities, by Family Income
2. (TR#37M) Marriage in Cross-Cultural Perspective
3. (TR#38M) Childcare Arrangements by Employed Mothers for Children under Age of 5
4. (TR#39M) Years Married and Sexual Frequency
5. (TR#40M) Census Figures Predict Shift in Household Composition
6. (TR#41M) Fertility among Married American Women

VIDEOS/MOVIES

Love and Courtship

CNN Video II. *Marriage Survey.* A survey of 459 women conducted by a University of Michigan sociology professor suggests that long-term dating does not guarantee a happy marriage. Instead, romantic love seems to be the key. Those who felt "head-over-heels" in love just prior to getting married—and who sustained romantic feelings—were happiest. Contrary to popular belief, there was no correlation between length of dating and marital satisfaction. Available from A&B Video Library.

The Familiar Face of Love. 1990. Looks at how we choose our mates and for what reasons. Discusses falling in love and features Dr. John Money discussing a love map—a mental blueprint of the ideal relationship we carry within us. 47 min. Available from FML.

When Harry Met Sally. 1989 (Color) Starring Billy Crystal and Meg Ryan, this movie is about a man and woman who have a genuine friendship but try to keep it from becoming a romantic attachment. 95 min. Available at video rental stores.

Diversity in American Families

Love and Sex. Hosted by Phil Donahue, this program takes viewers to a male strip club and a gay rights march, into a hospital room where a teenage mother is giving birth, and into the classroom. Love, monogamy, hetero- and homosexuality are covered. Includes doctors from the Masters & Johnson Institute and Kinsey Institute. 52 min. Available from A&B Video Library and FHS.

CNN Video II. *Gay Marriages.* Topic of gay marriages is explored. According to a CNN/Time Magazine poll, most people don't approve of gay marriages. Available from A&B Video Library.

Silent Pioneers: Gay and Lesbian Elders. Eight elderly gays and lesbians discuss their long-term relationships with persons of the same sex. Challenges many stereotypes about homosexuals and shows that they have long-standing, deep-rooted commitments. Among those interviewed, one male couple has been together for 55 years. 30 min. Available from FML.

Child Care

Dumping Kids in Day Care. In this specially-adapted Phil Donahue program, several ex-spouses face off to talk about the difficulties they have encountered since divorce, especially in regard to not having the time and energy to meet the needs of their own children. 28 min. Available from A&B Video Library and FHS.

Latch-Key Families. Some ten million American youngsters of school age are now latch-key children. Looks at how to provide for the physical safety and emotional needs of such children. 23 min. Available from A&B Video Library and FHS.

Divorce and Remarriage

An American Stepfamily. Examines the problems of conflicting loyalties and rivalries, dealing with former spouses, and the three categories of kids—his, hers, and theirs. 26 min. Available from A&B Video Library and FHS.

Children of Divorce. According to this specially-adapted Phil Donahue program, studies are now making it clear that children of divorce almost never recover totally from the pain, confusion, guilt, and displacement that their divorcing parents have inflicted on them; instead, they continue into adulthood to evince academic, behavioral, and psychological problems. 28 min. Available from A&B Video Library and FHS.

Irreconcilable Differences. 1984. (Color) Starring Ryan O'Neal and Shelley Long as a couple who marry and prosper, then lose sight of what is important to them. Their ten-year-old daughter sues them for divorce. (PG) 117 min. Available at video rental stores.

Say Good-bye Again: Children of Divorce. Documentary examines divorce from a child's point of view. Three families are studied over a two-year period to reveal how children in different age groups deal with the divorce process. 26 min. Available from A&B Video Library. Also at vido rental stores:
Beaches
Kramer vs. Kramer
The War of the Roses

The Dark Side of Family Life

Abused Wives. Specially-adapted Phil Donahue program tells of a marriage marked by a constant pattern of abuse. The wife of a former chief enforcement officer of the Securities and Exchange Commission is interviewed. 28 min. Available from A&B Video Library and FHS.

The Burning Bed. 1984. (Color) Farrah Fawcett plays a battered wife who sets her ex-husband on fire one night after living with his beatings for a number of years. Based on a true story by Faith McNulty. 100 min. Available at some video rental stores.

Child Abuse. Deals with the delicate subject of sexually and physically abused children. A therapist who works with sex offenders describes the common characteristics of offenders; a clinical social worker trained to talk with sexually abused children discusses the effects of abuse on the child. 19 min. Available from A&B Video Library and FHS.

Childhood Physical Abuse. Covers the range of problems in the area of physical abuse of children, including the ways in which abuse should be dealt with and how the physical abuse of children can be prevented. 26 min. Available from A&B Video Library and FHS.

Childhood Sexual Abuse. Looks at the ways in which adult women learn to work out the problems caused by their sexually abusive fathers, and how they seek to protect their own children from a recurrence of the pattern. 26 min. Available from A&B Video Library and FHS.

No More Secrets. Discusses the long-term damage that results from sexual abuse, offers the personal stories of children and of adults who were abused as children. 24 min. Available from A&B Video Library and FHS.

The Future of Marriage and Family

Family and Survival. Less than 5% of American households fit the profile of the traditional nuclear family. Broken homes, battered wives, estranged children, corporate nomads—these are today's commonplaces. 52 min. Available from A&B Video Library and FHS.

SPEAKER SUGGESTIONS

1. An anthropologist to discuss marriage and family in cross-cultural perspective.

2. A colleague who is conducting innovative research on some aspect of marriage and family life.

3. A judge or lawyer who practices in family or domestic relations court to discuss divorce in your city or state.

4. A family therapist to talk about family-related violence and treatment therapies for offenders.

POP QUIZ QUESTIONS

True-False

F   1. The term "family" is defined the same in virtually all societies.

F   2. Many nuclear families include grandparents, aunts, uncles, and cousins.

T   3. Sexual fidelity within marriage is considered to be important in most human groups.

F   4. Many societies do not use marriage and family to establish descent and inheritance.

T   5. Rules of endogamy specify that people must marry within their own group.

T   6. According to functionalists, the family is universal because it fulfulls functions essential to the well-being of society.

F   7. Industrialization of American society strengthened the family unit.

T   8. In the United States, love and marriage are channeled by age, education, social class, race, and religion.

T   9. Currently, the average age of an American bride is the oldest it has been in recorded history.

F 10. Most people who divorce do not choose to remarry.

ESSAY QUESTIONS

1. Describe some of the main variations found in marriage and families across cultures.
2. Compare and contrast functional, conflict, and symbolic interactionist perspectives on marriage and family.
3. Discuss the family life cycle, noting the importance of social class at each point in the cycle.
4. Identify the unique characteristics of African-American, Hispanic-American, and Asian-American families. State how the family life in each of these groups differs according to social class.
5. Analyze the major trends in American families and explain what has happened in the larger society to produce such trends.
6. Summarize the major problems experienced by families, including divorce, remarriage, and abuse.

CHAPTER
17

Education: Transferring Knowledge and Skills

CHAPTER SUMMARY

Industrialized societies have become credential societies; employers use diplomas and degrees to determine who is eligible for jobs, even when these qualifications may be irrelevant to the particular work. In earlier societies, education was synonymous with acculturation—the transmission of culture from one generation to the next. Today, education is no longer the same as informal acculturation, for the term now refers to a group's formal system of teaching knowledge, values, and skills. Educational systems in Great Britain, Japan, the former Soviet Union, and the United States are described. Functionalists emphasize the functions of education, including teaching knowledge and skills, transmitting cultural values, social integration, gatekeep-ing, and promoting personal and social change. Conversely, conflict theorists view education as a mechanism for maintaining social inequality and reproducing the social class system. Accordingly, they stress such matters as the way in which education reflects the social structure of society (the correspondence principle), unequal funding of schools, culturally biased IQ tests, tracking, and the hidden curriculum. In contrast, symbolic interactionists examine classroom interaction. Ways in which schools can be improved are explored. The Coleman Report, compensatory education, busing, the National Report Card, and the Rutter Report are discussed regarding problems in schools and possibilities for improvement in American education.

CHAPTER OUTLINE

I. Today's Credential Society
   A. A credential society is where employers use diplomas and degrees to determine job eligibility. The sheer size and consequent anonymity of American society is a major reason why credentials are required. Diplomas/degrees often serve as sorting devices for employers.
   B. Without the right credentials, a person will not get hired despite the person's ability to do the job better than someone else.
II. The Development of Modern Education
   A. In earlier societies, education was synonymous with acculturation (transmission of culture from one generation to the next), not with a separate institution. In societies where a surplus developed, a separate institution arose. During the Dark Ages, only the monks and a handful of the wealthy and nobility could read and write. Industrialization caused a need to be able to read, write, and work with figures because of the new machinery and new types of jobs.
   B. Mandatory education laws requiring children to attend school to a specified age or a particular grade level were enacted in all U.S. states by 1918. As industrialization progressed, education came to be essential to the well-being of society. As this trend continued, in-

dustrialized groups eventually developed the credential society.
III. Education in Cross-Cultural Perspective
   A. Education (no longer the same as informal acculturation) refers to a group's formal system of teaching knowledge, values, and skills.
   B. In Great Britain, the primary factory sorting students into different educational paths is social class. Children of the elite attend exclusive schools and universities; children of the lower classes attend public schools, from which they enter the labor force at age 16. Some middle-class parents pay for their children to attend private schools, but middle-class students are likely to attend regional (not elite) universities. From a conflict perspective, the educational system maintains the social class system.
   C. Japanese education reflects a group-centered ethic. Children in grade school work as a group, mastering the same skills/materials; cooperation and respect for elders (and positions of authority) is stressed. College admission procedures are based on test scores; only the top scorers are admitted, regardless of social class. The Japanese reward schoolteaching with high pay and prestige.

D. In the former Soviet Union, after the Revolution of 1917, the government insisted that socialist values dominate education, seeing education as a means to undergird the new political system. With the country still largely agricultural, education remained spotty; by 1950, only about half of Soviet young people were in school, and most of these came from the elite. The Soviets continued to work toward universal education, and the launching of Sputnik in the 1950s demonstrated that the Soviets had become effective in teaching mathematics, engineering, and the natural sciences.

IV. Education in the United States
   A. In the years following the American Revolution, the founders of the republic believed formal education should be the principal means for creating a uniform national culture. Standard texts would instill patriotism and teach principles of republican government. In the early 1800s, instead of an educational system there was a jumble of schools administered by separate localities, with no coordination. Children of the wealthy attended private schools; children of the lower classes (and slaves) received no formal education.
   B. Horace Mann, a Massachusetts educator, proposed that common schools be established throughout his state; the idea spread throughout the country. Industrialization and universal education occurred at the same time. Since the economy was undergoing fundamental change, political and civic leaders recognized the need for an educated work force. They also feared the influx of foreign values and looked on public education as a way to Americanize immigrants.
   C. As a result, education became more accessible in the United States than any other country. Today a larger proportion of the population attend colleges and universities in the United States than in any other industrialized country in the world. Almost 60% of all high school graduates now enter college, the highest rate in American history.

V. The Functionalist Perspective; Providing Social Benefits
   A. Manifest functions (intended consequences) of education include:
      1. Teaching knowledge and skills
      2. Cultural transmission of values
      3. Social integration—helping to mold students into a more or less cohesive unit
      4. Gatekeeping—determining who will enter what occupations (social placement—funneling people into various positions)—and tracking (sorting students into different educational programs on the basis of real or perceived abilities)
      5. Promoting personal change through critical thinking
      6. Promoting social change through fostering research
      7. Replacing family functions (e.g., sex education)
   B. Latent functions include matchmaking (people finding a future spouse in school), social networking, and helping stabilize employment (keeping unskilled individuals out of the labor market).

VI. The Conflict Perspective: Maintaining Social Inequality
   A. The educational system is a tool used by those in the controlling sector of society to maintain their dominance.
   B. The hidden curriculum is unwritten rules of behavior and attitude (e.g., obedience to authority, conformity to cultural norms) taught in school in addition to the formal curriculum. Values/work habits taught to help students "prepare for life" are merely devices to teach the middle and lower classes to support the capitalist class.
   C. Public schools are largely financed by local property taxes; there are rich and poor school districts. Unequal funding stacks the deck against minorities and the poor.
   D. IQ (intelligence quotient) tests not only measure intelligence but also culturally acquired knowledge; they focus on mathematical, spatial, symbolic, and linguistic abilities. Intelligence consists of more than these components; thus, IQ tests favor the middle class and discriminate against minorities and students from lower classes.
   E. The correspondence principle is how schools correspond to (reflect) the social structure of society. The educational system's agreement with the status quo perpetuates society's prevailing inequalities. The American educational system promotes capitalism and maintains existing social inequalities.
   F. Regardless of ability, children of the wealthy are usually placed in college-bound tracks and children of the poor in vocational tracks. Whites are more likely to complete high school, go to college, and get a degree than African and Hispanic Americans. The education system helps pass privilege (or lack thereof) across generations.

VII. The Symbolic Interaction Perspective: Teacher Expectations and the Self-Fulfilling Prophecy
   A. Symbolic interactionists study face-to-face interaction inside the classroom.
   B. The Rist research (participant observation in an African-American grade school with an African-American faculty) found tracking begins with teachers' perceptions. After eight days—and without testing for ability—teachers divided the class into fast, average, and slow learners; social class was the basis for the assignments. Students from whom more was expected did the best; students in the slow group were ridiculed and disengaged themselves from classroom activities; over the next few years, it stuck. The child's journey through school was preordained from the eighth day of kindergarten, a self-fulfilling prophecy (Robert Merton's term for an originally false assertion that becomes true simply because it was predicted).
   C. The Rosenthal/Jacobson experiment showed that teacher expectations were based on what they had been told about their students. Those who had been labeled as "spurters" made more progress than other students simply because teachers expected them to, and encouraged them more—another example of a self-fulfilling prophecy.
   D. Teachers' backgrounds result in their being pleased when middle-class students ask probing questions but not when lower-class students do. George Farkas found students scoring the same on course matter may receive different grades: females get higher grades, as

do Asian Americans. Some students signal that they are interested in what the teacher is teaching; teachers pick up these signals.

VIII. How Can We Improve Schools?
  A. The Coleman Report: In 1966, James Coleman published a report on American education indicating that assumptions about why whites outscore African Americans in school were inaccurate. He concluded the reason was not related to teaching techniques, class size, expenditures per student, etc.—but rather to social class. His findings gave support to compensatory education and busing.
  B. Compensatory education (programs designed to supplement background of lower-class children) began with Head Start. Results of these programs have been difficult to measure.
  C. Coleman found low-income African Americans attending middle-class, predominantly white schools score higher than similar students who attend mainly poor, African-American schools. He believed this was due to a changed peer culture: low-income students in middle-class environments could pick up study habits and more positive attitudes toward education. Busing—one of the most controversial measures ever to take place in American public education—was implemented to overcome neighborhood racial and social class segregation. After several years,

Coleman turned against busing because he saw it as a stimulus to "white flight."
  D. The National Report Card: Test scores in the United States have declined during the past 20–30 years. Three reasons may be: different people being tested (more students now from poor academic backgrounds); flashy distractions (TV and video games); and a decline in the quality of education. Social promotion (passing students even if they have not mastered basic materials) has produced an increase in functional illiterates—high school graduates who have difficulty with basic reading and math. America 2000 (a 1991 report) set forth the goal of world-class standards for student achievement: they would have to demonstrate competency in challenging subject matter. Critics fear such proposals will result in a standardized national curriculum.
  E. The Rutter report observed that because schools are unequal (based on social class of the students), a school's quality cannot be judged by looking at student achievement. Regardless of social class or personal abilities, students who attended schools where teachers challenge students intellectually and expect them to do well (as well as rewarding them for doing so) get better results (i.e., setting up a positive self-fulfilling prophecy).

LEARNING OBJECTIVES

After reading and studying Chapter 17, the student should be able to:

1. Explain why the United States has become a credential society.
2. Describe the development of modern education.
3. Outline the major differences in the educational systems of Great Britain, Japan, and the former Soviet Union.
4. Discuss the beginning of universal education in the United States.
5. List and briefly explain the manifest and latent functions of education.
6. Explain why conflict theorists state that education maintains social inequality.
7. Summarize symbolic interaction research regarding teacher expectations and the self-fulfilling prophecy.
8. State the conclusions of the Coleman Report and describe the relationship between this report and compensatory education and busing in the United States.
9. Explain why education in the United States has been given a "failing grade."
10. List positive factors in the learning environment which The Rutter Report states can improve schools and set up a positive self-fulfilling prophecy.

KEY TERMS

acculturation
compensatory education
correspondence principle
credential society
cultural transmission
education

functional illiterate
gatekeeping
hidden curriculum
latent functions
mandatory education laws
manifest functions

minimum competency tests
self-fulfilling prophecy
social placement
social promotion
tracking

KEY PEOPLE

Randall Collins
Caroline Persell, Sophia Catsambio, and
   Peter Cookson
Robert Rosenthal and Lenore Jacobson
James Coleman

Samuel Bowles
Ray Rist
George Farkas
Michael Rutter

CLASS DISCUSSION QUESTIONS

1. Do you think there are many instances in which the diploma or degree a person earns is irrelevant to the job for which they are hired? Can you give examples?
2. Would you pursue a college degree just for the sake of knowledge if the career you want to pursue did not require any type of credential?
3. Do all societies tend to have compulsory education requirements?
4. Have you attended school in a country other than the United States? If yes, in what ways was it similar to U.S. education? In what ways was it different?
5. Why do you think universal education has been so important in the United States?
6. What American values were you taught as a part of your earlier educational experiences?
7. How powerful do you think the influence of a person's peers is in the U.S. educational structure?

8. Based on schools you have attended, can you give examples of the gatekeeping function of education?
9. Do you think that schools have a hidden curriculum which perpetuates existing social inequalities? Why or why not?
10. Is it possible for IQ tests to accurately measure a person's intelligence without being culturally biased? Why or why not?
11. From your own experiences, have you seen the self-fulfilling prophecy in action in education?
12. Did your kindergarten or earliest school experiences determine how the rest of your educational experience would proceed?
13. If you were serving on a commission to determine how to improve American education, what types of changes would you suggest? Why?

PROJECTS

1. Interview a number of students at your college who are not enrolled in your introductory sociology course to determine what they expect to gain by graduating from college. Develop a set of questions to determine what type of credentials they hope to obtain and what they perceive to be the relationship, if any, between the courses they are currently taking and their career plans. Present your findings to the class.
2. Write a paper comparing the educational systems of other societies with American education. For example, many articles and books are available which compare the Japanese and American systems, especially regarding the relationship between education and employment.
3. Look for examples of the hidden curriculum at your academic

institution. Are certain norms and values being encouraged even if they are not overtly discussed? If you are attending a private, church-related institution, are the beliefs and values of that church included either overtly or covertly in the academic courses you are taking? Present your findings to the class or in a term paper.
4. Conduct library research on the Coleman Report, compensatory education, busing, recent studies of SAT scores, the Rutter Report, or similar reports to determine what suggestions have been made for changing American education and how effective (or ineffective) some of these approaches have been. Create your own suggestions for changes to present to the class.

TRANSPARENCIES

1. (TR#37) Educational Achievement in the United States
2. (TR#38) The Funneling Effects of Education: Race, Ethnicity, and Education
3. (TR#39) Educational Expenditures and Student Scores

TRANSPARENCY MASTERS

1. (TR#42M) How Much Will You Earn? Income and Education
2. (TR#43M) National Results of the Scholastic Aptitude Test (SAT)

VIDEOS/MOVIES

Education in Cross-Cultural Perspective

To Sir With Love. 1967. (Color) Starring Sidney Poitier as a teacher in a rough, lower socioeconomic level school in London where he gradually earns respect from his students. 105 min. Available at some video rental stores.

CNN Video II. *Examination Hell in Japan: Career Mobility.* Japanese students go through examination hell, knowing that unless they are admitted to a few select institutions, their mobility/life chances will be drastically restricted. Available from A&B Video Library.

Head of the Class. This *Sixty Minutes* segment shows three- and four-year-olds in Japan doing homework for hours each day so they will get into the best kindergarten. Mothers drive their children to do more and better. There is no time to waste and no time to play. The goal of the whole learning process is to gain admission to college, which assures a job commensurate with the exclusivity of the school. 14 min. Available from FHS.

Cultural Transmission of Values

Dead Poets Society. 1989. (Color) Robin Williams, playing a charismatic English teacher at a New England prep school, inspires his students but not always in the "right" direction. 128 min. Available at video rental stores.

Social Integration

Fast Times at Ridgemont High. 1982. Although largely just for entertainment, this movie shows the peer culture at work in high schools. The students of a Southern California high school spend most of their time at the mall and thinking about sex. Based on a factual book. 115 min. Available at video rental stores.

The Hidden Curriculum

Public Education: It's a Bull Market. 1991. Takes a critical look at the influential role that big business plays in public education in America. Hidden agendas include influencing students' opinions on nuclear energy and pesticides, creating a desire for products while supplying news or information, and "adoption" programs in which schools are given high-tech equipment in return for promoting that company's products to students and to other schools. 30 min. Available from FML.

The National Report Card: Falling Test Scores

CNN Video II. *National Testing.* The federal government wants to develop national tests by 1993 that would be taken at 4th, 8th, and 12th grades in five core subjects. This would entail the development of a national curriculum, however, and some experts feel that to develop such a curriculum is difficult and not desirable. Opponents of a national curriculum say that it's not fair to impose uniform standards on widely divergent communities. Available from A&B Video Library.

How Can We Improve Schools?

Stand and Deliver. 1987. (Color) Shows a tough, demanding teacher in an East L.A. barrio school who motivates his students to achieve. Based on a true story. (PG) 105 min. Available at video rental stores.

What Should We Do in School Today? 1992. Explores some of the most pressing issues facing educators today in terms of curriculum, discipline, teacher evaluations, and drop out rates. Visits four schools around the country that are trying to solve these problems. 22 min. Available from FML.

CNN Video II. *Endangered Teachers.* Violence against public school teachers has risen alarmingly. Report profiles a teacher whose student dropped LSD into his coffee; the trauma was so great that he has yet to return to the classroom. A math teacher recounts how he was hit over the head with a bottle; yet another teacher, and his class, were held at gunpoint by a high school student. The National School Safety Center says 5,000 teachers are assaulted every month; 1,000 of them seriously enough to require medical attention. The need to establish discipline in the schools is mentioned. Available from A&B Video Library.

SPEAKER SUGGESTIONS

1. An education professor to discuss American education now and into the 21st century.
2. A sociology of education professor to discuss current research based on functionalist, conflict, or symbolic interactionist perspectives.
3. A testing and evaluation specialist to discuss ways in which test makers attempt to prevent bias in the construction of test questions.
4. An educator or political leader at the local, state, or national level who has served on an educational commission attempting to improve the quality of education.

POP QUIZ QUESTIONS

True-False

T 1. Credentials are important in American society because of its size and degree of anonymity.

T 2. There was no separate social institution called education in earlier societies.

F 3. IQ is the primary factor that sorts British students into different educational paths.

F 4. From a functionalist perspective, teaching knowledge and skills is a latent function of education.

F 5. The American and Japanese educational systems both focus on individualism.

T 6. Conflict theorists believe the powerful use the educational system to maintain their dominance.

F 7. Symbolic interactionists state that the expectations of teachers do not have a significant impact on students from lower-income backgrounds.

T 8. According to Rist's study, a child's journey through school is preordained from the eighth day of kindergarten.

T 9. The Coleman Report gave strong support to compensatory education and busing.

T 10. Some researchers believe that social promotion was a factor in the increase in the amount of functional illiteracy in the United States.

ESSAY QUESTIONS

1. Describe the development of education in the United States and compare the American system with that of Great Britain, Japan, and the former Soviet Union.

2. Summarize the functionalist perspective on the social benefits provided by education. Explain why the functions of education have grown in the past decades.

3. Contrast the functionalist and conflict perspectives on education.

4. Explain how a self-fulfilling prophecy may arise out of a student's educational experience. Describe the role played by teachers in this process.

5. Discuss what makes some schools more effective than others, and note ways in which schools can be improved.

CHAPTER

18

Religion: Establishing Meaning

CHAPTER SUMMARY

The goal of the sociological study of religion is to analyze the relationship between society and religion and to gain insight into the role that religion plays in people's lives. Durkheim identified the essential elements of religion as beliefs and practices that separate the profane from the sacred and unite its adherents into a moral community. According to the functionalist perspective, religion meets basic human needs such as answering questions about ultimate meaning, emotional comfort, social solidarity, guidelines for everyday life, social control, adaptation, support for the government, and social change. Functionalists also believe religion has two main dysfunctions: war and religious persecution. Symbolic interactionists focus on how religious symbols communicate meaning and how ritual and beliefs unite people into a community. Conflict theorists see religion as a conservative force that serves the needs of the ruling class by reflecting

and reinforcing social inequality. Unlike Marx, who asserted that religion impedes social change by encouraging people to focus on the afterlife, Weber saw religion as a powerful force for social change. The world's major religions include Judaism, Christianity, Islam, Hinduism, Buddhism, and Confucianism. Just as different religions have distinct teachings and practices, so within a religion different groups contrast sharply with one another. Sociologists have identified cults, sects, churches, ane ecclesiae as distinct types of religious organizations. Secularization of religion and of culture has occurred in many societies, including the United States. Religion in America is characterized by diversity, pluralism and freedom, competition, commitment, privacy, and tolerance. Even in countries where a concerted effort was made to eliminate it, religion has continued to thrive. Religion apparently will continue to exist as long as humanity does.

CHAPTER OUTLINE

I. What Is Religion?
   A. According to Durkheim, religion is the beliefs/practices separating the profane from the sacred, uniting adherents into a moral community. Sacred refers to aspects of life having to do with the supernatural that inspire awe, reverence, deep respect, or deep fear. Profane refers to the ordinary aspects of everyday life.
   B. He found religion to be defined by three elements: beliefs that some things are sacred; practices (rituals) concerning things considered sacred; and a moral community (people united by their religious practices) resulting from the beliefs and practices.
II. The Functionalist Perspective
   A. Religion performs certain functions: answering questions about ultimate meaning (the purpose of life, why people suffer); emotional comfort; social solidarity; guidelines for life; social control; adaptation; support for the government; and social change (on occasion, as in the case of the civil rights movement in the 1960s).
   B. A functional equivalent of religion is a substitute serv-

ing the same functions (e.g., psychotherapy); some are difficult to distinguish from a religion. Although the substitute may perform similar functions, its activities are not directed toward God, gods, or the supernatural.
   C. War and religious persecution are dysfunctions of religion.
III. The Symbolic Interactionist Perspective
   A. Religions use symbols to provide identity and social solidarity for members. For members, these are not ordinary symbols, but sacred symbols evoking awe and reverence, which become a condensed way of communicating with others.
   B. Rituals are ceremonies or repetitive practices helping unite people into a moral community. Some are designed to create a feeling of closeness with God and unity with one another.
   C. Symbols, including rituals, develop from beliefs. Religious beliefs not only include values but also a cosmology (unified picture of the world).
   D. Religious experience is a sudden awareness of the su-

pernatural or a feeling of coming in contact with God. Some Protestants use the term born again to describe people who have undergone a religious experience.

E. Shared meanings that come through symbols, rituals, and beliefs unite people into a moral community, which is powerful—not only because it provides the basis for mutual identity, but also because it establishes norms that govern the behavior of members.

IV. The Conflict Perspective

A. Karl Marx called religion the "opium of the people" because he believed that the workers escape into religion. Conflict theorists are highly critical of religion because it diverts the energies of the oppressed from changing their circumstances.

B. Religious teachings and practices reflect a society's inequalities. Gender inequalities are an example: when males completely dominated U.S. society, women's roles in churches and synagogues were limited to "feminine" activities, a condition which is beginning to change.

C. Religion reflects the interests of those in power by teaching that the existing social arrangements of a society represent what God desires.

V. Religion and the Spirit of Capitalism

A. Weber saw religion as a powerful force for social change, observing that European countries industrialized under capitalism. Thus, religion held the key to modernization (transformation of traditional societies into industrial societies).

B. Weber stated the following conclusions: (1) the spirit of capitalism (desire to accumulate capital as a duty, as an end in itself) is a radical departure from the past; (2) religion (a Calvinistic belief in predestination) is the key to why the spirit of capitalism developed in Europe; and (3) a change in religion (from Catholicism to Protestantism) led to a change in thought and behavior (the Protestant ethic), which resulted in the "spirit of capitalism."

C. Today the spirit of capitalism and the Protestant ethic are by no means limited to Protestants (e.g., the Japanese).

VI. The World's Major Religions

A. The Origin of Judaism is traced to Abraham, who lived about 4,000 years ago in Mesopotamia. Contemporary Judaism in the United States has three main branches: Orthodox (adheres to the laws espoused by Moses), Reform (more liberal, uses the vernacular in religious ceremonies, and has reduced much of the ritual); and Conservative (falling somewhere between) Judaism. The history of Judaism is marked by conflict and persecution.

B. Christianity developed out of Judaism and is based on the belief that Christ is the messiah God promised the Jews. During the first 1,000 years of Christianity, there was only one church organization, directed from Rome; during the 11th century, Greek Orthodoxy was established. In the Middle Ages, the Roman Catholic church, aligned with the political establishment, grew corrupt, touching off the Reformation led by Martin Luther in the 16th century. Today there are over one billion Christians, divided into hundreds of groups.

C. Islam (whose followers are known as Muslims) began in the same part of the world as Judaism and Christianity; like the Jews, Muslims trace their ancestry to Abraham. The founder, Muhammad, established a theocracy—a government based on God being the ruler, his laws the statutes of the land, and priests his earthly administrators. After Muhammad's death, a struggle for control split Islam into two branches that remain today: the Shi'ite (more conservative, inclined to fundamentalism—belief that true religion is threatened by modernism and that faith as it was originally practiced should be restored) and the Sunni (generally more liberal).

D. Hinduism, the chief religion of India, goes back about 4,000 years, but has no specific founder or canonical scripture (texts thought to be inspired by God). Several books expound on the moral qualities people should strive to attain. Hindus are polytheists (believe there are many gods) and believe in reincarnation. Some Hindu practices—such as child marriage and suttee (cremating a widow along with her deceased husband) have been modified as a result of social protest.

E. About 600 BC, Siddhartha Gautama founded Buddhism, which emphasizes self-denial and compassion. Buddhism is similar to Hinduism in that the final goal is to escape from reincarnation into nonexistence of blissful peace.

F. Confucius (China 551–479 BC) urged social reform and developed a system of morality based on peace, justice, and universal order. The basic moral principle of Confucianism is to maintain jen (sympathy or concern for other humans). Originally, Confucianism was atheistic; however, as the centuries passed, local gods were added to the teachings, and Confucius himself was declared a god.

VII. Types of Religious Organizations

A. A cult is a new religion with few followers; all religions began as cults. Cults often begin with the appearance of a charismatic leader (exerting extraordinary appeal to a group of followers). Each cult's message is seen as a threat to the dominant culture. The cult demands intense commitment, and its followers confront a hostile world.

B. A sect is larger than a cult, but still feels substantial hostility from and toward society. At the very least, members of sects remain uncomfortable with many of the emphases of the dominant culture; nonmembers feel uncomfortable with sect members. Sects usually are loosely organized, emphasize personal salvation, an emotional expression of one's relationship with God, and recruitment of new members (evangelism). If a sect grows, its members tend to become respectable in society, and the sect is changed into a church.

C. A church is a large, highly organized religious group with little emphasis on personal conversion and formal, sedate services. The religious group is highly bureaucratized (including national and international offices that give directions to local congregations). Most new members come from within the church—from children born to existing members—rather than from outside recruitment.

D. An ecclesia is a religious group so integrated into the dominant culture that it is difficult to tell where one begins and the other leaves off. Ecclesiae also are called state religions. The government and religion work together to try to shape the society. There is no recruitment of members, for citizenship makes everyone a member. The majority of the society belong to the religion in name only.

E. A denomination is a "brand name" within a major religion (e.g., Methodist). On occasion a large group within a church may disagree on some aspects of the church's teachings (but not its major message) and break away to form its own organization.

F. Four major patterns of adaptation occur when religion and the culture in which it is embedded find themselves in conflict: (1) the society rejects the religious group, even trying to destroy it; (2) the religious group rejects the dominant culture and withdraws from it geographically (e.g., the Mormons moved to what is today the state of Utah); (3) the members of a religion reject the dominant culture and withdraw socially although they continue to live in the same geographical area; or (4) a cult or sect rejects only specified elements of the prevailing culture.

VIII. Secularizaton

A. Secularization of religion is the replacement of a religion's other-worldly concerns with concerns about this world. It occurs when religion's influence is lessened (both on a society's institutions and on individuals). Cultures become secularized when other social forces replace the functions traditionally fulfilled by religion. The secularization of religion may explain why Christian churches have splintered into so many groups: changes in social class of the members may create different needs, thereby failing to meet the needs of those whose life situation has not changed. Secularization also results from modernization—the industrialization of society, urbanization, mass education, wide adoption of technology and the transformation of *Gemeinschaft* to *Gesellschaft* societies. Religious explanations become less significant as people turn to answers provided by science, technology, modern medicine, and so on.

B. Secularization of culture is the process by which culture becomes less influenced by religion. For example,

in Iran religious leaders have risen in opposition to secularization and tried to force the clock back. Historically, religion permeated American culture, but today, American culture has been secularized, although personal religious involvement among Americans has not diminished.

IX. The Main Characteristics of Religion in the United States

A. Diversity (no state church, no ecclesia, and no single denomination that dominates the country).

B. Pluralism and freedom.

C. Competition (from many religions).

D. Commitment.

E. Privacy (religious commitment is a private pattern).

F. Toleration (for religious beliefs other than one's own).

G. Fundamentalist revival.

H. The electronic church (televangelists reach millions of viewers and raise millions of dollars; some have been unscrupulous, but some independent fundamentalist groups now subscribe to the electronic church and pay a fee in return for having "name" ministers piped "live" into their local congregation).

I. Characteristics of members of American churches:
   a. Region: membership is highest in the Midwest and South, with the east not far behind.
   b. Social class: each religious group draws members from all social classes, although some are top heavy and some are bottom heavy. People who change social class are also likely to change their denomination.
   c. Age: membership rate increases steadily with age.
   d. Race and ethnicity: all major religious groups in the United States draw from various racial and ethnic groups; however, persons of Hispanic or Irish descent are likely to be Roman Catholics, those of Greek origin to belong to the Greek Orthodox church, while African Americans are likely to be Protestants and belong to Baptist and fundamentalist sects.

X. The Future of Religion

A. Marx was convinced religion would crumble when the workers threw off the chains of oppression; however, after communist countries were established (and despite persecution) people continued to be religious.

B. Others believed science would replace religion; however, science cannot answer questions about four concerns many people have: the existence of God; the purpose of life; morality; and the existence of an afterlife. As a result, science simply cannot replace religion, and religion will last as long as humanity lasts.

LEARNING OBJECTIVES

After reading and studying Chapter 18, the student should be able to:

1. Define religion and explain Durkheim's essential elements of religion.
2. Describe the functionalist perspective on religion, including

the functional equivalents of religion, and the dysfunctions of religion.
3. Explain what aspects of religion are focused on by symbolic interactionists.
4. Identify the conflict perspective on religion and note the influence of Marx on this perspective.

5. Describe the relationship (as seen by Weber) between religion and the spirit of capitalism.
6. Outline the key characteristics of each of the world's major religions.
7. Define cult, sect, church, and ecclesia, and describe the process by which some groups have moved from one category to another.
8. Explain what is meant by secularization. Note how this process occurs in religion and in culture.
9. State the major characteristics of religion in America.
10. List the characteristics of people who are members of religious groups in the United States.
11. Analyze the future of religion. State whether or not you agree with the author's assertion that "religion will last as long as humanity lasts," and defend your answer.

KEY TERMS

animism
antisemitism
born again
charisma
charismatic leader
church
civil religion
cosmology
cult
denomination

ecclesia
fundamentalism
functional equivalent
modernization
monotheism
polytheism
profane (the)
Protestant ethic (the)
reincarnation
religion

religious experience
rituals
sacred (the)
sect
secular
secularization of culture
secularization of religion
spirit of capitalism (the)
state religion

KEY PEOPLE

Emile Durkheim
Karl Marx
Ernst Troeltsch

Ian Robertson
Max Weber

CLASS DISCUSSION QUESTIONS

1. Does the fact that sociologists do not seek to verify or to make value judgments about religious beliefs mean that they have no religious beliefs of their own? Why or why not?
2. What does the word "profane" mean to you? Do sociologists define it in the same way?
3. What purposes or functions do you think religion serves in societies?
4. What examples can you give of functional equivalents of religion?
5. Are religious symbols visible on your campus? In your city? If so, what do they represent?
6. Do you tend to agree with the functionalist or conflict perspective on religion? Why?
7. Do you agree with Max Weber's idea that religion can produce social change?
8. Has immigration to the United States contributed to the presence of more of the world's major religions in this country? If yes, can you give examples?
9. Do you agree that the word cult conjures up bizarre images in the minds of many individuals? Is this an accurate assessment?
10. Why is it difficult for groups, such as the Amish, to preserve the culture of their ancestors?
11. Do you feel that decisions by the U.S. Supreme Court, such as the one stating that "separation of church and state" prohibits public prayer at public school graduation ceremonies, contribute to the secularization of culture? Why or why not?
12. What role do you think religion plays in the lives of most Americans today?
13. Have you watched televangelists' programs? If so, how do they appeal to viewers? How has the electronic church changed U.S. religion?
14. Why are people who change their social class also likely to change their religious denomination?
15. Why do you think religion did not wither away as Marx predicted that it would?

PROJECTS

1. If you grew up attending religious services, describe the characteristics of that religion as a sociologist might. Has attending college produced any changes in your religious involvement? If yes, how?

2. Gather literature or attend services of religious organizations in your city. Analyze the data you have collected using the functionalist, conflict, and symbolic interactionist perspectives. For example, does the organization offer answers to questions about the purpose of life, why people suffer, and the existence of an afterlife? Are religious symbols, rituals, and beliefs discussed? Are issues pertaining to social inequalities addressed? For a class discussion or semester project, organize the literature and your notes so they can be shared with other students, and present your findings and conclusions in oral or written form.

3. Analyze a number of religious programs on television produced by major televangelists. Keep a log of the programs you watch, who is on the program, and answer the following questions: What type of message do they convey to their viewing audience? Do they blend patriotic and religious themes together? Do they ask for contributions from their viewers? In return, do they offer memberships, partnerships, or other indications that one "belongs" to their organization? Present your findings to the class or in a term paper.

TRANSPARENCIES

1. (TR#40) A Cult-Sect-Church-Ecclesia Continuum
2. (TR#41) Religious Preference of Americans

TRANSPARENCY MASTERS

1. (TR#44M) Average Income and Religious Affiliation
2. (TR#45M) Church and Synagogue Membership by Region
3. (TR#46M) Age and Church or Synagogue Membership

4. (TR#47M) Religion and Indicators of Social Class
5. (TR#48M) Profiles of American Religions
6. (TR#49M) Religious Beliefs and Educational Attainment

VIDEOS/MOVIES

The Long Search. A series of thirteen films that examines the world's religions: (1) *Protestant Spirit*—sects in the United States and the influence of black religious experience; (2) *Hinduism: 330 Million Gods;* (3) *Buddhism: Footprint of the Buddha—India;* (4) *Catholicism: Rome, Leeds and the Desert;* (5) *Islam: There Is No God but God;* (6) *Orthodox Christianity: The Rumanian Solution;* (7) *Judaism: The Chosen People;* (8) *Religion in Indonesia: The Way of the Ancestors;* (9) *Buddhism: The Land of the Disappearing Buddha—Japan;* (10) *African Religions: Zulu Zion;* (11) *Taoism: A Question of Balance—China;* (12) *Alternate Life Styles in California: West Meets East;* and (13) *Reflections on the Long Search.* Each film is approximately 53 min. Available from BBC.

Judaism

Exodus. 1960. (Color) Depicts the exodus of a group of Jews from Europe to Israel after World War II. Shows Israel's struggle for independence from British control and tensions that arose between the Arabs and the Jews. 213 min. Available at video rental stores.

Present Memory. 1992. Shows what it's like to be Jewish in America and reflects the viewpoints of a wide variety of people, including immigrants and native born, young and old, assimilated and alienated, and ordinary and famous. The film is divided into three segments to allow for discussion. 88 min. Available from FML.

Jacoba: The Heroism of an "Ordinary" Woman. 1990. Tells the story of a Jewish family successfully hidden from the Nazis and local Dutch collaborators by Jacoba Omvlee, a devout Calvinist, in a small Dutch village. Draws attention to the painful events of the Nazi era and the heroism displayed across religious lines. 63 min. Available from FML.

Yentl. 1983. (Color) Starring Barbra Streisand as a young woman in Eastern Europe at the turn of the century who disguises herself as a boy in order to fulfill her dream and get an education. (PG) Available at video rental stores.

Christianity

Ben-Hur. 1959. (Color) Includes Jewish and Christian themes and ends in a dramatic chariot race. 212 min. Available at some video rental stores.

The Cardinal. 1963. (Color) An Irish American's rise from the priesthood to the College of Cardinals. 175 min. Available at some video rental stores.

Elmer Gantry. 1960. (Color) A revivalist minister who predates modern televangelists but has many of the negative characteristics exhibited by some of those recently discredited. 145 min. Available at some video rental stores.

Islam

The Five Pillars of Islam. Discusses the essential principles on which Islam rests—its five pillars—and puts them into historical context. The program shows the huge international mosaic of Moslem believers, and the conflict between traditional teaching and the effects of industrialization. 30 min. Available from FHS.

Hinduism

The Ganges. The mother of rivers, the birthplace of Hinduism, the holy of holies of nearly a billion people; this program tells about the development of the rich panoply of ancient and modern cultures—Asian, Arabic, European, African, Hindu, Buddhist, Moslem, and Christian—found in India today. 45 minutes. Available from FHS.

Gandhi. 1982. (Color) Describes the life and times of Mohandas K. Gandhi, a charismatic leader who rose from the position of a simple lawyer to become a nation's leader and a worldwide symbol of peace and understanding. 188 min. Available at video rental stores.

Buddhism

Buddha in the Land of the Kami (7th–12th Centuries). The history of Japan past and present is the story of the kami, the supernatural, not quite godlike spirits who underlie the Japanese-ness of Japan. Includes the creation myth of Japan, explains the kami concept, the arrival of Buddhism and how modern-day Japan still is greatly influenced by the kami concept and Buddhism. 53 min. Available from FHS.

Types of Religious Organizations

Amish Riddle. 1992. Shows another side of the Amish in Pennsylvania. Focuses on them as dynamic people who have modified their rules to enable them to prosper while shunning mod-

ern conveniences that may pull the community apart. 50 min. Available from FML.

CNN Video II. *Born Again Bikers.* A group of born-again bikers meets in British Columbia. Many are reformed alcoholics and drug addicts. They now attempt to get others to change, using the streets as their ministry. Available from A&B Video Library.

Pray TV. 1982. (Color) A newly ordained, idealistic minister becomes involved with a dynamic televangelist who does not share those ideals. 100 min. (Not rated) Available at video rental stores.

The Future of Religion

CNN Video II. *Religious Revival.* The collapse of Communism has seen a strong revival of religion in Russia. Rituals once banned by the Party now are performed. Baptisms are conducted en masse due to great demand. A priest says that people have been starving for spiritual food and are flocking to churches. Under Communism, thousands of Christians were persecuted and priests were arrested. In 1990, both Soviet and Russian Parliaments enacted Freedom of Conscience laws allowing free worship. Available from A&B Video Library.

SPEAKER SUGGESTIONS

1. A colleague whose specialty is in sociology of religion to discuss current research.
2. A colleague from the philosophy department or academic area of your institution which teaches world religion courses.
3. A leader of campus ministries or a local minister to conduct a discussion on religion among college students.

POP QUIZ QUESTIONS

True-False

F 1. Sociologists seek to verify or disclaim individual faiths and to make value judgments about religious beliefs.

T 2. Emile Durkheim divided all aspects of life into the sacred and the profane.

F 3. Symbolic interactionists emphasize the functions of religion.

T 4. According to functionalists, war and religious persecution are dysfunctions of religion.

T 5. Karl Marx thought that the oppressed used religion as a drug to help them forget their misery.

T 6. According to Max Weber, religion held the key to modernization.

F 7. Polytheists believe there is only one God.

T 8. All religions began as cults.

F 9. State religions are called "churches."

F 10. In recent years mainstream denominations in the United States have gained members while fundamentalist groups have shrunk.

ESSAY QUESTIONS

1. Compare and contrast functionalist and conflict perspectives on the purpose of religion in societies and in the lives of individuals.
2. Using the symbolic interactionist perspective, explain how religious symbols, rituals, and beliefs help to forge a community of like-minded people.
3. Create a chart which demonstrates the major similarities and differences in the major world religions. Write a brief summary of conclusions which can be drawn from the chart.
4. Discuss the major types of religious organizations. Explain why some can coexist side-by-side with other groups and why some cannot.
5. Describe the secularization of religion and state how an understanding of this process can help explain why Christian churches in the United States have splintered into so many groups.
6. Outline the main characteristics of religion in America. State the impact of these characteristics on the future of religion.

C H A P T E R

19

Medicine: Health and Illness

CHAPTER SUMMARY

Sociologists view health as intimately related to society—to such matters as cultural beliefs, a country's stage of development, lifestyle, and social class. Cultural beliefs and practices determine what people consider to be health and illness. The sick role excuses people from normal responsibilities but obligates them to get well in order to resume those responsibilities. As measured by life span, Americans are healthier than they formerly were. Medicine in the United States has become a commodity, developing into America's largest business enterprise. The Carnegie study and subsequent funding of medical schools in the early 1900s encouraged professionalization of medicine. A monopoly on medicine by physicians approved by the medical establishment resulted. Fearing the advent of socialized medicine, the medical establishment at first resisted Medicare and Medicaid and then, after these programs began, found them to be a gold mine. Current issues in medical and health care include medical care as a commodity, malpractice suits and defensive medicine, inequality in distribution of physicians and health care facilities, depersonalization, sexism, medicalization of society, controversy about death—including the right to die—and problems related to health insurance. Current major threats to health are AIDS, smoking, alcohol abuse, and disabling environments. Alternatives to the current health-care system include the use of preventive medicine and holistic medicine (people take responsibility for their own health, rather than being passive recipients of illness and disease). Change, if it comes, is likely to be slow.

CHAPTER OUTLINE

I. The Sociological Perspective on Health and Illness
  A. Health is a human condition measured by four components: physical, mental, social, and spiritual. Rather than thinking of people as either healthy or unhealthy, it is useful to think of them as healthier in some areas and less healthy in others. Very few people are entirely healthy; that is, not many people are at peak performance in all four areas.
  B. Health is affected by cultural beliefs. In Western culture a person who hears voices and sees visions might be locked up; in a tribal society, such an individual might be a shaman ("witch doctor"—the healing specialist who attempts to control the spirits thought to cause a disease or injury). The four components of health all reflect a particular culture or even a specific group within a culture. The sociological significance of the cultural relativity of health is that people's definitions of health influence their attitudes and behavior. The effects of cultural beliefs on health can be illustrated by anorexia nervosa. This condition depends on the belief that thin is beautiful, a belief not shared in many parts of the world. As cultural beliefs change over time, so do a group's definitions of what makes people healthy.
  C. Within the same society, subcultural patterns and lifestyle produce specific patterns of health and illness. For example, although Nevada and Utah are adjacent states with similar levels of income, education, medical care, etc., the death rate is much higher in Nevada. This is because Utah is inhabited mostly by Mormons, who encourage conservative living and disapprove of the consumption of tobacco, alcohol, and caffeine.
  D. Social class makes a considerable difference in people's chances for good health: people with more money get sick less often and, if they do get sick, are able to pay for more adequate medical treatment than the poor.
  E. On a global scale there is an intimate connection between society and health. Heart disease and cancer are "luxury" diseases of the rich First World (a person has to live long enough to get them). Most people in Third World nations die from diseases that industrialized nations have brought under control. International stratification in medical care also is a fact of global life. Third World nations have little money to spend on health care and lag far behind industrialized nations in such care. Infant mortality rates are much higher in Third World countries and life spans are much shorter. Many dis-

eases that ravage the populations of the poorer countries could be brought under control if their meager funds were spent on public health.

F. The well role refers to a person feeling well and being able to do all of her or his ordinary activities. Functionalist Talcott Parsons identified three elements of its opposite—the sick role: the individual is not held responsible for being sick; is exempt from normal responsibilities; and agrees that the role is undesirable (he or she will seek competent help for the illness and will cooperate in getting well). Often there is ambiguity between the well role and the sick role because most situations are not clear-cut examples such as having a heart attack. A decision to claim the sick role typically is more of a social than a physical matter. Parents and physicians are the primary mediators between children's feelings of illness and the right to be released from responsibilities. Gender and age are significant factors in determining reactions to a worker's claim to the sick role. Social groups define the conditions under which people are "allowed" to be sick and legitimately excused from ordinary responsibilities.

II. Historical Patterns of Health

A. Heart disease and cancer account for 60% of all U.S. deaths. AIDS and homicide are 11th and 12th in terms of leading causes.

B. Were Americans healthier in the past? That is difficult to answer because many diseases on which information is now gathered routinely were previously not even recognized. If being healthier is measured by life span, then Americans are healthier than their ancestors.

C. When it comes to mental health, no rational basis for comparisons exists. Perhaps there were fewer mental health problems in the past; however, it is also possible that there is greater mental health today than in the past.

III. Medicine in the United States

A. The Professionalization of Medicine

1. In the 1700s, a person learned to be a physician by becoming an apprentice or simply hanging out a shingle to proclaim that he was a physician. During the 1800s, a few medical schools opened and there was some licensing; the schools categorically denied admission to Jews, women, and African Americans. In 1906 the American Medical Association examined the 160 medical schools in the United States and found only 82 acceptable. The Carnegie Foundation funded a study by Abraham Flexner to visit every medical school and make recommendations for change. Its report had a profound impact on American medicine because it recommended that admission and teaching standards be raised and that philanthropies fund the most promising schools.

2. The result was the professionalization of medicine, which refers to the development of medicine into a field for which education becomes rigorous and in which physicians undergo a rigorous education, claim an understanding of illness, regulate themselves, assert that they are performing a service for society, and take authority over clients.

B. The professionalization of medicine led directly to medicine becoming a monopoly. Laws restricted medical licenses to graduates of approved schools; only graduates of these schools were eligible to be faculty members who trained the next generation of physicians; and one group gained control over American medicine and set itself up as the medical establishment. American medicine always had a fee-for-service approach, but now it came under the control of a select group of men. Physicians set their own fees and had no competition. Although the poor received services from some physicians and hospitals, many remained without medical care. The medical association fought all proposals for government-funded medical treatment, including Medicare (government-sponsored medical insurance for the elderly) and Medicaid (government-paid medical care for the poor) until the physicians saw how lucrative these payments could be. The medical establishment consists not only of physicians, but also of nurses, hospital personnel, pharmaceutical companies, druggists, manufacturers of medical technology, and corporations that own hospitals.

C. Some researchers have found that the lower the social class, the higher the proportion of serious mental problems. As compared with middle- and upper-class Americans, the poor have less job security, lower wages, unpaid bills and insistent bill collectors, more divorce, greater vulnerability to crime, more alcoholism, etc. Such conditions deal severe blows to their emotional well-being. Social inequalities also mark the treatment of mental problems. Private mental hospitals serve the wealthy (and those who have good insurance) while state hospitals are reserved for the poor. The rich are more likely to be treated with various forms of psychotherapy, the poor with medication.

IV. Issues in Health and Health Care

A. In the United States, medicine is viewed as a commodity (to be purchased by those who can afford it), not a right. The total national health bill now is $11.60 of every $100 of the gross national product.

B. Prior to this century, doctors had four main treatments (purging, bleeding, blistering, and vomiting); today, science and technology have made marvelous advances, diagnoses are more accurate, and treatments are more effective. However, medicine remains imprecise and doctors make mistakes, just like people in other occupations. Malpractice suits have made physicians more aware of how they practice medicine: physicians practice defensive medicine—seeking consultations with colleagues and ordering additional lab tests—simply because a patient may sue. Defensive medicine greatly increases the cost of medicine.

C. Medicare and Medicaid have brought health care to millions who otherwise would go without, yet the adequacy of health care is still an issue. Few poor people have a personal physician and often wait in crowded public health clinics to receive care. Some find it difficult to locate a doctor who will accept them because many states are slow to pay or pay less than what physicians charge. When hospitalized, the poor are often in under-staffed/underfunded public hospitals, treated by rotation interns who do not know them and cannot follow up on their progress.

D. Depersonalization is the practice of dealing with people as though they were cases and diseases, not individuals. Many patients get the impression that they have been trapped by a cash machine—that the physician is impatiently counting the minutes and tabulating dollars while talking to the patient. Although students begin medical school with lay attitudes and want to "treat the whole person," as they progress through school, their feelings for patients are overpowered by the need to be efficient.

E. Women and men are treated differently regarding certain types of surgery. Women are less likely to be given heart surgery and if they are, they are more likely to die from the surgery because they are in more advanced stages of heart disease. They may receive unnecessary surgery, such as total hysterectomy, as some male doctors hold a biased attitude toward the female reproductive system. Male dominance of medicine in the United States underlies this sexism (only 18% of American physicians are women). Today, women earn 36% of all American medical degrees and in the next few years are expected to comprise 40% of medical school graduates.

F. Medicalization is the transformation of something into a matter to be treated by physicians. Examples include balding, weight and diet, wrinkles, and insomnia—there is nothing inherently medical in such conditions. Symbolic interactionists stress that medicalization is based on arbitrary definitions, part of a cultural way of looking at life that is bound to a specific historical period. Functionalists view medicalization as functional for the medical establishment and for patients who have someone to listen to their problems and are sometimes helped. Conflict sociologists assert that this process is another indication of the growing power of the medical establishment, and that as physicians medicalize more aspects of life, their power and profits increase.

G. Today, it is much more difficult than in the past to determine when someone is dead. In the past a person was considered to be dead if he or she was not breathing and had no heartbeat. With modern technology, machines can perform most bodily functions and thus force a new, narrower definition of death. Brain death means that although the body is still alive (i.e., its tissues and organs are maintained), it produces no brain waves and thus, there is no living person inside the body.

H. Some people belive that physicians should practice euthanasia—mercy killing—and help patients die if they request death to relieve insufferable pain or to escape from an incurable disease ("assisted suicide"). Others believe that this should never occur, or that euthanasia should be allowed only in specific circumstances. A living will (that people in good health sign to make clear what they wish medical personnel to do should they become dependent on artificial life-support systems) is an attempt to deal with this issue.

I. Health Insurance
1. Private health insurance and government-funded health care have contributed to the spiraling cost of care. At first they set no upper limits on tests or treatment, leaving the physician alone to make these decisions. As costs rose, insurance companies took four steps to try to control prices: (a) introduced or increased deductibles; (b) instituted coinsurance requiring the patient to pay a fixed portion of the cost of each hospital stay or medical treatment; (c) began utilization reviews (medical personnel review claims to determine whether a treatment was warranted); and (d) introduced "capping" (setting the maximum amount to be paid for each procedure).

2. Health maintenance organizations (HMOs) and diagnostic-related groups are two recent attempts to contain medical costs. HMOs are based on paying a predetermined fee to certain physicians to take care of the medical needs of employees. Since physicians are paid a set fee for the year, to make a profit they must be efficient and avoid unnecessary procedures. HMOs lower expenses, but patients complain about the lack of choice of physicians and hospitals, and some patients believe they are rushed out of hospitals before they have recovered.

3. The federal government classified all illnesses into 468 diagnostic-related groups and specified the exact amount it would pay for the treatment of each. Hospitals could make a profit only if they moved patients through the system quickly. Although the average hospital stay dropped immediately, some patients are discharged before being fully ready to go home, and others are refused admittance because they might cost the hospital money instead of making it a profit.

V. Threats to Health
A. AIDS (Acquired Immune Deficiency Syndrome) is probably the most pressing issue in American (and global) health. Its exact origin is unknown. In the United States, AIDS first appeared in the male homosexual population; it then passed on to the heterosexual population; others were infected with AIDS through blood transfusions. AIDS is now among the top five killers of American women of childbearing age. It is predicted that by the year 2000, as many women as men will have AIDS. AIDS has become the leading cause of death among American men between the ages of 25–44. AIDS is a global problem, and the majority of new cases are likely to be in Asia. Several drugs, such as AZT and DDI, have been found to slow the progress of AIDS, but no cure has yet been found.

B. Drugs
1. Cigarette smoking accounts for one out of every six deaths in the United States. Nicotine is an addictive drug. Smoking doubles a person's risk of heart attack and causes progressive emphysema.

2. Alcohol is the standard recreational drug in the United States. The average American drinker consumes about 39 gallons of alcoholic beverages per year. 10% of drinkers drink 50% of all the alcohol consumed in the United States. Problems associated with alcohol consumption include: drunken drivers are responsible for about half of the 49,000 fatalities in automobile accidents each year; pregnant women

who drink are more likely to give birth to children with birth defects; and alcohol abuse costs over $11 billion a year in medical expenses in the United States.

C. A disabling environment is one that is harmful to health. Some occupations have high health risks which are evident (e.g., mining, riding bulls in a rodeo, etc.). In others, the risk becomes evident only years after people have worked at what they thought was a safe occupation (e.g., laborers who worked with asbestos). The greenhouse effect refers to a warming of the earth that may change the globe's climate, melt its polar ice caps, and flood the earth's coastal shores. Use of fluorocarbon gases is threatening the ozone shield (the protective layer of the earth's upper stratosphere that screens out a high proportion of the sun's ultraviolet rays). In humans, this high-intensity ultraviolet radiation causes skin cancer.

VI. The Search for Alternatives
A. Many of the threats to health are preventable. Individuals can exercise regularly, eat nutritious food, maintain sexual monogamy, and avoid smoking and alcohol abuse in order to prevent disease. Preventive medicine is an alternative to intervention after the fact.
B. Holistic medicine is an approach to medical care centered on the idea that a person's body, feelings, attitudes, and actions are all intertwined and cannot be segregated into systems. From this perspective, the patient is viewed in terms of lifestyle and total environment. Change in medical treatment is likely to be slow because it flies in the face of established cultural practices and threatens vested interests in the current practice of medicine.

LEARNING OBJECTIVES

After reading and studying Chapter 19, the student should be able to:

1. Define health from a sociological perspective and explain what is meant by the cultural relativity of health.
2. Describe the ways in which subcultural patterns and social class produce specific patterns of health and illness.
3. Compare First and Third World nations regarding the types of diseases which are most likely to be found in each.
4. Identify the three elements of the sick role and explain why everyone is not given the same right to claim this role.
5. Answer the question, "Were Americans healthier in the past?"
6. Discuss the professionalization of medicine in the United States and list the characteristics of physicians which resulted from this process.
7. Explain what is meant by the monopoly of medicine and note the effect such monopolization had on the cost of medical care.
8. Describe the relationship between mental illness and social class.
9. Outline and briefly explain the major issues in U.S. health and health care.
10. Discuss these threats to health: disease, drugs, and disabling environments.
11. Analyze the prospects for change in medicine which might be possible through preventive and holistic medicine.

KEY TERMS

depersonalization
disabling environment
dumping
epidemiology
euthanasia

fee for service
health
Health Maintenance Organization (HMO)
holistic medicine
living will

medicalization
professionalization of medicine
shaman
sick role

KEY PEOPLE

Talcott Parsons
Thomas Szasz
Jack Haas and William Shaffir
Jan Howard

Abraham Flexner
Sue Fisher
Erich Goode

CLASS DISCUSSION QUESTIONS

1. What does the word "health" mean to you? How do sociologists use the term?
2. What American cultural beliefs do you think contribute to the problem of anorexia nervosa?
3. What types of lifestyles do you think may contribute to higher rates of illness?
4. Why do you think Americans with more money do not get sick as often as those with less money?

5. Can you explain why heart disease and cancer might be called "luxury" diseases?

6. Have you ever taken the "sick role" when you were not actually sick? Is being "sick" more acceptable than not wanting to go to work or school?

7. Do you think Americans are healthier—or sicker—than they used to be? Why?

8. Would you be willing to receive medical treatment from a person who just proclaimed that he or she was a doctor? Why did medicine become professionalized?

9. Do you think it was essential for the well-being of mothers and children that physicians took control over childbirth? Why or why not?

10. Does your physician work on a fee-for-service basis? What are some other methods of payment?

11. Do you agree that people in the lower social classes have greater mental problems? Why or why not?

12. Should medical care in the United States be treated as a commodity or as a right?

13. What are some examples of defensive medicine? Can you see why some physicians believe defensive medicine is necessary?

14. If you were a patient in a hospital, would you resent being referred to as "the gallbladder in Room 324"? Why does this type of practice often occur in medicine?

15. Do you think sexism would still exist in U.S. medicine if at least 50% of the physicians were women? Why or why not?

16. Do you believe people have a "right to die"? Why is it now difficult to determine when an individual dies?

17. Do you have health insurance? In what ways has health insurance contributed to the spiraling cost of medicine?

18. Do you think the practice of "dumping" by hospitals is ethical? Why or why not?

19. How devastating do you think the AIDS virus is going to become before a cure is found?

20. In your opinion, why do many people keep smoking even when they know that cancer and other diseases are directly related to their smoking?

21. Have you worked in a disabling environment? What kinds of hazards were involved?

22. In regard to health, do you agree with the old statement that "an ounce of prevention is worth a pound of cure"?

PROJECTS

1. For small group discussions or a term project, conduct library research on how American cultural beliefs influence one's perceptions of health. For example, you may wish to learn more about the cultural factors involved in eating disorders such as anorexia nervosa. Collect advertisements for weight-reduction products, diet drinks, or clothing and look for appearance norms of slimness which are reinforced to sell these products. Several books will assist you in preparing your report: Banner, Lois. *American Beauty.* NY: Knopf, 1983; Faludi, Susan. *Backlash: The Undeclared War Against American Women.* NY: Crown, 1991. Seid, Roberta Pollack. *Never Too Thin: Why Women Are at War with Their Bodies.* NY: Prentice Hall, 1989. Wolf, Naomi. *The Beauty Myth: How Images of Beauty Are Used Against Women.* NY: Morrow, 1991. Create a visual presentation with the ads and draw conclusions from your readings.

2. For small group or class discussion, interview a number of your friends and acquaintances to determine situations in which they take the "sick role." Find out whether any of them take off "mental health days" as well as days when they are ill. Determine how they approach professors or employers to tell them they are not going to be in class or at work. Compare your findings with those of classmates.

3. If you are planning a career in the medical field, you may wish to explore the history of professionalization for your area (e.g., physicians, dentists, nurses, medical technicians, physical therapists, etc.). Find information on the following: When did professionalization first occur in this field? What type of requirements were placed on those who planned to enter the profession? What types of regulatory groups—such as the American Medical Association—were created to determine standards and to enhance this field? Write a paper comparing your research to the discussion in your text.

4. Keep a journal of television, radio, and print media ads for doctors, hospitals, and facilities which offer "cures" for drug abuse, alcoholism, overeating, and mental disorders. Analyze the methods used to acquire patients, the frequency of and cost factors in running the ads, etc. (You do not need to know how much the ads themselves cost.) If several major hospitals are in competition with each other, determine how they attempt to show that their facilities, medical staff, and patient services are superior to the others. Present your log and a written analysis to the class. If you have videotaped some of the ads, show them as well.

5. Find examples of current malpractice lawsuits. Determine what the issues are in the suit. Relate your findings to the discussion in your text, and discuss them in small groups or in class discussion.

6. Prepare "pro" and "con" arguments for a debate on the right to die. Analyze recent legal cases, such as those of a medical doctor, known to some as "Doctor Death," who helped terminally-ill patients commit painless suicide. Present your arguments in a class debate or term paper.

TRANSPARENCIES

1. (TR#42) The Soaring Cost of Medical Care: The Amount the Average American Pays Each Year

2. (TR#43) Women with AIDS

3. (TR#44) AIDS in the United States

TRANSPARENCY MASTERS

1. (TR#50M) Infant Mortality Rates
2. (TR#51M) Distribution of AIDS by Means of Transmission, 1982–1991

3. (TR#52M) Health Status of Three Societies

VIDEOS/MOVIES

The Cultural Relativity of Health

Eating Disorders. Covers the personality profiles of the likeliest anorexia patients; explains their inability to acknowledge that they are thin enough; shows how anorexia develops and demonstrates its symptoms; and explores with some anorexics how they were cured. 26 min. Available from A&B Video Library and FHS.

The Monopoly of Medicine

Health Care on the Critical List: Containing Medical Costs. 1985. Describes the spiraling costs of health care and discusses whether it is possible to contain these costs. Concludes that the way we pay for health care affects how hospitals are run, how doctors practice medicine, and ultimately how patients are treated. 58 min. Available from FML.

Mental Illness and Social Inequality

Learning to Cope. Tension and anxiety are common elements in the human condition. Stress affects all people and learning to deal with periodic crises and regular transitions is a life-long process. This film introduces seven people who have successfully learned to cope. 25 min. Available from A&B Video Library.

Men, Depression, and Desperation. Members of the "stronger sex" can be overwhelmed by crisis—death, divorce, job loss—and seek escape through isolation, drugs, or even suicide. Dr. Herbert Freudenberger joins Phil Donahue to help men find ways to acknowledge, express, and come to grips with crisis. 28 min. Available from A&B Video Library and FHS.

Issues in Health and Health Care

CNN Video II. *Medical Malpractice.* One out of every three doctors has been sued at least once. All physicians expect to be sued at some point; as a consequence, they practice defensive medicine. Legislation has been proposed that would take most medical malpractice cases out of litigation and into binding arbitration. Malpractice reformers also call for a limit on damages that can be awarded. The medical establishment supports the legislation; many lawyers do not, claiming that limiting awards is unconstitutional. Available from A&B Video Library.

CNN Video II. *Affluent Hospital.* A new, $157 million-dollar hospital affiliated with the University of Southern California in Los Angeles opens directly across from a 57-year-old university-affiliated hospital serving the poor living in the L.A. barrio. Critics say that the new hospital symbolizes much that is wrong with American medicine: the disparity between the proliferation of specialists serving the upper classes and the dearth of doctors available to the poor. Available from A&B Video Library.

Who Lives, Who Dies: Rationing Health Care. 1989. This documentary shows that the American health care system is failing a large part of the population. One out of six Americans has no coverage and cannot afford basic care. They must rely on public clinics whose funding is shrinking. Poor children are at greatest risk. The system typically denies routine preventive care to millions, but then gives dying patients useless care they do not want. Includes a discussion of organ transplants where huge sums of money are spent for the relatively few. 58 min. Available from FML.

Controversy about Death

Defining Life: Should One Help a Loved One Die? 1992. What does one do when a terminally-ill loved one asks for help in committing suicide? This video shows the case of Bertram Harper, who was charged with murder for abetting the suicide of his terminally-ill wife and prosecuted in a landmark trial in Detroit, Michigan, in 1991. Although the court found him innocent, many questions still exist regarding this important issue. Two other similar cases also are documented. 26 min. Available from FML.

Euthanasia. 1990. Advances in modern technology have made it possible to postpone and control death and to sustain life almost indefinitely. This has raised a host of ethical questions that society must address. When does it become morally legitimate to pull the plug? Should a patient be guided to an easy death? What are the legal, moral and ethical implications of euthanasia? This video provides a good background for a discussion on the "right to die" issue. 44 min. Available from FML.

Threats to Health

CNN Video II. *AIDS: The Second Decade.* "AIDS and Women: Part II." Explores the question of whether women—and thus their babies—face additional biological and cultural obstacles in fighting AIDS. In the United States, more than 2,500 babies (1991 data) have been born infected with the AIDS virus; some women don't know they can transmit the disease to their unborn children. Discusses issues related to AIDS testing and to children with AIDS. 3.10 min. Available from A&B Video Library. Other videos available from the A&B Video Library include: *AIDS: Our Worst Fears; AIDS: The Epidemic's Second Decade; AIDS, the Family, and the Community; AIDS: The Women Speak; Kids with AIDS; Women with AIDS.*

Videos available from the A&B Video Library include: *Alcohol and the Family: Breaking the Chain; Cocaine: The End of the Line; Cracking a Craving; Drug and Alcohol Rehabilitation; Dying to be Sober; Kids Out of Control; The Power of Addiction.*

Perspectives: Health Care in Other Countries
CNN Video II. *Soviet Medical Care.* Describes the poor condition of medical care in Post-communist Russia. The government spends less than one percent on women and children's medical care, and half of the state's budget on military. Russian doctors are paid less than factory workers and are unable to procure needed drugs and medical equipment. While medical care is free in Russia, the quality is substandard. 2.55 min. Available from A&B Video Library.

Borderline Medicine: Comparing U.S. and Canadian Health Care. 1991. With the U.S. struggle to control soaring health care costs and 37 million Americans not covered by health insurance, the Canadian system of national health insurance looks attractive. This video explores both systems and includes comments by health care experts and business leaders such as Lee Iacocca on the medical and financial implications of both systems. 58 min. Available from FML.

SPEAKER SUGGESTIONS

1. A representative of your local, county, or state medical association to discuss the importance of his or her organization in regulating physicians.
2. A physician or social worker who practices in a public mental health facility or hospital to discuss mental illness and social issues.
3. Attorneys who regularly represent plaintiffs or defendants in medical malpractice litigation.

4. A colleague who teaches medical ethics at a medical school in your area to discuss physician-patient relations and/or issues relating to death and dying.
5. A social worker from an AIDS treatment center or hospice to discuss the "human face" of AIDS today.
6. A holistic practitioner to discuss how their emphasis is different from those of traditional medical practitioners.

POP QUIZ QUESTIONS

True-False
T 1. What people define as health varies from culture to culture.
T 2. Americans with more money do not get sick as often as those with less money.
F 3. The sick role is based on the conflict perspective.
F 4. Throughout history, a license has been required to practice medicine in the United States.
T 5. The American Medical Association initially fought every proposal for government-funded medical treatment.
F 6. In the American medical system, medicine is viewed as a right which should be available to everyone.
T 7. The medicalization of society refers to the process of

turning something that was not previously considered medical into a medical matter.
T 8. AIDS is now among the top five killers of American women of childbearing age.
F 9. Rates of cigarette smoking and alcohol use both have gone down in the United States because people have become aware of the health hazards associated with each.
T 10. Practitioners of holistic medicine place emphasis on the whole person, making their approach different from dominant medical practices.

ESSAY QUESTIONS

1. Discuss the sociological perspective of health and illness, including problems with defining health and the role that culture plays in health and illness.
2. Describe how the practice of medicine has changed in the United States from the earliest years to the present. Note how the professionalization and monopolization of medicine have impacted the quality and cost of health care in this country.

3. Analyze one of these health care issues from the functional, conflict, or symbolic interactionist perspective: malpractice suits and defensive medicine, depersonalization, sexism in medicine, or the medicalization of society.
4. Explain why it has become difficult to define death and discuss the controversy over the right to die.
5. Identify some of the major threats to health in the United States and note what might be done to lessen these problems.

CHAPTER

20

Population and Urbanization

CHAPTER SUMMARY

Demography is the study of the size, composition, growth, and distribution of human populations. Many demographers are convinced that the world is on a collision course with its food supply. Today, the basic cause of famine is the maldistribution of food rather than world overpopulation; however, the fact remains that the Third World population is growing at three times the rate of the First World. People in the Third World have many more children than people in the First and Second World because children play a very different role in Third World cultures. To project population trends, demographers use three demographic variables: fertility, mortality, and migration. Urbanization, the process by which an increasing proportion of a population lives in cities, represents the greatest mass migration in human history. About half of the entire world population now lives in cities; in the United States, the figure is about 80 percent. Three major models have been proposed to explain how cities expand: the concentric-zone, sector, and multiple-nuclei models. Some people find a sense of community in cities; others find alienation. To develop community in the city, people personalize their shopping, identify with sports teams, and even become sentimental about objects in the city. An essential element in determining whether someone finds community or alienation in the city is that person's social networks. Noninvolvement is generally functional for urbanites, but it impedes giving help in emergencies. American cities are subject to constant change, including the transition from white to minority leadership, the movement from the city to the suburbs, and the psychological separation of city and suburbs. Gentrification and the renaissance of downtown areas may point to the revitalization of American cities as suburban areas now are aging and experiencing problems similar to those of the cities.

CHAPTER OUTLINE

I. Population: Demography is the study of the size, composition, growth, and distribution of human populations. Many fear the world is becoming overcrowded and the planet will be marked by chronic famine and mass starvation.

II. The Specter of Overpopulation: Thomas Malthus wrote *An Essay on the Principle of Population* (1798) stating the Malthus theorem—population grows geometrically while food supply increases arithmetically; thus, if births went unchecked, population would outstrip food supply.

   A. New Malthusians believe Malthus was correct because an average of 200,000 people are born each day. The world population is following an exponential growth curve (where numbers increase in extraordinary proportions): 1837, one billion; 1927, two billion; 1957, three billion; 1972, four billion; and 1984, five billion.

   B. Anti-Malthusians are more optimistic—they do not believe that people blindly reproduce until there is no room left, and cite three stages of the demographic transition in Europe as an example. Stage 1, a fairly stable population (high birth rates offset by high death rates); Stage 2, "population explosion" (high birth rates

and low death rates); and Stage 3, population stability (low birth rates and low death rates). They assert this transition will happen in the poorer countries, which currently are in the second stage. Population shrinkage (a country's population becomes smaller because birth rate and immigration are too low to replace those who die and emigrate) has occurred in Europe.

   C. Who is correct? Only the future will prove the accuracy of either the projections of the New Malthusians or the Anti-Malthusians.

   D. Why are there famines? Anti-Malthusians point out that the amount of food produced for each person in the world has increased: famines are not the result of too little food production, but result from maldistribution of existing food. The New Malthusians counter that the world's population continues to grow and the earth may not be able to continue to produce sufficient food.

III. Population Growth: Three reasons why poor nations have so many children are (1) the status that parenthood provides; (2) the community supports this view; and (3) children are considered to be economic assets (the parents rely on the children to take care of them in their old age). People in First World countries see children as economic liabilities.

A. Demographers use population pyramids (graphic representations of a population, divided into age and sex) to illustrate a country's population dynamics (e.g., Mexico's doubling rate is only 28 years). A declining standard of living may result in political instability followed by severe repression by the government.

B. Estimated population growth is based on three demographic variables:

1. Fertility, measured by the fertility rate (number of children an average woman bears), is sometimes confused with fecundity (number of children a woman theoretically can bear). To compute a country's fertility rate, demographers use crude birth rate (annual number of births per 1,000 people).

2. Mortality is measured by the crude death rate (number of deaths per 1,000 people); some countries, such as Mexico, have high infant mortality rates (death rate of children during their first year). The life expectancy of Americans (number of years an average newborn can expect to live) has steadily increased; however, the human life span (maximum length of life) has not increased because of eventual degeneration of the body's vital organs.

3. Migration is measured by the net migration rate (difference between the number of immigrants moving in and emigrants moving out per 1,000 population); it may be voluntary or forced. Over one million enter the United States each year; many enter illegally. Push factors make people want to leave where they are living (e.g., persecution, lack of economic opportunity); pull factors attract people (e.g., opportunities in the new locale).

C. The growth rate equals births less deaths, plus net migration. In every country that industrializes, the growth rate declines.

D. Inaccuracies in government statistics and the fact that people unexpectedly change their behavior make it difficult to forecast population growth; thus, demographers formulate several predictions simultaneously, each depending on different assumptions: no one anticipates the United States will experience either population shrinkage or zero population growth.

IV. Urbanization is the process by which an increasing proportion of a population lives in cities.

A. Small cities with massive defensive walls existed as far back as 10,000 years ago; cities on a larger scale originated about 3500 B.C. as a result of the development of more efficient agriculture and of a surplus. A city is a place in which a large number of people are permanently based and do not produce their own food. Today's rapid urbanization not only means that more people live in cities, but also that today's cities are larger; about 150 of the world's cities contain at least one million people; by the year 2000 this number will have doubled; some areas are so crowded that cities run into one another, forming a megalopolis (a conglomeration of cities and their suburbs, forming an interconnected urban area).

B. In 1790, only about 5% of Americans lived in cities; by 1920, 50% of the U.S. population lived in urban areas; today, 80% of Americans live in urban areas, and about 190 U.S. cities have more than 100,000 inhabitants. The U.S. Census Bureau divided the country into 283 metropolitan statistical areas (MSAs)—which consist of a central city and the urbanized counties that are linked to it. Half of the entire U.S. population lives in just 39 MSAs.

V. Models of Urban Growth: Robert Park coined the term human ecology to describe how people adapt to their environment, such as their changing use of land (also known as "urban ecology"); human ecologists have constructed three models which attempt to explain urban growth patterns:

A. Ernest W. Burgess proposed the concentric-zone model, which views the city as a series of zones emanating from its center, with each characterized by a different group of people and activity: Zone 1, central business district; Zone 2, in transition with deteriorating housing and rooming houses; Zone 3, area to which thrifty workers have moved to escape the zone in transition, yet maintain access to work; Zone 4, more expensive apartments, single-family dwellings, and exclusive areas where the wealthy live; and Zone 5, commuter zone consisting of suburban areas or satellite cities that have developed around rapid transit routes.

B. The sector model sees urban zones as wedge-shaped sectors radiating out from the center. A zone might contain a sector of working-class housing, another sector of expensive housing, a third of businesses, and so on, all competing with one another for the same land. For example, when poor immigrants move into a city, they settle in the lowest-rent area available and, as their numbers grow, begin to encroach on adjacent areas. As the poor move closer to the middle class, the middle class leave, expanding the sector of lower-cost housing.

C. The multiple-nuclei model views the city as comprised of multiple centers or nuclei, each of which focuses on a specialized activity (e.g., retail districts, automobile dealers, etc.).

D. Critique of the models: cities are complex, and no single model yet developed does justice to this complexity; the models do not make allowances for the extent to which elites influence the development of cities.

VI. Experiencing the City

A. Louis Wirth argued that the city undermines kinship and neighborhood, which are the traditional bases of social control and social solidarity: Urban dwellers live in anonymity, their lives marked by segmented and superficial encounters which make them grow aloof from one another and indifferent to other people's problems. This is similar to the idea that *Gemeinschaft* (a sense of community that comes from everyone knowing everyone else) is ripped apart as a country industrializes, and *Gesellschaft* (societies characterized by secondary, impersonal relationships which result in alienation) replaces it.

B. Some sociologists use the term urban village to refer to an area of the city that people know well and in which they live, work, shop, and play.

C. Herbert Gans identified five types of people who live in the city: (1) cosmopolites—intellectuals and professionals, students, writers, and artists who live in the inner city to be near its conveniences and cultural benefits; (2) singles—young, unmarried people who come seeking jobs and entertainment; (3) ethnic villagers—live in tightly knit neighborhoods that resemble villages and small towns, united by race and social class; (4) the deprived—the very poor, the emotionally disturbed, and the handicapped who live in neighborhoods more like urban jungles than urban villages; and (5) the trapped—who consist of four subtypes: those who could not afford to move when their neighborhood was invaded by another ethnic group; downwardly mobile persons who have fallen from a higher social class; elderly people who have drifted into the slums because they are not wanted elsewhere and are powerless to prevent their downward slide; and alcoholics and drug addicts.

D. The city is divided into worlds that people come to know down to the smallest detail; city people create a sense of intimacy for themselves by personalizing their shopping (by frequenting the same stores and restaurants, people become recognized as "regulars"); spectator sports also engender community identification; city dwellers develop strong feelings for particular objects and locations in the city such as trees, buildings, rivers, lakes, parks, and even street corners.

E. City planners usually take an outsider's point of view regarding demolition of buildings/landmarks, which may have special meaning to residents of an area; insiders' views often are in sharp contrast to those of the outsiders who make plans for changing an area.

F. An essential element in determining whether someone finds community or alienation in a city is that person's social networks; community is found in relationships, not in buildings and space.

G. Urban dwellers follow a norm of noninvolvement—such as the use of a newspaper or a Walkman to indicate inaccessibility for interaction—to avoid encounters with people they do not know; use a variety of filters to prevent unwanted stimuli from reaching them, including unlisted telephone numbers, telephone answering machines, and post office boxes instead of revealing home addresses.

H. The more bystanders there are to an incident, the less likely people are to help because people's sense of re-

sponsibility becomes diffused. The norm of noninvolvement and the diffusion of responsibility may help urban dwellers get through everyday city life, but they are dysfunctional in situations like the murder of Kitty Genovese, because people do not provide assistance to others.

VII. The Changing City

A. One of the most significant changes in urban politics is the transition of power from white to minority leadership; peaceful management of the city is in the best interests of a city's elite—whether that elite be white or minority—so many groups have avoided confrontational politics and worked instead toward building coalitions.

B. Suburbanization—the movement frm the city to the suburbs—has had a profound effect on American cities. Although people have moved for over 100 years to towns next to the cities in which they worked, what is new today is the speed and extent to which people have left the city. Central cities lost residents, businesses, and jobs, causing the cities' tax base (which supports essential city services and schools) to shrink; people left behind were those with limited financial means. Suburbanites prefer the city to keep its problems to itself and fight movements to share suburbia's revenues with the city.

C. The downtown areas of many American cities are experiencing a renaissance; many people are returning to live in the city. Gentrification—the displacement of the poor by the relatively affluent who buy rundown properties and restore them—improves the appearance of urban neighborhoods; however, the existing residents are displaced as newcomers with more money start to buy up the neighborhood and increase property values.

1. American suburbs have increasing problems—including a deteriorating infrastructure, a rising crime rate, and in many suburbs, a "taxpayers' revolt," but suburbanization continues strong, and it is unlikely to change because of increasing fear of the inner city, improved transportation and communication, and decentralization of industry.

2. "Edge cities" are now developing. These are not consistent with any city's political boundaries but consist of a clustering of shopping malls, hotels, office parks, and residential areas near the intersection of major highways.

LEARNING OBJECTIVES

After reading and studying Chapter 20, the student should be able to:

1. Discuss the key issues in the debate between New Malthusians and Anti-Malthusians regarding the specter of overpopulation.

2. Explain why people in poor nations have so many children and note the implications of different rates of population growth.

3. State the three demographic variables used in estimating population growth.

4. Define the following terms: fertility rate, fecundity, crude birth rate, crude death rate, mortality rate, life expectancy, life span, net migration rate, immigrants, and emigrants.

5. Describe the process of urbanization and outline the history of how cities came into existence.

6. Discuss the three models of urban growth and critique the models.

7. Explain why many people feel a sense of alienation as a result of living in larger urban areas.
8. List and briefly describe the five different types of people who live in the city as identified by sociologist Herbert Gans.
9. Describe ways in which city people create a sense of intimacy for themselves in large urban areas.

10. Explain why the norm of noninvolvement and the diffusion of responsibility which help urban dwellers get through everyday city life may be dysfunctional in some situations.
11. Outline the major changes facing American cities regarding urban politics, suburbanization, and gentrification.

KEY TERMS

city
community
crude birth rate
crude death rate
demographic equation
demographic transition
demographic variables
demography
exponential growth curve

fecundity
fertility rate
gentrification
human ecology
life expectancy
life span
Malthus theorem
megalopolis
Metropolitan Statistical Area (MSA)

net migration rate
population pyramid
population shrinkage
suburb
suburbanization
urban networks
urbanization
zero population growth

KEY PEOPLE

Thomas Malthus
Ernest Burgess
Chauncey Harris and Edward Ullman

Robert Park
Homer Hoyt
Herbert Gans

CLASS DISCUSSION QUESTIONS

1. Why are many people in the Western world so concerned about the prospects of an overcrowded world?
2. Are you surprised to learn that another fifteen to twenty thousand people will be born in the time it takes you to read Chapter 20?
3. In your opinion, are the New Malthusians or the Anti-Malthusians most accurate in their assessment of population growth?
4. Do you agree with conflict theorists that swollen populations in developing nations may cause a change in the precarious balance of world power? Why or why not?
5. Does the world produce enough food to feed everyone? If yes, then why do people die of hunger?
6. Can you explain why a declining standard of living poses the danger of political instability? Could this ever occur in the United States?
7. Why do you think it would be difficult to estimate population growth?
8. Do you believe that industrialization has increased the life span? Why or why not?
9. Should there be a limit to the number of immigrants allowed into the United States? Should individuals who are HIV-positive be allowed to enter the country? Why or why not?

10. Can you explain why growth rates decline as countries industrialize?
11. Were you aware of zero population growth before taking this class? Do you know of groups in the United States which encourage this level of growth?
12. What type of growth pattern appears to have occurred in your hometown? In the city where you are attending school?
13. What type of opportunities do cities provide for you? What kinds of problems do they have?
14. How are the experiences of people different in large cities as compared with small communities?
15. Can you find examples of each of Gans's types of urban dwellers in your own city?
16. From your own experiences, what are some ways you have created your own little world within a large city context? Or within a large university setting?
17. If you were a city planner, would you find it useful to determine how people living in an area felt about a change before proposing that the change be made?
18. What are some examples of the "norm of noninvolvement" and the diffusion of responsibility on campus? In this city?
19. Will your life be affected by changes now occurring in American cities? If yes, in what ways?

PROJECTS

1. Do additional reading on population-related issues and provide extra information to your discussion group or the class. In addition to the sources at the end of the chapter, you may

wish to read some of the following: (a) Alonso, William (ed.). *Population in an Interacting World.* Cambridge: Harvard University Press, 1987; (b) Bogue, Donald. *The Population of the United States: Historical Trends and Future Projections.* NY: Free Press, 1985; (c) Easterlin, Richard A., and Eileen M. Crimmins. *The Fertility Revolution: A Supply-Demand Analysis.* Chicago: University of Chicago Press, 1985; (d) Kammeyer, Kenneth C., and Helen Ginn. *An Introduction to Population.* Chicago: Dorsey, 1986; and (e) Weeks, John. *Population: An Introduction to Concepts and Issues.* 4th ed., Belmont: Wadsworth, 1989.

2. Analyze a specific city in which you have lived or visited. Think of cities that have developed along the lines of the concentric-zone, sector, or multiple-nuclei models. Next think about the processes of urbanization, suburbanization, and gentrification that have occurred in the area where this city is located. What are the dynamics of this city and the problems of living or visiting there? Present your findings for class discussion or in written form. You may wish to do a visual presentation in which you draw the specifics for the city or cities you studied. Additional resources to assist in

writing your conclusions include: (a) Feagin, Joe R., and Robert Parker. *Building American Cities: The Urban Real Estate Game.* Englewood Cliffs: Prentice Hall, 1990; (b) Geist, William. *Toward a Safe and Sane Halloween and Other Tales of Suburbia.* NY: Time Books, 1985; (c) Jackson, Kenneth T. *Crabgrass Frontier: The Suburbanization of the United States.* NY: Oxford University Press, 1985; (d) Lyons, Larry. *The Community in Urban Society.* Philadelphia: Temple University Press, 1987; (e) Nelson, Kathryn P. *Gentrification and Distressed Cities: An Assessment of Trends in Intrametropolitan Migration.* Madison: University of Wisconsin Press, 1988; and (f) Smith, Neil, and Peter Williams (eds.) *Gentrification of the City.* Boston: Allen and Unwin, 1986.

3. For small group or class discussion, think of the type of city you would like to live in if it could have every feature which you desired, but none of the problems which exist in many cities today. What would this model city look like? What would it take to bring such a city into existence?

TRANSPARENCIES

1. (TR#45) Country of Birth of Immigrants to the United States
2. (TR#46) Growth Rates and Doubling Times for the World, the Five Continents, and Major Countries
3. (TR#47) Population Growth for 1750–2100: World, Less-Developed Regions, and "European," More-Developed Regions

4. (TR#48) Progress of Depression Cohort, Baby Boom Cohort, and Baby Bust Cohort through U.S. Population. Age-Sex Pyramid: 1960–2050 (Part A)
5. (TR#49) Progress of Depression Cohort, Baby Boom Cohort, and Baby Bust Cohort through U.S. Population. Age-Sex Pyramid: 1960–2050 (Part B)

TRANSPARENCY MASTERS

1. (TR#53M) World Population Growth over 2000 Years
2. (TR#54M) The Demographic Transition
3. (TR#55M) Why the Poor Need Children
4. (TR#56M) How Fast Is the World's Population Growing?
5. (TR#57M) Worldwide Urbanization

6. (TR#58M) Total Population Projections for the United States: 1970–2100, Assuming a Constant Fertility Rate of 2.11 Births per Woman
7. (TR#59M) Megalopolis in the Year 2000
8. (TR#60M) Patterns of Urban Spatial Differentiation

VIDEOS/MOVIES

Population Growth

Increase and Multiply. 1989. In Asia, Africa and Latin America, women give birth to an average of nine children each. Because of political pressures, the United States cut $88 million earmarked for family planning in the Third World. Filmed in Kenya, Zimbabwe, China, Guatemala and Mexico, this documentary shows in human terms the consequences of withdrawing family planning support. 55 min. Available from FML.

CNN Video II. *Hispanic Ecogap.* Aspen Institute report on status of Hispanics in the United States. While the number of Hispanics is booming, their economic status is declining. Some in the United States fear consequences on U.S. culture of a large-scale influx of Hispanics. Problems Hispanics face in the United States are discussed. Available from A&B Video Library.

Experiencing the City

Bright Lights, Big City. 1988 (Color) Starring Michael J. Fox and Kiefer Sutherland, this movie shows a young Midwesterner

whose life starts coming apart when he gets to New York City and gets caught up in drugs and nightlife. (R) 110 min. Available at video rental stores.

The Out-of-Towners. 1970. (Color) Starring Jack Lemmon and Sandy Dennis, this old movie shows a worst-case scenario of visiting New York City. Everything possible that can go wrong, does go wrong, and no one is willing to help them. 97 min. Available at some video rental stores.

Suburbanization and the Inner City

CNN Video II. *A Marshall Plan for the Inner City?* Urban League calls for a "Marshall Plan" to help inner-city African Americans reach parity with whites. Available from A&B Video Library.

Survival of a Small City: A Documentary on Urban Renewal. 1989. Filmed over a seven-year period, this film shows South Norwalk, Conn. before and after "revitalization." Follows a neighborhood as it struggles to reverse deterioration; shows the consequences of urban renewal, gentrification, and the dissolution of the old community. Deals with a number of issues brought up in the chapter, including: What is a city? Is it the people who live there, or a collection of buildings? Do city planners have the best interests of residents in mind?

What happens to residents after gentrification? 65 min. Available from FML.

SPEAKER SUGGESTIONS

1. A demographer to discuss global or national population trends.
2. A colleague who specializes in urban sociology to discuss current research in the field.

3. An urban planner from your city to talk about how long-range plans are developed.

POP QUIZ QUESTIONS

True-False

F 1. Sociologists have proven that the New Malthusian's projections of world growth trends are correct.

T 2. Conflict theorists believe that Western leaders' concerns about world population growth really are concerns about the balance of world power.

T 3. The amount of food produced for each person in the world has increased.

F 4. The main reason that people in poor nations have so many children is because they do not have effective contraceptives available to them.

T 5. Mexico's current population will double in 28 years.

T 6. Fecundity is the potential number of children that women are capable of bearing.

T 7. The growth rate declines in every country that industrializes.

T 8. Development of more efficient agriculture is essential to the development of cities.

F 9. Gemeinschaft societies are characterized by secondary, impersonal relationships.

T 10. Sociologists believe that urban dwellers divide the city into little worlds which they may come to know down to their smallest details.

ESSAY QUESTIONS

1. Analyze the arguments of Thomas Malthus, the New Malthusians and the Anti-Malthusians regarding whether the world is on a collision course with its food supply. Describe the majority problems caused by overpopulation.
2. Describe how demographers estimate population growth and note why they often make several projections of growth for the same group.

3. Trace the beginnings of world urbanization and of urbanization in the United States. Briefly describe the three major models which have been proposed to explain how cities expand.
4. Explain why alienation is a problem in large urban areas and discuss ways in which people attempt to develop community in the city.
5. Describe the future prospects for these cities.

CHAPTER
21

Collective Behavior and Social Movements

CHAPTER SUMMARY

Collective behavior is characterized by large numbers of people becoming emotionally aroused and engaging in extraordinary behavior, in which the usual norms do not apply. It includes violent acts—such as lynchings—and nonviolent acts—such as rumors, panics, fads, and fashions. Early explanations (such as the theories of Charles Mackay, Gustave LeBon, Robert Park, and Herbert Blumer) centered on some form of "madness" in which the individual was transformed by the crowd. Contemporary explanations (such as those of Ralph Turner and Lewis Killian, and Richard Berk) emphasize the rationality of the crowd and see collective behavior as directed toward a goal, even if it is cruel and destructive. Urban riots (such as the 1992 Los Angeles riot after the Rodney King verdict) are seen as being precipitated by a particular event, in a context of general social resentment and deprivation. Panics, rumors, fads, fashion and urban legends are also collective behavior. Social movements usually involve more people, are more prolonged, are more organized, and focus on social change. Four types of social movements, three levels of membership, and three publics of social movements are discussed. The life course of social movements is analyzed. Deprivation theory and mass society theory are used to explain why people join social movements. Resource mobilization theory accounts for why some social movements never get off the ground while others enjoy great success. Social movements seldom solve social problems because they focus on problems deeply embedded in society which do not lend themselves to easy solutions.

CHAPTER OUTLINE

Collective behavior is characterized by large numbers of people becoming emotionally aroused and engaging in extraordinary behavior, in which the usual norms do not apply.

I. Early Explanations: The Transformation of the Individual

A. In 1892, Charles Mackay concluded that when people were in crowds, they sometimes "went mad" and did "disgraceful and violent things;" just as a herd of cows will stampede, so people can come under the control of a "herd mentality."

B. Based on Mackay's idea, Gustave LeBon wrote *The Psychology of the Crowd,* stating that the individual is transformed by the crowd: In a crowd, people feel anonymous, not accountable for what they do; they develop feelings of invincibility, believing that together they can accomplish anything; their capacity for critical thought is swept away as they are caught up in the crowd's collective mind, making them highly suggestible; this paves the way for contagion—something like collective hypnosis—which releases the destructive instincts that society has so carefully repressed.

C. To LeBon's analysis, Robert Park added social unrest—which is transmitted from one individual to another; circular reaction is Park's term for the back-and-forth communication between the members of a crowd whereby a "collective impulse" is transmitted.

D. Using symbolic interaction theory and synthesizing both LeBon's and Park's ideas, Herbert Blumer identified five stages of collective behavior: (1) a background condition of social unrest—when people's routine activities are thwarted or when they develop new needs that go unsatisfied; (2) an exciting event occurs—one so startling that people become preoccupied with it; (3) people engage in milling—the act of standing or walking around as they talk about the exciting event—and circular reaction sets in; (4) a common object of attention emerges, and normal reasoning goes out the window as people get caught up in the collective excitement; (5) stimulation of the common impulses occurs as people's attention becomes fixed on certain ideas, and they attain a sense of collective agreement about what they should do. Social contagion—a collective excitement passed from one person to another—becomes the mechanism that stimulates these common impulses. The end result is an acting crowd—an excited group that collectively moves toward a goal, which may be constructive or destructive.

    E. Both LeBon and Blumer saw the crowd as transforming the individual, causing people to get so caught up in events that they no longer think and are vulnerable to suggestions that release their basest impulses; both analyses became highly influential and Blumer's analysis is used today in police manuals on crowd behavior.

II. The Contemporary View: The Rationality of the Crowd

    A. Critique of LeBon and Blumer: Contemporary sociologists stress that people are not transformed by the crowd into nonthinking beings but, rather, that people who commit even "cruel and destructive" acts need to be viewed as thinking people; rationality of the crowd becomes more visible when cultural options are factored into the analysis (e.g., when lynching was a cultural option in the South it was used; however, now that it is no longer a cultural option, mobs do not "go mad" and lynch people).

    B. Ralph Turner and Lewis Killian noted that human behavior is regulated by the normative order—socially approved ways of doing things that make up our everyday life—but when an extraordinary event occurs and existing norms do not cover the new situation, people develop new norms to deal with the problem (emergent norms). Five kinds of crowd participants are: the ego-involved—feel a high personal stake in the event, the concerned—have a personal interest in the event, but less than the ego-involved; the insecure—have little concern about the issue but have sought out the crowd because it gives them a sense of power and security; the curious spectators who are inquisitive and may cheer the crowd on even though they do not care about the issue; and the exploiters who do not care about the issue but use it for their own purposes (e.g., hawking food or T-shirts). The concept of emerging norms is important because it points to a rational process as the essential component of collective behavior.

    C. Richard Berk pointed out that people use a minimax strategy (trying to minimize their costs and maximize their rewards) whether in small groups or in crowds; the fewer the costs and the more rewards that people anticipate, the more likely they are to carry out a particular act.

    D. Examining a particular lynching, Clark McPhail concluded that the behavior was rational because kidnapping the accused was a well-planned event, and was an "invitational lynching"—the local media provided directions to the event. Based on that lynching, it is possible to conclude that people in crowds do things that they ordinarily would not do (they are encouraged by the support of others) but their activities are rationally coordinated in the attempt to reach whatever goals they set.

III. Other Forms of Collective Behavior

    A. The Los Angeles rioting which erupted after the verdict in the Rodney King trial demonstrates that urban riots are usually caused by frustration and anger at deprivation; frustration at being kept out of the mainstream society—limited to a meager education, denied jobs and justice, and kept out of good neighborhoods—builds to such a boiling point that it takes only a precipitating event to erupt in collective behavior; it is not only the deprived who participate in the riots, and the event that precipitates a riot is much less important than the riot's general context.

    B. The panic which occurred following the broadcast of H. G. Wells's *War of the Worlds* demonstrates that to anyone who is in a panic the situation is far from humorous. Panic is behavior that results when people become so fearful that they cannot function normally; this is why it is against the law to shout "Fire!" in a public building when no such danger exists—if people fear immediate death, they will lunge toward the nearest exit in a frantic effort to escape (e.g., the Beverly Hills Supper Club fire in Kentucky in 1977, in which 165 people died trying to get out of the two exits). Sociologists have found that not everyone panics in these situations, and some employees—such as some of those at the supper club—engage in role extension—the incorporation of additional activities into a role—to try to help people to safety.

    C. Rumors—information for which there is no discernible source and which is usually unfounded—are part of everyday life; they fill in missing information. People want to know about conditions that will have an impact on them, so when hard information is lacking, the void provides fertile ground for rumors. Larger work settings typically have rumors; however, in smaller settings, gossip—false, distorted, or blatantly untrue information of a more personal nature than a rumor—apparently serves the same purpose. Most rumors are short-lived and arise in a situation of ambiguity, only to dissipate when they are replaced either by another rumor or by factual information. A few rumors have a long life because they hit a responsive cord (e.g., rumors of mass poisoning of soft drink products that spread to many countries). Three main factors in why people believe rumors are that they: (1) deal with a subject that is important to an individual; (2) replace ambiguity with some form of certainty; and (3) are attributed to a creditable source.

    D. A fad is a temporary pattern of behavior that catches people's attention, while fashion is a more enduring version of the same. John Lofland identified four types of fads: object fads—such as the hula hoop or pet rocks; activity fads—such as eating goldfish or playing Trivial Pursuit; idea fads—such as astrology; and personality fads—such as Elvis Presley, Vanna White, and Michael Jordan. Fashion is a pattern of behavior that catches people's attention and which lasts longer than a fad. Most often thought of in terms of clothing fashions, it can also refer to hairstyles, home decorating, design and colors of buildings, and language.

    E. Urban legends are stories with an ironic twist that sound realistic but are false. Jan Brunvand, who studied the transmission of urban legends, concluded that: urban legends are passed on by people who think that the event happened to someone such as a "friend of a friend;" the stories have strong appeal and gain credibility from naming specific people or local places; and they are "modern morality stories," with each teaching a moral lesson about life.

Social movements involve unusual behavior, but usually involve more people, are more prolonged, are more organized, and focus on social change, as compared with collective behavior.

IV. Understanding Social Movements: The Case of the Nazis
  A. Social movements have six main characteristics: social unrest provides fertile ground for them; they express dissatisfaction with current conditions and promise something better; they are highly organized; they attract committed followers, including a core of "true believers; they attempt to change social conditions; and they potentially lead to extensive social change, even the transformation of society.
  B. The Nazis' development of the Third Reich and their belief that the Germans were a race of supermen is used to demonstrate how social movements get started and then take on a life of their own. Germany was in turmoil after World War I as a result of losing the war and financial chaos. Hitler promised to bring back prosperity and pride, to put people back to work, and to end hyperinflation, and the Nazis began to gain power. Hitler formed a secret organization within the Nazi party—the SS—which became the inner core of "true believers" who were assigned to carry out his dream of a pure Aryan nation. He built up an army, brought inflation under control, ended the breadline, and started the country on the road to prosperity. Laws were passed forbidding Aryans and Jews to intermarry, as well as forcing Jews out of government positions, teaching, and medicine; massive killings and internment in concentration camps was implemented in the name of racial purity. Few social movements in history have had as much impact as the Nazis did; the human destruction they perpetrated is mind-boggling. Not all social movements share these characteristics equally, and though few do so, social movements nevertheless have the potential to transform society—for good or for evil.
  C. Dehumanization is the process of reducing people to objects not deserving the treatment accorded humans. It involves four main characteristics: increased emotional distance from others; an emphasis on following orders; inability to resist pressures; and a diminished sense of responsibility. Symbolic interactionists stress that the essence of dehumanization is a label classifying people as less than human (e.g., the Nazis' use of labels was extremely effective). Today, war exalts treachery, bribery, and killings, and awarding medals to soldiers serves to glorify actions for which they would in other contexts be imprisoned.
  D. Propaganda, in its broad sense, is the presentation of information in the attempt to influence people; in its narrow sense, it is one-sided information used to try to influence people. It is used to influence public opinion—how people think about some issue—and is a regular part of modern life. Advertising is a type of propaganda, for it is not only an organized attempt to manipulate public opinion but also a one-sided presentation of information that distorts reality.

V. Breadth, Types and Tactics of Social Movements
  A. Social movements include such diverse activities as millenarian movements (based on the prophecy of coming social upheaval), the American civil rights movement of the 1960s, and the worldwide charismatic movement among Christians. Cargo cults—a social movement in which South Pacific islanders destroyed their possessions in the anticipation that their ancestors would send items by ship—are an interesting example of social movements.
  B. Many recent social movements are huge in scale and focus on broad concerns, some dealing with global matters.
  C. David Aberle classified social movements according to the type and amount of social change they seek. Of his four categories, two types seek to change people: alterative social movements seek to alter only particular aspects of people (e.g., the Women's Christian Temperance Union); while redemptive social movements seek to change people totally (e.g., a religious social movement that stresses conversion). Two types seek to change society: reformative social movements seek to reform only one part of society (e.g., animal rights or the environment); transformative social movements seek to change the social order itself and to replace it with their own version of the ideal society (e.g., revolutions in the American colonies, France, Russia, and Cuba).
  D. Tactics of social movements are best understood by examining levels of membership, publics they address, and their relationship to authorities. Three levels of membership are inner core (the leadership that sets goals, timetables, etc.); people committed to the goals of the movement, but not to the same degree as members of the inner core; and people who are neither as committed nor as dependable. Three types of publics are sympathetic (sympathize with goals of movement but have no commitment to movement), hostile (keenly aware of group's goals and want the movement stopped), and people who are unaware of or indifferent toward the movement. The movement's relationship to the authorities is important in determining tactics: If authorities are hostile to a social movement, aggressive or even violent tactics are likely; if authorities are sympathetic, violence is not likely; if a social movement is institutionalized, accepted by the authorities and given access to resources they control, the likelihood of violence is very low.
  E. Social movements have a life course, that is, they go through five stages as they grow and mature: (1) initial unrest and agitation; (2) mobilization (a relatively large number of people demand that something be done about the problem; leaders emerge during this stage); (3) organization (a division of labor with leadership that makes policy decisions and a rank and file that actively supports the movement); (4) institutionalization (as the movement becomes bureaucratized and leadership passes to career officials who may care more about their position in the organization than about the movement itself); and (5) organizational decline and possible

resurgence (some movements cease to exist; others become reinvigorated with new leadership from within or from coming into conflict with other social movements fighting for the opposite side of the issue—e.g., social movements relating to abortion).

VI. Why People Join Social Movements
  A. Deprivation Theory: People who are deprived of things deemed valuable in society—whether money, justice, status, or privilege—join social movements with the hope of redressing their grievances. This is a beginning point for looking at why people join social movements; however, it is even more important to look at relative deprivation theory—the belief that people join social movements based on their evaluations of what they think they should have compared with what others have. Absolute deprivation is peoples' actual negative condition; relative deprivation is what people think they should have relative to what others have, or even compared with their own past or perceived future. Improved conditions fuel human desires for even better conditions, and thus can spark revolutions.
  B. Mass Society Theory: William Kornhauser proposed mass society theory—based on the assumption that social movements offer a sense of belonging to people who have weak social ties. Mass society—an industrialized, highly bureaucratized, impersonal society—makes many people feel isolated and, as a result, they are attracted to social movements because they offer a sense of belonging. Doug McAdam (who studied those involved in civil rights movements) found, however, that many who participate in social movements have strong family and community ties, and joined such movements to right wrongs and overcome injustice, not because of isolation. The most isolated (the homeless) generally do not join anything—except food lines.

VII. The Success and Failure of Social Movements
  A. Resource mobilization—the mobilization of resources such as time, money, and people's skills—is a critical factor that enables social movements to make it past the first stage of agitation.
  B. Seldom do social movements actually solve problems because they find it necessary to appeal to a broad constituency and, to do so, they must focus on large-scale issues which are deeply embedded in society. Such broad problems do not lend themselves to easy or quick solutions; however, social movements make valuable contributions to solving problems, for they highlight areas of society to be changed.

LEARNING OBJECTIVES

After reading and studying Chapter 21, the student should be able to:

1. Discuss early explanations of collective behavior and note how these explanations focused on the transformation of the individual.
2. Contrast early explanations with contemporary theories about collective behavior.
3. Explain the emergent norm theory of Turner and Killian and the minimax strategy of Berk.
4. Discuss the question, "Can collective behavior really be rational?"
5. Describe other forms of collective behavior, including riots, panic, rumors, fads and fashions, and urban legends.
6. State the major reasons why social movements exist.
7. Identify the functions of dehumanization and propaganda in social movements.
8. List the four types of social movements, the three levels of membership found in such movements, and the three publics which each movement has.
9. Describe the characteristics of recent social movements and identify some of their major concerns.
10. Compare deprivation theory and mass society theory as explanations of why people join social movements.
11. State the key ingredients which contribute to the success or failure of social movements.

KEY TERMS

acting crowd
alternative social movement
cargo cult
circular reaction
collective behavior
collective mind
emergent norms
fad
fashion
gossip

mass society
mass-society theory
millenarian movement
milling
minimax strategy
normative order
panic
propaganda
public opinion
redemptive social movement

reformative social movement
relative social movement
relative deprivation theory
resource mobilization
riot
role extension
rumors
social movement
transformative social movement
urban legend

KEY PEOPLE

Charles Mackay
Robert Park
Ralph Turner and Lewis Killian
David Aberle

Gustave LeBon
Herbert Blumer
Richard Berk
William Kornhauser

CLASS DISCUSSION QUESTIONS

1. What examples can you think of where ordinary, law-abiding citizens have engaged in collective behavior of a violent nature?
2. Why do people often use "madness" or mental illness as an explanation for the behavior of others?
3. Have you ever been in a crowd which was transformed so that it did something its members normally would not do as individuals?
4. In your opinion, are people who engage in crowd behavior acting rationally or irrationally?
5. In what way is yelling for a referee's blood at a football game similar to shouting for real blood as a member of a lynch mob?
6. Do you think riots can be caused by media coverage of certain events? Why or why not?
7. What factors do you feel contribute to urban riots in the United States?
8. Why is it illegal to shout "Fire!" in a public building if no such danger exists?
9. How frequently do you hear rumors? Why are most rumors short-lived?
10. What examples can you give of current fads and fashions? How long do you think they will last?
11. Are you aware of urban legends in your hometown? On campus?
12. Have you participated in a social movement? Why do social movements exist?
13. Would you predict an increase in the number of social movements in the United States in the future? Why or why not?
14. Can you explain how the Nazis were successful in their takeover of Germany in spite of the fact that their actions seem so reprehensible today?
15. How successful do you think animal rights and environmental activist groups will be?
16. Why do you think people join social movements?
17. Do you think social movements actually solve problems? Why or why not?

PROJECTS

1. Attend a crowd gathering at your school or in the city. You may wish to go to a highly promoted rock or heavy-metal concert, a major sporting event, or some kind of protest or political rally. Keep notes on your observations about the number present, their appearance, what types of behavior occurred, and what the relationship is between what you see and what is discussed in this chapter. Discuss your observations in small groups, with the entire class, or in a written paper.
2. Analyze a current fad or fashion by going to a number of stores which specialize in the type of merchandise needed for the fad or fashion. To whom does the merchandise appeal? How is it marketed and advertised? Keep notes on your observations, and present your findings to the class.
3. Meet with a spokesperson for a social movement, such as animals rights or environmental activists. Find out about the pros and cons of the issues currently being discussed by the group. What types of changes do they hope to see take place? How do they get backers and new members? What tactics do they use? At what point in its life course is this particular social movement? Why would someone join this movement? Present your findings to the class or in a term paper.

VIDEOS/MOVIES

The Contemporary View: The Rationality of the Crowd

The Bonfire of the Vanities. 1990. (Color) Shows collective behavior as angry mobs demand that justice be done in the case of a wealthy, white Wall Street tycoon who is accused of seriously injuring a black youth in a hit-and-run automobile accident. (R) 125 min. Available at video rental stores.

CNN Video II. *Los Angeles Riots.*

Social Movements

Born on the Fourth of July. 1989. (Color) Starring Tom Cruise in the role of a real-life Vietnam veteran, who joined the Marines and came home from the Vietnam War paralyzed. After he got over his medical ordeal, he became an anti-war activist and led a social movement protesting the war. (R) 144 min. Available at video rental stores.

King: A Filmed Record . . . Montgomery to Memphis. 1970. (Black/White) Documents the social movement led by Dr. Martin Luther King from 1955 until his death in 1968. A compilation of news footage. 153 min. Available at some video rental stores.

Norma Rae. 1979. (Color) A New York City labor organizer is gradually successful in getting Norma Rae, played by Sally

Field, to see the benefits of unionization. Depicts a social movement to get better wages for workers in a textile mill in the South. (PG) 113 min. Available at video rental stores.

Those Who Know Don't Tell. 1991. Documents the history of the struggle to rid the workplace of occupational hazards, and uses union songs and interviews to tell the story of labor activists and those within the medical profession who became their advocates. Describes the social movement which pressed for occupational safety. 29 min. Available from FML.

SPEAKER SUGGESTIONS

1. University or city police officers who are responsible for crowd control to discuss their methods.
2. A colleague who has conducted research on riots, such as the Los Angeles riot of 1992.
3. A spokesperson for a social movement on your campus or in your community. [If you choose to have abortion discussed, you may wish to have both sides presented, but on separate days.]

POP QUIZ QUESTIONS

True-False

T 1. When people can't figure something out, they often resort to some form of "madness" as the explanation.

F 2. Collective behavior often arises without any forewarning or previous social unrest.

F 3. Contemporary sociologists state that people who commit cruel and destructive acts are nonthinking, irrational people.

F 4. The precipitating event is the most important factor in explaining why riots occur.

T 5. Sociologists who have studied panics found that many people continue to perform their roles during the panics.

F 6. Social movements involve fewer people and less organization than collective behavior.

F 7. Most social movements are organized for evil purposes.

F 8. Propaganda always is assumed to involve lies and distortions.

T 9. Some social movements set out to change people, while others want to change society.

T 10. Relative deprivation theory is based on what people *think* they should have relative to others.

ESSAY QUESTIONS

1. Compare and contrast the theories of Mackay, LeBon, Park, and Blumer on collective behavior.
2. Describe contemporary theories of collective behavior, especially those of Turner and Killian, and Berk. Explain why they believe that collective behavior is rational.
3. Discuss riots, panic, rumors, fads and fashions, and urban legends as different types of collective behavior.
4. Explain why social movements exist, and describe the role of dehumanization and propaganda in these movements.
5. Describe the seven propaganda techniques and analyze the extent to which these techniques are used in advertising today.
6. List and briefly discuss the types of social movements and the reasons why people join social movements.

C H A P T E R

22

Social Change, Technology, and the Environment

CHAPTER SUMMARY

Social change, the alteration of culture and society over time, is a vital part of social life. Social change has included four social revolutions; the change from *Gemeinschaft* to *Gesellschaft* society; the transformation of society by capitalism; and the impact of industrialization on the Third World and on social institutions in the United States. Theories of social change include: evolutionary theories, cyclical theories, conflict theories, and modernization. William Ogburn's processes of social change are innovation, discovery, and diffusion. There are four types of technology: primitive, industrial, postindustrial, and a new technology still to emerge. Technology is a driving force in social change, and it can shape an entire society by changing existing technology, social organization, ideology, values, and social relationships. Effects of the automobile and the computer on American society are analyzed. Major concerns about the computer focus on the potential for its abuse—for the invasion of privacy, the integration of misinformation into computerized records, and as an instrument for social control. Social change and the natural environment are explored in terms of environmental degradation in the past, environmental problems in the First, Second and Third World countries, the environmental movement, and environmental sociology. Harmony between technology and the natural environment is now needed.

CHAPTER OUTLINE

I. A Review of Social Change
    A. Social change is the alteration of culture and societies over time. There have been four social revolutions: the domestication of plants and animals, from which pastoral and horticultural societies arose; the invention of the plow, leading to agricultural societies; the industrial revolution; and now the information revolution, resulting in postindustrial societies.
    B. This has been accompanied by a change from *Gemeinschaft* (daily life centers on intimate and personal relationships) to *Gesellschaft* (people have fleeting, impersonal relationships) societies.
    C. Karl Marx identified capitalism as the basic reason behind the change in traditional societies. He focused his analysis on the means of production (factories, machinery, tools): those who owned them dictated the conditions under which workers would work and live. Max Weber saw religion as the core reason for the development of capitalism: as a result of the Reformation, Protestants no longer felt assured that they were saved by virtue of church membership and concluded that God would show visible favor to the elect. This belief encouraged Protestants to work hard and be thrifty. An economic surplus resulted, stimulating industrialization.

    D. Technological changes have led to new understandings of disease and the export of Western medicine to Third World nations, bringing them to the second stage of the demographic transition—reduced death rates but continuing high birth rates. Rapidly increasing populations strain Third World resources, leading to widespread hunger and starvation. Masses of peasants around the world are fleeing to urban areas; now almost half of the world's population lives in urban areas—most in squalor.
    E. A world system began to emerge in the 16th century, and in the 18th and 19th centuries, capitalism and industrialization extended the economic and political ties among the world's nations. Today, these ties are global, yielding a form of international stratification in which the industrialized countries of the First World dominate all the others. Dependency theory asserts that because the Third World countries have become dependent on the First World, they are unable to develop their own resources.
    F. Alignments between nations must shift to accommodate changing realities. The new world order will build on the current system of international stratification. The world's industrial giants (the United States, Canada, Great Britain, France, Germany, Italy, and Japan) are intent on deciding how they will share the world's markets, and on regulating

global economic and industrial policy to guarantee their own dominance, including continued access to cheap raw materials from the Second and Third Worlds. Even so, these industrial giants are feeling pressure to promote economic growth in the Third World.

G. Industrialized societies change so fast that life today bears few similarities to life 100 years ago. Social change has transformed social institutions in the United States: the family has grown more fragile, modern medicine and hospitals have changed radically, new religions have arisen and old ones splintered, and fundamental changes have occurred in gender relations, in racial and ethnic relations, and in attitudes toward the elderly.

II. Theories of Social Change

A. Evolutionary theories are unilinear or multilinear. Unilinear theories assume that all societies follow the same path, evolving from simple to complex through uniform sequences; however, these theories have been discredited, and seeing one's own society as the top of the evolutionary ladder is now considered unacceptably ethnocentric. Multilinear theories assume that different routes can lead to a similar stage of development, thus, societies need not pass through the same sequence of stages to become industrialized. Both unilinear and multilinear theories assume the idea of progress—that societies evolve toward a higher state—however, because of the crises in Western culture today, the assumption of progress has been cast aside and evolutionary theories have been rejected.

B. Cyclical theories examine great civilizations, not a particular society; they presume that societies are like organisms—they are born, reach adolescence, grow old, and die. Arnold Toynbee proposed the life course of civilizations: at first, they are able to meet challenges, yet when a civilization has become an empire, the ruling elite loses its capacity to keep the masses in line "by charm rather than by force," and the fabric of society is then ripped apart. Pitirim Sorokin proposed that civilizations can be distinguished by how they define the nature of reality: ideational (stresses faith and spirituality) or sensate (presuming reality to be located in "things" that are apparent to the mind) culture. Oswald Spengler proposed that Western civilization was on the wane; some analysts think the crisis in Western civilization may indicate he was right.

C. Marx viewed social change as a dialectical process—in which a thesis (the status quo) contains its own antithesis (opposition), and the resulting struggle between the thesis and its antithesis leads to a new state or synthesis. Thus, the history of a society is a series of confrontations in which each ruling group creates the seeds of its own destruction (e.g., capitalism sets workers and capitalists on a collision course).

D. Modernization (the change from agricultural to industrial societies) produces sweeping changes in societies. Modern societies are larger, more urbanized, and subject to faster change. They stress formal education and the future and are less religiously oriented. They have smaller families, lower rates of infant mortality, and higher life expectancy; they have higher incomes and

more material possessions. The transition to the postindustrial era seems to be leading toward a new type of society that rejects much of what modern society takes for granted.

III. Social Change and Technology

A. William Ogburn identified three processes of social change: (1) inventions, which can be either material (computers) or social (capitalism); (2) discovery, which is a new way of seeing things; and (3) diffusion—the spread of an invention or discovery from one area to another. Ogburn coined the term cultural lag to describe the situation in which some elements of a culture adapt to an invention or discovery more rapidly than others.

B. There are three types of technology: primitive (adaptation of natural items for human use); industrial (uses machines powered by fuels); and postindustrial (centers on information, transportation, and communication).

C. Five ways in which technology can shape an entire society are:

1. Transformation of existing technologies (e.g., the computer is rendering the typewriter practically obsolete).

2. Changes in social organization (e.g., introduction of factories changed the nature of work: people gathered in one place to do their work, were given specialized tasks, and became responsible for only part of an item, not the entire item).

3. Changes in ideology (e.g., just as changes in technology stimulated the development of communism, changes in technology are bringing about its end).

4. Transformation of values (e.g., if technology is limited to clubbing animals, strength and cunning are valued; if technology requires abstract thought, abstract thought is valued).

5. Transformation of social relationships (e.g., as men went to work in the factories, family relationships changed; as more women work outside the home, family relationships again are changing).

D. The automobile is an example of technological change. The automobile has pushed aside old technology (the horse and buggy); it has changed the shape of cities; it has changed rural life, providing farmers a better lifestyle but drying up old villages; it has changed architecture (drive-up windows, etc.); it has changed courtship practices and sexual norms; and it has had a major effect on the lives of women, giving them the opportunity to "go shopping" and exert greater control over the family budget.

E. The computer is another example, changing education, medicine, the military and war, the workplace, and personal relations between people. Shoshana Zuboff found that computerization of the workplace makes personal relationships less important, and gives managers greater ability for surveillance of workers without depending on face-to-face supervision. Computers also have resulted in "deskilling," reducing the skills necessary to do a job (e.g., a master baker who is replaced by an unskilled employee who needs only to press a button to start the mixing process).

F. Concerns about computers include loss of jobs (for some

jobs, computers are better than people), invasion of privacy (privacy is threatened by the vast amounts of personal information stored in computers); and the use which individuals, corporations, and even the government make of the information so stored.

G. Telecommunications have contributed to the shrinking of the world—in both space and time. National boundaries mean nothing to telecommunications, and information can no longer be contained: even during the Tiananmen Square massacre in Beijing, Chinese students faxed reports to Americans, and telecommunications was one of the many factors that contributed to the collapse of the Soviet empire.

IV. Social Change and the Natural Environment

A. Environmental degradation did not begin with industrialization: some early civilizations actually destroyed themselves by ignorant treatment of the environment. Examples include the Mesopotamian civilization and the great Mayan civilization of Central America.

B. Environmental problems today include: (1) depletion of the ozone layer; (2) acid rain (burning fossil fuels releases sulfur dioxide and nitrogen oxide, which react with moisture in the air to become sulfuric and nitric acid); (3) the greenhouse effect (buildup of carbon dioxide in the earth's atmosphere, allowing light to enter but inhibiting the release of heat) believed to cause (4) global warming (which may melt the polar ice caps, inundate the world's shorelines, cause climate boundaries to move about 400 miles north, and make many animal and plant species extinct); (5) clearing of tropical rain forests for lumber, farms, and pastures resulting in the extinction of numerous animal and plant species; and (6) the threat of nuclear pollution through accidents or nuclear attack.

C. Pollution was treated as a state secret in the former Soviet Union. With protest stifled, no environmental protection laws to inhibit pollution, and production quotas to be met, environmental pollution was rampant. For the most part, the protests which occurred after dissolution of the Soviet Union fell on deaf ears, and pollution continues because of the Second World's rush to compete industrially with the West, the desire to improve its standard of living, and the lack of funds to purchase expensive pollution controls.

D. The combined pressures of population growth and almost nonexistent environmental regulations destine the Third World to become the earth's major source of pollution. Some First World companies use Third World countries as a garbage dump for hazardous wastes and for producing chemicals no longer tolerated in their own countries.

E. Concern about the world's severe environmental problems has produced a worldwide social movement. In some countries, the environment has become a major issue in local and national elections (e.g., Germany, Great Britain, and Switzerland). This movement often transcends social class, gender, and race, and generally seeks solutions in education, legislation, and political activism.

F. Environmental sociology examines the relationship between human societies and the environment. Its basic assumptions include: (1) the physical environment is a significant variable in sociological investigation; (2) humans are but one species among many that are dependent on the environment; (3) because of intricate feedbacks to nature, human actions have many unintended consequences; (4) the world is finite, so there are potential physical limits to economic growth; (5) economic expansion requires increased extraction of resources from the environment; (6) increased extraction of resources leads to ecological problems; (7) these ecological problems place restrictions on economic expansion; and (8) the state creates environmental problems by trying to create conditions for the profitable accumulation of capital.

G. If we are to have a world that is worth passing on to the coming generations, we must seek harmony between technology and the natural environment. As a parallel to development of technologies, we must develop a greater awareness of their harmful effects on the planet, systems of control giving more weight to reducing technologies' harm to the environment than to lowering costs, and mechanisms to enforce rules for the production, use, and disposal of technology.

LEARNING OBJECTIVES

After reading and studying Chapter 22, the student should be able to:

1. Describe the four major social revolutions which have occurred.

2. Explain evolutionary and cyclical theories of social change, and note why these theories generally are not considered to be useful today.

3. State the major assumptions of conflict and modernization theories regarding social change.

4. Identify and define Ogburn's three processes of social change, and explain what is meant by "cultural lag."

5. Using the automobile or the computer as an example, explain how technology transforms society.

6. State the major concerns about computers.

7. Describe ways in which telecommunications has created global social change.

8. Discuss the environmental degradation which has occurred in the past and note the extent of environmental problems today.

9. Describe the environmental problems of the Second and Third World countries. State ways in which First World countries may have contributed to these problems.

10. Discuss the goals and activities of the environmental movement.

11. List the assumptions of environmental sociology.

12. Describe some of the actions which would be necessary to reach the goal of harmony between technology and the environment.

KEY TERMS

acid rain
alienation
diffusion
discovery
environmental sociology

greenhouse effect
industrial technology
invention
job deskilling
job multiskilling

new technology
postindustrial technology
primitive technology
social change
technology

KEY PEOPLE

Pitirim Sorokin
Karl Marx
William Ogburn
Celene Krauss

Oswald Spengler
Max Weber
Shoshana Zuboff

CLASS DISCUSSION QUESTIONS

1. Have you had specific times when you found yourself hoping that technology "really works?" For example, when you are boarding an airplane or entering a hospital for surgery?
2. Do you have a better grasp of how social change occurs in society as a result of taking this course?
3. Does social change usually produce progress in societies?
4. How do you think technology will change society in the future?
5. Can you give examples of recent inventions, discoveries, and diffusion in the United States?
6. Do you think cultural lag is a major problem in the United States? Why or why not?
7. Using television as an example, can you explain how technology has had a great impact on social life?
8. Do you think computers ultimately will make our lives easier or more complicated? Why?
9. Is today's concern with the environment a passing fad or will this issue become a focal point in the 21st century? Why?
10. In your opinion, is it possible for there to be harmony between technology and the environment? Why or why not?

PROJECTS

1. Explore in greater depth the relationship between social change and technology. You may wish to select a specific type of technology and analyze possible consequences. For example, look at the impact of robotics on society. One researcher is programming robots to deliver meal trays to hospital patients and pick them up when the person has finished. (What effect does this have on employees at the hospital? On the patients?) Or focus on the depiction of futuristic worlds in which technology prevails over humans as shown in motion pictures. Present your findings in small group or class discussions or in the form of a term paper.
2. For small group discussion, analyze what your life would be like without technology such as telephones, computers, cars, airplanes, etc. Suppose you still had all of the statuses and responsibilities you currently have, but not have technology. Would it be possible to fulfill all of your obligations?
3. If you have been in a position that involved working with machines more than with people, you may wish to do an analysis of how that position affected you personally. In what way is working with machines different from working with other people? To help you prepare for a presentation or paper, you may wish to read: Zuboff, Shoshana. *In the Age of the Smart Machine: The Future of Work and Power.* 1988. New York: Basic Books. Write a paper explaining the tasks involved in your position and the social and psychological aspects of that type of work.
4. Collect data on environmental activist groups on your campus and in your city. What types of issues are they most interested in? How do they go about making their beliefs known to elected officials? How do they recruit new members and donors to their cause? Present your findings to the class or in a paper.

TRANSPARENCIES

1. (TR#50) A Typology of Traditional and Modern Societies

VIDEOS/MOVIES

Social Change and Technology

Robocop. 1987. (Color) This futurist movie depicts a police officer in Detroit who is killed in the line of duty and then transformed into an ultrasophisticated cyborg by the corporation which now runs the police department. He seeks revenge on the people who killed him. Shows a view of life in the future which is pretty bleak and ugly. (R) 103 min. Available at video rental stores.

Robocop 2. 1990. (Color) In this sequel to *Robocop,* the cold-blooded corporate czar and drug kingpin attempts to end Robocop's existence while a better cyborg cop is being made to take its place. (R) Available at video rental stores.

Westworld. 1973. (Color) In this adult vacation resort of the future, robots wait on everyone until one of the robots malfunctions and chaos reigns supreme. (PG) 88 min. Available at some video rental stores.

Futureworld. 1976. (Color) In this sequel to *Westworld,* the robots continue to try to take over. (PG) 104 min. Available at some video rental stores.

The Terminator. 1984. (Color) A cyborg is sent here from the future to kill a seemingly innocent woman. (R) 108 min. Available at video rental stores.

Terminator 2: Judgment Day. 1991. (Color) In this sequel to *The Terminator,* the cyborg from the future returns to protect the savior of humanity from another terminator. (R) 136 min. Available at video rental stores.

Social Change and the Natural Environment

Environment at Issue. 1992. Discusses potentially devastating environmental problems faced by Americans, including acid rain, depletion of the ozone layer, global warming, and smog. Also looks at the heated debate over environmental action now occurring in this country and analyzes the debate over environmental legislation in southern California. 22 min. Available from FML.

The China Syndrome. 1979. (Color) Starring Jane Fonda, Jack Lemmon, and Michael Douglas, this movie depicts an attempted cover-up of an accident at a California nuclear plant. (PG) 123 min. Available at video rental stores.

Environmental Problems in the Second World

Black Triangle. 1992. The "black triangle," the corner of eastern Europe where Poland, Czechoslovakia and East Germany meet, is Europe's most polluted region. East Germany has Europe's biggest concentration of uranium mines outlined by slag heaps which loom over local towns. In northern Czechoslovakia vast open coal mines stretch as far as the eye can see. Power stations emit thick sulphurous smoke, defoliating the forests. With the relaxation of government controls in the East bloc, the miners and local residents are able to express their opposition to dangerous practices for the first time. 52 min. Available from FML.

Environmental Problems in the Third World

Halting the Fires. 1991. The Brazilian government, through Operation Amazon, has been supporting exploitation of natural resources. Many destructive activities, such as cattle ranching, are not economically viable without the subsidies the government provides. The film focuses on ranchers, miners, rubber tappers, loggers, and others whose activities affect the environment. 52 min. Available from FML.

South Africa: The Wasted Land. 1991. Documents the link between South Africa's Apartheid policy and its rapidly eroding environment. Severe overcrowding of its black population into the barely life-sustaining "homeland" areas has caused the land to be over-grazed and severely eroded. Because the homelands are deprived of electricity, trees are cut for fuel, leaving the soil more vulnerable to erosion. The black homelands have been the dumping grounds for toxic waste. When asbestos mines were closed in the seventies, they were not properly sealed. Now black families live in the midst of poisonous waste. 52 min. Available from FML.

The Environmental Movement

CNN Video II. *Toxic Battle.* In a small farming town near Los Angeles, California, residents (mostly Mexican-American migrant workers) protest plans to place a giant toxic waste incinerator 5 miles outside of town. Jesse Jackson charges the chemical waste company with environmental racism. In one of several attempts to block the incinerator, a lawsuit is filed against the company, alleging that the civil rights of the Spanish-speaking residents have been violated because public information about the project was disseminated only in English. The company counters that "pollution doesn't discriminate." Available from A&B Video Library.

The Energy Alternative Series: A Global Perspective. 1991. Series investigates innovative solutions to prevent worldwide ecological disaster. Includes *Changing the Way the World Works,* which concentrates on how less energy can be used to give the world's consumers the things they want; *The Rich Get Richer,* which focuses on tough, innovative laws and fresh initiatives worldwide which help contain energy consumption and pollution; and *Power to the People,* which focuses on the developing world where the energy debate is carried on against a background of grinding poverty. 52 min. each. Available from FML.

CNN Video II. *Earth First.* Start 1:12:04 end 1:14:22. Profile of Earth First, a militant environmental group, including its founder Dave Foreman. Focuses on government charges against Foreman and four associates that they conspired to sabotage nuclear plants; the government also charged the group with damaging ski lifts and sawing through power poles. Earth First claims that the government is trying to silence the movement. Available from A&B Video Library.

SPEAKER SUGGESTIONS

1. A colleague whose research has involved social change in various types of societies.
2. An expert from the computer science department or from a local high tech industry to talk about computers of the future.
3. An environmental specialist such as a person with the Environmental Protection Agency or the Occupational Safety and Health Agency to discuss environmental concerns and work hazards in your city or state. If your college or university has

an official designated to deal with hazardous waste on campus, etc., you may wish to have this person meet with your class.
4. A spokesperson for an environmental activist group on campus or in your city to talk about local issues and how they are working with the administration or governmental agencies to deal with these concerns.
5. A colleague whose area of specialization is environmental sociology.

POP QUIZ QUESTIONS

True-False

T   1. Attempts are underway to create a new world order based on the current system of international stratification.

T   2. Evolutionary theories are based on the idea that societies evolve toward a higher state.

F   3. Max Weber viewed social change as a dialectical process.

T   4. Invention is the combination of existing elements and materials to form new ones.

F   5. Industrial societies are based on information, transportation, and communication.

T   6. The automobile shifted basic values and changed the way people look at life.

F   7. Computers are likely to bring about "teacherless" classrooms and "doctorless" medicine in the future.

T   8. Job deskilling occurs when machines tell workers what to do.

F   9. Environmental degradation first occurred at the beginning of industrialization.

F   10. Environmental sociologists study environmental problems but are not environmental activists.

ESSAY QUESTIONS

1. Describe the four social revolutions and explain the consequences of these revolutions on people.
2. Compare and contrast earlier theories of social change, including evolutionary and cyclical theories, with conflict and modernization theories.
3. Discuss the relationship between social change and technology in society. Give specific examples of how a new technology can change many aspects of the lives of people.
4. Outline some of the major issues involving the environment today. Look at the problem from the standpoint of First, Second, and Third World countries, and explain why environmental issues must be viewed as a global concern.
5. Describe the activities of the environmental movement and of environmental sociologists in regard to seeking harmony between technology and the natural environment.

Appendix

VIDEO DISTRIBUTORS

Allyn & Bacon Video Library (A&B Video Library)
160 Gould Street
Needham Heights, MA 02194-2310

British Broadcasting Company (BBC)
630 Fifth Avenue
New York, NY 10020

Churchill Films (CF)
662 North Robertson Blvd.
Los Angeles, CA 90069

Films for the Humanities & Sciences (FHS)
P. O. Box 2053
Princeton, NJ 08543-2053

Films, Inc. (FI)
1213 Wilmette Avenue
Wilmette, IL 60091

Filmmakers Library, Inc. (FML)
124 East 40th Street, Suite 901
New York, NY 10016

Harper and Row Media
Harper/Collins Publishers, Inc.
10 East 53rd Street
New York, NY 10022

PBS Video
475 L'Enfant Plaza, SW
Washington, DC 20024

SOCIOLOGY

A Down-to-Earth Approach

James M. Henslin

Southern Illinois University, Edwardsville

Allyn and Bacon

Boston   London   Toronto   Sydney   Tokyo   Singapore

Editor in Chief Social Sciences: Susan Badger
Senior Editor: Karen Hanson
Developmental Editor: Hannah Rubenstein
Series Editorial Assistant: Marnie Greenhut
Editorial-Production Service: Susan McNally
Text Designer: Glenna Collett
Copyeditor: Deborah Fogel
Photo Research: Sharon Donahue
Cover Administrator: Linda Dickinson
Composition Buyer: Linda Cox
Manufacturing Buyer: Megan Cochran

Allyn and Bacon
A Division of Simon & Schuster, Inc.
160 Gould Street
Needham Heights, Massachusetts 02194

Credits

Chapter 1: *Early Ocean Park,* 1976 by Jane Golden from *The Big Picture: Murals of Los Angeles.* Photographs by Melba Levick, Commentaries by Stanley Young. Copyright © 1988 by Thames and Hudson Ltd., London. By permission of Little, Brown and Company.

Chapter 2: *Thanksgiving,* 1972 by Malcah Zeldis. Oil on board, 18 × 24″. Photo courtesy of the artist.

Chapter 3: *Wrapping it Up at the Lafayette,* 1974 by Romare Bearden (1914–1990), American, collage, acrylic, lacquer, 122 × 91.5 cm. The Cleveland Museum of Art, Mr. & Mrs. William H. Marlatt Fund, 85.41. Courtesy Estate of Romare Bearden.

Chapter 4: *Subway Graffiti, Quilt #3,* 1987 by Faith Ringgold. Acrylic paint on canvas with pieced, printed, dyed fabric, 60 × 84″ © Faith Ringgold. Collection of the artist.

Chapter 5: *The Making of a Fresco/The Building of a City Fresco,* 1931 by Diego Rivera (1886–1957), Mexican. San Francisco Art Institute. Photograph by Don Beatty © 1983.

Chapter 6: *Quilting Time,* 1986 by Romare Bearden, (1914–1990), American. Mosaic tesserae, 289 × 425 × 318 cm. © The Detroit Institute of Arts, Founders Society. Purchase with funds from the Detroit Edison Company. Courtesy Estate of Romare Bearden.

Chapter 7: *Sign of the Watchmaker* from the Girard Foundation Collection in the Museum of International Folk Art, a unit of the Museum of New Mexico.

Chapter 8: *Tie Cez,* 1977 by Red Grooms. Mixed media, 46 × 46 × 9″. Collection Nancy & Alan Saturn, Nashville, TN © 1992 ARS, New York.

Chapter 9: *The Flower Carrier,* 1935 by Diego Rivera. Oil and tempera on masonite, 48 × 47¾″. San Francisco Museum of Modern Art. Albert M. Bender Collection. Gift of Albert M. Bender in memory of Caroline Walter.

Chapter 10: *Living Room,* 1981 by Red Grooms. Oil on canvas, 28 × 44″. Collection of Red Grooms, New York © 1992 ARS, New York.

Chapter 11: *Piero Letters,* 1991 by Alan Feltus. Oil on linen. Courtesy Forum Gallery, New York.

Chapter 12: *Wedding,* 1973 by Malcah Zeldis. Oil on board, 23 × 27″. Photo courtesy of the artist.

Chapter 13: *Mecklenburg Morning,* 1987 by Romare Bearden. Collage and watercolor, 15 × 23″. Courtesy Estate of Romare Bearden and ACA Galleries, New York.

Chapter 14: *Builders,* 1980 by Jacob Lawrence. Gouache on paper, 34¼ × 25⅜″. Courtesy Safeco Insurance Company, Seattle. Photograph by Chris Eden.

Chapter 15: *Miss Liberty Celebration,* 1987 by Malcah Zeldis. Oil on corrugated cardboard, 54½ × 36½″. National Museum of American Art, Washington, D.C., Art Resource, New York.

Chapter 16: *Tar Beach,* 1988 by Faith Ringgold. Acrylic paint on canvas with pieced tie-dyed fabric, 74 × 68½″. © Faith Ringgold. Collection of Guggenheim Museum.

Chapter 17: *School Bell Time,* by Romare Bearden. Courtesy Estate of Romare Bearden and Kingsborough Community College, City University of New York, Brooklyn, New York.

Chapter 18: *Oracion,* 1989 by Orlando Agudelo-Botero. Multi-media on papier d'Arches, 29 × 41″. Courtesy of Engman International.

Chapter 19: *Shaman,* 1979 by Frank Howell. Photograph courtesy of The Studio of Frank Howell, Santa Fe, New Mexico.

Chapter 20: *Black Manhattan,* 1969 by Romare Bearden. Collage on paper and synthetic polymer on board, 25⅜ × 21″. Schomburg Center for Research in Black Culture, Arts & Artifacts Division, The New York Public Library, Astor Lenox and Tilden Foundations. Photograph by Frank Stewart. Courtesy Estate of Romare Bearden.

Chapter 21: *Dialogo de los Sordos* by Orlando Agudelo-Botero. Multi-media painting on papier d'Arches. Courtesy of Engman International.

Chapter 22: *Calypso's Sacred Grove,* 1977 by Romare Bearden from the *Odysseus Collages.* Collage on board, 12 × 15″. Israel Museum, Jerusalem. Courtesy Estate of Romare Bearden.

Continued on page xvi

ISBN 0-205-13754-7   92-41575
                            CIP

Printed in the United States of America

10 9 8 7 6 5 4 3 2 1   97 96 95 94 93 92

Brief Contents

PART I   THE SOCIOLOGICAL PERSPECTIVE

1 The Sociological Perspective   *1*
2 Culture   *30*
3 Socialization   *56*
4 Social Structure and Social Interaction: Macrosociology and Microsociology   *86*
5 How Sociologists Do Research   *112*

PART II   SOCIAL GROUPS AND SOCIAL CONTROL

6 Social Groups: Societies to Social Networks   *138*
7 Bureaucracy and Formal Organizations   *164*
8 Deviance and Social Control   *190*

PART III   SOCIAL INEQUALITY

9 Stratification in Global Perspective   *218*
10 Social Class in American Society   *246*
11 Inequalities of Gender   *278*
12 Inequalities of Race and Ethnicity   *308*
13 Inequalities of Age   *342*

PART IV   SOCIAL INSTITUTIONS

14 The Economy: Money and Work   *370*
15 Politics: Power and Authority   *400*
16 The Family: Our Introduction to Society   *428*
17 Education: Transferring Knowledge and Skills   *464*
18 Religion: Establishing Meaning   *494*
19 Medicine: Health and Illness   *526*

PART V   SOCIAL CHANGE

20 Population and Urbanization   *558*
21 Collective Behavior and Social Movements   *590*
22 Social Change, Technology, and the Environment   *626*

Contents

████████████████████ **PART I**   **THE SOCIOLOGICAL PERSPECTIVE** ████████████████████

1   **The Sociological Perspective**   **1**

The Sociological Perspective   **2**
Seeing the Broader Social Context
Sociology and the Other Sciences   **4**
The Natural Sciences ■ The Social Sciences ■ The Goals of Science
▓ *Down-to-Earth Sociology:* An Updated Version of the Old Elephant Story   *6*
The Development of Sociology   **7**
▓ *Down-to-Earth Sociology:* Enjoying a Sociological Quiz: Sociological Findings versus Common Sense   *7*
Auguste Comte ■ Herbert Spencer ■ Karl Marx ■ Emile Durkheim ■ Max Weber
The Role of Values in Social Research   **12**
Verstehen and Social Facts   **13**
Weber and Verstehen ■ Durkheim and Social Facts ■ How Social Facts and Verstehen Fit Together
Sociology in North America   **15**
Theoretical Perspectives in Sociology   **16**
Symbolic Interactionism ■ Functional Analysis ■ Conflict Theory ■ Levels of Analysis: Macro and Micro ■ Putting the Theoretical Perspectives Together
Applied and Clinical Sociology   **25**
▓ *Perspectives:* Sociology in a World of Turmoil   *26*
Summary   *27*
Suggested Readings   *28*

2   **Culture**   **30**

What Is Culture?   **32**
Culture and Taken-for-Granted Orientations to Life ■ Practicing Cultural Relativism

Components of Culture   **35**
▓ *Down-to-Earth Sociology:* Communicating across Cultural Boundaries   *36*
The Symbolic Basis of Culture ■ Language
▓ *Perspectives:* Miami—Language and a Changing City   *39*
Gestures ■ Values, Norms, and Sanctions ■ Folkways and Mores
Subcultures and Countercultures   **41**
Values in American Society   **42**
▓ *Perspectives:* Why Do Native Americans Like Westerns?   *44*
Value Clusters ■ Value Contradictions and Social Change ■ Emergent Values ■ Reactions to Changes in Core Values ■ Values as Blinders ■ "Ideal" versus "Real" Culture
Cultural Universals   **47**
▓ *Thinking Critically about Social Controversy:* Are We Prisoners of Our Genes?   *48*
Animals and Culture   **49**
Do Animals Have Language?
Cultural Diffusion and Cultural Leveling   **53**
Summary   *54*
Suggested Readings   *55*

3   **Socialization**   **56**

What is Human Nature?   **58**
Feral Children ■ Isolated Children
▓ *Down-to-Earth Sociology:* Heredity or Environment? The Case of Oskar and Jack, Identical Twins   *59*
Institutionalized Children ■ Deprived Animals ■ Bringing It All Together

iv

The Social Development of the Self, Mind, and Emotions *63*
Cooley and the Looking-Glass Self ■ Mead and Role Taking ■ Piaget and the Development of Thinking ■ Freud and the Subconscious ■ The Sequential Development of Emotions ■ Socialization into Emotions ■ The Self and Emotions as Social Constraints on Behavior

Socialization into Gender *70*
Gender, the Family, and Sex-Linked Behaviors ■ Gender Images in the Mass Media

Agents of Socialization *73*
■ *Perspectives:* Manhood in the Making *74*
The Family ■ Religion ■ The School ■ Peer Groups
■ *Perspectives:* Caught Between Two Worlds *77*
The Mass Media ■ The Workplace

Resocialization *79*
Involuntary Resocialization: Total Institutions ■ Voluntary Resocialization

Socialization Through the Life Course *80*
The Life Course ■ Distinctive Life-Course Patterns

Are We Prisoners of Socialization? *84*

Summary *85*

Suggested Readings *85*

4   Social Structure and Social Interaction: Macrosociology and Microsociology *86*

Levels of Sociological Analysis *88*
Macrosociology and Microsociology

Social Structure: The Macrosociological Perspective *89*
■ *Down-to-Earth Sociology:* College Football as Social Structure *90*
Culture ■ Social Class ■ Social Status ■ Roles ■ Groups

Social Institutions *95*
Changes in Social Structure ■ What Holds Society Together?

The Microsociological Perspective: Social Interaction in Everyday Life *99*
■ *Perspectives:* The Amish—*Gemeinschaft* Communities in a *Gesellschaft* Society *100*
Symbolic Interaction ■ Dramaturgy: The Presentation of Self in Everyday Life ■ Ethnomethodology: Discovering Background Assumptions ■ The Social Construction of Reality

The Need for Both Microsociology and Macrosociology *109*

Summary *110*

Suggested Readings *111*

5   How Sociologists Do Research *112*

What is a Valid Sociological Topic? *114*

Common Sense and the Need for Sociological Research *114*

A Research Model *115*
Selecting a Topic ■ Defining the Problem ■ Reviewing the Literature ■ Formulating a Hypothesis ■ Choosing a Research Method ■ Collecting the Data ■ Analyzing the Results ■ Sharing the Results

Six Research Methods *119*
Surveys
■ *Down-to-Earth Sociology:* Loading the Dice *121*
Secondary Analysis ■ Documents ■ Participant Observation (Fieldwork) ■ Experiments ■ Unobtrusive Measures
■ *Down-to-Earth Sociology:* The Hawthorne Experiments *128*
Deciding Which Method to Use
■ *Thinking Critically about Social Controversy:* Counting the Homeless *129*

Ethics in Sociological Research *131*
The Brajuha Research ■ The Humphreys Research

How Research and Theory Work Together *133*
A Final Word: When the Ideal Meets the Real

Summary *136*

Suggested Readings *136*

PART II   SOCIAL GROUPS AND SOCIAL CONTROL

6   Social Groups: Societies to Social Networks *138*

Social Groups and Societies *140*

The Transformation of Societies *141*
Hunting and Gathering Societies ■ Pastoral and Horticultural Societies ■ Agricultural Societies ■ Industrial Societies ■ Postindustrial Societies

■ *Perspectives:* A Tribal Mountain People Meets Postindustrial Society *147*

Groups within Society *149*
Primary Groups ■ Secondary Groups ■ In-Groups and Out-Groups ■ Reference Groups ■ Social Networks

Group Dynamics *154*
Group Size ■ Leadership

■ *Down-to-Earth Sociology:* How Group Size Affects Willingness to Help Strangers   *157*
Conformity to Peer Pressure: The Asch Experiment ■ Obedience to Authority: The Milgram Experiment ■ Groupthink and Decision Making ■ Preventing Groupthink
Summary   *162*
Suggested Readings   *163*

7   Bureaucracy and Formal Organizations   164

The Rationalization of Society   *166*
The Contribution of Max Weber ■ Marx on Rationalism
Formal Organizations and Bureaucracy   *168*
Formal Organizations ■ The Essential Characteristics of Bureaucracies ■ "Ideal" versus "Real" Bureaucracy ■ Dysfunctions of Bureaucracies
Voluntary Associations   *175*
The Functions of Voluntary Associations ■ The Problem of Oligarchy
Careers in Bureaucracies   *178*
The Corporate Culture: Consequences of Hidden Values
■ *Down-to-Earth Sociology:* Maneuvering the Hidden Culture—Women Surviving in the Male-Dominated Business World   *179*
Humanizing the Corporate Culture
■ *Perspectives:* Managing Diversity in the Workplace   *181*
Quality Circles ■ Employee Stock Ownership ■ Small Work Groups
■ *Down-to-Earth Sociology:* Self-Management Teams   *183*
Developing an Alternative: The Cooperative   *184*
The Japanese Corporate Model   *184*
■ *Perspectives:* Bottom-Up Decision Making in Japanese Corporations   *186*
■ *Down-to-Earth Sociology:* Home on the Range—Japanese-Style   *187*

Summary   *188*
Suggested Readings   *188*

8   Deviance and Social Control   190

Gaining a Sociological Perspective of Deviance   *192*
The Relativity of Deviance
■ *Perspectives:* Deviance in Cross-Cultural Perspective   *193*
Social Control ■ How Norms Make Social Life Possible ■ Comparing Biological, Psychological, and Sociological Explanations
The Symbolic Interactionist Perspective   *197*
Differential Association Theory
■ *Perspectives:* When Cultures Clash—Problems in Defining Deviance   *198*
Control Theory ■ Labeling Theory
The Functionalist Perspective   *200*
How Deviance Is Functional for Society ■ Strain Theory: How Social Values Produce Crime ■ Illegitimate Opportunity Theory: Explaining Social Class and Crime
The Conflict Perspective   *204*
Class, Crime, and the Criminal Justice System
Reactions to Deviants   *205*
Sanctions ■ Labeling: The Saints and the Roughnecks ■ The Trouble with Official Statistics ■ Degradation Ceremonies ■ Imprisonment
Reactions by Deviants   *210*
Primary, Secondary, and Tertiary Deviance ■ Neutralizing Deviance ■ Embracing Deviance
The Medicalization of Deviance: Mental Illness   *213*
Neither Mental nor Illness? ■ The Homeless Mentally Ill
The Need for a More Humane Approach   *215*
■ *Down-to-Earth Sociology:* Taking Back Children from the Night   *215*
Summary   *216*
Suggested Readings   *217*

PART III   SOCIAL INEQUALITY

9   Stratification in Global Perspective   218
What Is Social Stratification?   *220*
Systems of Social Stratification   *221*
Slavery ■ Caste: India and South Africa ■ Class
■ *Perspectives:* Social Stratification among Polish Jews   *226*
Clan and Class as Parallel Forms of Social Stratification
Gender and Social Stratification   *227*
What Determines Social Class   *228*
Karl Marx: The Means of Production ■ Max Weber: Power, Property, and Prestige

Why Is Social Stratification Universal?   *230*
The Functionalist View of Davis and Moore: Motivating Qualified People ■ Tumin: A Critical Response ■ Mosca: A Forerunner of the Conflict View ■ The Conflict View: Class Conflict and Competition for Scarce Resources ■ Toward a Synthesis
Comparative Social Stratification   *233*
Social Stratification in Great Britain ■ Social Stratification in the Former Soviet Union
Maintaining National Stratification   *235*
Why Not Total Exploitation?

Global Stratification: The Three Worlds *237*
The First World ■ The Second World ■ The Third
World ■ Imperfections in the Model
How the World's Nations Became Stratified *240*
Imperialism and Colonialism ■ World System Theory ■
Dependency Theory ■ Culture of Poverty ■ Evaluating
the Theories
Maintaining Global Stratification *242*
Neocolonialism ■ Multinational Corporations
■ *Perspectives:* The Patriotic Prostitute *243*
Summary *244*
Suggested Readings *245*

10 **Social Class in American
Society** *246*

What is Social Class? *248*
Measures of Social Class
Dimensions of Social Class *249*
Wealth ■ Power ■ Prestige ■ Status Inconsistency
Social Class in Industrial Society *258*
Updating Marx: Wright's Model ■ Updating Weber:
Gilbert's and Kahl's Model ■ Social Class in the Automobile
Industry ■ Life Chances ■ Physical and Mental Health ■
Below the Ladder: The Homeless
Consequences of Social Class *265*
Family Life ■ Values and Attitudes ■ Political
Involvement ■ Religion ■ Education ■ The Criminal
Justice System
Social Mobility *267*
Intergenerational, Structural, and Exchange Mobility ■
Social Mobility in the United States ■ Costs of Social
Mobility
■ *Thinking Critically about Social Controversy:* Upward Mobility
for American Workers—A Vanishing Dream? *269*
Where is Horatio Alger?
Poverty in the United States *271*
Drawing the Line: What Is Poverty? ■ Who Are the
Poor? ■ Children in Poverty: A New Social Condition?
■ *Thinking Critically about Social Controversy:* Children in
Poverty *273*
Short-Term and Long-Term Poverty ■ Individual versus
Structural Explanations of Poverty
Summary *276*
Suggested Readings *276*

11 **Inequalities of Gender** *278*

Why Are Males and Females Different? *280*
Biology or Culture? The Continuing Controversy
■ *Thinking Critically about Social Controversy:* Biology versus
Culture *282*
An Emerging Position in Sociology? ■ The Question of
Superiority

Women as a Minority Group *285*
Cross-Cultural Gender Inequality: Sex-Typing of Work ■
Cross-Cultural Gender Inequality: Prestige of Work ■ The
Genesis of Female Minority Status
Gender Inequality in American Society *289*
Fighting Back: The Rise of Feminism ■ Gender Inequality
in Education: Creating Sex-Linked Aspirations
■ *Down-to-Earth Sociology:* Making the Invisible Visible—The
Deadly Effects of Sexism *291*
Gender Inequality in Everyday Life
Gender Inequality in the Workplace *294*
Women in the Work Force ■ Discrimination in Hiring ■
The Pay Gap
■ *Perspectives:* Sexual Harassment in Japan *298*
The "Mommy" Track ■ Sexual Harassment
■ *Down-to-Earth Sociology:* Women on Wall Street—From
Subtle Put-Downs to Crude Sexual Harassment *301*
**Gender Inequality and Violence: The Case of
Murder** *302*
**Why Don't Women Take Over Politics and
Transform American Life?** *303*
Changes in Gender Relations *305*
Glimpsing the Future—With Hope *305*
Summary *306*
Suggested Readings *307*

12 **Inequalities of Race and
Ethnicity** *308*

**Basic Concepts in Race and Ethnic
Relations** *310*
Race: Myth and Reality ■ Ethnic Groups ■ Minority
Groups
Prejudice and Discrimination *313*
■ *Perspective:* Clashing Cultures *313*
When Prejudice and Discrimination Don't Match ■ The
Extent of Prejudice
Theories of Prejudice *316*
■ *Thinking Critically about Social Controversy:* Racism on
College Campuses *316*
Psychological Perspectives ■ Sociological Perspectives:
Functionalism, Conflict, and Symbolic Interaction
Individual and Institutional Discrimination *320*
Patterns of Intergroup Relations *322*
Genocide ■ Population Transfer ■ Internal
Colonialism ■ Segregation ■ Assimilation ■ Pluralism
**Race and Ethnic Relations in the United
States** *325*
The Dominance of White Anglo-Saxon Protestants ■ White
Ethnics ■ African Americans ■ Hispanic Americans
(Latinos)
■ *Down to Earth Sociology:* The Illegal Travel Guide *331*
■ *Perspectives:* The Browning of America *332*
Asian Americans ■ Native Americans

■ *Thinking Critically about Social Controversy:* Whose
   History?   *337*
Principles for Improving Ethnic Relations   *339*
Summary   *339*
Suggested Readings   *340*

13   Inequalities of Age   *343*

Social Factors in Aging   *344*
   Aging among Abkhasians ■ Aging in Industrialized Nations
■ *Down-to-Earth Sociology:* Applying Life Expectancy
   Figures   *347*
The Symbolic Interactionist Perspective   *348*
   Self, Society, and Aging ■ The Relativity of Aging:
   Cross-Cultural Comparisons ■ Ageism in American
   Society ■ The Mass Media: Purveyor of Symbol and Status
The Functionalist Perspective   *354*
   Disengagement Theory ■ Activity Theory

The Conflict Perspective   *356*
   Social Security Legislation ■ Rival Interest Groups
■ *Down-to-Earth Sociology:* Changing Sentiment about the
   Elderly   *357*
■ *Thinking Critically about Social Controversy:* Social
   Security—Fraud of the Century?   *358*
   Fighting Back: The Gray Panthers
Problems of Dependency   *360*
   Nursing Homes
■ *Down-to-Earth Sociology:* Pacification—Turning People into
   Patients   *362*
   Elder Abuse ■ The Question of Poverty
The Sociology of Death and Dying   *365*
   Effects of Industrialization ■ Death as a Process ■ Suicide
   and the Elderly ■ Hospices
Summary   *368*
Suggested Readings   *368*

PART IV   SOCIAL INSTITUTIONS

14   The Economy: Money and Work   *370*

The Transformation of Economic Systems   *372*
   Hunting and Gathering Economies: Subsistence ■ Pastoral
   and Horticultural Economies: The Creation of Surplus ■
   Agricultural Economies: The Growth of Trade ■ Industrial
   Economies: The Birth of the Machine ■ Postindustrial
   Economy: The Information Age
**The Transformation of the Medium of
   Exchange**   *376*
   Earliest Mediums of Exchange ■ Medium of Exchange in
   Agricultural Economies ■ Medium of Exchange in Industrial
   Economies ■ Medium of Exchange in Postindustrial
   Economies
World Economic Systems   *378*
   Capitalism ■ Socialism ■ Ideologies of Capitalism and
   Socialism ■ Criticisms of Capitalism and Socialism
■ *Down-to-Earth Sociology:* Selling the American Dream—The
   Creation of Constant Discontent   *381*
   The Systems in Conflict and Competition ■ The Future:
   Convergence?
The Inner Circle of Capitalism   *384*
   Corporate Capitalism ■ Interlocking Directorates ■
   Multinational Corporations
Work in American Society   *387*
   Three Economic Sectors ■ Women and Work ■ The
   Underground Economy ■ Patterns of Work and Leisure
Applying Sociological Theories   *392*
   The Funtionalist Perspective ■ The Conflict
   Perspective ■ The Symbolic Interaction Perspective
■ *Perspectives:* Who is Unemployed?   *395*
The Future of the U.S. Economy   *397*

Summary   *398*
Suggested Readings   *399*

15   Politics: Power and
      Authority   *400*

Micropolitics and Macropolitics   *402*
Power, Authority, and Coercion   *402*
   Authority and Legitimate Violence ■ Traditional
   Authority ■ Rational-Legal Authority ■
   Charismatic Authority ■ Authority as Ideal Type ■
   The Transfer of Authority
Types of Government   *409*
   Monarchies: The Rise of the State ■ Democracies:
   Citizenship as a Revolutionary Idea ■ Dictatorships and
   Oligarchies: The Seizure of Power
The American Political System   *411*
   Political Parties and Elections ■ Democratic Systems in
   Europe ■ Voting Patterns
■ *Perspectives:* Immigrants—Ethnicity and Class as the Path to
   Political Participation   *416*
   The Depression as a Transforming Event ■ Lobbyists and
   Special-Interest Groups ■ PACs and the Cost of Elections
Who Rules America?   *419*
   The Functionalist Perspective: Pluralism ■ The Conflict
   Perspective: Power Elite and Ruling Class ■ Which View
   Is Right?
**War: A Means to Implement Political
   Objectives**   *422*
   Is War Universal? ■ Why Do Nations Go to War? ■
   How Common Is War? ■ Costs of War ■ War and
   Dehumanization

■ *Perspectives:* Nations versus States—Implications of a New
World Order   *425*
A Coming World Order?   *426*
Summary   *426*
Suggested Readings   *427*

**16   The Family: Our Introduction to
Society   428**

**Marriage and Family in Cross-Cultural
Perspective   430**
Defining Family ■ Variations across Cultures ■ Common
Cultural Themes
**Marriage and Family in Theoretical
Perspective   434**
The Functionalist Perspective: Functions and
Dysfunctions ■ The Conflict Perspective: Gender, Conflict,
and Power
■ *Thinking Critically About Social Controversy:* The Second
Shift—Strains and Strategies   *437*
The Symbolic Interactionist Perspective: Marital
Communication
The Family Life Cycle   440
The Ideological Context: Love and Courtship
■ *Perspectives:* East Is East and West Is West—Love and
Arranged Marriages in India   *441*
Marriage
■ *Down-to-Earth Sociology:* Why Do People Become Jealous?
A Sociological Interpretation   *442*
Childbirth ■ Child Rearing ■ The Family in Later Life
Diversity in American Families   446
African-American Families ■ Hispanic-American Families
(Latinos) ■ Asian-American Families ■ One-Parent
Families
■ *Perspectives:* Peering beneath the Facade—Problems in the
Korean-American Family   *450*
Families without Children ■ Blended Families ■
Homosexual Families
Trends in American Families   451
Postponing Marriage ■ Cohabitation ■ Child Care
Divorce and Remarriage   455
Problems in Measuring Divorce ■ Children of Divorce ■
The Ex-Spouses ■ Remarriage
Two Sides of Family Life   458
Abuse: Battering, Marital Rape, and Incest ■ Families
That Work
The Future of Marriage and Family   461
Summary   *462*
Suggested Readings   *462*

**17   Education: Transferring
Knowledge and Skills   464**

Today's Credential Society   466
The Development of Modern Education   *467*

Education in Cross-cultural Perspective   *468*
Great Britain ■ Japan ■ The Former Soviet Union
Education in the United States   *471*
The Beginning of Universal Education
**The Functionalist Perspective: Providing Social
Benefits**   *472*
Teaching Knowledge and Skills ■ Cultural Transmission of
Values ■ Social Integration ■ Gatekeeping ■ Promoting
Personal Change ■ Promoting Social Change ■ Replacing
Family Functions ■ Other Functions
**The Conflict Perspective: Maintaining Social
Inequality**   *477*
The Hidden Curriculum ■ Stacking the Deck: Unequal
Funding
■ *Down-to-Earth Sociology:* Kindergarten as Boot
Camp   *478*
Discrimination by IQ: Tilting the Tests ■ The
Correspondence Principle ■ The Bottom Line:
Reproducing the Social Class Structure
■ *Thinking Critically about Social Controversy:* The
"Cooling-Out" Function of Higher Education   *483*
**The Symbolic Interactionist Perspective: Teacher
Expectations and the Self-Fulfilling
Prophecy**   *484*
The Rist Research ■ The Rosenthal/Jacobson
Experiment ■ How Do Teacher Expectations Work?
How Can We Improve Schools?   *487*
The Coleman Report ■ Compensatory Education ■
Busing ■ The National Report Card: Falling Test
Scores ■ The Rutter Report
■ *Down-to-Earth Sociology:* Positive Peer Pressure and the
Problem of Drugs   *491*
■ *Thinking Critically about Social Controversy:* Improving
America's Schools   *491*
Summary   *493*
Suggested Readings   *493*

**18   Religion: Establishing
Meaning   494**

What Is Religion?   *496*
The Functionalist Perspective   *497*
Functions of Religion ■ Functional Equivalents of
Religion ■ Dysfunctions of Religion
The Symbolic Interactionist Perspective   *499*
Religious Symbols ■ Rituals ■ Beliefs ■ Religious
Experience ■ Community
The Conflict Perspective   *502*
Opium of the People ■ A Reflection of Social
Inequalities ■ A Legitimation of Social Inequalities
Religion and the Spirit of Capitalism   *504*
The World's Major Religions   *505*
Judaism ■ Christianity ■ Islam ■ Hinduism ■ Buddhism ■
Confucianism

Types of Religious Organizations   *510*
Cult ■ Sect ■ Church
■ *Down-to-Earth Sociology:* Mass Shortage   *513*
Ecclesia ■ Variations in Patterns ■ A Closer Look at Cults
and Sects
■ *Perspectives:* Religion and Culture in India   *514*
Secularization   *515*
The Secularization of Religion
■ *Down-to-Earth Sociology:* Bikers and Bibles   *517*
The Secularization of Culture ■ 518
**The Main Characteristics of Religion in the United
States**   *520*
Diversity ■ Pluralism and Freedom ■ Competition ■
Commitment ■ Privacy ■ Toleration ■ Fundamentalist
Revived ■ The Electronic Church ■ Characteristics of
Members
The Future of Religion   *523*
Summary   *524*
Suggested Readings   *525*

**19   Medicine: Health and
          Illness   526**

**The Sociological Perspective of Health and
          Illness   528**
Defining Health ■ The Cultural Relativity of Health ■ The
Sick Role

Historical Patterns of Health   *532*
Physical Health ■ Mental Health
Medicine in the United States   *534*
The Professionalization of Medicine ■ The Monopoly of
Medicine
■ *Thinking Critically about Social Controversy:* Midwives
and Physicians: The Expanding Boundaries of a
Profession   *536*
■ *Thinking Critically about Social Controversy:* In the Care of
Strangers—The Hospital in American Society   *536*
Mental Illness and Social Inequality
Issues in Health and Health Care   *539*
Medical Care as a Commodity ■ Malpractice Suits and
Defensive Medicine ■ Inequality in Distribution ■
Depersonalization: The Cash Machine ■ Sexism in
Medicine
■ *Down-to-Earth Sociology:* The Doctor Nurse Game   *543*
Medicalization of Society ■ Controversy about Death
■ *Thinking Critically about Social Controversy:* The Legalization
of Euthanasia   *545*
Health Insurance
Threats to Health   *546*
Disease ■ Drugs ■ Disabling Environments
The Search for Alternatives `   *552*
Treatment or Prevention? ■ Holistic Medicine
■ *Perspectives:* Health Care in Other Countries   *553*
Summary   *556*
Suggested Readings   *556*

PART V   SOCIAL CHANGE

**20   Population and
          Urbanization   558**

Population   *560*
The Specter of Overpopulation   *560*
Thomas Malthus: Sounding the Alarm ■ The New
Malthusians ■ The Anti-Malthusians ■ Who Is
Correct? ■ Why Are There Famines?
Population Growth   *565*
Why the Poor Nations Have So Many Children ■
Implications of Different Rates of Growth ■ Estimating
Population Growth: The Three Demographic Variables ■
Industrialization and the Demographic Equation ■ Problems
in Forecasting Population Growth
■ *Perspectives:* Where the United States Population Is
Headed   *572*
Urbanization   *574*
The City in History   *574*
Models of Urban Growth   *576*
The Concentric-Zone Model ■ The Sector Model ■ The
Multiple-Nuclei Model ■ Critique of the Models
Experiencing the City   *578*
Alienation

■ *Perspectives:* Urbanization in the Third World   *579*
Community ■ Types of Urban Dwellers ■ Urban
Sentiment
■ *Down-to-Earth Sociology:* Giving Access Information—The
Contrasting Perspectives of Males and Females   *583*
Insiders' and Outsiders' Views: Implications for Urban
Planners ■ Urban Networks ■ Urban Overload ■
Diffusion of Responsibility
The Changing City   *585*
Urban Politics: The Transition to Minority
Leadership ■ Suburbanization ■ Trends in Suburbs and
Cities
Summary   *588*
Suggested Readings   *589*

**21   Collective Behavior and Social
          Movements   590**

Collective Behavior   *592*
**Early Explanations: The Transformation of the
          Individual**   *593*
Charles Mackay: The "Herd Mentality" ■ Gustave LeBon:

How the Crowd Transforms the Individual ■ Robert Park: Social Unrest and Circular Reaction ■ Herbert Blumer: The Acting Crowd ■ Comparing LeBon and Blumer

The Contemporary View: The Rationality of the Crowd   *595*
Critique of LeBon and Blumer: More Than a Creature of the Crowd ■ Ralph Turner and Lewis Killian: Emergent Norms ■ Richard Berk: Minimax Strategy ■ Can Collective Behavior Really Be So Rational? ■ The Anatomy of a Lynching

Other Forms of Collective Behavior   *599*
Riots ■ Panics ■ Rumors ■ Fads and Fashions ■ Urban Legends

Social Movements   *605*

Understanding Social Movements: The Case of the Nazis   *605*
Why Social Movements Exist ■ Dehumanization: Why Normal People Do Evil Things ■ Propaganda and Advertising: Manufacturing and Selling Ideas

Breadth, Types, and Tactics of Social Movements   *609*
Breadth of Social Movements

■ *Down-to-Earth Sociology:* "Tricks of the Trade"—The Fine Art of Propaganda   *610*
New Social Movements ■ Types of Social Movements ■ Tactics of Social Movements ■ The Life Course of Social Movements

■ *Thinking Critically About Social Controversy:* Which Side of the Barricades? Abortion as a Social Movement   *614*

Why People Join Social Movements   *616*
Deprivation Theory ■ Mass Society Theory

The Success and Failure of Social Movements   *617*
Resource Mobilization

Summary   *618*

Suggested Readings   *619*

22   Social Change, Technology, and the Environment   *620*

Social Change: A Review   *622*
The Four Social Revolutions ■ From *Gemeinschaft* to *Gesellschaft* ■ The Transformation of Society through Capitalism ■ Effects of Industrialization on the Third World ■ Globalization and Dependency ■ Shifts in International Stratification ■ Changes in the Social Institutions of the United States

Theories of Social Change   *624*
Evolutionary Theories ■ Cyclical Theories ■ Conflict Theory ■ Modernization

Social Change and Technology   *628*
Ogburn's Processes of Cultural Innovation ■ Types of Technology ■ How Technology Transforms Society ■ An Extended Example: Effects of the Automobile ■ An Extended Example: Effects of the Computer ■ Concerns about Computers ■ Telecommunications and Global Social Change

Social Change and the Natural Environment   *640*
Environmental Degradation in the Past

■ *Perspectives:* Lost Tribes, Lost Knowledge   *644*
The Environmental Problem Today ■ Environmental Problems in the Second World ■ Environmental Problems in the Third World ■ The Environmental Movement

■ *Thinking Critically about Social Controversy:* Ecosabotage   *644*
Environmental Sociology ■ The Goal of Harmony between Technology and the Environment

Summary   *646*

Suggested Readings   *647*

Boxes

■ DOWN-TO-EARTH SOCIOLOGY

An Updated Version of the Old Elephant Story   *6*
Enjoying a Sociological Quiz: Sociological Findings versus
  Common Sense   *7*
Communicating across Cultural Boundaries   *36*
Heredity or Environment? The Case of Oskar and Jack,
  Identical Twins   *59*
College Football as Social Structure   *90*
Loading the Dice   *121*
The Hawthorne Experiments   *128*
How Group Size Affects Willingness to Help
  Strangers   *157*
Maneuvering the Hidden Culture: Women Surviving in the
  Male-Dominated Business World   *179*
Self-Management Teams   *183*
Home on the Range—Japanese-Style   *187*
Taking Back Children from the Night   *215*
Making the Invisible Visible—The Deadly Effects of
  Sexism   *291*
The Illegal Travel Guide   *331*
Applying Life Expectancy Figures   *347*
Changing Sentiment about the Elderly   *357*
Pacification—Turning People into Patients   *362*
Selling the American Dream—The Creation of Constant
  Discontent   *381*
Why Do People Become Jealous? A Sociological
  Interpretation   *442*
Kindergarten as Boot Camp   *478*
Positive Peer Pressure and the Problem of Drugs   *491*
Mass Shortage   *513*
Bikers and Bibles   *517*
Midwives and Physicians—The Expanding Boundaries
  of a Profession   *536*

■ PERSPECTIVES

Sociology in a World of Turmoil   *26*
Miami—Language and a Changing City   *39*
Why Do Native Americans Like Westerns?   *44*
Manhood in the Making   *74*
Caught between Two Worlds   *77*
The Amish—*Gemeinschaft* Communities in a *Gesellschaft*
  Society   *100*
A Tribal Mountain People Meets Postindustrial
  Society   *147*

Managing Diversity in the Workplace   *181*
Bottom-Up Decision Making in Japanese
  Corporations   *186*
Deviance in Cross-Cultural Perspective   *192*
When Cultures Clash—Problems in Defining
  Deviance   *198*
Social Stratification among Polish Jews   *226*
The Patriotic Prostitute   *243*
Sexual Harassment in Japan   *298*
Clashing Cultures   *313*
The Browning of America   *332*
Who Is Unemployed?   *395*
Immigrants Ethnicity and Class as the Paths to Political
  Participation   *416*
Nations versus States—Implications of a New World
  Order   *425*
East Is East and West Is West—Love and Arranged
  Marriages in India   *441*
Peering beneath the Facade—Problems in the
  Korean-American Family   *450*
Religion and Culture in India   *514*
Health Care in Other Countries   *553*
Where the United States Population Is Headed   *572*
Urbanization in the Third World   *579*
Lost Tribes, Lost Knowledge   *644*

■ THINKING CRITICALLY ABOUT SOCIAL CONTROVERSY

Are We Prisoners of Our Genes?   *48*
Counting the Homeless   *129*
Upward Mobility for American Workers—A Vanishing
  Dream   *269*
Children in Poverty   *273*
Biology versus Culture   *282*
Racism on College Campuses   *316*
Social Security—Fraud of the Century?   *358*
The Second Shift—Strains and Strategies   *437*
The "Cooling-Out" Function of Higher Education   *483*
Improving America's Schools   *491*
In Care of Strangers—The Hospital in American
  Society   *536*
The Legalization of Euthanasia   *545*
Which Side of the Barricades? Abortion as a Social
  Movement   *614*
Ecosabotage   *644*

Preface

If you like to watch people and try to figure out why they do what they do, you will like sociology. If you like variety and surprises, sociology will provide them. As you study sociology, you will see how society has become part of your own consciousness, influencing everything you do. You will also see that many of your assumptions about life are unfounded. Over and over in this book, you will see that the "common sense" you are told to depend on comes up short when compared with the findings of sociologists. For example, did you know that what you see is partly determined by language? Or that stereotypes help to produce the very characteristics that are stereotyped in the first place?

Part of sociology's attraction is its fascinating combination of breadth and focus. Sociology is so broad that it includes an analysis of how industrialization is changing the face of the world, yet so focused that a couple's quarrels find their way into sociological scrutiny. From how people become presidents to how they become homeless, from why women are treated as second-class citizens to why people commit suicide—all are part of sociology.

Much to their dismay, instructors who believe that sociology can stimulate a fresh way of looking at the world often hear students complaining about their sociology textbook. These complaints are often well founded, for many texts are cumbersome and ponderous. Given the excitement—and enchantment—of sociology, this just shouldn't be. On the contrary, an introductory sociology textbook should impart some of the joy of discovering a new way of perceiving the social world.

Writing style, then, is critical in introducing sociology to a new generation. In this text, I ask you to participate in the exciting venture of discovering how social groups influence your behavior—including how you look at the world and yourself. As you read this book, you will see how the social environment penetrates your very being, how your opinions and attitudes are a reflection of your experiences, how remarkably different you would be had you been reared in a different family, social class, race, gender, or culture. The joy of self-discovery while exploring society is part of the excitement of sociology.

As you gain an overview of sociology (studying what are called social structure and social interaction), you will be introduced to classic works of early founders such as Durkheim, Weber, and Marx, as well as current sociological investigations. You will see the all-encompassing effects of racism, as well as how bureaucracies shape our experiences. You will understand how social institutions affect our lives, as well as how people become deviants. You will see how the world economic race, especially our competition with Japan and Europe, affects your future.

There is no reason that an overview of the principles of sociology should get lost in a morass of abstractions that impede learning. Consequently, I have made liberal use of examples from everyday life, so that sociological principles, concepts, and theories are presented in a "down-to-earth" fashion. Similarly, to help you see the world in broader perspective, I have also included many cross-cultural and multicultural materials. Their value is two-fold. On the one hand, they provide interesting and illustrative contrast, which helps you understand other ways of life. On the other hand, the comparisons challenge you to see yourself differently. That, in my opinion, is one of the objectives of an introduction to sociology.

These, then, are the goals that I have tried to reach in writing this introductory text. Initial classroom testing of these materials has elicited very positive response from students. Only you, however, can tell me if I have succeeded.

I find sociology the most interesting of all subjects offered in college—as I hope you will. It is my wish that your introduction to sociology provides a new way of looking at the social world. I would be happy to hear from you concerning your reactions to this introductory venture into sociology. If you wish, you may write to me at:

James M. Henslin
Department of Sociology
Southern Illinois University
Edwardsville, IL 62026

ACKNOWLEDGMENTS

Although writing this text engulfed my life for longer than I care to recall, it represents the contributions of many people. First, I owe a debt of gratitude to the fine reviewers whose perceptive comments have improved its presentation. I was pleased with the efforts they put into the reviewing process, and I have done my best to accommodate their suggestions. I wish to thank:

Sandra L. Albrecht
The University of Kansas

Kenneth Ambrose
Marshall University

Karren Baird-Olsen
Kansas State University

Linda Barbera-Stein
The University of Illinois

John K. Cochran
The University of Oklahoma

John Darling
University of Pittsburgh—Johnstown

Nanette J. Davis
Portland State University

Lynda Dodgen
North Harris Community College

Obi N. I. Ebbe
State University of New York—
    Brockport

David O. Friedrichs
University of Scranton

Norman Goodman
State University of New York—Stony
    Brook

Donald W. Hastings
The University of Tennessee—
    Knoxville

Charles E. Hurst
The College of Wooster

Mark Kassop
Bergen Community College

Alice Abel Kemp
University of New Orleans

Diana Kendall
Austin Community College

Gary Kiger
Utah State University

Abraham Levine
El Camino Community College

Ron Matson
Wichita State University

Armand L. Mauss
Washington State University

Robert Meyer
Arkansas State University

W. Lawrence Neuman
University of Wisconsin—Whitewater

Laura O'Toole
University of Delaware

Phil Piket
Joliet Junior College

Adrian Rapp
North Harris Community College

Walt Shirley
Sinclair Community College

Marc Silver
Hofstra University

Susan Sprecher
Illinois State University

Stephen R. Wilson
Temple University

Larry Weiss
University of Alaska

Stuart Wright
Lamar University

Douglas White
Henry Ford Community College

Second, I also am indebted to the capable staff of Allyn & Bacon—especially to Karen Hanson, who gave such positive feedback to the early manuscript; to Susan Badger, who initiated the project; to Deborah Fogel, for thorough copyediting; to Susan McNally for coordinating the project; and to those fine people in the art and production departments.

Finally, I cannot adequately express my appreciation to Hannah Rubenstein. If I were to compile a list of characteristics I desired in a development editor, it would include intelligence and dedication, of course. Those I received in abundance. By themselves, that would have been adequate. The surprise was the remarkable insight, and the humor under pressure—all wrapped up in a tireless worker who insisted on perfection. It was my privilege, Hannah.

It is with this goal—of making the introductory course in sociology an enjoyable, challenging, and eye-opening experience—that I have written this book. It is my privilege that you have selected *Sociology: A Down-to-Earth Approach* to use in your teaching. I will also count it a privilege if you will share your teaching experiences, including any suggestions for improving the text. I am not averse to receiving criticisms, for they allow me to see matters in a different light and to improve my efforts.

I wish you the very best in your teaching, and it is my sincere hope that this text contributes to that success. I look forward to hearing from you.

James M. Henslin
Department of Sociology
Southern Illinois University
Edwardsville, Illinois 62026

Continued from page ii

Abbreviations

Bettmann Archive (BA); Courtesy of Cable News Network, Inc. (CNN); Gamma-Liaison (GL); The Granger Collection, New York (GC); Photo Researchers, Inc. (PRI); The Picture Group (PG); Stock, Boston (SB); Tony Stone Worldwide/Chicago Ltd. (TSW); Wide World Photos (AP/WWP); Woodfin Camp & Associates (WCA).

Interior Photo Credits

Ch. 1: 3: Kenneth R. Good. 9: (GC). 10: (BA). 11: (BA). 12 (top, left): Doranne Jacobson. 12 (top, right): Richard Pasley/(SB). 12 (bottom): (BA). 15: (GC). 18: University of Chicago Library. 22: Shelby Lee Adams. *Ch. 2:* 33 (left): Alexandra Avakian/(WCA). 33 (right): Sepp Seitz/(WCA). 42: Alon Reininger/Contact/(WCA). 43 & 47: Bob Daemmrich/(SB). 48: Alain Eurard/(PRI). 49: Francois Gohier/(PRI). 52: Reprinted by permission of the publishers from *The Chimpanzees of Gombe* by Jane Goodall, Cambridge, MA: Harvard University Press © 1986 by the President and Fellows of Harvard College. 54: George Merillon/(GL). *Ch. 3:* 60: William Snyder/(GL). 62: Martin Rogers/(TSW). 64: Richard Hutchings/(PRI). 69: Moradabroi/Reflex/(PG). 75: Bob Daemmrich/(SB). 76 (top): (CNN). 76 (bottom): Jean-Yves Ruszniewski/(PRI). 78: Bob Daemmrich/(SB). 81: (GC). *Ch. 4:* 89: Peter Menzel/(SB). 92: Kent Gavin/Syndication International, Ltd. 93: Michael Freeman. 94: Bob Daemmrich/(SB). 96: Andy Levin/(PRI). 97 & 98: Michael Freeman. 102 (left): Alain Eurard/(PRI). 102 (right): Tom McHugh/(PRI). *Ch. 5:* 114: Andrew Popper/(PG). 117: Bob Daemmrich/(SB). 122: Will & Demi McIntyre/(PRI). 124 (top): Bob Crandall/(PG). 124 (bottom): George Riley/(SB). 130: Joe Sohm/(SB). 134: Ellis Herwig/(SB). *Ch. 6:* 140: Karen Kasmauski/(WCA). 141: "The Man Who Flew Into Space From His Apartment," by Ilya Kabakov, 1981–88. Collection of Musee National d'Art Moderne, Centre Georges Pompidou, Paris. Photo courtesy Ronald Feldman Fine Arts, New York. 143: M.P. Kahl/(PRI). 148: Jeffry W. Myers/(SB). 150: Susan Kuklin/(PRI). 151 (top): Bill Strode/(WCA). 151 (bottom): (AP/WWP). 152: Merillon-Saussier/(GL). 154: Peter Southwick/(SB). 155: Susan Kuklin/(PRI). 157: (AP/WWP). *Ch. 7:* 167: (GC). 168 (top): Doranne Jacobson. 168 (bottom): Art Resource, NY. 169: Doranne Jacobson. 173 (both): Courtesy, March of Dimes Birth Defects Foundation. 174: Tomas Muscionico/Contact/(WCA). 176: UPI/Bettmann. 179: Richard Sobol. 180: Bob Daemmrich/(SB). 185: Karen Kasmauski/(WCA). *Ch. 8:* 192: Kenneth R. Good. 195: (AP/WWP). 199: Tony O'Brien/(PG). 203: UPI/Bettmann. 206: Bob Daemmrich/(SB). 209 & 212: Baverel Didier/(GL). *Ch. 9:* 221 (left): Nathan Benn/(SB). 221 (right): Bob Daemmrich/(SB). 223: (GC). 224: Robert Caputo/(SB). 227: Dilip Mehtz/Contact/(WCA). 230: UPI/Bettmann. 232: (AP/WWP). 234: Chuck O'Rear/(WCA). 235: (GC). 239: Mario Ruiz/(PG). 241: (CNN). 243: Natsuko Utsumi/(GL). *Ch. 10:* 249: Carl Purcell/(PRI). 251: Charles Gupton/(TSW). 252: Steve Kagan/(GL). 254: Cynthia Johnson/(GL). 256: (AP/WWP). 257: Lori Grinker/Contact/(WCA). 262: Karen Kasmauski/(WCA). 265: Chris Brown/(SB). 269: (AP/WWP). 272: Lester Sloan/(WCA). 274: Selby Lee Adams. *Ch. 11:* 280: Jennifer James/(GL). 286: Mike Yamashita/(WCA). 287: Michael Freeman. 289: Library of Congress. 292: (GC). 295: Richard Hutchings/(PRI). 296: John Carter/(PRI). 299: Nancy J. Pierce/(PRI). 302: © Orlando Sentinel/(GL). 304: (AP/WWP). *Ch. 12:* 311 (left): (AP/WWP). 311 (right): UPI/Bettmann. 312: Rina Castelnuovo/Contact/(WCA). 313: © 1990 Sacha Hartgers/Focus/Matrix. 320: UPI/Bettmann. 324: (AP/WWP). 327: (AP/WWP). 333 & 336: Alon Reininger/Contact/(WCA). 337: Charles Herbert/(PRI). *Ch. 13:* 349: Suzanne Murphy/(TSW). 351: Shelby Lee Adam. 352: Michael Freeman. 354: Jerry Wachter/(PRI). 355: Alon Reininger/Contact/(WCA). 360: (AP/WWP). 361: Andy Levin/(PRI). 363: (CNN). 364 (left): Robert Daemmrich/(TSW). 364 (right): Stephanie Maze/(WCA). 366: (CNN). *Ch. 14:* 372 & 378 (top): Doranne Jacobson. 378 (bottom): John Elk/(SB). 379: (GC). 382: (CNN). 390: (Kermani/(GL). 393: (TSW). 394: Ted Clutter/(PRI). 396: C. Ursillo/(PRI). *Ch. 15:* 403: Brown Brothers. 404: (AP/WWP). 405: S. Maze/(WCA). 406 & 407: (GC). 410 & 411: (AP/WWP). 415: Brad Market/(GL). 416: Alon Reininger/Contact/(WCA). 423: Jasmin Krpan/(GL). *Ch. 16:* 434: Mike Yamashita/(WCA). 444: Doranne Jacobson. 446: Will & Demi McIntyre/(PRI). 447: Blair Seitz/(PRI). 448: Sisse Brimberg/(WCA). 449: Mike Yamashita/(WCA). 452: Alon Reininger/Contact/(WCA). 458: (CNN). *Ch. 17:* 469: Diane M. Lowe/(SB). 471: Deborah Copaken/Contact/(WCA). 472: (GC). 476: Jim Harrison/(SB). 482: Robert McElroy/(WCA). 486: Karen Kasmauski/(WCA). 488: Jacques Chenet/(WCA). *Ch. 18:* 498: (AP/WWP). 500: (GC). 502: Owen Franken/(SB). 503: (CNN). 508: Nabeel Turner/(TSW). 509: Jehangir Gazdar/(WCA). 510 & 517: (AP/WWP). 518: Robert Harding Picture Library. 521: Courtesy Religious News Service. *Ch. 19:* 531 (left): David Austen/(SB). 531 (right): Bob Daemmrich/(SB). 534: (GC). 539: Olivier Rebbot/(SB). 544: Detroit News/(GL). 547: Leah Melnick/Impact Visuals. 549: Rob Crandall/(PG). 551: (GC). 555: Alon Reininger/Contact/(WCA). *Ch. 20:* 562 (left): D. Savin/Petit Format/(PRI). 562 (right): Marc & Evelyne Bernheim/(WCA). 567: Doranne Jacobson. 570: Tony O'Brien/(PG). 571: Steve Starr/(SB). 574: (GC). 579: Mike Mazzaschi/(SB). 581: Frederica Georgia/(PRI). 582: Gerd Ludwig/(WCA). 583: Steve Leonard/(TSW). 587: Rafael Macia/(PRI). *Ch. 21:* 592, 598 & 599: (AP/WWP). 600: Alexandra Avakian/(WCA). 601: (AP/WWP). 607: (GC). 611 & 615: (AP/WWP). *Ch. 22:* 622: (AP/WWP). 625: (GC). 628: Dilip Mehta/Contact/(WCA). 629: James King Holmes/Science Photo Library/(PRI). 632: (GC). 637: Lawrence Migdale/(PRI). 641: Stan Wayman/(PRI). 642: Georg DeKeerle/(GL). 643: Catherine Ursillo/(PRI). 644: K. Buysse/(GL).

About the Author

James M. Henslin, who was born in Minnesota, graduated from high school and junior college in California and from college in Indiana. He earned his Master's and doctorate in sociology at Washington University in St. Louis, Missouri. His primary interests in sociology are the sociology of everyday life, deviance, social psychology, and the homeless. Among his more than a dozen books is *Down to Earth Sociology* (Free Press), now in its seventh edition, a book of readings that reflects these sociological interests. He has also published widely in sociology journals, including *Social Problems* and *American Journal of Sociology*.

While a graduate student, James Henslin taught at the University of Missouri at St. Louis. After completing his doctorate, he joined the faculty at Southern Illinois University, Edwardsville, where he is Professor of Sociology. He requests the introductory course, teaching it several times each year. He says, "I've always found the introductory course enjoyable to teach. I love to see students' faces light up when they first glimpse the sociological perspective and begin to see how society has become an essential part of how they view the world."

Henslin enjoys spending time with his family, reading, and fishing. His two favorite activities are writing and traveling. He especially enjoys living in other cultures, for this brings him face to face with behaviors that he cannot take for granted, experiences that "make sociological principles come alive."

CHAPTER 1

Jane Golden, Early Ocean Park,
1976

The Sociological Perspective

THE SOCIOLOGICAL PERSPECTIVE
  Seeing the Broader Social Context
SOCIOLOGY AND THE OTHER SCIENCES
  The Natural Sciences ■ The Social Sciences ■ The
  Goals of Science ■ *Down-to-Earth Sociology:* An
  Updated Version of the Old Elephant Story
THE DEVELOPMENT OF SOCIOLOGY
  Down-to-Earth Sociology: **Enjoying a Sociology
  Quiz—Sociological Findings versus Common
  Sense** ■ Auguste Comte ■ Herbert Spencer ■
  Karl Marx ■ Emile Durkheim ■ Max Weber
THE ROLE OF VALUES IN SOCIAL RESEARCH
VERSTEHEN AND SOCIAL FACTS
  Weber and Verstehen ■ Durkheim and Social

Facts ■ How Social Facts and Verstehen Fit
Together
SOCIOLOGY IN NORTH AMERICA
THEORETICAL PERSPECTIVES IN SOCIOLOGY
  Symbolic Interactionism ■ Functional
  Analysis ■ Conflict Theory ■ Levels of Analysis:
  Macro and Micro ■ Putting the Theoretical
  Perspectives Together
APPLIED AND CLINICAL SOCIOLOGY
  Perspectives: **Sociology in a World in Turmoil**
SUMMARY
SUGGESTED READINGS

Even from the dim glow of the faded red-and-white exit sign, its light barely reaching the upper bunk, I could see that the sheet was filthy. Resigned to another night of fitful sleep, I reluctantly crawled into bed—tucking my clothes firmly around my body, like a protective cocoon.

The next morning, I joined the long line of disheveled men leaning against the chain-link fence. Their faces were as downcast as their clothes were dirty. Not a glimmer of hope among them.

Speaker Sug. #1: A case worker from a shelter for the homeless.

No one spoke as the line slowly inched forward. When my turn came, I was handed a styrofoam cup of coffee, some utensils, and a bowl of semi-liquid that I couldn't identify. It didn't look like any food I had seen before. Nor did it taste like anything I had ever eaten.

My stomach fought the foul taste, every spoonful a battle. But I was determined. "I will experience what they experience," I kept telling myself. My stomach reluctantly gave in and accepted its morning nourishment.

The room was eerily silent. Hundreds of men were eating, but each was sunk deeply into his own private hell, his head aswim with disappointment, remorse, bitterness.

As I stared at the styrofoam cup holding my solitary post-breakfast pleasure, I noticed what looked like teeth marks. I shrugged off the thought, telling myself that my long weeks as a sociological observer of the homeless were finally getting to me. "That must be some sort of crease from handling," I concluded.

I joined the silent ranks of men turning in their bowls and cups. When I saw the man behind the counter swishing out styrofoam cups in a washtub of water, I began to feel sick at my stomach. I knew then that the jagged marks on my cup really had come from a previous mouth.

How much longer did this research have to last? I felt a deep longing to return to my family—in a world of clean sheets and healthy food.

THE SOCIOLOGICAL PERSPECTIVE

Project 1

L. Obj. 1: Explain the importance of the sociological perspective in understanding human behavior.

CDQ 1: What do you think you may learn from looking at your own world in a different light? How can the sociological perspective be useful for you?

Why were these men so silent? Why did they receive such despicable treatment? What was I doing in that homeless shelter? (After all, I hold a respectable, secure professional position, and I have a home.) And why were there no women among them?

Sociology offers a perspective, a view of the world. The **sociological perspective** (or imagination) provides a look at unfamiliar worlds, as above, *and* a fresh look at familiar worlds. In this text you will find yourself in the midst of motorcycle gangs in the United States, Nazis in Germany, chimpanzees in Africa, and warriors in South America. But you will also find yourself looking at your own world in a different light. Sometimes this sociological journey will make you smile as you see worlds that seem bizarre to you. At other times it may make you uncomfortable, especially if it makes you question your familiar world.

The sociological perspective not only provides a different way of looking at life, including our own comfortable, taken-for-granted worlds, but also is designed to provide an understanding of why people are the way they are. As we look at other worlds, or our own, the sociological perspective casts a light that enables us to gain a new vision of social life. In fact, this is what many find the major value of sociology.

The sociological perspective certainly has been a motivating force in my own life. Ever since I took my first introductory course in sociology, I have been enchanted by the perspective that sociology offers. I have thoroughly enjoyed both observing other groups and questioning my own assumptions of life. I sincerely hope that the same happens to you.

You won't have to stay at homeless shelters to gain an understanding of the homeless; sociologists have already done that. You won't have to ride with a motorcycle gang to understand why its members take pride in being dirty, or why they despise women; sociologists have already done that, too. Through their findings, which we will review in this book, you should gain an understanding of why some people are racists, sexists, or killers—while others work hard to eliminate such problems.

Seeing the Broader Social Context

The sociological perspective, then, opens a window onto the broader social context. To find out why people do what they do, it looks at **social location,** or where people are located in history and society. It focuses on their culture, social class, gender, religion, age, and education. At the center of the sociological perspective is the relationship of one group to another. For example, when sociologists examine how growing up as a female in today's society affects female ideas of what women can attain in life, they in turn look at how those ideas affect not only marriage today but also men's ideas of what *they* can expect.

sociological perspective: an approach to understanding human behavior by placing it within its broader social context

social location: people's group memberships because of their location in history and society

Sociologist C. Wright Mills (1959) said that the sociological perspective "enables us to grasp history and biography and the relationship between the two within society . . . to grasp what is happening to (people) as minute points of the intersection of biography and history within society."

What this means is that people's social experiences—the groups to which people belong and their particular experiences within those groups—underlie what people feel and what they do. If they belonged to different groups—or had different experiences in those groups—their attitudes and behavior would be different too. In short, in the sociological view people don't do what they do because of some sort of internal mechanism, such as instincts. Rather, external influences—people's experiences—become internalized, become part of an individual's thinking and motivations.

An example will make this point obvious. If we were to take a newborn baby away from its American parents today and place that infant with the Yanomamo Indian tribe in the jungles of South America, you know that when that child begins to speak, his or her sounds will not be in English. You also know that the child will not think like an American. He or she will not grow up wanting credit cards, for example, or designer jeans, a new car, and the latest video game. Equally, the child will unquestioningly take his or her place in Yanomamo society—perhaps as a food gatherer, a hunter, or a warrior—and will not even know about the world left behind at birth. And, whether male or female, that child will grow up, not debating whether to have one, two, or three children but assuming that it is natural to want a dozen children.

People around the globe take their particular world for granted. Something inside us Americans tells us that hamburgers are delicious, small families attractive, and designer clothing desirable. Yet something inside the Sinai Desert Arab tribes tells them that warm, fresh camel's blood makes a fine drink and that everyone should have a large family and wear flowing robes (Murray 1935; McCabe and Ellis 1990). And that something certainly isn't an instinct. As sociologist Peter Berger (1963) phrased it, that "something" is "society within us."

Although obvious, this point frequently eludes us. We often think and talk about people's behavior as though it is caused by their sex, their race, or some other factor transmitted by their genes. The sociological perspective helps us to escape from this cramped personal view by exposing the broader social context that underlies human behavior. It helps us to see the links between what people do and the social settings that shape their behavior.

society: a term used by sociologists to refer to a group of people who share a culture and a territory

Applying the sociological perspective to human behavior means to consider the broad social context in which people's lives take place. Just as the Yanomamo of South America set the general guidelines that influence their children, so do all groups around the world.

SOCIOLOGY AND THE OTHER SCIENCES

L. Obj. 2: Define sociology and compare it with the other social sciences.

Just as humans today have an intense desire to unravel the mysteries around them, people in ancient times also attempted to understand their world. Their explanations, however, were not based only on observations, but were mixed with magic and superstition as well.

To satisfy their basic curiosities about the world around them, humans gradually developed **science,** systematic methods used to study the social and natural worlds, as well as the knowledge obtained by those methods. **Sociology,** the scientific study of society and human behavior, is one of the sciences that modern civilization has developed.

A useful way of comparing these sciences—and of gaining a better understanding of sociology's place—is to first divide them into the natural and the social sciences.

The Natural Sciences

The **natural sciences** are the intellectual and academic disciplines designed to comprehend, explain, and predict the events in our natural environment. The endeavors of the natural sciences are divided into specialized fields of research according to subject matter, such as biology, geology, chemistry, and physics. These are further subdivided into even more highly specialized areas, with a further narrowing of content. Biology is divided into botany and zoology, geology into mineralogy and geomorphology, chemistry into its inorganic and organic branches, and physics into biophysics and quantum mechanics. Each area of investigation examines a particular "slice" of nature (Henslin 1993).

Essay #1

Project 2

CDQ 2: What types of subjects might interest political scientists? Economists? Anthropologists? Psychologists? Sociologists?

The Social Sciences

People have not limited themselves to investigating nature. In the pursuit of a more adequate understanding of our world, people have also developed fields of science that focus on the social world. These, the **social sciences,** examine human relationships. Just as the natural sciences are an attempt to objectively understand the world of nature, the social sciences are an attempt to objectively understand the social world. Just as the world of nature contains ordered (or lawful) relationships that are not obvious but must be discovered through controlled observation, so the ordered relationships of the human or social world, too, are hidden, and must be revealed by means of controlled and repeated observations.

Like the natural sciences, the social sciences are divided into specialized fields based on their subject matter. These divisions are anthropology, economics, political science, psychology, and sociology. And the social sciences, too, are subdivided into further specialized fields, whose branches are named for their particular focus. Thus, anthropology is divided into cultural and physical anthropology; economics has macro (large-scale) and micro (small-scale) specialties; political science has theoretical and applied branches; psychology may be clinical or experimental; and sociology has its quantitative and qualitative branches.

Since our focus is sociology, let us contrast sociology with each of the other social sciences. Note that the differences elaborated here are not always this clear in practice, for as they conduct their research social scientists do much that blurs the distinctions between their disciplines.

Political Science. *Political science* focuses on politics and government. Political scientists study the ways in which people govern themselves: the various forms of government, their structures, and their relationships to other institutions of society. Political scientists are especially interested in how people attain ruling positions in their society, how they then maintain those positions, and the consequences of their activities for

science: the application of systematic methods to obtain knowledge and the knowledge obtained by those methods

sociology: the scientific study of society and human behavior

natural sciences: the intellectual and academic disciplines designed to comprehend, explain, and predict events in our natural environment

social sciences: the intellectual and academic disciplines designed to understand the social world objectively by means of controlled and repeated observations

those who are governed. In studying a system of government with a constitutional electorate, such as that of the United States, political scientists are also deeply concerned with voting behavior.

Economics. *Economics* also concentrates on a single social institution. Economists study the production and distribution of the material goods and services of a society. They want to know what goods are being produced at what rate and at what cost, and how those goods are distributed. They are also interested in the choices that determine production, for example, the factors that lead a society to produce a certain item instead of another.

Anthropology. *Anthropology,* in which the primary focus is on preliterate peoples, is the sister discipline of sociology. The chief concern of anthropologists is to understand *culture,* a people's total way of life. Culture includes (1) the artifacts a group produces, such as tools, art, and weapons; (2) the group's structure, that is, the hierarchy and other patterns that determine its members' relationships to one another; (3) a people's ideas and values, especially a belief system and how it affects people's lives; and (4) the group's forms of communication, especially language. The anthropologists' traditional focus on past societies and contemporary preliterate peoples is now giving way somewhat to the study of groups in industrialized settings. Anthropologists who focus on modern societies are practically indistinguishable from sociologists.

Psychology. The focus of *psychology* is on processes that occur *within* the individual, within the "skin-bound organism." Psychologists are primarily concerned with mental processes: intelligence, emotions, perception, and memory. Some concentrate on attitudes and values; others are especially interested in personality, in mental aberration (psychopathology, or mental illness), and in how individuals cope with the problems they face.

Sociology. *Sociology* has many similarities to the other social sciences. Like political scientists, sociologists study how people govern one another, especially the impact of various forms of government on people's lives. Like economists, sociologists are extremely concerned with what happens to the goods and services of a society—but sociologists place their focus on the social consequences of production and distribution. Like anthropologists, sociologists study culture; they have a particular interest in the social consequences of material goods, group structure, and belief systems, as well as in how people communicate with one another. Like psychologists, sociologists are also concerned with how people adjust to the difficulties of life.

   Given these overall similarities, then, what distinguishes sociology from the other social sciences? Unlike political scientists and economists, sociologists do not concentrate on a single social institution. Unlike anthropologists, sociologists focus primarily on industrialized societies. And unlike psychologists, sociologists stress factors *external* to the individual to determine what influences people. In succeeding chapters, these distinctions will become clearer. The Down-to-Earth Sociology box on page 6 revisits an old fable about how members of different disciplines perceive the same subject matter.

CDQ 3: What does the updated version of the old elephant story tell you about the relationship between the social sciences?

The Goals of Science

The first goal of each science is to *explain* why something happens. The second goal is to make **generalizations**, that is, to go beyond the individual case and make statements that apply to a broader group or situation. For example, a sociologist wants to explain not only why Mary went to college or became an armed robber but also why people with her characteristics are more likely than others to go to college or to become armed robbers. To achieve generalizations, sociologists and other scientists

generalization: a statement that goes beyond the individual case and is applied to a broader group or situation

DOWN-TO-EARTH SOCIOLOGY

An Updated Version of the Old Elephant Story

It is said that in the recent past five wise men and women, all blindfolded, were led to an elephant. Each was asked to explain what they "saw." The first, a psychologist, feeling the top of the head, said, "This is the only thing that counts. All feeling and thinking takes place inside here. To understand this beast, we need study only this."

The second, an anthropologist, tenderly touching the trunk and the tusks, said, "This is really primitive. I feel very comfortable here. Concentrate on these."

The third, a political scientist, feeling the gigantic ears, said, "This is the power center. What goes in here controls the entire beast. Concentrate your studies here."

The fourth, an economist, feeling the mouth, said, "This is what counts. What goes in here is distributed throughout the body. Concentrate your studies on this."

Then came the sociologist (of course!), who, feeling the entire body, said, "You can't understand the beast by concentrating on only one part. Each is but part of the whole. The head, the trunk and tusks, the ears, the

mouth—all are important. And so are the parts of the beast that you haven't even mentioned. We must remove our blindfolds so we can see the larger picture. We have to see how everything works together to form the entire animal."

Pausing for emphasis, the sociologist added, "And we also need to understand how this creature interacts with similar creatures. How does their life in groups influence their behaviors?"

I wish I could conclude this fable by saying that the psychologist, the anthropologist, the political scientist, and the economist, dazzled upon hearing the wisdom of the sociologist, amidst gasps of wonderment threw away their blindfolds and, joining together, began to examine the larger picture. But, alas and alack! Upon hearing this sage advice, each stubbornly bound their blindfolds even tighter to concentrate all the more on the single part. And if you listened very, very carefully you could even hear them saying, "The top of the head is mine—stay away from it." "Don't touch the tusks." "Take your hand off the ears." "Stay away from the mouth—that's my area."

Project 3

CDQ 4: What common sense notions did you learn as you were growing up? What sociologists agree with them?

Project 4

patterns: recurring characteristics or events

common sense: those things that "everyone knows" are true

look for **patterns,** recurring characteristics or events. The third scientific goal is to *predict,* to specify what will happen in the future in the light of current knowledge.

To attain these goals, scientists must rely not on magic, superstition, or common beliefs but on conclusions based on systematic studies. They need to examine evidence with an open mind, in such a way that it can be checked by others. Secrecy, prejudice, and other biases, with their inherent closures, go against the grain of science.

Sociologists and other scientists also move beyond **common sense,** those ideas that prevail in a society that "everyone knows" are true. Just because "everyone" knows something is true does not make it so. "Everyone" can be mistaken, today just as easily as when common sense dictated that the world was flat, or that the sun rotated around the earth, or that no human could ever walk on the moon.

As sociologists and other social scientists examine people's assumptions about the world, their findings may contradict commonsense notions about social life. The Down-to-Earth Sociology box on page 7 provides a number of examples.

Sometimes the explorations of sociologists take them into nooks and crannies that people would prefer remain unexplored. A sociologist might, for example, study how people make decisions to commit a crime or to cheat on their spouse. Because sociologists want above all to understand social life, they can neither rely on unfounded assumptions nor cease their studies because people feel uncomfortable. With all realms of human life considered legitimate avenues of exploration by sociologists, their findings sometimes challenge even cherished ideas.

As they examine how groups operate, sociologists often confront prejudice and attempts to keep things secret. It seems that every organization, every group, nourishes a pet image that it presents to the public. Sociologists are interested in knowing what is really going on behind the scenes, however, so they peer beneath the surface to get past that sugarcoated image of suppressed facts (Berger 1963). This approach sometimes brings sociologists into conflict with people who feel threatened by that information—which is all part of the adventure, and risk, of being a sociologist.

THE DEVELOPMENT OF SOCIOLOGY

Just how did sociology begin? Has it always been around? Or is it relatively new?

In some ways it is difficult to answer these questions. By the time Jesus Christ was born, the Greeks and Romans had already developed intricate systems of philosophy about human behavior. Even preliterate peoples made observations about their tribal lives and were most likely aware, for example, which classes of people were more privileged and powerful. They also analyzed *why* life was as it was, but in doing so they often depended on magic, superstition, or explanations based on the positions of the stars.

Simple assertions of truth—or observations mixed with magic or superstition or the stars—are not adequate. *All science requires the development of theories that can be proved or disproved by systematic research.*

This fact simplifies the question of the origin of sociology, for measured by this standard sociology is clearly a recent discipline. It emerged about the middle of the nineteenth century when European social observers began to use scientific methods to test their ideas. Three factors combined to lead to the development of sociology.

The first was social upheaval in Europe. By the middle of the nineteenth century, Europe found itself experiencing the effects of the Industrial Revolution. This change from agriculture to factory production brought violent changes to people's lives. Masses of people, forced off the land, moved to the cities in search of work. There they were met with anonymity, crowding, filth, and poverty. Their ties to the land, to the generations that had lived there before them, and to their way of life were abruptly broken. The city greeted them with horrible working conditions: low pay, long, exhausting hours, dangerous work, bad ventilation, and much noise. To survive, families had to permit their children to work in these same conditions, some of them even chained to factory machines to make certain they did not run away.

No area of people's lives was left untouched, not even their personal relationships.

L. Obj. 3: Discuss how and why sociology emerged as a science in the middle of the nineteenth-century in Europe.

CDQ 5: Why do you think the timing was "ripe" in Europe for sociology to develop? Do you think the timing is "ripe" in the United States today for a resurgence of interest in sociology?

Project 5

DOWN-TO-EARTH SOCIOLOGY

Enjoying a Sociology Quiz—Sociological Findings versus Common Sense

Some findings of sociology support commonsense understandings of social life, while others contradict them. Can you tell the difference? If you want to enjoy this quiz fully, before turning the page to check your answers complete *all* the questions.

1 True/False The earnings of American women have just about caught up with those of American men.

2. True/False People on city streets at night are less helpful and friendly than people on city streets during the day.

3. True/False When faced with natural disasters such as floods and earthquakes, people panic and social organization disintegrates.

4. True/False Revolutions are more likely to occur when conditions are consistently bad than when they are improving rapidly.

5. True/False Most people on welfare are lazy and looking for a handout. They could work if they wanted to.

6. True/False Most American Roman Catholics oppose birth control.

7. True/False Compared with men, women touch each other more while they are conversing.

8. True/False Compared with women, men maintain more eye contact while they are conversing.

9. True/False Because of the rapid rise in the divorce rate in the United States, American children are much more likely to live in a single-parent household now than they were a century ago.

10. True/False The first statement *is* true, but what about the second? Each year the federal government computes an official poverty line, used to determine who is eligible for welfare and food stamps. Most welfare families live in poverty for at least five years.

11. True/False The more available alcohol is (as measured by the number of places to purchase alcohol per one hundred people), the more alcohol-related injuries and fatalities occur on American highways.

12. True/False Couples who live together before marriage usually report higher satisfaction with their marriages than couples who do not live together before marriage.

DOWN-TO-EARTH SOCIOLOGY

Sociological Findings versus Common Sense—Answers to the Sociology Quiz

1. False. The income gap has narrowed only slightly. Full-time working women earn on average only about 65 percent of what full-time working men earn; this low figure is actually an improvement, for in the 1970s women's incomes averaged about 60 percent of men's.

2. False. Using objective tests of helpfulness and friendliness (asking directions, planting a lost billfold, and so on), sociologists found that the opposite was true (Melbin 1988).

3. False. Following such disasters people develop *greater* cohesion, cooperation, and social organization to deal with the catastrophe.

4. False. Just the opposite is true. When conditions are consistently bad people are more likely to be resigned to their fate, while rapid improvement causes their aspirations to outrace their circumstances, which can increase frustration and foment revolution.

5. False. The vast majority of people on welfare are children, the old, the sick, the mentally and physically handicapped, or young mothers with few skills. Less than 2 percent meet the common stereotype of an able bodied male—and many of these are actively looking for jobs.

6. False. About 80 percent of American Roman Catholics favor birth control.

7. False. Men touch each other more during conversations (Whyte 1989; Henley, Hamilton, and Thornell 1985).

8. False. Female speakers maintain considerably more eye contact with their conversational partners (Henley and Hamilton 1985).

9. False. Strange as it may sound, the proportion of children who live with one parent is roughly the same today as it was one hundred years ago. A century back, many parents died at an early age, leaving only one parent to rear the children. Advances in public health and medicine, which have increased longevity, have greatly reduced this source of one-parent families—though a much higher divorce rate has made up the difference.

10. False. The usual pattern is for families to move in and out of poverty as divorce occurs, as wage earners lose a job or are rehired, when additional children are born, and so on. Only about 4 percent of American families stay below the poverty line for five consecutive years (Duncan and Morgan 1979; Ruggles 1989, 1990).

11. False. Counties in which alcohol is more readily available do not experience more alcohol-related injuries and fatalities, according to findings by researchers who compared the number of alcohol outlets per population in California counties with the alcohol-related highway injuries and fatalities in those same counties (Kohfeld and Leip 1991).

12. False. The opposite is true, perhaps because many couples who marry after cohabiting are less committed to marriage in the first place—and a key to marital success is firm commitment to one another. (Cf. Larson 1988.)

Today it is understood that many relationships are casual and fleeting, involving no more than a perfunctory greeting to, for example, a bank teller or a supermarket clerk. Life was not always like this, however; before the Industrial Revolution people had few impersonal relationships. As historian Peter Laslett (1984) put it, "There were no hotels, hostels, or blocks of flats for single persons, very few hospitals and . . . almost no young men and women living on their own." Individuals were permanently embedded in social circles in which their own reputations, as well as that of their family, were well known.

With the successes of the American and French revolutions, in which the idea that individuals have inalienable rights caught fire, the political systems in other countries slowly began to give way to more democratic forms. As the traditional order was challenged, religion lost much of its force as the unfailing source of answers to life's perplexing questions. Each fundamental social change further undermined traditional explanations of human existence.

When tradition reigns supreme, it provides a ready answer: "We do this because it has always been done this way." Such societies offer minimal encouragement for original thinking. Since the answers are already provided, there is little impetus to search for explanations. Sweeping change, however, does the opposite: by upsetting the existing order, it encourages questioning and demands answers.

And the rapid, turbulent social change engulfing nineteenth-century Europe begged for explanation.

The French Revolution of 1789 overthrew not only the aristocracy, but upset the entire social order. With change so extensive, and the past no longer a sure guide to the present, Auguste Comte (1798–1857) began to analyze how societies change, thus ushering in the modern science of sociology.

The second factor that encouraged the development of sociology was the development of imperialism. The Europeans had been successful in conquering many parts of the world. Their new colonial empires, stretching from Asia through Africa to North America, exposed them to radically different cultures. Those contrasting ways of life raised questions about why cultures differed.

The third factor was the success of the natural sciences. Advances in chemistry and physics, for example, had begun to transform the world. Given this strong emphasis on searching for answers in the physical world, it seemed logical to apply the method developed by the natural sciences—objective, systematic observations to test theories—to the social world as well.

Auguste Comte

This idea of applying the scientific method to the social world, known as **positivism,** was apparently first proposed by Auguste Comte (1798–1857). With the French Revolution still fresh in his mind, Comte left the small, conservative town in which he had grown up and moved to Paris. The changes he himself experienced, combined with those France underwent in the revolution, led Comte to become fascinated with the twin problems of social order and social change (which he called "social statics" and "social dynamics"). What holds society together, he wondered, so that it is able to function as a cohesive whole? What brings social order instead of anarchy or chaos? And then, once society does become set on a particular course, what causes it to change? Why doesn't it always continue in the direction it began?

As he pondered these questions, Comte concluded that the right way to answer them was to apply the scientific method to social life; just as it had revealed the absolute and immutable law of gravity so would this method uncover the laws that underlie society. A new science was needed, based on positivism, which would apply the social principles it would discover to social reform. Comte called this new science *sociology*— "the study of society" (from the Greek *logos*, "study of," and the Latin *socius*, companion, "being with others").

Essay #2

L. Obj. 4: Identify and explain the theoretical perspectives of Auguste Comte, Herbert Spencer, Karl Marx, Emile Durkheim, and Max Weber.

K.P.: Auguste Comte

positivism: the application of the scientific approach to the social world

K.P.: Herbert Spencer

K.P.: Karl Marx

K.P.: Emile Durkheim

CDQ 6: What do we know about suicide today that confirms some of Durkheim's assumptions of over 100 years ago? In what ways has our knowledge of suicide grown beyond that of Durkheim's day?

Project 6

Unfortunately, Comte did not take his own advice. He never conducted scientific investigations. Nevertheless, because he developed this idea and coined the term sociology, he is often credited with being the founder of sociology.

Herbert Spencer

Herbert Spencer (1820–1903), who grew up in England, is sometimes called the second founder of sociology. He too believed that society operates according to fixed laws. Spencer was convinced that societies evolve in the same manner as animal species. As generations pass, the most capable and intelligent ("the fittest") members of a society survive, while the less capable die out. Thus, over time, societies steadily improve.

Spencer called this principle "the survival of the fittest." Although Spencer coined this phrase, it is usually attributed to his contemporary, Charles Darwin, who later proposed that living organisms evolve over time in order to survive the conditions of their environment. Because of their similarities, Spencer's views of the evolution of societies became known as *social Darwinism.*

Unlike Comte, Spencer did not think sociology should guide social reform. In fact, he was convinced that no one should intervene in the evolution of society. The fittest members didn't need any help. They would always survive on their own and produce a more advanced society unless misguided do-gooders got in the way and helped the less fit survive. Consequently, Spencer's ideas—that charity and helping the poor were wrong, whether carried out by individuals or by the government—appalled many. Not surprisingly, wealthy industrialists, who saw themselves as "the fittest" (superior), found Spencer's ideas attractive. And not coincidentally, his views also assuaged any feelings of guilt they might have had for living like royalty while people around them starved.

Like Comte, Spencer was more of a social philosopher than a sociologist. Also like Comte, Spencer did not conduct scientific studies, but simply developed ideas about society and based his conclusions on those ideas. Eventually, after gaining a wide following in England and the United States, Spencer's ideas about social Darwinism were discredited.

Karl Marx

Karl Marx (1818–1883), a third individual who influenced sociology, also left his mark on world history. Marx's influence has been so great that even that staunch advocate of capitalism, *The Wall Street Journal,* has called him one of the three greatest modern thinkers (the other two being Sigmund Freud and Albert Einstein).

Like Comte, Marx thought that people should take active steps to change society. Marx, who came to England after being exiled from his native Germany for proposing revolution, believed that the key to human history was **class conflict.** According to Marxist theory, the *bourgeoisie* (the controlling class of capitalists who own the means to produce wealth) are locked in inevitable conflict with the *proletariat* (the exploited class, the mass of workers who do not own the means of production). This bitter struggle can end only when members of the working class unite in revolution and throw off their chains of bondage. The result will be a classless society, one free of exploitation in which all individuals will work according to their abilities and receive according to their needs (Marx and Engels 1848, 1967).

It is important to note that Marxism is not the same as communism. Although Marx stood firmly behind revolution as the only way for the proletariat to gain control of society, he did not develop the political system called communism, which was a later application of his ideas (and rapidly changing ones at that). Indeed, Marx himself felt disgusted when he heard debates about his insights into social life. After listening to some of the positions attributed to him, he even declared, "I am not a Marxist" (Dobriner 1969:222).

Karl Marx (1818–1883) believed that the roots of human misery lay in the exploitation of the proletariat, or propertyless working classes, by the capitalist class which owned the means of production. Social change, in the form of the overthrow of the capitalists by the proletarians, was inevitable from Marx's perspective. While Marx did not consider himself a sociologist, his ideas have profoundly influenced many in the discipline, particularly conflict theorists.

Unlike Comte and Spencer, Marx did not think of himself as a sociologist. He spent years studying in the library of the British Museum in London, where he wrote widely on history, philosophy, and, of course, economics and political science. Because of his insights into the relationship between the social classes, especially the class struggle between the "haves" and the "have-nots," many sociologists today continue to claim Marx as a significant early sociologist. He also introduced one of the major perspectives in sociology, conflict theory, which is discussed below.

Emile Durkheim

Emile Durkheim (1858–1917), who was born and reared in eastern France, was educated in both Germany and France. Durkheim received the first academic appointment in sociology in a French university, teaching first at the University of Bordeaux in 1887, and moving to the more prestigious Sorbonne in 1906 (Coser 1977).

Durkheim insisted on rigorous research. In a study still quoted today, he compared the suicide rates of several European countries. He (1897/1966) found that each country's suicide rate is different and that it remains remarkably stable year after year. He also found that different groups within a country have their own rate of killing themselves. For example, Protestants, the wealthy, males, and the unmarried killed themselves at a higher rate than did Catholics, Jews, the poor, females, and the married. From this, Durkheim drew the original and highly insightful conclusion that suicide is actually quite a different phenomenon than its commonsense interpretation would suggest. Suicide, he said, is not simply a matter of an individual here and there deciding to take his or her own life for personal reasons. Rather, *social factors underlie suicide,* and this is what keeps those rates fairly constant year after year.

Durkheim identified **social integration,** the degree to which people are tied to their social group as a key social factor in suicide. He found that people with weak social ties were more likely to commit suicide. This factor explained the higher suicide rate among Protestants, males, the wealthy, and the unmarried. Protestantism, Durkheim argued, encourages greater freedom of thought and action; males are more independent than females; wealthy people have greater choices in life; and the unmarried are less socially integrated than those bound by the ties and responsibilities of marriage. In other words, the level of social integration among these groups is not high enough to hold them back from suicide.

Durkheim also noted that although strong social bonds help to protect people from suicide, in some instances bonds that are very strong can encourage suicide. To illustrate this type of suicide, which he termed *altruistic suicide,* Durkheim used the example of grieving people who kill themselves following the death of a dearly loved spouse. Their own feelings are so integrated with those of their spouse that they prefer death rather than life without the one who gave meaning to life. Another example of altruistic suicide is the Japanese kamikaze pilots in World War II, whose missions were to ram their bomb-laden planes into enemy ships.

Almost one hundred years later, Durkheim's work is still quoted because of its scientific rigor and excellent theoretical interpretations. (The topic of theories is covered below.) Durkheim's research was so thorough that its principles apply equally to contemporary life: People who are less socially integrated continue to have a higher rate of suicide. Those same categories of people that Durkheim identified— Protestants, males, the wealthy, and the unmarried—are still more likely to kill themselves than are others.

Durkheim was concerned about the tendency of modern society to increase anomie, and thereby suicide. By **anomie,** Durkheim meant a lack of social integration—a feeling of being out of place, of not belonging, of having lost a sense of direction or purpose in life. Industrial societies, he said, encourage anomie by their **division of labor.** When people's tasks are divided by occupational specialties, they may feel isolated, no more than small cogs in an unfamiliar wheel that continues to grind them down.

The great French sociologist Emile Durkheim (1858–1917) contributed many important concepts to the discipline of sociology. His systematic study comparing suicide rates among several countries revealed an underlying social factor: People were more likely to commit suicide if their ties to others in their communities were weak. Durkheim's identification of the key role of social integration on social life remains central to sociology today.

class conflict: Marx's term for the struggle between the proletariat and the bourgeoisie

social facts: Durkheim's term for the patterns of behavior that characterize a social group

social integration: the degree to which people feel a part of social groups

anomie: Emile Durkheim's term for lack of social integration—a feeling of being out of place, of not belonging, of having lost a sense of direction or purpose in life

division of labor: Emile Durkheim's term for the allocation of people into occupational specialties

Emile Durkheim used the term anomie *to refer to the lack of a sense of intimate belonging. Durkheim believed that people in modern societies were in danger of feeling isolated, especially as a result of the strict division of labor characteristic of modern life. In contrast, members of traditional societies, who till the soil and work alongside family and neighbors, experience a high degree of social integration—the opposite of anomie.*

Max Weber (1864–1920) was another early sociologist who left a profound impression on sociology. He used cross-cultural and historical materials in order to determine how extensively culture affects people's orientations to life and to trace the causes of societal change.

Like Comte, Durkheim (1893/1933) proposed that sociologists actively intervene in society. To overcome anomie, he suggested that new social groups be created. Standing somewhere between the state and the family, those groups would help meet the need for a sense of belonging that the impersonality of industrial society was eroding. Central to all of Durkheim's studies was the idea that human behavior cannot be understood simply in individualistic terms, that it must be understood within its larger social context.

Max Weber

Max Weber (1864–1920) (Mahx VAY-ber), a German sociologist and a contemporary of Durkheim's, also held professorships in the new academic discipline of sociology. He was a renowned scholar who, like Marx, wrote in several academic fields. He agreed with much of what Marx wrote, but he strongly disagreed that economics is the central force in social change. Weber (1904/1958) instead saw religion as playing that role. He theorized that the belief systems provided by Roman Catholicism and Protestantism differed so radically that Roman Catholics would hold onto traditional ways of life, while Protestants were more likely to embrace change. To test his theory, Weber compared the economic development of several countries with the level of dominance of Protestantism or Catholicism within those countries. His conclusion—that Protestantism encourages greater economic development and in fact was the central factor in the rise of capitalism in those countries—was controversial, and is still debated by scholars today (Dickson and McLachlan 1989). Weber's analysis of the significance of religion is discussed in more detail in Chapters 7 and 18.

THE ROLE OF VALUES IN SOCIAL RESEARCH

Weber also raised another issue that remains controversial among sociologists when he declared that sociology should be **value free.** By this, he meant that a sociologist's **values,** personal beliefs about what is good or worthwhile in life and the way the world ought to be, should not affect his or her social research. Weber wanted **objectivity,** total neutrality, to be the hallmark of sociological research. If it were not, he said, sociological research would be contaminated.

Objectivity as an ideal value is not a matter of debate in sociology. All sociologists agree that objectivity is a proper goal, in the sense that sociologists should not distort data to make them fit preconceived ideas or personal values, and that research reports must accurately reflect actual, not desired findings. On the other hand, it is equally clear that no sociologist can escape values entirely. Like everyone else, sociologists are members of a particular society at a given point in history and are therefore infused with values of all sorts, which inevitably play a role in their research. For example, values are part of the reason that one sociologist chooses to do research on the Mafia, while another turns a sociological eye on kindergarten students. To overcome the distortions that values can cause, sociologists stress *replication,* that is, the repetition of a study by other researchers to see how the results compare. If values have unwittingly influenced research findings, replication by other sociologists should uncover this and correct the problem.

In spite of this consensus, however, the proper role of values in sociology is still hotly debated. The problem especially concerns ideas about the proper *purposes* and *uses* of sociological research. On these, there is much disagreement. Regarding the purposes of sociology, some sociologists take the position that sociology's proper role is to advance understanding. Sociologists should gather data on any aspect of social life in which they are interested and then use the best theory available to interpret their findings objectively. Others are convinced that it is the responsibility of sociologists to explore harmful social arrangements of society—to investigate what causes poverty, crime, war, and various forms of human exploitation.

Regarding the uses of sociology, those who say that understanding is sociology's proper goal take the position that the purpose of social research should be to add to the sum of scientific knowledge about human life. That knowledge then belongs to the scientific community and to the world and can be used by anyone for any purpose. In contrast, those who say that sociology should explore harmful social arrangements take the position that sociological knowledge should be used to reform society. They say that social arrangements should be studied for the purpose of improving social life— alleviating human suffering and making society a better place to live.

Although the sociological debate about the proper role of values is infinitely more complicated than the argument presented here—few sociologists take such one-sided views—the above sketch does identify its major issues. Perhaps sociologist John Galliher (1991) best expresses the majority position.

> Some argue that social scientists, unlike politicians and religious leaders, should merely attempt to describe and explain the events of the world but should never make value judgments based on those observations. Yet a value-free and nonjudgmental social science has no place in a world that has experienced the Holocaust, in a world having had slavery, in a world with the ever-present threat of rape and other sexual assault, in a world with frequent, unpunished crimes in high places, including the production of products known by their manufacturers to cause death and injury as has been true of asbestos products and continues to be true of the cigarette industry, and in a world dying from environmental pollution by these same large multinational corporations.

VERSTEHEN AND SOCIAL FACTS

Weber and Verstehen

Weber also stressed that one cannot understand human behavior simply by looking at statistics. Those cold numbers may represent people's activities, he said, but they must be interpreted. In contrast, we need to use **Verstehen** (a German word meaning "to understand"). Perhaps the best translation of this term is "to grasp by insight." By emphasizing *Verstehen,* Weber meant that the best interpreter of human action is

---

K.P.: Max Weber

CDQ 7: Can religion bring about social change? Did the teachings of religious leaders such as Dr. Martin Luther King, Jr. lead to social change in the United States?

Essay #3

L. Obj. 5: State the key issues in the sociological debate about the proper role of values in sociology.

CDQ 8: Do you think it is possible for a researcher's preconceived ideas or personal values to interfere with his or her research on capital punishment? Abortion? Euthanasia (mercy killing)?

L. Obj. 6: Explain what Max Weber meant by **Verstehen** and Emile Durkheim meant by social facts.

value free: the view that a sociologist's personal values or biases should not influence social research

values: ideas about what is good or worthwhile in life; attitudes about the way the world ought to be

objectivity: total neutrality

Verstehen: a German word used by Weber that is perhaps best understood as "to have insight into someone's situation"

CDQ 9: How can **Verstehen** help us to understand why homeless men in a shelter might be silent while college students often are noisy and sometimes boisterous?

someone who "has been there," someone who can understand the feelings and motivations of the people they are studying. In short, we must pay attention to what are called **subjective meanings,** the ways in which people interpret their own behavior. We can't understand what people do, Weber insisted, unless we look at how people themselves view and explain their behavior.

To better understand this term, let's return to the homeless in the opening vignette. Why were the men so silent? Why were they so unlike the noisy, sometimes boisterous college students in their dorms and cafeterias?

Verstehen can help explain this. When I interviewed men in the shelters (and in other settings, homeless women), they talked about their despair. As someone who knows—at least on some level—what the human emotion of despair is, you are immediately able to apply it to their situation. You know that people in despair feel a sense of hopelessness. They are filled with dissatisfaction and have little desire to experience life intensely. The future looks bleak, hardly worth plodding toward. Consequently, what is there worth talking about anyway? Who wants to hear another hard-luck story?

Contrast this scene with the animated conversations of any college cafeteria. College students represent the opposite end of the spectrum. To be sure, college has its ups and downs, but college life indicates a hopeful future. All of life lies ahead. The world beckons with accomplishments yet unknown—career, marriage, children. There is much to talk about, and among friends who share similar aspirations, you are interested in what others have to say. But the homeless? They live among detached, disinterested strangers, further dragged down by contact with others whose bleak lives of despair indicate a hopeless future.

By applying *Verstehen*—your understanding of what it means to be human and to face various situations in life—you gain an understanding of people's behavior, in this case the silence, the lack of communication, among the homeless.

Durkheim and Social Facts

In contrast to Weber's use of Verstehen, or subjective understandings, Durkheim stressed what he called *social facts*. By this term, he meant the patterns of behavior that characterize a social group. (Note however that Weber did not disagree about the significance of social facts, for they are the basis of his conclusions about Protestantism and capitalism.) That movie attendance is higher on weekends, that June is the most popular month for weddings, that suicide is most common among people sixty-five and over, and that more births occur on Tuesdays than any other day of the week—these are all social facts.

Social facts, said Durkheim, must be interpreted using social facts. In other words, each pattern reflects some underlying condition of society. People all over the country don't just coincidentally decide to do things in a similar way, whether seeing a movie or committing suicide. If that were the case, in some years weekends would be the most popular time for moviegoing, while in other years it would be Mondays and Tuesdays; in some years middle-aged people would be the most likely to kill themselves, in other years, young people, and so on. Patterns that hold true year after year, however, indicate that as thousands and even millions of people make their individual decisions, they are responding to conditions in their society. It is the job of the sociologist, then, to uncover social facts and then to explain them through other social facts—in the above instances, patterns of the work week, the school year, conditions of the aged, and the social organization of medicine respectively.

CDQ 10: Do you know why more Americans are born on Tuesday than any other day of the week? How can a combination of social facts and Verstehen be useful in explaining this phenomenon?

How Social Facts and Verstehen Fit Together

Social facts and Verstehen go hand in hand. As a member of American society, you know immediately why Fridays are more popular for moviegoing than Wednesdays, for

subjective meanings: the meanings that people attach to their own behavior

you have personally experienced the routines of our work week that make Friday evenings so attractive for dates and other social activities. In the same way, you know how June weddings are related to the end of the school year and how this month, now locked in tradition, common sentiment, and advertising, carries its own momentum. As for suicide among the elderly, covered in depth in Chapter 13, you probably already have a sense of the greater despair that Americans of this age feel.

But do you know why more Americans are born on Tuesday than any other day of the week? One would expect Tuesday to be no more common than any other day, and that is how it used to be. But no longer. To understand what happened, we need a combination of social facts and Verstehen. Three social facts are relevant: First, as discussed in Chapter 19, technological developments have made the hospital a dominating force in the American medical system. Second, current technology has made delivery by cesarean section safer. Third, the medical establishment is controlled by males who have profit as a top goal. As a result, an operation that used to be reserved for emergencies has become so routine that one-fourth of all American babies are now delivered in this manner, five times the rate of 1970 (*Statistical Abstract* 1991: 91). To these social facts, then, we add Verstehen. In this instance, it is understanding the preferences of mothers-to-be to give birth in a hospital, and the perceived lack of alternatives. Consequently, physicians schedule large numbers of deliveries for their own convenience, with most finding that Tuesdays fit their week best.

SOCIOLOGY IN NORTH AMERICA

Transplanted to American soil in the late nineteenth century, sociology first took root at the University of Chicago and at Atlanta University, then an all-black school. From there, academic specialties in sociology spread throughout American higher education. The growth was gradual, however. Although the first department of sociology in North America opened in 1892 at the University of Chicago, it was not until 1922 that McGill University gave Canada its first department of sociology. Harvard University did not open its department of sociology until 1930, and the University of California at Berkeley, which now has one of the strongest departments in the nation, did not follow until the 1950s.

At first, sociology in the United States was dominated by the department at the University of Chicago, founded by Albion Small (1854–1926), who also founded the *American Journal of Sociology* and was its editor from 1895 to 1925. Still preeminent in the field, the journal continues to be published at the University of Chicago. Members of this first sociology department whose ideas continue to influence today's sociologists include Robert E. Park (1864–1944), Ernest Burgess (1886–1966) and George Herbert Mead (1863–1931), who developed the symbolic interactionist perspective to be examined below.

W.E.B. Du Bois (1868–1963), an African American who completed his education at the University of Berlin, created a sociological laboratory at Atlanta University in 1897. His lifetime research interest was relations between whites and African Americans in the United States, and he published a book on this subject every year between 1896 and 1914. At first, Du Bois was content simply to collect and interpret objective data. Later, frustrated at the continuing exploitation of blacks, Du Bois turned to social action and helped found the National Association for the Advancement of Colored People (NAACP). Continuing to battle racism both as a sociologist and as a journalist, he finally embraced revolutionary Marxism. He later moved to Ghana, where he is buried (Stark 1989).

Like Du Bois, and following the advice of Comte, many of the early North American sociologists combined the role of sociologist with that of social reformer. They saw society, or parts of it, as corrupt and in need of serious reform. During the 1920s and

L. Obj. 7: Trace the development of sociology in the United States from its origins at the University of Chicago to its present-day perspectives.

K.P.: Albion Small

K.P.: W. E. B. Du Bois

CDQ 11: Why were some early American sociologists more interested in social reform or activism than others? Do you think sociologists today are more interested in academic pursuits or social reform?

W.E.B. Du Bois (1863–1963) spent his lifetime studying relations between whites and African Americans. Like many early North American sociologists, Du Bois combined the role of academic sociologist with that of social reformer.

1930s Park and Burgess not only studied prostitution, crime, drug addiction, and juvenile delinquency but also offered suggestions for how to alleviate these social problems.

During the 1940s, the sociology departments at Harvard, Michigan, Wisconsin, and Columbia universities challenged the preeminent position of the University of Chicago. At the same time, the academic emphasis shifted from social reform to social theory. Talcott Parsons (1902–1979), for example, developed abstract models of society that exerted great influence on sociology. These models of how the parts of society harmoniously work together did nothing to stimulate social activism.

Robert K. Merton (b. 1910) stressed the need for sociologists to develop **middle-range theories,** explanations that tie together many research findings but avoid the sweeping generalizations that attempt to account for everything. Such theories, he claimed, are preferable because they can be tested. Grand theories, on the other hand, while attractive because they seem to account for so much of social life, are of little value because they cannot be tested. Merton (1968) developed a middle-range theory of crime and deviant behavior (discussed in Chapter 8) that explains how American society's emphasis on attaining material wealth increases crime.

C. Wright Mills (1916–1962) deplored the theoretical abstractions of this period, which he said were accompanied by empty research methods. Mills (1956) urged sociologists to get back to social reform, seeing imminent danger to freedom in the coalescing of interests of the power elite—the wealthy, the politicians, and the military. After his death, the turbulence in American society in the 1960s and 1970s, fueled by the Vietnam War, also disturbed American sociology. As interest in social activism revived, Mills's ideas became popular among a new generation of sociologists.

The Present.   Since the 1970s, American sociology has not been dominated by any one theoretical orientation or by any single concern. Three theoretical frameworks are most commonly used, as we shall see below, and social activism remains an option for sociologists. Some sociologists are content to study various aspects of social life, interpret their findings, and publish these findings in sociology journals. Others direct their research and publications toward social change and actively participate in community affairs to help bring about their vision of a more just society.

During the past two decades, the activities of sociologists have broadened. Once just about the only occupation open to a graduate in sociology was teaching. Although most sociologists still enter teaching, the government has now become their second-largest source of employment. Many other sociologists work for private firms in management and planning positions. Still others work in criminology and demography, in social work, and as counselors. Sociologists put their training to use in such diverse efforts as tracking the spread of AIDS and helping teenage prostitutes escape from pimps. This book will later look more closely at some of these applications of sociology.

At this point, however, let's concentrate on a better understanding of sociological theory.

THEORETICAL PERSPECTIVES IN SOCIOLOGY

Facts never interpret themselves. They must always be interpreted by being placed into a framework. That conceptual framework is called a theory. A **theory** is a general statement about how some parts of the world fit together and how they work. It is an explanation of how two or more facts are related to one another. By providing a framework in which to fit observations, each theory interprets reality in a distinct way.

Three major theories have emerged within the discipline of sociology: symbolic interactionism, functionalism, and conflict theory. Let us first look at the main elements of these theories and then apply each theory to the question of why the divorce rate in the United States is so high.

K.P.: Robert K. Merton

K.P.: C. Wright Mills

TR#1: Major Theoretical Perspectives in Society

L. Obj. 8: Explain the major differences in the three major theoretical perspectives: symbolic interactionism, functional analysis, and conflict theory.

Project 7

TR#1M: American Marriage, American Divorce

middle-range theories: explanations of human behavior that go beyond a particular observation or research but avoid sweeping generalizations that attempt to account for everything

theory: a general statement about how some parts of the world fit together and how they work; an explanation of how two or more facts are related to one another

TABLE 1.1 Major Theoretical Perspectives in Sociology

Perspective	Usual level of analysis	Focus of analysis	Key terms	Applying the perspectives to the divorce rate of the United States
SYMBOLIC INTERACTIONISM	Microsociological—examines small-scale patterns of social interaction	Face-to-face interaction; how people use symbols to create social life	Symbols Interaction Meanings Definitions	Industrialization and urbanization change marital roles and lead to a redefinition of the nature of love, marriage, children, and divorce
FUNCTIONALISM (also called Structural Functionalism)	Macrosociological—examines large-scale patterns of society	Relationships among the parts of society; how these parts are *functional* (have beneficial consequences) or *dysfunctional* (have negative consequences)	Structure Functions (manifest and latent) Dysfunction Equilibrium	As social change erodes the traditional functions of the family, family ties are weakened and the divorce rate increases
CONFLICT THEORY	Macrosociological—examines large-scale patterns of society	The struggle for scarce resources by groups in a society; how dominant elites use power to control the less powerful	Inequality Power Conflict Competition Exploitation	When men control economic life, the divorce rate is low because women have few alternatives; the rising divorce rate reflects a shift in the balance of power between men and women

Symbolic Interactionism

We can trace the origins of **symbolic interactionism** to the Scottish moral philosophers of the eighteenth century, who noted that people evaluate their own conduct by comparing themselves with others (Stryker 1990). In the United States, a long line of thinkers added to this analysis, including the pioneering psychologist William James (1842–1910) and the educator John Dewey (1859–1952), who analyzed how people use symbols to encapsulate their experiences. This theoretical perspective was brought into sociology by sociologists Charles Horton Cooley (1864–1929), William I. Thomas (1863–1947), and George Herbert Mead (1863–1931), who added an analysis of how symbols lie at the basis of the self-concept (a question discussed in Chapter 3).

For symbolic interactionists, symbols are vital for social life. First, symbols lie at the root of the self-concept; we symbolize our own selves to ourselves, that is, we perceive ourselves in certain ways—such as young, appealing, and personable—and act accordingly. Second, without symbols our social relations would be limited to the animal level, for we would have no mechanism for perceiving others in terms of relationships (aunts and uncles, employers and teachers, and so on). Strange as it may seem, only because we have symbols can we have aunts and uncles, for it is these symbols that define for us what such relationships entail. Third, without symbols we could not coordinate our actions with others; we would be unable to make plans for a future date, time, and place. Unable to specify times, materials, sizes, or goals, we could not build bridges and highways. Without symbols, there would be no books, movies, or musical instruments. We would have no schools or hospitals, no government, no religion. In short, as symbolic interactionists point out, symbols make social life possible.

DCQ 12: Do you behave differently around relatives than around your closest friends? How would symbolic interactionists interpret your behaviors?

symbolic interactionism: a theoretical perspective in which society is viewed as composed of symbols that people use to establish meaning, develop their views of the world, and communicate with one another

George Herbert Mead (1863–1931) is one of the founders of symbolic interactionism, a major theoretical perspective in sociology. He taught at the University of Chicago, where his lectures were very popular. He wrote very little, however, and after his death his students compiled his lectures into an influential book, Mind, Self, and Society.

Speaker Sug. #3: A marriage or family researcher or therapist.

Essay #4

CDQ 13: How do we learn that "true love" is emotionally satisfying and that it will keep us constantly "turned on"?

Symbolic interactionists analyze how our definitions of ourselves and others underlie our behaviors. For example, if you think of someone as an aunt or uncle, you behave in a certain way, but if you think of that person as a boyfriend or girlfriend, you behave in quite another way. In a sense, we are different persons as we change our behaviors to match changing circumstances. It is as though we are on a stage, switching roles to suit our audience.

This topic will be examined in detail in Chapter 4, which features the work of sociologist Erving Goffman. For now, keep in mind that symbolic interactionists primarily examine face-to-face interaction, looking at how people work out their relationships and make sense out of life and their place in it.

Applying Symbolic Interactionism.   Now let's see how symbolic interactionism can explain the high American divorce rate (Henslin 1992) in terms of how changing symbols (meanings) have changed people's expectations and behavior.

1. *Emotional satisfaction*   In the earlier part of this century, symbolic interactionists observed that the basis for family solidarity was changing. As early as 1933, sociologist William F. Ogburn noted that personality was becoming more important in mate selection. Then in 1945, sociologists Ernest Burgess and Harvey Locke found that family solidarity was coming to depend more and more on mutual affection, understanding, and compatibility. What these sociologists had observed was a fundamental shift in American marriage: Husbands and wives were coming to expect—and demand—greater emotional satisfaction from one another.

   As this trend intensified, intimacy became the core of marriage. At the same time, as society grew more complex and impersonal, Americans came to see marriage as a solution to the tensions society produced (Lasch 1977). This new form, "companionate marriage," contributed to divorce, for it often placed a heavier burden on couples than they could carry (Zakuta 1989). Consequently, sociologists say, marriage has now become an "overloaded institution."

2. *The love symbol*   One reason our expectations of marriage are so high is our symbol of love. We learn that "true love" is emotionally satisfying, that it will keep us constantly "turned on." To the surprise of people in other cultures, Americans learn to commit to a lifelong relationship on the basis of what often turn out to be only transitory emotions (Bumiller 1992). Such unrealistic expectations attached to this love symbol set people up for crushed hopes, for when dissatisfactions enter marriage, as they inevitably do, spouses tend to blame one another for what they see as the other's failure. Their engulfment in the symbol of love at the time of marriage blinds them to the basic unreality of their expectations.

3. *The meaning of children*   The perception of childhood has recently undergone a deep historical shift with far-reaching consequences for the contemporary American family (Henslin 1992a). In medieval European society children were seen as miniature adults, and there was no sharp separation between the worlds of adults and children (Aries 1962). Boys were apprenticed at about age seven, while girls at the same age learned the homemaking duties associated with the wifely role. In the United States, just three generations ago children "became adults" when they graduated from eighth grade and took employment. Ideas about childhood have now undergone such a fundamental change that from miniature adults children have been culturally fashioned into impressionable, vulnerable, and innocent beings.

4. *The meaning of parenthood*   These changed notions of childhood have had a corresponding impact on our ideas of good parenthood. Today's parents are expected not only to provide unending amounts of affection, love, and tender care but also to take responsibility for ensuring that their children "reach their potential." As child rearing lasts longer and is more demanding, and emotional ties between parents and children become more intense, the family has been thrust into even greater "emotional overload" (Lasch 1977).

5. *Marital roles*   In earlier generations, newlyweds knew what they could legitimately expect from each other, for the respective responsibilities and privileges of husbands and wives were clearly defined. In contrast, today's much vaguer guidelines leave couples to work out more aspects of their respective roles on their own. Many find it difficult to figure out how to divide up responsibilities for work, home, and children. Worse, many spouses are not sure if they are adequately fulfilling their marital role, because there is little agreement on what that role entails.

6. *Perception of alternatives*   While the above changes in marriage expectations were taking place, another significant social change was under way: More and more women began taking jobs outside the home. As they earned paychecks of their own, many wives began for the first time to see alternatives to remaining in unhappy marriages. Symbolic interactionists consider the perception of an alternative an essential first step to making divorce possible.

7. *The meaning of divorce*   As these various factors coalesced—greater expectations of emotional satisfaction and changed marital and parental roles, accompanied by a new perception of alternatives to an unhappy marriage—divorce steadily increased. (Figure 1.1 shows the increase in divorce in the United States, from practically zero in 1890 to the current 1.2 million divorces a year. The plateau for both marriage and divorce since 1975 is probably due to increased cohabitation.)

   Moreover, as divorce became more common, its meaning changed. Once a symbol of almost everything negative—failure, irresponsibility, even immorality and social stigma—divorce became infused with new meanings—personal change, opportunity, even liberation. And as this symbolic change from failure to self-fulfillment reduced the stigma of divorce, it set the stage for divorce on an even larger scale.

8. *Changes in the law*   The law, itself a powerful symbol, began to reflect these changed ideas about divorce. Where previously divorce was granted only when the most rigorous criteria, such as adultery, were met, legislators now made "incompatibility" legitimate grounds for divorce. Some states even pioneered "no-fault" divorce, in which couples could work out their arrangements without accusations. In turn, easier divorce laws further contributed both to an increase in the rate of divorce and a corresponding decrease in the stigma attached to it.

In Sum.   Thus, symbolic interactionists explain divorce in terms of the changing symbols (or meanings) associated with both marriage and divorce. Changes in people's

CDQ 14: Have you decided how you wish to divide up family responsibilities with a marriage partner?

CDQ 15: Do you think divorce should be readily available in a society?

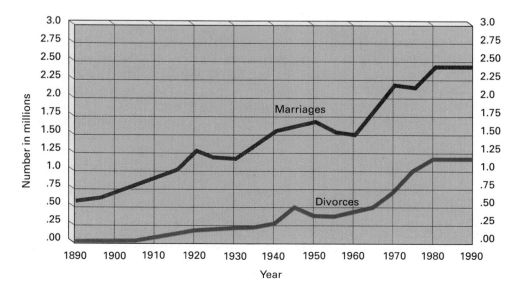

FIGURE 1.1   American Marriage, American Divorce. *(Source: Statistical Abstract of the United States,* 1991: Tables 128, 135 for 1960 to 1989; earlier editions for earlier years.)*

ideas—about divorce, marital satisfaction, love, the nature of children and parenting, and the roles of husband and wife—have put extreme pressure on married couples. No single change is *the* cause, but taken together, these changes provide a strong "push" toward divorce.

Are these changes good or bad? Central to symbolic interactionism is the position that to make a value judgment about change (or anything else) requires a value framework from which to view the change. Symbolic interactionism provides no such value framework. In short, symbolic interactionists can analyze social change, but they cannot pass judgment on that change.

Functional Analysis

Functional analysis, also known as *functionalism* and *structural functionalism,* is rooted in the origins of sociology (Turner 1978). Auguste Comte and Herbert Spencer used an organic analogy, analyzing society as a kind of living organism. Just as a biological organism has interrelated tissues and organs that function together, they wrote, so does society. Like an organism, if society is to function smoothly, its various parts must work together in harmony.

Emile Durkheim saw society as composed of many parts, each with its own function. When all the parts of society fulfill their functions, society is in a "normal" state. If they do not fulfill their functions, society is in an "abnormal" or "pathological" state. To understand society, then, functionalists say that we need to look at both *structure*—how the parts of a society are related to one another—and *function*—how each part contributes to society.

Robert K. Merton dismissed the organic analogy but continued the essence of functionalism, the image of society as a whole composed of interrelated parts. Merton used the term *functions* to refer to the beneficial consequences of people's actions that help to maintain the equilibrium of a social system. In contrast, *dysfunctions,* are consequences that undermine a system's equilibrium.

Functions can be either manifest or latent. Merton called an action intended to help a system's equilibrium a *manifest function.* For example, suppose the tuition at your college is doubled. The intention, or manifest function, of such a sharp increase may be to raise faculty salaries and thus recruit better faculty. Merton pointed out that people's actions can also have *latent functions,* unintended consequences that help a system adapt. Let us suppose that the tuition increase worked, that the quality of the faculty improved so greatly that your college gained a national reputation overnight. As a result, it was flooded with new applicants and was able to expand both its programs and its campus. The expansion contributed to the stability of your college, but it was unintended. Therefore, it is a latent function of the tuition increase.

Sometimes human actions have the opposite effect, of course, and hurt the system. Because such consequences are usually unintended, Merton called them *latent dysfunctions.* Let's assume instead that doubling the tuition backfired, that half the student body couldn't afford the increase and dropped out. With this loss of income, the college had to reduce salaries and lay off faculty. They managed to get through one year this way, but then folded. Because these results were not intended and actually harmed the social system (in this case the college) they represent a latent dysfunction of the tuition increase.

In Sum. From the perspective of functional analysis, then, the group is a functioning whole, with each part contributing to the welfare of the whole. Whenever we examine a smaller part, we need to look for its functions to see how it is related to the larger unit. This basic approach can be applied to any social group, whether an entire society, a college, or even a group as small as the family.

CDQ 16: Can you think of **any** good reason for your school to double the amount of tuition you currently are paying?

functional analysis: a theoretical framework in which society is viewed as composed of various parts, each with a function that, when fulfilled, contributes to society's equilibrium; also known as functionalism and structural functionalism

Applying Functional Analysis.   Now let's apply the principles of functional analysis to divorce. To account for the divorce rate in the United States, functionalists stress that industrialization and urbanization undermined the traditional functions of the family, namely economic production; the socialization of children; care of the sick and elderly; recreation; sexual control of family members; and reproduction. Let us see how each of these basic functions changed.

CDQ 17: Using functional analysis, what do you think accounts for the divorce rate in the United States today?

1. *Economic production*   Prior to industrialization, the family constituted an economic team. Most families found the availability of food uncertain, and family members had to cooperate in producing what they needed to survive. When industrialization moved production from home to factory, it disrupted the family team and weakened the bonds that tied family members together. Especially significant was the transfer of the husband/father to the factory, for this move separated him from the family's daily routine. In addition, the wife/mother and children now contributed less to the family's economic survival.

2. *Socialization of children*   At the same time as sweeping economic changes occurred, the government, which had grown larger, more centralized, and more powerful, usurped many family functions. To name just one example, local agencies removed educational responsibility from the family and in so doing also assumed much of the responsibility for socializing children. To make certain that families went along with this change, states passed laws requiring that children attend school and threatened parents with jail if they did not comply.

3. *Care of the sick and elderly*   As the central government expanded and its agencies multiplied, care of the aged changed from a family concern to a government obligation. With new laws governing medical schools and hospitals, institutionalized medicine grew more powerful, and medical care gradually shifted from the family to outside medical specialists.

4. *Recreation*   As more disposable income became available to Americans, business enterprises sprang up to compete for that income. This cost the family much of its recreational function, for much entertainment and "fun" changed from home-based, family-centered activities to attendance at paid events.

5. *Sexual control of members*   Even the control of sexuality was not left untouched by the vast social changes that swept the country. Traditionally, sexual relations within marriage were sanctioned as legitimate, those outside marriage considered illicit. Although this sexual control was always more ideal than real, for even among the Puritans matrimony never did enjoy a monopoly over sexual relations (Smith and Hindus 1975), it is now considerably weaker than it used to be. The "sexual revolution" of the past few decades has opened many alternatives to marital sex (Forrest and Singh 1990).

6. *Reproduction*   On the surface, the only family function that seems to have been left untouched is reproduction. Neither government nor private agency has removed it. Yet even this vital and seemingly inviolable function has not gone unchallenged. A prime example is the greater number of single women who are having children. Figure 1.2 shows that in the United States unmarried women now account for one-quarter of all births—and that the same trend is common in the industrialized world. (Japan is the only exception.) Even private agencies have taken over some of the family's control over reproduction. A married woman, for example, can get an abortion without informing her husband, and some high schools distribute condoms.

TR#2M: Percentage of a Country's Births to Unmarried Mothers

A Glimpse of the Past.   To see how sharply family functions have changed, it may be useful to take a glimpse of family life in the 1800s.

> When Phil became sick, he was nursed by Ann, his wife. She cooked for him, fed him, changed the bed linen, bathed him, read to him from the Bible, and gave him his medicine. (She did this in addition to doing the housework and taking care of their six

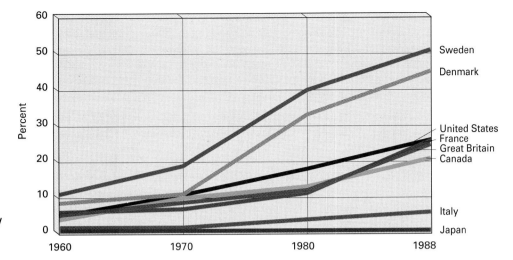

FIGURE 1.2 Percentage of Births to Unmarried Mothers by Country. *(Source: Statistical Abstract of the United States, 1991; 1440.)*

children.) Phil was also surrounded by the children, who shouldered some of his chores while their father was sick.

When Phil died, the male neighbors and relatives made the casket while Ann, her mother, and female friends washed and dressed the body. Phil was then "laid out" in the front parlor (the formal living room), where friends, neighbors, and relatives viewed him, paying their last respects. From there friends moved his body to the church for the final message, and then to the grave they had dug.

As you can see from this event, the functions of the family were diverse, covering many aspects of life and death that are now handled by outside agencies. Not only did the care of the sick take place almost exclusively within the family, but death was also

Sociologists who use the functionalist perspective stress that the traditional functions of the family have been undermined by social forces such as industrialization and urbanization, leading to dysfunctions, or a weakening of family ties. One traditional function of the family that has been largely replaced by strangers is attendance to the dead. Wakes in the home, once a universal practice among Christian families in America, are becoming increasingly rare—although still evident in certain parts of the country, as in this scene of an open casket in the living room of a family in Kentucky.

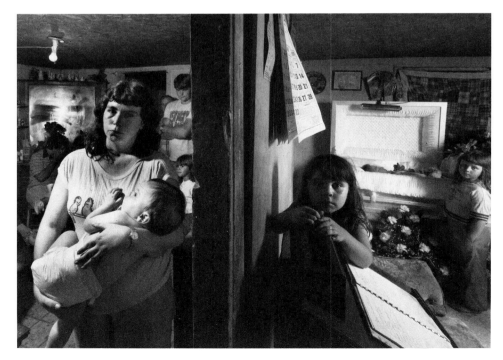

a family affair—from preparing the body to burying it. Now we assume that such functions *properly* belong to specialized agencies, and few of us can even imagine preparing the body of a close relative for burial. Such an act may even seem grotesque, almost barbarous, for our current customs also guide our feelings, another fascinating aspect of social life, but one, regrettably, that we do not have time to pursue. (Chapter 3, however, returns to the topic of emotions.)

In Sum.   The family has lost many of its traditional functions, while others are presently under assault. From a functionalist perspective, these changes have weakened the family unit. The fewer functions that family members have in common, the fewer their "ties that bind." This erosion of family functions has made the family more fragile and an increase in divorce in a context of high social strain inevitable. Thus, functionalists attribute the high divorce rate in the United States to a weakening or loss of family functions, which previously had held a husband and wife together in spite of whatever strain they experienced.

Conflict Theory

Conflict theory provides a third and sharply different perspective on social life. When Karl Marx, the founder of conflict theory, witnessed the effects of the Industrial Revolution that transformed Europe, he saw that peasants who had left the land to seek work in urbanizing areas were put to work by the new industrialists at wages that barely provided enough to eat. Shocked by the suffering and exploitation he witnessed, Marx began to analyze society and history.

As Marx developed **conflict theory,** he concluded that the key to all human history is class struggle. In each society, some small group controls the means of production and exploits all those who do not. In industrialized societies the struggle is between the **bourgeoisie,** the small group of capitalists who own the means to produce wealth, and the **proletariat,** the mass of workers exploited by the bourgeoisie. The capitalists also control politics, so that when workers rebel the capitalists are able to call on the power of the state to control them (Angell 1965).

When Marx made his observations, capitalism was in its infancy and workers were at the mercy of their employers. Workers had none of what we take for granted today—the right to strike, minimum wages, eight-hour days, coffee breaks, five-day work weeks, paid vacations and holidays, medical benefits, sick leave, unemployment compensation, Social Security. His analysis reminds us that these benefits came not from generous hearts, but from workers who, often violently, forced concessions from their employers.

Unlike Marx, conflict sociologists do not always focus on the struggle between the bourgeoisie and the proletariat. Some use conflict theory in a much broader sense. Ralf Dahrendorf (b. 1929) sees conflict as inherent in all relations that have authority. He points out that **authority,** or power that people consider legitimate, runs through all layers of society—whether small groups, a community, or the entire society. People in positions of authority try to enforce conformity, which in turn creates resentment and resistance. The result is a constant struggle throughout society to determine who has authority over what (Turner 1978).

Another sociologist, Lewis Coser (b. 1913), expanded the ideas of conflict even further. He points out that conflict is especially likely to develop among people in close relationships because they are connected by a network of responsibilities, power, and rewards. When people in a close relationship change something—whether their activities or goals—the arrangements that have been so carefully worked out among them are easily upset. Consequently, we can think even of close relationships as a balancing act of power, of maintaining and reworking a particular distribution of responsibilities and rewards.

conflict theory: a theoretical framework in which society is viewed as composed of groups competing for scarce resources

bourgeoisie: Karl Marx's term for capitalists, those who own the means to produce wealth

proletariat: Marx's term for the exploited class, the mass of workers who do not own the means of production

authority: power that people consider legitimate

In Sum.   Unlike the functionalists who view society as a harmonious whole, with its parts working together, conflict theorists see society as composed of groups competing for scarce resources. Although alliances or cooperation may prevail on the surface, beneath that surface is a struggle for power. Marx focused on struggles between the bourgeoisie and proletariat, but today's conflict theorists have expanded this perspective to include smaller groups and even basic relationships.

Applying Conflict Theory.   Applying conflict theory's emphasis on competition and exploitation to divorce, a sharply contrasting picture emerges. Conflict theorists look at men's and women's relationships in terms of basic inequalities—men dominate and exploit, while women are dominated and exploited. They also point out that marriage reflects the basic male-female relationship of society and is one of the means by which men maintain their domination and exploitation of women.

The Historical Record.   Conflict theorists stress that for millennia women have been passed by one male, the father, to another, the husband (Dobash and Dobash 1981). Just as the law allowed fathers to discipline daughters, so it allowed husbands to discipline their wives—and that included beating them. In society after society, women have traditionally been assigned the role of taking care of the personal needs of men— their fathers, husbands, and brothers—and the home has been the place in which they were relegated to lifetime servitude. Because marriage still reflects these millennia-old patterns of female subordination, it remains the basic arena for the ongoing struggle between the sexes. Power and inequality, then, are the keys to understanding the current divorce rate.

> **CDQ 18**: Is the assumption of conflict theory that women have always been assigned the role of taking care of the personal needs of men still valid today? Why or why not?

Different Experiences of Marriage.   Because of their unequal statuses, say conflict theorists, men and women experience marriage quite differently (Bernard 1992; Roache 1992). If a woman's main role in life is to be a wife and mother, the search for security to carry out this role guides her mate selection (Greer 1972). Women with this goal are more anxious than males about dating, mate selection, and the outcome of marriage. In contrast, males, who find their basic security in the workplace, are less concerned about the marital relationship. The consequence is an unequal balance of power in marriage, for wives are more dependent on its outcome and invest more in the relationship (Firestone 1970).

Fundamental Change in the Struggle.   Today, the relationships between men and women are undergoing a fundamental change. By making it easier to meet basic survival needs outside marriage, industrialization has fostered a culture in which men and women can overcome their historical social roles and power relationships (Firestone 1970). As females increasingly participate in social worlds beyond the home, they refuse to bear burdens previously accepted as inevitable and feel able to throw off the shackles of marriage should they become intolerable (James 1971).

At the center of today's marriage, then, is a struggle for power (Bernard 1992). Recent increases in the number of women working outside the home and in women's organizations advocating changes in male-female relationships have upset traditional imbalances of rights and obligations. Conflict in marriage is primarily due to husbands' resentment of their decreasing power and wives' resentment of their husbands' reluctance to share marital power.

In Sum.   Conflict theorists see marriage as reflecting a society's basic inequalities between males and females. Higher divorce rates result from changed male-female relationships, especially as wives attempt to resolve basic inequalities and husbands resist those efforts. From the conflict perspective, the increase in divorce is not a sign that marriage has weakened but rather a sign that women are finally making headway in their historical struggle with men.

Levels of Analysis: Macro and Micro

A major difference between the theoretical orientations described above is their level of analysis. The functionalist and conflict perspectives focus on **macro-level analysis;** that is, they examine large-scale patterns of society. In contrast, the symbolic interactionist perspective tends to focus more on **micro-level analysis,** on **social interaction,** or what people do when they are in one another's presence.

Let's return to the example of homelessness to make this distinction between micro and macro levels clearer. In studying the homeless, symbolic interactionists would focus on what they say and what they do. They would analyze what homeless people do when they are in shelters and on the streets, focusing especially on their communications, both their talk and their **nonverbal interactions** (how they communicate by gestures, silence, use of space, and so on). The observations that I made earlier about despair and silence of the homeless, for example, would be areas of interest to symbolic interactionists.

This micro level, however, would not interest functionalists and conflict theorists. They would focus instead on the macro level. Functionalists would examine how changes in the parts of society are related to homelessness. They might look at how changing relationships in the family (smaller, more divorce) and economic conditions (higher rents, inflation, fewer unskilled jobs, loss of jobs overseas) cause homelessness because people are unable to find jobs and do not have a family unit to fall back on. For their part, conflict theorists would stress the struggle between social classes, especially how the policies of the wealthy push certain groups into unemployment. That, they would point out, accounts for the disproportionate number of African Americans who are homeless. Chapter 4 explains the distinctions between macro and micro levels of analysis in more detail.

Putting the Theoretical Perspectives Together

Which theoretical perspective should we use to study human behavior? Which level of analysis is the correct one? As you have seen, each theoretical perspective provides a different and often sharply contrasting picture of our world. No theory or level of analysis encompasses all of reality. Rather, by focusing on different features of social life, each provides a distinctive interpretation. Consequently, it is necessary to use all three theoretical lenses to analyze changes in United States society. By putting the contributions of each perspective and level of analysis together, we gain a more comprehensive picture of social life.

As you can also see, the sociological perspective leads to an entirely different understanding of divorce than the commonsense understanding of "They-were-simply-incompatible." To take this larger view of human events, which is the sociological perspective, gives us a different way of viewing social life. This will become even more apparent in the following chapters as we explore topics as broad as sexism and as highly focused as a kindergarten classroom.

APPLIED AND CLINICAL SOCIOLOGY

In analyzing sociology as it relates to social change, sociologists Paul Lazarsfeld and Jeffrey Reitz (1989) divide sociology into three phases. First, as we have already seen, when sociology began it was indistinguishable from attempts to reform society. The primary concern of early sociologists was to make the world a better place. The point of analyzing social conditions was to use the information to improve social life. Albion Small, one of the first presidents of the American Sociological Society (1912–1913), said that the primary reason for the existence of sociology was its "practical application to the improvement of social life." Sociologists, he said, should use science to gain

L. Obj. 9: Compare micro level and macro level analyses and state which level of analysis is utilized by each of the major theoretical perspectives.

CDQ 19: How do you think that micro- and macro-level analyses can contribute to our knowledge of homelessness?

Essay #5

macro-level analysis: an examination of large-scale patterns of society

micro-level analysis: an examination of small-scale patterns of society

social interaction: what people do when they are in one another's presence

nonverbal interaction: communication without words through gestures, space, silence, and so on

knowledge and then use that knowledge to "realize visions" (Fritz 1989). This first phase of sociology lasted until the 1920s.

During the second phase, it became the goal of sociologists to establish sociology as a respected field of knowledge. To this end they sought to develop an autonomous sociology, that is, a sociology independent of any concrete social action. This goal was soon achieved, and within a generation sociology was incorporated into almost every college and university curriculum in the United States. This period is characterized by an emphasis on **pure** or **basic sociology,** aimed at making discoveries about life in human groups, but not at making changes in those groups. World War II marked the end of this phase.

pure or basic sociology: socio-logical research whose only pur-pose is to make discoveries about life in human groups, not to make changes in those groups

During the third and current phase, there has been an attempt to merge sociologi-cal knowledge and practical work. Dissatisfied with "knowledge for the sake of knowl-edge," sociologists increasingly desire to use their sociological knowledge to bring about social change, to make a difference in social life. The final results of this phase

---

P E R S P E C T I V E S
Cultural Diversity Around the World

Sociology in a World in Turmoil

The sociological perspective emphasized in this text does not come "naturally," and in some cases it is even vigor-ously resisted. People often have good reason to remain closed-minded. If they can keep social arrangements un-examined, their "old way" of doing things is not threat-ened. In contrast, by explaining how the various parts of society work together, sociology opens the possibility of liberating change.

This point was driven home by Mikhail Gorbachev, the former head of the former Soviet Union. When he declared *perestroika,* the "reconstruction" of his nation, Gorbachev committed himself to developing a new struc-ture for Soviet society. This required an objective, "out-side" view of the structure that existed at the time. To harness winds of change, people must take a new look at old things. Otherwise, how can they break out of the perspectives they hold?

Consequently, one of Mikhail Gorbachev's first initia-tives in higher education was to authorize graduate stu-dents to come to the United States. To study what? Engineering? Chemistry? Computer science? Physics? En-glish? None of these. It was to study *sociology.*

This graduate exchange between the former Soviet Union and the United States was worked out between the American Sociological Association and its Soviet counter-part. Soviet students were placed in fifteen sociology pro-grams around the United States. In addition, what was then the Soviet Union began to set up sociology depart-ments in its own universities.

At this radical juncture in history, the world is poised between opportunity and potential disaster. Economic markets and technology are being globalized (see Chap-ter 14). So is democracy. As traditional social orders are swept away, sociology has the potential to provide an understanding of these events—of the opportunities that

the world's societies face, as well as the land mines that can destroy those opportunities.

Sociology often makes people uncomfortable, how-ever, for as sociologists analyze the interconnections be-tween the parts of a society, they also expose its under-belly. Ruling parties become upset when sociologists show how a society's interconnections produce its social problems. For example, sociologists point out how social injustices are built into American society. They stress how as a result of social arrangements some groups are de-prived of opportunity, income, and education, thus in-creasing their chances of being malnourished, getting sick, dying young, getting divorced, having their children become juvenile delinquents or getting involved in drugs, and their adults committing street crimes. Such analysis challenges people's comfortable assumptions about why "those people" do what "they" do—and about their own place in society.

Closed societies feel especially threatened by sociol-ogy. For example, after the Tiananmen Square massacre, China moved away from sociology, for its leaders did not want to be confronted with social analysis. They wanted no one to question their social arrangements. Chinese students of sociology in the United States and elsewhere became suspect upon returning home.

In contrast, societies that want to understand them-selves tend to welcome sociology, for sociological analy-sis of relations at work, school, and home, relations be-tween ethnic groups, discrimination against women, the effects of social class, provides useful knowledge. In short, sociologists bring a society's interconnections into the open, where they can be examined. From this process arises the possibility of productive social change, which is the promise of sociology in a world in turmoil.

Source: Based on Boden, Giddens, and Molotch, 1990 and the author's interviews with Chinese graduate students studying so-ciology in the United States.

are not yet known, but the emphasis on applying sociology has gained much momentum in just the past few years.

Efforts to synthesize sociological knowledge and practical results are known as **applied sociology.** This term refers to the attempt to use sociology to solve problems. Applied sociologists work in a variety of settings, recommending practical changes that can be implemented. Often a business firm hires a sociologist to solve a problem in the workplace. Some sociologists conduct research for government commissions or agencies investigating social problems such as pornography, crime, violence, or environmental pollution.

Perhaps the best-known applied sociologist is Rosabeth Moss Kanter of Harvard University, who has published a number of studies of work organizations. In her popular book, *Men and Women of the Corporation,* a study of an industrial firm with more than fifty thousand employees, Kanter analyzed basic relationships between workers. Her findings, if management wished to apply them, could be used to bring about change in the corporation.

Some applied sociologists are evaluative; that is, as in Kanter's study, they make recommendations for change based on their findings. Others become directly involved in bringing about social change. This type of applied sociology is called **clinical sociology.** Clinical sociologists work in a variety of social settings. Those who work in industrial settings may try to change work conditions to reduce job turnover. Others work with drug addicts and ex-convicts; still others are family counselors who try to change basic relationships between a husband and wife or between children and their parents.

The Future.   Sociology is now swinging full circle. From an initial concern with improving society, sociologists switched their focus to developing abstract knowledge. Currently sociologists are again seeking ways to apply their findings. These efforts have gained momentum in recent years, and the future is likely to see much more applied sociology (see Perspectives box on page 26). Many departments of sociology now offer courses in applied sociology, and some offer specialties, and even internships, in applied sociology at both the graduate and undergraduate levels.

These changes are taking sociology closer to its starting point. They provide renewed contact with the discipline's roots, promising to invigorate sociology as they challenge us to grasp a vision of what society can become—and what sociology's role can be in that process of change.

CDQ 20: Does the sociology department at your school offer applied sociology courses? Would you be interested in taking such courses?

applied sociology: the use of sociology to solve problems—from the micro level of family relationships to the macro level of crime and pollution

clinical sociology: the direct involvement of sociologists in bringing about social change

SUMMARY

1. Sociology offers a perspective, a view of the world. This sociological perspective stresses that people's social experiences—the groups to which they belong and their particular experiences in those groups—underlie their behavior.

2. *Science* is the application of systematic methods to obtain knowledge and the knowledge obtained by those methods. Science has three goals: to explain, to generalize, and to predict. The sciences are divided into the *natural sciences,* those that focus on nature, and the *social sciences,* those that study human behavior. Scientific explanations often confront the obstacles of tradition, magic, superstition, and common sense.

3. Because *sociology,* the scientific study of society

and human behavior, has many forerunners, it is difficult to state precisely when it began. If systematic research and the testing of theories are taken as the standards, then sociology is very recent. The birth of sociology was accelerated by the upheavals of the Industrial Revolution. Early sociologists include Auguste Comte, Herbert Spencer, Karl Marx, Emile Durkheim, and Max Weber.

4. An unresolved issue in sociology is the role of values in social research. Weber believed social research should be value free. Sociologists agree on the ideal of objectivity, but disagree concerning the proper purposes and uses of sociology.

5. Weber proposed Verstehen, the concept of "grasping by insight" or subjective understandings, as a basic sociological approach, while Durkheim stressed what he called social facts. Verstehen and social facts combine to produce an understanding of social life.

6. Academic specialties in sociology first appeared in the late 1800s at the University of Chicago and at Atlanta University. Since the 1970s, American sociology has not been dominated by any one theoretical orientation or by any single concern. Social reform, a goal of early sociologists, is currently seen as simply one option for sociologists.

7. Facts must always be interpreted. A theory is a general statement about how two or more facts are related to one another. Three primary theoretical frameworks are utilized by sociologists: symbolic interactionism, functional analysis, and conflict theory. In this chapter the example of divorce was used to illustrate how each theory provides a unique interpretation of reality.

8. Symbolic interactionists focus on the meanings that underlie people's lives. They examine how people use symbols to develop and share their views of the world. Symbolic interactionists usually focus on the micro level.

9. Functionalists stress that society is made up of various parts. When working properly, each part contributes to the stability of the whole, fulfilling a function that contributes to society's equilibrium. They also apply these ideas to groups within society. Functionalists focus on the macro level.

10. Conflict theorists stress inequalities and regard society as composed of groups competing for scarce resources. These groups may form alliances or cooperate with one another, but underneath this surface harmony lies a basic competitive struggle to gain control over scarce resources. Conflict theorists also focus on the macro level.

11. Because no theory encompasses all of reality, sociologists use all three theoretical lenses. With each perspective focusing on certain features of social life and each providing its own interpretation, their combined insights provide a more comprehensive picture of society.

12. Applied sociologists use sociology to solve social problems, studying human behavior and organizations in a variety of settings to yield practical results. Applied sociology ranges from working on such broad problems as environmental pollution to improving family relationships. The current direction in sociology is toward more applied sociology.

SUGGESTED READINGS

Berger, Peter L. *Invitation to Sociology: A Humanistic Perspective.* New York: Doubleday, 1963. This delightful analysis of how sociology applies to everyday life is highly recommended.

Charon, Joel M. *Symbolic Interactionism: An Introduction, an Interpretation, an Integration.* Englewood Cliffs, N.J.: Prentice Hall, 1985. As it lays out the main points of symbolic interactionism, this book provides an understanding of why symbolic interactionism is important in sociology.

Henslin, James M., ed. *Down to Earth Sociology: Introductory Readings.* 7th ed. New York: The Free Press. 1993. This collection of readings about everyday life is designed to broaden the reader's understanding of society, and of the individual's place within it.

Homans, George Caspar. *Coming to My Senses: The Autobiography of a Sociologist.* New Brunswick, N.J.: Transaction Books, 1984. Homans emphasizes how being born into one of Boston's most privileged families shaped his orientations.

Merton, Robert K. *Social Theory and Social Structure.* New York: The Free Press, 1968. This classic work on functionalism covers the theory's main points, but is perhaps best read by advanced students.

Mills, C. Wright. *The Sociological Imagination.* New York: Oxford University Press, 1959. This classic work provides an overview of sociology from the framework of conflict theory.

Straus, Roger, ed. *Using Sociology.* Bayside, N.Y.: General Hall, 1985. The author examines how applied and clinical sociology are used in the practical world.

Turner, Stephen Park, and Jonathan H. Turner. *The Impossible Science: An Institutional Analysis of American Sociology.* New-bury Park, Calif.: Sage, 1990. After tracing the history of American sociology from the Civil War, the authors reflect on its future.

Journals

Clinical Sociology Review and *Sociological Practice Review* are two journals that report the experiences of sociologists who work in a variety of applied settings, from peer group counseling and suicide prevention to recommending changes to school boards.

About a Career in Sociology

The following pamphlets or brochures are available free of charge from the American Sociological Association: 1722 N Street, N.W., Washington, D.C. 20036 (202) 833-3410.

Careers in Sociology. American Sociological Association. What can you do with sociology? You like the subject and would like to major in it, but . . . This pamphlet provides information about jobs available for sociology majors.

Majoring in Sociology: A Guide for Students. American Sociological Association. This brochure provides an overview of the programs offered in sociology departments, possible areas of specialization, and how to find information on jobs.

Huber, Bettina J. *Embarking Upon a Career in Sociology with an Undergraduate Sociology Major.* American Sociological Association. This brochure, designed for undergraduate sociology majors who are seeking employment, discusses how to identify interests and skills, pinpoint suitable jobs, prepare a resume, and handle an employment interview.

Ferris, Abbott L. *How to Join the Federal Workforce and Advance Your Sociological Career*. American Sociological Association. This pamphlet gives tips on how to find employment in the federal government, including information on how to prepare a job application.

Miller, Delbert C. *The Sociology Major as Preparation for Careers in Business*. American Sociological Association. What careers can a sociology major pursue in business or industry? This brochure includes sections on job prospects, graduate education, and how to practice sociology in business careers.

CHAPTER 2

Malcah Zeldis, Thanksgiving, *1972*

Culture

WHAT IS CULTURE?
    Culture and Taken-for-Granted Orientations to Life ■ Practicing Cultural Relativism

COMPONENTS OF CULTURE
    The Symbolic Basis of Culture ■ *Down-to-Earth Sociology:* **Communicating across Cultural Boundaries** ■ Language ■ Gestures ■ *Perspectives:* **Miami—Language and a Changing City** ■ Values, Norms, and Sanctions ■ Folkways and Mores

SUBCULTURES AND COUNTERCULTURES

VALUES IN AMERICAN SOCIETY
    Perspectives: **Why Do Native Americans Like Westerns?** ■ Value Clusters ■ Value Contradictions

and Social Change ■ Emergent Values ■ Reactions to Changes in Core Values ■ Values as Blinders ■ "Ideal" versus "Real" Culture

CULTURAL UNIVERSALS
    Thinking Critically about Social Controversy: **Are We Prisoners of Our Genes? Sociobiology**

ANIMALS AND CULTURE
    Do Animals Have Language?

CULTURAL DIFFUSION AND CULTURAL LEVELING

SUMMARY

SUGGESTED READINGS

I had never felt heat like this before. If this was northern Africa, I wondered what it must be like closer to the equator. The sweat poured off me as the temperature soared to 110 degrees Fahrenheit.

As we were herded into the building—without air conditioning—hundreds of people lunged toward the counter at the rear of the building. With body crushed against body, we waited as the uniformed officials behind the windows leisurely examined each passport. It was at times like this that I wondered what I was doing in Africa. This was my big trip, the one I had dreamed of since I was a child. I had the summer off from teaching and enough money to travel for three months in Europe—if I hitchhiked and lived simply. Why hadn't I let Europe be enough? But, no, I had to try to pack it all in, and when I realized that Africa was so close to Europe—just a few miles from southern Spain—the allure was too great to pass up.

When I had arrived in Morocco, I found the sights that greeted me exotic—not far removed from my memories of *Casablanca, Raiders of the Lost Ark,* and other movies that over the years had become part of my collective memory. The men,

CDQ 1: When we travel to another country, why is it important for us to be aware of the culture in that society?

31

women, and even the children did wear those strange garments—white robes that reached down to their feet. What was especially striking was the fact that the women were almost totally covered. In spite of the heat, every woman wore not only a full-length gown, but also a head covering that reached down over the forehead and a veil that covered her face from the nose down. All you could make out were their eyes—and every eye the same shade of brown.

And how short everyone was! The Arab women looked to be on average 5 feet, and the men only about three or four inches more. As the only blue-eyed, blonde six-footer around, wearing jeans and a pullover shirt, in a world of white-robed short people, I stood out like a sore thumb. Everyone stared. No matter where I went, they stared. Wherever I looked, I found brown eyes staring intensely at me. Even staring back at those many dark brown eyes didn't accomplish anything. It was so different from home, where, if you caught someone staring at you, the person would immediately look embarrassed and glance away.

And lines? The concept apparently didn't even exist. Buying a ticket for a bus or train meant pushing and shoving toward the ticket man (always a man—no women were visible in any public position), who just took the money from whichever out-stretched hand he decided on.

And germs? That notion didn't seem to exist here either. Flies swarmed over the food in the restaurants and the unwrapped loaves of bread in the stores. Shopkeepers would considerately shoo off the flies before handing me a loaf. They also had home delivery of bread. I still remember a bread vendor finally delivering an unwrapped loaf to a woman standing on a second-floor balcony. She first threw her money to the bread vendor, and he then threw the unwrapped bread up to her. Only his throw was off. The bread bounced off the wrought iron balcony railing and landed in the street filled with people, wandering dogs, and the ever-present burros. The vendor simply picked up the loaf and threw it again. This certainly wasn't his day, for again he missed. But the man made it on his third attempt. And the woman smiled, satisfied, as she turned back into her apartment, apparently to prepare the noon meal for her hungry family.

As I stood in the oppressive heat of the Moroccan-Algerian border, the crowd had once again become unruly. Another fight had broken out. And once again, the little man in uniform appeared, shouting and knocking people aside as he forced his way to the little box nailed onto the floor. Climbing onto the box, he would shout at the crowd, his arms flailing about him. The people would become silent. But just as soon as the man would leave, the shoving and shouting would begin as the people again clamored around the officials.

The situation had become unbearable. Pressed body to body, the man behind me had decided that this was a good time to take a nap. Determining that I made a good support, he placed his arm against my back and leaned his head against his arm. Sweat streamed from my back at the point that his arm and head touched me.

Finally, I realized that I had to abandon American customs. I pushed my way forward, forcing my frame into every space I could make. At the counter, I shouted in English. The official looked up at the sound of this strange tongue, and, thrusting my long arms over the heads of three persons, I shoved my passport into his hand.

WHAT IS CULTURE?

What is culture? The concept is sometimes easier to grasp by description than by definition. For example, suppose you meet a young woman who has just arrived in the United States from India. That her culture is different from yours is immediately evident to you. You first see it in her clothing, jewelry, makeup, and hairstyle. Next you hear it in her language. It then becomes apparent by her gestures. Later, you will hear her express unfamiliar beliefs about the world and opinions about what is valuable or worth-while in life. All these characteristics are indicative of **culture,** the language, beliefs, values, norms, behaviors, and even material objects that are passed from one generation to the next.

In northern Africa, I was surrounded by a culture quite alien to my own. It was evident in everything I saw and heard. The **material culture**—such things as jewelry, art, buildings, weapons, machines, and even eating utensils, hairstyles, and clothing—provided a sharp contrast to what I was used to seeing. There is nothing inherently "natural" about material culture. That is, it is no more natural (or unnatural) to wear gowns on the street than it is to wear jeans.

I also found myself immersed in a contrasting **nonmaterial culture,** that is, a group's ways of thinking (its beliefs, values, and other assumptions about the world) and doing (its common patterns of behavior, including language, gestures, and other forms of interaction). North African assumptions about crowding to buy a ticket and staring in public are examples of nonmaterial culture. So are American assumptions about not doing either of these things. Like material culture, neither custom is "right." People simply become comfortable with the customs they learn during childhood, and—as in the case of my visit to northern Africa—uncomfortable when their basic assumptions about life are challenged.

Culture and Taken-for-Granted Orientations to Life

To develop a sociological imagination, it is essential to understand how culture affects people's lives. While meeting someone from a different culture may make us aware of culture's pervasive influence, attaining the same level of awareness regarding our own culture is quite another matter. *Our* speech, *our* gestures, *our* beliefs, and *our* customs are usually taken for granted. We assume that they are "normal" or "natural," and we almost always follow them without question. As anthropologist Ralph Linton (1936) said, "The last thing a fish would ever notice would be water." So it is with people: except in unusual circumstances, the effects of our own culture generally remain imperceptible to us.

Yet culture's significance is profound; it touches almost every aspect of who and what we are. We came into this life without a language, without values and morality, with no ideas about religion, education, war, money, friendship, love, relatives, rights

Project 1

CDQ 2: Why are we more comfortable with the customs we learn during childhood, and uncomfortable when our basic assumptions about life are challenged?

material culture: the material objects that distinguish a group of people, such as their art, buildings, weapons, utensils, machines, hairstyles, clothing, and jewelry

nonmaterial culture: a group's ways of thinking (including its beliefs, values, and other assumptions about the world) and doing (its common patterns of behavior, including language and other forms of interaction)

Americans take it for granted that if they can afford it (an important qualification) the supply of food is plentiful. In the former Soviet Union, however, this cultural assumption does not exist. Shortages have long been a fact of life, both under communism and since its demise.

Essay #1

and obligations, use of space, and so on. We possessed none of these fundamental orientations that we take for granted and that are so essential in determining the type of people we are. Yet at this point in our lives we all have them. Sociologists call this culture *within* us. These learned and shared ways of believing and of doing (another definition of culture) penetrate our beings at an early age and quickly become part of our taken-for-granted assumptions concerning normal behavior. *Culture becomes the lens through which we perceive and evaluate what is going on around us.* Seldom do we question these assumptions, for, like water to a fish, the framework from which we view life remains largely beyond our ordinary perception.

The rare instances in which these assumptions are challenged, however, can be upsetting. Although as a sociologist I should be able to look at my own culture "from the outside," my trip to Africa quickly revealed how fully I had internalized my own culture. My upbringing in Western industrialized society had given me strong assumptions about aspects of social life that had become deeply rooted in my being—staring, hygiene, and the use of social space—subjects to which I ordinarily gave no thought. But in Africa those assumptions were useless for the purpose of daily life. No longer could I count on people to stare only surreptitiously, to take precautions against invisible microbes, or to stand in an orderly way one behind the other on the basis of time of arrival to obtain a service.

As you can tell from the opening vignette, I personally found these different assumptions upsetting, for they violated my basic expectations of "the way people *ought* to be"—though I did not even know I held these expectations until they were so abruptly challenged. When my nonmaterial culture failed me—when it no longer enabled me to make sense out of the world—I experienced a disorientation known as **culture shock.** In the case of buying tickets, the fact that I was several inches taller than most Moroccans and thus able to outreach almost everyone helped me to adjust partially to their different ways of doing things. But I never did get used to the idea that pushing ahead of others was "right," and I always felt guilty when I used my size to receive preferential treatment.

The fundamental influence culture exerts on our lives fascinates sociologists. By examining more explicitly just how profoundly culture affects everything we are, this chapter will serve as a basis from which you can start to analyze your previously unquestioned assumptions of reality and thus help you gain a different perspective on social life and your role in it.

CNN: Effects of Losing and Regaining a Culture among Native-American Women

culture shock: the disorientation that people experience when they come in contact with a fundamentally different culture and can no longer depend on their taken-for-granted assumptions about life

In Sum.   To avoid losing track of the ideas under discussion let's pause for a moment to summarize, and in some instances clarify, the principles we have covered.

1. There is nothing "natural" about material culture. Arabs wear gowns on the street and feel that it is natural to do so; Americans do the same with jeans.
2. There is nothing "natural" about nonmaterial culture; it is just as arbitrary to stand in line as it is to push and shove.
3. Culture penetrates deep into the recesses of our spirits, becoming a taken-for-granted aspect of our lives.
4. Culture provides the lens through which we see the world and obtain our perception of reality.
5. Culture provides a "behavioral imperative"; that is, culture tells us what we ought to do in various situations. It provides the basis for our decision making.
6. Culture also provides a "moral imperative"; that is, by internalizing a culture, people learn ideas of right and wrong. (I, for example, believed deeply that it was unacceptable to push and shove to get ahead of others.)
7. Coming into contact with a radically different culture challenges people's basic assumptions of life. (I experienced culture shock when I discovered that cultural ideas about the use of space and hygiene no longer worked.)
8. Although the particulars of culture differ from one group of people to another,

culture itself is universal. That is, all people have culture. There are no exceptions. A society cannot exist without developing shared, learned ways of dealing with the demands of life.

9. All people act on the basis of **ethnocentrism,** using their own culture as the yardstick for judging the ways of others. All of us learn that our own group's ways are good, right, and superior to other ways of life.

10. The universal tendency to ethnocentrism is both functional and dysfunctional. It is functional because it creates in-group solidarity, which is essential to social life. Ethnocentrism can also be dysfunctional, however, for it can lead to harmful discrimination against other groups.

Practicing Cultural Relativism

Rather than using one's own culture as a standard to judge another culture, to practice **cultural relativism** is to try to understand a culture on its own terms. It is to look at how the various elements of a culture fit together, without judging those elements as superior or inferior to one's own way of life. The Down-to-Earth Sociology box on page 36 illustrates this point.

Cultural relativism presents a challenge to ordinary thinking, for we tend to use our own culture to judge another. For example, Americans may have strong feelings against raising bulls for the sole purpose of stabbing them to death in front of crowds shouting "Olé!". According to cultural relativism, however, bullfighting must be viewed strictly within the context of the culture in which it takes place—*its* history, *its* folklore, *its* ideas of bravery, and *its* ideas of sex roles.

As an American, you may still regard bullfighting as wrong, of course, since your culture, which lies deep within you, has no history of bullfighting. Americans possess culturally specific ideas about cruelty to animals, ideas that have evolved slowly and match other cultural elements. Consequently, practices that once were common in some areas—cock fighting, dog fighting, bear-dog fighting, and so on—have been gradually weeded out (Bryant 1993).

None of us can be entirely successful at practicing cultural relativism; we simply cannot help viewing a contrasting way of life through the lens that our own culture provides. Cultural relativism, however, is an attempt to mute that lens and thereby appreciate other ways of life rather than simply asserting, "Our way is right."

COMPONENTS OF CULTURE

The Symbolic Basis of Culture

Sociologists sometimes refer to nonmaterial culture as **symbolic culture** because a central component is the symbols that people use to communicate. A **symbol** is something to which people attach meaning and which they then use to communicate. Symbols are the basis of culture. They include language, gestures, values, norms, sanctions, folkways, and mores. Let's look at each of these components of symbolic culture.

Language

The primary way in which people communicate with one another is through **language**—a system of symbols that can be put together in an infinite number of ways for the purpose of communicating abstract thought. Each word is actually a symbol, a sound to which we have attached a particular meaning so that we can then use it to communicate with one another. Language itself is universal to all human groups, but there is nothing universal about the meanings given to particular sounds. Thus, in different cultures the same sound may mean something entirely different—or may have no meaning at all.

CDQ 3: Do you think that fan or spectator behavior at sports events and patriotic gatherings is an example of ethnocentrism? Why?

CNN: Culture Classes

L. Obj. 2: Differentiate between ethnocentrism and cultural relativism.

Speaker Sug. #2: A curator from a museum with a collection of artifacts from other countries.

L. Obj. 3: Discuss the symbolic components of culture, including language and gestures.

CNN : Changing U.S. Population and Bilingual Education

cultural relativism: understanding a people in the framework of its own culture

ethnocentrism: the use of one's own culture as a yardstick for judging the ways of other individuals or societies, generally leading to a negative evaluation of their values, norms, and behaviors

symbolic culture: another term for nonmaterial culture

symbol: something to which people attach meaning and then use to communicate with others

language: a system of symbols that can be combined in an infinite number of ways and can represent not only objects but also abstract thought

DOWN-TO-EARTH SOCIOLOGY

Communicating across Cultural Boundaries

When viewed from afar, cultural differences among human groups may be only a matter of interest. But when there is **culture contact,** that is, when people come into contact with people from different cultures, those differences can lead to problems in communication.

It is not only travelers who face this problem. Increasingly, business has become international, making cultural differences a practical problem for businesspeople. And at times, even highly knowledgable and experienced firms don't quite manage to break through those cultural barriers. General Motors, for example, was very successful in marketing its automobile, the Nova, in the United States. When they decided to export that success south of the border, they were perplexed when the car sold very, very slowly. Finally, someone let them in on the secret: In Spanish, "No va" is an entire sentence that means, "It does not go."

Not all results are negative, of course, and businesspeople are also able to capitalize on cultural differences. For example, Japanese women are highly embarrassed by the sounds they make in public toilets. To drown out the offensive sounds, they flush the toilet an average of 2.7 times a visit (Iori 1988). This wastes water, however, and that creates its own problems. Some enterprising American saw moneymaking possibilities in this and developed a battery-powered device that is mounted next to the toilet. When the woman activates the device,

it emits a 25-second flushing sound. Although a toilet-sound duplicator may seem useless for our culture, the Japanese government and private companies are buying about three thousand of these devices a month.

Cultural differences go beyond the humorous and are sometimes life-and-death matters. AIDS is a case in point. About two million Americans are infected with the AIDS virus, and AIDS has become the leading cause of death for Hispanic Americans and African Americans in New York. Part of the effort to reduce its spread involves advertising. Every good public relations campaign must meet its target audience "on its own turf"—if it fails to speak its language it will be worthless. Cultural differences have become significant in this campaign against AIDS (Navarro 1989). In Hispanic culture, sexual practices are considered more private matters than they are in our general culture. Consequently, when officials in New York City encouraged Hispanic women to cooperate in a survey of their knowledge and practices regarding AIDS, the typical response was, "What right do you have to inquire about my sexual practices?"

Even in such a serious matter, however, cultural differences often erupt in humor. In this same campaign, officials translated an anti-AIDS poster into Spanish. They were very proud of their efforts to penetrate the culture—until someone pointed out that no one could understand the meaning of the slogan, which translated to something like "A rubber is a friend in your pocket."

CDQ 4: What would your life be like if you had not learned a language? How would you communicate with others if you were hearing-impaired?

Essay #2

Project 2

Language Allows Human Experience to Be Cumulative.   By means of language one generation is able to pass significant experiences on to the next and allow that next generation to build upon experiences it may not itself undergo. This building process enables humans to modify their behavior in the light of what previous generations have learned. Hence the central sociological significance of language: *Language allows culture to develop by freeing people to move beyond their immediate experiences* (Hertzler 1965; Henslin 1975).

Without language, human culture would be little more advanced than that of the lower primates. People would be limited to communicating by some system of grunts and gestures, which would greatly shorten the temporal dimension of human life and limit communication to a small time zone surrounding the immediate present: events now taking place, those which have just taken place, or those which will immediately take place—a sort of "slightly extended present." You can grunt and gesture, for example, that you want a drink of water, but in the absence of language how could you share ideas concerning past or future events? There would be little or no way to communicate to others what event you had in mind, much less the greater complexities that humans communicate—ideas and feelings about events.

Speaker Sug. #3: Someone who works with hearing-impaired children.

Language Provides a Social or Shared Past.   Even without language an individual would still have memories of experiences and events. Those memories, however, would be extremely limited, for people associate experiences with words and then use words to recall the experience. Such memories as would exist in the absence of language would also be highly individualized, for they could be but rarely and incompletely communicated to others, much less discussed and agreed upon. With language, however, events can be codified, that is, attached to words and then brought back to the present through those words.

Language Provides a Social or Shared Future.   Language also extends the temporal dimension forward. When people talk about past events, they are able to understand how they will or should act in similar circumstances. Through words they share meanings that allow them to decide to pursue certain courses of action in future situations. Because language enables people to agree with one another concerning times, dates, and places, it also allows them to plan activities with one another.

Think about it for a moment. Without language how could people ever plan future events? How could they possibly communicate goals, purposes, times, and plans? Whatever planning could exist would have to be limited to extremely rudimentary communications, perhaps to an agreement to meet at a certain place when the sun is in a certain position. But think of the difficulty, perhaps impossibility, of conveying just a slight change in this simple arrangement, such as "I can't make it tomorrow."

Language Allows Shared Perspectives or Understandings.   Our ability to speak, then, allows us a social past and future; these two vital aspects of our humanity represent a watershed that distinguishes us from animals. But speech does much more than this. When humans talk with one another, they are exchanging ideas about events, that is, exchanging perspectives. Their words are the embodiment of their experiences, distilled and codified into a readily exchangeable form, mutually intelligible for people who have learned that language. Talking about events allows people to arrive at shared understandings that form the essence of social life.

Language Allows Complex, Shared, Goal-Directed Behavior.   Common understandings further enable people to establish a *purpose* for getting together. Let us suppose that you want to go on a picnic. You use speech not only to plan the picnic but also to decide on reasons for the picnic—which may be anything from "because it's-a-nice-day-and-shouldn't-be-wasted-studying" to "because-it's-the-fourth-of-July." Language permits you to blend individual activities into an integrated sequence. In other words, through discussion you decide who will drive; who will bring the wienies, the potato chips, the soda; where you will meet, and so on. Only because of language can you participate in such a common (in American culture) yet complex event.

Language and Perception: The Sapir-Whorf Hypothesis.   In the 1930s, two anthropologists, Edward Sapir and Benjamin Whorf, became intrigued when they noted that the Hopi Indians of the southwestern United States had no words to distinguish between the past, the present, and the future. English, in contrast, as well as German, French, Spanish, and so on, distinguish carefully just when something takes place. From this observation Sapir and Whorf developed the hypothesis that thinking and perception are not only expressed through language but actually shaped by language. They concluded that because language has embedded in it a way of looking at the world, learning a language involves learning not only words but also a particular way of thinking and perceiving (Sapir 1949; Landes 1983; Garrison 1990; Whorf 1961).

The implications of the **Sapir-Whorf hypothesis,** which alerts us to how extensively language affects us, are far-reaching. *The Sapir-Whorf hypothesis reverses common sense:* It indicates that rather than objects and events forcing themselves onto our consciousness, it is our very language that determines our consciousness, and hence our perception, of objects and events. Eskimos, for example, have many words for snow. As Eskimo children learn their language, they learn distinctions between types of snowfalls that are imperceptible to non–Eskimo speakers. Others might learn to see heavy and light snowfalls, wet and dry snowfalls, and so on; but not having words for

K.P.: Edward Sapir

K.P.: Benjamin Whorf

CDQ 5: Why do you think language has become a political and a social issue in the United States and Canada?

Sapir-Whorf hypothesis: Edward Sapir and Benjamin Whorf's hypothesis that language itself creates a particular way of thinking and perceiving

"fine powdery," "thicker powdery," and "more granular" snowfalls actually prevents them from perceiving snow in the same way as Eskimos do.

Humans characteristically try to make sense of their world by classifying their experiences. Those classifications (or words) in turn direct perception. Just as in the snow example above, if you learn to classify students as "dweebs," "dorks," "nerds," "brains," and so on, you will perceive a student who asks several questions during class or remains after class to talk about a lecture in an entirely different way than will someone who does not know these classifications.

In Sum. The significance of language is that it takes us beyond the world of apes, foraging and roving bands, and allows culture to develop. Language frees us from the present by providing a past and a future, giving us the capacity to share understandings about the past and develop common perceptions about the future, as well as establishing underlying purposes for our current activities. Consequently, as in the case of the picnic, each individual is able to perform a small part of a larger activity, aware that others are carrying out related parts. In this way a series of separated, isolated activities becomes united into a larger whole.

Language also allows us to expand our connections far beyond our immediate, face-to-face groups, so that our *individual* biological and social needs become part of the activities of extended networks of people. This development in turn leads to far-flung connections with our fellow humans, facilitating, for example, the cooperative actions ultimately responsible for our worldwide networks of production and distribution. Although language by no means *guarantees* cooperation among people, language is an *essential* precondition of collaboration. Without language, extended cooperative human endeavors simply could not exist (Malinowski 1945; Hertzler 1965; Blumer 1966).

Learning language means not just learning words but also acquiring the perceptions embedded in them. In other words, language both reflects and shapes cultural experiences. The United States is currently experiencing sharp increases in immigration. In cities such as Miami and Los Angeles, half or more of the residents speak Spanish as their first language. Precisely because language is such a primary shaper of experience and culture, difficulties arise among people who live among each other but do not share a language as illustrated in the Perspectives box on page 39.

It would be difficult to overemphasize the significance of language for social life. On it is predicated our entire way of life, although, like most aspects of culture, its *linguistic base* is usually invisible to us.

CDQ 6: How do gestures help you to communicate your emotions to other people? Give specific examples.

Project 3

Gestures

Humans also use their bodies to communicate with one another through **gestures.** While people in every culture of the world use gestures, their meaning may change completely from one culture to another.

Gestures are useful shorthand for communicating messages without using words. North Americans, for example, communicate a succinct message by raising the middle finger in a short, upward stabbing motion. I wish to stress "North Americans," for that gesture does not convey that message in southern Mexico, South America, or most other parts of the world.

I was once surprised to find that this particular gesture was not universal, having internalized it to such an extent that I thought everyone knew what it meant. When I was comparing gestures in Mexico, however, this gesture drew a blank look from friends. After I explained its intended meaning, they laughed and showed me their rudest gesture—placing the hand under the armpit. To me, they simply looked as if they were imitating a monkey, but to them the gesture meant "Your mother is a whore," absolutely the worst possible insult in that culture.

Gestures thus not only facilitate communication but, since they differ around the world, can also lead to misunderstandings, embarrassment, or worse. Once in Mexico,

gestures: the ways in which people use their bodies to communicate with one another

for example, I raised my hand to a certain height to indicate how tall a child was. My hosts began to laugh. It turned out that Mexicans have a more complicated system of hand gestures to indicate height: one for people, a second for animals, and a third for plants. (See Figure 2.1). What had amused them was that I had ignorantly used the plant gesture to indicate the child's height.

To get along in another culture, then, it is important to learn the gestures of that culture. If you don't you will not only fail to achieve the simplicity of communication that gestures allow but you will also miss much of what is happening, run the risk of appearing foolish, and possibly offend people. In many cultures, for example, you would provoke deep offense if you were to offer food or a gift with your left hand, because the left hand is reserved for dirty tasks, such as wiping after going to the bathroom. Left-handed Americans visiting Arabs please note!

P E R S P E C T I V E S
Cultural Diversity in U.S. Society

Miami—Language and a Changing City

In the years since Castro seized power in Cuba, the city of Miami has been transformed from a quiet southern city to a Latin American mecca. Few things better capture Miami today than its ethnic divisions, especially its long-simmering fight over language: English versus Spanish. The 1990 census found that half of the city's 358,548 residents have trouble speaking English—possibly the highest proportion in any large American city. Ten years ago, at 30 percent, the figure was high. Today's 50 percent who have difficulty communicating in English reflects the recent influx of Hispanic and Creole-speaking Haitian immigrants.

As this chapter stresses, language is a primary means by which people learn—and communicate—their social world. Consequently, language differences in Miami reflect a community not just of huge cultural diversity but of people who live in separate worlds. Sandra Laurin, a community college student, put it this way. "Everyone is in their own little group: the Haitians in their group, the Spanish in theirs, the Anglos in theirs." As classmate Nicole Allen added, "Language is a big barrier. It's so hard to communicate with everybody, you just don't bother."

Although the ethnic stew makes Miami culturally one of the richest cities in the United States, the language gap sometimes creates anger and misunderstanding. The aggravation of Anglos—tinged with hostility—is seen in the bumper stickers reading "Will the Last American Out Please Bring the Flag?"

But Hispanics, now a majority in Miami, are equally frustrated. Many feel Anglos should be able to speak at least some Spanish. Nicaraguan immigrant Pedro Falco, for example, is studying English and wonders why more people won't try to learn his language. "Miami is the capital of Latin America," he says. "The population speaks Spanish."

In the past ten years, Miami's population grew only 3.4 percent, but its Spanish-speaking population grew 15 percent, making the city 62 percent Hispanic. Throughout the United States, 83 percent of residents speak English at home, but only 25 percent of Miami residents do so.

What's happening in Miami, says University of Chicago sociologist Douglas Massey, is what happened in cities such as Chicago at the beginning of the century. Then, as now, the rate of immigration exceeded the speed with which new residents learned English, creating a pile-up effect in the proportion of non–English speakers. Becoming comfortable with English is a slow process, he points out, whereas immigration is fast.

Language and cultural flare-ups sometimes make headlines in the city. The Hispanic-American community was outraged in 1991 when an employee at the Coral Gables Board of Realtors lost her job for speaking Spanish at the office. And in 1989, protesters swarmed a Publix supermarket after a cashier was fired for chatting with a friend in Spanish.

David Lawrence, Jr., publisher of the *Miami Herald,* the area's dominant newspaper, sees the language gap as "a challenge and opportunity." Lawrence now publishes *El Nuevo Herald,* a Spanish-language edition with a circulation of one hundred thousand that has become a favorite of the Cuban elite. "The key to making any community work is obviously communication," notes Lawrence. "While lots of people, including myself, work hard to learn Spanish, part of being successful is being able to communicate in English."

Massey expects the city's proportion of non–English speakers to rise with continuing immigration. But he says that this "doesn't mean in the long run that Miami is going to end up being a Spanish-speaking city." Instead, Massey believes, bilingualism will prevail. "Miami is the first truly bilingual city," he says. "The people who get ahead are not monolingual English speakers or monolingual Spanish speakers. They're people who speak both languages."

Source: Copyright 1992, *USA Today.* Reprinted by permission.

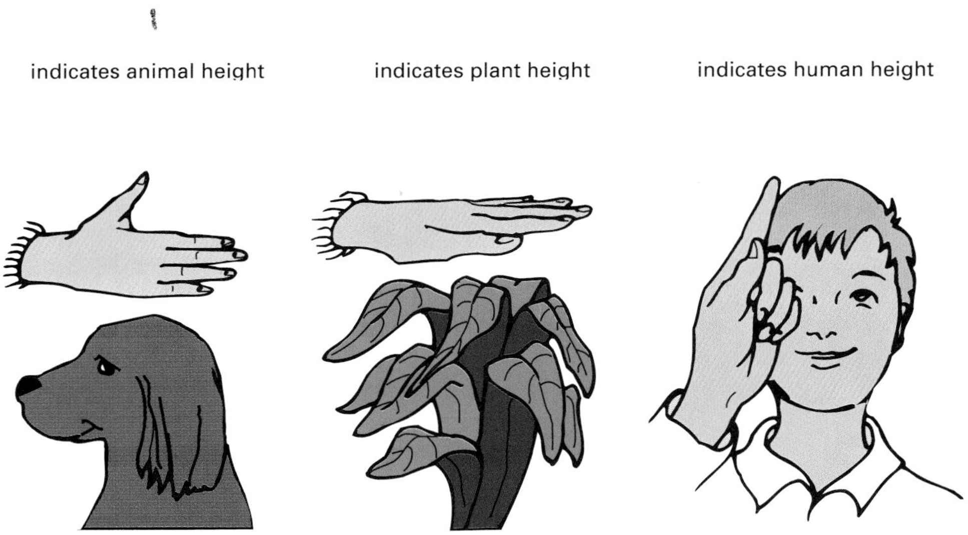

indicates animal height   indicates plant height   indicates human height

FIGURE 2.1   Gestures to Indicate Height

CDQ 7: Do you think there are any universal gestures? If so, give examples.

L. Obj. 4: Define the following terms: values, norms, sanctions, folkways, mores, and taboos.

values: the standards by which people define what is desirable or undesirable, good or bad, beautiful or ugly

norms: the expectations, or rules of behavior, that develop out of values

Now suppose for a moment that you are visiting southern Italy. After eating one of the best meals in your life you are so pleased that when you catch the waiter's eye, you smile broadly and use the standard American "A-OK" gesture of putting your thumb and forefinger together and making a large "O." The waiter looks horrified, and you are struck speechless when the manager asks you to leave. What have you done? Nothing on purpose, of course, but in that culture that gesture refers to a part of the human body that is not mentioned in polite company (Ekman et al. 1984).

Is it really true that there are no universal gestures? There is some disagreement on this point. Ethologists, researchers who study biological bases of behavior, claim that expressions of anger, pouting, fear, and sadness are built into our biology and are universal (Eibl-Eibesfeldt 1970:404). They point out that even infants who are born blind and deaf, who have had no chance to learn these gestures, express themselves in the same way. Anthropologists, in contrast, claim that no gestures are universal. They point out that even the gesture of nodding the head up and down to indicate "yes" is not universal, since in some parts of the world, such as areas of Turkey, nodding the head up and down means "no" (Ekman et al. 1984).

While this matter is not yet settled, we can note that at least almost all gestures vary around the world. It is also significant that gestures can create emotions. Some gestures are so associated with emotional messages that the gesture itself summons up an emotion. For example, my introduction to Mexican gestures took place at a dinner table. It was evident that my husband-and-wife hosts were trying to hide their embarrassment at actually using this obscene gesture at their dinner table. And I felt the same way—not about *their* gesture, of course, which meant absolutely nothing to me—but about the one I was teaching them.

Values, Norms, and Sanctions

To learn a culture is to learn people's **values,** their ideas of what is desirable in life (Williams 1960; 1970). Values are the standards by which people define good and bad, beautiful and ugly. To uncover people's values is to learn a great deal about them, for values underlie their preferences, guide their choices, and indicate what they hold worthwhile in life.

Every group develops both values and expectations concerning the right way to reflect them. Sociologists use the term **norms** to describe those expectations, or rules of behavior, that develop out of a group's values. They use the term **sanction** to refer to positive or negative reactions to the ways in which people follow norms. **Positive sanction** refers to an expression of approval given for following a norm, while **negative sanction** denotes disapproval for breaking a norm. Positive sanctions can be material, such as a money reward, a prize, or a trophy, but in everyday life they usually consist of hugs, smiles, a clap on the back, soothing words, or even handshakes. Negative sanctions can also be material—a fine is one example—but they, too, are more likely to consist of gestures, such as frowns, stares, harsh words, or raised fists. Being awarded a raise at work is a positive sanction, indicating that the norms clustering around work values have been followed, while being fired is a negative sanction, indicating the opposite. The North American finger gesture discussed above is, of course, a negative sanction.

Folkways and Mores

Norms that are not strictly enforced are called **folkways.** We expect people to comply with folkways, but we are likely to shrug our shoulders and not make a big deal about it if they don't. If someone insists on passing you on the left side of the sidewalk, for example, you are unlikely to take corrective action—although if the sidewalk is crowded and you must move out of the way, you might give the person a dirty look.

Other norms, however, are taken much more seriously. We think of them as essential to our core values, and we insist on conformity. These are called **mores** (MORE-rays). A person who steals, rapes, and kills has violated some of society's most important mores. As sociologist Ian Robertson (1987:62) put it

> A man who walks down a street wearing nothing on the upper half of his body is violating a folkway; a man who walks down the street wearing nothing on the lower half of his body is violating one of our most important mores, the requirement that people cover their genitals and buttocks in public.

It should also be noted that what are folkways to one group in society may constitute mores to another. Although a male walking down the street with the upper half of his body uncovered is deviating from a folkway, a female doing the same thing is violating accepted mores. In addition, the folkways and mores of a subculture (the topic of the next section) may be the opposite of the general culture. For example, to walk down the sidewalk in a nudist camp with the entire body uncovered would not violate the mores of that subculture—but, rather, conform to *their* folkways.

A **taboo** refers to a norm so strongly ingrained even the thought of its violation is greeted with revulsion. Eating human flesh and having sex with one's parents are examples of such behaviors (Benales 1973; Read 1974; Henslin 1993f).

SUBCULTURES AND COUNTERCULTURES

All groups, no matter what their size, have their own values, norms, and sanctions. Most groups are microcosms of the larger society to which they belong and thus reflect its values. Obvious examples are the Girl Scouts of America, the Future Farmers of America, and the Chamber of Commerce. In contrast, the values and related behaviors of some groups are so distinct that they set its members off from the general culture. Sociologists use the term **subculture** to refer to such groups. American society contains thousands of subcultures, some as broad as the way of life we associate with teenagers, others as narrow as those represented by skateboarders and boating enthusiasts. Occupations are a rich source of subcultures, and many of them develop a special language marking out their distinctive experiences. Thus cabdrivers (Davis 1959; Henslin 1967, 1993a), artists (McCall 1980), pool hustlers (Polsky 1967), police

CDQ 8: How do your family and friends use positive and negative sanctions to get you to do what they want?

CDQ 9: What are the folkways in a fast-food restaurant? What about in an expensive, "white tablecloth" restaurant with tuxedoed waitpersons?

CDQ 10: How do the values, norms, and sanctions of your fraternity, sorority, or other social club differ from those of the general culture?

L. Obj. 5: Compare and contrast dominant culture, subcultures, and countercultures.

sanction: an expression of approval or disapproval given to people for upholding or violating norms

positive sanction: a reward given for following norms, ranging from a smile to a prize

negative sanction: an expression of disapproval for breaking a norm, ranging from a mild, informal reaction such as a frown to a formal prison sentence

folkways: norms which are not strictly enforced

mores: (MORE-rays) norms that are strictly enforced because they are thought essential to core values

taboo: a norm so strong that it brings revulsion if it is violated

subculture: the values and related behaviors of a group that distinguish its members from the larger culture; a world within a world

*The norms and values of countercul-
ture groups are at odds with the dominant culture. Many youth gangs
provide members with a sense of belonging but at the same time isolate
them from the dominant culture because of clashing norms and values.*

(Pepinsky 1980), prostitutes (Davis 1971), thieves (Sutherland 1937), and construction
workers (Haas 1972) form subcultures. So do sociologists (Tiryakian 1971; Prus 1980),
who, as you are learning, also have developed a unique language for carving up the
world. Each subculture, *a world within the larger world* of the dominant culture, has a
distinctive way of looking at life (Gordon 1947; Komarovsky and Sargent 1949).

Unlike a subculture, in which a group carves out its own identity but remains
compatible with the dominant culture, the values of some groups set their members
in opposition to the dominant culture. Sociologists use the term **counterculture** to
describe such groups. Heavy metal adherents who glorify satanism, hatred, cruelty,
rebellion, sexism, violence, and death, are an example of a counterculture (Mace 1986).
Note that motorcycle enthusiasts—who emphasize personal feedom and speed, while
maintaining the accepted cultural value of success—form part of a subculture; on the
other hand, the members of an outlaw motorcycle gang—who also stress freedom and
speed, but add the values of dirtiness and despising women and work—form part of a
counterculture (Watson 1988).

We shall focus on norm violators in Chapter 8, which looks at deviance and social
control. At this point, let's examine the values of our larger society.

VALUES IN AMERICAN SOCIETY

As you well know, the United States is a **pluralistic society,** made up of many
different groups. We have numerous religious, racial, and ethnic groups, as well as
countless interest groups centering on such divergent activities as collecting dolls and
hunting animals. This state of affairs makes the job of specifying American values
difficult. Nonetheless, sociologists have tried to identify the underlying core values that
cut across the many groups that make up our society.

Essay #3

counterculture: a group whose
values place its members in opposition to the values of the
broader culture

pluralistic society: a society
made up of many different
groups

Sociologist Robin Williams (1965) identified the following core values in American society:

1. *Achievement and success*   Americans place a high value on personal achievement, especially outdoing others. This value includes the concept of getting ahead at work and school, and with it the goal of attaining wealth, power, and prestige.

2. *Individualism*   Americans have traditionally prized success through individual efforts and initiative. They cherish the value that in our system an individual can rise from the bottom to the very top of society. If someone does not "make it" or fails to "get ahead" to the degree that others expect, Americans generally find fault with that individual, rather than with the social system for placing roadblocks in his or her path. They tend to judge the person as having failed either through lack of ability or lack of application.

3. *Activity and work*   Americans expect people to work hard and to be busily engaged in some activity even when not at work. Work is an end in itself, and, as Williams says, "It is no accident that the business so characteristic of the culture can also be spelled "busyness."

4. *Efficiency and practicality*   Americans award high marks for getting things done efficiently. Even in everyday life, Americans consider it important to do things as fast or as well as possible, and constantly seek changes to increase efficiency.

5. *Science and rationality*   Americans have a passion for applied science, for using science to control nature—to tame rivers and harness winds—and to develop new technology. This value forms a smaller part of the larger American view of the universe as a highly ordered place.

6. *Progress*   Americans expect continued, rapid technological change. They believe that they should constantly build "more and better" gadgets and attain an ever-increasing national product. They also anticipate that all change be toward some vague ideal called "progress."

7. *Material comfort*   Americans expect a high level of material comfort. This comfort includes not only nutrition, medical care, and housing, but also late-model cars and recreational playthings—from boats and motor homes to computer games. In recent years, Americans have expressed massive dissatisfaction with economic conditions that have put adequate medical care and housing out of the reach of so many. We shall cover these topics in Chapters 10, 14, and 19.

8. *Equality*   It is impossible to understand Americans without first being aware of the central role that the value of equality plays in their lives. Equality of opportunity, an important concept in the ideal culture discussed below, has significantly influenced United States history and continues to mark relations between the groups that make up American society.

9. *Freedom*   This core value, too, pervades American life. It underscored the American Revolution, and Americans today bristle at the suggestion of any limitation on personal freedom. The Perspectives box highlights some startling research on this core value and Native Americans.

10. *Democracy*   By this term, Americans refer to the supremacy of majority rule, to the right of everyone to express an opinion, and to government by representative institutions. This value is so far-reaching that Americans fought World War I under the slogan, "Make the World Safe for Democracy."

11. *Humanitarianism*   According to Williams, Americans emphasize helpfulness, personal kindness, spontaneous aid in mass disasters, and organized philanthropy. This value includes not only sympathizing with victims of disaster or oppression, but also to opening pocketbooks and purses to provide them with food and other material needs.

12. *Racism and group superiority*   According to Williams, Americans value some groups more than others and have done so throughout their history. The institution of slavery in earlier American society is the most notorious example. We shall examine the consequences of sexism and racism in Chapters 11 and 12.

K.P.: Robin Williams

L. Obj. 6: List the core values in American society as identified by Robin Williams

CDQ 11: What do you consider to be an "adequate" education? Is this the same for everyone?

Essay #4

Humanitarianism is one of the core values sociologists have identified in American culture.

In an earlier publication (Henslin 1975), I updated Williams's analysis by adding the following three values.

13. *Education*   Americans are expected to go as far in school as their abilities and finances allow. Over the years, the definition of an "adequate" education has changed sharply, and today the expectation of a college education is held as an appropriate goal for almost all Americans. Some even view people who have an opportunity for higher education and who do not take it as doing something "wrong," not merely making a bad choice, but somehow involved in an immoral act.

14. *Religiosity*   There is a feeling that "every true American ought to be religious." This does not mean that everyone is expected to join a church or synagogue, but that everyone ought to acknowledge a belief in a Supreme Being and follow some set of matching precepts. This value is so pervasive that Americans stamp "In God We Trust" on their money and declare in their national pledge of allegiance that they are "one nation under God." We shall examine this value in Chapter 18.

15. *Romantic love and monogamy*   Americans feel that the only proper basis for marriage is romantic love. Songs, literature, mass media, and "folk beliefs" all stress this value, and sometimes include the theme that "love conquers all." Similarly, the idea that the only proper form of marriage is that of one man to one woman overwhelmingly predominates in American society. When the Mormons challenged this value in the 1800s, they were driven out of several states. They finally settled in what was then a wilderness, but even there the federal government would not

PERSPECTIVES

Cultural Diversity in U.S. Society

Why Do Native Americans Like Westerns?

American audiences (and even German, French, and Japanese) have devoured westerns. In the United States, it is easy to see why Anglos might like this genre, for it is they who seemingly defy odds and emerge victorious. It is they who are portrayed as heroically taming a savage wilderness, who fend themselves from cruel, barbaric Indians intent on their destruction. But why would Indians like westerns?

Sociologist JoEllen Shively, a Chippewa who grew up on Indian reservations in Montana and North Dakota, found that westerns are so popular that Native Americans bring bags of paperbacks into taverns to trade with one another. They even call one another "cowboy."

Intrigued, Shively decided to investigate the matter by showing a western movie to adult Native Americans and Anglos in a reservation town. To select the movie, Shively (1991) previewed over seventy westerns and then chose a John Wayne movie, *The Searchers,* because it focuses not only on conflict between Indians and cowboys but also shows the cowboys defeating the Indians. The viewers were matched on education, age, income, and percentage of unemployment. After the movie, she had the viewers fill out questionnaires and interviewed them.

Shively found something surprising: *all* Native Americans and Anglos identified with the cowboys; *none* identified with the Indians.

The ways in which Anglos and Native Americans

identified with the cowboys, however, were quite different, for each projected a different fantasy onto the story. While Anglos saw the movie as an accurate portrayal of the Old West and a justification of their own status in the social system, Native Americans saw it as embodying a free, natural way of life. In fact, Native Americans said that they were the "real cowboys." By this, they referred to their idealization of freedom and being "one's own man."

Shively concludes:

> In westerns, Indians express the ways in which they are different from the dominant society through one of the core myths of the dominant society. . . . To express their real identity—a combination of marginality on the one hand, with a set of values which are about the land, autonomy, and being free—they (use) a cultural vehicle (that is) written for Anglos about Anglos, but it is one in which Indians invest a distinctive set of meanings that speak to their own experience, which they can read in a manner that affirms a way of life they value, or a fantasy they hold to.

In other words, values, not ethnicity, are the central issue. If a Native American film industry were to portray Native Americans with the same values as the Anglo movie industry projects onto cowboys, then Native Americans would identify with their own group. Thus, says Shively, Native American viewers make cowboys "honorary Indians," for the cowboys express their values of bravery, autonomy, and toughness.

let them practice polygyny (one man having more than one wife). Utah's statehood was even made conditional on its acceptance of monogamy (Anderson 1942, 1966). In some respects this value has changed somewhat; Americans now tolerate more than one spouse—but still only one at a time, a marital practice sometimes called "serial monogamy."

Value Clusters

As you can see, values are not independent units; **value clusters** come together to form a larger whole. In the value cluster surrounding success, for example, we find hard work, education, efficiency, material comfort, and individualism all bound up together. Americans are expected to go far in school, to work hard afterwards, to be efficient, and then to attain a high level of material comfort, which, in turn, demonstrates success. Success is considered attributable to the individual's own efforts, the lack of success to his or her own faults.

L. Obj. 7: Explain what is meant by value clusters and value contradictions.

Value Contradictions and Social Change

Not all values fall into neat, integrated packages. Some, indeed, conflict with one another, leading to **value contradictions.** For example, the value that stresses group superiority comes into direct conflict with the values of democracy and equality. There simply cannot be full expressions of democracy, equality, racism, and sexism at the same time. Something has to give. One way in which Americans have sidestepped this particular contradiction in the past is to say that the values of democracy and equality apply only to certain groups. The contradiction was bound to surface over time, however, and so it did in this case. Americans have responded by continuing to stress the values of equality and democracy, while extending these values to more groups.

As society changes, then, some values are challenged and undergo modification. Although the Civil War put an end to slavery, this did not mean the end of some of the values that belonged to its cluster. Values that support racial superiority have only gradually been modified. Values of male supremacy in American society have also changed slowly as they have been challenged by conflicting values of equality. It is precisely at the point of value contradictions that one can see a major force for social change in a society.

Emergent Values

Because values are dynamic, changing over time, a core value can not only shrink in significance, while another takes on greater emphasis, but new values also evolve. Four interrelated core values now appear to be emerging in the United States: leisure, physical fitness, self-fulfillment, and the environment.

16. *Leisure* The emergence of leisure as a value is reflected in the phenomenal growth of a recreational infrastructure—from computer games, boats, and motor homes, to sports arenas, vacation homes, and a gigantic travel and vacation industry (Caplow 1991; Hamilton 1991). Table 2.1 illustrates the growth from 1970 to 1989 in the numbers of Americans who pursue recreational activities. This value can also be seen in the increasing concern for "retirement benefits," sometimes even expressed by college graduates as they apply for their first job.

17. *Physical fitness* Physical fitness is not a new American value, but the increased emphasis on it is moving it into the core. This trend can be seen in the "natural" foods craze; brew bars, obsessive concerns about weight and diet; the many joggers, runners, cyclists, and backpackers; and, of course, the mushrooming of health clubs and physical fitness centers.

18. *Self-fulfillment* This value is reflected in the "human potential" movement, a preoccupation with becoming "all one can be," "self-help," "relating," and "personal development." This process sometimes takes the form of "consciousness

Project 4

L. Obj. 8: Discuss the emergent values in American society and analyze why core values do not change without meeting strong resistance.

CDQ 12: Why do some college graduates ask about "retirement benefits" when they apply for their first job? Do you plan to ask this question?

value clusters: a series of interrelated values that together form a larger whole

value contradictions: values that conflict with one another; to follow the one means to come into conflict with the other

TABLE 2.1   Leisure in the United States

Number of participants (in millions)	1970	1980	1989
Amateur softball players	16	30	41
Bowlers	52	72	71
Golfers	11	15	25
Major league baseball attendance		44	56
Opera attendance	5	11	
Recreational boats owned	9	12	1
Visitors to national parks and national recreation areas			283
		$17	$44

Note: These figures reflect not only increases in the recreational pursuits of Americans, but also changing tastes in recreation. Note the slight decline that followed the sharp increase in the number of bowlers.
Source: *Statistical Abstract of the United States* 1980, Table 417; 1991, Tables 386, 395, 403, 404.

raising," of "getting in contact with one's inner being." In some instances it is called the "new age movement." Whatever its name, it represents a profound change regarding what one ought to expect out of life.

19. *Concern for the environment*   During most of American history, the environment was seen as a challenge—a wilderness to be settled, forests to be chopped down for farms and building materials, rivers and lakes to be fished, and animals to be hunted. The lack of concern for the environment that characterized earlier Americans is illustrated by the near extinction of the bison and the extinction in 1914 of the passenger pigeon, a bird previously so numerous that its annual migration would darken the skies for days. Today, Americans have developed a genuine, and hopefully long-term, concern for the environment, as illustrated by pressures that citizen groups have put on Congress to improve the quality of the country's air and water, a federal list of endangered species that merit special protection, and the requirement that construction projects file environmental impact statements. We shall return to this emergent value in Chapter 22.

These four emergent values form their own interrelated value cluster. Americans have come to a point in their economic development where millions of people are freed from long hours of work, and millions more are able to retire from work when they can still expect decades of life ahead of them. Concern for the environment is similar to concerns about physical fitness and self-fulfillment—for each is now viewed as an essential part of life that should be improved or come close to "its potential." This emergent value of environmental concern is also related to the current stage of United States economic development, a point that becomes clearer when we note that people focus and act on environmental concerns only after basic needs are met. At this point in their development, for example, Third World nations, which we shall study in Chapter 14, have a much more difficult time "affording" this value. These four values, then, are a logical response to new needs and interests resulting from fundamental changes in American society.

Reactions to Changes in Core Values

Core values do not change without meeting strong resistance from traditionalists who hold them dear. Consequently, many people are upset at the changes swirling around them, seeing their way of life challenged and their future growing insecure. A major criticism of these emerging values is that they encourage individualism at the cost of social responsibility. By encouraging people to be self-indulgent, it is argued, they cannot but neglect the needs of others; and these new values will therefore break down community, and, ultimately, undermine the family, religion, and the economy (Bellah et al. 1985; Etzioni 1982; Schur 1976). The new concern for the environment is also under attack, but for quite different reasons. Among the traditionalists who are threatened by this emergent value are hunters, builders, and businesspeople who feel that their rights are being trampled on by extremists.

Values as Blinders

Values and their supporting beliefs paint their own picture of reality, as well as forming a view of what life *ought* to be like. Because Americans value individualism so highly, for example, they tend to see people as free to pursue whatever legitimate goals they desire. This value blinds them to the many social circumstances that impede people's efforts. The dire consequences of family poverty, parents' lack of education, and dead-end jobs tend to drop from sight. Instead, Americans cling to the notion that anyone can make it—with the right amount of effort. And to prove it, dangled before their eyes are success stories of individuals who have succeeded in spite of huge handicaps.

"Ideal" versus "Real" Culture

Many of the norms that surround cultural values are only partially followed. Differences always exist between what a group holds out as its cultural ideal and what its members actually do. Consequently, sociologists use the term **ideal culture** to refer to the ideal values and norms of a people, to the goals they hold out. The idea of success, for example, is part of ideal culture. Americans glorify academic progress, hard work, and the display of material goods as signs of individual achievement. What people actually do, however, usually falls short of the cultural ideal. Sociologists call the norms and values that people actually follow **real culture.** Compared with their capacities, for example, most people don't go as far as they could in school or work as hard as they can.

Sociologists have identified concern for the environment as an emerging value in the United States.

CDQ 13: Do you think that values can be blinders? If yes, give examples.

Project 5

CULTURAL UNIVERSALS

With the amazing variety of human cultures around the world, are there any **cultural universals**—values, norms, or other cultural traits that are found everywhere?

Anthropologist George Murdock (1945) sought to answer that question. After combing through data gathered by anthropologists on hundreds of groups around the world, he drew up a list of customs concerning courtship, cooking, family, funerals, games, laws, music, myths, incest taboos, and toilet training.

While such activities are present in all cultures, however, *the specific customs clearly differ from one group to another.* There is no universal form of the family, no universal way of disposing of the dead. Similarly, specific games, rules, songs, stories, and methods of toilet training differ from one culture to another.

Even incest is defined differently from group to group. For example, the Mundugumors of New Guinea extend the incest taboo so far that seven of every eight women are ineligible marriage partners (Mead 1950). Other groups go in the opposite direction and allow some men to marry their own daughters (La Barre 1954). In certain circumstances, some groups even require that brothers and sisters marry one another (Beals and Hoijer 1965). The Burundi of Africa even insist that, to remove a certain curse, a son have sexual relations with his mother (Albert 1963). Such sexual relations are allowed only for special people (royalty) or in a special situation (such as that of a lion hunter before a dangerous hunt), however, and no society permits generalized incest for its members.

In short, although there are universal human activities (speech, music, storytelling, disposing of the dead, preparing food, and so on), there is no universally accepted way

L. Obj. 9: Define cultural universals and state whether, in actuality, they exist or not.

K.P.: George Murdock

ideal culture: the ideal values and norms of a people, the goals held out for them

real culture: the norms and values that people actually follow

cultural universal: a value, norm, or other cultural trait that is found in every group

Cultural universals are those values, norms, rites, customs, or other cultural traits which are found in all societies. One such cultural universal is marriage.

CDQ 14: Are humans programmed by their genes to behave in certain ways? Why or why not?

sociobiology: a framework of thought that views human behavior as the result of natural selection and considers biological characteristics to be the fundamental cause of human behavior

of doing any of them. Humans have no biological imperative that results in one particular form of behavior throughout the world. As indicated in the Thinking Critically section below, a few sociologists do take the position that genes significantly influence human behavior, although almost all sociologists disagree with this view.

THINKING CRITICALLY ABOUT SOCIAL CONTROVERSY

Are We Prisoners of Our Genes? Sociobiology

A controversial view of human behavior called **sociobiology** provides a sharp contrast to the view presented in this chapter. Instead of looking at human behavior as shaped by culture, sociobiology stresses natural selection as responsible for humans' particular biological characteristics, which shape human behavior.

According to Charles Darwin (1859), natural selection is based on four principles. First, reproduction occurs within a natural environment. Second, the genes of a species, the basic units of life that contain the individual's traits, are passed on to offspring. These genes have a degree of random variability; that is, different characteristics are distributed among the members of a species. Third, because the members of a species possess different characteristics, some members have a better chance of surviving in the natural environment than do others—and of passing their particular genetic traits to the next generation. Fourth, over thousands of generations, those genetic traits that aid survival in the natural environment tend to become common in a species, while those that do not tend to disappear.

Natural selection is used to explain the physical characteristics of plants and animals. It is also used to explain the behavior of animals: Over countless generations instincts emerged. Edward O. Wilson (1975), an insect specialist, claims that the principles of natural selection that led to human physical characteristics also led to human behavior as well. Human behavior, he said, is no different from the behavior of cats, dogs, rats, bees, or mosquitoes—it has been bred into *homo sapiens* through evolutionary principles.

Wilson deliberately set out to create a storm of protest, and he succeeded. He claims that religion, competition and cooperation, slavery and genocide, war and peace, envy and altruism—all can be explained through sociobiology. He provocatively adds that because human behavior can be explained in terms of genetic programming, the new discipline of sociobiology will eventually absorb sociology—as well as anthropology and psychology.

Obviously, most sociologists find Wilson's position totally unacceptable. Not only is it a direct attack on their discipline, it bypasses the essence of what sociologists focus on: humans designing their own cultures, developing their own unique ways of life. Sociologists do not deny that genetic principles underlie human behavior, at least not in the sense that it takes a highly developed brain to develop human culture, that abstract thought could not exist if we did not have a highly developed cerebral cortex.

But sociologists find the claim that human behavior is due to genetic programming to be quite another matter (Lewontin et al. 1984). Pigs act alike because they don't have a cerebral cortex, and instincts control their behavior. So it is for fleas, spiders, deer, elephants, and so on. But humans are far from being driven simply by instincts. Humans have abstract thought. They communicate symbolically. They discuss principles that underlie what they do. They decide on rational courses of action. They develop reasons and purposes and goals. They consider, reflect, and make choices.

In short, sociologists stress that we are not prisoners of our genes, and that is precisely why around the world we have developed so many fascinating, contrasting ways of life.

Why do sociologists discredit the sociobiologists' claim that all human behavior can be traced to genetic programming? Are you aware of any research that would be considered sociobiological in nature? Describe that research, and discuss whether or not you believe it poses a valid challenge to the sociological premise that humans have no biological imperative that results in a particular form of behavior that is common around the world.

ANIMALS AND CULTURE

Do Animals Have Culture? Let us digress for a moment to follow a fascinating and related issue: Do animals have culture? According to our definition of culture as a learned way of life that is passed on to others, it would seem that they could not. They certainly could not if animal behavior is entirely under the control of *instincts*, inherited patterns of behavior common to all normal members of a species. Instinctual behaviors, such as the distinctive nest building of a Baltimore oriole, are not learned. By definition, then, they do not constitute culture.

The basic sociological question, then, is this: Are there any behaviors that animals teach each other across generations—even though those behaviors may appear to be due to instincts? The answer to this question was revealed in a rather surprising way. Eight-year-old Jane Goodall decided that when she grew up she would go to Africa and live with wild animals. Not many adults are able to live out their childhood fantasies, but in 1957, when she was a twenty-two-year-old secretary in London, a schoolfriend invited her to visit her parents' farm in Kenya, Africa. Later, in Nairobi, she met Louis Leakey, a world-renowned anthropologist and paleontologist. When Leakey learned of Goodall's interest in animals, he hired her as a secretary.

Leakey had been working just across the border where he was collecting fossils in an area called the Olduvai Gorge. He invited her to go on a dig with him there, and on that trip he asked her if she would like to study some chimpanzees living on the shores of a lake. Leakey explained that because the remains of early humans were often found on lakeshores it was possible that "an understanding of chimpanzee behavior today might shed light on the behavior of our stone age ancestors" (Van Lawick-Goodall 1971).

Bear in mind that Goodall had no college degree, much less a Ph.D., nor did she have any training in fieldwork. Secretarial training was not exactly preparation for studying wild animals. Also, the "lake site" was in the remote jungle eight hundred miles from Nairobi—and working there would require her to live in isolation for years. Yet Goodall eagerly accepted the famous anthropologist's invitation. An obstacle to their plans arose, however, for when Tanzanian officials learned that a young woman was planning to live in the jungle by herself, they refused to grant a permit for the work. Only when Goodall's mother agreed to live with her did they issue the permit. Before Goodall (1971) left, she spent three weeks on an uninhabited island in Lake Victoria, which, she says, taught her "a good deal about such things as note-taking in the field, the sort of clothes to wear, the movements a wild monkey will tolerate in a human observer and those it will not."

Afterwards, she went on to her destination. At first, things didn't go well. While her mother remained in the camp on the shores of Lake Tanganyika, Goodall would spend her days unsuccessfully searching for chimpanzees. She was seldom even able to catch a glimpse of the wary chimps, who made sure they kept their distance from this strange intruder. You can imagine the frustration Goodall felt each evening, telling her mother that another day's effort had yielded nothing.

Goodall persisted, however, and about six months later the situation changed abruptly. That day began like all the preceding ones, just another big disappointment. When Goodall spotted some chimpanzees through her binoculars, she tried to sneak up on them. All she found were empty branches of a fruit tree (1971).

L. Obj. 10: Answer the question, "Do animals have culture?"

Speaker Sug. #4: An anthropologist or ethologist who has worked in primate labs or done field research with chimps or gorillas.

K.P.: Jane Goodall

Essay #5

Instead of assuming the answer, scientists have increasingly studied animals to observe the extent to which their behavior is learned, and not simply transmitted genetically.

The same old feeling of depression clawed at me. Once again the chimpanzees had seen me and silently fled. Then all at once my heart missed several beats.

Less than twenty yards away from me two male chimpanzees were sitting on the ground staring at me intently. Scarcely breathing, I waited for the sudden panic-stricken flight that normally followed a surprise encounter between myself and the chimpanzees at close quarters. But nothing of the sort happened. The two large chimps simply continued to gaze at me. Very slowly I sat down, and after a few more moments, the two calmly began to groom one another.

As I watched, still scarcely believing it was true, I saw two more chimpanzee heads peering at me over the grass from the other side of a small forest glade: a female and a youngster. They bobbed down as I turned my head toward them, but soon reappeared, one after the other, in the lower branches of a tree about forty yards away. There they sat, almost motionless, watching me.

About ten minutes later, as the sun was going down, the two chimps stopped their grooming. One stood and carefully looked Goodall over. Then the two turned and slowly walked away.

Goodall was naturally elated by this unexpected event. It was almost as if the chimps had given her an invitation to get to know them. Goodall practically ran down the mountainside to tell her mother about this exciting breakthrough. The exultation she felt at that moment made the depression and despair of the past months seem as nothing. After this overture, the chimpanzees gradually let Goodall get close to them. Eventually she made friends with the band, and over the next ten years she practically lived with them. Slowly she learned to understand how they communicated, and eventually she was able to participate in their gestures, hoots, and facial expressions. She continued her research for the next thirty years, living in a house made of "concrete blocks with a thin, corrugated tin roof and thatch, no running water, and windows covered in mesh to keep the baboons out" (Walters 1990).

The exotic nature of this fieldwork apart, what did Goodall actually learn that might help us decide whether animals have culture? Goodall noticed that, amazingly, the chimps made and used **tools;** they actually modified objects and used them for specific purposes. The tool itself was very simple, but tool it was. The chimps would first pick a blade of grass, then strip off its leaves and lick one end. Next they would poke the sticky end into a nest of termites. After waiting a bit, they would pull it out covered with termites, then savor the taste as they licked off the stick.

Encouraged by Goodall's discovery, scientists began trying to determine the extent of **animal culture**—learned, shared behavior among animals. They separated infant animals from their parents and others of their species to determine which behaviors remained constant. The surprise, of course, was not the behaviors that animals raised in isolation continued to have in common with their species. These were to be expected. And, indeed, squirrels raised in isolation still bury nuts, and spiders still spin distinctive webs. The surprise was the behaviors that did *not* continue. For example, although many birds raised in soundproof chambers will sing the songs unique to their species, a bullfinch raised with canaries will sing like a canary (Eibl-Eibesfeldt 1970).

One of the more interesting findings was that even the mating behavior of some animals is learned. Mating certainly appears as instinctual as cats bathing themselves, but it is not. For generations, zookeepers have been disappointed that many of their captives did not reproduce. Gorillas, for example, are notorious for not mating in captivity. The keepers constantly had to replenish their supply of these animals from the wild. When there was a seemingly endless supply of wild animals, and numerous hunters made their living by capturing them alive, the situation was a minor nuisance. With increasing numbers of endangered species, however, coupled with growing international restrictions on capturing and importing animals, it has become a major problem. In one of the more humorous footnotes to scientific endeavors to understand the extent of animal culture, zookeepers in Sacramento, California, noted that young gorillas seemed to want to mate, but didn't seem to know how (Stark 1989). To solve the

tool: an object that is modified for a specific purpose

animal culture: learned, shared behavior among animals

problem, they showed them a movie—of two adult gorillas mating. The lesson turned out to be a success.

Goodall's research and subsequent experiments answer our question: On a rudimentary level animal culture exists. Although the principle has been established, however, we do not yet know the particulars. What animals? What specific behaviors are learned? The initial answers, enticing though they may be, only point to further provocative questions.

Do Animals Have Language?

A related question that has intrigued scientists and nonscientists alike is whether or not animals have language. Do those barks and meows your pets make constitute language?

Social scientists think of language as more complex than mere sounds, as symbols that can be infinitely strung together to communicate abstract thought. Animal sounds, however, appear to be much like infant cries. Although a baby will cry when in pain, the cry of distress that brings a parent running is not language. It is merely a biological response to pain, similar to reflexes.

Social scientists, then, seem to be in agreement that animals do not have language. For the most part, that is true. Animals do not even have the vocal apparatus necessary for the complex sounds that make up language. But not all animals are incapable of learning language.

In a remarkable series of experiments, researchers have tried to teach chimpanzees to talk. In the earliest of these efforts, a husband and wife team at Indiana University tried to "humanize" a baby chimp, Gua. For nine months, the Kelloggs (1933) raised Gua together with their own infant son, Donald. Gua and Donald grew very close, and they would hold hands and hug one another. They would also imitate one another: Like Donald, Gua began to push a baby buggy, but, to the parents' surprise, Donald began to make the chimp "barking" sound for food, to carry objects in his mouth, and even to scrape the wall with his teeth (1933:144–145). At the end of the experiment eighteen-month-old Donald could respond appropriately to 68 words and phrases, while sixteen-month-old Gua could respond to 58. Gua did not learn to speak, and Donald's speech development was retarded—which may be why the Kelloggs ended their experiment.

Researchers began to theorize that the absence of chimpanzee speech might be due not to lack of intelligence (the inability to learn speech), but rather to the inability to make the sounds of speech. Noticing that chimps in the wild use many more hand signals than vocal signals, Allen and Beatrice Gardner (1969), psychologists at the University of Nevada, tested this idea by trying to teach a gestural language instead of a verbal one (Fleming 1974). Their first pupil was Washoe, a female chimpanzee who was born in the wild. In 1966, when Washoe was one year old, her language training began. Washoe was like a human baby. She slept a lot, had just begun to crawl, and her daily routine centered on diapers and bottles. The Gardners tried to teach Washoe American Sign Language, a system of communication in which hand gestures correspond to individual words. They never spoke in her presence, and they played a lot of games that promoted interaction between Washoe and themselves.

The Gardners were greatly encouraged when Washoe began to learn some of the signs, and they were elated when she began to generalize, to apply a sign learned in one situation to other situations. For example, they taught her the sign for "open" using three particular doors in the house trailer she lived in. Washoe transferred that sign to all doors, drawers, containers, the refrigerator, and even the water faucet.

Within a year, Washoe had become inventive and was putting signs together in the equivalent of simple sentences. She even made up combinations, such as joining the sign for "give me" with "tickle" to indicate that she wanted to be tickled. At the end of four years, Washoe could use 160 signs.

CDQ 15: Have you had a pet with which you could communicate? Do social scientists think that animals have language?

Jane Goodall's research demonstrated that animals have a primitive culture; that is, they teach one another behavior that is transmitted across generations. Such culture is very limited, however, because, unlike humans, animals do not have language.

The Gardners then transferred Washoe to the care of Roger Fouts, a graduate student who was moving to the University of Oklahoma to continue his studies in animal communication. When Washoe arrived, she did something that showed both the extent of her ability to understand language and her creativity with language. Up till then Washoe had been raised apart from other monkeys and had only once before seen one of her own kind. Now, as she joined other monkeys, she was taught the sign for "monkey." She used this sign correctly. But in referring to a particular monkey who had threatened her when she arrived, she would add the sign for "dirty." Previously, she had used "dirty" only for feces or for something that had become filthy, but now she would call him only "dirty monkey."

Washoe did just what my son would do at that age: When he didn't like a particular food, he would say, "It tastes like poop!"—a phrase we definitely had not taught him. Later, like a spoiled child, Washoe would use this sign for teachers who refused to grant her wishes.

While Fouts continues his work at the University of Oklahoma, other researchers are conducting various communication studies with chimpanzees in a number of laboratories. Especially encouraging results have come from a team of researchers headed by Duane Rumbaugh of Georgia State University (Fleming 1974). Their pupil, Lana, has learned to operate a keyboard consisting of fifty keys with a colored background and a white geometric shape on each key to represent a word. The keyboard is attached to a computer, and each shape that Lana selects is flashed on a screen, leaving a permanent record of all Lana's interactions with it. Lana uses this system to ask for all of her food and drink, toys, a look outside, and even movies, music, and human companionship.

At the same research center Sue Savage-Rumbaugh reports how she learned that one chimp, Kanzi, missed his friend, Austin, who would visit him at bedtime. Kanzi typed the symbols for "Austin" and "TV." When she played him a videotape of Austin,

Kanzi made some relaxing sounds and then settled into his nest for the night (Eckholm 1985). Kanzi also makes statements about actions by others. He not only asks to be tickled but also asks one person to tickle another while he watches. And then he asks the second to tickle the first.

Many scientists, however, are skeptical of these reports and claim that the chimps are not using real language (Eckholm 1985). Herbert S. Terrace of Columbia University, for example, asks, "Is it anything more than a sophisticated way of asking for things? Dogs can make symbols to ask to go outside. But this is different from what a child does when it names something."

Savage-Rumbaugh, too, is somewhat perplexed by something else she discovered. She found that chimpanzees that can punch the symbol for apple do not have the ability to pick an apple out of a group of objects when a human punches the symbol for apple. "It is hard to believe they couldn't reverse themselves. If they could name it," she wonders, "why couldn't they give it to me?"

Another intriguing experiment has been going on for the past thirteen years, in this case with a parrot. At Northwestern University Irene Pepperberg has taught Alex, an African Gray parrot, to name eighty objects, such as wool, walnut, and shower; to identify the color of objects; and to tell how many objects there are in groups up to six. Unconvinced, skeptics reply that the only thing that distinguishes Alex from pigeons taught to peck buttons for food is that his responses sound like English (Stipp 1990).

To answer the question of whether or not animals have the capacity for language, we must wait for more evidence. That evidence is now being collected. What we currently have, however, are data with intriguing implications.

CULTURAL DIFFUSION AND CULTURAL LEVELING

Project 6

For most of human history, cultures had little contact with one another. Communication was limited and travel slow. Consequently, in their relative isolation groups of people developed highly distinctive ways of life in response to the particular situations they faced. The characteristics they developed that distinguished one culture from another tended to change little over time.

Except in rare instances of extreme isolation, however, there was always *some* contact with other groups. Those contacts led to groups learning from one another, "borrowing" culture, and adapting it to their own situations. While such borrowing sometimes included nonmaterial culture, it was usually limited to material culture, such as copying the superior weapons of another group. Social scientists refer to the transmission of cultural characteristics from one group to another as **cultural diffusion.**

Today, of course, the situation is vastly different. Air travel has made it possible to journey halfway across the globe in a matter of hours. In the not so distant past, a trip from the United States to Africa was so unusual that only a few hardy Americans made it. Now hundreds of thousands make the trip each year. Communication has been similarly transformed. Until a century ago, communication was limited to hearing face-to-face speech and to rather primitive forms of sending messages: visual signals such as smoke and light reflected from mirrors, sending the written word from hand to hand, and so on. People in distant parts of the United States did not hear about the end of the Civil War until weeks and months after it was over. Today's electronic systems of communication transmit messages across the globe in a matter of seconds, and we can find out almost instantaneously what is happening on the other side of the world.

In fact, we are being united by travel and communication to such an extent that there almost is no "other side of the world" anymore. One result of this communications revolution is **cultural leveling,** a process in which cultures become similar to one another as expanding industrialization brings not only technology but also Western

CDQ 16: Can you think of examples of cultural diffusion in the United States? What about types of food? Music? Arts and crafts? Clothing?

Essay #6

culture contact: encounter between people from different cultures, or contact with some parts of a different culture

cultural diffusion: the spread of cultural characteristics from one group to another

cultural leveling: the process by which cultures become similar to one another, and especially by which Western industrial culture is imported and diffused into developing nations

The widespread adoption of rock music, both American and British, around the world is an example of cultural diffusion, *or the transmission and adoption of an aspect of one culture by another. When the Berlin Wall fell, Germans invited the British rock group Pink Floyd to stage a concert featuring songs from their album "The Wall."*

culture to the rest of the world. Japan, for example, is no longer a purely Eastern culture. It has adapted not only Western economic production but also Western forms of dress, music, and so on. These changes, superimposed on Japanese culture, have turned Japan into a blend of Western and Eastern cultures.

Cultural leveling is apparent to any traveler. Perhaps its most blatant example is the Golden Arches of McDonald's, which welcome today's visitors to Tokyo, Paris, London, Madrid, and even Moscow. In remote parts of the world, young people who know no English gyrate to the sounds of American rock music. While this activity does not in itself mark the end of their own traditional cultures, it will inevitably result in some degree of cultural leveling, some blander, less distinctive way of life—American culture with French, Japanese, and Bulgarian accents, so to speak. Although the "cultural accent" remains, something is lost forever.

SUMMARY

1. All human groups have culture—language, beliefs, values, norms, behavior, and even material objects that are passed on from one generation to the next. Material culture consists of objects such as art, buildings, clothing, and tools. Nonmaterial (or symbolic) culture refers to a group's ways of thinking and patterns of behavior. Ideal culture refers to a group's ideal values and norms, to the goals a people hold out for themselves; real culture refers to people's actual behavior, which usually falls short of their cultural ideal.

2. We all perceive and evaluate the world through the lens of our own culture. In confronting a culture that challenges our basic orientations, we are likely to experience a disorientation known as culture shock. People are naturally ethnocentric; that is, they use their own culture as the yardstick for judging the ways of others. In contrast,

those who embrace cultural relativism try to understand a different culture on its own terms. Extensive culture contacts, caused especially by expanded industrialization, have brought about rapid cultural diffusion. This process in turn is leading to cultural leveling, a process in which many groups are tending to adopt Western culture.

3. Language is the essence of culture, for it allows us to move beyond the present and to possess a shared past, future, and other common perspectives. Also deeply embedded in language are ways of perception, as indicated by the Sapir-Whorf hypothesis. Consequently, language forms the basis of human social life, for it allows human experience to be cooperative, extended, and cumulative. Gestures are universal to the extent that all people around the world use them. While ethologists claim that some gestures are also universal in their meaning, anthropologists disagree, stressing that, like other aspects of culture, the meaning of a gesture changes from one group to another. Consequently, a gesture that in one culture is meaningless may have a quite different meaning when used in another culture.

4. All groups have values, or standards by which they define what is desirable or undesirable. A group's values reveal a great deal about the group, since they indicate what its members hold to be worthwhile in life. All groups also develop norms, that is, rules or expectations about behavior, as well as positive sanctions to show approval of people who follow their norms, and negative sanctions to show disapproval of those who do not. Norms that are not strictly enforced are called folkways, while mores are norms that demand absolute conformity and are regarded as essential core values.

5. A subculture is a group whose values and related behaviors distinguish its members from the general culture, while a counterculture holds values opposed to those of the dominant culture.

6. Values are not independent units but are clustered together to form a larger whole. Value contradictions in a society indicate areas of social tension, which are also likely points of social change. Nineteen core American values were identified, four of which are defined as in the process of emerging. Changes in a society's fundamental values meet opposition from people who hold strongly to traditional values.

7. Although all human groups have customs concerning cooking, funerals, and so on, the specifics vary from one culture to another. In the sense that these activities occur everywhere, they constitute cultural universals. In the sense that no specific behaviors are the same everywhere, however, there are no cultural universals.

8. To the extent that some animals teach their young certain behaviors, animals also have culture. No animals, however, have language in the sociological sense of the term, although some animals apparently do have the capacity to learn language.

SUGGESTED READINGS

Chagnon, Napoleon A. *Yanomamö: The Fierce People.* 3rd ed. New York: Holt, Rinehart & Winston, 1983. This fascinating account of a preliterate people whose customs are extraordinarily different from ours will help you to see the arbitrariness of choices that underlie human culture.

Harris, Marvin. *Good to Eat: Riddles of Food and Culture.* New York: Simon & Schuster, 1986.

Harris, Marvin. *Cannibals and Kings: The Origins of Cultures.* New York: Random House, 1977.

To read Harris's books is to read about cultural relativism. Using a functional perspective, this anthropologist analyzes cultural practices that often seem bizarre to outsiders. He interprets those practices within the framework of the culture being examined.

Kephart, William M. *Extraordinary Groups: An Examination of Unconventional Life-Styles.* 3rd ed. New York: St. Martin's Press, 1987. The author provides insights into seven different subcultures: the Old Order Amish, the Oneida Community, the Father Divine movement, Gypsies, the Shakers, the Mormons, and modern communes.

Mahmoody, Betty. *Not Without My Daughter.* New York: St. Martin's Press, 1987. An American woman who married an Iranian and was practically held captive by him and his family in Iran, tells her story, which illustrates the profound cultural differences that people learn to accept as the "natural" way of doing things—as well as how difficult it is to unlearn what becomes one's taken-for-granted perception of the world.

Muehlbauer, Gene, and Laura Dodder. *The Losers: Gang Delinquency in an American Suburb.* New York: Praeger, 1983. By examining the youth subculture—especially its values and norms—the author explains why many suburbs are experiencing juvenile delinquency.

Spindler, George, Louise Spindler, Henry T. Trueba, and Melvin D. Williams. *The American Cultural Dialogue and Its Transmission.* Bristol, Penn.: Falmer Press, 1990. The authors analyze values central to American culture: individuality, freedom, community, equality, and success.

Tucker, David M. *The Decline of Thrift in America: Our Cultural Shift from Saving to Spending.* Westport, Conn.: Praeger, 1990. Tucker traces the change in American values from thrift to spending and consumption, indicating how this change has affected American competitiveness in world markets.

Van Lawick-Goodall, Jane. *In the Shadow of Man.* Boston: Houghton Mifflin, 1971. Goodall presents a fascinating first-person account of her research with wild chimpanzees.

Yinger, Milton J. *Countercultures: The Promise and Peril of a World Turned Upside Down.* New York: Free Press, 1982. The author examines the rise and maintenance of countercultures, showing them as important elements—whether creative or destructive—in the process of social change. The countercultures presented include goodness, beauty, the disadvantaged, politics, economics, religion, education, families, and sex norms.

Journal

Urban Life is a sociological journal that focuses on social interaction, and contains many detailed studies of the culture of small, off-beat groups.

CHAPTER 3

Romare Bearden, Wrapping It Up at the Lafayette, *1974*

Socialization

WHAT IS HUMAN NATURE?
Feral Children ■ Isolated Children ■ *Down-to-Earth Sociology:* **Heredity or Environment? The Case of Oskar and Jack, Identical Twins** ■ Institutionalized Children ■ Deprived Animals ■ Bringing It All Together

THE SOCIAL DEVELOPMENT OF THE SELF, MIND, AND EMOTIONS
Cooley and the Looking-Glass Self ■ Mead and Role Taking ■ Piaget and the Development of Thinking ■ Freud and the Subconscious ■ The Sequential Development of Emotions ■ Socialization into Emotions ■ The Self and Emotions as Social Constraints on Behavior

SOCIALIZATION INTO GENDER
Gender, the Family, and Sex-Linked Behaviors ■ Gender Images in the Mass Media

AGENTS OF SOCIALIZATION
The Family ■ *Perspectives:* **Manhood in the Making** ■ Religion ■ The School ■ Peer Groups ■ *Perspectives:* **Caught between Two Worlds** ■ The Mass Media ■ The Workplace

RESOCIALIZATION
Involuntary Resocialization: Total Institutions ■ Voluntary Resocialization

SOCIALIZATION THROUGH THE LIFE COURSE
The Life Course ■ Distinctive Life-Course Patterns

ARE WE PRISONERS OF SOCIALIZATION?

SUMMARY

SUGGESTED READINGS

The old man was horrified when he found out. Life never had been good since his daughter had lost her hearing when she was just two years old. She couldn't even talk—just fluttered her hands around trying to tell him things. Over the years, he had gotten used to that. But now . . . he shuddered at the thought of her being pregnant. No one would be willing to marry her, he knew that. And the neighbors, their tongues would never stop wagging. Everywhere he went, he could hear people talking behind his back.

If only his wife were still alive, maybe she could come up with something. What should he do? He couldn't just kick his daughter out into the street.

After the baby was born, the old man tried to shake his feelings, but they wouldn't let loose. Isabelle was a pretty name, but every time he looked at the baby he felt sick to his stomach.

He hated doing it, but there was no way out. His daughter and her baby would have to live in the attic.

Unfortunately, this is a true story. Isabelle was discovered in Ohio in 1938 when she was about six and a half years old, living in a dark room with her deaf-mute mother. Isabelle couldn't talk, but she did use gestures to communicate with her mother. An inadequate diet and lack of sunshine had given Isabelle a disease called rickets. Her legs

> were so bowed that as she stood erect the soles of her shoes came nearly flat together, and she got about with a skittering gait. Her behavior toward strangers, especially men, was almost that of a wild animal, manifesting much fear and hostility. In lieu of speech she made only a strange croaking sound (Davis 1988:77).

When the newspapers reported this case, sociologist Kingsley Davis decided to find out what happened to Isabelle after her discovery. We'll come back to that later, but first let's use the case of Isabelle to give us some insight into what human nature is.

WHAT IS HUMAN NATURE?

For centuries, people have been intrigued with the question of what is human about human nature. How much of people's characteristics comes from "nature" (heredity) and how much from "nurture" (the **social environment,** contact with others)? Scientists have made many attempts to unravel this matter (see the Down-to-Earth Sociology box on page 59). One way to answer this question would be to examine people who have been raised without human contact. Although ethics forbid us to conduct such an experiment, some insight into human nature may be gleaned from feral, isolated, and institutionalized children.

Feral Children

Over the centuries, the discovery of **feral** (wild) **children** has been reported from time to time. Supposedly, these children were abandoned or lost by their parents at a very early age and then raised by animals. In at least one instance, a feral child, known as the wild boy of Aveyron, was studied by contemporary scientists (Itard, 1962). This boy, who was found in the forests of France in 1798, walked on all fours and pounced on small animals, devouring them uncooked. He could not speak, and he gave no indication of feeling the cold. Other reports of feral children have claimed that upon discovery, these children acted like wild animals: They could not speak; they bit, scratched, growled, and walked on all fours; they ate grass, tore ravenously at meat, and drank by lapping water; and they showed an insensitivity to pain and cold (Malson 1972).

Most social scientists today dismiss the significance of feral children, taking the position that children cannot be raised by animals and that children found in the woods were reared by their parents as infants but abandoned, probably because they were retarded. But what if this were not the case? Could it be that by nature, when untouched by society, we would all be like feral children?

Isolated Children

Cases like Isabelle's surface from time to time. Because they are well documented, what can they tell us about human nature? We can first conclude that humans have no natural language, for Isabelle, and others like her, are unable to speak.

But maybe Isabelle was not normal. Perhaps Isabelle was retarded, as most scientists claim feral children are, and could not go through the normal stages of development that depend on biology, not society. As noted, Kingsley Davis followed up on this case. After Isabelle was discovered, she scored practically zero on an intelligence test. Apparently, she was severely retarded.

Heredity or Environment? The Case of Oskar and Jack, Identical Twins

Identical twins share exact genetic heredity. One fertilized egg divides to produce two embryos. If heredity is the cause of personality (or of people's attitudes, temperament, and basic skills), then identical twins should be identical not only in their looks but also in these characteristics.

The fascinating case of Jack and Oskar helps us unravel this mystery. From their experience, we can see the far-reaching effects of the environment—how social experiences override biology.

Jack Yufe and Oskar Stohr are identical twins born in 1932 to a Jewish father and a Catholic mother. They were separated as babies after their parents divorced. Oskar was reared in Czechoslovakia by his mother's mother, who was a strict Catholic. When Oskar was a toddler, Hitler annexed this area of Czechoslovakia (the Sudetenland), and Oskar learned to love Hitler and to hate Jews. He became involved with the Hitler Youth (a sort of Boy Scout organization designed to instill the "virtues" of patriotism, loyalty, obedience—and hatred).

Jack's upbringing provides an almost total contrast. Reared in Trinidad by his father, he learned loyalty to Jews and hatred of Hitler and the Nazis. After the war, Jack emigrated to Israel, where, at the age of 17, he joined a kibbutz. Later, Jack served in the Israeli army.

Nine years after World War II ended, in 1954, the two brothers met. It was a short meeting, and Jack had been warned not to tell Oskar that they were Jews. Twenty-two years later, in 1979, when they were forty-seven years old, social scientists at the University of Minnesota who were interested in the question of nature and nurture brought them together again. These researchers figured that since Jack and Oskar had the same genes, whatever differences they showed would have to be due to the environment—to their different social experiences.

Not only were Oskar's and Jack's attitudes toward the war, Hitler, and Jews different, so, too, were their other basic orientations to life. In their politics, for example, Oskar is quite conservative, while Jack is more liberal. Oskar turned out to be domineering in his attitude toward women, while Jack is more accepting of feminism. Oskar enjoys leisure, while Jack is a workaholic. And, as you can predict, Jack is very proud of being a Jew. Oskar, however, won't even mention it.

That would seem to settle the matter. But there is another side to the findings. The researchers also found that Oskar and Jack both like sweet liqueur and spicy foods, excelled at sports as children but had difficulty with math, and have the same rate of speech. Each even flushes the toilet both before and after using it.

Heredity or environment? How much influence does *each* have? The question is not yet settled, but at this point it seems fair to conclude that the *limits* of certain physical and mental abilities are established by heredity (such as ability at sports and mathematics), while such basic orientations to life as attitudes are the result of the environment. We can put it this way: For some parts of life, the blueprint is drawn by heredity; but even here the environment can redraw those lines. For other parts, the individual is a blank slate, and it is entirely up to the environment to determine what is written on that slate.

Source: Based on Begley 1979; Chen 1979.

At least that is what people first thought. But when Isabelle was given intensive language training, a surprising thing happened. She progressed through the learning stages that are characteristic of the first six years of life in the proper order and in rapid succession. In only two months, Isabelle was able to speak in short sentences. In just about a year, she could identify printed words, write a few words, do simple addition, and retell stories after hearing them. Seven months later, she had a vocabulary of almost two thousand words. It took only two years for Isabelle to reach the intellectual level normal for her age. She then went on to school, where she was "bright, cheerful, energetic . . . and participated in all school activities as normally as other children" (Davis 1988:78).

As discussed in the last chapter, language is the key to human behavior. Without language, people have no mechanism for developing thought. Unlike animals, humans have no instincts that take the place of language. If an individual lacks language, he or she lives in an isolated world, a world of internal silence, without shared ideas, without connections to others.

Without language, there can be no culture—no shared way of life—and culture is the key to what people become. Each of us possesses a biological heritage, but this heritage does not determine specific behaviors, attitudes, or values. It is our culture that superimposes the specifics of what we become on our biological heritage.

Institutionalized Children

But what is also required if a child is to develop into what we consider a healthy, balanced, intelligent human being is stimulating interaction with others.

A couple of generations ago, when we had a much higher death rate, orphanages dotted the United States. Children raised in orphanages tended to be smaller than other children, to have difficulty establishing close bonds with others, and to have lower IQs—if they survived, that is, for their death rates were much higher than average (Spitz 1945). These orphanages were not Dickensian institutions where ragged children were beaten and denied food. The children were kept clean and given simple but nutritious food. Nevertheless, the contrast with today's standards is remarkable. Here is an account of a good orphanage in Iowa during the 1930s.

> Infants up to the age of two years were housed in the hospital, then a relatively new building. Until about six months, they were cared for in the infant nursery. The babies were kept in standard hospital cribs that often had protective sheeting on the sides, thus effectively limiting visual stimulation; no toys or other objects were hung in the infants' line of vision. Human interactions were limited to busy nurses who, with the speed born of practice and necessity, changed diapers or bedding, bathed and medicated the infants, and fed them efficiently with propped bottles (Skeels 1966).

Although everyone knew that the cause of mental retardation was biological ("They're just born that way"), two psychologists who consulted in this Iowa orphanage, H. M. Skeels and H. A. Dye (1939), began to suspect that the absence of stimulating social interaction was the basic problem, not some biological incapacity on the part of the children. To test their controversial idea, they placed thirteen infants whose mental retardation was so obvious that no one wanted to adopt them in Glenwood State School, an institution for the mentally retarded. Each infant, then about nineteen months old, was assigned to a separate ward of mentally retarded women ranging in mental age from five to twelve and in chronological age from eighteen to fifty. The women were quite pleased with this arrangement. They not only did a good job taking care of the infants' basic physical needs—diapering, feeding, and so on—but

Human interaction is essential to the development of traits such as intelligence, cooperative behavior, friendliness—and happiness. This Romanian orphan, one of thousands abandoned by parents unable to take care of them under the totalitarian regime of Nicolae Ceausescu, has virtually none of the outside stimuli necessary to human development.

they also loved to play with the children, to cuddle them, and to shower them with constant attention. There was even considerable competition among the women to see which ward would have "its baby" walking or talking first. One women would become:

> particularly attached to him (or her) and figuratively "adopted" him (or her). As a consequence, an intense one-to-one adult-child relationship developed, which was supplemented by the less intense but frequent interactions with the other adults in the environment. Each child had some one person with whom he (or she) was identified and who was particularly interested in him (or her) and his (or her) achievements (Skeels 1966).

The researchers left a control group of twelve infants, also retarded but higher in intelligence, at the orphanage, where they received the usual care. Two and a half years later, Skeels and Dye tested all the children's intelligence. Their findings were startling: Those assigned to the retarded women had gained an average of twenty-eight IQ points while those who remained in the orphanage had lost thirty points.

What happened after these children were grown? Did these initial differences matter? Twenty-one years later, Skeels and Dye did a follow-up study. Those in the control group that had remained in the orphanage averaged less than third grade in education. Four still lived in state institutions, while the others held low-level jobs. Only two had married. In contrast, the average level of education for the thirteen individuals in the experimental group was twelve grades (about normal for that period). Five had completed one or more years of college. One had not only earned a B.A. but had gone on to graduate school. Eleven had married. All thirteen were self-supporting and had higher-status jobs or were homemakers (Skeels 1966). The attention that the retarded "mothers" had lavished on "their" babies had achieved startling benefits.

Other researchers have reported similar findings. William Goldfarb (1945) compared forty children sent to foster homes soon after birth with forty children who spent the first two years of their lives in institutions before being sent to foster homes. The institutionalized children suffered intellectually (scored lower on IQ tests), socially (were more aggressive), and emotionally (they were described as "cold").

Apparently, then, characteristics that we take for granted as being basic "human" traits—such as high intelligence, cooperative behavior, and friendliness—result from early close relations with other humans. The pathetic story of Genie underscores the point that intelligence and the ability to establish close bonds with others in later life are dependent on early interactions.

In 1970, California authorities found Genie, a thirteen-and-a-half-year-old girl who had been kept locked in a small room since she was twenty months old. Apparently her father (seventy years old when Genie was discovered) hated children, and had probably caused the death of two of Genie's siblings. Her fifty-year-old mother was partially blind and frightened of her husband. Genie could not speak, did not know how to chew, was unable to stand upright, and could not straighten her hands and legs. On intelligence tests, she scored at the level of a one-year-old. After intensive training, Genie learned to walk and use simple sentences (although they were garbled). Her language remained primitive, and at the age of twenty-one, Genie went to live in a board-and-care home for adults who cannot live alone (Pines 1981).

A final lesson can be gained by looking at animals that have been deprived of normal interaction.

Deprived Animals

In the last chapter, we saw that animals cannot have a social or shared past or future. Because they lack language to expand their time zones into the past and future, they have no way to communicate ideas and purposes about events not visually present. At the same time, we also saw that some animal behavior that we assume is instinctual

CDQ 3: Can you make a comparison between monkeys and human infants raised in isolation?

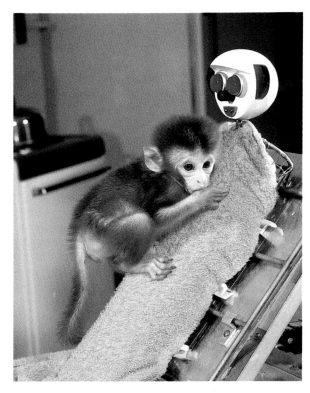

Like humans, monkeys also need interaction to thrive. Those raised under conditions of total isolation are unable to interact satisfactorily with others. In this photograph, we see one of the monkeys described below. When purposely frightened by the experimentor, the monkey has taken refuge in the soft terrycloth draped over an artificial "mother."

K.P.: Harry and Margaret Harlow

is actually learned. Let's take another look at animals, this time those that have been deprived of normal learning.

In a series of experiments with rhesus monkeys, psychologists Harry and Margaret Harlow demonstrated the importance of early learning. The Harlows (1962) raised baby monkeys in isolation. They gave each monkey two artificial mothers, shown in the photograph above. One "mother" was only a wire frame with a wooden head, but it did have a nipple from which the baby could nurse. Although the frame of the other "mother" had no bottle, it was covered with soft terry cloth. For their food, the baby monkeys had to go to the wire frame. But when the Harlows (1965) frightened the babies with a large mechanical bear or dog, the babies did not run to the wire frame "mother"; they would cling pathetically to their terry cloth "mother." The Harlows drew the significant conclusion that infant-mother bonding is due not to feeding but rather to what they termed "intimate physical contact." To most of us, this phrase means cuddling.

It is also significant that the monkeys raised in isolation were never able to adjust to monkey life. The experimenters placed them with other monkeys when they were grown. But because they didn't know how to enter into "monkey interaction"—to play and to engage in pretend fights—they were rejected by the other monkeys. Neither did they know how to engage in sexual intercourse, in spite of futile efforts to do so. The experimenters designed a special device, which allowed some females to become pregnant. After giving birth, however, the monkeys were "ineffective, inadequate, and brutal mothers . . . [who] violently rejected their babies when they attempted maternal contact, and frequently struck their babies, kicked them, or crushed the babies against the cage floor" (1965).

In another experiment, the Harlows (1965) divided baby monkeys into three groups. In the first group, each monkey was raised in total isolation, seeing no living being other than itself. In the second, each baby was allowed to be only with its mother. In the third, the baby monkeys were raised only with other baby monkeys.

After these monkeys were grown, they, too, were placed with adult monkeys. And again the Harlows observed what happened. The monkeys that had been raised in total isolation were the most abnormal. They would cower in the corner, avoid contact with others, and would not defend themselves. Those raised with just the mother were not much better adjusted. Those raised only with other baby monkeys, however, made a fairly good adjustment. As infants, they had obtained comfort and security by clinging to one another, and while they were growing up they had played together. From this experiment the Harlows concluded that interaction with peers is essential to normal development.

In one of their many other experiments, the Harlows varied the length of time for which baby monkeys were isolated. They found that those isolated for short periods of time (about three months) were able to overcome the effects of their isolation, whereas those isolated for longer periods (six months or more) were subsequently unable to adjust to normal monkey life. In other words, the longer the isolation, the more difficult it is to overcome its effects. There may also be a critical learning stage that, if missed, may be impossible to overcome. That may have been the case with Genie.

Because humans are not monkeys, we must always be careful about extrapolating from animal studies to human behavior. The Harlow experiments, however, strongly corroborate what we know about the effects on children of being raised in isolation.

Bringing It All Together

Apparently, warm, intimate interaction is essential to vital aspects of human development: biological, mental, emotional, moral, and social growth. Or, as psychologist Urie Bronfenbrenner (1992) says, to develop properly, "Kids need people who are crazy about them." Usually, loving, concerned parents provide this kind of interaction for their children.

Somewhat more radically, we can claim that babies do not "naturally" develop into human adults. Although their bodies certainly get bigger, if raised in isolation they become little more than big animals. They can't experience or even observe relations between people (the "connections" we call brother, sister, parent, friend, teacher, and so on). They aren't "friendly" in the accepted sense of the term, nor do they cooperate with others. They do not think in terms of a past and a future. Indeed, they do not appear to think at all in any meaningful way.

In short, to develop into adults with the characteristics that we take for granted as "human," children need to be surrounded by people who care for them. Only then can they develop into social adults within the limits set by their biology, for it is through human contact that people learn to be members of the human community. This interaction is what sociologists have in mind when they say, "Society makes us human."

THE SOCIAL DEVELOPMENT OF THE SELF, MIND, AND EMOTIONS

Let's now turn our attention to **socialization,** the process by which we learn the ways of society (or of particular groups). As you will see, this process is so fundamental to our identity that it even shapes the way we think and feel.

Cooley and the Looking-Glass Self

Back in the 1800s, sociologist Charles Horton Cooley (1864–1929) wondered how human infants develop a **self**—the ability to see themselves "from the outside." Cooley saw the self as our interpretation of how others see us, the ability to contemplate our existence, to project ourselves into the past, into the future, and into various situations in life. Cooley concluded that this unique aspect of "humanness" is *socially created;*

Essay #2

TR#2: Theories of Human Development

L. Obj. 2: Define socialization.

K.P.: Charles Horton Cooley

CDQ 4: Is it possible to define yourself apart from the other people in your life? Do you have a totally unique identity that is not tied to others?

socialization: the process by which people learn the characteristics of their group—the attitudes, values, and actions thought appropriate for them

self: the concept, unique to humans, of being able to see ourselves "from the outside"; to gain a picture of how others see us that is, our sense of self develops from interaction with others. He coined the term **looking-glass self** (1902) to describe the process by which a sense of self develops, which he summarized in the following couplet:

> Each to each a looking-glass
> Reflects the other that doth pass.

The looking-glass self contains three elements.

1. *We imagine how we look to others.* For example, we may think that others see us as tall and slim or short and fat.
2. *We interpret others' reactions.* We come to conclusions about how others evaluate us. Do they like us being tall and slim? Do they dislike us for being short and fat?
3. *We develop a self-concept.* As we interpret the reactions of others, we develop feelings and ideas about ourselves. A favorable reflection in the "social mirror" leads to a positive self-concept, a negative reflection to a negative self-concept.

Interestingly, the development of the self does *not* depend on accurate evaluations. Even if we grossly misjudge how others think about us, those misjudgments become part of our self-concept. In fact, some people regularly misinterpret the evaluations of others, and it is quite common for people to interpret neutral statements and actions incorrectly as negative. Extreme cases of such behavior are called paranoids. Sociologist Fred Goldner (1985) has also identified an opposite, much rarer type—individuals whom he calls "pronoids," persons who interpret everything, even criticism, as a positive reaction.

It is important to note that *the development of self is an ongoing, lifelong process.* Although the self-concept begins in childhood, it continues to develop throughout life. We continually involve ourselves in the three steps of the looking-glass self, and our ongoing interpretations of others' reactions modify the self. This process applies to all stages of life, even to old age. Significantly, then, the self is never a finished product but is always in process.

Mead and Role Taking

Sociologist George Herbert Mead (1863–1931), who taught at the University of Chicago, was also interested in how the self develops. He agreed with Cooley's idea that the self develops during social interaction. He added that play is critical to the development of a self. In play, children learn to **take the role of the other,** that is, to put themselves in someone else's shoes—to understand how someone else feels and thinks and to anticipate how another person will act.

Project 2

K.P.: George Herbert Mead

looking-glass self: a term coined by Charles Horton Cooley to refer to the process by which our self develops through internalizing others' reactions to us

taking the role of the other: putting oneself in someone else's shoes; understanding how someone else feels and thinks and thus anticipating how that person will act

According to the American sociologist George Herbert Mead, the self develops through three stages of role-taking—imitation, play, and games. This young girl is in the play stage, in which she pretends to take the role of a doctor.

Young children attain this ability only gradually (Coser 1977; Mead 1934). In a simple experiment psychologist J. Flavel (1968) asked fourteen-year-olds and eight-year-olds to explain a board game to a group of their peers. They were asked to explain it to some who were blindfolded and to others who were not. The eight-year-olds gave the same instructions to everyone, while the fourteen-year-olds gave more detailed instructions to those who were blindfolded. The younger children could not yet take the role of the other, while the older children could.

In developing this ability, children are first able to take only the role of **significant others,** individuals who significantly influence their lives, such as parents or siblings. By playfully assuming their roles, such as dressing up in their parents' clothing, children cultivate the ability to put themselves in the place of these significant others.

As the self gradually develops, children internalize the expectations of more and more people. The ability to take on roles eventually extends to being able to take the role of an abstract entity, "the group as a whole." To this, our understanding of how "most" people think of us, Mead gave the term **generalized other.**

Mead stressed that the development of the self through role taking goes through three stages.

1. *Imitation*   Children under three can only mimic others. They do not yet have a sense of self separate from others, and they can only imitate people's gestures and words. (This first stage is actually not role taking, but it prepares the child for it.)
2. *Play*   During the second stage, from the age of about three to five or six, children pretend to take the roles of specific people. They might pretend that they are a firefighter, a wrestler, the Lone Ranger, Supergirl, Batman, and so on. They also like costumes at this stage and enjoy dressing up in their parents' clothing, or tying a towel around their necks to "become" Superman or Wonder Woman.
3. *Games*   The third stage, that of organized play, or team games, begins roughly with the early school years. The significance for the self is that to play these games the individual must be able to take multiple roles, that is, be able to take the role of everyone on the team. One of Mead's favorite examples was that of a baseball game, in which each player must be able to take the role of all the other players. To play baseball, then, the child must know not only his or her own role but must also be able to anticipate who will do what when the ball is hit or thrown.

Mead also distinguished between the "I" and the "me" in the development of the self. The "*I*" is *the self as subject,* the active, spontaneous, creative part of the self. In contrast, the "*me*" is *the self as object,* made up of attitudes internalized from our interactions with others. Mead chose pronouns to indicate these two aspects of the self because in our language "I" is the active agent, as in "I shoved him," while "me" is the object of action, as in "He shoved me." Mead stressed that the individual is not only a "me"—like a robot passively absorbing the attitudes of others but, rather, the "I" actively makes sense of those attitudes; that is, people react to their social environments—evaluating the reactions of others and organizing them into a unified whole.

Mead also drew a conclusion that some find startling—that *not only the self but also the human mind is a social product.* Mead stressed that we cannot think without symbols. But where do these symbols come from? Only from society, which gives us our symbols by giving us language. If society did not provide the symbols, we would not be able to think and thus would not possess what we know as a mind. Mind, then, like language, is a product of society.

Piaget and the Development of Thinking

To the informal observations and theorizing of Cooley and Mead, Swiss psychologist Jean Piaget (1896–1980) added rigorous observation and testing of children to learn

CDQ 5: What were your favorite childhood games? When did you first become aware that games have rules and other players to deal with?

CDQ 6: Why do you think it was important for Piaget to add rigorous observation and testing of children to the informal observations and theorizing of Cooley and Mead?

K.P.: Jean Piaget

significant other: an individual who significantly influences someone else's life

generalized other: taking the role of a large number of people

how the thinking process developed (Piaget 1950, 1954; Phillips 1969). Piaget's research was prompted by his observation that when young children take intelligence tests, they give *consistently* wrong answers, while older children are able to give the expected answer. Piaget concluded that younger children use the same incorrect rule in arriving at their answers. In that case some normal process of development must underlie the way in which children acquire reasoning skills.

To test this idea, Piaget began to study how the minds of children mature, or, as he put it, their cognitive development. Piaget discovered that children pass through four stages: (1) sensorimotor, (2) preoperational, (3) concrete operational, and (4) formal operational. (If you equate the term **operational** with abstract thought, Piaget's findings will be easier to understand.)

At each stage, children develop new rules of reasoning, thinking skills that allow them to go on to the next stage. As will be apparent, a considerable range of mental abilities exists within each stage, and the reasoning skills that characterize the beginning or middle of a stage will be quite different from those evident at the end of a stage.

Let us look at these four stages of cognitive development.

1. *The sensorimotor stage*

During this stage, roughly the first two years of life, understanding is limited to direct contact with the environment. It is based on sucking, touching, listening, seeing. Infants do not think in any sense that we understand, and during the first part of this stage they do not even know that their bodies are separate from the environment. Indeed, they have yet to discover that they have toes. Neither can infants recognize cause and effect. That is, they do not know that their actions cause something to happen.

During the earlier parts of this stage, what is "out of sight" is literally "out of mind." Infants are not aware that objects have a permanent existence. (Piaget called this **object permanence**.) If you show an infant a piece of candy, he or she will reach for it. But if you then place the candy under a napkin in full sight of the infant, he or she will make no attempt to reach for it. As far as the infant is concerned, if it cannot be seen, it does not exist. At about ten months of age, however, infants discover permanent existence: Hide the candy, and they will reach for it.

2. *The preoperational stage*

During this stage, lasting roughly from age two to seven, children *develop the ability to use symbols.* Symbols, especially those provided by language, allow them to experience the world without having direct contact with it. At this stage children can tell the difference between objective reality and their own ideas. For example, they know that dreams are "not real."

At this stage children do not yet understand common concepts, however, such as numbers, size, speed, weight, volume, or causation. Although they can count, they do not really understand the concept of numbers. For example, if you spread out six flowers and six pennies, a child can count to six and will say that the flowers and pennies are equal in number. But if you then place the pennies in a single pile, the child will say there are more flowers than pennies. Pile the flowers together and spread the pennies out, and the child will say there are more pennies than flowers (Phillips 1969).

The child also cannot yet take the role of the other. In an experiment similar to Flavel's with the blindfolded students, Piaget asked preoperational children to describe a clay mountain range and found that they could do so. But when he asked them to describe how the mountain range looked from where another child was sitting, they could not do so. They could only repeat what they saw from their view. Children at this stage do not yet have the ability to take the role of the other.

3. *The concrete operational stage*

From the age of about seven to twelve, children's reasoning abilities are much more developed. But their reasoning remains *concrete.* They can understand numbers, causation, and speed, and they are able to take the role of the other and

operational: Piaget's term for abstract reasoning skills

object permanence: Piaget's term for children's ability to realize that objects continue to exist even when they are not visible

participate in team games, but without concrete examples they are unable to talk about such concepts as truth, honesty, or justice. They can explain why Jane's answer was a lie, but they cannot describe what truth itself is.

4. *The formal operational stage*

After the age of about twelve, children are capable of abstract thinking. They can talk about concepts, come to conclusions based on general principles, and use rules to solve abstract problems. During this stage, they are likely to become young philosophers (Kagan 1984). The questions they ask are no longer just the simple, "Why can't I do it?" variety (although they do continue such questioning!), but are likely to take the form, "If X is true, then why doesn't Y follow?" For example, children at the concrete operational stage might have said, "That is wrong!" in response to a televised depiction of American slavery. Now, however, they are more likely to ask, "If our country was founded on equality, how could there have been slavery?"

As emphasized in Chapter 2, the content of culture varies from group to group. These differences in content are significant in human thinking. Although individuals differ in the speed with which they pass through the four stages that Piaget identified, apparently children everywhere go through them in the same order. The *content* of their reasoning, however, differs markedly. For example, Americans learn to think of the abstract concepts of democracy and freedom in one way; the Chinese will use those same concepts in quite a different way, while in the jungles of South America the Yanomamo will never learn such ideas.

Researchers have concluded that not everyone reaches the fourth level of cognitive development (Kohlberg and Gilligan 1971). Many adults, they believe, are unable to reason abstractly because most of their thinking is stuck in the concreteness of the third stage. Two factors may be responsible. First, *biology* may set limits on an individual's capacity for cognitive development; that is, some people may be by nature more intelligent than others. Second, *social* experiences develop the capacity of some people for abstract thought, while limiting that development in others. For example, since the college experience is built around the fourth stage, college students increase their mental ability to manipulate principles and concepts (abstract reasoning).

Along with the development of the mind and the self comes the development of emotions. Let us look at how theorists explain this development.

Freud and the Subconscious

In Vienna at the turn of the century, Sigmund Freud (1856–1939) founded psychoanalysis, a technique for treating emotional problems through long-term, intensive exploration of the subconscious mind. We shall look at that part of his thought that applies to the development of personality.

K.P.: Sigmund Freud

Freud believed that personality consists of three elements. The child is born with the first, an **id,** Freud's term for inborn drives for self-gratification. The id of the newborn is evident in cries of hunger or pain. The pleasure-seeking id operates thoughout life, demanding the immediate fulfillment of basic needs: attention, safety, food, sex, aggression, and so on.

But the id's drive for immediate and complete satisfaction runs directly against the needs of other people. Society has norms and other constraints designed to control the id, and as the child comes up against those constraints (usually represented by parents), he or she must adapt to survive. To help adapt to these social forces, a second component of the personality emerges, which Freud called the **ego.** The ego is the balancing force between the id and the demands of society that suppress it. The ego also serves to balance the id and the **superego,** the third component of the personality, more commonly called the conscience.

The superego represents *culture within us,* the norms and values that we have internalized from our social groups. As the *moral* component of the personality, the

id: Freud's term for the individual's inborn basic drives

ego: Freud's term for a balancing force between the id and the demands of society

superego: Freud's term for the conscience, the internalized norms and values of our social groups

superego gives us feelings of guilt or shame when we break social rules, or pride and self-satisfaction when we follow them.

According to Freud, when the id gets out of hand, we follow our desires for pleasure and break society's norms. When the superego gets out of hand, we become overly rigid in following those norms, finding ourselves in a straitjacket of rules that inhibit our lives. The ego then comes into play, trying to prevent either the superego or the id from dominating. In the emotionally healthy individual, the ego succeeds in balancing these conflicting demands of the id and the superego. In the maladjusted individual, however, the ego cannot control the inherent conflict between the id and the superego, and the result is internal confusion and problem behaviors. It is beyond our scope to go into detail concerning these troubles, but that is what Freud spent his life trying to unravel.

Sociological Evaluations.   Sociologists react negatively to most of Freud's analysis (Bush and Simmons 1990; Epstein 1988). They object to the view that inborn and unconscious motivations are the primary reasons for human behavior, for this view denies the central tenet of sociology: that social factors such as social class, religion, and education shape people's behaviors. Feminist sociologists have been especially critical of Freud, noting that what is "male" is viewed as "normal" in his analysis, that feminine experiences are filtered through the model of male dominance, and therefore females are viewed as inferior, castrated males (Gilligan 1982; Chodorow 1990).

CDQ 7: Why do most sociologists react negatively to most of Freud's analysis? Can you think of some experts who may still rely on Freudian analysis today?

The Sequential Development of Emotions

Researchers have found that the development of human emotions parallels the growth in reasoning skills discovered by Piaget. Emotions, too, develop in the same orderly sequence (Kagan 1984). During the first three to four months, an infant has what we might call "emotional reflexes," registering surprise, joy, distress, and excitement without learning. Surprisingly, fear is not one of these emotional reflexes.

Between the ages of four and ten months, however, fear appears, as does anger. During the second year, many other emotions appear, including sadness (at the loss of a familiar object), anxiety (at not being able to do what was asked), and affection or tenderness. In line with Cooley's and Mead's theories, a child of this age shows no indication of perceiving others as having separate identities. The child also does not exhibit a sense of self; for example, he or she will look behind a mirror to find the person who must be there.

By the age of four, children show guilt and shame, indicating that a sense of self is developing, for these emotions require an awareness of being judged by others. By the age of five children also display pride, humility, envy, and jealousy—emotions that indicate greater "self-awareness." As they develop the ability to take the role of the other, by age six or seven children express emotions that indicate a judgment of the self in comparison with qualities that others possess. That is, they exhibit feelings about their relative abilities, attractiveness, honesty, bravery, dominance, and popularity.

By puberty children can express the entire range of emotions, including those that require abstract thought. An example of an emotion requiring abstract thought is a feeling of sympathy toward a group that one does not know, such as the Moravians. Who are the Moravians? That is precisely the point. One must first be capable of identifying the group, and then be capable of sympathizing with their problems—and that requires abstract thought.

L. Obj. 4: Analyze the relationship between socialization into emotions and social control in society.

Socialization into Emotions

As we have seen, socialization provides the particulars that go into human reasoning. Emotions, too, are not simply the results of biology. They also depend on socialization (Hochschild 1975; Pollak and Thoits 1989; Charon 1992).

Socialization plays a key role both in the kinds of emotions we feel and in how we express these emotions. Thus each culture has its own "norms of emotions" that determine the nature and expression of feelings.

This conclusion may sound strange. Don't all people get angry? Doesn't everyone cry? Don't we all feel guilt, shame, sadness, remorse, happiness, fear? What has socialization to do with emotions?

Let's start with the obvious. Certainly people around the world all feel these particular emotions, but the way in which they are expressed varies from one social group to another. This variation becomes evident when we compare cultures. Let's consider, for example, the case of very close male friends reunited after a separation of several months. Americans in this situation might shake hands vigorously or even give each other a little clap on the back. Japanese might bow, while Arabs will kiss. Note how the expression of emotions is dependent on culture and on one's location (in this case, gender) within the culture. A good part of childhood socialization centers on learning to express emotions correctly, for each culture has "norms of emotion" that demand conformity (Clark 1991).

Differences in expressing emotions are also evident within the same culture. For example, college professors probably show their pleasure at having done well, such as having given a good lecture, with a simple smile. In contrast, football players show their pleasure at having done well, such as having made a touchdown, by jumping up and down, throwing the ball to the ground, shouting, lifting one another into the air, clapping one another on the shoulders, or patting one another's rear. But there is something much deeper going on here, for the difference is not limited to display. Because their socialization differs, these individuals actually experience different emotions. The college professor *feels* satisfaction, contentment, or pride at a job well done. In contrast, the football player *feels* an intense triumph that borders on pure ecstasy.

As you know, our emotions are also influenced by those of others. For example, we are likely to feel sad (or happy) when around sad (or happy) people. But there is a deeper level in which our immediate environment influences our emotions. From it, we get clues regarding how to *label* our internal states. This labeling then affects what we actually feel. In an interesting, although ethically questionable, experiment, psychologists Stanley Schachter and Jerome Singer (1962) injected three groups of volunteers with epinephrine, a synthetic adrenalin, which causes the heart to pound and the hands to tremble. The first group, who did not know what the drug would do, were put together with people who acted euphoric—bouncing around, happily wadding paper into balls, and hooking shots into the wastebasket. These subjects reported feelings of euphoria and also began to show happiness. The second group, who were put together with people who acted angry, reported that they experienced anger. Some of the third group, who were told what the drug would do, were placed with people who acted angry, others with people who acted euphoric. These subjects did not report emotions, only physical reactions.

CDQ 8: Do you think all people feel the same emotions? Does socialization have anything to do with emotions?

Project 3

Finally, in some cultures people learn to experience emotions quite unlike ours. For example, the Ifaluk, who live on the Western Caroline Islands of Micronesia, refer to two forms of anger: *Song* is "justified anger," what you feel when someone does something wrong against you; while *nguch* refers to less justifiable anger, what you feel when someone seriously lets you down but hasn't done anything against you (Kagan 1984). It is difficult for Americans to grasp this distinction, for we have learned to call both feelings "anger." Another example from the same group may help to demonstrate how culture teaches people what emotions to feel. The Ifaluk word *fago* applies to feelings provoked by seeing someone suffer or in need of help, something close to what we refer to as sympathy or compassion. But they also use this term to describe their feelings when they are around someone who has high status, someone who is highly admired or respected. To us, these are two distinct emotions, and they require distinct terms. If we were to move to their society as adults we probably would never understand their emotions, while if we moved there as young children we would learn to feel as they do.

In short, socialization determines not only how we express our emotions, but also what emotions we feel. Because feelings are a significant part of our lives, to understand emotions is to broaden our understanding of human behavior in general. Let's look at how even our anticipation of emotions influences what we do.

The Self and Emotions as Social Constraints on Behavior

CDQ 9: Are you free to do whatever you want? Why or why not?

Most socialization is intended to turn us into conforming members of society. The self and emotions are essential to this process, for both serve as social constraints on our behavior. Although we like to think we are "free," consider for a moment just some of the factors that influence how we act: the expectations of friends, parents, and teachers; college rules; and federal and state laws. Suppose, for example, that for some reason, such as a moment of intense frustration or a devilish desire to shock people, you wanted to tear off your clothes and run naked down the street, what would stop you?

The answer is your socialization—*society within you*. Your experiences in society have resulted in a self that thinks along certain lines and feels particular emotions. This keeps you in line. Thoughts such as, "What would happen if I got caught?" "Would I be sent to jail?" "Would I be kicked out of school?" represent a sense of self, an awareness of the self in relationship to others. Your social mirror is also likely to reflect another important element of socialization, "What would my friends (family, teachers, acquaintances) think if they found out?" "How would I *feel* if they were to find out?" The fear of consequent shame and embarrassment is especially potent. Contemplating your act might even make you think about how you would feel *while* you were nude and cause you to conclude that the feeling of embarrassment (or shame) would be too great. In fact, socialization into emotions is so effective that you might well experience embarrassment just thinking about running nude in public! By socializing us into emotions, then, society sets up effective controls over our behavior.

Speaker Sug. #2: A colleague who specializes in gender-related research.

L. Obj. 5: Describe ways in which gender socialization channels human behavior.

gender socialization: the ways in which society sets children onto different courses in life purely *because* they are male or female

SOCIALIZATION INTO GENDER

Another primary way in which society channels our behavior is by **gender socialization.** By expecting different behaviors from people *because* they are male or female, the social group clearly nudges boys and girls in separate directions from an early age, laying down a foundation of contrasting orientations to life that carry over from childhood into adulthood. As a result of intensive and extensive socialization into gender, most men and women act, think, and feel according to the lines laid down by their culture as appropriate for their sex.

How do people learn "gender appropriate" orientations to life? How do societies convince their men and women that certain activities are "masculine," others "feminine," and on that basis proper for them or not? Of the many areas of our society that convey this message, we shall look at just two: the family and the mass media. Chapter 11 examines the broader issue of gender inequality.

Gender, the Family, and Sex-Linked Behaviors

We spend much of the time that follows birth learning what our assigned gender role requires. Our parents are the first significant others who teach us our part in this symbolic division of the world. Sometimes they do so self-consciously, perhaps by bringing into play pink and blue, colors that have no meaning in themselves but have social associations with gender. But our parents' own gender orientations are so firmly established that they also teach us gender roles without being aware of what they are doing.

CDQ 10: How did your family instruct you in what it means to be a girl or boy?

In what has become a classic study, psychologists Susan Goldberg and Michael Lewis (1969) explored this aspect of gender socialization by recruiting mothers along with their six-month-old infants into their laboratory, supposedly to observe the infants' development. Secretly, however, the researchers also observed the mothers. They found that the mothers kept their female children closer to them and that they touched and spoke more to their daughters. By the time the children were thirteen months old, the girls were more reluctant than the boys to leave their mothers. They stayed closer to their mothers during play, and they returned to them sooner and more often than did boys of the same age. When a barrier was set up to separate the mothers, who were holding toys, from their children, the girls cried and motioned for help more than the boys, who attempted to circumvent the barrier more actively. Goldberg and Lewis concluded that in our society mothers unconsciously reward female children for being passive and dependent and male children for being active and independent.

Project 4

Teaching males to be more active and express greater independence continues during childhood. Preschool boys are allowed to roam farther from home than their preschool sisters, and they are subtly encouraged to participate in more rough-and-tumble play—even to get dirtier and to be more defiant (Henslin 1993b).

The process that begins in the family is completed as the child is exposed to other aspects of society (Thorne 1990). Schools, for example, continue to sort males and females into different occupations solely on the basis of their sex. Expecting male and female students to be different, teachers nurture the "natural" differences they find. One result is that boys and girls develop different aspirations in life, a topic which we shall examine in Chapter 11.

Gender Images in the Mass Media

The mass media reinforce society's expectations of gender in many ways, through children's books, television, music, and newspapers.

L. Obj. 6: Identify the major ways in which cultural stereotypes of the sexes are perpetuated in the mass media.

Children's Books. In 1972, a research team led by sociologist Lenore J. Weitzman examined the children's books that had won the American Library Association's prestigious Caldecott Award for the best illustrations. Because women in the United States represent about 51 percent of the population, it would be reasonable to expect about half the characters in illustrated children's books to be female. The researchers, however, found females virtually invisible. Almost all told stories about male adventures and featured boys, men, and even male animals. (For every female animal, ninety-five male animals were depicted!) Girls were portrayed as passive and doll-like, boys as active and adventuresome. Most of the girls were depicted as trying to please their brothers and fathers, while the boys, in contrast, engaged in tasks requiring independence and self-confidence.

CDQ 11: What examples can you give of gender stereotyping in the media?

Following this study, feminists began a campaign to change this situation. They compiled lists of books they felt presented more positive images of females, such as *An Annotated Bibliography of Nonsexist Picture Books for Children* and *Little Miss Muffet Fights Back*. They even formed publishing companies to produce nonsexist books and attempted to "sensitize parents and teachers to the sexually biased and stereotyped content of the books being read by and to the nation's children" (Williams et al. 1987). Their goal was to have "Dick . . . speak of his feelings of tenderness without embarrassment and Jane . . . reveal her career ambitions without shame or guilt."

The results? To see what had changed, Allen Williams and other sociologists looked at the Caldecott Award winners of the 1980s. They found that females had become more visible, but in only one third of the books was a girl the central character. The pictures still conformed to traditional stereotypes. Girls were more likely to be shown indoors and as dependent, submissive, and passive, while males were more likely to be outdoors and shown as independent, competitive, and active. The researchers (1987) came to the following conclusion:

> . . . females appear to have begun to move outside the home, but not into the labor market. . . . the most telling finding is the near unanimity in conformity to traditional gender roles. Not only does Jane express no career goals, but there is no adult female model to provide any ambition. One woman in the entire 1980s collection of twenty-four books has an occupation outside the home, and she works as a waitress at the Blue Tile Diner. How can we expect Dick to express tender emotions without shame when only two adult males in this collection of books have anything resembling tender emotions and one of them is a mouse?

CNN: Kids TV Sexism

CDQ 12: How does television serve as an agent of gender socialization?

Television. Television also reinforces stereotypes of the sexes. Children's shows overwhelmingly feature more males than females. In cartoons, males outnumber females by four or five to one. A consistent message is that "men are born with more ambition than women" (Morgan 1982, 1987). The consequence? Children who watch more television do more sex-typing than children who spend less time in front of this electronic socializer (Rothschild 1984; Kimball 1986).

Where children's television leaves off, adult television picks up, continuing the message of male dominance. Numerous studies show that women are underrepresented in adult programming (Signorielli 1983, 1990). While there are some exceptions—Murphy Brown is depicted as stronger than her weak, sniveling boss—females are more likely to be portrayed as passive and indecisive. Men are much more likely to dominate women than the other way around. When women *are* shown to be strong, the message is likely to be mixed: In soap operas the villains are likely to be successful, strong women, while "good" women are depicted as vulnerable and naive (Benokraitis and Feagin 1986). In commercials, women's voices are rarely used as the voice-over. The significance is not lost on viewers, for the more television people watch, the more they tend to have restrictive ideas about women's role in society (Signorielli 1989, 1990).

Music. Music also perpetuates our cultural stereotypes of the sexes. Many songs directed toward teenagers give boys the message that they should dominate male-female relationships, that it is their personal failure if a girl is not submissive to them. In contrast, these same songs tell girls that they should be sexy, dependent, and submissive—and that they can control boys by manipulating the boys' sexual impulses (Stockard and Johnson 1980). In a study of how the sexes are portrayed on MTV, researchers found that three quarters of rock videos show only male performers (Vincent et al. 1987). Of those that do show females, 10 percent portray violence against women and 74 percent either "put women down" or "keep them in their place." Perhaps the most damning finding, however, is that in rock videos females are generally irrelevant, presented simply as decorations, background ornaments for male action.

Newspapers.   Researchers have found that newspapers perpetuate similar images. A study of 5,500 stories in eight newspapers showed that men are main characters eleven times more often than women. Whether in front-page stories, editorials, the business section, or the sports pages, men are more likely to be featured. When a story does feature a woman, it has smaller headlines and is shorter. When men are quoted, they are characterized by occupation and experience, while women, who are seldom quoted, are often identified by personal information, such as their clothing and physical description (Davis 1982). For every photo of a woman, about two photos of men are run (Luebke 1989). In the *Washington Post,* one of the nation's most influential and supposedly progressive papers, stories on men outnumber those on women nearly four to one (Blackwood 1983).

In Sum.   All of us are born into a society in which "male" and "female" are significant symbols. Sorted into separate groups from childhood, girls and boys come to have sharply different ideas of themselves and of one another, beginning within the family and later reinforced by other social institutions. Each of us learns the meanings our society associates with the sexes, and these symbols become integrated into our picture of the world—a picture that forces an interpretation of the world in terms of gender. To see how this principle applies to socialization in other cultures, see the Perspectives box on page 74.

Thus do gender messages shape our world of ideas. Mostly beneath our level of awareness, these messages mold the ways in which we see females and males. The net result is that gender serves as a primary basis for **social inequality,** giving privileges and obligations to one sex while denying them to the other, an issue we shall examine in detail in Chapter 11.

AGENTS OF SOCIALIZATION

Of the many agents of socialization that prepare us to take our place in society, we shall examine the family, religion, school, peers, mass media, and workplace. They are significant because they contribute to our self-concept, emotions, and reasoning abilities, as well as to our attitudes toward others.

L. Obj. 7: List and describe the influence of each agent of socialization on individuals.

Essay #3

The Family

Around the world, the first group to have a major impact on humans is the family. Unlike some animals, we cannot survive by ourselves, and as babies we are utterly dependent on our family. Our experiences in the family are so intense that they have a lifelong impact on us. They lay down our basic sense of self, establishing our sense of identity, our initial motivations, values, and beliefs (Gecas 1990). The family gives us ideas about who we are and what we deserve out of life. It is in the family that we begin to think of ourselves as strong or weak, smart or dumb, good-looking or ugly—or somewhere in between. And as noted above, here we begin the lifelong process of defining ourselves as female or male.

The Family and Social Class.   Researchers have documented the significance of social class in determining the initial values and orientations that children learn. Consider the difference between the upbringing of a child whose parents own a factory that employs several thousand people and that of another from a one-parent family surviving on meager welfare payments and purchasing groceries with food stamps. To see how far-reaching, yet subtle, social class is, let us compare how working-class and middle-class parents rear their children.

Sociologist Melvin Kohn (1959, 1963, 1976, 1977, 1983) found that the main concern of working-class parents is their children's outward conformity. They want their

TR#3M: Socialization Values

CDQ 13: Do you agree with the finding that middle-class parents do not focus on teaching obedience, neatness, and cleanliness to their children as much as working-class parents do? Why or why not?

social inequality: a state in which privileges and obligations are given to some but denied to others

PERSPECTIVES
Cultural Diversity Around the World

Manhood in the Making

The basic presupposition of the sociological perspective on gender is that differences between the sexes are due entirely, or almost entirely, to socialization. Some analysts consider the possibility that biology may account for some differences in men's and women's behavior, possibly even for attitudinal differences, but if it does, they assume that its influence is minor. Without in any way intending to try to resolve this issue, the following materials illustrate how vastly different masculinity is conceived in diverse cultures.

Anthropologist David Gilmore wanted to find out if there were universal elements to the idea of masculinity. He surveyed anthropological data on cultures in southern Spain, the United States, Canada, Britain, Mexico, Sicily, Micronesia, Melanesia, equatorial Africa, aboriginal South America, South Asia, East Asia, the Middle East, New Guinea, and ancient Greece. He found four basic elements associated with masculinity: (1) not being like females (to be called feminine is an insult), (2) matching or outdoing other males (which takes such forms as fighting, drinking, and gaining wealth), (3) personal accomplishment (especially sexual prowess, but also being able to withstand adversity and pain), and (4) "bigness" (of sexual organ, body, wealth, or possessions). He also found a consistent theme running through these elements—unlike femininity, masculinity does not come naturally, but must be attained. Masculinity is validated by reputation.

If Gilmore's sample of cultures had ended with these groups, we might conclude that regardless of how the specifics of the world's various expressions of masculinity may differ, they reflect a universal inherited predisposition, some inborn, underlying structure. Gilmore's sample, however, included two cultures where ideas of manliness differ sharply.

The first exception is Tahiti in the South Pacific. Tahitian males and females are similar to one another in both characteristics and roles. Both men and women are expected to be passive, yielding, and to ignore slights. Neither competitively strives for material possessions. Their blurred sex roles are manifested in the following ways: There is no expression of gender in their language, not even pronouns; children's names are not sex-specific; labor is not divided on the basis of gender.

The Semai of Central Malaysia are the second exception. The Semai, a racially mixed group of Malays, Chinese, and other people who have passed through their forest enclaves, also lack the differentiation between the sexes that most societies esteem. Their core value is not to make anyone feel bad, which means not denying or frustrating anyone. To do so could anger the spirits, which might take vengeance on the entire village. Consequently, the Semai have no contests or sporting competitions that might make a losing person feel bad. No one can give orders to another, for that might make the other feel bad. For the same reason, they can't resist someone's sexual advances. The Semai say that adultery, whether a man's or a woman's, is "just a loan." Nor are they to nag another person for sex, for that, too, would be aggressive. Not concerned about family lines, they love and treat all children well, regardless of paternity. Children may not be disciplined, for that might make them feel bad, and if a child says that he or she does not feel like doing something, that is the end of the matter. If the Semai, either men or women, encounter danger, they run away and hide without shame. Women become headmen, but less often than men, and men can become midwives, but rarely do. The one gender distinction that the Semai appear to make is that the men do the hunting.

Although Gilmore's survey of cultures failed to find a universal, he did confirm a significant sociological principle—that in each human group manhood (or in the exceptional cases of the Tahitians and the Semai, personhood) is a culturally imposed ideal to which men must conform whether or not they find it personally congenial. That we can also apply to cultural ideals of femininity.

Source: Based primarily on Gilmore 1990, but also on Epstein 1988 and Rhode 1990.

---

children to be obedient, neat, and clean, to follow the rules, and to stay out of trouble. They are likely to use physical punishment to make their children obey. In contrast, middle-class parents focus on developing their children's curiosity, self-expression, and self-control. They show greater concern for the motivations for their children's behavior and are less likely to use physical punishment than to reason with their children or to withdraw privileges and affection.

Kohn was not satisfied with simply documenting these differences. Just *why* should working-class and middle-class parents rear their children so differently? From his sociological imagination, Kohn knew that life experiences of some sort held the key. Kohn found this key in the world of work, a world in which blue-collar and white-collar workers have very different experiences. Blue-collar workers are usually supervised very closely. Their bosses expect them to do exactly as they are told. Since blue-collar parents expect their children's lives to be similar to their own, they draw upon these experiences as they rear their children. Consequently, they stress obedience and conformity. Middle-class parents, in contrast, especially those in management and the professions, experience a much freer workplace. They have greater independence, are encouraged to be imaginative, and advance by taking the initiative. Expecting their children to work at similar jobs, they, in turn, socialize them into these qualities—which they assume will be essential to their well-being.

Kohn had found only part of the key, however. What still puzzled him was that the class differences in child rearing were only tendencies. Not all working-class or middle-class parents treat their children alike; instead, some working-class parents act more like middle-class parents, and vice versa. As Kohn probed this puzzle, the pieces fell into place. He found that the parents' specific type of job was even more important than their social class. Many middle-class office workers, for example, have little freedom and are closely supervised. Kohn found that such workers follow the working-class pattern of child rearing, for they stress outward conformity. In contrast, some blue-collar workers, such as those who do home repairs, have a good deal of freedom. These workers follow the middle-class model in rearing their children (Pearlin and Kohn 1966; Kohn and Schooler 1969).

Families are a primary agent of socialization. Social class and occupational status of parents are key determinants in the initial values and orientations that children learn.

Religion

Although not everyone is raised in a religious, or even a "somewhat" religious, family, religion plays a significant role in the socialization of most Americans. Religion especially influences morality, becoming a key component in people's ideas of right and wrong. Religion is so important to Americans that 69 percent are official members of a local congregation, while during a typical week 43 percent of Americans attend a religious service (*Statistical Abstract* 1991:76). Religion is significant even for persons reared in nonreligious homes, for religious ideas pervade American society, providing basic ideas of morality that become significant for us all.

The influence of religion extends to other areas of our lives as well. For example, participation in religious services teaches us not only beliefs about the hereafter but also ideas about the dress, speech, and manners appropriate for formal occasions. Religion is so significant that we shall treat this social institution in a separate chapter.

The School

As discussed in Chapter 1, functionalists analyze how the parts of a social system fit together, stressing that each contributes to the whole. Each part has manifest and latent functions. The **manifest function,** or intended purpose, of formal education is not difficult to identify. Schooling is intended to transmit the skills and values thought appropriate for earning a living and for being a "good citizen." Accordingly, our schools teach reading, writing, arithmetic, and so on. Teachers also stress such values as managing money and voting.

Our schools also have several **latent functions,** unintended consequences that help the social system. First, by placing children under the direct control of teachers— people who are not their friends, neighbors, or relatives—schooling broadens their social horizons. It exposes them to new attitudes, values, and ways of looking at the world. Second, as children move beyond a world in which they may have been the almost exclusive focus of doting parents, they learn to be part of a large group of people of similar age. Third, children learn universality—that the same rules and the same sanctions apply to everyone, regardless of who their parents are or how special they may be at home. Fourth, children gradually come to realize that their behavior is recorded in permanent, official records that will have important and lasting conse-

CDQ 14: What did you learn in school in addition to academics—such as history, English, or calculus? Were some of the things you learned part of the hidden curriculum?

manifest function: the intended consequences of people's actions designed to help some part of a social system

latent functions: the unintended consequences of people's actions that keep a social system in equilibrium

Schools, which transmit skills and values, are key agents of socialization.

CDQ 15: What influence does your peer group have on your choice in clothes? Music? Entertainment? Can you think of other areas?

Project 6

peer group: a group of individuals roughly the same age linked by common interests

quences. Such latent functions help prepare the child to take a role in the world beyond the family.

The Perspectives box on page 77 explores the socialization of a Mexican-American writer who as a schoolchild learned to become an American. Only as an adult did he painfully realize that as a consequence of his school socialization, he thereby lost many of the values and ways of looking at the world unique to his Hispanic heritage.

Sociologists have also identified a *hidden curriculum* in our schools. By this, they refer to values that are not explicitly taught but form an inherent part of a school's activities. The wording of math problems and stories intended to teach English grammar, for example, bring lessons in patriotism, democracy, justice, and honesty—all characteristics the community deems desirable for its students to become "good citizens" and to take their place in the work force.

As conflict theorists point out, the hidden curriculum means that our schools in effect teach young people the prevailing "correct" attitude toward the economic system (Marger 1987). In other words, when schools teach young people to think that our economic system is basically just, it simultaneously teaches them to think that social problems such as poverty and homelessness have nothing to do with economic power, oppression, and exploitation.

Peer Groups

As a child's experiences with agents of socialization broaden, the influence of the family lessens. Entry into school marks only one of many steps in this transfer of allegiance. The formal aspects of school are themselves but a piece of this picture, one of the most significant aspects of education being a child's exposure to peer groups. A **peer group** is a group of individuals roughly the same age who are linked by common interests. Examples of peer groups, which exert such profound influence on children, are friends, clubs, gangs, and "the kids in the neighborhood."

As you probably well know from personal experience, peer groups are compelling. It is almost impossible to go against a peer group, whose cardinal rule seems to be "conformity or nothing." Three basic reasons underlie the immense power of peer groups. First, they are based on common interests, which represent issues critical for

Schools are important agents of socialization. In addition to teaching knowledge and skills—the manifest functions of education—they also initiate us into the acceptable attitudes, values, and roles of the larger culture (the latent functions of education). Thus wealthy children attending private schools not only learn knowledge and skills but are also taught how to assume their place in the economic system.

the individual at the moment. Second, they provide guidelines for vital aspects of life. Although a group of teenagers may seem to be "simply" shooting baskets or shopping, they are always doing much more than that. For example, they are also reacting to one another's expression of the self, and they are also in all likelihood talking about the opposite sex. As they engage in these "side activities"—which may be the most significant part of what they are doing—peer groups form norms that their members then enforce on one another. Third, peer groups are voluntary. As such, they hold the threat of expulsion: If you don't do what the others want, they will make you an "outsider," a "nonmember," an "outcast." For preteens and teens just learning their way around in the world, it is not surprising that the peer group is king. Consequently, next to the family, the peer group is the most powerful socializing force in society.

PERSPECTIVES
Cultural Diversity in U.S. Society

Caught between Two Worlds

Just as an individual is socialized into becoming a member of a culture, so a person can lose a culture through socialization. If you are intensely exposed to a new culture as an adult, as older immigrants are, you can selectively adopt aspects of the new culture without entirely relinquishing your native culture. The first remains dominant, the second an enriching addition. If the immersion occurs as a child, however, the second culture may vie for dominance with, or supplant entirely, your native heritage. This, in turn, can lead to inner turmoil. To cut ties with your first culture—one way of handling the conflict—can create a sense of loss that is recognized only later in life.

Richard Rodriguez, a literature professor and essayist who was born in the 1950s to working-class Mexican immigrants, has written extensively about this problem. Wanting their son to be successful in the adopted land, his parents named him Richard instead of Ricardo. While the Spanish-English hybrid name indicated the parents' aspirations for their son, it was also a portent of the conflict Richard would experience.

Like other children of Mexican immigrants, Richard's first language was Spanish—a rich mother tongue that provided his orientation to the world. Until the age of five, at which time he entered the public school system, he knew but fifty words in English. He described what happened when he began school.

> The change came gradually but early. When I was beginning grade school, I noted to myself the fact that the classroom environment was so different in its styles and assumptions from my own family environment that survival would essentially entail a choice between both worlds. When I became a student, I was literally "remade"; neither I nor my teachers considered anything I had known before as relevant. I had to forget most of what my culture had provided, because to remember it was a disadvantage. The past and its cultural values became detachable, like a piece of clothing grown heavy on a warm day and finally put away.

Like millions of immigrants before him, whose parents spoke German, Polish, Italian, and so on, English and education eroded family and class ties. But for Rodriguez, they also ate away at his racial and ethnic ties. For him, language and education were not simply devices that eased the transition to the dominant culture. Instead, they transformed Richard into a *pocho,* "a Mexican with gringo aspirations." They slashed at the roots that had given him life.

Facing such inner turmoil, some withdraw from the new culture—one clue to the high dropout rate of Hispanic Americans from educational institutions. Others cut ties with their family and cultural roots and wholeheartedly adopt the new culture. Rodriguez took the second course. He performed well in his new language, so well, in fact, that he went to Stanford University and then became a graduate student in English at the University of California at Berkeley. He was even awarded a Fulbright fellowship to study English Renaissance literature at the British Museum.

But the past wouldn't let him alone. Prospective employers were impressed with his knowledge of Renaissance literature. But at job interviews, they would ask if he would teach the Mexican novel in translation and be an adviser to Hispanic-American students. Rodriguez was haunted by the image of his grandmother, the culture he had left behind, the language to which he was now a stranger.

Richard Rodriguez represents millions of immigrants—not just those of Hispanic origin but millions from other cultures, too—who want to be a part of the United States without betraying their past. They fear that to integrate into American culture is to lose their roots. They are caught between two cultures, each beckoning, each offering rich rewards.

Source: Based on Richard Rodriguez 1975, 1982, 1990, 1991.

Peer groups are second only to the family in terms of their role as agents of socialization. Among adolescents, peer groups are the single most important socializing force.

For example, it is almost exclusively the peer group that sets the standards. If your peers listen to rap, heavy metal, rock and roll, country, folk, gospel, classical, or any other kind of music, it is almost inevitable that you also prefer that kind of music. It is the same for clothing styles and dating standards. Peer influences also extend to behaviors that violate social norms. If your peers are college-bound and upwardly striving, that is most likely what you will be; but if they use drugs, cheat, and steal, you are likely to do so, too.

Project 7

CDQ 16: What television programs and movies have you seen recently that you would not want your own children to see? Why?

The Mass Media

The **mass media,** forms of communication directed to large audiences, also socialize us. Radio and television, newspapers and magazines do not merely entertain us; as noted above concerning gender socialization, they also shape our attitudes, values, and other basic orientations to life.

Television has become the dominant medium, and watching television is a favorite activity of Americans. The average adult watches fifteen hours of television a week (Robinson 1990). American schoolchildren now spend more time in front of a television than they do in school, and most children spend more time watching television than interacting with their parents (Singer 1983; Singer and Singer 1983). Many American parents even use this medium as an electronic babysitter—although the values presented on it may sharply conflict with their own. They apparently do not realize this inconsistency, or else seriously underrate the power of television as a socializing agent.

Since most American children are exposed to so much television, it is not surprising that some social analysts have become concerned about the *content* of what children see. As Joshua Meyrowitz (1984) has pointed out, to use television as an electronic babysitter

> is equivalent to a broad social decision to allow young children to be present at wars and funerals, courtships and seductions, criminal plots and cocktail parties . . . television exposes children to many topics and behaviors that adults have spent several centuries trying to keep hidden from them.

mass media: forms of communication directed to huge audiences

Violence on television has become a special concern. Researchers have found that by the age of eighteen the average American has watched about 18,000 people being strangled, stabbed, shot, poisoned, blown up, drowned, run over, beaten to death, or otherwise ingeniously done in (Messner 1986). The big question, of course, is: What effects does televised violence have on its viewers? Perhaps it simply drains off aggressive impulses through fantasy. Researchers have probed this question for decades, with mixed results. Increasingly, however, studies indicate that a heavy diet of televised violence does promote aggressive behavior in children (Singer 1983; Singer and Singer 1983). Studies in the United States, Poland, Finland, and Australia have identified a circular path: Both boys and girls who experience a heavy diet of televised violence are more aggressive, while aggressive children are less popular with their peers and spend more solitary time watching more violent programs (Eron 1982).

The Workplace

Another major agent of socialization that comes into play somewhat later in life is the workplace. Here we rub shoulders with a group of people who become influential in forming our values and orientations. Those initial jobs that we take—part-time work after school and in college—are much more than a way to earn a few dollars. They are like school itself. From them, we learn not only a set of skills but also matching attitudes and values. And just as peer groups play a significant role at school, here, too, we form friendships that teach us a perspective on the world as well as on work.

To become committed to a field of work is the end result of a long process of socialization. Sociologist Wilbert Moore (1968) found that career socialization involves four phases. First comes *career choice,* the selection of some field of work and preparation for it. Second is *anticipatory socialization,* the process of learning to play a role before entering it, a sort of mental rehearsal for some future activity. As a person identifies with a role, he or she becomes aware of some of its expectations and rewards, which supposedly makes it easier to move into the new role (Bush and Simmons 1990). Anticipatory socialization may involve reading novels about people who work in one's chosen career, talking to them, or taking a summer internship. The third phase is *conditioning and commitment.* This refers to the act of going to work, finding that many dull or unpleasant tasks are associated with the work, and yet committing to that occupation. The fourth is *continuing commitment,* sticking with the work in spite of difficulties or alternatives that may arise.

An interesting aspect of work as a socializing agent is that the more you participate in a line of work, the more the work becomes a part of your self-concept. Eventually you come to think of yourself so much in terms of the job that if someone asks you to describe yourself, you are likely to include the job in your initial self-description by saying, "I am a teacher, accountant, nurse" or whatever.

RESOCIALIZATION

The term **resocialization** refers to the process of learning new norms, values, attitudes, and behaviors. Resocialization usually involves only a modification of existing orientations to life, but in some instances it may require learning a radically different perspective. Let us begin this topic with a look at total institutions.

Involuntary Resocialization: Total Institutions

Relatively few of us experience the powerful mechanism Erving Goffman (1961) called the **total institution.** He coined this term to refer to a place in which people are cut off from the rest of society and where they come under almost total control of the officials who run the place. Boot camp, prisons, concentration camps, some mental hospitals, some religious cults, and some boarding schools, such as West Point, are total institutions.

CDQ 17: In what way is your college education a part of your career socialization?

L. Obj. 8: Define the term resocialization and give examples of involuntary and voluntary resocialization.

Essay #4

Speaker Sug. #3: A therapist who works in a total institution.

K.P.: Erving Goffman

CDQ 18: Do you think prisons should have a severe resocialization process? Why or why not?

resocialization: the process of learning new norms, values, attitudes, and behaviors

total institution: a place in which people are cut off from the rest of society and are almost totally controlled by the officials who run the place

A person entering a total institution is greeted with a **degradation ceremony** (Garfinkel 1956), an attempt to remake the self by stripping away the individual's current identity and stamping a new one in its place. This may involve fingerprinting, photographing, shaving the head, and banning the person's **personal identity kit** (items such as jewelry, hairstyles, clothing, and other body decorations used to express individuality). Newcomers are ordered to strip, examined (often in humiliating, semi-public settings), and then given a uniform to designate their new status. (For prisoners, the public reading of the verdict and being led away in handcuffs by armed police also form part of the degradation ceremony.)

Total institutions are extremely effective in stripping away people's personal freedom. They are isolated from the public (the walls, bars, or other barriers not only keep the inmates in but also keep outsiders from interfering). They suppress preexisting statuses (inmates learn that their previous roles such as spouse, parent, worker, or student mean nothing, and that the only thing that counts is their current role). Total institutions suppress the norms of "the outside world," replacing them with their own rules and values and their own interpretation of life that must be learned in order to survive. They also closely supervise the entire lives of the residents—eating, sleeping, showering, recreation are all standardized. Finally, they control information, helping the institution to shape the inmates' ideas and "picture" of the world. This includes control of rewards and punishment. (Under conditions of deprivation, simple rewards for compliance such as sleep, a television program, a letter from home, a little extra food, or even a cigarette, act as powerful incentives in controlling behavior.) The institution correspondingly holds the power to punish rule breaking—often severely, such as by solitary confinement, or "not seeing" what other inmates do when they want to get even for something.

No one leaves a total institution unscathed, for the experience leaves an indelible mark on the individual's self that colors the way he or she sees the world. Many people who have gone through boot camp talk about it as one of the most significant experiences of their lives, and as the passing years dim its harshness, may even remember it with fondness. Boot camp is brutal, but swift. Prison, in contrast, is brutal and prolonged, and few former prisoners recall that experience with fondness. Neither recruit nor prisoner, however, has difficulty in pinpointing how the institution affected the self.

Voluntary Resocialization

Not all resocialization is involuntary, as it is in total institutions. In its most common form, resocialization occurs each time we learn something contrary to our previous experiences. For example, a new boss who insists on a different way of doing things resocializes you. Your participation is voluntary to the extent that if you don't like her rules, you may quit—as many people do in such situations. Such resocialization is mild, however, ordinarily but a slight modification of procedures.

Voluntary resocialization can, however, be as intense as the resocialization that occurs in total institutions. Psychotherapy and joining a religion are two instances in which the individual is exposed to ideas that contrast and even conflict with his or her previous ways of looking at the world. If these ideas "take," not only does the individual's behavior change, he or she also learns a fundamentally different way of looking at life.

SOCIALIZATION THROUGH THE LIFE COURSE

Our lives can be thought of as a sort of trajectory: Like a bullet passing through a series of surfaces, we go through life touching, and being touched by, a series of events. As noted earlier, the self is never a finished product for each point in the life course confronts us with fresh issues to be resolved (Bush and Simmons 1990), chal-

CDQ 19: Have you, in essence, agreed to participate in voluntary resocialization as a result of your enrollment in college?

L. Obj. 9: Discuss socialization through the life course by summarizing each of the stages. Note the major criticisms of this perspective.

degradation ceremony: a term coined by Harold Garfinkel to describe an attempt to remake the self by stripping away an individual's self-identity and stamping a new identity in its place

personal identity kit: items people use to decorate their bodies

lenges that require a reorientation of the self. Thus, we are always in the process of becoming.

As emphasized in the following discussion, it is not age that is most significant for determining what a person becomes but the social events that the individual experiences (Baltes 1979). Let us look briefly, then, at socialization across the life course. (Cf. Clausen 1973; Erikson 1950; Gordon 1972; Gould 1972; Levinson 1978; Pearlin and Lieberman 1979.)

The Life Course

Childhood (Birth to Age Twelve). Like the other developmental points in our lives, childhood is more than a biological stage. As discussed in the previous chapter, the culture in which we are raised shapes our fundamental orientations to life. Each of us lives in a particular society at some specific point in history, and that social context lays a framework over our biology. Although a child's biological characteristics (such as youth and dependency) are universal, the social experiences of the child (what others expect of the child) are not. In short, what a child "is" differs from one society to another.

To understand this point better, let's take a look at childhood in the past, so that you can see how different your childhood would have been if you had grown up then. When historian Philippe Ariès (1965) examined European paintings from the Middle Ages, he noticed that children were always dressed up in adult clothing. If children were not stiffly posed for a family portrait, they were depicted as engaging in adult activities. Ariès concluded that at that time and in that place childhood was not regarded as a special time of life. Rather, the Europeans considered children miniature adults. Ariès also pointed out that boys were apprenticed at very early ages. At the age of seven, for example, a boy might leave home for good to learn to be a jeweler or a stonecutter. A girl, in contrast, stayed home until she married, but by the age of seven she had to do her daily share of household tasks.

Rather than some idyllic period of tranquillity in which adults loved and protected children (the Western ideal), childhood used to be harsh. Another historian of childhood, Lloyd DeMause (1975), has documented the nightmare of childhood in ages past. To beat children used to be *the norm*. Parents who did not beat their children were considered neglectful of their social duty to keep them off the road to hell. Even teachers were expected to beat children, and one nineteenth-century German schoolteacher methodically recorded every beating he administered. His record shows 124,000 lashes with a whip, 911,527 hits with a stick, 136,715 slaps with his hand, and 1,115,800 cuffs across the ears. This expectation of beating was so general that even future kings didn't escape brutal punishment. Louis XIII, for example, "was whipped every morning, starting at the age of two, simply for being 'obstinate,' and was even whipped on the day of his coronation at the age of nine" (McCoy 1985:392).

To keep children in line, parents and teachers also felt it their moral duty to use psychological terror. They would lock children in dark closets for an entire day and frighten them with tales of death and hellfire. It was common to terrify children into submission by forcing them to witness gruesome events.

> A common moral lesson involved taking children to visit the gibbet [an upraised post on which executed bodies were left hanging from chains], where they were forced to inspect rotting corpses hanging there as an example of what happens to bad children when they grow up. Whole classes were taken out of school to witness hangings, and parents would often whip their children afterwards to make them remember what they had seen (DeMause 1975).

And some of us are concerned about what today's children see on television!

Obviously, times have changed. To treat a child this way now would horrify the neighbors and land the parents in jail. Young children today are not even allowed to work for wages except in special, highly controlled situations, much less can they be beaten. The current view is that children are tender and "innocent." Parents are

As we progress through the life course, expectations of what our roles and responsibilities are change from one life stage to another. In contemporary Western societies such as the United States, children are viewed as innocent and in need of complete protection from adult demands such as work and self-support. Historically and cross-culturally, however, ideas of childhood vary. In 15th-century Europe (Sir Walter Raleigh and son, artist unknown), for instance, children were viewed as miniature adults who assumed adult roles at the earliest opportunity.

Essay #5

CDQ 20: Is childhood defined in the same way in all societies? If you were given the choice, would you choose to grow up in the society in which you were reared?

expected to guide their physical, emotional, and social development while providing them with care, comfort, and protection. Now that is quite a change.

CDQ 21: Why is adolescence a difficult period of transition for some of us?

Adolescence (Ages Thirteen–Seventeen).   Adolescence is an even more recent social invention. Only during this century, in fact, was the word coined (Hall 1904). Previously, society did not mark out the teenage years as a distinct time of life. People simply passed from childhood into early adulthood, with no stopover.

The Industrial Revolution first brought the changes that marked out the teenage years as special. With economic change came material surpluses that allowed millions of teenagers to remain outside the labor force, while at the same time, the demand for education increased. The convergence of these two forces created a new gap between childhood and full adulthood. Someone later coined the term *adolescence* to mark this period as a special age.

Biologically equipped for both work and marriage but commonly denied both, adolescents suffer much inner turmoil. With no initiation rites to ground the self-identity and mark their passage into adulthood as in preliterate societies (Gilmore 1990), adolescents in the industrialized world must "find" themselves on their own. With social influences pulling in contrary directions, most adolescents feel inner disturbances.

Attempting to carve out an identity distinct from both the "younger" world being left behind and the "older" world still out of bounds, adolescents develop their own standards of clothing, hairstyles, language, music, and other claims to separateness (McAlexander and Schouten 1989). While these outward forms are readily visible, we usually fail to realize that adolescence, with all its trappings, is a social creation: It is contemporary society, not biological age, that makes these years a period of turmoil.

Early Adulthood (Ages Eighteen–Twenty-Nine).   If society invented adolescence as a special period in life, can it also invent other periods? Historian Kenneth Keniston suggested it could. He noted that American society seems to be adding a period of prolonged youth to our life course, in which post-adolescents continue to postpone adult responsibilities and are "neither psychological adolescents nor sociological adults" (Keniston 1960:3). From the end of high school through extended education, including vocational schools, college, and even graduate school, many Americans remain free from adult responsibilities, such as a full-time job, marriage, and home ownership. This period of extended preparation before "settling down" is early adulthood.

Somewhere during early adulthood, individuals gradually ease into adult responsibilities. They finish school, take a full-time job, engage in courtship rituals, get married—and go into debt. The self is considerably more stable during the latter part of this period than it was during adolescence, and this period is typically one of high optimism.

Middle Adulthood (Ages Thirty–Thirty-Nine).   The next period, middle adulthood, ends around the age of 40. Most people in middle adulthood are much surer of themselves and of their goals in life than before. As with any point in the life course, however, the self can receive severe jolts—in this case from such circumstances as divorce or being fired (Dannefer 1984). It may take years for the self to stabilize after such ruptures.

Because of recent social change, middle adulthood poses a special challenge for American women, who increasingly have been given the message that they can "have it all." They can be superworkers, superwives, and supermoms—all at the same time. During middle adulthood many come face to face with reality—too many conflicting pressures, too many demands to be satisfied—and find that something has to give. Women's attempts to resolve this dilemma are often compounded by another hard reality—that their husbands learned long ago through gender socialization, that child care and housework are not "masculine." In short, adjustments continue in this and all phases of life.

Later Adulthood (Ages Forty–Sixty-Five).   The age of 40 marks the transition to a different view of life, an attempt to evaluate the past and to come to terms with what lies ahead. People compare what they have accomplished with how far they had hoped to get. Many do not like the gap they see between where they are now and where they had planned to be. Looking at the years ahead, most people conclude that they are not likely to get much farther, that their job or career is likely to consist of "more of the same." Health and mortality also begin to loom large as individuals feel physical changes in their own bodies and watch their parents become frail, ill, and die. The consequence is a fundamental reorientation in thinking—*from time since birth to time left to live* (Neugarten 1976). This combination of concerns centering on attainment and mortality is commonly termed the "mid-life crisis."

Life at this point, however, is far from filled only with such concerns. Many people find this to be the most comfortable period of their entire lives in which they enjoy job security and a higher standard of living than ever before, a bigger house (perhaps paid for), newer cars, and more exotic vacations. The children are grown, the self is firmly planted, and fewer upheavals are likely to occur.

As they anticipate the next phase of life, however, most people do not like what they see.

Old Age and Death (Age Sixty-Six to Death).   In American society, this phase, which marks the end of the life course, begins around the mid-sixties. A comparison with preindustrial society, however, may be enlightening. First, because of their much shorter lifespan, people in preindustrial societies considered old age to begin in the forties. Second, persons considered old in preindustrial societies were also likely to be accorded high respect. Since adult roles changed very little from one generation to the next, the elderly were thought to have accumulated knowledge valuable to the young. The elderly might also hold almost all the wealth and power, which wouldn't exactly hurt their status either.

Our situation stands in marked contrast. First, the longer lifespan brought about by industrialization has delayed the onset of old age. This change is welcome, for it has been accompanied by an improvement in general health. The second major distinction, however, is less welcome, for the elderly in industrialized societies have undergone **social devaluation,** that is, they are considered to have less social value than other age groups (Achenbaum 1978). Because knowledge in industrialized societies becomes quickly outmoded, the elderly are often viewed as people who "once" knew something worthwhile, whom time has now passed by. Set in their ways, they live in the past and forever offer useless advice. Today such cruel cultural images are offset by more flattering stereotypes, such as that of the "sweet grandmother," the "helpful grandfather," and, increasingly, the "happy retirees" who have the time and money to travel, enjoy other leisure activities, and have fun.

In addition to coming to terms with cultural stereotypes, during this stage of life people also grapple with the idea of their own death. Because we have a self and can reason abstractly, we can contemplate death. Initially it is something "out there," but as people see their friends die and their own bodies no longer functioning as before, death becomes less abstract. Increasingly, people feel that "time is closing in" on them. In Chapter 13, where we focus on this latter stage of life, we shall examine people's reactions to knowing that they do not have long to live.

Distinctive Life-Course Patterns

Sociologist Alice Rossi (1974), found the life-course model outlined above inadequate. She noted that human experience is much more diverse than the model suggests (Epstein 1988). Rossi pointed out that recent conclusions about mid-life are very subjective and not as generalizable as the proponents of the model suggest. By this she means that the model is based on "look-alike" respondents, who all grew up in the

CDQ 22: Why do you think some people in later adulthood focus more on the time they have left to live rather than the time since their birth?

CDQ 23: Can you give examples of positive and negative stereotypes about older adults? Do you think these will change in the future?

K.P.: Alice Rossi

social devaluation: a reduction in the value or social worth placed on something or someone

same distinctive historical period—the 1920s and 1930s. Consequently, the Great Depression, World War II, and the Korean War left their mark on all of them. Rossi contrasted this group with today's middle-aged men who grew up in a historical period of growing prosperity. These men found greater opportunities and fairly easy promotions, allowing them to achieve beyond their parents' dreams. The model, then, fails to recognize how deeply people's experiences are grounded in the unique events of their particular society.

According to Rossi, not to account adequately for the effects of society on the life course causes the model to fail both men and women. Because our life course is not merely the outcome of our biology but also a reflection of our social experiences, social change is like a hammer beating out the contours of the "typical" life course. For example, the life course of today's women cannot but differ markedly from that of their grandmothers. Because contemporary women's roles in society have been transformed, not only their self-concepts but also the "critical points" of their "typical" life course have changed radically.

To continue the analogy of the trajectory, then, large-scale events determine some of the "surfaces" that will touch the individual's life. Sociologist C. Wright Mills (1959), for example, pointed out how wars and depressions, as well as peace and economic booms, leave their mark on people. They may cause people to postpone marriage and having children, or to rush into them; to be pushed into careers early, or kept out of them altogether. Other characteristics of society that distinguish life-course patterns are age group, race, gender, and social class (Cain 1979; Persell 1977; Sales 1978; Simmons et al. 1979). An individual's relationship to power is also significant (Gecas 1990). Each different social location leads to contrasting experiences in life and thus to major differences in life transitions. Age certainly plays a key role, of course, but as sociologist Glen Elder (1975:167) puts it, "Birth, puberty, and death are biological facts in the life course, but their meanings in society are social facts or constructions."

L. Obj. 10: Explain why human beings are not prisoners of socialization.

CDQ 24: Will human beings become robots because of socialization?

ARE WE PRISONERS OF SOCIALIZATION?

From our discussion of socialization, you might conclude that sociologists think of people as little robots: The socialization goes in, and the behavior comes out. People cannot help what they do, think, or feel, for everything is simply a result of their exposure to socializing agents.

Sociologists do *not* think of people in this way (Wrong 1961; Meltzer, Petras, and Reynolds 1975; Couch 1989). Although socialization is powerful, and profoundly affects us all, we have a self. Laid down in childhood and continually modified by later experience, the self is dynamic. It is not a sponge that passively absorbs influences from the environment but a vigorous, essential part of our being that allows us to act upon our environment.

Indeed, it is precisely because individuals are not little robots that their behavior is so hard to predict. The countless reactions of the many people important to us merge in each person—as discussed earlier, even twins do not receive identical reactions from others. As the self develops, we internalize or "put together" these innumerable reactions, producing a unique whole that we call the individual. And, each unique individual uses his or her own minds to reason and to make choices in life.

In this way, each of us is actively involved even in the social construction of the self. For example, although our experiences in the family lay down the basic elements of our personality, including fundamental orientations to life, we are not doomed to keep those orientations if we do not like them. We can purposely expose ourselves to groups and ideas that we prefer. Those experiences, in turn, will have their own effects on our self. In short, in spite of the powerful influences we experience, within the limitations of the framework laid down by society we can change even the self. And that self—along with the options available within society—is the key to our behavior.

SUMMARY

1. How much of people's characteristics come from "nature" (heredity) and how much from "nurture" (the social environment)? Observations of feral, isolated, and institutionalized children help answer this question, as do experiments with monkeys that have been isolated during infancy. All of these studies indicate that language and intimate interaction are essential to the development of what we consider to be human characteristics.

2. Humans are born with the *capacity* to develop a self, but the self is socially constructed; its content depends on social interaction. According to Charles Horton Cooley's concept of the looking-glass self, the self develops as the direct result of others' reactions. George Herbert Mead identified the ability to take the role of the other as essential to the development of the self. Mead concluded that even the mind is a social product.

3. Jean Piaget identified four stages in the development of the ability to reason: (1) sensorimotor, (2) preoperational, (3) concrete operational, and (4) formal operational. Sigmund Freud identified the id, ego, and superego as the essential components of personality. Our emotions, which develop in an orderly sequence, are also important components of our behavior.

4. Gender socialization, that is, sorting males and females into different roles on the basis of their being male or female, is a primary means of controlling human behavior. A society's ideals of sex-linked behaviors are reinforced by its social institutions. Anthropologists have identified two societies that apparently have little gender discrimination: the Tahitians of the South Pacific and the Semai of Central Malaysia.

5. The main agents of socialization are family, religion, school, peer group, the mass media, and the workplace. Each has its particular influences in socializing us into becoming full-fledged members of society. Only some of us experience the total institution, an agent of resocialization.

6. Socialization occurs throughout life, and each stage of the life course has its characteristic patterns. Industrialization has created fundamental changes in our view of the life course. The divisions presented here are childhood, adolescence, early adulthood, middle adulthood, later adulthood, and old age.

7. Although socialization lays down the basic self and establishes other frameworks (institutions, social class, gender, and so on) within which we live our lives, humans are not robots but rational beings who consider options and make choices.

SUGGESTED READINGS

Ariès, Philippe. *Centuries of Childhood: A Social History of Family Life.* New York: Vintage Books, 1965. This pathbreaking study of childhood in the Middle Ages provides a sharp contrast to child-rearing patterns in modern society.

Curtiss, Susan. *Genie: A Psycholinguistic Study of a Modern Day "Wild Child."* New York: Academic Press, 1977. The psycholinguist who worked with Genie for several years presents the details of a girl who was locked in a small room for twelve years.

Elkin, Frederick, and Gerald Handel. *The Child and Society,* 4th ed. New York: Random House, 1984. This classic overview of the socialization of children emphasizes social class, race, sex, and place of residence as significant factors in socialization.

Gilligan, Carol. *In a Different Voice: Psychological Theory and Women's Development.* Cambridge, Mass.: Harvard University Press, 1982. Gilligan examines the different ways in which males and females are socialized, focusing on the consequences for their relationships.

Gilmore, David D. *Manhood in the Making: Cultural Concepts of Masculinity.* New Haven, Conn.: Yale University Press, 1990. A survey of societies around the world aimed at determining if masculinity is constant; contains fascinating anthropological data.

Mead, George Herbert. *Mind, Self and Society from the Standpoint of a Social Behaviorist.* Ed. Charles W. Morris. Chicago: University of Chicago Press, 1962. (Originally published in 1934.) Put together from notes taken by Mead's students, this book presents Mead's analysis of how mind and self are products of society.

Piaget, Jean, and Barbel Inhelder. *The Psychology of the Child.* New York: Basic Books, 1969. The authors provide an overview of Piaget's experiments and conclusions about the thought processes of children.

Wilson, Clinty C., II, and Felix Gutierrez. *Minorities and Media: Diversity and the End of Mass Communication.* Beverly Hills, Calif.: Sage, 1985. This book analyzes the mass media as socializing agents, exploring how the media shape ideas about African Americans, Hispanic Americans, Native Americans, and Asian Americans.

CHAPTER 4

Faith Ringgold, Subway Graffiti, Quilt #3, *1987*

Social Structure and Social Interaction

LEVELS OF SOCIOLOGICAL ANALYSIS
   Macrosociology and Microsociology
SOCIAL STRUCTURE: THE MACROSOCIOLOGICAL
   PERSPECTIVE
      Down-to-Earth Sociology: **College Football as Social
      Structure** ■ Culture ■ Social Class ■ Social
      Status ■ Roles ■ Groups
SOCIAL INSTITUTIONS
   Changes in Social Structure ■ What Holds Society
   Together?
THE MICROSOCIOLOGICAL PERSPECTIVE:
   SOCIAL INTERACTION IN EVERYDAY LIFE

Symbolic Interaction ■ *Perspectives:* **The Amish—
Gemeinschaft Communities in a *Gesellschaft*
Society** ■ Dramaturgy: The Presentation of Self in
Everyday Life ■ Ethnomethodology: Uncovering
Background Assumptions ■ The Social
Construction of Reality
THE NEED FOR BOTH MICROSOCIOLOGY AND
   MACROSOCIOLOGY
SUMMARY
SUGGESTED READINGS

My curiosity had gotten the better of me. When the sociology convention finished, I climbed aboard the first city bus that came along. I didn't know where the bus was going, and I didn't even know where I was going to spend the night.

"Maybe I overdid it this time," I thought as the bus began winding down streets I had never seen before. Actually, since this was my first visit to Washington, D.C., I hadn't seen any of the streets before. I had no direction, no plans, not even a map. I carried no billfold, just a driver's license shoved into my jeans for emergency identification and a $10 bill tucked into my socks. My goal was simple: If I see something interesting, I'll get off and check it out.

"Nothing but the usual things," I mused, as we passed row after row of apartment buildings and stores. I could see myself riding buses the entire night. Then something caught my eye. Nothing spectacular—just groups of people clustered around a large circular area where several streets intersected.

I climbed off the bus and made my way to what turned out to be Dupont Circle. I took a seat on a sidewalk bench and began to observe. As the scene came into focus, I noted several street corner men drinking and joking with one another. One of the men broke from his companions and sat down next to me. As we talked, I mostly listened.

As night fell, the men said that they wanted to get another bottle of wine. I contributed. They counted their money and asked if I wanted to go with them.

Although I felt a churning inside—emotions combining hesitation and fear—I heard a confident "Sure!" coming out of my mouth. As we left the circle, the three men began to cut through an alley. "Oh, no," I thought. "That's not what I had in mind."

I had but a split second to make a decision. I found myself continuing to walk with the men, but holding back half a step so that none of the three was behind me. As we walked, they passed around the remnants of their bottle. When my turn came, I didn't know what to do. I shuddered to think about the diseases lurking within that bottle. I made another decision. In the semidarkness I faked it, letting only my thumb and forefinger touch my lips and nothing enter my mouth.

When we returned to Dupont Circle, the men finished their new bottle of Thunderbird. I couldn't fake it in the light, so I passed, pointing at my stomach to indicate that I was having problems.

Suddenly one of the men jumped up, smashed the emptied bottle against the sidewalk, and thrust the jagged neck in a menacing gesture. He stared straight ahead at another bench, where he had spotted someone with whom he had some sort of unfinished business. As the other men told him to cool it, I moved slightly to one side of the group—ready to flee, just in case.

LEVELS OF SOCIOLOGICAL ANALYSIS

Macrosociology and Microsociology

L. Obj. 1: Differentiate between macrosociology and microsociology.

CDQ 1: Why do you think that most people avoid street people? How might sociologists analyze street people?

L. Obj. 2: Indicate which levels of analysis are most likely to be used by functionalists, conflict theorists, and symbolic interactionists.

macrosociology: analysis of social life focusing on broad features of social structure, such as social class and the relationships of groups to one another; an approach usually used by functionalist and conflict theorists

microsociology: analysis of social life focusing on social interaction; an approach usually used by symbolic interactionists

social interaction: what people do when they come together

On this sociological adventure, I almost got myself in over my head. Fortunately, it turned out all right. The man's "enemy" didn't look our way, the broken bottle was set down next to the bench "just in case he needed it," and until dawn I was introduced to a life that up to then I had only read about.

Sociologists Elliot Liebow (1967) and Elijah Anderson (1978) have written fascinating accounts about men like these. Although street corner men may appear to be disorganized, simply coming and going as they please and doing whatever feels good at the moment, these sociologists have analyzed how *social structure* affects their lives; that is, how the characteristics of groups and society influence their behavior. Below, we shall examine this concept in detail.

Sociologists use two levels of analysis. The first, **macrosociology,** places the focus on broad features of social structure. Macrosociology investigates large-scale social forces and the effects they have on entire societies and the groups within them. Sociologists who use this approach analyze such things as social class and how groups are related to one another. If macrosociologists were to analyze street corner men, for example, they would stress that these men are located at the bottom of the American social class system. Their low status means that many opportunities are closed to them: The men have few skills, little education, hardly anything to offer an employer. As "able-bodied" men, however, they are not eligible for welfare. That means that they must hustle to survive. As a consequence, they spend their lives on the streets.

Conflict theory and functionalism, both of which focus on the broader picture, are examples of this macrosociological approach. In these theories, the goal is to examine the large-scale social forces that influence how groups are organized and positioned within a social system.

The second approach sociologists use is **microsociology.** Here the emphasis is placed on **social interaction,** what people do when they come together. Sociologists who use this approach are likely to focus on the men's survival strategies ("hustles"); their rules for dividing up money, wine, or whatever other resources they have; their relationships with girlfriends, family, and friends; where they spend their time and what they do there; their language; their pecking order; and so on. With its focus on face-to-face interaction, symbolic interaction is an example of microsociology.

A form of symbolic interaction that is sometimes used to analyze individual behavior is *exchange theory*. This perspective, developed by sociologist George Homans (1958, 1961), looks at human behavior in terms of rewards and costs. Exchange theorists assume that the basic motivation in human behavior is seeking pleasure and avoiding pain. Thus, people do what they do to gain the maximum rewards (such as money, approval, and recognition) and to minimize costs (such as punishment, withdrawal of approval, loss of money).

Although the emphases of macrosociology and microsociology differ, with each yielding a distinctive perspective, together they provide a more complete understanding of social life. We cannot adequately understand street corner men, for example, without using macrosociology. It is essential that we place the men within the broad context of how groups in American society are related to one another—for, as with ourselves, the social class of these men helps to shape their attitudes and behavior. Nor can we adequately understand these men without microsociology, for their everyday situations also form a significant part of their lives.

To better grasp these two contrasting approaches in sociology, and their relative contributions to our understanding of social life, let's take a look at each. As we do so, you may find yourself feeling more comfortable with one approach than the other. That is what happens with sociologists. For reasons of personal background and professional training, sociologists find themselves more comfortable with one approach. Consequently, they tend to use it in their research. Both approaches, however, are necessary for a full understanding of society.

SOCIAL STRUCTURE: THE MACROSOCIOLOGICAL PERSPECTIVE

Why do street corner people act as they do? Why do most of us avoid them? Why, perhaps, are most of us at least somewhat intimidated by them?

To better understand human behavior, we need to look first at how social structure *establishes limits on our behavior*. **Social structure** is the framework of society that is already laid out before you are born; it is the patterned relationships among people, such as the relationships between students and teachers common in a particular school. As the Down-to-Earth Sociology box on page 90 stresses, social structure also refers to group relationships that persist over time.

Because the term social structure may seem vague, consider first how you personally experience social structure in your everyday life. As I write this, I do not know

Essay #1

L. Obj. 3: Discuss social structure and explain why one's location in this structure affects that person's perceptions, attitudes, and behaviors.

Essay #2

social structure: the relationship of people and groups to one another; the characteristics of groups—all of which give direction to and set limits on behavior

Sociologists use two levels of analysis to study social life—macrosociological and microsociological. When studying street corner men or the homeless (or other social phenomena), sociologists who use the macrosociological level study how broad forces, such as the economy and the system of social class operating in a society, have contributed to existing conditions. Sociologists who use the microsociological level to study social life analyze how people in groups interact in everyday situations.

DOWN-TO-EARTH SOCIOLOGY

College Football as Social Structure

To gain a better idea of what social structure is, think of college football (Cf. Dobriner 1969). You know the various positions on the team: center, guards, tackles, ends, quarterback, and running backs. Each is a *status;* that is, each is a recognized social position. For each of these statuses, there is a *role;* that is, each of these positions has particular expectations attached to it. The center is expected to snap the ball, the quarterback to pass it, the guards to block, the tackles to tackle or block, the ends to receive passes, and so on. Those role expectations guide each player's actions; that is, the players try to do what their particular role requires. Since not everyone plays the role in precisely the same way, different *role performances* result. Each quarterback, for example, has a particular "style" of play.

Let's suppose that football is your favorite sport and you never miss a home game at your college. Let's also suppose that you graduate and move across the country. Five years later you return to your campus for a nostalgic visit. The climax of your visit is the biggest football game of the year. When you get to the game, you might be surprised to see a different coach, but you are not sur-

prised that each of the playing positions is occupied by people you don't know. All the players you knew have graduated, and their places have been filled by others.

This scenario exactly mirrors *social structure,* which is a framework around which a group exists. In the football example, that framework consists of the coaching staff and the eleven playing positions. The game depends not on any particular individual, but rather on the positions that the individuals occupy. When someone leaves a position, the game can go on because someone else takes it over and plays the role. The game will continue even though not a single individual remains the same from one period of time to the next. Notre Dame's football team endures today even though Knute Rockne, the gipper, and his teammates are long dead.

Even though you may not play football, you nevertheless live your life within a clearly established social structure. Society determines the statuses, roles, and so on, that its members will play—and when you were born, those essential components of social structure were already in place. You take your particular positions in life, others do the same, and society goes about its business. Although the specifics change with time, the game—whether of life or of football—goes on.

who you are. I do not know if you are African American, white, Hispanic American, Native American, Asian American. I do not know your religion. I do not know if you are young or old, tall or short, male or female. I do not know if you were reared on a farm, in the suburbs, or in the inner city. I do not know if you went to a public high school or an exclusive prep school. But I do know that you are in college. And that, alone, tells me a great deal about you.

CDQ 2: If people know that you are in college, what does that tell them about you?

From that one piece of information, I can assume that the social structure of your college is now shaping what you do. For example, let us suppose that today you felt euphoric over some great news. I can be fairly certain (not absolutely, mind you, but relatively certain) that when you entered the classroom, social structure overrode your mood. That is, instead of shouting at the top of your lungs and joyously throwing this book into the air, you entered the classroom fairly subdued and took your seat.

The same social structure influences your instructor, even if, on the one hand, he or she is facing a divorce or has a parent or child dying of cancer, or, on the other, has just been awarded a promotion or a million dollar grant. The instructor may feel like either retreating into seclusion or celebrating wildly, but it is most likely that he or she will conduct class. In short, personal feelings and desires tend to be overridden by social structure.

CDQ 3: Do you feel uncomfortable if you enter a crowded classroom and find that someone has already placed their books or coat on the chair in which you usually sit? Why or why not?

Just as social structure influences you and your instructor, so it also establishes limits for street corner people. They, too, find themselves in a specific social location in the American social structure—although at quite a different point. Consequently, they are affected differently—and nothing about their social location leads them to take notes or to lecture. Their behaviors are as logical an outcome of where they find themselves in the social structure as are your own. It is just as "natural" in their position in the social structure to drink wine all night as it is for you to stay up studying all night for a critical examination. It is just as "natural" for you to nod and say, "Excuse me," when you enter a crowded classroom late and have to claim a desk on which someone has already placed books or a coat as it is for them to break off the head of a wine bottle and glare at an enemy.

In short, people learn certain behaviors and attitudes because of their location in the social structure (whether privileged or deprived or in between), and they act accordingly. This is equally true of street corner people. *The difference is not in biology (race, sex, or any other supposed genetic influences on behavior), but in people's location in the social structure.* Switch places with the street corner people and watch your behaviors and attitudes change!

To better understand the social structure, which so critically affects who we are and what we are like, let us look in turn at each of its major components: culture, social class, social status, roles, groups, and institutions.

Culture

Essay #3

Chapter 2 looked in detail at how culture affects us. At this point, let's simply review the main impact of culture, the largest envelope that surrounds us. Sociologists use the term culture to refer to a group's language, beliefs, values, behaviors, and even gestures. Culture also includes the material objects used by a group. In short, culture is our social inheritance, what we learn from the people around us. Culture is the broadest framework that determines what kind of people we become. If we are reared in Eskimo, Japanese, Russian, or American culture, we will grow up to be like most Eskimos, Japanese, Russians, or Americans. On the outside, we will look and act like them; and on the inside, we will think and feel like them.

L. Obj. 4: Define the following concepts: culture, social class, social status, roles, groups, and social institutions.

Social Class

Societies are not unidimensional, and to understand people fully we must examine the particular social location they hold down in life. The major groups in American society are based on income, education, and occupational prestige. Large numbers of people who have similar amounts of income and education and who work at jobs that are roughly comparable in prestige make up a **social class**. Chapter 10 examines the American social class structure in detail. For now, it is sufficient to say that social classes are one of the chief components of the social structure of our society, that our ideas, attitudes, and behaviors largely depend on our particular social class. So it is with the street corner people, whose class standing is considered by all to be undesirable.

Speaker Sug. #1: A colleague who has been conducting cross-cultural research.

CDQ 4: In what ways are our ideas, attitudes, and behaviors dependent on the social class to which we belong?

CDQ 5: What do you think of when you hear the word "status?" What do sociologists mean when they use this term?

Social Status

When you hear the word "status," you are likely to think of prestige. These two words are welded together in common thinking. Sociologists, however, use **status** in a different way: to refer to the position that an individual occupies. That position may have a great deal of prestige, as in the case of a judge or an astronaut, or it may carry very little prestige, as in the case of a gas station attendant or a hamburger flipper at a fast-food restaurant. The status may also be looked down on, as in the case of a street corner man, an ex-convict, or a bag lady.

All of us occupy several positions at the same time. You may be simultaneously a son or daughter, a worker, a date, and a student. Sociologists use the term **status set** to refer to all the statuses or positions that you occupy. Obviously your status set changes as your particular statuses change; for example, if you graduate from college and take a full-time job, get married, buy a home, have children, and so on, your status set changes to include the positions of worker, spouse, homeowner, and parent.

The significance of statuses is that, like other aspects of social structure, they are part of our basic framework of living in society. The example above of students and teachers doing what others expect of them in spite of their temporary moods is an

social class: a large number of people with similar amounts of income and education who work at jobs that are roughly comparable in prestige

status: the position that someone occupies in society or a social group

status set: all the statuses or positions that an individual occupies

Each of us occupies several statuses. Princess Diana, for instance, is, among others, a wife, a mother, and Princess of Wales. Because she married into the Royal Family, her status as Princess of Wales is an achieved rather than an ascribed status. The woman touching Princess Diana's feet is a member of the Untouchable caste in India. Her caste status is ascribed, or involuntary.

CDQ 6: Why do some people wear wedding rings? What are some reasons for not wearing a ring?

Project 1

CDQ 7: What is your master status?

ascribed statuses: positions an individual either inherits at birth or receives involuntarily later in life

achieved statuses: positions that are earned, accomplished, or involve at least some effort or activity on the individual's part

status symbols: items used to identify a status

master status: a status that cuts across the other statuses that an individual occupies

illustration of how statuses affect our actions—and those of the people around us. Our statuses—whether daughter or son, worker or date, serve as guides for our behavior.

Ascribed Statuses and Achieved Statuses. The first type, **ascribed statuses,** are involuntary. You do not ask for them, nor can you choose them. Some you inherit at birth, such as your race, sex, and the social class of your parents, as well as your statuses as female (male), daughter (son), niece (nephew), and granddaughter (grandson). Others you involuntarily receive later in life. These are related to the life course discussed in Chapter 3, the biological passages that label someone a teenager, a young adult, middle aged, old, and so on.

The second type, **achieved statuses,** are voluntary. These you earn or accomplish. As a result of your efforts you become a student, an athlete, a scout, a friend, a spouse, a rabbi, minister, priest, or nun. Or, for lack of effort (or effort that others fail to appreciate), you become a school dropout, a former friend, an ex-spouse, a defrocked priest or nun. In other words, achieved statuses can be either positive or negative, both college president and bank robber represent achieved statuses.

The distinction between ascribed and achieved statuses is not always as simple as the definitions might suggest. For example, an individual might be a college student or athlete not because of his or her efforts, but because of the parents' influence in keeping that person in a private college or on the athletic team. In addition, some ascribed statuses can be changed into achieved statuses. For example, through education a poor person may move into a social class different from that ascribed at birth. Similarly, someone who was born rich might move into a lower social class through some blunder resulting in the loss of the family fortune.

The significance of social statuses for understanding human behavior is that each status provides guidelines for how people are to act and feel. Like other aspects of social structure, they set limits on what people can and cannot do. Because social statuses are an essential part of the social structure, they are found within all human groups.

Status Symbols. People who are very pleased with their particular social status may want others to recognize that they occupy that status. To gain this recognition, they use **status symbols,** signs that identify a status. For example, people wear wedding rings to announce their marital status; uniforms, guns, and badges to proclaim that they are police officers (and to not so subtly let you know that their status gives them authority over you); and "backward" collars to declare that they are Lutheran ministers or Roman Catholic or Episcopalian priests.

Because achievement and success are major American values, many people who have "made it" are not content to sit and privately look at their brimming bank accounts. Instead, they want to shout to the world that they have succeeded—so they drive BMWs and buy "vanity" license plates.

Some social statuses are negative, and so, therefore, are their status symbols. The scarlet letter in Nathaniel Hawthorne's book by the same title is one example. Another is the CONVICTED DUI bumper sticker that some counties require convicted drunk drivers to display if they wish to avoid a jail sentence.

All of us use status symbols to announce our statuses to others and to help smooth our interactions in everyday life. You might consider your own status symbols. For example, how does your clothing announce your statuses of sex, age, and college student?

Master Statuses. A **master status** is one that cuts across the other statuses that you hold. Some master statuses are ascribed. An example is your sex. Whatever you do, people perceive you as a male or as a female. If you are working your way through college by flipping burgers, people see you not only as a burger flipper and a student but as a *male* or *female* burger flipper and a *male* or *female* college student. Other master statuses are race and age.

Some master statuses are achieved. If you become very, very wealthy (and it does not matter if your wealth comes from an invention or the lottery—it is still *achieved* as far as sociologists are concerned), your wealth is likely to become a master status. No matter what else, people are likely to say, "She is a very rich burger flipper." (Or more likely, "She's very rich, and she used to flip burgers!")

Similarly, individuals who become disabled or disfigured find, to their dismay, that their condition becomes a master status. For example, a person whose face is extremely scarred, will be seen through this unwelcome master status no matter what else that individual may do in life, no matter what he or she may accomplish. Persons confined to wheelchairs can attest to how "Disabled" becomes a master status, how it overrides all their other statuses and determines others' perceptions of everything they do.

Although our statuses usually fit together fairly well, sometimes a contradiction or mismatch between statuses occurs; this is known as **status inconsistency.** A fourteen-year-old college student is an example of status inconsistency. So is a forty-year-old married woman on a date with a nineteen-year-old college sophomore.

From these examples you can understand an essential aspect of social statuses: Like other components of social structure, they come with a set of built-in *norms* (that is, expectations) that provide guidelines for behavior. When statuses mesh well, as they usually do, we know what to expect of people. Status inconsistency, however, upsets our expectations. In the examples above, how are you supposed to act? Are you supposed to treat the fourteen-year-old as you would a young teenager or as you would your college classmate? The married woman as the mother of your friend or as a classmate's date?

Roles

> All the world's a stage
> And all the men and women merely players.
> They have their exits and their entrances;
> And one man in his time plays many parts. . .
> 　　　　　　　　William Shakespeare
> 　　　　　　　　*As You Like It,* Act II, Scene 7

Like Shakespeare, sociologists, too, see roles as essential to social life. When you were born, **roles**—the behaviors, obligations, and privileges attached to a status—were already set up for you. Society was waiting with outstretched arms to teach you how it expected you to act as a boy or a girl. And whether you were born poor, rich, or somewhere in between, certain behaviors, obligations, and privileges were attached to each status.

The difference between role and status is that you *occupy* a status, but you *play* a role (Linton 1936). For example, being a son or daughter is your status, but your right to receive food and shelter from your parents—as well as their expectations that you be respectful to them—is your role.

Our roles are a sort of fence that helps keep us doing what society wants us to do. That fence leaves us a certain amount of freedom, but for most of us that freedom doesn't go very far. Suppose a female decides that she is not going to wear dresses—or a male that he will not wear suits and ties—regardless of what anyone says. In most situations they probably won't. When a formal occasion comes along, however, such as a family wedding or a funeral, they are likely to cave in to norms that they find overwhelming. Almost all of us stay within the fences that mark out what is "appropriate" for our roles. Most of us are little troubled by such constraints, for our socialization is so thorough that we usually *want* to do what our roles indicate is appropriate.

The sociological significance of roles is that they are an essential component of culture. They lay out what is expected of people, and as individuals throughout society perform their roles, those roles mesh together to form this thing called society. As

Master statuses overshadow our other statuses. The noted physicist and writer Stephen Hawking is severely disabled by Lou Gehrig's disease. For many, his master status is that of a disabled person. Because of his incredible. achievements in the face of his disability, however, many of his friends, colleagues, and readers of his works think of him simultaneously as a great physicist.

CDQ 8: Why are our roles a sort of fence that keeps us doing what society wants us to do?

status inconsistency: a contradiction or mismatch between statuses

role: the behaviors, obligations, and privileges attached to a status

Shakespeare put it, people's roles provide "their exits and their entrances" on the stage of life. In short, roles are remarkably effective at keeping people in line—telling them when they should "enter" and when they should "exit," as well as what to do in between.

The section on social interaction will examine roles in more detail. For now, let us turn to groups, another major component of social structure.

Groups

A **group** consists of people who regularly and consciously interact with one another. Ordinarily, the members of a group share similar values, norms, and expectations. Just as our actions are influenced by our social class, statuses, and roles, so, too, the groups to which we belong represent powerful forces in our lives. In fact, *to belong to a group is to yield to others the right to make certain decisions about our behavior.* If we belong to a group, we assume an obligation to act according to the expectations of other members of that group.

CDQ 9: What are the rules of some of the groups to which you belong that must be followed or you will no longer be in "good standing?"

Although this principle holds true for all groups, some groups merely wield influence over small segments of our behavior. If you belong to a stamp club, for example, their influence probably extends to your attendance at meetings and display of knowledge about stamps. Other groups, however, control many aspects of our behavior. The family is an example. When parents say to their fifteen-year-old daughter, "As long as you are living under my roof, you had better be home by midnight," they show their expectation that their children, as members of the family, will conform to their ideas about many aspects of life, in this instance their views on curfew. They are saying that so long as the daughter wants to remain a member of the household her behavior must conform to their expectations.

group: people who regularly and consciously interact with one another

involuntary memberships: (or involuntary associations) groups in which people are assigned membership rather than choosing to join

voluntary memberships: (or voluntary associations) groups to which people belong

To belong to any group is to relinquish to others at least *some* control over our lives. Those social groups that provide little option to belong are called **involuntary memberships** (or involuntary associations). These include our family and the sexual, ethnic, and racial groups into which we are born. Groups to which we choose to belong are called **voluntary memberships** (or voluntary associations). These include the scouts, professional associations, church groups, clubs, and work groups. If we want to remain members in good standing, we must conform to what people in those groups expect of us. Both voluntary and involuntary memberships are vital in affecting who

Social groups to which we choose to belong are called voluntary memberships.

we are, for our participation in them shapes our ideas and orientations to life. Chapter 6 focuses on the topic of groups in detail.

SOCIAL INSTITUTIONS

At first glance, the term "social institution" may appear far removed from our personal lives. The term seems so cold and abstract. In fact, however, **social institution,** society's standard ways of meeting its basic needs, refers to concrete and highly relevant aspects of our lives. For example, the *family* constitutes a social institution. So does *religion,* with its sacred books, clergy, and worship, as does the *law,* with its police, lawyers, judges, courts, and prisons. The term also covers *politics,* including broken campaign promises, Congress, and the president. It includes the field of *economics,* which determines whether new plants open and old ones close, as well as whether people work for a living or draw unemployment, welfare, or a pension. *Education,* with its teachers and students, colleges and universities, is a social institution, too. The term also embraces the world of *science,* with its test tubes and experiments and its interviewers and questionnaires, and that of *medicine,* with its doctors and nurses and hospitals and patients, as well as the Medicare and Blue Cross and Blue Shield that those patients struggle to pay for. Finally, the term social institution applies to the *military,* with its generals and privates and tanks and planes, and the entire war game that at times threatens to become too real.

To understand these nine social institutions is to realize how profoundly our lives are affected by social structure. Much of their influence lies beyond our ordinary awareness. For example, because of the way our economic order is arranged, it is considered normal to work eight hours a day for five days every week. There is nothing inherently natural about this pattern, however. Its regularity is only an arbitrarily imposed temporal arrangement for work and leisure and personal concerns. Yet this one aspect of a single social institution has the most far-reaching effects on how we structure our free time and activities, how we deal with our family and friends, how we meet our personal needs and nonwork obligations, and even on how we view our own place in society as a whole.

Each of the other social institutions has similarly far-reaching effects. By weaving the fabric of our society, they establish the context in which we live, shaping almost everything that is of concern to us. Social institutions are so significant that if ours were different we, too, would be different. We certainly could not remain the same, for our ideas and attitudes and other orientations to the social world, and even to life itself, would be different.

The Functionalist Perspective. Functionalists believe that social institutions exist because they perform vital functions for society. No society, they point out, is without social institutions. A group may be too small to have people specializing in education, science, or the military, but it will have established ways of teaching skills and ideas to the young and some mechanism of self-defense. Every society must meet its basic needs (or **functional requisites**) to survive; and according to functionalists, that is the purpose of social institutions.

What are those basic needs? Functionalists have identified five **functional requisites** that each society must fulfill if it is to survive (Aberle et al. 1950; Mack and Bradford 1979).

1. *Replacing members* If a society does not replace its members, it will soon no longer exist. Because reproduction is so fundamental to a society's existence, all groups have developed some version of the family unit. The family functions to control people's sex drive and to maintain orderly reproduction. The family also gives the newcomer to society a sense of belonging by providing a "lineage," an account of how he or she is related to others.

CDQ 10: Why are social institutions so important in everyone's life?

Essay #4

L. Obj. 5: Compare and contrast functionalists' and conflict theorists' views regarding social institutions.

social institutions: the standard means by which society meets its basic needs

functional requisites: the major tasks that a society must fulfill if it is to survive

2. *Teaching new members*   People who are born into a society must also be taught what it means to be a full-fledged member. To accomplish this, each society establishes elaborate devices to ensure that its newcomers are socialized early on into the group's basic expectations. As the primary "bearer of culture," the family is essential to this process, but other institutions, such as church and school, aid in meeting this functional requisite.

3. *Producing and distributing goods and services*   Every society must obtain and distribute basic resources, from food and clothing to shelter and education. Consequently, every society establishes an *economic* institution, a means of producing such resources along with routine ways to distribute them.

4. *Preserving order*   Societies always face two threats of disorder: one internal, the potential of chaos, and the other external, the possibility of being conquered. To defend themselves against external conquest they develop some means of defense, some form of the military. To protect themselves from internal threat, they develop some system of policing themselves, ranging from formal organizations of armed groups to informal systems of gossip.

5. *Providing a sense of purpose*   For people to cooperate with one another and willingly give up self-centered, short-term gains in favor of working with and for others, they need a sense of purpose. They need to be convinced that it is worth sacrificing for the common good. Societies develop different ways of establishing such belief systems, but a primary one is religion, which attempts to answer questions about ultimate meaning. All of a society's institutions are actually involved in meeting this functional requisite, for the family provides one part of an interrelated set of answers about the sense of purpose, the school another, and so on.

The Conflict Perspective.   The views of conflict theorists stand in marked contrast to those of functionalists. Conflict theorists agree that social institutions were originally designed to meet basic survival needs; however, they do not see social institutions as working harmoniously for the common good. On the contrary, conflict theorists believe that social institutions of every society are controlled by an elite that manipulates them expressly to maintain its own privileged position of wealth and power (Domhoff 1983, 1990, 1991; Useem 1988).

From a functionalist perspective, society meets five key functional requisites for its members. Providing a sense of purpose is one of the major functions of the social institution of religion.

Social institutions, one of the major components of social structure, include all of the organized functions in a society, including the economy, family, education, politics, medicine, and religion. From a conflict perspective, social institutions such as the economy are controlled by an elite that manipulates the system for its own advantage. These male boardmembers, according to conflict theorists, represent the interests of such an elite.

Conflict theorists point out that in American society a fairly small group of people has garnered the lion's share of the nation's wealth. Members of this elite sit on the boards of major corporations and of the country's most prestigious universities. They use campaign contributions and personal contacts to control the nation's lawmakers. Consequently, it is they who make the major decisions in this society: to go to war or to refrain from war, to raise or to lower taxes, to raise or to lower interest rates, to pass laws that favor or impede moving capital, technology, and jobs out of this country.

In recent years, feminist sociologists (both female and male) have used conflict theory to gain a better understanding of gender relations. Their basic insight is that gender is an element of social structure itself, not simply a characteristic of individuals (Hess 1990). In other words, throughout the world males and females form separate groups that have differential access to society's resources. Gender relations are examined in Chapter 11.

In Sum.   Conflict theorists regard our social institutions as having a single primary purpose—to preserve the social order—which they interpret as preserving the wealthy and powerful in their privileged positions.

Changes in Social Structure

This enveloping system that we call social structure, which so powerfully affects our lives, is not static. Our culture changes as it responds to new technology, to influences from abroad, and to evolving values. Our current "globalization" brings us into extensive contact with other cultures, exerting profound change in our basic orientations to life. Nor do social classes remain immune to the winds of change, for shifts in education, the work force, and relationships between racial and ethnic groups bring with them a shifting membership. Similarly, groups that did not exist, such as the IRS, come into being, and afterwards wield extraordinary power over our lives.

What Holds Society Together?

As will be discussed in depth in Chapter 6, sociologists define *society* as a people who share a culture and a territory. If a society contains many different groups and undergoes extensive social change, how does it manage to stay together? Many sociologists have grappled with the question of how societies manage to stay intact. Let us examine two main answers their efforts have yielded.

Mechancial and Organic Solidarity.   Sociologist Emile Durkheim (1893, 1933) found the key to **social cohesion**—the degree to which members of a society feel

CDQ 11: How do societies manage to stay together in spite of the presence of many competing groups and extensive social change?

K.P.: Emile Durkheim

L. Obj. 6: Use Durkheim's concepts of mechanical and organic solidarity and Tönnies' typology of *Gemeinschaft* and *Gesellschaft* to explain what holds societies together.

social cohesion: the degree to which members of a group or society feel united by shared values and other social bonds

united by shared values and other social bonds—in what he called **mechanical solidarity.** By this term Durkheim meant that people develop a collective consciousness when they perform the same or similar tasks. Think of an agricultural society, in which everyone is involved in planting, cultivating, and harvesting. Members of this group have so much in common that it is possible for them to know what most others feel like. This shared consciousness, or sense of identity and fate, unites them into a common whole.

As societies increase in size, however, their **division of labor** (how they divide up tasks) becomes more specialized. Instead of almost everyone doing the same jobs, some become jewelers, while others become artists, authors, shopkeepers, soldiers, and so on. Rather than splitting society apart, the division of labor makes people depend on one another's activities. Durkheim called this new form of solidarity based on interdependence **organic solidarity.** To see why he used this term, think about how you depend on your teacher to guide you through this introductory course in sociology, just as your teacher depends on you and other students to keep his or her job. The two of you are like organs in the same body. Although each of you performs different tasks, your dependence on one another creates a form of unity.

The significance of the change from mechanical to organic solidarity is that people no longer cooperate with one another because they *feel* alike (mechanical solidarity), but because they *depend* on one another's activities for their own survival (organic solidarity). In the past, societies tolerated little diversity in thinking and attitudes, for their unity depended on similar thinking. In contrast, modern societies tolerate many differences among people but still manage to work as a whole. While both past and present societies are based on social solidarity, the types of solidarity are remarkably different in each case.

Gemeinschaft and Gesellschaft.   Ferdinand Tönnies (1887, 1988) also tackled this question. He, too, saw major shifts in social structure and was alarmed at the new type of society he saw emerging. Tönnies used the term **Gemeinschaft** (Guh-MINE-shoft), "intimate community," to describe the traditional type of society in which life is intimate, a community in which everyone knows everyone else and people share a sense of togetherness. In such a society people toe the line because they are acutely sensitive to the opinions of others and know that if they deviate, others will gossip and damage their reputation. Although their lives are sharply controlled by the opinions of others, they draw comfort from being part of an intimate group.

Tönnies saw that industrialization was tearing at this intimate fabric of village life, that a new type of society was emerging. In this new society, made up increasingly of strangers and impersonal, short-term relationships, personal ties, family connections, lifelong friendships, and giving aid to one another were growing less important. Instead individual accomplishments and self-interests were being emphasized. Tönnies called this new type of society **Gesellschaft** (guh-ZELL-shoft), "impersonal association." As much as anyone might hate it, in *Gemeinschaft* society informal mechanisms such as

K.P.: Ferdinand Tönnies

CNN: The Amish People

mechanical solidarity: a collective consciousness that people experience as a result of performing the same or similar tasks

division of labor: the splitting of society's tasks into specialties

organic solidarity: a collective consciousness based on the interdependence brought about by the division of labor

Gemeinschaft: a type of society in which life is intimate; a community in which everyone knows everyone else and people share a sense of togetherness

Gesellschaft: a type of society dominated by impersonal relationships, individual accomplishments, and self-interest

Modern societies, in which people live and work among strangers, are largely Gesellschaft in nature. Many would argue that even though the United States and France are both highly industrialized nations, the United States is more thoroughly Gesellschaft than France. There, many people continue to live in small rural villages, where they gather to socialize in neighborhood cafes. Such cafes represent Gemeinschaft—or intimate community—in microcosm.

gossip had been effective in controlling people. In this new world of *Gesellschaft,* however, gossip was of little use, and to keep people in line society had to depend on more *formal* agencies, such as the police and courts.

In Sum.   Both Durkheim and Tönnies documented a fundamental change in the social structure. What they regretfully noted was the passing of a major form of social life, one unlikely ever to be seen again. Note that whether the terms used are *Gemeinschaft* and *Gesellschaft* or mechanical solidarity and organic solidarity, they indicate that social structure sets limits on what we do, feel, and think. In short, social structure is at the basis of what kind of people we become. The Perspectives box on page 100 describes one of the few remaining *Gemeinschaft* societies in the United States.

THE MICROSOCIOLOGICAL PERSPECTIVE: SOCIAL INTERACTION IN EVERYDAY LIFE

As noted earlier, the macrosociological approach stresses the broad features of society. In contrast, the microsociological approach has a narrower focus, placing its emphasis on face-to-face *social interaction,* or what people do when they are in the presence of one another.

Symbolic Interaction

For symbolic interactionists, the most significant part of life in society is social interaction. They are especially interested in the symbols that people use to define their worlds. They want to know how people look at things and how that, in turn, affects their behavior.

Stereotypes in Everyday Life.   When you first meet someone, you cannot help noticing certain highly visible and distinctive features, such as the person's sex, race, age, and physical appearance. Despite your best intentions, your first impressions are shaped by the assumptions you make about such characteristics (Snyder 1991). Those assumptions not only affect your ideas about the person, but also how you act toward that person. Even more significantly, your behavior in turn shapes the way that person acts toward you.

To test this hypothesis, Mark Snyder (1991), a psychologist, gave a number of college men a Polaroid snapshot of a woman, supposedly taken just moments before, and told them that they would be introduced to her after they talked with her on the telephone. Actually, the photograph, which showed either a physically attractive or unattractive woman, had been prepared before the experiment began. The one given to the subject had been chosen at random.

Stereotypes of physical attractiveness came into play even before each man spoke to the woman he was going to meet. As he gave each man the photograph, Snyder asked him what he thought the woman would be like. The men who had been given the photograph of an attractive woman said they expected to meet a poised, humorous, outgoing woman. The men who had been given a photo of an unattractive woman described the person they were going to meet as awkward, serious, and unsociable.

These stereotypes then influenced the men's behavior. As each man talked on the telephone to the woman he was expecting to meet, the stereotype affected his style of getting acquainted. Men who had been shown the photograph of an attractive woman were warm, friendly, humorous, and highly animated. Those who had been shown the photograph of an unattractive woman were cold, reserved, and humorless.

These differences, in turn, changed the women's behavior. Those who (unknown to them) were believed to be attractive responded to the men in a warm, friendly, and sociable manner, while those who were perceived as physically unattractive became

L. Obj. 7: State the key assumptions of the symbolic interactionist perspective regarding social life.

Speaker Sug. #2: A symbolic interactionist to talk about how research is conducted at the microsociological level.

Essay #5

TR#3: Self-Fulfilling Stereotypes

Speaker Sug. #3: A cartoonist who draws satirical or political cartoons to discuss use of exaggerated traits (stereotypes).

CDQ 12: How do our first impressions about a person affect our ideas about the person? How we will act toward the person? The way that person subsequently will act toward us?

PERSPECTIVES
Cultural Diversity in U.S. Society

The Amish—*Gemeinschaft* Communities in a *Gesellschaft* Society

American society exhibits all the characteristics Ferdinand Tönnies identified as those of a *Gesellschaft* society. Impersonal associations pervade everyday life. Local, state, and federal governments regulate many activities. Impersonal corporations hire people not based on long-term, meaningful relationships, but on their value to the bottom line. Similarly, when it comes to firing workers, the bottom line takes precedence over personal relationships. And, perhaps even more significant, millions of Americans do not even know their neighbors.

Within the United States, a handful of small communities exhibit characteristics that depart from those of the larger society. One such example is the Old Order Amish, followers of a sect that broke away from the Swiss-German Mennonite church in the late 1600s, settling in Pennsylvania around 1727. Today, more than 130,000 Old Order Amish live in the United States. The largest concentration, about 14,000, reside in Lancaster County, Pennsylvania. The Amish can also be found in about twenty other states and in Ontario, Canada, but 70 percent live in just three states: Pennsylvania, Ohio, and Indiana. The Amish, who believe that birth control is wrong, have doubled in size in just the past two decades.

To the nearly five million tourists that pass through Lancaster County each year, the quiet pastures and almost identical white farmhouses, simple barns, horse- or mule-drawn carts, and clothes calmly flapping on lines to dry convey a sense of peace and wholeness reminiscent of another era. Just sixty-five miles from Philadelphia, "Amish country" is, in many ways, a world away.

The Amish faith rests upon separation from the world, taking Christ's Sermon on the Mount literally, and obedience to the church's teachings and leaders. This rejection of worldly concerns, Donald Kraybill writes in *The Riddle of Amish Culture,* "provides the foundation of such Amish values as humility, faithfulness, thrift, tradition, communal goals, joy of work, a slow-paced life, and trust in divine providence."

The village life that Tönnies identified as fostering *Gemeinschaft* communities—and which he correctly predicted was fast being lost to industrialization—is very much alive among the Amish. The Amish make their decisions in weekly meetings, where, by consensus, they develop a set of rules, or *ordnung,* that guide their behavior.

Religion and the discipline that it calls for is the glue that holds these communities together. Brotherly love and the welfare of the community are paramount values. Most Amish farm on plots of one hundred acres or less, keeping their farms small so that horses can be used instead of tractors and neighbors can pitch in with the chores. In this way, intimacy—a sense of community—is maintained.

The Amish are bound by countless other communal ties, including language (a dialect of German known as Pennsylvania Dutch), a distinctive style of plain dress that has remained unchanged for almost three hundred years, and church-sponsored schools. Nearly all Amish marry, and divorce is forbidden. The family is a vital ingredient in Amish life; all major events take place in the home, including weddings and funerals, worship services, even births. Most Amish children attend church schools only until the age of thirteen. To go to school beyond the eighth grade would expose them to "worldly concerns" and give them information considered of no value to farm life. The Amish pay local, state, and federal taxes, but they pool their resources to fund their own welfare system, and therefore do not pay Social Security taxes. They won the right to be left out of the Social Security system only after drawn-out court battles. They believe that all violence is bad, even in personal self-defense, and register as conscientious objectors during times of war.

The Amish cannot, of course, resist all change. Instead, they attempt to adapt to change in ways that will cause the least harm to their core values. Because of land shortages and encroaching urbanization, some young Amish men cannot find farms. Some have turned to farm-related businesses, cottage industries, and woodworking trades. They go to great lengths to avoid leaving the home. The Amish believe that when the husband works away from the home, all aspects of life, from the marital relationship to the care of the children, seem to change—certainly an excellent sociological insight. They also believe that if a man receives a paycheck he will think that his work is of more value than his wife's. For the Amish, intimate, or *Gemeinschaft,* society is absolutely essential to their way of life.

Source: Based on Bender 1990; Hostetler 1980; Jones 1990; Kephart 1987; Kraybill 1989; Raymond 1990; Ruth 1990; Ziegenhals 1991.

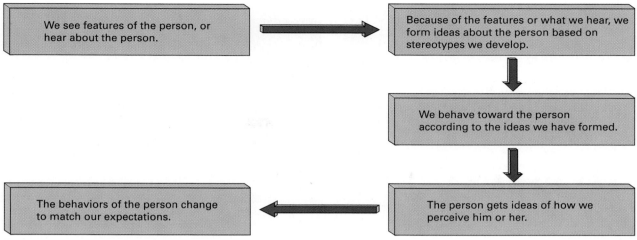

FIGURE 4.1   Self-Fulfilling Stereotypes

cool, reserved, and humorless. In short, *stereotypes tend to bring out the very kinds of behavior that fit the stereotype.*

A number of experiments have been conducted to see how stereotypes of gender, race, ability, and intelligence influence people (Snyder 1991). In one, a welding instructor in a vocational training center was told that five men in his training program had unusually high aptitude. Although the five had actually been chosen at random and knew nothing about the experiment, their performances changed radically. They were absent less often than other workers, learned the basics of welding in about half the usual time, and scored ten points higher than the other trainees on a welding test. The difference was noted even by the other trainees, who singled these five out as their preferred coworkers. The men were no different in their initial abilities, but the instructor's behavior brought about a change in their performance.

Chapter 17 explores in detail the work of two psychologists at Harvard University, Robert Rosenthal and Lenore Jacobson (1968). Let's just note here that they told teachers at an elementary school that certain of their students were exceptional and could be expected to show dramatic improvement in intellectual achievement during the coming school year. The children had actually been chosen at random. But the same phenomenon occurred. The "gifted" children made a dramatic improvement on their tests, outperforming their "less gifted" classmates.

In short, stereotypes that people hold influence their expectations and behavior which, in turn, *produce behaviors that conform to the stereotypes.* (see Figure 4.1)

Personal Space.   Another area of interest to symbolic interactionists is how people use personal space. Each of us surrounds ourselves with a "personal bubble" that we go to great lengths to protect. We open the bubble to intimates—to close friends, children, parents, and so on—but are careful to keep most people out of this space. In the hall, we might walk with books clasped in front of us (a strategy often chosen by females); we carefully line up at the drinking fountain, making certain there is space between us (we don't want to touch the person in front of us, and we don't want to be touched by the person behind us).

At times we extend our personal space. In the library, for example, you may place your coat on the chair next to you—claiming that space for yourself even though you are not using it. If you want to really extend your space, you might even spread books in front of the other chairs, keeping the whole table to yourself by giving the impression that others have just stepped away.

L. Obj. 8: Explain how stereotypes influence an individual's expectations and behavior.

Project 2

Among the many aspects of social life that sociologists with a microsociological focus study is personal space. What do you see in common in the above two photos?

K.P.: Edward Hall

Anthropologist Edward Hall (1959, 1966) studied the use of personal space in several cultures. He found that the amount of space people prefer varies from one culture to another. South Americans, for example, like to be closer when they speak to others than do persons reared in the United States. Hall (1959) recounts a conversation with a man from South America who had attended one of his lectures.

> He came to the front of the class at the end of the lecture to talk over a number of points made in the preceding hour. . . . We started out facing each other and as he talked I became dimly aware that he was standing a little too close and that I was beginning to back up. Fortunately I was able to suppress my first impulse and remain stationary because there was nothing to communicate aggression in his behavior except the conversational distance. His voice was eager, his manner intent, the set of his body communicated only interest and eagerness to talk. . . .
>
> By experimenting I was able to observe that as I moved away slightly, there was an associated shift in the pattern of interaction. He had more trouble expressing himself. If I shifted to where I felt comfortable (about twenty-one inches), he looked somewhat puzzled and hurt, almost as though he were saying, "Why is he acting that way? Here I am doing everything I can to talk to him in a friendly manner and he suddenly withdraws. Have I done anything wrong? Said something that I shouldn't?" Having ascertained that distance had a direct effect on his conversation, I stood my ground, letting him set the distance.

As you can see, in spite of his training and extensive knowledge of other cultures, Hall still felt uncomfortable in this conversation. He first interpreted the invasion of his personal space as possible aggression, for people get close (and jut out their chins and chests) when they are hostile. But when he realized that was not the case, Hall resisted his impulse to move.

After Hall (1969) analyzed situations like this, he observed that Americans use four different "distance zones."

1. *Intimate distance* This is the zone that the South American unwittingly invaded. It extends to about 18 inches from our bodies. We reserve this space for lovemaking and wrestling, comforting and protecting.
2. *Personal distance* This zone extends from 18 inches to 4 feet. We reserve it for friends and acquaintances and ordinary conversations. This is the zone in which Hall would have preferred to conduct his conversation with the South American.
3. *Social distance* This zone, extending out from us about 4 to 12 feet, marks impersonal or formal relationships. We use this zone for such things as job interviews.

4. *Public distance*   This zone, extending beyond 12 feet, marks an even more formal relationship. It is used to separate dignitaries and public speakers from the general public.

Let us now turn to dramaturgy, a special area of symbolic interactionism.

Dramaturgy: The Presentation of Self in Everyday Life

It was their big day, two years in the making.

Jennifer Mackey wore a white wedding gown adorned with an 11-foot train and 24,000 seed pearls that she and her mother had sewn onto the dress. Next to her at the altar in Lexington, Kentucky, stood her intended, Jeffrey Degler, in black tie. They said their vows, then turned to gaze for a moment at the four hundred guests.

That's when groomsman Daniel Mackey collapsed. As the shocked organist struggled to play Mendelssohn's "Wedding March," Mr. Mackey's unconscious body was dragged away, his feet striking—loudly—every step of the altar stairs.

"I couldn't believe he would die at my wedding," the bride said (Hughes 1990).

Sociologist Erving Goffman (1922–1982) added a new twist to symbolic interactionism when he developed **dramaturgy** (or dramaturgical analysis). By this term he meant that social life was like drama or the stage. Goffman stressed that birth ushers us onto the stage of everyday life, that our socialization (discussed in detail in the previous chapter) really consists of learning to perform on that stage.

Everyday life, he said, involves playing our assigned roles. We have **front stages** on which to perform them, as did Jennifer and Jeffrey. (By the way, Daniel Mackey didn't really die—he had just passed out from the excitement of it all.) But we don't have to look at weddings to find front stages. Everyday life is filled with them. Where your teacher lectures is a front stage. And if you make an announcement at the dinner table, you are using a front stage. In fact, you spend most of your time on front stages, for a front stage is wherever you deliver your lines. We also have **back stages,** places where we can let our hair down. When you close the bathroom or bedroom door for privacy, for example, you are entering a back stage. Similarly, a "teachers' lounge" is a back stage, where teachers can relax from their classroom performances.

The same setting can serve as both a back and a front stage. For example, when you get into your car by yourself and look over your hair in the mirror or check your makeup, you are using the car as a back stage. But when you wave at friends or give that familiar gesture to someone who has just cut in front of you in traffic, you are using your car as a front stage.

Everyday life provides many roles. A person may be a daughter or a son, a student, a teenager, a shopper, a worker, a date, and so on. While a role lays down the basic outline for a performance, it allows a great deal of freedom. The particular emphasis or interpretation that an individual gives a role, the person's "style," is known as **role performance.** Take your role as son or daughter as an example. You may play the role of ideal daughter or son, being very respectful, coming home at the hours your parents set, and so forth. Or that description may not even come close to your particular role performance.

Ordinarily our roles are sufficiently separated that conflict between them is minimized. Occasionally, however, what is expected of us in one role is incompatible with what is expected of us in another role. This problem, known as **role conflict,** makes us very uncomfortable, as illustrated in the diagram below on role strain and role conflict, in which family, friendship, student, and work roles come clashing together. Usually, however, we manage to avoid role conflict by segregating our roles, which in some instances may require a high-wire balancing act.

Sometimes the *same* role presents inherent conflict, a problem known as **role strain.** Suppose that you are exceptionally prepared for a particular class assignment. When your instructor asks an unusually difficult question, you may find yourself knowing the answer when no one else does. If you want to raise your hand, yet don't want to

K.P.: Erving Goffman

L. Obj. 9: Name the sociologist who originated the dramaturgical perspective and outline the key components of this view of everyday life.

CDQ 13: What are your "front stages" on which you are expected to perform? What are your "back stages" where you can let your hair down?

CDQ 14: Does everyone experience role conflict at one time or another? What about role strain?

TR#4: Role Strain and Role Conflict

dramaturgy: an approach, pioneered by Erving Goffman, analyzing social life in terms of drama or the stage; also called dramaturgical analysis

front stage: where performances are given

back stage: where people rest from their performances, discuss their presentations, and plan future performances

role performance: the ways in which someone performs a role within the limits that it provides; showing a particular "style" or "personality"

role conflict: conflicts that someone feels *between* roles because the expectations attached to one role are incompatible with the expectations of another role.

role strain: conflicts that someone feels *within* a role

make your fellow students look bad, you will experience role strain. The difference between role conflict and role strain is that role conflict is conflict *between* roles, while role strain is conflict *within* a role.

At the center of our performances in everyday life is the self and how we want others to think of us. We use our roles to communicate to others ideas that we want them to form about us. Goffman calls these efforts to manage the impressions that others receive of us **impression management.**

To communicate information about the self, we use three types of **sign-vehicles:** the social setting, our appearance, and our manner. The **social setting** is the place where the action unfolds. This is where the curtain goes up on your personal performances, where you find yourself on stage playing parts and delivering lines. A social setting might be an office, dorm, living room, church, gym, or bar. It is wherever you interact with others. Your social setting includes **scenery,** the furnishings you use to communicate messages, such as desks, blackboards, scoreboards, couches, and so on. If you allow yourself to be seen in certain places but not in others, you are using settings to manage the impressions others receive about you.

The second sign-vehicle is **appearance,** or how we look when we play our roles. Appearance includes **props,** which are like scenery, but they decorate the person rather than the setting. The teacher has books, lecture notes, and chalk, while the football player wears a special costume called a uniform. Although few of us carry around a football, we all use makeup, hairstyles, and clothing to communicate messages about ourselves. Props and other aspects of appearance serve as a sort of grease for everyday life: By letting us know what to expect from others, they tell us how we should react. Think of the messages that props communicate. Some people use clothing to say that they are college students, others that they are old; some that they are clergy, others that they are prostitutes. Similarly, people use different brands of cigarettes, liquor, and automobiles to convey messages of the self.

The third sign-vehicle is **manner,** the attitudes we demonstrate as we play our roles. We use manner to communicate information about our feelings and moods. By communicating anger or indifference, sincerity or good humor, for example, we indicate to others what they can expect of us as we play our roles. To try to make certain that the social setting is correct, that our manner is what people expect, and that our appearance is right is a characteristic of all role players. It becomes especially apparent,

---

impression management: the term used by Erving Goffman to describe people's efforts to control the impressions that others receive of them

sign-vehicles: the term used by Goffman to describe the ways in which a person communicates information about the self: social setting, appearance, and manner

social setting: the place where the action of everyday life unfolds

scenery: the furnishings of a social setting that people use to communicate messages about the self

appearance: how an individual looks when playing a role

props: personal items used to communicate messages about the self

manner: the attitudes that people show as they play their roles

---

FIGURE 4.2   Role Strain and Role Conflict

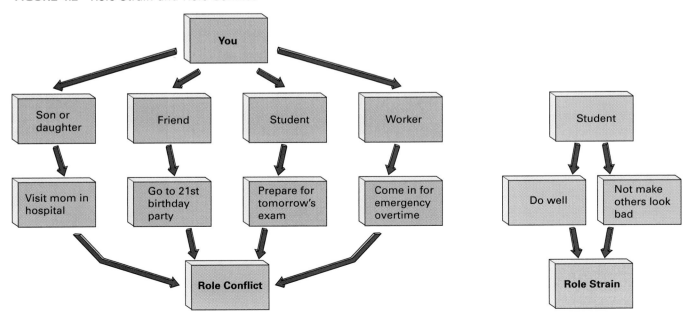

however, when we look at teenagers who are just beginning to date. For some reason, they are likely to take several showers a day, to stand before a mirror for hours combing and recombing their hair, and to change and rechange their clothing. In spite of our best efforts to manage the impressions that others receive of us, however, we sometimes fail. One of my favorite television scenes is of the character Molly Dodd trying to impress a date. She went to the "powder room," a backstage fix-up place reserved for women, where she did the usual things. Satisfied that she looked good, she made a grand entrance, with exaggerated movements and an expectant smile on her face—all the while trailing a long piece of toilet paper from her shoe. The scene is humorous because it highlights the fact that an incongruity of elements creates **embarrassment,** which in dramaturgical terms is a feeling that results when a performance fails.

To show ourselves as adept role players is a chief requirement for receiving positive recognition from others, something that we all covet. To accomplish this, said Goffman, we often use **teamwork,** whereby two or more people who are interested in the success of a performance work together to make certain that the performance goes off as planned. When a performance doesn't come off quite right, however, it may require **face-saving behavior.** We may, for example, ignore someone's flaws in performance, which Goffman defines as **tact.** Suppose your teacher is about to make an important point. Suppose also that her lecturing has been outstanding and the class is hanging on every word. Just as she pauses for emphasis, her stomach lets out a loud growl. She might then use a face-saving technique by remarking, "I was so busy preparing for class that I didn't get breakfast this morning." It is more likely, however, that both class and teacher will simply ignore the sound, both giving the impression that no one heard a thing—a face-saving technique called **studied nonobservance.** This allows the teacher to make the point, or as Goffman would say, it allows the performance to go on.

The following incident illustrates how critical role playing is to our success in life:

> Jim went to the college doctor with some mild complaint. While Jim was talking to him, the doctor opened a medical book and looked up the symptoms. He said that Jim probably had so and so, but that he might have such and such. Then the doctor opened another book, checked the index, and said he would give Jim a prescription for a certain medicine as it would cover either illness.
>
> Jim nodded, took the prescription, and left. He couldn't help wondering about this doctor, however. He had never seen a physician do that. He shrugged the feeling off, however, pleased that the doctor had also read to him the warnings about the drug.

Perhaps this physician was competent, but sufficiently lacking in confidence to want to double-check his conclusions in medical books. In fact physicians often face the same problem of not knowing for certain what ailment a patient really has, but to do their double-checking they generally make an excuse to leave the room so as to do it in private. Giving the impression of confidence is at least as important as competence—and is one of the chief lessons students learn in medical school (Haas and Shaffir 1993).

Actually, this doctor was not competent. Jim later went to him with a sliver embedded fairly deeply in his thigh.

> He looked at Jim's thigh and agreed that he had a sliver there all right. He then recommended that Jim go see a surgeon in town. Jim replied that he had come to have the doctor take care of it. The doctor said that to remove the sliver would require surgery and that he didn't do surgery. Jim replied that it wouldn't really be surgery, just removing a sliver. The doctor agreed to try.
>
> He then placed a bright light above Jim's thigh, sterilized the area, and surrounded it with gauze—just as one would expect a doctor to do. As he tried to remove the sliver, however, the doctor began to sweat profusely. Digging deep, but only able to retrieve part of the sliver, he announced that he could go no further, that Jim would

CDQ 15: Why is showing ourselves as adept role players a chief requirement for receiving positive recognition from others?

embarrassment: in dramaturgical terms, the feelings that result when a performance fails

teamwork: the collaboration of two or more persons interested in the success of a performance to manage impressions jointly

face-saving behavior: techniques used to salvage a performance that is going sour

tact: in dramaturgical terms, ignoring a flaw in someone's performance

studied nonobservance: a face-saving technique in which people give the impression that they are unaware of a flaw in someone's performance

have to go to the other doctor. Jim reassured him that he could handle it, saying that he had every confidence in him. The doctor continued and, after some difficulty, managed to remove the sliver.

This doctor was eventually fired, for he had violated basic expectations: that physicians not only be competent but also *show* competence (Haas and Shaffir 1991).

Ethnomethodology: Uncovering Background Assumptions

L. Obj. 10: State the major assumptions of ethnomethodology and of the social construction of reality.

As discussed in Chapter 1, symbolic interactionists stress that the events of life do not come with built-in meanings. Rather, we give meaning to things by classifying them; we interpret what happens to us by placing objects and events into frameworks provided by our culture.

Ethnomethodologists study how people make sense of everyday life. They try to uncover people's basic assumptions as they interpret their world. To better understand **ethnomethodology,** consider the word's three basic components. "Ethno" means folk or people; "method" means how people do something; "ology" means "the study of." Putting them together, then, *ethno/method/ology* means "the study of how people do things." Specifically, ethnomethodology is the study of how people use common-sense understandings to make sense out of their lives.

Let us suppose that when Jim had the sliver in his thigh the college doctor had not only suggested that he go to another physician, but also, taking out a pair of scissors, that he give Jim a haircut. That would have violated basic assumptions about what doctors are supposed to do. Although this physician did not do things quite properly, he did at least listen to his patient's medical problems and prescribe medicines. We all expect that of doctors. Haircuts, on the other hand, are simply not part of our expectations.

CDQ 16: Why would we be shocked and surprised if a physician gave us a haircut? (Except as preparation for brain surgery, of course!)

K.P.: Harold Garfinkel

Our basic expectations about the way life is and the way things ought to work (what ethnomethodologists call **background assumptions**) underlie our daily lives. Exactly how these background assumptions work is what ethnomethodologists try to discover. The founder of ethnomethodology, sociologist Harold Garfinkel, conducted some interesting exercises to get at these "folk" ways of making sense out of life. These common understandings of the way society ought to operate lie so deep in our consciousness that we are seldom aware of them, for almost everyone fulfills them unquestioningly. Thus, your doctor does not offer you a haircut, even if he or she is good at cutting hair and you need one!

Project 3

To uncover our background assumptions (also called basic rules), Garfinkel (1967) asked his students to act as though they did not understand the basic rules of social life. Some tried to bargain with supermarket clerks; others would inch closer to people and stare directly at them. They were met with surprise, bewilderment, even anger.

One of the more interesting exercises that Garfinkel's students conducted was to act as though they were boarders in their own homes. When they returned from class, they addressed their parents as "Mr." and "Mrs.," asked permission to use the bathroom, sat stiffly, were extremely courteous, and spoke only when spoken to. The other family members were stupefied (Garfinkel 1967).

> They vigorously sought to make the strange actions intelligible and to restore the situation to normal appearances. Reports (by the students) were filled with accounts of astonishment, bewilderment, shock, anxiety, embarrassment, and anger, and with charges by various family members that the student was mean, inconsiderate, selfish, nasty, or impolite. Family members demanded explanations: What's the matter? What's gotten into you? . . . Are you sick? . . . Are you out of your mind or are you just stupid?

ethnomethodology: the study of how people use background assumptions to make sense of life

background assumptions: deeply embedded common understandings, or basic rules, concerning our view of the world and of how people ought to act

In another exercise, students took words and phrases literally (Garfinkel 1967). For example, when one student asked his girlfriend what she meant when she said that she had a flat tire, she became hostile.

What do you mean, "What do you mean?"? A flat tire is a flat tire. That is what I meant. Nothing special. What a crazy question!

Another conversation went like this.

Acquaintance: How are you?
Student: How am I in regard to what? My health, my finances, my schoolwork, my peace of mind, my . . . ?
Acquaintance (red in the face): Look! I was just trying to be polite. Frankly, I don't give a damn how you are.

Students who are given the assignment to break background assumptions can be highly creative. The children of one of my students were surprised one morning when they came down for breakfast to find a sheet spread across the living room floor. On it were dishes, silverware, burning candles—and ice cream. They, too, wondered what was going on—but they dug eagerly into the ice cream before their mother could change her mind.

Another sociologist, Robert Lauer, also asked his students to put Garfinkel's ideas into practice. One of them gave new meaning to the phrase "laundering money" by going to a local laundromat and putting dollar bills into the washing machine and dryer. Fellow patrons didn't say much; they just called the police. It turned out that there is no law against washing money, but this student nonetheless became rather eager to explain just what he was doing.

In Sum. Ethnomethodologists explore background assumptions, a basic part of our taken-for-granted world that underlie our behavior and are violated only with risk. They are an essential part of the social structure that, deeply embedded in our minds, give us basic directions for everyday life. Although we are seldom aware of how extensively our background assumptions guide us through our daily lives, they are constantly present.

The Social Construction of Reality

Usually we assume that reality is something "out there" that hits us in the face. *It* is something that independently exists, and we must deal with it. Symbolic interactionists, however, point out that we define our own reality and then live within those definitions. Our definitions are so important that what we define as real is, for us, real. As sociologist W. I. Thomas said, in what has become known as the **Thomas theorem,** "If people define situations as real, they are real in their consequences."

Consider the following example:

I was driving a cab in St. Louis to gather data for my dissertation. To understand the cab drivers' world better, I participated in their activities both on the job and after work. One of their favorite after-work activities was craps, a dice game played for money. They played this game almost every night, using the used-car lot next door to the cab headquarters.

Although these cabbies knew exactly what the odds were for any combination on the dice, they would change their bets depending on *who* was shooting and with *whom* they were betting. For example, if a shooter was "hot" (making several winning points in a row), a cabbie might refuse a bet offered by that shooter, yet make the same bet with someone else that the shooter would not make his point (Henslin 1967).

The belief, illogical to most of us, that the person with whom you place bets can influence the dice, was real to these men. Although the same numbers would make a bettor win or lose, if a shooter was "hot" many would not bet directly against him. Yet they would make the identical bet with someone else—and be especially eager to take a bet if *that* person had been losing.

The cabbies also used a variety of other techniques to try to control the dice. They would throw the dice "hard" if they wanted a higher total, "soft" if they wanted a lower number. Shooters also called for their numbers, saying for example, "Six it!"

Essay #6

CDQ 17: Is reality something "out there" that hits us in the face?

K.P.: W. I. Thomas

Thomas theorem: an interpretation of the social construction of reality summarized in William I. Thomas's statement: "If people define situations as real, they are real in their consequences."

or "Eight it, dice," usually snapping their fingers at the instant they uttered the phrase. If a shooter dropped a die, he always set the dice down, then picked them up before throwing. To fail to do this, they believed, would result in a bad throw.

As far as these cabbies were concerned, gestures and words affected the dice. *Objective* reality is one thing, for the dice will follow odds that can be calculated precisely. The men knew these odds. But *subjective* reality (their definition of the situation) overrode these considerations, and they changed their bets accordingly.

CDQ 18: Do you believe that germs pose a threat to your well-being because you know for a fact that germs are real or because you were taught that they were real?

While you may not shoot craps and may not believe that gestures can influence the outcome of a throw of dice, your life, too, is affected by the **social construction of reality.** That is, what you believe to be real depends on what you have learned in society. For example, it is likely that you believe that germs pose a threat to your well-being and that you therefore take some precautions to avoid exposure to them. Your perception and behavior result not from the fact that germs are real but *because you grew up in a society that teaches they are real.* It is not the reality of microbes that impresses itself upon us, but society that impresses the reality of microbes upon us. To better see what this means, consider the following incident:

> On a visit to Morocco, in Northern Africa, I decided to buy a watermelon. When I indicated to the street vendor that the knife he was going to use to cut the watermelon was dirty (encrusted with filth would be more apt), he was very obliging. He immediately bent down and began to wash the knife in a puddle on the street. I shuddered as I looked at the passing burros, freely defecating and urinating as they went. Quickly, I indicated by gesture that I preferred my melon uncut after all.

For that vendor, germs did not exist. For me, they did. And each of us acted according to our definition of the situation.

Microbes, of course, *objectively* exist, and whether or not germs are part of our thought world makes no difference to whether we are infected by them. Our behavior, however, does not depend on the *objective* existence of something but rather on our *subjective interpretation,* on our definition of reality.

We are influenced by our own society's definitions to such an extent that we are seldom aware of how extensively our actions depend on them. The definitions that we learn from our culture underlie not only what we do but also what we perceive, feel, and think. Let me provide an example common to our society, although one that is difficult for males to identify with.

A gynecological nurse, Mae Biggs, and I did research on pelvic examinations. Reviewing about 14,000 cases, we looked at how the medical profession constructs social reality in order to define the examination of the vagina as nonsexual (Henslin and Biggs 1993). This desexualization is accomplished by painstakingly controlling the sign-vehicles—the setting, appearance, and manner.

The pelvic examination unfolds much as a stage play does. I will use "he" to refer to the physician because only male physicians participated in this study. Perhaps the results would be different with female gynecologists.

> *Scene one* (Person)   In this scene, the doctor responds to the patient as a person. He maintains eye contact with her, calls her by name, and discusses her problems in a professional manner. If he decides that a vaginal examination is necessary, he tells a nurse, "Pelvic in room 1." By this statement, he is announcing that a major change will occur in the next scene.
> *Scene two* (From Person to Pelvic)   This scene is the depersonalizing stage. In line with the doctor's announcement, the patient begins the transition from a "person" to a "pelvic." The doctor leaves the room, and a female nurse enters to help the patient make the transition. The nurse prepares the "props" for the coming examination and answers any questions the woman might have.

the social construction of reality: what people define as real because of their background assumptions and life experiences

What occurs at this point is essential for the social construction of reality, for *the doctor's absence at this point removes even the suggestion of sexuality.* The act of undressing in front of him could suggest either a striptease or intimacy, thus undermining the reality in the process so carefully being defined, that of nonsexuality.

The patient also wants to remove any hint of sexuality in the coming interaction, and during this scene she may express concern about what to do with her panties, perhaps muttering to the nurse, "I don't want him to see these." Most women solve the problem by either slipping their panties under their clothes or placing them in their purse.

Scene three (Pelvic)   This scene opens with the doctor entering the room. Before him is a woman lying on a table, her feet in stirrups, her knees tightly together, and her body covered by a drape sheet. The doctor seats himself on a low stool before the woman, tells her, "Let your knees fall apart" (rather than the sexually loaded, "Spread your legs"), and begins the examination.

The drape sheet is critical in this process of desexualization, for it *dissociates the pelvic area from the person:* The physician, bending forward and with the drape sheet above his head, can see only the vagina, not the patient's face. The vagina is thus dramaturgically transformed into an object for analysis, dissociated from the individual. Similarly, if the doctor examines the patient's breasts, he also dissociates them from her person by examining them one at a time, with a towel covering the unexamined breast. Like the vagina, each breast becomes an isolated unit dissociated from the person.

In this critical scene, the patient cooperates in being an object, becoming for all practical purposes a pelvis to be examined. She withdraws eye contact, from the doctor for certain but usually from the nurse as well, is likely to stare at the wall or at the ceiling, and avoids initiating conversation.

Scene four (From Pelvic to Person)   In this scene the patient becomes "repersonalized." The doctor has left the examining room; the patient dresses and takes care of any problems with her hair and makeup. Her reemergence as person is indicated by such statements as, "My dress isn't too wrinkled, is it?", indicating a need for reassurance from the nurse that the metamorphosis from "pelvic" back to "person" has been completed satisfactorily.

Scene five (Person)   In this scene, the patient is once again treated as a person rather than an object. The doctor makes eye contact with her and addresses her by name. She, too, makes eye contact with the doctor, and the usual middle-class American interaction patterns are followed. She has been fully restored.

To an outsider to our culture, the custom of single and married women going to a male stranger for a vaginal examination might seem strange. But not to us. We assume that such behavior is normal, and females in our society are encouraged to participate in this process *because they have been taught that such examinations are nonsexual in nature.* To achieve that definition of reality is a social process, brought about by such techniques as those just outlined.

In Sum.   It is not just pelvic examinations, germs, and craps that make up our definitions of reality. Rather, *all of our reality is socially constructed.* As sociologists Peter Berger and Thomas Luckmann (1967) point out, the members of a society agree on definitions of what is going on and then cooperate to maintain those definitions. Symbolic interactionists stress that this is actually what society consists of—our definitions and our interactions based on them.

THE NEED FOR BOTH MACROSOCIOLOGY AND MICROSOCIOLOGY

As noted earlier in this chapter, to understand social life adequately, we need both microsociology and macrosociology. Each makes a vital contribution to our understanding of human behavior, and our understanding would be vastly incomplete without one or the other.

To illustrate this point, consider the research on two groups of high school boys conducted by sociologist William Chambliss (1993). Both groups attended Hannibal High School. One group was composed of eight promising young students, boys who came from "good" families and were perceived by the community as "going somewhere." Chambliss calls this group the "Saints." The other group consisted of six

K.P.: Peter Berger

K.P.: Thomas Luckmann

L. Obj. 11: Indicate why both macrosociology and microsociology are necessary for a full understanding of social life.

CDQ 19: If you were a sociologist conducting a study on juvenile offenses, would you use microsociology, macrosociology, or both? Why?

lower-class boys who were seen as going down a dead-end road. Chambliss calls this group the "Roughnecks."

Both groups were seriously delinquent. Both skipped school, drank a lot, and committed criminal acts, especially fighting and vandalism. The Saints were actually the more delinquent. They were truant much more often, and they committed more acts of vandalism. Yet it was the Saints who had the good reputation, while the Roughnecks were seen by teachers, the police, and the general community as no good and heading for trouble.

These reputations followed the boys throughout life. Seven of the eight Saints went on to graduate from college. Three studied for advanced degrees: One finished law school and became active in state politics, one finished medical school and set up a practice near Hanibal, and one went on to gain a Ph.D. The four other college graduates entered managerial or executive training with large firms. After the parents of one Saint divorced, he failed to graduate from high school on time and had to repeat his senior year. Although this boy tried to go to college by attending night school, he never finished. He was unemployed the last time Chambliss saw him.

In contrast, only four of the Roughnecks even finished high school. Two of these boys did exceptionally well in sports and received athletic scholarships to college. They both graduated from college and became high school coaches. Of the two others who graduated from high school, one became a small-time gambler and the other disappeared "up north" where he was last reported to be driving a truck. Of the two who did not complete high school, each was last heard of serving time in state penitentiaries for separate murders.

To understand what happened to the Saints and the Roughnecks, we need to grasp *both* social structure and social interaction. That is, we need both macrosociology and microsociology. Using macrosociology, we can place these boys within the larger framework of the American social class system. This context reveals how opportunities open or close to people depending on their membership in the middle or lower social class, and how different goals are instilled in youngsters as they grow up in these vastly different groups. We can then use microsociology to follow their everyday lives. We can see how the Saints used their "good" reputations to skip classes repeatedly and how their access to automobiles allowed them to transfer their troublemaking to different communities and thus prevent damage to their local reputations. In contrast, lacking access to automobiles, the Roughnecks were highly visible. Their lawbreaking activities, limited to a small area, readily came to the attention of the community. Microsociology also reveals how their respective reputations opened doors of opportunity to the first group of boys while closing them to the other.

Thus we need both kinds of sociology, and both will be stressed in the following chapters.

SUMMARY

1. Sociologists analyze social structure because it forms an envelope around us, establishing limits on our behavior. The major components of social structure are culture, social class, statuses, roles, groups, and institutions. Sociologists use two levels of analysis. In macrosociology the focus is placed on large-scale features of social structure, while in microsociology the focus is on social interaction. Functionalists and conflict theorists tend to use a macrosociological approach, while symbolic interactionists are more likely to use a microsociological approach.

2. Our location in the social structure affects our perceptions, attitudes, and behaviors. Our culture, social class, social statuses, roles, groups, and social institutions

lay down our fundamental orientations to life. Culture lays the broadest framework, while social class, based on our economic position in society, unites us with similarly minded people. Each of us receives ascribed statuses at birth; later we occupy achieved statuses, all of which serve to control our behavior. Our behaviors and orientations are further influenced by the roles we play, our membership in groups, and our experiences with the institutions of our society. These components of society work together to help maintain social order.

3. Functionalists view social institutions as established ways of meeting universal group needs. Conflict theorists, in contrast, look at social institutions as the primary

means by which the elite maintains its privileged position.

4. Social structure is not static; it changes. Over time, new statuses, roles, and groups emerge. Membership of social classes changes, as do social institutions. Culture itself adjusts to changing technologies and ideas, at times undergoing huge shifts. Emile Durkheim invented the terms mechanical solidarity and organic solidarity to pinpoint a major shift in the nature of social cohesion. Ferdinand Tönnies analyzed how *Gemeinschaft* (intimate community) was being replaced by *Gesellschaft* (impersonal associations).

5. In contrast to functionalist and conflict theorists, who as macrosociologists focus on the "big picture," symbolic interactionists tend to be microsociologists. For them the most significant aspect of social life is social interaction. Symbolic interactionists analyze the symbols that people use to define their worlds. They examine how people look at things and how that in turn affects their behavior.

6. Stereotypes are assumptions of what people are like. When we first meet people, we classify them according to our perceptions of their visible characteristics and our stereotypes of those characteristics. Those assumptions guide our behavior, which, in turn influences others to behave in ways that reinforce our stereotypes.

7. Symbolic interactionists examine how people use physical space. Each of us is surrounded by a "personal bubble," which we very carefully protect. Because people from other cultures have "personal bubbles" of varying sizes, interaction between people from different cultures can be problematic. Americans typically use four different "distance zones": intimate distance, personal distance, social distance, and public distance.

8. Erving Goffman developed the theory of dramaturgy (or dramaturgical analysis), which analyzes everyday life in terms of the stage. At the core of this analysis are the impressions we attempt to make on others. For that, we use the sign-vehicles of setting, appearance, and manner. Our performances often call for teamwork and face-saving behavior.

9. In studying how we make sense of everyday life, ethnomethodologists try to uncover our background assumptions. These form the basic core of our reality, and we base our actions on what we define as real. Because our perceptions are rooted in the social structure and in interaction with others, sociologists use the term the social construction of reality.

10. Both microsociology (a focus on social interaction) and macrosociology (a focus on social structure) are necessary for us to understand social life fully, because each in its own way adds to our knowledge of human experience.

SUGGESTED READINGS

Couch, Carl J. *Social Processes and Relationships: A Formal Approach.* Dix Hills, N.Y.: General Hall, 1989. This analysis covers a wide range of processes and relationships, including bargaining, negotiating, solidarity, accountability, authority, romance, and tyranny.

Ebaugh, Helen Rose Fuchs. *Becoming an Ex: The Process of Role Exit.* Chicago: University of Chicago Press, 1988. To become a former "something," especially when that "something" was important to you, can be an excruciating experience that wrenches the self-concept. The author analyzes this process by looking at ex-nuns, divorce, losing custody of one's children, and so on.

Fields, Mamie Garvin, and Karen Fields. *Lemon Swamp and Other Places.* New York: Free Press, 1985. The second author is a sociologist who has recorded her grandmother's oral history. By providing rich details of an African-American woman's life, this book fills a valuable niche in our understanding of life in American society.

Goffman, Erving. *The Presentation of Self in Everyday Life.* New York: Doubleday, 1959. This is the classic statement of dramaturgical analysis; it provides a different way of looking at everyday life.

Gouldner, Helen, and Mary Symons Strong. *Speaking of Friendship: Middle-Class Women and Their Friends.* New York: Greenwood Press, 1987. Drawing on extensive interviews, the author explores the significance of friendship for middle-class American women.

Hatfield, Elaine, and Susan Sprecher. *Mirror, Mirror. . .: The Importance of Looks in Everyday Life.* Albany, N.Y.: SUNY Press, 1986. All of us consider appearance to be very important in everyday life. You may be surprised, however, at just how significant good looks are for determining what happens to us.

Helmreich, William B. *The Things They Say Behind Your Back: Stereotypes and the Myths Behind Them.* New Brunswick, N.J.: Transaction, 1984. Spiced with anecdotes and jokes, yet sensitively written, the book explores the historical roots of stereotypes. The author also illustrates how stereotypes help produce behavior that reinforces them.

Karp, David A., and William C. Yoels. *Sociology and Everyday Life.* Itasca, Illinois: F. E. Peacock, 1986. The authors examine how social order is constructed and how it provides the framework for our interactions.

Smith, Charles W. *Auctions: The Social Construction of Value.* New York: Free Press, 1989. The author details the ins and outs of this everyday event, based on participant observation.

Tönnies, Ferdinand. *Community and Society (Gemeinschaft und Gesellschaft),* with a new introduction by John Samples. New Brunswick, N.J.: Transaction, 1988. Originally published in 1887, this classic work focuses on social change, and provides insight into how society influences personality. Rather challenging reading.

Journals

The following three journals feature articles on symbolic interactionism and analyses of everyday life: *Qualitative Sociology, Symbolic Interaction, Urban Life.*

CHAPTER 5

Diego Rivera, The Making of a
Fresco/The Building of a City
Fresco, *1931*

How Sociologists Do Research

WHAT IS A VALID SOCIOLOGICAL TOPIC?

COMMON SENSE AND THE NEED FOR SOCIOLOGICAL RESEARCH

A RESEARCH MODEL
1. Selecting a Topic ■ 2. Defining the Problem ■ 3. Reviewing the Literature ■ 4. Formulating a Hypothesis ■ 5. Choosing a Research Method ■ 6. Collecting the Data ■ 7. Analyzing the Results ■ 8. Sharing the Results

SIX RESEARCH METHODS
Surveys ■ *Down-to-Earth Sociology:* **Loading the Dice** ■ Secondary Analysis ■ Documents ■ Participant Observation (Fieldwork) ■ Experiments ■ Unobtrusive Measures ■ *Down-to-Earth Sociology:* **The Hawthorne Experiments** ■ Deciding Which Method to Use ■ *Thinking Critically about Social Controversy:* **Doing Controversial Research—Counting the Homeless**

ETHICS IN SOCIOLOGICAL RESEARCH
The Brajuha Research ■ The Humphreys Research

HOW RESEARCH AND THEORY WORK TOGETHER
A Final Word: When the Ideal Meets the Real

SUMMARY

SUGGESTED READINGS

Renée had never felt fear before, at least not like this. It had begun as a vague feeling that something wasn't quite right. Then she had felt it creep up her spine, slowly tightening as it clawed its way upwards. Now it was like a fist pounding inside her skull.

Renée never went anywhere with strangers. Hadn't her parents hammered that into her head since she was a child? And yet here she was at nineteen, in a car with a man she didn't know. He had seemed nice enough at first. And it wasn't as though he was some stranger on the side of the road or anything.

Renée had met George at Patricia's party, attracted by the dark eyes that seemed to light up his entire face when he smiled. When he asked her to dance, Renée felt flattered. He was a little older, a little more sure of himself than most of the guys she knew. Renée liked that; it seemed a sign of maturity. As the evening wore on and he continued to be attentive to her, it seemed natural to accept his offer to take her home.

But then they passed the turn to her dorm. When Renée told him he had missed it, he mumbled a reply about "getting something." And as he continued driving, heading off into the country, that clawing feeling at the back of her neck began.

His eyes, now cold, almost pierced the darkness as he looked at her. "It's time to pay, babe," he said, and grabbed at her blouse.

Renée won't talk about that night. She doesn't want to remember anything that happened after that.

L. Obj. 1: Describe how sociologists go about selecting a topic for their research.

CDQ 1: Do you think some aspects of human behavior—such as date rape—should be off-limits for sociological research? Why or why not?

WHAT IS A VALID SOCIOLOGICAL TOPIC?

Sociologists research just about every area of human behavior. On the macro level, they study such broad matters as war (Cuzzort 1989), voting patterns (Piven and Cloward 1988), race relations (Wilson 1987), and city growth and development (Logan and Molotch 1987). On the micro level, they study such individualistic matters as waiting in public places (Schwartz 1991), meat packers at work (Thompson 1991), interactions between people on street corners (Whyte 1991), and even how people decorate their homes for Christmas (Caplow 1991). What happened to Renée in our opening vignette? Is that, too, a valid topic for sociologists to research? If so, how should we research this topic?

As discussed in Chapter 1, sociologists study social interaction. Although rape is an emotional topic, and consists of someone forcing himself on someone else, it meets the definition of people doing things with one another (in this case, *to* someone). As discussed in Chapter 1 also, no human behavior is ineligible for sociological research— whether that behavior is routine or unusual, respectable or reprehensible, free or forced. The question of *how* to do research, however, is a little more complicated, and needs to be examined in greater detail.

L. Obj. 2: Explain why common sense is an inadequate source of knowledge about human behavior.

COMMON SENSE AND THE NEED FOR SOCIOLOGICAL RESEARCH

First, why do we need sociological research? Why can't we simply depend on common sense, on "what everyone knows." As noted in Chapter 1 (page 7 and the Down-to-Earth Sociology box), supposedly commonsense ideas may or may not be true. Common sense, for example, tell us that the rape was a significant event in Renée's life.

Just about any aspect of human behavior can be the subject of sociological investigation. Today, many sociologists are investigating the impact of AIDS on society.

And common sense also tells us that rape has ongoing effects, that it can trigger fears and anxieties, and that it can make a woman distrust men in general.

While these particular ideas are accurate, however, we still need social research to test them, because not all commonsense ideas are true. After all, common sense tells some people that women's revealing clothing is one reason that men rape. To others, common sense indicates that men who rape are sexually deprived. Research, however, does not support either of these ideas. Studies show that men who rape don't care what a women wears. (Most rapists don't even care who the woman is; she is simply an object for their drives for power and sexual satisfaction.) And rapists may or may not be sexually deprived—as are men who do not rape. Many rapists have a wife or girlfriend with whom they have an ongoing sexual relationship.

If neither provocative clothing nor sexual deprivation is the underlying cause of rape, then what is? While we may want to know why men rape, we might also want to know how many women are raped or what their reactions are. Or we may want to know something entirely different about rape. That, of course, brings us to the need for sociological research.

Regardless of the particular question that we want to answer, the point is that we want to move beyond guesswork and common sense. We want to *know* what really is going on. And for accurate answers, we need sociological research. Let us look, then, at how sociologists do their research.

CDQ 2: What are some of the common-sense notions about rape that have been proven untrue?

A RESEARCH MODEL

As shown in Figure 5.1, eight basic steps are involved in scientific research. As you look at each of these steps, be aware that this is an ideal model. Although it identifies the primary elements of social research, in some research these steps are collapsed, in others their order may be changed, while in still others one or more steps may even be omitted.

TR#5: The Research Model

Essay #1

Project 1

1. Selecting a Topic

The first step is to select a topic. What is it that you want to know more about? Many sociologists simply follow their curiosity, their drive to know. They become interested in a particular topic, and they pursue it. In Chapter 1, for example, I explained in detail how I became interested in homelessness. Sometimes, sociologists choose a topic because a government agency or private source has made funding available. Sometimes, a particular social problem such as rape has become a pressing issue, and the sociologist wants to gather data that will help people better understand it—and perhaps to solve it.

L. Obj. 3: Identify the eight steps in a research model.

CDQ 3: Do you think it is possible that sociologists might have a problem with objectivity if their research is funded by a governmental agency, such as the Department of Defense, or by a private source, such as a multinational corporation? Are there ways they could circumvent such a problem?

2. Defining the Problem

The second step is to define the problem, to specify exactly what you want to learn about the topic. My interest in homelessness grew until I wanted to learn about homelessness across the nation. Ordinarily, sociologists' interests are much more focused than this. They develop a researchable question to focus on a specific area or problem. For example, they may want to compare the work experiences, the relative isolation, or the attitudes of homeless women and men. Or they may want to know *why* men rape.

3. Reviewing the Literature

The third step is to review the literature to see if the question has already been answered. Nobody wants to reinvent the wheel. In addition, a review of what has been written on the topic can stir ideas, further refining the problem to be investigated.

Speaker Sug. #1: A social science reference librarian to explain the various sources of data.

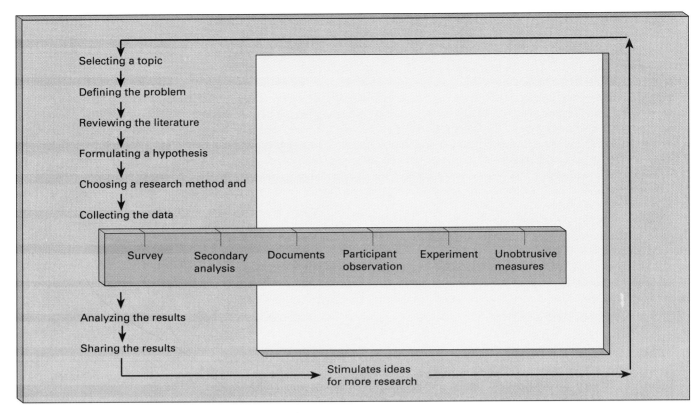

FIGURE 5.1 The Research Model (*Source:* Modification of Fig. 2-2 of Schaefer 1989)

TR#4M: Terms Commonly Used in Sociological Research

L. Obj. 4: Define the following terms: hypothesis, operational definition, validity, reliability, content analysis, and replication.

hypothesis: a statement of the expected relationship between variables according to predictions from a theory

variable: a factor or concept thought to be significant for human behavior, which varies from one case to another

operational definitions: the ways in which the variables in a hypothesis are measured

research method: (or research design) one of six strategies or procedures sociologists use to collect data: surveys, documents, secondary analysis, participant observation, experiments, and unobtrusive measures

validity: the extent to which operational definitions measure what was intended

4. Formulating a Hypothesis

The fourth step is to formulate a **hypothesis,** a statement of what you expect to find according to predictions from a theory. A hypothesis predicts a relationship between or among **variables,** factors that change, or vary, from one person or situation to another. For example, the statement "Men who are more socially isolated are more likely to rape than are men who are more socially integrated" is a hypothesis. Hypotheses need **operational definitions,** that is, precise ways to measure their variables. In this example, we would need operational definitions for three variables: social isolation, social integration, and rape.

5. Choosing a Research Method

The means by which sociologists collect data are called **research methods.** Sociologists have developed six basic research methods, outlined below, from which they select the method that will best answer the particular questions they want to solve.

6. Collecting the Data

The next step is to gather the data. Sociologists take great care to assure both the validity and reliability of their data. **Validity** refers to the extent to which operational definitions measure what they are intended to measure. In other words, we would need to be certain that we were really measuring social isolation, social integration, and rape and not something else.

Validity is a persistent problem for researchers. In this example, just how should we measure social isolation and integration? Can we simply get a measure of how frequently an individual interacts with others? Don't we also have to measure how much the individual identifies or feels a part of other people, a much more difficult matter? Even an operational definition for rape is not as simple to determine as it may seem. For example, there are various degrees of sexual assault. Look at Table 5.1, which lists a variety of unwanted sexual activities forced upon college women. Deciding which of these acts constitute rape for the purposes of specific research is an example of the difficulty of developing operational definitions. Certainly not all of these acts are rape, and, therefore, not all of those who performed them are rapists. In other words, we must be extremely careful that we know precisely what we are measuring.

CDQ 4: Why is an operational definition for rape not as simple to determine as it might seem?

Reliability refers to the extent to which studies yield consistent results. Inadequate operational definitions and sampling (covered below) will undermine reliability. For example, if our measure of rape is adequate and other researchers apply it to the same group of people we studied, they would include the individuals whom we included and exclude those whom we excluded. Clear measures, however, are just the first step toward reliability. Even though our operational definitions are clear and other researchers can follow them, we won't know that our study is reliable until other research produces similar results.

Project 2

7. Analyzing the Results

After the data are gathered, it is time to analyze them. Sociologists have specific techniques for doing this, each of which requires special training. They range from statistical tests (of which there are many, each with its own rules for application) to **content analysis,** which involves examining the content of something in order to identify its themes—in this case perhaps magazine articles or television programs about rape, or even diaries kept by women who have been raped. If a hypothesis has been part of the research—and not all social research makes use of hypotheses—it is during this step that it is tested.

reliability: the extent to which data produce consistent results

content analysis: the examination of a source, such as a magazine article, a television program, or even a diary, to identify its themes

Many sociologists are fascinated by the social institution of the family and choose to specialize in this area. Potential topics of investigation are infinite, but for a research project to be fruitful, the area of investigation should be as focused as possible.

TABLE 5.1   Learning to Read a Table

Date Rape and Other Unwanted Sexual Activities Experienced by Undergraduates

These are the results of a survey of 380 women and 368 men enrolled in introductory psychology courses at Texas A&M University. Percentages add up to more than 100 because often more than one unwanted sexual activity occurred on one date.

Unwanted sexual activity	Women who reported this had happened to them (%)	Men who reported they had done this (%)
He kissed without tongue contact	3.7	2.2
He kissed with tongue contact	12.3	0.7
He touched/kissed her breasts through her clothes	24.7	7.3
He touched/kissed her breasts under her clothes	22.6	13.1
He touched her genitals through her clothes	28.8	15.3
He touched her genitals under her clothes	28.4	13.9
He performed oral sex on her	9.9	8.8
He forced her to touch his genitals through his clothes	2.9	0.7
He forced her to touch his genitals under his clothes	5.8	2.2
He forced her to perform oral sex on him	2.5	4.4
He forced her to have sexual intercourse	20.6	15.3

Source: Muehlenhard and Linton 1987:190.

A table is a concise way of presenting information. Because sociological findings are often presented in tabular form, it is important to understand how to read a table. Tables contain six elements: title, headnote, headings, columns, rows, and source. When you understand how these elements work together, you know how to read a table.

1. The *title* states the topic of a table. It is located at the top of the table. What is the title of this table? Please determine your answer before looking at the correct answer below.

2. The *headnote* is not always included in a table. When it is, it is located just below the title. Its purpose is to give more detailed information about how the data were collected or how data are presented in the table. What are the first seven words of the headnote of this table?

3. The *headings* of a table tell what kind of information is contained in the table. There are three headings in this table. What are they?

4. The *columns* in a table present vertically arranged information, usually consisting of numbers. What is the fourth number in the second column and the second number in the third column?

5. The *rows* in a table present information arranged horizontally. What is the unwanted sexual activity listed in the second row?

6. The *source* of a table, usually listed at the bottom, provides information on where the data shown in the table originated.

Often, as in this instance, the information is specific enough for you to consult the original source. What is the source for this table?

Some tables are much more complicated than this one, but all follow the same basic pattern. To apply these concepts to a table with more information, see pages 414, 454, and 474.

Answers

1. Date rape and other unwanted sexual activities experienced by undergraduates
2. These are the results of a survey
3. Unwanted sexual activity, women who reported this had happened to them, and men who reported they had done this
4. 22.6; 0.7
5. He kissed with tongue contact
6. A 1987 article by Muehlenhard and Linton (listed in the bibliography of this text)

8. Sharing the Results

Now it is time to wrap up the research, or, if it is a broad project, at least some part of it. In this step the researchers write a report that shares their findings with the scientific community. The report includes a review of the above steps to help others judge the research results. It also shows how the findings are related to the literature, the body of existing research. When the research is published, usually in a scientific journal or a book, it then "belongs" to the scientific community. It is available for **replication;** that is, others can repeat the study to test its findings. In this way, research slowly builds, adding finding to finding.

Let us look in greater detail at the fifth step and examine the research methods that sociologists use.

SIX RESEARCH METHODS

Sociologists use six research methods (or research designs) for gathering data: surveys, secondary analysis, documents, participant observation, experiments, and unobtrusive measures. To understand these strategies better, let's continue our example of rape. As we do so, note how the questions to be answered affect the choice of method. Common to many research methods is determining what "average" is in order to provide a yardstick for comparison. Three measures of average are discussed in Table 5.2 on page 120.

Surveys

Let us suppose that your goal is to know how many women are raped each year. For this purpose the **survey** in which people are asked to answer a series of questions, would be an appropriate method. Before using this method, however, you must deal with the practical matter that faces all researchers—matching your goal to your resources. Limitations on money and time help to determine your **population,** the target group that you will study. Ideally, you may want to learn about all the females in the world. Obviously, however, your resources are unlikely to permit such a study, and you must narrow your population. Could you survey all American females? That population, too, lies far beyond your resources. How about the females in a particular state, or county, or city? Even so much smaller a target group is likely to demand huge resources. Instead, let us assume that your resources allow you only to investigate rape on your college campus.

Let us suppose that your college enrollment is large, making it impractical to survey all female students. Now you must select a **sample,** individuals from among your target population. How you choose a sample is critical, for the choice will affect the results of your study. For example, to survey only freshman females—or only seniors, or only those enrolled in introductory sociology courses, or only those in advanced physics classes—will produce unrepresentative results in each case.

To be able to generalize your findings to the entire campus, you must select a sample that is truly representative of the campus. What kind of sample will allow you to do this?

The best is a **random sample.** This does *not* mean that you stand on some campus corner and ask questions of whomever happens to walk by. In a random sample, everyone in the population has the same chance of being included in the study. In this case, since the population is every female enrolled in classes at your college, all such females—whether freshmen, sophomores, juniors, seniors, or graduate students—must have the same chance of being included in your study. Equally, such factors as a woman's major, her grade point average, or whether she is a day or evening or full- or part-time student must not affect her chance of being part of your sample.

replication: the repetition of research in order to test its findings

survey: the collection of data by having people answer a series of questions

population: the target group to be studied

sample: the individuals intended to represent the population to be studied

random sample: a sample in which everyone in the target population has the same chance of being included in the study

TABLE 5.2 Three Ways to Measure "Average"

Mean

The term "average" seems clear enough. As you learned in grade school, to find the average you add a group of numbers and then divide the total by the number of cases that were added. For example, assume that the numbers below represent men convicted of rape who are incarcerated in seven different prisons

321
229
57
289
136
57
1,795

The total is 2,884. Divided by 7 (the number of cases), the average is 412. Sociologists call this form of average the *mean.*

The mean can be deceptive because it is strongly influenced by extreme scores, either low or high. Note that six of the seven cases are less than the mean. Two other ways to compute averages are the median and the mode.

Median

To compute the second average, the *median,* first arrange the cases in order—either from the highest to

the lowest or the lowest to the highest. In this example, that arrangement will produce the following distribution:

57
57
136
229
289
321
1,795

Then look for the middle case, the one that falls halfway between the top and the bottom. That figure is 229, for three numbers are lower and three numbers higher. When there is an even number of cases, the median is the halfway mark between the two middle cases.

Mode

The third measure of average, the *mode,* is simply the cases that occur the most often. In this instance the mode is 57, which is way off the mark. Because the mode is often deceptive, and only by chance comes close to either of the other two averages, sociologists seldom use it. In addition, it is obvious that not every distribution of cases has a mode. And if two different numbers appear with the same frequency, you can have more than one mode.

CDQ 6: Is there a problem with asking research subjects, "What do you think should be done to rapists?" and listing only castration and execution as possible options? Why or why not?

stratified random sample: a sample of specific subgroups of the target population in which everyone in the subgroups has an equal chance of being included in the study

respondents: people who respond to a survey, either in interviews or in self-administered questionnaires

questionnaires: a list of questions to be asked

How can you get a random sample? First you need a list of all the currently enrolled female students. To select your sample from this list, you can use one of two would assign a number to each name on the list and then use random numbers to determine which particular names are to become part of your sample. (Random numbers are available on tables in statistics books, or they can be generated by a computer.)

Because a random sample truly represents the population—in this case female students at your college—you can generalize your findings to all the female students on your campus, whether they were included in the sample or not.

Social scientists have developed a variation of this sampling technique that you might want to consider. Suppose you want to compare the experiences of freshmen, sophomores, and so on. If so, you could use a **stratified random sample.** You would first subdivide your list of female college students into freshmen, sophomores, and so on, and then use random numbers to select subsamples from each class.

After you have decided on your population and sample, your next task is to make certain that your questions are neutral. Your questions must allow **respondents,** people who respond to a survey, to express their own ideas. Otherwise, you will end up with biased answers—and biased findings are worthless. (The Down-to-Earth Sociology box on page 121 gives examples of biased findings.) For example, if you were to ask, "What do you think should be done to rapists?" and list only castration and execution as possible options, you would not be taking accurate measurements of people's opinions. Similarly, if you were to begin a question with, "Don't you agree that rapists . . . ?" (deserve the death penalty, should not have so many appeals, and so on), you would be tilting the results toward agreement with the position being stated. The wording of **questionnaires,** then, the list of questions to be asked, can also affect research results.

Sociologists not only strive to ask questions that reduce bias; they are also concerned about how questionnaires are administered (carried out). There are two basic

DOWN-TO-EARTH SOCIOLOGY

Loading the Dice

The methods of science lend themselves to distortion, misrepresentation, and downright fraud. Consider the following information. Independent surveys show that

- Americans overwhelmingly prefer a Toyota to a Chrysler.
- Americans think that cloth diapers are better for the environment than disposable diapers.

Now look at the results of two other surveys, which are every bit as factual as the first. These show that

- Americans overwhelmingly prefer a Chrysler to a Toyota.
- Americans think that disposable diapers are better for the environment than cloth diapers.

Obviously such opposites cannot both be true. Is one the truth, the other a misrepresentation? Actually, both sets of findings are misrepresentations, although each does come from surveys conducted by "independent" researchers. The problem is that the so-called independence of the researchers is less than it seems.

It turns out that some consumer researchers load the dice. Hired by firms that have a vested interest in the outcome of the research, they deliver the results their clients are looking for. There are five basic ways of loading the dice.

1. *Choose a biased sample.* For example, if you were to ask unemployed union workers who trace their job loss to Japanese imports if they prefer a Chrysler or a Toyota, the answers are fairly predictable. (However, sociologists can never simply make such an assumption without doing research, for respondents continually surprise researchers.)

2. *Ask biased questions.* Even if researchers choose an unbiased sample, they can phrase their questions in such a way that most people see only one logical choice. The diaper survey cited above is a case in point. When the disposable diaper industry paid for the survey, the researchers used an excellent sample, but worded the question as follows: "It is estimated that disposable diapers account for less than 2 percent of the trash in today's landfills. In contrast, beverage containers, third-class mail and yard waste are estimated to account for about 21 percent. Given this, in your opinion, would it be fair to ban disposable diapers?"

Is it surprising, then, that 84 percent of the respondents (the actual results) answered that disposable diapers are better for the environment than cloth diapers? Similarly, when the cloth diaper industry funded its own survey, the wording of the questions loaded the dice the opposite way.

Consider the following findings, also from "independent" researchers, and every bit as factual as those cited above.

- Seventy-nine percent of Americans think that roach disks are effective in killing roaches.

- American college students overwhelmingly prefer Levi's 501 to the jeans of any competitor.

The researchers for Black Flag used the following question: "A roach disk . . . poisons a roach slowly. The dying roach returns to the nest and after it dies is eaten by other roaches. In turn, these roaches become poisoned and die. How effective do you think this type of product would be in killing roaches?" This question is obviously designed to channel people's thinking toward a predetermined answer—quite contrary to the standards of scientific research.

The researchers for Levi's loaded the dice even more obviously: In asking a sample of students which clothes would be the most popular in the coming year, their list of choices included no other jeans but Levi's 501.

3. *Discard undesirable results.* Researchers can simply keep silent about findings they find embarrassing, or they can even continue to survey samples until they find one that matches what they are looking for.

As stressed in this chapter, research must be objective before it can be considered scientific. Obviously, none of the above results qualifies. The underlying problem with the research cited here—and with so many similar surveys that are bandied about in the media—is that survey research has become big business. Simply put, the vast sums of money offered by business have corrupted many researchers.

The beginning of the corruption is subtle. Paul Light, associate dean of the Hubert Humphrey Institute at the University of Minnesota, put it like this: "A funder will never come to an academic and say, 'I want you to produce finding X, and here's a million dollars to do it.' Rather, the subtext is that if the researchers produce the right finding, more work—and funding—will come their way." He adds, "Once you're on that treadmill, it's hard to get off."

4. *Misunderstand the subjects' world.* This route can lead to errors every bit as great as those cited above. Even researchers who use an adequate sample and word their questions properly can end up with skewed results. For example, surveys show that 80 percent of Americans are environmentalists. Most Americans, however, are probably embarrassed to tell a stranger otherwise. Today, that would be like being against the flag, motherhood, and apple pie.

5. *Analyze the data incorrectly.* Even when researchers strive for objectivity, the sample and wording are correct, and respondents answer the questions honestly, the results can still be skewed—the researchers simply err in their calculations, such as entering incorrect data into computers.

The first three sources of bias constitute intentional, inexcusable fraud. The fourth and fifth sources of bias reflect sloppiness—which is no excuse in science.

Source: Based on Babbie 1985, Hunt 1986, Reynolds 1982, and Crossen 1991.

techniques for administering questionnaires. The first is for the respondents to fill them out. Although such **self-administered questionnaires** allow a larger number of people to be sampled at a relatively low cost, the researcher using this method loses control, because the conditions under which the questionnaires were filled out are unknown. For example, someone could influence the respondents' answers. In the second technique, the researcher asks the questions directly, either face to face or by telephone. The advantage of this method, called an **interview,** is that the researcher retains control of the situation—especially making certain that each question is asked in precisely the same way. This method has disadvantages, too, however. Not only does it limit the number of questionnaires that can be completed, while increasing the cost, but it can also result in **interview bias,** effects that interviewers can have on respondents that bias their answers. For example, respondents may be willing to write an anonymous answer but not to express the same opinion to another person directly. Respondents also sometimes try to make their answers match what they think an interviewer wants to hear.

In some cases, **structured interviews** work best. This type of interview uses **closed-ended questions,** questions followed by a list of possible answers. The advantages of structured interviews are that they are faster to administer and make it easier for the answers to be *coded* (categorized) so that they can be fed into a computer for analysis. The primary disadvantage is that respondents are limited to the answers already on the questionnaire, which may or may not match their own opinions. For other research, **unstructured interviews** work better. Here the interviewer poses a series of **open-ended questions,** which people answer in their own words. The primary advantage of unstructured interviews is that they allow respondents to express the full range of their opinions. The major disadvantage is that it can be difficult to compare one set of answers with another. For example, how would you compare these answers to the question, "What do you think causes rape?"

> "They haven't been raised right."
> "I think they must have had problems with their mother."
> "We ought to kill every one!"
> "They're all sick."
> "They're just *.*.* bastards!"

Research on rape also brings up another significant issue. You may have been wondering if your survey of rape victims would be worth anything even if you rigorously followed scientific procedures. Would a rape victim really give honest answers? Would she even admit to a stranger that she had been raped?

If you were simply to walk up to female strangers on the street and ask if they had ever been raped, there would understandably be little basis for taking your findings seriously. It is therefore vital for researchers to establish **rapport,** a feeling of trust,

self-administered question-naires: questionnaires filled out by respondents

interview: direct questioning of respondents

interview bias: effects that interviewers have on respondents that lead to biased answers

structured interviews: a form of interview that uses closed-ended questions

closed-ended questions: questions followed by a list of possible answers to be selected by the respondent

unstructured interviews: a form of interview that uses open-ended questions

coding: categorizing data

open-ended questions: questions that a respondent is able to answer in his or her own words

rapport: a feeling of trust between researchers and subjects

Sociologists who conduct surveys sometimes use interviews to collect data, conducted either by telephone or in person. One potential pitfall of the interview is interview bias. *This occurs when respondents alter their responses to fit what they think the interviewer wants to hear or do not fully reveal what they really think in the presence of the interviewer.*

with their respondents, especially when it comes to sensitive topics, areas about which people may feel embarrassment or other deep emotions.

We know that once rapport is gained (for example, by first asking nonsensitive questions), victims will talk to researchers about rape. To go beyond police statistics, researchers conduct national crime surveys in which they interview a random sample of 100,000 Americans, asking them if they have been victims of burglary, robbery, and so on. After gaining rapport, the researchers then ask questions about rape. They find that rape victims do share their experiences with them, yielding results that parallel the official statistics (Shim and DeBerry 1988).

Such surveys have uncovered significant variables that determine whether or not a woman will report a rape to the police. The first is age. Females below the age of twenty are the least likely to report the attack, while those between thirty-five and forty-nine are the most likely to report rape. Race and acquaintanceship are also significant: African-American victims are more likely to call the police if they are raped by someone they know, while white victims are more likely to report the rape when they are attacked by a stranger (Shim and DeBerry 1988).

While we may assume that such different reactions to rape represent contrasting experiences of African-American and white females in American life, to interpret such findings scientifically we need a theory and hypotheses that pinpoint those experiences. These have yet to be developed.

Secondary Analysis

In **secondary analysis,** another research method, the researcher analyzes data that have already been collected by other researchers. For example, if you were to examine the basic data gathered by the interviewers who conducted the national crime survey just mentioned, you would be doing secondary analysis.

Ordinarily, researchers prefer to gather their own data, but lack of resources, especially money, may limit those possibilities. In addition, existing data may contain a wealth of information, not pertinent to the goals of the original study, which can be analyzed for other purposes.

While this approach can solve problems of access, it poses its own problems. How can a researcher who did not directly carry out the research be sure that the data were systematically gathered, accurately recorded, and that biases were avoided? That may be an impossible task, especially when the original data were gathered by numerous researchers, not all of whom were equally qualified.

Documents

The use of **documents,** written sources, is a third research method employed by sociologists. To investigate social life, sociologists examine such diverse sources as books, newspapers, diaries, bank records, police reports, household accounts, immigration files, and records kept by various organizations.

To apply this method to the study of rape, you might examine police reports. These might reveal what proportion of complaints result in arrest, what proportion of all arrests are for rape, how many of the men arrested for rape are brought to trial, what proportion are convicted, how many receive probation, how many are imprisoned, and so forth. If those were your questions, police statistics would be valuable.

But for other questions those records would be useless. If you wanted to know about the social and emotional adjustment of rape victims, for example, they would tell you nothing. Other documents, however, might lend themselves to answering this question. A campus rape crisis center, for example, might have records that would provide key information. Diaries kept by rape victims would yield important insights into their reactions, especially how their attitudes and relationships with others change over time. If you couldn't locate such diaries, you might contact rape victims and ask

CDQ 7: If you were to walk up to female strangers on the street and ask if they had ever been raped, what type of response would you most likely receive? Why is rapport essential for good research?

Essay #3

CDQ 8: Why do most researchers prefer to gather their own data rather than relying on data collected by other researchers?

secondary analysis: the analysis of data already collected by other researchers

documents: written sources

Sociologists investigating rape may wish to examine documents kept by Rape Crisis Centers, which log the number of calls and visits made by rape victims.

CDQ 9: Can you think of reasons why a rape crisis center might be unwilling to cooperate with a researcher who wanted to talk with rape victims at the center?

CDQ 10: Do you think a male researcher could conduct participant observation research at a rape crisis intervention center? Why or why not?

Sociologists who put themselves directly into the research setting to discover their information engage in participant observation.

participant observation: (or fieldwork) research in which the researcher *participates* in a research setting while observing what is happening in that setting

them to keep diaries. Again, the rape crisis center might be the key in eliciting victims' cooperation. Their personnel might ask clients to keep such diaries. To my knowledge, no sociologist has yet studied rape in this way.

Of course, I am presenting an ideal situation in which the rape crisis center is opening its arms to you. In actual fact, the center might not cooperate at all, neither asking victims to keep diaries nor even letting you near its records. Access, then, is another problem researchers face constantly. Simply put, you can't study a topic unless you can gain access to it.

Participant Observation (Fieldwork)

In the fourth method, **participant observation,** the researcher *participates* in a research setting while *observing* what is happening in that setting. My research with the homeless, mentioned in Chapter 1, is an example of participant observation.

How is it possible to study rape by participant observation? Obviously, this method does not apply to being present during a rape. Rape, however, is a broad topic, and many questions about rape cannot be answered as adequately by any other method.

Let's continue to suppose that your interest is in how rape victims adjust to this traumatic event. You want to know what they think about themselves. You would like to learn how the rape has affected their behavior and their orientations to the world. For example, has their victimization affected their hopes and goals, their dating patterns, their ideas about men and their ability to form intimate relationships? Participant observation can provide detailed answers to such questions.

Now let's go back to your campus again, assuming, for the sake of argument, that it has a rape crisis intervention center. Such a setting lends itself to participant observation, for here you can observe rape victims from the time they first report the attack to their later participation in counseling. With good rapport, you may even be able to spend time with victims outside this setting, observing other aspects of their lives. Their statements and other behaviors may be the key that helps you unlock answers about their attitudes and other orientations to life.

As you may have noticed, the researcher's personal characteristics are extremely important in participant observation. For example, could a male researcher conduct such research? Technically, the answer is yes. Properly introduced and with the right demeanor, male sociologists could do this research. But given the topic, which specifically centers on the emotions of females who have been brutally victimized by males, female sociologists may be better suited to conduct such research, and thus more likely to achieve results. Here again, however, our commonsense suppositions regarding how likely female rape victims are to disclose information to male versus female interviewers are just that—suppositions. Research alone will verify or refute these assumptions. In conducting research, then, sociologists must be aware of how such variables as their sex, age, race, personality, and even height and weight can affect their findings

(Henslin 1990a). Although these variables are important in all research methods, they are especially important in participant observation.

Participant observers face a problem with **generalizability,** the ability to apply their findings to larger populations. Most of their studies are exploratory in nature, documenting in detail what people in a particular setting are experiencing and how they are reacting to those experiences. Although such research suggests that other people who face similar situations will react in similar ways, it is difficult to know just how far the findings apply beyond their original setting. The results of participant observation can, however, stimulate hypotheses and theories and be tested in other settings using other research techniques.

CDQ 11: Do you think that pornography creates attitudes that favor rape?

Experiments

A fifth research method is the **experiment.** The classic method of the natural sciences, it is however seldom used by sociologists, because they are generally interested in broad features of society and social behavior, or in the detailed workings of some social group, neither of which easily lend themselves to an experiment. The social sciences most likely to use this method are psychology and **social psychology,** a field that blends parts of psychology and sociology; these disciplines focus on small-scale variables that are suited to the rigorous control required by the experimental method.

The basic purpose of an experiment is to identify causal relationships, to find out what is the cause and what is the effect. Ordinarily, experiments are used to test a hypothesis. Experiments involve **independent variables,** those factors that cause a change in something, and **dependent variables,** those factors that are changed. Before an experiment can take place, the researcher must accurately measure the dependent variable. Then, after introducing the independent variable, the researcher must measure the dependent variable again to see what changes have occurred. This procedure is illustrated in Figure 5.2.

Suppose you want to test the hypothesis that pornography creates attitudes that favor rape. Suppose also that you have access to a laboratory on campus and that some males have volunteered for your experiment. Three conditions must be fulfilled in order to demonstrate cause and effect. First, there must be a **correlation** between the two variables; that is, they must occur together. In this case, there must be both exposure to pornography *and* a measurement of attitudes toward rape. Second, the independent variable must precede the dependent variable. In this case, if a change in attitude occurs before the men see the pornography, the pornography cannot be the cause of the change. Third, the change cannot be due to a third variable. If it is, it is called a **spurious correlation.** To illustrate spurious correlations, Table 5.3 explores the relationship of marijuana smoking and cocaine use.

generalizability: the extent to which the findings from one group (or sample) can be generalized or applied to other groups (or populations)

experiment: the use of control groups and experimental groups and dependent and independent variables to test causation

social psychology: an academic discipline that attempts to blend parts of psychology and sociology

independent variable: a factor that causes a change in another variable, called the dependent variable

dependent variable: a factor that is changed by an independent variable

correlation: the simultaneous occurrence of two or more variables

spurious correlation: the correlation of two variables actually caused by a third variable; there is no cause-effect relationship

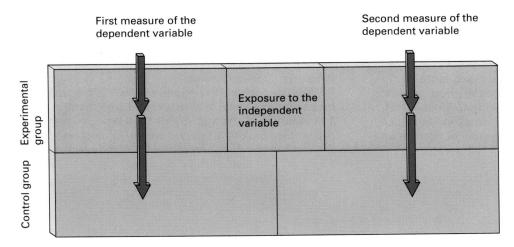

First measure of the dependent variable

Second measure of the dependent variable

Exposure to the independent variable

Experimental group

Control group

FIGURE 5.2 The Experiment

TABLE 5.3   Cause, Effect, and Spurious Correlations

To better understand causation and spurious correlations, let us consider marijuana smoking and the use of cocaine.

1. If two variables exist together, they are correlated.

Correlation

(1) Marijuana smoking ⟺ Cocaine use

2. Often people mistake correlation for causation, however, in this instance concluding that marijuana smoking causes cocaine use.

(2) Marijuana smoking ⟹ Cocaine use

There is nothing about smoking marijuana to cause someone to use cocaine, however.

3. In addition to correlation, causation also requires temporal priority; in other words, the independent variable must precede the dependent variable. In this example, marijuana smoking, the independent variable, *often* precedes cocaine use, the dependent variable. But not always. Although most North American cocaine users may have smoked marijuana before using cocaine, some used cocaine before they smoked marijuana; and some have never smoked marijuana. Many South Americans commonly chew coca leaves but do not smoke marijuana.

That leaves us with two possible explanations: Some people's cocaine use is caused by marijuana, and other people's cocaine use is caused by something else.

(3) Marijuana smoking ⟹ Cocaine use
    Other causes ⟹

That is possible. But science searches for the simplest explanations. In this instance, we would look for some underlying third variable that would explain the use of cocaine for both those who used marijuana first and for those who did not. Moreover, the explanation would be even more powerful if that third variable could also account for the smoking of marijuana.

4. Sociologists have identified subculture as that underlying third variable: If cocaine or any other drug is used in a person's subculture, that person is likely to use that drug. If most people in that subculture first smoke marijuana and later use some form of cocaine, the person is likely to follow that same path.

(4) 3rd variable ⟹ Marijuana smoking
    (subculture) ⟹ Cocaine use

Subculture also explains marijuana smoking. In short, sociologists have found that the best predictor of whether or not someone is going to smoke marijuana is whether or not that person's friends smoke marijuana. It is the same with the use of cocaine and other drugs.

5. Although subculture is a powerful variable, helping to account for such behaviors as the use of illegal drugs, shoplifting, vandalism and other forms of juvenile delinquency, dropping out of school, and becoming a member of a motorcycle gang, it is not a complete explanation. Human behavior, unlike that of an amoeba or the action of heat on some object, is infinitely complicated. What social forces produce a drug-using subculture?

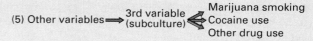

(5) Other variables ⟹ 3rd variable (subculture) ⟹ Marijuana smoking / Cocaine use / Other drug use

6. The complexity of this issue can be seen by noting that some individuals in a drug-using subculture may not themselves use drugs. This indicates that even more underlying variables (such as family values) are at work.

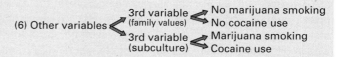

(6) Other variables ⟹ 3rd variable (family values) ⟹ No marijuana smoking / No cocaine use
                       3rd variable (subculture) ⟹ Marijuana smoking / Cocaine use

To close this discussion, let's consider this piece of information. Probably an even larger number of cocaine users first ate butter, milk, chocolate, and meat, took aspirin, and smoked cigarettes than first smoked marijuana. Why do you think that people do not mistake these spurious correlations for causation?

More on Correlations

Correlation simply means that two or more variables are present together. The more often they are found together, the greater the strength of their relationship. To indicate that strength, sociologists use a number called a *correlation coefficient.* If two variables are *always* related, they have what is called a *perfect positive correlation.* The number 1.0 represents this correlation coefficient. Nature has some 1.0s, such as the lack of water and the death of trees. 1.0s similarly apply to the human physical state, such as the absence of nutrients and the absence of life. But social life is much more complicated than physical conditions, and there are no 1.0s in human behavior.

In contrast, if two variables have a *perfect negative correlation,* it means that when one variable is present, the other is always absent. The number −1.0 expresses this correlation coefficient.

Weak positive correlations of 0.1, 0.2, 0.3, and 0.4 mean that one variable is associated with another only 1 time out of 10, 2 times out of 10, 3 times out of 10, and 4 times out of 10. In other words, in most instances the first variable is *not* associated with the second, indicating a weak relationship. The greater the correlation coefficient, the stronger the relationship. A strong relationship may indicate a causal relationship. Testing the relationship between variables is the goal of some sociological research.

Spurious correlations are especially troublesome. To make certain that unknown variables are not reponsible for whatever changes are observed, experimenters take many precautions. If, for example, you were to test the hypothesis that pornography creates attitudes that favor rape, your independent variable would be pornography, while your dependent variable would be attitudes toward rape. After measuring the men's attitudes toward rape, you could then have them watch pornography. Afterwards, you could again measure the men's attitudes. Could you then test your hypothesis and safely conclude that the pornography the men saw caused whatever change occurred in their attitudes?

Unfortunately, it is not that simple. How did you select the men? Are they somehow more prone to suggestion than other men? Or perhaps something happened on campus that affected the results. For example, was there a brutal rape that was widely publicized? Or something could have happened in the community to bias the results. For example, was a campaign against pornography launched about the same time?

To guard against spurious correlations, the effects of unknown third variables, you can randomly divide your subjects into two groups. By making certain that each person has an equal chance of becoming a member of either group, personal characteristics, such as "suggestibility," are distributed between the groups. Then you measure the dependent variable, in this case attitudes toward rape, of each group of men. To one group, called the **experimental group,** you introduce the independent variable, in this case violent pornographic movies. The other men, the **control group,** are not exposed to the independent variable; that is, they are not shown these movies. You then measure the dependent variable again in both groups of men. In this way, the effects of unknown third variables are "washed out"; that is, you can assume that, whatever such variables may be, they have had the same effects on both groups. Any changes in the dependent variable among the experimental group can now be attributed to what only that group received, namely, the independent variable.

Because there is always some chance that unknown third variables (called underlying variables) have not been evenly divided among the groups, you would need to replicate (retest) your results by doing the exact same experiment with other groups of men. You can be certain that other experimenters will do so. The Down-to-Earth Sociology box on page 128 describes a set of famous experiments undertaken in the 1920s, in which several surprising underlying third variables were uncovered.

Can—or should—such a powerful research method as the experiment be used to study rapists? Some might say that we should randomly divide convicted rapists into two groups and then castrate the men in one group (the experimental group). After their release from prison, we could then observe whether the rearrest rate for rape was lower among the experimental group than among the control group. Thus, we would know if castration is an effective strategy for reducing rape. Properly carried out, such a procedure could meet the rigorous demands of an experiment. And the results would be of value to society. Social scientists are bound by a code of ethics and legal constraints, however, that would make such an experiment questionable at best.

Researchers, however, might carry out other experiments on rapists without ethical or legal problems, for example if the independent variable were therapy instead of castration. Convicted rapists could be assigned to experimental and control groups randomly to assure that individual characteristics (number of convictions, education, rural and urban backgrounds, religion, race, age, and so on) would be evenly distributed between the groups. The experimental group would receive some particular form of therapy, the control group no therapy. We would have to assume that, except for the therapy, the prison and post-prison experiences had equal effects on the men. And differences in the rearrest rates for rape could then be attributed to the independent variable, the therapy. Such results, if positive (that is, if they did not *increase* rape), would provide valuable guidelines for dealing with rapists.

Other independent variables that could be considered are length of imprisonment,

CDQ 12: Why is it necessary to have a control group as well as an experimental group when conducting experiments?

experimental group: the group of subjects exposed to the independent variable in a study

control group: the group of subjects not exposed to the independent variable in a study

different forms of punishment, and degrees of isolation. Frankly, no one yet knows how to successfully change a rapist into a nonrapist, and such rigorous experiments are badly needed.

Essay #4

Unobtrusive Measures

The final method we shall consider is that of **unobtrusive measures,** the process of observing social behavior in people who do not know they are being studied. For example, social researchers have studied the level of whisky consumption in a town that was officially "dry" by counting empty bottles in trash cans, the degree of fear induced by ghost stories by measuring the shrinking diameter of a circle of seated children, and the popularity of exhibits at Chicago's Museum of Science and Industry by the wear on tiles in front of the various exhibits (Webb 1966).

How could we use unobtrusive measures to study rape? We could observe rapists in prison when they do not know that they are being watched. For example, we could arrange for the leader of a therapy group for rapists to be called out of the room. During his absence, social researchers could use a one-way mirror to observe the men's interactions and tape recorders to record what they say. This would probably tell us more about their real attitudes than most other techniques. Professional ethics, however, would likely prohibit this application of unobtrusive measures.

> **unobtrusive measures:** the observation of people who do not know they are being studied

---

DOWN-TO-EARTH SOCIOLOGY

The Hawthorne Experiments

The purpose of sociological research is to determine how variables influence human behavior. One famous research attempt, now a classic in sociology, drives home how necessary it is to accurately identify the true independent and dependent variables.

In the mid-1920s, a series of studies was carried out at the Hawthorne plant of the Western Electric Company near Chicago. The management wanted to know how different levels of lighting affected productivity. Several groups of female employees participated in the Relay Room Experiments. In the control room, the level of lighting was held constant as the women worked, while in the test room the lighting was varied. To everyone's surprise, output increased in *both* locations. In the test room, productivity remained high even when the lights were dimmed to about the level of moonlight—so low that workers could barely see what they were doing!

To solve this mystery, management called in a team of researchers headed by Elton Mayo of the University of Chicago. This team tested thirteen different work conditions, and they got the same results. When they changed the workers' pay from hourly wages to piece work, productivity increased. When they served refreshments, output again went up. When they added two five-minute rest periods, productivity jumped. When they changed the rest periods to two ten-minute periods, again output increased. When they let the workers go home early, they found the same result. Confused, the researchers then restored the original conditions, offering none of the added benefits. The result? Even higher productivity.

The situation became even more confusing when male workers were observed in the Bank Wiring Room Study. Here, the researchers did not change the work conditions at all. They simply observed the men while they worked and interviewed them after work. But instead of there being no change in productivity, as might have been expected, productivity *decreased.*

None of this made sense. In the Relay Room Experiments, why would both higher and lower lighting make productivity go up? Why would both longer and shorter breaks increase worker output? And why should productivity be still higher when conditions were returned to their original state? And in the Bank Wiring Room Study, why would productivity decrease without any change in work conditions?

Mayo concluded that the results were due to the research itself. Aware that they were being studied and pleased at the attention paid to them, the female workers responded by increasing their efforts. The male workers, in contrast, reacted by becoming suspicious about why the researchers were observing them. They feared that an increase in productivity would increase the amount they were expected to produce each day, or that it might even cost some of them their jobs. Consequently, they deliberately decreased their output.

The Hawthorne research is important—not for its findings on worker productivity, but for what it revealed about the research process itself. Today, social researchers carefully monitor the *Hawthorne effect,* the change in subjects' behavior that occurs when they know they are being studied.

Source: Based on Roethlisberger and Dickson 1939; Mayo 1966; Baron and Greenberg 1990.

Deciding Which Method to Use

Four primary factors underlie a researcher's choice of method. First, as mentioned earlier, resources are critical, and researchers must always match methods to available resources. For example, although they may prefer to conduct a survey, they may find that finances will not permit it and instead turn to the study of documents. Second, as also noted earlier, access to subjects is crucial. If persons in a sample live in remote parts of the country, researchers may have to conduct a telephone survey or mail questionnaires even if they would prefer face-to-face interviews. The third factor concerns the purpose of the research, the questions that the researcher wishes to answer. Each method is better for answering some questions than for others. Participant observation, for example, is a good method for uncovering people's real attitudes, while experiments work better for resolving questions of cause and effect. Fourth, the researcher's background or training comes into play. In graduate school, sociologists study all the methods but are able to practice only some of them. Consequently, following graduate school they generally feel most comfortable using the methods in which they have had the most training and tend to do so during their career. Thus, researchers who have been trained in **quantitative techniques,** which emphasize precise measurement, numbers, and statistics, are more likely to use surveys, while researchers who have been trained in **qualitative techniques,** which emphasize describing and interpreting people's behavior, lean toward participant observation. In the Thinking Critically section below, you can see how significant the choice of research method is, and how sociologists can find themselves in the midst of controversy for applying rigorous research methods.

L. Obj. 7: Enumerate the four primary factors involved in a researcher's choice of research method.

L. Obj. 8: Differentiate between quantitative techniques and qualitative techniques.

THINKING CRITICALLY ABOUT SOCIAL CONTROVERSY

Doing Controversial Research—Counting the Homeless

What could be simpler, or more inoffensive, than counting the homeless? As sometimes happens, however, even basic research lands sociologists in the midst of controversy. This is what happened to sociologist Peter Rossi and his associates.

It happened this way. There was a dispute between advocates for the homeless and the federal government. The advocates said that there were about three million Americans homeless, while the government said there were about one-twelfth this number, only about a quarter of a million. Each side accused the other of gross distortion—the one to place undue pressure on Congress, the other to keep the public from knowing how bad the situation really was.

Only an accurate count could clear up the picture, for both sides were only guessing at the numbers. Peter Rossi and the National Opinion Research Center decided to carry out an accurate count. They had no vested interest in supporting one side or the other, only in answering this question honestly.

The challenge was immense. No federal, state, county, or city registers exist from which to add up names, and only some of the homeless stay at shelters. The *population* was evident, America's homeless. A *survey* would be appropriate, but how do you survey a *sample* of this population? And for *validity,* to make certain that they were counting only people who were really homeless, the researchers needed a good definition of homelessness. To include people who weren't really homeless would destroy the study's *reliability.* The researchers wanted results that would be consistent if others were to *replicate,* or repeat, the study.

To settle the problem of definition, the researchers used the criterion of "literally homeless," persons "who do not have access to a conventional dwelling and who would be homeless by any conceivable definition of the term." Because a national count would cost about $6 million, the researchers decided to count just the homeless in Chicago.

quantitative techniques: research in which the emphasis is placed on precise measurement, the use of statistics and numbers

qualitative techniques: research in which the emphasis is placed on describing and interpreting people's behavior

Simply counting the number of homeless people who sleep in shelters or eat in soup kitchens will not yield an accurate picture of the total number of homeless Americans. For Rossi and his associates, this was only a starting point.

By using a stratified random sample, they were able to generalize to the entire country. The cost was still high, however—about $600,000.

To generalize about the homeless who sleep in shelters, the researchers used a stratified random sample of the city's shelters. For the homeless who sleep in the streets, vacant buildings, and so forth, they used a stratified random sample of the city's blocks. To make absolutely certain that their count was accurate, the researchers conducted two surveys. At night, trained teams visited the shelters and searched the alleys, bridges, and vacant houses.

Many found the results startling. On an average night, Chicago has 2,722 homeless persons. Because people move in and out of homelessness, between 5,000 and 7,000 are homeless at some point during the year. On warm nights, only two out of five sleep in the shelters, and even in winter only three out of four do so. The median age is forty, 75 percent are men, and 60 percent are African Americans. One in four is a former mental patient, one in five a former prisoner. A homeless person's income from all sources is less than $6 a day. Projecting these findings to the entire nation results in a national figure of about 350,000 homeless people.

The reactions were predictable. While government officials rubbed their hands in glee, stunned homeless advocates began a sniping campaign, denying the findings.

Remember that Rossi and associates had no interest in proving which side in the debate was right, only in getting reliable figures. Using impeccable methods, this they did.

The researchers had no intention of minimizing the problem of homelessness. They stressed that several hundred thousand Americans are so poor that they slip through the welfare system, sleep in city streets, live in alleys and shelters, eat out of garbage cans, are undernourished, and suffer from severe health problems. In short, these people live hopeless, despairing lives.

It is good to *know* for certain how many such persons there are. Even though the number is far less than the homeless advocates had estimated, this information can serve their cause. Since there are fewer homeless people than many had thought, the problem is more manageable. It means that if we have the national resolve, we can put our resources to work with greater certainty of success.

Nevertheless, as in this instance, people whose positions are not supported by research are not pleased, and they tend to take potshots at the researchers. This, of course, is one of the risks of doing sociological research, for sociologists never know whose toes they will step on. (*Source:* Based on Anderson 1986; Coughlin 1988; Hechinger 1988; Lochhead 1988; Rossi 1989; Rossi, Fisher, and Willis 1986; Rossi and Wright 1989; Rossi, Wright, Fisher, and Willis 1987; Stanley 1984.) ■

ETHICS IN SOCIOLOGICAL RESEARCH

In addition to choosing an appropriate research method, a sociologist must also bear in mind the matter of ethics. Sociologists cannot just do any type of research that they might desire. Their research must meet their profession's ethical criteria, which center on basic assumptions of science and morality (American Sociological Association 1989; Fichter and Kolb 1989). Research ethics require openness (sharing findings with the scientific community), honesty, and truth. Ethics clearly forbid the falsification of results or plagiarism, that is, stealing someone else's work. Another basic ethical guideline is that research subjects should not be harmed by the research. Ethics further require that the anonymity of people who provide private, sometimes intimate, and often potentially embarrassing or otherwise harmful information be preserved. Finally, although not all sociologists are in agreement about this, it is generally considered unethical for researchers to misrepresent themselves.

The Brajuha Research

Sociologists take these ethical criteria seriously. To illustrate the extent to which sociologists will go to protect their respondents, consider the research conducted by Mario Brajuha. Brajuha, a graduate student at the State University of New York at Stony Brook, was doing participant observation of restaurant work (Brajuha and Hallowell 1986). He lost his job as a waiter because the restaurant where he was working burned down. The fire turned out to be of "suspicious origin," and it was intensively investigated. During their investigation, detectives learned that Brajuha had taken extensive field notes, and they asked to see them. Brajuha refused. The district attorney then subpoenaed the notes. Brajuha still refused to hand them over. The district attorney then threatened to send Brajuha to jail. By this time, Brajuha's notes had become rather famous, and unsavory characters, perhaps those who had set the fire, also began to wonder what was in them. They, too, demanded to see them— accompanying their demands with threats of a different nature. Brajuha unexpectedly found himself in a very disturbing double bind.

For two years Brajuha steadfastly refused to hand over his notes, even though he had to appear at numerous court hearings and became filled with intense anxiety, until finally, the district attorney dropped the subpoena. Happily, when the two men under investigation for setting the fire died, so did the threats to Brajuha, his wife, and his children.

The Humphreys Research

Sociologists agree on the necessity to protect respondents, and they applauded the professional manner in which Brajuha handled himself. There is less than complete agreement, however, on the requirement that researchers not misrepresent them-

Speaker Sug. #3: A specialist in ethics from your department or the schools of business, law, or medicine.

L. Obj. 9: Describe the major ethical issues involved in sociological research; briefly demonstrate these issues by use of the Brajuha research and the Humphreys research as examples.

Essay #5

CDQ 13: Do you think Mario Brajuha should have turned over his participant observation field notes when detectives asked him to do so?

K.P.: Mario Brajuha

Project 3

CDQ 14: How would you feel if you learned that a researcher was conducting observations in a restroom you frequently use? Was Humphrey's research ethical?

K.P.: Laud Humphreys

selves, and sociologists who have violated this norm have exposed themselves to ethical controversy. The following example has forced social researchers to rethink and refine their ethical stance.

Laud Humphreys (1970; 1971; 1975), a classmate of mine at Washington University in St. Louis, was an Episcopal priest who decided to become a sociologist. For his Ph.D. dissertation Humphreys decided to study homosexuals. Specifically, he wanted to focus on social interaction in "tearooms," places where some male homosexuals go for quick, anonymous oral sex.

Humphreys found that some restrooms in Forest Park, just across from the campus, were tearooms. He first did a participant observation study, just hanging around these restrooms. He found that three people were always involved, the two having sex and a third person—called a "watchqueen"—who stayed on the lookout for police and other unwelcome strangers. Humphreys took the role of watchqueen, watching not only for strangers but also observing what the men did. He systematically recorded these encounters, and they became part of his dissertation.

Humphreys decided, however, that he also wanted to know more about the regular lives of these men. Impersonal sex in tearooms was a fleeting encounter, and the men must spend most of their time doing other things. What things? With whom? And what was the significance of the wedding rings that many of the men wore? Humphreys then hit upon an ingenious technique. Many of the men parked their cars near the tearooms. After observing an encounter, he would leave the restroom and record the license number of the man's car. Through the help of a friend in the St. Louis police department, Humphreys then obtained each man's address. About a year later, Humphreys arranged for these men to be included in a medical survey conducted by some of the sociologists on our faculty. Disguising himself with a different hairstyle and clothing, and driving a different car, he visited some of these men at their homes. He then interviewed them, supposedly for the medical study.

Humphreys said that no one recognized him—and he did obtain the information he was looking for: family background, social class, health, religion, employment, and relationship with wife. He found that most of the men were in their mid-thirties and had at least some college education. Surprisingly, the majority were married, and a higher proportion than in the general population turned out to be Roman Catholic. Moreover, these men led very conventional lives. They voted, mowed their lawns, and took their kids to Little League games.

Humphreys also found that although most of the men were committed to their wives and families, their sex life was far from satisfactory. Many reported that their wives were not aroused sexually or were afraid of getting pregnant because their religion did not allow them to use birth control. Humphreys concluded that these were heterosexual men who were using the tearooms for an alternative form of sex which, unlike affairs, was quick (taking no time away from their families), inexpensive (zero cost), and nonthreatening (the encounter required no emotional involvement to compete with their wives). If a wife had discovered her husband's secret sex life, of course, it would have been devastating to their relationship. And today, tearoom encounters present a much greater threat, for Humphreys conducted his research before the arrival of AIDS. Anyone participating in tearooms today risks death—both for himself and, by transmitting AIDS, also for his sexual partners, wife included.

This study stirred controversy among sociologists and nonsociologists alike (Goodwin, Horowitz, and Nardi, 1991). Humphreys was severely criticized by many sociologists, and a national columnist even wrote a scathing denunciation of "sociological snoopers" (Von Hoffman 1970). Concerned about protecting the identity of his respondents, Humphreys kept a master list in a safe deposit box. As the controversy grew more heated, however, and he feared that the names might be subpoenaed (a court case was being threatened), he gave me a list to take from Missouri to Illinois, where I had begun teaching. (It could have been some other list of respondents. I was told not to examine it, and I did not.) When he called and asked me to destroy it, I burned it in my backyard. Humphreys had a contract to remain at Washington University as an assistant professor, but he was fired before he could begin teaching. (Although other reasons were involved, his research was a central issue. There was even an attempt by one professor to have his Ph.D. revoked.)

Was the research ethical? That question is not easily decided. Although many sociologists sided with Humphreys and his book reporting the research won a highly acclaimed award, the criticisms mounted. At first Humphreys vigorously defended his position, but five years later, in a second edition of his book (1975), he stated that he should have identified himself as a researcher.

HOW RESEARCH AND THEORY WORK TOGETHER

As discussed, sociological research is based on the sociologist's interests, the availability of subjects, appropriate methods, and ethical considerations. But the value of research is also related to sociological theory. On the one hand, as sociologist C. Wright Mills (1959) so forcefully argued, research without theory is of little value, simply a collection of meaningless "facts." On the other hand, if theory is unconnected to research it is abstract and empty, unlikely to represent the way life really is. Research and theory, then, are interdependent, and sociologists combine them in their work.

They do this in three major ways. First, as stressed in Chapters 1 and 2, sociologists use theory to interpret data. Functionalism, symbolic interaction, and conflict theory are frameworks that sociologists use to interpret research findings. Second, theory helps to generate research. As sociologists develop hypotheses from theory, they identify areas that need to be explored further to test those hypotheses. Third, research helps to generate theory. When research findings do not fit a theory, they indicate that the theory needs to be modified.

Research findings that contradict a theory can also indicate that the data are inaccurate, that more research needs to be done. If a study were to show little relationship between poverty and abduction/rape by strangers, it would fly in the face of several sociological theories that are firmly based on existing studies. Consequently, if contradictory results came in, the research would be suspect and more research would need to be carried out. Theory and research then, go hand in hand, each feeding the other.

A Final Word: When the Ideal Meets the Real

Although one can list the ideals of research, real-life situations often force sociologists to settle for something that falls short of the ideal. For example, ideally you might want to interview a random sample of rapists under model conditions for your rape study. But the real world is seldom so cooperative. First, there is no list of the population, rapists, that would allow each rapist the same chance of being included in your sample. That eliminates random samples. Second, many rapists have never been caught. Let us suppose that by chance, such as some sort of unusual contact, you were able to include an uncaught rapist or two in your sample. How could you know what they represent? Why would you assume that one or two individuals would in any way be representative of the vast numbers of men who have never been caught for this act? Consequently, the typical dilemma that social researchers confront is either not to study what they want to study, or to do so under less than ideal conditions.

Now suppose you are driven by what sociologist Peter Berger (1963) identifies as the essence of the sociological pursuit, an intense desire to know more about social life. You *really* want to learn more about rapists. Then imagine you find a prison warden who welcomes your research. Should you turn that invitation down because it is less than ideal? Not on your life! You are well aware that imprisoned rapists do not represent

Essay #6

Project 4

L. Obj. 10: Discuss how research and theory work together. Note reasons why most research must be conducted under less than ideal circumstances.

K.P.: C. Wright Mills

CDQ 15: Why do you think sociologists often end up conducting research under less than ideal conditions?

K.P.: Peter Berger

the population of rapists in a scientific sense, that many rapists are not included in the prison—the uncaught, those who did the act but for a variety of reasons are found not guilty, and those who are found guilty but placed on probation. Nevertheless, you jump at the chance, for this is your opportunity to learn about rapists, and whatever you learn will be more than is already known.

K.P.: Diana Scully and Joseph Marolla

Such was the experience of Diana Scully and Joseph Marolla (1985). These two sociologists had the opportunity to interview rapists in prison, and they took it. The conditions may have been less than ideal, but their research expanded our knowledge about men who rape (Scully 1990). For example, they discovered something that goes against common sense—that most rapists are not sick, at least not in the sense that they are overwhelmed by uncontrollable urges. Rather, Scully and Marolla found that rapists are men for whom rape is rewarding. These men feel good while they rape. Or they feel good after they rape. They even find pleasure in anticipating the rape. Some plan their rapes, sometimes with other like-minded individuals. Some even rape with friends on a regular basis, such as on weekends, using rape as a form of recreation. Others rape spontaneously. Some men even use rape to get even with an enemy ("revenge rape"). Others simply take an unexpected opportunity, such as the man in the following example who was robbing a woman on a local supermarket parking lot.

> I wasn't thinking about sex. But when she said she would do anything not to get hurt, probably because she was pregnant, I thought, "why not?" (Scully and Marolla 1985)

Another man pinpointed how power was combined with sex in his rapes (p. 259).

K.P.: Elton Mayo

> Rape gave me the power to do what I wanted to do without feeling I had to please a partner or respond to a partner. I felt in control, dominant. Rape was the ability to have sex without caring about the woman's response. I was totally dominant.

To discover that most rapists engage in calculated behavior—that the motivating force is power not passion—the criminal pursuit of pleasure not mental illness—is part of the thrill of the sociological quest. Such findings not only add to our storehouse of "facts," they also contribute to sociological theory, enabling us to understand situations that go far beyond the particulars that generated the "facts." For example, because of this research we might theorize about "normal learning." We could assume that some otherwise normal individuals, through exposure to atypical situations, learn that rape is rewarding. With weak internal controls (controls inside the individual, such as conscience) and weak external controls (those located in the social groups to which they

Sociologists Diana Scully and Joseph Marolla interviewed rapists in prisons and reported their findings in a paper published in a sociological journal.

TABLE 5.4   Profiling the Rapist

Researchers have found that rapists vary in certain distinctive features. The following summaries, prepared with Linda Henslin, are based on studies of rapists who have been caught. These findings are an example of secondary analysis, a reexamination of data produced by other researchers, in this case Cohen, Seghorn, and Calmas 1969; Finkelhor and Yllo 1985; Hotchkiss 1978; Hills 1980; Athens 1980; Scully and Marolla 1985. These profiles of ten "types" of rapists show that many different motivations underlie rape (Henslin 1993c). The proportion of rapists within each type, as well as what other types may exist, is not known.

"More sociological" means that social influences on the motivations of the rapist are more prominent, while "more psychological" means that more deeply embedded, individualized influences are the more evident. The distinction should become clear as you compare these types.

More Sociological

1. *The recreational rapist* uses rape to engender a sense of male camaraderie. He joins friends to collectively participate in a dangerous activity. As sociologists Diana Scully and Joseph Marolla (1985) discovered, a man may make a date with a victim and without her knowledge drive her to a predetermined location where his friends are waiting to rape her. One man said that this practice was so much a part of his group's recreational routine that they had rented a house just for this purpose.

2. For *the political rapist,* the victim is merely a substitute for his enemy. The goal is to make a political statement, with the female victims merely pawns in a game played by men trying to get back at other men. Much of the raping done by soldiers in wartime is of this type. They feel an intense hatred of the enemy. By raping "the enemy's women," they show contempt for the enemy and declare their own superiority (Schwendinger and Schwendinger 1983).

3. *The opportunist* does not set out to rape. Rather, he unexpectedly sees an opportunity and grabs it. Not uncommonly, the rape occurs while he is committing a robbery or burglary. An example is given on p. 134.

4. *The date rapist* (or acquaintance rapist) is perhaps the most common type of rapist. Contrary to stereotypes, most date rape does not occur between relative strangers on first dates, but between couples who have known each other for about a year (Muehlenhard and Linton 1987). As Table 5.1 shows, a study of female undergraduates in introductory psychology courses found that about 21 percent had been forced to have intercourse against their will.

5. *The husband rapist,* contrary to many myths, is a "real" rapist. This case is not simply a matter of a husband being too insistent on having sex. After interviewing wives who had been raped, sociologists David Finkelhor and Kersti Yllo (1985) found that some marital rape is brutal, and some wives had to flee in terror of their lives and sanity.

More Psychological

6. *The revenge rapist,* like the political rapist, uses rape to get even with someone. It may be his victim with whom he is angry, but sometimes she is merely a substitute. An example is a man who went to collect some money that another man owed him. On finding the man was not home

> I grabbed her [the man's wife] and started beating the hell out of her. Then I committed the act. I knew what I was doing. I was mad. I could have stopped but I didn't. I did it to get even with her and her husband (Scully and Marolla 1985).

7. *The generally violence-prone rapist* is a man who has found rape just one of many violent ways to approach life. He sees the world itself as a violent affair. If he is going to get anything, he must take it—violently wresting it from others. And that includes sex. This man does not hesitate to use whatever violence he sees as necessary. Unlike the woman hater and sadist (below), however, his pleasure in rape is rooted in the sex rather than the violence, and he uses no more violence than is necessary to make a woman submit.

8. *The Walter Mitty rapist* is generally passive and submissive in most areas of life, but he carries an unrealistic image of masculinity. He uses rape to bridge the gap between what he perceives men ought to be and how he perceives himself. As part of his fantasy, he sees his victim as outwardly protesting but inwardly enjoying being raped—for he considers himself an outstanding sex partner. Carrying his fantasy one step further, he sometimes calls his victim the next day to try to make a date with her.

9. *The woman hater* has been severely hurt by some woman who is very important to him. This hurt has left an unhealed emotional wound and created a hatred of women. Rape gives him a feeling of power over women. He is likely to verbally degrade and to physically injure his victim in retaliation for his unhealed hurt.

10. *The sadist* also beats his victim, but unlike the woman hater he has no negative feelings toward women in particular. Rather, he has learned to receive pleasure by inflicting pain on others, and women are merely handy outlets for him. By raping women, he is able to combine the pleasure he receives from inflicting pain with the pleasure he receives from the sex act.

The question of what makes some type "more sociological" or "more psychological" could be debated endlessly. It is apparent, for example, that types 5 and 6 could just as well be classified at the lower end of the "more sociological" category. Note also the overlap between the types. For example, a date rapist or a husband rapist could also be a woman hater or a violence-prone individual.

Speaker Sug. #4: A colleague who has conducted research on rape or other violent criminal conduct.

belong, such as social ties), these men then rape. The specifics of the learning process, as well as the particulars of the internal and external controls, are yet to be discovered. Moreover, for some men, it is the ties to their social groups that foster rape—for their subculture encourages rape as a "manly" act. Table 5.4 provides two sets of profiles on rapists. One set categorizes types of rapists by the sociological influences that motivate them. The second set categorizes types of rapists by psychological motivation. At some point the Scully/Marolla study will stimulate sociological theorizing about rapists. And then sociologists will test those theories. And so sociology moves slowly onward, adding one small unit of data and theory to another.

And that is exactly what sociology needs more of—imaginative, and sometimes daring, research conducted in an imperfect world under less than ideal conditions. This is what it is all about. Sociologists study what people do—whether their behaviors are pleasing to others or whether they disgust them and arouse them to anger. In either case, the application of research methods takes us beyond common sense and allows us to penetrate surface realities so we can better understand social life.

SUMMARY

1. Any human behavior is a valid sociological topic, even disreputable behavior. Rape is such an example.

2. Common sense is highly limited and its insights often incorrect. Social research is therefore needed if we are truly to understand human behavior.

3. The basic research model consists of eight basic steps (see Figure 5.1).

4. Sociologists use six research methods (or research designs) for gathering data: surveys, documents, secondary analysis, participant observation, experiments, and unobtrusive measures. In this chapter the study of rape was used as an example to discuss the advantages and disadvantages of each method. The choice of research method depends on the research questions to be answered, the researcher's access to potential subjects, the resources available, the researcher's training, and ethical considerations.

5. Ethics is of fundamental concern to sociologists, who are committed to protecting their subjects from harm. Sociologists are supposed not to misrepresent themselves or their research. The Brajuha research on restaurants and the Humphreys research on "tearooms" both raised ethical issues.

6. Theory without research is not likely to represent real life, while research without theory is merely a collection of meaningless "facts." Theory and research go hand in hand: Research findings cause theory to be modified, while theory points to areas of social life that need to be researched.

7. Real-life situations often force sociologists to conduct research in less than ideal conditions. But research conducted in an imperfect world stimulates the sociological theorizing by which sociology combines data and theory.

SUGGESTED READINGS

Babbie, Earl R. *The Practice of Social Research.* Belmont, Calif.: Wadsworth, 1985. This "how-to" book of sociological research describes the major ways in which sociologists gather data and the logic that underlies each method.

Burgess, Robert, ed. *Studies in Qualitative Sociology: Reflections on Field Experience,* London: JAI Press, 1990. First-person accounts by sociologists provide an understanding of the problems and rewards of fieldwork.

Holmstrom, Lynda Lyttle. *The Victims of Rape: Institutional Reactions.* New Brunswick, N.J.: Transaction, 1983. The writer follows rape victims as they come in contact with the police, hospitals, and courts, illustrating how these contacts are often devastating to the victim.

Hunt, Morton M. *Profiles of Social Research: The Scientific Study of Human Interaction.* New York: Russell Sage/Basic Books, 1986. This text provides a clear, concise introduction to research methods.

Jorgensen, D. L. *Participant Observation: A Methodology for Human Studies.* Newbury Park, Calif.: Sage, 1989. The book explains the value of participant observation and summarizes interesting studies. From it, you may understand why *you* are uniquely qualified for doing participant observation.

Merton, Robert K., Marjorie Fiske, and Patricia L. Kendall. *The Focused Interview: A Manual of Problems and Procedures* 2nd ed. New York: The Free Press, 1990. Specific interviewing techniques are outlined; of value primarily to more advanced students.

Reynolds, Paul D. *Ethics and Social Science Research.* Englewood Cliffs, N.J.: Prentice Hall, 1982. The author explores ethical dilemmas confronted by social researchers.

Scully, Diana. *Understanding Sexual Violence: A Study of Convicted Rapists.* Boston: Unwin Hyman, 1990. The author's examination of the rationalizations of rapists helps us understand why some men rape and what they gain from it.

Smith, Carolyn D., and William Kornblum. *In the Field: Readings on the Field Research Experience.* New York: Praeger, 1989. These sociologists' first-person accounts of their experiences of fieldwork help bring the research process to life.

Webb, Eugene J., Donald T. Campbell, Richard D. Schwartz, Lee Sechrest, and Janet Below Grove. *Unobtrusive Measures: Nonreactive Research in the Social Sciences.* Chicago: Houghton Mifflin, 1981. The clear overview of unobtrusive measures also contains concise summaries of a great deal of research.

Whyte, William Foote, and Kathleen King Whyte. *Learning from the Field: A Guide from Experience,* Beverly Hills, Calif.: Sage, 1984. Focusing on the extensive field experience of the senior author, this book provides insight into the critical involvement of the self in this research method.

Writing Papers for Sociology

The Sociology Writing Group. *A Guide to Writing Sociology Papers.* 2nd ed. New York: St. Martin's Press, 1991. The guide takes students through all the steps in writing a sociology paper, from choosing the initial assignment to turning in a finished paper. The steps are explained in detail with many examples.

Cuba, Lee J. *A Short Guide to Writing about Social Science.* Glenview, Ill.: Scott, Foresman, 1988. The author summarizes the various types of social science literature, presents guidelines on how to organize and write a research paper, and explains how to prepare an oral presentation.

Romare Bearden, Quilting Time, *1985*

Societies to
Social Networks

SOCIAL GROUPS AND SOCIETIES

THE TRANSFORMATION OF SOCIETIES

Hunting and Gathering Societies ■ Pastoral and Horticultural Societies ■ Agricultural Societies ■ Industrial Societies ■ Postindustrial Societies ■ *Perspectives:* **A Tribal Mountain People Meets Postindustrial Society**

GROUPS WITHIN SOCIETY

Primary Groups ■ Secondary Groups ■ In-Groups and Out-Groups ■ Reference Groups ■ Social Networks

GROUP DYNAMICS

Group Size ■ Leadership ■ *Down-to-Earth Sociology:* **How Group Size Affects Willingness to Help Strangers** ■ Conformity to Peer Pressure: The Asch Experiment ■ Obedience to Authority: The Milgram Experiment ■ Groupthink and Decision Making ■ Preventing Groupthink

SUMMARY

SUGGESTED READINGS

*J*ohnny smiled as his finger tightened on the trigger. The explosion was pure pleasure to his ears. His eyes glistened as the bullet ripped into the dog. With an exaggerated swagger, Johnny walked away, surrounded by five buddies, all wearing Levi's, Air Jordans, and jackets emblazoned with the logo of Satan's Servants.

Johnny had never felt as if he belonged. His parents were never home much, and when they were, all they did was have one drunken quarrel after another. Many times he had huddled in a corner while the police separated his parents and handcuffed his father. One of Johnny's recurring memories was of his father being taken away in a police cruiser. School was a hassle, too, for he felt that the teachers were out to get him and that most of his classmates were jerks. It wasn't unusual for Johnny to spend most of his time in detention for disrupting classes and fighting during lunch period.

Johnny didn't want to be a loner, but that seemed to be what fate held in store. He once tried a church group, but that lasted just one meeting. He was lousy at skateboarding and had given that up after the guys laughed at him. It was the same with baseball and other sports.

But Satan's Servants—now that was different. For the first time in his life, Johnny felt welcome—even appreciated. All the guys got in trouble in school, and none of them got along with their parents. He especially liked the jackets, with the skull and crossbones and "Satan's Servants" emblazoned on the back. And finally, with the "Satan's Servettes," there were girls who looked up to him.

The shooting assured Johnny, now known as JB, of a firm place in the group. The old man wouldn't bother them anymore. He'd get the message when he found his dog.

When they returned to the abandoned building, which served as their headquarters, Johnny had never felt so good in his entire life. This was what life was all about. "There isn't anything I wouldn't do for these guys," he thought, as they gathered around him and took turns pointing the pistol.

SOCIAL GROUPS AND SOCIETIES

L. Obj. 1: Explain why groups are so important to individuals and to societies.

CDQ 1: What would your life be like if you were not a member of any group?

Speaker Sug. #1: A social scientist who has recently traveled or lived in the former Soviet Union.

group: in a general sense, people who have something in common and who believe that what they have in common is significant; also called a social group

society: people who share a culture and a territory

Groups are the essence of life in society. Workers in a corporation form a group, as do neighbors on a block. The family is a group, as are the Los Angeles Lakers basketball team. Group membership can encourage or inhibit freedom, improve or destroy quality of life. The groups to which we belong can give us feelings of well-being—or of bitterness and despair. They help to determine our goals and values, how we feel about ourselves, and even how we feel about life itself. Groups can provide a sense of purpose in life—or withdraw even the spark that makes life seem worthwhile. Just as Johnny found a sense of belonging in Satan's Servants, others find the same in the Scouts, in church and synagogue, in sports, in the family, at work.

Sociologists define **group** in many different ways. Albion Small, mentioned in Chapter 1 as an early North American sociologist at the University of Chicago, used group in a very broad sense to mean people who have some sort of relationship so that they are thought of together (Small 1905). Other sociologists use a much narrower definition, but as sociologists Michael Olmsted and Paul Hare (1978) pointed out, "An essential feature of a group is that its members have something in common and that they believe what they have in common makes a difference." This shall be our general definition of group, and more specific types of groups will be defined below as they are introduced.

Society, which consists of people who share a culture and a territory, is the largest and most complex group that sociologists study. The values, beliefs, and cultural artifacts of society profoundly affect the smaller groups within it. In the former Soviet Union, for example, hundreds of underground artists' groups formed, all of which shared opposition to the Soviet state. The members of one art movement, called "Apartment Art," visually depicted how stifling life was for the millions of Russians forced to live several families or more to one apartment. Because no one knew who

Whether small or large, groups are the essence of life in society.

As a society—the largest and most complex type of group—changes, so too do the smaller groups that form the society. Until the collapse of communism in the former Soviet Union, many artists were forced to work underground. In this photograph, the artist Ilya Kabakov, a member of a now-defunct underground art movement called "Apartment Art," depicts his version of life in a typical Russian apartment under communism. Many people shared small flats and often one or more flat members were spies for the government. In "The Man Who Flew Into Space From His Apartment," Kabakov illustrates a fantasy of escape from the terrible tensions these crowded and suspicious living conditions created.

was a government spy, an atmosphere of paranoia and unhappiness—which the artists tried to depict—was often present.

Now that the communist government responsible for the spying has collapsed, the impetus for the formation of these artists' groups is gone. These groups will either disband or refocus their artistic perception on social change and continuing problematic features of national life. Similarly, thousands of other groups in the former Soviet Union must also adapt to changing circumstances, for they, too, had defined themselves by the conditions of their society. As any society changes, then, so do the nature and types of its groups.

Later on, this chapter looks at the major types of groups in industrialized societies and the dynamics that occur within them. But first, let's trace the evolution of the largest social groups—societies—from those based on the simplest form of social organization to those based on increasingly complex social arrangements. Thus, before investigating the different types of contemporary groups and their dynamics, we need to examine how contemporary society came into being. How did the United States, for example, become an industrialized nation with literally millions of groups? Why has an overpowering emphasis on consumption emerged as a key cultural value in American society?

THE TRANSFORMATION OF SOCIETIES

When societies modernize, the types and nature of their groups are transformed. For instance, in hunting and gathering societies, age and gender provide virtually the only bases for group membership other than the tribe itself. As a result, the simplest societies contain few distinct groups. Contrast this with industrialized societies, which are fragmented into countless groups. Here, in addition to groups based on age and sex, we also find groups based on religion, ethnicity, neighborhoods, professional sta-

Essay #1

TR#6: The Social Transformation of Society

L. Obj. 2: Trace the transformation of societies through the five stages of development, and note the degree of social inequality present in each stage.

CDQ 2: Do you think you would like to live in a society in which age and gender were virtually the only bases for group membership? Why or why not?

tus, political affiliation, sports and recreation, and even opinions—for instance pro-choice and pro-life groups. Enveloping these many smaller groups, however, is the larger group known as society—which, by its particular characteristics and conditions, gives shape to these smaller groups.

In tracing the development of societies from their earliest beginnings, the next section examines the major characteristics of hunting and gathering societies, pastoral and horticultural societies, agricultural societies, industrial societies, and postindustrial societies. (The evolution of societies is portrayed in Figure 6.1.) Group patterns (social structure) that predominate in one society may be quite different in another. The ways in which groups determine our basic orientations to life will become more apparent as we examine societies of the past and see how our own society emerged.

Hunting and Gathering Societies

The simplest societies are called **hunting and gathering societies.** As the name implies, these groups depend on hunting and gathering for their survival. The men do the hunting (of animals), the females the gathering (of plants). Beyond this basic division of labor by sex, there are few social divisions. The groups usually have a **shaman,** or priest, but they, too, must help procure food. Although these groups give greater prestige to the male hunters, the women gatherers contribute more food to the group.

In addition to gender, the major unit of organization is the family. Most members are related by ancestry or marriage. Because the family is the only distinct social institution in these societies, it fulfills functions divided among many specialized institutions in modern societies. The family distributes food to its members, educates its children (especially in food skills), nurses the sick, and so on.

Because an area cannot support a large number of people who hunt animals and gather plants (they do not plant, only gather what is already there), hunting and gathering societies are small, usually consisting of only twenty-five to forty members. They are also nomadic, moving from one place to another as the food supply of an area gives out. Seldom do they construct permanent settlements, although they may return to a specific area after it has regenerated.

These groups are usually peaceful and place high value on sharing food, which is essential to their survival. The high risk of destruction of the food supply however—by

Project 1

CDQ 3: Why do you think the male hunters have more prestige in hunting and gathering societies even though the women gatherers contribute more food to the group?

hunting and gathering society: a society dependent on hunting and gathering for survival

shaman: a priest in a preliterate society

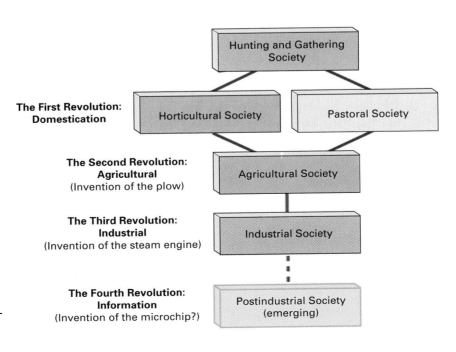

The First Revolution:
Domestication

The Second Revolution:
Agricultural
(Invention of the plow)

The Third Revolution:
Industrial
(Invention of the steam engine)

The Fourth Revolution:
Information
(Invention of the microchip?)

FIGURE 6.1 The Social Transformations of Society

The simplest form of societies are called hunting and gathering societies.

disease, drought, famine, and pestilence—makes their death rate very high. An individual has only about a fifty-fifty chance of surviving childhood (Lenski and Lenski 1987).

Hunters and gatherers are the most egalitarian of all types of societies. Because what the people hunt and gather are perishable, they can't accumulate possessions. Consequently, no one becomes wealthier than anyone else. There are no rulers, and most decisions are arrived at through discussion. Because their needs are simple and they do not accumulate material possessions, hunters and gatherers also have the most leisure of all human groups (Lee 1979; Sahlins 1972).

All human groups were once hunters and gatherers, and until several hundred years ago such societies were still fairly common. Now, however, only a few remain, such as the pygmies of central Africa, the San of the Namibian desert, and the aborigines of Australia. Sociologists Gerhard and Jean Lenski (1987) pointed out that modern societies have increasingly taken over the areas on which such groups depend for their food. They suggested that the few remaining hunting and gathering societies will soon disappear from the human scene.

Pastoral and Horticultural Societies

In earlier millennia (the estimate is about ten thousand to twelve thousand years ago), hunting and gathering societies branched in one of two directions. Very gradually, over thousands of years, some groups found that they could tame and breed some of the animals they hunted—primarily goats, sheep, cattle, and camels—others that they could cultivate plants.

The key to understanding the first branching is the word *pasture;* **pastoral societies** are based on the *pasturing of animals.* Pastoral societies developed in arid regions, where lack of rainfall made it impractical to build life around crops. Groups that took this turn remained nomadic, for they followed their animals to fresh pasture. The key to understanding the second branching is *horticulture,* or plant cultivation. **Horticultural societies** are based on the *cultivation of plants by the use of hand tools.* No longer having to abandon an area as the food supply gave out, these groups developed permanent settlements.

We can call the domestication of animals and plants the *first social revolution.*

CDQ 4: Why are hunting and gathering societies the most egalitarian of all types of societies?

CDQ 5: What types of advances had to occur before permanent settlements could develop?

CDQ 6: What was the first social revolution?

pastoral society: a society based on the pasturing of animals

horticultural society: a society based on the cultivation of plants by the use of hand tools

Although the **domestication revolution** was extremely gradual, it represented a fundamental break with the past and changed human history.

Horticulture apparently first began in the fertile areas of the Middle East. Primitive agricultural technology—hoes and digging sticks (to punch holes in the ground for seeds)—gradually spread to Europe and China. Apparently these techniques were independently invented in Central and South America, although they may have arrived there through **cultural diffusion** (the spreading of items from one culture to another) due to contacts yet unknown to us.

These discoveries of animal husbandry and plant cultivation were fundamental to the development of human society. They led to a series of interrelated changes, summarized below, that altered almost every aspect of human life. *First,* the human group became larger, for the more dependable food supply could support more people. *Second,* a more dependable food supply created a surplus—more food than was necessary for survival. *Third,* the food surplus allowed a specialized division of labor to develop: Some individuals became full-time priests, others the makers of jewelry, and so on. *Fourth,* the food surplus also stimulated trade, bringing more contact between groups. *Fifth,* as a result of the trade in surpluses, groups began to accumulate objects they considered valuable, such as gold, jewelry, utensils, and a greater variety of food. *Sixth,* material goods and trade created conditions for feuds and wars, for groups now had animals, pastures, croplands, and their growing possessions to fight about. *Seventh,* war in turn let slavery enter the human picture, for people found it convenient to let captives from the battles do their drudge work.

Eighth, some individuals accumulated more surplus goods than others. *Ninth,* this disparity led to the beginnings of social inequality, as some families (or clans) accumulated more wealth than others. Social stratification remained limited, however, for the surplus was limited, and the differences in wealth were not yet great enough to create social classes and castes. *Tenth,* wealth became hereditary as individuals passed on their few possessions to their descendants. *Eleventh,* as power became concentrated, forms of leadership changed and chiefs emerged.

Note that the central pattern that runs through this sequential transformation is the change *from greater to lesser equality.* The fundamental significance of this change was that where people were located within a society came to be increasingly significant in determining what happened to them in life.

Agricultural Societies

About five to six thousand years ago came the *second social revolution,* much more sudden and dramatic than the first. The **agricultural revolution** was brought about by the invention of the plow, an invention with such far-reaching effects that it produced a new type of society. This new **agricultural society** was based on large-scale agriculture, which depended on plows drawn by animals. Compared with hoes and digging sticks, the use of animals to pull plows was immensely efficient. More nutrients were returned to the soil as the ground was turned up, and much more land could be farmed by a smaller number of people. The result was a huge agricultural surplus, which allowed more people to engage in activities other than farming—to develop the things popularly known as "culture," such as philosophy, art, literature, and architecture. The changes during this period in history were so profound that they are sometimes referred to as "the dawn of civilization." Not only the plow but also the wheel, writing, and numbers were invented. The eleven developments outlined above, some of which were only tendencies during the earlier period, grew more pronounced.

One of the most significant changes was the growth of social inequality. When the agricultural surplus allowed the population to increase beyond anything previously known, cities developed. Groups began to be distinguished by greater or lesser possessions, and what had earlier been only a tendency now became a pronounced feature of social life. As conflict theorists point out, an elite gained control of the surplus resources

CDQ 7: Why do you think discoveries related to animal husbandry and plant cultivation were fundamental to the development of human societies?

CDQ 8: When did the second social revolution occur and what were its characteristics?

CDQ 9: What factors contributed to the growth of social inequality in agricultural societies?

domestication revolution: the first social revolution, based on the domestication of plants and animals, which led to pastoral and horticultural societies

cultural diffusion: the spread of items from one culture to another

agricultural revolution: the second social revolution, based on the invention of the plow, which led to agricultural societies

agricultural society: a society based on large-scale agriculture, dependent on plows drawn by animals

and wielded them to reinforce their own power. This concentration of resources and power was the precursor of the state, or the political institution, for to protect their privileged positions, the elite surrounded themselves with armed men to maintain their position. Next the elite levied taxes upon groups who had now become their "subjects," which opened the door to oppression.

No one knows exactly how it happened, but sometime during this period females also became subjugated to males. Sociologist Elise Boulding (1976) theorized that this change occurred because men were in charge of plowing and the cows. When metals were developed, men took on the new job of attaching the metal as tips to the wooden plows and doing the plowing. As a result,

CDQ 10: Why do you think females became subjugated to males during the agricutural period?

> the shift of the status of the woman farmer may have happened quite rapidly, once there were two male specializations relating to agriculture: plowing and the care of cattle. This situation left women with all the subsidiary tasks, including weeding and carrying water to the fields. The new fields were larger, so women had to work just as many hours as they did before, but now they worked at more secondary tasks. . . .This would contribute further to the erosion of the status of women.

Although Boulding's theory hasn't been proven, it matches the available evidence. As new evidence comes to light, we must expect to modify the theory.

Industrial Societies

Just as the agricultural revolution was based on a single invention, so was the much later *third revolution*. This, too, was sudden, dramatic, and turned society upside down. The **Industrial Revolution** began in Britain, where in 1765 the steam engine was first used to run machinery. Before this time some machines had harnessed nature (such as wind and water mills), but most had depended on human and animal power. This new source of energy led to the development of what is called **industrial society,** one that *harnesses machines powered by fuels to do its work.*

CDQ 11: What factors in Britain contributed to the development of industrial society?

The early steam-driven machines were soon replaced by internal combustion engines and by electric motors. Atomic power eventually became part of the picture—at first more a feature of publicity campaigns concerning its potential for changing social life than reality and, more recently, looming in the public consciousness as a menace to life itself.

Change feeds change. One invention stimulates another, because each invention incorporates elements from things already invented. Most inventions are merely a reassembling of elements or an adaptation of them, but a technological breakthrough, going far beyond what has existed, spawns hundreds and thousands of new adaptations.

As sociologist William F. Ogburn (1922; 1961) observed people adapting to technology, he concluded that a certain amount of time is required before people change their patterns in response to technological change. He called this interval **cultural lag.** In other words, industrial societies are always playing catch-up: Nonmaterial culture (values, beliefs, folkways, and how we relate to one another) always trails the more rapidly changing material culture (technology). Critics of this view point out that the process is not always so one-sided and that changes in the nonmaterial culture, such as values, also stimulate change in the material culture (Barber 1959).

CDQ 12: In what ways do you think "change feeds change?"

K.P.: William F. Ogburn

CDQ 13: How has technology changed your life from that of your parents and grandparents? What about computers? Telephone answering machines? Car phones?

CDQ 14: Why did social inequality become even more pronounced during the first stage of industrialization?

Let us look at some of the social changes that followed industrialization. This new form of production was far more efficient than anything the world had seen. Just as its surplus was greater, so were its social consequences. The eleven primary changes ushered in by agricultural and horticultural societies were accentuated even more, and with a much more dependable food supply and even greater surplus, the population boomed.

Social inequality became even more pronounced too, especially during the first stage of industrialization. The individuals who first utilized the new technology accumulated great wealth, their riches in many instances outrunning the imaginations of kings.

industrial revolution: the third social revolution, occurring when machines powered by fuels replaced most animal and human power

industrial society: a society based on the harnessing of machines powered by fuels

cultural lag: William F. Ogburn's term for the situation in which nonmaterial culture lags behind changes in material culture

Gaining an early position in the markets, they were able not only to control the means of production (factories, machinery, tools), but also to dictate the conditions under which people could work. A huge surplus of labor had already developed at this time, for feudal society was breaking up and masses of people were thrown off lands they and their ancestors had farmed as tenants for centuries. Moving to the cities, these landless peasants had no choice but to steal, starve, or work for starvation wages (Chambliss 1964; Michalowski 1985).

At that time, workers had no legal rights to safe, or even humane, working conditions; nor had they the right to unionize to improve them. The law considered employment to be a private contract between the employer and the individual worker. If workers banded together to ask for higher wages or to improve some condition of their work, they were fired. If they returned to the factory, they were arrested for trespassing. In the United States—where striking was illegal—strikers were beaten or shot by private police, and even by the national guard.

As American workers gradually won their demands for better working conditions, however, wealth spread to ever larger segments of society. Eventually, home ownership became common, as did the ownership of automobiles and an incredible variety of consumer goods. Beyond the imagination of social reformers, in the latter stages of industrial societies the typical worker enjoys a high standard of living in such terms as health care, longevity, and access to libraries and education.

The progression of industrialization to some extent reversed the earlier pattern of lessening equality. Universal indicators of increasing equality include better housing and a vast increase in consumer goods; the abolition of slavery; the shift from monarchies to more representative political systems; the automatic right to vote for all those over a specified age; and greater rights for women.

Another significant development during this period was a dramatic transformation in social institutions. As explained in Chapter 4, ascribed statuses gave way to achieved statuses as the intimacy and community of *Gemeinschaft* society yielded to the more formal, distant relationships of *Gesellschaft* society. And as analyzed in Chapter 1, the traditional functions of the family were eroded by other social institutions. Economic production moved from the family to work settings outside the home, some responsibility for the socialization of children was transferred to schools, medical treatment of the sick and injured was taken over by hospitals, care of the aged passed to nursing homes, and home recreation yielded to organized sports, electronic entertainment, and the mass media.

CDQ 15: Do you agree that the type of society in which you live is fundamental to the type of person you will become? Why or why not?

It is difficult to overstate the sociological principle that the type of society we live in is the fundamental reason that we become who we are. To see how industrial society affects your life, note that you would not be taking this course if it were not for industrialization. Clearly you would not have your car, clothing, home, telephone, stereo, computer, or electric lights, but neither would you hold your particular attitudes and aspirations for the future. Probably no aspect of your life would be the same, for you would be locked into agricultural or horticultural standards and their entire way of life. The Perspectives box on page 147 investigates how the Hmong, a group from an agricultural society in Southeast Asia, are adapting to their sudden immersion in the postindustrial society of the United States.

Postindustrial Societies

L. Obj. 3: Describe the characteristics of postindustrial society, and indicate some of the major changes occurring in such societies.

Change is so fundamental to human social life, and the forces set in motion during the previous period so potent, that a new type of society is once again emerging. Some social analysts have noted that the basic trend in advanced industrial societies is away from production and manufacturing to service industries. The United States was the first country to have more than 50 percent of its work force employed in service industries—health, education, research, the government, counseling, banking and investments, sales, law, and the mass media. Australia, New Zealand, western Europe,

PERSPECTIVES
Cultural Diversity in U.S. Society

A Tribal Mountain People Meets Postindustrial Society

What happens when a proud, tribal people from an agricultural society is suddenly transplanted to a postindustrial society? Perhaps no group is better able to exemplify the struggle to adapt to another type of society quite so well as the Hmong people from the northeastern highlands of Laos in Southeast Asia.

When United States forces withdrew from Vietnam and the North Vietnamese took over Laos in 1975, about one hundred thousand Hmong emigrated to the United States, mainly to California, Minnesota, and Wisconsin. The Hmong had fought loyally on the side of the United States against the North Vietnamese, sustaining a casualty rate five times that of United States forces. Part of a huge wave of immigration of some 850,000 postwar Southeast Asian refugees, this little-known people had distinctive needs that often went unmet by overwhelmed resettlement officials.

In Laos, the Hmong were tribal mountain dwellers whose agricultural life was light years removed from the world they encountered in the United States. They had no knowledge of cars, telephones, televisions, not even plumbing or electricity. They did not even have a written language until American and French missionaries invented one in the mid-1950s.

Resettled to American cities, the Hmong abruptly confronted a totally bewildering way of life for which their tribal, agricultural culture had left them quite unprepared. Many did not understand what locks were for, or the purpose of light switches. They had never seen a stove, and refugee workers would find them huddled around open fires in their living rooms. Some tried to make inside gardens by bringing in soil from the outside and spreading it around the living room floor. The Hmong used the toilet to wash rice—a logical adaptation of "water bowl" from their culture—but were perplexed when the rice disappeared if the toilet was accidentally flushed.

Perhaps the most poignant story of all is told by Sgt. Marvin Reyes of the Fresno city police: One night he pulled over a driver who was jerking his way through an intersection. The driver would stop, suddenly dart a few feet, then stop again. Figuring that the man was drunk, the officer was astonished when the Hmong driver said that he had been told to stop at every red light. It was late; the stoplight was blinking.

Not knowing English compounded the Hmong's problems. One Hmong man who dared to make his way through the labyrinth of the city to look for work carefully copied down the name of his street in case he got lost.

When he did lose his way, he showed the paper to a police officer. It read: ONE WAY.

The resettlement of the Hmong in cities across the United States proved a failure, for by isolating individuals, it undermined the clan and tribal bonds on which Hmong identity is based. The youth, knowing more English, began to take on greater authority, while Hmong women began to assert new, culturally unfamiliar independence.

In the face of this threat to traditional authority and social organization, tribal leaders stepped in. Selecting the San Joaquin Valley in California because of its similarity to the agricultural lands they had left behind, Hmong leaders organized mass migrations to this area. Lacking the skills to use modern, mechanized agriculture and suffering from a huge language barrier, the Hmong resorted to welfare and cheap housing in refugee ghettos. The unannounced home visits by government agents checking on welfare eligibility made many Hmong suspicious of outsiders.

With land in California so expensive, some Hmong leaders began to search the country for a different home base. They found that the lakes and trees of rural Burke and McDowell counties in North Carolina also reminded them of home. Since land is much cheaper there, about six hundred Hmong settled in these counties, buying land and homes. With low welfare support available in this state, the Hmong quickly picked up the work ethic. "Work—that is what America is all about," says Kue Chaw, the leader of this group.

As they make their perilous adjustment—holding on to what they can of their old way of life while changing what they must to survive in their new land—the Hmong are attempting to maintain their tribal closeness. So far, they have succeeded to an amazing degree; Hmong who travel to a strange town can look in the telephone book for a Hmong name and be welcomed into that family home even if they do not know the family. "This keeps us alive as a people, as a clan," say the Hmong.

Yang Dao, the first Hmong to earn a Ph.D., says that the Hmong must shake off their refugee status. He says, "We must start thinking like Hmong Americans. Take the best of Laos and the best of America and live like that."

Certainly the new identity destined to arise from this mixing of cultures will be sociologically interesting, another part of the cultural diversity that makes up the American folkscape.

Source: Based on Meredith 1984; Jones and Strand 1986; Spencer 1988; Mitchell et al. 1989; Cerhan 1990; Snider 1990; Trueba, Jacobs, and Kirton 1990.

CDQ 16: Do you think your career will be in information, services, and/or high technology? Will your career be characteristic of those found in postindustrial societies?

Speaker Sug. #2: A colleague in computer science or engineering to talk about what lies "beyond the postindustrial society"

CDQ 17: What changes do you think will occur in American society as a result of the information revolution?

Project 2

postindustrial society: a society based on information, services, and high technology, rather than on raw materials and manufacturing
information revolution: the fourth social revolution, based on technology that processes information

and Japan soon followed. The term **postindustrial society** refers to the new type of society that is emerging—one *based on information, services, and high technology,* rather than on raw materials and manufacturing (Bell 1973; Lipset 1979; Toffler 1980).

The basic component of the postindustrial society is information. People who offer services either provide or apply information of one sort or another. Teachers pass on knowledge to students, repair technicians use knowledge to service technological gadgets, while lawyers, psychiatrists, physicians, bankers, pilots, and interior decorators sell their specialized knowledge of law, the mind, the body, money, aerodynamics, and color schemes to clients. Unlike factory workers in an industrial society, they don't *produce* anything. Rather, they transmit or utilize knowledge to provide services that others are willing to pay for.

As reviewed above, early technological developments brought wrenching changes to past cultures. What will happen to ours? It may be that social analysts in years to come will speak of the current changes as the *fourth revolution.* Often called the **information revolution,** it is based on technology that processes information. Specifically, the computer chip is the primary technological change in the history of industrialized society. That tiny device is transforming society and with it, our social relationships. Its miniaturized circuitry allows many people to work at home, others to talk to people in distant cities and even other countries while they drive their automobiles. Because of it, we can peer farther into space than ever before. And because of it, millions of children spend countless hours struggling against video enemies, at home and in the arcades. The list of changes ushered in by this one technological advance is practically endless.

Our developing postindustrial society is also witnessing other fundamental changes; for example the field of biomedicine is poised on the threshold of an unfamiliar world. Surgeons can now operate on babies before they are born; and the consequences of gene splicing are making reality out of former science fiction. What will happen when gene splicers "create" new life forms, an almost inevitable result of their new capacity?

The main sociological question, however, is not which single invention will ultimately be credited as "the" cause of the new society but rather what the social consequences will be. How will our relationships at home, in the neighborhood, at school, at work, and in church and synagogue change? How will these changes cause us to

A hallmark of postindustrial societies is the information revolution, which is based on the computer chip.

think differently of ourselves? In what ways will they change our world view? We can see, for example, that family members are now less likely to eat their meals together, certainly not a factor that strengthens their bonds; that many people are content to watch television preachers, certainly not a factor to strengthen their ties to the local church; that many office workers, spending long hours focused on computer screens, feel isolated from their coworkers (Zuboff 1991); and that more people work at home, further weakening their ties with office colleagues (although perhaps strengthening their bonds with family members).

We can safely (perhaps) predict that science and education will grow in importance, for knowledge and its application are essential to this emerging type of society. It also seems that the widespread dissemination of knowledge will serve as a buffer between the individual and the state, providing even greater freedom and equality. For the more people are aware of comparable conditions in other countries, the harder it is for the state to enslave their minds and bodies. Some believe that the information revolution (satellites, television, video recorders, and the Xerox machine for quickly multiplying messages) lie at the essence of the breakdown of the Soviet empire. If information can no longer be restricted to a small controlling elite, how can you control the masses— except through brute force?

The full implications of the information explosion are still unknown, as is the shape the emerging society will take. But just as the larger group called society has historically exerted a fundamental force on people's thinking and behavior, so will it in its new form. As society is transformed, we, too, shall be swept along with it, even as our attitudes about the self and life are transformed.

GROUPS WITHIN SOCIETY

Essay #2

Sociologist Emile Durkheim viewed small groups as standing between the individual and the larger society. He said that if it were not for small groups, we would feel oppressed by that huge, amorphous entity known as society. We would experience **anomie,** the term Durkheim (1933) coined to refer to feelings of detachment, of rootlessness, of not belonging. By establishing intimate relationships and offering a sense of meaning and purpose to life, small groups serve as a sort of lifeline that helps to prevent anomie. Sometimes, as with Johnny's group in our opening vignette, small groups stand in opposition to the larger society, but in most instances they reinforce society's major values.

Before we look at the types of groups that make up our society—primary, secondary, in-groups and out-groups, social networks, and reference groups—we should distinguish between a group and an aggregate. An **aggregate** is a collection of people who have similar characteristics. For example, all college females who wear glasses are an aggregate, as are all males over six feet tall. Unlike groups, the individuals who make up an aggregate neither interact with one another nor take one another into account. Although the word *group* is sometimes used to refer to an aggregate, to avoid confusion in this book *group* will be used as defined earlier.

Project 3

L. Obj. 4: Define each of the following: primary groups, secondary groups, in-groups, out-groups, reference groups, and social networks.

K.P.: Charles H. Cooley

Primary Groups

In the opening vignette, Johnny never felt as though he belonged anywhere until Satan's Servants welcomed him. It was with them that he found friendship, admiration, and the close, intimate, face-to-face relationships that he valued. That is what sociologist Charles H. Cooley calls a **primary group.** As Cooley (1909) put it:

> By primary groups I mean those characterized by intimate face-to-face association and cooperation. They are primary in several senses, but chiefly in that they are fundamental in forming the social nature and ideals of the individual. The result of intimate association, psychologically, is a certain fusion of individualities in a common whole . . . .

anomie: feelings of not belonging, of being detached or uprooted

aggregate: people who have similar characteristics

primary group: a group characterized by intimate, long-term, face-to-face association and cooperation

CDQ 18: How do primary group relationships become fused into the individual's identity? Can you think of examples in your own life?

CDQ 19: Do you think all primary groups function positively? Why or why not?

Primary groups such as the family play a key role in our sense of self.

CDQ 20: Why do secondary groups tend to break down into primary groups? Can you give examples from your own membership in groups?

secondary group: compared with a primary group, a larger, relatively temporary, more anonymous, formal, and impersonal group based on some interest or activity, whose members are likely to interact on the basis of specific roles

What does Cooley mean by a "fusion of individualities in a common whole"? He means that a person's self becomes identified with

> . . .the common life and purpose of the group. Perhaps the simplest way of describing this wholeness is by saying that it is a "we"; it involves the sort of sympathy and mutual identification for which "we" is the natural expression. One lives in the feeling of the whole and finds the chief aims of [one's] will in that feeling.

In other words, the cooperative, intimate, long-term, face-to-face relationships provided by the primary group are so significant that the group becomes fused into the individual's identity. It is difficult, if not impossible, for the individual to separate his or her self from the primary group, for the self and the group merge into a "we."

Because primary groups, such as the family, friendship groups, and gangs mold our basic perspectives and ideals, Cooley calls them the "springs of life." As people internalize the views of their primary groups, those views become the lens through which they view life. Even as adults, no matter how far they may have come from their childhood selves, early primary groups remain "inside" people, where they continue to form part of the perspective from which they look out on the world.

Primary groups are essential to an individual's psychological well-being. Humans have an intense need for ongoing, cooperative, face-to-face associations that provide feelings of self-esteem. By offering a sense of belonging, a feeling of being appreciated, primary groups are uniquely equipped to meet this basic need.

Primary Groups That Fail.   Not all primary groups function positively, however. Some fail to provide the self-satisfactions that their members seek. Such groups, like Johnny's family, for example, are dysfunctional.

Three types of dysfunctions can be identified. First, the members of a primary group may quarrel and humiliate one another instead of providing reinforcement and support. (Note, however, that some members, such as those who dominate a family, may find personal rewards in such behavior.) Second, a primary group, such as the one Johnny joined, may purposely set itself against society. (Note, however, that as with Satan's Servants, the group may be dysfunctional for society but highly functional for its members.) The third dysfunction occurs when an essential primary group breaks down throughout society. An example would be if families in general were no longer to provide the essential benefits of a primary group. Some analysts think that this has already happened to the American family; others believe that the family is simply changing, but that it will continue to serve as an essential and beneficial primary group.

Secondary Groups

Compared with primary groups, **secondary groups** are larger, relatively temporary, more anonymous, formal, and impersonal. Such groups are based on some interest or activity, and their members are likely to interact on the basis of specific roles, such as president, manager, worker, or student. Examples are a college classroom, the American Sociological Association, a factory, or the Democratic party.

As we have seen in hunting and gathering societies and the early stages of agricultural and horticultural societies the entire society formed a primary group. In contrast, in industrial societies secondary groups have multiplied and become essential to our welfare. Over the course of our lives, we all join a variety of secondary groups. They are part of the way we get our education, make our living, and spend our money and leisure.

Although contemporary society could not function without secondary groups, such groups fail to satisfy deep needs for intimate association. Consequently, *secondary groups tend to break down into primary groups*. For example, at school and work we tend to form friendship cliques which provide such valued interaction that if it weren't

Relationships in secondary groups are more formal and temporary than those in primary groups. Often, members of secondary groups, such as workers in a large company, will form smaller primary groups.

for them we sometimes feel that school or work "would drive us crazy." Just as small groups serve as a buffer between us and the larger society, so the primary groups we form within secondary groups serve as a buffer between us and the demands that secondary groups place on us.

CDQ 21: In what ways are sports teams examples of in-groups and out-groups?

In-Groups and Out-Groups

Sometimes group membership is defined as much by what people are *not,* as by what they are; in other words, the antagonisms that some groups feel toward other groups are an integral part of their identity. Groups toward which individuals feel loyalty are called **in-groups,** those toward which they feel antagonisms, **out-groups.** For Johnny, Satan's Servants was an in-group, while the police, teachers, welfare workers, and all those associated with school represented out-groups.

The sociological significance of this fundamental division is twofold. First, in-groups provide a sense of identification or belonging, give feelings of superiority, and command loyalty. In-groups can therefore exert a high degree of control over their members. Johnny's shooting of the dog is such an example.

in-groups: groups toward which one feels loyalty

out-groups: groups toward which one feels antagonisms

During the Persian Gulf War, the Iraqi delegates to the United Nations formed a distinct out-group.

Second, the symbols of antagonism, even hatred, that out-groups represent help to reinforce the loyalty of members to their in-group. As a consequence, the members of an in-group may go to extremes, and may even be willing to face death to help destroy the out-group. With each seeing their own cause as just and their own group as virtuous, members of the Arab Brotherhood, for example, are willing to sacrifice their lives as they pursue the destruction of Israel, while extremists in Israel are equally dedicated to weakening the Arabs. Most relationships flowing from in-group–out-group relations, however, are much milder than this. More common are loyalties to sports teams that produce rivalries between nearby towns or colleges, in which the most extreme act is usually the invasion of the out-group's territory to steal a mascot, paint a rock, or uproot a goal post.

Sociologist Robert K. Merton (1968) identified a double standard that in-group loyalties and out-group antagonisms produce. The behaviors of one's in-group come to be looked at as virtues, while those same behaviors by members of an out-group are viewed as vices. For example, men who see women as members of an out-group may define an aggressive male employee as assertive, but an aggressive female employee as pushy; a male who doesn't speak up as "knowing when to keep quiet," but his female counterpart as too timid to make it in the business world.

K.P.: Robert K. Merton

CDQ 22: How do reference groups exert influence over people's behavior? What do you do if you have two reference groups that clearly conflict with each other?

reference group: Herbert Hyman's term for the groups we use as standards to evaluate ourselves

Reference Groups

Suppose you have just received a good job offer. It pays double what you hope to make even after you graduate from college. Your prospective employer says that you have to make up your mind within three days. And you will have to drop out of college now if you accept the job. As you consider the matter, thoughts like this may go through your mind: "My friends will say I'm a fool if I don't take the job . . . but Dad and Mom will practically go crazy. They've made sacrifices for me, and they'd be so disappointed if I didn't finish college. They've always said I've got to get my education first, that good jobs will always be there. . . . But, then, I'd like to see the look on the faces of those neighbors who said I'd never amount to much!"

This is an example of how people use **reference groups,** the groups we use as standards to evaluate ourselves. Your reference groups may include family, the Scouts,

The German neo-Nazis depicted here are an example of a reference group—the groups we use as standards to evaluate ourselves.

the members of a church or synagogue, your neighbors, teachers, classmates, and coworkers. Your reference group does not have to be one you actually belong to; it may include a group to which you aspire. For example, if you are thinking about going to graduate school, graduate students or members of the profession you want to join may form your reference group as you evaluate your grades or writing skills.

Reference groups exert tremendous influence over people's behavior. For example, if you want to become, say, the president of a corporation, or perhaps a rock musician, you will change your behavior in either case to match what you think others (the reference group) expect of you. In the first case, you might have your hair cut fairly short, start dressing more formally, use more formal speech, read *The Wall Street Journal,* take business and law courses, try to obtain a "fast-track" job, and join the local chamber of commerce. In the second, you might let your hair grow long (or perhaps shave your head), wear three earrings in one ear or perhaps in your nose, dress in ways your parents and many of your peers consider outlandish, read *Rolling Stone,* drop out of college, and hang around clubs and rock groups.

Sociologically, it is interesting to note that people often have reference groups that clearly conflict with each other. In the above example, if you wanted to become a corporate officer and had grown up in an Amish home, you would be likely to experience intense internal conflict, for the Amish strongly disapprove of such activities for their children. They ban high school and college education, three-piece suits, *The Wall Street Journal,* and corporate employment. Similarly, if you wanted to become a soldier and had been raised by dedicated pacifists, you would also be likely to experience deep conflict, as such parents are likely to hold quite different aspirations for their child and to disapprove of violence on principle.

Many of us experience conflicting reference groups as a regular part of life, given the pluralistic and highly mobile nature of American society. For some of us, then, the "internal recordings" that play contradictory messages are simply one cost of social mobility in an industrialized society.

Social Networks

Social networks, people linked by various social ties, have become highly significant in contemporary society. Your friends are part of your social network. So are your acquaintances and "friends of friends." If you become a sociologist, the sociologists you know will be part of your social network.

A primary characteristic of social networks is that they supply their members with valuable information. If an engineer (truck driver, babysitter, or mathematician) is fired, he or she is likely to make use of his or her social networks, perhaps calling friends, acquaintances, and others in the field to see if they know of any openings. Networks not only offer sources of information, they also provide socioemotional support, self-esteem, and even courage to face the rigors of everyday life (Statham, Miller, and Mauksch 1988). In some instances, as with a primary group, just knowing that they are there is a help.

Think of a social network as contacts that expand outward from yourself, gradually encompassing more and more people. Suppose that you want a summer job related to your major but can't get a foot in the door anywhere. You contact your major adviser, who hardly knows you, and she gives you some general information and suggests you check the want ads. Not exactly much help. But as you are talking, your adviser discovers that you come from the same little town in Ohio as she does, and that you have acquaintances in common. Your adviser then makes a few calls, one of the persons she calls also makes a few calls, and you are soon put in contact with someone who is hiring. From this single contact you have tapped into an extensive social network, part of which will eventually become your own.

A social network is not a one-way street, and in getting your job you have built up obligations, which you may later be called on to fulfill. Perhaps after you are estab-

CDQ 23: What kinds of valuable information do you get from social networks at school? If you are employed, from social networks at work?

social networks: the social ties radiating outward from the self, that link people together

The relationships we establish early in life may well serve us later in life, as is the case of these members of a social network of Harvard alumni.

lished in your field, you may get a telephone call to help find a summer job for the child of one of your major adviser's friends, for you have now become part of this network.

Sociologically, the significance of networks is that they tend to perpetuate social inequality. Simply put, some people's networks are more important than others'. Suppose, for example, that you want to be a physician. Let's make the reasonable assumption that social networks play a significant role in deciding which applicants get into medical schools. It is simply likely that your social network will be more efficient if you are the son or daughter of a physician.

Because most jobs are secured through social networks (Lin, Ensel, and Vaughn 1981), it is a truism that *who* you know is more important than *what* you know. This social fact is precisely what many females have run up against as they have tried to get good jobs: The "old boy" network tends to keep the best positions moving in the direction of friends and acquaintances, as well as friends of those friends and acquaintances—and these are not likely to be females (Hall 1987; McPherson and Smith-Lovin 1982, 1986; Abramson 1992).

The term **networking,** now accepted in popular speech, refers to the conscious use or even cultivation of networks, contacts people think will be helpful to them, usually for career advancement (Speizer 1983). Hoping to establish a circle of acquaintances that will prove valuable to them, people go to parties, join clubs, become members of churches or synagogues, and become active politically. Because of the obstacles posed by the "old boy" network, many females have begun developing specifically female occupational networks to further their careers.

GROUP DYNAMICS

L. Obj. 5: Explain what is meant by group dynamics, and indicate how group size affects interaction.

networking: the process of consciously using or cultivating networks for some gain

group dynamics: the ways in which individuals affect groups and the ways in which groups affect individuals

Now that we have surveyed the types of groups that make up society, let's look at what happens within groups, especially the ways in which individuals affect groups and the ways in which groups affect individuals. These reciprocal influences are known as **group dynamics.** We shall first discuss the differences that the size of the group makes and then examine the effects of the group on conformity, leadership, and decision making.

Before turning to focus on small groups, it is worth defining first what sociologists mean by this term. A **small group** is one that is small enough for everyone in it to interact directly with all the other members. Small groups can be either primary or secondary. Relatives at a family reunion and workers who take their breaks together represent primary small groups, while shoppers in a boutique and passengers on a public bus are examples of secondary small groups.

Group Size

Writing at the turn of the century, sociologist Georg Simmel (1858–1918) noted the significance of group size. He used the term **dyad** for the smallest possible group, consisting of two persons. Dyads, he noted, which include marriages, love affairs, and close friendships, show two distinct qualities. First, they are the most intense or intimate of human groups. Because only two persons are involved, the interaction is focused exclusively between one and the other. Many find this quality of dyads extremely satisfying, especially in the dyad of marriage; others feel threatened by this quality. Second, because they require the continuing active participation and commitment of both members, dyads are by definition the most unstable of social groups. If one member loses interest, the dyad collapses. In larger groups, in contrast, even if one member withdraws the group will continue, for its existence does not depend on a single member (Simmel 1950).

A **triad** is a group of three persons. A married couple with their first child is a common example of a triad. In spite of the difficulties couples usually experience adjusting to the birth of their first child—and hardly an aspect of their relationship goes untouched (Rubenstein 1992)—a child typically strengthens the marriage. Simmel uncovered the basic principle at work here, namely, triads are basically stronger than dyads. Like dyads, triads are also intense relationships, for interaction is shared by only three persons; but because interaction is shared with an additional person, the intensity lessens.

As Simmel also pointed out, triads, too, are inherently unstable. Because relationships among a group's members are seldom neatly balanced, they encourage the formation of a **coalition,** in which some group members align themselves against others. In a triad, it is not uncommon for two members to feel strong bonds with one another, leading them to act as a dyad and leaving the third feeling hurt and excluded.

The general principle is that *as a small group grows larger its intensity, or intimacy, decreases and its stability increases.* To see why, look at Figure 6.2 on page 156. The addition of each person to a group greatly increases the connections among people. In a dyad, there is only one relationship; in a triad, three; in a group of four, six; in a group of five, ten; if we expand the group to six, we have fifteen relationships; while a group of seven yields twenty-one relationships. If we continue adding members to the groups in this figure, we would soon be unable to follow the connections, for a group of eight has twenty-eight possible relationships, a group of nine thirty-six relationships, a group of ten forty-five, and so on. It is not only the increased size and number of relationships that make larger groups more stable. As groups grow, they tend to develop a more formal social structure to accomplish their goals. For example, more formal tasks are agreed upon, leaders emerge (see below), and more specialized roles come into play, ultimately resulting in the familiar formal offices of president, secretary, and treasurer.

The dynamics of group size have fascinating implications for social life. One such implication is the effect on people's willingness to help one another. In general, the smaller the group, the more people are willing to stick their necks out for strangers, as illustrated in the Down-to-Earth Sociology box on page 157. A second implication is a phenomenon that you have probably observed firsthand, and perhaps have reflected on. When a group is very small, its members behave very informally toward one another. As the group increases in size, however, its members grow more formal. A

K.P.: Georg Simmel

CDQ 24: How are your communications different when you are talking with one other person than when you are talking with two other people?

Essay #4

CDQ 25: Why do some couples experience difficulties adjusting to the birth of their first child? Can you think of ways to prevent this problem?

TR#7: The Multiplying Effects of Group Size on Relationships

Group size has a significant influence on how people interact. When a group changes from a dyad (two people) to a triad, the relationships among each of the participants undergoes a shift.

small group: a group small enough for everyone to interact directly with all the other members

dyad: the smallest possible group, consisting of two persons

triad: a group of three persons

coalition: the alignment of some members of a group against others

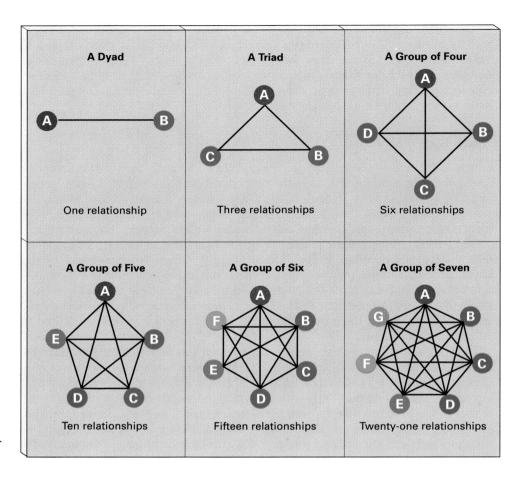

FIGURE 6.2 The Incremental Effects of Group Size on Relationships

leader: someone who influences the behaviors of others

instrumental leader: an individual who tries to keep the group moving toward its goals; also known as a task-oriented leader

degree of intimacy is lost, for no longer can the members assume that the others are "insiders" in sympathy with what they say. Now they must take a "larger audience" into consideration, and instead of merely "talking," they now begin to "address" the group. As their language becomes more formal, their body language stiffens too.

The third aspect of group dynamics is also one that you have likely observed many times. In the very early stages of a party, when only a few people are present, almost everyone talks with everyone else. As others arrive, however, the guests soon break into smaller groups. This sometimes dismays partygivers, who may want their guests all to mix together, and even make a nuisance of themselves trying to achieve *their* ideas of what a group should be like. The division into small groups is inevitable, however, for it follows the basic sociological principles we have just reviewed. Because the addition of each person rapidly increases connections (in this case, "talk lines"), it makes conversation more difficult. The guests therefore break into smaller groups in which they can not only see one another, but also, unlike in the larger group, comfortably interact directly with each person.

Leadership

All groups, no matter what their size, have leaders, though they may not hold a formal position in a group. A **leader** is simply someone who influences the behaviors of others. Some people are leaders because of their personalities, but leadership involves much more than this, as we shall see.

Groups have two types of leaders (Bales 1950, 1953; Cartwright and Zander 1968). The first is easy to recognize as a leader. This person, called an **instrumental leader**

DOWN-TO-EARTH SOCIOLOGY

How Group Size Affects Willingness to Help Strangers

Imagine you are taking a class with social psychologists John Darley and Bibb Latane (1968), who ask you to discuss the topic of adjusting to college life with other students. When you arrive, they tell you that to make things totally anonymous you will sit unseen in a booth and participate in the discussion over an intercom. You are to speak when your microphone comes on. The professors say that they will not listen in, and they leave.

You find the format somewhat strange, to say the least, but you participate. The other students, whom you have not seen, begin to freely exchange ideas, and you find yourself becoming wrapped up in the various problems they are sharing. One student even mentions how frightening he has found college because of his history of epileptic seizures. Soon after, this individual begins to breathe heavily into the microphone. Then he stammers and cries for help. A crashing noise follows; and you imagine him lying helpless on the floor. Then there is nothing but an eerie silence. What do you do?

It turns out the researchers staged the whole thing. No one had a seizure. In fact, no students were in other booths. Everything, except your comments, was on tape.

Some participants were told they would be discussing the topic with one other student, others with two, others with three, and so on. Darley and Latane found that all students who thought they were part of a dyad rushed out to help. If they thought they were part of a triad, only 80 percent went to help—and they were slower in leaving the booth. In six-person groups, only 60 percent went to see what was wrong—and they were even slower in doing so.

Darley and Latane concluded that in the dyad, the students clearly knew it was up to them. The professor was gone, and if they didn't help there would be no help. In the triad, students felt less personal responsibility, while in the larger groups they felt a *diffusion of responsibility:* It was no more up to them than it was up to anyone else.

Group size, then, affects our attitudes and behaviors in ways that ordinarily are invisible to us.

(or task-oriented leader) is an individual who tries to keep the group moving toward its goals. Such a leader tries to keep group members from becoming sidetracked, reminding them of what they are trying to accomplish. The **expressive leader** (or socioemotional leader), in contrast, is not usually recognized as a leader, but he or she certainly is. This person is likely to crack jokes, to offer sympathy, or to do other things that help lift the group's morale. Both types of leadership are essential: the one to keep the group on track, the other to increase harmony and minimize conflicts.

It is difficult for one person to be both an instrumental and an expressive leader, for these roles are contradictory. Because instrumental leaders are task-oriented, they sometimes create friction as they prod the group to get on with the job. Their actions often cost them popularity. Expressive leaders, in contrast, being peacemakers who stress personal bonds and the reduction of friction, are usually more popular (Olmsted and Hare 1978).

Let us suppose that the president of your college has asked you to head a task force to determine how the college can reduce sexual discrimination on your campus.

> **expressive leader:** an individual who increases harmony and minimizes conflict in a group; also known as a socioemotional leader

During the aborted August 1991 coup against the government of Mikhail Gorbachev, Boris Yeltsin, then president of the Russian Republic and now leader of the Commonwealth of Independent States became the instrumental leader of the former Soviet Union.

Project 4

CDQ 27: Do you prefer an authoritarian, democratic, or laissez-faire leadership style when you are the group leader? How about when you are a follower?

L. Obj. 7: State the reasons why researchers have concluded that democratic leaders are more effective than authoritarian ones.

CDQ 28: Are some leaders simply "born?" Why or why not?

leadership styles: ways in which people express their leadership

authoritarian leader: a leader who leads by giving orders

democratic leader: a leader who leads by trying to reach a consensus

laissez-faire leader: an individual who leads by being highly permissive

The position requires you to be an instrumental leader. However, you can obviously adopt a number of **leadership styles,** or ways of expressing yourself as a leader. The three basic styles are that of **authoritarian leader,** one who gives orders; **democratic leader,** one who tries to gain a consensus; and **laissez-faire leader,** one who is highly permissive. Which should you choose?

Social psychologists Ronald Lippitt and Ralph White (1958) carried out a classic study of these three leadership styles. Boys, matched for IQ, popularity, physical energy, and leadership, were assigned to "craft clubs" made up of five youngsters each. Adult males trained in the three leadership styles then rotated among the clubs, each playing all three styles to control possible effects of their individual personalities.

The authoritarian leaders assigned the children tasks and set the working conditions. They also praised or condemned their work arbitrarily, giving no explanation for why it was good or bad. The democratic leaders held group discussions and outlined the steps necessary to reach the group's goals. They also suggested alternative approaches to these goals and let the children work at their own pace. When they evaluated the children's projects, they gave "facts" as the bases for their decisions. The laissez-faire leaders were very passive. They gave the group almost total freedom to do as they wished. They stood ready to offer help when asked but made few suggestions. They did not evaluate the children's projects, either positively or negatively. While all this action was taking place, four researchers peered through peepholes, taking notes and making movies.

The results? Each leadership style produced different reactions. The boys who had authoritarian leaders became either aggressive or apathetic. Although both the aggressive and apathetic boys showed strong dependence on the leader, the aggressive ones also became hostile toward him. The boys also showed a high degree of internal solidarity. Compared with this group, the boys who had democratic leaders were more personal and friendly, more "group-minded," and looked to one another for mutual approval. They did less scapegoating, and when the leader left the room they continued working at a steadier pace. The boys with laissez-faire leaders asked more questions, but they made fewer decisions. They were notable for their lack of achievement.

The researchers concluded that the democratic style of leadership worked best. Those conclusions may have been colored by ideology, however, as the research was conducted by persons who themselves favored a democratic style of leadership; and it was conducted during a highly charged political period (Olmsted and Hare 1978). It should also be noted that different conditions demand different leadership styles. It would be difficult, for example, to run a large army if decisions had to be discussed and agreed upon. For such groups, an authoritarian style of leadership seems to be more effective. In contrast, a small group of therapists may work well under democratic leadership.

Given this information, then, what style of leadership would you choose if you were taking over the president's task force? At least you should now know that an authoritarian style, while it can be effective, will likely create hostility, and that a laissez-faire style is likely to produce few results. Keeping in mind the earlier materials on instrumental and expressive leadership, you might also wish to encourage some "light" behavior.

You may have noted that only males were involved in this experiment. It is interesting to speculate how the results might differ if the experiment were repeated with groups of girls and male and female leaders, groups of boys and male and female leaders, and groups of both girls and boys with male and female leaders. Perhaps you will become the sociologist to do this.

Finally, let's consider what kind of people become leaders. Are some leaders simply "born"? No sociologist would agree with such a premise, but we do know that personal characteristics are significant. Not surprisingly, more talkative persons who express determination and self-confidence are more likely than others to become leaders. Perhaps surprising, however, is the fact that physical characteristics are important;

taller persons and those judged better-looking are more likely to be vaulted into leadership (Stodgdill 1974; Crosbie 1975).

Much more subtle factors are also involved. For example, where you sit in a group makes a difference. Social psychologists Lloyd Howells and Selwyn Becker (1962) formed groups of five persons each who did not know one another. They seated them at a rectangular table, three on one side and two on the other. Their findings are startling: Although only 40 percent of the people sat on the two-person side, 70 percent of the leaders emerged from that side. The explanation is that more interactions are directed to persons across a table than to persons next to a speaker.

Conformity to Peer Pressure: The Asch Experiment

How influential are groups in people's lives? As we shall see, they wield a surprising amount of influence over attitudes and behaviors. Let us look first at *conformity* in the sense of going along with your peers. They have no authority over you, only the influence that you allow.

Imagine that you are taking a course in social psychology with Dr. Solomon Asch and that you have agreed to participate in an experiment. As you enter his laboratory, you see seven chairs, five of them already filled by other students. You are given the sixth. Soon the seventh person arrives. Dr. Asch stands at the front of the room next to a covered easel. He explains that he will first show a large card with a vertical line on it, then another card with three vertical lines. All each of you has to do is tell him which of the three lines is identical to the line on the first card (see Figure 6.3).

Dr. Asch then uncovers the first card with a single vertical line and the comparison card with the three lines. The correct answer is easy, for one of the lines is obviously too tall, another too short, and one exactly right. Each person, in order, states his or her answer aloud. The six before you all answer correctly, as do you when it is your turn. The second trial is just as easy, and you begin to wonder what is the point of your being here. Then something unexpected happens on the third trial. Just as before, it is easy to tell which lines match. The first student, however, gives a wrong answer. The second gives the same incorrect answer. So do the third and the fourth. By now you are wondering what is wrong. How will the person next to you answer? You can hardly believe it when he, too, gives the same wrong answer. Then it is your turn,

Essay #6

L. Obj. 8: Demonstrate the importance of peer pressure to conformity by analyzing the Asch experiment.

Speaker Sug. #4: A psychologist conducting research on conformity, peer pressure, groupthink, or other appropriate social psychological topics.

CDQ 29: How influential do you think groups are in people's lives? Does the Asch experiment correspond wth your thoughts?

K.P.: Solomon Asch

Project 5

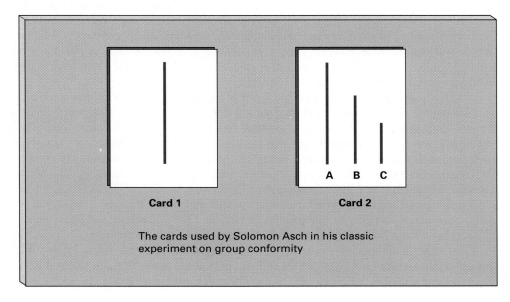

Card 1   Card 2

The cards used by Solomon Asch in his classic experiment on group conformity

FIGURE 6.3 Asch's Cards (*Source:* Asch 1952:452–453.)

and you give what you know is the right answer. The seventh person also gives the same wrong answer. On the next trial, the same thing happens. You know the choice of the other six is wrong, yet they give what to you are obviously wrong answers. You don't know what to think. Why aren't you seeing things the same way they are? Sometimes they do, but in twelve trials they don't. Something is seriously wrong, and you are no longer sure what to do. . . .

When the eighteenth card is finished, you feel relief. The experiment is finally over, and you are ready to bolt for the door. Dr. Asch walks over to you with a big smile on his face, thanks you for participating in the experiment, and then explains that you were the only real subject in the experiment! The other six were all stooges! "I paid them to give those answers," he says. Now you feel real relief. Your eyes weren't playing tricks on you after all.

What were the results? Asch (1952) tested fifty people. About 33 percent gave in to the group about half the time and gave what they knew to be wrong answers. Another 40 percent also gave wrong answers, but not as often. And 25 percent stuck to their guns and always gave the right answer. I don't know how I would do on this test (if I knew nothing about it in advance), but I like to think that I would be part of the 25 percent. You probably feel the same way. But why should we feel that we wouldn't be like *most* people?

The results are disturbing. In our "land of individualism," the group is so powerful that most people are willing, at least to some extent, to say things that they know do not match objective reality. And this was simply a group of strangers! How much more can we expect the group to enforce conformity when it consists of friends, people we value highly and depend on for getting along in life? Again, perhaps you will become the sociologist to run that variation of Asch's experiment, and perhaps to use female subjects.

Obedience to Authority: The Milgram Experiment

Let us define *obedience* as compliance with persons in authority. To what degree are people obedient? Do they continue to obey even in extreme situations in which they might seriously hurt others?

Imagine now that you are taking a course with Dr. Stanley Milgram (1963, 1965), a former student of Dr. Asch's. Let us also assume that you did not take part in Dr. Asch's experiment and have no reason to be wary of these experimenters. You appear in the laboratory to participate in a study on punishment and learning. A second student arrives, and you draw lots for the roles of "teacher" and "learner." You are to be the teacher, he the learner. You are glad that you are the teacher when you see that the learner's chair has protruding electrodes and resembles an electric chair. Dr. Milgram shows you the machine you will run. You see that one side of the control panel is marked "Mild Shock, 15 volts," the center says "Intense Shock, 350 Volts," while the far right side reads, "DANGER: SEVERE SHOCK."

"As the teacher, you will read aloud a pair of words," explains Dr. Milgram. "Then you will repeat the first word, and the learner will reply with the second word. If the learner can't remember the word, you press this lever on the shock generator. The shock will serve as punishment, and we can then determine if punishment improves memory." You nod, now extremely relieved that you haven't been designated a learner.

"Every time the learner makes an error, increase the punishment by 15 volts," Dr. Milgram says. Then, seeing the look on your face, he adds, "The shocks can be extremely painful, but they won't cause any permanent tissue damage. I want you to see." You then follow him to the "electric chair," and Dr. Milgram gives you a shock of 45 volts. "There. That wasn't too bad, was it?" "No," you mumble.

The experiment begins. You hope for the learner's sake that he is bright, but unfortunately he turns out to be rather dull. He gets some answers right, but you have to keep turning up the dial. Each turn of the dial makes you more and more uncomfort-

Essay #7

L. Obj. 9: Explain the following about the Milgram experiment: purpose of study, how it was conducted, conclusions reached, and why the methodology was questioned.

K.P.: Stanley Milgram

CDQ 30: How would you have reacted if you had been a student in Dr. Stanley Milgram's class when he conducted his experiments on obedience to authority?

able. You find yourself hoping that he won't miss another answer. But he does. When he received the first shocks, the learner let out some moans and groans, but now he is screaming in agony. He even protests that he suffers from a heart condition. *How far do you continue turning that dial?*

By now, you have probably guessed that there was no electricity attached to the electrodes and that the "learner" was a stooge, only pretending to feel pain. The purpose of the experiment, of course, was to find out at what point people refuse to participate. Does anyone actually turn the lever all the way to DANGER: SEVERE SHOCK?

Milgram was motivated to do this research because the slaughter of so many Jews, Gypsies, and others designated by the Nazis as "inferior" required the cooperation of "good people" (Hughes 1993). The fact that millions of ordinary people did nothing to stop the deaths seemed bizarre, and Milgram wanted to see how ordinary, intelligent Americans might react to an analogous situation.

Milgram was upset by what he found. Many "teachers" broke into a sweat and protested to the experimenter that this was inhuman and should be stopped. But when the experimenter, who sat by calmly, supposedly recording how the "learner" was performing, replied that the experiment must go on, this assurance from the "authority" ("scientist, white coat, university laboratory") was enough for most "teachers" to continue, even though they were free to leave. Even some who were "reduced to twitching, stuttering wrecks" continued to follow orders.

Milgram did eighteen of these experiments, using many subjects in each (Miller 1986). He used both males and females, put some teachers and learners in the same room, where the teacher could see the suffering, and had some learners not give verbal feedback, only pound and kick on the wall during the first shocks and then go silent. On some occasions he even added a second "teacher," this one a stooge who refused to go along with the experiment. The results varied from situation to situation. The highest proportion of "teachers" who pushed the lever all the way to 450 volts—65 percent—occurred when there was no verbal feedback from the learner. Of those who could turn and look at the learner, 40 percent turned the lever all the way. But only 5 percent carried out the severe shocking when the stooge-teacher refused to comply, a result that bears out some of Asch's results.

Milgram's experiment raised a ruckus in the scientific community. Not only were social researchers surprised, and disturbed, at the results, they were also alarmed at Milgram's methods. Recall that in Chapter 5 we reviewed the ethics of social research. Milgram's experiments became a stormy basis for rethinking research ethics. They stimulated associations of social researchers to adopt or revise codes of ethics and universities to require that subjects be informed of the nature and purpose of social research. Not only did researchers agree that to reduce subjects to "twitching, stuttering wrecks" was unethical, but almost all deception was banned.

The results of the Asch and Milgram experiments, however, still leave us with the disturbing question: "How far would *I* go in following authority?" Truly the influence of the group extends beyond what most of us imagine.

Groupthink and Decision Making

Among the disturbing implications of the Asch and Milgram experiments is the power of what is called **groupthink,** a narrowing of thought by a group of people. Sociologist Irving Janis used this term (1972) to refer to situations in which a group of people think alike and any suggestion of alternatives becomes a sign of disloyalty, there being only one correct answer. Even moral judgments must be put aside, for the welfare of the group depends on the particular course of action on which it has decided.

Groupthink is especially dangerous when it characterizes government officials. The options narrow, then finally disappear, and the officials are unable to see anything beyond what has already been decided on. They interpret all subsequent events in the

L. Obj. 10: Discuss groupthink, and explain how it can be dangerous for a society.

Project 6

CDQ 31: Do you feel that groupthink has disturbing implications for individuals and for societies? Why or why not?

K.P.: Irving Janis

groupthink: Irving Janis's term for a narrowing of thought by a group of people, leading to the perception that there is only one correct answer, in which the suggestion of alternatives becomes a sign of disloyalty

framework of the "right" answer, that is, what the group has determined to be the reasonable thing to do.

From the results of the Asch and Milgram experiments, you can see how group-think can develop. Suppose you are a member of the president's inner circle. When a discussion is first held about some critical matter, various options are presented. Eventually, these are narrowed to only a few choices, and at some point everyone seems to agree on what now seems "the only possible course of action." At that juncture, expressing doubts will bring you into direct conflict with *all* the other important people in the room, while actual criticism may mark you as not being a "team player." So you keep your mouth shut, with the result that each step you take along with the group commits you—and them—more and more to the "only" course of action.

United States history provides a fertile field of examples of groupthink: The refusal of President Roosevelt and his chiefs of staff to believe that the Japanese might attack Pearl Harbor and the subsequent decision to continue operations as usual; President Kennedy's invasion of Cuba; the policies of Presidents Kennedy, Johnson, and Nixon in Vietnam; and the Iran-Contra scandal of President Reagan's administration. Options in each case closed as officials committed themselves to a single course of action, which it became the equivalent of disloyalty to question. Those in power plunged ahead, no longer able to see different perspectives, no longer even trying to objectively weigh evidence as it came in, interpreting everything as supporting the one correct decision. Like Milgram's subjects, they became mired deeper and deeper in actions that as individuals they would have considered unacceptable, and found themselves pursuing policies they personally found morally repugnant.

Groupthink is one of the dangers that faces any government, for leaders already tend to be isolated at the top and can easily become cut off from information that does not coincide with their own opinions. Leaders in their turn often foster groupthink by surrounding themselves with an inner circle that closely reflects their own views.

Preventing Groupthink

Perhaps the key to preventing the mental captivity and paralysis caused by groupthink is the widest possible circulation, especially among top officials, of research that has been freely engaged in by social scientists, and information that has been freely gathered by media reporters. In addition, it might be useful to pass a law requiring the president of the United States to consult regularly with at least two advisers known to disagree violently with his or her views.

If this conclusion comes across as an unabashed plug for sociological research and the free exchange of ideas, it is. Giving free rein to diverse opinions is an essential deterrent to groupthink, which—if not prevented—can lead to the destruction of a society and, in today's world of sophisticated weapons, the mass destruction of the earth's inhabitants.

SUMMARY

1. On their way to postindustrial society, humans passed through four types of societies: hunting and gathering, pastoral or horticultural, agricultural, and industrial. This journey was marked by four social revolutions: domestication, agricultural, industrial, and information.

2. Hunting and gathering societies provided the greatest social equality. The root of the transition to social inequality was the accumulation of a food surplus, made possible through more efficient agricultural techniques. This

surplus was also a stimulus for the subordination of women by men and the development of the state, the rule of some over others. The general historical pattern of increasing inequality was eventually broken as workers in industrial societies demanded a greater share of the developing surplus.

3. Each social revolution brings with it sweeping social changes that upset the basic arrangements of society. Changes in culture usually follow technological change, a phenomenon known as cultural lag. The principal sociological concern in the case of each social revolution, including the current information revolution, is the social consequences of the transition.

4. By standing between the individual and the larger society, small groups help prevent anomie. A small group consists of individuals who are in contact with one another, who take one another into account, and who are aware that they have something significant in common. An aggregate, in contrast, is simply a number of people who have similar characteristics.

5. Small groups are divided into primary, secondary, in-groups and out-groups reference groups, and networks. The cooperative, intimate, long-term, face-to-face relationships provided by the primary group are so fundamental to social life that this group becomes an integral part of each member's identity. When primary groups function well, they provide a high level of satisfaction for their members; when they dysfunction, they fail to meet their members' basic needs.

6. Secondary groups are larger, relatively temporary, and more anonymous, formal, and impersonal than primary groups. Secondary groups have become essential to social life in industrial society. Secondary groups, such as those provided by work and school environments, tend to break down into primary groups, in which people's more intimate needs can be satisfied.

7. In-groups provide a sense of identification or belonging, give feelings of superiority, command loyalty, and exert a high degree of control over their members. Out-groups help create an identity for in-groups by showing them what they are *not*. As symbols of antagonism, out-groups sometimes provide the basis for extreme behavior.

8. Social networks consist of social ties that link people together. These contacts, expanding outward from the individual, are significant for establishing opportunities. They also tend to perpetuate social inequality.

9. Reference groups, groups used as standards to evaluate ourselves, exert significant control over people's lives. Having contradictory reference groups results in internal conflict.

10. Group dynamics concerns the ways in which individuals affect groups and the ways in which groups affect individuals. Group size is a significant aspect of group dynamics. Dyads, consisting of two persons, provide the most intense or intimate relationships, but they are also the most unstable type of human group. In triads, groups of three people, the presence of a third person fundamentally alters relationships among group members. Due to the tendency to form coalitions, triads are also unstable. As a small group grows larger, its intensity decreases and its stability increases.

11. A leader, someone who influences the behaviors of others, can be either instrumental or expressive. Both types of leaders are essential to the functioning of groups. The instrumental leader, who tries to keep the group moving toward its goals, is usually less popular than the expressive leader, who focuses on creating harmony and raising the group's morale. There are three main leadership styles: authoritarian (giving orders), democratic (trying to gain a consensus), and laissez-faire (being highly permissive). An authoritarian style appears to be more effective in emergency or highly regimented situations, a democratic style works best for most situations, and a laissez-faire style is usually ineffective. In determining who becomes a leader, not only personal characteristics but also social situations as simple as seating arrangements are influential.

12. The Asch experiment demonstrates the awesome influence of peer groups over their members, while the Milgram experiment shows how powerfully people are influenced by authority. Groupthink, encouraged by the isolation of political leaders, is a fascinating group dynamic that poses serious threats to society's well-being. To overcome it requires the freest possible circulation of contrasting ideas.

SUGGESTED READINGS

Homans, George. *The Human Group*. New York: Harcourt, Brace, 1950. Homans develops the idea that all human groups share common activities, interactions, and sentiments and examines various types of social groups from this point of view.

Janis, Irving. *Victims of Groupthink*. Boston, Mass.: Houghton Mifflin, 1972. Janis analyzes the captivity of thought: how groups become cut off from alternatives, interpret evidence in light of their preconceptions, and embark on courses of action that they should have seen as obviously incorrect.

Kephart, William M. *Extraordinary Groups: The Sociology of Unconventional Life-Styles*. 3rd ed. New York: St. Martin's, 1987. The author documents the effects of groups on their members' lives by examining Gypsies, the Amish, the Shakers, the Father Divine movement, and others.

Mills, Theodore M. *The Sociology of Small Groups*. Englewood Cliffs, N.J.: Prentice Hall, 1984. Mills provides an overview of research on small groups, focusing on the interaction that occurs within them (group dynamics).

Peters, Thomas J., and Robert H. Waterman, Jr. *In Search of Excellence: Lessons from America's Best Run Companies*. New York: Warner, 1982. Developing the thesis that successfully managed companies follow eight basic principles, the authors illustrate how those principles work in the corporate world.

Whyte, William H. *The Organization Man*. New York: Simon & Schuster, 1956. Although this book was written at midcentury, its analysis of how bureaucracies reward conformity and stifle creativity is still insightful.

Unknown, Sign of the Watchmaker, *contemporary folk art*

Bureaucracy and Formal Organizations

THE RATIONALIZATION OF SOCIETY
The Contribution of Max Weber ■ Marx on Rationalization

FORMAL ORGANIZATIONS AND BUREAUCRACY
Formal Organizations ■ The Essential Characteristics of Bureaucracies ■ "Ideal" versus "Real" Bureaucracy ■ Dysfunctions of Bureaucracies

VOLUNTARY ASSOCIATIONS
The Functions of Voluntary Associations ■ The Problem of Oligarchy

CAREERS IN BUREAUCRACIES
The Corporate Culture: Consequences of Hidden Values ■ *Down-to-Earth Sociology:* **Maneuvering the Hidden Culture—Women Surviving the Male-Dominated Business World**

HUMANIZING THE CORPORATE CULTURE
Perspectives: **Managing Diversity in the Workplace**

MODIFYING BUREAUCRACIES
Quality Circles ■ Employee Stock Ownership ■ Small Work Groups ■ *Down-to-Earth Sociology:* **Self-Management Teams**

DEVELOPING AN ALTERNATIVE: THE COOPERATIVE

THE JAPANESE CORPORATE MODEL
Perspectives: **Bottom-Up Decision Making In Japanese Organizations** ■ *Down-to-Earth Sociology:* **Home on the Range—Japanese-Style**

SUMMARY

SUGGESTED READINGS

This was the most exciting day Joan could remember. Her first day at college. So much had happened so quickly. Her senior year had ended with such pleasant memories: the prom, the graduation—how proud she had felt at that moment. But best of all had been the SAT scores. Everyone, especially Joan, had been surprised at the results—she had outscored everyone in her class. "Yes, they're valid," her adviser had assured her. "You can be anything you want to be."

Those words still echoed in Joan's mind. "Anything I want to be," she thought.

Then came the presidential scholarship! Full tuition for four years. Beyond anything Joan had ever dreamed possible. She could hardly believe it, but it was really hers.

"Next, please!" Joan's reverie was interrupted as she reached the head of the line. "Your number 3 card, please."

Joan looked startled. "My what?" she asked.

"Your number 3 card," said the clerk, with more than a hint of exasperation.

"I don't know what that is," Joan replied, beginning to feel a little foolish.

The irritation in the clerk's voice was now quite noticeable: "You can't get your schedule approved without your number 3 card. Where is it?"

"I don't have one," said Joan, feeling her face redden at the sound of a snicker behind her.

"Then you'll have to go to Forsyth Hall and get one. Next!"

Joan felt thoroughly confused. She had waited in line for an hour. Somehow she had missed the instructions to get a number 3 card in Forsyth before going to Rendleman Building for course approval. Dejected, she crossed the quadrangle to Forsyth and joined a double line of students stretched from the building into the courtyard.

But nobody told Joan that this was the line for paying tuition. Number 3 cards were issued in the basement.

You can understand Joan's dismay. Things could have been clearer—a lot clearer. The problem is that many colleges must register thousands of students, most of whom are going to start classes on the same day. To do so, they have broken the registration process into tiny bits, with each piece making a small contribution to getting the job done. Of course, as Joan found out, things don't always go as planned.

This chapter looks at how society is organized to "get its job done." As you read, you may be able to trace the source of some of your frustrations to this social organization, as well as see how your welfare depends on it.

THE RATIONALIZATION OF SOCIETY

L. Obj. 1: Explain what is meant by the "rationalization of society," and differentiate between the views of Max Weber and Karl Marx on this process.

CDQ 1: What does "rationality" mean to a sociologist? What does "rationality" mean to you in everyday usage?

K.P.: Max Weber

CDQ 2: Why do you think a traditional orientation in society would stand in the way of industrialization?

As discussed in Chapter 6, over the course of history societies have undergone transformations so extensive that whole new types of societies have emerged. A major development in addition to these transformations, which also leaves an indelible mark on our lives, is **rationality**—the acceptance of rules, efficiency, and practical results as the right way to approach human affairs. Let's examine how this approach to life—which we today take for granted—came about.

The Contributions of Max Weber

As sociologist Max Weber (1864–1920) made a survey of world history, he concluded that the hallmark of the world's groups and nations had been a **traditional orientation** to life—the idea that the past is the best guide for the present. In this view, what exists is good because it has passed the test of time. Customs—and relationships based upon them—have served people well and should not be lightly abandoned. A central orientation of a traditional society is to protect the status quo. Change is viewed with suspicion, and comes but slowly, if at all.

Such a traditional orientation stands in the way of industrialization, which requires rationality and the willingness—even eagerness—to change. If a society is to industrialize, then, a deep-seated shift must occur in people's thinking—from wanting to hold onto things as they are to seeking the most efficient way to accomplish matters. Practical consequences must replace the status quo, while rule-of-thumb methods give way to explicit rules and procedures for measuring results. This change is fundamental, requiring an entirely different way of looking at life that flies in the face of human history and is opposed to the basic orientation of all human societies until the time of industrialization. How, then, did what Weber called the **rationalization of society**—a widespread acceptance of rationality and a social organization largely built around this idea—come about?

Weber's answer to this puzzle has been the source of controversy ever since he first proposed it in his highly influential book, *The Protestant Ethic and the Spirit of*

rationality: the acceptance of rules, efficiency, and practical results as the right way to approach human affairs

traditional orientation: the idea, characteristic of feudal society, that the past is the best guide for the present

rationalization of society: a widespread acceptance of rationality and a social organization largely built around this idea

Capitalism (1904–1905). Weber's primary clue was that capitalism thrived only in certain parts of Europe. If he could determine why this was so, he should be able to discover the root of this fundamental change in human society. As Weber pursued the matter, he concluded that religion must hold the key, for it was in Protestant countries that capitalism flourished, while Roman Catholic countries held onto tradition and were relatively untouched by capitalism. But why should Roman Catholics have continued to hold onto the past, while Protestants embraced change, welcoming the new emphasis on practical results? Because, Weber said, there were essential differences between the two religions. Roman Catholic doctrine emphasized the acceptance of present arrangements, not change: "God wants you where you are. You owe primary allegiance to the Church, to your family, to your community and country. Accept your lot in life and remain rooted."

But Protestant theology was quite different, Weber argued, especially Calvinism, a religion he was intimately familiar with from his mother. Calvinists (followers of the teachings of John Calvin, 1509–1564) believed that before birth people are destined to go either to heaven or to hell—and they would not know to which until after their deaths. Weber believed that this doctrine imposed tremendous strain, filling Calvinists with an anxiety that pervaded their everyday lives. Salvation became their chief concern in life; and they wanted to know *now* where they were going after death.

To resolve their spiritual dilemma, Calvinists came up with an ingenious solution: God did not want his chosen ones to be ignorant of their destiny. Consequently, He would bestow signs of approval on those He had predestined for heaven. But what signs? The answer, they claimed, was found not in mystical, spiritual experiences, but in tangible achievements that people could see and measure. The sign of God's approval became success in life: Those whom God had predestined for heaven, He would bless with visible success.

This idea transformed Calvinists' lives, serving as an extraordinary motivation to work hard. Because Calvinists also believed that thrift is a virtue, their dedication to work led to an accumulation of money. Calvinists could not spend the excess on themselves, however, for to purchase items beyond the basic necessities was considered sinful. **Capitalism,** the investment of capital in the hope of producing profits, became an outlet for their excess money, while the success of those investments became a further sign of God's approval. Worldly success, then, became transformed into a spiritual virtue, and other branches of Protestantism, although less extreme, adopted the creed of thrift and hard work. Consequently, said Weber, Protestant countries embraced capitalism.

Now, what has this to do with rationalization? Simply put, capitalism demands rationalization, the careful calculation of practical results. If profits are your goal, you must compute income and expenses. You must calculate inventories and wages, the cost of producing goods and how much they bring in. You must determine "the bottom line." In such an arrangement of human affairs, efficiency, not tradition, becomes the drum to which you march. Traditional ways of doing things, if inefficient, must be replaced, for what counts are the results.

Marx on Rationalization

Another sociologist, Karl Marx, looked at the same problem and came up with entirely the reverse interpretation of events. He, too, noted that tradition had given way to rationality. Unlike Weber, however, Marx attributed this fundamental change in people's way of thinking not to religion but to capitalism itself. The development of capitalism, he said, caused people to change their way of thinking, not the other way around. It was the new form of production that broke down traditional relationships, uprooting the old ways of doing things. Because capitalism was much more efficient, when people saw the results they altered their ideas. Rationality, argued Marx, was the result of economics, the material forces of production.

Until the 1500s, the world's societies had a traditional orientation to life. Change was viewed with suspicion and came slowly. With the rise of capitalism, however, the pace of change accelerated.

CDQ 3: Why did Max Weber believe that religion could be a force for social change in societies? Do you think this idea is still valid today?

CDQ 4: How did worldly success become transformed into a spiritual value for the Calvinists? Do we view worldly success in the same way now?

CDQ 5: Can you state in your own words the ways in which Karl Marx's views on the development of capitalism differed from those of Max Weber?

K.P.: Karl Marx

capitalism: the investment of capital in the hope of producing profits

Max Weber wrote that the rise of capitalism and the type of society it produced—one based on rationality versus tradition—emerged in response to the Protestant ethic, especially the Calvinist doctrine of predestination. Karl Marx saw things differently. He believed that capitalism itself was responsible for the breakdown of traditional society and the rise of rationality.

formal organization: a secondary group designed to achieve explicit objectives

Who is correct? Weber, who concluded that Protestantism produced rationality, which then paved the way for capitalism? Or Marx, who concluded that capitalism produced rationality? No analyst has yet reconciled these two opposing themes to the satisfaction of sociologists: The two views still remain side by side.

FORMAL ORGANIZATIONS AND BUREAUCRACY

Regardless of whether Marx or Weber was right about its cause, rationality was a totally different way of thinking that came to permeate society. This new orientation transformed the basic way in which society was organized. The resulting rationalization of society includes the widespread existence of formal organizations, predominantly in the form of bureaucracies.

Formal Organizations

Rationality brought the proliferation of **formal organizations,** secondary groups designed to achieve explicit objectives. Unlike primary groups, formal organizations have a defined structure, including a set of officers, whose task it is to keep the organization moving toward its objectives.

Prior to industrialization, formal organizations existed, but they were few in number. The guilds formed in western Europe during the twelfth century are such an example. Groups of people who performed the same type of work became highly organized, controlling their craft in a local area by setting prices and standards of workmanship (Bridgwater 1953). Much like modern unions, guilds also prevented craftsmen from other localities from encroaching on their area. Probably the best example of an early formal organization is the army, with its structure of senior officers, junior officers, and ranks. Formal armies, of course, go back to early history.

With industrialization, however, secondary groups became common. Today we take their existence for granted and, beginning with grade school, all of us spend a good deal of time in them. Formal organizations tend to develop into bureaucracies, and in general, the larger the formal organization, the more likely it is to be bureaucratic.

Guilds, such as the one depicted in Rembrandt's Syndics of the Drapers Guild *represented one of the few types of formal organizations in existence before the advent of industrialization. Like modern unions, guilds were organizations that represented the interests of workers in a specific area. The men depicted in Rembrandt's painting created drapes— an important commodity before people had central heating.*

The Essential Characteristics of Bureaucracies

Although the army, the post office, a college, and General Motors may not seem to have much in common, they are all bureaucracies. As Weber (1947) analyzed them, the essential characteristics of a **bureaucracy** are as follows:

1. *A hierarchy with assignments flowing downward and accountability flowing upward*   The organization is divided into clear-cut levels. Each level assigns responsibilities to the level beneath it, while each lower level is responsible to the level above for fulfilling those assignments. The bureaucratic structure of a typical university is shown in Figure 7.1.

2. *A division of labor*   Each member of a bureaucracy has a specific task to fulfill, and all of the tasks are then coordinated to accomplish the purpose of the organization. In a college, for example, a teacher does not run the heating system, the president does not teach, and a secretary does not evaluate textbooks. These tasks are accomplished by being distributed among persons who have been trained to do them.

3. *Written rules*   In their attempt to become efficient, bureaucracies stress written procedures. In general, the longer a bureaucracy exists and the larger it grows, the more written rules it has. The rules of some bureaucracies cover just about every imaginable situation. In my university, for example, the rules are bound in handbooks: separate ones for faculty, students, administrative workers, and perhaps others that I do not even know exist. The basic rule generally becomes, "If there isn't a written rule covering it, it is allowed."

4. *Written communications and records*   Records are kept of much of what transpires in a bureaucracy. ("Fill that out in triplicate.") Consequently, workers in bureaucracies spend a fair amount of time reading and writing memos to one another. They also produce written reports detailing their activities. My university, for example, requires that each faculty member fill out quarterly reports summarizing the number of hours per week spent on specified activities as well as an annual report listing what was accomplished in teaching, research, and service—all accompanied by copies of publications, testimonies to service, and written teaching evaluations from each course. These materials go to committees whose task it is to evaluate the relative performance of each faculty member.

Essay #1

L. Obj. 2: State the definition of formal organizations, and list the essential characteristics of bureaucracies.

CDQ 6: Why do you think formal organizations are necessary in contemporary societies?

CDQ 7: Does this college/university have all of the essential characteristics of bureaucracy? Can you give specific examples?

TR#5M: The Bureaucratic Structure of a University

bureaucracy: a formal organization with a hierarchy of authority; a clear division of labor; emphasis on written rules, communications, and records; and impersonality of positions

Armies, with their strict hierarchies, division of labor, written rules, written communications and records, and impersonality, exhibit all of the characteristics Weber identified as essential to bureaucracies.

5. *Impersonality*   It is the office that is important, not the individual who holds the office. Consequently, members of a bureaucracy owe allegiance to the office, not to particular persons. If you work in a bureaucracy, you become a small cog in a large machine. Each worker is a replaceable unit, for many others are available to fulfill each particular function. For example, when a professor retires or dies, someone else is appointed to take his or her place.

These five characteristics not only help bureaucracies reach their goals but also allow them to grow and endure. One bureaucracy in the United States, the postal service, has become so large that one out of every 150 employed Americans now works for it (Frank 1990). If the head of a bureaucracy dies, retires, or resigns, the organization continues, ordinarily hardly skipping a beat, for unlike a "mom and pop" operation, the functioning of each unit and each person in those units does not depend on the individual who heads the organization.

"Ideal" versus "Real" Bureaucracy

L. Obj. 3: Describe the difference in "ideal" versus "real" bureaucracy.

CDQ 8: Do you agree that real bureaucracies differ from their ideal image? If so, how?

Just as people often act quite differently than the norms say they should, however, so it is with bureaucracies. The characteristics of bureaucracies identified by Weber are **ideal types**; that is, they are a composite of characteristics based on many specific examples. Think of a judge at a dog show. He or she has a mental image of what a particular breed of dog should look like, and judges each dog according to that perfect mental image. No particular dog will have all the characteristics, but all dogs of that breed put together have them. Thus, a particular organization may be ranked high or low on some characteristic and still qualify as a bureaucracy. Instead of labeling a particular organization as a "bureaucracy" or "not a bureaucracy," it probably makes more sense to think in terms of the *extent* to which an organization is bureaucratized (Hall 1963; Udy 1959).

As with culture, the real nature of a bureaucracy often differs from its ideal image. The actual lines of authority ("going through channels"), for example, may be quite different from those portrayed on organizational charts, such as that shown in Figure 7.1. For example, suppose that before being promoted, the university president taught in a certain department. As a result, friends from that department may have direct access to him or her. In giving their "input" (ranging from opinions about how to solve problems to personal grievances or even gossip), these individuals may skip their chairperson or even the dean of their college altogether.

Project 2

L. Obj. 4: Discuss the major dysfunctions of bureaucracies, and give examples of each type of problem.

CDQ 9: Have you encountered some of the dysfunctions of bureaucracies?

CDQ 10: Why do some workers experience bureaucratic alienation? Do you think there is anything organizations can do to keep this from happening? If so, what?

Dysfunctions of Bureaucracies

Although no other form of social organization in modern society has been found to be more efficient in the long run, as Weber recognized, his model accounts for only part of the characteristics of bureaucracies. They also have a dark side. As Joan in the opening vignette discovered, bureaucracies do not always operate smoothly. They slip up, and individuals sometimes get hurt. Probably all of us have been frustrated by red tape—what bureaucrats call "correct procedures." Other dysfunctions, which we shall now examine, are alienation, trained incapacity, goal conflict, goal displacement, engorgement, and incompetence.

Bureaucratic Alienation.   As you may have sensed from reading the characteristics of bureaucracies, they sometimes leave individual needs unfulfilled. Many workers find it disturbing to deal with others in terms of roles and functions rather than as individuals. Similarly, they may dislike writing memos instead of talking to people face to face.

Because employees must deal with one another in such formal ways, and because they constantly perform routine tasks, in large organizations workers often begin to feel more like objects than people, or, as Weber (1978) put it, "only a small cog in a

ideal type: composite of characteristics based on many specific examples ("ideal" in this case means an objective description of the abstracted characteristics)

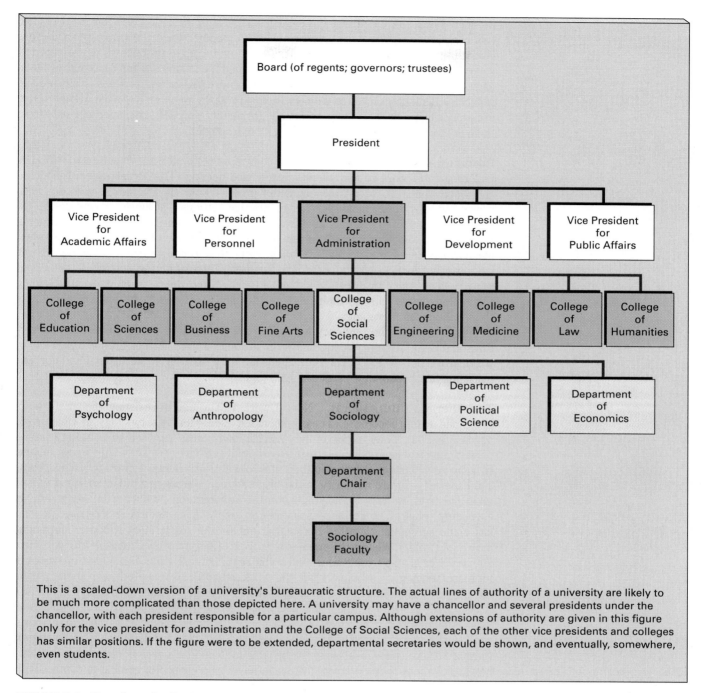

This is a scaled-down version of a university's bureaucratic structure. The actual lines of authority of a university are likely to be much more complicated than those depicted here. A university may have a chancellor and several presidents under the chancellor, with each president responsible for a particular campus. Although extensions of authority are given in this figure only for the vice president for administration and the College of Social Sciences, each of the other vice presidents and colleges has similar positions. If the figure were to be extended, departmental secretaries would be shown, and eventually, somewhere, even students.

FIGURE 7.1 Drawing of a Typical College Bureaucracy

ceaselessly moving mechanism which prescribes to [them] an endlessly fixed routine . . ." In addition, workers may feel that no one cares about them and that they are misfits in their surroundings.

Marx termed these reactions **alienation** and attributed them to the fact that workers were cut off from the finished product of their labor. Although restricting workers to repetitive tasks made for efficient production, he argued that it also reduced their satisfaction by limiting their creativity and sense of contribution to the finished

alienation: a feeling of power-lessness and normlessness; the experience of being cut off from the product of one's labor

product. Marx concluded that the underlying cause of alienation was that workers had lost control over their work because they no longer owned their own tools. Before industrialization, individual workers used their own tools to produce an entire product, such as a chair or table. Now the capitalists owned the machinery and tools and assigned each worker only a single step or two in the entire production process. Relegated to repetitive tasks disassociated from the actual product, workers had a diminished sense of responsibility for what they produced. Ultimately they felt estranged not only from their products but from their whole work environment.

Resisting Alienation.   Alienation, of course, is not a pleasant experience. Workers understandably want to feel useful, valued, and needed. They want to feel respected and worthwhile. To resist the alienation produced by bureaucracies, workers form primary groups. They band together in informal settings—at lunch, around desks, for a drink after work. There they give one another approval for jobs well done and express sympathy for the shared need to put up with cantankerous bosses, repetitive tasks, meaningless routines, and endless rules. Here they relate to one another not just as workers, but as people who value one another. They laugh and tell jokes, talk about their families, their problems, their goals, and, often, their sexual interests. Adding this multidimensionality to their work relationships restores their sense of being persons rather than mere cogs.

Sociologically, the tendency for workers to personalize their work areas with pictures and personal items is not simply an interesting trait. Rather, it is another way in which workers strive to overcome alienation—by claiming to be individuals, not just machines functioning at a particular job.

The Alienated Bureaucrat.   Not all workers succeed in resisting alienation, however, and some become extremely alienated (see Merton's typology in Chapter 8, pages 201–202). They remain in the organization because they see no viable alternative or because they have "only so many years until retirement." They hate every minute of it, however, and it shows—in their attitudes toward clients, toward fellow workers, and especially toward authority in the organization. The alienated bureaucrat does not take initiative, will not do anything for the organization beyond what he or she is absolutely required to do, and uses rules to justify doing as little as possible. If Joan had come across an alienated bureaucrat behind the registration window, she might have been told, "What's the matter with you? Everyone else manages to get their number 3 card, why can't you? Can't you read? I don't know what kind of students they are sending us nowadays." If the worker had been alienated even more, he or she might even have denied knowledge of where to get a number 3 card.

In spite of poor attitude and performance, alienated workers often retain their jobs, either because they may have seniority, or know the written rules backwards and forwards, or threaten expensive, time-consuming, and embarrassing legal action if they are fired. They are likely to be shunted off into small bureaucratic corners, however, where they do trivial tasks and have little chance of coming in contact with the public. This treatment, of course, only alienates them further.

Trained Incapacity.   Because of their specialties and the narrow corner of the organization that they hold down, workers often develop a **trained incapacity,** thinking only in terms of their own activity and unit and failing to grasp the larger goals of the organization. Sometimes this is a mere blind spot that can be remedied by communication between units, but at times trained incapacity can develop to the point where persons in one unit do not even care what happens to other units. At such a point the goals of the organization are impeded.

The city administration of New York City provides an example. It is divided into many units, some specializing in paving streets, others in laying sewer pipes, and so on. On occasion, only a few days after the street pavers have finished laying a street,

CDQ 11: How does trained incapacity impede the goals of an organization? Have you ever encountered this problem?

trained incapacity: a bureaucrat's inability to see the goals of the organization and to function as a cooperative, integrated part of the whole, caused by the highly specific nature of the tasks he or she performs

along come the installers of sewer pipe to rip up the fresh asphalt. All it would take is a few telephone calls to coordinate the work of the two units, but neither one seems to care. Each is doing precisely what is required of it, without regard for the other, providing a marvelous example of trained incapacity.

Goal Conflicts. Sometimes a bureaucracy creates **goal conflicts,** situations in which the goals of one unit conflict with those of the organization as a whole. Unionized workers, for example, often care little about the company's "bottom line," demanding raises whether the year was profitable or not. This attitude is sometimes fed by managers, who have themselves replaced the goal of "the bottom line" with the sole aim of feathering their own nests. Stockholders of public corporations, who see corporate managers continuing to vote themselves fat raises and bonuses in spite of decreased profits, frequently complain about such behavior.

Goal Displacement. Bureaucracies sometimes take on a life of their own, adopting new goals in a process called **goal displacement.** Thus, even when the goal of the organization has been achieved and there is no longer any reason for it to continue, continue it does. A good example is the National Foundation for the March of Dimes, organized in the 1930s to fight polio, a crippling disease that strikes without warning (Sills 1957). The origin of polio was a mystery to the medical profession, and the public was alarmed and fearful. All sorts of rumors ran rampant about its cause. Everyone knew someone who had been crippled by this disease. Overnight, a healthy child would be stricken. Parents were fearful because no one knew whose child would be next. The March of Dimes began to publicize individual cases, being especially effective by strategically placing posters of a child on crutches near cash registers in almost every store in America. The American public took the goals of the organization to heart and contributed heavily.

The organization raised money beyond its wildest dreams. Then during the 1950s, when the famous Salk vaccine for polio was developed, the threat of polio was wiped out almost overnight. The public breathed a collective sigh of relief. What then? Did the organization fold? After all, its purpose had been fulfilled. But, as you know, the March of Dimes is still around. Faced with the loss of their jobs, the professional staff that ran the organization quickly found a way to keep the bureaucracy intact by pursuing a new enemy—birth defects. Their choice of enemy is particularly striking, for it is doubtful that we will ever run out of birth defects—and thus unlikely that these persons will ever run out of jobs.

goal conflict: goals that conflict with one another, in this context, those of a unit in a formal organization and those of the organization as a whole

goal displacement: a goal displaced by another, in this context, the adoption of new goals by an organization; also known as *goal replacement*

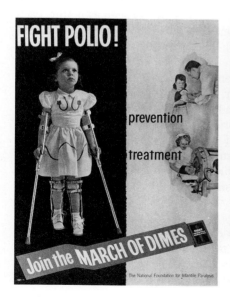

The March of Dimes was formed to fight polio in the 1930s. When a vaccine for the disease was found in the 1950s, the organization created new goals—fighting birth defects. This process of adopting new goals in the face of the demise of an organization is called goal displacement.

Under the totalitarian regime of Nicolae Ceausescu, which was overthrown in 1989, the government bureaucracy grew to incredible proportions. In his quest to house this bureaucracy, Ceausescu virtually bankrupted the country by pouring funds into bureaucratic monuments such as the one depicted in this photograph.

CDQ 12: Why do bureaucracies have an almost irresistible tendency to keep on growing? Can you give examples from your own experience?

CDQ 13: What is the Peter Principle? Do you agree with it? Why or why not?

bureaucratic engorgement: the tendency for bureaucracies to keep on growing

Peter Principle: a bureaucratic law, according to which the members of an organization are promoted for good work until they reach their level of incompetence, the level at which they can no longer do good work

Bureaucratic Engorgement.   Finally, bureaucracies have an almost irresistible tendency to keep on growing, a phenomenon known as **bureaucratic engorgement.** Always there are more tasks to be performed, related areas requiring expansion, more staff, more lines of authority. Moreover, what has come to be known as Parkinson's Law comes into play: "Work expands to fill the time available for its completion" (Parkinson 1957). Because workers cannot go home when they finish a task, but must wait until the end of their shift, they stretch out the work. If they don't look busy, someone will question the need to keep them employed or else will dump more work on them—neither desirable alternatives. Consequently, no matter what the amount of work assigned, employees try to look busy and more employees are always needed. New employees, of course, must be trained—taught the formal and informal ropes, familiarized with the employee benefit programs, and so on—all of which requires even more work for the current staff.

This tendency to expand is fed by the bureaucrats' basic assumption that their importance depends on size—of their budget, their staff, their office. And clearly, the larger the better. All units seem shorthanded, and no unit can quite accomplish all desired tasks without additional personnel. Since bigger is always seen as better, each unit seeks more employees, no unit returns money to the central administration, and each unit asks for a larger budget for the coming year, parading a long list of justifications for its perennial request.

As an example, my own sociology department, like every other in the university, carefully budgets expenditures during the year, periodically checking that it is not overspending, and then goes on a furious spending binge at the end of the year to make certain that every last cent is spent. Otherwise, the department chair fears, the administration will conclude that the department needs less money and will therefore cut next year's budget. Like every other department too, on demand it can produce an instant list of why it needs another two or three faculty members to have a viable program. In a different situation, of course, such as an accreditation hearing, the department will argue that its program is highly viable as it now is!

Bureaucratic Incompetence.   In a tongue-in-cheek analysis of bureaucracies, Laurence J. Peter proposed what has become known as **the Peter Principle:** Each employee of a bureaucracy is promoted to his or her *level of incompetence* (Peter and Hull 1969). People who perform well in a bureaucracy come to the attention of those higher up the chain of command and are promoted. If they again perform well, they are again promoted. This process continues until finally they are promoted to a level at which they can no longer handle the responsibilities well; this is their level of incompetence. There they hide behind the work of others, taking credit for what those under their direction accomplish. Although the Peter Principle contains a grain of truth, if it were generally true, bureaucracies would be staffed entirely by incompetents, and none of these organizations could succeed. In reality, bureaucracies are remarkably successful.

A particular incompetence is built into bureaucracies, however, that of difficulty in dealing with exceptional cases. As long as everything fits within the rules, a bureaucracy can roll along. But when it confronts the unusual, it seems unable to adjust, for that case is not covered by the rules. For example, assume that you have the delightful opportunity to study in Europe for a semester and you want your subscription to *The Intellectual Monthly* suspended for that period. You are likely to find that your choices are either to cancel your subscription (for a partial refund) or to keep the copies coming during your absence. The bureaucracy is set up to handle changes of address and cancellations, not suspensions. You may protest all you want about how you like the magazine and how you don't want to quit your subscription, but your protests are likely to be met with the answer, "I'm sorry, but we are not equipped to handle such requests." On the more positive side, given enough such requests the magazine will write a new rule to cover these cases, for it would rather change its procedures than lose many customers.

The Problem with the Bottom Line. Bureaucracies whose goal is to produce profit have little difficulty computing their bottom line. But what about organizations with different goals? How do they determine their success or failure? For example, if teaching is the goal of an organization, the number of students can be counted, the number of credit hours computed, and, based on these, the relative contributions of each department calculated. But are these really the goals of a teaching organization? As every teacher will say, the *quality* of teaching is what counts, not the number of students who are taught.

If that is the case (and I personally subscribe wholeheartedly to this premise, of course, for it arises from the particular position I hold—my attitude would likely be quite different if I were a long-term administrator), how do we calculate the "bottom line" in teaching? Most nonprofit organizations, including government agencies, face this difficulty. Most solve it by issuing annual reports that inflate their accomplishments but keep the bottom line, whatever it is, blurry indeed. The university is no exception.

Essay #3

VOLUNTARY ASSOCIATIONS

To get its work done, then, society organizes itself. In sharp contrast to the small groups studied in Chapter 6, bureaucracies have become the dominant form of organization for large, task-oriented groups. Yet in the United States, even more common than bureaucracies are voluntary associations: Let us examine their essential characteristics.

Back in the 1830s, a Frenchman traveled across the United States, observing the customs of this new nation. Alexis de Tocqueville wrote a book about his observations, *Democracy in America* (1835), which became widely read in Europe and in the United States and is still quoted for its insights into the American character. As an outsider, de Tocqueville was able to see patterns that those immersed in them could not. One of de Tocqueville's observations was that Americans joined a lot of **voluntary associations,** groups made up of volunteers who organize on the basis of some mutual interest.

Over the years, Americans have maintained this pattern and are extremely proud of it. A visitor entering any of the thousands of small towns that dot the landscape will

CDQ 14: Why are Americans so involved in voluntary associations? Are you involved in them?

Project 3

voluntary association: a group made up of volunteers who have organized on the basis of some mutual interest

Voluntary organizations are extremely popular in the United States. In this photograph, members of the Women's Volunteer Ambulance Association stand ready to offer their services.

be greeted with a highway sign proclaiming which volunteer associations that particular town has: Girl Scouts, Boy Scouts, Kiwanis, Lions, Elks, Eagles, Knights of Columbus, Chamber of Commerce, Junior Chamber of Commerce, Future Homemakers of America, Future Farmers of America, American Legion, Veterans of Foreign Wars, and perhaps a host of others. One form of voluntary association is so prevalent that a separate sign usually indicates which varieties are present in the town: Roman Catholic, Baptist, Lutheran, Methodist, Episcopalian, and so on. Not listed on these signs are many other voluntary associations, such as political parties, unions, professional associations, health clubs, the American Civil Liberties Union, the National Right to Life, the National Organization for Women, Alcoholics Anonymous, Gamblers Anonymous, Association of Pinto Racers, and Citizens United For or Against This and That.

Americans love voluntary associations, using them to express a wide variety of interests, goals, opinions, and even dissatisfactions. Some groups are local, consisting of only a few volunteers; some are national, with a paid professional staff; and others are in between. Some are temporary, organized to accomplish a particular task such as arranging the next Fourth of July fireworks. Others, such as the Scouts and the Democratic and Republican political parties, are permanent, large, secondary organizations with clear lines of command; and they are also bureaucracies.

Functions of Voluntary Associations

L. Obj. 5: Indicate the functions of voluntary associations, and explain how the problem of oligarchy occurs in such organizations.

CDQ 15: Do you think that voluntary associations meet people's basic needs? Why do these organizations typically have a high turnover rate?

K.P.: Robert Michels

CDQ 16: Why do the majority of members allow the iron law of oligarchy to occur in an organization?

Whatever their form, voluntary associations are so numerous because they meet people's basic needs. People do not *have* to belong to these organizations. They join because they obtain benefits from their participation. Functionalists have identified seven functions of voluntary associations.

1. Voluntary organizations advance the particular interests they represent. For example, adults who are concerned about children's welfare volunteer for the Scouts because they think that this group is superior to the corner pool hall. In short, voluntary associations get things done, whether ensuring that fireworks are purchased and shot off or that people become familiar with the latest legislation affecting their occupation.
2. Voluntary groups also offer people an identity, for some, even a sense of purpose in life. As in-groups, they provide their members with a feeling of togetherness, of belonging. This function becomes extremely important for some individuals, who become so wrapped up in voluntary associations that their participation becomes the center of their lives.

3. Voluntary associations help to govern the nation and to maintain social order. Groups that help "get out the vote" or assist the Red Cross in coping with disasters are obvious examples.

Note that the first two functions apply to all voluntary associations. In a general sense, so does the third. Although few organizations are focused on politics and the social order, taken together, voluntary associations are a significant part of the American social order. They help to incorporate individuals into the general society, and by allowing the expression of desire and dissent, voluntary associations help to prevent anomie.

Sociologist David Sills (1968) identified four other functions, which apply only to some voluntary groups.

4. Some voluntary groups mediate between the government and the individual, for example by providing a way in which people can put pressure on lawmakers.
5. Some voluntary groups provide training in organizational skills, helping individuals climb the occupational ladder.
6. Some voluntary groups help disadvantaged groups and bring them into the political mainstream. The National Association for the Advancement of Colored People (NAACP) is an example of such a group.
7. Finally, some voluntary groups challenge society's definitions of "normal" and socially acceptable. These groups, usually labeled extremist, can represent any interest. Ranging from the Ku Klux Klan to Greenpeace, they force officials to react, for they challenge society's established boundaries and indicate directions of social change.

Voluntary associations, then, represent no single interest or purpose. They can be reactionary, brought screaming into the present as their nails claw the walls of the past, or they can lead the vanguard for social change, announcing their vision of a world to come. In spite of their amazing diversity, however, a thread does run through all voluntary associations. That thread is mutual interest, for whatever a group's particular interest, it provides the basic reason for that particular voluntary association's existence.

Although mutual interests determine a group's purpose, the specific motivations of its members differ. Some join because of their conviction concerning the stated purpose of the organization, but others become members for quite other reasons, such as the chance to make contacts that will help them politically or professionally—or even to be closer to some special person of the opposite sex.

With motivations for joining voluntary associations and commitment to their goals so varied, these organizations typically have a high turnover. Some people move in and out of groups almost as fast as they change clothes. Within each organization, however, is an inner core of individuals who stand firmly behind the group's goals, or at least are firmly committed to maintaining the organization itself. If this inner core loses commitment, the group is likely to fold.

The Problem of Oligarchy

Rather than losing its commitment, however, this inner core is likely to grow ever tighter, becoming convinced that most members can't be counted on and that it can trust only the smaller group to make the really important decisions. To see this principle at work, let us look at the Veterans of Foreign Wars (VFW).

Sociologists Elaine Fox and George Arquitt (1985) studied three local posts of the VFW, a national organization of former American soldiers who have served in foreign wars. The constitution of the VFW, founded in 1913, is very democratic, giving every member of the organization the right to be elected to positions of leadership. Fox and

Essay #4

CDQ 17: In what ways will bureaucracy affect your career?

K.P.: Rosabeth Moss Kanter

CNN: Glass Ceiling

L. Obj. 6: Identify the consequences of hidden values in the corporate culture, especially noting their impact on women and minority participants.

CDQ 18: Do you agree with Rosabeth Moss Kanter's assessment of who gets ahead in a large corporation? Why or why not?

Arquitt found three types of VFW members: the silent majority (members who rarely show up), the rank and file (members who show up, but mainly for drinking), and leaders (those have been elected to office or appointed to committees). Although the leaders of the posts are careful not to let their attitudes show, they look down on the rank and file, viewing them as a bunch of ignorant boozers. Yet the leaders know that their power rests on these members, for it is they who vote the leaders into office. Consequently, the leaders walk a thin line when interacting with the rank and file, carefully concealing how much they dislike their drinking and their ignorance of matters affecting the welfare of veterans.

Because the leaders can't stand the thought that such persons might represent them to the community and at national meetings, a curious situation arises. Although the VFW constitution makes rank-and-file members fully eligible for top leadership positions, they never become leaders. In fact, the leaders are so effective in keeping their own group in leadership that even before an election is held they can specify who is going to be their new post commander. "You need to meet Jim," the sociologists were told. "He's the next post commander after Sam does his time." At first the researchers found this puzzling. How could the elite be so sure? As they investigated further, however, they found that leadership is effectively decided behind the scenes. The elected leadership appoints members to chair key committees. Since the individuals in these positions become the focus of attention, the members become aware of their accomplishments, and the top leaders come from this subgroup. The inner core, then, maintains control over the entire organization simply by appointing members of their inner circle to these positions.

Like the VFW, most organizations are run by only a few of their members. Building on the term *oligarchy,* a system in which many are ruled by a few, sociologist Robert Michels (1876–1936) coined the phrase **the iron law of oligarchy** to refer to the way in which formal organizations inevitably come to be dominated by a small, self-perpetuating elite. The majority of the members become passive, and an elite inner group keeps itself in power by passing the leading positions from one clique member to another. What many have found depressing about the iron law of oligarchy is that it applies even to organizations strongly committed to democratic principles. Even American political parties, supposedly the backbone of the nation's representative government, have fallen prey to it. Run by an inner group that may or may not represent the community, they, too, pass their leadership positions from one elite member to another. The iron law of oligarchy is not without its limitations, of course. Members of the inner group must remain attuned to the opinions of the other members, regardless of their personal feelings. If the oligarchy gets too far out of line, its members run the risk of a grass-roots rebellion that would throw them out of office. It is this threat that often softens the iron law of oligarchy by making the leadership responsive to the membership.

CAREERS IN BUREAUCRACIES

Since you are likely to end up working in a bureaucracy, let's look at how its characteristics may affect your career. The findings of sociologist Rosabeth Moss Kanter are of special interest here, for her research on bureaucracies is as popular with businesspeople as with sociologists.

The Corporate Culture: Consequences of Hidden Values

Who gets ahead in a large corporation? While we might like to think that success is the logical consequence of hard work, intelligence, and dedication, many factors other than merit underlie salary increases and promotions. After studying the inside workings

CDQ 19: What attempts have been made to humanize the corporate culture? Do you think they have been successful?

L. Obj. 7: Evaluate the major approaches to humanizing the corporate culture.

L. Obj. 8: Explain how quality circles, employee stock ownership, and small work groups have been used to modify bureaucratic organizational structure.

the iron law of oligarchy: Robert Michels's phrase for the tendency of formal organizations to be dominated by a small, self-perpetuating elite

corporate culture: the orientations that characterize corporate work settings

of a large corporation, Kanter (1977) identified the ways in which the **corporate culture,** the orientations that characterize corporate work settings, determines an individual's corporate fate. Her understanding of corporate culture also provides a behind-the-scenes glimpse of the dynamics of bureaucracy, so vital to our lives, but so seldom readily visible.

As mentioned above, the iron law of oligarchy characterizes formal organizations, and corporations are no exception to this principle. As Kanter (1977, 1983; Kanter and Stein 1979) documented, the tight inner group that heads a corporation represents not only the goals of the organization but also values that are not relevant to—and may even conflict with—those goals, such as preserving the dominance of persons like themselves. This corporate elite provides better access to information, networking, and "fast tracks"—for workers who are like themselves, usually white and male.

Because females and minorities do not match these "hidden values" of the corporate culture, they are treated differently. (Discrimination on the basis of sex and race will be examined in detail in Chapters 11 and 12.) Sometimes they are "showcased," put in highly visible positions with little power in order to demonstrate to the public and affirmative action officials how progressive the company is (Benokraitis and Feagin 1991). Often they are shunted into "slow-track" positions, jobs where promotions are slow because accomplishments in these areas seldom come to the attention of top management. As the Down-to-Earth Sociology box below illustrates, even ideas are judged not on their merits, but according to *who* expresses them—and if the person is female, the idea is much less likely to be taken seriously.

Kanter also found that a corporation's "hidden values" have enormous and pervasive effects on the attitudes and work performance of employees. Those who fit into

Sociologist Rosabeth Moss Kanter has written extensively about life in corporations, including such titles as Men and Women of the Corporation, The Change Masters, *and* When Giants Learn to Dance.

DOWN-TO-EARTH SOCIOLOGY

Maneuvering the Hidden Culture—Women Surviving the Male-Dominated Business World

I work for a large insurance company. Of its twenty-five hundred employees, about 75 percent are women. Only 5 percent of the upper management positions, however, are held by women.

I am one of the more fortunate women, for I hold a position in middle management. I am also a member of the twelve-member Junior Board of Directors, of whom nine are men and three are women.

Recently one of the female members of the board suggested that the company become involved in Horizons for Tomorrow, a program designed to provide internships for disadvantaged youth. Two other women and I spent many days developing a proposal for our participation.

The problem was how to sell the proposal to the company president. From past experiences, we knew that if he saw it as a "woman's project" it would be shelved into the second tier of "maybes." He hates what he calls "aggressive bitches."

We three decided, reluctantly, that the proposal had a chance only if it were presented by a man. We decided that Bill was the logical choice. We also knew that we had to "stroke" Bill if we were going to get his cooperation.

We first asked Bill if he would "show us how to present our proposal." (It is ridiculous to have to play the role of the "less capable female" in the 1990s, but, unfor-tunately the corporate culture sometimes dictates this strategy.) To clinch matters, we puffed up Bill even more by saying, "You're the logical choice for the next chairmanship of the board."

Bill, of course, came to our next planning session, where *we* "prepped" *him* on what to say.

At our meeting with the president, we had Bill give the basic presentation. We then backed *him* up, providing the background and rationale for why the president should endorse the project. As we answered the president's questions, we carefully deferred to Bill.

The president's response? "An excellent proposal," he concluded, "an appropriate project for our company."

To be successful, we had to maneuver through the treacherous waters of the "hidden culture" (actually not so "hidden" to women who have been in the company for a while). The proposal was not sufficient on its merits, for the "who" behind a proposal is at least as significant as the proposal itself.

"We shouldn't have to play these games," Laura said, summarizing our feelings.

But we all know that we have no choice. To become labeled "pushy" is to commit "corporate suicide"—and we're no fools.

Source: Written by an insurance executive in Henslin's introductory sociology class who chooses to remain anonymous.

the elite mold and are given greater opportunity to advance come to think of themselves as having superior abilities and as more committed to the company. As a consequence, they tend to outperform others and to become more committed. In contrast, those judged to be outsiders, who find opportunities closing up, come to think poorly of themselves, to become less committed to the organization, and to work at a level beneath their capacity. This powerful role of hidden values in producing attitudes and work performance is not readily visible, however, either to outside observers or even to the employees themselves. What people perceive is that employees with superior performances and greater commitment to the company are promoted, not how the structure of opportunity within the corporation has produced a self-fulfilling prophecy ("those who look like us, the elite, outperform others").

Kanter also found that attitudes and behavior are shaped by the level that people reach in the organization. In general, the higher people go, the higher their morale ("This is a good company. They recognize my abilities."). Reaching a high level also tends to make people more helpful to subordinates and less rigid in their style of leadership. The morale of people who don't get very far in the organization, however, is understandably likely to be lower, for they are frustrated. A less apparent consequence of blocked opportunity, however, is that such people are likely to be rigid supervisors and close defenders of whatever privileges they have. The Perspectives box on page 181 on Managing Diversity in the Workplace explores a recent corporate trend toward addressing the needs of those who have traditionally been powerless, or absent altogether, from the corporation.

There are two levels in a bureaucracy, then: The first is readily visible and the second underlies what we perceive. Because workers in a corporation are likely to see only the first level, they usually ascribe differences in behaviors and attitudes to individual personalities. Although the second level, the effects of the corporate culture, usually remains below employees' awareness, it molds how they think and, by extension, the quality of their work.

CDQ 20: Do you think conflict theorists are correct in their assumption that the basic relationship between workers and owners is confrontational regardless of how the work organization is structured?

L. Obj. 9: Describe the role of cooperatives, or collectives, in providing an alternative to bureaucracy.

HUMANIZING THE CORPORATE CULTURE

Bureaucracies, with all of their faults, have transformed societies by harnessing people's energies to stated goals and monitoring progress to those goals. Weber (1946)

Some corporations have begun to humanize the work setting by instituting such benefits as onsite daycare.

PERSPECTIVES
Cultural Diversity in U.S. Society

Managing Diversity in the Workplace

About thirty years ago, Title VII of the Civil Rights Act of 1964 banned employment decisions that discriminate on the basis of race, color, religion, sex, and national origin. To avoid legal penalties, companies created affirmative action programs. These programs became highly controversial, for they were seen by some as a form of reverse discrimination. Both praised and condemned, affirmative action programs remain in effect.

"Affirmative action will die a natural death," declares Roosevelt Thomas, president of the American Institute for Managing Diversity, a nonprofit research center affiliated with Morehouse College. "The focus today is diversity. Diversity means the condition of being different," Thomas adds, "and being different is not what affirmative action was about."

Since the passage of Title VII, the United States has undergone a major demographic shift. California will soon have a population 50 percent Hispanic American and nonwhite. More than half of the nation's work force now consists of minorities, immigrants, and women; white, native-born males, though still dominant, have become a statistical minority. In addition, about 80 percent of new workers are not white males.

Affirmative action relied heavily on assimilation. As described in Chapter 12, *assimilation* refers to the process by which minorities are absorbed into the dominant culture. Generally, assimilation involves relinquishing distinctive cultural patterns of behavior in favor of those of the dominant culture. Two, three, four generations ago, people who emigrated to this country routinely changed their names to help them enter the mainstream as soon and as completely as possible.

In contrast, the huge successes of the women's movement and civil rights activism have helped Americans to appreciate their differences, even to celebrate them. This change is transforming the workplace, for people who are comfortable and proud of being different are much less amenable to assimilation. "You don't have to aspire to be a white male or a member of the dominant group," says Thomas. "People are willing to be part of a team, but they won't jump into the melting pot anymore."

Diversity in the workplace is much more than skin color. Diversity also refers to gender, age, religion, social class, sexual orientation, and even to military experience.

Realizing that assimilation is probably not the way of the future, companies as diverse as Pacific Bell, IBM, Ford, and 3M have begun programs called "Managing Diversity" or "Valuing Diversity." The goals of these programs are threefold: (1) to uncover and root out biases and prejudices about people's differences, (2) to increase awareness and appreciation of people's differences, and (3) to teach "people skills," especially communication and negotiation skills, for working with diverse groups.

Is there a bottom line to these programs? They do have a practical side—to develop leaders who can put a team of diverse people together so they can cooperatively and efficiently reach corporate goals.

Applying the Theoretical Perspectives. From a *functionalist* pespective, we would say that programs in managing diversity are an adjustment in the economic system. They will help meet needs caused by changing demographics within the nation and new international relations that require American corporations to be more competitive. From a *symbolic interaction* perspective, we would say that these programs reflect a change in symbols—that they illustrate how being different from the dominant group now has a different meaning than it used to. These programs not only reflect that change, they also foster further change in the meaning of diversity. From a *conflict* perspective, we would say that the key term in managing diversity programs is not diversity, but *managing.* No matter what they are called, these programs are merely another way to exploit labor.

What do you think?

Source: Based on Petrini 1989; Thomas 1990; Galagan and Savoie 1991; Piturro and Mahoney 1991.

---

predicted that because bureaucracies are so efficient and have the capacity to replace themselves indefinitely, they would come to dominate social life. More than any prediction in sociology, this one has withstood the test of time (Rothschild and Whitt 1986).

Bureaucracies appear likely to remain our dominant form of social organization, and most of us, like it or not, are destined to spend our working lives in bureaucracies. Many people have become concerned about the negative side of bureaucracies, however, and would like to make them more humane. **Humanizing a work setting** means organizing it in such a way that it develops rather than impedes human potential. Among the characteristics of more humane bureaucracies are (1) the availability of opportunities on the basis of ability and contributions rather than personal characteristics; (2) a more equal distribution of power; and (3) less rigid rules and more open

humanizing a work setting: organizing a workplace in such a way that it develops rather than impedes human potential

decision making. In short, more people are involved in making decisions, their contributions are more readily recognized, and individuals feel freer to participate.

Can bureaucracies adapt to such a model? Contrary to some popular images, bureaucracies are not necessarily synonymous with unyielding, unwieldy monoliths. There is nothing in the nature of bureaucracies that makes them *inherently* insensitive to changing cultural needs or prevents them from humanizing corporate culture.

But the United States is in intense economic competition with other nations, especially Japan and western Europe, and it would be difficult to afford costly changes. To humanize corporate culture, however, does not necessarily involve huge expense. Kanter (1983) compared forty-seven companies that were rigidly bureaucratic with competitors of the same size that were more flexible in their approach. It turned out that the more flexible companies were the more profitable—probably because their greater flexibility encouraged greater company loyalty and productivity.

Essay #5

Project 4

L. Obj. 10: Compare and contrast the Japanese and United States corporate organizational models.

CDQ 21: What factors contributed to the huge economic success of Japan since World War II?

K.P.: William Ouchi

Quality Circles

In light of such findings, many corporations have taken steps to humanize their work settings, motivated not by any altruistic urge to make life better for their workers but by the self-interested desire to make their organization more efficient and competitive. About two thousand American companies—from the smallest to the largest—have begun to reform their work organizations. Some have developed "quality circles," which consist of perhaps a dozen workers and a manager or two who meet regularly to try to improve the quality of both the work setting and the company's products. To date, however, over half of these companies report that quality circles have yielded few benefits. Part of the reason may be that many companies set up quality circles for reasons of publicity, not intending to take employee suggestions seriously (Horn 1987; Saporito 1986).

Employee Stock Ownership

Many companies provide an opportunity for their employees to purchase the firm's stock at a discount or as part of their salary, depending on the company's profitability. About eight thousand American companies are now partially owned by their employees, but because each employee typically owns only a tiny amount of stock in the company, such "ownership" is practically meaningless. In about one thousand of these companies, however, the employees own the majority of the stock. Evidence has recently emerged that, on average, companies with at least 10 percent of their stock owned by employees are more profitable than other firms, probably because the workers are more committed and managers take a longer-term view (White 1992).

Even though the employees are the owners, this still does not mean that working conditions and employee-management relations are automatically friction-free. It seems, rather, that profitability is the key. Unprofitable firms pressure their employee-owners a great deal, creating resentment and tensions between workers and managers. Profitable companies show fewer tensions of this kind and resolve problems more quickly (Russell 1985; Horn 1987; Newman 1987).

Small Work Groups

Pioneered in the computer industry to increase productivity and cut down on absenteeism, small work groups, or self-managed teams, are now utilized by one in five employers in the United States, up from one in twenty just a decade ago. The results have been extraordinary, for employees who work in small groups not only feel a greater sense of loyalty to the company, work harder, and reduce their absenteeism, but small work groups also stimulate creative ideas and imaginative solutions to problems. Workers in these groups react more quickly to the threats posed by technological change and competitors' advances. No less a behemoth than IBM has found that people work more effectively in a small group than in a distant, centralized command structure (Larson and Dolan 1983; Drucker 1992).

Applying materials discussed in the last chapter helps to explain these results. The small work group establishes primary relationships among its members, and workers' identities become tied up with their group. Rather than being lost in a bureaucratic maze, here their individuality is appreciated, their contributions more readily recognized. The group's successes become the individual's successes—as do its failures reflect negatively on the individual. As a consequence of their expanded personal ties, workers make more of an effort. The results have been so good that in what is known as "worker empowerment," some self-managed teams even replace bosses in controlling everything from schedules to hiring and firing (Lublin 1992). For a glimpse of how self-management teams can make a difference, see the Down-to-Earth Sociology box below.

Conflict Perspective.   Conflict theorists point out that the basic relationship between workers and owners is confrontational regardless of how the work organization is structured (Edwards 1979; Derber and Schwartz 1988). Each walks a different path in life, the one exploiting workers to extract a greater profit, the other trying to resist that exploitation. Since their basic interests are fundamentally opposed, these critics argue, employers' attempts to humanize the work setting for their employees are mere window dressing, an attempt to conceal their fundamental exploitation of workers. If humanization of the work setting is not camouflage, then it is worse—an attempt to manipulate workers into active cooperation in their own exploitation.

DOWN-TO-EARTH SOCIOLOGY

Self-Management Teams

Probably the hottest thing going in large work organizations is small groups where workers have greater control—and responsibility—for their work. As the text mentions, such teams generally increase productivity and improve morale. Few settings have shown such dramatic change as the Chrysler plant at New Castle, Indiana.

With its high absenteeism and low productivity, Chrysler had just about given up on this rundown, aging factory. Worker alienation was evident throughout the plant. One forty-eight-year-old said, "I missed work when I wanted to miss work. Sometimes I just stayed home and got drunk." This worker, who makes $17.26 an hour, says that when a machine broke down, "We just sat around drinking coffee, waiting for the bosses to fix the problem." Workers felt especially lucky when a breakdown lasted all day.

In a last-ditch effort, Chrysler divided the plant into seventy-seven self-management teams. Workers were renamed "technicians," and line supervisors became "team advisers." More than window dressing, the new names reflected a change in relationships. Because their authority was reduced, some bosses quit, while that device so hated by workers, the time clock, disappeared. The teams now assign tasks, confront sluggish workers, order repairs, and talk to customers. They can even alter their work hours, but for that they must consult with a labor-management steering committee.

The results? Daily absenteeism was cut by more than half, dropping from 7 percent to 3 percent. Union grievances plummeted from one thousand a year to a mere thirty-three. Production costs shrank as defects per million parts made at the plant tumbled from three hundred to twenty. Needless to say, Chrysler is pleased.

Although the introduction of teams into work settings is seldom this dramatic, the results have been so positive that in the next decade probably half of American industry will adopt some form of self-managed teams. Some say such a modification is long overdue, that the day of bosses making all the decisions and breathing down workers' necks is long past. Others hope that the change has come in time to make a fundamental difference in the competitive position of the United States in the newly developed global marketplace.

Source: Based on Drucker 1992; Larson and Dolan 1983; Lublin 1992.

DEVELOPING AN ALTERNATIVE: THE COOPERATIVE

In the 1970s, many Americans, especially those opposed to capitalism and what they considered to be the deadening effects of bureaucracy, began to seek an alternative organizational form. They began to establish collectives, organizations owned by members who collectively make decisions, determine goals, evaluate resources, set salaries, and assign work tasks. These tasks are all carried out without a hierarchy of authority, for all members can participate in the decisions of the organization. Since the 1970s, about five thousand cooperatives have been established.

As sociologists Joyce Rothschild and Allen Whitt (1986) pointed out, cooperatives are not new, but were introduced into the United States during the 1840s. Cooperatives attempt to achieve a particular social good (such as lowering food prices and improving food quality) and to provide a high level of personal satisfaction for their members as they accomplish that goal. Because all members can participate in decision making, cooperatives spend huge amounts of time in deciding even routine matters. The economic results of cooperatives are mixed. Many are less profitable than private organizations, others more so. A few have been so successful that they have been bought out by bureaucratic corporations.

CDQ 22: Do you believe the Japanese corporate model could be transplanted to the United States? Why or why not?

THE JAPANESE CORPORATE MODEL

The Japanese have developed a form of the corporate model that has stimulated great interest in the United States and around the world. How were the Japanese able to arise from the defeat of World War II, including the nuclear destruction of two of their main cities, to become such a huge economic force in today's world? Some analysts trace part of the answer to the way in which their corporations are organized.

William Ouchi (1981), who analyzed the Japanese system of corporate organization in order to try to determine how it has contributed to the country's economic success, pinpointed five major ways in which it differs from the system in the United States.

Hiring and Promotion. In *Japan,* college graduates hired by a corporation are thought of as a team working toward the same goal, namely, the success of the organization. They are all paid about the same starting salary, and they are rotated through the organization to learn its various levels. Not only do they work together as a team, they are also promoted as a team. Team members always cooperate with one another, for the welfare of one represents the welfare of all. They also develop intense loyalty to one another and to their company. Only in later years are individuals singled out for recognition. When there is an opening in the firm, outsiders are not even considered.

Project 5

In the *United States,* an employee is hired on the basis of what the firm thinks that individual can contribute. Employees try to outperform others, regarding salary and position as a sign of success. The individual's loyalty is to himself or herself, not to the company. Advancements may be made within the corporation, but outsiders are often brought in.

Lifetime Security. In *Japan* lifetime security is taken for granted. Once hired, employees can expect to work for the same firm for the rest of their lives. Similarly, the firm expects them to be loyal to the company, to stick with it through good and bad times. On the one hand, employees will not be laid off or fired; on the other hand, they do not go job shopping, for their career—and many aspects of their lives—are wrapped up in this one firm.

In the *United States* lifetime security is unusual, being limited primarily to some

The Japanese corporate model differs from the U.S. corporate model in several key ways, including its greater emphasis on employee and employer commitment, training, and collective decision-making. Members of Japanese corporations work—and exercise—as a team.

college professors (who receive what is called *tenure*). A company is expected to lay off workers in slow times, and if it reorganizes it is not unusual for whole divisions to be fired. Given this context, workers are expected to "look out for number one," and that includes job shopping and job hopping, seeking better pay and opportunities elsewhere.

Almost Total Involvement. In *Japan* work is like a marriage: The employee and the company are committed to each other. The employee supports the company with loyalty and long hours of dedicated work, while the company, in turn, supports its workers with lifetime security, health services, recreational activities, sports and social events, and perhaps a home mortgage or even a home. Involvement with the company does not stop when the workers leave the building. They are likely to associate with company employees both on and off the job, to spend evenings with coworkers in places of entertainment, and perhaps to be part of a company study or exercise group.

In the *United States*, the work relationship is assumed to be highly specific. An employee is hired to do a specific job, and employees who have done their jobs have thereby fulfilled their obligation to the company. The rest of their hours are their own. They go home to their private lives which are highly separated from the firm.

Broad Training. In *Japan*, employees move from one job to another within the corporation. Not only are they not stuck doing the same thing over and over for years on end, but they gain a broader picture of the corporation, of its goals and approaches, its particular problems, and the way in which whatever job they are assigned fits into the broad picture.

In the *United States*, employees are expected to perform one job, to do it well, and then to be promoted upward to a job with more responsibility. Their understanding of the company is largely tied to the particular corner they occupy, and it may be difficult for them to see how their job fits into the overall picture.

Collective Decision Making. In *Japan,* decision making is a lengthy process, as illustrated in the Perspectives box on page 186. The Japanese think it natural that after

PERSPECTIVES
Cultural Diversity Around the World

Bottom-Up Decision Making in Japanese Organizations

When an important decision is to be made in a Japanese company, everyone who will feel its impact becomes involved. To decide where to locate a new plant, for example, or how to change a manufacturing process, may involve sixty to eighty people. A team of three will talk to each of these persons, carefully noting their opinions and concerns. When a modification comes about because of those opinions and concerns, the team then contacts each person again. This process continues until consensus is reached.

Let's look at what happens when a Japanese bank wants to make a major decision. First, the youngest and newest member of the department involved is given the job of writing a proposal that will be sent to the president. The proposal must lay out the one "best" alternative. First, the young person must figure out what alternatives are acceptable to the boss. To do so, he (almost exclusively a "he") talks to everyone, paying special attention to those who know the boss best. From this, he gets a good idea of what would be acceptable, but because he cannot completely figure out from others what the boss wants, he must add his own thoughts.

This is how variety enters the process. The company tries to socialize employees into a set of values and beliefs so common that all experienced employees would likely come up with similar ideas. Too much homogeneity, however, would lead to a loss of vitality and change, which is why the youngest person is assigned the job of writing the proposal.

While doing this, the young person will sometimes make a number of errors. He may suggest things that are technically impossible or leave things out. Even though the errors are costly in time and money, some of his suggestions will turn out to be good ideas. "Letting a young person make one error of his own is believed to be worth more than one hundred lectures in his education as a manager and worker.

"Ultimately a formal proposal is written and then circulated from the bottom of the organization to the top. At each stage, the manager in question signifies his agreement by affixing his seal to the document. At the end of (this) process, the proposal is literally covered with the stamps of approval of sixty to eighty people."

How can such a cumbersome process possibly work? It works only because it takes place within a common culture, a "framework of an underlying agreement on philosophy, values, and beliefs. These form the basis for common decision premises that make it possible to include a very large number of people in each decision."

Source: Adapted from Ouchi, 1981.

lengthy deliberations, to which each person to be affected by a decision contributes, everyone will agree on which suggestion is superior. This process broadens decision making, allowing workers to feel that they are an essential part of the organization, not simply cogs in a giant wheel.

In the *United States,* the individual who has responsibility for the unit in question does as much consulting with others as he or she thinks necessary and then makes the decision.

Adaptations and Cultural Difference.   The contrast between the systems is remarkable. If a single thread can be said to run through the Japanese corporate cloth, it is cooperation combined with group orientation. The American thread is a contrasting color, that of intense individualism and competition. Because of Japan's recent economic success, it has been suggested that the Japanese system should be transplanted to American soil. It needs to be noted, however, that both systems depend on their own cultural base; in other words, they do not stand alone but are each part and parcel of an integrated whole. To make the Japanese system work in the United States, therefore, would require changing vital elements of American work culture, for the success of their system depends on an acceptance of cooperation and the supremacy of the group as the correct approach to life. Any attempt to simply transplant the Japanese system intact would be futile, for it would run directly against deeply ingrained competitive aspects of American culture—from spelling bees in grade schools to high school and college sports. Perhaps grafting is a better approach. Without disrupting our culture, we can graft onto our system the parts of the Japanese model that we see as desirable.

American corporate leaders have come to see the benefits of the Japanese style, one of which is that the average income in Japan is higher than it is in the United States (Hartig 1990). Reluctantly, American management has begun the grafting process. Some elements, like group hiring and group promotions, for example, are being rejected outright as too foreign to American culture. Greater involvement in making decisions, however, appears more compatible. The GM Saturn plant in Spring Hill, Tennessee, is a notable example of grafting in this area. Organized with the goal of developing a team spirit, the plant attempts to involve workers more in decisions by stressing "cooperation between members of the United Auto Workers union and white-collar engineers and plant managers" (White and Guiles 1990). This approach, if it improves quality and productivity, may encourage further grafting experiments. The Down-to-Earth Sociology box below describes the experience of the workers of a Japanese-owned ranch in Montana.

Not everything about the Japanese system is good, however. One element is so unfair that, from the American perspective it's hard to imagine how the Japanese tolerate it. At the age of sixty, workers are suddenly let go. While early retirement may sound attractive, the problem is that retirement income does not begin until workers reach sixty-five. Accordingly, older workers face five years without support, having to depend on savings, part-time, low-paying work, and family and friends to get by until their retirement pay begins. In addition, the status of women in the Japanese corporations remains extremely weak; the vast majority of female Japanese workers are locked out of career-track positions (Brinton 1989).

DOWN-TO-EARTH SOCIOLOGY

Home on the Range—Japanese-Style

Many Americans have become alarmed about what some call the "Japanese invasion." By this, they refer to the vast amounts of goods made in Japan and imported into the United States and to the amount of property on these shores purchased by the Japanese. Some even say that Japan lost World War II but won the peace.

In imported goods, the Japanese presence has been especially visible in electronics and automobiles. In the purchase of property, hotels and beachfront homes stand out. Not so apparent are other purchases, such as the Lazy 8, a famous 77,000-acre spread near Dillon, Montana.

Besides the American xenophobia (fear of strangers, in this case, domination by the Japanese) surrounding the purchase, what is interesting sociologically is the application of the Japanese management style to a ranch in the old West. After paying $12.6 million for the Lazy 8, the new owners studied the operation from the bottom up. They found the American way of ranching with orders going from the ranch house to the bunk house, too "boss-centered." They then began to apply Japanese-style consensus management.

"Each week, the Lazy 8 cowpunchers mosey into a barn for 'an open forum discussion.' The cowboys talk about 'calving goals' and 'fundamental principles' with Ed Fryer, the ranch's thirty-nine-year-old foreman.

" 'We try to combine everybody's experience to reach our goals,' says Mr. Fryer, a tall, lean man in faded Levi's, who sounds somewhat more like a manager of a Toyota plant than a cow boss."

How is this new management style working? Cowboys have traditionally been loners, and many did not take too well to this change. About half simply quit. The rest have made the adjustment. Now each of the ranch's 2,800 head of cattle is tracked on the ranch computer from birth to slaughterhouse.

Why do the Japanese want to own a ranch in the old West? Two reasons. First, they have a fascination with anything from the old West. Western movies are an especially big hit in Japan. The second is somewhat more practical. In Japan, $20 a pound for beef is not unusual. In fact, the Japanese don't flinch at spending $50 a pound for the best cuts.

With even ranches in the old West giving in to the new management style, can any area of business life be immune? Is this change, then, perhaps the cutting edge of the future?

Source: Based on Richards 1990; Carlton and Barsky 1992; Grossman and McCarthy 1992.

SUMMARY

1. A major transition has occurred in the way people think—from a tradition-based desire to protect time-honored ways to rationality, a concern with efficiency and practical results. Weber traced the rationalization of society to Protestantism, while Marx attributed it to capitalism.

2. Formal organizations, secondary groups designed to rationally achieve explicit objectives, have proliferated in industrial society. Their most common form is a bureaucracy, which Weber characterized as having a hierarchy, a division of labor, written rules, written communications, and impersonality. These characteristics allow bureaucracies to be efficient and enduring, but Weber described an ideal type, a composite that may not accurately describe any actual organization.

3. In Weber's view, the impersonality of bureaucracies tends to produce alienation among workers—the feeling that no one cares about them and that they do not really belong in their surroundings. In Marx's view, alienation is somewhat different—workers are separated from the product of their labor because they participate in only a small part of a large process and have lost control over their work because they no longer own their own tools. Workers resist alienation by forming primary groups at work and by personalizing their work areas. Other dysfunctions of bureaucracies are trained incapacity, goal conflict, goal displacement, engorgement, and incompetence.

4. Voluntary associations are groups made up of volunteers who organize on the basis of some mutual interest. These associations further mutual interests, provide a sense of identity and purpose, help to govern and maintain order, mediate between the government and the individual, give training in organizational skills, help disadvantaged groups gain political power, and challenge established boundaries.

5. The leadership of voluntary associations is likely to perpetuate itself, a tendency Michels called the iron law of oligarchy. The VFW provides a case study of how this process works.

6. Although much of corporate culture is invisible, such as its hidden values, it greatly affects its members. Opened opportunity creates positive feelings about the self and the organization, as well as improving performance, while blocked opportunity creates negative feelings about the self and the organization, thereby decreasing performance. Those most likely to experience opened opportunity are those who match the hidden values of the corporate elite. Morale and style of leadership are influenced by the level one achieves in an organization.

7. To humanize a work setting is to organize it in such a way that it develops rather than impedes human potential. Among the characteristics of more humane bureaucracies are expanded opportunity on the basis of ability and contributions rather than personal characteristics, power more evenly distributed, and less rigid rules and more open decision making. Attempts to modify bureaucracies include quality circles and small work groups. Employee ownership plans give workers a greater stake in the outcomes of their work organizations. Cooperatives have been established as an alternative to bureaucracies.

8. The Japanese corporate model contrasts sharply with the American model in its hiring and promotion practices, lifetime security, involvement of workers, broad training of workers, and collective decision making. Transplanting this model to the United States requires that it be modified because it is founded on a series of cultural elements unlike those in the United States.

SUGGESTED READINGS

Ferguson, Kathy E. *The Feminine Case Against Bureaucracy.* Philadelphia: Temple University Press, 1984. Documenting how bureaucracies are male bastions of power and prestige, Ferguson illustrates the relative disadvantage they provide females.

Fucini, Joseph J., and Suzy Fucini. *Working for the Japanese: Inside Mazda's American Auto Plant.* New York: Free Press, 1990. The authors report on how American workers at the wholly-owned Japanese auto plant in Flat Rock, Michigan, have found that the team system requires them to sacrifice individual interests to the welfare of the group.

Kaminer, Wendy. *Women Volunteering: The Pleasure, Pain, and Politics of Unpaid Work from 1830 to the Present.* Garden City, New York: Anchor, 1984. The book summarizes 150 years of female participation in volunteer associations.

Kanter, Rosabeth Moss. *The Change Masters: Innovation for Productivity in the American Corporation.* New York: Simon & Schuster, 1983. By examining the basis of their capacity for innovation, the author explains why some corporations are more successful than others, illustrates how sociology is useful in solving practical problems, and explains how Americans can become more competitive.

Matyko, Alexander J. *The Self-Defeating Organization: A Critique of Bureaucracy.* New York: Praeger, 1986. The author explains that bureaucracies face a crisis because their hierarchical structure is too authoritarian for contemporary orientations.

Ouchi, William. *Theory Z: How American Business Can Meet the Japanese Challenge.* Reading, Mass.: Addison-Wesley, 1981. Contrasting the American and Japanese corporate models, the author shows how features of the Japanese model can be adapted to meet changing needs in the United States.

Parkinson, C. Northcote. *Parkinson's Law.* Boston: Houghton Mifflin, 1957. While this exposé of the inner workings of bureaucracies is delightfully satirical, if what Parkinson analyzes were generally true, bureaucracies would always fail.

Rothschild, Joyce, and J. Allen Whitt. *The Cooperative Workplace: Potentials and Dilemmas of Organizational Democracy and Participation.* New York: Cambridge University Press, 1986. Exploring the movement toward a more cooperative workplace, the authors discuss the advantages and pitfalls of such reforms.

CHAPTER 8

Red Grooms, Tie Cez, *1977*

Deviance and Social Control

GAINING A SOCIOLOGICAL PERSPECTIVE
OF DEVIANCE

The Relativity of Deviance ■ *Perspectives: Deviance in Cross-Cultural Perspective* ■ Social Control ■ How Norms Make Social Life Possible ■ Comparing Biological, Psychological and Sociological Explanations

THE SYMBOLIC INTERACTIONIST PERSPECTIVE

Differential Association Theory ■ *Perspectives: When Cultures Clash—Problems in Defining Deviance* ■ Control Theory ■ Labeling Theory

THE FUNCTIONALIST PERSPECTIVE

How Deviance Is Functional for Society ■ Strain Theory: How Social Values Produce Crime ■ Illegitimate Opportunity Theory: Explaining Social Class and Crime

THE CONFLICT PERSPECTIVE

Class, Crime, and the Criminal Justice System

REACTIONS TO DEVIANTS

Sanctions ■ Labeling: The Saints and the Roughnecks ■ The Trouble with Official Statistics ■ Degradation Ceremonies ■ Imprisonment

REACTIONS BY DEVIANTS

Primary, Secondary, and Tertiary Deviance ■ Neutralizing Deviance ■ Embracing Deviance

THE MEDICALIZATION OF DEVIANCE: MENTAL ILLNESS

Neither Mental nor Illness? ■ The Homeless Mentally Ill

THE NEED FOR A MORE HUMANE APPROACH

Down-to-Earth Sociology: **Taking Back Children from the Night**

SUMMARY

SUGGESTED READINGS

*I*n just a few moments I was to meet my first Yanomamo, my first primitive man. What would it be like? . . . I looked up (from my canoe) and gasped when I saw a dozen burly, naked, filthy, hideous men staring at us down the shafts of their drawn arrows. Immense wads of green tobacco were stuck between their lower teeth and lips making them look even more hideous, and strands of dark-green slime dripped or hung from their noses. We arrived at the village while the men were blowing a hallucinogenic drug up their noses. One of the side effects of the drug is a runny nose. The mucus is always saturated with the green powder and the Indians usually let it run freely from their nostrils. . . . I just sat there holding my notebook, helpless and pathetic. . . .

The whole situation was depressing, and I wondered why I ever decided to switch from civil engineering to anthropology in the first place. (Soon) . . . I was covered with red pigment, the result of a dozen or so complete examinations. . . . These examinations capped an otherwise grim day. The Indians would blow their noses into their hands, flick as much of the mucus off that would separate in a snap of the wrist, wipe the residue into their hair, and then carefully examine my face, arms, legs, hair, and the contents of my pockets. I said (in their language), "Your hands are dirty"; my comments were met by the Indians in the following way: They would "clean" their hands by spitting a quantity of slimy tobacco juice into them, rub them together, and then proceed with the examination. (Napoleon Chagnon 1977)

GAINING A SOCIOLOGICAL PERSPECTIVE OF DEVIANCE

So went Napoleon Chagnon's eye-opening introduction to the Yanomamo tribe of the rain forests of South America. His ensuing months of fieldwork continued to bring surprise after surprise, and often Chagnon (1977) could hardly believe his eyes—or his nose.

Where would we start to list the deviant behaviors of these people? Appearing naked in public? Using hallucinogenic drugs? Letting mucus hang from one's nose? Rubbing hands filled with mucus, spittle, and tobacco juice over a frightened stranger who doesn't dare to protest? Perhaps. But it isn't this simple, for first we must deal with the question of what deviance is.

The Relativity of Deviance

Sociologists use the term **deviance** to refer to a violation of norms. This deceptively simple definition takes us to the heart of the sociological perspective of deviance, which sociologist Howard S. Becker (1966) identifies this way: *It is not the act itself, but the reactions to the act, that make something deviant.* In other words, people's behaviors must be viewed from the framework of the culture in which they take place. To Chagnon, the behaviors were frighteningly deviant, but to the Yanomamo they represented normal, everyday life. What was deviant to Chagnon was *conforming* to the

L. Obj. 1: Explain why deviance is difficult to define.

CDQ 1: What does the word "deviance" mean to you? Do sociologists use this term in the same way?

K.P.: Howard Becker

deviance: the violation of rules or norms

From a sociological perspective, deviance is relative. In U.S. culture, for instance, taking drugs is considered deviant. Among the Yanomamo Indians, however, the normal route to initiation into manhood is accomplished through the administration of hallucinogens by a shaman, or holy man.

Yanomamo. From their viewpoint of life, you *should* check out strangers as they did—and nakedness is good, as are hallucinogenic drugs and letting mucus be "natural."

Chagnon's abrupt introduction to the Yanomamo allows us to see the *relativity of deviance,* a major point made by symbolic interactionists such as Howard S. Becker (1966) and Malcolm Specter and John Kitsuse (1977, 1980). As the Perspectives box below illustrates, because different groups have different norms, *what is deviant to some is not deviant to others.* This principle holds *within* a society as well as across cultures. Thus acts perfectly acceptable in one culture—or in one group within a society—may be considered deviant in another culture, or in another group within the same society.

What is similar about the following people: a college student cheating on an exam and a mugger lurking on a dark street; a child molester and a drunk; a jaywalker and a rapist; a killer and someone who breaks in line ahead of you? To a sociologist, these very different behaviors are all examples of deviance, for each is a violation of rules, or norms. Sociologists use the term **deviants** to refer to people who violate rules—whether the infraction is as minor as jaywalking or as serious as murder.

Unlike the general public, sociologists use the term *deviance* nonjudgmentally, to refer to acts to which people respond negatively. When sociologists use this term, it does not mean that they agree that an act is bad, just that others judge it negatively.

CDQ 2: Do you agree that a college student who cheats on an exam is, in some ways, similar to a mugger on a dark street?

deviants: people who violate rules, as a result of which others react negatively to them

---

PERSPECTIVES
Cultural Diversity Around the World

Deviance in Cross-Cultural Perspective

Anthropologist Robert Edgerton (1976) reports how differently human groups react to similar behaviors. Of the many examples he provides, let's look at suicide and sexuality to illustrate how a group's *definitions* of a behavior, not the behavior itself, determine whether or not it will be considered deviant.

Suicide. In some societies, suicide is seen not as deviance but as a positive act, at least under specified conditions. In traditional Japanese society, hara-kiri, a ritual disembowelment, was considered the proper course for disgraced noblemen or defeated military leaders. Similarly, kamikaze pilots in World War II who crashed their explosives-laden planes into United States warships were admired for their bravery and sacrifice. Traditional Eskimos approved the suicide of individuals no longer able to contribute their share to the group. Sometimes an aged father would hand his hunting knife to his son, asking him to drive it through his heart. For a son to refuse this request would be considered deviant.

Sexuality. Norms of sexuality vary so widely around the world that many behaviors considered normal or desirable in one society are considered deviant in another. The Pokot people of northwestern Kenya, for example, place high emphasis on sexual pleasure and fully expect that both a husband and his wife will reach orgasm. If a husband does not satisfy his wife, he is in serious trouble.

Pokot men often engage in adulterous affairs, and should a husband's failure to satisfy his wife be attributed to his adultery, when her husband is sleeping the wife will bring in female friends and tie him up. The women will then shout obscenities at him, beat him, and, as a final gesture of their utter contempt, slaughter and eat his favorite ox before releasing him. His hours of painful humiliation are assumed to make him henceforth more dutiful concerning his wife's conjugal rights.

Official versus Covert Norms. People can also become deviants for failing to understand that the group's official sexual norms may not be its real norms. As with many groups, the Zapotec Indians of Mexico expect sexual activity to take place exclusively between husband and wife. Yet the *only* person in one Zapotec community who had had no extramarital affairs was considered deviant. Evidently these people have a covert, commonly understood norm that married couples will engage in discreet extramarital affairs, for when a wife learns that her husband is having an affair she does the same thing. One Zapotec wife, however, did not follow this informal pattern. Instead, she continually threw her virtue up in her husband's face—and claimed headaches. Worse, she also informed all other husbands and wives in the village who their spouses' other partners were. As a result, this virtuous woman was condemned by everyone in the village. In other words, the official norms do not always represent the real norms—another illustration of the gap between ideal and real culture.

K.P.: Erving Goffman

To sociologists, then, all of us are deviants of one sort or another, for we all violate norms from time to time.

To be considered deviant, a person may not even have to do anything. Sociologist Erving Goffman (1963) used the term **stigma** to refer to attributes that discredit people. These attributes can range from physical deformities, blindness, deafness, mental retardation, and obesity—characteristics that violate norms of appearance and ability—to the color of one's skin or membership within given groups, such as prostitutes, relatives of criminals, or victims of AIDS. Once a person is stigmatized, the discrediting attribute defines that person's master status (recall from Chapter 4 that a person's master status supersedes all other statuses that a person occupies). Thus, even if, as in the case of basketball player Magic Johnson or tennis champion Arthur Ashe, you are a world-class athlete, dedicated father, and successful businessperson, once you are stigmatized as an AIDS victim, your other statuses fall away into the shadows and your master status becomes that of "Person with AIDS."

In Sum.   In sociology, the term deviance refers to all violations of social rules, regardless of their seriousness. The term is not a judgment about the behavior. Deviance is relative, for what is conforming behavior in one group may be deviant in another. As symbolic interactionists stress, if we are to understand people, we must understand the meanings that they give to events. Consequently, we must consider deviance from *within* a society's or group's own framework, for it is *their* meanings that underlie their behavior.

Speaker Sug. #1: A criminologist to discuss current issues in his or her field.

Social Control

Who Defines Deviance?   If deviance does not lie in the act, then, but in social definitions, where do those definitions come from? Why is something defined as deviant by one group but not by another? And whose definitions dominate? To answer these questions, let's look first at areas of agreement between functionalists and conflict theorists, then at how these views diverge.

Let's consider a preliterate society (a society without a written language) first. The Yanomamo, for example, have passed through a unique history. For survival, they have faced and solved a set of problems, and these solutions, having become part of their norms, are now an essential part of their way of life. They have developed ways to investigate strangers and to protect themselves from enemies. They are a small group, with strong social bonds, and close agreement on the way life is to be lived. To follow these norms is conformity, to violate them deviance.

CDQ 3: Why do you think it is more difficult to maintain social control in industrialized societies such as the United States?

CDQ 4: Do you agree with the conflict view that the group that holds power must always fend off groups that desire to replace it? If so, give examples.

Industrialized societies, in contrast, are made up of many competing groups, each with its own history of problems and with its own solutions. Each group also claims a unique identity, a way of life that distinguishes it from other groups in the same society, and its members share these ideas about the way the world is and ought to be. Each group has also developed norms that support its orientations to life. These norms, along with both formal and informal means of enforcing them, constitute a system of **social control.** Thus, because they participate in the same general culture, the groups in a pluralistic society agree on many things; yet due to their particular histories, they may differ sharply on many others—to the extent that what one group may consider right, another may consider wrong.

Up to this point in the analysis, functionalists and conflict theorists are in basic agreement about social control. But now they diverge.

stigma: "blemishes" that discredit a person's claim to a "normal" identity

social control: formal and informal means of enforcing norms

Functionalism and Social Control.   Functionalists stress how the various segments of the population in a pluralistic society coexist. As each enforces its own norms on its members, the groups attain a more or less balanced state. Although tensions between them may appear from time to time, the balancing of these tensions produces the whole that we call society. If a group threatens to upset the equilibrium, efforts are made to restore balance. For example, in a pluralistic society the central government often plays a mediating role between groups. In the United States, the executive, legislative, and judicial branches of the government mediate the demands of the various groups that make up society, preventing groups whose basic ideas deviate from those held by most members of society from taking political control (Riesman 1950). This view of mediation and balance among competing groups is broadly representative of what may be called the **pluralistic theory of social control.**

Conflict Theory and Social Control.   Conflict theorists, in contrast, stress that each society is dominated by a particular group and that the basic purpose of social control is to maintain the current power arrangements. Consequently, society is made up not of groups in balance, but rather of competing groups uneasily held together. The group that holds power must always fend off groups that desire to replace it and take over the society themselves. When another group does gain power, it, too, will immediately try to neutralize competing groups. Some groups are much more ruthless than others; for example, before World War II the Nazis in Germany and the Communists in the Soviet Union systematically eliminated individuals and groups they deemed a threat to their vision of the ideal society. Other dominant groups may be less ruthless, but they, too, are committed to maintaining power.

In American society, for example, although political power is not as naked as it is in dictatorships, conflict theorists note that an elite group of wealthy, white males maintains power by working behind the scenes to control the three branches of government (Domhoff 1983, 1991). These men make certain that their interests are represented in the day-to-day decisions of Congress, by the nominees to the United States Supreme Court, and by the presidential candidates of the two major political parties. Thus, it is this group's views of capital and property, the basis of their power, that are represented in the laws of society. This means that **official deviance**—the statistics on victims, lawbreakers, and the outcomes of criminal investigations and sentencing—centers on maintaining their interests.

Thus, conflict theorists stress, the state's machinery of social control represents the interests of the wealthy and powerful (Hall 1952). It is this group that determines the basic laws whose enforcement is essential to preserving its own power. Other norms, such as those that govern informal behavior (chewing with a closed mouth, appearing in public with combed hair, and so on), may come from other sources, but they simply do not count for much. Although they influence everyday behavior, they do not determine prison sentences.

From a conflict perspective, the elite in power decide who is deviant based not on the act itself but on its effects on their own interests. Thus, conflict theorists would claim that the arrest and conviction for drug trafficking of former Panamanian President Manuel Noriega occurred not because the United States government truly cared about his illegal drug activities, but because they decided he was no longer a reliable ally.

CDQ 5: According to conflict theorists, what group controls American society? Do you agree? Why or why not?

CDQ 6: What would life be like if you could never predict what others were going to do?

How Norms Make Social Life Possible

Regardless of the origin of a group's norms, or whose interests they represent, *norms make social life possible by making behavior predictable.* Consequently, every group within a society, and even human society itself, depends upon norms for its existence. Only because we can count on most people most of the time to meet the expectations of others can social life as we know it exist.

What would life be like if you could not predict what others would do? Imagine for a moment that you have gone to a store to purchase milk. . . .

> Suppose that the clerk says: "I won't sell you any milk. We are overstocked with soda, and I'm not going to sell anyone milk until our soda inventory is reduced."
>
> You don't like it, but you decide to buy a case of soda. At the checkout, the clerk says, "I hope you don't mind, but there's a $5 service charge on each fifteenth customer." You, of course, are the fifteenth.
>
> Just as you start to leave, another clerk stops you and says, "We're not working anymore. We're having a party." Suddenly a stereo begins to blast, and everyone in the store is dancing. "Oh, good, you've brought the soda," says one clerk, who takes your package and passes sodas all around.

pluralistic theory of social control: the view that society is made up of many competing groups, whose interests manage to become balanced

official deviance: a society's statistics on lawbreaking; its measures of victims, lawbreakers, and the outcomes of criminal investigations and sentencing

But life is not like this. You can depend on a grocery clerk selling you milk as long as it is in stock and that is what you want. You can also depend on paying the same price as everyone else. And you can depend on the clerks not to give a party in the store and force you to attend. Why can you depend on this? Because we are socialized to follow norms, to play the basic roles as society indicates we should.

Without norms we would have social chaos. Norms regulate our behavior; they dictate how we play our roles and how we interact with others. In short, norms allow **social order,** a group's usual and customary social arrangements, those upon which we depend and on which we base our lives. This is precisely the reason that deviance is often seen as so threatening, for it undermines predictability, the foundation of social life. Consequently, human groups develop a system of *social control,* formal and informal means of enforcing norms.

Comparing Biological, Psychological, and Sociological Explanations

Since norms are essential for society, why do people violate them? To better understand the reasons, it is useful to know first how sociological explanations differ from biological and psychological ones, and then to examine how the three sociological perspectives explain deviance.

Psychologists and *sociobiologists* explain deviance by looking for answers *within* individuals. They assume that something in the makeup of an individual leads him or her to become deviant. By contrast, sociologists look for answers in factors *outside* the individual. They assume that something in the environment influences people to become deviant.

Biological explanations focus on **genetic predispositions** toward deviance such as juvenile delinquency and crime (Lombroso 1911; Sheldon 1949; Kretschmer 1925; Glueck and Glueck 1956; Wilson and Hernstein 1985; Kamin 1975, 1986; Rose 1986). Biological explanations include (but are not restricted to) the following three theories: (1) intelligence—low intelligence leads to crime; (2) the "XYY" theory—an extra Y chromosome in males leads to crime; and (3) body type—persons with "squarish, muscular" bodies are more likely to commit **street crime,** acts such as mugging, rape, and burglary.

None of these theories has held up. Some criminals are very intelligent, and most persons of low intelligence do not commit crimes. Most criminals have the normal "XY" chromosome combination, and most persons with the XYY combination do not become criminals. Criminals run the range of the body types exhibited by humanity, and most people with "squarish, muscular" bodies do not become street criminals. In short, these supposedly "causal" characteristics are also found among the general population of persons who do not commit crimes.

This finding, however, does not rule out the possibility that biological factors influence deviance. Advances in biology have renewed interest in this issue, and some of the findings are intriguing. Psychiatrist Dorothy Lewis (1981), for example, compared the medical histories of delinquents and nondelinquents. She found that delinquents had significantly more head injuries. Then she matched the delinquents by the seriousness of their crimes. When she compared their medical histories, she found that the more violent delinquents—those incarcerated for murder, assault, and rape—also had more head injuries than boys locked up for lesser violence such as fights and threats with weapons. Many of the injuries had occurred before the age of two.

The answers, then, are not yet in, and we must await more research. Even if biological factors are involved in some forms of deviance, from a sociological perspective the causes of deviance cannot be answered by biology alone. Biological factors are always mediated through the social environment. That is, shaping mechanisms of various sorts affect different categories of people in different ways. For example, some of the expectations of the masculine role in American society—to be braver, tougher,

Project 1

L. Obj. 2: Compare and contrast biological, psychological, and sociological explanations of deviance.

CDQ 7: What are some recent examples of biological explanations for deviant behavior? Do you think they are valid? (e.g., PMS, high testosterone levels, etc.)

social order: a group's usual and customary social arrangements, on which its members depend and on which they base their lives

genetic predispositions: inborn tendencies, in this context, to commit deviant acts

street crime: crimes such as mugging, rape, and burglary

more independent, and less tolerant of insult—increase the likelihood that males will become involved in violence.

Psychological explanations of deviance focus on abnormalities in the individual personality, on what are called **personality disorders**. The supposition is that deviating individuals have deviating personalities (Kalichman 1988; Stone 1989; Heilbrun 1990), that various unconscious devices drive people to deviance. Neither specific negative childhood experiences nor particular personalities, however, have been linked with deviance. For example, children who had "bad toilet training," "suffocating mothers," or "emotionally aloof fathers" may become embezzling bookkeepers—or good accountants. Just as students, teachers, and bus drivers represent a variety of bad—and good—childhood experiences, so do deviants. In short, from a sociological perspective there is no inevitable outcome of particular childhood experiences.

Sociologists, in contrast, search for factors outside the individual. First, they stress that because deviance is relative there is no reason to expect that internal factors within individuals will account for deviance. For example, **crime** is the violation of norms that have been written into law. Since one society may pass a law against some behavior while another society passes no such law, why should we expect to find anything constant within people to account for a behavior that is conforming in one society and deviant in another?

Second, sociologists look for social influences that "recruit" some people rather than others to break norms. To account for why people commit crimes, for example, sociologists examine such external influences on them as socialization, subcultural membership, and social class. *Social class,* a concept discussed in depth in the next two chapters, refers to people's relative standing in terms of education, occupation, and especially income and wealth.

To see how sociologists study deviance, let's contrast the three sociological perspectives—symbolic interactionism, functionalism, and conflict theory—looking at how each theory accounts for criminal behavior.

THE SYMBOLIC INTERACTIONIST PERSPECTIVE

As we examine symbolic interaction, it will become more evident why sociologists are not satisfied with explanations rooted in biology and personality. A basic principle of symbolic interactionism is that each of us interprets social life through the symbols that we learn from the groups to which we belong. Let's consider the extent to which membership in a group influences people's behaviors and views of the world, also a focus of the Perspectives box on page 198.

Differential Association Theory

Sociologist Edwin Sutherland located the source of deviant behavior in socialization, or social learning. He coined the term **differential association** to indicate that whether people deviate or conform is influenced most by the groups with which they associate (Sutherland 1947; Sutherland and Cressey 1974). People who associate with groups oriented toward deviant activities learn what Sutherland called an "excess of definitions" of deviance. Consequently, they are more likely than members of other groups to engage in deviant activities. On the most obvious level, boys and girls who join Satan's Servants learn a way of looking at the world that is more likely to get them in trouble with the law than boys and girls who join the Scouts.

Although the norms that distinguish most groups from the general society vary only slightly from the dominant norms—they are more likely to be variations in appearance, manner, or belief than different attitudes toward such extreme behaviors as murder— some groups do teach their members to violate the dominant norms of society. Demographers Allen Beck, Susan Kline, and Lawrence Greenfeld (1988) documented just

CDQ 8: Do you think that an individual's childhood experiences inevitably cause that person to behave in a certain way? Why or why not?

Essay #1

CDQ 9: How are sociological explanations of deviance different in focus from psychological ones?

Essay #2

L. Obj. 3: State the key components of the symbolic interactionist perspective on deviance, and briefly explain differential association theory, control theory, and labeling theory.

K.P.: Edwin Sutherland

CDQ 10: Do you agree that teenage gangs are an example of differential association theory? Why or why not?

personality disorders: the view that a personality disturbance of some sort causes an individual to violate social norms

crime: the violation of norms that are written into law

differential association: Edwin Sutherland's term for the ways in which association with some groups results in learning an "excess of definitions" of deviance, and, by extension, in a greater likelihood that their members will become deviant

PERSPECTIVES
Cultural Diversity in U.S. Society

When Cultures Clash— Problems in Defining Deviance

In November 1989, sixteen-year-old Tina Isa, who lived with her parents in an apartment on the south side of St. Louis, was stabbed six times by her father, Zein, a Palestinian-born grocer who brought his family to the United States in 1985. Her mother, Maria, held Tina down as Zein ended his daughter's life.

In an eerie twist, the entire murder was captured on tape. For two years, the Isa household had been bugged by the FBI, which was monitoring Mr. Zein for possible illegal activities on behalf of the Palestinian Liberation Organization. While the surveillance unit was not staffed the night the murder occurred, Tina's screams and her parents' shouts in Arabic telling her to "die quickly" were clearly recorded—and ultimately replayed to a horrified jury.

Tina, the youngest of the Zein's seven children and the only daughter remaining at home, had clashed constantly with her parents and siblings. They strongly disapproved of her playing soccer and tennis on high school teams and of being on the cheerleading squad. Her job at a fast-food restaurant infuriated them, and when Tina went to her junior prom, her family followed her and forcibly brought her home.

Tina's mother is Roman Catholic; the rest of the Isa family is Muslim. None had assimilated into American culture like Tina. During their parents' murder trial, her sisters blamed Tina for her own murder, claiming that she had long brought shame to the family and that the parents had just done their duty. At their trial, Tina's parents showed no remorse. Sentenced to die by lethal injection, Maria Isa told the judge, "My daughter was very disrespectful and rebellious. We should not have to pay with our lives for something she did."

After Zein and Maria Isa were sentenced to death, Nocolas Gavrielides, who was born and raised in Jerusalem and is now an anthropology professor at the State University of New York, testified that the way Tina lived had offended her father's sense of honor. The parents were especially concerned that Tina would not remain a virgin and thus be unable to marry a relative of one of their sons-in-law. "Everyone growing up in the Middle East knows that being killed is a possible consequence of dishonoring the family," said Professor Gavrielides.

But others disagree, including Victor Le Vine, professor of Jewish and Near Eastern Studies at Washington University in St. Louis. "This is certainly aberrant behavior," he said. "Palestinians and other Arab refugees in the United States would regard it with horror."

In April 1985 the residents of Fresno, California, were confronted with a less shocking, but in some ways similar incident. Having decided that it was time to marry, a young Hmong refugee named Kong Moua went to a local college campus along with a group of friends and forced the girl he had selected as his mate to his house. He then had sex with her.

In the Hmong culture, Kong Moua had performed *zij poj niam,* marriage by capture. While this method of obtaining a marriage partner is not the only, or even the most frequent, way of marrying among traditional Hmong, neither is it a rare occurrence. Universal to Hmong courtship is the idea that men appear strong, women resistant and virtuous.

The apparent sincerity of Kong Moua presented a dilemma to the judge who heard his case. Under the United States legal system, Kong Moua had committed two crimes: kidnap and rape. Given Moua's cultural background, however, the judge felt uncomfortable simply applying American law. In an attempt to balance matters, he allowed Moua to plead to a lesser charge of false imprisonment, thus giving the court the leeway "to get into all these cultural issues and try to tailor a sentence that will fulfill both our needs and the Hmong needs." Moua was ordered to pay $1,000 to the girl's family and serve a ninety-day jail term.

What is the proper reaction when cultures clash? When the norms of the culture in which people were raised violate the norms of their host society, what should the proper reaction be? It is obvious that the United States cannot allow murder and rape just because of where a person was raised. But should the full force of the law be applied in such cases? If not, how can we justify two types of application?

Source: Based on Treen, Bell, and McGuire 1992; *New York Times,* October 28, 1991; and Sherman 1988.

how significant the family is in this regard. Using a representative sample of the 25,000 delinquents confined in high-security state institutions nationwide, they found that significant numbers have a relative who has been in prison: 25 percent a father, 25 percent a brother or sister, 9 percent a mother, and 13 percent some other relative. Apparently families involved in crime tend to set their children on a lawbreaking path.

The neighborhood is also likely to be influential, for sociologists have long observed that delinquents tend to come from neighborhoods in which their peers are involved in

According to differential association theory, the most influential factor in whether or not—as well as how—we deviate is the group or groups with which we associate.

crime (Miller 1958; Wolfgang and Ferracuti 1967). Sociologist Ruth Horowitz (1983; 1987), who did participant observation of a Chicano neighborhood in Chicago, discovered how the concept of "honor" can propel young men to deviance. The formula is simple. An insult is defined as a threat to one's manliness. Honor requires a man to stand up to an insult. Not to stand up to someone is to be less than a real man. Suppose that you were a young man growing up in this neighborhood. You would likely do a fair amount of fighting, for you would see many statements and acts as infringing on your honor; and you would be around other young men who felt the same way about their honor. You probably would make certain that you had access to a gun, for words and fists won't always do. Along with members of your group, you would define fighting, carrying guns, and shooting quite differently than do most people in American culture.

Studies of the Mafia also show a relationship between killing, manliness, and honor. *To kill is a primary measure of one's manhood.* Not all killings are accorded the same respect, however, for "the more awesome and potent the victim, the more worthy and meritorious the killer" (Arlacchi 1980). Some killings are very practical matters. A member of the Mafia who gives information to the police, for example, has violated the Mafia's *omerta* (the vow of secrecy its members take). Such an offense can never be tolerated, for it threatens the very existence of the group. This example further illustrates just how relative deviance is. While the act of killing is deviant to the larger society, *not* to kill after certain rules are broken, such as "squealing" to the cops, is the deviant act for this group.

As symbolic interactionists stress, people are not merely pawns in the hands of others, destined by group membership to think and behave in the precise way their group wants. Rather, individuals *help to produce their own orientations to life.* Their choice of association, for example, helps to shape the self. For instance, one college student may join a feminist group that is trying to change the treatment of females in college; another may associate with a group of women who shoplift on weekends. Their choice of groups points them in two different directions. The one who associates with shoplifters may become even more oriented toward deviant activities, while the one who joins the feminist group may develop an even greater interest in producing social change.

Control Theory

Sociologist Walter C. Reckless (1973), who developed **control theory,** stresses that everyone experiences "pushes" and "pulls" (temptations) toward deviances such as crime. Two control systems work against these pushes and pulls. The *inner control* system is the individual's capacity to withstand these pressures. Inner controls include internalized morality—conscience, ideas of right and wrong, and reluctance to violate religious principles. Inner controls also include fears of punishment, feelings of integ-

CDQ 11: How can the concept of "honor" propel a person to deviance? Can you give examples?

K.P.: Walter Reckless

CDQ 12: What are some of the "pushes" and "pulls" a student experiences when he or she is thinking about cheating on an exam? What types of controls work against these forces?

control theory: the idea that two control systems—inner controls and outer controls—work against our pushes and pulls toward deviance

K.P.: Travis Hirschi

CDQ 13: Do you agree that acts are deviant only because people label them as such? Why or why not?

rity, and the desire to be a "good" person (Hirschi 1969; Rogers 1977). The *outer control* system involves groups—such as family, friends, and the police—that influence a person to stay away from crime. Control theory is sometimes classified as a functional theory, because when outer controls operate well, the individual conforms to social norms and thereby does not threaten the status quo. Because symbols and meanings are central to this theory, however, it can also be classified as a symbolic interactionist theory.

As sociologist Travis Hirschi (1969) noted, the more people feel bonded to society, the more effective are their inner controls. Bonds are based on *attachments* (having affection and respect for others), *commitments* (having a stake in society that you don't want to risk, such as a respected place in your family, a good standing at college, a good job), *involvements* (putting time and energy into approved activities), and *beliefs* (holding that certain actions are morally wrong).

The likelihood that someone will deviate from social norms, for example by committing a crime, depends on the strength of these two control systems relative to the strength of the pushes and pulls toward the deviance. If the control systems are weak, deviance results. If they are strong enough, however, the person does not commit the deviant act.

Labeling Theory

Labeling theory, which focuses on the significance of the labels (names, reputations) given to people, also represents the symbolic interactionist perspective. According to labeling theory, acts are deviant only because people label them as such. Thus, the young Hmong man, whose attempt to "capture" a wife is recounted in the Perspectives box on page 198, is not seen as deviant by traditional Hmong. Perhaps some of his own relatives had married in this manner. They would label his behavior as desirable and expected, and perhaps even applaud him for it. In American society, however, different labels—those of kidnapper and rapist—are appropriate. Consequently, symbolic interactionists analyze the significance of labels in determining how people react to others. Labeling theory is discussed below on pages 206–207.

In Sum.   Symbolic interactionists examine how people's definitions of the situation underlie their deviation or conformance to social norms. Differential association theory focuses on the effects of group membership, while control theory emphasizes how people balance pressures to conform and to deviate.

THE FUNCTIONALIST PERSPECTIVE

Essay #3

L. Obj. 4: Discuss the major reasons why functionalists view deviance as functional for society.

K.P.: Emile Durkheim

CDQ 14: Can you give examples of social values which generate crime in the United States?

labeling theory: the view, developed by symbolic interactionists, that the labels people are given affect their own and others' perceptions of them, thus channeling their behavior either into deviance or into conformity

How Deviance Is Functional for Society

Most of us are upset by deviance, especially crime, and assume that society would be better off without it. The classic functionalist theorist Emile Durkheim (1933, 1964) came to a surprising conclusion, however. Deviance, including crime, he said, is functional for society, for it contributes to the social order. From the functionalist perspective, deviance performs three main functions.

1. *Deviance clarifies moral boundaries and affirms norms.* A group's ideas about how people should act and think mark its *moral boundaries.* Deviant acts challenge those boundaries. To call a deviant member to account, saying in effect, "You broke a valuable rule, and we cannot tolerate that," affirms the group's norms and clarifies the distinction between conforming and deviating behavior. To deal with deviants is to assert what it means to be a member of the group.

2. *Deviance promotes social unity.* Affirming the group's moral boundaries by reacting to deviants develops a "we" feeling among the group's members. In saying,

"You can't get by with that," the group collectively affirms the rightness of its own ways.

   3. *Deviance promotes social change.* Groups do not always agree on what to do with people who push beyond their acceptable ways of doing things. Some group members may even approve the behavior. Boundary violations that gain enough support become new, acceptable behaviors. Thus, deviance may also force a group to rethink and redefine its moral boundaries, helping groups, and whole societies, to change their customary ways.

Strain Theory: How Social Values Produce Crime

Functionalists argue that crime is a *natural* part of society, not an aberration or some alien element in our midst. Indeed, they say, some crime represents values that lie at the very core of society. This concept sounds strange at first. To understand how the acceptance of cultural values can generate crime, consider what sociologists Richard Cloward and Lloyd Ohlin (1960) identified as the crucial problem of the industrialized world: the need to locate and train the most talented persons of every generation— whether born in wealth or in poverty—so that they can take over the key technical jobs of modern society. When children are born, no one knows which ones will have the abilities to become dentists, nuclear physicists, or engineers. To get the most able and talented people to compete with one another, society tries to motivate *everyone* to strive for success. It does this by arousing discontent—making people feel dissatisfied with what they have so that they will try to "better" themselves.

Merton's Typology.   Sociologist Robert K. Merton (1956, 1968) developed **strain theory** to analyze what happens when large numbers of people are socialized into desiring **cultural goals** (the legitimate objectives held out to everyone, such as owning material possessions) while withholding from many access to the institutionalized means of achieving those goals. By **institutionalized means,** Merton meant the socially and legally acceptable ways by which people achieve goals, such as gaining an education or acquiring a good job. Anomie results when some members of society find themselves cut off from the institutionalized means. Due to racism, sexism, and social class, for example, some people are denied access to the approved ways of achieving cultural goals. For example, large numbers of people who want to succeed find their path to highly paid, prestigious jobs blocked because they grew up in poverty and received an inferior education.

   As shown in Table 8.1, Merton identified five types of responses to anomie. The first is actually a nondeviant response: conformity. Merton noted that by far the most common reaction to the goals that a society sets before its people is to *conform,* to use conventional, legitimate means to strive to attain them. In industrialized societies,

K.P.: Robert Merton

TR#6M: Merton's Typology of Individual Adaptation to Anomie

L. Obj. 5: Describe Merton's strain theory, and list and briefly explain the five types of responses to anomie.

CDQ 15: Is it possible for anyone who wants to gain an education or acquire a good job to do so in the United States? Why or why not?

CDQ 16: Why do you think most people take legally and socially acceptable actions to get ahead even if there might be a "shortcut" outside the law?

strain theory: Robert Merton's term for the strain engendered when a society socializes large numbers of people to desire a cultural goal (such as success) but withholds from many the approved means to reach that goal; one adaptation to the strain is crime, the choice of an innovative means (one outside the approved system) to attain the cultural goal

cultural goals: the legitimate objectives held out to the members of a society

institutionalized means: approved ways of reaching cultural goals

TABLE 8.1   Merton's Typology of Individual Adaptation to Anomie

Modes of Adaptation	Culture Goals	Institutionalized Means
Conformity	+ *	+
Innovation	+	−
Ritualism	−	+
Retreatism	−	−
Rebellion	±	±

*A + indicates acceptance, a − rejection, and a ± rejection of prevailing values and substitution of new values.

most people try for the best jobs, a good education, and so on. If well-paid jobs are unavailable, they take less desirable jobs and keep on looking. If they are denied access to Harvard or Stanford, they go to a state university. Others take night classes and attend vocational schools. In short, most people take legally and socially acceptable actions to get ahead. The remaining four types of responses are deviant. Individuals turn to *innovation* when they accept the goals of society but use illegitimate means to achieve them. Drug dealers, for instance, accept the goal of achieving wealth but reject the legitimate avenues for doing so. Embezzlers, robbers, and con artists are other examples of what Merton called innovators.

CDQ 17: Have you ever engaged in ritualism? For example, have you suffered "burnout" as a student but continued to attend classes?

Some people who find their way blocked become discouraged and give up on achieving cultural goals, but nonetheless cling to conventional rules of conduct. Merton called this type of response *ritualism.* While not seeking to excel or advance in position, ritualists nonetheless follow the rules of their job, sometimes with a vengeance. Teachers who suffer from "burnout" but continue to go through the motions of classroom performance after their idealism is shattered and abandoned are examples of ritualists. Their response is considered deviant because they cling to the job although they have actually abandoned the goal, in this instance stimulating young minds and, possibly, making the world a better place.

People who choose the third deviant path, *retreatism,* reject both cultural goals and the institutionalized means of achieving them. Those who drop out of the pursuit of success by way of alcohol or drugs are retreatists. Such people do not even try to appear as though they share the goals of their society.

The final type of deviant response identified by Merton is *rebellion.* Rebels, like retreatists, reject both society's goals and its institutionalized means, convinced that the society in which they live is corrupt. Unlike retreatists, however, they seek to replace existing goals with new ones. Revolutionaries are the most committed type of rebels.

Merton's theory has held up under examination. Sociologists have found that anomie is higher among the lower social classes, which fits the fact that these classes have less access to the institutionalized means to success (Bell 1957; Tumin and Collins 1959; Killian and Grigg 1962). Sociologists Chien Huang and James Anderson (1991) found that people in the lower classes perceive more obstacles to their goals and are more likely to give up on cultural values. In contrast, because they perceive fewer obstacles to their success, people in the upper classes are more committed to the dominant social values.

Strain theory underscores the main sociological point about deviance, namely, that deviants, including criminals, are not pathogenic individuals, but the product of society itself. Due to their social location, some people experience greater pressures to deviate from society's norms. Simply put, if a society emphasizes the goal of material success, groups deprived of access to this goal will be more involved in property crime.

L. Obj. 6: Identify the relationship between social class and crime by using the illegitimate opportunity theory and perspectives on white-collar crime.

Speaker Sug. #2: A police officer who investigates robberies, burglaries, drug dealing, and other street crimes.

Illegitimate Opportunity Theory: Explaining Social Class and Crime

That different social classes have unequal access to institutionalized means to success is also relevant to one of the more interesting sociological findings in the field of deviance: Different social classes have distinct styles of crime. Let us look first at the poor.

Functionalists point out that industrialized societies have no trouble socializing the poor into desiring material success. Like others, they, too, are bombarded with messages urging them to purchase everything from designer jeans to new cars. Television portrays vivid images of the middle class enjoying luxurious lives, reinforcing the myth that all full-fledged Americans can afford the goods and services portrayed on programs and offered in commercials (Silberman 1978).

The school system, however, which constitutes the most common route to success, fails the poor. It is run by the middle class, and when the children of the poor

Among the five types of responses to anomie that sociologist Robert Merton identified, Malcolm X's response would fall into the category of rebellion—in which a person rejects both society's goals and the culturally-sanctioned means of achieving those goals. Malcolm X rejected society's goals, but as a revolutionary, sought to create new ones in their place.

enter it, already at an educational disadvantage, they confront a bewildering world for which their background ill prepares them. Their grammar and nonstandard language, their ideas of punctuality and neatness, their lack of preparation in paper-and-pencil skills—all are removed from those of their new environment (Henslin, Henslin, and Keiser 1976). Facing these barriers, the poor drop out of school in larger numbers than their more privileged counterparts. Educational failure, in turn, closes the door on many legitimate avenues to financial success.

Not infrequently, however, a different door opens to them, one that sociologists Richard Cloward and Lloyd Ohlin (1960) called **illegitimate opportunity structures.** Woven into the texture of life in urban slums, for example, are robbery, burglary, drug dealing, prostitution, pimping, gambling, and other remunerative crimes, commonly called "hustles" (Liebow 1967; Anderson 1978, 1990; Sullivan 1989). For many of the poor, the "hustler" is a role model—glamorous, powerful, the image of "easy money," one of the few people in the area who approximates the cultural goal of success. For some, then, such illegal income-producing activities are functional, drawing the poor into certain types of property crime in disproportionate numbers.

White-Collar Crime.   Other social classes are not crime-free, of course, but for the more privileged classes a different illegitimate opportunity structure makes other *forms* of crime functional. Rather than mugging, pimping, and burglary, the more privileged encounter "opportunities" for income tax evasion, bribery of public officials, securities violations, embezzlement, false advertising, and price fixing. Sociologist Edwin Sutherland (1949) coined the term **white-collar crime** to refer to crimes that people of respectable and high social status commit in the course of their occupations.

Although the general public seems to think that the lower classes are more crime-prone, numerous studies show that white-collar workers also commit many crimes (Cressey 1953; Dowie 1977; Clinard et al. 1979; Weisburd, Wheeler, and Waring 1991). The difference in public perception has much to do with visibility. While crimes

CDQ 18: Do you think television shows and movies have glamorized illegitimate opportunity structures? Can you give examples?

K.P.: Richard Cloward and Lloyd Ohlin

Project 2

CDQ 19: Why are white-collar crimes available only to people of respectable and high social status?

illegitimate opportunity structures: opportunities for remunerative crimes woven into the texture of life

white-collar crime: Edwin Sutherland's term for crimes committed by people of respectable and high social status in the course of their occupations; for example, bribery of public officials, securities violations, embezzlement, false advertising, and price fixing

CNN: Crime Costs

CDQ 20: What types of crimes are most costly? Can you explain why it is difficult to answer this question?

committed by the poor are given much publicity, the crimes of the more privileged classes seldom make the evening news and go largely unnoticed. Yet white-collar crimes are very costly (Moore and Mills 1990). The cost of "crimes in the suites" (as opposed to crimes in the streets) may total about $200 billion a year. This is about *eighteen* times the cost of all the street crimes committed in the United States (Simon 1981; Gest and Scherschel 1985). These figures refer only to dollar costs. No one has yet figured out a way to compare, for example, the suffering of a rape victim with the pain experienced by an elderly couple who lose their life savings to white-collar fraud.

In terms of dollars, perhaps the most costly crime in recent times is the plundering of the United States savings and loan industry. Corporate officers, who had the trust of their depositors, systematically looted these banks of billions of dollars. The total cost may be as high as $500 billion—a staggering $2,000 for every man, woman, and child in the entire country (Kettl 1991; Newdorf 1991). Of the thousands involved the most famous culprit was Neil Bush, son of the president of the United States and an officer of Silverado, a Colorado savings and loan. Bush approved loans totaling $100 million to a company in which he secretly held interests, an act that helped bankrupt his firm (Tolchin 1991). Future generations will continue to suffer from the wholesale looting of this industry. The interest alone will be exorbitant (at 5 percent a year's interest on an increased national deficit of $500 billion would be $25 billion, at 10 percent $50 billion). Since the government does not pay its debt, but merely borrows more to keep up with the compounding interest, this extra $500 billion will double in just a few years. As the late Senator Everett Dirkson once said, "A billion here and a billion there, and pretty soon you're talking about real money."

CDQ 21: Why do you think the media typically considers white-collar crime to be less newsworthy than street crime?

Although white-collar crime is not as dramatic as a street killing or an abduction and rape—and therefore usually considered less newsworthy—it too can involve physical harm, and sometimes death (Reiman 1990). With the act clandestine and often a long lag between the act and the injury, the harm is difficult to measure. For example, although Dow Corning knew for twenty years that its silicone breast implants might leak, the company concealed that information. In the ensuing years, thousands of women suffered from ruptured implants, which apparently caused illnesses ranging from arthritis-type joint pain to severely swollen abdomens—and perhaps even increased their risk of cancer (Ingersoll 1992; Burton 1992; Burton, Ingersoll, and Rigdon 1992; Burton and McMurray 1992; McMurray 1992; Woods and Arnold 1992). Similarly, many unsafe working conditions, the result of executive decisions to put profits ahead of workers' safety, claim about one hundred thousand American lives each year—about *five* times the number of people killed each year by street criminals (Simon and Eitzen 1986; FBI 1990).

In Sum.   Functionalists conclude that a high crime rate is an integral part of industrialized society. To socialize people into the conspicuous consumption discussed in Chapter 14 (page 374) is to fuel the desire for possessions. Much crime, then, is the consequence of socializing people of all social classes into equating success with material possessions, while denying the lower classes the means to attain that success. People from different social classes encounter different opportunity structures.

Essay #4

L. Obj. 7: Explain the conflict view of the relationship between class, crime, and the criminal justice system.

THE CONFLICT PERSPECTIVE

Class, Crime, and the Criminal Justice System

Have you ever wondered what is going on when you read that top-level executives who defraud the public of millions through price fixing, insider trading, or stock manipulation receive only small fines and suspended sentences? In the same newspaper, furthermore, you may read that some young man who stole an automobile worth $5,000 was sentenced to several years in prison. How can a legal system that is supposed to provide "justice for all" be so inconsistent? According to conflict theorists, this question is central to the analysis of crime and the **criminal justice system**—the police, courts, and prisons that deal with people who are accused of having committed crimes.

Conflict theorists look at power and social inequality as the primary characteristics of every society. They see the most fundamental division in industrial society as that between the few who own the means of production and the many who do not, those who sell their labor and the privileged few who buy it. Those who buy labor, and thereby control workers, make up the **capitalist class;** those who sell their labor form the **working class.** Toward the most depressed end of the working class is the **marginal working class,** people with few skills whose jobs are low-paying, part-time, seasonal, or subject to unexpected layoffs (Carter and Clelland 1979). This class is marked by unemployment and poverty, and from its ranks come most of the prisoners in the United States. Desperate, these people commit street crimes, and because their crimes threaten the social order, they are severely punished.

According to conflict theorists, the idea that the law is a social institution that operates impartially and administers a code shared by all is simply a cultural myth promoted by the capitalist class. They see the law rather as an instrument of repression, a tool designed to maintain the powerful in their privileged position (Spitzer 1975; Jacobs 1978; Beirne and Quinney 1982). Because the working class holds the potential of rebelling and overthrowing the current social order, its members are arrested, tried, and imprisoned when they get out of line.

For this reason, the criminal justice system does not focus on the owners of corporations and the harm they do to the masses with their unsafe products, wanton pollution, and price manipulations but instead directs its energies against violations by the working class (Gordon 1971; Platt 1978; Coleman 1989). The violations of the capitalist class cannot be totally ignored, however, for if they became too outrageous or oppressive, the working class might rise up in revolution. To prevent this, a flagrant violation by a member of the capitalist class is occasionally prosecuted. The publicity given to the case helps to stabilize the social system by providing visible evidence of the "fairness" of the criminal justice system.

Usually, however, the powerful bypass the courts altogether, appearing instead before some agency with no power to imprison (such as the Federal Trade Commission). Most cases of illegal sales of stocks and bonds, price fixing, restraint of trade, collusion, and so on are handled by "gentlemen overseeing gentlemen," for such agencies are invariably directed by people from wealthy backgrounds who sympathize with the intricacies of the corporate world. It is not surprising, then, that the typical sanction is a token fine. In contrast, however, the property crimes of the masses are handled by courts that do have the power to imprison. The burglary, armed robbery, and theft by the poor not only threaten the sanctity of private property but, ultimately, the positions of the powerful.

From the perspective of conflict theory, then, the small penalties imposed for crimes committed by the powerful are typical of a legal system designed to mask injustice, to control workers, and, ultimately, to stabilize the social order. From this perspective, law enforcement is simply a cultural device through which the capitalist class carries out self-protective and repressive policies (Silver 1977).

REACTIONS TO DEVIANTS

Whether it be cheating on a sociology examination or holding up a liquor store, any violation of norms invites reaction. Reactions to deviance consist both of the responses of others (with sanctions, labeling, degradation ceremonies, or imprisonment) and of people's reactions to their own deviant behaviors.

CDQ 22: Do you think the American legal system provides equal justice for all? Why or why not?

CDQ 23: Is it possible for the powerful to bypass the courts altogether? Why or why not?

Essay #5

L. Obj. 8: Describe the reactions to deviants, and state why official statistics may not accurately reflect the nature and extent of crime in America.

TR#10: Classification of Norms

criminal justice system: the system of police, courts, and prisons set up to deal with people who are accused of having committed a crime

capitalist class: the wealthy who own the means of production and buy the labor of the working class

working class: those who sell their labor to the capitalist class

marginal working class: the most desperate members of the working class, who have few skills, little job security, and are often unemployed

CDQ 24: What types of sanctions do you think are most effective? Why?

Sanctions

As discussed in Chapter 2, people do not strictly enforce folkways but become very upset when mores are broken. Disapproval of deviance, called **negative sanctions,** ranges from frowns, gossip, and crossing people off guest lists to fines, imprisonment, exile, and capital punishment. **Positive sanctions,** in contrast—from smiles and informal words of approval to formal awards—are used to reward people for conforming to norms. Getting a raise is a positive sanction, being fired a negative sanction. Getting an A in basic sociology is a positive sanction, getting an F a negative one.

Most negative sanctions are informal. You will probably merely stare when someone dresses in what you consider inappropriate clothing, or just gossip if a married person you know spends the night with someone other than his or her spouse. Whether you consider the breaking of a norm simply an amusing matter that warrants no severe sanctions or a serious infraction that does, however, depends on your perspective. If a woman appears at your college graduation ceremonies in a swimsuit, you may stare and laugh, but if it is *your* mother you are likely to feel that different sanctions are appropriate. Similarly, if it is *your* father who spends the night with an eighteen-year-old college freshman, you are likely to do more than gossip.

Reacting to deviance is vital to the welfare of groups, for groups must maintain their boundaries if they are to continue to claim a unique identity. As we shall see in the next section, reactions to deviance also have far-reaching consequences for people's lives.

TR#7M: Delinquent Acts

Speaker Sug. #3: A representative of a "deviant" or dissident group to talk about the impact of labeling on individuals and groups.

K.P.: William Chambliss

Labeling: The Saints and the Roughnecks

For two years, sociologist William J. Chambliss (1973) observed two groups of adolescent lawbreakers in Hannibal High School. As noted in Chapter 4, he called one group the "Saints," the other the "Roughnecks." The members of these two groups were some of the most delinquent boys in the school. Both groups were "constantly occupied with truancy, drinking, wild parties, petty theft, and vandalism." As Chambliss catalogued their offenses, however, he noted that the Saints committed more criminal acts than the Roughnecks. Yet their teachers looked on the Saints as "headed for success" and the Roughnecks as "headed for serious trouble." Moreover, by the time they

negative sanctions: punishments or negative reactions to deviance

positive sanctions: devices for rewarding desired behavior

As symbolic interactionists stress, humans categorize their experiences and then act on the basis of their classifications. The classifications, or stereotypes, developed by teachers, police, and others in authority can have far-reaching effects on people's lives, as illustrated by the Saints and the Roughnecks described in the text. How do you think high school teachers classify these students?

finished high school, not one Saint had been arrested, while the Roughnecks were in constant trouble with the police.

Why did the community see these boys so differently? Chambliss concluded that this double vision was due to their family background, especially to social class. As symbolic interactionists emphasize, social class is a powerful symbol that vitally affects people's perceptions and behavior. The Saints came from respectable, middle-class families, while the Roughnecks came from less respectable, working-class families. Because of their respective backgrounds, teachers and other authorities expected good, law-abiding behavior from the Saints but trouble from the Roughnecks. And like the rest of us, both teachers and police see what they expect to see.

Social class also had a practical effect in making one group more *visible* than the other. Because the Saints had automobiles, they were able to make their drinking and vandalism inconspicuous by spreading it around neighboring towns. Without cars, the Roughnecks could not even make it to the edge of town. Day after day, the Roughnecks hung around the same street corners, where their boisterous behavior made them conspicuous, drew the attention of police, and, not incidentally, confirmed the ideas that the community had of them.

Another significant factor was also at work. The boys' different social backgrounds had equipped them with distinct *styles of interaction*. When police or teachers questioned them, the Saints were apologetic and penitent. They also showed respect for authority, perhaps the most important factor in winning the authorities over to their side (Westley 1953; Werthman and Piliavin 1981). In fact, their deferential behavior elicited such positive reactions that they escaped serious legal problems. In contrast, the Roughnecks' attitude was "almost the polar opposite." They expressed open hostility to the authorities, and even when they pretended to show respect, the veneer was so thin that it fooled no one. Consequently, while the police simply let the Saints off with warnings, they came down hard on the Roughnecks, interrogating and arresting them when they had the chance.

This study provides an excellent illustration of the labeling theory described earlier in this chapter. As noted, the labels given to people affect how others perceive them and how they perceive themselves, thus channeling their behavior either into deviance or into conformity. In this case, all but one of the Saints went on to college, after which one became a doctor, one a lawyer, one a Ph.D., and the others business managers. In contrast, only two of the Roughnecks went to college, both on athletic scholarships, after which they became coaches. The other Roughnecks did not fare so well. Two of them dropped out of high school, later became involved in separate killings, and received long prison sentences. Once became a local bookie, and no one knows the whereabouts of the other.

While a lifetime career is not determined by a label alone, the Saints and the Roughnecks nevertheless did live up to the labels that the community gave them. You can easily see in this case how labels opened and closed the doors of opportunity. Being labeled a "deviant" (certainly a far from nonjudgmental term in everyday life!) can lock people out of conforming groups and force them into almost exclusive contact with people who have similar labels.

The Trouble with Official Statistics

Both the findings of symbolic interactionists concerning the authorities' reactions to such groups as the Saints and the Roughnecks and the conclusions of conflict theorists that the criminal justice system exists to serve the ruling elite demonstrate the need for caution in interpreting official crime statistics. Statistics are not tangible objects, like produce in a supermarket, waiting to be picked up. They are a human creation, produced within a specific social and intellectual context for some particular purpose.

According to official statistics, working-class boys clearly emerge as much more delinquent than middle-class boys. Yet, as we have just seen, *who actually gets arrested*

Project 3

CDQ 25: Why are we more likely to believe that a statement is true if we are presented with statistics to "prove" it?

K.P.: Harold Garfinkel

CDQ 26: Do you think degradation ceremonies can have a long-term harmful impact on the persons subjected to such activities?

Project 4

Speaker Sug. #4: A jail or prison official to discuss problems in the criminal justice system.

TR#8: Growth in the American Prison Population

TR#9: Characteristics of American Prisoners

TR#8M: Crime Clock

CDQ 27: What do you think contributes to the high rate of recidivism in the United States?

police discretion: routine judgments by the police concerning whether to arrest someone or to ignore a matter

degradation ceremonies: rituals designed to strip an individual of his or her identity as a group member; for example, a court martial or the defrocking of a priest

recidivism rate: the proportion of persons who are rearrested

for what is directly affected by social class, a point that has far-reaching implications. As symbolic interactionists point out, the police use a symbolic system as they enforce the law. Their ideas of "typical criminals" and "typical good citizens," for example, permeate their work. The more a suspect matches their ideas of the "criminal profile," the more likely that person is to be arrested (Werthman and Piliavin 1981). **Police discretion,** the decision whether or not to arrest someone or even to ignore a matter, is a routine part of police work (Wilson 1981). Consequently, official crime statistics always reflect these and many other biases.

Degradation Ceremonies

When someone wanders far from a group's standards, the reaction to the deviant is likely to be harsh. In some instances, groups attempt to mark an individual indelibly as a DEVIANT for all the world to see. In Nathaniel Hawthorne's *The Scarlet Letter,* for example, Hester Prynne was forced to stand on a platform in public wearing a scarlet A sewn on her dress to mark her as an adulteress. Furthermore, she was expected by the community to wear this badge of shame every day for the rest of her life.

Sociologist Harold Garfinkel (1956) called such formal attempts to mark an individual with the status of an outsider **degradation ceremonies.** The individual is called to account before the group, witnesses denounce him or her, the offender is pronounced guilty, and, most important in sociological terms, steps are taken to *strip the individual of his or her identity as a group member.* Following a court martial, for example, officers found guilty stand at attention before their peers while the insignia of rank are ripped from their uniforms. A priest may be defrocked before a congregation, a citizen forced to wear a prison uniform. These procedures indicate that the individual is no longer a member of the group—no longer able to command soldiers, to preach or offer sacraments, to vote or to move about freely. Although Hester Prynne was not banished from the group physically, her degradation ceremony proclaimed her a *moral* outcast from the community, the scarlet A marking her as "not one" of them.

Imprisonment

Today, we don't make people wear scarlet letters, but we do remove them from society and make them wear prison uniforms. The prison experience follows a degradation ceremony involving a public trial and the public pronouncement that the person is "unfit to live among regular, law-abiding people" for some specified period of time.

Imprisonment is an increasingly popular reaction to crime. Each year more than a quarter of a million Americans are sent to prison, and as Table 8.2 shows, between 1970 and 1989 the number of Americans in prison more than tripled. About half of prison inmates are African Americans; about 95 percent are males (see Table 8.3). As noted earlier in this chapter, because social class funnels some people into the criminal justice system and others away from it, official statistics on social class and crime are inherently biased.

Among the many problems with imprisonment is that prisons fail to teach their clients to stay away from crime. Within just six years of their release from prison 69 percent are rearrested, most within just three years (Zawitz 1988). Some researchers have found that the **recidivism rate** (the proportion of persons who are rearrested) in the United States runs as high as 85 to 90 percent (Blumstein and Cohen 1987). Those given probation—released into the community under the court's supervision— do no better, for within 3 years 62 percent are arrested for a felony or have a disciplinary hearing for violating their parole (Langan and Cunniff 1992).

Perhaps an underlying reason for this high recidivism rate is that Americans do not agree on *why* people should be put in prison. There appears to be widespread agreement that offenders should be imprisoned, but not on the reasons for doing so. Let's examine the four primary reasons for imprisoning people.

TABLE 8.2 Growth in the American Prison Population

Number of Federal and State Prisoners	
1970	196,000
1975	241,000
1980	316,000
1985	481,000
1989	675,000

Note: To better understand the significance of this phenomenal growth, it is useful to compare it with the change in the general population during this period. Between 1970 and 1989, the population of the United States grew 20.6 percent, while the prison population grew more than eleven times as fast, increasing by 240 percent. If the number of prisoners had increased at the same rate as the general population, there would be 236,378 people in prison, only 35 percent of the actual numbers.

Source: Statistical Abstract of the United States 1991: Table 334.

TABLE 8.3 Characteristics of American Prisoners

Characteristic	Percent
Age	
Under 18	0.5
18–24	26.7
25–34	45.7
35–44	19.4
45–54	5.2
55–64	1.6
65 and over	0.6
Race	
White	49.7
African American	46.9
Other Races	3.4
Sex	
Male	95.6
Female	4.4

Note: The category "White" includes persons of Hispanic descent.

Source: Statistical Abstract of the United States 1991: Table 335.

Retribution. The purpose of **retribution** is to right a wrong by making offenders suffer or pay back what they have stolen. The offense is thought to have upset a moral balance; the punishment is an attempt to restore that balance (Cohen 1940). Attempts to make the punishment "fit the crime," such as sentencing someone who has stolen from a widow to work a dozen weekends in a geriatric center for the poor, are rooted in the idea of retribution.

> **retribution:** the punishment of offenders in order to restore the moral balance upset by the offense

Deterrence. The purpose of **deterrence** is to create fear so that others won't break the law. The belief underlying deterrence is that if people know that they will be punished, they will refrain from committing the crime. Sociologist Ernest van den Haag

> **deterrence:** creating fear so people will refrain from breaking the law

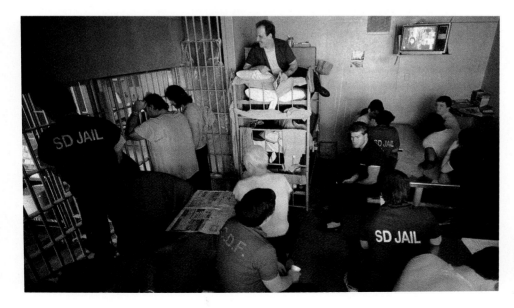

Overcrowding and the possibility of violence among inmates are just two of the problems created by the rising number of people imprisoned each year.

(1975), a chief proponent of deterrence, believes, like many Americans, that the criminal justice system is too soft. He advocates that juveniles who commit adult crimes be tried as adults, that parole boards be abolished, and that prisoners be forced to work.

Does deterrence work? Evidence is mixed, but those who claim that it does not like to recall an example from the 19th century. When English law meted out the death penalty for pickpockets, other pickpockets looked forward to the hangings—for people whose attention was riveted on the gallows made easy victims (Hibbert 1963). At this point, no firm evidence resolves the issue.

Rehabilitation.   **Rehabilitation** switches the focus from punishing offenders to re-socializing them so that they can become conforming citizens. One example of rehabilitation is teaching prisoners skills they can use to support themselves in respectable occupations after their release. Other examples include providing college courses in prison, encounter groups for prisoners, and **halfway houses**—community support facilities where ex-prisoners supervise many aspects of their own lives, such as household tasks, and still report to authorities.

Incapacitation.   **Incapacitation** means removing offenders from circulation. "Nothing works," some say, "but we can at least keep them off the streets." Criminologist James Q. Wilson (1975, 1992) supports incapacitation, calling it the only policy that works. He proposes what he calls "added incapacitation," increasing an offender's sentence each time he or she is convicted of a crime.

In the United States, the public is fearful of crime and despairing of solutions. Increasing dependence on prisons (see Table 8.2) may indicate that Americans are throwing up their hands as far as criminals are concerned and just trying to "keep them off the streets." It may also indicate attempts at retribution and deterrence. It certainly does not indicate efforts toward rehabilitation, for American prisons are basically simply holding tanks, offering few, if any, programs of rehabilitation.

As stated, an underlying reason for the high recidivism rate in the United States may be that Americans cannot make up their minds about the basic purpose of imprisonment. Perhaps if agreement could be established on its purpose, recidivism could be reduced. If the goal is to be retribution, creative solutions could be developed to make the punishment fit the crime; if it is deterrence, swift punishments could be designed that would strike terror into the heart of potential offenders; if it is to be rehabilitation, creative and effective programs could provide viable alternatives to a life of crime; and if it is incapacitation, more severe sentencing could be imposed. As it now is, confusion about purposes reigns.

REACTIONS BY DEVIANTS

People not only react to the deviant behaviors of others; they also react to their own violations of norms. Their own reactions can set them on paths that help propel them into or divert them from deviance.

Primary, Secondary, and Tertiary Deviance

Sociologist Nanette Davis (1978), who interviewed young women to find out how they had become prostitutes, noted that they had experienced a gradual slide from sexual promiscuity to prostitution. Their first acts of selling sex were casual. A girl might have run away from home and "turned a few tricks" to survive—or she might have done so to purchase a prom dress. At this point, the girls were in a stage of deviance that sociologist Edwin Lemert (1972) calls **primary deviance**—fleeting acts that do not become part of the self-concept. The young women did not think of themselves as prostitutes. As one girl said, "I never thought about it one way or another."

CDQ 28: Why can't Americans make up their minds about the basic purpose of imprisonment?

Project 5

L. Obj. 9: Distinguish between primary, secondary, and tertiary deviance. Give examples of each.

rehabilitation: the resocialization of offenders so that they can become conforming citizens

halfway house: community support facilities where ex-prisoners supervise many aspects of their own lives, such as household tasks, but continue to report to authorities

incapacitation: the removal of offenders from "normal" society; taking them "off the streets"

primary deviance: Edwin Lemert's term for acts of deviance that have little effect on the self-concept

Girls who prostitute themselves for a longer time, however, have to come to terms with their activities. They incorporate a deviant identity into their self-concept and come to think of themselves as prostitutes. When this occurs, they have entered **secondary deviance.**

The movement from primary to secondary deviance may be gradual. Through *self-labeling,* bit by bit the deviance becomes part of the self-concept. Often, however, the reactions of others facilitate this transition. For example, if a young woman is arrested for prostitution, it is difficult for her to define her activities as "normal," as she might in primary deviance. A face-to-face confrontation with a formal system that publicly labels her a sexual deviant challenges self-definitions. (Self-jarring labels can also be informal, as indicated by such terms as "nut," "queer," "pervert," and "whore.") One of the effects of such powerful labels is that they tend to lock people out of conforming groups and bring them in contact with other deviants.

There is yet another stage, one that few deviants reach. In **tertiary deviance,** deviant behavior is normalized and *relabeled* nondeviant (Kitsuse 1980; Weitz 1984). Although none of the women in Davis's sample had reached this stage, other prostitutes have. They have formed an organization called COYOTE (Call Off Your Old Tired Ethics), which has chapters in several states. This group takes the position that prostitution is a useful activity, a reasonable occupational choice, and that legislation should allow prostitutes to operate without interference from the government (Jenness 1990).

Neutralizing Deviance

Most people resist deviant labels and prefer to be known as conforming members of society, not outsiders. Even many people who are heavily involved in activities condemned by society consider themselves conformists. When sociologists Gresham Sykes and David Matza (1988) studied a group of delinquents, they found that in spite of their vandalism, fighting, drinking, and attacks on people these boys successfully resisted the labels that people tried to pin on them. As Sykes and Matza probed further, they found that the boys used five **techniques of neutralization,** or rationalizations, in an attempt to deflect society's norms.

Denial of Responsibility.   The youths frequently said, "I'm not responsible for what happened because . . ." and then were quite creative about causes. The act may have been an "accident," or they may see themselves as "victims" of society, with no control over what happened—like billiard balls shot around the pool table of life.

Denial of Injury.   Another favorite explanation of the boys was, "What I did wasn't wrong because no one got hurt." They would define vandalism as "mischief," gang fighting as a "private quarrel," and stealing cars as "borrowing." They might acknowledge the illegality of something they did but claim that it was "just having a little fun."

Denial of a Victim.   Sometimes the boys thought of themselves as avengers. To vandalize a teacher's car is only to get revenge for an unfair grade; to steal is to even the score with "crooked" store owners; to attack someone is justified retaliation against someone who threatened them. In short, when the boys accepted responsibility and even admitted that someone did get hurt, they rationalized that the people "deserved what they got."

Condemnation of the Condemners.   Another technique the boys used was to deny the right of others to pass judgment on them. They might accuse people who point their fingers at them of being "a bunch of hypocrites": the police are "on the take," teachers have "pets," and parents cheat on their taxes. In short, they say, "Who are *they* to accuse *me* of something?"

L. Obj. 10: Summarize these reactions by deviants: neutralizing deviance and embracing deviance.

K.P.: Gresham Sykes and David Matza

secondary deviance: Edwin Lemert's term for acts of deviance incorporated into the self-concept, around which an individual orients his or her behavior

tertiary deviance: the "normalization" of acts considered deviant by mainstream society; relabeling the acts as nondeviant

techniques of neutralization: ways of thinking or rationalizing that help people deflect society's norms

Appeal to Higher Loyalties.   A final technique the boys used to justify antisocial activities was to consider loyalty to the gang more important than following the norms of society. They might say, "I had to help my friends. That's why I got in the fight." Not incidentally, the boy may also have shot two members of the rival group as well as a bystander!

The identification of these five techniques of neutralization has implications far beyond the case of these boys, for it is not only delinquents who try to neutralize the views of the broader society. Look again at these five techniques: (1) "I couldn't help myself"; (2) "Who really got hurt?"; (3) "Don't you think she deserved that, after what *she* did?"; (4) "Who are *you* to talk?"; and (5) "I had to help my friends—wouldn't you have done the same thing under those circumstances?" Don't such statements have a familiar ring? All of us attempt to neutralize the moral demands of society, for such rationalizations help us sleep at night.

Embracing Deviance

Although most people resist being labeled deviant, there are those who revel in a deviant identity. Some teenagers, for example, make certain by their clothing, choice of music, and hairstyle that no one misses their purposeful status as outside adult norms. Their status among fellow members of a subculture, within which they are inveterate conformists, is vastly more important than any status outside it.

One of the best examples of a group that embraces deviance is motorcycle gangs. Sociologist Mark Watson (1988) did participant observation with outlaw bikers. He rebuilt Harleys with them, hung around their bars and homes, and went on "runs" (trips) with them. He concluded that outlaw bikers see the world as "hostile, weak, and effeminate," while they pride themselves on looking "dirty, mean, and generally undesirable," and take great pleasure in provoking shocked reactions to their appearance. Holding the conventional world in contempt, they also pride themselves on get-

Members of motorcycle gangs such as the Hell's Angels actively embrace deviance.

ting into trouble, laughing at death, and treating women as lesser people whose primary value is to provide them with services—especially sexual ones. Outlaw bikers also look at themselves as losers, a factor that becomes interwoven in their unusual embrace of deviance.

In Sum. Reactions to deviants vary from such mild sanctions as frowns and stares to such severe responses as imprisonment and death. Some sanctions are formal—court hearings, for example—although most are informal, as when friends refuse to talk to each other. One sanction is to label someone a deviant, which can have powerful consequences for the person's life, especially if the label closes off conforming activities and opens deviant ones. The degradation ceremony, in which someone is publicly labeled "not one of us," is a powerful sanction.

People also react to their own deviant behaviors. As long as they commit deviant acts but still think of themselves as conformists, they are in primary deviance. When they incorporate deviance into the self-concept, they are in secondary deviance. And when they "normalize" acts considered deviant by their society, relabeling them nondeviant, they are in tertiary deviance. To try to neutralize negative reactions to their deviant behaviors, people use a variety of techniques, ranging from condemning the condemner to claiming that no one was hurt. Although most people resist the labels that others try to place on them, some people, like outlaw bikers, embrace deviance.

THE MEDICALIZATION OF DEVIANCE: MENTAL ILLNESS

Another way in which society deals with deviance is to "medicalize" it. Let us look at what that entails.

Neither Mental nor Illness?

To *medicalize* something is to make it a medical matter, to classify it as a form of illness that properly belongs in the care of physicians. For the past hundred years or so, especially since the time of Sigmund Freud (1856–1939), the Viennese physician who founded psychoanalysis, there has been a tendency toward the **medicalization of deviance.** In this view, deviance, including crime, is a sign of mental sickness. Rape, murder, stealing, cheating, and so on are external symptoms of internal disorders, consequences of a confused or tortured mind.

Thomas Szasz (1970, 1986, 1989, 1990), a renegade in his profession of psychiatry, argued that *mental illnesses are neither mental nor illnesses. They are simply problem behaviors.* Some forms of so-called "mental" illnesses have organic causes; that is, they are physical illnesses that result in unusual perceptions and behavior. Some depression, for example, is caused by a chemical imbalance in the brain, which can be treated by drugs. The depression, however, may show itself as crying, long-term sadness, and the inability to become interested in anything. When a person becomes deviant in ways that disturb others, and these others cannot find a satisfying explanation for why the person is "like that," they conclude that a "sickness in the head" causes the inappropriate, unacceptable behavior.

All of us have troubles. Some of us face a constant barrage of problems as we go through life. Most of us continue the struggle, encouraged by relatives and friends, motivated by job, family responsibilities, and life goals. Even when the odds seem hopeless, we carry on, not perfectly, but as best we can.

Some people, however, fail to cope. Overwhelmed by the challenges of daily life, they become depressed, uncooperative, or hostile. Some strike out at others, while some, in Merton's terms, become retreatists and withdraw into their apartments or homes and won't come out. These are *behaviors, not mental illnesses,* said Szasz. They may be inappropriate coping devices, but they are coping devices, nevertheless, not

Essay #6

L. Obj. 11: Explain what is meant by the medicalization of deviance. Give the major arguments that could be presented "for" and "against" the medicalization of deviance.

K.P.: Thomas Szasz

CDQ 29: Is there such a thing as "mental illness?" If we embraced Szasz's idea, what kinds of changes would have to be made in society?

medicalization of deviance: the view of deviance as a medical matter, a symptom of some underlying illness that needs to be treated by physicians

mental illnesses. Thus, Szasz concluded, "mental illness" is a myth foisted on a naive public by a medical profession that uses pseudoscientific jargon to expand its area of control and force nonconforming people to accept society's definitions of "normal."

Szasz's extreme claim forces us to look anew at the forms of deviance called mental illness. He directed the analysis of behavior that people find bizarre away from causes hidden deep in the unconscious, placing the focus instead on how people learn behavior that others find inappropriate. To ask, "What is the origin of inappropriate or bizarre behavior?" then becomes similar to asking, "Why do women steal?" "Why do men rape?" "Why do teenagers cuss their parents and stalk out slamming doors?" The answers depend on people's particular experiences in social life. In short, some sociologists find Szasz's renegade analysis refreshing because it indicates that mental illness does not underlie bizarre behaviors—or deviance in general.

The Homeless Mentally Ill

Speaker Sug. #5: A mental health specialist to describe some of the problems brought on by deinstitutionalization.

Regardless of whether or not Szasz is right, we do incarcerate people whose behaviors we deem bizarre in mental hospitals. Psychiatrists working in mental hospitals have noticed that most patients adjust fairly well to hospital routines, and that the longer patients are cut off from the outside community, the more difficult it is for them to readjust to it later. During the 1960s, the psychiatric profession, working with state budget planners who wanted to save money, came up with the idea of **deinstitutionalization.** Mental patients would be released into the community, where their needs would be met by a network of outpatient services. Ongoing counseling and medicine would then enable these former patients to make the adjustment to living in the community again.

CDQ 30: Can you give examples of problems which may have been brought on by deinstitutionalization?

With the approval of politicians, the doctors began to open the doors of the nation's mental hospitals. The trouble was, the network of outpatient services was not set up. Patients were simply released into the streets. In perhaps the most notorious case, patients from Houston hospitals were placed in a van and dumped in front of the Greyhound bus station—located on skid row.

Consider how you would survive if you were abruptly dumped onto skid row without warning and without money. You and I would doubtless have a hard time making it, but not nearly as hard a time as those whose coping skills are already extremely fragile.

The bizarre thinking of many of the homeless is often attributed to their being former mental patients. Consider Jamie, who sits on the low wall surrounding the landscaped open-air eating area of an exclusive restaurant.

> Jamie appeared unaware of the stares elicited by her many layers of mismatched clothing, her dirty face, and the ever-present shopping cart overflowing with her meager possessions.
>
> Every once in a while Jamie would pause, concentrate, and point to the street, slowly moving her finger horizontally. I asked her what she was doing.
>
> "I'm directing traffic," she replied. "I control where the cars go. Look, that one turned right there," she said, now withdrawing her finger.
>
> "Really?" I said.
>
> After a while she confided that her cart talked to her.
>
> "Really?" I said again.
>
> "Yes," she replied. "You can hear it, too." At that, she pushed the shopping cart a bit.
>
> "Did you hear that?" she asked.
>
> When I shook my head, she demonstrated again. Then it hit me. She was referring to the squeaking wheels!
>
> I nodded.

When I left Jamie, she was pointing to the sky, for, as she told me, she also controlled the flight of airplanes. To most of us, Jamie's behavior and thinking are bizarre. They simply do not match any reality we know.

deinstitutionalization: the release of mental patients from institutions into the community pending treatment by a network of outpatient services

In Jamie's case, there may be an underlying organic cause to her behavior, such as a chemical imbalance. Other homeless people, however, may have no psychiatric history, yet exhibit strange behaviors, for *just being on the streets can cause mental illness*—or whatever we want to label socially inappropriate behaviors that we find difficult to classify.

Place yourself in the situation of the homeless. Suppose that you had no money, no place to sleep, no bathroom, did not know *if* you were going to eat, much less where, had no friends or anyone you could trust, and lived in constant fear of rape and violence. Wouldn't that be enough to drive you "over the edge"? Maybe, maybe not. But it is certainly enough for some people.

All of these conditions bring severe consequences, but consider just the problems involved in not having a place to bathe. (Shelters are often so dangerous that the homeless prefer to take their chances sleeping in public settings.) You will try at first to wash in the toilets of gas stations, bars, the bus station, or a shopping center. But you are dirty, and people stare when you enter, and they call the management when they see you wash your feet in the sink. You are thrown out, and told in no uncertain terms to never come back. So you get dirtier and dirtier. Eventually you come to think of being dirty as a fact of life. Soon, maybe, you don't even care. No longer do the stares bother you—at least not as much.

No one will talk to you, and you withdraw more and more into yourself. You begin to build a fantasy life. You talk openly to yourself. People stare, but so what? They stare anyway. Besides, they are no longer important to you. Perhaps, like a small child, you begin to imagine that you can control vehicles by pointing at them. Eventually you become convinced of it.

The point is that *homelessness and mental illness are reciprocal:* Just as "mental illness" can cause homelessness, so the trials of being homeless, of living on cold, hostile streets, can lead to unusual and unacceptable thinking and behaviors.

THE NEED FOR A MORE HUMANE APPROACH

As Durkheim (1893, 1958:68) pointed out, deviance is inevitable—even in a group of saints.

CDQ 31: What do you think would be a more humane approach to dealing with deviance in the United States?

DOWN-TO-EARTH SOCIOLOGY

Taking Back Children from the Night

Lois Lee is a sociologist who isn't afraid to take a stand—or to apply her sociological training to social problems. Lee did her master's thesis on the pimp-prostitute relationship, her doctoral dissertation on the social world of the prostitute. After receiving her Ph.D. from United States International University in 1981, Lee began to work with adult prostitutes. They told her, "You know, it's too late for you to help us, Lois. You've got to do something about these kids. We made a choice to be out here . . . a conscious decision. But these kids don't stand a chance."

Lee began by taking those teenagers who were prostituting themselves, into her home, where she lives with her husband and baby son. In three years, she brought back 250. Lee then founded "Children of the Night," which reaches the kids by means of "a twenty-four-hour hotline, a street outreach program, a walk-in crisis center, crisis intervention for medical or life-threatening situations, family counseling, job placement, and foster home or group placement." By providing alternatives to prostitution and petty crime, Lee estimates that Children of the Night has helped over five thousand young runaways and prostitutes get off the streets.

Lee's work has brought her national recognition and a presidential award. She credits her success to sociology, especially to the sensitivities to the relationships between groups that her discipline has given her. She says that her sociological training helped her "to understand and move safely through intersecting deviant worlds, to relate positively to police and caretaking agencies while retaining a critical perspective, to know which game to play in which situation."

As Lee remarked during a CBS interview, "I know what the street rules are, I know what the pimp game is, I know what the con games are, and it's up to me to play that game correctly. . . . It's all sociology. That's why when people call me a social worker I always correct them."

Source: Based on Buff 1987.

> Imagine a society of saints, a perfect cloister of exemplary individuals. Crimes, properly so called, will there be unknown; but faults which appear [invisible] to the layman will create there the same scandal that the ordinary offense does in ordinary [society].

With deviance inevitable, one measure of a society is how it treats its deviants. Deinstitutionalization certainly says little good about American society. Nor do its prisons. Filled with the poor, they are warehouses of the unwanted, reflecting patterns of broad discrimination in the larger society. White-collar criminals continue to get by with a slap on the wrist while street criminals are severely punished. Some deviants, failing to meet current standards of admission to either prison or mental hospital, take refuge in shelters and cardboard boxes in city streets. Although no one has *the* answers, it does not take much reflection to see that there are more humane approaches than these.

With deviance inevitable, the larger issues are how to protect people from deviant behaviors that are harmful to themselves or others, to tolerate those that are not, and to develop systems of fairer treatment for deviants. In the absence of the fundamental changes that would bring about a truly equitable social system, some sociologists have begun to confront street deviance head on. Lois Lee, for example, who has found sociology a useful tool for these endeavors, provides a striking example of applied sociology in her work with deviants, described in the Down-to-Earth Sociology box on page 215. In the end, however, such efforts are, unfortunately, Band-Aid work, for what is needed is a more humane social system, one that would prevent the social inequalities that are the focus of the next five chapters.

SUMMARY

1. Deviance is a broad concept, for it refers to the breaking of any norm, whether wearing inappropriate clothing or committing rape and murder. Deviance is relative; what people consider deviant varies from one culture to another and from group to group within the same society. Consequently, symbolic interactionists stress that acts are not inherently deviant, but are deviant only when they provoke negative reactions.

2. Where do the definitions of conforming or deviant behavior come from? Functionalists view them as the outcome of a balancing of the interests of the various groups that make up a society. Conflict theorists take the position that the group in power imposes its definitions on the other groups. Because norms allow society to exist by bringing predictability to human behavior, deviance is often seen as threatening.

3. Why do people deviate? Biologists and psychologists look for reasons within people, such as genetic predispositions or personality disorders; sociologists look for explanations in social relations. To explain crime, symbolic interactionists use differential association and control theory. Functionalists point out that deviance, including crime, is functional for society and an inherent part of any social group. They also use strain theory and illegitimate opportunity structures to argue that widespread socialization into norms of material success is responsible for much of the property crime committed by the poor. Conflict theorists

stress that society is divided into a capitalist class that hires labor and a working class that sells its labor. The marginal working class receives low pay, is desperate, and commits highly visible property crimes. The ruling class directs the criminal justice system, using it to punish the crimes of the poor while it diverts its own criminal activities away from the criminal justice system

4. Deviance results in negative sanctions. Labeling theory, developed by symbolic interactionists, stresses that the labels people are given affect their own and others' perceptions of them, channeling their behavior either into deviance or conformity. The effects of social class in determining which labels people are given is illustrated by the case study of the Saints and the Roughnecks. Both the conclusions of symbolic interactionists—that the police operate with a large measure of discretion—and those of conflict theorists—that the legal system is controlled by the capitalist class—cast doubt on the accuracy of official crime statistics. Some groups use degradation ceremonies to impress on their members that certain violations will not be tolerated. These ceremonies involve accusations, judgment, and stripping the individual of group membership. Imprisonment is motivated by retribution, deterrence, rehabilitation, and incapacitation.

5. Primary, secondary, and tertiary deviance refer to stages in people's reactions to their own disapproved behaviors. Many people succeed in neutralizing the norms of society and are able to commit deviant acts while thinking of themselves as conformists. Such people use five techniques of neutralization. Although most people resist labels of deviance, some embrace deviance.

6. The medical profession has attempted to medicalize many forms of deviance, claiming that they represent mental illnesses. Szasz disagreed, claiming that mental illness does not exist. The plight of mentally ill homeless people illustrates how problems in living can lead to bizarre behavior and thinking. With deviance inevitable, the larger issues are how to protect people from deviances that are harmful to themselves and others, to tolerate those that are not, and to develop systems of fairer treatment for deviants.

SUGGESTED READINGS

DiUlio, John J., Jr. *Governing Prisons: A Comparative Study of Correctional Management*. New York: The Free Press, 1990. In a proposal called "constitutional management," the author argues that America's prisons can be made safe and humane through a new governing system that "employs prison managers who are strong enough to control the inmates yet obliged to control themselves."

Jackson, Bruce. *Outside the Law: A Thief's Primer*. New Brunswick, N.J.: Transaction, 1972. An insider's perspective explains what it is like making a living by cracking safes and passing bad checks.

Kephart, William M., and William W. Zellner. *Extraordinary Groups: An Examination of Unconventional Life-Styles*. 4th ed. New York: St. Martin's Press, 1991. The authors present an overview of the Old Order Amish, Oneida Community, Gypsies, Shakers, Hasidim, Father Divine Movement, Mormons, and Jehovah's Witnesses.

Marx, Gary T. *Undercover: Police Surveillance in America*. Berkeley, Calif.: University of California Press, 1988. This insider's perspective on police operations has an especially insightful section on why some police who do undercover work tend to "become" what they are investigating.

Matza, David. *Delinquency and Drift*. New Brunswick, N.J.: Transaction, 1990. This analysis of how the delinquent subculture reflects the standards of conventional society explains how the drift toward delinquency is sometimes unwittingly aided by the enforcers of the social order.

Prus, Robert, and Styllianoss Irini. *Hookers, Rounders, and Desk Clerks*. Salem, Wis.: Sheffield, 1988. An account of the underground life of a hotel describes how the social worlds of prostitutes, pimps, thieves, strippers, and hotel personnel intersect.

Rafter, Nicole Hahn. *Partial Justice: Women, Prisons, and Social Control*. 2nd ed. New Brunswick, N.J.: Transaction, 1990. The author documents the development of separate prisons for women, the goal of reform in women's prisons, and current concerns to produce more than "partial justice."

Schur, Edwin M. *Labeling Women Deviant: Gender, Stigma, and Social Control*. New York: Random House, 1984. Using the perspective of labeling theory, the author examines the process by which females are devalued and "female deviance" produced.

Szasz, Thomas S. *The Myth of Mental Illness*. Rev. ed. New York: Harper & Row, 1986. Szasz takes the controversial position that mental illness is a myth, a mere label used by the medical establishment to broaden its control.

Weisburd, David, Stanton Wheeler, and Elin Waring. *Crimes of the Middle Classes: White-Collar Offenders in the Federal Courts*. New Haven, Conn.: Yale University Press, 1991. In examining the diversity of crime that comes under the term "white collar," the author explores the relationship of harm and blame to court sentences.

Diego Rivera, The Flower Carrier,
1935

Social Stratification in Global Perspective

WHAT IS SOCIAL STRATIFICATION?

SYSTEMS OF SOCIAL STRATIFICATION

Slavery ■ Caste: India and South Africa ■ Class ■ *Perspectives:* **Social Stratification among Polish Jews** ■ Clan and Class as Parallel Forms of Social Stratification

GENDER AND SOCIAL STRATIFICATION

WHAT DETERMINES SOCIAL CLASS?

Karl Marx: The Means of Production ■ Max Weber: Property, Prestige, and Power

WHY IS SOCIAL STRATIFICATION UNIVERSAL?

The Functionalist View of Davis and Moore: Motivating Qualified People ■ Tumin: A Critical Response ■ Mosca: A Forerunner of the Conflict View ■ The Conflict View: Class Conflict and Competition for Scarce Resources ■ Toward a Synthesis

COMPARATIVE SOCIAL STRATIFICATION

Social Stratification in Great Britain ■ Social Stratification in the Former Soviet Union

MAINTAINING NATIONAL STRATIFICATION

Why Not Total Exploitation?

GLOBAL STRATIFICATION: THE THREE WORLDS

The First World ■ The Second World ■ The Third World ■ Imperfections in the Model

HOW THE WORLD'S NATIONS BECAME STRATIFIED

Imperialism and Colonialism ■ World System Theory ■ Dependency Theory ■ Culture of Poverty ■ Evaluating the Theories

MAINTAINING GLOBAL STRATIFICATION

Neocolonialism ■ Multinational Corporations ■ *Perspectives:* **The Patriotic Prostitute**

SUMMARY

SUGGESTED READINGS

John F. Kennedy was born in Brookline, Massachusetts, on May 29, 1917. The son of Joseph Patrick Kennedy and Rose Fitzgerald Kennedy, he was one of ten children. His paternal grandfather, Patrick J. Kennedy, who had immigrated from Ireland in 1847, had made a fortune in the saloon business and had served in both houses of the Massachusetts State Legislature. His maternal grandfather, John F. ("Honey Fitz") Fitzgerald, had been mayor of Boston. Neither John (known as Jack) nor his three brothers and six sisters ever attended public schools. Jack went to Riverside Country Day School, an exclusive school for children of the wealthy in Brookline, Massachusetts. His high school years were spent at Choate School in Wallingford, Connecticut. He began college at Princeton University and graduated from Harvard University in 1940.

Joseph Patrick Kennedy, who contributed substantially to the presidential campaign of Franklin Delano Roosevelt, was appointed chairman of the Securities and Exchange

Commission in 1933 and American ambassador to Great Britain in 1937. He set up a trust fund so that each of his children would receive $100,000 at the age of twenty-one. He made plans for his eldest son, Joseph Patrick Kennedy, Jr., to become president of the United States. After Joe, Jr., was killed in World War II, his father decided that the next eldest son, Jack, could be groomed for the presidency instead. Joseph Kennedy first had him run for the Senate. After winning the presidential election in 1960, Jack appointed his younger brother Bobby attorney general of the United States. Jack's youngest brother, Edward (Teddy), then took Jack's Senate seat.

When Mary Petrovitch signed into the hospital, she paid with a "green card," the state voucher that guarantees the hospital a government-approved payment for each medical procedure. Her delivery was normal, and in three days she went home with her new daughter, Kim.

Kim attended Thomas Mann Elementary and Thomas Jefferson High. During her early years, Kim didn't even realize that she was poor, for everyone in the projects had about the same income, and all her neighbors bought groceries with food stamps. As time went on, however, Kim became more and more aware of differences between herself and others in society. During high school, where she attended classes with students from more privileged backgrounds, this distinction was always in her mind. She became determined to make her life different: She would go to college and make something of herself.

During the end of her junior year, Kim fell in love. She never made it back to high school. Instead, the earnings from her two part-time jobs went to rent and payments for their "almost new" car. On the day that she would have graduated, Kim checked into the hospital to have her first baby. She paid with a green card.

WHAT IS SOCIAL STRATIFICATION?

L. Obj. 1: Define social stratification and briefly discuss the four major systems of social stratification.

CDQ 1: How does social class help to explain why you are in college and how many children you plan to have?

Project 1

The distance between Jack Kennedy and Kim Petrovitch illustrates the heart of social stratification, for to talk about social stratification is to refer to inequalities between people. Their inequalities are obvious: wealth versus poverty, private versus public schools, and power versus powerlessness. One was born to a life of privilege, the other to deprivation. In short, the son of a Kennedy and the daughter of a Petrovitch have far from equal chances in life—and that is what social stratification is all about.

It is important to emphasize at the outset that social stratification does not simply refer to individuals. It is a *way of ranking large groups of people into a hierarchy that shows their relative privileges.* **Social stratification** is a system in which people are divided into layers according to their relative power, property, and prestige.

Jack Kennedy, for example, was not only part of his family, but also part of a larger group of people who come from similarly privileged backgrounds. Their backgrounds are so similar, in fact, that members of this group share values, attitudes, and lifestyles. They even tend to think alike and to vote for the same candidates for political office. It is the same with Kim and her mother; the millions of people who come from backgrounds like hers also share similar life chances. They, too, tend to think alike. With their chances of success so much slimmer, most of their attitudes contrast sharply with those of the Kennedys. And when it comes to voting, neither Kim, her mother, nor others in their circumstances are likely even to show up at the polls (Gilbert and Kahl 1982, 1987). In other words, society is stratified into layers, and each layer has its own characteristics.

Just as it did for Kim Petrovitch and Jack Kennedy, the layer of society into which you were born has vitally affected your life. Membership in your layer, which sociologists call *social class,* even helps explain why you are in college and how many hildren

social stratification: the division into layers of nations or of people according to their relative power, property, and prestige

Social stratification exists in virtually all societies.

you plan to have. Social class will continue to exert its powerful hold on you throughout your life, as you will see from this and the following chapter.

How do the various layers that make up society develop?

SYSTEMS OF SOCIAL STRATIFICATION

Every society stratifies its members in some form. Some, like the agricultural societies studied in Chapter 6, draw firm lines that separate group from group, while others, like hunting and gathering societies, show much greater equality. Regardless of its forms, however, the existence of social stratification is universal. There are four major systems of social stratification: slavery, caste, class, and clan.

Slavery

Types, Causes, and Conditions of Slavery.   **Slavery,** whose essential characteristic is *ownership of some people by others,* has been common throughout world history. The Greeks and Romans had slaves, as did the ancient Africans. Slavery was least common among nomadic peoples, especially hunters and gatherers, and most common among agricultural peoples (Landtman 1968).

Contrary to popular assumption, slavery was not usually based on racism, but on one of three other factors. The first was debt. In some cultures, an individual who could not pay a debt could be enslaved by the creditor. The second was a violation of the law. Instead of being killed, a murderer or thief might be enslaved by the family of the victim as compensation for the loss he or she had caused. The third was war and conquest. When one group of people conquered another, it was often convenient to enslave at least some of the vanquished (Starna and Watkins 1991). Historian Gerda Lerner (1986) notes that through this practice the first slaves were women. When premodern men raided a village or camp, they killed the men, raped the women, and then brought the women back as slaves. The women were valued for sexual purposes, for reproduction, and for extra labor.

One of the most notable examples of slavery occurred roughly twenty-five hundred years ago in Greece, when it was not yet a nation but a collection of city-states. A city that became powerful and conquered another city would enslave some of the vanquished. Both slaves and slaveholders were Greek. Similarly, when Rome became the supreme power of the Mediterranean area about two thousand years ago, following the custom of the time the Romans enslaved some of the Greeks they had conquered.

CDQ 2: Why do you think slavery has been common throughout world history? Who benefits from a system of slavery?

CDQ 3: Why were women some of the first slaves?

slavery: a form of social stratification in which some people own other people

Some of these slaves, more educated than their conquerors, served as tutors in Roman homes. Slavery, then, was a sign of defeat in battle, of a criminal act, or of debt, not the sign of some supposedly inherently inferior status.

The world has witnessed many different types of slavery. *In some cases, slavery was temporary.* After serving a set number of years, a slave might be free to return to his or her home country. Slaves of the Israelites were set free in the year of jubilee, which occurred every fifty years. Roman slaves ordinarily had the right to buy themselves out of slavery. They knew what their purchase price was, and some were able to meet this price by striking a bargain with their owner and selling their services to others. Such was the case with some of the educated Greek slaves. In most instances, however, slavery was lifelong. Some criminals, for example, became slaves when they were given life sentences as oarsmen on Roman war ships. There they served until death, which under this exhausting service often did not take long.

Slavery was not necessarily inheritable. In most places, the children of slaves were automatically slaves themselves. But in some instances, the child of a slave who served a rich family might even be adopted by that family, becoming an heir who bore the family name along with the other sons or daughters of the household. In ancient Mexico, the children of a slave were always free (Landtman 1968:271).

Slaves were not necessarily powerless and poor. In almost all instances, slaves owned no property and had no power. Among some slaveholding groups, however, slaves could accumulate property and even rise to high positions in the community. Occasionally, a slave might even become wealthy, loan money to the master, and end up owning slaves himself or herself (Landtman 1968). Such instances, however, were not typical.

Slavery in the New World.   **Indentured service** represents a fuzzy line between a contract and slavery (Main 1965; Elkins 1968). Many persons who desired to start a new life in the American colonies were unable to pay their passage. Ship captains would carry them on credit, depending on someone to "buy their paper" when they arrived. This arrangement provided passage for the penniless, payment for the ship's captain, and servants for wealthier colonists for a set number of years. During that specified period, the individuals had to serve their master—and could be captured and forcibly returned if they ran away. At the end of the period of indenture, the individuals became full citizens, able to live where they chose and free to sell their labor.

When the colonists found that there were not enough indentured servants to meet their growing need for labor, they tried to enslave Indians. This attempt failed miserably. Among other reasons, when Indians escaped they knew how to survive in the wilderness and were able to make their way back to their tribe. The colonists then turned to Africans, who were being brought to North and South America by the British, Dutch, English, Portuguese, and Spanish.

Given this context, some analysts conclude that racism in America developed out of slavery. Finding it profitable to make people slaves for life, American slave owners developed an **ideology,** a system of beliefs that justifies current (or potential) social arrangements to support what they wanted. Essential to an ideology that would justify lifelong slavery was the view that the slaves they imported from Africa were inferior to themselves. Some concluded that the slaves were not even fully human. Others said that they were locked into a childlike, helpless state, which meant that they needed to be taken care of by superior people—white colonists, of course. In either case, the colonists developed elaborate justifications for slavery on the presumed superiority of one race and inferiority of another.

Later on, to make slavery even more profitable, slave states passed laws that made slavery *inheritable;* that is, the babies born to slaves became the property of the slave owners (Stampp 1956). These children could be sold, bartered, or traded. To strengthen their control, slave states passed laws making it illegal for slaves to marry, to be away from the master's premises without carrying a pass, to hold meetings, or to learn to read (Lerner 1972).

CDQ 4: Why do you think people would "sell" themselves into indentured service? Can you think of any circumstances in which you would be willing to do the same?

L. Obj. 2: Describe the characteristics of slavery, and note the uses of slavery in the New World.

CDQ 5: What type of ideology is necessary to justify the existence of slavery?

indentured service: a contractual system in which someone sells his or her body (services) for a specified period of time in an arrangement very close to slavery, except that it is voluntarily entered into

ideology: beliefs about human life or culture that justify social arrangements

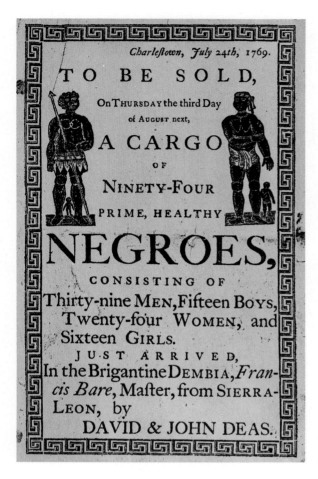

Slavery is an age-old system of social stratification.

Patterns of legal discrimination did not end after the Civil War. For example, until 1954 the states operated two separate school systems. Even until the 1950s, to keep the races from "mixing," it was illegal in Mississippi for a white and an African American to sit together on the same seat of a car! The reason there was no outright ban on both races being in the same car was to allow for African-American chauffeurs.

Common Characteristics of Slavery. The practice of slavery, then, differed markedly from one region or time to another. However, whether slavery was the outcome of debt, punishment, conquests, or racism; whether it was permanent or temporary; whether it was inheritable or not, a slave was the property of another person, and a legal system dictated by slave owners enforced the slave's status. Slavery was a major divide between people, marking those who were free (and thus entitled to certain privileges by the law) and those who were slaves (and not so entitled).

Caste: India and South Africa

The second system of social stratification is caste. In a **caste system** of social stratification, status is determined by birth and is lifelong. In sociological terms the basis of a caste system is ascribed status, which is discussed in Chapter 4. Achieved status cannot change an individual's place in this system. People born into a low-status group will always have low status, no matter how much they personally may accomplish in life.

L. Obj. 3: Distinguish between caste and class systems. Give examples of each.

Speaker Sug. #1: A researcher studying global stratification or caste systems.

caste system: a form of social stratification in which individual status is determined by birth and is lifelong

In a caste system of stratification, status is determined at birth and is lifelong. Members of lower castes suffer deprivation in virtually all aspects of life, including education.

Societies with this form of stratification try to make certain that the boundaries between castes remain firm. They practice **endogamy,** marriage within their own group, and prohibit intermarriage. To prevent contact between castes, they even develop elaborate rules about *ritual pollution,* teaching that contact with inferior castes contaminates the superior caste.

CDQ 6: What do you think has contributed to the caste system lasting for almost three thousand years in India?

TR#9M: India's Caste System

CDQ 7: Why do the caste systems in India and South Africa appear to be breaking down?

India.   India provides the best example of a caste system of social stratification. Based not on race but on religion, it has existed for almost three thousand years. India's four main castes, or *varnas,* are depicted in Table 9.1. The four main castes are subdivided into thousands of specialized subcastes, or *jati,* with each *jati* performing a specific occupation. For example, knife sharpening is done only by members of a particular subcaste.

The lowest caste, the Hartijans, are actually so low that they are beneath the caste system altogether. The Hartijans, along with some of the Shudras, make up India's "untouchables." If someone of a higher caste is touched by one of them, that person becomes unclean. In some cases, a person is contaminated even by the shadow of an untouchable. Early morning and late afternoons are therefore especially risky, for the long shadows of these periods pose a danger to everyone higher up the caste system. Consequently, Hartijans are not even allowed in some villages during these times. For those contaminated, their religion specifies **ablution,** or washing rituals, to restore purity (Lannoy 1975).

endogamy: marriage within one's own group

ablution: a washing ritual designed to restore ritual purity

TABLE 9.1   India's Caste System

Caste	Occupation
Brahmins	priests or scholars
Kshatriyas	nobles and warriors
Vaisyas	merchants and skilled artisans
Shudras	common laborers
Hartijans	the outcastes; degrading labor

Although India's caste system was officially abolished in 1949, the force of centuries-old practices cannot be so easily eliminated, and the caste system remains part of everyday life in India.

South Africa.   Up to the present, South Africa provided another example of social stratification based on caste. Europeans of Dutch descent, a numerical minority called Afrikaners, controlled the government, the police, and the military to enforce their ideas of proper social stratification in a system they called **apartheid** (ah-PAR-tate), the separation of the races. By law there were four different racial castes: Europeans (whites), Africans (blacks), Coloureds (mixed races), and Asians. On the basis of caste, the law specified where people could live, work, and go to school.

After decades of trade sanctions, sports boycotts, and worldwide negative publicity, however, Afrikaners are reluctantly dismantling their caste system. They have already eliminated some of its most objectionable features (such as the production of passes on demand by black Africans), integrated most public facilities, and begun to allow some black representation in politics. Because South African apartheid originated much more recently than India's caste system, is less buttressed by religion, and is accepted by only a minority of the people, it should prove easier to remove.

India's caste system, too, is finally breaking down. Probably because India's traditions are based on religion and not on race, the world community has tolerated it. In contrast to apartheid, the breakdown of caste in India is due to industrialization and urbanization, for it is difficult to maintain caste divisions in crowded and anonymous cities (Robertson 1976).

An American Racial Caste System.   Before leaving the subject of caste, note that when slavery in the United States ended, it was replaced by a *racial caste system,* in which birth marked a person for life (Berger 1991). Race determined a person's status in all social relationships with members of the other racial group. In this system, *all* whites were considered higher than *all* African Americans. Even in the earlier parts of this century, long after slavery was ended, this attitude persisted. When whites met African Americans on a southern sidewalk, the latter had to move aside. And as in India, the upper caste feared pollution from the lower, insisting on separate hotels, restaurants, and even toilets and drinking fountains in public facilities.

Class

As we have seen, stratification systems based on slavery and caste are rigid. The lines marking the divisions between people are so firm that, theoretically at least, there is no movement from one group to another. As you are born, so you remain for the rest of your life.

In constrast, a **class system** is much more open, for it is based primarily on money or material possessions. It, too, begins at birth, when an individual is ascribed the status of his or her parents, but, unlike caste and slavery, social class may change due to what the individual achieves (or fails to achieve) in life. In addition, there are no laws specifying occupations on the basis of birth or prohibiting marriage between the classes.

A major characteristic of a class system, then, is its relatively fluid boundaries. A class system allows **social mobility,** that is, movement up or down the class ladder. The potential for improving one's social circumstances, or class, is one of the major forces that drives people to go far in school and to work hard. As the Perspectives box on page 226 illustrates, a class system certainly does not guarantee ease of movement, nor equality of opportunity, for the structural features of society limit movement both up and down the class ladder. As in the case of Kim Petrovitch, the family background that an individual inherits at birth may determine disprivileges that give the child little chance of climbing very far—or, as in the case of Jack Kennedy, it may provide privileges that make it almost impossible to fall down the class ladder.

CDQ 8: Would you rather be born into a caste or class system? Why?

CDQ 9: Do you believe that social mobility still exists in the United States? Why or why not?

apartheid: the separation of races as was practiced in South Africa

class system: a form of social stratification based primarily on the possession of money or material possessions

social mobility: movement up or down the social class ladder

PERSPECTIVES

Cultural Diversity Around the World

Social Stratification among Polish Jews

The stratification of the Jews in Stoczek, Poland, between World Wars I and II provides a rich contrast with stratification in the United States. The four sources of social status for the Jews were occupation, wealth, learning, and lineage. In general, people were located at the same point on all four scales.

The first source of status, occupation, was divided into men of labor (about 60 percent) and businessmen (about 39 percent). About 1 percent were learners, who did not work. Learners devoted themselves full time to studying the *Torah,* the Jewish law as written in the first five books of the Old Testament. Learners were supported by their wives or by their parents-in-law. High respect was given to a man who devoted his life to learning.

Wealth, the second base of prestige, had three acceptable uses. First, a person should eat well, dress well, and enjoy other pleasures; but anyone who spent money only on such things was considered a "pig." To be rich *and* command respect also required the use of money for doing good deeds (*mitzvot*) for the needy. To give money to those who needed it, rather than to those who could repay, was a sign of having a true "Jewish heart." Doing a good deed for an orphan, for example, deserved greater credit than doing a similar deed for a self-supporting person. In addition to gaining honor and respect, the doer of good deeds also stored up credit with God for the afterlife. The third use of money was to purchase status for one's children—to educate one's sons or to marry one's daughters into a better lineage.

The third source of status, learning, referred to studying the *Torah.* Unlike education, learning was not an activity completed at some point, but rather a lifelong endeavor. Learning was a goal in itself, not a means to obtaining material benefits. It was the equivalent of "refinement," and was to be pursued with love and joy. To sit up late at night studying, after a long day's work, brought prestige in the community. The advice and opinions of a learned man were highly valued.

The fourth source of status, lineage, was the first thing to be established when strangers met or when people talked about a third person. People were accorded high prestige if they were descendants of learned, wealthy, and charitable ancestors. By itself, however, the connection was insufficient; individuals had to live up to their lineage by being learned and charitable themselves. Those who did not were seen as having squandered their inheritance.

These four sources of social status translated into three social classes. At the top of the social pyramid were people with much learning, wealth, and a reputation for giving to the needy. Next came the middle class, consisting of shopkeepers and traders who had some means and some learning. At the bottom of the social scale were the plain Jews—workers and craftsmen who had little learning and little money.

In Stoczek, it was important for all the people to know their place and to act with proper respect toward those with higher status. To fail to do so was seen as insolence, and such persons were looked down upon by the entire community. Social status was so significant that there were no friendships between adults of different classes, and status even determined where a man would sit in the synagogue. Reserved for men of highest status were the seats nearest to the eastern wall—those closest to Jerusalem.

Although anyone was supposed to be able to move up the class ladder through attaining wealth or learning, class membership was, for the most part, hereditary. Women who guided their children to love learning or to do good deeds were given higher status, as were those who were very religious and did good deeds themselves. A woman whose father was a rabbi or scholar was also accorded higher status, as was a woman who encouraged her husband to *mitzvot* or supported him so he could devote all his time to learning. Women were not allowed to worship alongside the men in the synagogue, but were permitted only in the balcony or some other separate place.

The world depicted by this stratification system was erased by Hitler in his systematic—and largely successful—campaign to destroy European Jewry.

Source: Based on Heller 1953, 1991.

Clan and Class as Parallel Forms of Social Stratification

clan system: a form of social stratification in which individuals receive their social standing through belonging to an extended network of relatives

While class systems are characteristic of industrialized societies, in partially industrialized societies two systems may coexist as parallel forms of social stratification. While social classes develop in the cities, large portions of the population remain stratified along more traditional lines. The model in the rural areas is the **clan system,** in which the individual's status depends on lineage linking him or her to an extended network of relatives. The individual's welfare depends on this greatly extended family. If the clan is high in the stratification system, so is the individual.

As in the caste system, clan membership is determined by birth and is lifelong. Unlike the caste system, however, the clan system permits marriage to cross clan lines. Marriage is even sometimes used to forge alliances between clans, for marriage in traditional societies brings with it specified obligations between the in-laws. Interclan marriage thus establishes special relationships between clans.

Arab countries provide an example of parallel class and clan social stratification. Birth signals membership into a clan, and as in a family, the clan's resources—whether few or many—become the individual's. Allegiance to the clan is a lifelong obligation, and clan membership largely determines relations between people. Industrialization, however, is blurring the lines between clans. It is especially in the cities that the traditional lines are breaking down, but even here the clan continues to play a significant role, as we can see from the following example.

> The Sultan clan consists of about 150 individuals, who occupy a dozen neighboring houses in Kuwait City. To survive the Iraqi occupation of Kuwait in 1989–90, members of this clan pooled their resources for the common good. Those in the appliance business bribed officers with food processors, microwave ovens, and televisions; while those in the hotel business secreted away huge amounts of steak and shrimp from the hotel, which they shared with clan members. Together they plotted—and obtained— the release of one of their members who had been imprisoned and were able to smuggle him into Saudi Arabia (Horwitz 1991).

Project 2

L. Obj. 4: State the relationship between gender and social stratification.

Speaker Sug. #2: A gender specialist conducting research on Third World women.

GENDER AND SOCIAL STRATIFICATION

As already noted, every society is stratified, although the type of stratification may vary from one society to another, and even within the same society over time. On occasion, social researchers thought that they had discovered an exception to the universality of stratification. For example, sociologist Gunnar Landtman (1968) was impressed when he saw practically no differences among the Kiwi Papuans of New Guinea (1968:5–6).

> [E]very man is on a footing of equality with all the rest, and no one has any authority over his fellows. Every man does the same work and no one employs servants. . . . Custom also requires anyone to come and assist a fellow-villager for a day or two, if he is engaged in some particularly arduous work. An invitation to this effect is always accepted, although no payment is given. . . .The building of a house and other greater enterprises are always undertaken in common, assistance being given by those who will not benefit directly from the work when completed. . . .There are no rich and no poor people, because hardly any property exists such as would constitute difference in wealth.

Gender stratification in the division of labor has been found in all societies.

As Landtman probed more deeply, however, he found that beneath these surface similarities lay deep divisions. He discovered that some men had much more influence than others. Greater prestige was given to great warriors ("who have killed many people and captured many heads"), successful hunters and harpooners, renowned sorcerers, and men able to entertain more guests (which required more wives to do more gardening, fishing, and cooking). Similarly, some men were looked down on, especially idlers, widowers who had not remarried, and those with physical or mental disabilities.

As you may have noticed, Landtman refers only to men. Women were also part of the Kiwi stratification system, of course, but they were placed into a totally separate category, in which all of them were subservient to the men. This gender gulf was so great that Landtman (1968) observed this about the group that had at first appeared so equal.

It is an everyday episode of village life, when the families are returning from their garden work, to see the wife almost staggering under her burden of three or four baskets of garden produce, firewood, etc., on her back, and in many cases a little baby right on top, while her husband proudly walks in front, carrying only his bow, arrows, and stone-headed club, and possibly a firebrand, at which he lights his pipe.

Although in no society is gender the sole basis for stratifying people, gender discrimination cuts across all systems of social stratification (Huber 1990). In slavery, gender may be used to assign individuals their tasks. In a caste system, within each caste a woman's status is lower than a man's. Similarly with class and clan, gender invariably creates a significant distinction between people—and always in favor of the males. In short, no matter what system a society may use to divide people into different layers, gender is always an essential part of those distinctions within each layer. Gender is so significant in human relations that a separate chapter is devoted to this topic (Chapter 11). Race and age, other significant bases for social stratification, will be examined in Chapters 12 and 13.

WHAT DETERMINES SOCIAL CLASS?

A disagreement arose in the early days of sociology concerning the meaning of social class in industrialized nations. Let us compare how Marx and Weber saw the matter.

Karl Marx: The Means of Production

As discussed in Chapter 1, when Karl Marx (1818–1883) carried out his social analysis societies were in upheaval. The feudal system had broken up and masses of peasants had moved from their traditional lands and occupations to cities. With large numbers of displaced peasants competing for few jobs, only a pittance was offered for labor. Workers dressed in rags, went hungry, and slept under bridges and in hovels, while the factory owners built mansions, hired servants, and lived in the lap of luxury. Seeing this disparity between poverty and wealth, Marx concluded that social class depends on a single factor—the **means of production**—the tools, factories, land, and investment capital used to produce wealth (Marx 1844/1964; Marx and Engels 1848/1967).

Marx argued that the distinctions people often make between themselves—such as clothing, speech, education, or relative salary—are superficial matters that camouflage the only real significant dividing line: People (the **bourgeoisie**) either own the means of production or they (the **proletariat**) work for those who do. This is the only distinction that counts, for these two classes make up modern society. In short, according to Marx, it is the relationship to the means of production that determines social class.

Marx did recognize that other groups were part of industrial society: farmers and peasants; a **lumpenproletariat** (marginal people such as migrant workers, beggars, vagrants, and criminals); and a middle class (self-employed professionals). Marx did not consider these groups social classes, however, for they lacked **class consciousness**—a common identity based on their position in the means of production. They did not see themselves as exploited workers whose plight could be solved only by collective action. Consequently, Marx thought of these groups as insignificant in the coming workers' revolution that would overthrow capitalism.

Marx saw class consciousness as the essential basis of the unity of workers. As capital becomes more concentrated, he claimed, the two classes will become increasingly hostile (Anderson, 1974). The proletariat will perceive capitalism as the common source of their oppression and will unite and throw off the chains of their oppressors. Through revolution, workers will take control of the means of production and usher in a classless society, where no longer will the few grow rich at the expense of the

---

CDQ 10: Can you think of any society in which women are at the top of the system of social stratification? In what ways does gender discrimination cut across all systems of social stratification?

K.P.: Karl Marx

L. Obj. 5: Identify the basic assumptions of Karl Marx regarding what determines one's social class.

CDQ 11: Do you agree with Marx that social class depends on a single factor—the means of production? Why or why not?

means of production: the tools, factories, land, and investment capital used to produce wealth

bourgeoisie: Karl Marx's term for the people who own the means of production

proletariat: Karl Marx's term for the people who work for those who own the means of production

lumpenproletariat: Karl Marx's term for marginal people such as migrant workers, beggars, vagrants, and criminals

class consciousness: Karl Marx's term for awareness of a common identity based on one's position in the means of production

many. What holds back the workers' unity and their revolution, however, is *false consciousness,* the mistaken identification of workers with capitalists.

Until the workers usher in this classless society, the only distinction worth mentioning is whether a person is an owner or a worker. That decides everything else, for property determines people's lifestyles, shapes their ideas, and establishes their relationships with one another.

Max Weber: Property, Prestige, and Power

Max Weber (1864–1920) became an outspoken critic of Marx's view. Weber said that property is far from being the sole basis of a person's position in the stratification system. Economics is not the whole picture, he argued. On the contrary, three elements—property, prestige, and power (the three P's)—determine social class (Gerth and Mills 1958; Weber 1968). (Weber used the terms "class," "status," and "power," but many contemporary sociologists find "property," "prestige," and "power" to be clearer terms. If you wish, you can substitute "wealth" for "property.")

Property, said Weber, is certainly significant in determining a person's standing in society. On that he agreed with Marx. But, he argued, property is only one of three essential elements. Some powerful people, such as managers of corporations, for example, *control* the means of production although they do not *own* them. If managers can control property for their own benefit—awarding themselves huge bonuses and magnificent perks—it makes no practical difference that they do not own the property that they so generously use for their own benefit.

Prestige, the second element in Weber's analysis, is often derived from property, for people tend to look up to the wealthy. Prestige, however, is also based on other factors. An Olympic gold medalist or a daredevil who does some stunning feat are two examples. Even though such persons do not own property, they may be given high prestige. Moreover, some people even exchange their prestige for property. For example, they might be paid for saying that they start their day with "the breakfast of champions." In other words, property and prestige are not one-way streets: Although property can bring prestige, prestige can also bring property.

Power, the third element of social class, is the ability to control others, even over their objections. Certainly, Weber agreed, property is a major source of power, as Marx said. But it is not the only source. Position, for example, can also lead to power. A notable example is J. Edgar Hoover, who headed the FBI for forty-eight years, from 1924 to 1972. He wielded such enormous power that during his latter years even presidents Johnson and Kennedy were fearful of him. Hoover's power, however, did not come from ownership of property, for he lived simply and did not accumulate property. Rather, his power derived from his position as the head of this powerful government agency. Not only did he direct a well-trained secret police, he also maintained files on presidents and members of Congress documenting their sexual indiscretions, files they knew he could leak to the public.

Like prestige, then, property and power are also not one-way streets. As in the case of Hoover, position can bring power. In addition, position can also bring property. The wealthy former presidents of Mexico, who were raised in poverty but managed to put away many millions of dollars during their single six-year term in office, provide clear examples of how position can be used to accumulate vast property. It is, of course, unnecessary to go south of the border to find examples of politicians of humble origin using their position to gain property.

CDQ 12: Do you think that Marx's notion of a classless society is possible? Why or why not?

K.P.: Max Weber

L. Obj. 6: Explain why Max Weber was critical of Marx's perspective, and summarize Weber's views regarding social class position.

CDQ 13: Are property (wealth), prestige, and power central ingredients of the American class structure? Why or why not?

CDQ 14: Can you give examples of how property can bring prestige and how prestige can bring property?

CDQ 15: Do you think politicians should use their positions to gain property?

Max Weber identified three elements of social class—property, prestige, and power. J. Edgar Hoover, Director of the FBI for 48 years, lacked great wealth but possessed enormous power.

In Sum. Marx claimed that a person's social class depends solely on his or her position in relationship to the means of production—as a member of either the bourgeoisie or the proletariat—while Weber argued that social class is a combination of property, prestige, and power.

WHY IS SOCIAL STRATIFICATION UNIVERSAL?

Project 3

TR#12: Differing Explanations of Social Stratification

K.P.: Kingsley Davis and Wilbert Moore

L. Obj. 7: State the basic assumptions of functionalists like Davis and Moore, and present Tumin's criticisms of this viewpoint.

What is it about social life that makes all societies stratified? At the very least, why are there not *some* societies that are not stratified? We shall first consider the explanation proposed by functionalists, which has aroused a good deal of controversy in sociology, followed by criticisms of this position. We then explore explanations by conflict theorists.

The Functionalist View of Davis and Moore: Motivating Qualified People

As explained in Chapter 1, functionalists take the position that whatever characterizes a society is functional for that society; in other words, a group's particular characteristics represent historical adaptations that contribute to its survival. Since social inequality is universal, then, it must be extremely functional for society. In applying this principle, sociologists Kingsley Davis and Wilbert Moore (1945, 1953) concluded that stratification is inevitable for the following reasons:

1. Society must make certain that its positions are filled.
2. Some positions are more important than others.
3. The more important positions must be filled by the more qualified people.
4. To motivate the more qualified people to fill these positions, society must offer them greater rewards.

Let us look at some examples to flesh out the functionalist position. The positions of college president, chief executive officer of a corporation, and general of an army are deemed much more important for society than are those farther down the line of command in each institution—students, assembly-line workers, and privates. They are more important in the sense that decisions made by those who fill these top positions affect many people. Any mistakes they make carry implications for a large number of students, workers, and privates—their careers, pay checks, and, in some cases, even life and death.

Positions with greater responsibility also require greater accountability. College presidents, CEOs, and army generals are accountable for how they perform—to boards of control, stockholders, and the leader of a country, respectively. How can society motivate highly qualified people to enter such high-pressure positions? What keeps people from avoiding them and seeking only less demanding positions?

The answer, said Davis and Moore, is that society offers greater rewards for its more responsible, demanding, and accountable positions: higher salaries and benefits and greater prestige. Thus, a salary of $1 million, country club membership, a private jet, and a limousine may be necessary to get the most highly qualified persons to compete with one another for a certain position, while a $30,000 salary without fringe benefits is enough to get hundreds of persons to compete for some other, lower position. Similarly, higher rewards are necessary to recruit people to positions that require rigorous training.

The functionalist argument is simple and clear. Society works better if its most qualified people hold its most important positions. For example, to get highly talented people to become surgeons—to undergo many years of rigorous training and then cope with life-and-death situations on a daily basis, as well as withstand the Sword of Damocles known as malpractice suits—requires a high pay-off.

Tumin: A Critical Response

Note that the Davis-Moore thesis is an attempt to explain *why* social stratification is universal, not an attempt to *justify* social inequality. Note also that their view nevertheless makes many sociologists uncomfortable, for they see it as coming close to justifying social inequality.

Melvin Tumin (1953) was the first sociologist to point out what he saw as major flaws in the functionalist position, four of which are listed below:

First, how do you measure the importance of a position? If importance is measured by the rewards a position carries, the argument is circular. There must be an independent measure of importance to test whether the more important positions actually carry higher rewards. For example, how can it be logical to say that a surgeon is really more important to society than a garbage collector, when the garbage collector helps prevent contagious diseases that could wipe out an entire population?

Second, if stratification worked as Davis and Moore describe it, society would be a **meritocracy**; that is, all positions would be awarded on the basis of merit. Ability, then, should predict who goes to college. Instead, the best predictor of college entrance is family income. The more a family earns, the more likely their children are to go to college. Similarly, while some people do get ahead through ability and hard work, others simply inherit wealth and the opportunities that go with it. Moreover, a stratification system that places half the population above the other half solely on the basis of sex does not live up to the argument that talent and ability are the bases for holding important positions. In short, one look at people like Kim Petrovitch and John F. Kennedy shows that factors far beyond merit give people their relative positions in society.

Third, Davis and Moore place too much emphasis on money and fringe benefits. These aren't the only reasons people take jobs. Some jobs, such as college teaching, require many years of training and do not pay much, yet they have no shortage of

CDQ 16: What types of positions do functionalists think should be most highly rewarded in society? Do you agree?

K.P.: Melvin Tumin

CDQ 17: Can you explain how the Davis-Moore thesis could be used to justify social inequality?

CDQ 18: What arguments can you give to justify paying a surgeon more than a garbage collector? How about paying a garbage collector more than a surgeon?

CDQ 19: Do you agree with Tumin's idea that money and fringe benefits are not the only reasons people take jobs? Why or why not?

meritocracy: a form of social stratification in which all positions are awarded on the basis of merit

applicants. If money were the main motivator, why would people spend four years in college, then average another six or seven years pursuing a Ph.D.—only to earn slightly more than someone who works in the post office? Obviously college teaching offers more than monetary rewards: high prestige (most people in the community look up to people in this position), autonomy (college teachers have considerable discretion in their activities), rewarding social interaction (much of the job consists of talking to people), security (when given tenure, college teachers have a lifetime job), leisure and the opportunity to travel (professors work short days, enjoy several weeks' vacation during the school year, and have the entire summer off).

Fourth, if social stratification is so functional, it ought to benefit almost everyone. In actual fact, however, social stratification is *dysfunctional* to many. Think of the many individuals who could have made invaluable contributions to society had they not been born in a slum and had to drop out of school, taking a menial job to help support the family; or had they not been born female and assigned "women's work," ensuring that they could not maximize their mental abilities (Huber 1988).

Mosca: A Forerunner of the Conflict View

In 1896 Italian sociologist Gaetano Mosca wrote an influential book entitled *The Ruling Class.* In it, he argued that every society will be stratified by power, for three main reasons.

1. A society cannot exist unless it is organized. This means that there must be politics of some sort in order to coordinate people's actions and get society's work done.
2. Political organization always results in inequalities of power, for it requires that some people take leadership positions, while others follow.
3. It is human nature to be self-centered. Therefore, persons in positions of power will use their positions to bring greater rewards for themselves.

There is no way around these facts of life, said Mosca. Social stratification is inevitable, and every society will stratify itself along lines of power. Because the ruling class is well organized and enjoys easy communication among its relatively few members, it is extremely difficult for the majority they govern to resist (Marger 1987). Mosca's argument is a forerunner of explanations developed by conflict theorists.

The Conflict View: Class Conflict and Competition for Scarce Resources

Conflict theorists such as G. William Domhoff (1967, 1983, 1991), C. Wright Mills (1956), and Irving Louis Horowitz (1966) stress that conflict, not function, is the basis of social stratification. In short, every society has only limited resources to go around, and in every society groups struggle with one another for those resources. Whenever a group gains power, it uses that power to extract what it can from the groups beneath it. The dominant group takes control of the social institutions, using them to keep other groups weak and to preserve for itself the best resources. Class conflict, then, is the key to understanding social stratification, for society is far from being a harmonious system that benevolently distributes greater resources to society's supposedly more qualified members.

All ruling classes—whether slave masters or modern elites—develop an ideology to justify people's relative positions. This ideology not only helps prevent the ruling class from feeling guilty about possessing wealth in the midst of deprivation, but also affirms its position in power by seducing the oppressed into **false consciousness.** For example, the ideology encourages the oppressed to believe that their welfare depends on keeping society stable—so they support laws against their own interests and even sacrifice their children as soldiers in wars designed to support the entrenchment of the bourgeoisie.

Marx predicted that the workers would revolt. The day will come, he claimed,

K.P.: Gaetano Mosca

L. Obj. 8: Discuss Mosca's perspective on the universality of social stratification and explain why he is considered to be a forerunner of the conflict view.

L. Obj. 9: Compare Marx's early conflict-oriented perspective with that of later conflict theorists such as G. William Domhoff, C. Wright Mills, and Irving Louis Horowitz.

CDQ 20: Why is it necessary for all ruling classes to develop an ideology to justify people's relative positions? Can you think of examples?

Nelson Mandela, leader of the African National Congress (ANC), has spent his life fighting the white government of South Africa and the system of apartheid it developed to keep blacks from control of the country's resources.

when class consciousness will overcome ideology, and the workers, with their eyes finally opened, will throw off their oppressors. At first, this struggle for control of the means of production may be covert, showing itself only in such acts as industrial sabotage, but ultimately it will break out into open resistance. The struggle will be difficult, for the bourgeoisie control the police, the military, and even education (where they inculcate false consciousness in the workers' children).

Some conflict theorists have given a different focus to Marx's original emphasis. C. Wright Mills (1956), Ralf Dahrendorf (1959), and Randall Collins (1974, 1979), for example, stress that conflict between capitalists and workers is not the only important conflict in contemporary society. Groups within the *same class* also compete for scarce resources—for power, influence, wealth, education, housing, territory, and even prestige—whatever benefits society has to offer. This competition results in conflict between the young and the old, labor unions and business owners, producers and consumers, women and men, and racial and ethnic groups. Unlike functionalists, then, conflict theorists hold that just beneath the surface of what may appear to be a tranquil society lies overt conflict—uneasily held in check.

Toward a Synthesis

In spite of vast differences between the functionalist and conflict views, some social analysts have tried to synthesize them. Sociologist Gerhard Lenski (1966), for example, used the development of surpluses as a basis for reconciling the two views. He said that the functionalists are right when it comes to societies that have only basic resources and do not accumulate wealth. In hunting and gathering societies, the limited resources are channeled to people as rewards for taking on important responsibilities. The conflict theorists are right, however, when it comes to societies with a surplus. Because humans pursue self-interest, they struggle to control those surpluses, and a small elite emerges. To protect its position, the elite builds social inequality into the society, which results in a full-blown system of social stratification.

COMPARATIVE SOCIAL STRATIFICATION

Now that we have examined different systems of social stratification and considered why stratification is universal, let us look in turn at social stratification in Great Britain and in the former Soviet Union.

Social Stratification in Great Britain

Great Britain is often called England by Americans, but England is only one of the countries that make up the island of Great Britain. The others are Scotland and Wales. In addition, Northern Ireland is part of the United Kingdom of Great Britain and Northern Ireland.

Like other industrialized countries, Great Britain has a class system that can be divided into a lower, middle, and upper class. A little over half the population is in the lower or working class, while close to half the population is in the nation's very large middle class. That leaves a tiny upper class, which consists of perhaps 1 percent of the population. This 1 percent is powerful, highly educated, and so wealthy that it owns 43 percent of the entire nation's private capital and 81 percent of all corporate stock (Westergaard and Resler 1975).

Compared with Americans (who, regardless of their social background, are likely to claim that they are middle class), the British are extremely class-conscious. Like Americans the British recognize class distinctions on the basis of the type of car a person drives, or the stores that person patronizes. But the most striking characteristics of the British class system are language and education. Differences in speech still have a powerful impact on British life. Accent almost always betrays class, and as soon

CDQ 21: Is admission to law school or medical school largely based on competition within the same class? Why or why not?

K.P.: Gerhard Lenski

TR#11: The Percentage of a Country's Total income Going to the Poorest 20% of the Population for Selected Countries

L. Obj. 11: Compare and contrast social stratification in Great Britain, the former Soviet Union, and the United States.

CDQ 23: Why do you think most Americans are likely to claim they are middle class? Why are the British more class-conscious?

false consciousness: Karl Marx's term for the mistaken identification of workers with the interests of capitalists

The British remain far more class conscious than Americans. Perhaps that is why the British monarchy has lasted so long.

as someone speaks, the listener is aware of that person's class—and treats him or her accordingly.

Education is the primary way in which the British perpetuate their class system from one generation to the next. Almost all children go to neighborhood schools, but the children of Great Britain's more privileged 5 percent—who own *half* the nation's wealth—attend exclusive private boarding schools (known as "public" schools), where they are trained in subjects considered "proper" for members of the ruling class. An astounding 50 percent of the students at Oxford and Cambridge, the country's most prestigious universities, come from this 5 percent of the population. The effects of Great Britain's stratified education are striking, as sociologist Ian Robertson (1987) points out.

> To give one illustration of the influence of these schools, no fewer than eighteen former pupils of the most exclusive of them, Eton, have become prime minister. Imagine the chances of a single American high school producing eighteen presidents!

Project 4

Vladimir Ilyich Lenin (1870–1924) and Leon Trotsky (1879–1940) heeded Karl Marx's call for a classless society. They led a revolution in Russia to bring this about. They, and the nations that followed their banner, never claimed to have achieved the ideal of communism, in which all contribute their labor to the common good and receive according to their needs. Instead, they used the term socialism to describe the intermediate step between capitalism and communism, in which social classes are abolished but some individual inequality remains.

Although the socialist nations often manipulated the world's mass media to tweak the nose of Uncle Sam because of the inequalities in the United States, they, too, were marked by huge disparities in privilege—much more than they ever acknowledged to the outside world. Their major basis of stratification was membership in the Communist party. Party members were given greater access to the resources of the society than anyone else. Party membership was often the determining factor in deciding who would gain admission to the better schools or obtain the more desirable jobs. The equally qualified son or daughter of a nonmember would be turned down, for such privileges came with demonstrated loyalty to the Party.

Even the Communist party itself was highly stratified. Most members occupied a low level, having such assignments as spying on other workers. For their services, they might be given easier jobs in the factory or occasional access to special stores to purchase hard-to-find goods. A smaller number were mid-level bureaucrats with better than average access to resources and privileges. The top level consisted of a small elite: Party members who enjoyed not only power but also limousines, imported delicacies, vacation homes, and even servants and hunting lodges. In line with other stratification systems around the world, women held lower positions in the Party, as was readily evident in each year's May Day photos of the top members of the Party reviewing the weapons paraded in Moscow's Red Square. The top officials were always male.

Rather than eliminating social classes, then, the Communist revolution merely ushered in a different set of classes. An elite continued to rule from the top. Before the revolution the elite was based on inherited wealth; afterwards, it consisted of top party officials. Below this elite was a middle class, much smaller than ours, consisting of white-collar and other skilled workers. At the bottom was a mass of peasants and unskilled workers, very similar to the lower class before the revolution.

Struggling with a bloated bureaucracy, the gross inefficiencies of central planning, workers who did not see a personal stake in their assignments, and the allocation of 12 percent of the gross national product to the military (*Statistical Abstract* 1991:1489), the leaders of the USSR became increasingly frustrated as they saw the West continue to thrive. It added to their distress to see the prosperity of even the Japanese, the World War II adversary with whom they had arrogantly refused to make a peace treaty. Their ideology did not intend their citizens to be deprived, and in an attempt to turn things around, the later Soviet leadership initiated reforms, allowing elections with more than one candidate for an office (unlike earlier elections) and even encouraging private investment and ownership. The results of these reforms on their stratification system are yet to be seen.

MAINTAINING NATIONAL STRATIFICATION

Let us consider how social stratification is maintained within a nation. It is not difficult to understand that those at the top of society would wish to maintain their position. But how do they manage to do so?

The key lies in controlling the social institutions. Let's look first at the case of medieval Europe. At that time, land, which was owned by only a small group of people, was the primary source of wealth. With the exception of the clergy and some craftsmen,

CDQ 24: If you had lived in the former Soviet Union, where would you have wanted to be in their system of stratification? Why?

CDQ 25: How do you think those at the top of American society are able to maintain their positions? Will they always be able to do so?

Depicted in this French miniature, painted about 1450, is the coronation of 15-year-old Philip Augustus (1165–1223) as king of France by the Archbishop of Reims in 1179 or 1180. During his reign serfdom practically disappeared, cities and the merchant class grew prosperous, and Philip began the building of great cathedrals. The church's stamp of approval was essential for the legitimacy of the monarchy, with the right to rule passed from one generation to the next.

almost everyone was a peasant working for this small group of powerful landowners, called the aristocracy. The peasants farmed the land, took care of the cattle, and built the roads and bridges. Each year, they had to turn over a designated portion of their crops to their feudal lord. Year after year, for centuries, they did so.

Why didn't the peasants rebel and take over the land themselves? There were many reasons, not the least of which is that the army was controlled by the aristocracy. Coercion, however, only goes so far, for it breeds hostility and nourishes rebellion. How much more effective it is to get the people to *want* to do what the ruling elite desires. This is where ideology comes into play, and the aristocracy of that time used it to great effect. They developed the idea of the **divine right of kings,** teaching that the king's authority came directly from God. The king could delegate authority to nobles, who as God's representatives had to be obeyed, too. To disobey was a sin against God; to rebel meant a sentence to hell.

The control of ideas, then, can be remarkably more effective than brute force. Consequently, the elite in every society develops an ideology to justify its top position. To the degree that such ideology is accepted by the masses, those social arrangements are stable.

Although the particular ideology of medieval Europe no longer governs people's minds today, ideology itself has not lost its voice in maintaining stratification. Today, schools in every nation teach that the particular form of government common in the country—*whatever form of government that may be*—is the best. Each nation's schools also stress the virtues of governments past and present, not their vices. Religion also teaches that we owe obedience to authority, that laws are to be obeyed.

The control of information is a related method used by elites everywhere to maintain their positions of power. In dictatorships the control of information is accomplished through the threat of force, for dictators can—and do—imprison newspaper editors and reporters for printing reports critical of the ruling regime, sometimes even for publishing information unflattering to them (Timerman 1981). The ruling elites of democracies, lacking such power, accomplish the same purpose by manipulating the media through the selective release and withholding of information ("in the interest of national security"). But just as coercion has its limits, so does the control of information—especially given recently developed forms of communication (from satellite communications to modems and fax machines) that pay no respect to international borders.

Also critical in maintaining stratification are social networks—the social ties that link people together. As discussed in Chapter 6, social networks—contacts expanding outward from the individual that gradually encompass more and more people—supply valuable information and tend to perpetuate social inequality. Sociologist G. William Domhoff (1983, 1990) has documented that members of the elite move in a circle of power that multiplies their opportunities. As with the Kennedys in the opening vignette, these contacts with persons of similar backgrounds, interests, and goals allow the elite to pass privileges from one generation to the next. In contrast, as with the Petrovitches, the social networks of the poor perpetuate disprivilege.

Always underlying the maintenance of national stratification is control of the social institutions. The legal establishment enforces the laws passed under the influence of a society's elite. The elite also commands the police and military and can give orders to crush a rebellion—or even to run the post office if postal workers strike. As noted, however, force has its limits, and a nation's elite generally finds it preferable to maintain its stratification system by peaceful means, especially by influencing the thinking of its people.

L. Obj. 10: Explain why elites are not able to totally exploit other people in a given society.

divine right of kings: the idea that the king's authority comes directly from God

Why Not Total Exploitation?

What prevents a society's ruling elite from milking the other groups for everything it can? Why does industrialization create a large middle class, instead of ever harsher exploitation? As explained in Chapter 6, in the first stages of industrialization the elite is able to exploit workers mercilessly. However, advancing industrialization tends to distribute wealth, for skilled and educated workers are needed to handle the growing number of technical jobs (Lipset and Bendix 1959; Wallerstein 1974). In line with the functionalist argument, as people become skilled, they are in high demand and able to command greater resources. The result is a growing middle class.

A further limit to exploitation is the ruling class's desire to secure its position of privilege. It is perilous for an elite to always have to protect itself from poor people intent on toppling them, or to be continually hounded by strikes and industrial sabotage. Consequently, the elite finds it advantageous to buy off the lower classes, some through higher wages and better benefits, others through welfare and food stamps. In line with the conflict view of social stratification, benefits to the poor are far from altruistic. Rather, they are deliberate steps to reduce social tensions so as to protect the interests of the elite.

CDQ 22: Do you agree with the conflict perspective that the elite buys off the lower classes? If yes, what are some examples?

GLOBAL STRATIFICATION: THE THREE WORLDS

Just as the people within a nation are stratified into groups based on their relative power, prestige, and property, so are nations. The most common model divides nations into three groups according to how they rank in terms of wealth and economic development. Nations highest according to these criteria also rank highest in prestige and power. The differences between these groups of nations are so immense that it is as though their citizens live in different worlds. Consequently, nations are categorized as belonging to the First World, Second World, and Third World. ("First" does not mean better, but richer, having higher prestige, and, above all, being more powerful.) As we examine global stratification, we will stress basic relationships between these three groups of nations.

Project 5

TR#13: Income Inequality Around the World

L. Obj. 12: Describe the major characteristics of First World, Second World, and Third World nations, and name at least three countries which fit in each category.

The First World

The *First World* consists of the earth's most heavily industrialized nations: the United States and Canada in North America; Great Britain, France, Germany, Switzerland, and the other industrialized nations of western Europe; Japan in Asia; and Australia and New Zealand in the area of the world known as Oceania. Although there are variations in their economic systems (discussed in Chapter 14), these nations are capitalistic. With only about 25 percent of the earth's land and 15 percent of its people, these relatively few nations hold most of the world's wealth. Their wealth is so enormous, in fact, that even the poor in the First World live better and longer lives than do the average citizens of Third World nations. Table 9.2 shows the tremendous disparities in income among nations.

CDQ 26: Do the poor in First World nations live better and longer lives than the average citizens of Third World nations?

The Second World

The *Second World* consists of nations that are more or less industrialized and have been governed by socialism or communism: the nations of the former Soviet Union and its former satellites in eastern Europe (Poland, Czechoslovakia, Hungary, Romania, Bulgaria, and the Baltic Republics). These nations account for about 15 percent of the earth's land and 10 percent of its people. Inhabitants of the the Second World have a considerably poorer standard of living and lower incomes than those who live in the First World, but they are much better off than members of the Third World.

The term "more or less" industrialized is used because the industrialization of the second world nations is spotty. While most people in the Second World live and work in urban settings, compared with the First World a much higher proportion live on

Speaker Sug. #3: An expert on the former Soviet Union, Poland, Czechoslovakia, or other Second World countries.

TABLE 9.2   Income Inequality around the World

Nation	Income per person*	Nation	Income per person
First World Nations			
Switzerland	$28,660	France	$17,830
Japan	$23,290	Austria	$17,360
Finland	$23,153	Belgium	$16,390
Sweden	$20,880	Netherlands	$15,320
Denmark	$20,385	Australia	$14,440
United States	$19,840	Great Britain	$14,080
Canada	$19,020	Italy	$13,860
Germany	$19,000	Spain	$8,418
Second World Nations			
The former Soviet Union	$8,819	Romania	$5,107
Czechoslovakia	$7,870	Poland	$4,734
Hungary	$6,780	Cuba	$2,644
Bulgaria	$5,660		
Third World Nations			
Greece	$5,340	Bolivia	$600
Portugal	$3,906	Indonesia	$414
South Korea	$2,397	Togo	$390
Argentina	$2,134	Ghana	$380
Mexico	$2,076	Central African Republic	$376
Chile	$1,979	China	$360
Peru	$1,846	Kenya	$354
Costa Rica	$1,584	Pakistan	$338
Turkey	$1,263	India	$329
Belize	$1,250	Gambia	$230
Colombia	$1,190	Afghanistan	$220
Thailand	$1,170	Burma	$220
Cameroon	$1,010	Sierra Leone	$200
Cambodia	$960	Chad	$190
Congo	$930	Vietnam	$180
Swaziland	$900	Bangladesh	$180
Ivory Coast	$790	Nepal	$173
Morocco	$753	Madagascar	$156
Senegal	$705	Ethiopia	$121
Egypt	$630	Tanzania	$120
Angola	$620	Mozambique	$68
Oil-Rich Nations			
United Arab Emirates	$18,430	Oman	$5,900
Bahrain	$9,994	Saudi Arabia	$5,364
Qatar	$9,920		

* Variously listed as per capita gross national product and per capita income. Although the latest year available has been used, the years vary, usually 1987 to 1989.
Note: This listing shows just how inadequate the category Third World is, for Greece, Portugal, South Korea, and many Central and South American nations have little in common with such nations as Chad and Mozambique. An interim category, such as "Fourth World," to classify countries in the process of industrialization, would be helpful.
Source: *Statistical Abstract of the United States,* 1991: Table 1446 and *World Almanac and Book of Facts,* 1992.

farms. On such measures as access to electricity, indoor plumbing, automobiles, telephones, televisions, and even food, citizens of these nations rank lower than those in the First World but higher than those in the Third World. Production and distribution facilities are underdeveloped, resulting in the infamous shortages and long lines that Muscovite shoppers endure daily.

Haitians have endured corrupt leaders and persistent poverty for hundreds of years. Although Haitian slaves wrested power from their French colonial rulers in 1804, the country has been ruled by a small group of wealthy mulattos ever since. This leadership has plundered the nation's coffers while doing little for those they govern.

The Third World

The rest of the world's nations make up the *Third World,* where there is little industrialization, most people are peasant farmers living on farms or in villages, and living standards are low. These nations account for about 60 percent of the earth's land and about 75 percent of the world's people.

It is difficult to imagine the poverty that characterizes the Third World. Although wealthy nations have their pockets of poverty, as Table 9.2 shows, most people in the Third World live on less than $1,000 a year, in some cases considerably less. Most of them have no running water, indoor plumbing, central water supply, or access to trained physicians. Because modern medicine has cut infant mortality but not births (see Chapter 19), the world population grows fastest in these nations, thus placing even greater burdens on their limited facilities, and causing them to fall farther behind each year. The twin specters of poverty and death at an early age continuously stalk these countries.

Imperfections in the Model

This classification of nations into First, Second, and Third World is helpful in that it pinpoints gross differences among them, but it is also inadequate. A notable example of nations that do not fit these categories well is the oil-rich nations of the Middle East. These nations are not industrialized, but by providing the oil and gasoline that fuels the machinery of the industrialized nations, they have become wealthy. Consequently, to classify them as Third World nations glosses over significant material differences, for example, modern hospitals, extensive prenatal care, pure water systems, and high literacy. Kuwait, on whose formal behalf the United States and other industrialized powers fought Iraq in the Gulf War, is so wealthy that almost none of its citizens works. The government simply pays each a generous annual salary just for being citizens. Migrant workers from the Third World do most of the onerous chores that daily life requires, while highly skilled workers from the First World run the specialized systems that keep the nation's economy going and, apparently, fight its wars for them as well.

Speaker Sug. #4: An economist conducting research on development in First World and Third World countries.

CDQ 27: Do you think the governments of First World nations have any responsibility to help Second and Third World nations?

L. Obj. 13: Outline the major theories of how the world's nations became stratified.

HOW THE WORLD'S NATIONS BECAME STRATIFIED

The answer to how global stratification came about appears easy to answer. It would seem that the poorer nations must have fewer resources than the richer nations. As with so many other "obvious" answers, however, this one, too, falls short, for many of the Second and Third World nations are rich in natural resources, while one First World nation, Japan, has few. There are four competing theories that explain why the world's nations became stratified as they are.

Imperialism and Colonialism

CDQ 28: Did the United States gain its powerful position at the expense of other nations?

The first theory examines patterns of stratification that developed over centuries as European powers exploited weaker nations. In 1902, economist John Hobson (1858–1940) proposed a theory based on the surplus capital produced by industrialization. He argued that because the nations that industrialized lacked enough consumers in their own country to make it profitable to invest all excess capital there, and it was unprofitable to leave the capital idle, business leaders persuaded the government to take over other countries and lands. Because of pressures from manufacturers, financiers, investors, shippers, and exporters, who wanted to expand their markets and gain access to cheap raw materials, the government embarked on **imperialism,** the pursuit of unlimited geographical expansion.

The nations that industrialized first got the jump on the rest of the world in this regard. When industrialization began in Great Britain about 1750, then spread throughout western Europe, reaching the United States about 1825, these nations became the most powerful countries in the world. According to Hobson's theory, the reason Great Britain fought France, Spain, Portugal, Holland, and Germany was to control international markets in which to invest excess capital.

The industrialized nations then **colonized** weaker nations—invading them and exploiting their labor and natural resources. At one point, there was even a free-for-all among the industrialized European nations as they frantically rushed to divide up an entire continent. As Africa was sliced into pieces, even tiny Belgium got into the act and acquired the Congo. While the more powerful European nations would plant their national flags in a colony and send their representatives to directly run the government and administer the territory's affairs, the United States usually chose to plant corporate flags in the colony and let these corporations dominate the territory's government. Central and South America are prime examples of such "economic imperialism" on the part of the United States. No matter what the form, and whether it was benevolent or harsh, the purpose was the same—to exploit the nation's people and resources for the benefit of the "mother" country.

Western imperialism and colonization, then, shaped the Third World. In some instances, the industrialized nations were so powerful that they were able to divide their booty among themselves by drawing lines across a map and forming new states without regard for tribal or cultural considerations. Britain and France did just this in North Africa and parts of the Middle East, which is why the national boundaries of Libya, Saudi Arabia, Kuwait, and other nations are so straight. This legacy of European conquerors still erupts into tribal violence because tribes with no history of national identity were arbitrarily included within the same political boundaries.

World System Theory

K.P.: Immanuel Wallerstein

To explain how global stratification developed, Immanuel Wallerstein (1974, 1979, 1984), the major proponent of the second theory, focused on the interdependence of the earth's nations. He argued that since the sixteenth century a **world system** has been developing; that is, the world's countries have been increasingly tied together by economic and political connections.

imperialism: a nation's pursuit of unlimited geographical expansion

colonization: the process in which one nation takes over another nation, usually for the purpose of exploiting its labor and natural resources

world system: the way in which the world's countries are tied together by economic and political connections

Wallerstein identified four groups of interconnected nations. In the first group, the *core nations,* capitalism first developed (Britain, France, Holland, and later Germany). The economic advantage that capitalism gave these nations made them rich and powerful. The second group, nations on the *semiperiphery* (the countries around the Mediterranean), became highly dependent on trade with the core nations. Consequently, their own economies stagnated. The third group, the *periphery,* or fringe, consists of the eastern European countries. Primarily limited to selling cash crops to the core nations, their economies developed even less. The fourth group, which Wallerstein called the *external area,* includes most of Africa and Asia. These nations were left out of the development of capitalism and had few if any economic connections with the core nations.

Capitalism's relentless expansion, claimed Wallerstein, resulted in a **capitalist world economy** dominated by the core nations (to which Canada, the United States, Japan, and a few other highly industrialized nations were added). The new world economy forged economic and political connections between the core nations and others. This economy turned out to be so all-encompassing that today even the nations in the external area are being drawn into its commercial web.

CNN: Poverty

Globalization.   The extensive interdependence among the nations of the world that has come about through the expansion of capitalism is called **globalization.** Although the process of globalization has been under way for the past several hundred years, today's new forms of communication and transportation have greatly speeded it up. The interconnections are so extensive that no nation is able to live in isolation, and events in remote parts of the world now affect us all—sometimes immediately, for example when a revolution interrupts the flow of raw materials, at other times in a slow ripple effect, as when a change in some government's policy changes that country's ability to compete in world markets. All of today's societies, then, no matter where they are located in the world, are part of a global social system.

Dependency Theory

The third theory is sometimes difficult to distinguish from world system theory. **Dependency theory** attributes the lack of economic development in many nations, especially in the Third World, to the dominance of the world economy by the industrialized nations (Cardoso 1972; Furtado 1984). According to this theory, the First World nations turned other nations into their plantations and mines, planting or extracting whatever they needed to meet their growing appetite for commodities and exotic foods. As a result, many Third World nations began to specialize in a single cash crop. Brazil

capitalist world economy: the dominance of capitalism in the world along with the international interdependence that capitalism has created

globalization: the extensive interconnections among world nations resulting from the expansion of capitalism

dependency theory: the belief that lack of industrial development in Third World nations is caused by the industrialized nations dominating the world economy

Essential to globalization is a system of telecommunications that encircles the earth, connecting small human groups around the world into a single, encompassing system. Here we see how even a remote, preliterate people, the Gaviao Indians in Brazil's remote Amazon, are being incorporated into this system.

became the primary source for coffee; Panama, Nicaragua, Guatemala, and other Central American countries specialized in bananas (hence the term "banana" republics); Chile became the primary source of tin; and the Belgian Congo (Zaire) was turned into a gigantic rubber plantation. By becoming dependent on the industrialized nations, the Third World countries did not develop independent, vibrant economies of their own.

Culture of Poverty

K.P.: John Kenneth Galbraith

An entirely different explanation of global stratification was proposed by John Kenneth Galbraith (1979), a social economist. Building on the ideas of anthropologist Oscar Lewis (1966), Galbraith argued that some nations remained poor because they were crippled by a **culture of poverty,** a way of life that perpetuates poverty from one generation to the next. He explained it in this way: Most of the world's poor live in rural areas, where they barely eke out a living from the land. Their marginal life offers little room for error or risk, so they tend to stick closely to tried-and-true, traditional ways. Experimenting with new farming or manufacturing techniques is threatening, for if these fail they could lead to hunger or death. Their religion also reinforces traditionalism, for it teaches fatalism, the acceptance of their lot in life as God's will. The problem, Galbraith claimed, is not that the Third World nations lack resources but rather that their culture inhibits economic development.

Evaluating the Theories

CDQ 29: Can you explain why most sociologists agree with imperialism, world systems, or dependency theories more than with theories based on a culture of poverty?

Most sociologists find an explanation based on imperialism, world systems, or dependency theory preferable to one based on a culture of poverty, for they feel that Galbraith's theory places blame on the victim, the poor nations themselves. But even taken all together, these theories yield only part of the picture, as becomes apparent in looking at the example of Japan. After World War II, Japan was saddled with both a religion that stressed fatalism and a disadvantaged position in world markets. None of the theories described above would have led anyone to expect a devastated Japan, stripped of its military and colonies, to become an economic powerhouse able to turn the Western world on its head.

Each theory, then, yields but a partial explanation, and the grand theorist who will put the many pieces of this puzzle together has yet to appear.

MAINTAINING GLOBAL STRATIFICATION

L. Obj. 14: Explain how global stratification has been maintained.

Why are the same countries rich year after year, while the rest remain poor? Let us look at two explanations of how global stratification is maintained.

Neocolonialism

K.P.: Michael Harrington

Sociologist Michael Harrington (1977) observed that although the First World nations no longer invade a country and make it a colony, they control Third World nations through **neocolonialism.** This term means that the industrialized nations not only set the prices they charge for their manufactured goods but also control the international markets where they purchase the mineral and agricultural wealth of these Third World nations. Thus, the industrialized nations determine how much they will pay for tin from Bolivia, copper from Peru, coffee from Brazil, and so forth. Neocolonialism also means that First World nations move hazardous industries out of their own countries into Third World nations that, eager to get the employment, allow themselves to be used as dumping grounds for untreated factory waste (LaDou 1991).

The First World nations set up a cycle of indebtedness by selling weapons and other manufactured goods to the Third World nations, making these nations eternal

culture of poverty: a culture that perpetuates poverty from one generation to the next

neocolonialism: the economic and political dominance of Third World nations by First World nations

debtors and keeping them from developing their own industrial capacity. Because of these nations' huge debts, the industrialized countries are then able to dictate the terms of their trading relationships. Thus, although the Third World nations have their own governments—whether elected or dictatorships—they remain almost as dependent on the industrialized nations as they were when those nations occupied them. For an interesting example of neocolonialism today, see the Perspectives box below.

Multinational Corporations

A second way in which international stratification is maintained is through **multinational corporations,** companies that operate across many national boundaries. To get an idea of their huge size, and, therefore, the enormous power they wield, note that of the one hundred largest economic units in the world, fifty are nations and the other fifty are multinational corporations (Benson and Lloyd 1983). For more on multinational corporations, see Chapter 14.

In some cases, multinational corporations exploit Third World nations directly. A prime example is the United Fruit Company, which for decades controlled national and local politics in the Central American nations, running them as a fiefdom for the company's own profit while the United States marines waited in the wings in case the company's interests needed to be backed up. Most commonly, however, multinational

Project 6

Speaker Sug. #5: A business expert knowledgeable about the inner-workings of multinational corporations.

CDQ 30: Are you surprised to learn that of the one hundred largest economic units in the world, fifty are nations and the other fifty are multinational corporations? Why or why not?

multinational corporations: companies that operate across many national boundaries

---

P E R S P E C T I V E S
Cultural Diversity Around the World

The Patriotic Prostitute

> Holidays with the most beautiful women of the world. An exclusive tour by Life Travel . . . You fly to Bangkok and then go to Pattaya . . . Slim, sunburnt and sweet, they . . . are masters in the art of making love by nature, an art we European people do not know . . . In Pattaya costs of living and loving are low (from a Swiss pamphlet)

A new wrinkle in the history of prostitution is the "patriotic prostitute." These are young women who are encouraged by their governments to prostitute themselves to help the country's economy. Patriotic prostitution is one of the seediest aspects of global stratification. Some Third World nations encourage prostitution to help pay their national debts. A consequence is that perhaps 10 percent of all Thai women between the ages of fifteen and thirty have become prostitutes. Bangkok alone reports one hundred thousand prostitutes—plus two hundred thousand "masseuses."

Government officials encourage prostitution as a service to their country. In South Korea, prostitutes are issued identification cards that serve as hotel passes. In orientation sessions, they are told: "Your carnal conversations [sic] with foreign tourists do not prostitute either yourself or the nation, but express your

heroic patriotism." With such an official blessing, "sex tourism" has become big business. Travel agencies in Germany openly advertise "trips to Thailand with erotic pleasures included in the price." Japan Air Lines hands out brochures that advertise the "charming attractions" of Kisaeng girls, advising men to fly JAL for a "night spent with a consummate Kisaeng girl dressed in a gorgeous Korean blouse and skirt."

What the enticing advertising fails to mention is the misery underlying Third World prostitution. Many of the prostitutes are held in bondage. Some are forced to work for pimps to pay family debts. Some are kept under lock and key to keep them from escaping. The advertisements also fail to mention the incidence of AIDS among Third World prostitutes. Somewhere between 25 percent and 50 percent of Nairobi's ten thousand prostitutes appear to be infected.

Women's groups protest this international sex trade, deploring in particular its exploitation of the world's most impoverished and underprivileged women.

Source: Based on Gay 1985; Cohen 1986; Shaw 1987; O'Malley 1988; Srisang 1989.

As part of a global system of stratification, multinational corporations from the more powerful industrialized nations work closely with urban elites in the Third World nations. In return for the cooperation of a country's ruling elite, including its maintenance of a stable political system which aids the exploitation of the country's resources, the elite is paid off handsomely—as illustrated by these Saudis shopping for Rolls Royces, and matching cars for their sons.

corporations help to maintain international stratification simply by doing business. A multinational's interconnections may involve mining in several countries, manufacturing in many others, and running transportation and advertising networks around the globe. No matter where the particular profits are made, or where they are reinvested, the primary beneficiaries are First World nations, especially the one in which the multinational corporation has its central headquarters. As Michael Harrington (1977) stressed, the real profits are made in processing the products and in controlling their distribution—and these profits are withheld from the Third World.

KP: Michael Lipton

According to sociologist Michael Lipton (1979), multinational corporations work closely with an urban power elite of the Third World. This elite, which lives a sophisticated upper-class life in the major cities of its home country, sends its children to Oxford, the Sorbonne, or Harvard to be educated. The multinational corporations funnel investments to this small circle of power, whose members favor projects such as building laboratories and computer centers in the capital city, projects that do not help the vast majority of their people living in poor, remote villages where they farm small plots of land.

This, however, is not the full story. Multinational corporations also play a role in changing international stratification. This is an unintentional by-product of their worldwide search for cheap resources and labor. By moving manufacturing from First World countries with high labor costs to Third World countries with low labor costs, they not only exploit cheap labor but in some cases also bring genuine prosperity to those nations. Although in comparison with their counterparts in the First World these workers are paid a pittance, it is more than they can earn elsewhere. With new factories come opportunities to develop new skills and a capital base. This does not occur in all nations, but the "Asian tigers" in the Pacific Rim nations have developed a strong capital base and have begun to rival the older capitalist nations.

SUMMARY

1. Social stratification refers to a system of dividing large groups of people into layers, creating a hierarchy of relative privilege based on power, property, and prestige. Every society stratifies its members. There are four major systems of social stratification: slavery, caste, class, and clan.

2. The essential characteristic of slavery is that some people own other people. Initially, slavery was based not on race but on debt, punishment, or defeat in battle. Slavery could be temporary or permanent, and was not necessarily passed on to one's children. In North America slav-

ery was especially brutal. Slaves had no legal rights, and the system was gradually buttressed by a racist ideology. Some social analysts believe that slavery produced racism, rather than racism producing slavery.

3. In a caste system of social stratification, status is determined by birth and is lifelong. Societies with this form of stratification, such as India and South Africa, try to make certain that the boundaries between castes remain firm. People marry within their own group, develop rules about ritual pollution, and believe that contact with inferior castes make the superior caste "unclean."

4. Compared with slavery and caste systems, class-based stratification is much more open, for it is based primarily on money or material possessions. Industrialization encourages the formation of class systems. Partially industrialized nations may maintain their previous form of stratification, usually the clan, alongside the developing class system. In the clan system an individual's status depends on lineage that links him or her to an extended network of relatives. Gender discrimination cuts across all forms of social stratification.

5. Karl Marx argued that the only factor that determines social class is a person's relationship to the means of production. If you own them, you belong to the bourgeoisie; if you do not, you are one of the proletariat. When workers realize the common source of their misery, according to Marx, they will unite and rebel. At that time, they will found communism, a classless society. Ideology manipulated by the ruling class and false consciousness hinder this revolution. Max Weber disagreed, claiming that three elements dictate an individual's standing in society: property, prestige, and power.

6. Sociologists have proposed various answers to the question of why social stratification is universal. Gaetano Mosca argued that stratification is inevitable because every society must have leadership, and leadership always perpetuates inequality. Functionalists Kingsley Davis and Wilbert Moore argued that to attract the most capable persons to fill its important positions, society must offer them higher rewards. Melvin Tumin sharply criticized this view, while Gerhard Lenski suggested a synthesis between the functionalist and conflict perspectives.

7. What prevents contemporary ruling elites from totally exploiting those under them? First, there are limits to the effectiveness of brute force; second, industrialization builds a large middle class on which the elite depends; third, the elite finds it more expedient to buy off the lower classes. Comparing the systems of social stratification in Great Britain and the former Soviet Union helps us to better understand cross-cultural differences.

8. Nations, too, are stratified into groups based on their relative power, prestige, and property. The most common model divides nations into three groups: the First, Second, and Third Worlds. Four theories attempt to account for the advent of global stratification: imperialism and colonialism, world system theory, dependency theory, and a culture of poverty. Neocolonialism and multinational corporations help to maintain global stratification.

9. To maintain social stratification within a nation, the ruling class utilizes an ideology that justifies current arrangements, controls information, and, when all else fails, depends on brute force. The social networks of the rich and the poor also perpetuate social inequality.

SUGGESTED READINGS

Carter, Bob. *Capitalism, Class Conflict and the New Middle Class.* London: Routledge & Kegan Paul, 1985. Carter explains why capitalism was not overthrown by the workers' revolution as Marx predicted.

Freedman, Robert. *The Mind of Karl Marx: Economic, Political, and Social Perspectives.* Chatham, N.J.: Chatham House, 1986. A conflict theorist provides an overview of social stratification from his perspective.

Lane, David. *The End of Social Inequality: Class, Status and Power Under State Socialism.* Winchester, Mass.: Allen & Unwin, 1982. Lane analyzes social stratification in socialist societies.

Miles, Rosalind. *The Woman's History of the World.* Topfield, Mass.: Salem House, 1989. The author examines the importance of gender in human history.

Tumin, Melvin M. *Social Stratification: The Forms and Functions of Social Inequality.* 2d ed. Englewood Cliffs, N.J. Prentice Hall, 1985. A functionalist provides an overview of social stratification from his perspective.

United Nations. *World Economic Survey 1990: Current Trends and Policies in the World Economy.* New York: United Nations, 1990. This survey of the economic characteristics of the world's nations provides a detailed contrast between the rich and poor nations.

Voslensky, Michael. *Nomenklatura: The Soviet Ruling Class.* New York: Doubleday, 1984. A Soviet analyst provides an overview of social stratification in what is now the former Soviet Union.

Wills, David K. *Klass: How Russians Really Live.* New York: St. Martin's Press, 1986. An American sociologist provides an overview of social stratification in the former Soviet Union.

CHAPTER **10**

Red Grooms, The Living Room, *1981*

Social Class in American Society

WHAT IS SOCIAL CLASS?
Measures of Social Class

DIMENSIONS OF SOCIAL CLASS
Wealth ■ Power ■ Prestige ■ Status Inconsistency

SOCIAL CLASS IN INDUSTRIAL SOCIETY
Updating Marx: Wright's Model ■ Updating Weber: Gilbert's and Kahl's Model ■ Social Class in the Automobile Industry ■ Below the Ladder: The Homeless

CONSEQUENCES OF SOCIAL CLASS
Life Chances ■ Physical and Mental Health ■ Family Life ■ Values and Attitudes ■ Political Involvement ■ Religion ■ Education ■ The Criminal Justice System

SOCIAL MOBILITY
Intergenerational, Structural, and Exchange Mobility ■ Social Mobility in the United States ■ Costs of Social Mobility ■ *Thinking Critically about Social Controversy:* **Upward Mobility for the American Worker—A Vanishing Dream?** ■ Where Is Horatio Alger?

POVERTY IN THE UNITED STATES
Drawing the Line: What Is Poverty? ■ Who Are the Poor? ■ Children of Poverty: A New Social Condition? ■ *Thinking Critically about Social Controversy:* **Children in Poverty** ■ Short-Term and Long-Term Poverty ■ Individual versus Structural Explanations of Poverty

SUMMARY

SUGGESTED READINGS

Ah, New Orleans, that fabled city on the Gulf. Images from its rich past floated through my head—pirates, wealth, intrigue. So did memories from a pleasant vacation—the exotic French Quarter with odors of Creole food and sounds of earthy jazz drifting through the air.

The shelter for the homeless, however, brought me back to an unwelcome reality. The shelter was the same as those I had visited in the North—as well as the West and the East—only dirtier. The dirt, in fact, was the worst that I encountered during my research, and this was the only shelter to insist on payment to sleep in one of its filthy beds. The men looked the same—disheveled and haggard, wearing that unmistakable expression of despair—just like the homeless anywhere in the country. Except for the accent, you wouldn't know where you were. Poverty wears the same tired face, I realized. The accent may differ, but the face remains the same.

Now, just a block or so from the shelter, I felt indignation well up within me. I had become used to the sights of abject poverty. I had come to expect what I saw in the shelters and on the streets. Those no longer held surprises. But this was startling.

Huge posters mounted on the glitzy transparent plastic shelter covering the bus stop, advertising wares available nearby, glared at me obscenely out of joint with the reality of despair that I had just left. Almost life-sized pictures portrayed finely dressed men and women, proudly strutting elegant suits, dresses, jewelry, and furs. The prices were astounding—perhaps not to some, but certainly to the homeless I had just left.

A feeling of disgust swept over me as I looked at the display. "Something is cockeyed in this society," I thought, my mind refusing to stop juxtaposing the images in the ads with those of the suffering I had witnessed in the shelter. I felt nauseated—and surprised at the urge to deface the sketches and photos of these people in their finery.

Occasionally, the facts of social class in American life hit home with brute force. This was one of those moments. The disjunction that I felt in New Orleans was triggered by the ads, but it was not the first time that I had experienced this sensation. Whenever my research abruptly transported me from the world of the homeless to one of another social class, I felt unfamiliar feelings of disjointed unreality (Henslin 1990). Each social class has its own way of being, its own fundamental orientations to the world, and because these contrast so sharply the classes do not mix well.

WHAT IS SOCIAL CLASS?

To gain an understanding of social classes in American society, the first question we need to examine is what social class is. "There are the poor and the rich—and then there are you and I, neither poor nor rich." That is just about as far as most Americans' consciousness of social class goes. Let's try to flesh this out.

Our task is made somewhat difficult because sociologists have no clear-cut, accepted definition of social class. As noted in Chapter 9, conflict sociologists (of the Marxist orientation) see only two social classes: those who own the means of production and those who do not. The problem with this view, say most sociologists, is that it lumps too many people together. Physicians and corporate executives with incomes of $200,000 a year are lumped together with hamburger flippers working at McDonalds for $9,000 a year.

Most sociologists agree with Weber that there are more dimensions to social class than a person's relationship to the means of production. Consequently, most sociologists use Weber's dimensions and define a **social class** as a large group of people who rank close to one another in wealth, power, and prestige. These three elements separate people into different lifestyles, give them different chances in life, and provide them with distinct ways of looking at the self and the world. These elements will be examined in detail below. But let's first look at three different ways of measuring social class.

Measures of Social Class

Subjective Method. The **subjective method** is to ask people what their social class is. Although simple and direct, this approach is filled with problems. First, people may deny that they belong to any class, claiming, instead, that everyone is equal. Second, people may classify themselves according to their aspirations—to where they would like to be—rather than to where they actually are. Third, when asked to what class they belong, *nine out of ten Americans identify themselves as middle class* (Vanneman and Cannon 1987). This reply—more than likely prompted by the powerful American ideology of equality—effectively removes the usefulness of the subjective method.

Reputational Method. In the **reputational method,** people are asked what class others belong to, based on their reputations. Social anthropologist W. Lloyd Warner (1941, 1949) pioneered this method in a study of a community he called "Yankee City."

CDQ 1: Do you think most Americans are conscious of social class? Why or why not?

L. Obj. 1: Define social class and explain why sociologists do not agree on how many social classes there are.

L. Obj. 2: Compare the three ways of measuring social class.

Speaker Sug. #1: A social scientist conducting research on social class.

CDQ 2: Why do you think nine out of ten Americans identify themselves as middle class? Do you believe their assessment is correct?

K.P.: W. Lloyd Warner

social class: according to Weber, a large group of people who rank close to one another in wealth, power, and prestige; according to Marx, one of two groups: capitalists who own the means of production and workers who sell their labor

subjective method: (of measuring social class) a system in which people are asked to define their own social class

reputational method: (of measuring social class) a system in which people who are familiar with the reputations of others are asked to judge their social class

Most Americans identify themselves as middle class. How would you identify the people in this neighborhood block party?

Three of his colleagues, Allison Davis, Burleigh Gardner, and Mary Gardner (1941) used the reputational method to study Old City, a Southern town of ten thousand inhabitants. How they saw their town's social classes is depicted in Figure 10.1 on page 250. The value of this approach is that it provides an understanding of how people in a community see major social divisions. The primary disadvantage is that its use is limited to small communities where people know one another. As you can see from Figure 10.1, this method produces several different snapshots of a class system, for people see life from the perspectives of their own class.

Objective Method.   In the **objective method,** researchers rank people according to objective criteria such as wealth, power, and prestige. Although there is always the possibility that researchers will err in their measurement, this method has the advantage of letting others know exactly what measurements were made, so that they can test them.

In Sum.   Given the three choices of subjective, reputational, and objective methods to determine social class, sociologists use the objective method almost exclusively. The studies reported below are examples of the objective approach.

DIMENSIONS OF SOCIAL CLASS

Let us now turn to the three criteria most commonly used to measure social class: wealth, power, and prestige.

Wealth

The primary dimension of social class is wealth. **Wealth** consists of property and income. *Property* comes in many forms, such as buildings, land, animals, machinery, cars, stocks, bonds, businesses, and bank accounts. *Income* is money received as wages, rents, interest, royalties, or the proceeds from a business.

Distinction between Wealth and Income.   Wealth and income are sometimes assumed to be the same, but they are not. Some people have much wealth and little income. For example, a farmer may own much land, but with the high cost of fertilizers

CDQ 3: Can you explain why most sociologists use the objective method to determine social class?

L. Obj. 3: Outline and explain the dimensions of social class.

Project 1

Essay #1

CDQ 4: In your opinion, is it possible for a professional to have an annual income of over $150,000 a year and still have very little wealth?

objective method: (of measuring social class) a system in which people are ranked according to objective criteria such as wealth, power, and prestige

wealth: property and income

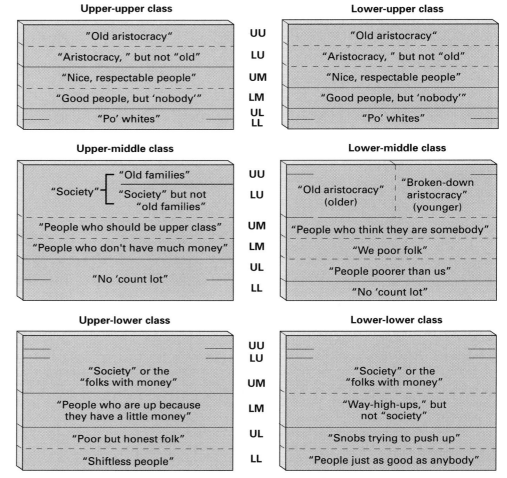

Upper-upper class

"Old aristocracy"	UU
"Aristocracy," but not "old"	LU
"Nice, respectable people"	UM
"Good people, but 'nobody'"	LM
"Po' whites"	UL LL

Lower-upper class

"Old aristocracy"	
"Aristocracy," but not "old"	
"Nice, respectable people"	
"Good people, but 'nobody'"	
"Po' whites"	

Upper-middle class

"Society" ⎡ "Old families" UU
         ⎣ "Society" but not LU
             "old families"
"People who should be upper class" UM
"People who don't have much money" LM
                                    UL
"No 'count lot"   LL

Lower-middle class

"Old aristocracy" (older) | "Broken-down aristocracy" (younger) UU / LU
"People who think they are somebody" UM
"We poor folk" LM
"People poorer than us" UL
"No 'count lot" LL

Upper-lower class

	UU LU
"Society" or the "folks with money"	UM
"People who are up because they have a little money"	LM
"Poor but honest folk"	UL
"Shiftless people"	LL

Lower-lower class

"Society" or the "folks with money"	
"Way-high-ups," but not "society"	
"Snobs trying to push up"	
"People just as good as anybody"	

FIGURE 10.1   How Social Class is Perceived by Different Groups.
Note: The classes listed at the top of each box (Upper-upper class, etc.) represent a sociological division in common use at the time of this research, a six-fold division that is sometimes still used.

(*Source:* Reprinted from page 65 of *Deep South: A Social-Anthropological Study of Caste and Class,* by Allison Davis, Burleigh B. Gardner, and Mary R. Gardner. Reprinted by permission of The University of Chicago Press. Copyright 1941 by the University of Chicago.)

and machinery, a little bad weather can cause the income to disappear. Others have much income and little wealth. For example, an executive with $150,000 annual income may actually be debt-ridden. Below the surface prosperity, he or she may be greatly overextended: unpaid bills for the children's exclusive private schools, the sports cars one payment away from being repossessed, and huge mortgage payments on the large home in the exclusive suburb. Typically, however, wealth and income go together.

Distribution of Wealth.   Who owns the wealth in the United States? One answer, of course, is "everyone." While that statement has some merit, it overlooks how that wealth is divided among "everyone." How are the two forms of wealth, property and income distributed among Americans?

Property.   Overall, Americans are worth a hefty sum, about $14 trillion (*Statistical Abstract* 1991; Table 762). Most of this wealth is in the form of real estate, corporate stocks, bonds, and business assets. As Figure 10.2 shows, this wealth is highly concentrated. The vast majority, 68 percent, is owned by only *10 percent* of the nation's families. How rich are they? This top 10 percent owns *50 percent* of the value of all real estate, *90 percent* of corporate stocks and business assets, and *95 percent* of bonds (Stafford et al. 1986). That leaves only 50 percent of the value of real estate, just 10

TR#10M: Distribution of Wealth of Americans

CDQ 5: Do you think property is pretty evenly distributed among the middle and upper classes in the United States? Why or why not?

Wealth in the United States is unequally divided, with a mere 0.5 percent of the population owning over a quarter of the nation's wealth.

percent of stocks and businesses, and only 5 percent of all bonds for the other 90 percent of Americans.

And these figures are only part of the picture of how concentrated American wealth is. The super-rich, *the wealthiest 0.5 percent of Americans, own 27 percent of the country's entire wealth.* In fact, about 325,000 families own 40 percent of all the corporate stock and business assets in the entire country (Stafford et al. 1986–87; *The Wall Street Journal,* July 28, 1986:38; *Statistical Abstract* 1990: Table 731).

Income.   How is income distributed in American society? Economist and Nobel laureate Paul Samuelson put it this way: "If we made an income pyramid out of a child's blocks, with each layer portraying $500 of income, the peak would be far higher than Mount Everest, but most people would be within a few feet of the ground" (Samuelson and Nordhaus 1989:644).

Actually, if each block were 1½ inches tall, the typical American would be only *4 feet off the ground,* for the average per capita income in the United States is about $17,000 per year. See Figure 10.3. The typical family does better than this, for its average annual income, from all working members, runs about $34,000. Yet compared

TR#15: The Concentration of U.S. Wealth

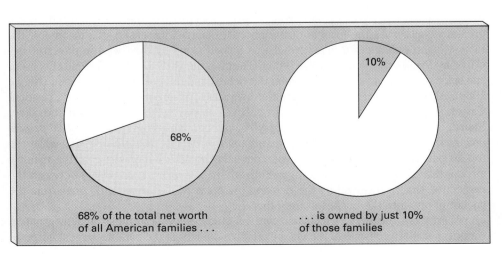

68% of the total net worth of all American families . . .

. . . is owned by just 10% of those families

FIGURE 10.2   Distribution of Wealth of Americans. (*Source: ISR Newsletter,* winter 1986–87:3.)

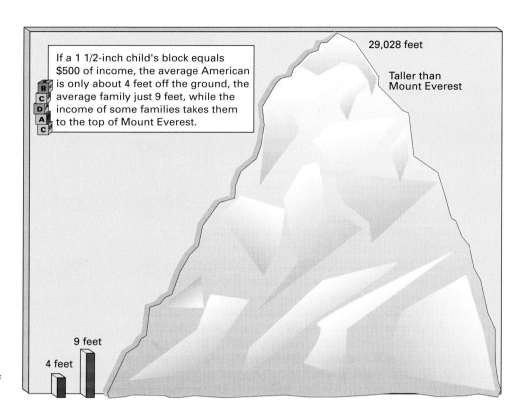

If a 1 1/2-inch child's block equals $500 of income, the average American is only about 4 feet off the ground, the average family just 9 feet, while the income of some families takes them to the top of Mount Everest.

29,028 feet

Taller than Mount Everest

9 feet

4 feet

FIGURE 10.3   The Division of Income in the United States

Thirty-seven-year-old William H. Gates III, founder and CEO of the Microsoft Corporation, is one of the richest men in America. His estimated worth is 7 billion dollars.

with the Mount Everest incomes of a few, the earnings of the typical American family bring it to only 9 feet off the ground (*Statistical Abstract* 1991: Tables 715, 732).

The fact that some Americans reach the top of Mount Everest while others live only 6 inches up the slope presents a striking image of the extremes of income in U.S. society. Another way to portray these differences is to divide the United States population into five equal sections, rank each one from highest to lowest income, and compare the results. As Table 10.1 shows, the top 20 percent acquires almost 45 percent of all income in the United States, while the bottom 20 percent receives less than 5 percent of the nation's income.

Beyond demonstrating social inequality, Table 10.1 illustrates five other striking features. First is the consistency of the income divisions through the years. There has been such little change over the past two generations that the divisions now are almost exactly as they were forty-five years ago, at the end of World War II. Second, for a period of about twenty-five years, from roughly 1945 to 1970, there was a trend toward greater equality: As the income of the poorest quintiles increased, the income of the richest quintile decreased. This trend was helped along by the "war on poverty" declared by President Johnson in the 1960s. Third, in the early 1970s this trend reversed, and since then the income gap between the richest and the poorest has widened (Niggle 1989). Although this trend toward greater inequality had already begun under President Carter, President Reagan's economic policies of the 1980s accentuated the slide. Fourth, the gains of the "war on poverty" have been wiped out; *the poorest 20 percent now receive the same small share of the national income as they did in 1945,* while the top 20 percent and the very top 5 percent take home a larger share of the nation's income than they did forty years ago. Fifth, there is a direct relationship between the respective shares received by the rich and the poor. Money apparently goes from the pocket of one into the pocket of the other.

Apart from the very rich, whom we will study below, the most affluent group in American society consists of the chief executive officers of the nation's largest corpora-

TABLE 10.1   The Percentage of the Nation's Income Received by Each 5th and the Top 5 Percent of America's Families Since World War II

Year	Lowest 5th	Second 5th	Middle 5th	Fourth 5th	Highest 5th	Top 5%
1989*	4.6	10.6	16.5	23.7	44.6	17.9
1985**	4.7	10.9	16.9	24.2	43.3	16.5
1980	5.1	11.6	17.5	24.3	41.6	15.3
1975	5.4	11.8	17.6	24.1	41.1	15.5
1970	5.4	12.2	17.6	23.8	40.9	15.6
1965	5.2	12.2	17.8	23.9	40.9	15.5
1960	4.8	12.2	17.8	24.0	41.3	15.9
1955	4.8	12.2	17.7	23.7	41.6	16.8
1950	4.5	12.0	17.4	23.5	42.6	17.0
1945	4.6	10.9	16.9	24.2	43.5	16.7

The distribution of United States income—salaries, wages, and other earnings—has shown little change in the past forty-five years, and our current distribution is almost exactly as it was forty-five years ago. However, the trend from 1945 to 1970 was toward greater equality, and since 1970 greater inequality.
*Latest year available.
**Because the 1985 data were not published, those shown here are the average of the 1984 and 1986 figures.
Source: Statistical Abstract of the United States, 1947, 1952, 1957, 1962, 1967, 1972, 1977, 1982, 1987, 1991.

tions. The *Wall Street Journal* ("The Boss's Pay," 1990) surveyed America's 325 largest companies to determine what they paid their CEOs. The median annual compensation, including salaries and bonuses, came to $1 million a year. (Median means that half the CEOs received more than this amount, and half less.) This figure does *not* include their stock options. Those who exercised options earned an *additional* $428,000. (Nor does this figure include their income from investments—interest, dividends, capital gains.)

Imagine how you could live with an income like this. And that is precisely the point. Beyond the numbers lies a reality that profoundly affects people's lives. The differences in wealth between those at the top and the bottom mean vast differences in lifestyles—from choosing, on the one hand, between the French Riviera and the Swiss Alps for spring break or choosing, on the other, whether to spend the little money that remains at the laundromat or on milk for your children. The divisions of wealth in American society represent not "mere" numbers, but choices that make real differences in people's lives.

Power

With wealth comes power. We see this principle at work in our homes, in our towns—whether big or small—even in our high schools. This does not mean that every wealthy person has a lot of power, of course. Some wealthy people are content to simply watch their investments grow, and celebrities in show business and sports who have made many millions may make decisions that affect few lives. In general, however, power tends to follow money.

On the national scene, it is no different. About one-third of United States senators are millionaires. During the 1960s and 1970s, three of the Rockefeller brothers became state governors, and one the vice president of the United States. As recounted in the opening vignette of Chapter 9, John F. Kennedy became president, while his brother Teddy became a senator and his brother Bobby attorney general of the United States. With the huge Kennedy wealth and powerful political connections, even a succession of scandals was not enough to make Ted Kennedy resign his Senate seat—or defeat him in subsequent elections. The presidency continues to exemplify the political dominance of millionaire, white males from families with "old money."

TR#11M: How the Pay Gap Grew in the Eighties

TR#12M: The Percentage of the Nation's Income Received by Each Fifth and the Top Five Percent of America's Families Since World War II

CDQ 6: Can you explain why U.S. income divisions have changed very little over the past 45 years?

CDQ 7: Do you believe that the tasks performed by chief executive officers of the nation's largest corporations merit them being paid over $1 million a year each? Why or why not?

CDQ 8: Do you agree that "power tends to follow money?" Can you give examples?

Project 2

Many of the nation's leaders come from wealthy backgrounds.

Secretary Mosbacher

The president

K.P.: C. Wright Mills

Concentration in the Hands of a Few.   Back in the 1950s, sociologist C. Wright Mills (1956) was criticized for insisting that power was concentrated in the hands of the few, for his analysis contradicted the powerful ideological myth of equality. As discussed in earlier chapters, Mills coined the term "power elite" to refer to those who make the big decisions in American society. He and others have stressed how wealth and power coalesce in a group of individuals who share ideologies and values, belong to the same private clubs, hire the same bands for their daughters' debutante balls, and vacation at the same exclusive resorts. These shared backgrounds, contacts, ideologies, and vested interests all serve to reinforce their view of the world and of their special place in it (Domhoff 1974, 1978).

Like many people, you may have said to yourself, "Sure, I can vote, but somehow the big decisions are always made in spite of what I might think. Certainly *I* don't make the decision to send soldiers to Vietnam, Grenada, Panama, or Kuwait. *I* don't decide to raise taxes. It isn't *I* who decide to change welfare benefits."

And then another part of you may say, "But *I* do it through my representatives in Congress." True enough—as far as it goes. The trouble is, it just doesn't go far enough. Such views of being a participant in the nation's "big" decisions are a playback of the ideology we learn at an early age—an ideology that Marx said is put forward by the elites to both legitimate and perpetuate their power (Marger 1987). Sociologists Daniel Hellinger and Dennis Judd (1991) call this the "democratic facade" that conceals where the real power in American society lies.

The concentration of wealth in the hands of the few means that those few wield extraordinary power in American society. As one social analyst pointed out, those 325,000 families that own 40 percent of all corporate stock and business assets in the entire country virtually control corporate America (Stafford et al. 1986–87).

K.P.: G. William Domhoff

Sociologist G. William Domhoff (1990), continuing in the tradition of Mills, argued that the power of this group is so extensive that no major decision of the United States government is made without their approval. He has analyzed how this minority controls both the nation's foreign and domestic policy and how it makes decisions—from establishing Social Security rates to determining taxes and trade tariffs—working behind the scenes with elected officials. While Domhoff's conclusions are controversial—and alarming—they certainly follow logically from the principle that wealth brings power, and extreme wealth brings extreme power.

Prestige

Occupations and Prestige.   Table 10.2 illustrates how people rank occupations according to **prestige** (respect or regard). From this table, you can see how your parents' occupations, those of your neighbors, and the one that you are striving for all stacked up. Because of the movement toward a global society, this table also shows how the rankings of Americans compare with the residents of sixty other countries.

Why do people give some jobs more prestige than others? If you look at Table 10.2, you will notice that the jobs at the top have four elements in common.

1. They pay more;
2. They require more education;
3. They entail more abstract thought;
4. They offer greater autonomy (freedom, or self direction).

If we turn this around, we can see that people accord *less* prestige to jobs that pay less, require less preparation or education, involve more physical labor, and are closely supervised.

One of the more interesting aspects of these rankings is that they are remarkably consistent across countries and over time. People in every country, for example, rank college professors higher than nurses, nurses higher than social workers, and social

Project 3

CDQ 9: Are firefighters really less important to society (and thus should earn less) than professional football players? What about if your house is on fire?

prestige: respect or regard

Successful novelists such as Toni Morrison are accorded a high level of occupational prestige. While many writers, even well-regarded ones, are not necessarily wealthy, the large number of sales of her books has made Morrison comparatively rich.

TABLE 10.2 Occupational Prestige: How the United States Compares with 60 Countries

Occupation	United States	Average of 60 Countries	Occupation	United States	Average of 60 Countries
Supreme Court Judge	85	82	Professional Athlete	51	48
College President	82	86	Undertaker	51	34
Physician	82	78	Social Worker	50	56
Astronaut	80	80	Electrician	49	44
College Professor	78	78	Secretary	46	53
Lawyer	75	73	Real Estate Agent	44	49
Dentist	74	70	Farmer	44	47
Architect	71	72	Carpenter	43	37
Psychologist	71	66	Plumber	41	34
Airline Pilot	70	66	Mail Carrier	40	33
Electrical Engineer	69	65	Jazz Musician	37	38
Civil Engineer	68	70	Bricklayer	36	34
Biologist	68	69	Barber	36	30
Clergy	67	60	Truck Driver	31	33
Sociologist	65	67	Factory Worker	29	29
Accountant	65	55	Store Sales Clerk	27	34
Banker	63	67	Bartender	25	23
High School Teacher	63	64	Lives on Public Aid	25	16
Author	63	62	Bill Collector	24	27
Registered Nurse	62	54	Cab Driver	22	28
Pharmacist	61	64	Gas Station Attendant	22	25
Chiropractor	60	62	Janitor	22	21
Veterinarian	60	61	Waiter or Waitress	20	23
Classical Musician	59	56	Bellhop	15	14
Police Officer	59	40	Garbage Collector	13	13
Actor or Actress	55	52	Street Sweeper	11	13
Athletic Coach	53	50	Shoe Shiner	9	12
Journalist	52	55			

Source: Treiman 1977, Appendices A and D; Nakao and Treas 1991.

workers higher than janitors. Similarly, the occupations that were ranked high back in the 1950s are still ranked high in the 1990s—and likely will be in future decades.

Table 10.2 reveals a disadvantage of the objective method of studying social stratification, namely, how do you rank a two-career family? Should you use only the husband's occupation, only the wife's, or average their scores (which would really represent neither occupation)? In addition, how do part-time workers fit in? Note also that although occupations are the primary source of prestige for most people, they are not the only source. Some gain fame (prestige) through inventions, feats (mountain climbing, Olympic gold medals), or even doing good to others (Mother Teresa).

Displaying Prestige. For prestige to be of value, people must acknowledge it. In times past, the ruling elite even passed laws to emphasize their higher status. In ancient Rome, only the emperor and his family were allowed to wear purple, while in France only the nobility could wear lace. In England, no one could sit while the king was on his throne. Some kings and queens required that subjects depart by walking backwards—so that they never "turned their back" on the "royal presence."

In spite of today's much greater equality and the absence of consumption laws that specify who can and cannot wear particular clothing or colors, the elite continues to enforce its prestige. Western kings and queens expect curtsies and bows, while their Eastern counterparts expect their subjects to touch their faces to the ground. The American president enters a room only after others are present (to show that *he* isn't the one waiting for *them*). If seated, the others rise when the president appears and remain standing until he is seated, or, if he is going to speak without sitting first, until

Debutante balls are one way of displaying prestige.

he signals (gives permission) for them to sit. Military officers surround themselves with elaborate rules about who must salute whom, while uniformed officers in the courtroom assure that everyone stands when judges enter.

Most people are highly conscious of prestige, a fact that advertisers well know and exploit relentlessly. Consequently, designers can charge more for a particular item of clothing not because it is of better quality but because it displays a particular label. Similarly, people buy cars not only for transportation, but also for the particular vehicle's prestige value. (How does a BMW compare with a Yugo—not for power, but for prestige?) People gladly spend many thousands of dollars more for a home with a "good address," that is, one in a prestigious neighborhood. For many, prestige is a primary factor in deciding which college to attend. Everyone knows how the prestige of a generic sheepskin from Regional State College compares with a degree from Harvard, Princeton, Yale, or Stanford.

Among the thousands of ways in which people demonstrate prestige (and power and wealth) is to make others wait. The following story is told about President Truman.

> One day Winthrop Aldrich, the president of the Chase Manhattan Bank, sat for a half hour outside the president's office in the White House. When someone drew to the president's attention that such a powerful, prestigious individual was waiting, Mr. Truman replied:
>
> "When I was a United States senator and headed the war investigation committee, I had to go to New York to see this fella Aldrich. Even though I had an appointment he had me cool my heels for an hour and a half. So just relax. He's got a little while to go yet" (Schwartz 1991).

Status Inconsistency

As discussed earlier, income and property usually go together, as do wealth and power. In fact, ordinarily a person ranks at the same point on all three dimensions of social class—wealth, power, and prestige. The homeless men in the opening vignette are an example—as were John F. Kennedy and Mary Petrovitch in the opening vignette of Chapter 9. Sometimes the match is not there, however, and someone has a mixture of high and low ranks, a condition called **status inconsistency.** This leads to some interesting situations.

CDQ 10: How does making other people wait demonstrate a person's prestige? When you have a doctor's appointment, do you wait for your doctor or does your doctor wait for you?

Essay #2

Sociologist Gerhard Lenski (1954, 1966) pointed out that each of us tries to maximize our **status,** our social ranking. Thus individuals who rank high on one dimension of social class but lower on others will expect people to judge them on the basis of their highest status. Others, however, concerned about maximizing their own position, may respond to them according to their lowest status.

Sociologist Ray Gold (1952) studied status inconsistency among apartment-house janitors. Since they had unionized, they made more money than some of the people whose garbage they carried out. Tenants became especially upset when they saw their janitors driving newer and more expensive cars than they did. Some would attempt to "put the janitor in his place" by making "snotty" remarks to him, and instead of addressing him by name, they would say, "Janitor." For their part, the janitors took secret pride in knowing "dirty" secrets about the tenants, gleaned from their garbage.

Individuals with status inconsistency, then, are likely to confront one frustrating situation after another. They claim the higher status, but are handed the lower. The sociological significance of this condition, said Lenski, is that such persons are likely to be more radical and approve political actions aimed against higher status groups. Sociologist Gary Marx (1967) decided to test Lenski's hypothesis. Realizing that American society places a higher value on its white members, he wondered if African-American bankers and physicians—whose prestige may thus be low relative to their incomes and occupations—would be politically more radical than black janitors. Of course, common sense tells us that janitors, who are much worse off financially, must be more radical than bankers and physicians. Using a national sample, Marx found that African-American bankers and physicians were, in fact, more radical than African-American janitors. (Because his study was done in the 1960s, however, and the relative status of African Americans has changed since then, we need a retest to see how the situation is today.)

Would this principle also apply to college professors? They, too, suffer from status inconsistency, for although their prestige is very high, as we saw in Table 10.2, their incomes are relatively low. Hardly anyone in society is more educated, and yet college professors don't even come close to the top of the income pyramid. In line with Lenski's prediction, the politics of most college professors are, indeed, left of center. This hypothesis may also hold true *among* academic departments, that is, the higher a department's pay, the less radical are its politics. Teachers in departments of business and medicine, for example, are among the most highly paid in the university—and they are also the most politically conservative. This hypothesis is also likely to hold true *within* departments, for in general, regardless of the department, higher-paid members are more conservative, lower-paid members more liberal. Although age is a highly significant variable (age generally brings more conservative views of life and older teachers generally earn more than younger ones) status inconsistency may be part of the explanation. Only testing, of course, can determine the validity of these observations.

SOCIAL CLASS IN INDUSTRIAL SOCIETY

The question of how many social classes there are in contemporary industrial society is a matter of debate. Sociologists have proposed various models, but no model has gained universal support. There are two main models: one that builds on Marx, the other on Weber.

Updating Marx: Wright's Model

As discussed in Chapters 1 and 9, Marx argued that there are just two classes—capitalists and workers—with membership based solely on a person's relationship to the means of production. Sociologist Eric Wright (1979, 1985) wrestled with Marx's concept of social classes, realizing that not everyone falls neatly into these two categories. First, Marx's categorization of "workers" is much too broad to be applicable to today's conditions. Top executives, managers, and supervisors especially stand out. Although they are technically workers because they do not own the means of production, they act more like capitalists. In addition, some workers are "semiautonomous employees" and have considerable control over money and what they do with their labor.

Second, the category "capitalist" is also too broad. Take, for example, someone who owns a factory that employs one thousand workers. The owner's decisions, good or bad, directly affect one thousand families. Now take a successful automobile mechanic, whose good neighborhood reputation as a kid who loved cars, working out of his own backyard, grows until he quits his regular job and builds a large building with six bays and an office. This mechanic is now a capitalist, for he employs five or six other mechanics and owns the tools and building (the "means of production"); but he has little in common with the factory owner, who controls the lives of one thousand workers. His activities—even his lifestyle and consciousness—are entirely different.

Wright resolved this problem by regarding some people as simultaneously members of more than one class, having what he called **contradictory class locations.** By this Wright meant that the person's position in the class structure generates contradictory interests. For example, the automobile mechanic turned business owner may want his mechanics to have higher wages, since he has directly experienced their working conditions for most of his own working life. At the same time, his own interests—remaining profitable and competitive with other repair services—cause him to resist pressures to raise wages.

Taking contradictory class locations into account, Wright then modified Marx's analysis and identified four classes: (1) *capitalists* (or owners), who own enterprises and employ others; (2) *petty bourgeoisie,* who own small businesses; (3) *managers,* who sell their own labor but also exercise authority over other employees; and (4) *workers,* who simply sell their labor to others. As you can see, this model allows finer divisions than the one Marx originally proposed, yet it maintains the primary distinction between employer and worker.

Updating Weber: Gilbert's and Kahl's Model

Sociologists Dennis Gilbert and Joseph Kahl (1987) developed a six-class model to describe the class structure of the United States and other capitalist countries. Think of their model, illustrated in Figure 10.4, as a ladder. Our discussion will start with the highest rung and move downward. In line with Weber, on each lower rung you find less wealth, less power, and less prestige. Note that in this model education is also a primary criterion of class.

The Capitalist Class.   Only about 1 percent of the population can be included among the super-rich who occupy the very top rung of the class ladder. Their power is so great that their decisions open or close jobs for millions of people. Through their ownership of newspapers, radio stations, and television companies, together with their generous contributions to political parties, this elite class even helps to shape the consciousness of the nation. Its members perpetuate themselves by passing on to their children their assets and influential social networks.

Old Money.   The capitalist class can be divided into "old" and "new" money (Aldrich 1988). People whose wealth has been in the family longer have greater prestige. Many people entering the capitalist class have found it necessary to cut moral corners, at least here and there. This "taint" to the money disappears with time, however, and the later generations of Kennedys, Rockefellers, Vanderbilts, Mellons, DuPonts, Chryslers, Fords, Morgans, Nashes, and so on are considered to have "clean" money

K.P.: Dennis Gilbert and Joseph Kahl

L. Obj. 5: Discuss Gilbert and Kahl's updated model of Weber's perspective.

TR#16: The American Social Class Ladder

CDQ 13: Do you think there is really any difference in "old" and "new" money in the United States? Why or why not?

contradictory class location: Erik Wright's term for a position in the class structure that generates contradictory interests

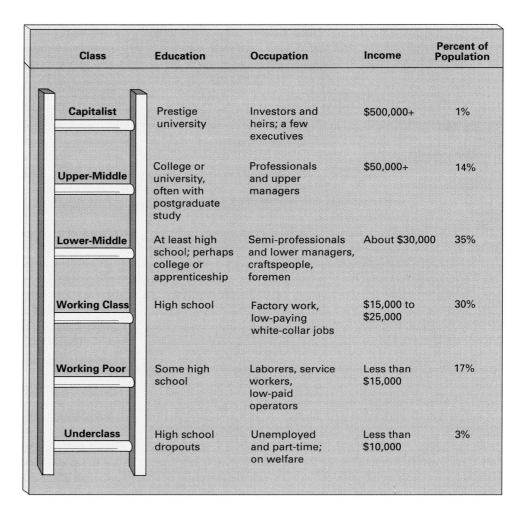

Class	Education	Occupation	Income	Percent of Population
Capitalist	Prestige university	Investors and heirs; a few executives	$500,000+	1%
Upper-Middle	College or university, often with postgraduate study	Professionals and upper managers	$50,000+	14%
Lower-Middle	At least high school; perhaps college or apprenticeship	Semi-professionals and lower managers, craftspeople, foremen	About $30,000	35%
Working Class	High school	Factory work, low-paying white-collar jobs	$15,000 to $25,000	30%
Working Poor	Some high school	Laborers, service workers, low-paid operators	Less than $15,000	17%
Underclass	High school dropouts	Unemployed and part-time; on welfare	Less than $10,000	3%

FIGURE 10.4 The American Social Class Ladder. (*Source:* Based on Gilbert and Kahl 1987.)

simply by virtue of the passage of time. Able to be philanthropic as well as rich, they establish foundations and support charitable causes. Subsequent generations attend prestigious prep schools and universities, male heirs are likely to enter law, and these old-money capitalists wield vast power as they protect their huge economic empires with extensive political connections and contributions (Domhoff 1983, 1990, 1991; Cookson and Persell 1985; Persell and Cookson 1986).

New Money. Those at the lower end of the capitalist class also possess vast sums of money and power, but it is new, and therefore suspect. Although these people may have made fortunes in business, the stock market, inventions, entertainment, or even sports, they have not gone to the right schools and lack the influential social networks that old money provides. Consequently, those with old money cannot depend on this newer group for adequate in-group loyalty. Their children, however, will ascend into the upper part of the capitalist class if they go to the right schools and marry old money.

The Upper-Middle Class. Of all the classes, the upper-middle is the one most shaped by education. Very few members of this class do not have at least a bachelor's degree, and many have postgraduate degrees in business, management, law, or medicine. These people manage the corporations owned by the capitalist class or else operate their own businesses or profession. As Gilbert and Kahl (1982) say, these positions may not grant prestige equivalent to a title of nobility in the Germany of Max Weber, but they certainly represent the sign of having "made it" in contemporary America. . . . Their income is sufficient to purchase houses and cars and travel that become public symbols for all to see and for advertisers to portray with words and pictures that connote success, glamour, and high style.

Consequently, parents and teachers push children to prepare themselves for upper-middle-class jobs. About 14 percent of the population belong to this class.

The Lower-Middle Class.

About 35 percent of the population belong to the lower-middle class. Members of this class follow orders on the job given by those who have upper-middle-class credentials. Their technical and lower-level management positions bring them a good living—albeit one constantly threatened by rising taxes and inflation—and they enjoy a generally comfortable, mainstream lifestyle. They usually feel secure in their positions and anticipate being able to move up the social class ladder.

The distinctions between the lower-middle class and the working class on the next lower rung are more blurred than those between other classes. As a result, these two classes run into one another. The prestige of lower-middle-class work is higher than that of the occupations of the working class, however, and their incomes are generally higher.

CDQ 14: Why do parents and teachers push children to prepare themselves for upper-middle-class jobs? Can everyone in the U.S. have such a job?

The Working Class.

This class consists of relatively unskilled blue-collar and white-collar workers who occupy highly routinized, closely supervised, manual and clerical jobs. Most of these workers have a high school education, their incomes are lower than those of the lower-middle class, and little prestige is attached to what they do. Their work is more insecure, and they are subject to layoffs during recessions. They feel vulnerable, but anticipate that layoffs will be temporary and that they will be able to support their families in a "simple but decent" manner. With only a high school diploma, the average member of the working class has little hope of climbing farther up the class ladder. Consequently, most concentrate on getting ahead by achieving seniority on the job rather than by changing their type of work. About 30 percent of the population belong to this class.

The Working Poor.

Members of this class, about 17 percent of the population, work at unskilled, low-paying temporary and seasonal jobs, such as share-cropping, migrant farm work, and day labor. Although many of the younger members of this class have high school diplomas, they are likely to have received them simply for putting in time and may be functionally illiterate, having difficulty reading even the want ads (see Chapter 17). The working poor are not likely to vote (Gilbert and Kahl 1987), for they feel that no matter what party is elected to political office it simply means "business as usual."

With little education, low and undependable income, and minimal prestige or even value placed on their work, the working poor live from paycheck to paycheck—when there is a paycheck, that is. Constantly in debt, many depend on food stamps to supplement their meager incomes. In old age they rely entirely on Social Security, since their jobs do not provide retirement benefits. Because they cannot save money or depend on steady work, members of this class run the risk of falling onto the lowest rung. High stress is part of their daily lives, and one of their greatest fears is ending up "on the streets."

CDQ 15: Why is the stress level so high among the working poor? Is this problem increasing in the 1990s?

The Underclass.

On the lowest rung, and with next to no chance of climbing anywhere, is the **underclass** (Wilson 1987; Ricketts and Sawhill 1988; Prosser 1991). Concentrated in the inner city, this group has little or no connection with the job market. Those who are employed, and some are, do only the most menial, low-paying, temporary work. Welfare is their main support and most members of other classes consider these people the ne'er-do-wells of society. Although life is the toughest in

underclass: a small group of people for whom poverty persists year after year and across generations

Migrant workers, who perform seasonal work at low wages, are members of the working poor.

this class, it is not hopeless and research shows that their children's chances of getting out of poverty are fifty-fifty (Gilbert and Kahl 1982:353). About 3 percent of the population fall into this class.

Social Class in the Automobile Industry

The example of the automobile industry aptly illustrates this social class ladder. The Fords, for example, own and control a manufacturing and financial empire whose net worth is truly staggering. Their power matches their wealth, for through their multinational corporation their decisions affect plants, production, and employment in many countries. The family's vast accumulation of money, not unlike its accrued power, is now several generations old. Consequently, Ford children go to the "right" schools, know how to spend money in the "right" way, and can be trusted to make family and class interests paramount in life. They are without question at the top level of the *capitalist* class.

Next in line come top Ford executives. Although they may have an income of several hundred thousand dollars a year (and some, with stock options and bonuses, earn well over $1 million annually), most are new to wealth and power. Consequently, they would be classified at the lower end of the capitalist class.

A husband and wife who own a Ford agency are members of the *upper-middle* class. Their income clearly sets them apart from the majority of Americans, and their reputation in the community is enviable. More than likely they also exert greater than average influence in their community, but their capacity to wield power is limited.

A Ford salesperson, as well as people who work in the dealership office, belongs to the *lower-middle* class. Although there are some exceptional salespeople, perhaps a few of whom make a lot of money selling prestigious, expensive cars to the capitalist class, salespeople at a run-of-the-mill local Ford agency are definitely lower-middle class. Compared with the owners of the agency, their income is less, their education is also likely to be less, and their work brings them less prestige.

A mechanic who repairs customers' cars is a member of the *working* class, although one who has risen in rank and now supervises the repair shop would be lower-middle class.

Window washers and janitors who are hired only during the busy season and then laid off, as well as those who "detail" used cars (making them appear newer by washing and polishing the car, painting the tires and floor mats, spraying "new car scent" into the interior, and so on) belong to the *working poor*. Their income and education are low, and the prestige accorded their work minimal.

Ordinarily, the *underclass* is not represented at all in the automobile industry. It is conceivable, however, that the agency might hire a member of the underclass, for the day or job only, to rake the grass or to clean up the used-car lot. In general, however, personnel at the agency do not trust members of the underclass and do not want to associate with them, even for a brief period. They prefer to hire someone from the working poor for such jobs.

Life Chances

Essay #4

CDQ 17: Why is money the single most significant factor in determining life chances?

The primary significance of social class is that it determines **life chances,** the probabilities concerning the fate an individual may expect in life. Obviously not everyone has the same chances in life, and in this society the single most significant factor in determining life chances is money. Simply put, if you have money, you can do a lot of things you can't do if you don't have it. The more money you have, the more control you have over your life, and the more likely you are to find life pleasant. Beyond this obvious point, however, lies a connection between social class and life chances that is not so evident. It is worth considering this matter in more detail.

A Matter of Life and Death.   Social class is so important to our lives that it even affects our chances of living and dying. The principle is simple: The lower a person's class, the more likely that individual is to die before the expected age. This principle holds true at all ages. Infants born to the poor are about *50 percent* more likely to die during their first year of life than are infants born into other classes (Gortmaker 1979). In old age—whether seventy or ninety—the poor are more likely to die of illness and disease. During both childhood and adulthood, the poor are also more likely to be killed by accident, fire, or homicide.

Speaker Sug. #2: A physician from a public, "charity" hospital or clinic in your city to talk about the problems of indigent patients.

CDQ 18: Why do you think people higher up the social class ladder tend to have better physical and mental health than those in the lower classes?

Physical and Mental Health

In addition to increased chances of dying earlier, a lower social class position adversely affects levels of physical and mental health during the life course. Part of the explanation for different death rates, for instance, lies in unequal access to medical care and nutrition. Medical care is expensive, and even with state-funded plans for the poor, the higher classes receive better medical treatment. Poorer people also suffer from inferior nutrition. It is difficult for them to afford balanced meals, and they are considerably less educated concerning nutrition. Their meals tend to be heavy in fats and sugars, neither of which is healthy. Table 10.3 contrasts typical diets of poorer and more affluent families.

Social class also affects mental health. Over and over, sociologists have found that the mental health of the lower classes is worse than that of the higher classes (Faris and Dunham 1939; Srole et al. 1978; Brown and Gary 1988; Ulrich et al. 1989). This difference reflects the greater stresses that those in the lower classes experience, such as unpaid bills, unemployment, dirty and dangerous work, the threat of eviction, unhappy marriages, and broken homes. Of course, people higher up the social class ladder also experience stress in daily life, but their stress is generally less and their coping resources greater. Not only can they afford vacations, psychiatrists, and counselors, but *their class position gives them greater control over their lives, a key to good mental health.*

TR#13M: Different Grocery Lists

Speaker Sug. #3: A psychiatrist who treats patients from diverse social classes to discuss the relationship between mental health/illness and social class.

life chances: the probabilities concerning the fate an individual may expect in life

TABLE 10.3 Different Grocery Lists

Lower income*	Higher income*
Refrigerated pizza	Melba toast
Pork rinds	Frozen Italian dinners (two foods)
Beef patties	Bottled grapefruit juice
Corn dogs	Frozen green beans
Frozen apple juice	Imported cheeses
Ramen noodles	Olive oil
Pizza mixes	Bottled water
Spiced lunch meat (e.g., Spam)	Fruit spreads
Hominy grits	Cranberry juice
Dried beans	Fresh mushrooms
Shortening (e.g., Crisco)	Liquid seasonings
Vienna sausage	Pure whipping cream
Powdered soft drinks (e.g., Kool-Aid)	Frozen carrots
Canned spinach	Nuts (cans or jars)
Canned peas	Frozen Italian dinners (one food)
Canned mixed vegetables	Exotic fruit juices
Cooking sauces (e.g., for Sloppy Joes)	Herbal tea
Instant coffee	Fresh cranberries
Sugar	Frozen yogurt
Powdered creamers	Caviar or canned lobster

The twenty items on this list are not the items that the groups buy the most, but those they buy most out of proportion to their representation in the population. The items are arranged in descending order. That is, items at the top of the list are most frequently purchased. Items at the bottom of the list, while purchased less, are still more likely to be purchased by the particular group.

*"Lower Income" is less than $5,000 annual income for each person in a family of two or more. "Higher Income" is $20,000 for each person in a family of two or more.

Source: Reprinted by permission of the *Wall Street Journal* © 1990 Dow Jones & Company, Inc. All Rights Reserved worldwide.

Below the Ladder: The Homeless

The homeless men described in the opening vignette of this chapter, and the women and children like them, are so far down the class structure that their position must be considered even lower than the underclass. Technically, the homeless are members of the underclass, but their poverty is so severe and their condition in life so despairing that we can think of them as occupying an unofficial rung below the underclass.

These are the people whom most Americans wish would just go away. Their presence on our city streets bothers passersby from the more privileged social classes—which includes just about everyone. "What are those obnoxious, foul-smelling people doing here, cluttering up my city?" appears to be a common response. Some people respond with sympathy and a desire to do something. But what? Almost all just shrug their shoulders and look the other way, despairing of a solution and somewhat intimidated by the presence of the homeless.

The homeless are the "fallout" of industrialization, especially of the postindustrial developments reviewed in Chapter 6. In another era, society would offer them work. Most would dig ditches, shovel coal, and run the factory looms, while some would explore and settle the West. Others would follow the lure of gold to California, Alaska, and Australia. Today, however, industrialized societies have little need of unskilled labor, and these people are left to wander aimlessly about the city streets.

CDQ 16: Do you think people are homeless because of their own personal habits or because of societal problems?

The homeless have virtually no property, power, or prestige.

CONSEQUENCES OF SOCIAL CLASS

As is apparent from our discussion of the class ladder—and of those who cannot climb even onto the first rung—social class makes fundamental differences to people's lives. Let's examine some of these implications of social class.

Family Life

Social class also has significant effects on family life. It influences married life, gender roles, and the nature of child rearing.

Marriage and Gender Roles. Marriages are more likely to fail in the lower social classes, and the children of the poor are thus more likely to grow up in broken homes. A primary reason is that insufficient income often creates tension, leading to fighting and, consequently, marital dissatisfaction. Also contributing to marital dissatisfaction are more rigid gender roles in the lower classes, where greater separation of activities by gender is deemed "proper."

Child Rearing. As discussed in Chapter 16, sociologist Melvin Kohn (1977) found significant class differences in child-rearing patterns. Lower-class parents are more concerned that their children conform to conventional norms and obey authority figures. Middle-class parents, in contrast, encourage their children to be more creative and independent, and tolerate a wider range of behaviors (except in speech, where they are not as tolerant of bad grammar and curse words).

Child rearing varies by class, Kohn concluded, primarily because the parents' occupations and respective visions of their children's futures differ markedly. Lower-class parents are closely supervised in their jobs, and they anticipate that their children will work at similar jobs. Consequently, they see a need for them to defer to authority. In contrast, parents from the more privileged classes work at jobs in which they enjoy greater creativity and self-expression. Anticipating similar work for their children, they encourage them to have greater freedom. Out of these contrasting orientations also

Project 4

L. Obj. 6: Examine the consequences of social class on life chances, physical and mental health, family life, values and attitudes, political involvement, religion, education, and the criminal justice system.

arise different ways of enforcing discipline; lower-class parents are more likely to use the stick, while the middle classes rely more on verbal persuasion.

Values and Attitudes

CDQ 19: Do you believe the government should intervene in the economy to make citizens financially secure? How do members of the working class feel about this?

Each social class can be thought of as a broad subculture with distinct approaches to life. As Marx would have said, the basic reason for class differences is people's relationship to the means of production. Consequently, social class has far-reaching effects on people's values and attitudes (Shingles 1989). For example, the working class feels much more strongly than other classes that the government should intervene in the economy to make citizens financially secure (Calloway and Tomaskovic-Devey 1989).

The capitalist class, in contrast, places stronger emphasis on family tradition—its ancestors, history, a sense of unity and even of purpose (or destiny) in life (Baltzell 1979; Aldrich 1989). Children in this class are more likely to need the approval of their parents in choosing a mate, for they learn that their choice affects not only them but the whole family unit, on which the mate will have an impact for generations to come. The capitalist class also emphasizes "breeding" and being "cultured." Although these terms refer to appropriate behavior in a variety of settings, such as proper speech and manners at formal gatherings, they also imply an attitude that encompasses life. There is simply a "right" way of doing things—and then there are the "other" ways, the customs of the lower classes.

CDQ 20: Why might the wealthy see designer labels as cheap and showy?

CDQ 21: Why do you think people in the lower classes are more likely to vote Democrat and those in the higher classes Republican?

Status Symbols. Status symbols, which reflect values and attitudes, vary with social class. Clearly, only the wealthy can afford certain items, such as yachts. But beyond affordability lies a class-based preference in status symbols. For example, Yuppies (young upwardly mobile professionals) are quick to flaunt labels and other material symbols to show that they have "arrived," while the rich, more secure in their status, often downplay such images. The wealthy see designer labels of the more "common" classes as cheap and showy. They, of course, flaunt their own status symbols, such as $20,000 Rolex watches.

Political Involvement

People in the lower classes are more likely to vote Democrat, those in the higher classes Republican. People understandably see political issues from their own corner in life, and the major political parties, like it or not, are seen as promoting different class interests. Political participation is not equal among the various social classes; in general, the higher the social class, the greater the political involvement (Gilbert and Kahl 1987). This principle applies not only to voting but also to working in political campaigns. This is one reason that the Republican party is able to win elections, although it has far fewer registered voters than the Democrats. (Forty-eight percent of American voters identify with Democrats, compared with only 41 percent who identify with Republicans, a difference of thirteen million voters—*Stastistical Abstract* 1991: Tables 452, 454.) Republicans are more likely to be well-to-do, and, thus, to campaign and vote.

People in the higher classes are more likely to be conservative on *economic* issues (favoring lower taxes and less government spending) and more liberal on *social* issues (favoring abortion, the Equal Rights Amendment, homosexual rights, legalized prostitution), while those from lower classes tend to be more liberal on economic issues and more conservative on social issues (Erikson, Luttberg, and Tedin 1980; Wolfinger and Rosenstone 1980; Syzmanski 1983).

Religion

CDQ 22: Can you give examples of how social class affects one's religion and education?

One area of social life that we might think would be unaffected by social class is religion. ("People are religious, or they are not. People are believers, or they are not.") This is not the case, however, for social class affects just about every aspect of religious orientation. First, members of the upper-middle class are more likely to attend church than are the lower classes. In fact, this pattern holds for all voluntary organizations— the lower classes are always less likely to belong or to participate. Second, as we shall discuss in Chapter 18, denominations broadly follow class lines. Episcopalians, for example, are much more likely to recruit from the middle and upper classes, while Baptists draw heavily from the lower classes. Methodists are more middle class, while most sects recruit almost exclusively from the lower classes. Patterns of worship also follow class lines: those that attract the lower classes have more spontaneous worship services and louder music, while those that draw mostly from the middle and upper classes are more restrained.

Education

TR#14: Percentage of Households with at Least One of Its Primary Family Members, 18–24 Years Old, in College

As shown in Figure 10.4, education levels increase in proportion to social standing. Parents in the more privileged classes push their children to do well in school, rewarding them for good grades and holding positive and negative role models before them. Because the American educational system is based on middle-class values, middle-class children feel more comfortable in school than their working-class counterparts, who are likely to find themselves in a strange environment and less pleasing to their teachers (Henslin, Henslin, and Keiser 1976). Consequently, children from the lower classes generally do less well and often drop out during their high school years (Wilson 1987).

As was apparent in the opening vignette of Chapter 9, the type of education also varies dramatically with social class. (This question is discussed more fully in Chapter 17.) Those who belong to the capitalist class bypass public schools entirely in favor of exclusive private schools, where their children are trained to take a commanding role in society. Some children of the upper-middle class attend less exclusive private schools, and with the exception of children who attend parochial schools, most of which are Roman Catholic, almost all children of the other classes go only to public schools.

The Criminal Justice System

Speaker Sug. #4: A public defender to speak on social class and the criminal justice system.

L. Obj. 7: Distinguish between the different types of social mobility and note some of the costs of such mobility.

CNN: Separate and Unequal

CDQ 23: Do you think everyone strives for upward social mobility? Why or why not?

Essay #5

If justice is supposed to be blind, it certainly is not when it comes to one's chances of being arrested (Hurst 1992). As discussed in Chapter 8, the white-collar crimes of the more privileged classes are likely to be dealt with outside the criminal justice system, while the street crimes of the lower classes are dealt with by the police. One consequence of this double standard is that members of the lower classes are far more likely to be on probation, on parole, or in jail. In addition, since people tend to commit crimes in or near their own neighborhoods, the lower classes are more likely to be robbed, burglarized, or murdered.

SOCIAL MOBILITY

No aspect of life, then, is untouched by social class. Because life is so much more comfortable in the more privileged classes, people strive for upward social mobility.

Intergenerational, Structural, and Exchange Mobility

Sociologists are especially interested in **intergenerational mobility,** the change that family members make in their social class from one generation to the next. Children are initially assigned the social class of their parents, but unlike the caste system we studied in the previous chapter, children can pass up their parents. If the child of a salesperson who works for an automobile agency, for example, goes to college, works as a salesperson in the agency during the summer, and eventually becomes the manager

intergenerational mobility: the change that family members make in social class from one generation to the next

upward social mobility: movement up the social class ladder

of the dealership, that person has experienced **upward social mobility.** Conversely, if a child of the agency's owner becomes an alcoholic, fails to get through college, and takes a lower-status job, he or she experiences **downward social mobility.**

Note that in these two examples, the mobility is directly attributable to the individual's behavior—hard work, sacrifice, and ambition on the one hand, versus indolence and alcohol abuse on the other. Some social mobility is due to such individual factors. But most sociologists consider the critical factor to be **structural mobility,** social changes that affect the status of large numbers of people. To understand what is meant by this term, think of the change from manual labor to factory machines and then to computers. To upgrade vast numbers of blue-collar jobs to white-collar positions makes millions of people upwardly mobile. The change in their status is due not to their individual efforts but to changes in the structure of society.

A third type of mobility is **exchange mobility.** This term refers to movement of people up and down the social class system, where, on balance, the system remains about the same. Suppose a working-class female goes to college and specializes in computers. After graduating, she lands a sales job with IBM, taking the place of a man who has been fired for not keeping up with his sales quota. This man grows despondent, nurses the bottle—and grudges—for several months, and then takes a job selling cars. In this example, one person has moved up to the lower-middle class while another has moved down to the working class. Seldom is exchange on a one-to-one basis, however; the term refers to general, overall movement of large numbers of people that leaves the class system basically untouched.

Social Mobility in the United States

How much movement is there on the American social class ladder? Studies of intergenerational mobility have focused on men, since the large numbers of women now in the work force are a relatively new phenomenon. Compared with their fathers, about one-half of all men have moved up, about one-third have stayed in the same place, and about one-sixth have moved down (Blau and Duncan 1967; Featherman and Hauser 1978; Featherman 1979). A major cause of this mostly upward trend is structural mobility, for most jobs in our society have been upgraded. By eliminating many blue-collar jobs and creating vast numbers of white-collar jobs, structural changes have made intergenerational mobility common.

If structural change has pushed the majority of workers into positions slightly ahead of their parents, though, it could also do the opposite. In other words, if the United States does not keep pace with global changes, its economic position may decline, resulting in fewer good jobs, lower incomes, and shrinking opportunities. In short, structural conditions can go either way, and vast mobility in the past is no guarantee for the future. A decline could thus lead to the frustrating position in which most Americans have slightly *less* status than their parents. Some social analysts think that this decline has already begun. The Thinking Critically section on page 269 illustrates some of the structural obstacles that Americans are currently facing.

Next to choosing one's parents (very wealthy, of course), the key to social mobility is education (Blau and Duncan 1967; Featherman and Hauser 1978; Sewell, Hauser, and Wolf 1980; Davis 1982). A person from the working poor who completes college, for example, makes an automatic jump in social class. As noted, however, members of the working poor are actually more likely to drop out of high school than those in the social classes above them.

Costs of Social Mobility

Social mobility can bring unexpected costs. Sociologists Richard Sennett and Jonathan Cobb (1988) studied working-class men and women in Boston who had made financial sacrifices so that their children could get ahead. The men worked long hours, were

---

CDQ 24: How much movement do you think there is on the American social class ladder?

K.P.: Jonathan Cobb

CDQ 25: What are some of the costs of social mobility? Can you give examples from your own experiences?

K.P.: Richard Sennett

---

downward social mobility: movement down the social class ladder

structural mobility: movement up or down the social class ladder that is attributable to changes in the structure of society, not to individual efforts

exchange mobility: about the same numbers of people moving up and down the social class ladder, such that, on balance, the social class system shows little change

seldom home, and, along with their wives, did without things to permit their children to finish high school and go on to college. The parents expected that their children would appreciate what they were doing for them, but to their dismay they found estrangement, lack of communication, bitterness, and confusion. Estrangement resulted because the father was seldom home and the children grew distant from him; lack of communication because the children's world of education was so remote from the parents' world that they no longer had much in common; bitterness because, instead of receiving appreciation for their deep sacrifice, the parents felt betrayal by this estrangement and lack of communication; and confusion, because, in their separate worlds, neither parents nor children understood one another.

THINKING CRITICALLY ABOUT SOCIAL CONTROVERSY

Upward Mobility for the American Worker—A Vanishing Dream?

Robert Middlecoff, a thirty-five-year-old Ohioan, spent most of the 1980s rebuilding furnaces at a metals foundry near Cleveland. When the plant closed in 1990, Middlecoff's $26,000-a-year job vanished with it. Today, while retraining himself for a career in computers, he and his wife live on her income of $15,400 and struggle to make their monthly mortgage payment of $611. Middlecoff worries about his chances of getting a new job in the computer field. He knows that even these jobs are scarce and that many employers look for college graduates to fill the positions.

Twenty-two years ago, Letitia Brown, daughter of a migrant worker, easily found work at an auto assembly plant in Flint, Michigan. Things are different now, however, for her son, Alphonse, who is caught in a spiral of intergenerational downward mobility. At twenty-eight, Alphonse has moved from one low-paying job to the next and has given up hope of joining the assembly line. Says his mother, "In Buick City, there's nobody left with less than thirteen or fourteen years' seniority. We're on our way back to being migrants."

Since 1979, out of twenty-one million manufacturing jobs, almost three million have disappeared—taking with them the dreams of upward mobility for millions of American workers like Robert Middlecoff and Alphonse Brown.

The hopes of many for upward mobility—even for stable employment—have been dashed by plant closings as the nation makes a wrenching adjustment to the postindustrial society. This demonstration took place in front of the corporate headquarters of General Motors in New York City.

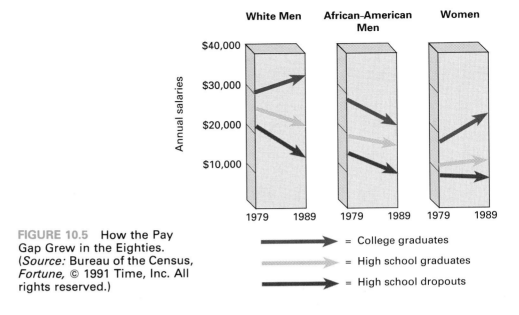

FIGURE 10.5   How the Pay
Gap Grew in the Eighties.
(*Source:* Bureau of the Census,
Fortune, © 1991 Time, Inc. All
rights reserved.)

This large-scale job displacement presents daunting challenges to American society. For generations, Americans considered a brighter future their birthright, and for
much of the period after World War II the nation's economy delivered. But today's
global economy is reserving its richest rewards for the highly educated or for those
working in jobs sheltered from foreign competition. The result is that millions of workers in the lower half of America's labor force are hitting a brick wall. They are doing
worse than they once did, or worse than their parents did, and working harder than
ever while falling further behind.

Despite the fact that United States manufacturers recorded a gain in productivity
during the 1980s, wages, adjusted for inflation, fell almost 2 percent during that decade.
Why did this happen? With foreign competition nipping at their heels, manufacturers
tried to translate productivity gains into lower product prices. Rising health care costs
also ate into workers' take-home pay. Also, unions grew weaker in the 1980s.

Hardest hit in this downward mobility spiral are those who either dropped out of
school or did not attend college. Following the usual pattern, African-American workers
have borne a heavier burden of widespread job displacement than have white workers.
The time between their losing a job and finding another has also been longer than that
for whites. Women are the only group of unskilled workers to post a gain. This seems
to be a bright spot—except that women still earn on average only 69 percent of what
men make.

What effect will this structural change in the economy have on you? If you graduate
from college with skills that can be applied to high technology, you're likely to fare well
and avoid the pain suffered by millions of unskilled workers. Figure 10.5 illustrates
how a college degree translates into higher earnings. Note that white males who
dropped out of high school in 1979 earned an averge of $20,000 (in 1989 dollars). Ten
years later, however, the picture for these men had turned gloomy, for by then their
income had dropped 24 percent. For white male graduates, however, the picture is
just the opposite. This group posted an 11 percent gain.

For African-American males, however, the picture is bleaker on all fronts. Wages
dropped for *both* college graduates and high school dropouts. This was probably because
of hiring freezes in the federal government and decreased emphasis on affirmative
action during the Reagan administration.

College, it appears, is worth the price of admission—at least for white males and
for all women. For African-American males, although the return on investment has

shrunk, college remains more attractive than the alternative of dropping out of high school or college. (*Source:* Based on Dentzler 1991; Fierman 1991; Kletzer 1991; Newman 1988; Nussbaum et al. 1992; O'Hare 1988; Olsen 1990.)

Where Is Horatio Alger?

The models of Horatio Alger did not die with the novels of an earlier America. They are alive and well in the psyche of Americans. From abundant, real-life examples of people from humble origins who climbed far up the social class ladder, Americans know that anyone can get ahead by *really* trying. In fact, they believe that most Americans, including minorities and the working poor, have an average or better than average chance of getting ahead—obviously a statistical impossibility (Kluegel and Smith 1986).

The accuracy of Horatio Alger is less important than the belief itself in *limitless possibilities for everyone.* Functionalists would stress that this belief is functional for society. On the one hand, it encourages people to compete for higher positions, or, as the song says, "to reach for the highest star." On the other hand, it places blame for failure squarely on the individual. If you don't make it—in the face of extensive opportunities to get ahead—the fault must be your own. The Horatio Alger belief helps to stabilize society, then, for since the fault is viewed as the individual's, not society's, current social arrangements are satisfactory. This reduces pressures to change the system.

POVERTY IN THE UNITED STATES

As illustrated in Figure 10.4, the working poor and underclass together form about 20 percent of the population of the United States. This percentage translates into a huge number, about fifty million people. Thus, poverty in the United States is a major public policy issue. The growing number of children in poverty poses an especially severe threat to this society.

Drawing the Line: What Is Poverty?

To define poverty, the United States government assumes that poor families spend one-third of their income on food and then multiplies a low-cost budget for food by three. Those whose incomes are lower than this amount are classified as below the poverty line. As sociologist Michael Katz observed (1989), this definition is unrealistic. It ignores changing standards of food consumption, does not allow for snacks, and assumes a careful shopper who cooks all meals at home and never has guests. Nevertheless, this is how the government draws the line that separates the poor from the nonpoor.

It is part of the magical sleight-of-hand of modern bureaucracy that a modification in this official measure of poverty instantly adds—or subtracts—millions of people from this category (Katz 1989; Ruggles 1990). Although the official definition of poverty does not make anyone poor, the way in which poverty is defined does have serious practical consequences. The government uses this definition to make choices about who will receive help and who will not. Based on this official definition of poverty, who in the United States is poor?

Who Are the Poor?

Race. Although two out of three poor people are white, in relationship to their numbers in the population racial minorities are much more likely to be poor. As Table 10.4 shows, only 10 percent of whites are poor, but 31 percent of African Americans and 26 percent of Hispanic Americans live in poverty.

CDQ 26: Do you agree that Horatio Alger belief helps to stabilize society? Why or why not?

L. Obj. 8: State the major characteristics of the poor in the United States. Indicate how the poverty line is drawn.

TR#14M: Percentage below the Poverty Line

CDQ 27: Why do you think that poverty in the United States is a major public policy issue?

Speaker Sug. #5: A supervisor from a welfare agency to discuss eligibility requirements and procedures for getting welfare benefits in your city.

Essay #6

CNN: New Poor

poverty line: the official measure of poverty calculated to include those whose incomes are less than three times a low-cost food budget

TABLE 10.4   Percentage of Americans Below the Poverty Line, by Race, Ethnicity, and Age+

	Whites	African Americans	Hispanic Americans
Overall	10.0	30.7	26.2
Elderly + +	10.0	32.2	22.4
Children + + +	14.1	43.2	35.5

+ In 1989, the poverty line was defined as an annual income of $6,311 for a single person, $8,076 for two persons, $9,885 for a family of three, $12,675 for a family of four, $14,990 for a family of five, and $16,921 for a family of six (*Statistical Abstract,* 1991, 430). To update these figures, add about $300 a year for one person, $375 for two, $450 for three, $600 for four, $700 for five, and $775 for six.

+ + The elderly are defined here as persons aged 65 and over.

+ + + Children are defined as persons under the age of eighteen. The poverty rate is *higher* for groups of younger children.

Source: Statistical Abstract of the United States, 1991: Tables 745, 746, 749.

Old Age.   As Table 10.4 also shows, old age has little effect on a person's likelihood of being poor, for the percentage of poor people over the age of sixty-five is practically the same as the overall percentage by race. A few years ago this was not the case, but changes in government policies concerning Social Security, subsidized housing, and subsidized food and medicine have significantly cut the rate of poverty among the elderly (see Chapter 13). Nevertheless, this consistency does mean that an elderly African American or Hispanic American is two or three times more likely to be poor than is an elderly white person.

Sex.   The greatest predictor of whether an American family is poor is not race, but the sex of the person who heads the family (U.S. Bureau of the Census, 1987). *Most poor families are headed by women* (Gimenez 1990). If a single-parent family is headed by a male, the poverty rate is 11 percent, close to the national average. If a female heads a single-parent family, however, that figure triples to 35 percent. The three major causes of this phenomenon, called **the feminization of poverty,** are divorce, births to unwed mothers, and the lower wages paid to women.

CDQ 28: What has contributed to the feminization of poverty in the United States? Can you give examples?

Project 5

CNN: Child Poverty

feminization of poverty: a trend in American poverty whereby most poor families are headed by women

The number of children living in poverty in the United States rose dramatically during the 1980s among all U.S. subgroups. Particularly hard hit have been Hispanic-American and African-American children. Fourteen percent of all white American children also live in poverty.

Children of Poverty: A New Social Condition?

Table 10.4 also shows that children are more likely to live in poverty than are adults in general or the elderly in particular. Note that this holds true regardless of race, but that poverty is much greater among minority children. More than one out of three Hispanic-American children and more than two out of every five African-American children are poor, astounding figures considering the wealth of this country and the supposed concern for children's well-being. This new, and tragic, aspect of poverty in the United States is the topic of the Thinking Critically section below.

THINKING CRITICALLY ABOUT SOCIAL CONTROVERSY

Children in Poverty

During the 1980s, children slipped into poverty faster than any other age group—and Hispanic-American children slipped the fastest. As Table 10.4 shows, more than one out of three Hispanic-American children are poor (a total of 2.6 million out of 7.2 million). The specific country of origin is significant; the child poverty rate is 48 percent for Puerto Ricans, 37 percent for Mexicans, 26 percent for Central and South Americans, and 24 percent for Cubans. Although the poverty *rate* grew fastest among Hispanic-American children, the proportion of African-American children who are poor, 43 percent, is still higher. At 14 percent, the poverty rate among white children is the lowest.

Why is child poverty growing fastest among Hispanic Americans? Several factors have been identified; among them low education and low-paying jobs among parents, an increase in divorce, an increase in households headed by females, discrimination, a greater likelihood that the head of the family is under thirty and a higher than average number of children in each household.

According to sociologist and United States Senator Daniel Moynihan, the overall increase in child poverty is due to a general breakdown in the American family, specifically a continuing increase in the rate of births outside marriage, which parallels the rate of child poverty. The overall rate of out-of-wedlock births, 26 percent, breaks down into 18 percent for whites and 64 percent for nonwhites. In 1960 only 5 percent of all children were born to unmarried mothers.

Regardless of causes—and there are many—the statement that children live in poverty can be as cold and meaningless as saying that their shoes are brown. Easy to overlook is the significance of this poverty. Poor children are more likely to die in infancy, to be malnourished, to develop more slowly, and to have more health problems. They are more likely to drop out of school, to become involved in criminal activities, and to have children while still in their teens—thus perpetuating the cycle of poverty.

Many social analysts—liberals and conservatives alike—are alarmed at the increase in child poverty in this country, believing that at the current overall rate child poverty represents a new social condition. They emphasize that it is time to stop blaming the victim, identify instead the structural factors that underlie child poverty, and relieve the problem by taking immediate steps to establish national programs of child nutrition and health care. Solutions, however, require fundamental changes: (1) removing obstacles to employment; (2) improving education; and (3) strengthening the family. To achieve these three fundamental changes, what specific programs would *you* recommend? (*Source:* Based on Cohen 1991; Duncan and Rodgers 1991; Lawton 1991; Moynihan 1991; Segal 1991; *Statistical Abstract of the United States,* 1991: Tables 746–749.)

While this may look like a scene from the Great Depression of the 1930s, it is not. This multigenerational gathering of male family members took place in a living room in Appalachia—in 1989.

Essay #7

L. Obj. 9: Contrast short and long-term poverty.

L. Obj. 10: Assess individual versus structural explanations of poverty.

Project 6

culture of poverty: the assumption that the values and behaviors of the poor make them fundamentally different from other people and that these factors are largely responsible for their poverty

Short-Term and Long-Term Poverty

In the 1960s Michael Harrington (1962) and Oscar Lewis (1966) suggested that some of the poor get trapped in a **culture of poverty.** Their assumption was that the values and behaviors of the poor "make them fundamentally different from other Americans, and that these factors are largely responsible for their continued long-term poverty" (Ruggles 1989:7).

Economist Patricia Ruggles (1989, 1990) wanted to see if this was true. Was there a self-perpetuating culture, transmitted across generations, which kept its members in poverty? If so, it would certainly confirm common stereotypes of the poor as lazy people who bring poverty on themselves. After studying national statistics, Ruggles found that about half the poor are *short-term poor;* that is, they move out of poverty within a few months, a year, or at most a few years. About half are *long-term poor,* whose poverty lasts at least eight years. Even most of the long-term poor will eventually move out of poverty, however, for contrary to popular belief, very few people pass poverty across generations. In fact, most children of the poor do not grow up to be poor. Only about 20 percent of those who are poor as children are still poor when they are adults (Corcoran et al. 1985; Sawhill 1988; Ruggles 1989).

Since the number of people in poverty remains fairly constant year after year, however, this means that in any given year about as many people move into poverty as move out of poverty. In addition, although most people who are poor today will not be poor in just a few years, about 1 percent of the American population—two and a half million people—remain poor year in and year out. They were poor twenty years ago, and they are poor today. Ruggles found that most of this group have three primary characteristics: they are African American, unemployed, and live in female-headed households. About half are unmarried mothers with children.

Individual versus Structural Explanations of Poverty

We have a choice of placing blame either on the poor or on social conditions. On the one hand, we can believe the stereotypes of people as poor because of their own inadequacies, such as laziness or lack of intelligence. On the other hand, we can look at social structure as the reason for poverty. Sociologists accept this second explanation of why people are poor—looking to such factors as inequalities in education and access to learning job skills, as well as other forms of discrimination and large-scale economic changes. For example, because American society now needs relatively few unskilled workers, large numbers of unskilled people are unemployed or work only at marginal jobs that pay poverty incomes (see Chapter 14). Others are held back by racial, ethnic, age, and gender discrimination. The sociological approach, then, is to examine the structural features of society that create poverty.

Occasionally even well-intentioned scholars, however, blame the poor for their poverty. Edward Banfield (1974), for example, argued that orientation to time helps to explain poverty. Banfield noticed that the poor are inclined toward immediate gratification, while the middle class opt for **deferred gratification,** that is, forgoing something in the present for the sake of greater gains in the future. From this, he concluded that the "present orientation" of the one keeps them in poverty, while the "future orientation" of the other keeps them out of poverty.

Let's take a closer look at life on the bottom and see how it is easy to mistake these behaviors as the cause rather than the consequence of people's class positions. As we have seen, poverty is brutal. The poor face more illnesses, accidents, malnourishment, street crimes, and unemployment than do members of other social classes. They have less education, less hope, and little or no control over what happens to them in life. Indeed, not knowing what is going to happen next is one of the primary characteristics of poverty. The future is a series of question marks, punctuated by one emergency after another.

Can a person living in poverty plan far ahead? How, when tomorrow may bring even more problems than today brought? From this perspective, the desire for immediate gratification can be seen to be *a consequence, not a cause,* of the situations that the poor face on a daily basis. Sociologist Elliot Liebow (1967), who studied African-American street corner men in Washington, D.C., noted that these men, who live in abject poverty, are just as concerned about the future as anyone—only they perceive their future accurately—and it looks bleak. Consequently, lacking any grounds for the promise of something better, they conclude that they may as well enjoy what they have at the moment, for tomorrow is not likely to bring any improvement. In other words, their immediate gratification is not the cause of their poverty, but an accurate reflection of their life situation.

Deferred gratification among the middle classes is equally a reflection of their life situation, for they have a surplus that they can deposit in a bank and retrieve safely at their leisure. As Liebow points out, the poor also save, but their savings come in a form invisible to the middle class: They buy material items such as musical instruments and watches, from which they can get practical use, and yet pawn in an emergency.

Poor people would love the chance to practice deferred gratification, but they have little or nothing to defer. If the daily reality of the middle class were an old car that runs only half the time, threats from the utility company to shut off the electricity and gas, and a choice between buying medicine, diapers, and food or paying the rent, their orientations to life would surely undergo a radical change. Again, the behaviors of the poor are driven by their poverty more than they are a cause of it.

As Marx and Weber pointed out, social class penetrates our consciousness, shaping our ideas of life and our proper place in society. When the rich look around, they see superiority, purpose, and control. In contrast, the poor see defeat, haplessness, and unpredictable forces. Each knows the dominant ideology, that their particular niche in life is due to their own efforts—that the reasons for success—or failure—lie solely with the self (Newman 1988; Shepelak 1989; Gatewood 1990; Hurst 1992). Like the fish not seeing water, people tend not to see the effects of social class on their own lives.

CDQ 29: Do you think a person living in poverty can plan far ahead? Why or why not?

CDQ 30: Why do you think people tend not to see the effects of social class on their own lives?

deferred gratification: forgoing something in the present in the hope of achieving greater gains in the future

SUMMARY

1. Sociologists do not agree on how many social classes there are. According to Karl Marx, there are only two: capitalists who own the means of production and workers who sell their labor. Most sociologists follow Max Weber's analysis and think of social classes as made up of wealth (property and income), power, and prestige. The three methods of measuring social class are subjective, reputational, and objective.

2. Several models of the class structure of industrial society have been proposed. Wright, who modified Marx, suggested a model of four classes: capitalists, managers, petty bourgeoisie, and workers. Gilbert and Kahl, whose model is used here, proposed six classes: capitalist, upper-middle, lower-middle, working class, working poor, and the underclass.

3. Wealth, power, and prestige are concentrated in the upper classes. The top 10 percent of American families own 68 percent of the wealth of the entire nation. If the highest income were the size of Mount Everest, the average American would stand but 4 feet off the ground. The distribution of wealth has changed little over the past couple of generations, and the poorest and richest quintiles in the nation now receive about the same share of the country's wealth as they did in 1945. The trend of the past two decades has been toward greater inequality of income.

4. The occupations with the greatest and lowest prestige have changed little over the decades, and are quite similar from country to country. Occupations that pay more and require more education and thinking are accorded greater prestige. Getting others to acknowledge one's prestige is a common endeavor. The social classes have different styles of status symbols.

5. Most people are status consistent; that is, they rank high or low on all three dimensions of social class. People who rank higher on some dimensions than on others are status inconsistent. In general, they want others to act toward them on the basis of their highest status. Concerned about their own ranking, however, people tend to interact on the basis of the others' lowest status. The frustrations of status inconsistency tend to produce political radicalism.

6. Social class membership leaves no aspect of social life untouched. Its primary significance is the determination of people's life chances. An individual's chances of dying early, receiving good health care and nutrition, becoming mentally ill, and getting divorced are all related to social class. Class membership also affects child-rearing patterns, values and attitudes, politics, religion, education, and involvement in the criminal justice system.

7. Three types of social mobility are intergenerational, exchange and structural. Most American men have a status higher than their fathers, largely due to structural mobility. An indication that upward social mobility has slowed down and will be less common in coming years is the flattening of family income in spite of the increase in two-income families. The future of social mobility depends on how the United States fares in the international markets. Parents who make sacrifices for the social class advancement of their children experience unexpected costs.

8. The Horatio Alger myth is functional for American society because it encourages people to strive to get ahead and places the blame for failure on individuals, not on society. Those most likely to be poor are racial minorities, children, and women. The elderly are no longer more likely than other members of society to be in poverty.

9. Some social analysts believe that characteristics of the poor, such as a desire for immediate gratification, cause poverty. Sociologists, in contrast, examine structural features of society, such as employment opportunities and discrimination, to find the causes of poverty. Sociologists generally conclude that life orientations are a consequence of one's position in the social class structure, not its cause.

SUGGESTED READINGS

Domhoff, G. William. *The Power Elite and the State: How Policy Is Made in America.* New York: Aldine de Gruyter, 1990. The author analyzes the network of social power that underlies the major social policy decisions of the United States—and the plans of the power elite for a world economic order.

Ehrenreich, Barbara. *Fear of Falling: The Inner Life of the Middle Class.* New York: Harper Collins, 1990. Ehrenreich dissects the middle class by examining a wide variety of sources, including films, child-rearing manuals, and even the "class cues" built into clothing, furniture, and shopping habits. She also explains why from the 1960s to the 1980s the professional middle class "retreated from liberalism" to a "meaner, more selfish outlook, hostile to the aspirations of those less fortunate."

Gatewood, Willard B. *Aristocrats of Color: The Black Elite, 1880–1920.* Bloomington, Ind.: Indiana University Press, 1990. Analyzing the rise and decline of the African-American upper class that developed after the Civil War, Gatewood focuses on marriage, occupations, education, religion, clubs, and relationships with whites and with African Americans of lower classes.

Gilbert, Dennis, and Joseph A. Kahl. *The American Class Structure: A New Synthesis.* 3rd ed. Homewood, Ill.: Dorsey Press, 1987. Two sociologists provide an overview of social stratification in the United States.

Himmelfarb, Gertrude. *Poverty and Compassion: The Moral Imagination of the Late Victorians.* New York: Knopf, 1991. This account of poverty and the system of charity in Victorian

England shows that the question of structural and individual causes of poverty is not new.

Hurst, Charles E. *Social Inequality: Forms, Causes, and Consequences*. Boston: Allyn & Bacon, 1992. Hurst analyzes social stratification in the United States.

Katz, Michael B. *The Undeserving Poor: From the War on Poverty to the War on Welfare*. New York: Pantheon, 1989. Katz looks at major changes in social policy regarding poverty and examines why Americans define poverty in terms of family, race, and culture rather than in terms of inequality, power, and exploitation.

Rodgers, Harrell R., Jr. *Poor Women, Poor Families*. Armonk, N.Y.: M. E. Sharpe, 1987. The author analyzes poverty among women, emphasizing how the picture has changed during the past thirty years.

Steinitz, Victoria Anne, and Ellen Rachel Solomon. *Starting Out: Class and Community in the Lives of Working-Class Youth*. Philadelphia: Temple University Press, 1986. Contrasting the experiences of youths in three working-class communities, the authors explore the high value placed on loyalty, responsibility, and interdependence.

Vanneman, Reeve, and Lynn Weber Cannon. *The American Perception of Class*. Philadelphia: Temple University Press, 1987. This overview of class consciousness among Americans emphasizes how the working poor perceive class.

Wilson, William Julius. *The Truly Disadvantaged: The Inner City, the Underclass, and Public Policy*. Chicago: University of Chicago Press, 1987. The author looks at how the conditions of the black urban poor have deteriorated and suggests what can be done to improve matters.

CHAPTER *11*

Alan Feltus, Piero Letters, *1991*

Inequalities of Gender

WHY ARE MALES AND FEMALES DIFFERENT?
Biology or Culture? The Continuing Controversy ■ *Thinking Critically about Social Controversy—Biology versus Culture* ■ An Emerging Position in Sociology? ■ The Question of Superiority

WOMEN AS A MINORITY GROUP
Cross-Cultural Gender Inequality: Sex-Typing of Work ■ Cross-Cultural Gender Inequality: Prestige of Work ■ The Genesis of Female Minority Status

GENDER INEQUALITY IN AMERICAN SOCIETY
Fighting Back: The Rise of Feminism ■ Gender Inequality in Education: Creating Sex-Linked Aspirations ■ *Down-to-Earth Sociology:* **Making the Invisible Visible—The Deadly Effects of Sexism** ■ Gender Inequality in Everyday Life

GENDER INEQUALITY IN THE WORKPLACE
Women in the Work Force ■ Discrimination in Hiring ■ The Pay Gap ■ The "Mommy Track" ■ Sexual Harassment ■ *Perspectives:* **Sexual Harassment in Japan** ■ *Down-to-Earth Sociology:* **Women on Wall Street—From Subtle Put-Downs to Crude Sexual Harassment**

GENDER INEQUALITY AND VIOLENCE: THE CASE OF MURDER

WHY DON'T WOMEN TAKE OVER POLITICS AND TRANSFORM AMERICAN LIFE?

CHANGES IN GENDER RELATIONS

GLIMPSING THE FUTURE—WITH HOPE

SUMMARY

SUGGESTED READINGS

The teenage girls crept cautiously through the jungle. Blending into the silent streams of dawn, machine guns at their sides, the shadowy figures quickly stepped across the narrow opening. Masked by the thick veil of foliage, they waited for those carrying the T-81 Chinese assault rifles. The last to cross were the three with rocket launchers.

"Ready?" whispered Kamir. Eyes glistening, the other young women nodded. Suddenly, the morning's silence was pierced by a lethal barrage. Panicked, the Sri Lankan troops tried to flee, only to be cut down by gunfire from all sides. Leaving the soldiers writhing in death agonies, the women slipped back into the jungle's cover, as silently as they had arrived.

The Tamils of Sri Lanka used to consider warfare to be "men's work." But all that changed when teenage girls joined Tamil separatists in their armed struggle for independence. Tamils traditionally believe that women should be demure, quietly blending into the background. But in the present circumstances, they have little time for such views. Maybe later.

What makes a man masculine and a woman feminine? The answer, stress most sociologists, is socialization into a culture's expectations concerning masculinity and femininity. The changes experienced by Tamil women, depicted here and featured in the opening vignette, vividly illustrate this point.

And then, again, maybe not. The Tiger women, as they are called, operate checkpoints twenty-four hours a day. They drive heavy trucks captured from the Indian army and take part in active combat. And like the Tiger men, each young woman wears a cyanide capsule around her neck. If capture is imminent, rather than being questioned by the enemy—and almost certainly raped and tortured—they bite into that capsule. (Based on an *Associated Press* report of March 29, 1990.)

Fierce revolution has ripped Tamil society apart. Of their traditional roles, relationships, and institutions nothing remains untouched. When the war ends, all will have to be reconstructed, a new culture astride the past and the present. What that new culture will be is not the subject here, although it would be fascinating to observe the transformation. What is significant for our purposes is the role that young Tamil women are playing in their revolution and the way in which the Tamil definition of "feminine" behavior has been transformed. We will return to this point later.

This chapter examines **gender stratification**—men's and women's unequal access to power, prestige, and property on the basis of sex. Gender stratification is especially significant because it cuts across all aspects of social life. No matter what social class people belong to, they are still stratified by gender (Huber 1990). We shall first try to understand why males and females are different from one another, next look at inequality between the sexes around the world, and then examine inequalities between men and women in American society in everyday life, education, and work. In examining male-female relationships, we shall review such topics as sexual harassment, unequal pay, and different patterns in murder, as well as consider why, since females make up more than 50 percent of the population, they don't take over American politics. We shall also review current changes in gender relationships.

L. Obj. 1: Define gender stratification and differentiate between sex and gender.

Essay #1

gender stratification: men's and women's unequal access to power, prestige, and property on the basis of their sex

sex: biological characteristics that distinguish females and males, consisting of primary and secondary sex characteristics

WHY ARE MALES AND FEMALES DIFFERENT?

When we consider how females and males differ, the first thing that usually comes to mind is **sex,** the *biological* characteristics that distinguish males and females. *Primary sex characteristics* consist of a vagina or a penis and other organs related to reproduction; *secondary sex characteristics* refer to the physical distinctions between males and females that are not directly connected with reproduction. Secondary sex characteristics become clearly evident at puberty when males develop more muscles, a lower voice, and more hair and height; while females form more fatty tissue, broader hips, and larger breasts.

Gender, in contrast, is a *social,* not a biological characteristic. Gender, which varies from one society to another, refers to what a group considers proper for its males and females. Whereas sex refers to male or female, gender refers to masculinity or femininity. In short, you inherit your sex, but you learn your gender as you are socialized into specific behaviors and attitudes. The sociological significance of gender is that it serves as a primary sorting device by which society controls its members. Ultimately, gender determines the nature of people's access to their society's system of power, property, and even prestige. Gender, then, is much more than what you see when you look at people. Like social class, reviewed in Chapter 10, gender is a structural feature of society.

Before examining inequalities of gender, let us consider why men and women differ socially. Are they, perhaps, just "born that way"?

Biology or Culture? The Continuing Controversy

Why do males and females act differently? For example, why are most males—unlike the Tamil—more aggressive than most females? Why do females tend to enter "nurturing" occupations such as nursing and child care in far greater proportions than males? To answer such questions, most people respond with some variation of, "They are just born that way."

Is this the correct answer? Certainly biology plays a significant role. Each individual begins as a fertilized egg. The egg, or ovum, is contributed by the mother, the sperm that fertilizes the egg by the father. At the very moment the egg is fertilized, the individual's sex is determined. Each person receives twenty-three pairs of chromosomes from the ovum and twenty-three from the sperm. The egg has an X chromosome. If the sperm that fertilizes the egg also has an X chromosome, the embryo becomes female (XX). If the sperm has a Y chromosome, it becomes male (XY).

Does this difference in biology account for differences in male and female behaviors? Does it, for example, make females more comforting and more nurturing, and males more aggressive and domineering? While almost all sociologists take the side of "nurture" in this "nature versus nurture" controversy, a few do not, as you can see from the Thinking Critically section on page 282.

Sociologists find most compelling the argument that if biology were the principal factor in human behavior, around the world we would find women to be one sort of person and men another. But consider the opening vignette. Certainly the emergence of female warriors in Tamil society was due to changes in their social conditions, not to changes in their biology. Sociologists who consider socialization to be the answer (whose position is summarized in the Thinking Critically section) point to such instances as conclusive evidence. Such examples are so self-evident, they say, that there is really little reason to continue the discussion. In contrast, other sociologists (whose positions are summarized in the same section) disagree sharply. They concede that the changed behavior of Tamil females was due to changed conditions, but claim that the Tamils represent only a specific, momentary *overcoming* of basic biological predispositions. Female warriors are not unknown to the world; they are just rare. When the revolution is over, as has happened in all previous instances in the world, the Tamil women will resume behaviors more in keeping with their biological predispositions.

Although this controversy is far from resolved, the dominant sociological position is that gender differences come about because every society in the world uses sex to mark its people for special treatment (Epstein 1988). Sorted into separate groups, males and females learn contrasting expectations in life and are given different access to their society's privileges. As symbolic interactionists stress, the visible differences of sex do not come with meanings built into them. Rather, society interprets those

Project 1

L. Obj. 2: Discuss the continuing controversy regarding biological and cultural factors which come into play in creating gender differences in societies.

CDQ 1: Which do you think is most significant in explaining why males and females act the way they do—biology or culture? Why?

gender: the social characteristics that a society considers proper for its males and females; masculinity or femininity

CDQ 2: Can you explain why gender is the primary division between people in every society? In what ways is this true in the United States?

physical differences, and males and females thus take their relative positions in life according to the meaning that a particular society assigns them.

In every society, gender is *the* primary division between people. Each society possesses its own set of expectations of what is appropriate for males and females. To try to guarantee *the differences that it expects,* each society socializes males and females into different behaviors and attitudes. Similarly, each society sets up barriers that provide unequal access on the basis of sex.

THINKING CRITICALLY ABOUT SOCIAL CONTROVERSY

Biology versus Culture—Culture Is the Answer

For sociologist Cynthia Fuchs Epstein, differences between men's and women's behavior are solely the result of social factors—socialization and social control. Her argument is as follows.

1. Just because an idea has been around for as long as anyone can remember does not mean that it is inevitable or based on physiology. Would anyone make the argument that antisemitism, child abuse, or slavery are biologically determined? Yet a new group of "experts," sociobiologists, "feel comfortable believing that the subordination of women is inevitable, programmed into human nature." This argument is simply a defense by the oppressors and is no more legitimate than the Nazis' argument that they were the master race and Jews inferior subhumans.

2. A reexamination of the anthropological record shows greater equality between the sexes in the past than we had thought. Women in earlier societies participated in small-game hunting, devised tools for hunting and gathering, and gathered food along with men.

3. Studies of current hunting and gathering societies also show that "both women's and men's roles have been broader and less rigid than those created by stereotypes. For example, the Agta and Mbuti are clearly egalitarian and thus prove that hunting and gathering societies exist in which women are not subordinate to men. Anthropologists who study them claim that there is a separate but equal status of women at this level of development."

4. If gender differences were due to physiology, wouldn't societies depend on "instinct" for their division of labor? Instead, however, the "types of work that men and women perform in each society are stipulated by the society, allowing few individuals to make choices outside the prescribed range." To keep women in line and males dominant, extensive social machinery has been developed—from a raised eyebrow to laws and social customs that separate men and women into "sex-appropriate" activities.

5. Biology does "cause" certain human behavior, but it is limited to reproduction or body structure that allows or inhibits social access, "such as playing basketball or crawling through a small space."

6. As studies show, once discrimination in occupations is removed, women "exhibit similar work force commitment and turnover rates." The cause of occupational differences is social discrimination, not biology.

7. The rising status of women in the United States and in other parts of the world invalidates the idea that women's subordination is constant and universal. Female crime rates are growing closer to those of males, again indicating a change in behavior due to social conditions, not a change in biology. Women are participating in "adversarial, assertive, and dominant behavior" at all levels of the judicial system. Not incidentally, their "dominant behavior" also shows up in scholarly female challenges to the biased views about human nature that have been proposed by male scholars.

In short, it has been social factors—socialization, exclusion from opportunity, disapproval, and other forms of social control—not "women's incompetence or inability to read a legal brief, to perform brain surgery, [or] to predict a bull market . . . that has kept them from interesting and highly paid jobs." Arguments "which indicate an evolutionary and genetic basis of hierarchy affixed to sex status" are simplistic. They "rest on a dubious structure of inappropriate, highly selective, and poor data, oversimplification in logic and inappropriate inferences by use of analogy." (*Source:* Epstein 1986, 1988, 1989.)

Biology versus Culture—Biology Is the Answer

Sociologist Steven Goldberg finds it astonishing that anyone should doubt "the presence of core-deep differences between men and women, differences of temperament and emotion we call masculinity and femininity." His argument, that it is not the environment but inborn differences that "give masculine and feminine direction to the emotions and behavior of men and women," is summarized below.

1. An examination of the original studies of societies from around the world shows that not one of the thousands of societies (past and present) for which evidence exists lacks patriarchy. Stories about past **matriarchies** (societies in which women dominate men) are simply myths; they don't make good history, and if you believe those you may as well believe the myths about cyclopes.

2. "All societies that have ever existed have associated political dominance with males and have been ruled by hierarchies overwhelmingly dominated by men."

3. In all societies, the highest status nonmaternal roles are associated with males.

4. Just as a six-foot woman does not prove the social basis of height, so exceptional individuals, such as a highly achieving and dominant woman, do not refute "the physiological roots of behavior."

5. The values, songs, and proverbs in every society "associate dominance with the male in male-female relationships and encounters."

6. Of the thousands of societies of which we have evidence, not a single one reverses male and female expectations. "Why," he asks, "does every society from that of the Pygmy to that of the Swede associate dominance and attainment with males?" The argument that males are more aggressive because they have been socialized that way is the equivalent of a claim that men can grow moustaches because boys have been socialized that way.

In other words, the world's patterns of socialization and social institutions have not developed independent of "psychophysiological tendencies." Rather, socialization and social institutions merely reflect—and sometimes exaggerate—those inborn tendencies. Societies around the world expect males to dominate because that is what their members observe. They then *reflect* this natural tendency in their socialization and social institutions.

In short, males "have a lower threshold for the elicitation of dominance behavior . . . a greater tendency to exhibit whatever behavior is necessary in any environment to attain dominance in hierarchies and male-female encounters and relationships." Males have "greater willingness to sacrifice the rewards of other motivations—the desire for affection, health, family life, safety, relaxation, vacation and the like—in order to attain dominance and status."

This principle does not apply to every male or every female but to statistical averages. And those averages, in large numbers, become determinative. Only one interpretation of the cross-cultural evidence of why these social institutions "always work in the same direction" is valid. Male dominance of society is simply "an inevitable social resolution of the psychophysiological reality." Any interpretation other than inborn differences is "wrongheaded, ignorant, tendentious, internally illogical, discordant with the evidence, and implausible in the extreme."

While this reality does lead to discrimination against women, whether or not one approves the results is not the point. The point is that this is the way humans are, regardless of how we feel about it or may wish it were different. (*Source:* Goldberg 1974, 1986, 1989.) ■

matriarchy: a society in which women dominate men

Speaker Sug. #1: A specialist in gender roles.

K.P.: Alice Rossi

An Emerging Position in Sociology?

Without losing sight of the social experiences that mold femininity and masculinity or taking the extreme position that biology determines human behavior, many sociologists acknowledge that biological factors may be involved. Alice Rossi (1977, 1984), a feminist sociologist and former president of the American Sociological Association, has suggested that women are better prepared biologically for "mothering" than are men, that women are more sensitive to such stimuli as the infant's soft skin or their nonverbal communications. Her basic point is that it is not necessary to take an either-or position. The issue is not biology *or* society; it is that nature provides biological predispositions, which are then overlaid with culture (Cf, Renzetti and Curran 1992).

This assumption is supported by a bizarre case, one that no ethical experimenter would dare to have attempted. The drama began in 1963, when seven-month-old identical twin boys were taken to a doctor for a routine circumcision (Money and Ehrhardt 1972). The inept physician, who was using electrocautery (a heated needle), turned the electric current too high and accidentally burned off the penis of one of the boys. You can imagine the parents' reaction of disbelief—followed by horror as the truth sank in.

CDQ 3: If it were impossible to tell whether your own newborn child was a male or female, how would you deal with the situation?

What can be done in a situation like this? The damage was irreversible. The parents were told that the child could never have sexual relations. After months of soul-wrenching agonies and tearful consultations with experts, the parents decided that their son should have a sex-change operation. When he was seventeen months old, surgeons used the boy's own skin to construct a vagina. The parents then gave the child a girl's name, dressed him in frilly clothing, let his hair grow long, and began to treat him as a girl. Later, physicians gave the child female steroids to promote female pubertal growth.

At first the results were extremely promising. When the twins were four and a half years old, the mother said (remember that the children are identical biological counterparts):

> One thing that really amazes me is that she is so feminine. I've never seen a little girl so neat and tidy. . . . She likes for me to wipe her face. She doesn't like to be dirty, and yet my son is quite different. I can't wash his face for anything. . . . She is very proud of herself, when she puts on a new dress, or I set her hair. . . . She seems to be daintier (Money and Ehrhardt 1972).

About a year later, the mother described how their daughter imitated her while their son copied his father.

> I found that my son, he chose very masculine things like a fireman or a policeman. . . . He wanted to do what daddy does, work where daddy does, and carry a lunch kit. . . . And [my daughter] didn't want any of those things. She wants to be a doctor or a teacher. . . . But none of the things that she ever wanted to be were like a policeman or a fireman, and that sort of thing never appealed to her. . . . I think it's nice if your boy wants to be a policeman or a fireman or something and the girl wants to do girl things like a doctor, or teaching, or something like that, and I've tried to show them that it's very good (Money and Ehrhardt 1972).

If the matter were this clear-cut, we could use this case to conclude that gender is entirely up to nurture. Seldom are things in life so simple, however, and a twist occurs in this story. In spite of her parents' coaching and the initially encouraging results, the twin whose sex had been reassigned did not adapt well to femininity Milton Diamond (1982), a medical researcher, reports that at age thirteen she was unhappy and having a difficult time adjusting to being a female. She walked with a masculine gait, and was called "cavewoman" by her peers.

We certainly need more evidence about this individual's life experiences to understand what we can learn from this case. At this point, we do not know to what degree biology influences male/female behavior, but we do know that biological distinctions are not a legitimate reason for social inequality.

The Question of Superiority

Let's consider a thorny question that people have debated through the ages: Which sex is superior? Since men have dominated societies, it is they who have come up with the "official" answers. It is not surprising, therefore, that they have identified their own sex as superior. Looking at the matter more objectively, however, we find that this is not an easy question to answer. In fact, there can be no answer unless we first rephrase the question to ask *in what ways*. It seems that males and females are both superior—but in different ways.

On the one hand, males are biologically superior to the extent that they are stronger and larger. This difference is considerable, for the average female is only two-thirds as strong as the average male (Gallese 1980). On the other hand, females are biologically superior in the sense that they outlive males. The average life expectancy of American females is about seventy-eight, while for males it is only about seventy. Although about 105 male babies are born for every 100 female babies in the United States, by the time those children reach the age of thirty-five there are as many females as males. At age seventy-five, for every male almost two females have survived (*Statistical Abstract* 1991:Table 13).

Females are intellectually superior to the extent that they generally begin to speak sooner than boys, to use sentences earlier, to score higher in tests of verbal fluency, and to do better in grammar and spelling. But boys are intellectually superior to the extent that they do better on spatial tasks and score higher on math (Bardwick 1971; Lengermann and Wallace 1985; Goleman 1987). Why such differences exist is a matter of debate among social scientists, a debate that, of course, takes us back to the problem discussed above, that of social learning versus inherited abilities (Holden 1987).

With neither sex biologically or socially superior, then, how is it that around the world males dominate human societies?

WOMEN AS A MINORITY GROUP

As noted, gender discrimination pervades every society, touching almost every aspect of social life. Consequently, even though women outnumber men, sociologists have found it useful to refer to women as a **minority group,** one that is discriminated against on the basis of physical characteristics. Sociologist Helen Hacker (1951), who was the first to apply this concept to women, noted that women are discriminated against economically, in education, in politics, and in everyday life. While some of the particulars of gender discrimination in our society have changed since Hacker's observation—women are no longer barred from jury duty, for example—gender inequality still exists in the areas she identified: jobs, education, politics, and everyday life.

Cross-Cultural Gender Inequality: Sex-Typing of Work

Before looking at gender inequality in American society, let's consider a brief overview of gender inequality around the world. Anthropologist George Murdock (1937), who surveyed 324 premodern societies around the world, found that in all of them activities are **sex-typed;** in other words, every society associates activities with one sex or the other. He also found that activities considered "female" in one society may be "male" activities in another society, and vice versa. In some groups, for example, taking care of cattle is women's work, while other groups assign this task to men.

Metalworking was the exception, being men's work in all the societies examined. Three other pursuits—making weapons, pursuing sea mammals, and hunting—were almost universally the domain of men, but in a few societies women were allowed to participate. Although Murdock found no particular work that was universally assigned to women, he did find that making clothing, cooking, carrying water, and grinding grain

CDQ 4: Why is it difficult to answer the question, "Which sex is superior?" What have you been socialized to believe?

L. Obj. 3: Explain why women are considered to be a minority group and summarize the theories of how this minority status occurred.

Essay #2

CDQ 5: Why do you think sociologists refer to women as a minority group?

K.P.: Helen Hacker

TR#19: Gender Allocation in Selected Technological Activities in 324 Societies

K.P.: George Murdock

CDQ 6: Can you give examples of sex-typed work in the U.S. today?

minority group: a group that is discriminated against on the basis of its members' physical characteristics

sex-typed: the association of behaviors with one sex or the other

When anthropologist George Murdock surveyed 324 premodern societies worldwide, he found that work activities in all of them were sextyped. In Somalia, women tend the livestock.

were commonly female tasks. In a few societies, however, such activities were regarded as men's work.

From Murdock's cross-cultural survey, we can conclude that there is nothing about anatomy that requires men and women to be assigned different work. Biology is not destiny when it comes to occupations; anatomy does not automatically sort men and women into different work. Rather, as we have seen, pursuits considered masculine in one society may be deemed feminine in another.

Cross-Cultural Gender Inequality: Prestige of Work

You might ask whether the division of labor between the sexes really illustrates social inequality. Could it be that Murdock's findings simply represent arbitrary forms of the division of labor, not gender discrimination.

That could be the case, except for this finding: *universally, greater prestige is given to male activities regardless of what these particular activities are* (Linton 1936; Rosaldo 1974). If taking care of cattle is men's work, then cattle care is given high importance and carries high prestige, but if taking care of cattle is women's work, it is considered less important and given less prestige. Or, to take an example closer to home, when delivering babies was "women's work," the responsibility of midwives, it was given low prestige. But when men took over this task, its prestige increased sharply (Ehrenreich and English 1973). In short, it is not the work that provides the prestige, but the sex with which the work is associated.

The Genesis of Female Minority Status

CNN : Women's Rights in Kenya: A Case of Cultural Lag

patriarchy: a society in which men dominate women

Some analysts question whether **patriarchy,** male dominance, is universal, speculating that in some earlier societies women may have dominated, or at least been equal, to men. Apparently the horticultural and hunting and gathering societies reviewed in Chapter 6 exhibited much less gender discrimination than do contemporary societies (Lerner 1986). In such societies, women are believed to have played a much more active role in all aspects of social life, and even to have contributed about 60 percent of the group's total food. After reviewing the historical record, however, historian and feminist Gerda Lerner (1986) concluded that "there is not a single society known where women-as-a-group have decision-making power over men (as a group)."

How did it happen, then, that around the world women and their activities came to be held in less esteem than men and male pursuits, and that in all societies women became systematically discriminated against in social life? Although the origin of patriarchy is unknown and can only be guessed at, two interesting theories have emerged. Both assume that patriarchy is universal and, accordingly, look to universal conditions to explain its origins. Each focuses on universal biological factors coupled with universal social factors.

Childbirth and Social Experiences.   The first theory points to the social consequences of biological differences in human reproduction (Lerner 1986; Hope and Stover 1987; Friedl 1990). In early human history, life was short and many children had to be born to reproduce the human group. Because only women get pregnant, carry a child nine months, give birth, and nurse, women were limited in movement and activities for a considerable part of their lives. To survive, an infant needed a nursing mother. With a child at her breast or in her uterus, or one carried on her hip or on her back, women were physically encumbered. Consequently, around the world women assumed tasks associated with the home and child care, while men took over the hunting of large animals and other tasks that required greater speed and absence from the base camp for longer periods of time (Huber 1990).

As a consequence, males became dominant. It was the men who left camp to hunt animals, who made contact with other tribes, who traded with these other groups, and who quarreled and waged war with them. It was also men who made and controlled the instruments of death, the weapons used for hunting and warfare. It was they who accumulated possessions in trade, who gained prestige by triumphantly returning with

Project 2

CDQ 7: Do you think that childbirth limits women's abilities to achieve on the level of men today? Why or why not?

One theory about the origins of patriarchy is that because of childbirth, women assumed tasks associated with home and child care, while men hunted and performed other tasks requiring greater strength, speed, and absence from home.

prisoners of war or with large animals to feed the tribe. In contrast, little prestige was given to the ordinary, routine, taken-for-granted activities of women—who are not seen as risking their lives for the group. Eventually, men took over society. Their weapons, items of trade, and knowledge gained in contact with other groups became sources of power. As they exerted their new power on women, women became second-class citizens, subject to male decisions.

CDQ 8: Do you believe that women should be involved in warfare? What about on the front lines of combat duty?

K.P.: Marvin Harris

Warfare and Physical Strength.   The second theory was put forward by anthropologist Marvin Harris (1977), who attributed patriarchy to the following universal conditions: (1) social—threats to the existence of human groups; and (2) biological—differences in the relative physical strength of males and females.

Harris argued that in prehistoric times, each small human group was threatened with annihilation from other groups. To survive, each group had to recruit members to fight enemies in dangerous, hand-to-hand combat. As you can imagine, the threat of injury and death made this recruiting process difficult. People had to be coaxed into bravery through promises of rewards and coerced through threats of punishment. Females, on average only 85 percent as large and only two-thirds as strong as men, found themselves at a huge disadvantage in hand-to-hand combat.

To encourage males to become the defenders and attackers, females became the reward. Males who did not live up to their group's expectations of bravery were banished from the tribe, while males who showed bravery were rewarded with sexual access to women. Some groups carried this idea to such an extent that only males who had proven their bravery by facing an enemy in combat were allowed to marry. Since some women were brawnier than some men, to exclude them from combat entirely might seem irrational. If women were to be the chief inducement for men to risk their lives, however, it was necessary to separate them from combat. To make the system work, men had to be trained from birth for combat, and women conditioned from birth to acquiesce in male demands.

According to this explanation, the reward for male bravery came at the direct expense of females. In almost all band and village societies, when men took control they assigned women the "drudge work": weeding, seed grinding, fetching water and firewood, carrying household possessions during moves, and routine cooking. Because men preferred to avoid these onerous tasks—and were able to do so if they had one or more wives—access to women proved an effective bait to induce men to fight.

Evaluating the Theories.   Which theory is correct? Remember that the answer is buried in human history and there is no way of testing either explanation. Either theory may be correct, patriarchy could have arisen due to some combination of the two, or some third theory may be the right one. For example, Frederick Engels proposed that patriarchy developed with the origin of private property (Lerner 1986). He could not explain why private property should have produced patriarchy, however. Gerda Lerner (1986) has suggested that patriarchy may even have had different origins in different places.

Whatever its ancient origins, patriarchy was surrounded with cultural supports to justify gender inequality. Men developed notions of their own inherent superiority—based on the evidence of their dominant position in society. They then consolidated their power, surrounded many of their activities with secrecy, and constructed elaborate rules and rituals to avoid "contamination" by the females whom they now openly deemed inferior.

As tribal societies developed into larger groups, men, enjoying their power and privileges, maintained their dominance long after hunting and hand-to-hand combat ceased to be routine, and even after large numbers of children were no longer needed to reproduce the human group. Male dominance in contemporary societies, then, is a continuation of a millennia-old pattern whose origin is lost in history.

Against enormous opposition from men, women finally won the right to vote in the United States in 1919. They first voted in national elections in 1920.

GENDER INEQUALITY IN AMERICAN SOCIETY

Gender inequality is not some accidental, hit-or-miss affair, but a structured part of each society. A society's institutions work together to maintain the particular group's customary forms of gender inequality. Custom, grounded in long history which both justifies and maintains arrangements of gender inequality, is only slowly giving way. Men, who are reluctant to abandon their privileged positions, use various cultural devices to keep women subservient. Let us first look at men's resistance to change in American society, then at some of these devices.

Fighting Back: The Rise of Feminism

Power yields tremendous privilege. Like a magnet, the elite in a society draws the best resources available. High positions bring privileged lifestyles and, just as important, allow the elite to feel like superior beings. Consequently, the powerful cling tenaciously to their positions and use social institutions to maintain their power.

In the United States, American women did not have the right to vote until 1920. They could not hold property in their own names, nor make legal contracts. They could neither testify in court nor serve on juries. Women did not even have the right to their own wages; instead, a woman's paycheck was handed over to her father or husband. In short, American women, like women around the world, were legally controlled by men, either fathers or husbands, and possessed few legal or social rights to self-determination.

How could the situation have changed so much that the above description sounds fictitious? As a group, American men are no exception to the general principle that people in power cling to their elite positions. Male privileges were not willingly surrendered. Rather, in both the United States and Europe women's rights were the fruits of a prolonged and bitter struggle (Barry 1986; Offen 1990). Toward the end of the

CDQ 9: Why have some people resisted changes in women's and men's roles in American society?

Essay #3

L. Obj. 4: Describe the major factors which led to the rise of feminism in the United States and note how successful this movement has been up to this point in time.

nineteenth century, American women directly confronted men, who first denied them the right to speak and then ridiculed them when they persisted in speaking in public. Leaders of the feminist movement, then known as suffragists, chained themselves to posts and to the iron grillwork of public buildings—and then went on talking while the police sawed them loose. When imprisoned, they continued to protest by going on hunger strikes. Threatened by such determination and confrontations, men spat on demonstrators for daring to question their place, slapped their faces, tripped them, pelted them with burning cigar stubs, and hurled obscenities at them (Cowley 1969).

In 1913, the agitation of American women so threatened the male establishment that the federal government summoned troops to Washington, D.C. In 1916, feminists formed the National Women's Party. In January 1917, they threw a picket line around the White House, which they picketed continuously for six months. On June 22, the pickets were arrested. Declaring their fines unjust, the women refused to pay them. Hundreds went to prison, including Lucy Burns and Alice Paul, two leaders of the National Women's Party. The extent to which these women had threatened male prerogatives is demonstrated by their treatment in prison.

> The guards from the male prison fell upon us. I saw Miss Lincoln, a slight young girl, thrown to the floor. Mrs. Nolan, a delicate old lady of seventy-three, was mastered by two men. . . . Whittaker (the Superindendent) in the center of the room directed the whole attack, inciting the guards to every brutality. Two men brought in Dorothy Day, twisting her arms above her head. Suddenly they lifted her and brought her body down twice over the back of an iron bench. . . . The bed broke Mrs. Nolan's fall, but Mrs. Cosu hit the wall. They had been there a few minutes when Mrs. Lewis, all doubled over like a sack of flour, was thrown in. Her head struck the iron bed and she fell to the floor senseless. As for Lucy Burns, they handcuffed her wrists and fastened the handcuffs over head to the cell door (Cowley 1969).

Although women enjoy fundamental rights today, gender inequality still pervades society and dearly affects women's welfare. The Down-to-Earth Sociology box on page 291 provides an example of how discrimination can become a life-and-death matter. Although women today continue to press for more rights and a greater share of society's power, the shape of the struggle has changed. Today's weapons are law suits, lobbying, and the mass media, while the battles are for scarce positions in good colleges and graduate schools, as well as for better jobs.

The goal of equality continues to elude women, however, for discrimination on the basis of gender remains a fact of life. From the conflict perspective, gender discrimination will end only when men as a class yield their power. The struggle will therefore continue, for like any group, men will not willingly give up their millennia-old positions of privilege.

Gender Inequality in Education: Creating Sex-Linked Aspirations

In education, too, a glimpse of the past sheds light on the present. About a century ago, leading men in education made what is to us the startling claim that women's wombs dominated their minds. This idea was so ingrained in our male-dominated culture that Dr. Edward Clarke, a member of Harvard University's medical faculty and its powerful Board of Overseers, issued the following warning about the dangers that education posed for women.

> A girl upon whom Nature, for a limited period and for a definite purpose, imposes so great a physiological task, will not have as much power left for the tasks of school, as the boy of whom Nature requires less at the corresponding epoch (Andersen 1988).

Clarke then urged young women to study only one-third as much as young men—and not to study at all during menstruation.

This quotation, which allows us to see into the mindset of earlier generations, reminds us how far we have come. However, today's schools still use sex to sort

Project 3

Essay #4

CNN: Girls' Education

L. Obj. 5: Discuss ways in which educational systems may perpetuate gender inequality.

Speaker Sug. #2: An affirmative action officer to discuss guidelines, policies, and procedures at your institution.

CDQ 10: Can you give examples of how today's schools still use sex to sort students into different activities?

DOWN-TO-EARTH SOCIOLOGY

Making the Invisible Visible— The Deadly Effects of Sexism

Medical researchers were perplexed. Reports were coming in from all over the country indicating that women, who live much longer than men, were twice as likely to die after coronary bypass surgery. Researchers at Cedars-Sinai Medical Center in Los Angeles checked their own records. They found that of almost 2,300 coronary bypass patients, 4.6 percent of the women died as a result of the surgery, compared with only 2.6 percent of the men.

Initial explanations had been based on biology. Coronary bypass surgery involves taking a blood vessel from one part of the body and stitching it to a coronary artery on the surface of the heart. This operation was supposedly more difficult to perform on women because of their smaller hearts and coronary arteries.

The researchers first tested this theory by measuring the amount of time that surgeons kept patients on the heart-lung machine while they operated. It turned out that women were kept on the machine for less time than men, indicating that the operation was not more difficult to perform on women.

As the researchers probed, a surprising answer slowly unfolded. It lay in neither biology nor lifestyle. Rather, the culprit was sexual discrimination on the part of the medical profession. The findings showed that compared with the males the females who had bypass surgery were older and their illnesses more severe.

Their physicians simply didn't take their chest pains as seriously as those of their male patients. Physicians, it turns out, are *ten* times more likely to give men exercise stress tests and radioactive heart scans. And they send male patients to surgery on the basis of abnormal stress tests but wait until a woman shows clear-cut symptoms of coronary heart disease before sending her to surgery. Being referred for surgery later in the course of the disease decreases the chances of survival.

In short, gender bias is so pervasive in our society that it operates beneath our level of awareness and can even be a matter of life or death. The doctors were unaware that they were discriminating. They had no intentions to do so. In what ways do you think gender bias affects your own perceptions and behavior?

Source: Based on Bishop 1990.

---

students into different activities (Weitzman 1984; Foley 1990). Expecting male and female students to be different, teachers still nurture the "natural" differences they find. Just as a century ago, they continue to perpetuate the gender inequalities of the existing social order. High school counselors and teachers continue to foster sex-linked aspirations by encouraging females to choose "feminine" occupations thought compatible with future husbands and children, and males to choose work more befitting the future roles for which they are being groomed. Girls are often steered into clerical jobs, males into business and the professions.

Even school sports help to produce sex-linked aspirations. Boys tend to become the football players, girls to join the drill team and drum majorettes (Foley 1990). As sociologist Carol Whitehurst (1977) put it, "The boys perform, the girls cheer." The boys' athletic programs, considered important for true "masculine" development, are widely publicized and amply funded, while girls' sports, considered peripheral to "feminine" development, are given less publicity and go underfunded. Although federal law (Title IX passed in 1975) prohibits sexual discrimination in education, many schools fail to make their sports programs equally accessible to male and female students.

K.P.: Carol Whitehurst

By the time they enter college, males and females differ considerably in their aspirations. Two extremes in bachelor's degrees highlight this distinction. Ninety-two percent of bachelor's degrees in home economics are awarded to females, while 95 percent of bachelor's degrees in military "science" go to males. Similarly, men earn 86 percent of bachelor's degrees in the "masculine" field of engineering, while women are awarded about 90 percent of bachelor's degrees in the "feminine" field of nursing (*Sociological Abstract* 1991:Table 284).

CDQ 11: Why do you think it is true that the further one climbs the educational ladder, the more the educational experience itself becomes a masculine endeavor?

The further one climbs the educational ladder, the more the educational experience itself becomes a masculine endeavor. Although females outnumber males at the undergraduate level, with each passing year of graduate work the proportion of females decreases—even in the fields in which females are already greatly underrepresented. For example, the proportion of females earning degrees in engineering shrinks from

The expectations of others, whether teachers, parents, or the media, help to produce sex-linked aspirations. This 1960s ad for a refrigerator assumes that women are the primary customers and that they will derive a feeling of self-worth from owning a fancy one.

14 percent at the bachelor's level to 8 percent at the doctoral level. Table 11.1 features graduate work in the sciences, where males outnumber females in all but two fields. This table illustrates sex-linking of aspirations and accomplishments, for in *all* scientific fields females are less likely than men to complete the doctoral program (*Sociological Abstract* 1991: Tables 265, 652). Note that the females' highest attrition rate occurs in engineering and mathematics, traditionally two strongly masculine fields. For more on gender and education, see Chapter 17.

L. Obj. 6: Describe the general devaluation of things feminine in American society.

Gender Inequality in Everyday Life

Of the many aspects of gender discrimination in everyday life that could be examined, we have space to look only at two: the general devaluation of femininity in American society and male dominance of conversation.

TABLE 11.1   Doctorates in Science, by Sex and Field

Field	Students Enrolled in Doctoral Programs		Doctorates Conferred		Female Attrition*
	Female	Male	Female	Male	
Engineering	13%	87%	8%	92%	38%
Physical Sciences	22%	78%	19%	81%	14%
Computer Sciences	25%	75%	18%	82%	28%
Agriculture	28%	72%	21%	79%	25%
Mathematics	29%	81%	18%	82%	38%
Biological Sciences	44%	56%	37%	63%	16%
Social Sciences	47%	53%	33%	67%	30%
Psychology	63%	37%	56%	44%	11%
Health Fields	75%	25%	57%	43%	24%

*The difference between the proportion of females enrolled in a program and the proportion granted doctorates divided by the proportion enrolled in the program. Data are from 1989, except for doctorates granted in health fields, which are from 1988.

Source: Statistical Abstract of the United States 1991:Tables 1009, 1010.

General Devaluation of Things Feminine. "Leaning against the water cooler, two men—both minor executives—are nursing their cups of coffee, discussing last Sunday's Giants game, postponing for as long as possible the moment when work must finally be faced.

"A vice president walks by and hears them talking about sports. Does he stop and send them back to their desks? Does he frown? Probably not. Being a man, he is far more likely to pause on his way and join in the conversation, anxious to prove that he, too, is 'one of the boys,' feigning an interest in football that he may very well not share at all. These men—all men in the office—are his troops, his comrades-in-arms.

"Now, let's assume that two women are standing by the water cooler discussing whatever you please: women's liberation, clothes, work, any subject—except football, of course. The vice president walks by, sees them, and moves down the hall in a fury, cursing and wondering whether it is worth the trouble to complain—but to whom?—about all those bitches standing around gabbing when they should be working. 'Don't they know,' he will ask, in the words of a million men, 'that this is an office?' " (Korda 1973:20–21).

Women routinely find themselves devalued as they encounter antagonistic attitudes on the part of men (Schur 1984). As indicated in the above scenario, women's capacities, interests, attitudes, and contributions are not taken as seriously as those of men. Masculinity is valued more highly, for it represents success and strength; while femininity is devalued, for it is perceived as failure and weakness.

During World War II, sociologist Samuel Stouffer noted the general devaluation of things feminine. In his classic study of combat soldiers, *The American Soldier,* Stouffer reported that officers used feminine terms as insults to motivate soldiers (1949).

> So the fear of failure [is part of] central and strongly established fears related to sex-typing. To fail to measure up as a soldier in courage and endurance was to risk the charge of not being a man. ("Whatsa matter, bud—got lace on your drawers?")

A generation later, to prepare soldiers to fight in Vietnam accusations of femininity were still used as a motivating insult. Drill sergeants would mock their troops by

CDQ 12: Do you agree that women's capacities, interests, attitudes, and contributions are not taken as seriously as those of men? Why or why not?

K.P.: Samuel Stouffer

saying, "Can't hack it, little girls?" (Eisenhart 1975). In the Marines, the worst insult to male recruits is to compare their performance to a woman's (Gilham 1989).

The same phenomenon occurs in male sports. Sociologist Douglas Foley (1990) notes that football coaches insult boys who don't play well by saying that they are "wearing skirts," and sociologists Jean Stockard and Miriam Johnson (1980), who observed boys playing basketball, heard boys who missed a basket called a "woman."

This name-calling is sociologically significant. As Stockard and Johnson (1980:12) point out, such insults embody the generalized devaluation of women in American society. As they noted, "There is no comparable phenomenon among women, for young girls do not insult each other by calling each other 'man.'"

Gender Inequality in Conversation.   As you may have noticed, gender inequality also shows up in everyday talk. Because men are more likely to interrupt a conversation and to control changes in topics, sociologists have noted that talk between a man and a woman is often more like talk between an employer and an employee than between social equals (Hall 1984; West and Garcia 1988; Smith-Lovin and Brody 1989; Tannen 1990). Even in college, male students interrupt their instructors more often than do female students, especially if the instructor is female (Brooks 1982). In short, conversations between men and women mirror their relative positions of power in society.

Derogatory terms and conversation represent only the tip of the iceberg, however, for as we have seen, underlying these aspects of everyday life is a structural inequality based on gender that runs throughout society. Let's examine that structural feature in the workplace.

GENDER INEQUALITY IN THE WORKPLACE

In many ways, gender discrimination is most visible in the workplace, where most Americans spend a huge portion of their lives. Here, some will be the victims of gender inequality, others its beneficiaries.

Women in the Work Force

In all industrialized nations, huge numbers of women enter the world of paid employment. Figure 11.1 documents this trend for the United States. Each decade since 1890

FIGURE 11.1   Women's and men's proportion of the American labor force. Note: Pre-1940 figures include women fourteen and over: figures for 1940 and after are for women sixteen and over. (*Source:* 1969 *Handbook on Women Workers,* 1969:10; *Manpower Report to the President,* 1971:203, 205; Mills and Palumbo, 1980:6, 45; *Statistical Abstract of the United States,* 1991:Table 636.)

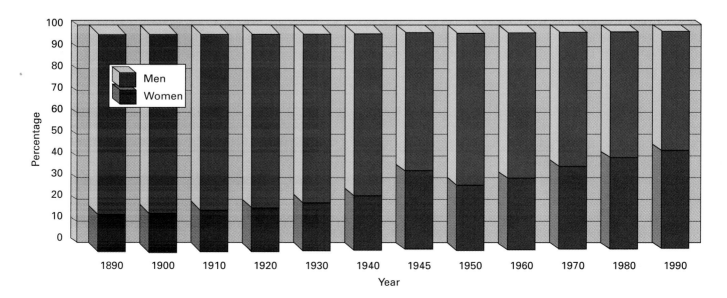

Researchers have found that gender inequalities emerge even in conversations. Among other patterns, they have found that men tend to interrupt and change topics more often than women.

women have made up an increasing proportion of the American labor force. This trend continued steadily until the period immediately following World War II, when millions of women left the factories and offices to return home as full-time wives and mothers. Not until twenty-five years later, in 1970, were women again as large a proportion of all workers as they were in 1945. Today, for every ten male workers, there are eight female workers.

Figure 11.2 shows American women's *labor force participation rate;* that is, the proportion of women sixteen and older who are in the labor force. At the turn of the century, only about one in five females was employed outside the home. By 1945, this rate had doubled. After World War II, however, it declined, not reaching that rate again until the early 1960s. June of 1978 was significant—for the first time in American history, 50 percent of all females aged sixteen and over were employed, at least part-time, outside the home. Today, the proportion is about three of every five women.

TR#18: Women's and Men's Proportion of the American Labor Force

TR#15M: What Proportion of American Women Work for Wages?

labor force participation rate: the proportion of the population or of some group sixteen years and older in the work force

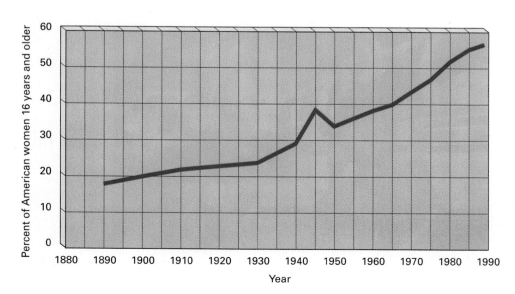

FIGURE 11.2 What proportion of American women work for wages? Note: American women sixteen years and older. (*Source: 1969 Handbook on Women Workers,* 1969:10; *Manpower Report to the President,* 1971:203, 205; Mills and Palumbo, 1980:6; *Statistical Abstract of the United States,* 1991: Table 632.)

Essay #5

Discrimination in Hiring

Although the law states that family responsibilities cannot be a factor in hiring, transfer, or promotion, and forbids employers from even enquiring about a prospective employee's family status, many firms get around the law. Fearing that her child's needs may interfere with a woman's ability to do her job, many employers discriminate against mothers—but not against fathers. Job recruiters use at least three strategies to get around the law and discover if a woman is married or a mother (Berkeley 1989). Knowing what firms are really doing may prove helpful in a future interview.

The On-the-Spot Strategy.   During a break in the job interview, a low-level employee asks the candidate what kind of health-insurance plan she wants: individual, husband-and-wife, or family coverage. Thinking that this means the company wants to hire her, the candidate answers, her reply revealing everything the company wants to know.

The Relaxed Lunch Strategy.   Recruiters take a prospective female employee to lunch at an expensive restaurant. With the candidate's guard down in this informal atmosphere, one of the recruiters might say, "What a hassle this morning! The car pool got messed up, and I was almost late for work. Anything like that ever happen to you?" Feeling relaxed among "people like herself," the candidate talks about the problems of being a working mother—and unknowingly ruins her chance for the job.

The Direct Approach.   Some recruiters openly flout the law and ask the woman about her family situation. This puts the candidate in a dilemma: Although she may know that they are violating the law by asking this question, to refuse to answer endangers her chances of getting the job. If she lies, the truth will be apparent at some point, and her deceit is likely to make relationships at work suffer.

The Pay Gap

Speaker Sug. #3: An economist who has studied the pay gap between women and men.

Once in the work force, men and women face different worlds—and the situation does not favor women. In science, females are excluded from the scientists' "inner circle" (Zuckerman, Cole, and Bruer 1991), while in the legal profession, even women who have graduated from quality law schools and received academic honors are only half as likely as men to receive partnerships in their legal firms (Spurr 1990).

Women earn less than men both in low-skilled job and in the professions. This pay gap exists even among women who perform the same work as their male counterparts.

Perhaps the persistent pay gap, which characterizes other industrialized nations as well (Brinton 1989; Rosenfeld and Kalleberg 1990; Sorensen 1990), is the best indicator of gender discrimination in the work world. If we consider all year-round, full-time workers in the nation, we find that women's wages average *only 69 percent* of men's (*Statistical Abstract* 1991:Table 736). Until the past few years, women's earnings hovered between 58 and 60 percent of men's, so that being paid only two-thirds of what men make is actually an improvement!

Could the pay gap be due to the fact that women tend to choose lower-paying jobs, such as grade-school teaching, whereas men are more likely to go into more lucrative fields such as business and engineering? Such an argument carries some merit. Researchers have found that perhaps half the pay gap is due to such factors, but that the balance is due to gender discrimination (Kemp 1990).

Economists Rex Fuller and Richard Schoenberger (1991) studied how gender discrimination works and how it leads to huge pay gaps. Because their research focused on gender inequality *within* the same occupation, eliminating the variable of career choice, it is especially valuable. These researchers examined the starting salaries of 230 business majors at the University of Wisconsin, of whom 47 percent were women. They found that the average female starting salary was 11 percent ($1,737) lower than that of the average male.

There could conceivably be valid reasons for this, of course. The female candidates might have been less qualified. Perhaps they received lower grades or did fewer internships—and therefore deserved lower salaries. To test this assumption, Fuller and Schoenberger examined the college records of these students. It turned out that the female students had actually earned higher grades and had done more internships than the men. In other words, women more highly qualified than men were offered lower salaries!

Having discovered a pattern of deep gender discrimination, Fuller and Schoenberger wondered what happened after these graduates were on the job. Would these initial starting salaries wash out, so that after a few years of employment the males and females would be earning about the same? To find out, they followed these graduates' careers. Five years later, the pay gap had grown even wider. Among the graduates still working full-time, the women now earned 14 percent ($3,615) less than the men.

Nor is a look at the national scene encouraging. As Table 11.2 shows, at all educational levels women earn less than men. This table also reveals that the average woman with a college degree earns *less* than the average man who has only a high school diploma. The pay gap, or gender penalty, translates into an astounding total. From this table you can compute that, earning $15,782 more a year, between the ages of twenty-five and sixty-five the average male college graduate will earn about $630,000

CDQ 14: Do you think the pay gap between men and women can be explained by the fact that women tend to choose lower-paying jobs than men? Why or why not?

K.P.: Rex Fuller and Richard Schoenberger

TABLE 11.2 Annual Earnings by Education

	High School		*College*		
	Dropout	*Graduate*	*1-3 years*	*Graduate*	*5+ years*
Male	$24,673	$29,852	$34,697	$44,456	$55,288
Female	$15,217	$19,069	$23,441	$28,674	$34,307
The Gender Penalty					
Earnings	$ 9,456	$10,783	$11,256	$15,782	$20,981
Percentage	38%	36%	32%	36%	38%

Note: These figures are mean money income for year-round, full-time workers twenty-five years old and over as of March 1989. I have arbitrarily added 10 percent to update the figures somewhat, an addition that does not affect the relativity of the earnings.

Source: Statistical Abstract of the United States, 1991:Table 740.

more than the average female college graduate. Could *you* use an extra half million or so?

The gender penalty persists both in low-skilled jobs and in the professions. Female lawyers in corporate settings make $40,000 less per year than do male lawyers (Hagan 1990). In colleges and universities, female Ph.D.'s earn about 23 percent less than male Ph.D.'s—and that holds true regardless of their field of work, their experience, the nature of their jobs, or the quality of their training (Andersen 1988). A survey of the 325 largest corporations in the United States showed that the average chief executive officer receives an annual salary of $1 million. These CEOs also earned another $400,000 from stock options. *Not one of these 325 CEOs is a female.* (*The Wall Street Journal,* April 18, 1990)

K.P.: Felice Schwartz

Felice Schwartz, president of Catalyst, a nonprofit research organization that focuses on women's issues in the workplace, surveyed female executives in the largest United States corporations (Lopez 1992). She found that women face a "glass ceiling" and "glass walls." The "glass ceiling" prevents women from advancing to top executive positions, while it lets men pass through. Thus in companies where about half of the professional employees are women, women hold fewer than 5 percent of the senior management positions. The "glass walls" are obstacles that keep women from moving laterally into core positions in marketing, production, and sales from which senior executives are tapped. Stereotyped as being better at providing "support," women are pushed into such positions as public relations and human resources—which do not provide the experience needed for jobs in top management.

In the upper ranks, the pay gap is maintained through an "old boys'" network. That is, a network of acquaintances brings access to jobs, promotions, and opportunities. Excluded from this network, female professionals find themselves at a disadvantage when it comes to professional opportunities (Andersen 1988). To combat this disadvantage, some female professionals are developing alternative networks to help

PERSPECTIVES
Cultural Diversity Around the World

Sexual Harassment in Japan

The public relations department had come up with an eye-catcher: Each month, the cover of the company's magazine would show a woman taking off one more piece of clothing. The men were pleased, looking forward to each new issue.

Six months later, with the cover girl poised to take off her tank top in the next edition, the objections of women employees had grown too loud to ignore. "We told them it was a lousy idea," said Junko Takashima, assistant director of the company's women's affairs division. The firm, Rengo, dropped the striptease act.

The Japanese men didn't get the point. "What's all the fuss about?" they wondered. "Beauty is beauty. We're just admiring the ladies. It's a wish, or maybe a hope. It's nothing serious. It just adds a little spice to boring days at the office."

"It's degrading to us, and it must stop," responded female workers, who, encouraged by the American feminist movement, have broken their long tradition of passive silence.

The Japanese have no word of their own to describe this situation, so they have borrowed the English phrase "sexual harassment." They are now struggling to apply it to their own culture. In Japan a pat on the bottom has long been taken for granted as a boss's way of getting his secretary's attention. But now the men no longer know how a woman will react.

Differing cultural expectations have led to problems when Japanese executives—always male—have been sent to overseas factories. A managing director of Honda learned this the hard way. During business meetings he repeatedly put his hand on the knee of an American employee. When she threatened to sue, he was transferred back to Japan.

The Japanese expectation that everyone will work together harmoniously does not make it easy for female employees. A woman who complains is viewed as violating corporate harmony. But women are speaking out, and discovering how to apply the Western concept "sexual harassment."

Source: Based on Graven 1990.

When Felice Schwartz suggested in 1989 that corporations offer working women with children the option of selecting a separate—and slower-paced—career track than that of childless women, controversy flared. Some said that instead of offering women the option of lowering their work aspirations in favor of family, employers should encourage males to share equally in family tasks. These critics of the "Mommy Track" also called for family-oriented benefits such as onsite daycare and parental leave for both parents.

their own careers (Cox 1986; Schwartz 1989), while others are suing for equal treatment (Pleck 1990).

The "Mommy Track"

Most wives invest more of themselves in their families than do their husbands. Wives are more likely to be the caretakers of the marriage, to nurture it through the hard times. Most wives also take greater responsibility for taking care of the children and spend considerably more time doing housework (see Chapter 16). Consequently, most employed wives face greater role conflict than do their husbands.

To help resolve this conflict, Felice Schwartz (1989) has suggested that corporations offer women a choice of two parallel career paths. The "fast track" consists of the high-powered, demanding positions that may require sixty or seventy hours of work per week. In addition to regular responsibilities, an executive on the fast track handles emergencies, attends unexpected and out-of-town meetings, and takes home a briefcase jammed with work at night and on weekends. With such limited time outside of work, family life often suffers. Women can choose this "fast track" if they wish. Or they may instead choose the proposed "mommy track," which would stress both career and family. Less would be expected of a woman on the "mommy track," for her commitment to the firm would be lower and her commitment to her family higher.

That, of course, say critics, is exactly what is wrong with such proposals. A "mommy track" will encourage women to be satisfied with lower aspirations and fewer promotions and confirm male stereotypes of female executives (Ehrlich 1989; Day 1990). To encourage women to withdraw from the hard-driving, competitive race to climb the corporate ladder would only perpetuate, or even increase, the executive pay gap. The "mommy track," conclude critics, would merely keep men in executive power by relegating women to an inferior position in corporate life.

Critics suggest that a better way of confronting the conflict between work and family is for husbands to take greater responsibilities at home and for firms to provide on-site day care, flexible work schedules, and parental leave without loss of benefits

CNN: Baby Boom

CDQ 15: Is the "mommy track" a good idea for women who want to get ahead at work and also have a family? Why or why not?

(Auerbach 1990; Deutsch 1990; Galinsky and Stein 1990; Hall 1990). Some maintain that the choice between family and career is artificial, that there are ample role models of family-oriented, highly successful women from Sandra Day O'Connor, Justice of the United States Supreme Court, to Ann Fisher, astronaut and physician (Ferguson and Dunphy 1991).

Sexual Harassment

Speaker Sug. #4: A lawyer who has represented clients in sexual discrimination or sexual harassment lawsuits.

CDQ 16: Do you think sexual harassment is an individual problem or a societal problem?

Many people see sexual harassment only in individual terms. They see a male, attracted to a female, making an advance, and the female responding as she wishes—accepting, rejecting, or giving some form of "maybe." According to this view, individuals are simply "doing what's natural." What's the problem? The sexual attraction could have taken place anywhere; it just happened to occur at work.

Until 1976, in fact, sexual harassment was literally unspeakable, for it had no name. Before then women considered this experience to be something that happened to them as individuals. They did not draw a connection between unwanted sexual advances and their subordinate positions at work. Heightened awareness of the structural basis of these problems, however, arose from the activities of feminist groups. As women discussed this problem, they gradually came to see sexual advances by men in more powerful positions at work as part of a structural problem of the workplace. They then developed the term **sexual harassment** to describe the use of a person's position to force unwanted sexual demands on someone (MacKinnon 1979). In line with symbolic interactionism, a change in consciousness resulted from a *symbolic reinterpretation of their experiences.* In short, when they had a name to refer to their experiences, they saw them in a different light. To see how this same reintrepretation is occurring in another culture, see the Perspectives box on page 298.

Sexual harassment may consist of a single encounter at work or a series of incidents. It may be a condition for being hired, retained, or promoted. Whether it consists of verbal sexual suggestions or "accidental" touching, at the core of sexual harassment is a power imbalance. Because the more powerful person has the capacity to fire, to demote, or to make life miserable the less powerful person finds it difficult to ward off sexual demands.

Sexual harassment is not an exclusively female problem; males, too, are victimized. In a study of 23,000 federal civil service workers, 42 percent of the females and 15 percent of the males reported that they had been sexually harassed (*Merit Systems Protection Board* 1981). In most instances, the harasser and the victim are of the opposite sex. When the harasser is the same sex as the victim, sexual harassment is far more likely to involve males than females.

CDQ 17: Can problems of sexual harassment be solved? What would you suggest be done?

Victims of sexual harassment have begun to fight back. They have demanded and received legal protection. The Equal Employment Opportunity Commission has broadened the definition of sexual harassment to include all unwelcome sexual attention that affects an employee's job conditions or creates a "hostile" working environment (Adler 1991). Some awards to victims of sexual harassment have run over $1 million. Some victims, however, have fought in court for several years at considerable expense, only to lose the case and then be ordered to pay the legal fees of those they had accused (*Congressional Quarterly Researcher* 1991). The legal concept has also become so fuzzy that in one case a female employee who was *not* asked for sexual favors while others were was ruled a victim of sexual harassment (Hayes 1991).

When the congressional hearings for Judge Clarence Thomas's confirmation to the United States Supreme Court were viewed by a national television audience in 1991, sexual harassment became a household term overnight. Sexual harassment has become a top item in executive education programs, and many companies are trying to develop precise written policies specifying exactly which behaviors are intolerable (Adler 1991; Lublin 1991). For an overview of gender discrimination and sexual harassment on Wall Street, see the Down-to-Earth Sociology box on page 301.

DOWN-TO-EARTH SOCIOLOGY

Women on Wall Street—From Subtle Put-Downs to Crude Sexual Harassment

Wall Street offers some of the best opportunities in corporate America for women to reap huge financial rewards, power, and prestige. Wall Street is also made up of an old boys' network where business is based on "personal relationships, prankish humor, and clannish favor-swapping."

Women who pursue Wall Street careers sometimes find that those personal relationships, humor, and favor-swapping are sexist to the core. Let us look at some of that sexism.

First, it is tough for a woman to break into Wall Street. Although women hold 40 percent of the jobs at Wall Street's ten largest securities firms, only 4 percent of partners and managing directors are women. At Goldman, Sachs & Co., Wall Street's most successful investment bank, only 4 of the 146 partners are women. And of the 26 directors of the New York Stock Exchange, only 2 are women.

Second, to find out if female job applicants might secretly favor marriage and family over a career, Wall Street recruiters often ask them questions that they don't ask male applicants. The way the matter is approached places women in a double bind. If they aren't married, recruiters want to know why—as though something were wrong with them. And if they are married, recruiters want to know if something is wrong with the marriage. After all, why are they seeking a job like this where they will have to do extensive traveling? There is no way to win. Men simply aren't asked the same kind of questions.

"Of course we ask women about family," respond many firms. "It's not fair to us to lose an employee to her family after we've spent a lot of money training her." As the chief executive of a major firm said, "We lose nearly 50 percent of the women we recruit out of business school, but only 4 percent of the men."

Third, once on the job, women run up against a broad range of offensive and discriminatory practices. At a high-level meeting at Oppenheimer, for instance, a senior executive turned to a female lawyer and said, "You should have told me to turn down the air conditioning. Your nipples are sticking out."

Fourth is the larger issue: Many of the men who run Wall Street simply don't believe that women belong in high-powered jobs. Jessica Palmer, who heads the capital markets group at Salomon Brothers, points out that men think of femininity and power as incompatible. "Does a chief executive want to take advice from a petite woman?" she asks. "She had better be better than her male colleagues."

The president of Bear Stearns perfectly illustrated the fundamental sexism that runs through Wall Street when he said that the reason that few women sell stocks and bonds is that if a woman were rejected she "would probably have to go to the ladies' room and dab her eyes."

Although to fight the prejudice and discrimination that engulf Wall Street is to risk getting blackballed in the securities industry, Wall Street women have begun to fight back. They now complain to supervisors and file charges in the courts. In one celebrated case, Teresa Contardo won a landmark victory against Merrill Lynch. The judge's decision read, "There existed in the office a male 'locker room' atmosphere in which the male workers engaged in lewd remarks and male birthdays were celebrated in the office in the presence of customers, with . . . a birthday cake in the shape of a phallus."

As the confirmation hearings for Supreme Court justice Clarence Thomas gave sexism and sexual discrimination national attention, and as many women are no longer willing to suffer in silence, Wall Street is trying to clean up its act. The New York Stock Exchange has declared that "all inappropriate pictures, pinups, and postcards" featuring nude women must be removed from the trading floor.

Discussion Questions

1. Many critics claim that concessions such as removing offensive pictures from offices only scratch the surface, and that the real problem is the deep-rooted gender discrimination that pervades Wall Street. How do you think the underlying discrimination can be dealt with?

2. In what ways do you think that the old boys' network influences gender relations in other occupations?

3. In what work settings have you experienced or seen sexism? Compare those experiences with those recounted here. What features do they have in common?

4. The old boys' network on Wall Street is being touched by the winds of social change. If it is ever completely dismantled, how do you think things will be different on Wall Street?

5. Not all women on Wall Street agree that the lewd behaviors recounted here constitute sexual harassment. Barbara Roberts, a former director at Dean Witter Reynolds, says that this is just part of the business culture. "If you're not comfortable with a certain level of lewdness, you shouldn't be here," she says. What do you think? Are these behaviors sexual harassment—or simply sexual customs that one gender is more comfortable with?

6. Finally, not all Wall Street women see sexual discrimination on Wall Street. Elaine Garzarelli, the top-rated stock market strategist for Shearson Lehman, says, "I think being a woman has helped me, actually, on Wall Street. The men seem to respect us as doing a very tedious job and really looking at the details. Women tend to do that. Women are very service oriented." What do you think?

Source: Based on Cohen, Power, and Siconolfi, 1991.

Out of the more than 170 serial killers estimated in the United States since 1977, there have been fewer than a dozen women. Aileen Wuornos is one of this as yet small group. Wuornos, a prostitute from Florida, was convicted of picking up as many as ten men and then shooting them.

L. Obj. 8: Distinguish between female and male patterns of violence, especially in the case of murder.

GENDER INEQUALITY AND VIOLENCE: THE CASE OF MURDER

Another area of gender inequality emerges when we examine patterns of murder. Around the world, without exception, males kill at a rate several times that of females (Daly and Wilson 1988). Although no theorist claims that all the differences in male and female killing are genetic, some do claim that males are born with a greater predisposition to kill (Daly and Wilson 1988). Like other aspects of male/female behavior, however, most sociologists trace patterns of murder to social experiences (Wolfgang 1958; Wolfgang and Ferracuti 1967; Athens 1980; Huff-Corzine et al. 1986).

CDQ 18: In what ways do the differences between male and female killers reflect their different experiences in the social world?

For decades, researchers have found consistent differences between male and female killers that reflect their different experiences in the social world (Wolfgang 1958; Ward, Jackson, and Ward 1969). Females who kill are more likely to kill at home; to kill an intimate, usually a male partner, in the midst of a domestic dispute; and to use a household implement such as a butcher knife. Males, who do the vast majority of killing, are more likely to kill strangers and acquaintances in public places, especially in and near bars.

Researchers hypothesized that as society changed these gender styles of killing would also change (Adler 1975; Simon 1975). They developed a "liberation hypothesis," namely, that as more women moved out of the home to public activities and places, their patterns of killing would become more like men's—they would kill more often, they would be more likely to use guns, and most of their victims, too, would be strangers and acquaintances.

K.P.: Nancy Jurik and Russ Winn

TR#16M: Male and Female Murderers: Their Characteristics and Victims

In testing this hypothesis, however, sociologists found that murder patterns continue to follow gender roles (Wilbanks 1983; Browne and Williams 1989). When sociologists Nancy Jurik and Russ Winn (1990) examined homicides in Phoenix, Arizona, they found that women, who committed only 7 percent of the murders, still followed traditional patterns. These gender differences are shown in Table 11.3.

Jurik and Winn did find, however, that patterns of gun usage support the liberation hypothesis. As Table 11.3 shows, female killers in the Phoenix area are just as likely as their male counterparts to use a gun. This finding may indicate that we are simply experiencing a cultural lag and that as women's roles broaden further, male and female murder patterns will eventually grow closer. Gender styles in murder persist, however, at least at this moment in our history.

TABLE 11.3 Male and Female Murderers: Their Characteristics and Victims

	Percentage	
	Males	*Females*
Killed someone in the home	42	85
Killed someone with whom one had an intimate relation-ship (includes spouses, lovers, and relatives)	18	58
Killed someone with whom there was a romantic interest	14	75
Killed a stranger	27	10
Killed someone with whom there was no history of prior conflict	71	40
Killed someone of another race	24	7
Planned the killing	45	27
If a codefendant, did the killing (the partner played only a helping role)	90	10
Used a household implement	3	10
Killed without a weapon	9	1
Killed with a gun	59	59

Source: Jurik and Winn 1990.

WHY DON'T WOMEN TAKE OVER POLITICS AND TRANSFORM AMERICAN LIFE?

The relative position of men and women in American society is illustrated nowhere better than in the area of politics, where men wield the power at all levels. This holds true for party leadership, elected office, appointed office, and the policy-making levels of the federal and state civil service.

Why don't women, who outnumber men, take political control of the nation? Nine million more women than men are of voting age (*Statistical Abstract* 1991:Table 450). Women, however, are vastly underrepresented in political decision making. As Table 11.4 shows, the higher the office the fewer the women. The handful of women who have served as governors and as mayors of large cities are exceptions to the dominant

L. Obj. 9: Explain why women historically have not taken over politics and transformed American life.

CDQ 19: Do you think a woman will be elected President of the United States during the next ten years? Twenty years?

TR#17: American Women in Political Office, 1990

K.P.: Marcia M. Lee

Project 5

TABLE 11.4 American Women in Political Office, 1990

	Percent and number held by women	
	Percent	*Number*
National Office		
United States Senate	2%	2
United States House of Representatives	7%	29
State Office		
Governors	6%	3
State legislature	18%	359
Local Office		
Mayors*	17%	151

Does not include women elected to the judiciary, appointed to state cabinet-level positions, elected to executive posts by the legislature, or members of a university board of trustees.
*Of cities with a population over 30,000.

Source: National Women's Political Caucus.

As of 1992, there were just two women in the U.S. Senate, three states headed by female governors, and one female Supreme Court Justice. However, many female candidates for Senate and Congressional seats, at both the state and Federal levels, won primary races in 1992, pointing to a growing trend toward greater participation by women in political life.

pattern in the American political arena. Why, in spite of their numerical majority, is women's political participation primarily confined to women's organizations or to work at the lowest level of political parties?

Marcia M. Lee (1977), a political scientist, concluded that two dilemmas underlie women's underrepresentation in elective office. The first is that women find the role of mother incompatible with that of politician. In a study of political activists in New York City, Lee found that being a parent kept neither men nor women from general participation in politics. In fact, women spent more time than men on political activities. Running for elective office was another matter, however. Where fathers felt free to run for office, mothers felt that the irregular hours required for campaigning would interfere with the care of their children and that they might be criticized for being a bad mother. In contrast, the fathers did not feel uncomfortable about their wives filling in for them at home during their campaigning, and they did not fear criticism about being a bad father. Unlike the women, the men found the role of politician perfectly compatible with the cultural expectations of husband and father.

Why can't women who want to be elected to office solve this dilemma by waiting until their children are grown and then taking up where they left off? Because, for the most part, seeking office is one of those experiences in life that, once forgone, is lost forever. For while the mothers stay at home caring for their children, their male peers, actively campaigning and serving in low-level offices, gain basic political know-how and indispensable political connections. By virtue of their experience, they are then deemed qualified by the political parties to build on their connections and to run for higher office.

The second dilemma is **marginality,** a state of belonging to two groups that have incompatible values and not feeling fully accepted and comfortable in either one (Githens and Prestage 1977). The worlds of women and politicians represent different ways of life, and the female politician becomes marginal to each. As she participates in the world of politics, her self-concept changes. No longer is she able to accept the "feminine" ways of her past—yet male politicians continue to view her as an outsider. The usual solution to marginality is to select one world and reject the other. In this case,

marginality: the condition of belonging to two groups whose values are incompatible with each other and not feeling fully accepted and comfortable in either

not to run for office is usually the simpler choice, as it avoids the severe threat to a woman's self-esteem posed by elected office, as well as the disorientation and personal isolation that it brings.

Additional factors contribute to the failure of American women to dominate politics in proportion to their numbers. For one, few women perceive themselves as a class of people whose domination is remediable by bloc or class political action. In addition, women are underrepresented in law and business, the careers from which most politicians come. Women are also hindered to the degree that an election campaign is considerably enhanced by a supportive spouse who plays an unassuming background role and provides solace, encouragement, and voter appeal—roles most men are extremely reluctant to adopt. Another structural barrier is that males already occupy the positions of power. Preferring to retain their bastions of privilege, these males seldom incorporate women into the centers of decision making or present them as viable candidates (Githens and Prestage 1977).

CDQ 20: What changes—if any—have you seen in the participation levels of women in politics in the past ten years?

CHANGES IN GENDER RELATIONS

As stressed in earlier chapters, the meaning of a symbol is not written in stone. So, the symbols of masculinity and femininity—and also relationships between the sexes—change over time. Although women and their social contributions continue to be downgraded, there is evidence of growing respect for the abilities of women. Since 1937 the Gallup Poll has asked random samples of Americans whether they would vote for a qualified woman nominated by their party for the presidency (Schaefer 1979; Gallup Poll 1987). In 1937 only one of three American men said that they would vote for such a woman. By 1955, this number had increased to one of two American men. Now about four of five Americans—both men and women—would vote for a woman for president, certainly a strong indication that the symbol of female is undergoing major change in our society.

Without doubt, the historical trend is toward greater equality between the sexes (Goode 1982; Chafetz 1984; Huber 1986). As we have seen, previous generations of women fought hard to win rights that are now taken for granted. The continuing struggle will center on breaking down structural barriers and gaining greater access to leadership and other positions of responsibility in such institutions as the military, education, business, and politics.

Essay #6

L. Obj. 10: Describe what the future looks like in terms of gender relations in the United States.

CDQ 21: Do you predict that there will be greater equality between the sexes in the future? Why or why not?

Project 6

Speaker Sug. #5: A representative from NOW, EMILY'S List, Eagle Forum, Concerned Women of America, or other advocacy group to talk about their perspective.

GLIMPSING THE FUTURE—WITH HOPE

The vast increase in the number of employed women, illustrated in Figures 11.1 and 11.2, will gradually force changes in gender images and gender relations. For example, as millions of children see both mothers and fathers leave for work and bring home paychecks, they will assume that a man is not the exclusive breadwinner and that a woman is more than a mother and a wife.

As women come to play a fuller role in the decision-making processes of our social institutions—the direction in which we are headed—further structural obstacles to women's and men's more equitable participation in society will give way. Stereotypes and role models, which lock men into exclusively male activities as they push women into roles considered feminine, will be broken. As structural barriers fall and more activities become desexualized, both men and women will be free to become involved in activities more compatible with their desires or proclivities as *individuals*.

As sociologist Janet Giele (1978) pointed out, the ultimate possibility is a new conception of the human personality. At present structural obstacles, accompanied by supporting socialization and stereotypes, cast men and women into fairly rigid molds along the lines that culture dictates. To overcome these obstacles and abandon traditional stereotypes is to give men and women new perceptions of themselves and one

K.P.: Janet Giele

another. As they develop a new consciousness of themselves and of their own potential, basic relationships between women and men will change.

Both females and males will then be free to feel and to express needs and emotions that present social arrangements deny them. Women are likely to perceive themselves as more in control of their environment and to explore this aspect of the human personality. Men are likely to feel and to express more emotional sensitivity—to be warmer, more affectionate and tender, and to give greater expression to anxieties and stresses that their gender now forces them to suppress. In the future we may discover that such "greater wholeness" of men and women entails many other dimensions of the human personality.

Certainly distinctions between the sexes will not disappear. There is no reason, however, for biological differences to be translated into social inequalities. The reasonable goal is appreciation of sexual differences coupled with equality of opportunity—which may well lead to a transformed society (Hubbard 1990; Offen 1990). If so, as sociologist Alison Jaggar (1990) observed, gender equality can become less a goal than a background condition for living in society.

SUMMARY

1. The term *sex* refers to biological distinctions between males and females. Sex consists of both primary and secondary sex characteristics. The term *gender,* in contrast, refers to what society considers proper behaviors and attitudes for its males and females. Sex distinguishes male and female, while gender separates masculinity and femininity.

2. Gender inequality refers to men's and women's unequal access to a society's power, property, and prestige. In the debate over whether differences between male and female behaviors are caused by inherited or learned characteristics (nature versus nurture), almost all sociologists are on the side of nurture. Each society establishes a structure that, on the basis of gender, permits or limits access to the group's privileges.

3. Asking the question which sex is superior merely offers a false choice, for each is superior in different ways. George Murdock surveyed information on premodern societies and found not only that all of them have sex-linked activities, but also that, universally, greater prestige is given to male activities. Two theories attempt to explain how women became a minority group in their own societies. One focuses on childbirth, the other on warfare.

4. Sociologists define women as a minority group. In reviewing gender inequalities in American society, the women's struggle for equality must be seen in historical and contemporary perspective. Schools tend to produce sex-linked aspirations. The higher the educational level, the more the sexes are sorted into "appropriate" fields of study. Two other aspects of gender inequality in everyday life are the general devaluation of femininity and male dominance of conversation.

5. The world of work has experienced a more or less steady trend of increasing women's participation in the work force over the last century. Continued discrimination is manifested in corporate hiring techniques, the pay gap, and sexual harassment. The pay gap, which characterizes all occupations, begins at the time of hiring and grows over the years. The average lifetime pay gap for college graduates is over $600,000 in favor of men. Sexual harassment is a structural problem caused by relative positions in the workplace. Murder continues to show traditional gender patterns, except for the use of guns.

6. American women have the numerical capacity to take over politics and transform society. Yet the higher the office, the fewer the women. Twin dilemmas for women in this area are the incompatibility of politics and motherhood and marginality, the fact that political office separates a woman from the culturally-dominant definitions of femininity.

7. Changing images of gender in American society indicate greater equality. The ultimate possibility is a new conception of the human personality, one that allows both males and females to pursue their individual interests unfettered by gender. If this ever occurs, it may well result in a transformed society.

SUGGESTED READINGS

Andersen, Margaret L. *Thinking About Women: Sociological Perspectives on Sex and Gender.* 2nd ed. New York: Macmillan, 1988. Andersen provides a wide-ranging overview of the social influences on the place of women in society.

Barry, Kathleen. *Susan B. Anthony: A Life or the Love of Women.* New York: The Free Press, 1986. Chronicles events in the life of the foremost nineteenth-century leader of the fight for women's rights and examines the international women's movement of that period.

Deegan, Mary Jo, and Michael Hill, eds. *Women and Symbolic Interaction.* Winchester, Mass.: Allen & Unwin, 1987. In their analysis of the feminine self, the authors stress that the self is the core basis for our interactions and for understanding our place in society.

Doane, Janice, and Devon Hodges. *Nostalgia and Sexual Difference: The Resistance to Contemporary Feminism.* New York: Methuen, 1987. The authors discuss the controversy over feminism, which has thoroughly divided both male and female Americans, despite the fact that its basic goal, equality, is a central American value.

Epstein, Cynthia Fuchs. *Deceptive Distinctions: Sex, Gender, and the Social Order.* New Haven, Conn.: Yale University Press, 1988. Epstein argues that the distinctions between the sexes are the social products of a sexist society and that they are used as barriers to deny equality.

Friedan, Betty. *The Feminine Mystique.* New York: Norton, 1963. The best-seller that captured the imagination of American women, galvanizing and inspiring the women's movement in the 1960s.

Lunneborg, Patricia W. *Women Changing Work.* Westport, Conn.: Greenwood Press, 1990. Based on interviews with women doing "men's jobs," the author distinguishes four major ways in which women are changing male-dominated work: a greater service orientation to clients, a more nurturing approach to coworkers, a more balanced lifestyle, and a different use of power in management.

Rhode, Deborah L., ed. *Theoretical Perspectives on Sexual Difference,* New Haven, Conn.: Yale University Press, 1990. Rhode examines sociological, anthropological, and psychological theories of sexual differences, emphasizing feminist theory.

Stolz, Barbara Ann. *Still Struggling.* Lexington, Mass.: D. C. Heath, 1985. Featuring the problems and struggles of working women with low incomes, the author presents the world from their perspective and analyzes the social factors that oppress them.

Tannen, Deborah. *You Just Don't Understand: Women and Men in Conversation.* New York: William Morrow, 1990. A psycholinguist documents the extent to which speech patterns of men and women are related to basic differences in their social worlds.

Zuckerman, Harriet, Jonathan R. Cole, and John T. Bruer. *The Outer Circle: Women in the Scientific Community.* New York: Norton, 1991. The authors explore the degree to which the exclusion of women from the "inner circle" of male-dominated science results in an alienation that has profound effects on their work.

Journals

The following four journals focus on the role of gender in social life: *Feminist Studies, Gender and Society, Sex Roles,* and *Signs: Journal of Women in Culture and Society.*

CHAPTER 12

Malcah Zeldis, Wedding, *1973*

Inequalities of Race and Ethnicity

BASIC CONCEPTS IN RACE AND ETHNIC RELATIONS
Race: Myth and Reality ■ Ethnic Groups ■ Minority Groups

PREJUDICE AND DISCRIMINATION
Perspectives: **Clashing Cultures** ■ When Prejudice and Discrimination Don't Match ■ The Extent of Prejudice

THEORIES OF PREJUDICE
Thinking Critically about Social Controversy: **Racism on Campus** ■ Psychological Perspectives ■ Sociological Perspectives: Functionalism, Conflict, and Symbolic Interaction

INDIVIDUAL AND INSTITUTIONAL DISCRIMINATION

PATTERNS OF INTERGROUP RELATIONS
Genocide ■ Population Transfer ■ Internal Colonialism ■ Segregation ■ Assimilation ■ Pluralism

RACE AND ETHNIC RELATIONS IN THE UNITED STATES
The Dominance of White Anglo-Saxon Protestants ■ White Ethnics ■ African Americans ■ Hispanic Americans (Latinos) ■ *Down-to-Earth Sociology:* **The Illegal Travel Guide** ■ *Perspectives:* **The Browning of America** ■ Asian Americans ■ Native Americans ■ *Thinking Critically about Social Controversy:* **Whose History?**

PRINCIPLES FOR IMPROVING ETHNIC RELATIONS

SUMMARY

SUGGESTED READINGS

The colonel was exhausted. He scowled as he looked at the long line facing him.

"Sometimes I wonder if it's worth the effort," he thought. "But someone's got to do it. They're short of men, and we all have to make sacrifices in war."

The colonel looked at the young man and woman standing in front of his desk—disheveled, unkempt hair, the man unshaven for weeks, both reeking a strong odor. The body odor was one of the worst parts of his job. That was why he always kept a fan blowing across his desk. At least it helped a little.

"I'm glad I don't have to touch them," the colonel thought, as he scratched his shoulder. His shoulder was acting up again. He could hardly wait to get home to Hilda. She would rub it, as she always did after a hard day's work. "If it weren't for my wife and kids, I don't know how I could keep going," he mused.

The colonel glanced at the pair again. "He seems strong enough. There's still some work in him," he thought. "But she's too weak." He motioned the young man to the right, the young woman to the left.

There was no doubt about the next seven. Four were old, two were young children, and one hobbled as he walked. "They wouldn't last a day. Just a waste of time," the colonel said to himself. He motioned them to the left.

The line seemed to stretch to eternity. Indeed, the line did stretch to eternity. The colonel was a member of the Schutzstaffel, the infamous Nazi SS. As a physician, he had been assigned to Auschwitz, the concentration camp that served a double purpose: mass extermination and the employment of slave labor (Rubenstein 1987). His job was not to heal, but to sort people into two groups. Children, the elderly, and the weak were sent to one door—from which they were transported to the gas ovens. Those who looked strong entered the other door, from which they emerged as factory slaves. They labored until they dropped from overwork and lack of nutrition, ordinarily just a matter of a few weeks.

While you and I are not likely to feel sympathy for the colonel—hurting shoulder or not—the fact is that quite ordinary people cooperated with the Nazi death machine (Hughes 1993). Perhaps through this chapter you will come to better understand how that could be.

BASIC CONCEPTS IN RACE AND ETHNIC RELATIONS

Race: Myth and Reality

With its almost six billion people, the world offers a fascinating variety of human shapes and colors. Skin color that is black, white, red (not really), yellow, and almost all hues of brown. Eyes in various shades of blue, brown, and green. Thick and thin lips. Straight hair, curly hair, kinky hair, black, white, red, and yellow hair—and, again, all hues of brown.

As humans spread throughout the world, their adaptations to diverse climate and other living conditions resulted in this fascinating variety of complexions, colors, and shapes. Genetic mutations added distinct characteristics to the peoples of the globe. In this sense the concept of **race,** a group with inherited physical characteristics that distinguish it from another group, is a reality. Humans do indeed come in a variety of colors and shapes.

In two senses, however, race is a myth, a fabrication of the human mind. The *first* fabrication is the idea that any one race is superior to another. All races have their geniuses—and their idiots. Like language, no race is superior to another. Adolf Hitler's ideas were extreme. He believed that a superior race, called the Aryans, was responsible for the cultural achievements of Europe. These tall, fair-skinned blonds—the "master race"—possessed the genetic stuff that made them inherently superior. (Never mind that Hitler was not a blond!) Consequently, the Aryans were destined to establish a higher culture and institute a new world order. This destiny required them to avoid the "racial contamination" that breeding with inferior races would engender and to isolate or destroy races that might endanger Aryan culture.

The colonel in our opening vignette, even though educated in one of the best medical schools of the time, bought that line. He gave up healing and began mass killing—all in the name of what was good for the "master race." Even many scientists of the time—not only in Germany but throughout Europe and the United States—espoused the idea of racial superiority. Not surprisingly, they considered themselves members of the supposedly superior race!

In addition to the myth of racial superiority, there is a *second* myth—that of the existence of a "pure" race. From the perspective of contemporary biology, humans show such a mixture of physical characteristics—in skin color, hair texture, nose shape, head shape, eye color, and so on—that "pure" races do not exist. Instead of falling into distinct types clearly separate from one another, human characteristics flow endlessly together. These minute gradations made arbitrary any attempt to draw definite lines.

Large groupings of people, however, can be classified by blood type and gene

Essay #1

L. Obj. 1: Distinguish between the concepts of race and ethnicity, and explain how race can be both a reality and a myth.

CDQ 1: Can you explain why race is in some ways a myth?

race: inherited physical characteristics that distinguish one group from another

Fanning hatred for Jews as a scapegoat for Germany's problems and preaching the superiority of the supposed racially pure Aryans, Adolf Hitler eventually put his ideas of race into effect. The result was the Holocaust, the wholesale and systematic slaughter of Jews and others deemed racially inferior. In the photo on the left, Hitler is addressing a group called "Hitler Youth," a sort of Boy Scouts dedicated to serving Hitler and his ideas. The photo on the right is of U.S. Senators visiting the concentration camp at Buchenwald after Germany's defeat in World War II, where they view a small part of the consequences of Hitler's racial ideas.

frequencies. Yet even this arrangement does not uncover "race." Rather, such classifications are so arbitrary that biologists and anthropologists can draw up listings showing any number of "races." Ashley Montagu (1964), a physical anthropologist, pointed out that some scientists have classified humans into only two "races" while others have found as many as two thousand. Montagu (1960) himself classified humans into forty "racial" groups.

This is not meant to imply that the *idea* of race is a myth. That idea is definitely very much alive. It is firmly embedded in our culture, a social reality that we confront daily (Rothenberg 1990). As noted in Chapter 4, sociologist W. I. Thomas observed that "if people define situations as real, they are real in their consequences." The fact that no race is superior or that biologically we cannot even decide how people should be classified into races is not what counts. What makes a difference for social life, rather, is that people *believe* these ideas, for *people act on beliefs, not facts.* As a result, we always have people like Hitler—and those like the colonel who agree with him. Most people, fortunately, do not believe in such extremes, yet most people also appear to be ethnocentric enough to believe, at least just a little, that their *own* race is superior to others.

Ethnic Groups

Whereas the term *race* refers to biological characteristics that distinguish one people from another, **ethnicity** and **ethnic** apply to cultural characteristics. Derived from the Greek *ethnos,* meaning "people" or "nation," these terms refer to people who identify with one another on the basis of common ancestry and cultural heritage. Their sense of belonging centers on country of origin, distinctive foods, dress, family names and relationships, language, music, religion, and other customs.

ethnic (and ethnicity): having distinctive cultural characteristics

Although this distinction between race and ethnicity is clear—one is biological, the other cultural—people often confuse the two. This confusion is due to the cultural differences people see *and* the way they define race. For example, many people consider the Jews a race—including many Jews. Jews, however, are more properly considered an ethnic group, for it is their cultural characteristics, especially religion, that bind them together. Wherever Jews have lived in the world, they have intermarried. Consequently, Jews in China may look mongoloid, while some Swedish Jews are blue-eyed blonds. This matter is even more strikingly illustrated in the case of the Ethiopian Jews, who look so different from European Jews that when they immigrated to Israel some felt that they could not *really* be Jews.

Minority Groups

Sociologist Louis Wirth (1945) defined a **minority group** as people who are singled out for unequal treatment and who regard themselves as objects of collective discrimination. Either physical (racial) or cultural (ethnic) differences can be the basis of the unequal treatment. Wirth added that discrimination excludes minorities from full participation in the life of their society.

Surprisingly, this term does not necessarily mean that a minority group is a numerical minority. For example, before India's independence in 1947, a handful of British colonial rulers collectively discriminated against millions of Indians, while under apartheid in South Africa a tiny white minority controlled and discriminated against the black majority. Accordingly, sociologists refer to those who do the discriminating not as the majority but, rather, as the **dominant group,** for they have greater power, more privileges, and higher social status.

Emergence of Minority Groups.   A group becomes a minority through the expansion of political boundaries by another group. As anthropologists Charles Wagley and Marvin Harris (1958) pointed out, small tribal societies contain no minority groups. (The exception is women, as discussed in Chapter 11.) In tribal societies everyone is "related," speaks the same language, practices the same customs, shares similar values, and belongs to the same physical stock. When one group expands its political boundaries, however, its action produces minority groups, as people with different customs, languages, values, and physical characteristics then become bound into a single political entity. A second way in which a group becomes a minority is by moving—or being transported—into a territory. A notable example is African-American slaves in the United States.

The dominant group almost always considers its privileged position to be due to its own innate superiority. Being in a position of political power—and unified by shared physical and cultural traits—the dominant group uses its position to discriminate against those with different—and supposedly inferior—traits.

Shared Characteristics.   Wagley and Harris identified five characteristics shared by minorities worldwide.

1. Membership in a minority group is an ascribed status; that is, it is not voluntary, but comes through birth (see Chapter 4).
2. The physical or cultural traits that distinguish minorities are held in low esteem by the dominant group.
3. Minorities are unequally treated by the dominant group.
4. Minorities tend to marry within their own group.
5. Minorities tend to feel strong group solidarity (a sense of "we-ness").

These conditions—especially when combined with collective discrimination—tend to create a shared sense of identity among minorities, and, in many instances, even a sense of common destiny.

CDQ 2: Why do you think people often confuse race and ethnicity?

Project 1

K.P.: Louis Wirth

L. Obj. 2: Define the term "minority groups" and identify five characteristics shared by minority groups worldwide.

K.P.: Charles Wagley and Marvin Harris

CDQ 3: Do you consider yourself to be a member of a minority group? Why or why not?

minority group: people who are singled out for unequal treatment, and who regard themselves as objects of collective discrimination

dominant group: the group with the most power, greatest privileges, and highest social status

PREJUDICE AND DISCRIMINATION

Although virtually all Americans are familiar with prejudice and discrimination, the United States certainly has no monopoly on these negative features of social life. On the contrary, they appear to characterize every society, regardless of size. The Perspectives box below recounts the prejudice and discrimination now rampant in Europe. In Northern Ireland, Protestants discriminate against Roman Catholics; in Israel, Ashkenazi Jews, primarily of European descent, discriminate against Sephardi Jews from Asian and African backgrounds; and in Japan, the Japanese discriminate against just about anyone who isn't Japanese, especially the Koreans and Ainu who live there (Spivak 1980; Fields 1986). In some places the elderly discriminate against the

CDQ 4: What examples can you give of situations where prejudice leads to discrimination?

L. Obj. 3: Differentiate between prejudice and discrimination and discuss reasons why prejudice and discrimination do not always match.

P E R S P E C T I V E S
Cultural Diversity Around the World

Clashing Cultures

"Africans and Italians don't mix," shouts Michele Corti, who has organized a protest against new housing for Arabs and Africans in Milan, Italy. "Milan is becoming the Bronx of Italy," he says.

Western European countries that once sent their huddled masses to the United States are now fending off the tired and poor from the Third World. When the economy of western Europe boomed, accompanied by plummeting birthrates (see Chapters 14 and 20), a need was created for immigrant labor. Workers from the Third World answered that need.

The result has been clashing cultures, accompanied by prejudice and discrimination—some of it mild, some violent, all of it ugly.

Heiko Baumert of Berlin, who sports tattoos of swastikas and storm troopers on his arms, says, "If you mix races in Germany, it never works." The young man next to him, with shaved head and black, steel-toed boots, adds, "We want to wake up Germans and pressure the state to kick the foreigners out."

"Foreigners Out" declare the graffiti on a nearby nightclub. The young men, numbering about three hundred, who have battled Africans in an adjoining block, say, "It is demagoguery to ignore the achievements of the Nazis."

In France, where immigrants from North Africa make up 8 percent of the population, the National Front was dismissed as a racist fringe group just a few years ago. The party's slogan, "Let's Make France for the French," has hit a national nerve. Jean-Marie Le Pen, the head of

the party, says, "If integration between Islamic immigrants and the French were possible, it would have happened already. We must make these people go back to their homes." Bruno Megret, the chief strategist of the National Front, adds, "France must be made racially pure. Racial integration corrupts. There is a worldwide cosmopolitan conspiracy that seeks to abolish national identity and infect the world with the AIDS virus." In 1992, the National Front carried 14 percent of votes nationwide.

Italy is home to a million immigrants, and thousands more are arriving weekly. In the city of Florence, residents have thrown bottles and set guard dogs on North Africans. "There is a long tradition in Italy of regarding anyone from outside your own village with suspicion," explains Roberto Formigoni, a vice president of the European Parliament.

The slowing economies of Europe have made the situation even more tense. In Austria, the birthplace of Hitler, the right-wing Freedom party has scored big gains on an anti-immigration platform.

And the immigrants? They are caught between two worlds. For many, their native country has become as foreign as their adopted land. With this upsurge in racism, however, their desire for a better life—which drew them from their homelands—is now tinged with fear. As Phung Tien, a thirty-year-old factory worker from Vietnam, who is living in Germany, succinctly expresses the matter, "I don't want to go home, but I don't want to die either."

Source: Based on Horwitz and Forman 1990; Forman and Carrington 1991; Gumbel 1992; Shlaes 1992.

Speaker Sug. #1: Individuals willing to discuss situations in which they have experienced prejudice and discrimination.

young, in others the young against the elderly. And, as discussed in Chapter 11, all around the world men discriminate against women.

As you can see from this list, **discrimination** is an *action*—unfair treatment directed against someone. When the basis of such discrimination is race, it is known as **racism,** but discrimination can be based on many characteristics other than race—including age, sex, height, weight, income, education, marital status, sexual orientation, disease, disability, religion, and politics. Discrimination is often the result of **prejudice**—a prejudging of some sort, usually in a negative way—which is an *attitude*. Positive prejudice exaggerates the virtues of a group, such as thinking that some group (usually one's own) is more capable than others. Most prejudice, however, is negative, a prejudgment that some groups are inferior.

When Prejudice and Discrimination Don't Match

Before you began reading this chapter, it is likely that you knew something very obvious: prejudiced people discriminate—at least if they have the chance—and nonprejudiced people do not. As you have seen over and over in this text, sociologists have disproved many of the things people commonly take for granted. So it is in this instance.

K.P.: Robert Merton

TR#17M: The Relationship between Attitudes and Actions

Back in 1934, when prejudice against the Chinese was more widespread than it is today and there were no laws against discrimination, sociologist Richard LaPiere designed a simple study. He and a Chinese couple traveled around the United States, staying or eating at over 250 hotels and restaurants. LaPiere waited six months and then wrote to all of these businesses asking if they were willing to serve "members of the Chinese race." Over 90 percent replied that they would not serve Chinese. Yet, on their entire trip, LaPiere and his friends *had been refused service only once.*

Sociologist Robert Merton (1949) found such inconsistencies fascinating. As he thought about the matter, Merton concluded that there were four possible connections between attitudes and actions. These are shown on Figure 12.1 and explained below.

1. *The All-Weather Bigot.* The all-weather bigot meets our expectations, for attitudes and actions are consistent: he or she is both prejudiced and discriminates. This person is likely to say, "Of course I discriminate—they deserve it."

2. *The Fair-Weather Bigot.* The fair-weather bigot's attitudes and actions do not match. Although this person is prejudiced against the minority, he or she does not discriminate. With today's civil rights legislation, the most common reason for such failure to discriminate is to avoid legal penalties. If in business, this person is likely to say, "I don't like them, but I can't turn them away."

3. *The Fair-Weather Liberal.* The fair-weather liberal's attitudes and actions don't match either. Although the fair-weather liberal believes in equal treatment, he or she discriminates. In the 1960s, when racial discrimination in hotels and restaurants was

discrimination: an *act* of unfair treatment directed against an individual or a group

racism: prejudice and discrimination on the basis of race

prejudice: an *attitude* or prejudging, usually in a negative way

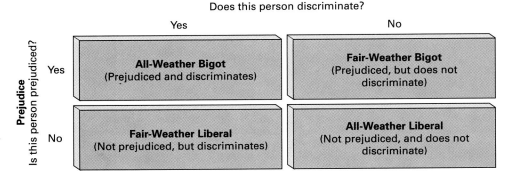

FIGURE 12.1 The Relationship between Attitudes and Actions. (*Source:* Merton 1949, 1976.)

legal—as well as the norm—fair-weather liberals were common. The *social structure* kept them in line, for anyone who refused to discriminate would lose both customers and social standing. Although restaurants today cannot bar minorities, they can give them slower service (Farrell and Jones 1988; Feagin 1991), and servers who are not prejudiced find themselves cooperating in this form of discrimination. They are likely to say, "What else can I do?"

4. *The All-Weather Liberal.* Like the all-weather bigot, this person's attitudes and behaviors are consistent. The all-weather liberal is neither prejudiced nor discriminates. He or she is likely to say, "Everyone should be treated equally. Anything less is un-American and immoral, and I would never be a part of it."

As we have seen, attitudes and behaviors do not always match. The fair-weather bigot, for example, does not discriminate despite being prejudiced—but only because doing so might incur such sanctions as legal penalties. And as we also saw in the case of fair-weather liberals, not everyone who discriminates is motivated by prejudice. Thus, although prejudiced people tend to discriminate and nonprejudiced people try to avoid discriminating, there is not always a one-for-one relationship; for the social environment, which creates prejudice in the first place, may encourage or discourage discrimination.

The Extent of Prejudice

Sociologists Lawrence Bobo and James Kluegel (1991) tested the extent to which non-Hispanic white Americans are prejudiced. Using a probability sample (from which we can generalize), they found that younger and more educated whites are more willing to have close, sustained interaction with other groups than are less educated and older whites. Details of their findings are shown in Figure 12.2. We must await a matching study to test the prejudices of African Americans, Hispanic Americans, Native Americans, and Asian Americans.

Perhaps you have noticed that people who are prejudiced against one racial or ethnic group are likely to be prejudiced against other groups. This principle was strikingly illustrated by the research of psychologist Eugene Hartley (1946), who asked people how they felt about various racial and ethnic groups. Besides blacks, Jews, and

CNN: Hate Crimes

TR#18M: Percentage of White Americans Who Believe That Different Races Should Live in Segregated Housing by Education

CDQ 5: Why do you think people who are prejudiced against one racial or ethnic group tend to be prejudiced against other groups as well?

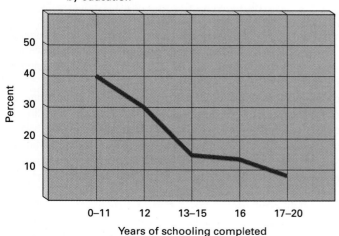

Percentage of white Americans who believe that different races should live in segregated housing, by education

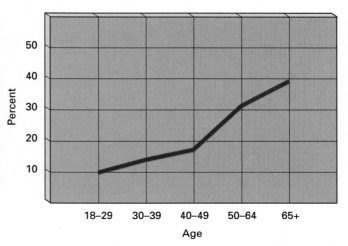

Percentage of white Americans who believe that racial intermarriage should be banned, by age

FIGURE 12.2 Social Distance. (*Source:* Bobo and Kluegel, 1991.)

so on, his list included the Wallonians, Pireneans, and Danireans—names he had made up. Most people who expressed dislike for Jews and blacks also expressed dislike for these three fictitious groups. The significance of Hartley's study is that prejudice does not depend on negative experiences with others. People can be, and are, prejudiced against people they have never met—and even against groups that do not exist!

THEORIES OF PREJUDICE

CNN: Racism on U.S. Campuses

If prejudice does not depend on negative experiences, then, what causes it? Social scientists have developed several theories to explain prejudice. In the following section we look at psychological theories, then at sociological explanations. First, however, we consider an issue with which some of you may already be familiar—that of racism on campus.

THINKING CRITICALLY ABOUT SOCIAL CONTROVERSY

Racism on College Campuses

African-American students were upset, and white students didn't understand why. The economics professor had said, "Not many blacks take my class. It's too tough for them." When he was accused of racism, he denied that he had a racial bone in his body, saying that he had worked hard for thirty-two years to integrate students from different racial backgrounds. "What I said is the truth," he added. When African-American students went to the administration, the professor apologized.

At the fraternity party, the men did a vaudeville skit in which they painted their faces and hands black and sang "Mammy." "It's just good fun," the fraternity president said to his critics. The college administration ruled that blackface skits are within the students' right of free speech. Another fraternity held a slave auction to raise money for the poor. Females were "sold" to the highest bidder. The slaves had to walk their "masters" to class, carry their books, and stand in lunch line for them. Each had SLAVE written on her forehead. When African-American students complained, the response was, "Don't make a big deal out of nothing. This is our annual fund-raising event for the poor. You're too sensitive."

The heat was on the university administration. A professor had written in his weekly column in the student newspaper that Puerto Rican students "traveled in packs" and spoke English only when they wanted to. When criticized, he replied that he had only written the truth, that it was time for minorities to be integrated into student life instead of remaining aloof.

When minority students went to the administration to demand that they "change the college environment," one of the trustees replied, "You should settle down and concentrate on your studies. I think that's the main reason your group isn't doing as well as the whites." The trustee later had to apologize.

The swastika scrawled on a wall, the burning of a cross in front of a predominantly African-American student dormitory, the use of racial slurs such as "nigger" and "kike," the mock hanging of a minority student—everyone knows that all these are blatant racism. But what about the specific events described above? One side, consisting of both minorities and whites, says that they are all racist. The other side defends them as nonracist. Both sides have adherents who say such events must be protected in the name of free speech.

What do you think? Are such incidents racist, and if so are they nevertheless defensible on the grounds of free speech? Should they be banned and the participants disciplined, or tolerated to preserve free speech? Are some minorities too sensitive? Are whites too insensitive? What should be done? Support your position by applying ideas from this chapter.

Now consider this: Why do some students consider an act racist, while others do not? If students at a party dress up as "cowboys and Indians," is their behavior racist? Is it racist only if Native American students object? What if Native American students participate?

Finally, to spell out the symbolic interactionist basis of the issue, in the last example is it the act—or the objection to the act—that makes it racist? (*Source:* Brodie 1989; Farrell and Jones 1988; Fitzgerald 1989; Greene 1989; Belknap 1991; Boulard 1991; Ruffins 1991.)

Psychological Perspectives

Frustration and Scapegoats.   In 1939 psychologist John Dollard and associates suggested that prejudice is the result of frustration. People who are unable to strike out at the real source of their frustration (such as low wages or unemployment) find someone else to blame. They view this **scapegoat**—the group they unfairly blame for their troubles—as having few good traits. In this way a racial, ethnic, or religious minority, which is by no means the true cause of these people's frustration, becomes a convenient—and safe—target on which to vent it.

Even mild frustration can increase prejudice, as three psychologists demonstrated in an ingenious experiment. Emory Cowen, Judah Landes, and Donald Schaet (1959) first measured their subjects' tendencies toward prejudice and then purposely frustrated them. They gave the subjects two puzzles to solve, but made sure that they did not have enough time to solve them. Then, after the subjects had worked furiously on the puzzles, the experimenters shook their heads in disgust and expressed disbelief that the subjects had not finished. A retest of the subjects showed higher scores indicating prejudice. They had directed their frustration outward, onto people who had nothing to do with their problem.

The Authoritarian Personality.   Have you ever wondered if personality is a cause of prejudice—if some people are more inclined to be prejudiced, and others more fair-minded? For psychologist Theodor Adorno, this was no idle speculation. Under Hitler, Adorno had seen the destructive effects of prejudice firsthand. With the horrors he had observed still fresh in his mind following his escape from the Nazis, Adorno wondered whether there was a certain type of individual who was more likely to fall for the racist utterances and policies of people like Hitler, Mussolini, and the Ku Klux Klan.

Adorno and his associates (1950) decided to test this idea. They developed three scales: a series of statements that measured ethnocentrism, antisemitism, and support for strong, authoritarian government. Testing about two thousand people, ranging from college professors to prison inmates, Adorno found that people who scored high on one scale also scored high on the other two. For example, people who agreed with antisemitic statements also agreed that it was good for a government to be highly authoritarian and that foreign ways of life posed a threat to the "American" way.

Adorno concluded that highly prejudiced people have an **authoritarian personality,** a similar psychological makeup characterized by a high degree of conformity, intolerance, insecurity, excessive respect for authority, and submissiveness to superiors. Such people see many threats to their world, are anti-intellectual, and antiscientific. They believe that things are either right or wrong and are disturbed by ambiguity, especially in matters of religion or sex. Adorno concluded that this type of personality is formed in children raised by bigoted, cold, and aloof parents who discipline them harshly. This early family socialization makes such children anxious when confronted by norms and values that differ from their own. Finding a scapegoat, people different from themselves whom they define as inferior, helps to assure them that their positions are right. In this way they avoid having to question their own ideas.

Adorno's research was provocative, and more than a thousand research studies followed. In general, these studies showed that people who are older, less educated,

L. Obj. 4: Compare psychological and sociological perspectives on prejudice. Indicate why sociologists believe psychological explanations are inadequate.

K.P.: John Dollard

CDQ 6: Why are people more likely to look for scapegoats in tough economic times? Can you think of examples?

K.P.: Theodor Adorno

scapegoat: an individual or group unfairly blamed for someone else's troubles

authoritarian personality: Theodor Adorno's term for people who are prejudiced and rank high on scales of conformity, intolerance, insecurity, excessive respect for authority, and submissiveness to superiors

less intelligent, and from a lower social class are more likely to be authoritarian. The research, however, did not support Adorno's ideas about the early socialization of people who rank high on these scales. In fact many believe that Adorno had measured consequences of low education, not socialization (Yinger 1965).

L. Obj. 5: Outline the functionalist, conflict, and symbolic interactionist perspectives on prejudice.

Sociological Perspectives: Functionalism, Conflict, and Symbolic Interaction

Sociologists find psychological explanations inadequate. They stress that the key to understanding prejudice is not the internal state of individuals, but how society is structured. Thus, sociological theories focus on the ways in which some environments foster prejudice, while others reduce it. These theories examine the problem from the functionalist, conflict, and symbolic interactionist perspectives.

Essay #2

Functionalism.   In a telling scene from a television documentary, journalist Bill Moyers interviewed Fritz Hippler, a Nazi intellectual who at the age of twenty-nine was put in charge of the entire German film industry. Hippler said that when Hitler came to power the Germans were not more antisemitic than the French, probably less so. It was one of his assignments to create antisemitism, which he did by producing movies that contained vivid scenes comparing Jews to rats—their breeding threatening to infest the population.

Why was Hippler told to create hatred? Prejudice and discrimination were functional for the Nazis. The Jews provided (1) a common enemy around which the Nazis were able to unite a Germany weakened by its defeat in World War I and bled by rampant inflation; (2) businesses, bank accounts, and other property they could confiscate; and (3) key positions (university professors, reporters, judges, and so on) in which they could place their own flunkies as they fired Jews. In short, making the Jews a target of hatred was functional for the Nazis because it helped unite the German people behind goals of nationalism and power. From the functionalists' point of view, consuming hatred in the end also showed its dysfunctional side, as the Nazi officials who were brought to trial at Nuremberg discovered.

To harness state machinery to hatred as the Nazis did—the schools, police, courts, mass media, and almost all aspects of the government—makes prejudice practically irresistible. Recall the identical twins featured in the Perspectives box on page 59. Oskar and Jack had been separated as babies. Jack was brought up as a Jew in Trinidad, while Oskar was raised as a Catholic in Czechoslovakia. Under the Nazi regime, Oskar learned to hate Jews, in spite of the fact that, unknown to himself, he was a Jew.

K.P.: Muzafer and Carolyn Sherif

That prejudice is functional and shaped by the social environment was dramatically demonstrated by psychologists Muzafer and Carolyn Sherif (1953) in a simple but ingenious experiment. In a boys' summer camp, they first assigned friends to different cabins and then made the cabin the basic unit of competition. Each cabin competed against the others in sports and for status. In just a few days, strong in-groups had formed, and even former lifelong friends were calling one another "cry baby" and "sissy" and showing intense dislike for one another.

CDQ 7: What do you believe is likely to happen when two groups are pitted against each other in an "I-win-you-lose" situation? What can we learn from the Sherif experiment?

The Sherif study illustrates two major points. First, the social environment can be deliberately arranged to generate either positive or negative feelings about people. Second, prejudice, one of the products of pitting group against group in an "I-win-you-lose" situation, is functional in that it creates in-group solidarity and out-group antagonisms. As usual, functionalists do not justify what they observe but, rather, dispassionately identify functions and dysfunctions of human action.

Conflict Theory.   Conflict theorists stress that the ruling class systematically exploits this principle that pitting group against group in a win-or-lose situation creates prejudice. It is in their own class interests for capitalists to split workers along racial or ethnic lines. If white and minority workers are united, they will demand higher wages and better working conditions. In contrast, groups that fear, distrust, or even hate one another will actively work against one another. To reduce solidarity is to weaken bargaining power, drive down costs, and increase profits. Thus the ruling class exploits racial and ethnic strife to produce a **split-labor market,** undermining the strength of workers by dividing them along racial, ethnic, or even gender lines (Reich 1972, 1981; Wilson 1978; Wright 1979).

Unemployment is a weapon that the ruling class uses to help maintain a split-labor market. If everyone were employed, the high demand for labor would put workers in a position to demand pay increases and better working conditions. Keeping some people unemployed, however, provides a **reserve labor force** from which owners can draw when they need to expand production temporarily. When the economy contracts, these workers are easily released to rejoin the ranks of the unemployed. Minority workers are perfect for the reserve labor force, for their presence is a constant threat to white workers with jobs (Willhelm 1980).

The consequences are devastating, say conflict theorists. Just like the boys in the Sherif experiment, African Americans, whites, Hispanic Americans, and so on, see themselves as able to make gains only at one another's expense. They therefore direct their frustration, anger, and hatred toward those whom they see as standing in their way. Pitted against one another, racial and ethnic groups learn to distrust one another instead of recognizing their common class interests and working for their mutual welfare (Szymanski 1976).

Symbolic Interaction.   While conflict theorists focus on the role of the capitalist class in exploiting racial and ethnic inequalities, symbolic interactionists examine how perception and labels produce prejudice.

How Labels Create Prejudice.   "What's in a name?" asked Romeo. In answer he declared, "That which we call a rose/By any other name would smell as sweet." This may be true of roses, but it does not apply to human relations. In that context, words are not simply meaningless labels. Rather, *the labels we learn color the way we see the world.*

Symbolic interactionists stress that labels are an essential ingredient of prejudice. Labels cause **selective perception,** that is, they lead people to see certain things and blind them to others. Through labels, people look at members of a group as though they were all alike. As sociologists George Simpson and Milton Yinger (1972) put it, "New experiences are fitted into old categories by selecting only those cues that harmonize with the prejudgment or stereotype."

Racial and ethnic labels are especially powerful. They are shorthand for emotionally laden stereotypes. The term *nigger,* for example, is not, like Romeo's rose, simply a neutral name. Nor are *honkey, spic, mick, kike, limey, kraut, dago,* or any of the other words people use to derogate ethnic groups. The nature of such words overpowers us with emotions, blocking out rational thought about the people they refer to (Allport 1954).

Symbolic interactionists stress that prejudiced people learn their prejudices in interaction with others. No one is born prejudiced, but at birth each of us joins some particular family and racial or ethnic group, where we learn beliefs and values. There, as part of our basic orientations to the world, we learn to like—or dislike—members of other groups and to perceive them positively or negatively. Similarly, if discrimination is the common practice, we learn to practice it routinely. Just as we learn any other attitudes and customs, then, so we learn prejudice and discrimination.

Stereotypes and Discrimination: The Self-Fulfilling Prophecy.   The stereotypes that we learn from our social environment both justify prejudice and discrimination and produce stereotypical behavior in those who are stereotyped. Let us consider Group X. Negative stereotypes characterize Group X as lazy and therefore appear to

CDQ 8: Do you feel that racial and ethnic groups in the United States can make gains only at one another's expense? Does the system have to be set up this way?

CDQ 9: Can you give examples of how we learn prejudices in interaction with others? Is there such a thing as a "harmless" joke?

Project 2

split-labor market: a term used by conflict theorists for the capitalist practice of weakening the bargaining power of workers by splitting them along racial, ethnic, sex, age, or any other lines

reserve labor force: the term used by conflict theorists for the unemployed, who can be put to work during times of high production and then discarded when no longer needed

selective perception: the ability to see certain points but remain blind to others

justify withholding opportunities from this group and placing its members in inferior positions. The result is a self-fulfilling prophecy. Denied jobs that require high dedication and energy, Group X members are confined to forms of "dirty work" seen as more fitting for "that type" of people. Since much dirty work is irregular, members of Group X are also liable to be readily visible—standing around street corners. The sight of their idleness then reinforces the original stereotype of laziness, while the discrimination that created the "laziness" in the first place passes unnoticed.

INDIVIDUAL AND INSTITUTIONAL DISCRIMINATION

L. Obj. 6: Compare and contrast individual and institutional discrimination. Give examples of each type.

Project 3

CDQ 10: Are individuals always aware that they are discriminating against other people? Are individuals who are being discriminated against always aware that this is occurring?

individual discrimination: the negative treatment of one person by another on the basis of that person's characteristics

institutional discrimination: negative treatment of a minority group that is built into a society's institutions

Sociologists stress that we need to move beyond thinking in terms of **individual discrimination,** the negative treatment of one person by another on the basis of race or ethnicity. While such behavior certainly creates problems for those who are targets, it is primarily a matter of one individual treating another badly. Focusing on human behavior at the group level, sociologists encourage us to think in broader terms, to examine **institutional discrimination,** that is, to see how discrimination is woven into the fabric of society.

Discrimination so pervades American society that it can occur without either the person doing the discriminating or those being discriminated against being aware of it. An example is coronary bypass operations. Mark Wenneker and Arnold Epstein (1989), two physicians, became suspicious that racial discrimination was a factor in this procedure. To test their suspicions, they studied all patients admitted to Massachusetts hospitals for circulatory diseases or chest pain. Comparing patients by their age, sex, race, income, and even whether the medical bill was paid by insurance, the researchers found that whites were 89 percent more likely to be given coronary bypass surgery. A national study of Medicare patients showed an even higher discrepancy—that whites were three times as likely as blacks to receive coronary bypass surgery (Winslow 1992). The particular interracial dynamics that cause medical decisions to be made on the basis of race are unknown at present. It is more than likely that physicians *do not intend* to discriminate. But in ways we do not yet fully understand, discrimination is somehow built into the medical delivery system. Race apparently works as gender does. Just as higher death rates for women following bypass surgery can be traced to the different attitudes physicians have toward their female patients (see Chapter 11, page 291), so race seems to be an unconscious basis for giving or denying access to advanced medical procedures. (For further analysis of the medical system, see Chapter 19.)

Because ideas of race and ethnicity are such a significant part of society, all of us are "properly" classified according to those ideas. This photo illustrates the difficulty such assumptions posed for Israel. The Ethiopians, although claiming to be Jews, looked so different from other Jews that it took several years for Israeli authorities to acknowledge this group's "true Jewishness."

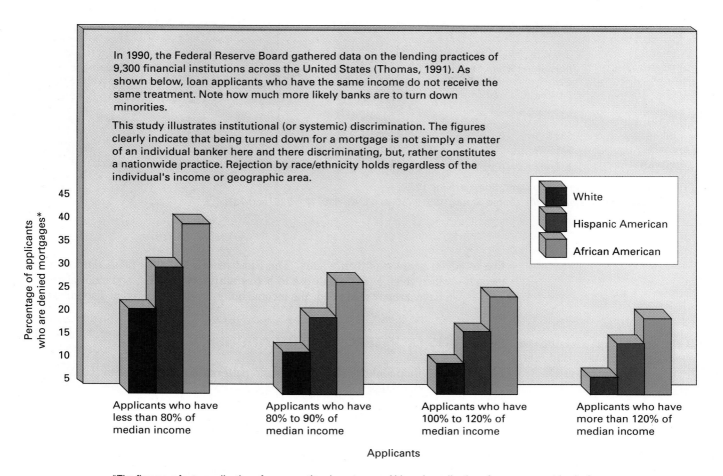

In 1990, the Federal Reserve Board gathered data on the lending practices of 9,300 financial institutions across the United States (Thomas, 1991). As shown below, loan applicants who have the same income do not receive the same treatment. Note how much more likely banks are to turn down minorities.

This study illustrates institutional (or systemic) discrimination. The figures clearly indicate that being turned down for a mortgage is not simply a matter of an individual banker here and there discriminating, but, rather constitutes a nationwide practice. Rejection by race/ethnicity holds regardless of the individual's income or geographic area.

Legend:
- White
- Hispanic American
- African American

Y-axis: Percentage of applicants who are denied mortgages*

X-axis (Applicants):
- Applicants who have less than 80% of median income
- Applicants who have 80% to 90% of median income
- Applicants who have 100% to 120% of median income
- Applicants who have more than 120% of median income

*The figures refer to applications for conventional mortgages. Although applications for government-backed mortgages had lower overall rates of rejection, the identical pattern showed up for all income groups. Median income refers to the income of each bank's local area.

FIGURE 12.3   Percentage of Applicants Who Are Denied Mortgages.*

As Figure 12.3 makes clear, institutional discrimination is readily visible in the area of economic well-being. Overall patterns of discrimination also show up when we examine income. As shown in Table 12.1, family incomes of (non-Hispanic) white Americans are substantially higher than those of African Americans and Hispanic Americans. The average Hispanic-American family income is only about 64 percent of the average white income; the income of the average African-American family is just 57 percent that of whites. Note from this table that the unemployment rate for African Americans runs almost two and a half times that of whites, while for Hispanic Americans it is about one and three-quarter times as high. As this table also shows, differences in the poverty rate are also considerable, two and a half times higher than whites for Hispanic Americans and over three times as high for African Americans.

What is the significance of these statistics? Behind these cold numbers are people who find themselves advantaged or disadvantaged on the basis of race or ethnicity. Just as social class helps to determine an individual's health (see Chapters 10 and 19), so do race and ethnicity (Krieger 1990). As Table 12.2 reflects, discrimination translates into life and death. Note that an African-American baby has *twice* the chance of dying in infancy as a white baby does, an African-American mother is more than three times as likely to die in childbirth as a white woman, and African Americans live

CNN: Banks/Blacks

TR#20: Race and Health

CDQ 11: Why do you think that an African-American baby has twice the chance of dying in infancy as a white baby does?

TABLE 12.1   Indicators of Relative Economic Well-Being, 1990*

	Median Family Income	Percentage of White Median Family Income	Unemployment Rate	Percentage of White Unemployment Rate	Percentage Below Poverty Line	Percentage Above the White Poverty Rate
Non-Hispanic						
White	$33,915		4.7%		10.1%	
Hispanic American	$21,769	64%	8.0%	170%	26.7%	258%
African American	$19,329	57%	11.3%	240%	31.3%	310%

*The reporting dates are inconsistent. Some are for 1989.
Source: Statistical Abstract of the United States, 1991: Tables 43, 45, 635, 721, 725, and 733.

L. Obj. 7: List and describe the six patterns of intergroup relations.

TR#21: Patterns of Intergroup Relations: A Continuum

Essay #3

CDQ 12: Do patterns of genocide still exist today? If yes, can you give examples?

five to seven years less than whites. The basic reason for all of these differences is income—which gives or denies access to better nutrition, housing, and medical care—and, as we have already examined, the income differences are rooted in discrimination.

PATTERNS OF INTERGROUP RELATIONS

In any society that contains minorities, basic patterns develop between the dominant group and the minorities. Those patterns are shown in Figure 12.4: genocide, population transfer, internal colonialism, segregation, assimilation, and pluralism. Let us look at each in turn.

Genocide

As has been observed repeatedly in this book, stereotypes (or labels) powerfully influence human behavior. Symbolic interactionists point out that labels are so powerful that they can even persuade people who have been taught from childhood that hurting others, much less killing them is wrong, to participate in mass murder.

This century's most notorious example is represented in the opening vignette, in which the colonel, educated in music, science, and in sensitivities to the social graces and feelings of others, perceives his participation in **genocide**—the systematic slaughter of an entire people—as an act of patriotism and self-sacrifice. Hitler's attempt to destroy all Jews required the cooperation of ordinary citizens. Those who turned on their neighbors and fellow citizens were not some strange beasts brought forth from the bowels of the earth but, rather, ordinary men and women who were taught to think

genocide: the systematic annihilation or attempted annihilation of a race or ethnic group

TABLE 12.2   Race and Health*

	Infant mortality	Maternal deaths	Life expectancy	
			Males	Females
White	8.5	5.9	72.6	79.1
African American	17.6	19.5	65.2	74.0

*The national data base used for this table does not list these figures for Hispanic Americans or other ethnic groups. White refers to non-Hispanic whites. The rate is the number per 1,000. Infant mortality is the number of deaths per year of infants under one year old per 1,000 live births.
Source: Statistical Abstract of the United States, 1991: Tables 105, 111, and 188.

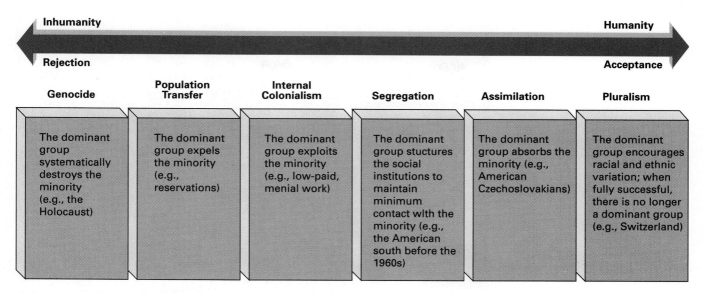

FIGURE 12.4   Patterns of Intergroup Relations: A Continuum

of Jews as *submenschen,* or subhuman. The result was the Holocaust, the slaughter of about six million Jews, a quarter of a million Gypsies, hundreds of thousands of Slavs, and unknown numbers of homosexuals and physically deformed or mentally ill persons—all of whom were defined as "subhumans." The slaughter occurred with the tacit complicity of ordinary German citizens (Hughes 1991).

The Holocaust is, unfortunately, not the only example of the use of labels to justify genocide. The United States government and American settlers did the same thing in referring to Native Americans as "savages." Labeling them clearly as something less than human made it easier to justify killing them. In this instance, as in so many, genocide was motivated by the settlers' desire to take over their resources. Although most Native Americans actually died from diseases brought by the settlers, against which they had no immunity (Kitano 1974; Schaefer 1979; Dobyns 1983; Thornton 1987), the settlers ruthlessly destroyed the Native Americans' food base (buffalos, crops) in order to weaken them so they could take over their lands. They also killed Native Americans who resisted the white settlers' advance toward the West. These policies resulted in the death of more than *90 percent* of Native Americans (Garbarino 1976; Thornton 1987).

During the 1800s, when most of this slaughter occurred, the same thing was happening in other places. In South Africa, the Boers, or Dutch settlers, looked upon the native Hottentots as jungle animals and totally wiped them out. In Tasmania, the British settlers ruthlessly stalked the local aboriginal population, hunting them for sport and sometimes even for dog food. You may wish to look at Perspectives box on page 641 to see how the genocide of native populations is continuing today.

Labels, then, are powerful forces in human life. Labels that dehumanize others help people to **compartmentalize**—to separate their acts from feelings or attitudes that would threaten their self-concept and make it difficult for them to participate in the act (Bernard, Ottenberg, Redl 1968). Thus, *whenever genocide is proposed or practiced, the targeted group is labeled as less than fully human.*

Population Transfer

Population transfer is of two types, indirect and direct. *Indirect* population transfer is achieved by making life so unbearable for members of a minority that they leave "voluntarily." Under the bitter conditions of czarist Russia, for example, millions of

compartmentalize: to separate acts from feelings or attitudes

population transfer: involuntary movement of a minority group

Amidst hysterical fears that Japanese Americans would sabotage industry and military installations on the West Coast, in the early days of World War II Japanese Americans were transferred to "relocation camps." Many returned home after the war to find that their property had been defaced or damaged.

Jews made this "choice." *Direct* transfer takes place when a minority is expelled. Examples include the expulsion of Jews and Arabs from Spain by King Ferdinand and Queen Isabella (who financed Columbus's voyage to America), the relocation of Native Americans to reservations, and the transfer of Americans of Japanese descent to relocation camps during World War II.

Internal Colonialism

In Chapter 9, the term colonialism was used to describe the exploitation of the Third World by the nations of the First World. Conflict theorists use the term **internal colonialism** to describe a society's policy of exploiting a minority group, using social institutions to deny the minority access to the society's full benefits (Blauner 1972). Slavery, reviewed in Chapter 9, is an extreme example of internal colonialism, while the historical pattern of white dominance of minorities is a more "routine" form. The South African system of *apartheid,* now in the fitful process of being dismantled, is another example. Although the dominant Afrikaners despised the minority, they found their presence necessary. As Simpson and Yinger (1972) put it, who else would do all the hard work?

Segregation

Segregation—the formal separation of racial or ethnic groups—accompanies internal colonialism. Segregation allows the dominant group to exploit the labor of the minority (butlers, chauffeurs, housekeepers, nannies, street cleaners) while maintaining social distance (Collins 1986). In the southern United States until the 1960s, by law African Americans and whites had to use separate public facilities such as hotels, schools, swimming pools, bathrooms, and even drinking fountains. In some states, laws also prohibited interracial marriage. In the North, segregation was more of an informal practice, although there, too, a scattering of laws prohibited interracial marriage, while the legal structure upheld residential segregation.

internal colonialism: the systematic economic exploitation of a minority group

Assimilation

Assimilation is the process by which a minority is absorbed into the mainstream culture. There are two types. In *forced* assimilation the dominant group refuses to allow the minority to practice its religion, speak its language, or follow its customs. Prior to the fall of the Soviet Union, for example, the dominant group, the Russians, required that Armenian schoolchildren be instructed in Russian and that Armenians honor Russian, not Armenian, holidays. *Permissible* assimilation, in contrast, permits the minority to adopt the dominant group's patterns in its own way and at its own speed. In Brazil, for example, an ideology favoring the eventual blending of diverse racial types into a "Brazilian stock" encourages its racial and ethnic groups to inter-marry.

Pluralism

A policy of **pluralism** permits or even encourages racial and ethnic variation. For example, the United States has followed a "hands-off" policy toward immigrant associations, foreign-language newspapers, and religion. Freedom of religion became such an important value in the United States that in 1972 sociologists Simpson and Yinger noted that "religious pluralism is now nearly fully the fact as well as the ideal." Today, as Muslim minarets adorn major American cities, we see even greater religious pluralism. Switzerland provides perhaps the most outstanding example of pluralism. The Swiss are a nation made up of three separate ethnic groups—French, Italians, and Germans—who have kept their own languages, and live peacefully in political and economic unity. None of these groups can properly be called a minority.

RACE AND ETHNIC RELATIONS IN THE UNITED STATES

TR#20M: Racial and Ethnic Groups in the United States

Essay #4

L. Obj. 8: Discuss the differences in experiences of White Anglo-Saxon Protestants (WASPs) and those of white ethnics in the United States.

Using these materials as background, we can now sketch an overview of race and ethnic relations in the United States. Like any overview, the information presented forms a composite, that is, a portrait of common characteristics.

The Dominance of White Anglo-Saxon Protestants

The term **WASP** stands for White Anglo-Saxon Protestant. In its narrow meaning WASP refers to Protestant Americans whose ancestors came from England, but in its broader sense it includes all white Protestants from western Europe. Because WASPs settled the original thirteen American colonies, it was they who also established the basic social institutions of what became the United States. Consequently, whatever their background, all subsequent immigrants confronted **Anglo-conformity**; they were expected to speak the English language and to adopt other Anglo-Saxon ways of life. American society was supposedly destined to become a modified version of England.

Table 12.3 shows the racial/ethnic background of Americans today. Note that Americans of English background are still the single most numerous ethnic group—although almost nudged out by Americans of German ancestry. Lacking an official royalty, and somewhat envious of European royal courts, in 1890 some WASPs established the Society of Mayflower Descendants to determine which families possessed the right "blood lines." Membership was limited to those who could trace their ancestry to the immigrants who arrived on the Mayflower. Around the same time, the Social Register Association began to publish the *Social Register*. To be listed in this book is to be deemed a member of the upper class, for only people with "old" money are included. Such organizations help isolate their members from the more "common" folk (Baltzell 1964).

assimilation: the process of being absorbed into the mainstream culture

pluralism: a philosophy that permits or encourages ethnic variation

WASP: a white Anglo-Saxon Protestant; narrowly, an American of English descent; broadly, an American of western European ancestry

Anglo-conformity: the expectation that immigrants to the United States would adopt the English language and other Anglo-Saxon ways of life

TABLE 12.3 Racial and Ethnic Groups in the United States

Racial or ethnic classification	Numbers of Americans
African American	31,571,000
Hispanic American*	20,505,000
Asian American	3,072,000
Chinese	894,000
Filipino	795,000
Japanese	791,000
Korean	377,000
Vietnamese	215,000
Native American	1,479,000
Jamaican	253,000
European ancestry	
English	49,596,000
German	49,224,000
Irish	40,166,000
French	12,892,000
Italian	12,184,000
Scottish	10,049,000
Polish	8,228,000
Dutch	6,304,000
Swedish	4,345,000
Norwegian	3,454,000
Russian	2,781,000
Czech	1,892,000
Hungarian	1,777,000
Welsh	1,665,000
Danish	1,518,000
Portuguese	1,024,000

*Hispanic Americans are also of European ancestry.

Source: *Statistical Abstract of the United States,* 1991: Tables 16, 21, 27, 48.

White Ethnics

Although WASP colonists identified with other whites, not all whites were considered equal. WASPs saw some groups as more "desirable citizens," others less so. The arrival in the United States of **white ethnics**—immigrants, primarily from western Europe, whose language and other customs differed from the WASPs—was greeted with negative stereotypes. For example, Irish immigrants were seen as dirty, lazy drunkards. Other white ethnics—Germans, Poles, Jews, Italians, and so on—were painted with similarly broad strokes. The WASP view was that if people came from another country and had different customs—especially religion or language—something was wrong with them.

Naturally, such attitudes placed great pressure on immigrants to blend into the mainstream culture. The children of most immigrants embraced the new way of life and quickly came to think of themselves as Americans rather than as Germans, French, Hungarians, and so on. They dropped their distinctive customs, especially their language, often seeing them as symbols of shame. This generation of immigrants was caught between two worlds, that of their parents from "the old country" and their new

white ethnics: white immigrants to the United States whose culture differs from that of WASPs

home. It was *their* children who made the easier adjustment, for they had fewer outmoded customs to discard.

These immigrants from western Europe assimilated into the mainstream American culture so successfully that many of their descendants are today only vaguely aware of their ethnic origins. Most can identify the country, but not the city or region. (With extensive interethnic marrying, many do not even know the countries from which their families originated—nor do they care.) In the past few decades, however, many of these people have rediscovered their roots, are developing an appreciation of their ethnic heritage, and are trying to trace family lines and recover a stronger ethnic identity.

African Americans

Chapter 9 analyzed how slavery resulted in a legacy of racism; Chapter 21 below details the lynchings that grew out of this fierce racism. Discrimination was so integral a part of American life that it was not until 1944 that the Supreme Court decided that African Americans could vote in southern primaries, and not until 1954 that they had the legal right to attend the same public schools as whites (Carroll and Noble 1977; Polenberg 1980). Well into the 1950s, the South was still openly—and legally—practicing **segregation.**

King's Leadership and Civil Disobedience. It was 1955, in Montgomery, Alabama. As specified by law, whites took the front seats of the bus, while African Americans went to the back. As the bus filled up, the middle section was needed by whites.

In that section sat a middle-aged African-American woman, Mrs. Rosa Parks. Ordinarily she would have shrugged her shoulders and moved to the back of the bus when more whites got on—as she had so many times before. But today she was tired and didn't feel like moving. So she stubbornly sat there while the bus driver raged and whites felt insulted. Her subsequent arrest touched off mass demonstrations, led fifty thousand blacks to boycott the city's buses for a year, and thrust an otherwise unknown preacher into an historic role.

Dr. Martin Luther King, Jr., who was later to meet his fate at the hands of whites as he participated in strikes by garbage workers in Memphis, Tennessee, took control. He organized car pools and preached nonviolence. Incensed at this radical organizer and at the stirrings in the normally compliant African-American community, segregationists also put their beliefs into practice—by bombing homes and dynamiting churches.

K.P.: Dr. Martin Luther King, Jr.

L. Obj. 9: Outline the history of the African-American experience in the United States. Discuss the role of leaders such as Dr. Martin Luther King, Jr. in creating social change.

Speaker Sug. #3: The Director of African-American, Hispanic-American, Asian-American, or Native-American Studies at your school.

segregation: the policy of keeping racial or ethnic groups apart

Shown here is Mrs. Rosa Parks being fingerprinted in Atlanta following her arrest in 1956 for refusing to give up her bus seat to a white. As detailed in the text, her arrest touched off a bus boycott that thrust Dr. Martin Luther King, Jr., to center stage in the civil rights movement—which eventually transformed American society.

Under King's leadership, **civil disobedience,** the act of deliberately but peacefully disobeying laws considered unjust, became a tactic widely used by civil rights activists to break down institutional barriers. Inspired by Mahatma Ghandi, who had played a critical part in winning India's independence from Britain, King (1958) based his strategy on the following principles.

1. Pursuing active, nonviolent resistance to evil.
2. Not seeking to defeat or humiliate opponents, but to win their friendship and understanding.
3. Attacking the forces of evil rather than the people who are doing the evil.
4. Being willing to accept suffering without retaliating.
5. Refusing to hate the opponent.
6. Acting with the conviction that the universe is on the side of justice.

Rising Expectations and Civil Strife.   The barriers came down slowly, but they did come down. Not until 1964 did Congress pass the Civil Rights Act, making it illegal to discriminate in hotels, theaters, and other public places. Then in 1965, Congress passed the Voting Rights Act, banning the literacy and other tests that had been used to keep eligible African Americans from voting.

Encouraged by such gains, African Americans then experienced what sociologists call **rising expectations;** that is, they believed better conditions would soon follow. The lives of the poor among them, however, changed little, if at all. Frustrations built, finally exploding in Watts in 1965, when people living in that African-American ghetto of central Los Angeles took to the streets in the first of what have been termed "the urban revolts." When King was assassinated on April 4, 1968, ghettos across the nation again erupted in fiery violence. Under threat of the destruction of America's cities, Congress passed the sweeping Civil Rights Act of 1968.

Continued Gains.   Since then, African Americans have made remarkable political and economic progress. They now hold about 6 percent of all elected offices in the state legislatures, three times what they held just ten years ago (Rich 1986; *Statistical Abstract* 1991: Tables 441, 447). In spite of this gain, however, their representation is still only half their proportion of the population. With their large number of votes, African Americans have been politically influential for several decades; the extent of their political prominence was highlighted when Jesse Jackson competed for the Democratic presidential nomination in 1984 and 1988. In 1989, this progress was further confirmed when L. Douglas Wilder of Virginia became the nation's first elected African-American governor (Perry 1990). The political prominence of African Americans came to the nation's attention again in 1991 at the televised Senate hearings held to confirm the appointment of Clarence Thomas to the Supreme Court. After grueling questioning concerning sexual harassment charges brought by a former employee, Thomas was confirmed as the nation's second African-American Supreme Court justice.

An integrated public school system has remained elusive, however. After the Supreme Court victory in 1954 that affirmed the right of equal access to public schools, many whites responded by leaving the cities for all-white suburbs. Other whites continued living where they were, but avoided integrated schools by sending their children to all-white private schools (Farley and Allen 1987; Scott 1988). "White flight" resulted in situations such as that in Atlanta, Georgia, where public schools actually became much more segregated after they were officially integrated—going from 55 percent white to only 10 percent white (Stevens 1980).

As their enrollment in colleges and in graduate and professional schools increased, more African Americans gained better-paying positions. A new middle class then emerged, which is now three times the proportion of the African-American population that it was in 1940. In terms of constant dollars (adjusted for inflation), African-American families with incomes of $50,000 or more increased from 1 out of 17 in 1967

Speaker Sug. #2: Official responsible at your college or university for increasing enrollment/retention of minority students, recruiting minority faculty members.

civil disobedience: the act of deliberately but peacefully disobeying laws considered unjust

rising expectations: the sense that better conditions are soon to follow, which, if unfulfilled, creates mounting frustration

to 1 out of 7 today. The odds of an African American becoming wealthy have increased tenfold since 1940 (Smith and Welch 1986; O'Hare et al. 1991). Many African Americans have been left behind, however. (See Tables 12.1 and 12.2.) One consequence of the continued discrimination and persistent poverty was the riots in South Central Los Angeles in 1992.

Race or Social Class? As opportunities continue to open up for educated middle-class African Americans, while the urban poor are stuck in a quagmire of poverty, some sociologists have suggested that the significant factor today is social class rather than race. Sociologist William Wilson (1978, 1987) argued that the African-American community is divided into two groups—those with money and those without. When the expansion of civil rights generated new opportunities, the middle class moved out of the ghettos. Just at that time, however, manufacturing jobs declined, and many blue-collar jobs were transferred to the suburbs. The removal of secure jobs along with the flight of the middle class left behind the impoverished, described by sociologists Douglas Massey and Mitchell Eggers (1990) as "an isolated and very poor community without the institutions, resources, and values necessary for success in modern society."

The result, claimed Wilson, was the creation of two worlds of African-American experience. One consists of those who are stuck in the ghetto. There they continue to live in poverty, confront violent crime daily, attend terrible schools, face dead-end jobs or welfare, and are filled with hopelessness and despair, combined with apathy or hostility. The other consists of those who have moved up the social class ladder, live in good housing in relatively crime-free neighborhoods, have well-paid jobs that offer advancement, and send their children to good schools. Their middle-class experiences and middle-class lifestyle have changed their views on life. Their aspirations and values have become so altered that they no longer have much in common with African Americans who remain poor. According to Wilson, then, social class is the major determinant of their quality of life.

Many sociologists point out that this analysis omits the vital element—discrimination—that still underlies the relative impoverishment of African Americans. (Cf. Feagin and Feagin 1986; Landry 1987; Feagin 1991; Keith and Herring 1991.) Some emphasize that gains have slowed and that at *all* levels, whether among factory workers, managers, or supervisors, income gaps still exist—with whites *always* on top (Oliver and Glick 1982; O'Hare 1991). Both Wilson and his critics agree that poverty is proportionately much greater among African Americans. It is Wilson's claim, however, that processes related to social class—not race—are mainly responsible for perpetuating this situation (Wilson 1981).

It is likely that both ethnic discrimination and a disadvantaged social status contribute to the conditions experienced by this largest minority group in the United States. It is also likely that African Americans who occupy an advantaged class position and enjoy greater opportunities face less discrimination.

In spite of the greater opportunities that have allowed many African Americans to become middle class, they remain worse off than whites on *all* indicators of well-being, including employment, poverty, housing, education, and even health and mortality. (See Tables 12.1 and 12.2) Sociologist William O'Hare et al. (1991) summarized the situation.

The gap between the well-being of blacks and whites is continuing evidence of the second-class status of African Americans. Black infants are twice as likely to die as are white infants. Black children are nearly three times more likely to live in a single-parent family or to live in poverty than are white children. Blacks are only half as likely to go to college; those who earn college degrees have incomes one-third less than do whites with the same education. And, while the number of affluent blacks has skyrocketed over the past decade, the net [average] wealth of black households is only one-tenth that of whites.

Essay #5

CNN: Separate and Unequal

TR#21M: Varying Explanations of Inequality by Race, Class, and Gender

CDQ 13: Do you agree with the idea that social class rather than race is the most significant factor in determining the life chances of African Americans in the United States today? Why or why not?

K.P.: William Wilson

Chicanos: Hispanic Americans whose country of origin is Mexico

Hispanic Americans (Latinos)

Numbers, Origins, and Location.   The second-largest ethnic group in the United States is the *Hispanic Americans*, or Latinos, people of Spanish origin. In addition to the fourteen to twenty million **Chicanos** (those whose country of origin is Mexico), this minority includes about two million Puerto Ricans, a million Cuban Americans, and about three million people from Central or South America, primarily Venezuela and Colombia. While most Chicanos live in the southwestern states, most Puerto Ricans live in New York City and Cuban Americans are concentrated in the Miami area.

Officially tallied at twenty-one million (see Figure 12.5), the actual number of people of Hispanic origin living in the United States is considerably higher and could reach twenty-five or twenty-seven million. No one knows for certain because, although the vast majority of Latinos are legal residents, large numbers have entered the country illegally. Such individuals, not surprisingly, avoid contact with both public officials and census forms. Each year more than one million persons are apprehended at the border or at points inland and deported to Mexico (Armstrong 1986), but perhaps as many as two or three million manage to enter the United States. Most migrate for temporary work and then return to their homes and families. (The Down-to-Earth Sociology box on page 331 explores this vast subterranean immigration.) Their immigration has been so extensive that although 85 percent of Chicanos in 1960 were born in the United States, today a majority of all Hispanic Americans are immigrants or the children of immigrants (Chavez 1990).

To gain an understanding of these numbers, note that roughly as many people of Hispanic origin live in the United States as there are Canadians in Canada. To midwesterners, such a comparison often comes as a surprise, for members of this minority are virtually absent from vast stretches of Middle America. Hispanic Americans, however, are bringing seismic changes to some areas of the country. As shown in Figure 12.6, three out of four are concentrated in just four states: California, Texas, New York, and Florida (Vega 1990). Florida's Dade County is nearly half Hispanic, while Los Angeles, New York City, and Houston are about one-quarter Hispanic. In the largest state, California, Hispanic Americans are expected to *outnumber* Anglos before the end of the century (Engardio 1988). And by the year 2015 their population is expected to top forty million, making them this nation's largest minority group (Corchado 1989). For changes in the ethnic composition of the United States, see the Perspectives box on page 332.

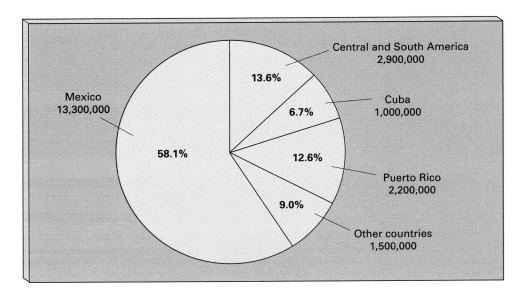

FIGURE 12.5 Country of Origin of the Hispanic American Population of the United States. (*Source:* The Hispanic Population of the United States: March 1990, Bureau of the Census.)

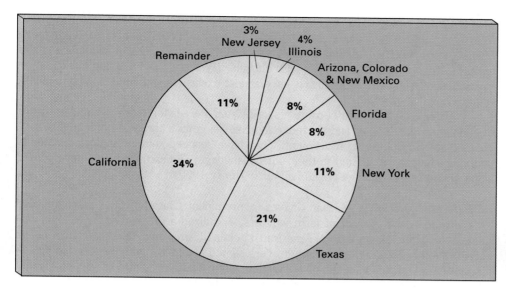

FIGURE 12.6 Geographic distribution of the Hispanic-American population. (*Source:* Bureau of the Census.)

DOWN-TO-EARTH SOCIOLOGY

The Illegal Travel Guide

Manuel was a drinking buddy of Jose's, a man I had met on an earlier trip to Mexico. At forty-five, Manuel can best be described as friendly, outgoing, and enterprising.

Manuel lived in the United States for seven years and speaks fluent English. Preferring his home town in Colima, Mexico, where he can pal around with his childhood friends, Manuel always seemed to have money and free time.

When Manuel invited me to go on a business trip with him, I quickly accepted. I never could figure out how Manuel made his living and how he was able to afford a car—a luxury that none of his friends had. As we traveled from one remote village to another, Manuel would gather a crowd and sell used clothing that he had heaped in the back of his older-model Ford station wagon.

While chickens ran in and out of the dirt-floored, thatched-roof hut, Manuel spoke in whispers to a slender man of about twenty-three. The sense of poverty was overwhelming. Juan, as his name turned out to be, had a partial grade school education. He also had a wife, four hungry children under the age of five—and two pigs, his main food supply. Although eager to work, he had no job—and no prospects of getting one, for there was simply no work available.

As we were drinking a Coke, the national beverage of the poor of Mexico, Manuel explained to me that he was not only selling clothing—he was also lining up migrants to the United States. For $200 he would take a man

to the border and introduce him to a "wolf," who, for another $200 would surreptitiously make a night crossing into the promised land.

When I saw the hope in Juan's face, I knew nothing would stop him. He was borrowing every cent he could from every relative to get the $400 together. He would make the trip although he risked losing everything if apprehended—for wealth beckoned on the other side. He personally knew people who had been there and spoke in glowing terms of its opportunities.

Looking up from the children playing on the dirt floor with the chickens pecking about them, I saw a man who loved his family and was willing to suffer their enforced absence, as well as the uncertainties of a foreign culture whose language he did not know, in order to make the desperate try for a better life.

Juan handed me something from his billfold, and I looked at it curiously. I felt tears as I saw the tenderness with which he handled this piece of paper—his passport to opportunity—a social security card made out in his name, sent by a friend who had already made the trip and who was waiting for Juan.

It was then that I knew that the thousands of Manuels scurrying about the face of Mexico and the millions of Juans they were transporting could never be stopped—for the United States held their only dream of a better life.

Source: James M. Henslin

The Spanish Language.   The Spanish language distinguishes Hispanic Americans from other ethnic minorities in the United States. Although not all of them speak Spanish, most can. It is estimated that half of all Hispanic-American adults are unable to speak English or can do so only with difficulty (Whitman 1987). Being fluent only in Spanish in a society where English is used almost exclusively presents a major obstacle to getting a well-paid job.

The use of Spanish has become a social issue. Perceiving the growing prevalence of Spanish in advertising and on radio and television as a threat, some Anglos have initiated an "English First" movement. They have succeeded in getting most states to consider a law to make English their official language; and sixteen states have passed some version of such a law (Whitman 1987; Henry 1990).

K.P.: Cesar Chavez

Politics and Disunity.   Cesar Chavez, a prominent Chicano leader who crusaded for years on behalf of migrant farm workers, organized a grape boycott in 1965 that carried the labor struggle into American kitchens. After five years of conflict, the boycott succeeded when the grape growers signed a contract with the Chavez group. Migrant farm workers gained further strength when they later affiliated with the largest national labor organization in the United States, the AFL-CIO.

P E R S P E C T I V E S
Cultural Diversity in U.S. Society

The Browning of America

Studies of population trends in the United States indicate a future that surprises many. Currently, almost one American in four defines himself or herself as Hispanic or nonwhite. If current trends in immigration and birth persist, by the year 2000 the population of Asian Americans will increase about 22 percent, that of Hispanic Americans about 21 percent, and that of African Americans about 12 percent. During this same period, whites are expected to increase by a puny 2 percent.

By the year 2020, the number of Hispanic Americans and nonwhites will double, to nearly 115 million, but the white population will show no increase at all (see Chapter 20). The year 2056, when someone born today will be in his or her sixties, is expected to be the watershed year, for then the "average" American will trace his or her descent to Africa, Asia, the Hispanic world, the Pacific Islands, Arabia—to almost anywhere but white Europe.

In some places, the future has already arrived. In the entire state of New York, 40 percent of elementary and secondary schoolchildren belong to an ethnic minority. In California, 51 percent of schoolchildren are Hispanic American and nonwhite: 31 percent Hispanic American, 11 percent Asian American, and 9 percent African American.

A truly multicultural society will pose unique problems and opportunities. For example, in 2056, when "minorities" are expected to outnumber whites, there will be a large number of retirees but dwindling numbers of workers who pay taxes to pay for their Social Security benefits. For race and ethnic relations, the significance is

that most of the retirees will be white, and most of the workers from today's minorities.

White Americans, who have enjoyed a privileged status in the United States, are unlikely to welcome this changed balance. Political backlashes of various sorts are likely. For example, the "English First" movement is a reaction to the growing influence of Spanish-speaking Americans. Similarly, African Americans, who feel that they have waited the longest and endured the most in the fight for equal opportunity, resist gains made by Hispanic Americans. They also feel that as affirmative action has been broadened to include even white women, it has become of less value for them.

Finally, this change will mean a rethinking of American history as citizens debate the source of the nation's successes and just what its "unalterable" beliefs and other national symbols are. No longer, for example, will the meaning of the Alamo and the West be clear. Did the Alamo represent the heroic action of dedicated Americans against huge odds—or the well-deserved death of extremists bent on wresting territory from Mexico? Was the West settled by individuals determined to find economic opportunity and freedom from oppression—or a savage conquest, just another brutal expression of white imperialism?

While we cannot predict the particulars, of one thing we can be certain—that the future will be challenging as the United States undergoes this fundamental transformation in its population.

Source: Henry 1990; Whitman 1987.

With the recent arrival of large numbers of Hispanics into the United States, the use of Spanish has become controversial. One issue is the use of Spanish in schools. Some feel that Spanish should be used in grade school to help assimilate the children of Hispanic immigrants, while others take the position that these children will assimilate better if instruction is given only in English.

Divisions of national origin and social class prevent political unity (Skerry and Hartman 1991). Hispanic Americans see national origin as highly significant; Puerto Ricans, for example, feel little in common with Chicanos, or with those from Venezuela, Colombia, or El Salvador. People from rural and urban areas also bring with them different cultural traditions. Nevertheless, the ability to appeal to a broad segment of voters has resulted since 1900 in the election of six Hispanic-American governors in three states: New Mexico, Arizona, and Florida (Chavez 1990). Although they make up 8 percent of the American population, Hispanic Americans hold only 1 to 2 percent of elected offices nationwide.

Social class divisions also make united action difficult. Like people of other ethnic backgrounds, huge gulfs exist among Hispanic Americans based on education and income. The half-million Cubans who fled Castro's rise to power in 1959, for example, were mostly well-educated, well-to-do professionals or businesspeople. In contrast, the one-hundred-thousand "boat people" from Cuba who arrived in 1980 were mostly lower-class refugees, people with whom the earlier arrivals would not even have associated in Cuba. The earlier arrivals, firmly established in Florida and in control of many businesses and financial institutions, continue to feel a chasm between themselves and the more recent immigrants.

Fragmented among themselves and discriminated against by Anglos, Hispanic Americans also find strong divisions between themselves and African Americans (Skerry and Hartman 1991). With sharply contrasting cultures and markedly differing ideas about life, the two minorities usually avoid each other. As Hispanic Americans have become more visible in American society and more vocal in their demands for equality, they have come face to face with African Americans also actively seeking change, who fear that Latino gains in jobs and at the ballot box will come at their expense (Chavez 1990).

Asian Americans

A Background of Discrimination.   It was December 7, 1941, a quiet Sunday morning destined to "live in infamy," as President Roosevelt described it. Wave after wave of Japanese bombers began their dawn attack on Pearl Harbor. Beyond their expectations, the pilots found the Pacific fleet anchored like sitting ducks.

This attack left behind not only destruction. It also changed the world political order by precipitating the United States into World War II. As the nation readied for war, no American was untouched. Many left home to battle overseas. Others left the farm to work in factories to support the war effort. All lived with the rationing of food, gasoline, coffee, sugar, meat, and other essentials.

This event, however, affected Americans of Japanese descent in a special way. Just as waves of planes had rolled over Pearl Harbor, so waves of suspicion and hostility rolled over the Japanese Americans. Overnight, they became the most detested ethnic group in the United States (Daniels 1975). Many Americans feared that Japan would invade the United States and that the Japanese Americans would fight on the Japanese side. They also feared that they would sabotage military installations on the West Coast. Although no Japanese American had been involved in even a single act of sabotage, on February 1, 1942, President Roosevelt signed Executive Order 9066, authorizing the removal of anyone considered a threat from certain military areas. All people on the West Coast who were *one-eighth Japanese or more* were imprisoned, being removed to what were euphemistically termed "relocation camps." They were charged with no crime. There were no indictments, no trials. Japanese ancestry was sufficient cause for being imprisoned.

This was not the first time that Asian Americans had met direct, overt discrimination. The Chinese had immigrated in large numbers between 1850 and 1880, and the presence of two hundred thousand immigrants, lured by gold strikes in the West and the need for unskilled workers, created among white workers the specter of cheap labor. Mobs and vigilante groups then intimidated the Chinese. For example, although 90 percent of the Central Pacific's labor force was Chinese, when the famous golden spike was driven at Promontory, Utah, in 1869 to mark the joining of the Union Pacific and the Central Pacific railroads, white workers physically prevented the Chinese from being present (Hsu 1971).

As fears of "alien genes and germs" grew, United States legislators passed anti-Chinese laws (Schrieke 1936). The 1850 California Foreign Miners' Act, for example, required the Chinese (and Hispanics) to pay a special fee of $20 a month—at a time when wages were only $1 a day. The chief justice of the California Supreme Court even ruled that Chinese testimony against whites was inadmissible in court, a disqualification that stood for almost twenty years (Carlson and Colburn 1972). In 1882 Congress passed the Chinese Exclusion Act, suspending all Chinese immigration for ten years. (Four years later, the Statue of Liberty was dedicated. The tired, the poor, and the huddled masses it was to welcome were obviously not Chinese.)

Spillover Bigotry.   When immigrants from Japan began to arrive, they encountered "spillover bigotry" from the exclusionary practices directed against the Chinese. They also confronted a stereotype that lumped Asians together, depicting them as lazy and untrustworthy. In 1913 California passed the Alien Land Act, prohibiting anyone ineligible for citizenship from owning land. Federal law, which had initially allowed only whites to be citizens, had been amended in the 1870s to extend that right to African Americans and some Native Americans—although most Native Americans were not granted citizenship in their own land until 1924 (Amott and Matthaie 1991). The Supreme Court repeatedly ruled that since Asians had not been mentioned in these amendments, they were prohibited from becoming citizens (Schaefer 1979). In 1943, Chinese residents were finally allowed to become citizens, but those born in Japan were excluded from citizenship until 1952.

Cultural and Ethnic Diversity. Contrary to stereotypes that prevail in our society, it is inaccurate to characterize Asian Americans as a single group. Asian Americans—the fastest-growing minority in the United States, growing at twenty times the rate of non-Hispanic whites (O'Hare and Felt 1991)—are diverse peoples divided by separate cultural heritages. The three largest groups of Asian Americans—persons of Chinese, Filipino, and Japanese descent—are concentrated in Los Angeles, San Francisco, Honolulu, and New York City. With its individual culture and history, each group faces its own problems. They, too, are divided by social class. Many of the Chinese living in the urban settlements known as "Chinatowns," for example, face the typical problems of ghetto poverty: poor health, a high suicide rate, poor working conditions, and substandard housing. Others are well off financially and live comfortably.

Why Have Japanese Americans Been So Successful? Of the ethnic groups we have discussed, the Japanese have been the most successful financially. Their average family income is about $3,000 a year higher than that of the general population. Three major factors appear to account for their success: family life, educational achievement, and assimilation into the mainstream culture.

The first factor, family life, gives Japanese Americans their basic strength, for the young are socialized into cultural values that stimulate cohesiveness and the motivation to succeed (Bell 1991). Most children grow up in close-knit families that stress self-discipline, thrift, and industry (Suzuki 1985). This early socialization within a framework of strict limits and constraints provides the basic impetus for the second and third factors.

The second factor is educational achievement. On average, both male and female Japanese Americans go farther in school than the general population. Japanese Americans are also about 50 percent more likely than the general population to become affluent professional and technical workers. Their educational and economic success in turn affords them better-than-average housing and health care.

Assimilation, the third ingredient in Japanese-American success, is indicated by the community's high intermarriage rate. About 63 percent of Japanese Americans marry non–Japanese Americans (Bell 1991), while 70 percent live in non-Japanese neighborhoods, and about 75 percent say one or both of their two best friends are not Japanese American. A sociologist who has studied these assimilation patterns, Darrel Montero (1980, 1981), suggested that Japanese Americans may be committing "ethnic suicide." In just two generations they have changed from a people considered "inassimilable" to a group that cuts its ethnic ties and intermarries extensively.

The Most Recent Immigrants. The most recent influx of Asian Americans came with the end of United States involvement in the war in Vietnam, when 130,000 refugees were evacuated to the United States. Scattered to various locations across the country upon their arrival, they were denied an avenue of adjustment used by previous immigrant groups, the ethnic community. On their own, however, the Vietnamese have begun to resettle in California and Texas, where they have established their own communities.

Researchers who followed a random sample of the original group that arrived in 1975 report that, overall, the Vietnamese have adjusted quite well (Montero 1979; Montero and Dieppa 1982). Researchers conducted five surveys, one every six months. Each survey found a larger proportion of the refugees working full-time, and earning higher incomes and a smaller proportion receiving government assistance.

Although the post-1975 arrivals, the "boat people," homeless refugees literally adrift at sea, came from lower social classes, they, too, have progressed remarkably well. Their children, who knew no English when they arrived, have done very well in school, with 79 percent earning As and Bs. Their math performance is especially outstanding, with 47 percent earning As ("Working Toward" 1985).

These initial findings indicate that the Vietnamese will do well in American society.

CDQ 15: Why do you think Japanese Americans have been held up as the model for success to other race and ethnic groups in the United States?

To help them adjust to their host society, immigrants often band together for support, publish newspapers in their native language, establish churches, shop in stores that sell foods from their homeland, and live near one another. Recent immigrants to the United States are following this pattern, as depicted in this photo of Koreatown in Los Angeles, California.

Because they have arrived so recently, however, patterns of prejudice, discrimination, and assimilation remain to be seen.

Native Americans

From Genocide to Containment.   How large was the Native American population when Columbus landed on these shores? Although some scholars say it was as high as eighteen million (Dobyns 1983), the best estimate appears to be about five million (Thornton 1987). After reaching a low of a quarter of a million around the turn of the century, Native Americans today number about one and three-quarter million (this figure includes Eskimos and Aleuts).

At first relations between the European settlers and the Native Americans were by and large peaceful. As more Europeans arrived, however, they began a relentless push westward. The original Native American population stood in the way of this expansion, and as described above, the Europeans embarked on a policy of genocide. The United States Cavalry was assigned the task of "pacification," which involved slaughtering tens of thousands of Native Americans. The acts of cruelty perpetrated by whites against Native Americans appear to be endless; two of the most grisly were the distribution of blankets contaminated with smallpox under the guise of a peace offering, and the Trail of Tears, a forced march of a thousand miles from the Carolinas and Georgia to Oklahoma. With only light clothing to wear on their midwinter march, four thousand Cherokees died. This act took place after the United States government changed its policy from genocide to population transfer and began to confine Native Americans to specified areas called reservations.

To implement population transfer, the government made treaties with individual tribes, granting them specified lands forever. These treaties were often broken as American settlers demanded more land and natural resources. In 1874, for instance, when gold was discovered in South Dakota's Black Hills, a flood of settlers began to invade reservation lands. When conflict erupted, the United States Cavalry was sent in—to no one's surprise, on the side of the settlers. The notorious defeat of General Custer at Little Big Born in 1876 was one of the consequences. The symbolic end to Native American resistance may have been the 1890 massacre at Wounded Knee,

Because most Native Americans live either on isolated reservations established by the U.S. government or in "Indian neighborhoods" in large cities, most other Americans are unaware of their presence in American society. Depicted here are Navajos practicing religious rites on an Arizona reservation.

South Dakota, where, of 350 Native Americans, the cavalry gunned down 300 men, women, and children (Kitano 1974; Thornton 1987).

Writing History: The Privilege of the Victor. As noted above, stereotypes and labels can be used to justify inhumane acts and to compartmentalize those acts so that they will not conflict with favorable definitions of the self. So it was in relation to the Native Americans, who were viewed as stupid, lying, thieving, murdering, pagan "savages" (Simpson and Yinger 1972). The plots of countless movies illustrate the ideology that to kill a dangerous savage was to make the world safer for civilized people. Similarly, American history texts were written by the victors. They labeled themselves "pioneers," not "invaders"; referred to their military successes as "victories" but those of the Native Americans as "massacres"; and called the seizure of Native American lands "settling the land," but the Native Americans' defense of their homelands against overwhelming numbers "treacherous" (Josephy 1970). This topic is explored in the Thinking Critically section.

CNN: Hispanic History

CDQ 16: Can you think of negative images of Native Americans in movies you have seen? What about positive images?

THINKING CRITICALLY ABOUT SOCIAL CONTROVERSY

Whose History?

History must always be told from someone's viewpoint, for it is a basic condition of human beings to perceive life from their own perspective. And since perspectives depend on experiences, the greater the differences in people's backgrounds and lives the more their perspectives differ.

As mentioned above, to the victors goes the privilege of writing history from *their* perspective, which, of course, contrasts sharply with that of the vanquished. Thus, Native Americans do not regard the defeat of General George Custer in quite the same way as do most history books. They are much more likely to see it as a victory over an armed group invading their land than as a massacre of an outnumbered, brave band of cavalrymen.

It is this issue of perspective that underlies the current controversy surrounding the teaching of history in American schools. The question of *what* should be taught was always assumed, for the school boards, teachers, and textbook writers were united by a common background of similar experiences. It was unquestioningly assumed, for example, that George Washington was the general-hero-founder of the nation. No question was raised about whether grade and high school curricula should mention that he owned slaves. In the first place, the white boards, teachers, and textbook writers were generally ignorant of such facts, and, secondly, upon learning of them, thought them irrelevant.

But no longer. The issue now is one of balance—how to make certain that the accomplishments of both genders and many racial/ethnic groups are included in teaching. Houghton Mifflin, one of the largest publishers in the United States, strove for such a balance in a recent series of grade school texts. The company was not motivated simply by fairness or the desire to present more thorough, accurate history. Rather, the state of California had passed stringent guidelines concerning gender and racial/ethnic balance—and for the first year alone $25 million in textbook sales was at stake.

The company's very attempt at fairness, however, made race and ethnicity more of an issue than ever and ended up satisfying few groups. For example, critics claimed, the publisher did not adequately stress the annihilation of other cultures by whites.

The issue of multiculturalism in textbooks is not limited to the instance of Houghton Mifflin and California. Rather, the matter is now central to school districts around the nation. Teachers, principals, school boards, and publishers are wrestling with a slew of problematic questions. How much space should be given to Harriet Tubman versus George Washington? How much stress should be placed on illegal immigration? Is there enough attention paid to discrimination against Asian Americans? Is the attempted genocide of American Indians sufficiently acknowledged? What about the contributions to American society of females and white minorities—Poles, Russians, and so on?

No one yet knows the answers. What is certain at this point is that the imagery of American society has changed—from a melting pot to a tossed salad. At the heart of the current issue is the fact that so many groups have retained separate identities, instead of fusing into one as was "supposed" to happen. The question being decided now is how much emphasis should be given to the salad as a whole, and how much to the cucumbers, tomatoes, lettuce, carrots, and so on.

The answers to the questions currently being addressed will bring forth new images of history, which does not consist merely of established past events, but also involves a flowing, winding, and sometimes twisted perception that takes place in the present. (*Source:* Glazer 1991; Hemp 1991; Woodward 1991.)

The Invisible Minority and Self-Determination. Native Americans can truly be called the invisible minority. Because about 50 percent live in rural areas and almost half in just three states—Oklahoma, California, and Arizona—most other Americans are hardly conscious of a Native American presence in American society (Thornton 1987). The isolation of many Native Americans on reservations further reduces their visibility.

The systematic attempts of past generations to destroy the Native Americans' way of life and their resettlement onto reservations continue to have deleterious effects. Of all American minorities, Native Americans are the worst off. Roughly two in five Native American families fall below the official poverty level, while their unemployment rate runs several times that of whites. Their life expectancy is about eight to ten years less than that of the nation as a whole, with one in four Native Americans dying before the age of twenty-five (the national average is one in seven). Their suicide rate is double the national average, while their rate of alcoholism is perhaps five times that of the general population. Taken as a whole, it seems fair to conclude that Native American life in the dominant white society is not a satisfying one (Schaefer 1979; Snipp and Sorkin 1986).

Given these conditions, it is not surprising that Native Americans want change. Central to their demands are the enforcement of United States government treaties and the right to self-determination, that is, the right to remain unassimilated in Anglo culture and to run their own affairs as a separate people. Perhaps the most significant development in this aspect of ethnic relations is *pan-Indianism,* an emphasis on common elements that run through their cultures in the attempt to develop a self-identification that goes beyond any particular tribe. This endeavor of working for the welfare of all Native Americans has increased self-pride and stimulated the development of national Native American organizations.

Two other major changes are occurring. The first is an extensive rate of intermarriage with other ethnic groups, primarily whites. The second is a large immigration to the city and once there, a clustering together into ethnic communities. As historian Russell Thornton (1987) noted, it is likely that Native Americans will adapt to the urban environment without losing their ethnic identity.

PRINCIPLES FOR IMPROVING ETHNIC RELATIONS

If a society can become devoted to creating prejudice and discrimination, as was the case in Nazi Germany, one can be organized to bring about racial and ethnic harmony. To achieve this goal, we certainly cannot pass laws against prejudice, for prejudice is a feeling or attitude. Although it is possible to outlaw discrimination, which is an act, does this do any good?

Not only do laws make discrimination more difficult—and thus bring behavior more in line with American ideals—but they also reduce prejudice. A series of national opinion polls shows that as institutional discrimination declined and contact between members of different ethnic groups increased, prejudice decreased (Harris 1978).

Increasing contact between ethnic groups is no guarantee that prejudice will decrease, however, for not all contact is positive. Recall the Sherif experiment with the boys at summer camp. Setting group against group clearly increases prejudice and discrimination, and must therefore be avoided. Social psychologist Gordon Allport (Pettigrew 1976) developed four guidelines that can serve to promote the type of intergroup contact that decreases prejudice.

1. The groups should possess equal status in the situation (interethnic housing, for example, should involve occupants from the same social class background).
2. The groups should be seeking common goals (for example, parents from different ethnic backgrounds meeting to try to improve their children's school).
3. The groups should feel the need to pull together to obtain their goals (to improve an integrated school system, for example, voters from the various ethnic groups must vote for a bond proposal).
4. Authority, law, and custom should support interaction between the groups (if legal authorities strongly stand behind school integration, for example, more positive interaction is likely).

Project 4

L. Obj. 11: State the major principles for improving ethnic relations.

CDQ 17: Do you believe that ethnic relations can be improved by passing laws against prejudice? What about laws against discrimination?

K.P.: Gordon Allport

pan-Indianism: the emphasis of common elements in Native American culture in order to develop a mutual self-identification and to work toward the welfare of all Native Americans

SUMMARY

1. In the sense that different groups of people inherit distinctive physical characteristics, race is a reality. The concept of race is a myth, however, in the sense of one race being superior to another and of there being pure races. The *idea* of race is powerful, shaping basic relationships between people. Whereas race refers to biology, the term *ethnic* refers to cultural characteristics. Minorities originate with the expansion of political boundaries or the movement of people into a political entity.

2. Prejudice refers to an attitude, discrimination to an act. The attitude and the act do not always match, for some people who are prejudiced do not discriminate, while

others who are not prejudiced do. Sociologists look beyond individual discrimination to institutional discrimination to discover how prejudice is woven into the fabric of society. Discrimination is such an integral part of our society that at times it occurs without the awareness of either the perpetrator or the object of the discrimination. The relative availability of coronary bypass surgery for whites and African Americans is an example.

3. Psychological theories of the origin of prejudice stress frustration (and resulting prejudice toward scapegoats) and authoritarian personalities. Sociological theories stress that different social environments increase or decrease prejudice. Conflict theorists look at how the ruling class exploits ethnic groups in an attempt to keep them disunited and thus hold down wages. Symbolic interactionists stress how labels create selective perception (by which the negative is perceived) and self-fulfilling prophecies (by which the negative is produced).

4. Dominant groups generally practice one of six policies toward minority groups: genocide, population transfer, internal colonialism, segregation, assimilation, and pluralism. Dehumanizing labels, which allow compartmentalization, are an essential element in genocide and other inhumane acts.

5. WASPs—White Anglo-Saxon Protestants—have dominated American society since colonial times. They have often discriminated against other whites, whose culture was different from theirs.

6. African Americans are the largest minority group in American society. Dr. Martin Luther King's civil disobedience campaign was highly significant in improving their status. Rising expectations in the 1960s led to urban riots and civil rights legislation. The gains that African Americans have made in recent years have led to the suggestion that social class membership is now more important than race in determining their life chances. This issue is an ongoing controversy in sociology.

7. Hispanic Americans, the second-largest minority, are characterized by the Spanish language and internal divisions of national origin and social class that prevent political unity.

8. Asian Americans, the fastest-growing minority in the United States, have in the past had special taxes levied against them and endured immigration laws barring their entrance to the United States. They, too, are not a single ethnic group but are marked by major ethnic divisions. Japanese Americans have been especially successful due to their pattern of strong family life, educational achievements, and assimilation. Recent immigrants from Vietnam have generally made good progress.

9. The relationship between whites and Native Americans have been characterized by treachery, cruelty, and broken promises. Having won the struggle, whites gained the privilege of writing the history of this relationship. This "invisible minority," the worst off of the minorities in American society, wants self-determination and still awaits the fulfillment of treaty obligations.

10. Four principles can be implemented to improve ethnic relations: equal status, common goals, solidarity, and institutional support. If this is the goal, it is essential to avoid pitting one ethnic group against another in a struggle for limited resources.

SUGGESTED READINGS

Allen, Irving Lewis. *Unkind Words: Ethnic Labeling from Redskin to WASP*. Westport, Conn.: Bergin & Garvey, 1990. Allen explores ethnic labeling in popular speech, showing how ethnic slurs reflect social change and the diversity and complexity of American society.

Bean, Frank D., and Marta Tienda. *The Hispanic Population of the United States*. New York: Russell Sage, 1988. Based on country of origin, the authors present an overview of Hispanic Americans.

Bloom, Jack M. *Class, Race, and the Civil Rights Movement*. Bloomington: Indiana University Press, 1987. The author analyzes the factors underlying the civil rights movement and its choice of tactics.

Brown, Dee. *Bury My Heart at Wounded Knee*. New York: Holt, Rinehart and Winston, 1971. Brown presents a vivid chronicle of major events in the relationship between whites and Native Americans from 1860 to 1890.

Deloria, Vine, Jr., and Clifford M. Lytle. *The Nations Within: The Past and Future of American Indian Sovereignty*. New York: Pantheon Books, 1984. The authors argue that Native American tribes are sovereign nations and that existing treaties are the proper basis of relations between them and the federal government.

Farley, Reynolds, and Walter R. Allen. *The Color Line and the Quality of Life in America*. New York: Russell Sage, 1987. The authors survey relations between whites and African Americans from 1900 to the 1980s.

Horwitz, Gordon J. *In the Shadow of Death: Living Outside the Gates of Mauthausen*. New York: The Free Press, 1990. How could the Nazi death camps, built in inhabited areas, coexist with the nearby population? Horwitz probes people's capacity to be neutral in the face of evil, to suspend moral judgment, and to cooperate with daily horror.

Irwin-Zarecka, Iwona. *Neutralizing Memory: The Jew in Contemporary Poland*. New Brunswick, New Jersey: Transaction, 1990. What does a nation do with collective memories of shame that can bitterly divide it? This book focuses on the cooperation of Poles in the killing of Jews during the Nazi occupation.

Jackson, James S., ed. *Life in Black America*. Newbury Park, California: Sage, 1991. Using the first representative sample of African Americans, the authors analyze their work, neighborhoods, family and religious life, joblessness, retirement, physical and mental health, race identity, political action, and life course.

King, Martin Luther, Jr. *Stride Toward Freedom: The Montgomery Story.* New York: Harper, 1958. King recounts his involvement in the events that propelled him into the leadership of one of the most significant social movements in American history.

Kitano, Harry H. L. *Japanese Americans: The Evolution of a Subculture.* 2nd ed. Englewood Cliffs, New Jersey: Prentice Hall, 1976. The author of this overview of the Japanese-American experience graduated from high school while in a relocation camp.

Myrdal, Gunnar. *An American Dilemma.* New York: Harper & Row, 1962. A sociologist from Sweden presents a highly influential analysis of race relations in American society.

Rapoport, Louis. *Stalin's War Against the Jews: The Doctors' Plot and the Soviet Solution.* New York: The Free Press, 1990. A trumped-up plot accusing Jews of attempting to poison the Soviet leadership was followed by a wave of antisemitic hysteria that swept through Russia, resulting in Jews being purged from the elite circles of the Soviet army and navy, the Communist party, and even the secret police.

Rodriguez, Clara. *Puerto Ricans: Born in the U.S.A.* Boston: Unwin Hyman, 1989. The author presents an overview of Hispanic Americans from Puerto Rico.

Thornton, Russell. *American Indian Holocaust and Survival: A Population History Since 1492.* Norman, Okla.: University of Oklahoma Press, 1987. This overview of Native Americans emphasizes relationships with whites and population changes.

CHAPTER 13

Romare Bearden, Mecklenburg Morning, 1987

Inequalities of Age

SOCIAL FACTORS IN AGING
Aging among Abkhasians ■ Aging in Industrialized Nations ■ *Down-to-Earth Sociology:* **Applying Life Expectancy Figures**

THE SYMBOLIC INTERACTIONIST PERSPECTIVE
Self, Society, and Aging ■ The Relativity of Aging: Cross-Cultural Comparisons ■ Ageism in American Society ■ The Mass Media: Purveyor of Symbol and Status

THE FUNCTIONALIST PERSPECTIVE
Disengagement Theory ■ Activity Theory

THE CONFLICT PERSPECTIVE
Social Security Legislation ■ Rival Interest Groups ■ *Down-to-Earth Sociology:* **Changing**

Sentiment about the Elderly ■ *Thinking Critically about Social Controversy:* **Social Security—Fraud of the Century?** ■ Fighting Back: The Gray Panthers

PROBLEMS OF DEPENDENCY
Nursing Homes ■ Elder Abuse ■ *Down-to-Earth Sociology:* **Pacification—Turning People into Patients** ■ The Question of Poverty

THE SOCIOLOGY OF DEATH AND DYING
Effects of Industrialization ■ Death as a Process ■ Suicide and the Elderly ■ Hospices

SUMMARY

SUGGESTED READINGS

I n the village of Tamish in [the ex-Soviet region of] Abkhasia, I raised my glass of wine to toast a man who looked no more than 70. "May you live as long as Moses (120 years)," I said. He was not pleased. He was 119.

With these words, Sula Benet (1971) began a report on the people of Abkhasia who commonly live to be 100, or even older. Even after spending months with the Abkhasians, Benet was unable to judge the older Abkhasians. He found that most work regularly—whether they are 70 or 107. They still have good eyesight, most still have their own teeth, they walk more than two miles a day, and are slim. The old women are dark-haired, slender, with fair complexions and shy smiles. A study of 123 people over 100 showed neither mental illness nor cancer.

The Abkhasians' perception of age is so different that they do not even have a word for "old people." The closest is a word designating persons over 100: "long living people."

Do the Abkhasians really live this long? Some researchers doubt it, and have challenged the accuracy of Benet's report (Haslick 1974; Harris 1990). One problem

343

is a lack of records—this people did not have a written language until after the Russian Revolution of 1917. Some investigators, however, have documented the Abkhasians' account through military records. They did find that a few Abkhasians were lying—some men claiming to be younger than they were. One man, who was going to marry, for example, said he was 95, but records indicated he really was 108.

SOCIAL FACTORS IN AGING

As discussed in Chapters 1 and 3, the nature of childhood can vary tremendously depending on whether a society views children as miniature adults just about ready for adult roles, or as vulnerable, dependent beings in need of long years of protection. Sociologists stress that this same principle applies to growing old. Age, too, is far from a matter of mere biology. As the Abkhasians illustrate, people's very chances of growing old are affected by the society in which they live. How, then, does society influence the aging process?

Aging among Abkhasians

Abkhasia is a mountainous region within the Georgian republic of the former Soviet Union. It is an agricultural society, with few inroads made by industrialization. While we cannot determine with certainty why the Abkhasians live so long, a few clues indicate the *social* nature of their longevity. The Abkhasians themselves give three reasons: their customs regarding sex, work, and diet (Benet 1971). Let us consider each in turn, and then add a fourth factor.

1. *Sexual Practices.*   First, the Abkhasians feel that sexual energy should be conserved. Their traditional age for marriage is thirty, and they believe that nothing sexual should occur before marriage. It is essential that a woman be a virgin at marriage. If not, she will be scornfully returned to her family. As you can well understand, it is not easy to follow this ideal, but the Abkhasians have a special cultural problem— even a woman's armpit is considered an erogenous zone, and all women must carefully keep them covered.

In marriage, sex is guiltless, a pleasure to be enjoyed as one of the good things in life. For the sake of one's health, however, marital sex should not be overdone. It is not uncommon for Abkhasian men to retain their sexual potency in old age, and some even father children after one hundred. About one of every seven or eight women over fifty-five still menstruates.

2. *Work.*   Work, the second explanation they give for their longevity, is an essential element of Abkhasian life. No Abkhasian "retires," for that status is unknown to them. They can't understand why anyone would want to "retire" from life.

From childhood until the end of life, the Abkhasians do what they are capable of doing. Early in childhood, they do "chores." A four-year-old might feed and water the chickens, for example. As adults, the men work the land or herd goats, while the women work at home and care for farm animals. Only with advancing age do the Abkhasians gradually decrease their activities: At about eighty some cut down on their work, while others slow down at about ninety. At that time a man may begin to stop plowing and lifting heavy loads, while a woman may cut down on her housework and cooking. Still, after the age of one hundred, the average Abkhasian works about four hours a day. The Abkhasians have a saying, "Without rest, you cannot work; without work, rest gives you no benefit."

3. *Diet and Eating Customs.*   Diet, the third reason the Abkhasians give for their longevity, has been investigated extensively. They consider overeating to be dangerous and regard overweight people as ill. When they see someone even a little overweight, they inquire about the person's health. Abkhasians take in almost 25 percent fewer calories than do the industrial workers in their state; at the same time they consume twice as much Vitamin C. They eat their food, which is served on platters and already cut into small pieces, with their fingers. They take only small bites and chew them slowly. All food is freshly prepared, for they regard leftovers as unhealthy.

Meals are eaten leisurely. The presence of guests is a special occasion, with toasts made to the virtues (real or imaginary) of each person present. Such meals may last several hours.

The Abkhasians eat meat only about once or twice a week. They prefer chicken, beef, and young goat. In the winter, they like a little pork. They do not like fish, although fish are plentiful in their area. Their meat, always freshly slaughtered, is broiled only until the blood stops running. Most of their diet consists of fresh fruits and vegetables, and includes large quantities of garlic. They eat cornmeal and goat cheese daily. They do not drink tea or coffee, but do drink wine at lunch and dinner and consume about two glasses of buttermilk a day. They never eat sugar, but do use honey.

4. *Social Integration—a Sense of Community.*   Researchers are impressed with the Abkhasians' approach to work and diet, but they doubt that their sexual practices contribute to their longevity. Researchers suggest a fourth factor, which the Abkhasians apparently take so much for granted that they are not aware of it: the strong sense of belonging and security that results from their approach to life.

From childhood, each individual is highly integrated in the group—and remains so throughout life. As people grow older, they remain active, valued, contributing members of their community. Consequently, the elderly never feel that they are a burden to anyone. They are never segregated or shunted off into some corner of society. Rather, they continue doing the same work (although less), playing the same games, and eating the same foods as younger Abkhasians. There is no sudden rupture between what they "were" and what they "are." (You never hear "I used to be a teacher [accountant, physician], but now I am retired.") The elderly neither vegetate, nor do they have the need to "fill time" with such activities as bingo or shuffleboard.

Their extraordinarily broad sense of kinship is an example of their integration into the group. Everyone who can be traced to the same ancestor is considered a brother or a sister, as are people who have the same last name. This means that each individual feels closely related to several hundred—or even thousand—other people, and that he or she can count on them for help.

With such reckoning of extended kinship beyond anything he had known, Benet thought that the Abkhasians were exaggerating. One day, when a friend, Omar, took him to another village, however, Benet found that they meant what they said.

> Omar began to introduce Benet to his brothers and sisters. After about twenty such introductions, Benet asked how many brothers and sisters he had. When Omar explained that in this village he had thirty, Benet kept his disbelief to himself.
>
> In one of the homes they visited, the host played a recording of Abkhasian epic poetry. When Benet expressed admiration of the poetry, Omar took the record from the player and handed it to him as a gift. Benet declined, saying, "Omar, you know it isn't yours." "Oh, yes, it is," replied Omar. "This is the home of my brother." Perplexed, Benet looked at the "brother," who said, "Of course he can give it to you. He is my brother."

In Sum.   Although it is impossible to specify precisely what leads to the longevity of the Abkhasians, clearly several social factors are involved. Their diet certainly contributes, as does their pattern of work, the leisure with which they approach life, and their sense of integration within their community. Conversely, although the precise mechanisms have not been isolated, the following social factors are likely to be a burden on people's health and help shorten life: isolation from family and community (a group of people who provide a sense of belonging and respect) and from meaningful activities

CDQ 1: Have you seen or heard recent news reports on the factors that contribute to longevity in the United States? What about diet? Work patterns? Leisure? A sense of belonging?

(from which one derives a sense of purpose in life); and the withdrawal of esteem (interaction based on respect and appreciation).

With this as background, let us look at the process of aging in modern, industrialized societies. As we do so, you may from time to time wish to make a mental note of the contrast with the Abkhasians.

Aging in Industrialized Nations

Along with other industrialized nations, the United States has experienced its own increase in longevity. As Figure 13.1 shows, the United States has witnessed a long, steady increase in life expectancy throughout this century. Public health measures, especially a safer water supply and developments in medicine—which have suppressed the killers of earlier years such as German measles, smallpox, diphtheria, and tuberculosis—have brought an uninterrupted march toward longer life.

To me, and perhaps to you, it is startling to realize that at the turn of this century the average American would not even see age fifty. Since then, life expectancy has increased so greatly that Americans born today can expect to live until their seventies or eighties. (To apply this change to yourself, see the Down-to-Earth Sociology box on page 347.) It is important to keep in mind, however, that people in industrialized societies are not living to age 120 or 150. Rather, because the diseases that kill people at younger ages are mostly under control, more people survive to later adulthood.

The term **graying of America** refers to the larger proportion of older persons in the United States population. Look at Figure 13.2 on page 348. In 1900, only 4 percent of Americans were aged sixty-five or over. Since then, their proportion of the population has *tripled*, and today almost 13 percent of Americans are aged sixty-five or over. Another way of looking at this is to note that American society has become so "gray" that there are now six and a half million more elderly Americans than teenagers (*Statistical Abstract* 1991: Tables 12, 13).

Visitors to Florida know that the elderly are not evenly spaced across the nation; the elderly in that state represent almost 18 percent of the population. The other states with the highest proportions of elderly are South Dakota, West Virginia, Arkansas, Rhode Island, Pennsylvania, and Iowa. The elderly make up between 14 and 15

CDQ 2: Are you surprised to learn that at the beginning of the twentieth century the average American would not live to age fifty? Why or why not?

TR#24: The Graying of America

TR#27M: Number of Elderly for 1950–2020

TR#28M: The Growth of the Population 65 Years and Over, 1900–2020

graying of America: the process by which older persons make up an increasing proportion of the United States population

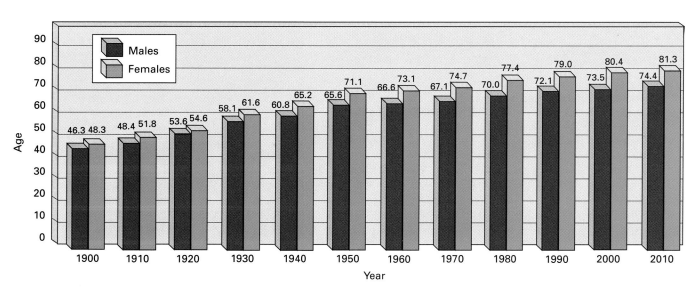

FIGURE 13.1   Life Expectancy by Year of Birth. (*Source: Statistical Abstract of the United States,* 1991; Table 105; *Historical Statistics of the United States, Colonial Times to 1970, Bicentennial Edition, Part I, Series B, 107–115.*)

percent of the population of these states. In contrast, in Texas, Colorado, Wyoming, and Utah the elderly make up only 8 to 10 percent of the population, while in Alaska their proportion is less than 4 percent (*Statistical Abstract* 1990: Table 28).

Worldwide Trends.   The United States is not alone in this trend. Rather, all industrialized nations are graying. Wherever industrialization comes, it brings health measures that allow a larger proportion of a population to reach an advanced age. As Table 13.2 shows, only 5.7 percent of the population in China, a nonindustrialized nation, are aged

TR#23: The Elderly in Cross-Cultural Perspective

DOWN-TO-EARTH SOCIOLOGY

Applying Life Expectancy Figures

You can apply the information in Figure 13.1 to your own family. If you are about twenty, your grandparents could have expected to live only to about sixty. If they made it past that, they beat the odds. Your own life expectancy at birth, however, jumped to about sixty-nine if you are a male and to about seventy-six if you are a female. You can see the projections for your own children.

Your life expectancy now is actually higher than it was at birth, for life expectancy increases with each year you survive—at least it does on paper. Actually, your own life span is determined by biology (inherited disease) and social factors (access to more nourishing food, better medical care, and lifestyle). As death takes its toll on people in high-risk occupations or on those who have less access to medical treatment because they are poor, for example, the life expectancy for survivors goes up because it leaves a larger proportion of people who have better access to good nutrition and medical care and who live less risky lives.

To gauge the current projections for your life expectancy, locate your age in the left column of Table 13.1. As these figures are only averages, they do not indicate how long any particular person will live, of course. Depending on genetics, lifestyle (including those associated with social class), and a bit of luck (such as avoiding AIDS, car accidents, and homicide)—your own life expectancy may be higher (or lower) than these averages.

As illustrated in Figure 13.1 and Table 13.1, gender is a critical factor in determining life expectancy. No matter in what year a person is born, the average female lives longer than the average male. Consequently, as more males die, with each year of advancing age females outnumber males by a larger margin. By age sixty-five and over, about two out of every three Americans are females.

As is also evident from this table, the racial or ethnic inequalities covered in Chapter 12 also have a significant impact on life expectancy. At every age (except eighty-five), and for both males and females, the life expectancy of whites is greater than that of African Americans. Although the sources from which these data were drawn do not provide precise information for other ethnic groups, you may apply these general principles: The life expectancy for Hispanic Americans falls in between the figures for African Americans and whites, that of Asian Americans is closer to whites, and for Native Americans it is lower than for African Americans.

TABLE 13.1   Average Years You Can Expect to Live

If you are:	African American		White	
Age	Male	Female	Male	Female
0	65.2	73.6	72.2	78.9
5	61.7	70.0	68.1	74.7
10	56.8	65.1	63.1	69.7
15	51.9	60.2	58.2	64.8
16	51.0	59.2	57.3	63.8
17	50.1	58.2	56.4	62.8
18	49.1	57.2	55.4	61.9
19	48.2	56.3	54.5	60.9
20	47.3	55.3	53.6	59.9
21	46.4	54.4	52.6	59.0
22	45.5	53.4	51.7	58.0
23	44.7	52.4	50.8	57.0
24	43.8	51.5	49.9	56.1
25	42.9	50.5	49.0	55.1
26	42.0	49.6	48.0	54.1
27	41.2	48.6	47.1	53.1
28	40.3	47.7	46.2	52.2
29	39.4	46.8	45.3	51.2
30	38.6	45.8	44.3	50.2
35	34.4	41.2	39.7	45.4
40	30.4	36.7	35.1	40.6
45	26.6	32.3	30.6	35.9
50	22.9	28.1	26.2	31.3
55	19.5	24.1	22.1	26.9
60	16.2	20.4	18.3	22.7
65	13.5	17.1	14.9	18.8
70	10.9	13.9	11.8	15.1
75	8.7	11.1	9.1	11.8
80	6.8	8.6	6.9	8.8
85	5.6	6.8	5.2	6.4

Source: Vital Statistics of the United States, 1987, Life Tables, II, Section 6, February 1990: Table 6-3.

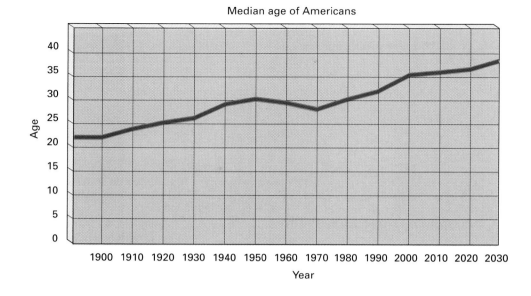

FIGURE 13.2 The Graying of America. (*Source: Statistical Abstract of the United States,* various editions. Figures for 1990 and projections are from the 1991 edition, Table 1435.)

sixty-five and over. Because its population is so huge, however, China has more aged people than any other country.

As the proportion of a nation's population over age sixty-five increases, a greater burden is placed on its younger citizens to pay for the benefits the elderly need. Table 13.2 also shows the proportion of their payrolls that several nations pay to fund benefits for the elderly. In spite of the common complaints of Americans that Social Security taxes are too high, this table shows that the United States rate is relatively low.

THE SYMBOLIC INTERACTIONIST PERSPECTIVE

In applying symbolic interactionism to aging, we will first consider what makes a person "old," and what it means to be old. We then look at how negative stereotypes of the elderly developed in American society and at the ongoing effects of the mass media on perceptions of aging.

Self, Society, and Aging

You can probably remember when you thought a twelve-year-old was "old"—and anyone older beyond reckoning, just "up there" someplace. You were probably five or six at the time. To a twelve-year-old, however, someone of twenty-one probably seems "old." At twenty-one, thirty may mark that line, and forty may seem "quite

Essay #2

L. Obj. 2: Discuss the major conclusions drawn by symbolic interactionists regarding aging.

CDQ 3: Can you explain what is meant by the statement that "age is relative?" Do you agree?

Stereotypes of the elderly as inactive people in ill health are inappropriate for the vast majority of Americans over 65. With higher life expectancy, most Americans can expect to live well past 65 and to enjoy years of active living—whether relaxing with grandchildren and great grandchildren, pursuing hobbies and volunteer work, continuing paid employment, or spending time at the beach.

old." And so it keeps on going, with "old" gradually receding from the self. To people who turn forty, fifty seems old; at fifty, the late sixties look old (not the early sixties, for at that point in accelerating years they don't seem too far away).

At some point, of course, an individual must apply the label "old" to himself or herself. Often, culturally sanctioned definitions of age force this label on people sooner than they are ready to accept it. In the typical case, the individual has become used to what he or she sees in the mirror. The changes have taken place very gradually, and each change, if not exactly taken in stride, has been accommodated. (Consequently, it comes as a shock, when meeting a friend one has not seen in years, to see how much that person has changed. At class reunions, *each* person can hardly believe how much older *the others* appear!)

If there is no single point at which people automatically cross a magical line and become "old," what, then, makes someone "old"? We can point to several factors that spur people to apply the label of old to themselves.

The *first* factor is biology. One person may experience "symptoms" of aging much earlier than another: wrinkles, balding, aches, inability to do certain things that he or she used to take for granted. Consequently, one person will feel "old" at an earlier or later age than others, and only at that time *adopt the role of an "old person,"* that is, begin to act the way old people in that particular society are thought to act.

CDQ 4: Why do you think some individuals feel "old" at an earlier age than other people?

TABLE 13.2   The Elderly in Cross-Cultural Perspective

Country	Total Population	Percentage over 65	Number over 65	Percentage of Payroll Taxes Paid to Support the Elderly
Sweden	9,000,000	18.0	1,600,000	19.95
Germany	78,000,000	15.0	11,700,000	18.7
Italy	58,000,000	14.7	8,500,000	25.21
France	56,000,000	14.1	7,900,000	14.8
Netherlands	15,000,000	12.9	1,900,000	19.0
United States	250,000,000	12.6	31,500,000	12.12
Japan	124,000,000	11.9	14,800,000	12.4
Canada	27,000,000	11.5	3,100,000	4.0
China	1,118,000,000	5.7	63,700,000	N/A

Sources: Statistical Abstract of the United States, 1991: Tables 1434, 1435, 1459; Special Report, 1989.

Personal history or biography is a *second* factor that influences when a person decides to "be" old. Someone may have an accident that limits mobility and makes that person feel old sooner than others. Or a woman may have given birth at sixteen to a daughter, who in turn has a child at eighteen. When this woman is thirty-four, she is a biological grandmother. It is most unlikely that she will begin to play any stereotypical role—spending the day in a rocking chair, for example—but *knowing* that she is a grandmother is bound to have an impact on her self-concept.

A *third* factor in determining when people label themselves old is gender roles. Sociologist Inge Bell (1976) who analyzed the impact of gender roles on aging in the United States, said:

> For [men], sexual value is defined much more in terms of personality, intelligence, and earning power than by physical appearance. Women, however, must rest their case largely on their bodies. Their ability to attain status in other than physical ways and to translate that status into sexual attractiveness is severely limited by the culture.

An indication of differences in age definitions for men and women, adds Bell, is that a man can reach farther down the age ladder in choosing a mate, while the female's choice is more limited to males her own age or older. Note that while this is the *typical* situation, many individuals depart from it. Although it is possible that Joan may marry someone ten years younger than herself, it is much more common for Bill and Henry to do so. This difference in "gender aging" makes the transition to age thirty (as well as to age forty, and so on) more difficult for females. Because of *social years* (the relative value the culture places on men's and women's ages), at age thirty a man is simply not considered as old as a woman at age thirty. Biology, again, has nothing to do with this socially constructed reality.

CDQ 5: Do you agree that there is a difference in the social aspects of "gender aging?" If so, give examples

The *fourth* factor is that cultures vary in the timetables they use to signal to their members when they are old. Since there is no automatic age at which people become "old," each society makes its own determination. The Abkhasians, for example, have set thirty as the traditional age for marriage—quite young by their standards, but a time when some Americans fret about wrinkles and other telltale signs of "advancing age." That, coupled with their expectations that people we consider advanced in age will continue to work and participate in their usual social activities, makes them see "old" quite differently than we do.

The timetables adopted by a given culture are not fixed, however. Just as the management of a railroad or bus line adjusts the timetable when travelers shift their vacation habits, so societies can adjust their expectations about the onset of old age. In Japan, for example, age sixty was so firmly marked as the beginning of old age that the Japanese had a special word for it. This term, *kanreki,* literally means "return of the calendar," a time at which people were expected to become dependent. At *kanreki,* it was acceptable to turn to one's children for support. Now that the Japanese have industrialized and established pension plans, however, they have advanced their idea of the onset of old age to sixty-five or seventy—the time of eligibility for pensions (Maeda 1980; Palmore 1985).

The Relativity of Aging: Cross-Cultural Comparisons

L. Obj. 3: Demonstrate by using cross-cultural comparisons that societies vary widely on their perceptions of what makes a person old, what it means to grow old, and how the elderly are viewed.

To pinpoint the extent to which being old involves factors beyond biology, and how each society infuses old age with its own particular meanings, let us look at three cross-cultural examples.

Anthropologists who studied the Tiwi, a group who inhabit an island off the northern coast of Australia, discovered something different about what it means to be old (Hart and Pilling 1983).

> Bashti looked in envy at Masta. Masta strutted just a bit as he noticed Bashti glance his way. He knew what Bashti was thinking. Had he not thought the same just twenty years earlier? Then he had no wife; now he had three. Then he had no grand hut. Now he did, plus one for each wife. Then he had no respect, no power, no wealth. Now he

As symbolic interactionists stress, by itself old age has no meaning. Rather, as with other stages in life, each society determines the meaning of old age, and offers roles to match. Shown here is a 104-year-old Thai woman in the village of Wang Lung. The role her society has ascribed for her is that of a caring, nurturing grandmother.

was looked up to by everyone. "Ah, the marvels and beauty of gray hair," Masta thought.

Bashti hung his head as he slouched toward the fringe of the group. "But my turn will come. I, too, will grow old," he thought, finding some comfort in the situation.

Why did Bashti wish to grow old, something that few people in the United States want to do? Traditional Tiwi society is a **gerontocracy,** a society run by the elderly. The old men are firmly entrenched in power and control everything. Their power is so inclusive, that the old men marry *all* the women—both young and old—leaving none for the young men. Only when a man is older and he has gained wealth and power is he able to marry. (In Tiwi society, females are the pawns, and aging is of no advantage to a woman.)

Traditional Eskimo society also provides a rich contrast to that of a modern, industrialized society such as the United States.

Shantu and Wishta fondly kissed their children and grandchildren farewell. Then sadly, but with resignation at the sacrifice they knew they had to make for their family, they slowly climbed onto the large slab of ice. The goodbyes were painfully made as the ice floe inched into the ocean currents. Shantu and Wishta would now starve. But they were old, and their death was necessary, for it reduced the demand on the small group's scarce food supply.

As the younger relatives watched Shantu and Wishta recede into the distance, each knew that their turn to make this sacrifice would come. Each hoped that they would be able to face it as bravely.

To grow old in traditional Eskimo society meant death, for no longer was one able to fulfill one's tasks. Survival was so precarious that all, except very young children, had to pull their own weight. The food supply was so limited that there was nothing left over to give to anyone who could not take an active part in the closely integrated tasks required for survival.

Finally, let's consider the meaning of age in traditional Chinese society.

Wong Fu bowed deeply as he met Ming Chau. When Ming Chau sat down, Wong Fu shyly took a seat at his side. Wong Fu had wanted to speak to Ming Chau for some time. Ming Chau was in his eighties, and his many years of experience had brought wisdom. Wong Fu was certain that Ming Chau would have the answer for his problem. He would remain silent until Ming Chau asked him about his family. Perhaps then he might be able to bring the matter up. If not, he would wait until the next time he was able to meet with Ming Chau.

gerontocracy: a society (or other group) run by the old

Because of biography or individual experiences—which depend greatly on social class—people apply the label "old" at different ages. This woman in eastern Kentucky shows the ravages of poverty—wrinkled forehead, and sunken cheeks due to lost teeth—that make some people age much faster than others.

Just as culture determines when old age begins, so it determines what that age category *means* for people. With the Tiwi, old age means power (matched by envy on the part of the younger); with the traditional Eskimos, resignation to a deliberate death; and among the Chinese, reverence, accompanied by respect from the younger. That does not, of course, exhaust the meanings of old age in these societies, but these are dominant emphases.

Symbolic interactionists stress that, by itself, old age has no particular meaning. There is nothing about adding years to one's life that automatically brings power, resignation, or respect. Indeed, as noted in relation to the Abkhasians, there is nothing inherent in the aging process that requires a people even to have a word for "old" (the Abkhasians use "long living" instead). The symbolic interactionist perspective, then, helps us to see that living a long life takes on whatever meanings a culture assigns it—and that from those meanings flow behaviors and attitudes typical to that culture. The meaning of aging may also change as a society changes. The modernization of China, for example, is resulting in less veneration of the elderly.

Let us now examine, from a symbolic interactionist perspective, how the meaning of aging has changed in American society.

Ageism in American Society

At first, the audience sat quietly as the developers explained their plans for a high-rise apartment building. After a while, people began to shift uncomfortably in their seats. Now they were showing open hostility.

"That's too much money to spend on these people," said one.

"You even want them to have a swimming pool?" asked another incredulously.

Finally, one young woman put it all in a nutshell when she asked, "Who wants all those old people around?"

When physician Robert N. Butler (1975, 1980) heard these responses to plans to construct an apartment building for senior citizens in a suburb of Washington, D. C., he came to realize how deeply feelings against the elderly run in our society. He coined the term **ageism** to refer to prejudice, discrimination, and hostility directed against people because of their age.

Why do we have such attitudes about the elderly? There was a time in our society when the word "old" suggested kindliness, wisdom, generosity, even graciousness and beauty. Now the adjective "old" has become an affront. We have *old and sick, old and poor, old and doddering, old and helpless, old and crabby, old and crotchety, old and*

Essay #3

K.P.: Robert Butler

CDQ 6: Why do you think prejudice, discrimination, and hostility are directed against people because of their age?

TR#26M: Myths About Aging

L. Obj. 4: Describe some of the negative stereotypes about the elderly and discuss ways in which the mass media perpetuate these ideas.

ageism: prejudice, discrimination, and hostility directed against people because of their age; can be directed against any age group

useless, and *old and dependent* (Cottin 1979). Take your choice. None is pleasant. In American society, old age conjures up images of ugliness, weakness, uselessness, dependence, and crankiness. Although old age means different things to different people, in general its image is negative, and none of us wants the label "old" applied to us.

As we have just seen, there is nothing inherent in old age to summon forth these meanings. Why, then, were the stereotypes of old age in American society once positive? And why did they become negative? Two answers have been proposed. The first focuses on industrialization. Historian Andrew Achenbaum (1978) found that in the early 1800s old people were valued for three principal reasons. First, reaching old age was in itself a rare enough accomplishment, so people admired the elderly and listened to their advice on how to stay alive. Second, old people were considered guardians of virtue and advised others on how to live a good life. Third, old people knew more about how to work productively than did the young. To quit working simply because of age was considered foolish, and young workers respected and learned from the elderly.

In the 1800s, social changes began to erode these bases of respect, ushering in a decline in the social value of the elderly. First, improved sanitation and medical care meant that more people reached old age, so age itself lost its distinction. Second, because industrialization changed ideas of morality and proper relationships, the opinions of the elderly became outmoded. Third, because of new techniques and machinery used in the changing workplace, old workers now knew less than the young about efficiency and productivity, and as a result managers began to retire old workers in favor of the young. Fourth, the growth of mass education took away the mystique that the elderly had superior knowledge (Cowgill 1974).

Sociologist Erdman Palmore (1985) and historian David Fischer (1977) suggested that a decline in the status of the elderly began before industrialization. Fischer noted that between 1770 and 1820 Americans underwent a shift in attitude toward the aged. For example, the proportion of children given the same names as their grandparents declined. One reason that the elderly lost status was that they became more numerous. Prior to the 1800s, death was common at any age, but as life expectancy lengthened and the proportion of Americans over sixty-five increased, death remained common only in old age. Thus, old age became linked with death.

K.P.: Erdman Palmore

K.P.: David Fischer

It is a basic principle of symbolic interaction that people perceive both themselves and others according to the symbols of their culture. Thus, as the meaning of old age was transformed—from usefulness to uselessness, from wisdom to foolishness, from an asset to a liability, and even to an association with death—not only did younger people see the elderly differently, but the elderly also saw themselves in a new light, for they, too, internalize dominant cultural symbols.

The Mass Media: Purveyor of Symbol and Status

Project 2

Chapter 11 examined the impact of the mass media on our ideas of gender and on relationships between men and women. The mass media likewise communicate implicit messages about the aged. These messages not only reflect the currently devalued status of the elderly in American society but also reinterpret and refine ideas. They tell us what people over sixty-five *should* be like as workers, consumers, family members, and so on. Like women, the elderly are underrepresented on television, in advertisements, and in the most popular magazines. Their omission implies a lack of social value. The covert message is that the elderly are "past their prime," are of little consequence, and can be safely ignored (Powell and Williamson 1985).

CDQ 7: How does a fear of growing old, especially as depicted in the mass media, promote sales of "anti-aging" products? Have you bought products which claim to help you keep your "youthful" appearance?

This message is not lost on television viewers, who internalize the media's negative symbols and go to great lengths to deny that they are growing old. The mass media then exploit fears of losing youthful vitality to sell hair dyes, skin creams, and innumerable other devices that supposedly avoid even the appearance of old age (Powell and Williamson 1985).

In Sum.   Biological age is only part of aging, for old age is also a matter of social definition. Different societies use distinct social timetables for determining when someone is old, and groups are likely to apply the label "old" in one way to females and quite another to males. In a society that fills the term "old" with negative meanings and stereotypes, people struggle against social pressures to define themselves as old. In contrast, members of societies that place a high value on being old may eagerly await and even embrace this status.

Essay #4

L. Obj. 5: Summarize the functional perspective on aging and explain disengagement theory and activity theory.

THE FUNCTIONALIST PERSPECTIVE

As explained in Chapter 1, functionalists examine how the various parts of society work together. We can consider an **age cohort,** people born at roughly the same time who pass through the life course together, as a component of society. As an age cohort in industrialized society nears retirement, it must make an accommodation with other parts of society if there is to be a smooth transition. For example, if the age cohort nearing retirement is large (a "baby boom" generation), many jobs will open at roughly the same time. If it is small (a "baby bust" generation), fewer jobs will open. In the one instance, the next age cohort will be offered many top positions; in the other instance, very few.

Two theories focus on the mutual adjustments necessary between those who are retiring and society's other components: disengagement theory and activity theory.

K.P.: Elaine Cumming

K.P.: William Henry

CDQ 8: Why do you think society encourages the elderly to hand over their positions voluntarily to younger people?

Disengagement Theory

Elaine Cumming and William Henry (1961) developed **disengagement theory** to explain how society prevents disruption by having the elderly vacate (or disengage from) their positions of responsibility. A situation in which only death or incompetence caused the elderly to leave their positions would be very disruptive. Consequently, society encourages the elderly to hand their positions over voluntarily to younger people. Even among the Abkhasians, the elderly gradually slow down. In industrialized societies the elderly are paid an income in return for giving up their positions to the younger. Thus, disengagement is a mutual agreement between two parts of society that facilitates a smooth transition of its positions of power and responsibility.

Cumming (1976) also examined disengagement from the individual perspective, pointing out that disengagement begins during middle age, long before retirement, when the individual senses that the end of life is closer than its start. The immediate consequence of this realization is not disengagement, however, but a feeling that time is limited and that priority must therefore be assigned to goals and tasks. In industrialized

age cohort: people born at roughly the same time who pass through the life course together

disengagement theory: the belief that society prevents disruption by having the elderly vacate (or disengage from) their positions of responsibility.

Age cohorts exert powerful effects on society. If larger than usual numbers of people are born within a few years of one another (a "baby boom") or fewer than usual (a "baby bust"), many adjustments have to be made in society—from hiring or laying off teachers in the early years to a surplus or scarcity of workers later, and finally, to relative difficulty or ease in providing pensions and medical care. During the 1950s the United States experienced a baby boom that is having such effects now. Some of the members of that boom are shown here.

societies, disengagement begins in earnest with the departure of children from the household, then with retirement, and eventually, widowhood.

This is the *typical* path for Americans, especially for men, as they gradually disengage from their usual activities. Since most women who are in their sixties today have not worked full-time, retirement is not part of their typical disengagement. As Cumming (1976) observed, this model also does not account for cases in which people are widowed before their last child leaves home, those who work past the usual retirement age, or those who have married late and still have children at home when they retire.

Activity Theory

What are the consequences for people as they disengage from their usual activities? That question is the focus of **activity theory,** which examines people's reactions to exchanging one set of roles for another. Although we could consider this theory under other perspectives, because the focus is how disengagement is functional or dysfunctional, it, too, can be considered from the functionalist perspective.

Researchers have found that satisfaction in old age is related to both level and type of activity. Older people who maintain a high level of activity tend to be more satisfied with life than those who do not (Neugarten 1972, 1977). Solitary activities and formal memberships, however, are not as important as informal activities, such as spending time with friends and acquaintances. The more that people find the new activities satisfying, the more they are pleased with life itself. In short, life satisfaction is higher for people who draw a sense of meaning and purpose from their activities and relationships.

Some researchers, however, say that the theory needs to take individual styles of adjustment into account. For example, Sociologist Jennie Keith (1982), who studied a French retirement community, found that some people are happy when they are very active, others when they are relatively inactive. That, of course, should come as no surprise, for this is precisely how it is with younger people. Just like other age groups, the elderly consist of people from varied backgrounds, and no single brush stroke can characterize them all.

activity theory: the belief that satisfaction during old age is related to a person's level and quality of activity

Why is old age a source of satisfaction for some, but of despair for others? Researchers have found that people's level and type of activity are significant factors. Some of the elderly obtain immense satisfaction and a sense of purpose from volunteer activities that help the younger generation, as does this man who is helping elementary school children with their homework.

THE CONFLICT PERSPECTIVE

CDQ 9: Do you believe all elderly people are happiest when they are very active? Why or why not?

L. Obj. 6: Explain why conflict theorists see social life as a struggle between groups for scarce resources and note how this impacts different age cohorts.

Project 3

Speaker Sug. #2: A Social Security administrator to discuss rules and regulations governing Social Security.

Conflict theorists, as explained, regard social life as a struggle between groups over scarce resources. At times, this struggle may require that groups cooperate with one another or that they form alliances. The bottom line, however, is that each group competes with the others to increase its own share of resources. With the components of society in competition with one another, conflict is ready to break out at any time.

From the conflict perspective, the guiding principles of social life are competition, disequilibrium, and change. So it is with society's age groups. Whether the young and old recognize it or not, they are part of a basic struggle that threatens to throw society into turmoil. The passage of social security legislation is an example of this struggle.

Social Security Legislation

In the 1920s, before Social Security provided an income for the aged, two-thirds of all citizens over sixty-five had no savings and could not support themselves (Holtzman 1963; Hudson 1978). The Great Depression made matters even worse, and in 1930 Robert C. Townsend, a social reformer, started a movement to rally older citizens into a political force. He soon had one-third of all Americans over sixty-five enrolled in his Townsend clubs, demanding benefits from the government (Holtzman 1963). His idea was for the federal government to impose a national sales tax of 2 percent to provide $200 a month for every person over sixty-five—the equivalent of about $1,800 a month today (Gordon 1987). Townsend tried to sell his idea by stressing that this measure would vastly increase spending and help the depressed economy by generating new business.

In 1934, the Townsend Plan went before Congress, and the Townsend clubs gathered hundreds of thousands of signatures on petitions in support of the plan. It was an election year, and Congress was particularly vulnerable to this grass-roots revolt by old people across the country. But the Townsend Plan frightened Congress because it called for such high payments to the elderly. Many were also afraid that it would remove the incentive to work and save for the future (Schottland 1963). Congress looked for a way to reject the plan without appearing to be opposed to old-age pensions. When President Roosevelt announced his own, more modest social security plan in June 1934, Congress embraced it.

This legislation required that workers retire at sixty-five. It did not matter how well people did their work, nor how much they needed an income. For decades, the elderly protested. Finally, in 1978 Congress raised the mandatory retirement age to seventy, and then eliminated it in 1986. Today, almost 90 percent of Americans retire by age sixty-five, but they do so voluntarily. They can no longer be forced out of their jobs simply because of their age.

CDQ 10: Did programs such as Social Security come into being as a result of the generosity of Congress and U.S. taxpayers?

Conflict theorists point out that the retirement benefits Americans have today are not the result of generous hearts in Congress. They are, rather, the result of a struggle between competing interest groups. As conflict theorists stress, equilibrium is only a temporary balancing of social forces, one that is always ready to come apart. Perhaps more direct conflict will emerge in the future. Let us consider that possibility.

Rival Interest Groups

TR#22M: Costs of Social Security

Will the future bring conflict between the elderly and the young? While violence is not likely to result, some form of conflict seems inevitable, for the interests of the young and the old are on a collision course. In an era of huge budget deficits, some suggest that the elderly are getting more than their share of society's resources. The huge costs of Social Security (Old Age and Survivors Insurance) have become a national concern. As Figure 13.3 shows, Social Security taxes were only $784 million in 1950,

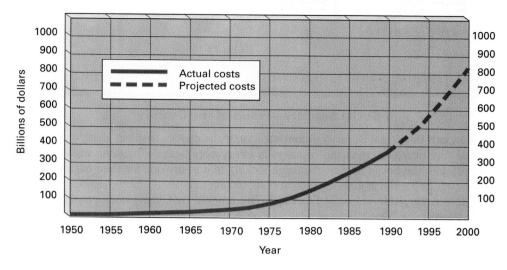

FIGURE 13.3 Costs of Social Security. (*Source: Statistical Abstract of the United States,* various years. Figures from 1970 on are from the 1991 edition, Table 592.)

but now they run *500* times higher. The Down-to-Earth Sociology box below examines stirrings of resentment that may become widespread.

Some form of conflict seems inevitable. As America grays, the number of people who collect Social Security grows, but the proportion of working people—those who pay for these benefits out of their wages—shrinks. Some see the shift in this **dependency ratio,** the number of workers compared with the number of Social Security recipients, as especially troubling. Presently, five working-age Americans pay Social Security taxes to support each person who is over sixty-five—but shortly after the turn of the century this ratio will drop to less than three to one, and by the year 2035,

> **dependency ratio:** the number of workers required to support one person on Social Security

---

DOWN-TO-EARTH SOCIOLOGY

Changing Sentiment about the Elderly

Just a few years back, there was widespread concern about the extensive poverty among America's elderly population. As noted in the text, Congress took effective measures, and the rate of poverty among the elderly dropped to the lowest of all age groups. At this point, is sentiment about the elderly changing?

There are indications that it is. Teresa Anderson (1985) recounted her resentment when she had to pay more than her parents for an identical room in the same motel. Her parents work, have no dependents, and own several pieces of property. According to her, something is wrong when people are automatically entitled to a "senior citizen discount," regardless of need.

Robert Samuelson (1988) went further. He pointed out that the total outlay for Social Security, Medicare, and other programs for the elderly is 20 percent more than our bloated bill for national defense. He proposed eliminating tax breaks for the elderly such as their extra standard deduction on federal income tax forms and their tax exemption on half their Social Security income. He also suggested that the cost-of-living adjustments in Social Security be reduced.

The medical ethicist Daniel Callahan (1987) went even further. He argued that limited medical resources may justify rationing medical care for the elderly. For example, considering costs, should we perform open-heart surgery on a person in his or her eighties, which might prolong life only two or three years—or should we use those same resources for a kidney transplant to a child, which might prolong life by fifty years?

Samuelson accused the elderly's powerful lobby, the American Association of Retired Persons (AARP), of using misleading stereotypes to take unfair advantage of the public and politicians. He said, "In the real world, the stereotypes of the elderly as sedentary, decrepit and poor have long vanished, but in politics the cliche is promoted and perpetuated. The elderly remain in a single group considered to be—as a result only of their age—especially vulnerable, needy and deserving." He then accused the AARP of outright hypocrisy: "They insist (rightfully) that age alone doesn't rob them of vitality and independence, while also arguing (wrongfully) that age alone entitles them to special treatment." They can't have it both ways, Samuelson believes.

What do you think?

to two to one. The following Thinking Critically section summarizes major problems with Social Security.

THINKING CRITICALLY ABOUT SOCIAL CONTROVERSY

Social Security—Fraud of the Century?

Each month the Social Security Administration mails checks to about thirty-five million retired Americans. Across the country, in every occupation, American workers dutifully pay into the Social Security system, looking to it to provide for their basic necessities—and, hopefully, a little more—in their old age.

How dependable is Social Security? The answer that some social analysts have come up with is, "Don't bet your old age on it."

The first problem is well known. Social Security is not like a bank account into which individuals make deposits, and then, when they need the money, draw it out. Instead, the money that current workers pay into Social Security is paid to retired workers. When these current workers retire, they will be paid not from their own savings, but from the contributions of others who are still working.

This system is like a chain letter—it works well as long as enough new people join the chain. If you join early enough, you will collect much more than you paid in—but if you get in toward the end, you are simply out of luck. And, say some conflict theorists, we are nearing the end of the chain, for the number of retirees has grown faster than the work force. When the number of workers supporting each retiree drops from five or six to just two, Social Security taxes may become so prohibitive that they would stifle the country's entire economy.

To address this problem, Social Security taxes were raised in 1977 and again in 1983. These increased revenues were intended to build up a Social Security surplus in the trillions of dollars—easing the burden on a future, smaller labor force.

The second problem with Social Security takes us to the root of the crisis, or, some say, fraud. In 1965 President Lyndon Johnson, bogged down in a horribly expensive war in Vietnam, wanted to conceal the war's true costs from the American public. To produce a budget that would hide the red ink, politicians hit upon an ingenious solution—they simply transferred the revenue from Social Security to the general fund (the general income of the United States government, most of which comes from income taxes). The confiscation went unnoticed by the American public, for it was accomplished simply by prohibiting the Social Security Administration from investing its revenues in anything but United States treasury bonds—a form of government IOUs. Suppose that you buy a $1,000 United States treasury bond (although they don't come that small). The government takes your $1,000 and gives you a document that says it owes you $1,000 plus interest on a certain date. This is just what happens with the money that American workers pay into Social Security. The Social Security Administration collects money from workers, pays the retired, and then hands the excess over to the United States government, which, in turn, gives out these gigantic IOUs that state the amount to be paid plus interest—all due at a later date. When these IOUs come due, instead of paying them the United States government simply exchanges them for more treasury bonds, in larger amounts, of course, since they include the interest that is never paid.

Now, if the government were running a surplus, the shenanigans might be OK. But the fact that the public's pension money is being appropriated by an organization with an annual deficit of $250 billion or $350 billion does not exactly inspire confidence.

This cyclical process is also used to help conceal the true extent of the government's debt from the American public, for the annual deficits announced by the government do *not* include these amounts confiscated from American workers. The Gramm-Rudman provisions, designed to limit the amount of federal debt, do *not* count the funds "borrowed" from Social Security. It is as though this particular government spending does not exist.

It's an ideal political money machine. The general fund gets fed by Social Security, and Social Security gets fed by workers, who think they're building up a retirement nest egg for themselves when the money is actually being spent by the federal government.

Will Social Security still be there when you retire? Some conflict theorists say that you should not count on it, for every year the government wipes the Social Security trust fund clean. The federal government now owes the fund about $15 trillion, which means that the national debt is several times its official figures. If this process continues, it is estimated that to support future retirees, Social Security taxes will have to be raised so high that they will eat up 45 percent of the income of American workers.

Will American workers stand for such huge taxes? Will there one day be a taxpayers' revolt that will leave millions of retirees without their monthly payments? How can the federal government be prevented from spending revenues designated for Social Security? Are the current arrangements legitimate—or is the system a gigantic fraud? (*Source:* Smith 1986; Smith 1987; Hardy 1991; and Gary North's financial newsletter, *Remnant Review.* Raw data in which Social Security receipts are listed as deficits can be found in the United States Treasury's *Monthly Treasury Statement of Receipts and Outlays,* the *Winter Treasury Bulletin,* and the *Statement of Liabilities and Other Financial Commitments of the United States Government,* all government publications.) ■

As shown in Figure 13.4, Medicare and Medicaid costs for the elderly have soared. Medicare and Medicaid now account for *82 percent* of all federal money spent on health care (*Statistical Abstract* 1990: Table 141). Because of this, some say that the health care of other age groups, especially children, is being shortchanged. Others fear that

TR#25: Health Care Costs for the Elderly and Disabled

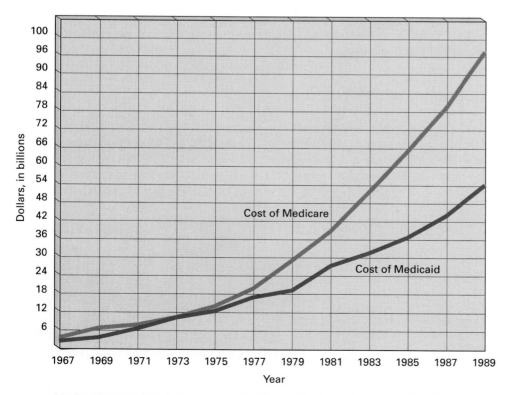

Medicaid is intended for the poor and is financed by federal, state, and local governments. Medicare is intended for the elderly and disabled and is financed by the federal government.

FIGURE 13.4   Health-Care Costs for the Elderly and Disabled. (*Source: Statistical Abstract of the United States,* various years. The figures for 1989 are from the 1991 edition, Table 148.)

Congress will be forced to "pick between old people and kids" (Davidson 1985). As the Down-to-Earth Sociology box on page 357 mentioned, proposals are already being made to trim programs for the elderly on the basis that they are "beyond the nation's ability to pay" (Otten 1988).

To protect their remarkable gains, as well as to demand new ones, older Americans have organized a powerful political lobby. The activities of this group, the American Association of Retired Persons (AARP) which boasts twenty-eight-million members, are running against other interest groups in society.

If there is going to be a showdown, it may not be far away. As the Thinking Critically section above also illustrates, the surplus that younger groups have begun to covet, asking that it be put to work *for them* by funding other federal programs (Malabre 1988), may be merely illusionary. Social Security may be part of a national con game in which American workers are the victims. This is one issue about which conflict theorists probably would prefer to be proven wrong.

Fighting Back: The Gray Panthers

The Gray Panthers illustrate the central position of conflict theorists—that competition for limited resources forms the basis of group relationships. Back in the 1960s, Margaret Kuhn (1990) decided that she was fed up with the disadvantaged position of the elderly. Taking her cue from the Black Panthers, an organization that was then striking fear into the hearts of many Americans, she founded the Gray Panthers. The purpose of this organization, which encourages people of all ages to join, is to work for the welfare of both old and young. On the micro level, the goal is to develop positive self-concepts. On the macro level, the goal is to build a power base that will challenge institutions that oppress the poor, whatever their age. The Gray Panthers have actively fought ageism, regardless of the age group that is on the receiving end of discrimination. One indication of their effectiveness is that their members are frequently asked to testify before congressional committees concerning pending legislation.

Before we close this chapter, let us look at problems of dependency and the sociology of death and dying.

PROBLEMS OF DEPENDENCY

As we examine problems of dependency, we need first to note that the elderly are not as isolated as stereotypes would lead us to believe. Half of all persons over sixty-five live within a half hour of a child. Forty percent see or talk to one of their children daily, 80 percent at least weekly, while only 6 percent do so less than once a month

Project 4

CDQ 11: Do you agree that Social Security may be part of a national con game in which American workers are the victims? Why or why not?

Speaker Sug. #3: A spokesperson for the Gray Panthers or the AARP to discuss current elder issues in your city or state.

K.P.: Margaret Kuhn

Essay #5

L. Obj. 7: State some of the problems of dependency, especially in regard to nursing homes, elder abuse, and poverty.

Speaker Sug. #4: A person from Meals on Wheels or other home-visitation programs which focus on the elderly.

K.P.: Ethel Shanas

As symbolic interactionists stress, the application of labels is not an automatic process. American elderly are resisting labels that stereotype them as inactive, nonproductive people who have nothing to contribute to society. Shown here is Maggie Kuhn, who founded the Gray Panthers for just this reason.

(*Statistical Abstract* 1989: Tables 42, 43). Four-fifths have a living brother or sister, and one-third see a sibling at least once a week. In addition, as can be seen from Table 13.3, most older males live with their wives. Because most wives outlive their husbands, however, the same is not true for most older women, a considerably larger proportion of whom live alone. Note that only a very small proportion of America's elderly live with relatives. The others live independently.

TR#23M: Differences in Age at Marriage

TR#24M: Where Do America's Elderly Live?

Project 5

CNN: Nursing Home Care

Nursing Homes

Nevertheless, some of the elderly are unable to maintain independence. About 5.3 percent of Americans over the age of sixty-five are in nursing homes at any one time (*Statistical Abstract* 1991: Tables 13, 179). With turnover, however—some residents return home after only a few weeks or a few months, others die after a short stay— perhaps 20 percent of elderly Americans spend at least some time in a nursing home. Nursing home residents are *not typical* of the elderly, however. They are likely to be quite ill, or over eighty, or never to have married and therefore without family to take care of them (Shanas 1979). What is life like for them?

It is difficult to say good things about nursing homes, even those that are run well. First, nursing care is so expensive (averaging about $25,000 a year) that of those without family, 70 percent go broke within just three months (Ruffenbach 1988). Nursing home residents tend to be "depressed, unhappy, and intellectually ineffective." They "possess a negative self-image, are docile, submissive, and have low interest in their surroundings" (Smith and Bengston 1979).

The literature, both popular and scientific, is filled with horror stories—reports of patients neglected, beaten, and otherwise maltreated. Of course, not all nursing homes are like that. On the contrary, most are probably at least halfway decent. Some even provide a pleasant decor and concerned help, but they still fall far short of being home (Butterworth 1990). Even in the decent ones, there is a tendency to strip away human dignity. Sociologist Sharon Curtin recounted this incident in one of the better nursing homes (1976).

Nursing home residents, most of whom are either very old or very sick, are not *typical of the elderly. Shown here is a Native American in an old age home at Pine Ridge Indian Reservation in South Dakota.*

> Miss Larson entered Montcliffe the last week of October . . . . Shortly after her admission, I arrived at 7 A.M. to find the night nurse indignant and angry. Miss Larson had climbed over the side rails during the night, and had been found in the bathroom. "She didn't ring or call out," said the nurse. . . . "Why, she might have been hurt, and she is so confused. I want the doctor to order me more sedation. We can't have her carrying on, and disturbing all the other patients. Finally, we had to put her in restraints and I repeated her sleeping pill. But she kept yelling all the same."
>
> I walked in the room and Miss Larson was indeed in restraints. . . . "Get me out of these!" she ordered. "How dare they try to stop me from getting out of bed. I always have to relieve myself at night; and they never answer my bell . . . . So I crawl over the edge; I've been doing it ever since I came to this place. . . ."
>
> Miss Larson was not confused; but in a place where all the patients are so sedated that they scarcely move a muscle during the night, she was counted a nuisance. I did

TABLE 13.3 Where Do America's Elderly Live?*

	Males	Females
Spouse	74%	40%
Alone	16%	41%
With Relatives	8%	18%
With Persons Who Are Not Relatives	2%	1%

*These figures refer to the noninstitutionalized population. About 4 percent of America's elderly live in nursing homes.

Source: Statistical Abstract of the United States, 1991: Table 63.

not want them to increase her sedation; barbiturates frequently make old people confused and disoriented. Even if she was a pain in the neck, I like her better awake and making some sense. The problem was she had no rights. She was old, sick, feeble. Therefore she must shut up, lie still, take what little was offered and be grateful. And if she did that, she would be a "good girl."

The elderly bitterly resent being treated like children—in an institution or anywhere else. They resist, as did Miss Larson, but resistance is usually fruitless. As the Down-to-Earth Sociology box below illustrates, the odds are stacked against elderly residents, for the institution holds the power.

Not everything about nursing homes is bad, of course. They do provide care for those who have no families, or are so sick that their families can no longer care for them. Sometimes nursing homes even help family relationships. One study of a well-run, middle-class nursing home revealed that 70 percent of residents and their children either had grown closer to one another or had been helped to maintain an already close relationship (Smith and Bengston 1979). In some cases, before admittance to the nursing home, their affection had been strained by the parent's physical or mental traumas. Professional care in the nursing home had improved the parent's condition, freeing the child or children to again provide emotional support to the parent. The other 30 percent simply continued their earlier pattern of alienation.

Elder Abuse

Like other social problems shrouded in secrecy, abuse of the elderly has been difficult to study. Researchers, however, have found that the practice is fairly extensive. About 3 or 4 percent of elderly Americans—about one million persons—are abused each year. Apparently about 10 percent of Americans are abused at some time during their older years. Abuse takes many forms other than hitting, including verbal abuse, emotional abuse, neglect, and financial exploitation (Clark 1986; Pillemer and Wolf 1987).

Who are the abusers? The conclusions are inconsistent. While researchers agree that most abusers are members of the elderly person's own family, they disagree about whether the abuser or the abused is the dependent person. Some researchers conclude

CNN: Elderly Abuse

CDQ 13: Why do you think abuse of the elderly is difficult to study?

CDQ 12: Under what circumstances do you think it might be necessary to place one of your loved ones in a nursing home? How would you feel about doing this?

DOWN-TO-EARTH SOCIOLOGY

Pacification—Turning People into Patients

In search of firsthand knowledge of what goes on in nursing homes, sociologist Timothy Diamond (1987) chose participant observation, taking a job as a nursing assistant. He had a preconceived notion of nursing home patients as a passive group of people—sitting in chairs, lying in bed, mostly motionless, the recipients of someone else's acts. He found, however, that this image is only partially true, that some patients actively struggle against the staff to shape their environment. But active resistance is the exception, for it is difficult to maintain a sense of self in a nursing home.

Diamond's observations revealed that nursing home staff routinely dehumanize their patients, referring to them as objects. Nursing assistants are assigned "beds" rather than patients; those who need help in eating are scornfully termed "feeders." The staff also describe the patients as "out of their minds" and "going through their second childhood."

As Diamond discovered, however, some patients fight back. First, they grumble. At 7 A.M., when they are awakened, one may complain, "Work all my life waiting for retirement, and now I can't even sleep in the mornings." Some become demanding, saying, "Where's my Social Security? Get me the administrator! I want my Social Security checks!"

Patients who yell to show their anger, however, are said to be "acting out." They are likely to be "chemically subdued" with tranquilizers until they become compliant. Most patients are engulfed by the identity thrust upon them as residents of nursing homes. Treated and charted as diseased individuals, they tend to become resigned to this final phase of their lives. As their ties to the social world diminish, they withdraw emotionally. They become isolated even from one another, and in a room where forty to fifty people are eating, one will hear little or no conversation, the result, according to Diamond, of "the overwhelming pacification process of patienthood that sweeps over them."

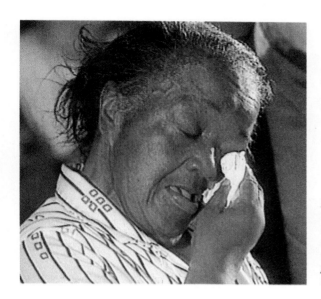

Recent research shows that abuse of the elderly is more common than had been thought. Like other forms of abuse, elderly abuse occurs behind closed doors and seldom becomes a public matter. Most abusers are family members.

that most elder abuse is a result of the stress produced from taking care of a person who is highly dependent and demanding (Douglass 1983; Gelman 1985). Others, however, contend that this explanation blames the victim—placing fault on the elderly person for creating stress. They conclude that the abuser is usually dependent on the elderly person—typically an adult child who remains dependent financially, and perhaps emotionally, on the elderly person whom he or she abuses (Pillemer 1985). Future research should provide the solution.

The Question of Poverty

The elderly live in nagging fear of poverty. Since they do not know how long they will live, nor what the rate of inflation will be, they are uncertain whether their money will last as long as they will. How realistic is this fear? While we cannot speak to any individual case, we can look at the elderly as a group.

An image of poor, neglected grandparents was used in earlier decades to promote programs to benefit elderly Americans. While it was an apt description during the 1960s and 1970s—for at that time the poverty rate of the elderly was greater than that of the general population—it is no longer broadly accurate. The expansion of federal programs for the elderly led to one of the greatest success stories of public policy. In 1959, 33 percent of Americans aged sixty-five and over were living below the poverty line. By 1975, this rate had plunged to 15 percent (Hudson 1978). From there, it dropped even further, to less than 12 percent today. As Table 13.4 shows, America's elderly are now *less* likely than the average American to be living in poverty.

TR#26: Sources of Income for Elderly Persons

CDQ 14: Are the fears of the elderly that they will end up living in poverty realistic? Why or why not?

TR#25M: Percentage below the Poverty Line

Age	Percentage below the Poverty Line
15 and under	20.1
16–21	15.3
22–44	10.3
45–54	7.4
55–59	9.7
60–64	9.5
65 and over	11.4
overall	12.8

Source: Statistical Abstract of the United States, 1991: Table 748.

TABLE 13.4   Percentage of Population below the Poverty Line

Just as at other stages in the life course, having money adequate for one's needs and desires makes life more pleasant and satisfying. This elderly woman who must live out of her car is not likely to find this time of her life satisfying. Income, however, is hardly the sole determiner of satisfaction during old age. As indicated in the text, integration in a community in which one is respected is also a critical factor. Thus, these elderly men, although poor, are likely to find this time of life much more satisfying than the isolated homeless woman.

While people are glad that the elderly are better off than they were, they are bothered that this improvement may have come at the cost of others. For example, as is also shown on Table 13.4, children are much more likely to be poor than are the elderly. Critics point to Figure 13.5, which shows that as the proportion of the elderly living in poverty decreased, the proportion of poor children increased. As the Down-to-Earth Sociology box on changing sentiment illustrated, such criticisms are likely part of an attempt to reduce federal benefits for the elderly. Consequently, advocates for the elderly, such as the Gray Panthers, take these criticisms seriously. Their position is that reducing the poverty of the elderly did not create poverty for anyone else and that the government should develop programs to reduce the poverty of all Americans.

Economic progress among the elderly has been uneven, leaving some subgroups worse off than others. Table 13.5 shows that patterns of earlier years generally follow people into old age. Note that the racial/ethnic patterns discussed in Chapter 12 also persist among the elderly: Hispanic Americans aged sixty-five and over are more than twice as likely as whites to be poor, while the poverty rate among elderly African Americans is over three times the white rate. This table also indicates a consequence of the pattern reviewed in Chapter 11, that of women earning less than men. Elderly

FIGURE 13.5 Trends in Poverty. (*Source: Congressional Research Service; Statistical Abstract of the United States,* 1991: Table 748.)

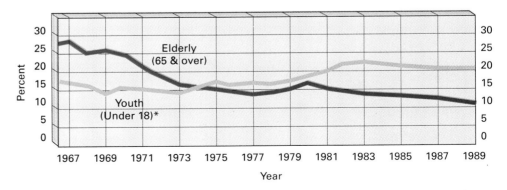

*Note: For some years the government figures for youth refer to persons under 18, for other years to persons under 16.

TABLE 13.5   The Elderly and Poverty

	Percentage below the Poverty Line
Race or ethnicity	
White	10.0
Hispanic American	22.4
African American	32.2
Head of family unit	
Male	6.1
Female	12.6
Living arrangements	
Living in Family	6.1
Living with Unrelated Persons	24.1

Source: Statistical Abstract of the United States, 1990: Table 746; 1991: Table 749.

women who head a family are twice as likely to be poor as older male heads of households. Finally, this table also demonstrates the significance of family. Elderly people who live with unrelated individuals are four times as likely to be poor as those who live in families.

THE SOCIOLOGY OF DEATH AND DYING

Although the term was not mentioned, Durkheim's analysis of suicide in Chapter 1 introduced the topic of the sociology of death and dying. This concluding section first examines the effects of industrialization on attitudes toward death, returns to the topic of suicide, considers death as a process, and looks at the role of hospices in today's society.

Effects of Industrialization

Like old age, death is more than a biological event; it, too, is shaped by culture. In preindustrial societies, the sick were taken care of at home, and they died at home. Because life was short, during childhood most people saw a sibling or parent die (Blauner 1966). As noted in Chapter 1, corpses were even prepared for burial at home.

Industrialization radically altered the circumstances of dying. With the coming of modern medicine, dying was transformed into an event to be managed by professionals in hospitals. Consequently, many people today have never personally seen anyone die. Fictional deaths on television are the closest most people come to witnessing death. In effect, dying has become an event that takes place behind closed doors—isolated, disconnected, remote.

In consequence, the process of dying has become strange to us—and perhaps more fearful as well. To help put on a mask of immortality, we hide from the fact of death. We have even developed elaborate ways to refer to death without using the word itself, which uncomfortably reminds us of our human destiny. We carefully construct a language of avoidance, terms such as "gone," "passed on," "passed away," "no longer with us," "gone beyond," "passed through the pearly gates," "at peace now."

As people grow older, however, death becomes a less distant event. The elderly see many friends and relatives die, and often much of their talk centers on those persons. Often, fears about dying concern more the "how" of death than death itself.

L. Obj. 8: Examine the effects of industrialization on the process of death and dying.

Essay #6

CDQ 15: Why do you think many people today have never personally seen anyone die?

The elderly are especially fearful of dying alone or in pain. One of their biggest fears is cancer, which seems to strike out of the blue.

Death as a Process

L. Obj. 9: Outline the five stages that people go through when they are told they have an incurable disease.

K.P.: Elisabeth Kübler-Ross

Psychologist Elisabeth Kübler-Ross (1969, 1981) found that coming face to face with one's own death sets in motion a five-stage process, which she discovered through her interviews with people who had been informed that they had an incurable disease.

1. *Denial* In this first stage, people cannot believe that they are really going to die. ("The doctor made a mistake. Those test results aren't right.") They avoid the topic of death and any situation that might remind them of it.
2. *Anger* In this second stage they acknowledge their coming death but see it as unjust. ("I didn't do anything to deserve this. So-and-so is much worse than I am, and he's in good health. It isn't right that I should die.")
3. *Negotiation* Next, the individual tries to get around death by making a bargain with God, with fate, or even with the disease itself. ("I need one more Christmas with the family. I never appreciated them as much as I should have. Don't take me until after Christmas, and then I'll go willingly.")
4. *Depression* In this stage, people are resigned to the fact that death is inevitable. They are extremely unhappy about it, however, and they grieve because their life is about to end and they have no power to change the course of events.
5. *Acceptance* In this final stage, people come to terms with the certainty of impending death. They still don't like it, but they now accept that this is how it is going to be. ("Life has to end some time, and this is when it's going to end for me.") During this period, they are likely to get their affairs in order—to make wills, pay bills, give instructions to children on what kind of adults they should become and of how they should take care of mommy (or daddy), and express regret at not having done certain things when they had the chance. Devout Christians are likely to talk about the hope of salvation and their desire to be in heaven with Jesus.

Kübler-Ross noted that not everyone experiences all these stages, nor necessarily in this precise order. Some people never come to terms with their death and remain in the first or second stages throughout the process of dying. Others may move back and forth, vacillating, for example, between acceptance, depression, and negotiation.

Suicide and the Elderly

CNN: Senior Suicide

L. Obj. 10: Give reasons for the high rate of suicide among the elderly.

In Chapter 1, we noted how Durkheim analyzed suicide as much more than an individual act. He stressed that social facts lead to each country having its own suicide rate, and that these rates remain quite stable year after year. It is the same with the age cohorts

As noted in the text, American elderly have the highest suicide rate of all age groups. Efforts to combat suicide include hot lines in which an elderly person contemplating suicide can talk to another elderly person (as shown here). As important as such efforts are, however, sociologically more significant would be the removal of structural barriers that prevent participation in activities the elderly find satisfying, as well as the removal of negative stereotypes.

TABLE 13.6 How Many Americans Kill Themselves Each Year?

Age	Rate (per 100,000)	Number of Deaths
10–14	1.4	169
15–19	11.3	2,016
20–24	15.0	2,832
25–34	15.4	6,783
35–44	14.8	5,414
45–54	14.6	3,636
55–64	15.6	3,368
65–74	18.4	3,345
75–84	25.9	2,528
85 and over	20.5	623

Source: Statistical Abstract of the United States, 1991: Tables 12, 126.

of a nation. As you can see from Table 13.6, of all age groups, Americans over sixty-five are the most likely to kill themselves. Much publicity has been given to adolescent suicide, and rightly so, but the suicide rate of those aged fifteen to nineteen is the lowest for all age groups except those younger than themselves. Suicide peaks between the ages of seventy-five and eighty-four, when it is more than double the rate for adolescents. Even though the rate declines after age eighty-four, it remains the second highest of all age groups.

Many social facts underlie the high suicide rate of the elderly—from a sense of hopelessness as life closes in to social isolation, failing health, the deaths of spouse and friends, pain, loneliness, and the prospect of nothing but more of the same. Even negative stereotypes make a contribution. Beyond motivation, however, lies the primary sociological point: Suicide rates of age cohorts represent social forces, and you can expect these rates to be little changed five to ten years from now.

CDQ 16: Can you explain why the elderly have a high suicide rate?

Hospices

In earlier generations, when not many people made it to age sixty-five or beyond, death at an earlier age was taken for granted—much as people take it for granted today that most people *will* see sixty-five. In fact, about 75 percent of deaths in the United States now occur after the age of sixty-five. This has led to a concern about the *how* of dying. Few elderly people want to burden their children with their own death; they want to die with dignity and with the comforting presence of friends and relatives. Hospitals, to put the matter bluntly, are awkward places in which to die. There, patients are surrounded by strangers in formal garb, in an organization that puts its routines ahead of their needs. In addition to their coldness and formality, hospitals are also extremely expensive.

Hospices emerged as a solution to these problems. Originating in Great Britain, hospices are intended to provide dignity in death, to reduce the emotional and physical burden on children and other relatives, to reduce costs, and to make people comfortable in what Elisabeth Kübler-Ross (1989) called the living-dying interval, that period between discovering that death is imminent and death itself. The term **hospice** originally referred to a place, but increasingly it refers to services that are brought into a dying person's home.

Perhaps a contrast between hospices and hospitals will make the distinction clearer. Whereas hospitals are dedicated to prolonging life, hospices are dedicated to bringing comfort and dignity to a dying person's last days or months. In the hospital

L. Obj. 11: Explain the functions of hospices in modern societies.

Speaker Sug. #5: A staff member or volunteer with a hospice in your area to discuss goals and treatment philosophies of these organizations.

hospice: a place, or services brought into someone's home, for the purpose of bringing comfort and dignity to a dying person

the patient is the unit, but in the hospice the unit changes to the dying person and his or her friends and family. In the hospital, the goal is to make the patient well; in the hospice it is to relieve pain and suffering. In the hospital, the primary concern is the individual's physical welfare; in the hospice, although medical needs are met, the primary concern is the individual's social—and in some instances, spiritual—well-being.

SUMMARY

1. Growing old is much more than a biological matter; what people are like when they are old also depends a great deal on the society in which they live. Cultural beliefs and attitudes affect the outlook and behaviors of the elderly—just as they do for everyone else. The example of the Abkhasians illustrates how culture—habits of work, diet, and social integration—even affects longevity.

2. Whenever a nation industrializes, the lifespan of its population increases. The United States has experienced an uninterrupted increase in longevity. Today, life expectancy at birth averages seventy-two for males and seventy-nine for females, and almost 13 percent of Americans are sixty-five or over. Sex and race or ethnicity have profound effects on life expectancy. An individual's life expectancy increases with each year that he or she lives.

3. The symbolic interactionist perspective can be applied to the topics of what makes a person old, what it means to grow old, negative stereotypes of the elderly, and the effects of the mass media. The application of the label "old" depends on four different factors: biological, biographical, gender-related, and cross-cultural. Cross-cultural patterns—for example, among the Tiwi, traditional Eskimos, and Chinese—demonstrate the role of society in determining what an individual experiences when he or she grows old. Industrialization has also profoundly affected the meaning of being old, while the mass media have created many negative messages about aging.

4. The functionalist perspective focuses on the withdrawal of the elderly from positions of responsibility. Disengagement theory emphasizes that retirement is a mutual agreement between the individual and society to ensure a smooth transition in positions of responsibility and power.

Activity theory examines the adjustment of the elderly to their disengagement. In general, elderly people who have a high level of activity are more satisfied with life than those who do not, but the quality of the activity is especially important.

5. The conflict perspective was applied to social security legislation and to age cohorts as rival interest groups. In light of the huge costs of Social Security, Medicare, and Medicaid, younger and older Americans may be on a collision course. The phenomenon of the Gray Panthers is also consistent with the notion of basic competition for scarce resources.

6. Problems of dependency include nursing homes, elder abuse, and poverty. On the negative side, nursing homes tend to strip away human dignity and to make their residents passive. On the positive side, nursing homes often provide a safety valve that allows parents and children to establish better relationships with one another. Abusers of the elderly are usually family members. Researchers don't agree on whether the abuser or the abused is the more dependent. In recent years, the poverty rate of the elderly has dropped below that of the rest of the nation. The elderly most likely to be poor are minorities and women.

7. Industrialization has changed our experience with death. The process of dying involves denial, anger, negotiation, depression, and acceptance. Age cohorts have quite stable rates of suicide, with the suicide rate of the elderly the highest of all age groups. Hospices are intended to provide dignity in death, to reduce the emotional and physical burden on relatives, to reduce costs, and to make people comfortable during the living-dying interval.

SUGGESTED READINGS

Butler, Robert N. *Why Survive? Being Old in America.* New York: Harper & Row, 1985. This scathing criticism of growing old in American society won a Pulitzer Prize.

Chambre, Susan Maizel. *Good Deeds in Old Age: Volunteering by the New Leisure Class.* Lexington, Mass.: Lexington Books, 1987. With larger numbers of Americans retiring each year and a high level of activity considered essential to good health, volunteer activities have become increasingly important.

DiGiulio, Robert C. *Beyond Widowhood.* New York: Free Press,

1989. Based on personal experience as well as research, the author presents a sensitive and moving analysis of the grieving process.

Hooyman, Nancy R., and H. Asuman Kiyak. *Social Gerontology: An Interdisciplinary Perspective.* Needham Heights, Mass.: Allyn & Bacon, 1988. The authors explore the aging process from the perspectives of sociology, psychology, social work, and nursing.

Kamerman, Jack B. *Death in the Midst of Life: Social and Cultural*

Influences in Death, Grief, and Mourning. Englewood Cliffs, N. J.: Prentic Hall, 1988. Kamerman examines people's reactions to the death of a loved one.

Marshall, Victor W., ed. *Later Life: The Social Psychology of Aging.* Beverly Hills, Calif.: Sage, 1986. Symbolic interactionists explore social aspects of aging.

Matthews, Sarah H. *Friendships Through the Life Course: Oral Biographies in Old Age.* Newbury Park, Calif.: Sage, 1986. Focusing on the importance of close social relationships in maintaining the health of the elderly, Matthews explores how the elderly see the significance of their friendships.

Pillemer, Karl A., and Rosalie S. Wolf, eds. *Elder Abuse: Conflict in the Family.* Dover, Mass.: Auburn House, 1987. This collection of readings presents an overview of this disturbing topic.

Journals

The Gerontologist and *Journal of Gerontology* each focus on issues of aging, while *Youth and Society: A Quarterly Journal* examines adolescent culture.

CHAPTER 14

Jacob Lawrence, Builders, *1980*

The Economy: Money and Work

THE TRANSFORMATION OF ECONOMIC SYSTEMS
Hunting and Gathering Economies: Subsistence ■ Pastoral and Horticultural Economies: The Creation of Surplus ■ Agricultural Economies: The Growth of Trade ■ Industrial Economies: The Birth of the Machine ■ Postindustrial Economy: The Information Age

THE TRANSFORMATION OF THE MEDIUM OF EXCHANGE
Earliest Mediums of Exchange ■ Medium of Exchange in Agricultural Economies ■ Medium of Exchange in Industrial Economies ■ Medium of Exchange in Postindustrial Economies

WORLD ECONOMIC SYSTEMS
Capitalism ■ Socialism ■ Ideologies of Capitalism and Socialism ■ Criticisms of Capitalism and Socialism ■ *Down-to-Earth Sociology:* **Selling the**

American Dream—The Creation of Constant Discontent ■ The Systems in Conflict and Competition ■ The Future: Convergence?

THE INNER CIRCLE OF CAPITALISM
Corporate Capitalism ■ Interlocking Directorates ■ Multinational Corporations

WORK IN AMERICAN SOCIETY
Three Economic Sectors ■ Women and Work ■ The Underground Economy ■ Patterns of Work and Leisure

APPLYING SOCIOLOGICAL THEORIES
The Functionalist Perspective ■ The Conflict Perspective ■ The Symbolic Interactionist Perspective ■ *Perspectives:* **Who Is Unemployed?**

THE FUTURE OF THE UNITED STATES ECONOMY

SUMMARY

SUGGESTED READINGS

The alarm pounded in Kim's ears. "Not Monday already," she groaned. "There must be a better way of starting the week." She pressed the snooze button on the clock (from Germany) to sneak another ten minutes' sleep. In what seemed just thirty seconds, the alarm shrilly insisted she get up and face the week.

Still bleary-eyed after her shower, Kim peered into her closet and picked out a silk blouse (from China), a plaid wool skirt (from Scotland), and leather shoes (from India). She nodded, satisfied, as she added a pair of simulated pearls (from Taiwan). Running late, she hurriedly ran a brush (from Mexico) through her hair. As Kim wolfed down a bowl of cereal (from the United States), topped with milk (from the United States), bananas (from Costa Rica), and sugar (from the Dominican Republic), she turned on her kitchen television (from Korea) to listen to the weather forecast.

Gulping the last of her coffee (from Brazil), Kim grabbed her briefcase (from Wales), purse (from Spain), and jacket (from Taiwan), and quickly climbed into her car (from Japan). As she glanced at her watch (from Switzerland), she hoped the traffic would be in her favor. She muttered to herself as she glimpsed the gas gauge at a street light (from Great Britain). She muttered again when she paid for the gas (from Saudi Arabia), for the price had risen once more. "My check never keeps up with prices," she moaned to herself as she finished the drive to work.

The office was abuzz. Six months ago, New York headquarters had put the company up for sale, but there had been no takers. The big news this Monday was that both a Japanese and a Canadian corporation had put in bids over the weekend. No one got much work done that day, as the whole office speculated about how things might change.

As Kim walked to the parking lot after work, she saw a "Buy American" bumper sticker on the car next to hers. "That's right," she said to herself. "If people were more like me, this country would be in better shape."

While the vignette may be slightly exaggerated, it is not too far from the experience of most Americans. Many of us are like Kim—using a multitude of products from around the world, and yet somewhat concerned about the declining competitive position of our own country. In terms of trade and products, the world has certainly grown much smaller in recent years. We live in a global economy, and this chapter focuses on the consequences of this fact for the future of the United States.

THE TRANSFORMATION OF ECONOMIC SYSTEMS

L. Obj. 1: Trace the transformation of the economic systems through each of the historical stages and state the degree to which social inequality existed in each of the economies.

In Mexico, the market is a bustling scene—farmers selling fruits and vegetables, as well as poultry, goats, and caged songbirds—others selling homemade blankets, serapes, huaraches, pottery, belts. Women bend over open fires cooking tacos, which their waiting customers wolf down with soft drinks. The market is a combined business and social occasion, as people make their purchases and catch up with each other on the latest gossip. Such scenes used to characterize the world, but now they are limited primarily to the Second and Third Worlds. The closest people come in the United States is a flea market or a bazaar.

Today, the term *market* means much more than such settings and activities. It has kept its original meaning of buying and selling, but it now refers to things much more

Although the term market *now refers to the mechanisms by which people establish value so they can exchange goods and services, its original meaning referred to a direct exchange of goods, as shown in this photo of a market in Chiapas, Mexico. In peasant societies, where such markets are still a regular part of everyday life, people find the social interaction every bit as rewarding as the goods and money that they exchange.*

impersonal. **Market,** the mechanism by which we establish values in order to exchange goods and services, today means the Dow Jones Industrial Average in New York City, and the Nikkei Average in Tokyo. Market also means the movement of vast amounts of goods across international borders, even across oceans and continents. Market means brokers taking orders for IBM, speculators trading international currencies, and futures traders making huge bets on whether oil, wheat, and pork bellies will go up or down—and, of course, making a purchase at the local food store.

People's lives have always been affected by the dynamics of the market, or as sociologists prefer to call it, the **economy.** Today, the economy, which many sociologists believe is the most important of our social institutions, differs radically from all but our most recent past. Economic systems have become impersonal and global. The products that Kim used in our opening vignette make it apparent that today's economy knows no national boundaries. The economy is essential to our welfare for it means inflation or deflation, high or low interest rates, high or low unemployment, economic recession or economic boom. The economy affects our chances of buying a new home, of having to work at a dead-end job or of being on a fast track in an up-and-coming company.

To better understand the economy of the United States and its relative standing in history, it is useful to review the historical stages that preceded it. These stages were discussed in some detail in chapter 6 (pp. 141–149), in which the Lenskis (1987) described how societies were transformed from those based on relatively simple organization to those with more complex organization. In the following section, we shall briefly examine the economic system of each type of society.

Hunting and Gathering Economies: Subsistence

The earliest human societies, *hunting and gathering societies,* had a simple **subsistence economy.** Groups of perhaps twenty-five to forty persons lived off the land, simply gathering what they could find, moving from place to place as their food supply ran low. Hunting added to these people's knowledge and skills as they developed weapons and learned to prepare and store meat. Because there was little or no excess food or other items, there was little trade with other groups. With no excess to accumulate, there was a high degree of social equality in this earliest type of economy.

Pastoral and Horticultural Economies: The Creation of Surplus

In pastoral and horticultural economies, people began to cultivate and breed animals. This development created a more dependable food supply, and, ultimately, a *surplus.* The creation of a surplus was one of the most significant events in human history, for it changed people's basic relationships. The food surplus allowed human groups to grow in size, to become more settled in a single place, and to develop a specialized division of labor. For the first time in human history, some individuals were able to devote their energies to tasks other than food production. Some became shamans, others leather workers, weapon makers, and so on. This newly developed division of labor had far-reaching effects on human life, for the items that were produced stimulated trade. The primary sociological significance of surplus and trade was that they fostered social *inequality,* for some members of the group were now able to accumulate more possessions than others. The effects of that change remain with us today.

Agricultural Economies: The Growth of Trade

The invention of the plow brought even greater surpluses to agricultural economies, magnifying the trends of the previous period. Even more people were freed from food production, more specialized divisions of labor followed, and trade expanded both in terms of the range of goods exchanged and the geographical distance over which trade

CDQ 1: How do you think people's lives today are affected by the American economy?

Speaker Sug. #1: An anthropologist who has studied nations in the various stages of economic development.

market: any process of buying and selling; on a more formal level, the mechanism that establishes values for the exchange of goods and services

economy: a system of distribution of goods and services

subsistence economy: the type of economy in which human groups live off the land with little or no surplus

occurred. As cities developed into trading centers, power passed from the heads of families and clans to a ruling elite. The result was even greater social, political, and economic inequality.

Industrial Economies: The Birth of the Machine

Industrial economies, which are based on machines powered by fuels, created a surplus unlike anything the world had seen. Following the invention of the steam engine in 1765, only a minority of people were needed for food production, and the vast surplus and accumulation of manufactured goods stimulated extensive trade between nations. The trend toward even greater social inequality continued during the early part of the Industrial Revolution, as some individuals found themselves able to exploit the labor of many others and to manipulate the political machinery for their own purposes. Later on, bloody battles occurred as workers unionized to improve their working conditions.

As the surplus produced by industrialization increased, the emphasis changed from the production of goods to their consumption. Sociologist Thorstein Veblen (1912) used the term **conspicuous consumption** to describe this fundamental change in people's orientations. By this term, Veblen meant that the Protestant ethic identified by Weber—an emphasis on hard work, savings, and a concern for salvation (discussed in Chapters 7 and 18)—had been replaced by an eagerness to show off wealth by the "elaborate consumption of goods."

Postindustrial Economy: The Information Age

In 1973, sociologist Daniel Bell noted the emergence of a new *postindustrial economy*. According to Bell, this type of economy has six characteristics: (1) extensive trade among nations; (2) a large surplus of goods; (3) a service sector so large that it employs the majority of workers; (4) a wide variety and quantity of goods available to the average person, (5) an "information explosion," and (6) a "global village," that is, technological advances that make possible instantaneous, worldwide communications.

Of these six characteristics, perhaps the two most striking hallmarks are the information explosion and the emergence of a global village. Today, news of political

---

K.P.: Thorstein Veblen

Project 1

CDQ 2: What examples of conspicuous consumption can you give?

K.P.: Daniel Bell

CDQ 3: Do you watch network or cable television newscasts? If yes, how are these broadcasts examples of the "global village?"

conspicuous consumption: Thorstein Veblen's term for a change from the Protestant ethic to an eagerness to show off wealth by the elaborate consumption of goods

---

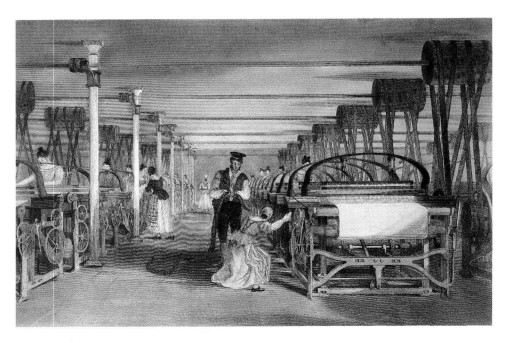

The Industrial Revolution not only changed the way people worked, but also altered social relationships. Shown here is a scene from an early stage of the Industrial Revolution, power loom weaving in a textile mill about 1834. Two vital aspects of this fundamental change are immediately evident: the infinitely greater productive power of the machine as opposed to hand work, and the employment of women.

and economic changes, instantaneously transmitted by satellite, not only affects prices on the New York Stock Exchange but reverberates on the Japanese Nikkei Stock Exchange as well. Because national boundaries now present less of a barricade than ever to the exchange of goods and information, the world has become far more accessible.

Consequences are especially visible in Europe, where the twelve nations of the European Community (EC)—Belgium, Denmark, France, Germany, Great Britain, Greece, Ireland, Italy, Luxembourg, the Netherlands, Portugal, and Spain—and the six nations of the European Free Trade Association (EFTA)—Austria, Finland, Iceland, Norway, Sweden, and Switzerland—have formed a unified economic and political entity. So far each nation remains sovereign and retains its own legislature, courts, and heads of state, but there is also a European Parliament, a European court, and, as proposed, a single military (Revzin 1990; Burke and Rafferty 1991). And just as following the formation of the United States the currencies of the individual states continued to circulate for a time, so do those of individual EC members as the EC develops a unified currency. The goal of political unity is expected to be reached within the next decade.

Continued Inequalities.   Although the postindustrial economy has brought a greater availability of goods, it has not resulted in social equality. As explained in Part III, the United States continues to be marked by a vast gap in income between the rich and the poor, men continue to earn considerably more than women, and whites are paid more than either African Americans or Hispanic Americans.

That this nation is *not* achieving economic equality in the postindustrial economy is apparent from a look at household income. Year after year, for example, the ethnic and racial gap remains. As Figure 14.1a shows, compared with whites, Hispanic Americans and African Americans are two-and-one-half to three times as likely to be below the poverty line; Figure 14.1b also illustrates that the median household income of whites is considerably higher than that of Hispanic Americans or African Americans.

Figure 14.2 shows income inequality in even starker terms: The richest fifth of Americans earn about *48 percent* of all the income in the United States, while the poorest fifth earn only about *4 percent.* In other words, income inequality in the postindustrial economy remains so great that the top fifth of the population averages *twelve times* as much income as the lowest fifth.

Two hallmarks of postindustrial economies are information and a global village. Just a few decades ago, the value of goods in what used to be "far off" Japan had little or no relevance to the West. Today, in contrast, with Japan an integrated part of a world market, economic events there are significant for the stock exchanges in New York, London, Zürich, Bonn, Paris, Brussels, Madrid, and so on. Shown here are floor traders at the Tokyo Stock Exchange.

CDQ 4: Why do you think the postindustrial economy has not resulted in social equality?

TR#27: Percentage of American Households below Poverty Line

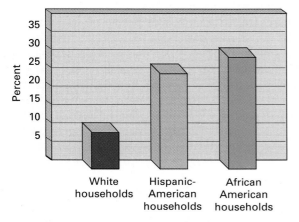

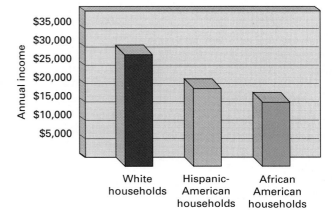

FIGURE 14.1   Percentage of American Households below the Poverty Line and Household Income 1989. (*Source: Statistical Abstract of the United States,* 1991: Table 748, 727.)

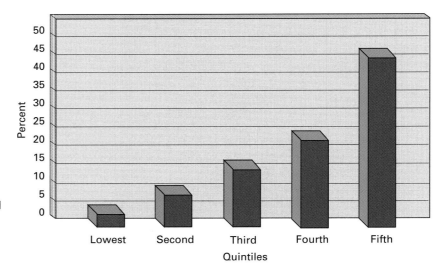

FIGURE 14.2 Percentage of the Entire Income of the United States Received, by Quintile, 1989. (*Source: Statistical Abstract of the United States,* 1991: Table 758.)

THE TRANSFORMATION OF THE MEDIUM OF EXCHANGE

As each type of economy evolved, so, too, did the **medium of exchange,** the means by which people value and exchange goods and services. As we review this transformation, you will see how the medium of exchange is vital to each society, both reflecting its state of development and contributing to it.

Earliest Mediums of Exchange

As noted, the lack of surplus in hunting and gathering and pastoral and horticultural economies meant that there was little to trade. Whatever trading did occur was by **barter,** the direct exchange of one item for another. The surplus that stimulated trade in the later types of economy led to different ways of valuing goods and services for the purpose of exchange. Let us look at how the medium of exchange was transformed.

Medium of Exchange in Agricultural Economies

Although bartering continued in agricultural economies, people increasingly came to use **money,** a medium of exchange by which items are valued. In most places, money consisted of gold and silver coins, their weight and purity determining the amount of goods or services that they could purchase. In some places people made purchases with **deposit receipts,** receipts that transferred ownership to a specified number of ounces of gold, bushels of wheat, or amount of other goods that were on deposit in a warehouse or bank. Toward the end of the agricultural period, deposit receipts became formalized into **currency** (paper money), each piece of paper representing a specific amount of gold or silver that could be redeemed from a central warehouse. Thus currency (and deposit receipts) represented **stored value,** and no more currency could be issued than the amount of gold or silver that the currency represented. Gold and silver coins continued to circulate alongside the deposit receipts and currency.

Medium of Exchange in Industrial Economies

With but few exceptions, bartering became a thing of the past in industrial economies. Gold was replaced by paper currencies, which, in the United States, could be exchanged for a set amount of gold stored at Fort Knox. This policy was called the **gold standard,** and as long as each dollar represented a specified amount of gold the number

medium of exchange: the means by which people value goods and services in order to make an exchange, for example, currency, gold, and silver

barter: the direct exchange of one item for another

money: a general term for a medium of exchange, currency being the most common form in our society

deposit receipts: a receipt stating that a certain amount of goods is on deposit in a warehouse or bank; the receipt is used as a form of money

currency: paper money

stored value: the backing of a currency by goods that have been stored

gold standard: paper money backed by gold

of dollars that could be issued was limited. By the end of this period, United States paper money could no longer be exchanged for gold or silver, resulting in **fiat money,** currency issued by a government that is not backed by stored value.

One consequence of the move away from stored value was that coins made of precious metals disappeared from circulation. In comparison with paper money, these coins were more valuable, and people became unwilling to part with them. Gold coins disappeared first, followed by the largest silver coin, the dollar. Then, as inferior metals (copper, zinc, and nickel) replaced the smaller silver coins, people began to hoard them, and silver coins also disappeared from circulation.

Even without a gold standard that restrains the issuing of currency to stored value, governments have a practical limit on the amount of paper money they can issue. In general, prices increase if a government issues currency at a rate higher than the growth of its **gross national product,** the total amount of a nation's goods and services. This condition, known as **inflation,** means that each unit of currency will purchase fewer goods and services. Governments try to control inflation, for it can be a destabilizing influence on society.

As you can see from Figure 14.3, as long as the gold standard limited the amount of currency, the purchasing power of the dollar remained relatively stable. When the United States departed from the gold standard in 1937, the dollar no longer represented stored value, and it plunged in value. As this figure so clearly shows, today's dollar is but a shadow of its former self, retaining only about 10 percent of its original purchasing power.

In the industrial economy, checking accounts held in banks became common. A *check* is actually a type of deposit receipt, for it is a promise that the writer of the check has enough currency on deposit to cover the check. The latter part of this period saw the invention of the **credit card,** a device that allows its owner, who has been preapproved for a set amount of credit, to purchase goods without an immediate exchange of money—either metal or currency. The credit card owner is later billed for the purchases.

TR#28: Declining Value of the Dollar

Speaker Sug. #2: An expert on finance to discuss the possibilities of a "moneyless" society.

CDQ 5: What medium of exchange do you most often use? Why?

fiat money: currency issued by a government that is not backed by stored value

gross national product: the amount of goods and services produced by a nation

inflation: an increase in prices

credit card: a device that allows its owner to purchase goods but to be billed later

debit card: a device that allows its owner to charge purchases against his or her bank account

Medium of Exchange in Postindustrial Economies

During the first part of the postindustrial economy, paper money circulates freely. Paper money then becomes less common as it is gradually replaced by checks and credit cards. The **debit card,** a device by which a purchase is charged against its owner's bank account, comes into being. Increasingly, spending means not an exchange of physical money—whether paper or coins—but rather the electronic transfer of numbers residing in computer memory banks. In effect, the new medium of exchange is itself a part of the information explosion.

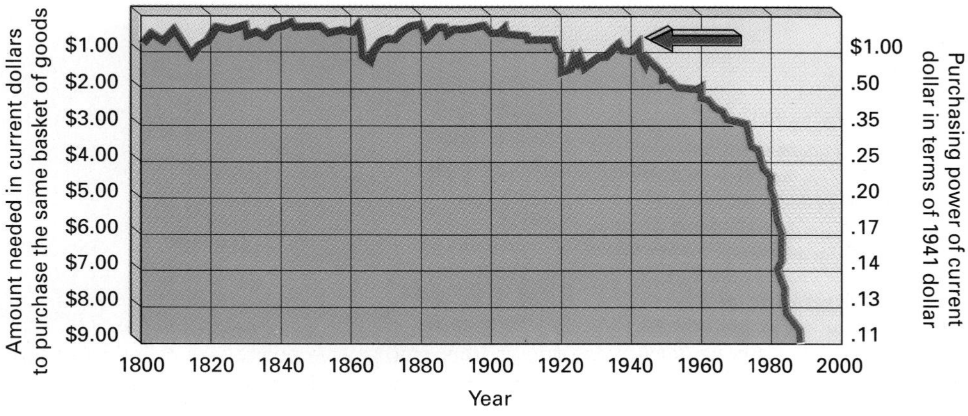

FIGURE 14.3 Declining Value of the Dollar. (*Source:* "Alternative Investment Market Letter," November 1991.)

Essential to the exchange of goods and services is a medium of exchange. With extensive travel a characteristic of today's global market, currencies must be able to be instantaneously exchanged, a function served by this "camel bank" in Jaisalmer, India. As a global economy continues to develop, it is possible that one day there will be a single world currency.

WORLD ECONOMIC SYSTEMS

Now that we have outlined the main economic changes in history—the transformation from the hunting and gathering economy to the postindustrial economy and changes in the mediums of exchange—let us compare capitalism and socialism, the two main economic systems in force today.

Capitalism

capitalism: an economic system characterized by the private ownership of the means of production, the pursuit of profit, and market competition

private ownership of the means of production: the possession of machines and factories by individuals, who decide what shall be produced

profit: the amount gained from selling something for more than it cost

market competition: the exchange of items between willing buyers and sellers

laissez-faire capitalism: unrestrained manufacture and trade (literally, "hands off" capitalism)

People who live in a capitalist society are immersed in details that blur its essentials. It is difficult to see beyond the local shopping mall and fast-food chains. If we distill the businesses of the United States to their basic components, however, we see that **capitalism** has three essential features: (1) **private ownership of the means of production** (individuals own the land, machines, and factories, and decide what shall be produced); (2) the pursuit of **profit** (selling something for more than it costs); and (3) **market competition** (an exchange of items between willing buyers and sellers).

Welfare (or State) Capitalism versus Laissez-Faire Capitalism. Many people believe that the United States is an example of true capitalism. True (or pure) capitalism, however, known as **laissez-faire capitalism** (literally meaning "hands off"), exists only when market forces are able to operate without interference from the government. Such is not the case in the United States, where many restraints to the laissez-faire model have been instituted. In the United States, the current form of capitalism is *welfare* (or *state*) *capitalism,* in which private citizens own the means of

An essential aspect of every society is economy, a system of exchanging goods and services. The boat vendors in Thailand provide an efficient means of getting fresh produce to eager consumers, where the goods are exchanged for cash. A similar exchange in American stores occurs, but, as part of the postindustrial society, the transaction is mediated through electronic numbers.

production and pursue profits, but do so within a vast system of laws designed to protect the welfare of the population.

Suppose, for example, that you have discovered what you think is a miracle tonic: It will grow hair, erase wrinkles, and dissolve excess fat. If your product works, you will become an overnight sensation—not only a multimillionaire, but also the toast of television talk shows.

Before you count your money—and your fame—however, you must reckon with **market restraints,** the laws and regulations of welfare capitalism that limit your capacity to sell what you produce. First, you must comply with local and state rules. You must obtain a charter of incorporation, business licenses, and a state tax number that allows you to make untaxed purchases. Then come the federal regulations. You cannot simply take your item to local stores and ask them to sell it; you must first seek approval from federal agencies that monitor compliance with the Pure Food and Drug Act. This means that you must prove that your product will not cause harm to the public. In addition, you must be able to substantiate your claims—or else face being shut down by state and federal agencies that monitor the market for fraud. Your manufacturing process is also subject to government regulation: state and local laws concerning cleanliness and state and federal rules for the storage and disposal of hazardous wastes.

Suppose that you succeed in overcoming these obstacles, your business prospers, and the number of your employees grows. Other federal agencies will monitor your compliance with regulations concerning racial and sexual discrimination, the payment of minimum wages, and the remittance of Social Security taxes. State agencies will also examine your records to see that you have paid unemployment compensation taxes on your employees and remitted sales taxes on items that you sell at retail. Finally, the Internal Revenue Service will constantly look over your shoulder. In short, the United States economic system is far from an example of laissez-faire capitalism.

To see how welfare or state capitalism developed in the United States, let us go back to the 1800s when capitalism in this country was considerably less restrained. At that time, you could have made your "magic" potion in your kitchen and sold it at any outlet willing to handle it. You could have openly advertised that it grew hair, erased wrinkles, and dissolved fat, for no agency existed to monitor your product or your claims. In fact, that is precisely what thousands of individuals did at that time, producing numerous "elixirs" with whimsical names such as "Grandma's Miracle Medicine" and "Elixir of Health and Happiness." One product could claim that it simultaneously restored sexual potency, purged the intestines, and made people more intelligent. People often felt better after drinking such tonics, for many elixirs were liberally braced with alcohol and even cocaine (Ashley 1975). Indeed, until 1903, a main ingredient of Coca-Cola was cocaine. To protect the public's health, in 1906 the federal government passed the Pure Food and Drug Act and began to regulate products.

The regulation of state capitalism was also accelerated by John D. Rockefeller's remarkable success in unregulated markets. After a ruthless drive for domination—which included drastically reducing rates for oil and then doubling them after driving out the competition, and in some instances sabotaging a competitor's pipelines and refineries—Rockefeller managed to corner the United States oil and gasoline market (Josephson 1949). With his competitors crippled or eliminated, his company, Standard Oil, was able to dictate prices to the entire nation. Rockefeller had achieved the capitalist's dream, a **monopoly,** the control of an entire industry by a single company.

Rockefeller had overplayed the capitalist game, however, for he had wiped out one of its essential components, competition. Consequently, to protect this cornerstone of capitalism, the federal government passed antimonopoly legislation and broke up Standard Oil. Today, the top firms of each industry—such as General Motors in automobiles and General Electric in household appliances—must obtain federal approval before acquiring another company in the same industry. If the government determines

L. Obj. 2: State the three essential features of capitalism and explain why "pure" capitalism does not exist.

Essay #2

CDQ 6: Can you think of any kind of business you could set up in the United States today in which you would not have to comply with rules and regulations?

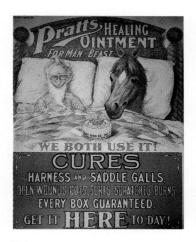

This advertisement from 1885 represents an earlier stage of capitalism, when individuals were free to manufacture and market products with little or no interference from the government. Today, the production and marketing of goods take place under detailed, complicated government regulations.

market restraints: laws and regulations that limit the capacity to manufacture and sell products

monopoly: the control of an entire industry by a single company

CDQ 7: Why do most people think that the U.S. economic system is capitalistic if, in reality, it is far from "pure" capitalism?

L. Obj. 3: Describe the three essential components of socialism and give reasons why "pure" socialism does not exist.

CDQ 8: How do you think an economic system which distributes resources according to a person's need, instead of financial ability to pay, would work in the U.S.?

divest: to sell off

socialism: an economic system characterized by the public ownership of the means of production, central planning, and the distribution of goods without a profit motive

market forces: the law of supply and demand

democratic socialism: a hybrid economic system in which capitalism is mixed with state ownership

that one firm dominates a market, and thereby unfairly restricts competition, it can force that company to **divest** (sell off) some of its businesses.

Another characteristic of welfare capitalism is that although the government fiercely supports competition, it establishes its own monopoly over "common good" items—those presumed essential for the common good of the citizens, such as soldiers, war supplies, highways, and sewers.

In Sum. As currently practiced, capitalism is far from the classical laissez-faire model. The economic system of the United States encourages the first two components of capitalism, the private ownership of the means of production and the pursuit of profit. But a vast system of government regulations both protects and restricts the third component, market competition. In addition, the government controls "common good" items.

Socialism

Socialism also has three essential components: (1) the *public* ownership of the means of production; (2) central planning; and (3) the distribution of goods without a profit motive.

In socialist economies, the government owns the means of production—not only the factories, but also the land, railroads, oil wells, and gold mines. Unlike capitalism, in which **market forces**—supply and demand—determine what shall be produced and the prices that will be charged, in socialism a central committee decides that the country needs X number of toothbrushes, Y toilets, and Z shoes. This group decides how many of each shall be produced, which factories will produce them, the prices that will be charged for the items, and where they will be distributed.

Socialism is designed to eliminate competition, for goods are sold at predetermined prices regardless of demand for an item. Profit is not the goal, nor is encouraging consumption of goods in low demand (by lowering the price), nor limiting the consumption of hard-to-get goods (by raising the price). Rather, the goal is to produce goods for the general welfare and to distribute them according to people's needs, not their ability to pay.

In a socialist economy everyone in the economic chain works for the government. The members of the central committee who determine production are government employees, as are the administrators who oversee production, the factory workers who do the producing, the truck drivers who move the merchandise, and the clerks who sell it. Although those who purchase the items work at entirely different jobs—in offices, on farms, in day-care centers—even they are government employees.

Just as capitalism does not exist in a pure form, neither does socialism (Horowitz 1989). Although the ideology of socialism calls for resources to be distributed according to need and not position, in line with the functionalist argument of social stratification presented in Chapter 9, socialist countries found it necessary to offer higher salaries for some jobs in order to entice people to take greater responsibilities. For example, factory managers always earn more than factory workers. By narrowing the huge pay gaps that characterize capitalist nations, however, socialist nations have been able to establish considerably greater equality of income.

Dissatisfied with the greed and exploitation of capitalism and the lack of freedom and individuality of socialism, some Western nations (most notably Sweden and Denmark) have adopted **democratic socialism,** or welfare socialism. In this form of socialism, both the state and individuals engage in production and distribution. While the government owns and runs the steel, mining, forestry, and energy concerns, as well as the country's telephones, television stations, and airlines (The *Wall Street Journal,* November 12, 1991), the retail stores, farms, manufacturing concerns, and most service industries remain in private hands.

Ideologies of Capitalism and Socialism

Capitalism and socialism not only have different approaches to the production and distribution of goods; each represents a distinct ideology.

Capitalists hold that market forces should determine both products and prices and that it is healthy for people to strive after profits. They believe that under such conditions people will seek to produce items that make a profit, and that the only items that will make a profit are those that are in demand. As the Down-to-Earth Sociology box below shows, the market also *creates* a demand for products. In short, market forces underlie the successful capitalist society. The potential for profit encourages people to develop and produce new products desired by the public, while workers are motivated to work hard so that they can make as much money as possible to purchase more goods.

In contrast, socialists believe that profit is immoral, that it represents *excess value* extracted from workers. Because an item's value represents the work that goes into it, there can be no profit unless workers are paid less than the value of their labor. Profit, then, represents an amount withheld from workers. To protect workers from this exploitation, socialists believe that the government should own the means of production, using them not for profit, but to produce and distribute items according to people's needs rather than their ability to pay.

Criticisms of Capitalism and Socialism

L. Obj. 4: State the major criticisms of capitalism and socialism. Explain why some theorists believe the two systems are converging.

The primary criticism leveled against capitalism is that it leads to social inequality. Capitalism, say its critics, produces a tiny top layer consisting of wealthy, powerful

DOWN-TO-EARTH SOCIOLOGY

Selling the American Dream—The Creation of Constant Discontent

Advertising is such an integral part of contemporary American life that it almost appears to be the natural state of people in this country to be deluged with ads. We open a newspaper or magazine and expect to find that a good portion of its pages proclaim the virtues of products and firms. We turn on the television and are assailed with commercials for about ten minutes of every half hour (except on public television). Some social analysts even claim that the purpose of television is to round up an audience to watch the commercials—making the programs a mere diversion from the medium's real objective of selling products!

A fascinating potential of advertising is its ability to increase our desire to consume products for which we previously felt no need whatsoever. American kitchens, filled with gadgets that slice and dice and machines that turn anything into a sandwich, attest to this power.

But advertising's power to make people gluttons for consumption goes beyond kitchen gadgets soon consigned to back drawers and later to garage sales. Many Americans today would not think of going out in public without first shampooing, rinsing, conditioning, and blow-drying their hair. Many also feel the need to apply an underarm deodorant so powerful that it overcomes the body's natural need to sweat. For many women, pub-

lic appearance also demands the application of foundation, lipstick, eye shadow, mascara, rouge, powder, and perfume. For many men, after-shave lotion is essential. And only after covering the body with clothing bearing suitable designer labels do Americans feel that they are presentable to the public.

Advertising also penetrates our consciousness to such a degree that it determines not only what we put on our bodies, what we eat, and what we do for recreation, but to a large degree also how we feel about ourselves. Our ideas of whether we are too tall, too short, too fat, too skinny, too hippy, too buxom, whether our hair is too oily or too dry, our skin too dark, too light, too hairy, or too rough are largely a consequence of advertising. As we weigh our self-image against the idealized pictures that constantly bombard us in our daily fare of commercials, we conclude that we are lacking something. Advertising, of course, assures us that there is salvation—another new product that promises to deliver exactly what we lack.

The creation of constant discontent—continual dissatisfaction with ourselves compared to perfect images that are impossible to match in real life—is, of course, intentional. And it leaves most Americans vulnerable to consuming more of the never-ending variety of products that the corporations have decided that we need—and that they are only too willing to sell.

CDQ 9: Can you think of examples of underemployment in your city? Do you know of anyone with a Masters or Ph.D. degree working in a fast food restaurant?

people, who exploit a vast bottom layer of unemployed and underemployed (**underemployment** is the condition of having to work at a job beneath one's training and abilities or being able to find only part-time work). Another major criticism is that the few who own the means of production and reap huge profits are able to influence legislation in favor of decisions that go against the public good merely to further their own wealth and power.

The primary criticism leveled against socialism is that it does not respect individual rights (Berger 1986). Others (in the form of some government body) control people's lives—making decisions about where they will live, where they will go to school, where they will work, how much they will be paid, and, in the case of China, even how many children they may have (Mosher 1983). Critics also argue that socialism is not capable of producing much wealth, so that its greater equality really amounts to giving almost everyone an equal chance to be poor.

The Systems in Conflict and Competition

These contrasting ideologies paint such different pictures—not only of the economy but also of the way the world "ought" to be—that proponents of each have come to see the other as inherently evil. Capitalists see socialists as violating basic human rights of freedom of decision and opportunity, while socialists see capitalists as violating basic human rights of freedom from poverty.

As a result of these opposing views, *each sees the other as a system of exploitation.* With each side painting itself in moral colors while viewing the other as a threat to its very existence, this century witnessed the world split into two main blocs. The West armed itself to defend capitalism, the East to defend socialism. The remaining "nonaligned" nations were often able to receive vast sums of economic and military aid by playing the West and the East off against one another.

In recent years, fundamental changes have taken place. The former Soviet Union, which headed the Eastern bloc of nations, concluded that its system of central planning had failed. Suffering from shoddy goods and plagued by shortages, its standard of living severely lagged the West (Newman 1991). Consequently, the former Soviet Union began attempting to reinstate market forces, including the private ownership of property and profits for those who produce and sell goods. Capitalism emerged victorious with the fall of the Berlin Wall in 1989, which precipitated the reunification of the two Germanys.

China watched in dismay as its one-time mentor abandoned basic premises of socialism (Szelenyi 1987). In 1989, at the cost of many lives and despite world opposition, Chinese authorities, in what is called the Tiananmen Square massacre, even put down an uprising by students and workers who were demanding greater freedom and economic reforms. In spite of these repressive measures, however, and while main-

Project 2

CNN: South China Part 1

underemployment: the condition of having to work at a job beneath one's level of training and abilities, or of being able to find only part-time work

Although capitalism and communism have been at each other's throats for three generations, an uneasy accord has apparently been reached. Capitalist countries have adopted a few features of socialism, and communist nations have adopted some features of capitalism, as shown here with Pepsi advertisements in China. Convergence theory points to a hybrid economic system in the future.

taining allegiance to Marxist-Leninist-Maoist principles, China has quietly instituted changes that encourage capitalism on a limited scale. Some Western (capitalist) enterprises have been allowed into the country, farmers can cultivate their own small plots on the communal farms, credit cards have come into use, and in peculiarly capitalist tradition, even bits of that symbol of China itself, the "Great Wall," are sold for profit as souvenirs. Such changes are likely to continue—until China, too, extensively modifies its economic system, perhaps even embracing capitalism (McGregor 1992).

The democratic socialist nations of western Europe have not remained untouched by the movement away from socialism. Sweden, for instance, provides its citizens remarkable "from-cradle-to-grave" security. No Swede need ever fear losing a car or house due to unemployment or illness. To pay for its extensive welfare system and to support their unprofitable state-run industries, Swedish citizens pay taxes in excess of 50 percent of their income. This tax rate has discouraged private investment, slowing Sweden's growth rate. As its international competitive position slipped, the Swedes encouraged capitalism (Meyerson 1992). They embarked on **privatization,** the selling of their state-run industries to private companies. By the end of 1991, Sweden had put thirty-five state-owned companies up for sale, including steel mills, mines, the national airline, the national food and health-care conglomerate, and even some of its forests. These companies employ 300,000 people, or about 7 percent of Sweden's work force, and have annual sales of $40 billion. The Swedish government plans to use the proceeds from the sale of these assets to reduce its foreign debt and to build more railways and highways (The *Wall Street Journal,* November 12, 1991).

At least in this point in history, capitalism speaks with a louder voice than does socialism. Capitalist economies, however, speak in a variety of accents, some more muted than others, with the versions in China, the republics of the former Soviet Union, Great Britain, Japan, Germany, Sweden, and the United States each differing markedly from one another.

The Future: Convergence?

Clark Kerr (1960, 1983) suggested that as nations industrialize they grow similar to one another. They develop comparable divisions of labor (such as professionals and skilled technicians), emphasize higher education, and urbanize extensively. Similar values also pervade the society, uniting its various groups. By themselves, these tendencies would make capitalist and socialist nations grow more alike, but some sociologists, such as William Form (1979), have pointed to another factor that brings these nations closer to one another in spite of their incompatible ideologies. They say that both capitalist and socialist systems have adopted features of the other. Known as **convergence theory,** this view points to a possible hybrid or mixed economy for the future.

Convergence theory is given support by the recent promotion of profit in socialist countries. It may be easier to understand convergence, however, by looking at what has happened to capitalism in the United States. Although the world sees the United States as the exemplar of capitalism, this nation, too, has adopted many socialist practices. Each such feature, viewed with alarm when first proposed, eventually became a firm part of the economic system, blurring its socialist base. Consider the following currently taken-for-granted aspects of the United States economic system: unemployment compensation (taxes paid by workers are distributed to those who no longer produce a profit); subsidized housing (shelter, paid for by the many, is distributed to the poor and elderly, with no motive of profit); welfare (taxes from the many are distributed to the needy); the minimum wage (the government, not the employer, determines the minimum that a worker shall be paid); and Social Security (as noted in Chapter 13, the retired do not receive what they paid into the system; instead, the money they receive is collected from current workers). These changes indicate that the United States has moved away from pure capitalism and, embracing some socialist principles, has produced its own version of a mixed type of economy.

CDQ 10: Do you agree that at this point in history, capitalism is speaking with a louder voice than socialism? Why or why not?

privatization: the selling of a nation's state-run industries to the private sector

convergence theory: the view that as capitalist and socialist economic systems each adopt features of the other, a hybrid (or mixed) economic system may emerge

By definition, democratic socialist economies (also called "mixed economies") are a mixed type. In addition to adopting national health care (socialized medicine), Great Britain also took over the nation's railroads and coal mines after World War II and ran the nation's airlines and television industry. Like Sweden, however, Great Britain later decided that it had traveled too far down the socialist path and privatized many of its state-run industries (Harrison and Bluestone 1988). Finding that when the state takes control of an industry, efficiency drops—for people do not work as hard when they have less personal stake in the outcome—Great Britain began the process of selling its airlines and television networks to private buyers; and many local authorities began offering for sale the housing they provide to the poor at low rents.

Perhaps, then, the tremendous upheavals now occurring in the world's economic systems indicate that the hybrid is closer than ever. On the one hand, not even staunch capitalists want a system that does not provide at least minimum support during unemployment, extended illness, and old age. On the other hand, socialist leaders have reluctantly admitted that profit is a basic motivator of economic behavior. If the convergence does occur, it is likely to make the world a safer place, for there will be no need for any group to paint its economic system in stark moral colors and swear to defend it to the last ounce of blood (Sakharov 1974). Such peace is relative, of course—by no means does it indicate the end of dictators and demagogues, violent nationalistic movements, regional ethnic conflicts, or oppression of all sorts.

THE INNER CIRCLE OF CAPITALISM

Essay #3

L. Obj. 5: Define corporate capitalism, oligopolies, interlocking directorates, and multinational corporations. Note the ways in which each of these has fundamentally altered the face of capitalism.

As we have seen, capitalism has undergone so many changes that its laissez-faire form is unrecognizable today. At this point, let us examine two further developments in capitalism: corporate capitalism and multinational corporations.

Corporate Capitalism

Corporations have fundamentally altered the face of capitalism. The **corporation,** a legal entity treated in law as an individual, is the joint ownership of a business enterprise, whose liabilities and obligations are separate from those of its owners. For example, each shareholder of General Motors—whether the owner of one or 100,000 shares—owns a portion of the company. As a legal entity, General Motors can buy and sell, sue and be sued, make contracts, and incur debts. The corporation, however, not its individual owners, is responsible for the firm's liabilities—such as paying its debts and fulfilling its contracts.

CDQ 11: How influential do you think major corporations are in American economic and political decision-making? In the global economy?

Corporations have so changed capitalism that the term **corporate capitalism** has emerged to indicate that giant corporations dominate the economic system. Of the hundreds of thousands of businesses and tens of thousands of corporations in the United States, a mere five hundred dominate the economy. Called the "Fortune 500" (derived from *Fortune* magazine's annual profile of the largest five hundred companies), these firms are so large that their annual profits represent one-quarter of the United States' entire gross national product (*Statistical Abstract,* 1990: Tables 690, 899).

One of the most significant aspects of corporations is the *separation of ownership and management.* Unlike most businesses, it is not the owners, those who own the company's stock, who run the day-to-day affairs of the company. Rather, a corporation is run by managers who are able to treat it *as though it were their own* (Cohen 1990). The result is the "ownership of wealth without appreciable control and control of wealth without appreciable ownership" (Berle and Means 1932). Sociologist Michael Useem (1984) put it this way.

> When few owners held all or most of a corporation's stock, they readily dominated its board of directors, which in turn selected top management and ran the corporation. Now that a firm's stock [is] dispersed among many unrelated owners, each holding a

corporation: the joint ownership of a business enterprise, whose liabilities and obligations are separate from those of its owners

corporate capitalism: the domination of the economic system by giant corporations

tiny fraction of the total equity, the resulting power vacuum allow[s] management to select the board of directors; thus management [becomes] self-perpetuating and thereby acquire[s] de facto control over the corporation.

Management determines its own salaries, sets goals and awards itself bonuses for meeting them, authorizes market surveys, hires advertising agencies, determines marketing strategies, and negotiates with unions. The management's primary responsibility to the owners is to turn in quarterly and annual profits. The greater the profit, the better their job performance (Useem 1984).

At the annual stockholders' meeting the owners consider broad company matters, the most important of which are deciding who will serve on the board of directors and selecting a firm to audit the company's books. As long as management reports a handsome profit, the stockholders simply rubber-stamp its recommendations. It is so unusual for this not to happen, that when it does not the outcome is known as a **stockholders' revolt.** The irony of this term is generally lost, but remember that in such cases it is not the workers but the owners who are rebelling!

The world's largest corporations wield immense economic and political power. Forming **oligopolies**—several large companies that dominate a single industry, such as olive oil, breakfast cereal, or light bulbs—they dictate pricing, set the quality of their products, and protect their markets. Oligopolies also use their wealth and connections for political purposes, especially to support legislation that gives them special tax breaks or protects their industry from imports. Oligopolies are tempted to abuse their power in more sinister ways as well. One notorious example of the abuse of power and position by an oligopoly came to light in 1973 when the International Telephone and Telegraph Company (ITT) joined the CIA in a plot to unseat Chile's elected government. After their attempt to bring about the economic collapse of Chile failed, they then plotted a coup d'état, which resulted in the assassination of the Chilean president, Salvador Allende (Sigmund 1977).

The top of the largest corporations forms what sociologist Michael Useem (1984) called the *inner circle*, a cohesive group of business leaders whose concerns extend beyond their own firms. Although members of that inner circle may compete with one another, their common interest in protecting the private ownership of property unites them. They support political candidates who stand firmly for capitalism, promote legislation favorable to big business, consult with high-level politicians, publicly defend free enterprise, and serve as trustees for foundations and universities.

Interlocking Directorates

One way in which the wealthy use corporations to wield power is by means of **interlocking directorates.** The elite sit on the boards of directors of not just one but several companies. Their fellow members on those boards also sit on the boards of other companies, and so on. Like a spider's web that starts at the center and then fans out in all directions, eventually the interlocking of directorates includes all the top companies in the country (Mintz and Schwartz 1985). As the chief executive officer of a firm in Great Britain, who also sits on the board of directors of half a dozen other companies, noted

> If you serve on, say, six outside boards, each of which has, say, ten directors, and let's say out of the ten directors, five are experts in one or another subject, you have a built-in panel of thirty friends who are experts who you meet regularly, automatically each month, and you really have great access to ideas and information. You're joining a club, a very good club (Useem 1984).

The resulting concentration of power minimizes competition, for a director is not going to approve a plan that will be harmful to another company in which he or she (mostly he) has a stake. The top executives of the top United States companies also meet together in recreational settings, where they renew their sense of solidarity, purpose, and destiny (Domhoff 1991).

CDQ 12: Can you foresee any problems occurring as a result of the same person sitting on the boards of directors of a number of companies?

stockholders' revolt: the refusal of a corporation's stockholders to rubber-stamp decisions made by its managers

oligopoly: the control of an entire industry by several large companies

interlocking directorates: the phenomenon of one person holding directorships in several companies

CNN: The Maquiladoras and the Job Controversy

Multinational Corporations

As seen in the opening vignette and as discussed in Chapter 9, corporations have outgrown national boundaries. As you can see from Table 14.1 of the world's largest twenty-five multinational corporations, the United States is home to ten, Japan is second with four, Britain, Germany, and Italy tie for third with three each, and South Korea and Switzerland each have one.

Since World War II, Americans became so accustomed to United States dominance in international business that they have come to consider it their inherent right to own property in other nations. To them, it seemed immoral of another nation to limit their ownership. A notable example occurred in 1938 when Mexico kicked out the United States oil companies and nationalized its oil industry—openly declaring that the oil in Mexico was Mexican treasure—Americans were deeply offended (Camp and Riley 1990). To Americans traveling in remote parts of the globe, advertisements for Coca-Cola and Kodak seemed a natural, and somehow satisfying, reminder of their nation's dominance and superiority.

Now that the shoe is partially on the other foot, Americans are seriously questioning the naturalness and rightness of multinational corporate ownership. When British, French, and Japanese companies purchase beachfront properties, hotels, farmland

CDQ 13: Why do you think there has been an outcry among some Americans about "foreign ownership" of large amounts of property in cities such as New York and Houston?

TABLE 14.1 The Top Twenty-Five Corporations in the World

Name	Country	Annual sales In $millions	Annual profits In $millions	Assets In $millions	Employees
1. General Motors	United States	125,126	(1,985)*	180,236	761,400
2. Royal Dutch/Shell	Britain/ Netherlands	107,203	6,442	106,349	137,000
3. Exxon	United States	105,885	5,010	87,707	104,000
4. Ford	United States	98,274	860	173,662	370,400
5. IBM	United States	69,018	6,020	87,568	373,816
6. Toyota	Japan	64,516	2,993	55,340	96,849
7. IRI	Italy	61,443	926	NA	419,500
8. British Petroleum	Britain	59,540	3,013	59,199	116,750
9. Mobil	United States	58,770	1,929	41,665	67,300
10. General Electric	United States	58,414	4,303	153,884	298,000
11. Daimler-Benz	Germany	54,259	1,041	44,982	376,785
12. Hitachi	Japan	50,685	1,476	49,455	290,811
13. Fiat	Italy	47,751	1,346	66,026	303,238
14. Samsung	South Korea	45,042	NA**	NA	NA
15. Philip Morris	United States	44,323	3,540	46,569	168,000
16. Volkswagen	Germany	43,710	651	41,892	268,744
17. Matsushita Electric Industrial	Japan	43,516	1,649	49,747	198,299
18. ENI	Italy	41,761	1,696	60,466	130,745
19. Texaco	United States	41,235	1,450	29,975	39,199
20. Nissan	Japan	40,217	808	36,402	129,546
21. Unilever	Britain/ Netherlands	39,971	1,636	24,806	304,000
22. Du Pont	United States	39,839	2,310	38,128	143,961
23. Chevron	United States	39,262	2,157	35,089	54,208
24. Siemens	Germany	39,227	913	41,142	373,000
25. Nestlé	Switzerland	33,359	1,634	27,859	199,021

*( ) indicates a loss for the year.
**NA indicates figures are not available.
Source: Fortune © 1991 Time, Inc. All rights reserved.

and motion picture companies in the United States, Americans feel as though they are being invaded. Offended at such a close presence of other nations, they question their motives, worry about foreign influence in the government, and become concerned about profits being taken out of their country and ending up in the hands of foreigners who care nothing for its well-being.

WORK IN AMERICAN SOCIETY

Let us now turn our focus on work in American society. To understand the present situation, we must first review the large-scale changes in what are called economic sectors.

Three Economic Sectors

Sociologists divide economic life into three sectors: primary, secondary, and tertiary. The proportion of a society's labor force in each of these sectors depends on its degree of industrialization. In the **primary sector,** workers extract natural resources from the environment. People who fish for a living or who mine copper work in the primary sector. So do hunters, cattle raisers, farmers, and lumberjacks. The primary sector is central to the preindustrial societies reviewed above. In the **secondary sector,** workers turn raw materials into manufactured goods. They package fish, process copper into electrical wire, and turn trees into lumber and paper. The secondary sector dominates industrial economies.

In contrast, the main focus of the **tertiary sector** is neither extracting raw materials nor turning them into products, but providing services. Some workers in the tertiary sector, such as computer repair technicians and automobile mechanics, install or service products. Others, such as nurses, private detectives, and masseuses, provide personal services. Although *most* of the labor force in postindustrial societies work in the tertiary sector, all three sectors exist side by side, as illustrated by a simple product like the common lead pencil. People who extract lead and cut timber work in the primary sector, those who turn the wood and lead into pencils are in the secondary sector, and those who advertise and sell the pencils work in the tertiary sector.

The change from primary to secondary to tertiary sectors evolved very slowly during most of history but has speeded up drastically in recent generations. The three generations that preceded us illustrate the speed of this most recent transition: During our great-grandparents' day, almost everyone in the United States worked in the primary sector, most of them at farming. During our grandparents' working lives, most Americans worked in the secondary sector, and about the time our parents went to work the scale tipped in favor of the tertiary sector. If you check your family history, you may find that the occupations of your ancestors mirror this transition.

One sign of our entry into the postindustrial society is the decline in blue-collar jobs. Sociologists Maxine Baca Zinn and Stanley Eitzen (1990) noted that "there are far fewer of these workers now because we have shifted from a labor-intensive society to a knowledge-intensive one. The need is for knowledge workers who design, control, and service products and who manage information, not operators who do unskilled, repetitive work." Social analyst Peter Drucker (1987) put it this way: "Yesterday's blue-collar workers in manufacturing were society's darlings; they are fast becoming stepchildren."

Farming provides a remarkable example of this transition, for which there is no parallel in history (Drucker 1987). Figure 14.4a shows the decline of employment in farming, where most of our ancestors once worked. As the number of farmers declined during the early and mid-1900s, manufacturing picked up the slack. During the 1800s, a typical farmer could produce only enough food for five people, while with today's powerful farming machinery and hybrid seeds he or she now feeds about eighty. In the

L. Obj. 6: Distinguish among the three economic sectors and describe the signs which mark a society's movement into the postindustrial stage.

CDQ 14: If a person was asking you for career advice and indicated that he or she wanted to be sure they had a job, what types of work would you be most likely to recommend? What would you not recommend?

K.P.: Maxine Baca Zinn and Stanley Eitzen

primary sector: that part of the economy that extracts raw materials from the environment

secondary sector: that part of the economy in which raw materials are turned into manufactured goods

tertiary sector: that part of the economy that consists of service-oriented occupations

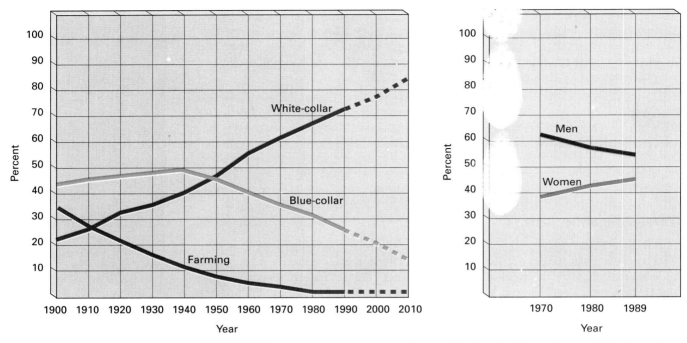

FIGURE 14.4 Percentage of United States Workers in Three Types of Work and Proportion of United States Workers by Sex. (*Source: Statistical Abstract of the United States:* 1991: Table 1461.)

1800s over 50 percent of the American work force was engaged in farming, but this figure has dropped to only about 1 percent today (*Statistical Abstract* 1990: Table 646).

Figure 14.4a also shows that a major transition occurred about 1960. Then, for the first time, most Americans worked in the tertiary sector. Although a postindustrial economy requires very few people to produce food or basic materials and fewer and fewer people to process them, the information explosion demands that large numbers of people work in the tertiary sector.

Women and Work

One of the major changes in the American work force has been a sharp increase in the number of women who work outside the home for wages. (For a discussion of sexual discrimination in the work setting, see Chapter 11; for dual-career marriages, see Chapter 16.) As you can see from Figure 14.4b, women have become an increasingly larger component of the American work force; today about 45 percent of workers are women. As shown in Figure 14.5, this percentage is one of the highest in the industrialized world.

How likely a woman is to work outside the home depends on several factors, especially her race and marital status. As Figure 14.6a shows, a larger proportion of African-American than white women is in the labor force. Note that the disparity has remained about ten percentage points. Figure 14.6b shows that marital status also underlies work. Single women are the most likely to work for wages; married women follow close behind; and divorced, widowed, and separated women are the least likely to be in the work force.

As with men, women's satisfaction with work increases if they have greater control over their work, find a sense of dignity on the job, and enjoy what they do. The stereotype of women as being more nurturing than men pervades the work setting, and researchers have found that men often take advantage of this stereotype to "dump"

K.P.: Peter Drucker

TR#29: Percentage of Americans in Three Types of Work

Essay #4

TR#30: Percentage of Married Women in the U.S. Labor Force, by Race

CDQ 15: What factors do you believe may contribute to women's satisfaction with work outside the home? With men's work-related satisfaction?

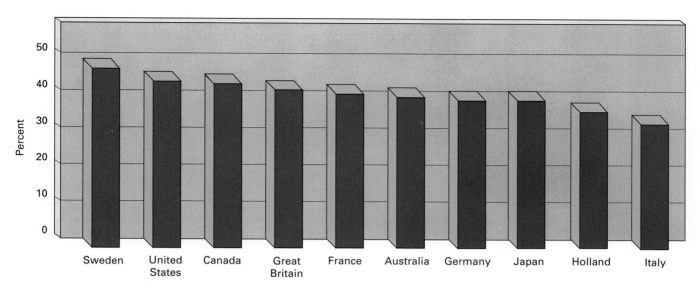

FIGURE 14.5   What Percentage of the Labor Force Is Female? (*Source: Statistical Abstract of the United States,* 1990: Table 1462; 1991: Table 1461.)

work they dislike onto their female coworkers. Women are apparently more concerned than men with maintaining a balance between their work and family lives (Statham, Miller, and Mauksch 1988).

The Quiet Revolution.   Figure 14.6b also shows that married women are the fastest-growing segment of paid labor. Since 1960, the proportion of married women in the labor force has almost doubled. In 1980, for the first time in United States history, as many married women worked at least part-time outside the home for wages as those who did not. Now it is three of five. Because the movement of wives and mothers from the home has been a gradual trend and represents such a fundamental shift—forcing changes in all family relationships—sociologists sometimes call it the **"quiet revolution."**

L. Obj. 7: Trace the development of the "quiet revolution" in the United States.

The Underground Economy

Taxes play a significant part in our lives—and no one except the Internal Revenue Service (IRS) seems to like them. Like people around the world, Americans try to avoid taxes. Recall, for example, the Boston Tea Party of 1773, when to protest taxes that the British had imposed on tea, a group of colonists, disguised as Native Americans, threw three ships' cargo of tea into Boston Harbor. While the colonists had to pay taxes on such items as imported tea, glass, and lead, they did not have to put up with income taxes. This form of taxation was not imposed until 1913 (Caplin 1962).

To avoid what they consider exorbitant taxes, many Americans underreport their income. This evasion takes two common forms. The first is to report income on full-time jobs, but not that earned from work done "on the side." An electrician who works for a factory, for example, may do home repairs on Saturdays but report none of this income to the IRS. The second is to hide part of one's regular income. A dentist, for example, might not report bills paid in cash.

Economic activities for which income is not reported are part of the **underground economy** (or informal economy). In addition to underreporting legal earnings, the underground economy also includes illegal activities that individuals cannot report even if they wanted to. Drug dealing is perhaps the largest source of illegal income. Unreported to the IRS are huge sums of money—*billions* of dollars per year—that flow from

CDQ 16: Do you know of examples of the underground economy in your hometown? Where you attend school?

quiet revolution (the): the fundamental changes in society that follow the movement of vast numbers of women from the home to the work force

underground economy: an exchange of goods and services that is not reported to the government

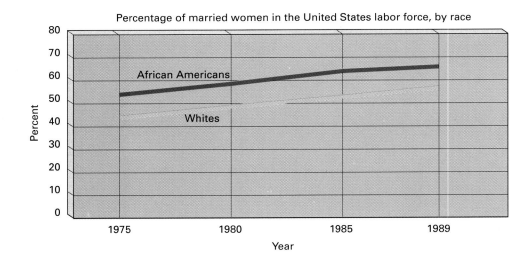

FIGURE 14.6 Percentage of Women in the United States Labor Force by Race and Marital Status. (*Source: Statistical Abstract of the United States,* 1991: Table 644, 641.)

users to sellers and their network of growers, importers, processors, transporters, and enforcers. So it is with income from gambling, theft, loan sharking, bribery, and extortion, as well as swindles or "scams" of almost every conceivable form. Similarly, few prostitutes report their income. As a twenty-year-old child-care worker who also works as a prostitute two or three nights a week said, "Why do I do this? For the money! Where else can I make this kind of money in a few hours. And it's all tax free" (author's files).

Because of its subterranean nature, no one knows the exact size of the underground economy. Estimates, however, place it at 10 to 20 percent of the regular economy (Simon and Witte 1982; Hershey 1988). Since the nation's official gross national product runs between $5 and $6 trillion, the underground economy may total anywhere between $500 billion and $1 trillion. Whatever its exact size, the underground economy represents a huge slice of income that escapes the scrutiny of the IRS and distorts the official statistics of the country's gross national product.

Patterns of Work and Leisure

Suppose that it is 1860 and you work for a textile company in Lowell, Massachusetts. When you arrive at work one day, you find that the boss has posted a new work rule: All workers will have to come in at the same time and remain until quitting time. Like the other workers, you feel outrage. You join them as they shout, "This is slavery!" and march out on strike, indignant at this preposterous demand (Zuboff 1991). What we take for granted today was new to the work scene less than 150 years ago. Until that time, workers came and left when they wanted. To see why, let's consider how patterns of work and leisure are related to the transformation of economies.

Hunting and gathering economies provided tremendous amounts of leisure. If people did not face some unusual event, such as drought or pestilence, it did not take long to gather what they needed for the day. In fact, *most of their time was leisure,* and the rhythms of nature were an essential part of their lives. Agricultural economies also allowed much leisure, for, at least in the Western hemisphere, work peaked in the spring, let up in the summer, and then peaked again in the fall. During the winter work was practically nonexistent, for by this time the harvest was in, animals had been slaughtered, food had been canned and stored, and a wood supply had been laid up. There remained just the household and a few animals to take care of.

Industrialization, however, brought fundamental change. No longer was time harnessed to seasonal rhythms, as it had been for all of human history. Now rhythms were dictated by bosses and machines. At first, workers insisted on moving to their traditional rhythms. After working for several weeks, a worker would disappear, only to reappear when money ran out. For many, enjoying leisure was considerably more important than amassing money (Weber 1904–1905). Bosses, wanting to profit from regular, efficient production, began to insist that all workers start work at the same time. To workers, that seemed like slavery. Today, in contrast, those work patterns artificially imposed on us have become part of our culture and are taken for granted.

Leisure refers to time not taken up by work or required activities such as eating and sleeping. It is not the activity itself that makes something leisure, but the purpose for which it is done. Consider driving a car. If you do it for pleasure, it is leisure, but if you are a traveling salesperson, an on-duty police officer, or commuting to the office, it is work. If done for enjoyment, horseback riding, reading a book, and target shooting are leisure—but these activities are work for jockeys, students, and soldiers in basic training.

Compared with early industrialization, workers today have more leisure. About one hundred years ago the work week was half again as long as today's, for then workers had to be at their machines sixty hours a week. When workers unionized, one of their first demands was a shorter work week. Experts disagree whether or not this pattern of more leisure has continued. Economist Juliet Schor (1991) claimed that the trend reversed itself during the 1960s. Her studies showed that Americans now work 138 hours a year more than they did in 1960 and that the American work year exceeds every industrialized nation except Japan. Economist Sar Levitan, however, said his studies showed that Americans have continued to gain leisure (Trost 1992). At this point, we must await further research to answer this question.

Patterns of leisure change with the life course, following the "U" curve shown on Figure 14.7. Young children enjoy the most leisure, but teenagers still have consider-

The underground economy, which escapes taxation, has become a significant part of the United States economy. Although most of the underground economy consists of unreported earnings from legal activities, it also includes income from illegal activities such as the cultivation and sale of marijuana. In Humboldt County, California, marijuana, though still illegal, has become the largest crop. Shown here is a member of the Drug Enforcement Administration in the never-ending task of uprooting marijuana plants.

CDQ 17: What leisure activities do you enjoy? Is leisure the same for everyone? Why or why not?

leisure: time not taken up by work or required activities such as eating and sleeping

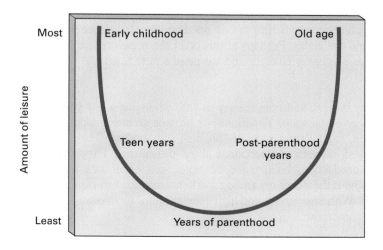

FIGURE 14.7 Leisure and the Life Cycle: The "U" Curve of Leisure.

ably more leisure than their parents. Parents with small children have the least leisure, but after the children leave home, leisure picks up again. After the age of sixty-five, the amount of leisure for adults peaks.

APPLYING SOCIOLOGICAL THEORIES

Before we close this chapter, let's see what pictures emerge when we apply the three theoretical perspectives of sociology to economic life.

Essay #5

L. Obj. 8: Contrast the functional and conflict perspectives on economic life.

Project 3

The Functionalist Perspective

Work, of course, is functional for society. It is only because people work that we have electricity, roads, hospitals, schools, automobiles, and homes. Beyond this obvious point, however, lies a basic sociological principle: *work binds us together.* Let us review Durkheim's principles of mechanical and organic solidarity introduced in Chapter 4.

Mechanical Solidarity.   In preindustrial societies, the primary sector provides social solidarity. Because people do similar work and directly share so many aspects of life, they look at the world in similar ways. Durkheim used the term **mechanical solidarity** to refer to the sense of unity—feeling as others feel and identifying with them—that comes from people doing similar activities.

Organic Solidarity.   As societies industrialize, however, this form of solidarity breaks down. It is replaced by **organic solidarity**—economic interdependence. As the secondary sector develops, the division of labor becomes highly specialized. Because people work at different occupations, they feel less solidarity with one another. Grape growers in California, for example, may feel little in common with manufacturers of aircraft in Missouri. Yet, even though the one may not identify with the other, like an organism each is part of the same economic system and depends on the others to fulfill their jobs.

As the tertiary sector expands in postindustrial society, so does organic solidarity. Now people who live in California or New York—or even Michigan—depend on workers in Tokyo to produce cars. Tokyo workers, in turn, depend on Saudi Arabian workers for oil, South American workers to operate ships, and workers in South Africa for palladium (for catalytic converters). As interdependence has grown, a disruption in some far part of the world now affects us (see Chapter 9). Though we do not feel unity with one another—in fact, we sometimes even feel hostility—interdependence wraps us all in the same economic package.

CDQ 18: Do economic cycles have any impact on you personally? Why or why not?

Work, then, as Durkheim analyzed it, is the basis of social solidarity around the world. Durkheim witnessed the change from mechanical to organic solidarity, from primary to secondary sectors, but he did not live long enough to see this process engulf the world, to get to the point at which Kim in our opening vignette depends for her daily life on workers around the globe. Perhaps at this point the term organic solidarity is inadequate to depict this sweeping change, and we need a new term like "superorganic solidarity."

mechanical solidarity: Durkheim's term for the unity that comes from being involved in similar occupations or activities

organic solidarity: the interdependence that results from people's mutual need that each fulfill his or her job

economic cycle: periods of economic "booms" (expansion) followed by periods of "busts" (contraction)

Economic Cycles.   Why is work sometimes easy to find, when just a few years later you can't pay someone to give you a job? Functionalists provide an interesting explanation for **economic cycles,** capitalism's cycle of "booms" and "busts." They say that booms occur when business owners are confident about the future. They then hire more workers, increase production, build more factories, and order raw materials. Money flows freely throughout the economy among workers, manufacturers, suppliers, salespeople, and planners. With easy credit and high consumption, expansion continues as though there were no tomorrow.

Functionalists stress the interdependence of nations, how the welfare of each depends on the work and products of many other nations. An example of the "superorganic solidarity" now developing is the reliance of Western nations on oil from North Yemen, depicted in this photo. Conflict theorists, in contrast, stress the exploitation of Third World nations by the First World and of workers by the country's elite who own the oil and live off their investments—and the sweat of workers.

The "boom" ends in overexpansion. Some segments of the economy feel it first. When sales of new homes slow, for example, the market becomes glutted as houses already under construction are completed. Builders then lay off workers and reduce prices. Bankers, frightened that people won't be able to pay back their loans, tighten up credit. Fearful of layoffs, workers cut their purchases, and inventory in many industries builds up. Producers then cancel expansion plans and cut production. With more layoffs, fewer raises, and factories made idle, a full-blown recession follows.

Functionalists, however, spot something beneath this gloomy picture of the recession wringing out excesses from the economy. In their view, easy credit had lured many individuals and businesses into heavy debt; and too much money was circulating, causing inflation to heat up. The foreclosures and bankruptcies transfer property to more prudent hands, and teach others valuable lessons. Inefficient factories close—and stay out of business—while efficient factories emerge from the recession leaner and even more competitive. For the particular businesses and workers who go bankrupt or barely make it, the cycle is dysfunctional—but not for the system itself.

As the recession continues, the Federal Reserve Board in Washington, which determines interest rates for the whole country, lowers interest rates to make borrowing easier and get more money circulating. This, in turn, stimulates demand, and as their excess inventory shrinks businesses increase production. Another boom period then follows, with high production and employment; and the cycle repeats itself.

To smooth out the business cycle, the Federal Reserve Board tries to raise interest rates before the top of the boom is reached (to cut expansion and prevent the buildup of excess inventory) and to lower interest rates before the boom bottoms out (to encourage consumption and increase expansion).

Although socialist economies don't experience this cycle, neither are they as productive (Berger 1986). Thus workers in a socialist economy do not face the tortures of unemployment and bankruptcy, but neither do they enjoy as high a standard of living as their counterparts in capitalist societies.

As conflict theorists stress, capitalist economies need a reserve labor force that can be put to work in boom times and laid off during economic downturns. A good example is silver mining in Idaho, depicted in this photo. When silver prices fall below the cost of producing silver, workers are laid off. This miner, and other members of the reserve labor force, will then survive on unemployment, and when that runs out, on low-paying, part-time work or welfare. When silver prices again rise, he will be called back to work, again putting in grueling hours like this—until the next reduction in silver prices leads to a repetition of the process.

CDQ 19: If people are willing to work harder and for lower wages if they think someone else is waiting to get their jobs, what impact do you think this has on unions?

L. Obj. 9: Give examples of the types of research conducted by symbolic interactionists regarding the economy.

Project 4

CDQ 20: Are you planning to enter a profession? What are its essential characteristics?

reserve labor force: conflict theorists' term for the unemployed

profession: an occupation characterized by rigorous education, a theoretical perspective, self-regulation, authority, and service (as opposed to a job)

The Conflict Perspective

Exploitation of Workers.   As usual, each theoretical perspective paints only part of the picture. Conflict theorists see the functionalists' view as too easily turned into a justification to exploit workers and make them endure hardships instead of organizing to change working conditions. In contrast to the solidarity and interconnections seen by functionalists, conflict theorists stress oppression, exploitation, and anomie as the essentials of work in a capitalist economy. They regard workers as exploited by those who own the means of production, mere tools to be used and then discarded when no longer useful. As workers labor to produce profits for the owners, they are ground down by their work, and their exhausted bodies are spewed out by an economic machine as soon as it no longer needs them.

Economic Cycles.   How does the conflict view of economic cycles differ from that of functionalists? Following their basic orientation, conflict theorists are not concerned with how booms and busts tune the capitalist machinery. Rather, they see the economic cycle as powered by greed, power, and exploitation. Because profit, not people's welfare, is the goal, capitalists overexpand to wring every bit of profit they can. When profits decrease, they pull back, laying off workers until they need them again. That people get hurt in this process is of no concern to them.

As noted in Chapter 12, conflict theorists also stress that capitalists maintain a **reserve labor force,** unemployed people whom they can hire for temporary work and then fire at will during the next economic downturn. People in dire need will work for low wages—happy to earn something—and they can be fired as soon as no longer needed. If workers knew the true extent of unemployment, however, it might feed discontent and destabilize society. Consequently, as the Perspectives box on page 395 shows, official statistics are manipulated to produce low unemployment figures.

Although economic recessions seem to hurt capitalists, and a few do go under, the reduction of excess inventory during recessions sets the scene for the wealthy to make even more money in the economic boom that follows. In addition, recessions help to depress wages. Workers find it difficult to demand higher pay when unemployment is high, for they know that the unemployed are willing to work for less. Owners also use recessions as an opportunity to replace strikers with nonunion employees, sometimes even to bust unions.

To capitalists, then, *full* employment, not unemployment, is the specter that haunts the economy. In an economy with full employment, workers would demand higher wages. Higher wages would reduce profits, which, as capitalists see the matter, is the purpose of the economy (Lekachman 1982).

The Symbolic Interactionist Perspective

As we apply this perspective, let us explore two different aspects of work: The characteristics that make work a profession and the way in which work affects an individual's perception of self and life.

Profession or Job? Work as Status Symbol.   Just what distinguishes a job from a **profession?** We know that selling hamburgers from a drive-in window is not a profession, but why isn't selling shoes? Sociologists identify five characteristics of professions (Etzioni 1969; Goode 1960; Greenwood 1962; Parsons 1954).

   1. *Rigorous education*   A high school education will not do. Nor will a six-week training course in cutting hair, or even a rigorous course in diesel repair. Today the professions require not only college but also graduate school. Ordinarily, those years are followed by an examination that determines whether or not someone will be allowed into the profession. From personal experience, I would like to add that this examination is one of the most significant parts of the educational ordeal. The gnawing threat of

PERSPECTIVES

Cultural Diversity in U.S. Society

Who Is Unemployed?

It is hard to believe that Amy and Peter are not officially part of the unemployed. After all, they have no jobs. In fact, they have no home. They are among the 350,000 homeless and jobless Americans sleeping in alleys and shelters for the destitute (Rossi, Wright, Fisher, and Willis 1987). That fact, however, is *not* enough to count them as unemployed.

To see how the calculation works, let us suppose that you lose your job. After six months' frustrating search for work you become so discouraged that you just stay home and stare blankly at the television. Amazingly, you are no longer counted as unemployed. As far as official statistics are concerned, to be unemployed you must be *actively* seeking work. If not, the government leaves you out of its figures. People without jobs who have not looked for work during the previous four weeks are simply not factored into the government's unemployment figures.

Now, let us suppose that you do keep on looking for work, but in the meantime your neighbor pays you to clean out her garage and rake the leaves. If you put in fifteen hours and report them you won't be counted, for the government figures that you have a job (Table 14.2). Now assume that you keep on looking for work, don't work, don't rake leaves for a few hours' pay, but can't pay your telephone bill. Again, you won't show up in the figures, for the Bureau of Labor Statistics counts only people it reaches in a random telephone survey. To get an accurate idea how many are unemployed, then, we need to add about 3 percent to the official unemployment rate (Myers 1992). If the Labor Department says it is 8 percent, the true rate is actually about 11 percent—a difference of about eight million people.

Granted these problems, certain patterns do show up year after year. As you can see from this table on unemployment, unemployment varies by race, education, and marital status. Whites are the least likely to be unemployed, African Americans the most likely; Hispanic Americans fall in between. You won't be surprised to see that the higher a person's education, the less the likelihood of unemployment; but you might be surprised to see that men are more likely to be unemployed than women—and that married people are the least likely to be unemployed, separated people the most likely, and that divorced workers fall in between. Although the particular percentages fluctuate with changing economic conditions, the patterns themselves hold from year to year.

TABLE 14.2 The Percentage of Americans Who Are Officially Unemployed

Category	Percent
Sex	
Males	7.3
Females	6.1
Race/Ethnicity	
Whites	6.5
African Americans	14.7
Hispanics	11.3
Ethnic Background of Hispanics	
Mexican	
Males	9.1
Females	10.8
Puerto Rican	
Males	11.1
Females	10.5
Cuban	
Males	6.5
Females	7.2
Other*	
Males	7.3
Females	8.4
Education	
1–3 years high school	9.1
4 years high school	5.6
1–3 years college	4.4
4 years college	3.5
5+ years college	3.0
Marital Status	
Married	4.9
Divorced	6.3
Separated	11.1

* Refers primarily to persons from Central or South America.

Note: Bureau of Labor Statistics reported in June 1992 as this book went to press showed an average increase of 1.2 percent in unemployment of males and females from those contained in *Statistical Abstract*. Accordingly, I have added 1.2 percent to the categories of ethnic background of Hispanics, education, and marital status. Consequently, figures for these three categories are approximate as not all would increase the same amount.

Sources: Statistical Abstract of the U.S., 1991: Tables 633, 636, 639, 643; Bureau of Labor Statistics, June 1992.

never knowing for certain if your years of preparation will allow you to enter your chosen profession hangs over your head like the sword of Damocles.

2. *Theory* The education is theoretical, not just "hands on." Instead of "Turn this nut, and it frees the main bolt that holds the carburetor," or, "Use more of an

Is this a profession or a job? We have no difficulty identifying this work as a job, for, although skilled, these seamstresses in Chinatown, New York, are easily replaced, require little training to perform these repetitive tasks, are low paid, and work under close supervision. As indicated in the text, however, in some instances the lines between jobs and professions blur and not all work is so easily categorized.

upward motion, and the hair will be smoother," heavy stress is placed on causes and processes. In other words, concepts or objects that cannot be seen are used to explain what can be seen. For example, in theology actions of God are used to explain human events. In medicine, microbes, viruses, and genetics are used to explain disease. In sociology, social structure and social interaction are used to explain human behavior.

3. *Self-Regulation*   Members of the profession claim that only they possess sufficient knowledge to determine the profession's standards and to certify those qualified to be admitted. As sociologist Ernest Greenwood (1962) put it, "Anyone can call himself a carpenter, locksmith, or metal-plater if he feels so qualified. But a person who assumes the title of physician or attorney without having earned it conventionally becomes an imposter." The group's members also determine who shall be decertified because of incompetence or moral problems. To kick someone out is always a serious matter—not only because it denies the individual the right to practice the profession but also because it reflects poorly on the group's original judgment, thus casting doubt on the claim to self-regulation.

4. *Authority over clients*   Members of a profession claim authority over clients on the basis of their specialized education and theoretical understanding. Unlike carpentry, in which any of us can see that the nail is bent, the matter is too complex for "lay people" to understand. Thus the members of the profession claim to know what is best for their clients. It is the clients' obligation to follow the professional's instructions.

5. *Service to society, not self-interest*   The public good lies at the heart of the profession. Although some car salespersons may make preposterous claims about serving the public good, we all know that they sell cars to make money. So it is with telephone installers, barbers, and so on. In contrast, the professions claim that their primary purpose is to serve the public. They exist "to provide service to whoever requests it, irrespective of the requesting client's age, income, kinship, politics, race, religion, sex and social status" (Greenwood 1962). As professionals fulfill what they call "the public trust," they, of course, are entitled to an income.

Obviously, this fifth criterion is the weakest. Today, we expect the basic motivation of a physician to be not far different from that of an automobile mechanic. While both physicians and automobile mechanics may want things to get better for their customers, most of us assume both do what they do for money.

Is it a profession or a job? In some ways, this is not an either/or matter. While we can identify the extremes—medicine is a profession and flipping burgers is not—we can also say that work is "more" or "less" professionalized. For example, we may wish to make the case that creating stained glass windows and painting landscapes are professions. We can measure them according to these five criteria and see that they rank higher on some than on others. So it is with other work. Using these guidelines, we can see that practicing law is less professional than practicing medicine, for law is low on theory and, in the public's mind at least, even more questionable on its claim to be doing a service for society.

Work Satisfaction.   Let us briefly examine a second aspect of work from the symbolic interactionist perspective—the question of what makes work satisfying. As is well known, pay is central to job satisfaction, for unless a person is independently wealthy, no matter how much he or she likes a job, if it does not pay enough to buy groceries or gasoline it will prove highly unsatisfying. Pay, however, provides only *the general context that makes work satisfying* (Jencks, Perman, and Rainwater 1988). The specific conditions that increase job satisfaction are good working relationships with others, autonomy (control over one's work), and a feeling of purpose and accomplishment (Kohn et al. 1990; Mortimer and Lorence 1989). When these characteristics are present, morale is high. When they are absent, work loses its lustre in spite of good pay.

THE FUTURE OF THE UNITED STATES ECONOMY

To try to glimpse the future, it is helpful to first review what is happening to the United States economy as it makes the transition to a postindustrial society (Harrington and Levinson 1988; Kuttner 1988). Of the many wrenching changes, perhaps the most significant is a declining standard of living. Social analysts Bennett Harrison and Barry Bluestone (1988) put it this way.

> The standard of living of American workers—and a growing number of their families—is in serious trouble. For every affluent "yuppie" in an expensive big-city condominium, working as a white-collar professional for a high-flying, high-technology concern or a multibillion dollar insurance company, there are many more people whose wages have been falling and whose families are finding it more and more difficult to make ends meet.

To see what they mean, look at Figure 14.8 on page 398, which apparently indicates a handsome increase in American wages. Translate these wages into constant dollars, however, and you strip away the illusion. American workers now makes *less* than they did in 1970. Harrison and Bluestone called this reduction *the great U-turn of American society.* They point out that from the end of World War II to about 1973 the standard of living of the average American worker rose steadily. Inflation-adjusted pay, unemployment and health insurance, paid vacations, and sick leave—all improved. Today, however, people don't just *feel* they are getting farther behind—they really are.

What brought about this decline in average earnings and standard of living? One explanation is a profit squeeze felt by American corporations. Profits declined due to a surge in imports and a decline in exports, which fell from a peak of nearly 10 percent of gross national product in 1965 to less than 6 percent now. In response, American businesses cut labor costs: They hired more temporary and part-time workers, forced concessions from labor unions, and canceled cost-of-living allowances. In addition, in recent years most new jobs have been in the lower-paying service industries—retail sales and fast-food outlets (Harrison and Bluestone 1988).

If these trends continue, the postindustrial world faces the disturbing potential of ending up with a *"two-thirds society,"* the term used by Peter Glotz (1986), the national secretary of the German Social Democratic Party, to describe a society divided into three layers. An upper third, consisting of well-educated and prosperous technocrats, will be in charge of society. In the middle third will be insecure workers who increasingly wear white rather than blue collars. The lowest third will consist of the unemployed and underemployed—the elderly of the lower classes, migrant workers, the

Speaker Sug. #3: A colleague who has conducted work satisfaction studies.

CDQ 21: If you are currently employed, what do you find most satisfying about your work? Least satisfying?

Speaker Sug. #4: An economist to give a forecast about the U.S. economy in the twenty-first century.

K.P.: Bennett Harrison and Barry Bluestone

TR#29M: Average Hourly Earnings of the U.S. Workers in Current Dollars

TR#30M: Occupations with the Highest Concentration by Race/Ethnicity/Gender

TR#31M: What Jobs Will Be Expanding Most: 1982–1995

L. Obj. 10: Discuss the "Great U-Turn" and analyze the possibilities for improvement in the U.S. economy.

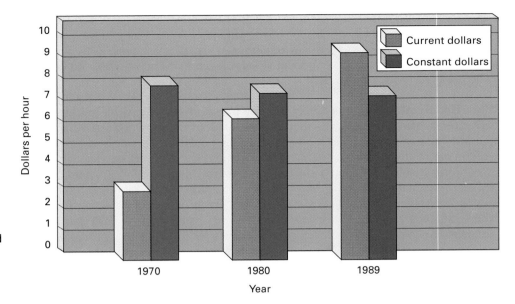

FIGURE 14.8 "Average Hourly Earnings of United States Workers in Current and Constant (1982) Dollars." (*Source: Statistical Abstract of the United States,* 1991: Table 673.)

CDQ 22: Do you believe Americans will be able to straighten out the great "U-turn?" Why or why not?

physically and mentally handicapped, teenagers who cannot find their way into the job market, and the homeless.

Will we be able to straighten out the great American U-turn? The economic fate of the United States is inextricably linked to many domestic events—economic planning, tax subsidies, savings rates, capital investments, labor relations, and the adoption of cost-saving techniques such as the "just in time" parts delivery system used in Japan. The competitiveness of industry even depends on such domestic factors as the quality of education, which, as we shall see in Chapter 17, is also in a troubled state. Beyond such domestic factors, however, lie worldwide events, especially the global demand for products and services. A worldwide economic slowdown would severely damage the economic engine of the postindustrial world, while a worldwide depression would cripple it. No one can say with certainty how such countervailing domestic and international forces will ultimately play out.

We can be reasonably sure, though, that the future will be wrenching (Hern 1988). Industries will continue to be ripped up in some parts of the nation so that they can be transplanted onto foreign shores, workers will be retooled, and families will be forced to migrate from declining regions to others in the hope of finding good jobs. Similar events occurred when the United States made the transition from an agricultural to an industrial economy, and earlier generations made the difficult adjustment. Based on the past, then, perhaps we should be cautiously optimistic as we approach the new economy.

SUMMARY

1. We have entered the era of the postindustrial economy, in which most people work in the tertiary sector. As global interconnections increase, they will force more vast changes in society. Past societies made fundamental transitions when they changed from the preindustrial, primary sector to the industrial, secondary sector.

2. The world's two main economic systems are capitalism and socialism. The United States system is not pure

capitalism, for it operates with market restraints and has adopted socialist features. Neither does socialism exist anywhere today in a pure form, for all socialist countries have adopted elements of capitalism. Each system is supported by an ideology that justifies its form of economy. Convergence theory suggests that the two economic systems are merging.

3. The corporation is fundamental to modern capitalism. The wealthy use interlocking directorates to help consolidate their power, and the largest multinational corporations are now world powers.

4. Functionalists point out that work is a fundamental source of social solidarity. Due to emerging global economic networks, workers around the world depend on one another. Functionalists see economic cycles as a result of built-in patterns of production, consumption, and credit, which lead to excess and must be wrung out of the economy.

5. Conflict theorists see economic cycles as the result of capitalists' uncaring, endless pursuit of profit. They stress that workers are exploited by systems that depend on profit, while capitalists keep in reserve a labor force of unemployed persons whom they use and then dismiss.

6. Symbolic interactionists have identified five primary features that distinguish professions from jobs: education, theory, self-regulation, authority, and service. Using these criteria, some occupations are "more" profes-

sional than others. Symbolic interactionists also analyze factors that lead to work satisfaction.

7. The large increase in the number of married women who work for pay has led to so many consequences that it is being called "the quiet revolution." The underground economy in the United States is so extensive that it undermines official economic statistics.

8. Leisure decreased as the economy changed from preindustrial to industrial. Today, the picture is mixed. The middle class, teenagers, and the elderly have more leisure, but many women find themselves doing "double duty," working in the office or factory by day and doing housework at night.

9. American society has made a great U-turn. Around 1970 wages, adjusted for inflation, began to decline. Underlying this decline is a corporate profit squeeze, caused by a decline in exports and an increase in imports. The future course of the postindustrial economy depends on both domestic and international events.

SUGGESTED READINGS

Bensman, David, and Roberta Lynch. *Rusted Dreams: Hard Times in a Steel Community.* New York: McGraw-Hill, 1987. The authors analyze plant closings in Chicago and illustrate some of the wrenching adjustments required by the change to a postindustrial economy.

Berger, Peter. *The Capitalist Revolution: Fifty Propositions About Prosperity, Equality, and Liberty.* New York: Basic Books, 1986. Berger's explanation of why capitalism is highly productive and why it enhances personal liberty is especially useful in light of changes in the Eastern bloc.

Cohen, Stephen S., and John Zysman. *Manufacturing Matters: The Myth of the Post-Industrial Economy.* New York: Basic Books, 1987. The authors argue that manufacturing remains essential to the United States economy.

Fucini, Joseph J., and Suzy Fucini. *Working for the Japanese: Inside Mazda's American Auto Plant.* New York: Free Press, 1990. Focusing on how Americans adjust to the "just in time" delivery system, mandatory overtime, and the Japanese "team system" emphasizing harmony and close cooperation, this book also looks at how Americans and Japanese resolve misunderstandings that arise from differences in language and culture.

Harrison, Bennett, and Barry Bluestone. *The Great U-Turn: Corporate Restructuring and the Polarizing of America.* New York: Basic Books, 1988. The authors investigate major changes taking place in the United States economy, focusing on the declining standard of living of the average American.

Marx, Karl. *Selected Writings in Sociology and Social Philosophy,* eds. Thomas B. Bottomore and Maximilian Rubel. New York: McGraw-Hill, 1964. Many Americans, unfamiliar with Marx's ideas, will benefit from this useful introduction, especially to Marx's analysis of social class and alienation.

Porter, Michael E. *The Competitive Advantage of Nations.* New York: Free Press, 1990. Based on research in ten countries, the author first examines how productivity is the key to a nation's competitive market position and then provides an explanation for the economic success of Japan and the decline of Great Britain.

Ritzer, George, and David Walczak. *Working: Conflict and Change.* 3rd ed. Englewood Cliffs, N.J. Prentice Hall, 1986. This analysis of work in American society emphasizes the transition to a postindustrial economy.

Rothschild, Joyce, and J. Allen Whitt. *The Cooperative Workplace: Potentials and Dilemmas of Organizational Democracy and Participation.* Cambridge, Mass.: Cambridge University Press, 1986. Focusing on the basic values that unite people in worker-owned and worker-run enterprises, the authors identify ten conditions that support democracy in organizations.

Statham, Anne, Eleanor M. Miller, and Hans O. Mauksch, eds. *The Worth of Women's Work.* Albany, N.Y.: State University of New York Press, 1988. The authors examine women's work, both unpaid housework and paid work in the labor force.

Womack, James P., Daniel T. Jones, and Daniel Roos. *The Machine that Changed the World.* New York: Macmillan, 1990. This analysis of the international automobile industry stresses how the Japanese revolutionized mass production.

Journals

Two journals that focus on issues presented in this chapter are *Work and Occupations* and *Insurgent Sociologist.*

CHAPTER *15*

Malcah Zeldis, Miss Liberty Celebration, *1987*

Politics: Power and Authority

MICROPOLITICS AND MACROPOLITICS

POWER, AUTHORITY, AND COERCION
    Authority and Legitimate Violence ■ Traditional Authority ■ Rational-Legal Authority ■ Charismatic Authority ■ Authority as Ideal Type ■ The Transfer of Authority

TYPES OF GOVERNMENT
    Monarchies: The Rise of the State ■ Democracies: Citizenship as a Revolutionary Idea ■ Dictatorships and Oligarchies: The Seizure of Power

THE AMERICAN POLITICAL SYSTEM
    Political Parties and Elections ■ Democratic Systems in Europe ■ Voting Patterns ■ *Perspectives:* **Immigrants—Ethnicity and Class as the Path to Political Participation** ■ The Depression as a Transforming Event ■ Lobbyists and Special-Interest Groups ■ PACs and the Cost of Elections

WHO RULES AMERICA?
    The Functionalist Perspective: Pluralism ■ The Conflict Perspective: Power Elite and Ruling Class ■ Which View Is Right?

WAR: A MEANS TO IMPLEMENT POLITICAL OBJECTIVES
    Is War Universal? ■ Why Nations Go to War ■ How Common Is War? ■ Costs of War ■ War and Dehumanization

A COMING WORLD ORDER?
    Perspectives: **Nations versus States—Implications for a New World Order**

SUMMARY

SUGGESTED READINGS

In the 1930s, George Orwell wrote *1984,* a book about a future in which the government, known as "Big Brother," dominates society, dictating almost every aspect of everyone's life. To even love someone is considered a sinister activity, a betrayal of the first love and unquestioning allegiance that all citizens owe Big Brother.

Two characters, Winston and Julia, fall in love. Because of Big Brother, they meet furtively, always with the threat of discovery and punishment hanging over their heads. When informers turn them in, expert interrogators separate Julia and Winston. They swiftly proceed to break their affection—to restore their loyalty to Big Brother.

Then follows a remarkable account of Winston and his tormentor, O'Brien. Winston is strapped so tightly into a chair that he can't even move his head. O'Brien explains that inflicting pain is not always enough, but that everyone has a breaking point, some worst thing that will push them over the edge.

O'Brien tells Winston that he has discovered his worst fear. Then he sets a cage with two giant, starving sewer rats on the table next to Winston, picks up a mask connected to the door of the cage and places it over Winston's head. In a quiet voice,

O'Brien explains that when he presses the lever, the door of the cage will slide up, and the rats will shoot out like bullets and bore straight into Winston's face. Winston's eyes, the only part of his body that he can move, dart back and forth, revealing his terror. Still speaking so quietly that Winston has to strain to hear him, O'Brien adds the rats sometimes attack the eyes first, but sometimes they burrow through the cheeks and devour the tongue. When O'Brien places his hand on the lever, Winston realizes that the only way out is for someone to take his place. But who? Then he hears his own voice sceaming, "Do it to Julia! . . . Tear her face off, strip her to the bones. Not me! Julia! Not me!"

Orwell does not describe Julia's interrogation, but when they see each other later they realize that having betrayed each other, they no longer care for each other. Big Brother has won.

Winston's crime was that he had given his loyalty to Julia, his lover, instead of to Big Brother, the overseeing, all-demanding, and all-controlling government. Winston's misplaced loyalty made him a political heretic, for it was the obligation of every citizen to place the state above all else in life. To preserve the state's dominance over the individual, Winston's allegiance had to be taken away from Julia. As you see in this paraphrase of an interrogation in George Orwell's *1984,* it was.

Although seldom this dramatic, *politics is always about power* and the prerogatives that come with it. Not many regimes would do what O'Brien, a dutiful government employee, did to Winston. But some would. And rulers are sometimes so ruthless that nothing is too extreme for them. Others do their best to please their citizens, convinced that in the general good is the good of all. Most probably fall somewhere in between.

L. Obj. 1: Define the following terms: micropolitics, macropolitics, power, authority, coercion, state, and revolution.

CDQ 1: From groups in which you participate, can you give examples to support the statement that "every group is political?"

Essay #1

power: the possession of enough authority to carry out one's will, even over the resistance of others

micropolitics: the exercise of power in everyday life, such as deciding who is going to do the housework

macropolitics: the exercise of large-scale power, the government being the most common example

authority: power that people accept as rightly exercised over them; also called legitimate power

coercion: power that people do not accept as rightly exercised over them; also called illegitimate power

MICROPOLITICS AND MACROPOLITICS

Although the images that come to mind when we think of politics are those of government—kings, queens, coups, dictatorships, running for office, voting—politics, in the sense of power relations, is also an inevitable part of everyday life (Schwartz 1990). As Weber (1968) said, **power** is the ability to carry out your will in spite of resistance, and in every group, large or small, some individuals have power over others. Symbolic interactionists use the term **micropolitics** to refer to the exercise of power in everyday life. Routine situations in which people jockey for power include employees' attempts to make a good impression on the new boss—who will decide which one of them will be promoted to manager—as well as an argument between a couple over which movie to see or efforts by parents to enforce their curfew on a reluctant daughter or son. *Every group, then, is political, for in every group there is a power struggle of some sort.*

In contrast, **macropolitics**—the focus of this chapter—refers to the exercise of large-scale power over a broad group. Governments, whether the dictatorship faced by Winston or the elected forms in the United States, Canada, and Germany, are examples of macropolitics. Let us turn, then, to macropolitics, considering first the matter of authority.

POWER, AUTHORITY, AND COERCION

For a society to exist, it must have a system of leadership. Some people will have to have power over others. As Max Weber (1947) pointed out, however, people can perceive power as legitimate or illegitimate. Weber used the term **authority** to refer to legitimate power—that is, power that people accept as right. In contrast, illegitimate power—**coercion**—is power that people do not accept as just.

Suppose that you are on your way to buy a CD player on sale for $250. As you approach the store, a man jumps out of the alley, throws an arm around your neck, and shoves a gun in your back. He demands your money. Frightened for your life, you hand it over. Now suppose instead that before you go to the CD sale first you have a final examination. As you drive there, traffic makes you late. Afraid you might miss the test, you step on the gas. As the needle hits eighty-five just a mile from campus, you see flashing blue and red lights in your rear-view mirror. Your explanation about the final examination doesn't faze the officer—nor the judge before whom you appear a few weeks later. She first lectures you on safety and then orders you to pay $50 court costs plus $10 for every mile an hour over sixty-five. You pay the $250.

The mugger, the police officer, and the judge all have power. The end result is also the same; in each case you part with $250 and go home minus a CD player. The difference is that the mugger has no authority. You don't consider him as having the *right* to do what he did. In contrast, you acknowledge that the officer has the right to stop you and that the judge has the right to fine you.

Authority and Legitimate Violence

K.P.: Max Weber

L. Obj. 2: Describe the three sources of authority identified by Max Weber. Indicate why these are "ideal types."

K.P.: Peter Berger

As sociologist Peter Berger observed, however, it makes little difference whether you pay the fine that the judge levies against you willingly or refuse. The court will get its money one way or another.

> There may be innumerable steps before its application [violence], in the way of warnings and reprimands. But if all the warnings are disregarded, even in so slight a matter as paying a traffic ticket, the last thing that will happen is that a couple of cops show up at the door with handcuffs and a Black Maria. Even the moderately courteous cop who hands out the initial traffic ticket is likely to wear a gun—just in case (Berger 1963).

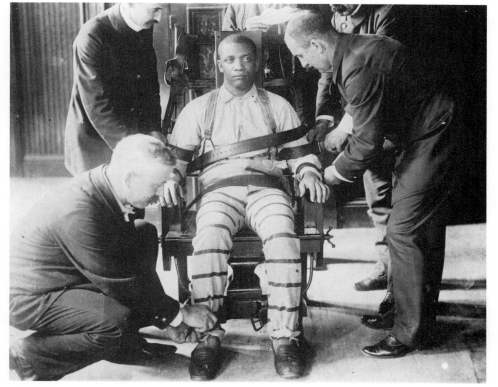

The ultimate foundation of any political order is violence. This is nowhere more starkly demonstrated than when a government takes human life. Shown in this 1910 photo from Sing Sing Prison is a man about to be executed.

TR#33: Definitions of Behavior as Practiced by the State and Private Citizens

CDQ 2: Do you agree that violence is the ultimate foundation of any political order? Why or why not?

CDQ 3: How stable do you think the U.S. government is? Is it true that the more a government is seen as legitimate, the more stable it is?

state: synonymous with government; the source of legitimate violence in society

revolution: armed resistance designed to overthrow a government

The **state,** then—a term synonymous with government—is the source of legitimate force in society. This point, made by Max Weber (1946, 1968)—that the state claims the exclusive right to use violence and the right to punish everyone else who does—is critical to our undertanding of macropolitics. If someone owes you a debt, you cannot imprison them or even forcibly take money from them. The state can. The ultimate proof of the state's authority is that you cannot kill someone because he or she has done something that you consider absolutely horrible—but the state can. As Berger (1963) summarized this matter, *"Violence is the ultimate foundation of any political order."*

Below, we shall explore the origins of the modern state, but first let us look at a situation in which the state loses legitimacy.

The Collapse of Authority. Sometimes the state oppresses its people, and they resist their government just as they do a mugger. The people cooperate reluctantly—but with a smile if that is what is required—while they eye the gun in the hand of the government's representatives. When the people get a chance, however, they work against the system. And, as they do with a mugger, if they are able they even take up arms to free themselves.

What some see as coercion, however, others may see as authority. Consequently, some people will remain loyal to a government, willingly defend it, perhaps even die for it, although others are ready to take up arms against it. In the absence of outside forces such as a defeat in war, *the more a government is seen as legitimate, the more stable it is.*

As a government loses its legitimacy—that is, as the people reject its right to rule over them—it becomes unstable. As public order breaks down, the government may compound the situation by becoming even more oppressive to try to reassert its control. The people, or a group of them, might then take up arms and try to overthrow the government. **Revolution,** armed resistance with the intention to overthrow a government, is not only a people's rejection of a government's claim to rule over them but also a rejection of its monopoly on violence. In a revolution, the people claim that right for themselves and if successful, they will establish a new state in which they have the right to monopolize violence.

The more that people see a government as legitimate, the more likely they are to cooperate with it, and the more stable it is. In 1989 in Beijing, China, students and workers protested the legitimacy of their government's power. The government then reasserted its authority through violence, massacring an unknown number of demonstrators. Shown here is a confrontational scene shortly before the massacre. With the people's withdrawal of legitimacy, this government may be ruling on borrowed time.

If leadership is more stable when people accept its authority, it is worth examining the sources of that authority. Just why do people accept power as legitimate? Max Weber (1968) identified three sources of authority: traditional, rational-legal, and charismatic. Let us examine each in turn.

Traditional Authority

Essay #2

Throughout the world's history, the most common form of authority has been traditional. **Traditional authority,** which is based on custom, is the hallmark of preliterate groups. In these societies, custom dictates basic relationships. For example, because of birth a particular individual becomes the chief, king, or queen. As far as members of that society are concerned, this is the right way to determine a ruler because "that is the way it has always been done."

Gender relations in preliterate groups are also based on traditional authority. The divisions between men and women are based on the past, with custom determining that a gulf should be maintained between them. Custom also dictates the specifics of their relationships. For example, in small villages in southern Spain and in a large part of Portugal, widows are expected to wear only black until they remarry—which generally means that they wear black for the rest of their lives. By law, a widow is free to wear any color she wishes, but not by tradition. Tradition decrees black, and she— along with her community—accepts the legitimacy of this authority. The force of tradition is so strong that if a widow were to violate the dress code, she would create a scandal. She would be seen as having profaned the memory of her deceased husband and would be ostracized by the "respectable" members of the community.

When traditional society changes, traditional authority is undermined. As a society industrializes, for example, new perspectives on life open up, and no longer does traditional authority go unchallenged. Thus, in contemporary southern Spain and parts of Portugal, you can see old women dressed in black from head to toe—and you immediately know their marital status. Younger widows, however, are likely to be indistinguishable from other women. Because large sections of these countries have industrialized, the more recently widowed find alternatives to the custom that ruled their ancestors for centuries.

Even in industrial and postindustrial societies, however, traditional authority never totally dies out (Schwartz 1990). Parental authority provides an excellent example. Parents exercise authority over their children *because* they have always had such authority. From generations past, we inherit the idea that parents are not only responsible for providing their children with food, shelter, and discipline, but also that they have the right to choose their children's doctors and schools, and to teach them religion and morality.

This traditional authority of parents over their children—unquestioned in most places in the world—has not gone completely unchallenged, however. Just as for the widows of Spain and Portugal, matters are no longer as clear-cut as they once were, and some Western societies debate the right of parents to spank their children. Sweden has even passed laws that forbid spanking, and Swedish authorities arrest parents who lay a hand on their children (Nilsson 1991).

Rational-Legal Authority

The second type of authority identified by Weber, **rational-legal authority,** is not based on custom but on written rules. "Rational" means reasonable, and "legal" means part of law. Thus "rational-legal" refers to matters agreed to by reasonable people and written into law (or regulations of some sort). The matters agreed to may be as broad as a constitution that specifies the rights of all members of the group, or as narrow as a contract between two individuals. The bureaucracies studied in Chapter 7 are based on rational-legal authority. Consequently, rational-legal authority is also called *bureaucratic authority.*

For centuries, widows in the Mediterranean area were expected to dress in black. Their long dresses were matched by black stockings, black shoes, and black head covering. Widows conformed to this socially defined expression of ongoing sorrow for the deceased husband not because of law, but because of custom. Today, however, as industrialization erodes traditional authority, few widows follow this practice.

CDQ 4: Do you believe that traditional authority eventually dies out in a society? Why or why not?

traditional authority: authority based on custom

rational-legal authority: authority based on law or written rules and regulations; also called bureaucratic authority

George Washington, shown here at the Constitutional Convention at Philadelphia in 1787, is an example of rational-legal authority. That is, he took office according to a system of rules that people had agreed on, in this case, the new Constitution of the United States.

CDQ 5: Does the President of your college or university have authority based on his or her reputation and personal characteristics? Why or why not?

Rational-legal authority derives from the position that an individual holds, not from the person who holds the position. In a democracy, for example, the president's authority comes from the office, as specified in a written constitution, not from his or her reputation or personal characteristics. Similarly, rational-legal authority subjects everyone—no matter how high the office—to the organization's written rules. In governments based on traditional authority the ruler's word may be law, but in those based on rational-legal authority the ruler's word is subject to the law.

Charismatic Authority

Over five hundred years ago, a farmer's daughter heard a voice urging her to go to war. Her king, Charles VII, had been prevented by the English from ascending to the French throne. The voice told her that God had a special assignment for her and that she should put on male clothing and recruit an army to fight on Charles's behalf. In 1429, Joan of Arc obeyed. She recruited an army, and her leadership had phenomenal results. She conquered cities and routed the English. Later that year, her visions were fulfilled as she stood next to Charles while he was crowned king of France (Bridgwater 1953).

CDQ 6: Who would you consider to be a charismatic leader today?

CDQ 7: Why do you think that the line of succession to the U.S. Presidency is so clearly spelled out in the 25th Amendment to the U.S. Constitution?

Joan of Arc is an example of **charismatic authority,** the third type of authority Weber identified. (*Charisma* is a Greek word that means a gift freely and graciously given [Arndt and Gingrich 1957].) A charismatic individual is someone to whom people are drawn because they see the individual as exceptionally gifted. Note that the armies did not follow Joan of Arc because it was the custom to do so, as in traditional authority. Nor did they risk their lives alongside her because she held a position defined by written rules, as in rational-legal authority. Instead, people followed her because they were drawn to her outstanding traits. They saw her as a messenger of God, fighting on the side of justice, and accepted her leadership because of these attractive qualities.

charismatic authority: authority based on an individual's outstanding traits, which attract followers

The Threat Posed by Charismatic Authority.   Charismatic leaders work outside the established political system. Because they rule neither by custom nor law, but by their personal ability to attract followers, they pose a threat to the established political order. Whereas a king owes allegiance to tradition and a president to the system of law, to what does a charismatic leader owe allegiance? Independent of the political structure, he or she can direct followers according to personal preference—which can include the overthrow of traditional and rational-legal authorities.

Because charismatic leaders pose a threat to the established order, traditional and rational-legal authorities are often quick to oppose them. If they are not careful, however, they can create a martyr, arousing even higher sentiment in favor of the charismatic leader and in opposition to themselves. Occasionally, the Roman Catholic church faces such a threat when a priest claims miraculous powers, a claim perhaps accompanied by amazing healings. As people flock to this individual, they bypass parish priests and the formal ecclesiastical structure. The transfer of allegiance to an individual in this way threatens the church bureaucracy. Consequently, the church hierarchy may encourage the priest to withdraw from the public eye, perhaps to a monastery to rethink matters. Thus the threat is defused, rational-legal authority reasserted, and the stability of the organization maintained.

Authority as Ideal Type

Weber's classifications—traditional, rational-legal, and charismatic—represent ideal types of authority. As noted in Chapter 7, ideal type does not refer to what is ideal or desirable, but to a composite of characteristics found in many real-life examples. In fact, then, a particular leader may be difficult to classify, as he or she may show a combination of characteristics.

A remarkable example occurred after Word War I, when Germany, still suffering the stinging humiliation of national defeat, was ravaged by high unemployment and hyperinflation. Many Germans of that period saw Adolf Hitler as a type of savior, destined to create a new Germany. At first, Hitler could attract only a few radicals.

Charismatic authority—wherein an individual is followed because others perceive that he or she possesses a special gift, perhaps even a touch from God—threatens both traditional and rational-legal authority. One of the best known examples of charismatic authority is Joan of Arc, who raised and led a French army against the English.

As his vision of a new Germany spread, however, it eventually encompassed the middle classes. Coming to see Hitler as having the ability to restore prosperity and pride to Germany, businessmen contributed to his campaign. After Hitler was elected, he used his power to suspend elections and have his decrees made law. As an elected official, Hitler was a rational-legal leader. But he was also charismatic, his speeches mesmerizing masses of Germans. He was able to instill such devotion in thousands of followers that they were willing to endure hardships, even to lay down their lives for him.

Another example is John F. Kennedy. As the elected head of the United States government, Kennedy, too, represented rational-legal authority. Yet his mass appeal was so great that his public speeches aroused large numbers of people to action. When in his inaugural address Kennedy said, "Ask not what your country can do for you, but what you can do for your country," millions of Americans were touched. When Kennedy proposed a Peace Corps to help poorer countries, thousands of idealistic young people volunteered for challenging foreign service.

Charismatic and traditional authority can also overlap, as is illustrated by the case of the Ayatollah Khomeini of Iran. Khomeini was a religious leader, holding the traditional position of ayatollah. His embodiment of the Iranian people's dreams, however, as well as his austere life and devotion to principles of the Koran, gave him such mass appeal that he was also a charismatic leader. Khomeini's followers were convinced that he had been given a gift from God, and his speeches could arouse tens of thousands of followers to action. In rare instances, then, traditional and rational-legal leaders possess charismatic traits. Instances of this are unusual, however, and most authority is clearly one type or another.

Note also that charismatic leaders can be good or evil. As mentioned, Hitler, the Ayatollah Khomeini, and John F. Kennedy can be classified at least partially as charismatic leaders. Joan of Arc, as well as Moses, Jesus Christ, and Muhammad, are pure charismatic leaders, for they held no office, either traditional or rational-legal, and yet each recruited ardent followers. Following the symbolic interactionists, we can see that people impute goodness or badness to a charismatic leader. Most Americans, for example, perceived Khomeini as bad, while Iranians saw him in a different light. In the case of Joan of Arc, the English and French had quite different views, the Egyptians certainly didn't see Moses in the same light as the Israelites did, and so on.

The Transfer of Authority

The orderly transfer of authority at the death, resignation, or incapacitation of a leader is critical for social stability. Succession is a greater problem in the case of charismatic authority than with either traditional or rational-legal authority. Under traditional authority, people know who is next in line. Under rational-legal authority, people may not know who the next leader will be, but they do know *how* that person will be selected. In both traditional and rational-legal systems of authority, the rules of succession are established.

Charismatic authority, however, presents a different problem. Because charismatic authority relies neither on custom nor law and is built entirely around a single individual, the death or incapacitation of a charismatic leader can mean a bitter succession struggle, which may result in the splintering or even disbanding of the group. To preserve the organization, some charismatic leaders make arrangements for an orderly transition of power by appointing a successor. This step still does not guarantee orderly succession, of course, for allegiance depends on the leader's personal characteristics, and there is no guarantee that the followers will perceive the designated heir in the same way as they did the charismatic leader. Another strategy is to construct an organization, supposedly to honor the memory of the charismatic founder, which then perpetuates itself with a rational-legal leadership. Weber used the term the **routinization of charisma** to refer to the transfer of authority from a charismatic leader to either

routinization of charisma: the transfer of authority from a charismatic figure to either a traditional or a rational-legal form of authority

traditional or rational-legal authority. Problems of succession are one reason that charismatic authority is inherently less stable than either traditional or rational-legal authority.

TYPES OF GOVERNMENT

In the following section, we shall compare and contrast monarchies, democracies, dictatorships, and oligarchies. As we do so, we shall also look at how the institution of the state arose, and how the idea of citizenship was revolutionary.

Monarchies: The Rise of the State

At this point, it is useful to look at the fundamental changes that have occurred in political systems, just as Chapter 14 reviewed the historical transformation of economic systems. Hunting and gathering societies were small and needed no extensive political system. They operated more like an extended family, with decisions being made as they became necessary. As surpluses developed and societies grew larger, however, there arose the need for more extensive and formalized decision making and control.

When cities developed—perhaps about 3500 B.C. (Fischer 1976)—they became centers of power. **City-states** came into being, with power radiating outward from a city like a spider's web. The city controlled the immediate area around it, but the areas between cities remained in dispute. Each city-state had its own **monarchy,** a king or queen whose right to rule was considered hereditary. If you drive through Spain, France, or Gemany, you can still see evidence of former city-states. In the countryside you will see only scattered villages. Farther on, your eye will be drawn to the outline of a castle on a faraway hill. As you get closer, you will see that the castle is surrounded by a city. Several miles farther, you will see another city, also dominated by a castle. Each city, with its castle, was once a center of power.

As city-states warred with one another, the victorious ones would extend their rule. Eventually, one city-state would be able to wield power over an entire region. Over time, after further conquests, and sometimes alliances, the size of these regions grew. As this happened, the people slowly developed an identity with the larger region (seeing distant inhabitants as a "we" instead of a "they"), and what we call the state—the political entity that claims a monopoly on the use of force within a territory—came into being.

Democracies: Citizenship as a Revolutionary Idea

Spain changed from a collection of independent city-states to a country when Queen Isabella and King Ferdinand, rulers of the two most powerful city-states, united their political power by marriage, and then together conquered the other Spanish city-states. The United States, which owes much of its origin to these two rulers, who personally financed Columbus's voyage, had no city-states. Each colony, however, like a city-state, was small and independent. After the American Revolution, the colonies united. With the greater strength and resources that came from political unity, they conquered almost all of North America, bringing it under the power of a central government.

The government formed by this new country was called a **democracy.** (Derived from two Greek words—*kratos,* power and *demos,* common people—democracy literally means "power to the people.") After successfully revolting against the British king, the founders of the new country were distrustful of kings. They wanted to place political decision making into the hands of the people. This was not the first democracy the world had seen, but such a system had been tried before only with smaller groups. Athens, a city-state of Greece, practiced democracy two thousand years ago, with each male above a certain age having the right to be heard and to vote. Members of Native American tribes were also able to elect a chief, and in some, women were able to vote.

city-state: an independent city whose power radiates outward, bringing the adjacent area under its rule

monarchy: a form of government headed by a king or queen

democracy: a system of government in which authority derives from the people, derived from two Greek words that translate literally as "power to the people"

The essence of a democracy is people being able to elect their leaders. Although the United States gave the world representative democracy, the right to vote was withheld from many on the basis of property, sex, and race. Only since the 1950s have restrictions been lifted that kept many African Americans from the voting booth. Over the years, they have slowly gained political power, as illustrated in this photo of L. Douglas Wilder, the first African American to be elected a state governor as he is sworn in as governor of Virginia in 1991.

Because of their small size, tribes and cities were able to practice **direct democracy.** That is, they were small enough for the eligible voters to meet together, express their opinions, and then vote publicly—much like a town hall meeting today. As populous and spread out as the United States was, however, direct democracy was impossible. Consequently, **representative democracy** was invented. Certain citizens (at first only white landowners) voted for men to represent them in Washington. Later the vote was extended to nonowners of property, African Americans, women, and others.

Today we take the idea of citizenship for granted. What is not evident to us is that the idea had to be conceived in the first place. There is nothing natural about citizenship—it is simply a way in which we choose to define ourselves. Throughout most of human history people were thought to belong to a clan, to a tribe, or even to a ruler. The idea of **citizenship**—that by virtue of birth and residence people have basic rights—is quite new to the human scene (Turner 1990).

Historically, people's rights were usually limited to sex and family position. The rights of a resident of France in the 1600s, for example, depended on whether the individual was a male or female, a peasant or a member of the nobility. There were *no overarching rights* that people possessed simply because they were French. In essence, everyone belonged to the king, and the king had power even of life and death over all his subjects.

The concept of representative democracy based on citizenship, perhaps the greatest gift the United States has given to the world, was revolutionary. Power was to be vested in the people themselves, and government was to flow from the people. The fact that at the time this concept was revolutionary is generally lost on us, but remember that its implementation meant the *reversal of traditional ideas, for the government was to be responsive to the people's wishes, not the people to the wishes of the government.* To keep the government responsive to the needs of its citizens, people had not only the right, but the obligation, to express dissent. In a widely quoted statement, Thomas Jefferson observed that

> a little rebellion now and then is a good thing. . . . It is a medicine necessary for the sound health of government. . . . God forbid that we should ever be twenty years without such a rebellion. . . . The tree of liberty must be refreshed from time to time with the blood of patriots and tyrants. It is its natural manure. (In Hellinger and Judd 1991)

The idea of **universal citizenship**—of *everyone* having the same basic rights by virtue of being born in a country (or by immigrating and becoming a naturalized citizen)—flowered very slowly, and came into practice only through fierce struggle. When the United States was founded, for example, that idea was still in its infancy.

CDQ 8: Do you believe that most U.S. citizens take the idea of citizenship for granted? Why or why not?

direct democracy: a form of democracy in which the eligible voters meet together to discuss issues and make their decisions

representative democracy: a form of democracy in which voters elect representatives to govern and make decisions on their behalf

citizenship: the concept that birth (and residence) in a country impart basic rights

universal citizenship: the idea that everyone has the same basic rights by virtue of being born in a country (or by immigrating and becoming a naturalized citizen)

Today, it seems inconceivable to us that any group should not have the right to vote, hold office, make a contract, or own property. For earlier generations of Americans, however, it seemed just as inconceivable that nonowners of property, women, African Americans, Native Americans, Japanese Americans, Chinese Americans, and many others should have such rights. Over the years, then, rights have been extended, and in the United States the concept of citizenship and its privileges now applies to all. No longer does property, sex, or race determine the right to vote, to testify in court, and so on. These characteristics do, however, influence whether or not one votes, as we shall see in the section on voting patterns below.

Dictatorships and Oligarchies: The Seizure of Power

Democracies and monarchies are not the only systems of government. In some countries, an individual seizes power, sometimes by killing the king, queen, or president, and then dictates his will onto the people. A government run by a single person who has seized power is known as a **dictatorship.** Sometimes an individual or a small clique seizes power, resulting in a form of government known as an **oligarchy.** The frequent coups in Central and South America, in which a few military leaders seize control, are examples of oligarchies. Although one individual may be named president, it is often a group of high-ranking officers, working behind the scenes, who make the decisions. If their designated president becomes uncooperative, they remove him from office and designate another.

Monarchies, dictatorships, and oligarchies can be benevolent, or they can be totalitarian. **Totalitarianism** refers to almost *total* control of a people by the government. As our opening vignette demonstrated, totalitarian regimes tolerate no opposing opinion. Nazi Germany is an example. Hitler's decisions could not be questioned, and they were to be carried out under penalty of death. He delegated power to a few close associates from his early days and kept the populace in tight control through the Gestapo, a ruthless secret police force that looked for any sign of dissent. Control was so total that spies watched moviegoers' reactions to newsreels, investigating those who were reported as not responding "appropriately" (Hipler 1987).

In totalitarian regimes, the names of those who rule change, but the techniques of control remain the same. Threats and terror force citizen compliance and allow the dictator to remain in power. A description of Nazi Germany could just as well be applied to the Soviet Union under Stalin, Uganda under Idi Amin, or Iraq under Saddam Hussein. The police, courts, armed forces, and entire government bureaucracy are directly accountable to the dictator. Individual rights, if they existed prior to the dictator, simply disappear, while if individual citizens dissent, they disappear.

People around the world find the ideas of citizenship and of representative democracy appealing. Those who have no say in their government's decisions, or face prison for expressing opinions different from those of their government, find in these ideas the hope for a brighter future. The rapid spread of information around the world today lets them know whether they are more or less privileged politically than others, a knowledge that produces pressure for greater citizen participation in government. It looks as though the future will continue to step up this pressure.

THE AMERICAN POLITICAL SYSTEM

At this point, let us turn to an overview of the American political system. We shall consider the two major political parties, compare the American political system with other democratic systems, examine voting patterns, analyze how the Great Depression of the 1930s transformed American politics, and examine the role of lobbyists and PACs.

Essay #4

Nicolae Ceausescu, shown here beneath his country's coat of arms as he waves to delegates to the Congress of the Communist Party in Bucharest in 1989, was an example of a totalitarian leader. He attempted to exert almost total control over the Romanian people, thinking that whatever he wished was right for Romania. When communist regimes in Europe fell shortly after this photo was taken, the people's rage at Ceausescu's oppression (torture and secret police, combined with vast luxuries for himself, family, and cronies) resulted in his execution.

CDQ 9: Why do people around the world find the ideas of citizenship and of representative democracy appealing?

Essay #5

Project 1

dictatorship: a form of government in which power is seized and held by an individual or small clique

oligarchy: power held by a small group of individuals; the rule of the many by the few

totalitarianism: a form of government that exerts almost total control over the people

Political Parties and Elections

After the founding of the United States, several political parties emerged to compete with one another. By the time of the Civil War, two parties were founded that came to dominate American politics (Burnham 1983): the Democrats, who in the public mind are often associated with poor, working-class people, and the Republicans, who are associated with people who are financially better off. Each party nominates candidates, and in preelections, called primaries, the voters decide which candidates will represent their party. Each candidate then campaigns, trying to appeal to the most voters. Table 15.1 shows how Americans align themselves with political parties.

Although the Democratic and Republican parties represent different philosophical principles, each appeals to such a broad membership that it is difficult to distinguish a conservative Democrat from a liberal Republican. The extremes, however, are easy to discern. Democrats and Republicans line up on opposite sides of legislation that transfers income from one group to another or that controls wages, working conditions, and competition. Deeply committed Democrats support all such legislation, while dyed-in-the-wool Republicans oppose it.

Those elected to Congress may cross party lines. That is, some Democrats vote for legislation proposed by Republicans, and vice versa. This happens because office-holders are bound to support their party's philosophy but not necessarily all its specific proposals. For example, Democrats may support the principle that the poor should have more income. During elections, they will make much of this issue. They may call Republicans callous representatives of the rich. The Republicans, in turn, have their own choice words to rouse emotions—and votes—perhaps calling an opponent misguided, or even, if the contest really heats up, un-American. When it comes to a specific bill, however, such as raising the minimum wage, not all Democrats or Republicans see it the same way. Some conservative Democrats may view the measure as unfair to small employers, or too costly, given the country's debt, and vote with the Republicans against the bill. At the same time, liberal Republicans—feeling that the proposal is just, or sensing a changing sentiment in voters back home—may side with its Democratic backers.

TABLE 15.1   How Americans Identify with Political Parties

	1960 (%)	1970 (%)	1980 (%)	1988 (%)
Democrats				
Strong Democrat	20	20	18	18
Weak Democrat	25	24	23	18
Independent Democrat	6	10	11	12
Total	51	54	52	48
Republicans				
Strong Republican	16	9	9	14
Weak Republican	14	15	14	14
Independent Republican	7	8	12	13
Total	37	32	35	41
Other				
Independent	10	13	13	11
Not Political	3	1	2	2
Total	13	14	15	13

Note: Due to rounding, the figures do not always total 100 percent.
Source: Statistical Abstract of the United States, 1991: Table 452.

Regardless of their differences, however, the Democrats and Republicans represent *different slices of the center.* Although they may promote different legislation, each party firmly supports such fundamentals of American society as free public education, a strong military, freedom of religion, speech, assembly, and, of course, capitalism—especially the private ownership of property. Minority parties that advocate radical change in these ideas can muster but few votes, and, accordingly, are short-lived and of little consequence in the American political system. Most Americans consider a vote for a minority party a waste. Of the few votes received by candidates of minority parties, some come from strong conviction, while others are a form of protest from people who do not like either of the candidates of the dominant parties.

Democratic Systems in Europe

We tend to take our political system for granted and assume that any other democracy looks like ours—even down to having two major parties. Such is not the case. To gain a comparative understanding, let us look briefly at the system generally followed in European nations.

Although both theirs and ours are democracies, there are fundamental distinctions between the two (Domhoff 1979, 1983; Lipset 1963). First, elections in most European countries are not based on a winner-take-all electoral system. In the United States, election results are determined by a simple majority. For example, if a Democrat wins 51 percent of the votes cast in an electoral district, he or she takes office. The Republican candidate, who may have won 49 percent, loses everything. In contrast, most European countries base their elections on a system of **proportional representation;** that is, the seats in the national legislature are divided according to the proportion of votes received by each political party. If one party wins 51 percent of the vote, for example, that party is awarded 51 percent of the seats; while a party with 49 percent of the votes receives 49 percent of the seats.

Second, proportional representation encourages minority parties, while the winner-take-all system discourages them. As we saw, the American system pushes parties to the center as they strive to obtain the broadest possible support required to win elections. For this reason, the United States has **centrist parties.** The proportional representation followed in most European countries means that if a party gets 10 percent of the voters to support its candidate, it will get 10 percent of the seats. This system encourages the formation of **noncentrist parties,** those that propose less popular or even offbeat ideas. For example, a party may make its central platform a return to the gold standard, or the retirement of all nuclear weapons and the shutting down of all nuclear power reactors.

Two main results follow from being able to win even just a few seats in the national legislature. First, if a minority party has officeholders, it gains access to the media throughout the year, receiving publicity that helps keep its issues alive. Second, the party may gain power beyond its numbers. Because many parties compete in the elections, no single party is likely to gain an absolute majority of the seats in the national legislature. To muster the required votes to make national decisions, then, the party with the most seats generally forms a **coalition government** by aligning itself with one or more of the smaller parties. On occasion, therefore, a party with only 10 or 15 percent of the seats may be a crucial factor in deciding key issues. It may even be able to make or break the coalition. Consequently, the minority party may be able to trade its vote on some particular issue for the larger party's support on another.

In some countries, governments call themselves democratic but hold closed elections in which only a single candidate is allowed to run for office. Since such elections violate the basic premises of democracy, the use of the word *democratic* in such cases bears no comparison with our sense of the term. Until recently, this situation pertained in the former Soviet Union. At this point, however, the people of this former totalitarian

CDQ 10: Do you think the Republican and Democratic parties actually are different from one another? If yes, in what ways?

proportional representation: an electoral system in which seats in a legislature are divided according to the proportion of votes each political party receives

centrist party: a political party that represents the center of political opinion

noncentrist party: a political party that represents marginal ideas

coalition government: a government in which a country's largest party aligns itself with one or more smaller parties

state are allowed a choice among candidates and are even able to dissent openly and criticize their elected leaders. This could change at any time, however, especially in the face of unsettling inflation and food shortages (Galuszka, Bremner, and Brady 1992).

Voting Patterns

Year after year, Americans show consistent voting patterns. From Table 15.2, you can see how voting varies by age, race/ethnicity, education, employment, and income. Note that the percentage of people who vote increases with age. Currently, people aged forty-five and over are twice as likely to vote as those between the ages of

Essay #6

L. Obj. 5: Describe American voting patterns and identify those most and least likely to vote in elections.

TR#32: Percentage of Americans Who Vote for President

CDQ 11: Why do you think the percentage of people who vote increases with age? Wouldn't younger people have more to gain?

TABLE 15.2   Percentage of Americans Who Vote for President

	1976	1980	1984	1988
Overall				
Americans Who Vote	59	59	60	57
Age				
18–20	38	36	37	33
21–24	46	43	44	38
25–34	55	55	55	48
35–44	63	64	64	61
45–64	69	69	70	68
65 and up	62	65	68	69
Race/Ethnic				
White (Non-Hispanic)	61	61	61	59
African American	49	51	56	52
Hispanic American	32	30	33	29
Education				
Grade School Only	44	43	43	37
High School Dropout	47	46	44	41
High School Graduate	59	59	59	55
College Dropout	68	67	68	65
College Graduate	80	80	79	78
Labor Force				
Employed	62	62	62	58
Unemployed	44	41	44	39
Income				
Under $5,000		38	39	35
$5,000 to $9,999		46	49	41
$10,000 to $14,999		54	55	48
$15,000 to $19,999		57	60	54
$20,000 to $24,999		61	67	58
$25,000 to $34,999		67	74	64
$35,000 and over		74	74	70*
Sex				
Male	60	59	59	56
Female	59	59	61	58

*For 1988, the percentage is an average of $35,000 to $49,900 and over $50,000.

Source: Statistical Abstract of the United States, 1991: Table 450; Current Population Reports, Series P-20, Vol. 440.

eighteen and twenty. This table also shows the significance of race in voting patterns. Non-Hispanic whites are more likely to vote than are African Americans, while Hispanic Americans are considerably less likely to vote than either. The difference is so great that whites are about twice as likely to vote as Hispanic Americans.

As with age, greater education too increases the likelihood of voting. People who finish college are about twice as likely to vote as those who complete only grade school. Employment and income also affect the probability that people will vote. People who make over $35,000 a year are twice as likely to vote as those who make less than $5,000. Finally, note that about the same proportion of males and females vote in presidential elections.

A crucial aspect of the socialization of newcomers to the United States has been the process of learning the American political system. The Perspectives box on page 416 details the key role of ethnicity in this process.

Social Integration.   How can we explain the voting patterns shown in Table 15.2? The people most likely to vote are older, more educated, affluent working whites, while those least likely to vote are poor, younger, ill-educated, unemployed Hispanic Americans. From these patterns, we can draw this principle: *The more that people feel they have a stake in the political system, the more likely they are to vote.* They have more to protect, and feel that voting can make a difference. In effect, people who have been rewarded by the political system feel more socially integrated. They vote because they perceive that elections directly affect their own lives and the type of society in which they and their children live.

Alienation.   In contrast, those who gain less from the system—in terms of education, income, and jobs—are more likely to be alienated. Such people feel that their vote will not affect their lives one way or another, that "next year will be more of the same regardless of who is president," that "all politicians do is lie to us." Similarly, minorities who feel that the American political system is a "white" system are less motivated to vote.

Voter Apathy.   Table 15.2 also indicates that a large proportion of people who have jobs, high education, and good incomes also stay away from the polls. Many people do not vote because of **voter apathy,** or indifference. Like the alienated, they feel that their vote will not affect the outcome. A common attitude is "What difference does my

CDQ 12: Do you vote regularly? Why does such a relatively small proportion of eligible voters actually vote in the United States?

voter apathy: indifference and inaction on the part of individuals or groups with respect to the political process

In some countries, people have taken up arms and are risking their lives to win the right to vote. In others, such as the United States where some of the people have had the right to vote since the 1700s and others since 1920, voting is taken for granted. Many feel that their vote will make little difference, and due to such voter apathy, a small number of eligible voters decide election results.

P E R S P E C T I V E S
Cultural Diversity in U.S. Society

Immigrants—Ethnicity and Class as the Path to Political Participation

That the United States is the land of immigrants is a truism; every schoolchild knows that since the English Pilgrims first landed on Plymouth Rock, successive groups—among them Germans, Scandinavians, Italians, Poles, and Greeks—crossed the Atlantic ocean to reach American shores.

Some, such as the Irish immigrants in the late 1800s and early 1900s, left to escape unendurable poverty and famine. Others, such as the Jews of czarist Russia, fled a government that singled them out for persecution. Some fled as refugees or asylum seekers from lands divided by war. Others, called *entrepreneurial immigrants,* sought economic opportunities absent in their native lands. Still others came as *sojourners,* immigrants who planned to return after a temporary stay. Finally, some left at the urging of their governments, who wished to use these immigrants' presence in the new land for their own country's interest (Portes and Rumbaut 1990).

Today, the United States witnesses its second large wave of immigration of the twentieth century. The first, in the early 1900s, in which immigrants came to account for 13.2 percent of the population, consisted largely of Europeans. Today, the mix of immigrants—currently about 6.2 percent of the population—is far more diverse, with the greatest number coming from South and Central American and Asian countries. As in the past, there is widespread concern that "too many" immigrants will alter the character of the United States. "Throughout the history of American immigration," wrote sociologists Alejandro Portes and Ruben Rumbaut, "a consistent thread has been the fear that the 'alien element' would somehow undermine the institutions of the country and lead it down the path of disintegration and decay."

Thus, both immigration and the fear of its consequences are central to the history of the United States. A widespread fear held by native-born Americans in the early part of the century was that immigrants would subvert the democratic system in favor of socialism or communism. Today, some fear that the primacy of the English language is threatened. In addition, the age-old fear that immigrants will supplant native-born Americans in the labor market remains strong. Finally, groups that have struggled for political representation fear that newer groups will gain political power at their expense.

But what in fact is the route to political participation by immigrants? According to Portes and Rumbaut, immigrants organize as a group on the basis of *ethnicity* rather than *class.* They do so in response to common problems, especially discrimination, incurred as an ethnic group. "The reaffirmation of distinct cultural identities . . . has been the rule among foreign groups and has represented the first effective step in their social and political incorporation," noted Portes and Rumbaut. "Ethnic solidarity has provided the basis for the pursuit of common goals through the American political system: by mobilizing the collective vote and by electing their own to office, immigrant minorities have learned the rules of the democratic game and absorbed its values in the process."

This pattern of banding together on the basis of ethnicity can be seen, for example, in the case of Irish immigrants in Boston. They built a power base that put the Irish in political control of the city, and, ultimately, saw one of their own sworn in as president of the United States.

As Portes and Rumbaut observed, "Assimilation as the rapid transformation of immigrants into Americans 'as everyone else' has never happened." Instead, all immigrant groups began by fighting for their own interests as Irish, Italians, German, and so on. Only when they had attained enough political power to overcome discrimination did they become "like everyone else"—that is, like others who had power.

Thus, only when a certain level of political power is achieved, when groups gain political representation somewhat proportionate to their numbers, does the issue of class grow in significance. This, then, is the path that immigrants follow in their socialization into the American political system.

Source: Portes and Rumbaut 1990; Prud 'Homme 1991; Salholz 1990.

---

one vote make when there are millions of votes?" Many of the apathetic see little difference between the two major political parties (Zipp 1985). The result is that two out of five eligible American voters do not vote for president, and that less than half the nation's eligible voters (about 46 percent) vote for members of Congress (*Statistical Abstract* 1991: Table 450).

The Depression as a Transforming Event

Until Franklin Delano Roosevelt (FDR) became president in 1932, the country's ruling philosophy was that the government should play as small a part as possible in people's lives. This belief extended to the economy. The proper role of local government was to run schools, make the community safe, and operate a small maintenance department for garbage, sewers, and streets; that of the federal government was to build highways and bridges, deliver the mail, and maintain a small armed force. Government, at whatever level, was to collect as few taxes as possible. The poor were the responsibility of family, church, and local community.

During what became known as the Great Depression of the 1930s, which followed the stock market's collapse in 1929, employment around the country collapsed too. About one in every four workers had no job, and many of those who did worked for subsistence wages. Some felt lucky to get $80 or $100 ($800 to $1,000 in today's dollars) for a month of hard labor.

These conditions transformed public opinion, and with it, the role of government in the economy. Previously, Americans had been convinced that only laziness kept people from work. Now they saw that millions desperately wanted to work, but no work was available. At this point, Americans began to develop a sociological imagination, for they caught a glimpse of the economic system itself. They began to see that having a job or being unemployed was not simply the result of individual traits such as initiative or the lack of it, but the consequence of the social system itself. They demanded that the government do something about the economy.

In 1932 Herbert Hoover, the Republican incumbent, was defeated, and Roosevelt, a Democrat, took office with the promise to change things. That he did. He took the view that it was the government's responsibility to oversee the country's economy. Among other things, he instituted federal work programs such as the Works Progress Administration (WPA) to build parks and civic buildings, and the Rural Electrification Association (REA) to bring electricity to the country's farms. Because he put people back to work, FDR was reelected in 1936, 1940, and 1944.

American politics was never the same again. Both Republicans and Democrats adopted the idea that, at least to some extent, private business *is* the government's business. Although each party expresses its own version of this philosophy, both nevertheless support payments to unemployed workers, the elderly, and the poor. Parties and candidates may propose specific changes in these programs, but any party that suggested dismantling unemployment insurance, Social Security, and welfare would have no chance of being elected.

Lobbyists and Special-Interest Groups

Suppose that as president of the United States, you want to make dairy products more affordable for the public in general and the poor in particular. As you check into the matter, you find that prices for milk and cheese are high because the government is paying dairy farmers over $1 billion a year in price supports (*Statistical Abstract* 1990: Table 1130). You therefore propose to eliminate these subsidies.

Immediately, large numbers of people leap into action. They send telegrams to your office, contact their senator and representatives, and call reporters for news conferences. The news media report that hardships will result from your proposed action and that across the land dairy farmers will be put out of business. The Associated Press distributes pictures of a farm family—their Holsteins grazing in the background—informing readers how this healthy, happy family of good Americans struggling to make a living will be destroyed by your proposal.

President or not, you don't have a chance of getting your legislation passed.

What happened? The dairy industry went to work to protect its special interests. A **special-interest group** consists of people who think alike on a particular issue and who can be mobilized for political action. The dairy industry is just one of thousands

Project 2

L. Obj. 6: Analyze the ways in which special-interest groups influence the political process.

CDQ 13: What are some of the special-interest groups in your city or state? Are you currently a member of any special-interest group?

special-interest group: a group of people who have a particular issue in common and can be mobilized for political action

of powerful special-interest groups that are able to protect their own interests without regard to the general welfare. If, as president, you propose that the federal government save $8 billion dollars a year by not subsidizing wheat, immediately the wheat industry will be nipping at your heels. If you propose to reduce medical costs by increasing competition among physicians, the American Medical Association (AMA) will spring into action.

Special-interest groups employ **lobbyists,** people paid to influence legislation on behalf of their clients. Lobbyists, who swarm the corridors of Capitol Hill, have become a major force in American politics. Members of Congress who are interested in being reelected—must pay attention to lobbyists, for they represent a bloc of voters who have a vital interest in the outcome of specific bills. Lobbyists can deliver votes to you—or to your opponent. In addition, they are well financed and can contribute huge sums to support or oppose your reelection.

Because so much money was being passed under the table by special-interest groups to members of Congress, in the 1970s legislation limited the amount that any individual, corporation, or special-interest group could give a candidate, and required all contributions over $1,000 to be reported. Special-interest groups immediately did an end sweep around the new laws by forming **political action committees** (PACs), organizations that solicit contributions from many donors—each contribution within the allowable limits—and then use the large total to influence legislation.

PACs have become a powerful influence in Washington, for they bankroll lobbyists and legislators. More than four thousand PACs disburse over $350 million (*Statistical Abstract* 1991: Tables 458, 459). A few PACs represent broad social interests such as environmental protection, but most stand for narrow financial concerns, such as the dairy, oil, banking, and construction industries. Those PACs with the most clout in terms of money and votes gain the ear of Congress.

PACs and the Cost of Elections

The huge costs of today's elections are one reason that lobbyists and PACs have become so important in Washington, as well as in state capitols. No longer are elections a matter of an individual having an idea about how government ought to be and then gathering support for that idea—if indeed they ever were. Instead, a candidate needs money—big money—to get elected. Suppose that you intend to run for the Senate. To have a chance of winning, you must not only shake hands around the state, be photographed hugging babies, and eat a lot of chicken dinners at local civic organizations, you must also send out hundreds of thousands of pieces of mail to solicit votes and financial support. Several such mailings may total millions of items. Television, essential for your campaign, will cost you thousands of dollars for a single ad. If you are an *average* candidate, you will spend $3.5 million on your campaign (*Statistical Abstract* 1990: Tables 429, 452).

Now suppose that the representatives of a couple of PACs pay you a visit. One says that his organization will pay for a mailing, while the other offers to buy some television and radio ads. Let us also suppose that it is only a few weeks from the election and the polls show you and your opponent neck and neck. When your campaign manager tells you that the election hangs in the balance and your war chest is empty, the offers by the PACs look very appealing. As you feel somewhat favorably toward their positions, you accept. Once elected, though, you owe them. When a piece of legislation that affects their interests comes up for vote, their representatives call you—at your unlisted number at home—and tell you how they want you to vote. It would be political folly to double-cross them.

It is said that the first duty of a politician is to get elected—and the second duty to get reelected. If you are an average senator, to finance your reelection campaign you must raise $1,600 *every single day* of your six-year term. It is no wonder that money has been dubbed the "mother's milk of politics" (Abramson and Rogers 1991).

CNN: Lobbying Money

CDQ 14: Why are elections so costly in the United States? Do you think they have to be?

lobbyists: people paid to influence legislation on behalf of their clients

political action committee: (PAC) an organization formed by one or more special-interest groups to solicit and spend funds for the purpose of influencing legislation

Criticism of Lobbyists and PACs. The major criticism leveled against lobbyists and PACs is that they force legislators to owe allegiance not to the people they represent, but to special-interest groups. While many object to them on these grounds alone, others are disturbed by the foreign influences that lobbyists bring to the legislative process. Japan is a case in point; it spends $100 million a year to pressure members of Congress to reduce quotas and duties on imports of televisions, automobiles, and so on (Judis 1990). Over one hundred former government officials have been hired to support Japanese interests in Washington. Toyota has formed its own PAC called Auto Dealers and Drivers for Free Trade, through which it funnels money to members of Congress (Tiffany 1990). Critics further argue that the playing field is not level, for Japan forbids foreigners to influence *its* legislation (Judis 1990).

Even if the United States were to allow lobbyists only for domestic interests—or perhaps even outlaw PACs altogether—special-interest groups would not disappear from the American political process. Before PACs, lobbyists walked the corridors of the Senate, they have always had access to Senate staff, and, since the time of Alexander Graham Bell they have carried the unlisted numbers of members of Congress. Lobbyists—for good or ill—play an essential role in the American political system.

WHO RULES AMERICA?

L. Obj. 7: Distinguish between the functionalist and conflict perspectives on who rules America.

With special-interest groups and their lobbyists and PACs, some wonder just who United States senators and representatives really represent. And most wonder what actually goes on behind the scenes in Washington and the state capitols. Do the people in general rule, or do special-interest groups? This question has led to a lively debate among sociologists. In previous chapters, we have discussed the contrasting views of sociologists on the control of American society, and this is an opportune moment to review them.

The Functionalist Perspective: Pluralism

Essay #7

TR#34M: Veto-Groups Model

CDQ 15: Do you agree with the functionalist or the conflict perspective on who rules America? Why?

Functionalists view the state as having arisen out of the basic needs of the social group. To protect themselves from would-be oppressors, people formed a government and gave it the monopoly on violence. Their continuing need, however, is to prevent the state from turning that force against themselves. To return to the example used earlier, states have a tendency to become muggers. Thus, people must perform a balancing act between having no government—which would lead to **anarchy,** a state in which disorder and violence reign—and having a government that protects them from violence, but may itself turn against them. When functioning well, then, the state is a balanced system that protects its citizens—from themselves and from government.

What keeps the government of the United States from turning against its citizens? Functionalists say that **pluralism,** a diffusion of power among many interest groups, prevents any one group from gaining control of the government and using it to oppress the people (Dahl 1961, 1982; Polsby 1959; Huber and Form 1973). The founders of the United States were determined that the government should not come under the control of any one group, or else they believed democracy would be doomed. To balance the interests of competing groups, the founders set up three branches of government—the executive (president), judiciary (courts), and legislature (Congress and House of Representatives). Each is sworn to uphold the Constitution, which guarantees rights to citizens, and each is able to nullify the actions of the other two. This system, known as **checks and balances,** was designed to ensure that power remains distributed and that no one branch dominates.

From the functionalist perspective, ethnic groups, women, farmers, factory workers, religious groups, bankers, bosses, the unemployed, coal miners, the retired, as well as the broader categories of the rich, middle class, and poor, are all parts of the

anarchy: a state of lawlessness or political disorder caused by the absence or collapse of governmental authority

pluralism: the diffusion of power among many interest groups, preventing any single group from gaining control of the government

checks and balances: the separation of powers among the three branches of U.S. government—legislative, executive, and judicial—so that one is able to nullify the actions of the other two, thus preventing the domination of any single branch

pluralist American society. They are among the many interest groups to which politicians must pay attention, for each has political muscle to flex at the polls. To be reelected, politicians promote legislation that benefits special-interest groups, or, at the very least, does not offend them. The competitive activities of these many interest groups prevent the dominance of any single group and balance the political system.

Thus, say functionalists, no one group rules America. Rather, in the pluralistic system power is widely dispersed among the many groups that make up American society (Dahl 1982; Marger 1987). As each group pursues its own interests, it is balanced by many other groups pursuing theirs. As special-interest groups negotiate with one another and reach compromises, conflict is minimized, and the resulting policies gain wide support. Consequently, no one group rules, and the political system is responsive to the people.

The Conflict Perspective: Power Elite and Ruling Class

Conflict theorists, in contrast, maintain that the thousands of special interest groups are only part of the superficial appearance of the American political system. Something quite different is going on inside the power structure (Hellinger and Judd 1991).

Conflict theorists do not deny that the lobbyists scurrying around Washington are an important feature of American political life. Lobbyists do promote specific legislation, but that is not where the *real* power lies. Those are only bits and pieces, laws passed for specific purposes. What really counts is the big picture, not its fragments. The important question is who holds the power that determines the overarching policies of the United States. For example, who determines how many Americans will be out of work by raising or lowering interest rates? Who sets policies that transfer jobs from the United States to countries with low-cost labor? Who makes policies that determine the rate of inflation? And the ultimate question of power: Who is behind decisions to go to war?

Power Elite.   C. Wright Mills (1956) took the position that the most important matters are not decided by lobbyists, nor even by Congress. Rather, the decisions that have the greatest impact on the lives of Americans—and people across the face of the globe—are made by a coalition of individuals whose interests coincide and who have access to the center of political power in the United States. Mills called them the **power elite,** and said that it is this group that rules America. As depicted in Figure 15.1, the power elite consists of the top leaders of the largest corporations, the most powerful generals and admirals of the armed forces, and certain elite politicians—the president, his cabinet, and select senior members of Congress who chair the major committees. It is they who wield power, who make the decisions that direct the country—and shake the world (Hourani 1987; Hellinger and Judd 1991).

Are the three groups that make up the power elite—the top political, military, and corporate leaders—equal in power? Mills said they were not, but for his choice of dominance he did not point to the president and his staff or even to the generals and admirals, but rather to the corporate heads. Because all three segments of the power elite view capitalism as essential to the welfare of the country, business interests, he said, come foremost in setting national policy.

Ruling Class.   Sociologist William Domhoff continued Mills's argument. Domhoff (1967, 1970, 1983, 1990) asserted that the United States is run by a ruling class composed of the wealthiest and most powerful individuals in the country. About 1 percent of Americans belong to the super rich, the powerful capitalist class studied in Chapter 10. Members of this class—who attend prestigious private schools, belong to exclusive private clubs, and are millionaires several times over—control America's top corporations and foundations, even the boards that oversee the major universities. And it is no accident that it is from this group that the president chooses most members of

L. Obj. 8: Compare and contrast the power elite perspective of C. Wright Mills with William Domhoff's ruling class theory.

K.P.: C. Wright Mills

TR#32M: Power in American Society: The Model Prepared by C. Wright Mills

TR#33M: Domhoff's View of the Structure of Power

K.P.: William Domhoff

power elite: C. Wright Mills's term for those who rule America: the top people in the leading corporations, the most powerful generals and admirals of the armed forces, and certain elite politicians

his cabinet and appoints the top ambassadors to the most powerful countries of the world.

As noted in Chapter 9, ruling classes help secure their position by promoting an ideology that supports current divisions of power and wealth (Marger 1987). The American power elite promotes the view that positions come through merit and that everyone has a chance to become rich. For the most part, the power elite keeps out of the public eye as much as possible, content to be active behind the scenes as its members make national policy decisions. In order to maintain their interests, however, a few members take prominent positions in the government.

Conflict theorists point out that we should not think of the ruling class as a group that meets together and agrees on specific matters. Rather, it consists of people whose backgrounds and orientations to life are so similar that they automatically share the same goals. The result is not complete unity, however, for at times the interests of one segment conflict with those of another. For example, leaders in banking and finance may want higher interest rates to attract foreign capital, while those in manufacturing will push for lower rates to promote expansion. One segment may want high tariffs on imports to protect its manufacturing interests, while another may favor low tariffs because it has moved its manufacturing operations overseas.

Although the ruling class has such occasional differences of opinion, its members generally see eye to eye. Their behavior stems not from some grand conspiracy to control the country, but, rather, from a mutual interest in solving the problems that face large businesses (Useem 1984). Able to ensure that the social policies it deems desirable for the country are adopted, this powerful group sets the economic and political conditions under which the rest of the country operates (Domhoff 1990). We shall return to this line of inquiry below.

Which View Is Right?

The functionalist and conflict views of power in American society cannot be reconciled. Either competing interests block the dominance of any single group, as functionalists assert, or a power elite oversees the major decisions of the United States, as conflict theorists maintain. Perhaps at the middle level of Mills's model, depicted in Figure 15.1, the competing interest groups do keep each other at bay, and none is able to dominate. If so, the functionalist view would apply to this level, as well as to the lowest level of power. Perhaps functionalists have just not looked high enough, and activities

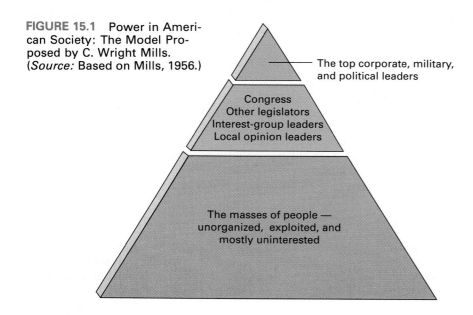

FIGURE 15.1 Power in American Society: The Model Proposed by C. Wright Mills. (*Source:* Based on Mills, 1956.)

The top corporate, military, and political leaders

Congress
Other legislators
Interest-group leaders
Local opinion leaders

The masses of people —
unorganized, exploited, and
mostly uninterested

at the peak remain invisible to them. If so, on that level lies the key to American power, the dominance that conflict theorists assert.

The answer, however, is not yet conclusive. For that, we must await more research, for nothing at this point determines the matter once and for all.

WAR: A MEANS TO IMPLEMENT POLITICAL OBJECTIVES

As we have noted, an essential characteristic of the state is that it claims a monopoly on violence. In some instances, the state uses violence to protect citizens from individuals and groups, at other times it turns violence against its own people. The state may also direct violence against other nations. **War,** armed conflict between nations (or politically distinct groups), is often part of national policy. Let us look at this aspect of politics.

Is War Universal?

While human aggression and individual killing characterize all human groups, war does not. War is simply *one option* that groups may choose for dealing with disagreements; but not all societies choose this option. The Mission Indians of North America, the Arunta of Australia, the Andaman Islanders of the South Pacific, and the Eskimos of the Arctic, for example, have procedures to handle aggression and quarrels, but they do not have organized battles that pit one tribe against another. These groups do not even have a word for war (Lesser 1968).

Why Nations Go to War

Why do nations choose war to handle disputes? Sociologists answer this question by focusing not on factors *within* humans, such as aggressive impulses, but by looking for *social* causes—conditions in society that encourage or discourage combat between nations.

Sociologist Nicholas S. Timasheff (1965) identified three essential conditions of war. The first is a cultural tradition of war. Due to experiences with war in the past, the leaders of a group see war as on option when they face conflict with other nations. The second is an antagonistic situation in which two or more states confront incompatible objectives. For example, each may want the same land or resources. The third is a "fuel" that heats the antagonistic situation to a boiling point, so that people cross the line from thinking about war to actually engaging in it. Timasheff identified seven such "fuels." He found that war is likely if a country's leaders see the antagonistic situation as an opportunity to achieve one of the following objectives:

1. Gain revenge or settle "old scores" from previous conflicts
2. Dictate their will to a weaker nation
3. Enhance their prestige, or save the nation's "honor"
4. Unite rival groups within their country
5. Protect or exalt their own position
6. Satisfy the national aspirations of ethnic groups, bringing under their rule "our people" who are living in another country
7. Forcibly convert others to religious and ideological beliefs

How Common Is War?

One of the contradictions of humanity is that people long for peace while at the same time they glorify war. The glorification of war can be seen by noting how major battles hog the center of a country's retelling of its history and how monuments to its generals are scattered throughout the land. From May Day parades in Moscow's Red Square

---

Project 3

L. Obj. 9: Discuss the major uses of war in societies. Analyze the costs and dehumanizing aspects of war.

Speaker Sug. #3: A military recruiter and/or peace activist to talk about war-related topics.

CDQ 16: Under what circumstances do you think the United States should engage in war? When should the U.S. not engage in war?

K.P.: Nicholas S. Timasheff

war: armed conflict between nations or politically distinct groups

Unlike human hopes, there is no end to war. Sorokin's survey indicates how extensively European nations have been involved in war. Shown here is one of the more recent conflicts, the shelling of Dubrovnik, Yugoslavia, after internal war broke out between rival ethnic groups following the dissolution of communist power.

to the Fourth of July celebrations in the United States and the Cinco de Mayo victory marches in Mexico, war and revolutions are interwoven into the fabric of daily life.

K.P.: Pitirim Sorokin

To find out how often war occurred in European history, sociologist Pitirim Sorokin (1937) counted the wars from 500 B.C. to A.D. 1925. He documented 967 wars, an average of one war every two to three years. Counting years or parts of a year in which a country was at war, at 28 percent Germany had the lowest record of warfare, while Spain's 67 percent gave it the dubious distinction of being the most war-prone. Sorokin found that Russia, the land of his birth, had experienced only one peaceful quarter-century during the previous one thousand years. Since the time of William the Conqueror, who took power in 1066, England was at war an average of fifty-six out of each one hundred years. As noted, Spain fought even more often. It is worth noting the history of the United States in this regard: Since 1850, it has intervened militarily around the world more than 150 times, an average of *more than once a year* (Kohn 1988).

Costs of War

One side-effect of the industrialization stressed in this text is a greater capacity to inflict death. For example, during World War I bombs claimed fewer than 3 of every 100,000 people in England and Germany. With technical advancements in human destruction, however, by World War II this figure increased a hundredfold, to 300 of every 100,000 civilians (Hart 1957). Our killing capacity has so increased since then that sociologist Hornell Hart (1957) estimated the death rate in a war fought with nuclear bombs at 100,000 per 100,000!

Although one might think that the massive loss of lives and property of two world wars would have taught the world's nations a lesson in peace, warfare continues as a common technique of pursuing political objectives. For about seven years, the United States fought in Vietnam—at a cost of 59,000 American and about 2 million Vietnamese lives (Herring 1989; Hellinger and Judd 1991). For nine years, the Soviet Union waged war in Afghanistan—with a death toll of about 1 million Afghanistani and perhaps 20,000 Soviet soldiers (Armitage 1989). An eight-year war between Iran and Iraq cost about

400,000 lives. The total exacted by Cuban mercenaries in Africa and South America is unknown. Also unknown is the number of lives—almost exclusively Iraqi—lost in the brief war against Iraq by international forces led by the United States, although the figure of 100,000 losses on the Iraqi side has been suggested by media reports. Israel and its Arab neighbors engage in a seemingly endless succession of "preemptive strikes" followed by "retaliatory measures." Meanwhile, on the broader front, the cold war thaws, then freezes again. Currently, it has thawed more than at any time since 1950, and the United States and the former Soviet Union have announced that their nuclear missiles are no longer aimed at each other's cities.

CDQ 17: Do you think that war inevitably causes dehumanization?

War and Dehumanization

War exacts many costs in addition to killing people and destroying property. One is its effect on morality. Exposure to brutality and killing often causes **dehumanization,** the process of reducing people to objects that do not deserve to be treated as humans.

As we review findings on dehumanization and see how it breeds callousness and cruelty, perhaps we can better understand how O'Brien in the opening vignette could have unleashed rats into someone's face, or how the colonel in the opening vignette of Chapter 12 could have unfeelingly sent people to their deaths. Physician-researchers Viola W. Bernard, Perry Ottenberg, and Fritz Redl (1971) identified four characteristics of dehumanization.

1. *Increased emotional distance from others* People stop identifying with others, no longer seeing them as having basic human qualities similar to themselves. Instead of people, they become subhumans, "the enemy," or objects of some sort.

2. *An emphasis on following procedures* Regulations become all-important. They are not questioned, for they are seen as a means to an end. People are likely to say, "I don't like this, but it is necessary to follow procedures," or, "We all have to die some day. What difference does it make if these people die now?"

3. *Inability to resist pressures* Fears of losing occupational security, losing the respect of one's group, or having one's integrity and loyalty questioned take precedence over individual moral decisions.

4. *A diminished sense of personal responsibility* People come to see themselves as only small cogs in a large machine. They are not responsible for what they do, for they are simply following orders. The higher-ups who give the orders are thought to have more complete or even secret information that justifies the acts. They think, "The higher-ups are in a position to judge what is right and wrong, but in my humble place, who am I to question these acts?"

In short, thinking of the enemy as an object removes the necessity to treat that enemy as a human being. Conscience grows numb, and even acts of torture become dissociated from a person's "normal self." Brutality and killing become simply actions to be done in order to accomplish a job. It is not the individual's responsibility to question whether or not the job should be done—that responsibility is limited, rather, to carrying out a duty. Torturing and killing are extremely unpleasant, but somehow they fit into the larger scheme of things—and someone has to do such "dirty work." Those who make the decisions are the ones who are responsible, not the simple soldier who follows orders.

K.P.: Tamotsu Shibutani

dehumanization: the act or process of reducing people to objects that do not deserve the treatment accorded humans

As sociologist Tamotsu Shibutani (1970) stressed, dehumanization is helped along by the tendency for prolonged conflicts to be transformed into a struggle between good and evil. The enemy, of course, represents evil in the equation. To fight against absolute evil sometimes requires the suspension of moral standards—for one is dealing with an abnormal situation, an enemy that is less than human and the precarious survival of good. War, then, exalts treachery, bribery, and killing—and medals are given to glorify actions that would be condemned in every other context.

As soldiers participate in acts that they, too, would normally condemn, they neutralize their morality. This behavior insulates them from acknowledging their behaviors as evil, which would threaten their self-concept and mental adjustment. Surgeons, highly sensitive to patients' needs in other medical situations, become capable of mentally removing an individual's humanity. By thinking of patients as mere "recipients of surgical techniques," surgeons are able to mutilate them just to study the results. They become capable of systematically recording the reactions of prisoners whom they have

---

PERSPECTIVES
Cultural Diversity Around the World

Nations versus States—Implications for a New World Order

There are about five thousand nations in the world today. What makes each a *nation* is that its people share a language, culture, territorial base, and political organization and history. A *state*, in contrast, claims a monopoly on violence or force over a territory. A state may contain many nations. The Kaiapo Indians are but one nation within the state called Brazil. The Penan people of Sarawak are but one nation within the state called Malaysia. The Chippewa and Sioux are two nations within the state called the United States. To nation peoples, group identity transcends political affiliation. The five thousand nations have existed for hundreds, some even for thousands, of years. In contrast, most of the world's 171 states have been around only since World War II.

Very few nations have ever been asked if they wished to become part of a state. They have been incorporated by force. Some states have far better records than others, but overall, no ideology, left or right, religious or sectarian, has protected nations or promoted pluralism much better or worse than any other. In fact, the twentieth century has probably seen more genocides and ethnocides (the destruction of an ethnic group) than any other.

All modern states are empires, and they are increasingly seen as such by nations. From Lithuania to Canada, the movement by nations pushing for power-sharing and autonomy demands that the world evolve a creative new kind of geopolitics or be gripped by ever worsening cycles of violence.

Clearly, the Palestinians who live within Israel's borders will not soon identify themselves as Israelis. But did you know that the Oromos in Ethiopia have more members than three-quarters of the states in the United Nations, and that they do not think of themselves as Ethiopians? The twenty million Kurds don't consider themselves first and foremost Turks, Iranians, Iraqis, or Syrians. There are about 130 nations in the former USSR, 180 in Brazil, 90 in Ethiopia, 450 in Nigeria, 350 in India. That so many nations are squeezed into so few states is, in fact, the nub of the problem.

In most states, power is in the hands of a few elites, who operate by a simple credo: Winner take all. They control foreign investment and aid, and use both to reinforce their power. They set local commodity prices, con-

trol exports, and levy taxes. The result is that powerless nations often provide most state revenues and receive few services in return. "Development" programs usually allow a state to steal from its nations, whether it be Indian land from North and South America or oil from the Kurds in Iraq. When nations attempt to resist this confiscation of their resources, open conflict results.

Nearly all debt in Africa, and nearly half of all other Third World debt, comes from the purchase of weapons by states to fight their own citizens. Most of the world's twelve million refugees are the offspring of such conflicts, as are most of the hundred million internally displaced people who have been uprooted from their homelands. Conflict theorists view most of the world's famine victims as nation peoples who are being starved by states that assimilate them while taking their food supplies. They also see most of the colonization, resettlement, and villagization programs sponsored by states as an attempt, in the name of progress, to bring nation peoples to their knees.

A vicious cycle forms. The appropriation of a nation's resources leads to conflict, conflict leads to weapons purchases, weapons purchases lead to debt, and debt leads to the appropriation of more resources—and the cycle intensifies.

Now that the cold war is over, the United States and the former USSR are pulling back on aid to many rulers of Third World states. This is likely to unleash more struggle by nations that sense an opportunity to win greater control over their future. The number of shooting wars may increase just at the time when arms makers and NATO and Warsaw Pact countries are trying to dump obsolete weapons and find markets for new ones.

If nations and states are to peacefully coexist, a political system that is built from the bottom up—one that gives autonomy and power to nation peoples—will have to evolve. Beyond this guiding principle, there is no single model. Weak states with strong nations may break into new states. Newly independent nations, after trying to make a go of it for a while, may later decide that it is to their advantage to be part of a larger political unit.

Of one thing we can be certain. The next twenty years will likely be bloody if the world cannot find a better way to answer the demands of its now emboldened nations.

Source: Reprinted with permission from *Mother Jones* magazine, © 1990, Foundation for National Progress.

immersed in vats of ice water in freezing weather, considering their deaths insignificant because the results might save the lives of their fighter pilots shot down over freezing water (Gellhorn 1959). A man can pause in the middle of torturing someone, take a call from his wife to plan dinner, and then calmly resume torturing his victim (Stockwell 1989).

Dehumanization does not always insulate the self from guilt, however, and its failure to do so can bring severe personal consequences. During the war, while soldiers are surrounded by army buddies who agree that the enemy is less than human and deserves inhuman treatment, such definitions ordinarily remain intact. After returning home, however, the dehumanizing definitions more easily break down. Many soldiers then find themselves seriously disturbed by what they did during the war. While most eventually adjust, some cannot, for example, the soldier from California who wrote this note before putting a bullet in his head (Smith 1980).

> I can't sleep anymore. When I was in Vietnam, we came across a North Vietnamese soldier with a man, a woman, and a three- or four-year-old girl. We had to shoot them all. I can't get the little girl's face out of my mind. I hope that God will forgive me . . . I can't.

CDQ 18: Do you foresee a world order developing in the future?

L. Obj. 10: Explain why some theorists believe that there is a possibility that global and economic unity could come about. Note the main strengths and limitations of this viewpoint.

CNN: Internal Conflicts within and among Developing Nations

A COMING WORLD ORDER?

The historical trend has been for states to grow larger and larger. Today, the worldwide flow of information, capital, and goods, has rendered national boundaries increasingly meaningless. As noted in Chapter 14, most European countries have formed an economic unit that supersedes their national boundaries. Similarly, the United Nations is designed to be a political entity that transcends national borders. Designed to moderate disputes between countries, the United Nations can also authorize the use of international force against individual nations—as it did against North Korea in 1950 and Iraq in 1990.

Will this process continue . . . until there is but one state or empire, the earth itself, under the control of one leader? That is a possibility, perhaps deriving not only from these historical trends but also from a push by a powerful group of capitalists who profit from global free trade (Domhoff 1990). Although the trend is in full tilt, even if it continues we are unlikely to see its conclusion during our lifetimes, for national boundaries and national patriotism will die only a hard death. At the same time as borders shift, as occurred with the breakup of the Soviet Union, previously unincorporated nations such as Lithuania and Azerbaijan have clamored for their independence and the right to full statehood. The Perspectives box on page 425 explores the rising tension between nations and states worldwide.

If such global political and economic unity does come about, it is fascinating to speculate on what type of government will result. If Hitler had had his way, his conquests would have resulted in world domination—by a world dictator and a world totalitarian regime. Fortunately, the tendency now is toward greater rights of citizens and greater political participation. If this trend continues—and it is a big "if"—and if a world order does emerge, the potential for human welfare is tremendous. If, however, we end up with totalitarianism, and the world's resources and peoples come under the control of a dictatorship or an oligarchy, the future for humanity could be extremely bleak.

SUMMARY

1. Every group is political, in the sense that power is always a factor. The essential nature of politics is power. The state claims a monopoly on the use of violence, and the ultimate foundation of any political order is violence. The basic human dilemma for citizens is how to establish a government that will protect them from violent groups and individuals but not use violence against them.

2. Weber identified three types of authority: traditional, based on custom; rational-legal, based on law and written procedures; and charismatic, based on an individual's outstanding personal characteristics. Historically, countries have moved from having traditional to rational-legal forms of authority. Charismatic authority threatens both other types. A central problem for all three types of authority is orderly succession, the transfer of leadership in such a way that it does not lead to social instability.

3. Four main forms of government are monarchies, democracies, dictatorships, and oligarchies. Democracies are based on the concept of citizenship, fairly new in world history. The concepts of democracy and citizenship, now finding worldwide appeal, are transforming global politics.

4. Because the United States has a winner-take-all electoral system, political parties must appeal to the center and minority parties make little headway. Many democracies in Europe have a system of proportional representation, which encourages the formation of minority, off-center political parties.

5. In general, the more that people feel they have a stake in the political system, the more likely they are to vote. Americans most likely to vote are whites, the elderly, the rich, the employed, and the highly educated.

6. A fundamental transformation in American politics occurred with the election of Franklin D. Roosevelt in 1932. The Great Depression and FDR's policies in response to it permanently altered political consciousness of Americans. Both Democrats and Republicans adopted the idea that private business is also the government's business.

7. Special-interest groups, with their lobbyists and PACs, play a significant role in American politics. Functionalists view them as part of the pluralistic nature of American politics. One reason PACs have become so important is the huge cost of national elections.

8. The question of who rules America has led to a lively debate among sociologists. Functionalists view the country's thousands of competing interest groups as balancing one another, with no single group dominating. Conflict theorists zero in on the top level of power, where they see a ruling elite consisting of the country's top political, military, and corporate leaders, with the latter's business interests dominant.

9. War, a means to implement political objectives, has been common in both European and United States history. Nicholas Timasheff identified three essential conditions of war: a cultural tradition, an antagonistic situation, and a "fuel" that ignites the antagonistic situation. A particularly high cost of war is dehumanization of the enemy, as a result of which people commit brutal acts that they would condemn in normal circumstances.

10. Are we on the threshold of an international world order? Historical trends and the merging interests of world business leaders indicate that the possibility is growing.

SUGGESTED READINGS

Amnesty International. *Amnesty International Report.* London: Amnesty International Publications, published annually. The reports summarize human rights violations around the world, listing specific instances country by country.

Creveld, Martin van. *The Transformation of War.* New York: The Free Press, 1990. The idea that war is rational—which has guided political affairs to the present—is outmoded. Any strategic planning based on this assumption, which the developed world continues to pursue, is disconnected from current realities.

Domhoff, G. William. *The Power Elite and the State: How Policy Is Made in America.* New York: Aldine de Gruyter, 1990. Domhoff develops the thesis that coalitions within the power elite shape the major policies of the United States.

Dye, Thomas R. *Who's Running America?* 5th ed. Englewood Cliffs, N.J.: Prentice Hall, 1990. To answer the title's question, the author presents an overview of America's power elite.

Mills, C. Wright. *The Power Elite.* New York: Oxford University Press, 1956. This classic analysis elaborates the thesis summarized in this chapter that American society is ruled by the nation's top corporate leaders, together with an elite from the military and political institutions.

Payne, James L. *The Culture of Spending.* San Francisco: Institute for Contemporary Studies, 1992. Using the "culture of the capital" (developing a "persuasion hypothesis") to explain why the United States Congress consistently spends more than it collects in taxes, Payne makes recommendations for changing this culture.

Randall, Vicky. *Women in Politics: An International Perspective.* 2nd ed. Chicago: University of Chicago Press, 1987. Randall compares the role of women in politics in both industrialized and developing nations.

Smoke, Richard, and Willis Harman. *Path to Peace: Exploring the Feasibility of Sustainable Peace.* Boulder, CO: Westview, 1987. The authors examine nine ways to avoid nuclear war, including possible actions by both government leaders and grass-roots movements.

Stiehm, Judith Hicks. *Arms and the Enlisted Woman.* Philadelphia: Temple University Press, 1988. The author presents an overview of American military policy regarding enlisted women.

Timasheff, Nicholas S. *War and Revolution.* Edited with a preface by Joseph F. Scheuer. New York: Sheed and Ward, 1965. A classic analysis; discusses the movement from peace to war, war to peace, and revolution to order.

Journals

Most sociology journals publish articles on politics. Two that focus on this area of social life are *American Political Science Review* and *Social Policy.*

CHAPTER 16

Faith Ringgold, Tar Beach, *1988*

The Family

MARRIAGE AND FAMILY IN CROSS-CULTURAL PERSPECTIVE
 Defining Family ■ Variations across Cultures ■ Common Cultural Themes

MARRIAGE AND FAMILY IN THEORETICAL PERSPECTIVE
 The Functionalist Perspective: Functions and Dysfunctions ■ The Conflict Perspective: Gender, Conflict, and Power ■ *Thinking Critically about Social Controversy:* **The Second Shift—Strains and Strategies** ■ The Symbolic Interactionist Perspective: Marital Communication

THE FAMILY LIFE CYCLE
 The Ideological Context: Love and Courtship ■ *Perspectives:* **East Is East and West Is West . . . Love and Arranged Marriage in India** ■ Marriage ■ *Down-to-Earth Sociology:* **Why Do People Become Jealous? A Sociological Interpretation** ■ Childbirth ■ Child Rearing ■ The Family in Later Life

DIVERSITY IN AMERICAN FAMILIES
 African-American Families ■ Hispanic-American Families (Latinos) ■ Asian-American Families ■ One-Parent Families ■ *Perspectives:* **Peering beneath the Facade—Problems in the Korean-American Family** ■ Families without Children ■ Blended Families ■ Homosexual Families

TRENDS IN AMERICAN FAMILIES
 Postponing Marriage ■ Cohabitation ■ Child Care

DIVORCE AND REMARRIAGE
 Problems in Measuring Divorce ■ Children of Divorce ■ The Ex-Spouses ■ Remarriage

TWO SIDES OF FAMILY LIFE
 Abuse: Battering, Marital Rape, and Incest ■ Families That Work

THE FUTURE OF MARRIAGE AND FAMILY

SUMMARY

SUGGESTED READINGS

On this wet afternoon, a dozen students, aged ten to twelve, are sitting in a circle at Kennedy Elementary School. They are all children of divorce. "It's called a support group," says the school counselor who meets with the children once a week. Despite the fact that divorce is now regarded as part of the American way of life, these children feel deep discomfort and alienation.

Tony earnestly explains, "Sometimes you are too scared to tell your friends. You might be ashamed." A girl named Flora stares at the floor and adds, "Sometimes they say they are just going on a trip. They lied." Says Helen, "After all, the divorce is as much ours as our parents'."

Any adult who has tried to explain a divorce to a happily married friend will understand what the kids call "the brick wall." Happy people do not know, and will not believe, that the phrase, "they fight" can mean a father who says, "If I see your mother, I'll kill her"—and means it. And having to carry messages can mean being used as cannon fodder in support-check battles.

Money is a big topic. "My father sends $350 a month, and I never get to see any of it," Billy says. "Last night he came over to pick up a lamp, and my mother said, 'Children, your father has just stolen a lamp.'"

The "divorced kids" find the parents' new relationships especially difficult. Julie says, "My mother had this man living in the house. I felt as if I was in the way. She would agree with him about things she would object to if it were just us. Mothers don't want to rock the boat with men." "My father wants to marry this woman," says Tony, "and he takes her kids out for doughnuts on Sunday mornings. It really upsets my younger sister; he never did that with us."

"Christmas is such a problem," says Janie. "You feel so guilty about the one you're not with." (Based on O'Reilly 1979)

CDQ 1: Do you think children are the real victims of divorce? Why or why not?

Although husbands and wives often hurt one another during divorce, children are the real victims. They feel helpless and betrayed, caught between two people they love—but who can't stand each other. For them, the future is uncertain, the present unbearable.

Many feel that the real tragedy of divorce is children suffering from their parents' mistakes. Ruptured relationships between husbands and wives and between parents and their children—accompanied by feelings of betrayal, guilt, and anxiety—are symptoms of a major upheaval in the family today. The American divorce rate, the highest in the industrialized world (Sorrentino 1990), is one aspect of marriage and family that we shall explore in this chapter.

MARRIAGE AND FAMILY IN CROSS-CULTURAL PERSPECTIVE

To better understand American patterns of marriage and family, let's first sketch a cross-cultural portrait. The perspective it yields will give us a context for interpreting what we experience in this vital social institution.

Essay #1

TR#37M: Marriage in Cross-Cultural Perspective

Speaker Sug. #1: An anthropologist to discuss marriage and family in cross-cultural perspective

L. Obj. 1: Explain why it is difficult to define the term "family."

CDQ 2: Are there some elements which are essential to marriage and family in all human groups?

Defining Family

"What is a family anyway?" asked William Sayres (1992) at the beginning of an article on this topic. By this question, he meant that although the family is so significant to humans that it is universal—every human group in the world organizes its members in families—the world's cultures display so much variety that the term *family* is difficult to define. For example, although the Western world regards a family as consisting of a husband, wife, and children, other groups have family forms, as shown on Table 16.1, in which men have more than one wife (**polygyny**) or women more than one husband (**polyandry**). To define the family as the approved group into which children are born overlooks the Mentawei of Indonesia, who require that a woman give birth to a child *before* she is allowed to marry. And what about the Banaro of New Guinea? Among this group a young woman must not only give birth before she can marry but cannot consider the father of her child as her future husband (Murdock 1949).

And so it goes. For just about every element, you might consider essential to marriage or family, some group has a different custom. Not even the sex of the bride and groom is unalterable. While in almost every instance the bride and groom are female and male, there are rare exceptions.

In some American Indian tribes, men and women who wanted to be the opposite sex could go through a ceremony (*berdache*) that would *socially* declare them so. Afterwards, they would perform the tasks associated with that sex (whether hunting for the "new" man or cooking for the "new" woman) *and* be allowed to marry—the husband and wife then being of the same biological sex (Amott and Matthaei 1991). Similarly,

polygyny: a marriage in which a man has more than one wife

polyandry: a marriage in which a woman has more than one husband

TABLE 16.1 Marriage in Cross-Cultural Perspective

	Traditional societies	*Modern societies*
Functions	Encompassing (see the 6 functions listed on pp 434–435.)	More limited (many functions now fulfilled by other social institutions)
Structure	Extended (marriage embeds the spouses in a kinship network)	Nuclear (marriage brings fewer obligations toward the spouse's kin)
Number of spouses at one time	Most have one-spouse (*monogamy*), while some have several (*polygamy*). Polygamy is of two types: *polygyny* (most common), two or more wives, and *polyandry* (rare), two or more husbands	One (*monogamy*)
Choice of spouse	Spouse selected by parents, usually the father	Relatively free choice made by the bride and groom
Couple's home	Couples most commonly reside with groom's family (*patrilocal residence*), less commonly with bride's family (*matrilocal residence*)	Couples establish new home (*neolocal residence*)
Line of descent	Most commonly figured from male ancestors (*patrilineal kinship*); less commonly from female ancestors (*matrilineal kinship*)	Figured from male and female ancestors equally (*bilateral kinship*)

in several parts of Africa women of nobility are allowed to marry other women. In these marriages, an unacknowledged lover fathers the children. The mother then follows the prevailing rights of fathers and gives the child her name, status, and property (Levi-Strauss 1956; Querlin 1965). And in the contemporary Western world, Denmark legalized homosexual marriages in 1992.

Even to say that the family is the unit in which children are disciplined and parents are responsible for their material needs doesn't work. For among the Trobriand Islanders, the wife's eldest brother is responsible for making certain that his sister's children are fed and are properly disciplined when they get out of line (Malinowski 1927). Finally, although sexual relationships might be assumed to characterize a husband and wife, the Nayar of Malabar never allow a bride and groom to have sex. In fact, they send the groom packing after a three-day celebration of the marriage—and never allow him to see his bride again (La Barre 1954). (In case you are wondering, the groom comes from another tribe, and Nayar women are allowed to have sex, but only with approved lovers—who can never be the husband. This system keeps family property intact—along matrilineal lines.)

Such remarkable variety means settling for a very broad definition. A **family** is a group of people who consider themselves related by blood, marriage, or adoption.

family: a group of people who consider themselves related by blood, marriage, or adoption; they usually live together

They usually live together—or, as in the case of grown children, at least have lived together.

We can classify families as **nuclear** (husband, wife, and children) and **extended** (including persons such as grandparents, aunts, uncles, and cousins in addition to the nuclear unit). There are also the **family of orientation** (the family in which an individual grows up) and the **family of procreation** (the family formed when a couple have their first child). (A person who is married but has not yet had a child is technically part of a couple, not a family.) Finally, regardless of its form, **marriage** can be viewed as a group's approved mating arrangements—usually marked out by a ritual of some sort (the wedding) to indicate the couple's new public status.

Variations across Cultures

To place marriage and family in greater cross-cultural perspective, let's look at variations in age at marriage, sexual relations, sexual exclusivity, child rearing, and divorce.

Age at Marriage.   Worldwide, most brides and grooms are fairly close in age. In some groups, however, the age gap is huge. In Siberia, for example, Chukchee young women of about twenty marry baby husbands (Levi-Strauss 1956). The bride nurses her little husband, who may be only two or three years old—and cares for him until he is old enough to fulfill his marital duties. The Chukchee feel that the parental care the wife gives her baby husband creates a lasting emotional bond between them as husband and wife.

Members of another group marry at an even younger age. The Tiwi of Northern Australia marry off their babies even before they are born (Hart and Pilling 1960). If a mistake is made in guessing the sex of the child, the father of a newborn simply selects a new bride or groom.

Sexual Relations.   Like the Nayar of Malabar, who prohibit sex between a husband and wife altogether, the Dani of New Guinea also practice sexual customs that vary considerably from those found in most societies (Heider 1972). Many husbands and wives do not even live in the same compound (group of huts). Of those who do, the men sleep in one part of the compound, the women in another. After the birth of a child, a Dani husband and wife abstain from sex for a long period of time—not just for a month or two, but for four or five years!

Most human groups consider sexual fidelity within marriage to be important. Some groups consider this so important that they kill offenders. Although cultural rules may require sexual fidelity for both husband and wife, in practice it is usually the straying wife, not the erring husband, who is killed. Traditional Eskimos provide a well-known exception to this expectation of fidelity (Ruesch 1959). A good host shares his wife with an overnight guest, and both husband and wife are offended if a guest is rude enought to turn down their hospitality. (This custom used to present a problem for anthropologists who did fieldwork among the Eskimos—perhaps not so much for moral reasons as because of the women's custom of making themselves erotic by rubbing their faces with blubber and perfuming themselves with urine poured over their hair.)

Note that having sex with the occasional anthropologist or other overnight guest takes place according to established norms. The wife is not following her own inclinations. Rather, she is *shared*—like property—by her husband.

Child Rearing.   Among some tribal groups, the father bears no responsibility for his children. Instead, as with the Trobriand Islanders and the Nayar mentioned above, those responsibilities go to the wife's eldest brother. An interesting consequence of assigning discipline and nurturing to the child's maternal uncle is that the children owe allegiance to him instead of to their father. Groups that practice this custom conceive of the family in a manner remarkably at odds with Western perception, for their family

CDQ 3: Why do you think marriage is a group's approved mating arrangement?

nuclear family: a family consisting of a husband, wife, and child(ren)

extended family: a nuclear family plus other relatives, such as grandparents, uncles and aunts, who live together

family of orientation: the family in which a person grows up

family of procreation: the family formed when a couple's first child is born

marriage: a group's approved mating arrangements, usually marked by a ritual of some sort

life revolves around the brother-sister relationship rather than the husband-wife relationship.

Divorce. The American divorce rate is certainly high, but it is puny compared with that of the Kanuri of Nigeria (Cohen 1971). In that group, half of all marriages don't even last four years. Some measurements indicate a divorce rate of 99 percent. Divorce is almost exclusively the man's prerogative, for to obtain a divorce a Kanuri man can simply say to his wife, "I divorce you" in front of witnesses. If he chooses, he can simply send his wife a letter instead. The divorce is not registered, nor is any further procedure required.

A Kanuri wife, however, cannot obtain a divorce so easily. She must manipulate her husband into divorcing her. Some wives pick a fight or burn the food. If that does not work, she may refuse to cook or to have sex. If even that fails, a wife might confront her husband in public, tear his robe, scream for the neighbors, and shout insults at him—saying that she will stop making a scene only if he grants a divorce. This tactic generally proves remarkably effective.

In Sum. The wide variety of patterns of marriage and family worldwide illustrates that there is no single way of "experiencing" marriage and family. Rather, in the course of its history, each group has adopted its own cultural patterns. As discussed in Chapter 2, however, humans tend to be enthnocentric, and when it comes to marriage and family, people tend not only to judge other forms as "different," but also as "wrong."

Common Cultural Themes

In spite of this diversity, several common themes do run through marriage and family. All societies use marriage and family to establish patterns of mate selection, descent, inheritance, and authority.

CDQ 4: Do all societies use marriage and family to establish patterns of mate selection, descent, inheritance, and authority? Why or why not?

Patterns of Mate Selection. Because who marries whom is related to the welfare of the community, each group establishes norms to govern who can and cannot marry one another. Norms specifying that people must marry within their own group are called **endogamy,** while rules specifying that people must marry outside their group are known as **exogamy.** Although some norms of mate selection are written into law, most are informal. Most African Americans marry African Americans, for example, although laws of endogamy prohibiting interracial marriages were repealed a couple of generations ago.

Patterns of Descent. How are you related to your father's father or to your mother's mother? The explanation is found in your society's **system of descent,** the pattern by which people trace kinship over generations. It certainly seems logical—and natural—to think of ourselves as related to people on both sides of the family, but this is only one of three logical ways to reckon descent. In the **bilateral** system, descent is traced on both the mother's and the father's side. In a **patrilineal** system, descent is traced only on the father's side, and children are not considered related to their mother's relatives. In a **matrilineal** system, descent is figured only on the mother's side, and children are not considered related to their father's relatives.

endogamy: the practice of marrying within one's own group

exogamy: the practice of marrying outside one's group

system of descent: how kinship is traced over the generations

bilateral: (system of descent) a system of reckoning descent that counts both the mother's and the father's side

patrilineal: (system of descent) a system of reckoning descent that counts only the father's side

matrilineal (system of descent): a system of reckoning descent that counts only the mother's side

Patterns of Inheritance. A primary reason that all societies regulate mate selection and descent is the desire to provide an orderly way of passing property and other rights to the next generation. Marriage and family—in whatever form is customary in a society—are used to trace descent and to compute rights of inheritance. In the bilateral system, property is passed to both males and females, in the patrilineal system only to males, and in the matrilineal system (the rarest form) only to females. Each system matches a people's ideas of justice and logic.

Patterns of Authority.   Historically, some form of **patriarchy,** a social system in which men dominate women, has formed a thread running through all societies. As noted in Chapter 11, there are no historical records of a true **matriarchy,** a social system in which women dominate men. Thus, all marriage and family customs developed within a framework of patriarchy. Although family patterns in the United States are becoming more egalitarian, many customs practiced today still point to their patriarchal origin. The division of household labor, discussed below (pages 436–439), is one such example. Naming patterns also reflect patriarchy. In spite of recent trends, the typical bride still takes the groom's last name, and children, too, are usually given the same last name as their father. (Different naming customs, however, do not signal equality. In Mexico and Spain, both highly patriarchal societies, children are given the last names of both parents.)

MARRIAGE AND FAMILY IN THEORETICAL PERSPECTIVE

A cross-cultural perspective, then, provides a broad context by which to view our own patterns of marriage and family. From it, we can see that our patterns are just one of a wide variety of patterns that humans have chosen. Yet another picture emerges when we apply the three sociological theories.

Essay #2

L. Obj. 2: Discuss the functionalist, conflict, and symbolic interaction perspectives regarding marriage and family.

patriarchy: male control of a society or group

matriarchy: female control of a society or group

The Functionalist Perspective: Functions and Dysfunctions

As noted in Chapter 1, functionalists stress that to survive, society must meet certain basic needs, or functions. When functionalists look at family, they examine how it contributes to the well-being of other parts of society. They also identify its dysfunctions.

Why the Family Is Universal.   As described in Chapter 1, the family serves six essential functions: (1) economic production; (2) socialization of children; (3) care of the sick and aged; (4) recreation; (5) sexual control; and (6) reproduction. For an overview of these functions, see page 21. Functionalists note that the fulfillment of

Because who marries whom is important for society—not simply for the bride and groom—the human group sets up rules about who should marry whom, and then channels its members into its expectations. The norms that surround these newlyweds in Java may differ from those in the West, but they function in the same way to channel mate selection, control sexuality, regulate child birth and inheritance, and so on.

these needs is so essential for the well-being of society that *the family is universal.* That is, to make certain that these functions are performed, every human group has found it necessary to adopt some form of the family. Although the form may vary markedly from one group to another, the functions are the same.

Functions of the Incest Taboo. Functionalists have noted that the **incest taboo**—rules specifying which people are too closely related to have sex or to marry— helps the family avoid role confusion, which in turn facilitates the socialization of children. Consider how legitimizing father-daughter incest would complicate family roles. First, it would disrupt father-daughter roles. If it were OK for fathers to have intercourse with their daughters, could their role still be that of disciplinarian? Or would it change to that of lover, which is quite a different matter? Second, it would disrupt wife-daughter roles. How should the wife treat her daughter—as a daughter, a rival, or as a subservient second wife? Similarly, should the daughter see her mother as a mother or as a rival wife? And her father as a father or as a lover? Third, it would disrupt husband-wife relationships. For example, would the wife be the husband's main wife, a secondary wife—or even "the mother of the other wife" (whatever role that might be)? Similar disruptions would occur with maternal incest (Henslin 1975).

By not allowing individuals to mate within the family, the incest taboo also forces people to look outside the family for marriage partners. Anthropologists theorize that exogamy was especially functional in primitive societies, for it forged alliances between tribes that would otherwise have killed each other off (Beals, Hoijer, and Beals 1977). Today, exogamy extends the individual's social networks beyond the nuclear family, building relationships with the spouse's family.

CDQ 5: Why is it considered necessary for individuals to look outside their own family for marriage partners?

Shifting Foundations of the Family. In addition to studying its functions, functionalists also identify the family's dysfunctions. As noted in Chapter 1, industrialization has made the family much more fragile by eroding its functions. To weaken the family's functions is to weaken the "ties that bind" and to remove the reasons for a family to struggle together against hardships. The consequence is higher divorce, and—as seen in our opening vignette—the pain experienced by the children of divorce. From the functionalist perspective, then, increased divorce does not represent "incompatible personalities" but a shifting foundation of the family itself.

Isolation and Emotional Overload. Functionalists also point out that, unlike the extended family, which is enmeshed in kinship networks, the nuclear family can depend on few people for material and emotional support. Because responsibilities are concentrated among fewer people, the members of a nuclear family are vulnerable to "emotional overload." Thus the loss of a job, extended illness, or death place tremendous strain on family members, tension that may lead to hostility and bitterness (Hartmann 1981; Christensen and Johnsen 1989; Zakuta 1989; DiGiulio 1992). In addition, the relative isolation of the nuclear family makes it easier for the "dark side" of families to emerge—incest and various other forms of abuse, matters that we shall examine later in this chapter.

The Conflict Perspective: Gender, Conflict, and Power

Conflict theorists focus on how the economic institution affects families. The sweeping economic changes reviewed in Chapter 6—such as the industrialization of an agricultural society—forced families to change. Similarly, the changes taking place in today's postindustrial society cannot leave families untouched. Let's look at how gender relations are changing.

CDQ 6: Do you tend to agree with the functionalist or the conflict perspective on the family? Why?

incest taboo: rules specifying the degrees of kinship that prohibit sex or marriage

Gender Relations in the Past. Conflict theorists stress that industrialization placed husbands and wives in such different domains of life that it even changed the character of men and women (Zinn and Eitzen 1990). Historian John Demos (1977) made the following observation.

> The man of the family now became the breadwinner in a special sense. Each day he went out to work: each night he returned. His place of work no longer bore any relation to his home environment. What he did at work was something of which other family members knew little or nothing. His position as husband and father was altered, if not compromised; he was now a more distant, less nurturant figure, but he had special authority, too, because he performed these mysterious activities that maintained the household.

Pushed into the marketplace and separated from the home, men focused on self-advancement and competition; women, in turn, emerged as guardians of the family and home. The ideal qualities of femininity became generosity, sensitivity to the needs of others, and self-sacrifice. This orientation, which has been called "The Cult of True Womanhood," had the effect of controlling women; it underlined the authority of the male as "head" of the family, making it the woman's duty to be submissive to her husband. The wife was to be a comforter and to maintain the home as a private refuge for the male who was exposed to the hardships of economic life (Zinn and Eitzen 1990).

The large number of wives entering the labor force in recent years is also having a profound impact on family roles. Wives are now expected to juggle both career and family at the same time as traditional expectations of male and female roles continue to dominate many aspects of the family. For instance, if a child becomes ill, who is expected to take over? In spite of equal work commitments it is far more often the wife than the husband who assumes this responsibility (Zinn and Eitzen 1990). Thus the gender inequality described in Chapter 11 shows up in basic husband-and-wife relationships in the home.

Power Struggles and Housework.   Among the consequences of married women working for pay is a reshuffling of power in the home. A husband who is the family's sole breadwinner tends to make most of the family's major decisions. When a wife goes to work for wages, however, along with her paycheck comes increased power in the family. Apparently a working wife no longer has to put up with her husband being so dominating, for her income gives her alternatives (Blumstein and Schwartz 1985; Doudna 1983).

In their study of heterosexual couples, Blumstein and Schwartz (1985) found that marital roles have changed so rapidly that couples find it difficult to know how to relate to each other. Previously, traditional roles provided clear answers in many areas of life that are now problematic: who should make the living, do the home repairs, clean the house, bathe the children, do the cooking, and initiate the sex. Today, couples must work out these areas of married life for themselves.

One result is an ongoing struggle between wives and husbands. To reconcile the demands of two jobs with a happy family life is the challenge that couples face—one whose solution is important, but often elusive. As Figure 16.1 shows, it is a rare husband who puts in as many hours doing housework as his wife. As this figure also illustrates, even husbands whose wives are full-time employees do little more housework than husbands whose wives are full-time homemakers. A study in the Netherlands showed identical patterns (Komter 1989).

Sociologist Arlie Hochschild (1989) pointed out that in the *typical* case, after returning home from an eight-hour day of work for wages, the wife puts in a "second shift" doing cooking, cleaning, and child care. She calculated the difference in time spent on housework and found that wives in two-paycheck families average fifteen hours' more work each week than their husbands. Over a year, that means that wives work an *extra month of twenty-four-hour days a year.* Not surprisingly, the burden of the second shift has created deep discontent among wives. Those problems, as well as how wives and husbands cope with them, are discussed in the Thinking Critically section on page 437.

CDQ 7: What is meant by the "second shift?" Do you think most two-paycheck families have worked out an equitable division of household work?

TR#34: Who Does the Housework?

K.P.: Arlie Hochschild

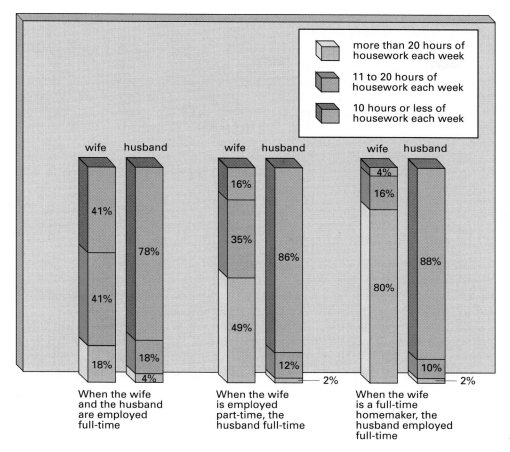

FIGURE 16.1 Who Does the Housework?* (*Source: Current Population Reports,* P-20, No. 418, *Marital Status and Living Arrangements,* March 1986.)

Hochschild (1989) quoted the one-sided nature of the second shift as satirized by Gary Trudeau in the Doonesbury comic strip.

> A 'liberated' father is sitting at his word processor writing a book about raising his child. He types: "Today I wake up with a heavy day of work ahead of me. As Joannie gets Jeffry ready for day care, I ask her if I can be relieved of my usual household responsibilities for the day. Joannie says, 'Sure, I'll make up the five minutes somewhere.'"

THINKING CRITICALLY ABOUT SOCIAL CONTROVERSY

The Second Shift—Strains and Strategies

Sociologist Arlie Hochschild (1989) wanted to find out what life was like in two-paycheck families. For nine years she and her research associates interviewed and reinterviewed fifty-odd families. Hochschild also did participant observation with a dozen of them. She "shopped with them, visited friends, watched television, ate with them, walked through parks, and came along when they dropped their children at day care." She even interviewed the child-care workers.

Hochschild noted that women have no more time in a day than when they stayed home, but that now there is twice as much to get done. Most wives and husbands in her sample felt that the second shift—the household duties that follow the day's work for pay—is the wife's responsibility. But as they cook, vacuum, and take care of the children after their job in the office or factory, many wives feel overtired, emotionally drained, and resentful. Not uncommonly, these feelings show up in the bedroom, where the wives show a lack of interest in sex.

It isn't that men do nothing around the house. But since they see household responsibilities as the wife's duty, they "help out" when they feel like it—or when they get nagged into it. And since most parents would rather tend to their children than clean house, men are more likely to "contribute" to the second shift by taking children to do "fun" things—to see movies, visit the zoo, and go for outings in the park. In contrast, the woman's time with the children is more likely to be "maintenance"—feeding and bathing them, taking them to the doctor, and so on.

The strains from working the second shift affect not only the marital relationship, but also the self-concept. Here is how Hochschild (1989) described one woman who tried to buoy her flagging self-esteem.

> After taking time off for her first baby, Carol Alston felt depressed, "fat," "just a housewife," and for a while became the supermarket shopper who wanted to call down the aisles, "I'm an MBA! I'm an MBA!"

In two cases the second shift presents little problem. In the first, about 20 percent of husbands actually do their share of work on the second shift. In the second case, the wife and the husband both feel that the second shift is the wife's responsibility, and she works the second shift more or less unquestioningly.

For most families, however, the second shift poses severe problems. Most wives feel strongly that the second shift should be shared, but many husbands disagree. Some wives feel that it is hopeless to try to get their husbands to change. They work the second shift, but they resent it. Others have a "showdown" with their husbands, some even giving the ultimatum, "It's share the second shift, or it's divorce." Still others try to be "supermom" who can do it all.

Men counter with strategies of their own. Some cooperate and cut down on their commitment to a career. Others lower their expectations of time to be spent alone with their wives and cut back on movies, seeing friends, doing hobbies.

Most men, however, engage in what Hochschild described as strategies of resistance. She identified the following:

Playing Dumb.   When they do household tasks, some men show incompetence. They can't cook rice without burning it; when they go to the store, they forget grocery lists; they can never remember where the broiler pan is. Hochschild did not claim that men do these things purposely, but, rather, that by withdrawing their mental attention from the task they "get credit for trying and being a good sport," but do it in such a way that they are not chosen next time.

Waiting It Out.   By waiting to be asked to do household chores, many men force their wives to take on the additional chore of the asking itself. Since many wives dislike asking because it feels like "begging," this strategy often works. Some men make this strategy even more effective by showing irritation or becoming glum when they are asked, discouraging the wife from asking again.

Needs Reduction.   The best example of this strategy is a father of two who explained that he never shopped because he didn't "need anything." He didn't need to iron his clothes because he "[didn't] mind wearing a wrinkled shirt." He didn't need to cook because "cereal is fine." As Hochschild observed, "Through his reduction of needs, this man created a great void into which his wife stepped with her 'greater need' to see him wear an ironed shirt . . . take his shirts to the cleaners . . . and cook his dinner."

Substitute Offerings.   Expressing appreciation to the wife for her being so organized that she can handle both work for wages and the second shift at home can be a substitute for helping. In this way, some husbands subtly encourage their wives to keep on working the second shift.

Hochschild (1991) is confident that such problems can be solved. Use the materials in this chapter and others to

1. Identify the underlying social causes of the problem of the second shift;
2. Identify, based on your answer to number 1, social solutions to this problem;
3. Determine how a working wife and husband might best reconcile this problem in their own marriage. ■

The Symbolic Interactionist Perspective: Marital Communication

Project 1

The Importance of Talk. As noted in Chapter 1, symbolic interactionists focus on the meanings that people give their relationships. Even if newlyweds have grown up in the same society, *she* has learned a world of feminine expectations, *he* a world of masculine ones. In marriage, the new couple must merge these two worlds, not an altogether easy task.

As sociologists Peter Berger and Hansfried Kellner (1992) noted, the primary means by which a couple unite their separate worlds is conversation. By talking about their experiences, a couple share their ideas and feelings. The more they talk to each other, the more their perceptions and ideas merge. Talking allows a couple to see things from increasingly closer perspectives, helping them to overcome the separateness that society has created by throwing males and females into different corners of life.

K.P.: Peter Berger and Hansfried Kellner

Two Marriages in One. Although symbolic interactionists have found that husband-wife talk brings spouses closer to one another, they also have found that huge gulfs remain. In a classic work, sociologist Jessie Bernard (1972) wrote that when researchers

K.P.: Jessie Bernard

> ask husbands and wives identical questions about the union they often get quite different replies. There is usually agreement on the number of children they have and a few other such verifiable items, although not, for example, on length of premarital acquaintance and of engagement, on age at marriage and interval between marriage and birth of first child. Indeed, with respect to even such basic components of the marriage as frequency of sexual relations, social interaction, household tasks, and decision making, they seem to be reporting on different marriages.

At first the researchers interpreted the differences as due to methodological inadequacies. They felt that if they had developed better ways to interview couples, the answers of husbands and wives would agree. Gradually, however, the researchers concluded that because husbands and wives hold down different corners of the marriage they actually perceive the marriage differently. In fact, their experiences contrast so sharply that *every marriage contains two separate marriages:* the wife's and the husband's.

With regard to sexual relations, for example, why—since the husband and wife are referring to the same instances of making love—wouldn't they agree on such a basic matter as how frequently they have sex? The answer lies in differing *perceptions* of lovemaking. It appears that in the typical marriage the wife desires greater emotional involvement from her husband, while the husband's desire is for more sex (Komter 1989; Barbeau 1992). When questioned about sex, then, the husband, feeling deprived, tends to underestimate it, while the wife, more reluctant to participate in sex because of unsatisfied intimacy needs, overestimates it (Bernard 1972).

CDQ 8: Can you explain why symbolic interactionists believe every marriage contains two separate marriages?

In Sum. Both functionalists and conflict theorists examine the macro level. Functionalists analyze how the family has grown more fragile as other social institutions have eroded its traditional functions. Conflict theorists examine how the family responds to economic change. They note that today's marriages are marked by a power struggle between husbands and wives because, while wives have entered the labor force in large numbers, traditional roles are only slowly giving way. In their focus on the micro level, symbolic interactionists observe family interaction. They note the central role that communication plays in the adjustment of husbands and wives to one another and the way in which talk is the primary means used to merge a husband's and wife's separate worlds.

THE FAMILY LIFE CYCLE

Project 2

Essay #3

Speaker Sug. #2: A colleague who is conducting innovative research on some aspect of marriage and family life

L. Obj. 3: Outline the major developments in each stage of the family life cycle.

CNN: Marriage Survey

CDQ 9: Do you think all societies share the American infatuation with romantic love? How is this notion promoted in the United States?

Thus far we have seen how widely the forms of marriage and family vary around the world and have examined marriage and family from the three sociological perspectives. We now turn the focus onto American society. Here, we discuss the family life cycle (especially courtship and romantic love), diversity and trends in American families, divorce, and remarriage. We shall also look at the "dark side" of families and, finally, examine what makes marriage work.

The Ideological Context: Love and Courtship

Romantic Love.   As noted in Chapter 2, romantic love is a paramount American value. Images of romance so pervade American culture—its folk stories, music, and mass media—that 80 percent of college students believe romantic love to be the single most important factor in marriage (Roper 1985). Ideas of romantic love provide the ideological context in which Americans seek their mates and form families.

Not all societies share this American infatuation with romantic love. For example, India, where parents arrange the marriages and the divorce rate is low, provides a marked contrast to these assumptions. The Perspectives box on page 441 shows that young people even *like* the idea that parents arrange their marriage. Such a view—just as in cultures where love is considered the ideal basis for marriage—depends on a set of assumptions about the way the world of marriage and family ought to operate.

In the United States, as in other Western societies, because love is thought essential to marriage, it plays a significant role in everyday life. Accordingly, social scientists have probed this concept with the tools of the trade—laboratory experiments, questionnaires, interviews, and systematic observations. One of the more interesting experiments was conducted by psychologists Donald Dutton and Arthur Aron (Rubin 1985), who discovered that fear breeds love. Across a rocky gorge, about 230 feet above the Capilano River in North Vancouver, a rickety footbridge sways in the wind. Another footbridge, a solid structure, crosses only ten feet above a shallow stream. An attractive female experimenter approached men who were crossing these bridges, asking if they would take part in her study of "the effects of exposure to scenic attractions on creative expression." She then showed them a picture, and they wrote down their associations. The researchers, who measured the sexual imagery in the men's stories, found that the men on the unsteady, frightening bridge were more sexually aroused than the men on the solid bridge. They were also more likely to call the young woman afterward—supposedly to get more information about the study.

This research, of course, was really about sexual attraction, not love. The point, however, is that romantic love is usually initiated by sexual attraction. We find ourselves sexually attracted to someone, spend time with that person, and discover mutual interests. If this pattern continues, we eventually label our feelings "love." Apparently, then, romantic love has two components. The first is emotional, a feeling of sexual attraction. The second is cognitive, a label that we attach to our feelings. If we do attach this label, we describe ourselves as being "in love."

East Is East and West Is West . . .:
Love and Arranged Marriage in India

After Arun Bharat Ram returned home with a degree from the University of Michigan, his mother announced that she wanted to find him a wife. Arun would be a good "catch" anywhere: twenty-seven years old, good education, good manners, intelligent, handsome—and heir to one of the largest fortunes in India. Nonetheless, Arun would not consider selecting a mate on his own.

Arun's mother already had someone in mind. Manju, who came from a solid, middle-class family, was also a college graduate. Both she and her parents had good reputations. Arun and Manju met in a coffee shop in a luxury hotel—along with both sets of parents. He found her pretty and quiet. He liked that. She was impressed that he didn't boast about his background.

After four more meetings, one with the two alone, the parents asked their children if they were willing to marry. Neither had any major objections.

Prime Minister Indira Ghandi and fifteen hundred other guests came to the wedding.

"I didn't love him," Manju says, "But when we talked, we had a lot of things in common." She then adds, "But now I couldn't live without him. I've never thought of another man since I met him."

Although India has undergone extensive social change, Indian sociologists estimate that about 95 percent of marriages are still arranged by the couple's parents. Today, however, as with Arun and Manju, modern couples have veto power over their parents' selection. Another innovation is that the couple are allowed to talk to each other before the wedding—unheard of just a generation ago.

The fact that arranged marriages are the norm in India does not mean that this ancient land is without a tradition of passion and love. Far from it. The *Kamasutra* is world-renowned for its explicit details about lovemaking, and the erotic sculptures at Khajuraho still startle Westerners today. Indian mythology extols the copulations of gods, and every Indian schoolchild knows the love story of the god Krishna and Radha, the beautiful milkmaid he found irresistible.

Why, then, does India have arranged marriages, and why does this practice persist today, even among the educated middle and upper classes?

Arranged marriage must be seen in the context of India's total culture, especially as one component of its caste system. As seen in Chapter 9, India's millennia-old caste system continues with but few modifications ushered in by law. Although public schools are open to all castes, and supposedly all government jobs also, the caste system remains intact. Arranged marriage, then, is one means by which parents ensure that young people do not marry outside their caste. If love were allowed to be the basis of marriage, the caste divisions might begin to crumble.

As a consequence of their very different histories, India and the United States have developed dissimilar cultures. Contrasting approaches to love and marriage are but one aspect of social life among many that distinguish each. In the United States, individual mate selection matches ideals of individuality and independence, two of the core cultural values described in Chapter 2, while the practice of arranged marriage in India matches ideals of proper relationships between caste members and of reciprocal obligations between parents and children.

To Indians, to practice unrestricted dating would be to trust important matters to inexperienced young people. It would encourage premarital sex, which, in turn, would break down family lines that virginity at marriage assures the upper castes. Consequently, Indian young people are socialized to think that parents have cooler heads, greater experience, and superior wisdom in these matters. In the United States family lines are much less important, and caste is an alien concept.

Even ideas of love differ. For Indians, love is a more peaceful emotion, based on long-term commitment and devotion to family. While Americans might follow them that far, Indians go one step farther and think of love as something that can be "created" between two people. To do so, one needs to arrange the right conditions. And in Indian culture, marriage is one of the right conditions that create love.

Thus, Indian and American cultures have produced not just different, but opposite, approaches to love and marriage. For Indians, marriage produces love—while for Americans, love produces marriage. Americans see love as having a mysterious element, a passion that "grabs" the individual. Indians see love as a peaceful feeling that develops when a man and a woman are united in intimacy and share common interests and goals in life.

Source: Based on Bumiller 1989; Cooley 1962; Gupta 1979; Loomis and Loomis 1965; Merton 1976; Prakasa and Rao 1979; Weintraub 1988; Whyte 1992.

Marriage

In the typical case, marriage in the United States is preceded by "love," but contrary to folklore, whatever love is, it certainly is not blind. That is, love does not hit anyone willy-nilly, as if Cupid had shot darts blindly into a crowd. If it did, since Americans consider love the proper basis for marriage, their marital patterns would be practically unpredictable. An examination of marital patterns in the United States, however, reveals that love is socially channeled. Even its related emotion, jealousy, has a social base, as discussed in the Down-to-Earth Sociology box below.

CDQ 10: Why do most individuals in the United States marry others who are similar in age, education, social class, race, and religion to themselves? How do people react when a person marries someone with very different characteristics from his or her own?

homogamy: the tendency of people with similar characteristics to marry one another

propinquity: spatial nearness

property: the rights, by law or custom, to act toward something in certain ways

erotic property: persons about whom one feels jealous

The Social Channels of Love and Marriage.   Love and marriage are channeled by age, education, social class, race, and religion (Tucker and Mitchell-Kerman 1990; Schoen and Wooldredge 1989; Schoen et al. 1989; Zinn and Eitzen 1990). For example, an African-American female with a college degree whose parents are both physicians is likely to fall in love and marry a black male slightly older than herself who has graduated from college, whose parents are both professionals. In contrast, a white female who is a high school dropout and whose parents are on welfare is likely to fall in love and marry a white male who comes from a background similar to hers. As with all social patterns, there are exceptions. Figure 16.2 illustrates one of the exceptions. About 0.4 percent of the 56 million married couples in the United States (about 220,000 couples) are racially mixed.

Sociologists use the term **homogamy** to refer to the tendency of people with similar characteristics to marry one another (South 1991). Homogamy occurs largely as a result of **propinquity,** or spatial nearness. That is, people who live near one another, or who associate with one another at school, church, or work, also tend to "fall in love" and marry one another. These persons are far from a random sample of the population, for social filters produce neighborhoods and churches that follow race and social class lines.

DOWN-TO-EARTH SOCIOLOGY

Why Do People Become Jealous? A Sociological Interpretation

One might wonder why sociologists would study jealousy, for it is usually considered a psychological matter. Sociologists have probed this emotion, however, and have found that jealousy, like love, follows *social* channels.

The *sociological* base of jealousy becomes apparent from the unique approach taken by sociologist Randall Collins (1989). He began by noting that **property** consists not only of material goods, but also of rights to act toward them in certain ways. For example, owning a car means having the right to drive it, to give someone else permission to drive it, to trade it, or even to beat it with a hammer.

Collins took the principle that property equals rights one step further and applied it to people. This idea may sound strange at first, but, as he indicated, in everyday life we refer to someone as "mine" (*my* father, mother, boyfriend, girlfriend) versus "not mine" (*your* brother, sister, husband, wife, and so on). By this, we refer to our rights—or lack of rights—concerning how we can act toward people. For example, if you refer to someone as "my" mother you probably expect her to comfort you when you have a problem, and perhaps, to loan you money when you are broke. If "your" mother did this for me, it would be kindness, or a favor, not a right that I had.

To this idea, Collins then added another concept—that some couples become each other's **erotic property.** By this, he did not mean to imply that they in any sense "own" each other, but rather that the relationship provides both partners with a right of sexual access. Each then feels the right to feel jealous toward the other. From this perspective, marriage in Western society is a way of declaring that a husband and wife have an exclusive mutual claim as each other's erotic property. Accordingly, a spouse will become jealous if a rival appears on the scene.

This principle holds cross-culturally, declared Collins, following whatever marital patterns a group may have. For example, the Toda, who live in Southern India (Murdock 1949), are poor and practice female infanticide, one consequence of which is a shortage of women. Because of it, Toda brothers marry the same wife. The brothers are not jealous of one another, because the wife is not the exclusive erotic property of just one husband, but of them all. The husbands, however, would all become jealous if their wife were to show an erotic interest in some other man.

Essential to jealousy among mates, then, is the quality of exclusive sexual access to erotic property. This points to the *sociological* basis of jealousy, for such relationships are *socially* determined, differing from one culture to another.

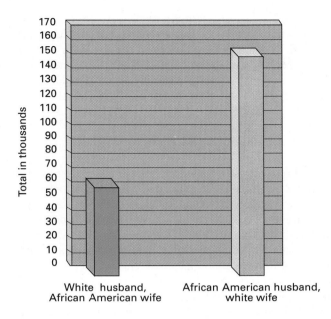

FIGURE 16.2 The Racial Background of Husbands and Wives in Marriages between Whites and African Americans. (*Source: Statistical Abstract of the United States,* 1991: Table 54.)

Childbirth

Sociologist Martin Whyte (1992), who interviewed wives in the greater Detroit area, found that marital satisfaction usually decreases with the birth of a child. To explain why, recall from Chapter 6 that a dyad (just two persons) provides greater intimacy than a triad (after adding a third person, interaction must be shared). To move from the theoretical to the practical, think about the practical implications of coping with a newborn—heavy expenses, less free time (feeding, soothing, and diaper changing), a lot less sleep, and a decrease in sexual relations (Rubenstein 1992). (See Table 16.2 for a summary of how often American couples make love.)

Sociologist Lillian Rubin (1976), who compared fifty working-class families with twenty-five middle-class families, found that social class significantly influences the way in which couples adjust to the arrival of children. The working-class couples had their first baby just nine months after marriage. These couples hardly had time to adjust to being husband and wife before they were thrust into the demanding roles of mother and father. The result was huge tension, financial problems, bickering, and interference from in-laws. The young husbands generally weren't ready to "settle down" and resented getting less attention from their wives. A working-class husband who became a father just five months after getting married made a telling statement to Rubin (1976) when he said, "There I was, just a kid myself, and I finally had someone *to take care of me*. Then suddenly, I had to take care of a kid, and she was too busy with him *to take care of me*" (italics added).

In contrast, Rubin found the middle-class parents much more prepared. They not only had more resources, they also postponed the birth of the first child allowing more

TABLE 16.2 How Often Do American Couples Make Love?

	Number of times per month			
Years together	*12 or more*	*4–12*	*1–4*	*1 or less*
0–2	45%	38%	11%	6%
2–10	27%	46%	21%	6%
10 or more	18%	45%	22%	16%

Source: Based on Blumstein and Schwartz, 1983.

time to adjust to each other. For them, on average, the first baby arrived three years after marriage. Similarly, in their study of middle-class couples, sociologists Brent Miller and Donna Sollie (1985) found that the greatest problem the newborn brought was disorderliness and unpredictability. To cope, the couples tried to become more flexible, patient, and organized. The newborn's arrival generally brought middle-class couples closer to one another, making them value their husband-wife relationship even more.

Child Rearing

Social class is also important in child rearing. As noted in Chapter 3, sociologist Melvin Kohn (1959, 1963, 1976, 1977) found that parents of each class socialize their children into the norms of their respective work worlds. Because members of the working class are more closely supervised and are expected to follow explicit rules laid down for them by others, their concern is less with their children's motivation and more with outward conformity. They are more apt to use physical punishment. In contrast, middle-class parents, who are expected to take more initiative on the job, are more concerned that their children develop curiosity, self-expression, and self-control. They are more likely to withdraw privileges or affection than to use physical punishment.

Often invisible to us is how the historical period sets the context of child rearing. An emerging pattern in the United States at this historical point is for fathers to be more active in child rearing (Greif 1985; Ehrensaft 1987, 1989). In addition to performing basic tasks such as putting their children to bed or feeding them, today's fathers are also more likely to participate in their children's intimate life—from joining in fantasy to helping them work out their fears.

Parents exhibit "gender styles" in parenting, especially in play. Researchers have found that fathers are more physical with young children than mothers, and much more

CDQ 12: What examples can you give of gender styles your parents exhibited when they were rearing you or your siblings?

As increasing numbers of women have taken jobs outside the home, fathers have become more involved in rearing their children. As a consequence, more and more children will observe and imitate role models different from those of the previous generation. Slowly, then, change occurs in basic relationships. The change is gradual, however, and at this point in history almost all American wives/mothers retain primary responsibility for the care of their children.

likely than their wives to wrestle and roughhouse with them (Easterbrooks and Goldberg 1984). Mothers, in contrast, tend to be more verbal and to play quieter games such as "peek-a-boo." Play is not a meaningless activity, and these distinct styles teach children both to associate different kinds of behaviors with each sex, and to adopt those themselves.

Birth order is also significant in child rearing. Firstborns tend to be disciplined more than children who follow, but they also receive considerably more attention (White, Kaban, and Attanucci 1979). When the next child arrives, the firstborn competes to maintain the attention. Researchers suggest that this instills in firstborns a greater drive for success, which is why they are more likely than their siblings to earn higher grades in school, to go to college, and to go further in college. Firstborns are even more likely to become astronauts, to appear on the cover of *Time* magazine, and to become president of the United States. Although subsequent children may not go as far, neither are they as intense about being successful, and they are more relaxed in their relationships (Forer 1976; Goleman 1985; Snow, Jacklin, and Maccoby 1981). Certainly these are not hard-and-fast rules, however. As with any description of general trends, many variations exist.

Some analysts are concerned that American children are pressured into growing up too quickly. Psychologist David Elkind (1981) coined the term "hurried child" to describe the process in which social pressures from the family, school, and the mass media encourage children to take on roles beyond their age. As a consequence, many children no longer look like children; they wear clothing, hairstyles, makeup, and jewelry that make them look older. Many analysts are especially concerned that young children are exposed to highly violent and explicitly sexual television programs, videos, and music. The consequences of "hurrying" children in this way are yet to be seen.

The Family in Later Life

The Myth of the Empty Nest. After the last child leaves home, the husband and wife are left, as at the beginning of their marriage, "alone together." This situation, sometimes called the **empty nest,** is thought to signal a difficult time of adjustment for women—especially those who have not worked outside the home—because they have devoted so much energy to a child-rearing role that is now gone. Sociologist Lillian Rubin (1992), however, who interviewed both career women and homemakers, found that the negative picture painted by the "empty nest" syndrome is largely a myth. Contrary to the stereotype, she found that women's satisfaction generally *increases* when the last child leaves home. Similar findings have come from other researchers, who report that most mothers feel relieved, finally able to spend more time on themselves (Whyte 1992). A typical statement was made by a forty-five-year-old woman, who leaned forward in her chair as though to tell Professor Rubin a secret.

> To tell you the truth, most of the time it's a big relief to be free of them, finally. I suppose that's awful to say. But you know what, most of the women I know feel the same way. It's just that they're uncomfortable saying it because there's all this talk about how sad mothers are supposed to be when the kids leave home.

Other sociologists report that many couples feel a renewed sense of companionship at this time (Kalish 1982). This closeness appears to stem from four causes: (1) the couple is free of the many responsibilities of child rearing; (2) they have more leisure; (3) their income is at its highest; (4) at the same time, their financial obligations are reduced.

Retirement. Many older people in the United States view giving up work as a welcome opportunity to do things they never had time for. For others—these whose sense of self-concept is intricately tied into their job—retirement poses a threat. Those forced into retirement face the loss of a valued role and become unwilling participants

CDQ 13: Do you think most parents experience the empty nest? Why or why not?

K.P.: Lillian Rubin

empty nest: a married couple's domestic situation after the last child has left home

in the social disengagement discussed in Chapter 13. Whether willing or reluctant to retire, one of the problems of the preretirement period is the frustrating task of trying to compute how long one's resources are likely to last based on one's life expectancy and determining a rough estimate of annual expenses in the face of unknown inflation.

Widowhood.   Women are more likely than men to face the problem of adjusting to widowhood, for not only does the average woman live longer than a man but she has also married a man older than herself. The death of a spouse is a wrenching away of identities that have merged through the years (DiGiulio 1992). Now that the one who had become an essential part of the self is gone, the survivor, as in adolescence, is forced once again to wrestle with the perplexing question, "Who am I?"

Sociologist Robert Atchley (1975) found that widowhood is less lonely and anxious for people who maintain active social lives, while sociologist Starr Hiltz (1989) found that adjustment is more difficult if the death was unexpected. Survivors who know that death is impending make preparations that smooth the transition—from arranging finances to psychologically preparing themselves for being alone. Saying goodbye and cultivating treasured last memories are important in adjusting to the death of an intimate companion.

DIVERSITY IN AMERICAN FAMILIES

It is important to note at the outset that there is no such thing as *the* American family. Rather, family life and characteristics vary widely throughout the United States. The significance of social class, stressed above, will continue to be evident as we examine diversity in families—race and ethnicity, one-parent families, childless families, blended families, and homosexual families.

African-American Families

Note that the heading is African-American *families,* not *the* African-American family. There is no such thing as *the* African-American family any more than there is *the* white family or *the* Hispanic-American family. The primary distinction is not between blacks

CDQ 14: Is there such a thing as the American family? Why or why not?

Essay #4

CDQ 15: In what ways are the experiences of African-American, Hispanic-American, and Asian-American families similar? In what ways are they different?

L. Obj. 4: State the unique problems experienced by African-American, Hispanic-American, and Asian-American families.

Sociologists have found that the empty nest is not so empty after all. Instead of being filled with regrets and loneliness after the last child leaves home, most married couples find a time of fulfillment, financial ease, leisure and a period of renewed acquaintanceship.

and whites, Hispanics and blacks, and so on, but between social classes, especially those who live in poverty and those who do not.

As with other groups, the family life of African Americans differs according to social class (Lerner 1979; Gatewood 1990). The upper, or capitalist, class is extremely concerned with maintaining family lineage. Following the class interests reviewed in Chapter 10—preservation of position of privilege and family fortune—they are especially concerned about the family background of those whom their children marry. To them, marriage is viewed as a merger of family lines. Children of this class marry later than children of other classes (Zinn and Eitzen 1990).

Middle-class African-American families focus on achievement and respectability. Both husband and wife are likely to work outside the home. Their concerns are that the family stay intact and that their children go to college, get good jobs, and marry well—that is, marry people like themselves, respectable and hardworking, who want to get ahead in school and pursue a successful career.

African-American families in poverty face all the problems that poverty brings. Because the men are likely to have few skills and to be unemployed, it is difficult for them to fulfill the cultural roles of husband and father. Consequently, these families are likely to be headed by a female and to have a high rate of unwed motherhood. Divorce and desertion are also more common than among other classes. Sharing scarce resources and stretching kinship are primary survival mechanisms. That is, people who have helped out in hard times are considered brothers or sisters, to whom one owes obligations as though they were blood relatives (Stack 1974).

African-American females are more likely than other racial groups to marry men who are less educated than they are themselves, who are unemployed, or who are divorced. The reason is a *marriage squeeze*, that is, among African Americans there are fewer unmarried males per one hundred unmarried females than is the case in other racial and ethnic groups. Because they can find fewer eligible partners, African-American women marry individuals with comparatively less desirable characteristics than they themselves possess (South 1991).

Like other groups, there is no such thing as the *African-American family. Social class is the significant factor that makes divorce, employment, number of children, and type of husband-wife roles more or less likely.*

Hispanic-American Families (Latinos)

The characteristics of Hispanic-American families follow the same general social class outline sketched above. Figure 16.3 compares the household formations of Hispanic Americans, African Americans, and whites. On the proportion of married couples and

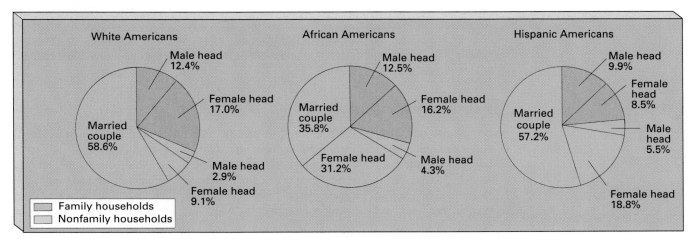

Note: White Americans refers to non-Hispanics.

FIGURE 16.3 Percentage of United States Households Headed by Males, Females, and Married Couples. (*Source: Statistical Abstract of the United States,* 1991: Table 58.)

More than any other characteristic, Hispanic Americans are set apart by their country of origin, and, often, by the use of Spanish. Researchers have found that Hispanic families tend to be larger than average, with the mother making most of the day-to-day decisions. Within this general context, including broad disapproval of divorce, social class is a primary factor in determining family specifics.

female-headed families, Hispanic Americans fall in between whites and African Americans, a relativity that holds for many social characteristics—education, income, poverty, infant mortality, sick days, unemployment, and so on.

A primary distinction among Hispanic Americans is their country of origin. Families from Cuba, for example, are more likely to be headed by a married couple than are those from Puerto Rico. What really distinguishes Hispanic-American families, however, is culture—especially the Spanish language, the Roman Catholic religion, a strong family orientation with a disapproval of divorce, and **machismo,** an emphasis on male strength and dominance. In Chicano families (those originating from Mexico), the husband-father plays a stronger role than in either white or African-American families (Vega 1990). He tends to be close to the younger children, more remote with the older ones (Mirande 1985). The wife-mother, while not having the prestige or status of the husband-father, makes most of the day-to-day decisions for the family and does the routine disciplining of the children. She is usually more family-centered than her mate, displaying more warmth and affection to her children. Hispanic-American families also tend to be more extended than either African-American or white families, and the sexual double standard—males allowed to be more sexually active than females—is also more likely to prevail.

As sociologist William Vega (1990) noted, more research is needed to ascertain whether these generalizations are accurate. As with all other groups, individual Hispanic-American families vary.

Asian-American Families

Sociologist Bob Suzuki (1985) pointed to cultural differences that distinguish Chinese-American and Japanese-American families from most others. Although they have adopted the nuclear family common in the United States, they have retained Confucian values that provide a distinct framework for family life: humanism, collectivity, self-discipline, hierarchy, wisdom of the elderly, moderation, and obligation. Obligation means that each individual owes respect to other family members and carries the responsibility never to bring shame on the family. Asian Americans tend to be more permissive than Anglos in child rearing and more likely to use shame and guilt rather than physical punishment to control their children's behavior.

Immigrants find that their old and new cultures clash, making it difficult for them to hold onto their old culture. Caught between two cultures—neither ready to give up

machismo: an emphasis on male strength and dominance

As detailed in this chapter, diversity is the hallmark of American families. "The American family" does not exist; rather, the United States has many types of families. Although ethnicity is one of the criteria by which we can analyze families, social class differences cut across ethnicity.

the old nor yet prepared to accept the new—family relationships sometimes suffer severely. Fractures in the Korean-American family are explored in the Perspectives box on page 450.

In Sum.   Social class and culture hold the key to understanding family life. Race by itself signifies little, if anything. The more resources a family has, the more it assumes the middle-class characteristics of a nuclear family consisting of husband, wife, and children. Compared with the poor, middle-class families have fewer children and unmarried mothers, and place greater emphasis on educational achievement and deferred gratification.

One-Parent Families

To understand single-parent families, consider the following five significant points. Poor persons, regardless of race or ethnicity, are more likely to form one-parent families. As we saw in Figure 16.3, one-parent families are three to seven times more likely to be headed by a female than a male. For almost all racial and ethnic groups, unwed motherhood has risen sharply—overall, one of every four American children is born to a woman who is not married (*Statistical Abstract* 1991: Table 92). As discussed in Chapter 11, females are paid less than males. Finally, the less educated earn less. The result of these converging factors is that one-parent families are overwhelmingly likely to be poor.

To understand the typical one-parent family, then, we need to view it through the lens of poverty; for that is its primary source of strain (Reimers 1984). The results are serious, not just for these parents and their children, but for society as a whole. Children from single-parent families are more likely to drop out of school, to become delinquent, to be poor as adults, to divorce, and to bear children outside marriage

Peering beneath the Facade—Problems in the Korean-American Family

The face that most Americans see is that of model citizens—hardworking, striving, studious people living in closely knit families. Another face has begun to peer out, however, one that shows serious cracks in the solidarity of Korean-American families—problems of quarrelling, wife abuse, divorce, and juvenile delinquency.

In a surprise twist, these family problems derive from the very characteristics that have helped Korean Americans adapt to their new homeland. As the pastor of the Korean Presbyterian Church in Beltsville, Maryland, tells his parishioners, "You work too hard. You must slow down, or your workaholism is going to cause mental and physical breakdowns." Many of his flock toil fourteen hours a day in their mom-and-pop stores. Not unlike his flock, the pastor himself worked several jobs to get through the seminary.

To understand the problem, consider the impact that American life is having on Korean immigrants. In Korea, the family is modeled after Confucian ideals of discipline and hierarchy: The husband-father is the undisputed head of the family, and his wife and children owe him unquestioning respect and obedience. Here, however, the cultures clash, and the traditional hierarchy of the Korean family is breaking down.

Wives in Korea rarely work, but among the immigrants about two-thirds do—usually putting in long hours alongside their husbands in the family business. In addition, the wives also take care of the home, make the dinner, and care for the children. Many wives feel guilty that they don't spend enough time with their children.

Although most Korean-born wives follow tradition and remain quietly respectful, some are no longer willing to accept their demure place behind their husbands. After getting their first taste of economic success, wives have begun to speak up. Their complaints about being overtired and lacking time for the children, however, are met with confusion and resistance. Already burdened by their own long hours at work, and frustrated by the difficult task of adjusting to a new culture, some husbands grow silent at their wives' behavior, refusing to address the issue at all. Others shout and break things. A few even turn to alcohol and violence.

All immigrants face the thorny problem of deciding what to keep of their old way of life. To shed one's lifelong culture tears at the heart, for it comes from childhood. In contrast, the new generation, born in the host country, has trouble understanding the ways of their parents. So Korean immigrants are finding what the millions of Italians, Germans, Irish, and others from hundreds of other countries experienced before them.

Source: Based on Mintz and Pae 1988; Sue and Wagner 1973; Suzuki 1985; Thomas and Znaniecki 1918; Young 1991; Whyte 1992.

themselves (Dornbusch et al. 1985; McLanahan 1985; Weisner and Eiduson 1986). The cycle of poverty should be apparent.

Families without Children

Couples without children may consider themselves "childless" or "child free," depending on whether the lack of a child is the result of unsolved infertility or choice. Sociologist Charlene Miall (1986) found that infertile couples often feel stigmatized. In the light of cultural expectations to be fertile, they find that people—sometimes even strangers—bring up the topic. To avoid being confronted with negative attitudes, such couples often avoid the topic of children and may even select friends on the basis of their attitudes toward childlessness.

And the child free? Why do they choose to go against the norm and not have children? Sociologist Kathleen Gerson (1985), who also investigated this issue, found that some women see their marriage as unstable and either do not believe their relationship can withstand the strains that a child would bring or think that it will break up before the child is grown. Others feel a child would be too expensive. Some career-oriented women consider that a child will bind them to the home, and that they will suffer from boredom and loneliness as a result. Other women feel that having a child will force them to give up career opportunities.

Both childless and child-free marriages are becoming more common. In 1976, only 13 percent of American women in their thirties did not have children. By 1988, this figure had jumped to 20 percent. The highest rate of voluntary childlessness is among Asian Americans and whites, the lowest among Hispanic Americans (Lang 1991). Among college-educated working women, a full 25 percent of those between thirty-five and forty-five do not have children (Lang 1991). More education, careers for women, effective contraception, abortion, the costs of rearing children, as well as changing attitudes toward children and goals in life—all contribute to this trend.

Blended Families

An increasingly significant type of family formation found in contemporary American society is that of the **blended family,** one whose members were once part of other families. Two divorced persons who marry and each bring their children into a new family unit become a blended family. With divorce more common, an increasing number of children spend some of their childhood years in blended families. One result is more complicated family relationships, exemplified by the following description written by one student.

> I live with my dad. I should say that I live with my dad, my brother (whose mother and father are also my mother and father), my half sister (whose father is my dad, but whose mother is my father's last wife), and two stepbrothers and stepsisters (children of my father's current wife). My father's wife (my current stepmother, not to be confused with his second wife who, I guess, is no longer my stepmother) is pregnant, and soon we all will have a new brother or sister. Or will it be a half brother or half sister?
>
> If you can't figure this out, I don't blame you. I have trouble myself. It gets very complicated around Christmas. Should we all stay together? Split up and go to several other homes? Who do we buy gifts for anyway? (author's files)

Homosexual Families

Although marriage between homosexuals is illegal in the United States, many homosexual couples live in monogamous relationships that they refer to as marriage. As a sign of change, Jerry Brown, former governor of California, in his bid for the 1992 Democratic presidential nomination said that he supported the legalization of homosexual marriages. In addition to the lack of legal support for their relationships, homosexual couples also face the stigma of a disapproved lifestyle. Here, too, social class is significant; and their relationships are given shape by the orientations and resources provided by education, occupation, and income or wealth.

Sociologists Philip Blumstein and Pepper Schwartz (1985) interviewed homosexual couples and found that their struggles are typical of heterosexual marriages, involving the usual concerns of housework, money, careers, problems with relatives, and sexual adjustment. About 13 percent of female homosexuals (*lesbians*) had sex outside the relationship during the two months before they were interviewed, while for male homosexuals the figure ran to over 50 percent. This level of infidelity could be part of the reason that their relationships, though tending to be more egalitarian than those of heterosexuals (Harry 1982), are also more likely to break up.

TRENDS IN AMERICAN FAMILIES

As is apparent from this discussion, patterns of marriage and family life in the United States are undergoing a fundamental change. Other indicators of this change, which we examine, include the postponement of marriage, cohabitation, child care for working parents, divorce, and remarriage.

CNN: Gay Marriages

CDQ 16: Do you think that marriages between homosexuals will be legalized in the United States during the next decade? Why or why not?

Essay #5

L. Obj. 6: Describe the current trends affecting marriage and family life in the United States.

blended family: a family whose members were once part of other families

The family is not easy to define. Images of a husband/breadwinner, wife/homemaker, and several children are far from adequate for today's realities. Although homosexuals cannot legally marry in any state, state laws differ on other aspects of family, as shown in this photo of two lesbians in California who have legally adopted a daughter.

Postponing Marriage

Figure 16.4 illustrates that for about sixty years the median age at first marriage dropped and the age gap between husband and wife also narrowed. In 1890 the typical wife was forty-nine months younger than her husband, but by 1950 the age gap had dropped to thirty months (it has now narrowed to twenty months). However, the

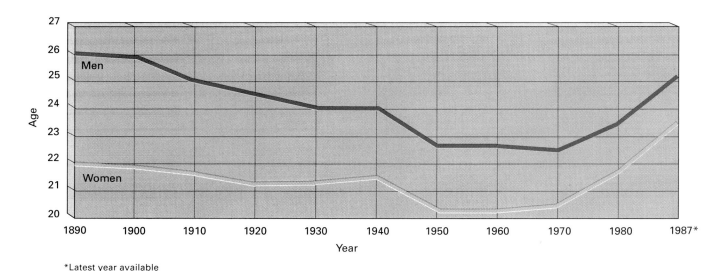

*Latest year available

FIGURE 16.4　The Median Age at which Americans Marry for the First Time. (*Source: Statistical Abstract of the United States,* 1991: Table 131, and earlier years.)

median age at first marriage for females began to increase after 1960, for males after 1970. *The average age of an American bride is now the oldest it has been at any time since accurate records were first kept.*

Why did such a remarkable change occur? The answer turns out to be very simple. Although young people have postponed the age at which they first marry, they have *not* postponed the age at which they first set up housekeeping together. In other words, the postponement in marriage has been offset by an increase in cohabitation. If cohabiting couples were counted as married, the rate of family formation and age at first marriage would show little change (Bumpass, Sweet, and Cherlin 1991). Let's look at this trend.

Cohabitation

As Figure 16.5 shows, **cohabitation,** adults living together in a sexual relationship without being married, has increased over *five times* in just two decades. Cohabitation has become so common that about half of the couples who marry have cohabited (Gwartney-Gibbs 1986). The rate of cohabitation in the United States, however, is lower than in Canada and in most European countries (Sorrentino 1990).

Commitment is the essential difference between cohabitation and marriage. While the assumption of marriage is permanence, cohabiting couples agree to remain together for "as long as it works out." Marriage requires public vows—and a judge to authorize its termination; cohabitation requires only that a couple move in together and move out when it's over. The difference is illustrated by a study of Swedish couples. Sociologists Neil Bennett, Ann Blanc, and David Bloo (1988) found that couples who cohabit before marriage are more likely to divorce than couples who do not first cohabit. The reason, they concluded, is that cohabiting couples have a weaker commitment to marriage and to relationships. That couples who live together prior to marriage are likely to have less successful marriages is also borne out in studies of American couples (Whyte 1992).

Americans have become much more tolerant of cohabitation. An indicator of changing attitudes is that when hiring executives, some corporations now pay for live-in partners to attend orientation sessions and also take them on house-hunting trips. Few

CDQ 17: Why have Americans become more tolerant of cohabitation?

cohabitation: the condition of living together as an unmarried couple

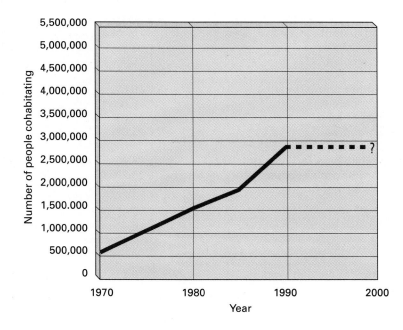

FIGURE 16.5 Cohabitation in American Society. (*Source: Statistical Abstract of the United States,* 1991: Table 53.)

companies do this, however, and almost all continue to exclude live-in partners from health insurance (*The Wall Street Journal,* January 11, 1989: B1). Some notable exceptions, include The Lotus Corporation and Ben & Jerry's, an ice cream company, both of which have policies offering the same benefits to heterosexual married workers and to gay and lesbian workers who have what the companies call "spousal equivalents."

Child Care

Through the centuries, the full-time care of American children fell automatically to the mother. Now that 59 percent of mothers work for wages, that assumption no longer holds (O'Connell and Bachu 1990). With so many mothers working, who is taking care of the children?

A study by the United States Bureau of the Census answers this question. As shown in Table 16.3, whether the mother is working full- or part-time has a considerable impact on child-care arrangements. The table contains several striking findings. First, a father is much more likely to take care of the children if his wife is working only part-time. Second, children whose mothers work full-time for wages are more likely to be cared for by nonrelatives. Third, mothers who work part-time are much more likely to take care of their children at work. Fourth, 0.4 percent of children whose mothers work full-time *take care of themselves,* even though they are under the age of five. Since there are 5,677,000 children under five whose mothers work full-time, (O'Connell and Bachu 1990), this percentage translates to about 23,000 children! In many cases, neighbors must look in on these little children at least occasionally.

The term "latchkey children" refers to young children whose parents are not home when the children leave for school, nor there when they return. They are given a key

TR#38M: Child-Care Arrangements by Employed Mothers for Children under Age of 5

CDQ 18: What are some of the unique problems of latchkey children? Were you a latchkey child when you were growing up?

TABLE 16.3   Child-Care Arrangements of Employed Mothers for Children under the Age of Five

	Mothers who are employed	
	Full-time	Part-time
Care in child's home (total)	24.2%	39.2%
By father	9.7%	24.5%
By grandparent	5.5%	4.4%
By other relative	2.9%	3.9%
By nonrelative	6.1%	6.4%
Care in another home (total)	38.8%	30.2%
By grandparent	8.8%	8.5%
By other relative	5.0%	4.1%
By nonrelative	25.0%	17.6%
Organized child-care facilities (total)	28.4%	17.6%
Day care or group center	19.2%	10.9%
Nursery school or preschool	9.2%	6.7%
In kindergarten	1.4%	0.4%
Child cares for self	0.4%	0.0%
Mother cares for child at work	6.7%	12.6%

Source: O'Connell and Bachu 1990: Table 1, Part B.

to let themselves in and then spend an hour (or several) alone before their parents return. This pattern has become so common that some grade schools are trying to alleviate the children's fears and dangers by extending school hours. Children are even given public-service numbers that they can call for reassurance.

As we have seen so many times in this book, social class vitally affects people's quality of life. So it does in relation to child care. As shown in Figure 16.6, for mothers who are employed, the higher the family income, the more likely that children under five are cared for in organized care facilities. We can safely assume that few of the 23,000 preschool children who take care of themselves have parents who can afford to purchase quality child care.

The problem of latchkey children and the inequities of child care exacerbated by social class are two of the primary reasons many people support national legislation for day care, which would set national standards of care and provide national funding.

DIVORCE AND REMARRIAGE

Problems in Measuring Divorce

You have probably heard that the American divorce rate is 50 percent, a figure popular with reporters. The statistic is true in the sense that each year about half as many divorces are granted as there are marriages performed. In 1989, for example, 2,404,000 marriages were performed in the United States and 1,163,000 divorces were granted (*Statistical Abstract* 1991: Table 135).

With these statistics, what is wrong with saying that the divorce rate is 50 percent? The real question is why these two figures should be compared in the first place. The couples who divorced do not—with rare exceptions—come from the group who married that year. The one set of figures has nothing to do with the other, so these statistics in no way establish the divorce rate.

What figures should we compare, then? Couples who divorce are drawn from the entire group of married people in the country. Since the United States has 55,750,000 married couples, and only 1,163,000 of them obtained divorces in 1989, the divorce rate is 2.1 percent, not 50 percent (*Statistical Abstract* 1991: Table 50). A couple's

TR#36M: Percentage of Children under Five by Employed Mothers, in Organized Care Facilities, by Family Income

Essay #6

L. Obj. 7: State why it is difficult to measure divorce accurately. Note some of the adjustment problems of children of divorce and of ex-spouses.

Speaker Sug. #3: A judge or lawyer who practices in family or domestic relations court to discuss divorce in your city or state

Project 3

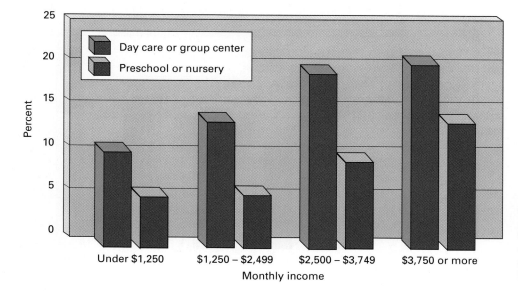

FIGURE 16.6 Percentage of Children under Five of Employed Mothers, in Organized Care Facilities, by Family Income. (*Source:* O'Connell and Bachu 1990: Erratum for Figure 2.)

TR#36: Divorce Rates in Selected Countries

CDQ 19: If you want to know your own chances of marital success, what variables should you consider?

chances of still being a married couple at the end of a year are 98 percent—not bad odds. Chances of marital success are much better than the mass media would lead us to believe.

Over time, of course, those annual 2.1 percentages add up. A third way of measuring divorce, then, is to ask, "For every thousand married persons, how many divorced persons are there?" As you can see from Figure 16.7, in just two decades this number *tripled*. As Table 16.4 illustrates, the United States has—by far—the highest divorce rate in the industrialized world (Sorrentino 1990). Although the divorce rate leveled off about 1981, and has even declined somewhat since then, the increase has been so great that sociologists Teresa Martin and Larry Bumpass (1989) estimated that as many as two-thirds of all couples getting married today may divorce.

If you want to know your own chances of marital success, you must consider many variables. One of the most significant is education, for the chances of marriage working out for people who have a college education are much better than average. The interesting exception is women with five or more years of college, among whom the divorce rate is second only to women who have not graduated from high school (Houseknecht and Spanier 1980). Because most of these divorces occur after graduate studies begin, sociologists Sharon Houseknecht, Suzanne Vaughan, and Anne Macke (1984) suggested that graduate education leads to a reevaluation of traditional marital roles and an unwillingness on the part of the women to sacrifice career ambitions to fulfill such roles. Factors that make marriage successful are summarized at the end of this chapter.

Children of Divorce

As was apparent in the opening vignette, divorce profoundly threatens a child's world. The number of American children involved in divorce today is huge—over one million each year (*Statistical Abstract* 1991: Table 133). Most divorcing parents become so wrapped up in their own problems that they are unable to prepare their children for the divorce—even if they knew how to do so in the first place. When the break comes, children become confused, insecure, and frightened of the future. For security, many cling to the unrealistic idea that their parents will be reunited (Wallerstein and Kelly 1992).

Research has confirmed the commonsense notion that time is a healer of emotions, for in a group of children of divorced parents, each year a larger proportion make a

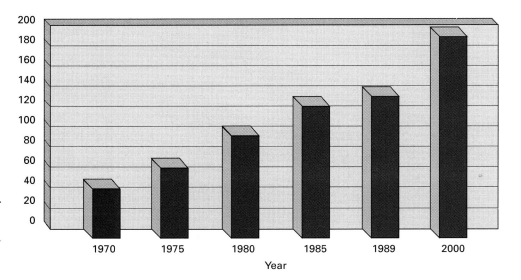

FIGURE 16.7 For Every Thousand Married Persons, How Many Divorced Persons Are There? (*Source: Statistical Abstract of the United States*, 1991: Table 51.)

TABLE 16.4   Divorce Rates in Ten Industrial Countries per Thousand

	1960	1970	1980	1988
United States	9.2	14.9	22.6	20.8
Denmark	5.9	7.6	11.2	13.1
Canada	1.8	6.3	10.8	12.6
Great Britain	2.0	4.7	12.0	12.3
Sweden	5.0	6.8	11.4	11.4
Germany	3.6	5.1	6.1	8.8
France	2.9	3.3	6.3	8.4
Netherlands	2.2	3.3	7.5	8.1
Japan	3.6	3.9	4.8	4.9
Italy	NA	1.3	0.8	2.1

Note: For United States and Germany, the last column is 1987.
Source: Statistical Abstract of the United States 1991: Table 1439.

better adjustment. Researchers have also found several factors that help children adjust to divorce. Adjustment is better if (1) both parents show understanding and affection; (2) the child lives with a parent who is making a good adjustment; (3) family routines are consistent; (4) the family has adequate money for its needs; and (at least according to preliminary studies) (5) the child lives with the parent of the same sex (Clingempeel and Reppucci 1982; Lamb 1977; Peterson and Zill 1986; Wallerstein and Kelly 1992).

The Ex-Spouses

Common emotions surrounding divorce are anger, depression, and anxiety, as well as relief and even persisting attachment to the former spouse. Women are more likely than men to feel that the divorce is giving them a "new chance" in life. In some cases, one spouse plans the divorce long before it occurs. Out of feelings of affection and concern, some even try to prepare the spouse for the divorce that only they know is coming. A few couples manage to remain friends through it all—but they are the exception. The spouse who initiates the divorce usually gets over it sooner (Kelly 1992; Stark 1989; Vaughan 1985).

Divorce does not necessarily mean the end of a couple's relationship. About half of divorced couples maintain at least monthly contact with their ex-spouses. For many couples, these "continuities," as sociologist Diane Vaughan (1985) called them, are necessary because of the needs of their children. For others, however, the continuities represent a lingering attachment (Masheter 1991). The former husband may help his former wife hang a picture and move furniture, for example, or she may invite him over for a meal. Some couples even continue to make love after their divorce.

After divorce, a couple's cost of living increases—two homes, two telephone and utility bills, and so forth. But the financial impact is very different for men than for women. Divorce often spells economic hardship for women, especially mothers of small children (Mauldin 1991). In 90 percent of divorce cases, mothers are awarded custody of their children. However, as we discussed in Chapter 11, most women earn less than men, and only about half the child support granted by the courts is paid in full. Sociologist Christine Grella (1990) found that in the first year following divorce the standard of living for women with dependent children drops 50 percent. Based on another sample, sociologist Lenore Weitzman (1985) found that the standard of living decreases 73 percent for women, while for former husbands it increases 42 percent.

You may wish to review pages 18–25 of Chapter 1, summarizing the basic reasons for the increase in the American divorce rate.

K.P.: Lenore Weitzman

CDQ 20: In your opinion, are people who get a divorce unhappy with the institution of marriage or with their current marriage partner? What do remarriage statistics reveal about this?

With most wives outliving their husbands and divorce becoming more common, extensive remarriage occurs in the United States. Because older females outnumber older males, older females are much more likely to be unmarried than are older males. As at earlier ages, many older Americans also marry for reasons of romantic love.

Project 4

Speaker Sug. #4: A family therapist to talk about family-related violence and treatment therapies for offenders

L. Obj. 8: Explain the statement that "family life can be very rewarding or very brutal" and give examples of abuse within the family setting.

CDQ 21: Can you explain why some sociologists refer to the family as "the cradle of violence?"

Remarriage

In spite of the number of people who emerge from the divorce court swearing, "Never again!" most do—and fairly soon at that. About four of every five divorced persons remarry, with an average lapse between divorce and remarriage of only three years. Most divorced people remarry other divorced people (London and Wilson 1988). As Table 16.5 shows, in almost half (46 percent) of all American marriages today, either the bride, the groom, or both have been married previously. You may be surprised to find that the women most likely to remarry are young mothers and those who have not graduated from high school; women without children and those with a college education are less likely to remarry (Glick and Lin 1986). The reason, apparently, is that the more educated and more independent can afford to be more selective—and also that they find fewer eligible males of their status who are still unmarried. In all categories, men are more likely than women to remarry, perhaps because they have a larger pool of potential mates from which to select.

How do those marriages work out? The divorce rate of remarried people *without* children is the same as that of first marriages. Those who bring children into their new marriage, however, are more likely to divorce again (White and Booth 1985). Sociologist Andrew Cherlin (1989) suggested that remarriages with children are more difficult because we have not developed norms to govern these relationships. For example, we lack satisfactory names for stepmothers, stepfathers, stepbrothers, stepsisters, stepaunts, stepuncles, stepcousins, and stepgrandparents. At the very least, these are awkward terms to use, but they also represent ill-defined relationships.

TWO SIDES OF FAMILY LIFE

Family life can be very rewarding or very brutal. Although most people find their experiences in marriage and family to be somewhere in between, the extremes inform us about the potential of family life as well as its dark side. Let's first look at situations in which marriage and family have gone seriously wrong and then try to answer the question of what makes marriage work.

Abuse: Battering, Marital Rape, and Incest

The dark side of family life refers to situations and events that the persons involved would rather keep in the dark. We shall look at battering, rape, and incest.

Battering. To determine the amount and types of violence in American homes, sociologists Murray Straus, Susan Steinmetz, and Richard Gelles interviewed nationally representative samples of American couples. They asked them about slapping, pushing,

TABLE 16.5 The Marital History of United States' Brides and Grooms

First marriage of bride and groom	54%
First marriage of bride, remarriage of groom	11%
First marriage of groom, remarriage of bride	11%
Remarriage of bride and groom	24%

Source: Statistical Abstract of the United States, 1991: Table 130.

kicking, biting, beating, and so on—even about attacking with a knife or gun (Straus 1980; Straus, Gelles, and Steinmetz 1980; Straus and Gelles 1988; Straus 1992).

They found that children are the most violent members of the family. During the year preceding the interview, two-thirds of them had physically attacked a brother or sister. Most acts of violence involved nothing more than shoving or throwing things, but one-third had kicked, bitten, or, in some instances, attacked with a knife or gun.

Although not all sociologists agree (Dobash et al. 1992), Straus concludes that husbands and wives are about equally likely to attack one another. When it comes to the effects of violence, however, sexual equality vanishes. (Straus 1980; Gelles 1980; Straus 1992). As Straus pointed out, even though *she* may throw the coffeepot first, it is generally *he* who lands the last and most damaging blow. Consequently, many more wives than husbands need medical attention because of marital violence. A good part of the reason, of course, is that most husbands are bigger and stronger than their wives, putting women at a disadvantage in this literal battle of the sexes.

Researchers have also found that violence between husbands and wives is not equally distributed among the social classes. Family violence, rather, follows certain "social channels," making some people much more likely to be abusers—or victims— than others. The highest rates of marital violence (Gelles 1980) are found among

- families with low incomes
- blue-collar workers
- people under thirty
- families in which the husband is unemployed
- families with above-average numbers of children
- families living in large urban areas
- minority ethnic groups
- individuals who have no religious affiliation
- people with low education

As Straus (1992) emphasized, although no single route leads to marital violence, sexual inequality legitimizes force and coercion. That is, the sexist structure of society described in Chapter 11 makes some men think that they are superior and have a right to force their will on their wives.

Marital Rape.   How common is marital rape? Sociologist Diana Russell (1980), who used a sampling technique that allows generalization, found that 12 percent of married women report that their husbands have raped them. Similarly, 10 percent of a representative sample of Boston women interviewed by sociologists David Finkelhor and Kersti Yllo (1983, 1989) reported that their husbands had used physical force to compel them to have sex. Finkelhor's and Yllo's in-depth interviews with fifty of these victims showed that marital rape most commonly occurs during separation or during the breakup of a marriage. They found three types of marital rape.

Nonbattering Rape.   (40 percent) The husband forces his wife to have sex, with no intent to hurt her physically. These instances generally involve conflict specifically over sex, such as the husband feeling insulted when his wife refuses to have sex.

Battering Rape.   (48 percent) In addition to sexually assaulting his wife, the husband intentionally inflicts physical pain to retaliate for some supposed wrongdoing on her part.

Perverted Rape.   (6 percent) These husbands, apparently sexually aroused by the violent elements of rape, force their wives to submit to unusual sexual acts. Anger and hostility can also motivate this type of rape. (The remaining 6 percent are mixed, containing elements of more than one type.)

K.P.: Murray Straus, Susan Steinmetz, and Richard Gelles

K.P.: Diana Russell

Incest.　Incest—sexual relations between relatives, such as brothers and sisters or parents and children—is most likely to occur in families that are socially isolated (Holder 1980). As with marital rape, sociological research has destroyed assumptions that incest is not common. Diana Russell (1986), who interviewed a probability sample (from which one can generalize) of 930 women in San Francisco, found that 16 percent were victims of incest before they turned eighteen. Russell used a very broad definition of incest, however, and included not only sexual intercourse but any unwanted sexual act—even an unwanted kiss. This information is not intended to minimize the problem of incest, which includes young victims and even forcible rape, but rather to point out the problem of operational definitions noted in Chapter 5.

Who are the offenders? Russell found that uncles are the most common offenders, followed by first cousins, then fathers (stepfathers especially), brothers, and, finally, relatives ranging from brothers-in-law to stepgrandfathers. There is little incest between mothers and sons.

Incest places enormous burdens on its victims. Finkelhor (1980) found that both male and female victims of incest have low self-esteem, and that boys victimized by older men are four times as likely as nonvictims to engage in homosexual activity. Incest victims who experience the most difficulty are those who have been victimized the most often, those whose incest took place over long periods of time, and those whose incest was "more serious," for example, sexual intercourse as opposed to sexual touching (Russell n.d.).

L. Obj. 9: List some of the characteristics which tend to be present in marriages that work. Explain why happy and unhappy couples approach problems differently.

CDQ 22: Is making a marriage last the same thing as having a happy marriage? Why or why not?

K.P.: Jeanette and Robert Lauer

incest: sexual relations between specified relatives, such as brothers and sisters or parents and children

Families That Work

After examining divorce and family abuse, one could easily conclude that marriages seldom work out. That would be far from the truth, however, for about two of every three married Americans report that they are "very happy" with their marriages (Cherlin and Furstenberg 1988; Whyte 1992). Let us, then, see if we can identify the key features that make marriages work.

What Makes Marriage Last?　As we have seen, social class makes a considerable difference to whether a marriage will last. Other important variables include age, residence, education, and religion. The chances of a marriage working out increase if

- the bride and groom are out of their teens
- the parents do not oppose the marriage
- the parents are not divorced
- the couple have known each other at least six months
- the couple were engaged before getting married
- the couple did not cohabit
- the bride is not pregnant
- the couple finish college
- the parents have money
- the couple have a good income
- the couple are from a rural area
- the couple agree on who should work outside the home
- the couple agree on how to handle the housework
- the couple are religious

(Bennett, Blanc, and Bloo 1988; Stinnett 1992; Whyte 1990).

What Makes Marriage Happy?　It is one thing for a marriage to last, another for it to be happy. To find out what makes marriage successful, sociologists Jeanette and Robert Lauer (1992) interviewed 351 couples who had been married fifteen years or longer. They found that in 51 of these marriages one or both spouses was unhappy but stayed together for religious reasons, family tradition, or "for the sake of the children." The study revealed that the 300 happy couples have the following eight factors in common.

1. They think of their spouse as their best friend.
2. They like their spouse as a person.
3. They think of marriage as a long-term commitment.
4. They believe that marriage is sacred.
5. They agree with their spouse on aims and goals.
6. They believe that their spouse has grown more interesting over the years.
7. They strongly want the relationship to succeed.
8. They laugh together.

Sociologist Nicholas Stinnett (1992) used interviews and questionnaires to study 660 families from all regions of the country. He found that happy families have the following six characteristics in common.

1. They spend a lot of time together.
2. They are quick to express appreciation.
3. They are committed to promoting one another's welfare.
4. They do a lot of talking and listening to one another.
5. They are religious.
6. They deal with crises in a positive manner.

The Lauers also found that happy and unhappy couples approach problems differently. Happy couples are determined to confront and work through problems, while unhappy couples ignore, avoid, or endure them. Finally, these studies show that happily married couples do *not* agree on equality—not in the sense of believing that marriage is a fifty-fifty proposition. Rather, their attitude is that "you have to be willing to put in *more* than you take out."

THE FUTURE OF MARRIAGE AND FAMILY

What can we expect of marriage and family in the future? Will the high divorce rate, increasing cohabitation, and the postponement of marriage eventually make marriage a thing of the past for most people?

Quite the contrary. After completing a study of marriage, sociologist Martin Whyte (1992) concluded that we should side with the optimists regarding the state of marriage in the United States. In spite of legitimate areas of concern—especially the likelihood that rates of family violence will remain high and that even larger numbers of children will live in poverty—marriage and family serve most people well. The vast proportion of Americans—between 90 and 95 percent—will continue to marry. So will most people who divorce, trying again for the satisfactions that eluded them the first time. If the percentage of Americans who marry does drop, it will not be a sign that Americans have forsaken marriage. Rather, it will only bring us back to the historical norm that was changed by the "marriage-happy" 1950s (Whyte 1992). We can safely assume that for the foreseeable future the vast majority of Americans will continue to reaffirm marriage as vital to their welfare.

Three trends are likely to continue. Cohabitation will increase, as will the age at first marriage and the number of women joining the work force. As more married women work for wages, it is likely that the marital balance of power will continue to shift in the direction of making husband-wife relationships more egalitarian.

Additional sociological research will provide a better understanding of the present and contribute to a better future. Such research can help move us beyond the distorted

CDQ 23: What do you predict will be the future of marriage and family in the United States? How will this affect your own decisions?

L. Obj. 10: Summarize research findings regarding the future of marriage and family in the United States.

pictures painted by cultural myths, "what everyone knows," and the negative views about marriage and family often promoted by the mass media. Research can also bring our own family life into sharper focus, allowing us to see better how our own experiences fit into the patterns of our culture. Finally, sociological research can help to answer the big question of how to formulate state and national legislation that will support and enhance family life.

SUMMARY

1. A cross-cultural perspective broadens our understanding of marriage and family. Remarkable variety exists around the world—from societies in which babies are married to those in which husbands and wives are barred from having sex with each other. Four universal themes in marriage are mate selection, descent, inheritance, and authority.

2. Functionalists point out that the family is universal because it performs functions essential for society; they see the erosion of these functions as the reason for the high American divorce rate. They also analyze how the incest taboo prevents role confusion and extends social networks. Conflict theorists focus on how changing economic conditions affect families, especially gender relations. The current power struggle over housework is a reflection of these changing conditions. Symbolic interactionists stress how people build meaning in their marital relationships.

3. The ideology of romantic love, assumed by contemporary Americans to be the proper basis for marriage, contrasts sharply with the practice of arranged marriages in India. Apparently romantic love, which follows social channels, has two components: emotional (sexual feelings) and cognitive (a label we give those feelings). The concept of exclusive sexual access to erotic property is the key to understanding jealousy. The life cycle of the American family encompasses marriage, childbirth, child rearing, and the family in later life.

4. Family diversity in American culture includes racial and ethnic differences, one-parent families, childless families, blended families, and homosexual families. The more resources a family has, the more it takes on middle-class characteristics. Families with more resources have fewer children and unwed mothers, and place greater emphasis on education and deferred gratification. One-parent families need to be viewed through the lens of poverty—for that is their primary source of strain.

5. Current trends favor the postponement of marriage, cohabitation, dual-career families, and greater use of child care. It is difficult to specify the divorce rate because there are many ways to measure it. Various studies have focused on children of divorce, relationships of ex-spouses, and why remarriages have a higher divorce rate.

6. The "dark side" of family life refers to violence, incest, and marital rape. Children are the most violent family members. Although husbands and wives are about equally violent, husbands inflict more severe injuries. Incest (usually a male violator and a female victim) and marital rape (which most frequently occurs during separation or the breakup of a marriage) are not uncommon.

7. Researchers have identified variables that help marriages last and be happy. There is reason for optimism concerning marriage and family in the United States. Most Americans are pleased with their marriages.

SUGGESTED READINGS

Bianchi, Suzanne M. *America's Children: Mixed Prospects.* Washington, D.C.: Population Reference Bureau, 1990. Bianchi explains why divorce, births to unmarried mothers, single-parent households, children living in poverty, mothers in the labor force, children in child care, and "latchkey children" will become even more common in American society.

Blumstein, Philip, and Pepper Schwartz. *American Couples: Money, Work, Sex.* New York: Pocket Books, 1985. The authors explore the adjustment patterns of heterosexual and homosexual couples.

Henslin, James M., ed. *Marriage and Family in a Changing Society.* 4th ed. New York: Free Press, 1992. The forty-nine readings in this collection provide an overview of marriage and family in American society.

Hochschild, Arlie. *The Second Shift: Working Parents and the Revolution at Home.* New York: Viking Penguin, 1989. Based on interviews and participant observation, the author provides an in-depth report on family life in homes where both husband and wife are employed full-time.

Millman, Marcia. *Warm Hearts and Cold Cash: The Intimate Dynamics of Families and Money.* New York: Free Press, 1991. Americans assume that people who belong to the same family owe one another certain emotions. The author analyzes how money becomes a measure of those emotional relationships, and, in turn, a substitute for the emotions themselves.

Mintz, Steven, and Susan Kellogg. *Domestic Revolutions: A Social History of American Family Life.* New York: Free Press, 1988. This highly readable overview of the changes American families have undergone from colonial times to the present also documents the diversity of American families.

Weitzman, Lenore J. *The Divorce Revolution.* New York: Free Press, 1985. The author examines effects of no-fault divorce laws on property settlements and the custody of children.

Yarrow, Andrew. *Latecomers: Children of Older Parents.* New York: Free Press, 1990. Exploring what it means to be one of the twenty million Americans born to parents over thirty-five. Yarrow examines the childhood, adolescence, and adulthood of such children and contrasts their experiences with those of children born to younger parents.

Journals

Journal of Comparative Family Studies, Journal of Divorce, Journal of Family and Economic Issues, Journal of Family Violence, Journal of Marriage and the Family, Journal of Family Issues, Family Relations, and *Marriage and Family Review* publish articles on almost every aspect of marriage and family life.

CHAPTER 17

Romare Bearden, School Bell Time, *1978*

Education: Transferring Knowledge and Skills

TODAY'S CREDENTIAL SOCIETY

THE DEVELOPMENT OF MODERN EDUCATION

EDUCATION IN CROSS-CULTURAL PERSPECTIVE
Great Britain ■ Japan ■ The Former Soviet Union

EDUCATION IN THE UNITED STATES
The Beginning of Universal Education

THE FUNCTIONALIST PERSPECTIVE: PROVIDING SOCIAL BENEFITS
Teaching Knowledge and Skills ■ Cultural Transmission of Values ■ Social Integration ■ Gatekeeping ■ Promoting Personal Change ■ Promoting Social Change ■ Replacing Family Functions ■ Other Functions

THE CONFLICT PERSPECTIVE: MAINTAINING SOCIAL INEQUALITY
The Hidden Curriculum ■ Stacking the Deck: Unequal Funding ■ *Down-to-Earth Sociology:* **Kindergarten as Boot Camp** ■ Discrimination by IQ: Tilting the Tests ■ The Correspondence

Principle ■ The Bottom Line: Reproducing the Social Class Structure ■ *Thinking Critically about Social Controversy:* **The "Cooling-Out" Function of Higher Education**

THE SYMBOLIC INTERACTIONIST PERSPECTIVE: TEACHER EXPECTATIONS AND THE SELF-FULFILLING PROPHECY
The Rist Research ■ The Rosenthal/Jacobson Experiment ■ How Do Teacher Expectations Work?

HOW CAN WE IMPROVE SCHOOLS?
The Coleman Report ■ Compensatory Education ■ Busing ■ The National Report Card: Failing Test Scores ■ The Rutter Report ■ *Down-to-Earth Sociology:* **Positive Peer Pressure and the Problem of Drugs** ■ *Thinking Critically about Social Controversy:* **Improving America's Schools**

SUMMARY

SUGGESTED READINGS

 endy still feels resentment when she recalls the memo that greeted her that Monday morning.

With growing concern about international competition for our products, the management is upgrading several positions. The attached listing of jobs states the new qualifications that must be met.

Wendy quickly scanned the list. The rumors had been right, after all. The new position the company was opening up—the job *she* had been slated to get—was among them.

After regaining her composure somewhat, but still angry, Wendy marched to her supervisor's office. "I've been doing my job for three years," she said. "You always gave me good evaluations, and you said I'd get that new position."

"I know, Wendy. You'd be good at it. Believe me, I gave you a high recommendation. But what can I do? You know what the higher-ups are like. If they decide they want someone with a college degree, that's just what they'll get."

"But I can't go back to college now, not with all my responsibilities. It's been five years since I was in college, and I still have a year to go."

The supervisor was sympathetic, but she insisted that her hands were tied. Wendy would have to continue working at the lower job classification—and stay at the lower pay.

It was Wendy's responsibility to break in Melissa, the newcomer with the freshly minted college degree. Those were the toughest two weeks Wendy ever spent at work—especially since she knew that Melissa was already being paid more than she was.

TODAY'S CREDENTIAL SOCIETY

L. Obj. 1: Explain why the United States has become a credential society.

Essay #1

K.P.: Randall Collins

CDQ 1: Do you think there are many instances in which the diplomas or degrees people earn are irrelevant to the jobs for which they are hired? Can you give examples?

Project 1

CDQ 2: Would you pursue a college degree just for the sake of knowledge if the career you want to pursue did not require any type of credential?

---

credential society: the use of diplomas and degrees to determine who is eligible for jobs, even though the diploma or degree may be irrelevant to the actual work

Sociologist Randall Collins (1979) observed that we have become a **credential society,** one in which employers use diplomas and degrees to determine who is eligible for a job. In many cases the diploma or degree is quite irrelevant for the particular work that must be performed. The new job that Wendy wanted, for example, did not actually change into a task requiring a college degree. Her immediate supervisor knew Wendy's capabilities well and was sure she could handle the responsibility just fine—but the new company policy required a credential that Wendy didn't have. Similarly, is a high school diploma necessary to pump gas or to sell shoes? Yet employers often require such credentials.

In fact, it is often on the job, not at school, that employees learn the particular knowledge or skills that a job requires. A high school diploma teaches no one how to pump gas or to be polite to customers. Melissa had to be taught the ropes by Wendy. Why, then, do employers insist on diplomas and degrees? Why don't they simply use on-the-job training?

One major reason credentials are required is the sheer size and consequent anonymity of American society. Diplomas and degrees serve as automatic sorting devices. Because employers don't know potential workers personally or even by reputation, they depend on schools to weed out the capable from the incapable. By hiring a college graduate, the employer assumes that the individual is a responsible person; for evidently he or she has shown up on time for numerous classes, has turned in scores of assignments, and has demonstrated basic writing and thinking skills. The specific job skills that a position requires can then be grafted onto this base certified by the college.

In other cases, specific job skills must be mastered before an individual is allowed to do certain work. As a result of accelerated rates of change in technology and in knowledge, simple on-the-job training will not do for physicians, engineers, and airline pilots. That is precisely why doctors so prominently display their credentials. Their framed degrees declare that they have been certified by an institution of higher learning, that they are qualified to work on our bodies.

Without the right credentials, you won't get hired. It does not matter that you can do the job better than someone else. You will never have the opportunity to prove what you can do, for you lack the credentials even to be considered for the job. This leads to some rather strange situations. For example, even though a college professor may have earned a Ph.D. and taught in a college for many years, he or she cannot teach in a high school without taking additional courses. Although high school teaching requires a lower degree, it also requires certification from a school of education. Some states have recently acknowledged this problem and now allow people with excellent backgrounds but no education credits "alternative routes" to teaching (Doyle, Cooper, and Trachtman 1991).

Credentialing is only one indicator of the central role that the educational institution plays in modern life. Before exploring the role of education in contemporary society, let us first look at how modern education developed and briefly outline education in several other parts of the world.

THE DEVELOPMENT OF MODERN EDUCATION

L. Obj. 2: Describe the development of modern education.

In earlier societies there was no separate social institution called education. There were no special buildings called schools, and no people who earned their living as teachers. Rather, as an integral part of growing up children learned what was necessary to get along in life. If hunting or cooking were the essential skills, then persons who already possessed those skills taught them. *Education was synonymous with* **acculturation,** the transmission of culture from one generation to the next—as it still is in today's preliterate groups.

In some societies, when a sufficient surplus developed—as in Arabia, China, North Africa, and classical Greece at the time of Aristotle—a separate institution developed. Some people then devoted themselves to teaching, while those who had the leisure—the children of the wealthy—became their students. In ancient China, for example, Confucius taught a few select pupils, while in Greece Aristotle, Plato, and Socrates taught science and philosophy to upper-class males. Such formal instruction stood in marked contrast to the learning of traditional skills such as farming or hunting, for it was clearly intended to develop the mind.

The flourishing of education during the period roughly marked by the birth of Christ, however, slowly died out. During the Dark Ages of Europe, the candle of enlightenment was kept burning by monks, who, except for a handful of the wealthy and nobility, were the only ones who could read and write. Although they delved into philosophy, the intellectual activities of the monks centered on learning Greek, Latin, and Hebrew so that they could read early texts of the Bible and the church fathers. Similarly, Jews kept formal learning alive as they studied the Torah.

Formal education, however, remained limited to those who had the leisure to pursue it. (In fact, *school* comes from the Greek work *scholē* meaning "leisure.") Industrialization transformed this approach to learning, for the new machinery and new types of jobs brought a general need to be able to read, to write, and to work accurately with figures—the classic three Rs of the nineteenth century (Reading, 'Riting, and 'Rithmetic).

Over time the amount of education considered necessary continued to expand. By 1918, all American states had **mandatory education laws** requiring children to attend school, usually until they had completed the eighth grade or turned sixteen, whichever came first. In the early 1900s in the United States, graduation from the eighth grade was considered to be a full education for most people (Bettelheim 1982). "Dropouts" at that time were students who did not complete grade school, and high school was thought of as a form of "higher" education. As you can see from Figure 17.1, in 1910 less than 3 percent of Americans had a college education, compared with 21 percent in 1989. As industrialization progressed and fewer people made their living from agriculture, formal education came to be thought of as essential to the well-being of society. As this trend continued, industrialized groups eventually developed what Collins called the credential society.

TR#37: Educational Achievement in the United States

CDQ 3: Do all societies tend to have compulsory education requirements?

Universal compulsory education still does not characterize much of the Third World. Even if they have mandatory attendance laws, they are not enforced. In some Third World countries, most children do not go beyond the first couple of grades. There are two basic reasons for this. First, they find little use for an education beyond the minimum required for working the land and taking care of the household, just as American farmers needed little education one hundred years ago. Second, these societies are extremely poor. As Table 9.2 on page 238 illustrated, the average income per person in some of these countries is less than 5 percent of the average American income. They simply cannot afford extensive formal education. As in the American past,

acculturation: the transmission of culture from one generation to the next

mandatory education laws: laws that require all children to attend school until a specified age or until they complete a minimum grade in school

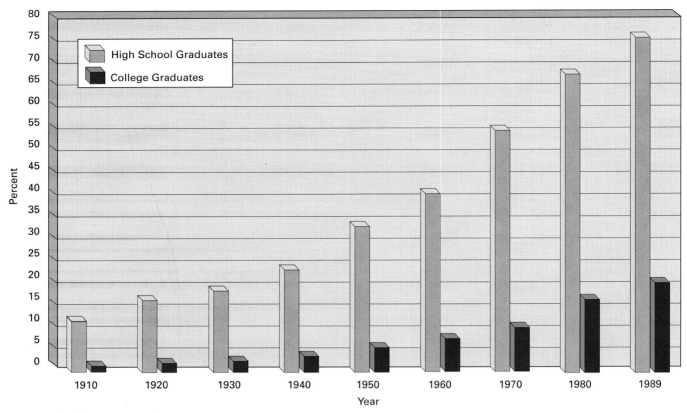

Percent

*Americans 25 years and over

FIGURE 17.1 Educational Achievement in the United States. (*Source:* National Center for Education Statistics, 1991: Table 8.)

L. Obj. 3: Outline the major differences in the educational systems of Great Britain, Japan, and the former Soviet Union.

CDQ 4: Have you attended school in a country other than the United States? If yes, in what ways was it similar to U.S. education? In what ways was it different?

education: a formal system of teaching knowledge, values, and skills

only the wealthy have either the means or the leisure for formal education—especially anything beyond the basics.

EDUCATION IN CROSS-CULTURAL PERSPECTIVE

Education, then, is no longer the same as informal acculturation, for the term now refers to a group's *formal* system of teaching knowledge, values, and skills. Before focusing on American society, let's look at this formal system in several other parts of the world.

Great Britain

As we saw in Chapter 9, distinctions between Great Britain's social classes are pronounced. Those distinctions are also reflected in the country's educational system, which results in one type of education for children of the elite and quite another for other children.

The primary factor that sorts British students into different educational paths is social class. Children of the elite attend exclusive grade schools, called "prep schools." From there, they progress to exclusive private boarding schools, called, confusingly, "public schools." Children of the lower social classes attend state elementary schools and high schools, from which they enter the labor force at age sixteen. Many middle-class children attend these state schools also, but some middle-class parents pay for their children to attend private high schools instead.

Although university education is free and the government pays students a stipend to attend them, almost all working-class students quit high school at age sixteen. Middle-class students are likely to attend regional universities, while students at Brit-

Compared with farming skills, formal education is considered a luxury of little use in an agricultural society. Basic mathematics and reading are valued, however, because of the necessity to figure expenses and profits. Some agricultural countries are so poor that they can afford neither classrooms nor regular teachers, and few of their children attend school. Shown here is a math lesson in Nepal, taught by a traveling teacher who tries to acquaint children with addition and subtraction. For many children, such lessons will be the extent of their formal education.

ain's most elite universities, Oxford and Cambridge, come almost exclusively from the country's elite.

From a conflict perspective, the educational system of Great Britain maintains the country's social class system. It makes certain that the ruling elite passes its privileges to its children, while it allows the most able and industrious members of the lower classes to be upwardly mobile. The system trains the vast majority of Britons for subservient positions—where they work for the ruling class.

Japan

A central sociological principle of education is that education reflects culture. Since a core Japanese value is solidarity with the group, competition among individuals is downgraded. For example, in the work force persons who are hired together work as a team. They all help make decisions, and they are even promoted collectively (Ouchi 1991). Japanese education reflects this group-centered ethic. Children in grade school work as a group, all mastering the same skills and materials. Teachers stress cooperation and respect for elders and others in positions of authority. By law, Japanese schools even use the same textbooks.

College admission procedures in Japan are also very different from those that prevail in the United States (Cooper 1991). Like the Scholastic Aptitude Test (SAT) required of American college-bound high school seniors, Japanese seniors who want to attend college must take a national test. Only the top scorers in Japan, however—rich and poor alike—are admitted to college. In contrast, even an American high school graduate who performs poorly on these tests can find some college to attend—as long as his or her parents can pay the tuition.

This Japanese practice poses a fascinating cultural contradiction. Although cooperation is a core Japanese value, students are admitted to college only on the basis of intense competition. Because this make-or-break process for young Japanese affects the course of their entire lives, each day after high school children of affluent parents attend cram schools (*juku*). The annual college admission tests have become a national obsession. Families and friends nervously stand on college campuses at midnight awaiting the outcome that seals their fate. The results are posted on flood-lit bulletin boards. Families shout in joy—or hide their faces in shame and disappointment, while

Project 2

CNN: Examination Hell in Japan: Career Mobility

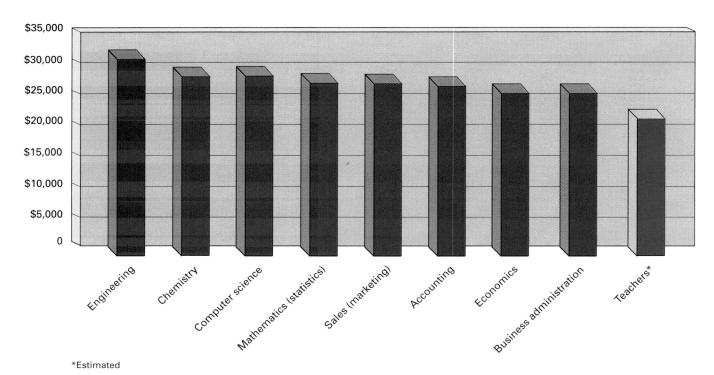

*Estimated

FIGURE 17.2 Starting Salaries of College Graduates—Public School Teachers Compared with Private Industry, 1990. (*Source: Statistical Abstract of the United States,* 1991: Table 239.)

reporters photograph the results and rush back to their papers with the news. The next day, entire neighborhoods are abuzz with the results (Rohen 1983; White 1987).

Just how highly do the Japanese value education? One way to tell how much a society values something is to see how much money it chooses to spend on it. By law, Japanese teachers are paid 10 percent more than the highest-paid civil service workers, putting teachers in the top 10 percent of the country's wage earners (Richburg 1985). In sharp contrast, as Figure 17.2 shows, the starting salaries of teachers in the United States are considerably less than those in other fields. Because the Japanese reward schoolteaching with both high pay and high prestige, each teaching opening is met by a barrage of eager, highly qualified applicants.

The Former Soviet Union

After the Revolution of 1917, the ruling Soviet Communist party attempted to upgrade the nation's educational system. At that time, as in most other countries, education was limited to the elite. The Revolution, meant to usher in social equality, was also intended to make education accessible to all. Just as the new central government directed the economy, so it directed the country's education. Following the sociological principle that education reflects culture, the government insisted that socialist values dominate education for it saw education as a means to undergird the new political system. As a result, schoolchildren were taught that capitalism was evil and that communism was the salvation of the world.

With the country still largely agricultural, education remained spotty for the next two decades. The Nazi invasion of the Soviet Union during World War II dealt a severe blow to the attempt to provide universal education, as military service disrupted the education of hundreds of thousands of young people. Even by 1950, only about half of Soviet young people were in school, and most of these came from the more privileged strata (children of the more educated and Party members) rather than from workers and peasants (Bell 1973; Grant 1979; Ballentine 1983; Matthews 1983; Tomiak 1983).

Eyeing the gains of the West, the Soviet leadership continued to struggle toward universal education, seeing education as a key to becoming a world power. Although the Soviet Union never succeeded in becoming a world industrial power—its power was based on military threat, not industrial might—its educational success did challenge the West. The launching of Sputnik in the 1950s caught Western leaders by surprise, forcing them to acknowledge how effective the Soviets had become in teaching mathematics, engineering, and the natural sciences.

With events changing so rapidly and so extensively in the former Soviet Union, it is risky to characterize anything about their educational system. However, because it is true of education everywhere, it is safe to conclude that Russia and each former Soviet republic will shape its educational system to reflect its own culture—to glorify its historical exploits and reinforce its values and world views. As these countries adopt some form of a competitive market system—destined to transform basic ideas about profit and private property—their educational systems will similarly reflect the changing culture.

EDUCATION IN THE UNITED STATES

Having looked briefly at education in other parts of the world, let us now turn to the educational system in the United States. As might be expected, we shall see how it, too, reflects the national culture.

The Beginning of Universal Education

In the years following the American Revolution, the founders of the new republic felt that formal education should be the principal mechanism for creating a uniform national culture out of its various component nationalities and religions. Thomas Jefferson and Noah Webster proposed a universal system of schooling based on standardized texts that would instill patriotism and teach the principles of republican government (Hellinger and Judd 1991). They reasoned that if the American political experiment were to succeed, it needed educated voters who were capable of making sound decisions.

Speaker Sug. #1: An education professor to discuss American education now and into the twenty-first century.

L. Obj. 4: Discuss the beginning of universal education in the United States.

CDQ 5: Why do you think universal education has been so important in the United States?

Shown here are Russian schoolgirls in Moscow. The ruling elite of the Soviet Union attempted to provide universal education for Soviet citizens, but, as in capitalist societies, the educational system of the former Soviet Union was stratified, with the best educational opportunities reserved for children of the ruling elite.

Several decades later, however, in the early 1800s, the United States still had no comprehensive school system. The country remained politically fragmented, with many of its states, as well as those that then were only territories, still thinking of themselves as near-sovereign nations.

The system of education reflected the political situation. In effect, there was no *system*, just a hodge-podge of independent schools administered by separate localities, with no coordination among them. Most public schools were supported by tuition, with a few poor children being allowed to attend free. Parochial schools were run by Lutherans, Presbyterians, Congregationalists, and Roman Catholics (Hellinger and Judd 1991). Children of the rich attended private schools. Most children of the lower classes—and all slaves—received no formal education at all. Only the wealthy could afford to send their children to college or, at that time, even to high school.

Horace Mann, an educator from Massachusetts, found it deplorable that the average family could not afford to send its children even to grade school. In 1837 he proposed that "common schools," supported through taxes, be established throughout his state. Mann's idea spread throughout the country, as state after state directed more of its resources to public education. It is no coincidence that universal education and industrialization occurred simultaneously. Seeing that the economy was undergoing fundamental change, political and civic leaders recognized the need for an educated work force. They also feared the influx of foreign values and looked on public education as a way to Americanize immigrants (Hellinger and Judd 1991).

As a result, education became more accessible in the United States than in any other country. Even today, a larger proportion of the population attend colleges and universities in the United States than in any other industrialized country in the world (Rubinson 1986). In fact, almost 60 percent of all high school graduates now enter college, the highest rate in American history (*Statistical Abstract* 1991: Table 261).

THE FUNCTIONALIST PERSPECTIVE: PROVIDING SOCIAL BENEFITS

As stressed in previous chapters, a central position of functionalism is that when the parts of society are working properly, each contributes to the well-being or stability of that society. The intended consequences of people's actions are known as **manifest functions**, while those that are not intended are called **latent functions**. As we

Essay #2

Speaker Sug. #2: A sociology of education professor to discuss current research based on functionalist, conflict, or symbolic interactionist perspectives.

L. Obj. 5: List and briefly explain the manifest and latent functions of education.

manifest functions: intended consequences of people's actions

latent functions: unintended consequences of people's actions

This 1893 photo of a school in Montana, taught by Miss Blanche Lamont, provides a glimpse into the past, when free public education, itself pioneered in the United States, was still in its infancy. In these one-room rural schools, a single teacher had charge of grades 1 to 8. Children were assigned a grade not by age but by mastery of subject matter. Occasionally, adults who wished to learn to read or to do mathematics would join the class. Attendance was sporadic, for the needs of the family's economic survival came first.

examine the functions of education, both its manifest and latent functions will become evident.

Teaching Knowledge and Skills

Education's most obvious manifest function is to teach knowledge and skills, whether those be the traditional three Rs or their more contemporary versions, such as computer literacy. Each society must train the next generation to fulfill its significant positions. From a functionalist perspective, this is the reason that schools are founded, parents support them, and taxes are raised to finance them.

Cultural Transmission of Values

At least as significant as teaching knowledge and skills is a function of education called **cultural transmission,** a process by which schools pass on a society's core values from one generation to the next. As discussed in Chapter 2, values lie at the center of every culture (see pages 42–45 for a summary of values that characterize American culture). In addition to responding to the demands of industrialization, the need to produce an informed electorate, and the desire to Americanize immigrants, how else does the United States educational system reflect—and transmit—cultural values?

Schools are such an essential part of American culture that it is difficult even to know where to begin. For example, the fact that instruction takes place almost exclusively in English, the dominant language of the society, reflects an intimate evolution from British institutions. Similarly, the architecture of school buildings themselves reflects Western culture, their often distinctive appearance identifying them as schools on sight, unlike, for example, the thatched-roof schools of some tropical societies.

Americans value "bigness," and this value is reflected in the American educational system. With 46 million students attending grade and high schools, and another 13 million enrolled in college, American education has become big business. Primary and secondary schools provide employment for 2.75 million teachers, while another 793,000 people teach in colleges and universities (*Statistical Abstract* 1991: Tables 232, 265). Millions more work as support personnel—aids, administrators, grounds keepers, janitors, secretaries, and clerks. Another several million earn their living in industries that service schools—from building schools to manufacturing pencils, paper, and desks.

To examine the way in which American education transmits American values, however, is more instructive than simply counting how many people are involved in the process. To illustrate this intricate interconnection between education and values, let's look at how the educational system transmits individualism, competition, and patriotism.

Individualism.   Individualism forms a thread that is integrally woven into the American educational system. Unlike their Japanese counterparts, American teachers and students seldom focus on teamwork. Where Japanese schools stress that the individual is only one part of a larger, integrated whole, American students learn that the individual is on his or her own. Pervasive but often subtle, such instruction begins in the early grades when teachers point out the success of a particular student. They might say, for example, "Everyone should be like José," or, "Why can't you be like María, who got all the answers right?" In such seemingly innocuous statements, the teacher thrusts one child ahead of the rest, holding the individual up for praise.

Competition.   The schools' emphasis on individualism and competition is a primary means by which they transmit essential American values. Competitive games in the classroom and the schoolyard provide an apt illustration. In the classroom, a teacher may line up one group, such as boys and girls, for a spelling bee, while on the playground children are encouraged to play hard-driving competitive games and sports. (In

CDQ 6: What American values were you taught as a part of your earlier educational experiences?

cultural transmission: in reference to education, the way in which schools transmit a society's culture, especially its core values

free play, boys are more likely than girls to choose directly competitive games [Thorne and Luria 1993].) The school's formal sports program—baseball, football, basketball, soccer, hockey, volleyball, and so on—pits team against team in head-to-head confrontations, driving home the lesson that the competitive spirit is highly valued. Although organized sports stress teamwork, the individual is held up for praise. The custom of nominating an "outstanding player" (emphasizing which of these persons is *the* best), as well as the tendency of sports writers to single out the exploits of particular persons, illustrates the continued dominance of individualism in team sports.

Patriotism.   Finally, like schools around the world, American schools feel a duty to teach patriotism. Consequently, American students are taught that the United States is the best country in the world; Russians learn that no country is better than Russia; and French, German, British, Spanish, Japanese, Chinese, Afghanistani, and Turkish students all learn the same about their respective countries. To instill patriotism, grade school teachers in every country extol the virtues of the society's founders, their struggle for freedom from oppression, and the goodness of the country's basic social institutions.

In the United States, grade school teachers wax eloquent when it comes to the exploits of George Washington—whether real or mythical (and each society tends to develop myths about its own early heroes). Throwing a silver dollar across the Potomac and chopping down the cherry tree are vivid memories many adults carry from their childhood classrooms—their hesitant suspicions about the waste of money or how such a good person could have chopped down a valued tree in the first place hushed by the teacher's stress on Washington's virtues: strength and accuracy in throwing the silver dollar, and honesty about the cherry tree.

Social Integration

Schools also perform the function of *social integration,* helping to mold students into a more or less cohesive unit. Indeed, as we just saw, forging a national identity by integrating immigrants into a common cultural heritage was one of the manifest functions of establishing a publicly funded system of education in the United States (Hellinger and Judd 1991). When children enter school, they come from many different backgrounds. Their particular family and social class may have taught them speech patterns, dress, and other behaviors or attitudes that differ from those generally recognized as desirable or acceptable. In the classroom and on the playground, those backgrounds take new shape. The end result is that schools help socialize students into the mainstream culture.

Peer culture is especially significant, for most students are eager to fit in. From their peers, they learn ideas and norms that go beyond their family and little corner of the world. Guided by today's powerful mass media, students in all parts of the country choose to look alike by wearing, for example, the same brands and styles of jeans, shirts, skirts, blouses, sneakers, and jackets. Parental influence rapidly declines as the peer culture encourages new behaviors and ideas, molding not only the youths' appearance but even their speech patterns and interaction with the opposite sex (Thorne and Luria 1993).

It is not just the school playground and peer culture, of course, that help to bring about social integration. The classroom itself is also highly significant in this process. As students salute the flag and sing the national anthem, for example, they become aware of the "greater government" and increase their sense of national identity. One of the best indicators of how education promotes political integration is the fact that millions of immigrants have attended American schools, learned mainstream ideas, and given up their earlier national and cultural identities as they became American (Violas 1978).

How significant is this integrative function of education? It goes far beyond similarities of appearance or speech. To forge a national identity is to stabilize the political

CDQ 7: How powerful do you think the influence of a person's peers is in the U.S. educational structure?

system itself. If people identify with a society's social institutions and *perceive them as the basis of their welfare* they have no reason to rebel. This function is especially significant when it comes to the lower social classes, the groups from which social revolutionaries would ordinarily be drawn. To get the lower classes to identify with the American social system *as it is* goes a long way to preserving the system as it is.

Gatekeeping

Gatekeeping, or determining which people will enter what occupations, is another major function of education. Credentialing, the subject of the opening vignette, is an example of gatekeeping. Because Wendy did not have the credentials, but Melissa did, education closed the door to the one and opened it to the other.

Essential to the gatekeeping function is **tracking,** the sorting of students into different educational programs on the basis of real or perceived abilities. Tests are used to determine which students should be directed into "college prep" programs, while others are put onto a vocational track. The impact is lifelong, for, like Wendy and Melissa, throughout adulthood opportunities for positions, advancement, and earnings are opened or closed on the basis of educational results.

Tracking begins in grade school, where on the basis of test results most students take regular courses, but some are placed in advanced sections of English and mathematics. In high school, tracking becomes more elaborate. In many schools, students are funneled into one of three tracks: general, college prep, or honors. All students who complete their sequence of courses receive a high school diploma and are eligible to go on to college. Those in the lowest track, however, are most likely to go to work after high school or at best to attend a community college; those in the highest track usually enter the more prestigious colleges around the country; and those in between most often attend a local college or regional state university.

As noted in Chapter 9, functionalists regard merit as the basis for gatekeeping, also known as **social placement.** Sociologists Talcott Parsons (1940), Kingsley Davis, and Wilbert Moore (1945), who pioneered this view, argue that a major task of society is to fill its positions with capable people. Some of those positions, however, such as that of physician, require high intellectual abilities and many years of arduous education. Consequently, to motivate capable people to postpone immediate gratification and submit to the educational demands, society holds out rewards of high income and prestige. Other jobs require far fewer skills and intellectual abilities and can be performed by persons of lesser intelligence. Thus, functionalists look on education as offering an opportunity for students with greater abilities and drive to get ahead and regard educational testing as a means of helping to determine people's abilities. As we shall see, conflict theorists sharply disagree.

Promoting Personal Change

Personal change is achieved through critical thinking. Although schools teach students the benefits of present social arrangements, they also teach them to "think for themselves"—to critically evaluate ideas and social life. One consequence is that the further people go in school, the more open they tend to be to new ways of thinking and doing things. People with more education tend to hold more liberal ideas, while those with less education tend to be more conservative.

Promoting Social Change

The educational institution also contributes to social change through fostering research. Most university professors are given time off from teaching so that they can do research. Their findings become part of the culture, a body of accumulated knowledge that stimulates social change.

Some of the results of academic research have had an explosive impact on society—literally, in the case of the atomic and hydrogen weapons that were developed

CDQ 8: Based on schools you have attended, can you give examples of the gatekeeping function of education?

gatekeeping: the process by which education opens and closes doors of opportunity; another term for the social placement function of education

tracking: the sorting of students into different educational programs on the basis of real or perceived abilities

social placement: a function of education that funnels people into a society's various positions

in part from university research. Other studies lead to gradual changes in daily life, such as new materials for clothing and homes. Nobody remains untouched by this function of education. For example, medical research conducted in universities across the world is partially responsible for the longer life span discussed in Chapter 13.

Replacing Family Functions

As society has changed, so have the functions of its various institutions. Many families, for example, now look to the schools to provide sex education. This has stirred controversy, for other families wish to keep sex education a family function and resent the schools for taking it over. Child care is another example. Grade schools do double duty as babysitters for parents who both work, or for single mothers in the work force. Child care has always been a latent function of formal education, for it was an unintended consequence of schooling. Now, however, since most families have two wage earners, child care has changed into a manifest function. Some schools even offer child care both before and after formal classes.

Other Functions

In addition to those just discussed, education fulfills many other latent functions. For example, because most students are unmarried, high schools and colleges effectively serve as *matchmaking* institutions. It is here that many young people find their future spouses. The sociological significance of this function of schools is that they funnel people into marriages with mates of similar social class background, interests, and educational level. Schools also establish *social networks*. Some older adults maintain friendship networks from high school and college, while others become part of business or professional networks that prove highly beneficial to their careers. Finally, schools also help to *stabilize employment*. Industrialized societies have little use for unskilled individuals. Schools keep part of the population out of the labor market, thereby reserving those positions for older workers.

One of the latent functions of higher education is to provide a network of friends and acquaintances. As with other networks, this network of Harvard alumni opens opportunities and provides a buffer against hard times.

THE CONFLICT PERSPECTIVE: MAINTAINING SOCIAL INEQUALITY

Conflict theorists offer a sharply different view of education. Unlike functionalists, who see education as a social institution that performs functions for the benefit of society, conflict theorists see the educational system as a tool used by those in the controlling sector of society to maintain their dominance.

The Hidden Curriculum

Sociologists use the term **hidden curriculum** to describe the set of unwritten rules of behavior and attitudes, such as obedience to authority and conformity to cultural norms, that are taught in the schools in addition to the formal curriculum. From a conflict perspective, the real purpose of education is to perpetuate, through the hidden curriculum, existing social inequalities. The values and work habits taught to help students "prepare for life," say conflict theorists, are merely devices to teach the middle and lower classes to loyally support the capitalist class. Members of the capitalist class need people to run their business empires, and they are more comfortable if their managers possess "refined" language and manners. Consequently, middle-class schools, whose teachers know where their pupils are headed, place high stress on "proper" English and "good" manners. Since few lower-class children will occupy managerial positions, teachers in inner-city schools that serve such students are more likely to allow ethnic and street language in the classroom. They do not view the children of the poor as needing "refined" speech and manners; they simply need to be taught to obey rules so that they can take their place in the closely supervised positions of low status for which they are destined (Bowles and Gintis 1976; Olneck and Bills 1980). From the conflict perspective, even kindergarten has a hidden curriculum, as the Down-to-Earth Sociology box on page 478 illustrates.

Stacking the Deck: Unequal Funding

Conflict theorists observe that funding for education is a scarce resource unequally distributed among rich and poor students, and even among different geographical regions. This inequality becomes readily visible when we look at Table 17.1. You can

Essay #3

L. Obj. 6: Explain why conflict theorists state that education maintains social inequality.

CDQ 9: Do you think that schools have a hidden curriculum which perpetuates existing social inequalities? Why or why not?

Project 3

hidden curriculum: the set of unwritten rules of behavior and attitudes, such as obedience to authority and conformity to cultural norms, which are taught in schools in addition to the formal curriculum

TABLE 17.1 State Ranking in Expenditures on Education, per Student

Rank	State	Expenditure	Rank	State	Expenditure	Rank	State	Expenditure
1.	New Jersey	$8,439	18.	Florida	$5,051	35.	Indiana	$4,126
2.	New York	$8,094	19.	Virginia	$5,000	36.	Texas	$4,056
3.	Connecticut	$7,934	20.	Illinois	$4,853	37.	Nebraska	$3,874
4.	Alaska	$7,252	21.	Kansas	$4,706	38.	Arizona	$3,853
5.	Rhode Island	$6,523	22.	Washington	$4,638	39.	Kentucky	$3,824
6.	Massachusetts	$6,170	23.	California	$4,598	40.	South Carolina	$3,731
7.	Maryland	$5,887	24.	Iowa	$4,590	41.	North Dakota	$3,581
8.	Delaware	$5,849	25.	Colorado	$4,580	42.	Tennessee	$3,503
9.	Wisconsin	$5,703	26.	Hawaii	$4,504	43.	Oklahoma	$3,484
10.	Pennsylvania	$5,670	27.	Georgia	$4,456	44.	Louisiana	$3,457
11.	Maine	$5,517	28.	Ohio	$4,394	45.	Alabama	$3,314
12.	Vermont	$5,418	29.	Nevada	$4,387	46.	South Dakota	$3,312
13.	Wyoming	$5,281	30.	North Carolina	$4,386	47.	Arkansas	$3,272
14.	New Hampshire	$5,149	31.	Missouri	$4,226	48.	Mississippi	$3,151
15.	Minnesota	$5,114	32.	New Mexico	$4,180	49.	Idaho	$3,037
16.	Oregon	$5,085	33.	Montana	$4,147	50.	Utah	$2,733
17.	Michigan	$5.073	34.	West Virginia	$4,146	AVERAGE		$4,890

Note: These are 1990 figures. They refer to the amount spent per student in grade school and high school.
Source: Statistical Abstract of the United States, 1991: Table 244.

DOWN-TO-EARTH SOCIOLOGY

Kindergarten as Boot Camp

Sociologist Harry Gracey (1991), who carried out participant observation in a kindergarten, found that the main function of kindergarten is to teach "the student role." He concluded that kindergarten is a sort of boot camp for the entire educational system. Here, tender students are drilled in the behaviors and attitudes deemed appropriate for the student role, which, he argued, is to follow classroom routines. The goal of kindergarten is to mold many individuals from diverse backgrounds into a compliant group that will, on command, unthinkingly follow classroom routines.

Kindergarten's famous "show and tell," for example, does not merely allow children to be expressive. It also teaches them to follow the teacher's direction. (It is the teacher who is in control, they who are to do what they are told.) The activity further demonstrates to children that they must talk only when they are asked to speak. ("It's 'your turn,' Jarmay.") The format also teaches children to request permission to talk ("Who knows what Letitia has?") by raising a hand and being acknowledged. Finally, the whole ritual teaches children to acknowledge the teacher's ideas as superior. (She is the one who has the capacity to evaluate students' activities and ideas.)

Gracey found a similar hidden curriculum in the other activities he observed. Whether it was drawing pictures, listening to records, snack time, or rest time, the teachers would quiet talkative students, even scolding them at times, while giving approval for conforming behaviors. In short, the message is that the teacher—and, by inference, the entire school system—is the authority.

The purpose of kindergarten, Gracey concluded, is to teach children to "follow orders with unquestioning obedience." To accomplish this, kindergarten teachers "create and enforce a rigid social structure in the classroom through which they effectively control the behavior of most of the children for most of the school day." This produces three kinds of students: (1) "good" students who submit to school-imposed discipline and come to identify with it; (2) "adequate" students who submit to the school's discipline but do not identify with it; and (3) "bad" students who refuse to submit to school routines. This third type is also known as "problem children." To bring them into line, a tougher drill sergeant, the school psychologist, is called in.

Learning the student role prepares children for grade school, where they "will be asked to submit to systems and routines imposed by the teachers and the curriculum. The days will be much like those of kindergarten, except that academic subjects will be substituted for the activities of the kindergarten."

Gracey adds that these lessons extend well beyond the classroom, that they prepare students for the routines of the work world, whether those be of the assembly line or the office. Mastering the student role prepares them to follow unquestioningly the routines imposed by "the company."

---

see here that for each of its students New Jersey spends three times what Utah does for its students. Note also that in terms of expenditure per student no southern state ranks in the top fourteen states, while nine southern states rank in the bottom seventeen. If you divide the list in the middle, you also can see that all eleven eastern states rank in the top half (actually, the top fourteen), while only two southern states rank in the top half and the other nine fall in the bottom half. There is more to such figures than meets the eye, however. Although higher expenditure is generally associated with higher educational quality, high spending does not necessarily produce quality education. The students from Iowa, for example, which ranks only twenty-fourth in expenditure, scored the highest on the SAT test. But this figure, too, is misleading, for compared with some other states not as many Iowan graduates take the test. Table 17.2 shows that expenditure on education and student achievement can even be negatively correlated.

Conflict theorists go beyond this observation, however. They stress that within the public school system of each state, unequal funding stacks the deck against minorities and the poor. Because public schools are largely supported by local property taxes, the more well-to-do communities (where property values are higher) have larger school budgets, while the poorer communities end up with much less to spend on their children. Consequently, the richer communities are able to offer higher salaries for teach-

TR#39: Educational Expenditures and Student Scores

TABLE 17.2 Educational Expenditures and Student Scores

Country	Money Spent per Student	Math Scores (8th Grade)	Math Scores (12th Grade)	Science Scores (Age 14)
		Rank	Rank	Rank
Sweden	$4,181	7	3	5
Canada	$3,665	3	4	3
United States	$3,232	6	6	7
Finland	$2,605	5	2	4
England	$2,502	4	5	6
Netherlands	$2,059	2	Not Available	2
Japan	$1,922	1	1	1

Note: The original source is inconsistent. It variously lists England, United Kingdom, or England and Wales, while Canada is sometimes listed as Canada, at other times as Ontario and British Columbia.

Source: Snyder and Hoffman, 1991.

ers (and take their pick of the most highly qualified and motivated candidates), as well as afford the latest textbooks, microcomputers, additional foreign-language and music instruction, and various other "culturally enriching experiences." Because American schools so closely reflect the social class system, then, the children of the privileged emerge from grade school best equipped for success in high school, and, in turn, come out of high school best equipped for success in college. The financial payoffs that are so unequally distributed are shown in Figure 17.3.

TR#42M: How Much Will You Earn? Income and Education

Speaker Sug. #3: A testing and evaluation specialist to discuss ways in which test makers attempt to prevent bias in the construction of test questions.

Discrimination by IQ: Tilting the Tests

How would you answer the following question?

A symphony is to a composer as a book is to a(n) _____.
___ paper
___ sculptor
___ musician
___ author
___ man

You probably had no difficulty coming up with "author" as your choice. Wouldn't any intelligent person have done so?

CDQ 10: Is it possible for IQ tests to accurately measure a person's intelligence without being culturally biased? Why or why not?

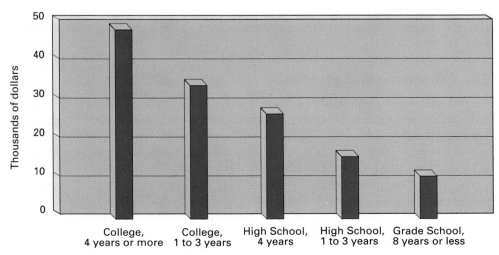

Note: These are median annual earnings for 1989.

FIGURE 17.3 How Much Will You Earn? Income and Education. (*Source: Statistical Abstract of the United States,* 1991: Table 723.)

In point of fact, this question raises a central issue in intelligence testing. Not all intelligent persons would know how to answer it, because it contains *cultural biases.* In other words, children from some backgrounds are more familiar with the concepts of symphonies, composers, sculptors, and musicians than are other children. Consequently, the test is tilted in their favor (Turner 1972; Ashe 1992).

Perhaps asking a different question will make the bias clearer. How would you answer this question?

If you throw dice and "7" is showing on the top, what is facing down?
___ seven
___ snake eyes
___ box cars
___ little Joes
___ eleven

How about this one?

Which word is out of place?
___ splib
___ blood
___ gray
___ spook
___ black

These last questions, suggested by Adrian Dove (n.d.), a social worker in Watts, are slanted toward a nonwhite, lower-class experience. It is surely obvious that these *particular* cultural biases tilt the test so that children from some social backgrounds will perform better than others.

So it is with IQ (intelligence quotient) tests that use words such as *composer* and *symphony.* A lower-class or minority child may have heard about rap, rock, or jazz but not about symphonies. In other words, IQ tests measure not only intelligence but also culturally acquired knowledge. The cultural bias built into the IQ tests used in schools is clearly *not* tilted in favor of the lower class.

A second inadequacy of IQ tests is that they focus on mathematical, spatial, symbolic, and linguistic abilities. Intelligence, however, consists of more than these components. The ability to compose music, to be empathetic to the feelings of others, or to be humorous or persuasive are also components of intelligence.

The significance of these factors, say conflict theorists, is that culturally biased IQ tests favor the middle classes and discriminate against minorities and students from lower-class backgrounds. These tests, used to track students, assign disproportionate numbers of minorities and the poor to noncollege tracks. This outcome, as we have seen, destines them for lower-paying jobs in adult life. Thus, conflict theorists view IQ tests as another weapon in the arsenal designed to maintain the social class structure over the generations.

The Correspondence Principle

Conflict sociologists Samuel Bowles and Herbert Gintis (1976) used the term **correspondence principle** to refer to the way in which schools correspond to (or reflect) the social structure of society. By this term, they meant that the educational system's almost point-for-point agreement with the status quo helps to perpetuate society's prevailing social inequalities. The list below provides some examples.

Society	Schools
capitalism/free enterprise	promote competition
social inequality	unequal funding of schools/track the poor to vocations
racial/ethnic prejudice	make minorities feel inferior/track minorities to vocations

correspondence principle: the sociological principle that schools correspond to (or reflect) the social structure of society

Society	Schools
bureaucratic structure of the corporation	authority structure of the classroom
need for submissive workers	make students submissive
need for dependable workers	promote punctuality
need to maintain armed forces	promote patriotism (to fight for capitalism)

Thus, conclude conflict theorists, the American educational system promotes capitalism and maintains existing social inequalities. It is designed to produce dependable workers who will not question their bosses, as well as some individuals who will go on to be innovators in thought and action but can still be counted on to be loyal to the capitalist system (Olneck and Bills 1980).

The Bottom Line: Reproducing the Social Class Structure

Conflict theorists point out that American education, like the British system, *reproduces the social class structure*. As we have seen, a basic proposition of conflict theory is that regardless of their abilities, children of the more well-to-do are likely to be placed in the college-bound tracks, children of the poor into the vocational tracks, and each to inherit matching life opportunities laid down before they were born.

To test this hypothesis, sociologist Samuel Bowles (1977) decided to find out whether test scores were more significant than family background in predicting college attendance. His results are shown in Figure 17.4. Of the *brightest* 25 percent of high school students, 90 percent of those from affluent homes go to college, while only 50 percent of those from low-income homes do so. When we look at the *weakest* students, social class, as opposed to ability, becomes even more visible. Twenty-six percent of such children from affluent homes go to college, while only 6 percent of children from poorer homes do so.

K.P.: Samuel Bowles

Chapters 10 and 12 reviewed how the American class system is related to race and ethnicity. To see how the educational system reproduces this aspect of the social class structure, look at Figure 17.5 on page 482, which shows the *funneling effect* of education. You can see that whites are more likely to complete high school, to go to college, and to get a bachelor's degree. African Americans and Hispanic Americans, in contrast, are not only more likely to drop out of high school, but those who do complete high school are less likely to go to college, and those who do go to college are considerably less likely to graduate. In short, whites are more likely to be funneled in one direction, African Americans and Hispanic Americans in another. The reasons have to do with the discrimination built into American society which we reviewed in earlier chapters and are far from the results of educational discrimination alone.

TR#38: The Funneling Effects of Education: Race, Ethnicity, and Education

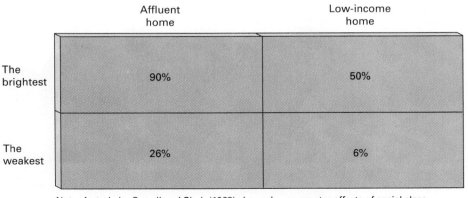

Student's background

FIGURE 17.4 Who Goes to College? The Role of Social Class and Personal Ability in Determining College Attendance. (*Source:* Bowles 1977.)

Note: A study by Sewell and Shah (1968) showed even greater effects of social class.

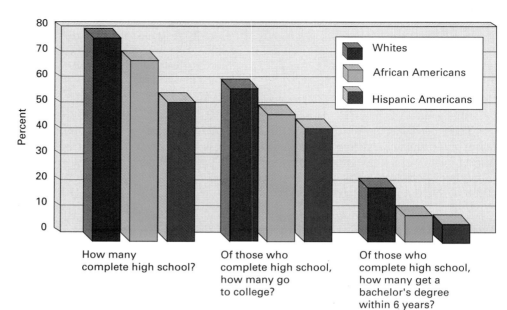

FIGURE 17.5 The Funneling Effects of Education: Race and Ethnicity. (*Source: Statistical Abstract of the United States,* 1991: Tables 258, 261, 288.)

K.P.: Caroline Persell, Sophia Catsambio, and Peter Cookson

The educational system, however, say conflict theorists, is an essential part of this process. It is designed to help the children of the privileged classes succeed, while impeding the progress of the children of the oppressed classes. They point out that most children of the less privileged—the poor and minorities—are funneled into community college vocational programs, where some are "cooled out" to accept a lesser status in life, as indicated in the Thinking Critically section on page 483. In contrast, children of the middle classes attend state universities and small private colleges. As sociologists Caroline Persell, Sophia Catsambis, and Peter Cookson (1992) pointed out, while in high school the offspring of the elite attend exclusive boarding schools, where their learning environment includes small classes, well-paid teachers, and even more books in the library. Not coincidentally, they also inherit a cozy social network between the school's college advisers and the admissions officers of the nation's most elite colleges. Some networks are so efficient that they enable half of such a school's graduating class to be admitted to Harvard, Yale, or Princeton (Persell and Cookson

Conflict theorists stress that a country's educational system is a primary means by which the ruling elite reproduces the social class structure, that is, maintains the social classes in their relative positions across generations and continues its own dominance of society. This fencing class at Lawrenceville Academy in New Jersey illustrates this principle, for these students are not learning useful skills but, rather, "gentlemanly" pursuits suitable to their class position.

1985). The educational system of the United States, then, helps to pass—and with-hold—privilege across the generations.

In Sum.   From the conflict perspective, the educational institution is a *tool of exploitation,* a mechanism for keeping the children of workers in their place, while helping the capitalist class to continue its domination of society. Conflict theorists stress that the appearance that education is available for all is misleading. Instead, the best education is reserved for children of the elite, which prepares them to take a dominant place in society; a middle level of education provides training for children of the middle class, who will serve the elite in managerial positions; and, except for the very brightest and most industrious, children of the poor are blocked from higher education (Bowles and Gintis 1976; Collins 1979; Apple 1982; Hurn 1985).

THINKING CRITICALLY ABOUT SOCIAL CONTROVERSY

The "Cooling-Out" Function of Higher Education

Sociologist Burton Clark found that most students who enter California's community colleges want to go on to study for a bachelor's degree. Although about two-thirds enroll in programs that permit them to transfer to a four-year college or university, only about one-third of these students actually do so.

Clark (1990) wanted to find out why one-third of the students change their minds. Why do they give up their original intention and accept a lower status? His research revealed that it was not so much that *they* change their minds as that the community college changes their minds for them. He referred to this process as "cooling out." Let's look at it.

First, preentrance testing funnels poorly qualified students into remedial classes, initiating a process of doubt about the reality of planning to go on for a higher degree. Significantly, the test results also become part of a folder that counselors use.

Second, a counselor meets with the students in order to "help students to accept their limitations" so they can "strive for success in worthwhile objectives that are within their grasp." The counselor begins to "gently" edge the students toward a "terminal program" by getting them to enroll in "proper" courses.

Third, the students take a course entitled, "Orientation to College," in which the goal is "to assist students to evaluate their own abilities and vocational choices." As part of the course, the students must do a "self-appraisal of fitness" for occupations.

The "evidence" gradually accumulates: test scores, course grades, and recommendations from teachers and counselors. This procedure is designed to "heighten self-awareness in relation to choice." Counselors then begin to encourage students to move from a transfer major to a one- or two-year program of vocational, business, or semiprofessional training.

Fourth, the students face a different classroom reality than that of high school, for no longer are they automatically passed. When they receive low grades, they are referred back to a counselor who asks the student to do more "self-assessment."

Finally, students who continue to do poorly are put on probation. A major effect of probation is the "slow killing off of lingering hopes" that students may still have of continuing for a bachelor's degree.

Why does Clark use the term "cooling out"? He argues that the process itself is kept hidden from the student and the community. The college advertises itself as a transfer college, yet most students never transfer to another college but instead are diverted to terminal programs. To cool out students—so that they feel good about themselves and the college—the school uses the following techniques.

Gradual Disengagement.   The process outlined above is designed to let the student only gradually become aware that original goals are inappropriate.

Objective Denial.   The objective record (in the counselor's folder) is designed to "speak for itself." It is not the college or counselor who is dictating a new choice, but the record that shows another choice of career to be more appropriate.

Alternative Achievement.   As students are diverted away from their original choice, an "alternative career" is made to appear not too different from the original goal. In this way, students do not "fail," but merely correct a "mistake."

Consolation.   Counselors try to be patient with the "overambitious." They gently teach them the value of alternative careers and console them about the lower status.

Clark found that dealing "softly" is essential to cooling out students. Counselors, for example, do not tell a student that he or she is not smart enough to become an engineer, an attorney, or a physician. Rather, counselors gradually steer them toward pursuits thought more appropriate to their abilities. If the cooling out is successful, the student will embrace the alternative career, find it a "more appropriate" choice than the original, while the underlying process of making that "right" choice will remain invisible to him or her.

Questions

1. Provide an alternative explanation for the points that Clark makes. (*Hint:* If you apply the functionalist perspective, the same points will look quite different.)

2. What do you think community colleges could do to increase the proportion of students who transfer to four-year colleges and do well there?   ■

CDQ 11: From your own experiences, have you seen the self-fulfilling prophecy in action in education?

Essay #4

L. Obj. 7: Summarize symbolic interaction research regarding teacher expectations and the self-fulfilling prophecy.

THE SYMBOLIC INTERACTIONIST PERSPECTIVE: TEACHER EXPECTATIONS AND THE SELF-FULFILLING PROPHECY

Whereas functionalists look at how education functions to benefit society and conflict theorists examine how education perpetuates social inequality, symbolic interactionists study face-to-face interaction inside the classroom. They have found that the expectations of teachers are especially significant for determining what students learn.

As noted, tracking—based on tests that have a social class bias—places students on different paths on the basis of their supposed abilities. To our understanding of how tracking works, symbolic interactionists add teacher expectations.

K.P.: Ray Rist

The Rist Research

In 1970, sociologist Ray Rist carried out participant observation in an exclusively African-American grade school with an African-American faculty. Rist found that tracking begins with the teacher's perceptions. After only eight days in the classroom, the kindergarten teacher felt that she knew the children's abilities well enough to assign them to three separate worktables. To Table 1, Mrs. Caplow assigned those she considered to be "fast learners." They sat at the front of the room, closest to her. Those whom she saw as "slow learners," she assigned to Table 3, located at the back of the classroom. She placed "average" students at Table 2, in between the other tables.

This pattern seemed strange to Rist. He knew that the children had not been tested for ability, yet the teacher was certain that she could differentiate between bright and slow children. Investigating further, Rist found that social class was the underlying basis for assigning the children to the different tables. Middle-class students were separated out for Table 1, children from poorer homes to Tables 2 and 3. The teacher paid the most attention to the children at Table 1, who were closest to her, less to Table 2, and the least to Table 3. As the year went on, children from Table 1 perceived that they were treated better and that they were better students. They became the leaders in class activities and even ridiculed children at the other tables, calling them "dumb." Eventually, the children at Table 3 disengaged themselves from many classroom activities. Not surprisingly, at the end of the year only the children at Table 1 had completed the lessons that prepared them for reading.

This early tracking stuck. When these students entered the first grade, their new teacher looked at the work they had accomplished and placed students from Table 1 at her Table 1. She treated her tables much as the kindergarten teacher had, and the children at Table 1 again led the class.

The children's reputations continued to follow them. The second-grade teacher reviewed their scores and also divided her class into three groups. The first she named the "Tigers," and, befitting their name, gave them challenging readers. Not surprisingly, the Tigers came from the original Table 1 in kindergarten. The second group she called the "Cardinals." They came from the original Tables 2 and 3. Her third group consisted of children she had failed the previous year, whom she called the "Clowns." The Cardinals and Clowns were given less advanced readers.

Rist concluded that *the child's journey through school was preordained from the eighth day of kindergarten!* What had occurred was a **self-fulfilling prophecy**, a term coined by sociologist Robert Merton (1949) to refer to an originally false assumption of what is going to happen that comes true simply because it was predicted. For example, if people believe an unfounded rumor that a bank is in trouble and, assuming that they won't be able to get their money out, all rush to the bank to demand their money, the prediction—although *originally false*—is now likely to be true.

In this case, of course, we are dealing with something more important than banking, the welfare of little children. As was the case with the Saints and the Roughnecks in Chapter 8, labels are powerful. They have a tendency to set people on courses of action that affect the rest of their lives. That, of course, is the significance of Rist's observations of these grade school children.

CDQ 12: Did your kindergarten or earliest school experiences determine how the rest of your educational experience would proceed?

The Rosenthal/Jacobson Experiment

During the course of our education, most of us have seen teacher expectations at work. On one level, we know that if a teacher expects higher standards, then we must perform at a higher level to earn good grades. Teacher expectations, however, also work in ways that we don't perceive, as Robert Rosenthal and Lenore Jacobson, two social psychologists, discovered. In what has become a classic experiment, Rosenthal and Jacobson (1968) tried out a new test in a San Francisco grade school. They tested the children's abilities and then told the teachers which students would probably "spurt" ahead during the year. They instructed the teachers to watch these students' progress, but not to let the students or their parents know about the test results. At the end of the year, they tested the students again and found that the IQs of the predicted "spurters" had jumped ten to fifteen points higher than those of the other children.

You might think that Rosenthal and Jacobson then became famous for developing a very valuable scholastic aptitude test. Actually, however, this "test" was another of those covert experiments. Rosenthal and Jacobson had simply given routine IQ tests to the children and had then *randomly* chosen 20 percent of the students as "spurters." These students were *no different* from any others in the classroom. A self-fulfilling prophecy had taken place: The teachers expected more of those particular students,

K.P.: Robert Rosenthal and Lenore Jacobson

self-fulfilling prophecy: Robert Merton's term for an originally false assertion that becomes true simply because it was predicted

From the way this room is furnished you can see the poverty of this school in Daufuskie Island, South Carolina. It is unlikely that the teachers will expect much of such students, or that the students will expect much of themselves. The low expectations of both will likely be satisfied.

K.P.: George Farkas

and the students responded. In short, expect dumb and you get dumb. Expect smart, and you get smart.

Although attempts to replicate this experiment have had mixed results (Pilling and Pringle 1978), a good deal of research confirms that when students are expected to do better than other students, they generally do (Seaver 1973; Snyder 1991).

How Do Teacher Expectations Work?

How do teacher expectations actually work? Observations of classroom interaction give us some idea (Leacock 1969; Rist 1970; Buckley 1991; Farkas 1991). The teacher's own middle-class background comes into play, for teachers are pleased when middle-class students ask probing questions. They take these as a sign of intelligence. When lower-class students ask similar questions, however, teachers are more likely to interpret those questions as "smart aleck." In addition, lower-class children are more likely to reflect a subculture that "puts down" intellectual achievements, an attitude that, communicated subtly, causes teachers to react negatively.

Sociologist George Farkas (1990a, 1990b), who led a team of researchers in probing how teacher expectations affect students' grades, added to this analysis. Using a stratified sample of students in a large urban school district in the Southwest and a survey of their teachers, the researchers found that students who scored similarly on tests over the course materials did not necessarily receive the same grade for the course. Specifically, females and Asian Americans averaged higher grades than males, African Americans, Hispanic Americans, and whites who had scored as well on the course work.

To explain this, the first conclusion most of us would jump to would be discrimination. In this case, however, such an explanation does not seem to work very well, for it is most unlikely that the teachers would be prejudiced against males and whites. Farkas suggested using symbolic interaction to interpret these unexpected results. He noted that some students "signal" to their teachers that they are "good students." The teachers pick up those "signals" and reward such persons with better grades. The "signals" that communicate "good student" are not surprising—greater docility (eagerness to cooperate and accept what the teacher says) combined with greater diligence (a show of effort and interest). In short, some students signal that they are interested in what the teacher is teaching and that they are "trying hard." Females and Asian Americans, the researchers concluded, are most likely to display these characteristics.

We do not yet have enough information on how teachers form their expectations, how they communicate them to students, or exactly how these expectations influence teacher-student interaction. Nor do we know very much about how students "signal" messages to teachers. Perhaps you will become the educational sociologist to shed more light on this significant area of human behavior.

HOW CAN WE IMPROVE SCHOOLS?

The question of how to improve schools in the United States has always been a matter of concern to educators and the public. It became a point of bitter controversy in the 1960s, however, and it has remained so ever since.

The Coleman Report

In 1966, sociologist James Coleman published a report on American education that created a furor. Congress had commissioned a study of educational opportunities and race. Coleman led a research team that gathered data from 4,000 schools, 68,000 teachers, and about 600,000 students. Everyone, including Coleman, expected that the study would show that whites outscored African Americans because of differences in the quality of their respective schools. Coleman, however, found that the usual assumptions—teaching techniques, library facilities, expenditure per student, class size, condition of buildings, and teacher training—made little or no difference. You can see why these findings created a stir, for they showed that what communities were spending their money on was irrelevant.

If the characteristics of the schools didn't account for the differences in test scores, then what did? Coleman found that the underlying reason was social class. In short, whites scored higher not because their schools were better, but because a larger proportion of them came from middle-class homes.

Unlike so many reports on education, Coleman's report did not collect dust on library shelves. It had an immediate and profound impact on national policy. Coleman's findings gave strong support to compensatory education and busing.

Compensatory Education

If lower-class homes failed to motivate and prepare children for educational success, then the schools had to do so. This effort would require **compensatory education**— educational programs designed to make up for what lower-class children lacked. The federally funded Head Start program, for example, was set up to bridge this gap by providing a "culturally enriching" experience—using the alphabet, books, music, "educational" toys and games—that would enable lower-class children to begin school on much the same footing as middle-class children.

The results of Head Start and other compensatory education programs have been difficult to measure. At first, studies indicated that these programs brought the children only temporary gains, which disappeared as they went through school (Cicerelli, Evans and Schiller 1969; Stanley 1973). Later studies, however, using more refined measurements, showed that compensatory education makes lasting differences. Students who have received compensatory education score higher on IQ tests, gain an improved self-image, and do better in school than students of similar background who have not (Lazar et al. 1977, 1982). Finally, although research is not yet conclusive, there are also indications that students who have received this type of education are less likely to become delinquent, single mothers, or unemployed (Berrueta-Clement et al. 1984).

Essay #5

CDQ 13: If you were serving on a commission to determine how to improve American education, what types of changes would you suggest? Why?

Speaker Sug. #4: An educator or political leader at the local, state, or national level who has served on an educational commission attempting to improve the quality of education.

Project 4

L. Obj. 8: State the conclusions of the Coleman Report and describe the relationship between this report and compensatory education and busing in the United States.

K.P.: James Coleman

compensatory education: educational programs designed to fill a gap in the background of lower-class children

The results of Head Start, a federally financed program designed to provide culturally enriching experiences to help prepare children of poverty for success in school, have proved difficult to measure. Consequently, arguments abound for both eliminating and expanding such programs as that shown here at a Cardinal Spellman Head Start classroom.

Busing

Coleman also found that low-income African-American students who attend middle-class, predominantly white schools score higher than similar students who attend poor, mainly African-American schools. Coleman suggested that this was due to a *changed peer culture;* the low-income students in middle-class schools pick up better study habits and more positive attitudes toward education. This finding stimulated one of the most controversial measures ever taken in American public education: busing. If segregated schools came about because of segregated neighborhoods, it was argued, desegregation could be accomplished by moving students to different schools. The result was a furor of marches, picketing, and even some violence.

Although racism often lay at the root of the opposition, there were also other reasons, primarily resistance to the disappearance of neighborhood schools. Up to this time, children attended the school closest to them, and parents had a fairly good idea of what went on in the classroom. But no longer. A child might live just across the street from a school, yet be bused to another school a half hour away. Many parents who did not express racist objections to integrated schools now felt discriminated against and took the position, "It is fine with me to bring low-income children into my child's school, but why do you have to bus my child across town when there is a school in my own neighborhood?"

By 1975, Coleman himself had turned against busing. He saw busing as a stimulus to "white flight," the movement of whites from the city to the suburbs. Not only had busing failed to bring about racial integration, but white flight had made many city schools more segregated than ever (Coleman 1975; Coleman, Hoffer, and Kilgore 1975). Even today, about four decades after the 1954 order by the Supreme Court to desegregate American schools, most white children attend schools that are mostly white, and most African-American children attend schools that are mostly African American.

Although busing has failed to bring about desegregation of the schools, it has led to some gains. For example, low-income African Americans and Hispanic Americans who attend predominantly white schools score higher than those who attend racially segregated schools. It appears, however, that once again social class is the key: Low-income minority students who attend low-income white schools are not likely to have higher scores, while low-income minority students who attend middle-class white schools are (Mahard and Crain 1983). Today, both white and minority parents, who can afford to, take their children out of lower-class schools and enroll them in private schools.

The National Report Card: Failing Test Scores

One of the more disturbing aspects of American education has been the decline in test scores during the past twenty to thirty years. The national averages on the Scholastic Aptitude Test (SAT) reached an all-time peak in 1963, then began to skid downhill (Powell and Steelman 1984). As you can see from Table 17.3, in 1963 the combined verbal and math scores were 973 (out of a possible 1,600 points). They then dropped year by year, reaching a low of 890 in 1980. After a slight recovery, they have again begun to decline.

These lower SAT scores have proved so unsettling that several recent presidents have summoned national commissions to try to find out their causes. Three main reasons have been proposed. The first—not so obvious—is that *different people are being tested*. As we have seen, the number of students attending high school and college has risen steadily. This means that more students from poor academic backgrounds now take the test. In earlier years, they would have dropped out of high school or not considered college (Owen 1985). In that case the real problem is inferior education for disadvantaged students, which results in their lower test scores (Murray and Herrnstein 1992).

The second explanation (at least for the decline in verbal scores) is somewhat more obvious—that flashy distractions have won the students' attention away from books (Ridgon and Swasy 1990). Most children find television and video games much more appealing than reading. Since children do less reading, they acquire fewer literary skills, a smaller vocabulary, and less rigor in thought and verbal expression—all of which are reflected in lower verbal scores.

The third explanation is the most obvious—that lower test results are due to a decline in the quality of American education. Many are convinced that the culprit is low standards: "frill" courses, less homework, fewer term papers, grade inflation, and unionized, burned-out teachers who are more interested in collecting a paycheck than in educating their students. An inner-city school in Chicago provides a remarkable example of low standards—the girl who placed third in the senior class ranked in the lowest 2 percent of the nation's graduates (Kotlowitz 1992).

In 1983, the National Commission on Excellence in Education concluded its investigation with a report entitled *A Nation at Risk*. Its main conclusion was that American education had deteriorated. Commission members were especially disturbed about **social promotion,** the practice of passing students from one grade to the next even though they have not mastered basic materials. An unfortunate result of social promotion is the increase in **functional illiterates,** high school graduates who have difficulty with basic reading and math. A few high school graduates cannot even understand want ads or figure out if they have been charged the right amount at the grocery store. Not surprisingly, this commission recommended that educational standards be raised. Top grades should be more difficult to attain, students should spend more time in school,

L. Obj. 9: Explain why education in the United States has been given a "failing grade."

TR#43M: National Results of the Scholastic Aptitude Test (SAT)

social promotion: the practice of passing students from one grade to the next even though they have not mastered basic materials

functional illiterate: a high school graduate who has difficulty with basic reading and math

TABLE 17.3 National Results of the Scholastic Aptitude Test (SAT)

	1963	1967	1970	1973	1975	1977	1980	1983	1985	1987	1990	1991
Verbal	——	466	460	445	434	429	424	425	431	430	424	422
Math	——	492	488	481	472	470	466	468	475	476	476	474
Total	973	958	948	926	906	899	890	893	906	906	900	896

Source: Powell and Steelman 1984; De Witt 1991; various editions of *Statistical Abstract of the United States.*

CNN: National Testing

and students should be required to take more courses in math, science, English, social studies, and computer science. They also recommended that schools recruit better-qualified teachers by paying higher salaries.

In 1989, President Bush took the unusual step of calling all fifty governors to Washington for an "education summit." The group's conclusion was that youngsters should "leave grades four, eight, and twelve having demonstrated competency in challenging subject matter including English, mathematics, science, history and geography." The problem, of course, is how to measure competency. A 1991 presidential report, *America 2000,* set forth the goal of "world-class standards" for student achievement. Critics fear that such proposals will result in a standardized national curriculum, with **minimum competency tests,** while supporters take the position that this is precisely what the United States needs to prepare for global competition (Cooper 1992; Finn 1992).

Although the reasons for the national decline in test scores are still a matter of debate, the material presented in this chapter indicates that American schools will do a better job—and test scores increase—if teachers expect, and demand, more of their students.

The Rutter Report

L. Obj. 10: List positive factors in the learning environment which The Rutter Report states can improve schools and set up a positive self-fulfilling prophecy.

K.P.: Michael Rutter

A study by British sociologist Michael Rutter et al. (1979) can help provide guidelines for improving the American school system. Rutter observed that because schools are unequal—some drawing more students from disadvantaged homes, others more from privileged homes—a school's quality cannot be judged merely by looking at the achievements of the students leaving it. Rather, it is the *gain* that the students of each school make that must be measured, and measured again over time. In a three-year study of twelve inner-city schools in London, Rutter's team of researchers observed classroom interaction, interviewed teachers, and compared the students' initial intake scores with their later achievement scores. They found that regardless of the students' background when they entered school—IQ, parents' occupation, and intake test scores—students learned more if they were in schools where *teachers*

1. Expected their students to do well
2. Stressed academic achievement
3. Regularly assigned homework
4. Regularly checked homework
5. Displayed the children's work
6. Required students to use the library
7. Spent more time teaching and less on nonteaching activities such as record keeping or assemblies
8. Interacted with the entire class
9. Included periods of quiet time in which the students worked in silence
10. Dealt with discipline problems *before* they became disruptions
11. Praised students for good work
12. Involved more students in school activities—such as homework monitor or participation in school assemblies (involvement in after-school activities and sports showed no difference)
13. Used lesson plans that were the product of group planning
14. Were monitored by the department
15. Arrived on time

Rutter found that, *regardless of social class or personal abilities,* students who attended schools with these characteristics learned more. Obviously, schools that fail to provide even a basic learning environment can teach little. A background assumption of this report, then, is that schools are not ruled by hoodlums who threaten students and teachers with weapons, and that students are not high on drugs. Some urban

minimum competency tests: national tests on which students must attain some minimum score

DOWN-TO-EARTH SOCIOLOGY

Positive Peer Pressure and the Problem of Drugs

Few people fail to recognize that drugs are a major problem in American schools, and that drug abuse cruelly robs many young people of an education. Many solutions have been tried, but few work. One that has proven successful uses solid sociological principles, for it is built on the significance of culture in influencing human behavior.

This program, Youth to Youth, was tried at Eastmoor Middle School in Columbus, Ohio, a school marked by the all-too-familiar combination of gangs, graffiti, vandalism, and drugs. In just four years, there was such a change that the school was acclaimed "drug free" by the Department of Education. (That does not mean that there are no drugs in the school, just that, relatively speaking, there are few.)

The transformation began when a physical education teacher, Helen Trautman, posted this notice: "Anyone interested in a drug-free group should come to room 207." Cooperating with teachers isn't exactly "cool" for early adolescents, so she didn't expect a large turnout. To her surprise, it was standing room only.

Youth to Youth does not lecture kids about the evils of drugs, a futile approach that has been tried too many times before. Instead, building on the principle that peer pressure is the key to adolescent behavior, the program attempts to make that pressure positive.

The centerpiece of the program is a Youth to Youth club. The club promotes social activities to divert students from drugs and provides peer support for coping with problems that often lead to drug use. In short, positive peer pressure makes it "cool" to avoid drugs, rather than to use them.

In the case of Eastmoor, the principal also helped make positive peer pressure work. By banning the wearing of gang colors, bandannas, and even T-shirts that promote beer or drugs, he helped to reduce the attraction of a lifestyle that favors drugs. Results were quickly evident. Fights were reduced by half, vandalism decreased, and test scores improved. The new test scores raised Eastmoor Middle School from twenty-sixth in Columbus schools to fifteenth.

Boosting self-esteem is another part of the program. For example, when club members are asked to finish this sentence: "I'm proud that I . . .", the task is met with a chorus of responses: "I'm proud that I'm loved." "I'm proud that I play football." "I'm proud that I'm drug free."

Not all students join Youth to Youth because they want to avoid drugs. Many come just for the social activities. Some, however, find that for the first time they are able to express openly their feelings about school, home, and adolescence. Many "get hooked" on the positive emphasis of the group and come to envision the potential of a better life ahead.

Of course, the dances, pizza parties, and skiing trips help; combined with the rest of the approach, they make drugs seem a lot less attractive by comparison. And that, after all, is what the program is all about.

Source: Based on Grunebaum et al., 1987; Hallinan and Williams 1990; Stout 1991.

schools in the United States are nothing more than expensive babysitting services, and as long as they remain such we can expect little from them. It is the students in such schools who want to learn, but cannot, who are shortchanged, not just for the present but for the rest of their lives (Toby 1992). The Down-to-Earth Sociology box above deals with this issue.

On the surface, these conclusions seem far from surprising: Spend as much time as possible on teaching, keep students involved in the classroom, enforce discipline, assign homework, hold students responsible for learning, reward good work—and why wouldn't students, regardless of their background, learn more? In short, teachers who challenge students intellectually, expect them to do well, and then reward them for doing so get better results. Sociologically, what they are doing is setting up a positive self-fulfilling prophecy. The Thinking Critically section below presents other specific proposals for improving schools.

CNN: Endangered Teachers

THINKING CRITICALLY ABOUT SOCIAL CONTROVERSY

Improving America's Schools

Critics and educators have put forward a number of proposals designed to improve the quality of America's schools. Note that these proposals are all based on the same background assumption: an adequate learning environment. As noted in this chapter, for the teaching-learning process to function adequately, students must first be guaranteed physical safety and freedom from fear so that their minds can be freed to learn. That basic requirement, it seems, would be a simple matter to accomplish *if* school administrators would refuse to tolerate threats, violence, drugs, and weapons of all sorts and expel students who threaten the welfare of others. In short, adults must first reclaim authority and provide basic safety if schools are to regain the capacity to teach. Only given the fulfillment of these conditions can such proposals as the following work.

Students

- Raise requirements for graduation from eighth grade and high school to include more math, science, and language courses
- Institute annual, rigorous competency testing
- Ban social promotion, allowing only students who pass competency tests to be promoted to the next grade
- Lengthen the school year to eleven months (the current short year is a legacy from an agricultural society that needed students to help on the farm in summer)

Teachers

- Require all those entering the teaching profession to pass minimum competency tests
- Require all teachers to pass minimum competency tests every two years
- Provide alternative routes to teaching for college graduates who have not taken education courses *but* have at least three years' employment in a related field—they, too, must pass the minimum competency tests
- Set starting salaries for teachers at 10 percent above the median starting salaries of other college graduates in the state—the 11-month teaching year and the increase in salary will make this a full-time job with full-time pay
- Appoint master teachers who have proven their excellence in the classroom to supervise new teachers—and reward them with a healthy bonus

Schools

- Give the parents of each student a voucher in the amount of the state's average cost per pupil (see Table 17.1)
- Allow the voucher to be spent on any school—public, private, or parochial—that meets the state's minimum standards
- Use the annual testing of students to evaluate how well a school is teaching, in terms of the overall *gain* in students' scores, not the overall scores
- Publish each school's report card (on its students' median ject matter) prominently in area newspapers so that parents can make an informed decision about where to spend their education vouchers

Questions

1. Which proposals do you think would work? Which ones do you think would not work? Why?

2. Implementing some of these proposals would mean breaking the public schools' current monopoly on education tax dollars. Who would be threatened by such proposals? What chance do you think such proposals would have of getting passed?

3. Experienced teachers vigorously object to proposals that they, too, be required to pass minimum competency tests. Why do you think they resist this idea?

4. Apply your sociological imagination to these proposals. For example, how might they affect relationships between the social classes? Note that if the voucher system were adopted, all income groups in each state would receive the same amount.

5. Finally, what sort of competition would spring up among schools? What kind of new schools do you think would come into being? Do you think the changes would be desirable? Why or why not?

SUMMARY

1. For most of the world's history, there was no separate, formal social institution of learning. Education and acculturation were the same. Today, however, formal education plays such a central role in modern life that industrialized societies have become credential societies; employers use diplomas and degrees to determine who is eligible for jobs, even though these qualifications may be irrelevant to the particular work.

2. Education always reflects and transmits culture, as seen in descriptions of the educational systems of Great Britain, Japan, and the Soviet Union. Individualism, competition, and patriotism are examples of core cultural values transmitted through education in the United States.

3. From the functionalist perspective, education is a means by which society is stabilized. Functions of education include teaching knowledge and skills, teaching values, social integration, gatekeeping, and promoting personal and social change. Functionalists also examine how schools are replacing traditional family functions.

4. Conflict theorists, in contrast, view education as a mechanism for maintaining social inequality and reproducing the social class system. Accordingly, they stress such matters as the way in which education reflects the social structure of society (the correspondence principle), unequal funding, tracking, the hidden curriculum, and biased IQ tests.

5. Symbolic interactionists are more likely to examine classroom interaction, for example, by studying how teacher expectations lead to self-fulfilling prophecies of student performance. The studies undertaken by Rist and Rosenthal/Jacobson illustrate this approach.

6. What makes some schools more effective than others is a matter of debate. The Coleman Report found that social class, not the characteristics of the schools themselves, was the most significant factor. This report supported compensatory education and busing. During the 1950s, national averages on the Scholastic Aptitude Test (SAT) rose, reaching an all-time peak in 1963. Since then, they have declined. The three main explanations for this decline are that American high schools now teach more people with poor academic backgrounds, that students read less because of competing activities, and that the quality of education in the United States has eroded. Schools can be improved by applying the findings of the Rutter Report, thus setting up a positive self-fulfilling prophecy.

SUGGESTED READINGS

Ballantine, Jeanne. *The Sociology of Education: A Systematic Analysis.* 2nd ed. Englewood Cliffs, N.J.: Prentice Hall, 1989. This overview of the sociology of education reviews many of the topics discussed in this chapter in greater depth.

Bloom, Allan. *The Closing of the American Mind: How Higher Education Has Failed Democracy and Impoverished the Souls of Today's Students.* New York: Simon & Schuster, 1987. This well-written, scathing denunciation of today's educational practices hit a national nerve and raced to the best-seller lists.

Boyer, Ernest L. *College: The Undergraduate Experience in America.* New York: Harper & Row, 1987. Based on interviews with both students and faculty, the author paints a critical picture of life on the college campus.

Howe, Quincy, Jr. *Under Running Laughter: Notes from a Renegade Classroom.* New York: Free Press, 1990. A tenured professor of classics recounts his experiences and describes the unorthodox techniques he used to teach "throwaway" adolescents in the inner city, aimed at turning their energies to constructive ends.

Kozol, Jonathan. *Savage Inequalities.* New York, N.Y.: Crown Publishers: 1991. Kozol presents a journalistic account of educational inequalities that arise from social class.

National Commission on Excellence in Education. *A Nation at Risk: The Full Account.* Cambridge, Mass.: USA Research, 1984. Prompted by a long decline in national scores on the Scholastic Aptitude Test, this national study analyzes what is wrong with the American educational system and makes suggestions for what can be done to correct it.

Oakes, Jeannie. *Keeping Track: How High Schools Structure Inequality.* New Haven, Conn.: Yale University Press, 1985. Oakes focuses on what is certainly one of the central problems in American education: the way in which educational tracking maintains social inequality.

Schoolland, Ken. *Shogun's Ghost: The Dark Side of Japanese Education.* Westport, Conn.: Bergin & Garvey, 1990. The author, a college teacher in Japan for five years, shatters the myth of excellence in Japanese education in his account of unruly classrooms, general lack of discipline and study habits, truancy, and rampant cheating on exams.

Trueba, Henry T., Lila Jacobs, and Elizabeth Kirton. *Cultural Conflict and Adaptation: The Case of Hmong Children in American Society.* Bristol, Penn.: Falmer Press, 1990. In examining problems of Hmong children living in California, the author probes the multiethnic challenges facing American schools.

U.S. Department of Education. *Schools that Work: Educating Disadvantaged Children,* Washington, D.C.: U.S. Government Printing Office, 1987. Can low-income, inner-city children really be educated? Or is such an attempt merely a waste of money? This report, analyzing successful public and private schools, indicates what can be done.

Journals

The following three journals contain articles that examine almost every aspect of education: *Education and Urban Society, Harvard Educational Review, Sociology of Education*

CHAPTER *18*

Orlando Agudelo-Botero, Oracion,
1989

Religion: Establishing Meaning

WHAT IS RELIGION?

THE FUNCTIONALIST PERSPECTIVE
Functions of Religion ■ Functional Equivalents of
Religion ■ Dysfunctions of Religion

THE SYMBOLIC INTERACTIONIST PERSPECTIVE
Religious Symbols ■ Rituals ■ Beliefs ■ Religious
Experience ■ Community

THE CONFLICT PERSPECTIVE
Opium of the People ■ A Reflection of Social
Inequalities ■ A Legitimation of Social Inequalities

RELIGION AND THE SPIRIT OF CAPITALISM

THE WORLD'S MAJOR RELIGIONS
Judaism ■ Christianity ■ Islam ■
Hinduism ■ Buddhism ■ Confucianism

TYPES OF RELIGIOUS ORGANIZATIONS
Cult ■ Sect ■ Church ■ *Down-to-Earth Sociology:*

Mass Shortage ■ Ecclesia ■ Variations in
Patterns ■ *Perspectives:* **Religion and Culture in
India** ■ A Closer Look at Cults and Sects

SECULARIZATION
The Secularization of Religion ■ *Down-to-Earth
Sociology:* **Bikers and Bibles** ■ The Secularization
of Culture

THE MAIN CHARACTERISTICS OF RELIGION
IN THE UNITED STATES
Diversity ■ Pluralism and Freedom ■
Competition ■ Commitment ■ Privacy ■
Toleration ■ Fundamentalist Revival ■
The Electronic Church ■ Characteristics of Members

THE FUTURE OF RELIGION

SUMMARY

SUGGESTED READINGS

With his mother's call, Tom's world had begun to crumble. Amidst sobs, she had told him that she had left his father. After twenty-two years, their marriage was over! Why? It just didn't make sense. Tom knew that his mother and father had problems, that they argued quite a bit. But they always had. And didn't every married couple? Where was he going to go for the summer? His parents had put the house up for sale, and each had moved to a small apartment. There was no home anymore.

Life seemed a little brighter when Tom met Amy in English class. She was the only one he could talk to about his feelings—Amy's parents had divorced three years before, and she understood. When Amy was invited to a meeting of the Unification church, Tom agreed to go with her.

The meeting was a surprise. Everyone was friendly, and everything was low-key. And everyone seemed so sure. They all believed that Judgment Day was just around the corner.

Amy and Tom found the teachings rather strange, but, since the people had been so friendly, they came back. After Tom and Amy attended meetings for about a month, they became good friends with Marcia and Ryan. Later they moved into an apartment house where Marcia, Ryan, and other Moonies lived. After a while, they dropped out of college and immersed themselves in a new life as Moonies.

WHAT IS RELIGION?

As we have seen in previous chapters, all human societies are organized by some form of the family, as well as by some kind of economic system and political order. These key social institutions are thus central to human existence. They touch on aspects of life that are essential to human welfare. This chapter examines religion, another universal social institution.

The goal of the sociological study of religion is to analyze the relationship between society and religion and to gain insight into the role that religion plays in people's lives. Sociologists do not seek to verify or disclaim individual faiths or to make value judgments about religious beliefs. As mentioned in Chapter 1, sociologists have no tools for deciding that one course of action is more moral than another, much less that one religion is "the" correct one or "more" correct than another. Religion is a matter of faith; sociologists deal with empirical matters, things they can observe or measure. Thus sociologists can measure the extent to which people are religious and can study the effects of religious beliefs and practices on social life. Sociologists can study how religion is organized and how systems of belief are related to culture, stratification systems, and other social institutions. (See Chapter 4 for a review of the elements of social structure.) Unlike theologians, however, they cannot evaluate the truth of a religion's teachings.

In 1912 Emile Durkheim published an influential book, *The Elementary Forms of the Religious Life,* in which he tried to identify the elements common to all religions. After surveying religions around the world, Durkheim discovered no specific belief or practice that they all shared. He did find, however, that all religions, regardless of their name or teaching, separate the sacred from the profane. By **sacred,** Durkheim referred to aspects of life having to do with the supernatural that inspire awe, reverence, deep respect, even fear. By **profane,** he meant aspects of life that are not concerned with religion or religious purposes but are instead part of the ordinary aspects of everyday life. Durkheim also found that all religions develop a community around their practices and beliefs. Durkheim (1965) summarized his findings in the following way.

> A religion is a unified system of beliefs and practices relative to sacred things, that is to say, things set apart and forbidden—beliefs and practices which unite into one single moral community called a Church, all those who adhere to them.

Thus, he argued, a **religion** is defined by three elements.

1. *Beliefs* that some things are sacred (forbidden, set off from the profane)
2. *Practices* (rituals) concerning the things considered sacred
3. *A moral community* (a church) resulting from a group's beliefs and practices

Durkheim used the word **church** in an unusual sense, to refer to any "moral community" centered on beliefs and practices regarding the sacred. In Durkheim's sense, *church* means a moral community of Buddhists bowing before a shrine, Hindus dipping in the Ganges River, and Confucianists offering food to their ancestors. Similarly, the term *moral community* does not imply morality in the sense familiar to most of us. Moral community simply means people united by their religious practices—and that would include Aztec priests who each day gathered around an altar to pluck out the beating heart of a virgin.

Project 1

L. Obj. 1: Define religion and explain Durkheim's essential elements of religion.

CDQ 1: Does the fact that sociologists do not seek to verify or to make value judgments about religious beliefs mean that they have no religious beliefs of their own? Why or why not?

K.P.: Emile Durkheim

CDQ 2: What does the word "profane" mean to you? Do sociologists define it in the same way?

sacred (the): Durkheim's term for things set apart or forbidden, which inspire fear, awe, reverence, or deep respect

profane (the): Durkheim's term for mundane elements of everyday life

religion: according to Durkheim, beliefs and practices that separate the profane from the sacred and unite its adherents into a moral community

church: a large, highly organized religious group with little emphasis on personal conversion and formal, sedate worship services

To gain an understanding of the sociological approach to religion, let's see what picture emerges when we apply the three theoretical perspectives.

THE FUNCTIONALIST PERSPECTIVE

Functions of Religion

In Durkheim's sense of religion—dividing the world into the sacred and profane and establishing rituals around those beliefs—religion is universal. The reason for its universality, say functionalists, is that religion meets basic human needs. Functionalists (Alpert 1939; Chalfant, Beckley, Palmer 1987; Galanter 1989; Glock and Stark 1965; O'Dea and Aviad 1983; Stack 1983; Tittle and Welch 1983) identify those needs as covering eight main aspects of life.

Questions about Ultimate Meaning. Around the world, religions provide answers to perplexing questions about ultimate meaning—such as the purpose of life, why people suffer, and the existence of an afterlife. Those answers give people a sense of purpose. Instead of seeing themselves buffeted by random events in an aimless existence, religious believers see their lives as fitting into a divine plan.

Emotional Comfort. The answers that religion provides about ultimate meaning also comfort people, by assuring them that there is a purpose to their suffering and allowing them to look forward to release from the pains of this life. Similarly, religious rituals that enshroud critical events as illness and death provide emotional comfort at such times of crisis. The individual knows that others care and can find consolation in following a familiar and prescribed pattern.

Social Solidarity. Religious teachings and practices unite believers into a community that shares values and perspectives ("we Jews," "we Christians," "we Muslims"). The religious rituals that surround marriage, for example, link the bride and groom with a broader community that wishes them well. So do other religious rituals, such as those that celebrate birth and mourn death.

Guidelines for Everyday Life. The teachings of religion are not only abstract. They also apply to people's everyday lives. For example, four of the Ten Commandments delivered by Moses to the Israelites concern God, but the other six contain instructions on how to live everyday life, including how to get along with parents, employers, and neighbors.

Social Control. In addition to providing guidelines for everyday life, religion also controls people's behaviors. Most norms of a religious group apply only to its members, but some set limits on nonmembers also. At times, for instance, religious teachings are even incorporated into criminal law. In the United States, for example, blasphemy and adultery were once statutory crimes for which offenders could be arrested, tried, and sentenced. Laws that prohibit the sale of alcohol before noon on Sunday—or even Sunday sales of "nonessential items" in some places—are another example.

Adaptation. Religion can help people adapt to new environments. For example, it is not easy for immigrants to adapt to the confusing customs of a new land. By maintaining the native language and familiar rituals and teachings, religion can provide continuity with an immigrant's cultural past.

The handful of German immigrants who settled in Perry County, Missouri, in the 1800s, for example, even brought their Lutheran minister with them. Their sermons and hymns continued to be in German, and their children also attended a school in

Essay #1

L. Obj. 2: Describe the functionalist perspective on religion, including the functional equivalents of religion, and the functions and dysfunctions of religion.

Speaker Sug. #1: A colleague whose specialty is in sociology of religion to discuss current research.

Project 2

CDQ 3: What purposes or functions do you think religion serves in societies?

CDQ 4: What examples can you give of functional equivalents of religion?

which the minister conducted classes in German. Out of this small group grew the Lutheran Church–Missouri Synod which, in spite of its name, is an international denomination that numbers almost three million persons. Little by little, this group's descendants and converts entered mainstream American culture. Today, except for Luther's basic teachings and some church practices, little remains of the past, for just as it helped the immigrants adapt to a new environment, so the religion itself underwent change.

Support for the Government.   Most religions provide support for the government. The American flag so prominently displayed in many churches represents this support. Governments reciprocate by supporting God as witnessed in the inaugural speeches of American presidents, which invariably ask God to bless the nation.

In some instances, the government sponsors a particular religion, bans all others, provides financial support for building churches and seminaries, and may even pay salaries to the clergy. The religions so sponsored are known as **state religions.** During the sixteenth and seventeenth centuries in Sweden the government sponsored Lutheranism, in Switzerland, Calvinism, and in Italy, Roman Catholicism. In other instances, even though no particular religion is sponsored by the government, religious beliefs are so established in a nation's life that the country's history and social institutions are sanctified by being associated with God. For example, though American officials may not belong to any particular religion, they take office by swearing that they will, in the name of God, fulfill their duty. Similarly, Congress is opened with prayer by its own chaplain, schoolchildren recite daily the pledge of allegiance (including the phrase, "one nation under God"), and coins bear the inscription, "In God We Trust." Sociologist Robert Bellah (1970) referred to this phenomenon as **civil religion.**

Social Change.   Although religion is often so bound up with the prevailing social order that it resists social change, there are occasions when religion spearheads change. In the 1960s, for example, the civil rights movement, which fought to desegregate public facilities and reduce racial discrimination at Southern polls, was led by

state religion: a government-sponsored religion

civil religion: Robert Bellah's term for the development of religion into such an established feature of a country's life that its history and social institutions become sanctified by being associated with God

Religion can promote social change, as was evident with the civil rights movement in the United States in the 1950s and 1960s. The foremost leader of this movement was Dr. Martin Luther King, Jr., a Baptist minister, shown in this 1963 photo making a speech in Washington, D.C. King's repetition of the phrase, "I have a dream," helped to make this speech memorable. He was referring to his dream of the end of racial discrimination, when "all God's children" would live in harmony and peace. Although King was assassinated on April 4, 1968, his dream lives on in the hearts of many.

religious leaders, especially leaders of African-American churches such as Martin Luther King, Jr. These churches served as the centers at which the rallies were organized (Morris 1984).

Functional Equivalents of Religion

The eight functions described above can also be fulfilled by other components of society. If another component fulfills most of these functions of religion—answering questions about ultimate meaning, providing guidelines for daily life, promoting social control and social change, and so on—sociologists call it a **functional equivalent** of religion. Thus, for some people, psychotherapy is a functional equivalent of religion. For others, a political party may be the substitute. For still others, humanism or transcendental meditation perform similar functions.

Some functional equivalents are difficult to distinguish from a religion (Luke 1985). For example, communism had its prophets (Marx and Lenin), sacred writings (all of Marx, Engels, and Lenin, but especially the *Communist Manifesto*), high priests (the heads of the Communist party), sacred buildings (the Kremlin), shrines (Lenin's body on display in Red Square), rituals (the annual May Day parade in Red Square), and even martyrs (Cuba's Che Guevara). Soviet communism, which was avowedly atheistic and tried to wipe out all traces of Christianity and Judaism from its midst, even tried to replace baptisms and circumcisions with state-sponsored rituals that dedicated the child to the state. The Communist party also produced rituals for weddings and funerals.

As sociologist Ian Robertson (1987) pointed out, however, there is a fundamental distinction between a religion and its functional equivalent. Although the substitute may perform similar functions, its activities are not directed toward God, gods, or the supernatural.

Dysfunctions of Religion

Functionalists also examine ways in which religion can be *dysfunctional*, that is, can bring harmful results. Two main dysfunctions are war and religious persecution.

War. History is filled with wars that were supposedly fought for religious reasons. Between the eleventh and fourteenth centuries, for example, Christian monarchs conducted nine bloody Crusades in an attempt to wrest control of the Holy Land from the Muslims. Unfortunately, such wars are not just a relic of the past, for even today Protestants and Catholics kill one another in Northern Ireland, while Jews and Muslims take up arms against one another in Israel.

Religious Persecution. Beginning in the 1200s and continuing into the 1800s, in what has become known as the Inquisition, Roman Catholic leaders burned convicted witches at the stake. In 1692, Protestant leaders in Salem, Massachusetts, did the same thing. (The last execution for witchcraft was in Scotland in 1722 [Bridgwater 1953].) Similarly, it seems fair to say that the Aztec religion had its dysfunctions—at least for the virgins offered to appease angry gods. In short, religion has been used to justify oppression and any number of brutal acts.

THE SYMBOLIC INTERACTIONIST PERSPECTIVE

As discussed in previous chapters, symbolic interactionists focus on the role of meaning in people's lives, especially the way in which symbols communicate meaning. Let's apply this perspective to religious symbols, rituals, and beliefs to see how they help to forge a community of like-minded people.

Essay #2

L. Obj. 3: Explain what aspects of religion are focused on by symbolic interactionists.

CDQ 5: Are religious symbols visible on your campus? In your city? If so, what do they represent?

functional equivalent: in this context, a substitute that serves the same functions (or meets the same needs) as religion, for example, psychotherapy

Ein erschröckliche geschicht/ so zu Derneburg in der Graff-schafft Reinstepn am Harz gelegen von drepen Jauberin unnd zwapen Mañen/ In etlichen tagen des Monats October Im 1 5 5 5. Jare ergangen ist.

Woodcuts (engraved blocks of wood coated with ink to leave an impression on paper) were used to illustrate books shortly after the printing press was invented. This woodcut commemorates a dysfunction of religion, the burning of witches at the stake. This particular event occurred at Derneburg, Germany, in 1555.

Religious Symbols

To see how significant religious symbols can be, suppose that it is about two thousand years ago and you have just joined a new religion. You have come to believe that a recently crucified Jew named Jesus is the Messiah, the Lamb of God offered for your sins. The Roman leaders are persecuting the followers of Jesus. They hate your religion because you and your fellow believers will not acknowledge Caesar as God.

Christians are few in number, and you are eager to have fellowship with other believers. But how can you tell who is a believer? Spies are all over. They have sworn to destroy this new religion, and you do not relish the thought of being fed to lions in the Coliseum.

You use a simple technique. While talking with a stranger, as though doodling absentmindedly in the sand or dust, you casually trace out the outline of a fish. Only fellow believers know the hidden symbolism—that each letter in the Greek word for fish matches the first letter of each word in the Greek sentence, "Jesus (is) Christ the Son of God." If the other person gives no response, you rub the outline out and continue the interaction as normal. If there is a response, you eagerly talk about your new faith.

All religions use symbols to provide identity and social solidarity for their members. For Muslims, the primary symbol is the crescent moon and star, for Jews the Star of David, for Christians the cross. For members, these are not ordinary symbols, but sacred symbols that evoke feelings of awe and reverence. In Durkheim's terms, religions use symbols to specify what is sacred and to separate the sacred from the profane.

A symbol is a condensed way of communicating. Worn by a fundamentalist Christian, for example, the cross says, "I am a follower of Jesus Christ. I believe that He is the Messiah, the promised Son of God, that He loves me, that He died to take away my sins, that He rose from the dead and is going to return to earth, and that through Him I will receive eternal life."

That is a lot to pack into one symbol—and it is only part of what the symbol means to a fundamentalist believer. To persons in other traditions of Christianity, the cross conveys somewhat different meanings—but to all Christians, the cross is a shorthand way of expressing many meanings. So it is also with the Star of David, the crescent moon and star, the cow (expressing to Hindus the unity of all living things), and the various symbols of the world's many other religions.

Rituals

Rituals, ceremonies or repetitive practices, are also symbols that help unite people into a moral community. Some rituals, such as the bar mitzvah of Jewish boys and Holy Communion of Christians, are designed to create in the devout a feeling of closeness with God and unity with one another. Rituals include kneeling and praying at set times, bowing, crossing oneself, singing, lighting candles and incense, a liturgy, Scripture readings, processions, baptisms, weddings, funerals, and so on.

Beliefs

Symbols, including rituals, develop from beliefs. The belief may be vague ("God is") or highly specific ("God wants us to prostrate ourselves and face Mecca five times each day"). Religious beliefs not only include *values* (what is considered good and desirable in life—how we ought to live) but also a **cosmology,** a unified picture of the world. For example, the Jewish, Christian, and Muslim belief that there is only one God, the Creator of the universe, who is concerned about the actions of humans and who will hold us accountable for what we do, is a cosmology. It presents a unifying picture of the universe.

Religious Experience

The term **religious experience** refers to a variety of experiences that seem to have in common a sudden awareness of the supernatural or a feeling of coming in contact with God. Some people undergo a mild version, such as feeling closer to God when they look at a mountain or listen to a certain piece of music. Others report a life-transforming experience, for example, St. Francis of Assisi, who became aware of God's presence in every living thing.

Some Protestants use the term **born again** to describe people who have undergone such a life-transforming religious experience. Such persons say that they came to the realization that they had sinned, that Jesus had died for their sins, and that God requires them to live a new life. Henceforth their worlds become transformed, they look forward to the Resurrection and a new life in heaven, and they see relationships with spouses, parents, children, and even bosses in a new light. They also report a need to make changes in how they interact with others, so that their lives reflect their new, personal commitment to Jesus as their "Savior and Lord." They describe a feeling of beginning life again, hence the term "born again."

Community

Finally, the shared meanings that come through symbols, rituals, and beliefs (and for some, a religious experience) unite people into a moral community. Persons in a moral community feel a bond with one another, for their beliefs and rituals bind them together while at the same time separating them from those who do not share their unique symbolic world. Mormons, for example, feel a "kindred spirit" (as it is often known) with other Mormons. So do Baptists, Jews, Jehovah's Witnesses, and Muslims with members of their respective faiths.

rituals: ceremonies or repetitive practices; in this context, religious observances or rites

cosmology: teachings or ideas that provide a unified picture of the world

religious experience: a sudden awareness of the supernatural or a feeling of coming in contact with God

born again: a term describing Christians who have undergone a life-transforming religious experience so radical that they feel they have become new persons

Symbolic interactionists stress that a basic characteristic of humans is that they attach meaning to objects and events and then use representations of those objects or events to communicate with one another. Some religious symbols are used to communicate feelings of awe and reverence. For Roman Catholics, few such symbols are as effective as St. Peter's Basilica in the Vatican, depicted here. Other symbols, such as the water used in baptism or the bread and wine used in communion, are more ordinary in nature but just as powerful (see photo on facing page).

As a symbol of their unity, members of some religious groups address one another as "brother" or "sister." "Sister Dougherty, we are going to meet at Brother and Sister Tedrick's on Wednesday" is a common way of expressing a message. The terms "brother" and "sister" are intended to symbolize a relationship so close that the individuals consider themselves members of the same family.

Community is powerful, not only because it provides the basis for mutual identity, but also because it establishes norms that govern the behavior of its members. Members either conform, or they lose their membership. In Christian churches, for example, an individual whose adultery becomes known, and who refuses to ask forgiveness, may be banned from the Church. He or she may be formallly excommunicated, as in the case of Catholics, or more informally discharged, as is the usual Protestant practice.

The removal of community is a serious matter for persons whose identity is bound up in the community. Sociologist John Hostetler (1980) reported the Amish practice *shunning*—ignoring an offender in all situations. Persons who are shunned are treated as though they do not exist (for if they do not repent by expressing sorrow for their act they have ceased to exist as members of the community). The shunning is so thorough that even family members, who themselves remain in good standing in the congregation, are not allowed to talk to the person being shunned.

CDQ 6: Do you tend to agree with the functionalist or conflict perspective on religion? Why?

L. Obj. 4: Identify the conflict perspective on religion and note the influence of Marx on this perspective.

K.P.: Karl Marx

THE CONFLICT PERSPECTIVE

In contrast to the functionalist and symbolic interactionist perspectives, the conflict perspective examines religion from the standpoint of the support it provides for the status quo, the way in which it helps to maintain social inequalities and the established order of power and politics.

Opium of the People

In general, conflict theorists are highly critical of religion. Karl Marx, an avowed atheist who believed that the existence of God was an impossibility, set the tone for conflict

theorists with his most famous statement on this subject.

> Religion is the sigh of the oppressed creature, the sentiment of a heartless world. . . .
> It is the opium of the people (Marx 1844, 1964).

By this statement, Marx meant that the oppressed (the workers), sighing for release from their suffering, escape into religion. They use religion as a drug to help them forget their misery. By providing false hope of happiness in a coming world, religion takes their eyes off their suffering in this one. It diverts their energies from changing their present circumstances.

A Reflection of Social Inequalities

Conflict theorists stress that religious teachings and practices reflect a society's inequalities. Gender inequality illustrates this point. When males completely dominated American society, American churches and synagogues ordained only men, limiting women to such activities as teaching children in Sunday school or preparing meals for congregational get-togethers, which were considered appropriate "feminine" activities.

As women's roles in the broader society changed, these changes then came to be reflected in their religious roles. First, many religious groups allowed women to vote. Then, as women attained prominent positions in the business world and professions, some Protestant and Jewish groups allowed women to be ordained. Similarly, just as women still face barriers in secular society, some congregations still refuse to ordain women. In some congregations the barriers remain so high that women are still not allowed to vote.

If we move beyond the local congregation, we see that national church organizations also reflect women's political position in general society. As discussed in Chapter 15, and as you know from your own observations, the higher the level in the American political structure, the fewer the women. Religious organizations are no exception to this cultural pattern, for there, too, the higher the level, the fewer the women. On national boards, it is a rare woman who holds membership, and the highest positions remain an almost exclusively male bastion of power.

A Legitimation of Social Inequalities

In addition to mirroring social inequalities of the larger society, conflict theorists say that religion also legitimates them. By this, they mean that religion, reflecting the interests of those in power, teaches that the existing social arrangements of a society represent what God desires. For example, during the Middle Ages Christian theologians decreed the "divine right of kings." This doctrine meant that God determined who would become king and set him on the throne. The king ruled in God's place, and it was the duty of a king's subjects to be loyal to him (and to pay their taxes). To disobey the king was to disobey God.

In what is perhaps the supreme technique of legitimating the social order, going even a step further than the "divine right of kings," the religion of ancient Egypt held that the Pharaoh was a god. The Emperor of Japan was similarly declared divine. If this was so, who could even question his decisions? How many of today's politicians would give their right arm for such a religious teaching!

Conflict theorists point to many other examples of the extent to which religion legitimates the social order. One of the more interesting took place in the decades before the American Civil War. Southern ministers used scripture to defend slavery, saying that it was God's will—while at the same time Northern ministers legitimated *their* regional social structure and used Scripture to denounce slavery as evil (Ernst 1988). In a not too dissimilar situation, the Dutch Reformed church of South Africa supported apartheid, teaching that God wants whites to rule blacks and that it is sinful for the races to mix. Similarly, Hinduism supports the Indian caste system by teaching that an individual who tries to change caste will come back in the next life as a member of a lower caste—or even as an animal.

People who are caught up in religious teachings tend not to see their social implications. Although it is readily apparent to non-Hindus that their teachings of caste and reincarnation legitimate social inequality, the connection remains invisible to most Hindus. In a similar fashion, most of the legitimating of social inequality that emanates from Judeo-Christian religions remains invisible to us.

RELIGION AND THE SPIRIT OF CAPITALISM

Max Weber disagreed intensely with the conflict perspective on religion, especially with Marx's position that religion merely reflects and legitimates the social order, and that religion impedes social change by encouraging people to focus on the afterlife, as discussed in Chapter 7. Weber saw the focus on the afterlife as a source of profound social change.

Like Marx, Weber personally observed the European countries industrialize in the embrace of capitalism. Weber was intrigued with the question of how these societies had broken out of their old restraints and traditional ways. Tradition is strong and holds people in check, yet entire societies were embroiled in this fundamental transformation. As he explored this problem, Weber concluded that religion held the key to **modernization**—the transformation of traditional societies to industrial societies.

Weber wrote *The Protestant Ethic and the Spirit of Capitalism* (1958, original 1904–1905) to explain his conclusions. Because Weber's argument was presented in Chapter 7 (pages 166–167), it is only summarized here.

> 1. Capitalism is not just a superficial change; it represents a fundamentally different approach to work and money. *Traditionally, people worked just enough to meet their basic needs, not so that they could have a surplus to invest.* The **spirit of capitalism** is a radical departure from the past, for it means that people accumulate capital not to spend it, but as an end in itself. They even consider it a duty to invest money in order to make profits, which, in turn, they reinvest to make more profits.
>
> 2. Why did the spirit of capitalism develop in Europe, and not, for example, in China or India, where the people had similar opportunities: population, intelligence,

L. Obj. 5: Describe the relationship (as seen by Weber) between religion and the spirit of capitalism.

CDQ 7: Do you agree with Max Weber's idea that religion can produce social change?

K.P.: Max Weber

modernization: the transformation of traditional societies into industrial societies

spirit of capitalism (the): Weber's term for the desire to accumulate capital as a duty—not to spend it, but as an end in itself

material resources, education, and so on? According to Weber, *religion was the key.* The religions of China and India, and indeed Roman Catholicism in Europe, encouraged a traditional approach to life, not thrift and investment. Capitalism appeared when religion changed.

   3. What was different about Protestantism, especially Calvinism? The followers of John Calvin could not depend on religion to be assured that they were saved. Not even being a member of the church or "feeling" saved was sufficient. Calvinists believed that God had predestined some people to heaven, others to hell, and that in this life you couldn't know where you were headed.

   4. This doctrine created intense anxiety: Am I predestined to hell or to heaven, people wondered? As Calvinists wrestled with this question, they concluded that each church member had a duty to prove that he or she was one of the elect, and to live as though he or she were predestined to heaven—for good works were a demonstration of salvation.

   5. This conclusion motivated Calvinists not only to lead highly moral lives, but also to work hard, not waste time, and be frugal—for idleness and needless spending were signs of worldliness. Weber called this approach to life the **Protestant ethic.**

   6. All the hard work, combined with religious restraints on spending money on luxuries (which were narrowly defined), resulted in an accumulation of capital that was invested.

   7. Thus, a change in religion (from Catholicism to Protestantism, especially Calvinism) led to a fundamental change in thought and behavior (the Protestant ethic), which resulted in the "spirit of capitalism." Thus capitalism originated in Europe, and not in places where religion did not encourage capitalism's essential elements: the accumulation of capital through frugality and hard work, and its investment and reinvestment.

Although Weber's analysis has been highly influential, it has not lacked critics (Marshall 1982). Hundreds of scholars have attacked it, some for overlooking the lack of capitalism in Scotland (a Calvinist country), others for failing to explain why the Industrial Revolution was born in England (not a Calvinist country), still others on many other points. Hundreds of other scholars have defended Weber's argument. There is currently no historical evidence that can definitively prove or disprove Weber's thesis.

Today the spirit of capitalism and the Protestant ethic are by no means limited to Protestants. American Catholics, for example, have about the same approach to life as do American Protestants. As we all know, the Japanese have embraced capitalism, and many say that they work harder and save more than those who come from countries imbued with the Protestant ethic. Certainly the Japanese are not Protestants, but as sociologist Robert Bellah (1957) noted, their religions also encourage hard work and success.

At this point in history, the Protestant ethic and the spirit of capitalism are not confined to any specific religion or even part of the world. Rather, they have become cultural traits that have spread to societies around the world (Greeley 1964; Yinger 1970).

THE WORLD'S MAJOR RELIGIONS

Of the thousands of religions in the world, most of the world's population practice one of the following six: Judaism, Christianity, Islam, Hinduism, Buddhism, and Confucianism. Let us briefly review each.

Judaism

The origin of Judaism is traced to Abraham, who lived about four thousand years ago in Ur and Haran in Mesopotamia. Jews believe that God (Jahweh) made a covenant with Abraham, setting aside his descendants as a chosen people and promising to make them "as numerous as the sands of the seashore" and give them a special land that

Essay #3

CDQ 8: Has immigration to the United States contributed to the presence of more of the world's major religions in this country? If yes, can you give examples?

L. Obj. 6: Outline the key characterics of each of the world's major religions.

Speaker Sug. #2: A colleague from the philosophy department or academic area of your institution which teaches world religion courses.

Protestant ethic (the): Weber's term to describe the ideal of a highly moral life, hard work, industriousness, and frugality

would be theirs forever. The sign of this convenant was the circumcision of male children, to be performed when a newborn was eight days old. Descent is traced through Abraham and his wife, Sarah, their son Isaac, and their grandson Jacob (also called Israel).

Joseph, a son of Jacob, was sold by his brothers into slavery and taken to Egypt. Following a series of hair-raising adventures, Joseph became Pharaoh's right-hand man. When a severe famine hit Canaan, where Jacob's family was living, Jacob and his eleven other sons fled to Egypt. Under Joseph's leadership, they were welcome. A subsequent Pharaoh, however, enslaved the children of Israel, and they served as slaves for about four hundred years.

Eventually a leader named Moses arose among the oppressed children of Israel. After finally persuading Pharaoh to let all the slaves, numbering at that time about two million, go, Moses led them into freedom. Before they reached their Promised Land, the children of Israel spent forty years in desert wanderings. Sometime during those years, Moses delivered the Ten Commandments from Mount Sinai.

Abraham, Isaac, Jacob, and Moses hold special positions of respect in Judaism. The events of their lives and the recounting of the early history of the Israelites are contained in the first five books of the Bible, called the *Torah*. The founding of Judaism marked a fundamental change in religion, for it was the first religion based on **monotheism,** the belief that there is only one God. Prior to Judaism, religions were based on **polytheism,** the belief that there are many gods. In Greek religion, for example, Zeus was the god of heaven and earth, Poseidon the god of the sea, Hades the god of the underworld, and Athena the goddess of wisdom. Other groups followed **animism,** believing that all objects in the world have spirits, many of which are dangerous and must be outwitted.

Contemporary Judaism in the United States comprises three main branches: Orthodox, Reform, and Conservative. Orthodox Jews adhere to the laws espoused by Moses. They eat only foods prepared in a designated manner (kosher), observe the Sabbath in a traditional way, and segregate males and females in their religious services. During the 1800s, a group that wanted to make their practices more compatible with the secular (nonreligious) culture broke from this tradition. This liberal group, known as Reform Judaism, mostly uses the vernacular (a country's language) in its religious ceremonies and has reduced much of the ritual. The third branch, Conservative Judaism, falls somewhere between the other two. No branch has continued polygyny (allowing a husband to have more than one wife), the original marriage custom of the Jews, which was outlawed by rabbinic decree almost a thousand years ago.

The history of Judaism is marked by conflict and persecution. The Israelites were conquered by Babylon, and again made slaves. After returning to Israel and rebuilding the temple, they were later conquered by Rome, and after their rebellion at Masada in A.D. 70 failed, they were dispersed for almost two thousand years into other nations. During those centuries, they faced prejudice, discrimination, and persecution (called **antisemitism**) by many peoples and rulers. The most horrendous example is Hitler's attempt to eliminate them as a people in the Nazi Holocaust of World War II. Under the Nazi occupation of Europe and North Africa, about six million Jews were slaughtered, hundreds of thousands dying in gas ovens constructed specifically for this purpose.

Central to Jewish teaching is the requirement to love God and do good deeds. Good deeds begin in the family, where each member has an obligation toward the others. Sin is a conscious choice to do evil, and must be atoned for by prayers and good works. Jews consider Jerusalem their holiest city, where the Messiah will one day appear bringing redemption for them all.

Christianity

Christianity, which developed out of Judaism, is also monotheistic. Christians believe that Jesus Christ is the Messiah whom God promised the Jews.

Jesus was born in poverty, and traditional Christians believe, to a virgin. Within

monotheism: the belief that there is only one God

polytheism: the belief that there are many gods

animism: the belief that all objects in the world have spirits, many of which are dangerous and must be outwitted

antisemitism: prejudice, discrimination, and persecution directed against Jews

two years of his birth, Herod, named King of Palestine by Caesar, who had conquered Israel, was informed that people were saying that a new king had been born. When Herod sent soldiers to kill Jesus, his parents fled with him to Egypt. After Herod died, they returned, settling in the small town of Nazareth.

About the age of thirty, Jesus began a preaching and healing ministry. His teachings challenged the contemporary religious establishment and as his popularity grew, the religious and political leaders plotted to have him killed by the Romans. Christians interpret the death of Jesus as a blood sacrifice for their sins. They believe that through his death they have peace with God and will inherit eternal life.

The twelve main followers of Jesus, called apostles, believed that Jesus was resurrected from the dead. They preached the need to be "born again," to convert, accept Jesus as Savior, give up selfish ways, and live a devout life. The new religion spread rapidly, and after initial hostility from imperial Rome—including the feeding of believers to the lions in the Coliseum—in A.D. 317 Christianity became the empire's official religion.

During the first thousand years of Christianity, there was only one church organization, directed from Rome. During the eleventh century, bitter disagreement over doctrine and politics led to the establishment of Greek Orthodoxy, which was headquartered in Constantinople (now Istanbul, Turkey). During the Middle Ages, the Roman Catholic church, aligned with the political establishment, grew corrupt. Some Church offices, such as that of bishop, were sold for a set price, and, in a situation that touched off the Reformation led by Martin Luther in the sixteenth century, the forgiveness of sins (including those not yet committed) could be purchased by buying an "indulgence."

Although Martin Luther's original goal was to reform the Church, not divide it, the Reformation began a splintering of Christianity. It coincided with the breakup of feudalism, and as the ancient political structure came apart, people clamored for independence not only in political but also in religious thought. Today, Christianity is the most popular religion in the world, with over one billion adherents. Christians are divided into hundreds of groups, some with doctrinal differences so slight that only members of the group can appreciate the extremely fine distinctions that, they feel, significantly separate them from others.

Islam

Islam, whose followers are known as Muslims, began in the same part of the world as Judaism and Christianity. Islam is the world's third monotheistic religion. It was founded by Muhammad, who was born in Mecca (now in Saudi Arabia) about A.D. 570. Muhammad married Khadija, a wealthy widow. About the age of forty, he reported that he had visions from God. These, and his teachings, were later written down in a book called the Koran. Few paid attention to Muhammad, although Ali, his son-in-law, believed him. When he found out that there was a plot to murder him, Muhammad fled to Medina, where he found a more receptive audience. There he established a *theocracy* (a government based on the principle that God is the ruler, his laws the statutes of the land, and priests his earthly administrators), and founded the Muslim empire. In A.D. 630 he returned to Mecca, this time as a conqueror (Bridgwater 1953).

After Muhammad's death, a struggle for control over the empire he had founded split Islam into two branches that remain today, the Sunni and the Shi'ite. The Shi'ite, who believe that the *imam* (the religious leader) is inspired as he interprets the Koran, are generally more conservative and inclined to **fundamentalism,** the belief that modernism threatens religion and that the faith as it was originally practiced should be restored. The Sunni, who do not share this belief, are generally more liberal.

Like the Jews, Muslims trace their ancestry to Abraham. Abraham fathered a son, Ishmael, by Hagar, his wife Sarah's Egyptian maid (Genesis 25:12). Ishmael had twelve sons, from whom a good portion of today's Arab world are descended. For them, Jerusalem is also a holy city. The Muslims consider the bibles of the Jews and the Christians to be sacred but take the Koran as the final word. They believe that the

fundamentalism: the belief that true religion is threatened by modernism and that the faith as it was originally practiced should be restored

The pilgrimage to Mecca, the city of Muhammad's birth, is a sacred duty of Muslims. Each year millions make the pilgrimage. Shown here is the mosque complex at Mecca.

followers of Abraham and Moses (Jews) and Jesus (Christians) changed the original teachings and that Muhammad restored their purity. It is the duty of each Muslim to make a pilgrimage to Mecca during his or her lifetime.

Unlike the Jews, the Muslims continue to practice polygyny. They place a limit on it, however, and a man is allowed to have only four wives.

Hinduism

Unlike the other religions described above, Hinduism has no specific founder. Going back about four thousand years, Hinduism is the chief religion of India. The term Hinduism, however, is Western, and in India the closest term is *dharma* (law). Unlike Judaism, Christianity, and Islam, Hinduism has no canonical scripture, that is, no texts thought to be inspired by God. Instead, several books, including *Brahmanas, Bhagavad-Gita,* and *Upanishads,* expound on moral qualities that people should strive after. They also delineate the sacrifices people should make to the gods.

Hindus are *polytheists;* that is, they believe that there are many gods. One of these gods, Brahma, created the universe. Brahma, along with Shiva (the Destroyer) and Vishnu (the Preserver), form a triad at the center of modern Hinduism. A central belief is *karma,* spiritual progress. There is no final judgment, but a cycle of life, death, and rebirth. Death involves only the body, and each person's soul is reincarnated, coming back in a form that matches the individual's moral progress in the previous life (which centers on proper conduct in following the rules of one's caste). If an individual reaches spiritual perfection, he or she has attained *nirvana.* This marks the end of the cycle of death and rebirth, when the soul is reunited with the universal soul. When this occurs, *maya,* the illusion of time and space, has been conquered.

Some Hindu practices have been modified as a consequence of social protest—especially child marriage and *suttee,* the practice of cremating a surviving widow along with her deceased husband (Bridgwater 1953). Other ancient rituals remain unchanged, such as *kumbh mela,* a purifying washing in the Ganges River, which takes place every twelve years, and in which millions participate.

From his review of world religions, Durkheim concluded that all religions have beliefs, practices, and a moral community. Part of Hindu belief is that the Ganges is a holy river and bathing in it imparts spiritual benefits. Each year, millions of Hindus participate in this rite of ablution.

Buddhism

About 600 B.C., Siddhartha Gautama founded Buddhism. (Buddha means the "enlightened one," a term Gautama was given by his disciples.) Gautama was the son of an upper-caste Hindu ruler in an area north of Benares, India. At the age of twenty-nine, he renounced his life of luxury and became an ascetic. Through meditation, he discovered the following "four noble truths," all of which emphasize self-denial and compassion.

1. Existence is suffering.
2. The origin of suffering is desire.
3. Suffering ceases when desire ceases.
4. The way to reach the end of desire is to follow the "noble eightfold path."

The noble eightfold path consists of

1. Right belief
2. Right resolve (to renounce carnal pleasure and to harm no living creature)
3. Right speech
4. Right conduct
5. Right occupation or living
6. Right effort
7. Right-mindedness (or contemplation)
8. Right ecstasy.

Buddhism is similar to Hinduism in that the final goal is to escape from **reincarnation** into nonexistence or blissful peace (Bridgwater 1953).

Buddhism spread rapidly. In the third century B.C., the ruler of India adopted Buddhism and sent missionaries throughout Asia to spread the new teaching. By the fifth century A.D., Buddhism reached the height of its popularity in India, after which it died out. Buddhism, however, had been adopted in Ceylon, Burma, Tibet, Laos, Cambodia, Thailand, China, Korea, and Japan, where it flourishes today.

reincarnation: in Hinduism and Buddhism, the return of the soul after death in a different form

As Durkheim pointed out, each religion has teachings about the sacred and profane and their relationship to one another. The goal of Buddhism is to escape reincarnation through denial of the self and compassion for others. In some areas, Buddhists practice fire walking, as depicted in this photo of a priest in Tokyo.

Essay #4

L. Obj. 7: Define cult, sect, church, and ecclesia, and describe the process by which some groups have moved from one category to another.

K.P.: Ernst Troeltsch

TR#40: A Cult-Sect-Church-Ecclesia Continuum

CDQ 9: Do you agree that the word cult conjures up bizarre images in the minds of many individuals? Is this an accurate assessment?

Confucianism

About the time that Gautama lived, K'ung–Fu-tsu (551–479 B.C.) was born in China. Confucius (his name strung together in English), a public official, was distressed by the corruption that he saw in government. Unlike Gautama, who urged withdrawal from social activities, Confucius urged social reform and developed a system of morality based on peace, justice, and universal order. His teachings were incorporated into writings called the *Analects*.

The basic moral principle of Confucianism is to maintain *jen*, sympathy or concern for other humans. The key to jen is to maintain right relationships—being loyal and placing morality above self-interest. In what is called the "Confucian Golden Rule," Confucius stated a basic principle for jen: to treat those who are subordinate to you as you would like to be treated by people superior to yourself. Confucius taught that right relationships within the family (loyalty, respect) should be the model for society. He also taught the "middle way," an avoidance of extremes.

Confucianism was originally atheistic, simply a set of moral teachings without reference to the supernatural. As the centuries passed, however, local gods were added to the teachings, and Confucius himself was declared a god. Confucius's teachings became the basis for the government of China. About A.D. 1000, the emphasis on meditation gave way to a stress on improvement through acquiring knowledge. This emphasis remained dominant until the twentieth century, by which time the government had become rigid, with approval of the existing order having replaced respectful relationships (Bridgwater 1953). Following the Communist revolution of 1949, political leaders attempted to weaken the people's ties with Confucianism.

TYPES OF RELIGIOUS ORGANIZATIONS

Just as different religions have distinct teachings and practices, so *within* a religion different groups contrast sharply with one another. Let's look at the types of religious organizations sociologists have identified: cult, sect, church, and ecclesia. The typology presented here is a modification of analyses by sociologists Ernst Troeltsch (1931), Liston Pope (1942), and Benton Johnson (1963). Figure 18.1 illustrates the relationship between each of these four types of religious organizations.

Cult

The word cult conjures up many bizarre images—shaven heads, weird music, unusual clothing, brainwashing, children estranged from their parents. Secret activities under cover of darkness, even images of ritual murder, may come to mind. In the opening vignette, Tom and Amy dropped out of college, and, to the dismay of their parents and friends, cut themselves off from their usual surroundings and activities.

Cults, however, are not necessarily weird, and few practice "brainwashing" or bizarre rituals. In fact, *all religions began as cults* (Stark 1989). A **cult** is simply a new or different religion, whose teaching and practices put it at odds with the dominant culture and religion. Cults often begin with the appearance of a **charismatic leader,** an individual who inspires people because he or she seems to have extraordinary qualities. **Charisma,** as noted in Chapter 15, refers to an outstanding gift. Finding something highly appealing about such an individual, people feel drawn to both the person and the message.

The most popular religion in the world today began as a cult. Its handful of adherents believed that an unschooled carpenter who preached in remote villages in a back-

cult: a new religion with few followers, whose teachings and practices put it at odds with the dominant culture and religion

charismatic leader: literally, someone to whom God has given a gift; more commonly, someone who exerts extraordinary appeal to a group of followers

charisma: literally, an extraordinary gift from God; more commonly, outstanding "magnetic" attraction

FIGURE 18.1   A Cult-Sect-Church-Ecclesia Continuum. *(Source:* Based on Troeltsch (1931), Pope (1942), and Johnson (1963).)

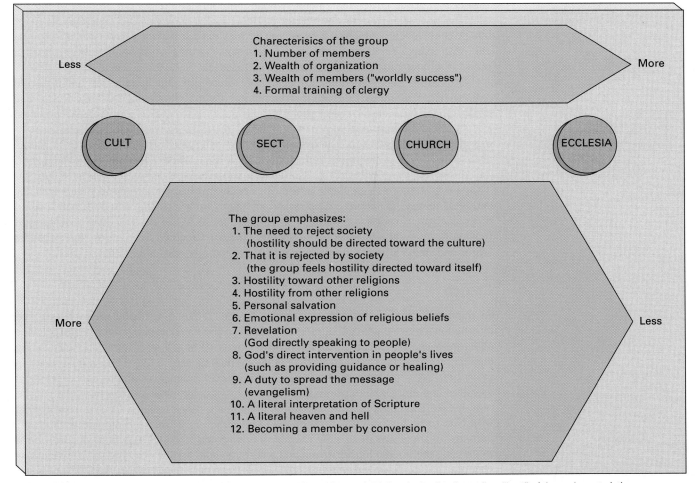

Note: Any religious organization can be placed somewhere on this continuum, based on its having "more" or "less" of these characteristics.

ward country was the Son of God, that he was killed and came back to life. Those beliefs made the early Christians a cult, set them apart from the rest of their society, and created intense antagonisms. Persecuted by both religious and political authorities, these early believers clung to one another for support, many cutting off associations with their unbelieving families and friends. To others, the early Christians must have seemed deluded and brainwashed.

So it was with Islam. When Muhammad revealed his visions and said that God's name was really Allah, he was alone. Only a few people believed him at first. To others, he must have seemed crazy, deranged.

Each cult (or new religion) meets with rejection from society. Its message is considered bizarre, its approach to life strange. Its members antagonize the majority, who are convinced that they have a monopoly on the truth. The new message may claim revelation, visions, visits from God and angels, some form of enlightenment, or seeing the true way to God. The cult demands intense commitment, and its followers, confronting a hostile world, pull into a tight circle, separating themselves from nonbelievers.

Most cults fail. Not many people believe the new message, and the cult fades into obscurity. Others, however, succeed and make history. Over time, large numbers of people may accept the message, and become followers of the religion. If this happens, the new religion changes from a cult to a sect.

Sect

A **sect** is a group larger than a cult, whose members still feel a fair amount of tension with the prevailing beliefs and values of the broader society. The sect may even be hostile to the society in which it lives. At the very least, its members remain uncomfortable with many of the emphases of the dominant culture, while nonmembers, in turn, tend to be uncomfortable with members of the sect.

Ordinarily, sects are loosely organized. They are still fairly small and have no national organization that directs their activities. Even if they belong to local or regional associations, individual congregations retain much control. Sects emphasize personal salvation and an emotional expression of one's relationship with God. Clapping, shouting, dancing, and extemporaneous prayers are hallmarks of sects. Like cults, sects also stress active recruitment of new members, an activity that some call evangelism.

If a sect grows, over time its members tend to make peace with the rest of society. They become more respectable in the eyes of the majority and feel much less hostility and little, if any, isolation. To appeal to the new, broader base, the sect shifts some of its doctrines, redefining matters to remove some of the rough edges that created tension between it and the rest of society. If a sect follows this course and becomes larger and more integrated into society, it has changed into a church.

Church

At this point, the religious group is highly bureaucratized—probably with national and international headquarters that give directions to the local congregations, enforce rules about who can be ordained, and control finances. (For a recruitment difficulty facing one church, see the Down-to-Earth Sociology box on page 513.) The group's worship service is likely to have grown more sedate, with much less emphasis on personal salvation and emotional expression. Written prayers, for example, are now likely to be read before the congregation, sermons to be much more formal, and the relationship with God to be less intense. Rather than being recruited from the outside by fervent, personal evangelism, most new members now come from within, from children born to existing members. Rather than joining through conversion—seeing the new truth—children may be baptized, circumcised, or dedicated in some other way. When older, children may be asked to affirm the group's beliefs in a confirmation or bar mitzvah ceremony.

sect: a group larger than a cult that still feels substantial hostility from and toward society

DOWN-TO-EARTH SOCIOLOGY

Mass Shortage

The largest denomination in the United States is facing a crisis. The Roman Catholic church, which numbers about 55 million Americans, has lost priests at a staggering rate. Over the past thirty years, the number of priests in training in high school and collegiate seminaries has dropped a whopping 89 percent—from 40,000 to less than 4,500. On top of this, many priests are turning in their collars. The Archdiocese of Chicago, the nation's largest Catholic jurisdiction, loses one priest every eighteen days.

The loss of priests is occurring just as the Catholic population in this country is swelling as a result of migration from Mexico and South America. Some feel that this combination of growing numbers of Catholics and shrinking numbers of priests may lead to a Mass shortage—not enough priests to celebrate Mass for all who wish to attend.

The reason for this crisis appears to be the Roman Catholic church's insistence on the celibacy of priests, a rule that went into effect with the First Lateran Council of 1123. Until then, priests could marry.

Many Roman Catholics say it is time to change. Perhaps the rule served a purpose in years past, but now it is dysfunctional. The priests complain of loneliness and denounce celibacy as unhealthy.

So far, the Pope has not budged. He says, "If we Catholics are being brought to our knees by the need for more priests, then that is a good position from which to pray for more clergy."

In the meantime, Madison Avenue–style pitches are being tried: direct mail, promotional films. But the efforts are showing puny results. Priests keep an eye out for young men who remain praying at their pews after other parishioners have headed for the parking lot. But when they are asked if they have considered becoming a priest, the issue of celibacy makes them "freeze, just like you whisked a knife to castrate them."

Some think that it is just a matter of time until the celibacy rule is changed. Others suggest that female priests are the answer.

Source: Based on Bridgwater 1953; Schoenherr, Young, and Vilarino 1988; Shannon 1991.

Ecclesia

Finally, some groups become so well integrated into a culture, and so strongly allied with their government, that it is difficult to tell where one leaves off and the other takes over. In these state religions, also called **ecclesia**, the government and religion work together to try to shape the society. There is no recruitment of members, for citizenship makes everyone a member. The majority of the society, however, may belong to the religion in name only. The religion is part of a cultural identification, not an eye-opening experience. In Sweden, for example, where Lutheranism is the state religion, most Swedes come to church only for baptisms, marriages, and funerals. As shown in the Perspectives box on page 514, the culture and the religion interpenetrate one another, and results can be extreme if the government makes changes that contradict the ecclesia.

Where cults and sects see God as personally involved and concerned with an individual's life, requiring an intense and direct response, an ecclesia's vision of God is more impersonal and remote. Church services reflect this view of the supernatural, for they tend to be highly formal, directed by ministers or priests who have undergone rigorous training in approved schools or seminaries and follow set routines.

Examples of ecclesia include the Church of England (whose very name expresses alignment between church and state), the Lutheran church in Sweden and Denmark, Islam in Iran and Iraq, Confucianism in China until this century, and, during the time of the Holy Roman Empire, the Roman Catholic church, which was the official religion for what is today Europe.

Variations in Patterns

Obviously, not all religious groups go through all of these stages. Some die out because they fail to attract enough members. Others, such as the Amish, remain sects. And since only a limited number of countries have state religions, very few religions ever become ecclesias.

ecclesia: a religious group so integrated into the dominant culture that it is difficult to tell where the one begins and the other leaves off; also called a state religion

PERSPECTIVES
Cultural Diversity Around the World

Religion and Culture in India

Religion and culture can be so interwoven that they totally blend into each other. As they interpenetrate, the religion reflects the culture and the culture reflects the religion. When religion is integral to a people's entire way of life, changing a cultural practice can threaten both the culture and the religion.

So it is in India, where Hinduism permeates the culture. A major teaching of Hinduism is that each person has a spiritual obligation to observe the caste system, that is, to function within the limits set by the caste into which he or she was born. According to Hindu belief, an individual who does this well will be born into a higher caste in the next incarnation.

What happens if the government says that caste arrangements discriminate against members of the lower castes and that a remedy must be sought in this life, and not postponed until a future reincarnation? In 1990 the Indian government did just that when it began an affirmative action program to give Hindus from lower, less privileged castes more government jobs.

To Hindus, this was no mere shuffling of government positions. It was a life-and-death matter, a threat to their fundamental belief system about the way the world is meant to be. To indicate how strongly they felt about the matter—and how much the new policy threatened their core values—150 upper-caste Hindu youths committed

suicide, many by dousing themselves with gasoline and setting themselves on fire (Sterba 1990).

The cow, worshiped as a sacred animal that represents the mother of life, is another integral feature of Indian religion and everyday life. To kill a cow is considered worse than to take a human life. The Indian constitution even includes a bill of rights for cows, and the government maintains "old age homes" for cows (Harris 1974). To Western thinking, it is irrational for 100 million cows to wander the countryside and cities while millions of people go to bed hungry and each day hundreds die of starvation. However, anthropologist Marvin Harris (1974), who analyzed the role of cattle in Indian life pointed out that the taboo against killing cows produces a net benefit to the society. The cattle, which live off humanly inedible products, provide not only milk and energy for plowing but extremely valuable dung—used for fertilizer, cooking fuel, and even mortar and flooring. The taboo also prevents farmers from killing the animals during times of drought. Because farmers depend on oxen for plowing and for transportation (pulling their carts), they must overcome a short-term view. If they killed their cattle during droughts, when they and their families are starving, they would be left without energy for farming after the monsoon rains come. As Harris (1974) noted, Westerners do not realize that farmers would rather eat their cows than starve, but that they will surely starve later if they do eat them.

In addition, such neat classifications as those in this typology are not perfectly matched in the real world. For example, some groups become churches but retain a few characteristics of sects, such as an emphasis on evangelism or a personal relationship with God. Some sects, such as the early Quakers, stressed a personal relationship with God, but shied away from emotional expressions of their beliefs. (They would quietly meditate in church, with no one speaking, until God gave someone a message to share with others.) Some sects, like the Amish, place little or no emphasis on recruiting others.

Finally, although all religions began as cults, not all varieties of a particular religion did so. For example, a **denomination**—a "brand name" within a major religion, for example, Methodism or Reform Judaism—may begin as a splinter group. Although splintering, or schism, usually gives birth to sects, on occasion a large group within a church may disagree with *some aspects* of the church's teachings (not its major message) and break away to form its own organization. An example is the Southern Baptist Convention, formed in 1845 to defend the right to own slaves (Ernst 1988).

A Closer Look at Cults and Sects

denomination: a "brand name" within a major religion, for example, Methodist or Baptist

As we have seen, because of their break with the past, cults and sects present an inherent challenge to the social order. Four major patterns of adaptation occur when religion and the culture in which it is embedded find themselves in conflict.

First, the society may reject the religious group entirely, or even try to destroy it. The early Christians are an example. The Roman emperor declared them enemies of Rome and determined that all Christians were to be hunted down and destroyed until not one was left alive. Even the memory of their heresy was to be removed from history.

In the second pattern, the religious group rejects the dominant culture and withdraws from it geographically. Believing that the survival of their religion is at stake, its members migrate. In some cases, they cannot tolerate the surrounding society and feel too uncomfortable to remain. In other cases, they face persecution and decide that they had better leave.

The Mormons provide an example of the latter type of migration. Their rejection of Roman Catholicism and Protestantism as corrupt, accompanied by their belief in polygyny, led to their persecution. In 1831, they left Palmyra, New York, and moved first to Kirtland, Ohio, and subsequently to Independence, Missouri. When the persecution continued, they moved to Nauvoo, Illinois. There a mob murdered the founder of the religion, Joseph Smith, and his brother Hyrum. The Mormons then decided to escape the dominant culture altogether by founding a community in the wilderness. Consequently, in 1847 they settled in the Great Salt Lake valley of what is today the state of Utah (Bridgwater 1953).

A third pattern is for the members of a religion to reject the dominant culture and withdraw socially. Although they continue to live in the same geographical area as others, they try to have as little as possible to do with nonmembers of their religion. They may withdraw into closed communities, like the Essenes, a Jewish sect that existed in the second century A.D.

Such is the case of the Amish, who, as noted in Chapter 4 (Perspectives box on the Amish, page 100), broke away from Swiss-German Mennonites in 1693. The Amish try to preserve the culture of their ancestors, a simpler time when life was uncontaminated by television, movies, automobiles, or electricity. To do so, they emphasize family life, traditional male and female roles, and live on farms, which they work with horses. They continue to wear the same style of clothing as their ancestors did three hundred years ago, to light their homes with oil lamps, and to speak German at home and in church. They also continue to reject electricity and motorized vehicles. They do mingle with non-Amish to the extent of shopping in town—where they are readily distinguishable by their form of transportation (horse-drawn carriages), clothing, and speech.

In the fourth pattern, a cult or sect rejects only specified elements of the prevailing culture; and neither the religion nor the culture is seriously threatened by the other. For example, religious teachings may dictate that immodest clothing—short skirts, swimsuits, low-cut dresses, and so on—is immoral, or that wearing makeup or going to the movies is wrong. Most elements of the main culture, however, are accepted. Although specified activities are forbidden, members of the religion are able to participate in most aspects of the broader society. They are likely to resolve this mild tension either by adhering to the religion or by "sneaking," doing the forbidden acts on the sly.

SECULARIZATION

Sociologists use the term **secularization of religion** to refer to the replacement of spiritual or "otherworldly" concerns with concerns about "this world." Secularization occurs when religious influence over life is lessened, both on a society's institutions and on individuals. (The term **secular** means "belonging to the world and its affairs.") Cultures, too, become secularized when other social forces replace the functions traditionally fulfilled by religion. Secularization is thus an important type of social change.

CDQ 10: Why is it difficult for groups, such as the Amish, to preserve the culture of their ancestors?

Essay #5

L. Obj. 8: Explain what is meant by secularization. Note how this process occurs in religion and in culture.

secularization of religion: the replacement of a religion's "otherworldly" concerns with concerns about "this world"

secular: belonging to the world and its affairs

The Secularization of Religion

The Splintering of American Churches.   The secularization of religion can explain a question that has perplexed many: Why have Christian churches splintered into so many groups? Why don't Christians have just one church, or at most several, instead of the hundreds of sects and denominations that dot the American landscape?

The simplest answer, of course, is that Christians have disagreed about doctrine (church teaching). As theologian and sociologist Richard Niebuhr pointed out, however, there are many ways of resolving doctrinal disputes besides splintering off and forming another religious organization. Niebuhr (1929) found that the answer lies more in *social* change than in *religious* conflict.

The explanation goes like this. As noted earlier, when a religion becomes more churchlike, tension between it and the main culture lessens. Quite likely, its founders and first members were poor, or at least not too successful in worldly pursuits. Feeling estranged from their general culture, they received a good part of their identity from the cult or sect. Their services and practices stressed differences between their values and cosmology and those of the dominant culture. They also probably stressed the joys of the coming afterlife, when they would be able to escape from their present pain.

As time passes, however, the group's values—such as respect for authority, frugality, the avoidance of gambling, alcohol, and drugs—may actually help the members to experience worldly success. As they become more middle-class and respectable in the eyes of society, they no longer experience the isolation or the hostility felt by the founders of their group.

As this change occurs, the group's teachings—in the official literature as well as in sermons—begin to center more on this world. Life's burdens don't seem as heavy, and the need for relief through an imminent afterlife doesn't seem as pressing. Similarly, the pleasures of the world no longer appear as threatening to salvation or to "true" belief. There follows an attempt to harmonize religious beliefs with the changing orientation to the culture.

Protestant sects such as the Church of the Nazarene and the Church of God provide examples. In their early years, they stressed that jewelry, makeup, and movies were worldly and that true believers had to separate themselves from such things. Over time, the groups became less vocal about movies, and then fell silent about them. Similarly, after initial protests, they gradually objected less and less to their younger members wearing makeup, which at first was "light," and barely discernible, and later became a "normal" amount. Finally came accommodation with the secular culture to such an extent that ministers' wives now dye their hair and wear makeup and jewelry. A sociological cycle has been completed, and what was formerly called the "Jezebel" has become a role model for young women. The teaching changes also, and one hears, "Outward appearances aren't really important. It's what's in your heart that counts."

This is just an example. The particulars vary from one group to another, for not many chose movies, makeup, and jewelry as central identifiers. But the process is the same. As a group becomes more middle-class, the worldly success of its members leads it to change its teachings.

While the secularization of a sect is occurring, however, one segment of the group remains dissatisfied: those members who have had less worldly success. They continue to feel estranged from the broader culture. For them, the tension and hostility remain real, making their group's gradual accommodation to the culture uncomfortable. They view the change as a "sellout" to the secular world.

In short, changes in social class create different needs. As a religious organization changes to meet the changing social status of some of its members, it thereby fails to meet the needs of those whose life situation has not changed. The Down-to-Earth Sociology box on page 517 describes a group whose needs are not met by established religious organizations, but by a small, evangelizing, sectlike group.

This, says Niebuhr, creates irreconcilable tension. The group whose needs are

DOWN-TO-EARTH SOCIOLOGY

Bikers and Bibles

The Bible Belt churchgoers in Eureka Springs, Arkansas, stare as Herbie Shreve, unshaven, his hair hanging over the collar of his denim vest, roars into town on his Harley Davidson. With hundreds of other bikers in town, it is going to be a wild weekend of drunks, nudity, and fights.

But not for Herbie. After pitching his tent, he sets up a table at which he offers other bikers free ice water and religious tracts. "No hard sell. They seek us out when it's the right time," says Herbie.

The ministry began when Herbie's father, a pastor, took up motorcycling to draw closer to his rebellious teenage son. As the pair rode around the heartland of America, they were often snubbed by fellow Christians when they tried to attend church. So Herbie's father hatched plans for a motorcycle ministry. "Jesus said, 'Go out to the highways and hedges,' and that always stuck with me," says the elder Mr. Shreve. "I felt churches ought to be wherever the people are."

They founded the Christian Motorcyclists Association (CMA), headquartered in Hatfield, Arkansas. It now has 33,000 members in more than 300 chapters in the United States and Canada. Members of the CMA call themselves "weekend warriors."

"Riding for the Son" is emblazoned on their T-shirts and jackets, which doesn't make for easy riding. In the midst of the nudity and drunkenness, they stand out.

No MCA member has ever been harmed by a biker. But they have come close. In the early days, bikers at a rally surrounded Herbie's tent and threatened to burn it down. "Some of those same people are friends of mine today," says the elder Mr. Shreve.

Stepping over a guy who had passed out in front of his tent, Herbie goes through the campground urging last night's carousers to join them by a lake for a Sunday service. Four years ago no one took him up on it. Today twenty bikers straggle down to the dock.

Herbie's brief sermon is plain-spoken. He touches on the biker's alienation—the unpaid bills, the oppressive bosses, the righteous church ladies "who are always mad and always right." He tells them that Jesus loves them, and that they can call him anytime. "I'll help fix your life," he says.

Some Christian groups make the conversion of others a primary goal. One such group is the Christian Bikers' Association, discussed in this box. Another is the Full Gospel Motorcycle Association, shown here joining hands in prayer before setting out to change tires, help stranded motorists, and preach the gospel. The bikers strike up conversations about their motorcycles, then change the topic to "how to reverse direction from the highway to hell to the highway to heaven."

They have several conversions this weekend. They give away more tracts—and a couple of the group come up to thank Herbie.

"You just stay at it. You don't know when their hearts are touched. Look at these guys," Herbie says, pointing to fellow CMA members. "They were all bikers headed for hell, too. Now they follow the Son."

Herbie gets on his Harley. In town, the churchgoers stare as he roars past, his long hair sweeping behind him.

Source: Based on Graham 1990; Shreve 1991.

not being met then splinters off, forming a sect in which its members feel more comfortable. This newly formed group again stresses its differences with the world, the need for more personal, emotional religious experience, and salvation from the pain of living in this world. The cycle then repeats itself.

The secularization of religion also occurs on a much broader scale. As a result of modernization—the industrialization of society, urbanization, mass education, wide adoption of technology, and the transformation of *Gemeinschaft* to *Gesellschaft* societies—people depend much less on traditional explanations of life (Berger 1967). Thus, religious explanations become less significant as people turn to answers provided by science, technology, modern medicine, and so on. Although the members of a religion, including its priests, ministers, and rabbis, depend upon religion less for answers to everyday questions and problems of living, many hold onto its rituals. This, of course, is one of the reasons that sects come into existence in the first place.

As societies modernize, people hold onto religious traditions, often blending religious practices with social change. Just as Shinto priests bless farmers' new oxen for plowing and transportation, so urban dwellers seek their blessings of new cars.

The Secularization of Culture

Just as a religion can be secularized, so can a culture. The term **secularization of culture** describes what happens when the influence of religion on a culture originally permeated by religion diminishes. Let's look at two examples.

Iran.   When a culture secularizes, religious leaders can rise in opposition and try to force the clock back. Islamic fundamentalism is a case in point. The Shah of Iran, Mohammad Reza Pahlavi, believed that adoption of Western ideas and separation of religion from politics were the keys to modernizing Iran (Fischer 1980; McCasland, Cairns, and Yu 1969). He introduced sweeping changes—restricting the authority of the religious leaders, allowing alcohol, and encouraging Western dress. No longer, for example, were women required to wear robes down to their feet, veils over their nose and face, and the *chador* (forehead covering).

Conservative Muslims were outraged. The Ayatollah Khomeini, an Islamic religious leader, saw Western ideas as a threat to traditional Islam, which holds, for example, that women are always to be modest—and that it is immodest for a woman to let a man other than her husband see her face. Khomeini took a public stand against the Shah's modernization policy, declaring that the West was controlled by Satan and that Western influences (music, dress, and other customs) were satanic. He fled to Paris, where, continuing to lead an ascetic life, he plotted the overthrow of the Shah. In 1979 his followers in Iran fomented a revolution, the Shah fled to the United States, and Khomeini took control of the country, determined to reshape the entire culture and even the government along the lines dictated by the Koran fourteen hundred years earlier.

To understand how fundamental this change was, note that boys and girls were not allowed to sit in the same classrooms, that it became a crime, punishable by law, for a woman to appear in public without her face hidden by a veil and chador, and that—as it had for hundreds of years before modernization—adultery again became punishable by death. The death penalty was no idle threat; under the Ayatollah's regime, adulterers were stoned to death. After the Ayatollah's death in 1989, Iran's leaders championed a freer attitude toward social and sexual contact between men and

secularization of culture: the process by which a culture becomes less influenced by religion

women (Associated Press, December 6, 1990). The first post-Khomeini elections, held in 1992, gave victory to moderate reformers who are expected to gradually ease some of the most severe restrictions, while keeping Iran Islamic and continuing restrictions on female attire (Waldman 1992).

The United States. The United States provides another example of the secularization of culture; but here the process was gradual, and religious leaders did little more than condemn it from time to time. To begin with, it must be remembered that, in spite of attempts to reinterpret history, the Pilgrims and most of the Founding Fathers of the United States were highly religious people. The Pilgrims were even convinced that God had guided them to found a new land, while many of the Founding Fathers felt that God had guided them to develop a new form of government.

The clause in the Constitution that guarantees the separation of church and state was not an attempt to keep religion out of government, but a (successful) device to avoid the establishment of a state religion like that in England. Here, people were to have the freedom to worship as they wished. The assumption of the founders was even more specific—that Protestantism represented the true religion.

The phrase in the Declaration of Independence, "All men are created equal," refers to a central belief in God as the Creator of humanity. A member of the clergy opened Congress with prayer. Many colonial laws were based on principles derived explicitly from the Old and the New Testaments. In some, blasphemy was listed as a crime, as was failing to observe the Sabbath. Similarly, adultery was a crime that carried the death penalty. Even public kissing between husband and wife was considered an offense, punishable by being placed in the public stocks (Frumkin 1967). In other words, religion permeated American culture. It was part and parcel of the way early Americans saw life. Their lives, laws, and other aspects of the culture all reflected their religious beliefs.

Today, however, American culture has been secularized; that is, the influence of religion on public affairs has greatly lessened. Laws are no longer passed on the basis of religious principles. In general, ideas of what is "generally good" have replaced religion as an organizing principle for the culture.

The causes of this secularization are many. One is science, which, as it advanced, developed explanations for many aspects of life that people previously attributed to God. Similarly, industrialization, urbanization, and mass education represented not just external changes but brought with them a more secular view of the world. One consequence is that such conditions as wealth and poverty, high and low intelligence, the election of one candidate and defeat of another, are attributed to natural processes, not to God's intervention or will.

Although the secularization of culture means that religion and culture are now farther apart than ever and that religion is less important in public life, personal religious involvement among Americans has not diminished. Ninety-four percent believe that there is a God, 77 percent believe there is a heaven, and 69 percent claim membership in a church or synagogue. On any given weekend, 43 percent of all Americans attend a church or synagogue (Gallup 1990; Woodward 1989; *Statistical Abstract* 1991: Table 76). The religious preferences of Americans are shown on Table 18.1.

To underscore the paradox of how religious participation has increased at the very same time as the culture has become secularized, we can note that the proportion of

CDQ 11: Do you feel that decisions by the U.S. Supreme Court, such as the one stating that "separation of church and state" prohibits public prayer at public school graduation ceremonies, contribute to the secularization of culture? Why or why not?

TR#41: Religious Preference of Americans

TABLE 18.1 Religious Preference of Americans

	Protestant	Catholic	Jewish	Other	None
Percentage who say they are:	56	28	2	4	10

Source: Statistical Abstract of the United States, 1991: Table 76.

Americans who belong to a church or synagogue is now *twice* as high as it was in 1900 and *four* times as high as in 1850 (Hout and Greeley 1987). Church membership is, of course, only a rough indicator of the significance that religion plays in someone's life, for some church members are not particularly religious, while many intensely religious persons—Abraham Lincoln, for one—never join a church.

Essay #5

L. Obj. 9: State the major characteristics of religion in America.

Speaker Sug. #3: A leader of campus ministries or a local minister to conduct a discussion on religion among college students.

L. Obj. 10: List the characteristics of people who are members of religious groups in the United States.

CDQ 12: What role do you think religion plays in the lives of most Americans today?

THE MAIN CHARACTERISTICS OF RELIGION IN THE UNITED STATES

With its hundreds of denominations and sects, how can we generalize about religion in the United States? What do these many religious groups have in common? It certainly isn't doctrine, but doctrine is not the focus of sociology. As stated at the beginning of this chapter, sociologists are interested in the relationship between society and religion, and the role that religion plays in people's lives. Sociologically, then, we can identify the following major characteristics of religion in American society.

Diversity

The United States has no state church, no ecclesia, and no single denomination that dominates the country. The largest single group is the Roman Catholic church, to which 28 percent of Americans belong. While twice as many Americans claim to be Protestants, those 56 percent are divided among hundreds of different religious organizations (*Statistical Abstract* 1991: Tables 76, 78).

Pluralism and Freedom

It is the government's policy not to interfere with religions. The government's position is that its obligation is to ensure an atmosphere in which people can worship as they see fit.

Competition

America's many religions compete for clients. Various congregations advertise in the Yellow Pages of the telephone directory and compete with one another to insert appealing advertising—under the guise of news—in the religious section of the Saturday or Sunday edition of the local newspapers.

Commitment

Americans are a deeply religious people, as demonstrated by the high proportion who believe in God and attend a church or synagogue. This religious commitment is underscored by generous support for religion and its charities. Each year Americans donate about $50 billion to religious causes (*Statistical Abstract* 1991: Table 79). To appreciate the significance of this huge figure, keep in mind that, unlike a country in which there is an ecclesia, those billions of dollars are not taxes but voluntary contributions that are the result of religious commitment.

Privacy

Americans consider religious commitment a private matter, not something to be paraded in public. They believe that religious observances should take place behind closed doors—either those of a church or one's own home. Publicly talking about religion—except for those who are paid to do so—is considered a violation of public manners. Americans even tend to view "street corner preachers" as mentally unbalanced (Hong and Dearman 1993).

Toleration

The general religious toleration can be illustrated by three prevailing attitudes (1) "All religions have a right to exist—as long as they don't try to brainwash anyone or bother me." (2) "With all the religions to choose from, how can anyone tell which one—if any—is true?" (3) "Each of us may be convinced about the truth of our religion—and that is good—but to try to convert others is a violation of the individual's dignity."

Fundamentalist Revival

During the past decade or so, mainstream churches have either lost membership or seen their attendance drop. Roman Catholics began to feel this pinch following the Pope's 1967 reiteration of the church's ban on birth control (Hout and Greeley 1987). Most American Catholics disagree with the Pope's position and practice birth control in spite of what their church teaches. They are also calling other positions into question, and attending services less often. Similarly, increasing numbers of Jews and Roman Catholics now marry outside their faith—a phenomenon almost unthinkable a generation or so ago.

While the mainstream denominations have shrunk or become weaker, fundamentalist churches have undergone something of a revival, probably for the reasons summarized on Figure 18.1 on page 511. Fundamentalist churches teach that the Bible is literally true and that salvation comes only through a personal relationship with Jesus Christ. They also decry what they see as the permissiveness of American culture: sex on television and in movies, abortion, corruption in public office, premarital pregnancy, cohabitation, and drugs. Their answer is firm, simple, and direct. People whose hearts are changed through religious conversion will change their lives. The approach of the mainstream churches, which offer a remote God and a corresponding lack of emotional involvement, fails to meet the basic religious needs of large numbers of Americans. The fundamentalist message apparently meets those needs.

The Electronic Church

What began as a ministry to shut-ins and those who do not belong to a church has blossomed into its own type of church. Its preachers, called "televangelists," reach millions of viewers and raise millions of dollars. Some of its most famous ministries are those of Robert Schuler (the "Crystal Cathedral") and Pat Robertson (the 700 Club). Its most infamous preachers are Jim Bakker and Jimmy Swaggert. Jim Bakker was sentenced to forty-five years in federal prison for misappropriation of funds (reduced to eighteen years on appeal) (Applefrome 1991), while Jimmy Swaggert lost his national television ministry (which brought in over $50 million a year) when revelations of his involvements with prostitutes became public.

Many local ministers view the electronic church as a competitor. They complain that it competes for the attention of their members and siphons off money that could go to good causes. The electronic church replies that its money does go to good causes and that through its conversions it feeds members into the local churches, strengthening, not weakening them.

An interesting combination of local congregations and the electronic church has emerged. Some independent fundamentalist groups now subscribe to the electronic church. They pay a fee in return for having "name" ministers piped "live" into their local congregation. They build services around these electronic messages, supplementing them with songs and adding other "local touches."

Characteristics of Members

About 69 percent of Americans belong to a church or synagogue. Let us look at the characteristics of people who hold formal membership in a religion.

Project 3

CDQ 13: Have you watched televangelists' programs? If so, how do they appeal to viewers? How has the electronic church changed U.S. religion?

TR#48M: Profiles of American Religions

TR#49M: Religious Beliefs and Educational Attainment

A recent innovation in American religion is the electronic church, consisting of millions of television viewers of religious programs. Some viewers belong to local congregations, but many do not. Pictured here is one of the more successful television preachers (also called televangelists), Robert Schuler, who has constructed a unique church he calls the "Crystal Cathedral" in Orange, California.

TABLE 18.2 Church and Synagogue Membership by Region

Midwest	South	East	West
72%	74%	69%	55%

Source: Statistical Abstract of the United States, 1991: Table 76.

TABLE 18.3 Age and Church or Synagogue Membership

Age	Membership
18–29	61%
30–49	66%
50 +	76%

Source: Statistical Abstract of the United States, 1991: Table 76.

TR#45M: Church and Synagogue Membership by Region

TR#47M: Religion and Indicators of Social Class

TR#44M: Average Income and Religious Affiliation

CDQ 14: Why are people who change their social class also likely to change their religious denomination?

Region. Membership is not evenly distributed around the country. As shown on Table 18.2, membership is highest in the Midwest and the South, with the East not far behind. In the West, membership is considerably lower than in the other regions, perhaps because the West is both the newest region in the nation and has the highest net migration. If so, when its residents have put down firmer roots, the West's proportion of religious membership will increase.

Social Class. Religion in the United States is stratified by social class. As can be seen from Figure 18.2, each religious group draws members from all social classes, but some are "top-heavy" and others "bottom-heavy." The most top-heavy are the Episcopalians and Jews, the most bottom-heavy the Baptists and Evangelicals. This figure is further confirmation that churchlike groups tend to appeal more to the successful, the more sectlike to the less successful.

Americans have a tendency to change their religion. About 40 percent of Americans currently belong to a denomination different from the one in which they were raised (Sherkat and Wilson 1991). People who change their social class are also likely to change their denomination. An upwardly mobile person is likely to seek a religion that draws more persons from his or her new social class. An upwardly mobile Baptist, for example, may become a Methodist or a Presbyterian. For Roman Catholics, the situation is somewhat different. Since each parish is a geographical unit, an individual who moves into a more affluent neighborhood may automatically transfer into a congregation that attracts a different social class.

FIGURE 18.2 Average Income and Religious Affiliation. (*Source:* Compiled from data in *Gallup Opinion Index,* 1987: 20–27, 29.)

Age. The chances that an American will belong to a church or synagogue vary by age. As shown on Table 18.3, younger adults are the least likely to belong, while membership rates increase steadily with age.

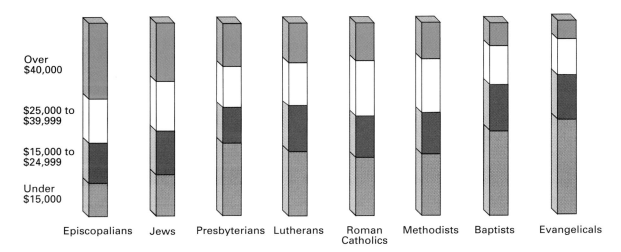

Race and Ethnicity.　It is common for religions around the world to be associated with race and ethnicity: Islam and Arabs, Judaism and Jews, Hinduism and Indians, and Confucianism and Chinese. Sometimes, as with Hinduism and Confucianism, a religion and a particular country are almost synonymous. Christianity is not associated with any one country, although it is associated primarily with Western culture.

All major religious groups in the United States draw from America's various racial and ethnic groups. Like social class, however, there is a clustering that connects religion with race and ethnicity. Persons of Hispanic or Irish descent are likely to be Roman Catholics, those of Greek origin to belong to the Greek Orthodox church. African Americans are likely to be Protestants, more specifically, to belong to Baptist and fundamentalist sects.

Although many churches are integrated, it is not without cause that Sunday morning between ten and eleven has been called "the most segregated hour in the United States." Blacks tend to belong to exclusively or largely African-American churches, while most whites see only whites in theirs. The segregation of churches is based not on law, but on custom.

TR#46M: Age and Church or Synagogue Membership

THE FUTURE OF RELIGION

Marx was convinced that religion would crumble when the workers threw off their chains of oppression. When the workers usher in a new society based on justice, he argued, there will no longer be a need for religion, for religion is the refuge of the miserable, and people will no longer be miserable. Religion will wither away, for people will see that thoughts about an afterlife are misdirected, and that they must put their energies into developing a workers' paradise here on earth (De George 1968).

After Communist countries were established, however, people continued to be religious. At first, the leaders thought they were simply a remnant that would eventually dwindle to nothing. Old people might cling to the past, but the young would give it up, and with the coming generation religion would be over.

The new Marxist states, avowing atheism, were not content to let this withering occur on its own, however; they began a concerted effort to eradicate religion from their midst. (Keep in mind that Marx said that he was not a Marxist. He did not advocate the persecution of religion, for he felt that religion would crumble on its own.) The Communist government in the Soviet Union declared that church buildings were state property and turned them into museums or office buildings. The school curriculum was designed to ridicule religion, and, as noted, a civil marriage ceremony was substituted for the religious ceremony (complete with an altar and a bust of Lenin), while a ceremony dedicating newborns to the state was even substituted for baptism. Ministers and priests were jailed as enemies of the state, and parents who dared to teach religion to their children were imprisoned or fired from their jobs, their children taken from them to be raised by the state where they would learn the "truth." In spite of such persecution, religion remained strong, even among many of the youth.

Another group of thinkers, who placed their faith not in socialism or communism but in science, foresaw a similar end to religion. As science advanced, it would explain everything. Science would transform human thought, and religion, which was merely mistaken prescientific thinking, would be replaced. For example, in 1966 Anthony Wallace, one the world's best known anthropologists, made the following observation.

> The evolutionary future of religion is extinction. Belief in supernatural beings . . . will become only an interesting historical memory. . . . doomed to die out, all over the world, as a result of the increasing adequacy and diffusion of scientific knowledge.

Marx, Wallace, and the many other social analysts who took this position were wrong. Religion thrives in the most advanced scientific nations, in capitalist and socialist

L. Obj. 11: Analyze the future of religion. State whether or not you agree with the author's assertion that "religion will last as long as humanity lasts," and defend your answer.

CDQ 15: Why do you think religion did not wither away as Marx predicted that it would?

CNN: Religious Revival

countries. It is evident that these analysts did not understand the fundamental significance that religion plays in people's lives.

Humans are inquiring creatures. They are aware that they have a past, a present, and a future. They reflect on their experiences to try to make sense out of them. One of the questions that people develop as they reflect on life is the purpose of it all. Why are we born? Since we have a future—at least in the sense of a tomorrow if we don't die today—can there also be a future after life is over? If so, where are we going, and what will it be like when we get there? Out of these concerns arises this question: If there is a God, what does God want of us in this life? Does God have a preference about how we should live?

Science cannot answer such questions. By its very nature, science cannot tell us about four main concerns that many people have: (1) the existence of God; (2) the purpose of life; (3) morality; and (4) the existence of an afterlife. About the first, science has nothing to say (no test tube has isolated God nor refuted God's existence); for the second, science can only provide a definition of life and describe the characteristics of living organisms (it has nothing to say about ultimate purpose); for the third, science can demonstrate the consequences of behavior but not the moral superiority of one action compared with another; for the fourth, again science can offer no information, for it has no tests that it can use.

Science simply cannot replace religion. Nor can political systems, as demonstrated by the experience of socialist and Communist countries. Science cannot even prove that loving your family and neighbor is superior to hurting and killing them. It can describe death and compute consequences, but it cannot dictate the *moral* superiority of any action, even in such an extreme example.

There is no doubt that religion will last as long as humanity lasts—or until humans develop adequate functional alternatives. And even though such alternatives had different names, wouldn't they, too, be a form of religion?

SUMMARY

1. Durkheim identified the essential elements of religion as beliefs and practices that separate the profane from the sacred and unite its adherents into a moral community. In general, sociologists still use this definition.

2. Functionalists find that religion is universal because it meets basic human needs, especially that of providing ultimate meaning. They have also identified dysfunctions and functional equivalents of religion. Symbolic interactionists focus on how religious symbols communicate meaning, how rituals and beliefs unite people into a community, how religion promotes values and provides a cosmology or picture of the world, and what people mean by a religious experience. Conflict theorists see religion as a conservative force that serves the needs of the ruling class by reflecting and reinforcing social inequalities.

3. There are six main religions in the world—Judaism, Christianity, Islam, Hinduism, Buddhism, and Confucianism—the first three of which are monotheistic.

4. Sociologists have identified cults, sects, churches, and ecclesias as distinct types of religious organizations. These types are differentiated by their size, wealth, training of clergy, relationship to society and other religions, conception of God and the afterlife, interpretation of Scrip-

ture, emphasis on conversion, emotional expression, and evangelism. All religions began as cults. Some disappear, some remain cults, while others develop into a sect, then a church, and, in rare instances, an ecclesia.

5. The secularization of religion helps to explain the splintering of Christianity into so many groups. As the members of a religion become more established, they become more at peace with their secular culture. Their religion then changes to reflect their new attitudes and social class. As it does so, however, it fails to meet the needs of those of its members who have not been upwardly mobile. Those persons then splinter off and form a religious group that they find more satisfying.

6. Unlike Marx, who saw religion as only a conservative force, Weber saw religion as a powerful force for social change. Weber argued that by creating anxiety about salvation, Calvinism encouraged frugality and the investment of savings, thus stimulating capitalism. Religion also leads to social change by creating tension with the social order.

7. Religion in America is characterized by diversity, pluralism and freedom, competition, commitment, privacy, toleration, a fundamentalist revival, and a new electronic church. Religious involvement varies by region, social class, and age. American congregations tend to be segregated by race and ethnicity.

8. Marxists and those who placed their faith in science predicted that religion would disappear. Instead, religion has thrived, even in countries where there was a concerted effort to eliminate it. With science and political systems an inadequate substitute, religion will apparently continue to exist as long as humanity does.

SUGGESTED READINGS

Berger, Peter. *The Sacred Canopy: Elements of a Sociological Theory of Religion.* New York: Doubleday Anchor, 1969. Applying the functionalist, symbolic interactionist, and conflict perspectives to the analysis of religion, the author synthesizes the writings of Emile Durkheim, Max Weber, and Karl Marx.

Haddad, Yvonne Yazbeck, and Adair T. Lummis. *Islamic Values in the United States: A Comparative Study.* New York: Oxford University Press, 1987. In recent years, large numbers of Muslims have immigrated to the United States and become American citizens. Like the millions of immigrants before them, they have brought their religion with them. The author examines the adaptation of Islam to its new environment.

Hunter, James Davidson. *Evangelicalism: The Coming Generation.* Chicago: University of Chicago Press, 1987. What will the evangelical churches be like in coming years? Since they will be shaped by those persons now being trained, the author focuses on persons studying for the ministry.

Lippy, Charles H., and Peter W. Williams, eds. *Encyclopedia of the American Religious Experience: Studies of Traditions and Movements.* New York: Charles Scribners Sons, 1988. This overview of religions in the United States focuses on their histories, as opposed to their teachings.

Smart, Ninian. *The World's Religions.* Englewood Cliffs, N.J.: Prentice Hall, 1989. The author presents a summary of the teachings and characteristics of religions around the world.

Stark, Rodney, and William Sims Bainbridge. *The Future of Religion: Secularization, Revival, and Cult Formation.* Berkeley, Calif.: University of California Press, 1985. This overview of trends in American religions argues that secularization is an impetus to religious revival and innovation.

Tec, Nechama. *When Light Pierced the Darkness: Christian Rescue of Jews in Nazi-Occupied Poland.* New York: Oxford University Press, 1986. Why did some Christians risk capture and cruel death to save Jews from the hands of the Nazis? The author is not only a sociologist but also a survivor of the death camps.

Journals

The following three journals publish articles that focus on the sociology of religion: *Journal for the Scientific Study of Religion, Review of Religious Research, Sociological Analysis: A Journal in the Sociology of Religion.*

CHAPTER 19

Frank Howell, Shaman, *1979*

Medicine: Health and Illness

THE SOCIOLOGICAL PERSPECTIVE OF HEALTH AND ILLNESS
   Defining Health ■ The Cultural Relativity of Health ■ The Sick Role

HISTORICAL PATTERNS OF HEALTH
   Physical Health ■ Mental Health

MEDICINE IN THE UNITED STATES
   The Professionalization of Medicine ■ The Monopoly of Medicine ■ *Down-to-Earth Sociology:* **Midwives and Physicians—The Expanding Boundaries of a Profession** ■ Mental Illness and Social Inequality ■ *Thinking Critically about Social Controversy:* **In the Care of Strangers—The Hospital in American Society**

ISSUES IN HEALTH AND HEALTH CARE
   Medical Care as a Commodity ■ Malpractice Suits and Defensive Medicine ■ Inequality in Distribution ■ Depersonalization: The Cash Machine ■ Sexism in Medicine ■ *Down-to-Earth Sociology:* **The Doctor-Nurse Game** ■ Medicalization of Society ■ Controversy about Death ■ *Thinking Critically about Social Controversy:* **Shall We Legalize Euthanasia?** ■ Health Insurance

THREATS TO HEALTH
   Disease ■ Drugs ■ Disabling Environments

THE SEARCH FOR ALTERNATIVES
   Treatment or Prevention? ■ *Perspectives:* **Health Care in Other Countries** ■ Holistic Medicine

SUMMARY

SUGGESTED READINGS

*T*erry Takewell (his real name) was a twenty-one-year-old diabetic who lived in a small trailer park in Somerville, Tennessee. When Zettie Mae Hill, Takewell's neighbor, found the unemployed carpenter drenched with sweat from a fever, she called an ambulance. Takewell was rushed to nearby Methodist Hospital, where, it turned out, he had an outstanding bill of $9,400. A directive in the emergency room told staff members to alert hospital supervisors if Mr. Takewell ever returned.

When the hospital administrator was informed of the admission, Takewell was already in a hospital bed. The administrator went to Mr. Takewell's room, helped him to his feet, and escorted him to the parking lot. There, neighbors found him under a tree and took him home.

Mr. Takewell died about twelve hours later.

Zettie Mae Hill is still torn up about it. She wonders if Mr. Takewell would be alive today if she had directed his ambulance to a different hospital. She said, "I didn't think a hospital would just let a person die like that for lack of money." (Based on Ansberry 1988)

THE SOCIOLOGICAL PERSPECTIVE OF HEALTH AND ILLNESS

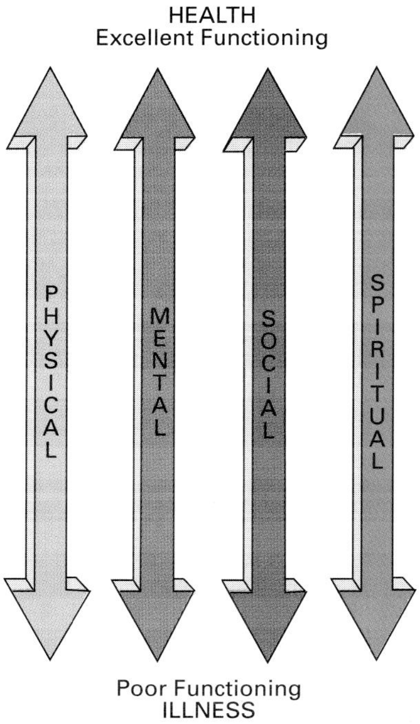

As the case of Mr. Takewell illustrates, health is much more than a biological matter. Sociologists view health as intimately related to society—to such matters as cultural beliefs, a country's stage of development, lifestyle, and social class.

Defining Health

The definition of health seems so obvious that the question does not merit being asked. We all know what health is—or do we?

Trying to define health is like reaching for a bar of soap in a bathtub—just as you think you have it in your hand, it manages to slip away. A commonsense definition of health is the absence of disease or injury, but that is like defining marriage by saying that it is the absence of singleness. It only says what it is *not,* not what it is.

When international health experts wrestled with this question back in the 1940s, they identified three components of **health:** physical, mental, and social (World Health Organization 1946). In consideration of the material covered in the previous chapter on religion, the spiritual dimension qualifies as a fourth component.

Figure 19.1 portrays this definition of health, which has several implications. First, rather than thinking of people as either healthy or unhealthy, it is useful to think of them as healthier in some areas and less healthy in others. A "certified" mentally ill person, for example, may be in fine physical shape, while a person who is physically ill may enjoy excellent mental health. Second, very few people are entirely healthy; that is, not many people are at peak performance in all four areas.

The Cultural Relativity of Health

Health, therefore, is a relative matter, as is most apparent in its mental and spiritual components. For example, in Western culture officials might lock up a person who hears voices and sees visions, while in a tribal society such an individual might be made a **shaman** ("witch doctor") for being in close contact with the gods. The social component is similarly relative. For example, does a person who fails to get along with others and causes huge problems at work necessarily demonstrate bad "social" health? Consider someone whose morals set her at odds with coworkers. She refuses to go along with padding a government payroll and threatens to blow the whistle. If some see her as a hero and others as a villain, what is her "social" health?

Even the physical component is relative. Suppose one morning you look in the mirror and see strange blotches covering your face and chest. Hoping against hope that it is not a serious disease, you rush to a doctor. If the doctor pronounced the words "dyschromic spirochetosis," your fears would be confirmed. Now, wouldn't everyone around the world draw the conclusion that the spots are a disease? No, not everybody. In one South American tribe this skin condition is so common that the few individuals who *aren't* spotted are seen as the unhealthy ones—and they are excluded from activities (Zola 1983).

Ultimately, then, a definition of health requires the symbolic interactionist perspective, which views health from the framework of a particular culture, or even of a specific group within a culture. The sociological significance of the cultural relativity of health is that people's definitions of health influence their attitudes and behavior.

HEALTH
Excellent Functioning

PHYSICAL   MENTAL   SOCIAL   SPIRITUAL

Poor Functioning
ILLNESS

FIGURE 19.1 A Continuum of Health and Illness.

health: a human condition measured by four components: physical, mental, social, and spiritual

shaman: the healing specialist of a preliterate tribe who attempts to control the spirits thought to cause a disease or injury; commonly called a witch doctor

To make the cultural relativity of health more visible, let us consider effects of cultural beliefs, lifestyle, social class, and international stratification.

Cultural Beliefs.   The effects of cultural beliefs on health can be illustrated by anorexia nervosa, a condition in which individuals—primarily young females—try to make themselves excessively thin by eating little and secretly vomiting much of what they do eat. Such a condition depends on the belief that thin is beautiful, a belief not shared in many parts of the world. For example, Arab men associate female beauty with greater weight than do Americans.

As cultural beliefs change over time, so do a group's definitions of what makes people healthy. Americans used to think, for example, that it was unhealthy for a woman to go to college because, as noted in Chapter 11, experts presumed a war between a woman's uterus and her brain over a limited supply of energy (Fisher 1986); that masturbation caused mental illness; and that cigarette smoking was good for health. (Lucky Strike used to advertise its cigarettes as soothing to the throat.)

Subcultural Patterns and Lifestyle.   Within the same society, subcultural patterns and lifestyle produce specific patterns of health and illness. Utah and Nevada provide a remarkable illustration. Though they are adjacent states with similar levels of income, education, medical care, urbanization, crime, and even climate (Fuchs 1981), Nevada's overall death rate is 47 percent higher than Utah's (*Statistical Abstract* 1991: Table 119). Nevadans are twice as likely to die from cancer and three times as likely to die from liver disease, homicide, and AIDS. Lifestyle accounts for the difference; Utah is inhabited mostly by Mormons, who encourage conservative living and disapprove of the consumption of tobacco, alcohol, and caffeine. Similarly, the Amish have lower rates of high blood pressure than do non-Amish people (Fuchs et al. 1990).

Effects of Social Class.   As Table 19.1 shows, social class also makes a considerable difference to people's chances for good health. On average, Americans with more money do not get sick as often as those with less money. And, as the case of Terry Takewell illustrates, poor people have a more difficult time gaining access to medical treatment—which further undermines their health.

International Stratification and Health Care.   The intimate connection between society and health is also apparent on a global scale. Heart disease and cancer, for example, are "luxury" diseases; that is, they characterize the rich First World. In the Third World, where few people live long enough to get cancer and heart disease, most people die from diseases that the industrialized nations have already brought under control.

Suppose, for example, that you had been born in a poor country located in the tropics. Instead of facing cancer or a heart attack in old age, during your much shorter

L. Obj. 1: Define health from a sociological perspective and explain what is meant by the cultural relativity of health.

Essay #1

CDQ 1: What does the word "health" mean to you? How do sociologists use the term?

CDQ 2: What American cultural beliefs do you think contribute to the problem of anorexia nervosa?

Project 1

L. Obj. 2: Describe the ways in which subcultural patterns and social class produce specific patterns of health and illness.

CDQ 3: What types of lifestyles do you think may contribute to higher rates of illness?

CDQ 4: Why do you think Americans with more money do not get sick as often as those with less money?

L. Obj. 3: Compare First and Third World nations regarding the types of diseases which are most likely to be found in each.

CDQ 5: Can you explain why heart disease and cancer might be called "luxury" diseases?

K.P.: Talcott Parsons

TABLE 19.1   Numbers of Days that People Were So Sick that They Cut Down on Their Usual Activities

Income	Days
Under $10,000	27
$10,000 to $20,000	18
$20,000 to $35,000	12
Over $35,000	10

Source: Statistical Abstract of the United States, 1991: Table 188.

life you would continually face illness and death from four major sources: malaria (from mosquitos), internal parasites (from contaminated water), diarrhea (from food and soil contaminated with human feces), and malnutrition. As the Third World develops economically, its population will likely trade these killers in and begin to worry about cancer and heart attacks instead.

International stratification in medical care is a fact of global life. Just like the poor in the United States, Third World countries have little money to spend on health care. They can afford neither the facilities to train many medical personnel nor expensive medicines and equipment. Consequently, they lag far behind the industrialized nations in terms of medical care. One consequence is huge disparities in infant mortality rates and life spans. As Figure 19.2 shows, less than 10 of every 1,000 babies born in the industrialized nations die before they are a year old. In contrast, in some Third World countries, such as Afghanistan, Angola, and Ethiopia 165 out of every 1,000 infants die before their first birthday. Similarly, whereas people in the First World can expect to live to the age of about 75, in many Third World countries—Afghanistan, Cambodia, Malawi, and Nigeria—life expectancy is less than fifty years (*Statistical Abstract* 1991: Table 1436).

Many diseases that ravage the populations of these poorer countries could be brought under control if their meager funds were spent on public health. Cheap drugs can prevent malaria, while safer water supplies and increased food production would go a long way toward eliminating the other major killers. Instead, however, these countries spend money on training a few doctors in the West, who then primarily serve the country's elite. The elite receive Western-style medical treatment—including high

FIGURE 19.2 Infant Mortality Rates.* *Source:* United Nations Department of International Economic and Social Affairs, Statistical Office; *Statistical Abstract of the United States,* 1991: Table 111; *Demographic Yearbook,* 1987 (United Nations).

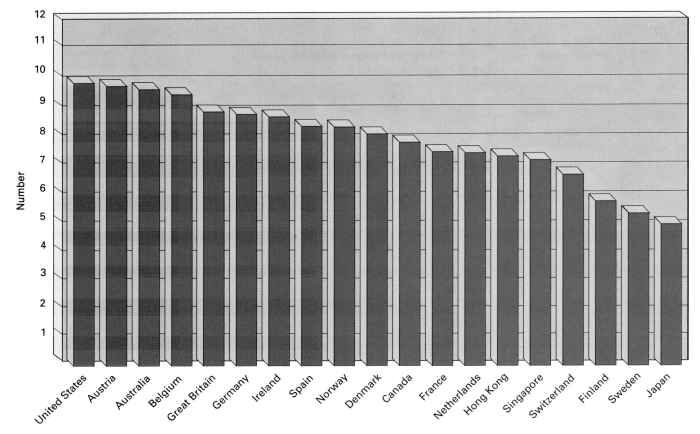

*Infant deaths (babies who die before one year of age) per thousand live births in nineteen industrialized countries.
Note: Figures are the latest available from each country — 1985, 1986, 1987.

 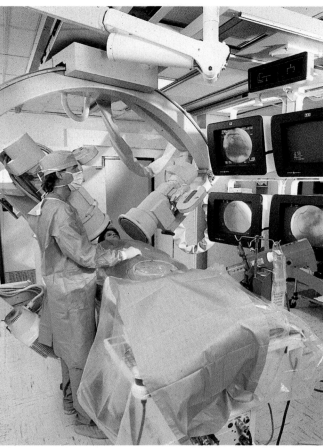

technology, from X-rays to life-support systems—while the poor go without even basic medical services, and continue to die at an early age due to lack of preventive health measures.

The Sick Role

Elements of the Sick Role.   Just as being sick is more than a biological matter, so is the role that surrounds illness. If you feel well and are able to do all of your ordinary activities, we can call your condition the *well role* (cf., Glik and Kronenfed 1989). Now assume that you have been laid low by a virus and are suffering from severe diarrhea and a fever of 104 degrees. No one will doubt that you are unable to perform your usual activities and that you should stay home from work or school, see a doctor, and take medicine. We can call this the **sick role.** Sociologist Talcott Parsons (1948, 1951, 1975), a functionalist, identified three elements of the sick role. First, the individual is not held responsible for being sick. Second, he or she is exempt from normal responsibilities. Third, the individual agrees that the role is undesirable, that he or she will seek competent help for the illness, and will cooperate in getting well.

Note that while the sick role excuses people from performing their usual responsibilities, it also obligates them to seek medical treatment and to follow the prescribed remedy for recovery. Not following a physician's orders, or failing to seek help—except for minor illnesses generally considered to pass on their own—violates this role. In such instances, the responsibility for the illness is transferred to the individual, and he or she is denied the right to claim sympathy from others or to be legitimately excused from normal routines.

International stratification in health care is starkly contrasted in these two photographs. The one on the left shows medical treatment in Papua, New Guinea. The items on the table represent the extent of medical technology available to most residents of the Third World.
The photo on the right, a catheterization laboratory in Austin, Texas, illustrates the medical technology available in the First World. Not all citizens of the First World, however, have equal access to such technology.

Project 2

sick role: a social role that excuses people from normal obligations because they are sick or injured, while at the same time expecting them to seek competent help and cooperate in getting well

CDQ 6: Have you ever taken the "sick role" when you were not actually sick? Is being "sick" more acceptable than not wanting to go to work or school?

Claiming the Sick Role.   Clear-cut events such as heart attacks and limb fractures occur infrequently. Rather, there is often ambiguity between the well role and the sick role. For example, suppose you feel "somewhat" ill and have only a slightly elevated temperature. Do you then "become" sick or not? That is, at what point do you claim the sick role? Such a decision is more a social than a physical matter. For example, if you are facing a test for which you are unprepared and are allowed to make it up, you are likely to call in sick. In fact, the more you think about the test and your lack of preparation, the worse you are likely to feel—thus legitimating to yourself your claim to the sick role. In contrast, if you are supposed to attend your best friend's birthday party, you are much less likely to play the sick role, though in both cases your physical condition is in fact the same.

Parents and physicians are the primary mediators between our feelings of illness and our right to be released from responsibilities. That is, they legitimate our claim to the sick role. For children, parents call the school to excuse the child's absence. The parents, of course, must be convinced of the genuine nature and severity of the illness—which often results in a tug-of-war between the child and the parents. As gatekeepers to this role, the parents must decide whether the child's symptoms are fake, real but not severe enough to warrant absence from school, or genuine and sufficiently serious to allow the child to play the sick role.

For adults, it is primarily physicians who legitimate the individual's claim to the sick role. The "doctor's excuse" amounts to written permission to play the sick role, removing the need for employers, teachers, and sometimes parents to pass judgment on the individual's claim.

Not everyone, however, is given the same right to claim the sick role. During participant observation of a pottery factory in England, sociologist Paul Bellaby (1990) noted that gender and age were significant in determining reactions to a worker's claim to this role. In this case, it was more acceptable for younger workers to call in sick. Other workers, and perhaps even management, were likely to understand that young workers would drink too much and not report for work because of a hangover. In contrast, both management and workers saw older workers as more settled and responsible; and they were expected to show up for work regardless of how they felt. Similarly, unmarried young women were allowed more claim to the sick role than older women—but less than young men. Older women were expected not to "give in to sickness," and to do the job in spite of ailments.

Thus, the social group defines the conditions under which people are "allowed" to be sick and legitimately excused from ordinary responsibilities (Freidson 1988). If they are so excused, the role requires them to cooperate in getting well so that they can return to their usual positions. Functionalists thus define the sick role as a device to ensure that people do not exploit illness and injury and return quickly to fulfill the responsibilities on which others depend.

HISTORICAL PATTERNS OF HEALTH

CDQ 7: Do you think Americans are healthier—or sicker—than they used to be? Why?

How have patterns of health and illness in the United States changed? And are Americans healthier—or sicker—than they used to be? The answers to these two questions take us into the field of **epidemiology,** the study of how medical disorders are distributed throughout a population.

Physical Health

epidemiology: the study of disease and disability patterns in a population

Leading Causes of Death.   The first question is fairly easy to answer, because the United States government maintains records that allow comparisons between different causes of death. As Figure 19.3 shows, half of the ten leading causes of death in 1900 do not even appear in the current top ten. On the other hand, heart disease and cancer

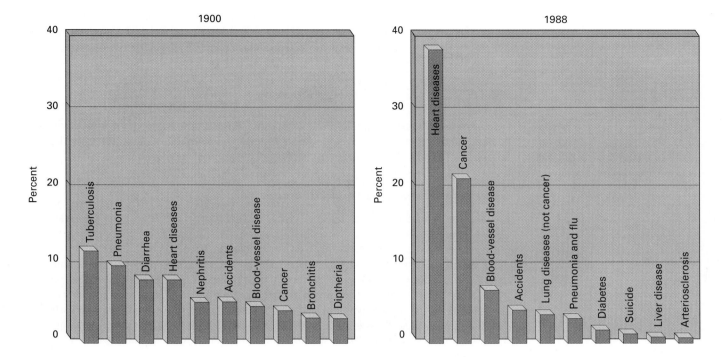

FIGURE 19.3   The Top Ten Causes of Death in American Society. (*Source:* National Center for Health Statistics, Division of Vital Statistics, National Vital Statistics System, *Statistical Abstract of the United States,* 1991: Table 119.)

have jumped to the top of the list, and now account for *60 percent* of all deaths. Not shown, but placing eleventh and twelfth, are AIDS and homicide. AIDS is discussed more fully later in this chapter.

Were Americans Healthier in the Past?   To determine if Americans are healthier today than in the past brings us face-to-face with the definitional problem just discussed. "Healthy" by whose standards? In addition, many diseases on which information is now gathered routinely were previously not even recognized. Mortality rates, however, provide the surest guide. If we assume that a group that lives longer is healthier—at least physically—than a group that has a shorter life span, we can conclude that contemporary Americans are healthier than their ancestors.

Some may see this conclusion as flying in the face of polluted air and water and high rates of smoking and cancer. And it does. Sometimes older people say, "When I was a kid, cancer wasn't around. I never knew anyone who died from cancer, and now it seems everyone does." What they overlook is that in the past much cancer went unrecognized. People were simply said to have died of "old age" or "heart failure." In addition, most cancers strike older people, and when most people die younger cancer has less chance of being a cause of death.

L. Obj. 5: Answer the question, "Were Americans healthier in the past?"

Mental Health

When it comes to mental health, no rational basis for comparisons exists. The elderly may paint a picture of a past with lower suicide rates, less mental illness, and so on, but we need measures of mental illness or mental health, not anecdotes. The idyllic past—where everyone lived in a happy home, married for life, and was at one with the universe—never existed. All groups have had their share of mental problems—and commonsense beliefs that the situation is worsening represent perceptions, not measured reality. Such perceptions of fewer mental problems in the past may be true, of course, but the opposite could also be true. The point is that we simply do not know.

MEDICINE IN THE UNITED STATES

Let's now look at medicine in the United States. This section will examine how medicine became a commodity and developed into America's *largest* business enterprise. First, though, we need to understand the professionalization of medicine.

The Professionalization of Medicine

Imagine that you are living in the American colonies in the 1700s and that you want to become a physician. There are no course prerequisites, no entry exams—in fact, there are no medical schools. You simply ask a physician to train you and assist with menial tasks in return for the opportunity to learn. When *you* think that you have learned enough, you hang out a shingle and thereby proclaim yourself a physician. The process was similar to the way in which someone becomes an automobile mechanic today. And like mechanics today, you could skip the apprenticeship if you wished, and simply hang out the shingle. If you could convince people that you were good, you made a living. If not, you turned to something else.

During the 1800s, a few medical schools opened, and there was some licensing. Medical schools then, however, were like religious sects today; they competed for clients and represented different claims on truth. That is, medical schools had competing philosophies about both the causes of illnesses and the most effective treatments. Jews, women, and African Americans were denied admission, training was short, often not even a high school diploma was required, there was no clinical training, and lectures went unchanged from year to year. Even Harvard University's medical school curriculum took only two school years to complete—and the school year in those days lasted only four months (Starr 1982; Rosenberg 1987).

In 1906 the American Medical Association (AMA) examined the 160 medical schools in the United States and found only 82 acceptable (Starr 1982). The AMA then

Essay #2

L. Obj. 6: Discuss the professionalization of medicine in the United States and list the characteristics of physicians which resulted from this process.

CDQ 8: Would you be willing to receive medical treatment from a person who just proclaimed that he or she was a doctor? Why did medicine become professionalized?

Project 3

Speaker Sug. #1: A representative of a medical association to discuss the importance of that organization in regulating physicians.

In the 1860s, medical care in the United States was a hit-or-miss affair run by untrained and poorly trained medical personnel who were unaware of germs. Conditions in hospitals were miserable, as illustrated by this lithograph showing a patient in Bellevue Hospital in New York City in 1860.

THE SICK WOMEN IN BELLEVUE HOSPITAL, NEW YORK, OVERRUN BY RATS.

asked the Carnegie Foundation to investigate the matter. Abraham Flexner, a renowned educator of the time, who was chosen to head the study, visited every medical school. Even the most inadequate opened their doors to him, for they thought that gifts from the Carnegie Foundation would follow (Rodash 1982). Flexner found glaring problems. The laboratories of some schools consisted only of "a few vagrant test tubes squirreled away in a cigar box." Other schools had libraries with no books.

What became known as the Flexner Report had a profound impact on American medicine. Flexner (1910) recommended that admission and teaching standards be raised and that philanthropies fund the most promising schools. As a result, those schools that were funded were able to upgrade their facilities and attract more capable faculty and students. Left with inadequate funds, most of the other schools became noncompetitive and had to close their doors.

The result was the **professionalization of medicine.** This process meant that physicians (1) underwent a rigorous education; (2) claimed a theoretical understanding of illness; (3) regulated themselves; (4) claimed that they were performing a service for society (rather than just following self-interest); and (5) took authority over clients (Goode 1960). (For differences between professions and jobs, see Chapter 14, pages 394–397.)

The Monopoly of Medicine

The professionalization of medicine led directly to medicine becoming a monopoly. Laws restricted medical licenses only to graduates of approved schools, and only graduates of those schools were eligible to become the faculty members who trained the next generation of physicians. In short, competition between philosophies of medicine and the education of physicians was curtailed as one group gained control over American medicine and set itself up as *the* medical establishment. As the Down-to-Earth Sociology box on midwives explains, physicians even took control over childbirth, previously considered a natural event to be handled by women.

American medicine always had a **fee-for-service** approach (the patient pays a physician to diagnose and treat), but it now came under the control of a select group of men. Only they were allowed to practice medicine. Only they knew what was right for people's health. Only they knew the secret language (Latin), which they would scribble on special pieces of parchment for translators (pharmacists) to decipher (Miner 1991).

American physicians were now in a position to turn their profession into the most lucrative in the country—for they set their own fees and had no competition. Eventually, however, there was a public outcry that the poor and elderly were unable to afford those fees. Although the poor received free services from many physicians and hospitals, many remained without medical care. The AMA systematically and bitterly fought every proposal for government-funded medical treatment. Physicians were convinced that government funding would "socialize" medicine, removing the fee-for-service approach and turning them into government employees.

After *Medicaid* (government-paid medical care for the poor) and *Medicare* (government-sponsored medical insurance for the elderly) were instituted in the 1960s, however, American physicians found that these programs did not lead to socialization. Instead, they found millions of additional customers, for persons who previously could not afford medical services now had their medical bills guaranteed by the government. As Figure 13.4 in Chapter 13, page 359, illustrates, these programs have become extremely expensive—and they put much wealth into physicians' pockets each year.

Like any other big business, the American medical establishment—consisting not only of physicians, but also of nurses, paraphysicians, hospital personnel, pharmaceutical companies, druggists, medical technology manufacturers, and especially the corporations that own hospitals—has launched a marketing campaign to drum up even more customers.

K.P.: Abraham Flexner

L. Obj. 7: Explain what is meant by the monopoly of medicine and note the effect such monopolization had on the cost of medical care.

CDQ 9: Do you think it was essential for the well-being of mothers and children that physicians take control over childbirth? Why or why not?

CDQ 10: Does your physician work on a fee-for-service basis? What are some other methods of payment?

Project 4

professionalization of medicine: the development of medicine into a field in which education becomes rigorous, and in which physicians claim a theoretical understanding of illness, regulate themselves, claim to be doing a service to society (rather than just following self-interest), and take authority over clients

fee for service: payment by a patient to a physician to diagnose and treat the patient's medical problems

Midwives and Physicians—The Expanding Boundaries of a Profession

Midwifery provides an example of the professionalization of medicine and an insight into the founding of the American medical establishment (Danzi 1989; Ehrenreich and English 1973; Rodash 1982; Wertz and Wertz 1981). It had been the custom in the United States, as in Europe and elsewhere, for midwives to deliver babies. Pregnancy and childbirth were considered natural events, for which women were best equipped to help women. It was also considered indecent for a man to know much about pregnancy, much less to be present during the delivery of a baby. Some midwives were trained, others were simply neighborhood women who had experience in childbirth. In many European countries, midwives were licensed by the state—as they still are. In the United States, physicians came to see midwives as business competitors. They wanted the profits that came with delivering babies, and some also felt that they could provide better service.

A major problem, however, was that few physicians knew anything about delivering babies. To learn, they first sneaked into the bedrooms where midwives were assisting births. To say "sneaked" is no exaggeration, for some physicians crawled in on their hands and knees so that the mother-to-be would not know a man was present. Many midwives refused to cooperate in this subterfuge, however, and the training of most physicians was limited to lessons with a mannequin. As physicians gained admission to childbirth, the issue of indecency persisted. At first the physician was limited to fumbling blindly under a sheet in a dark room, his head decorously turned aside.

As physicians gained expertise in childbirth and grew more powerful politically, they launched a bitter campaign against midwives, attacking them as "dirty, ignorant, and incompetent" and calling them a "menace to the health of the community." Using the new political clout of the American Medical Association, physicians succeeded in persuading many states to pass laws that made it illegal for anyone but a physician to deliver babies. Some states, however, continued to allow nurse-midwives to practice. The struggle is not yet over; today nurse-midwives and physicians still clash about who has the right to deliver babies.

Conflict theorists emphasize that this struggle was an attempt by males to gain control over what had been female work. They stress that political power was central to the physicians' success in expanding their domain. Without denying the political aspect, symbolic interactionists stress that the key to physicians' success in winning control over the delivery of babies was the redefinition of pregnancy and childbirth from a natural event to a medical condition. To eliminate midwives, physicians launched a campaign of definitions, stressing that it was a fallacy that pregnancy and childbirth were normal conditions. Their new definitions, which flew in the face of the millennia-old tradition of women helping women to have babies, transformed pregnancy and childbirth from a natural process to a "medical condition" that required the assistance of an able man. When this redefinition made childbirth "man's work," not only did the prestige of the work go up—so did the price.

Empty hospital beds are a bad investment, and filling them adds to the bottom line. Probably all of you have seen billboards urging people to choose a particular hospital or doctor's clinic for a specific medical need. But probably not all of you know that such medical marketing campaigns cost a *billion* dollars a year, or that special hospitals—or suites within hospitals—cater to the tastes of the rich. They offer not only fine furniture and textured wallpaper, but also gourmet meals served with linen napkins and real silverware (Lewin 1987). To see the role that hospitals have played in the professionalization of medicine, and how they, too, have contributed to the high cost of health care, see the Thinking Critically box below.

THINKING CRITICALLY ABOUT SOCIAL CONTROVERSY

In the Care of Strangers—The Hospital in American Society

In October 1810, Ezra Stiles Ely, a newly ordained Presbyterian minister, began to preach in the almshouse hospital of New York City. The few hospitals that existed then were places of last resort, for the sick were the responsibility of families, neighborhoods, and towns. People who were under the care of strangers were by definition adrift from family and community.

It took a strong stomach and high purpose for the young man to enter this "nest of moral and physical decay," where the destitute, the mentally ill, the syphilitics, and old and diseased prostitutes went to die. Ely was met with overpowering smells from bodies stowed in as thick as they could lie. Patients had to share beds, and on one such pallet he found two "abandoned" girls, thirteen and fifteen. A victim of typhus fever in another room had been allowed to lie dead for a full day among his fellow patients before being removed. In still another ward, the liberal use of vinegar and [the] burning [of] linen could not, as it was hoped, disguise the overpowering odor of impending death.

The rooms were too crowded for the sexes to be segregated—and Ely predicted the generation of another crop of paupers. Children circulated restlessly through the almshouse; they could not be kept to themselves, nor could the many young prostitutes be kept from "all intercourse with wicked men." Despite some efforts at classification, most wards were a hodgepodge of ages and sexes, of disabilities and ailments.

According to medical thinking of the time, moral depravity was a cause of physical illness. Syphilis, then practically incurable, was an example. So were the ravages of alcoholism. Persons suffering from such diseases were considered undeserving. They were left in the streets, locked in jails, or sent to almshouse hospitals.

But where were the deserving sick to go? There were hardworking men who were "stricken down with incapacitating illness . . . aged widows of irreproachable character who had spent a lifetime in piety and hard work" whose families couldn't care for them. To gain support for hospitals that would serve good people who had become ill through no fault of their own, fundraisers told contributors that such hospitals would discriminate between the deserving and the undeserving. Consequently, admission to these hospitals required "a written testimonial from a 'respectable' person attesting to the moral worth of the applicant."

For nurses, hospitals meant hard work, long hours, and low pay. A nurse's shift ran from 5:00 A.M. to 9:00 P.M. During those sixteen hours (six days a week), nurses not only dispensed medicines but also "scrubbed the floors, washed the sheets, and fetched dinner." Healthier patients had to pitch in, too, for there might be one nurse for seventy-five patients. At night, nurses were not on duty, and the less sick had to help those worse off. Physicians seldom appeared, but when they did they demanded total attention.

Hospitals were sources of disease and death. It was not yet known in the early 1800s that germs caused disease, and lack of hygiene made deaths from fevers and infections in hospitals so common that people referred to them as "hospitalism." The larger the hospital, the higher the death rate among patients. As the theory of germs came to be more widely accepted, surgeons began to wash before surgery, and the death rate from postoperative infections declined. The teaching staff of medical schools saw the advantage of being affiliated with hospitals and began to require clinical training of their students. As technology developed, hospitals became more dependent on X-ray machines and the like. The expense of such technology drove up the cost of patient care, making patients who could pay more important for the hospitals' welfare. In turn, patients who could pay expected the latest technology for their money. The result was a process that fed on itself: As hospitals offered more technology and medical care, patients demanded even more.

Following a national pattern of transferring social functions from family and neighborhood to institutional sites, hospitals came to be seen as places that offered care superior to that available at home. By 1910, the hospital had become a national institution, not just a refuge for the urban poor. Most towns of any size had their own hospital. Formerly under nonmedical (lay) control, power and authority passed to a professional management, which headed an increasingly complex, bureaucratic organization. Nurses became better trained, more disciplined, and more focused on patient care. Physicians came to look at hospitals as places where they could practice careers in surgery or other specialties.

The change in hospitals reflected the professionalization of medicine, mirroring both its advances and problems. Already by the 1920s, more technology and higher wages of hospital workers made the high cost of hospital care a public concern. In the forefront of the controversy were questions that have still not been resolved: Is the hospital to be the provider of medical care on the basis of need, or a profit-making enterprise like a department store? Does the hospital belong to the community, or is it simply part of the "marketplace of discrete and impersonal cash transactions"? Just what is the public's right to health care? (*Source:* Rosenberg 1987)

Mental Illness and Social Inequality

As physicians throughout the United States enlarged their domain, they also moved into the field of mental problems. Psychiatrist Thomas Szasz (1961) severely criticized this development, claiming that there is no such thing as a "mental" illness. People have "problems in living," he argued, not "mental" illnesses. In most cases there is no discernible organic illness, but if there is, it is a physical illness and needs to be treated by physical means. If there is not, then the individual has a problem in living that can be helped by many types of counselors.

Without taking a position on Szasz's provocative and controversial position, we can inquire if there are also social inequalities in mental health. Sociologist Leo Srole and his colleagues at Columbia University (1978) decided to explore whether a relationship exists between social class and mental health. Srole's researchers developed their own scale of symptoms, trained their own interviewers, and interviewed a representative sample of New Yorkers. They found an inverse correlation between mental problems and social class; in other words, the lower the social class, the higher the proportion of serious mental problems.

Sociologists have little difficulty understanding why people in the lower social classes have greater mental problems. These problems are part of a stress package that comes with poverty. Compared with middle- and upper-class Americans, the poor have less job security, lower wages, more unpaid bills and insistent bill collectors, more divorce, greater vulnerability to crime, more alcoholism, more violence, more physical illness, and less success in school. Such conditions certainly deal severe blows to people's emotional well-being.

Social inequalities also mark the treatment of mental problems. Private mental hospitals serve the wealthy (and those who have good insurance), while dreaded state hospitals are reserved for the poor. The rich are also more likely to be treated with "talk" therapy (various forms of psychotherapy), the poor with medication.

As noted in Chapter 8 (pages 214–215), the policy of deinstitutionalization carried out in the 1960s, which was intended to cut costs and integrate mental patients into the community, backfired. One consequence of deinstitutionalization is that the poor find it difficult to get admitted to mental hospitals—even though these are funded by the government. The following account of an incident I observed in a shelter for the homeless demonstrates the severity of this problem.

> Standing among the police, I watched the elderly, nude man, slowly put on his clothing. He had ripped the wires out of the electrical box, and then led the police a merry chase as he had run from room to room.
>
> I asked the officers where they were going to take him, and they replied, "To Malcolm Bliss" (the state hospital). When I said, "I guess he'll be in there for quite a while," they replied, "Probably for just a day or two. We picked him up last week—he was crawling under cars at a traffic light—and they let him out in two days."

The police then explained that one must be a danger to others or to oneself to be admitted as a long-term patient. Visualizing this old man crawling under cars in traffic and the possibility of electrocution in ripping out electrical wires with bare hands, I marveled at the definitions of "danger" that the psychiatrists must be using. Certainly a middle-class or rich person would receive different treatment, and would not, of course, be in this shelter in the first place.

CDQ 11: Do you agree that people in the lower social classes have greater mental problems? Why or why not?

Around the world, social class is the best predictor of lifestyles that create diseases (or avoid them), lead to short lives (or long ones), and deny (or open) access to the most advanced medical care available in a society. As you can see from this photo of a Caracas, Venezuela, slum, these children are exposed to social conditions that have a dramatic impact on their health.

ISSUES IN HEALTH AND HEALTH CARE

With this background, let's look at current issues in health and medical care in American society. We shall examine medical care as a commodity, malpractice and defensive medicine, inequality in medical delivery, depersonalization, sexism, medicalization, defining death, the right to die, and health insurance.

Medical Care as a Commodity

The case of Mr. Takewell illustrates a major sociological characteristic of the American medical system: *Medicine is viewed as a commodity, not a right* (Bodenheimer 1990). Like any other commodity, therefore, medicine is purchased by those who can afford it and withheld from those who cannot. The result is a *two-tier system of medical care,* one for those who can pay and another for those who cannot. The soaring cost of medical treatment has made medical treatment expensive not only for people like Terry Takewell, but also for many members of the middle class. The elderly in America are especially frightened of not being able to afford medical care.

And not without reason. As shown in Figure 19.4, in 1960 Americans paid $150 per person for a year's medical services. That cost now runs more than fifteen times as much, amounting to almost $2,500 for the average American. Expected to break $1 trillion sometime during the 1990s, the total national health bill now eats up $11.60 of every $100 of the gross national product (the country's entire income from all sources) (*Statistical Abstract* 1991: Table 136). To gain some idea of the enormity of this increase, consider that if the price of televisions had risen at this rate a seventeen-inch black-and-white television would now cost about $3,000 (*Consumer Reports,* January 1960).

L. Obj. 9: Outline and briefly explain the major issues in U.S. health and health care.

CDQ 12: Should medical care in the U.S. be treated as a commodity or as a right?

TR#42: The Soaring Cost of Medical Care: The Amount the Average American Pays Each Year

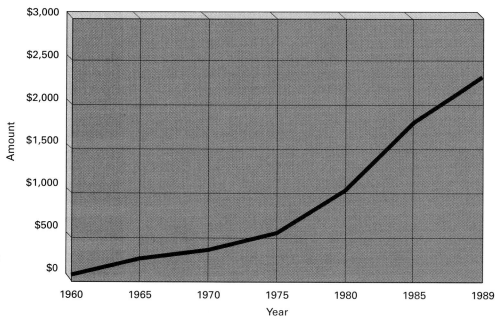

FIGURE 19.4   The Soaring Cost of Medical Care: The Amount the Average American Pays Each Year. (*Source:* Various editions of the *Statistical Abstract of the United States,* including 1991: Table 136.)

This phenomenal increase has not taken place because Americans are sicker than they used to be; rather, its causes are sociological. As discussed in Chapter 13, the fact that the proportion of the elderly, who are more likely to need medical treatment than other age groups, is increasing in the United States fuels the cost spiral (Fox 1989). More advanced—and expensive—technology is also part of the picture. At its foundation, however, is the "American way" of medicine, which regards medical care as a commodity to be sold at a profit to those who can afford it. We shall return to this issue—and its implications—throughout the chapter.

Malpractice Suits and Defensive Medicine

Some have said that prior to this century bumbling physicians may have killed more people than they ever helped. This may be true, especially considering that physicians didn't even wash their hands before performing surgery or delivering babies (they didn't know about germs). Doctors had four main treatments: (1) purging (feeding substances that cause diarrhea in order to get rid of "bad fluids"); (2) bleeding (opening a vein so that the "bad fluids" could drain out); (3) blistering (applying hot packs to cause burns so that the "bad" fluids—pus—could drain); and (4) vomiting (feeding substances that made people throw up the "bad" substances).

But now physicians are trained well, science and technology have made marvelous advancements, diagnoses are more accurate, and treatments are more effective than ever. Yet medicine remains imprecise, and like those who work in every other occupation, doctors, too, make mistakes. This—along with a legal system that encourages lawsuits and jurors willing to award huge sums—makes physicians mindful of malpractice suits as they practice medicine. In some extreme cases, physicians even wonder if a patient sought him or her out *in order to* instigate a lawsuit. One physician expressed his anxiety this way. "I'm looking for something else to do because medicine is no longer fun. Every time I treat a patient, I wonder if this is the one who is going to turn around and sue me" (author's files).

Project 5

CNN: Medical Malpractice

Speaker Sug. #3: Attorneys who regularly represent plaintiffs or defendants in medical malpractice litigation.

Essay 3

To protect themselves, physicians practice defensive medicine, seeking consultations with colleagues and ordering additional lab tests simply because a patient may sue. The purpose of these procedures is not to benefit the patient but to leave a paper trail that can be used in the doctor's defense. If a patient charges malpractice, the physician is then able to document that he or she did everything that reasonably could be done. Defensive medicine, of course, boosts the cost spiral even further. Medical tests and consultations are expensive, and they add huge amounts to the overall cost of medical care—as well as to physicians' profits. In addition, some tests are *intrusive,* that is, they harm the patient in some way. On the positive side, defensive medicine does uncover some maladies that would otherwise be overlooked.

CDQ 13: What are some examples of defensive medicine? Can you see why some physicians believe defensive medicine is necessary?

Inequality in Distribution

In general, medical care has improved. Medicare and Medicaid have brought health care to millions who otherwise would go without. In fact, in the course of a year a poor person is now slightly *more* likely than a middle-class person to see a physician. This sounds as though inequality in the treatment of physical illnesses has been solved, but given the data in Table 19.1 on page 531, showing that the poor are sick more often than other people, apparently the poor are still not seeing physicians often enough (Robert Wood Johnson Foundation 1983).

CNN: Affluent Hospital

There is also the matter of *adequacy* of health care. Unlike the other classes, few poor people have a personal physician, and while awaiting care they are likely to spend hours in crowded public health clinics. In addition, because many states are notoriously slow to pay, and pay less than physicians charge their middle-class patients, some poor people—including many young mothers with babies—find it difficult to locate a doctor who will accept them. Finally, when hospitalized, the poor are likely to find themselves in understaffed and underfunded public hospitals, where they are treated by rotating interns who do not know them and cannot follow up on their progress.

Depersonalization: The Cash Machine

One of the main criticisms leveled against the medical profession is **depersonalization,** the practice of dealing with people as though they were cases and diseases, not individuals. People want to know that they count, but current assembly-line medical practices make it difficult for patients to feel that they do. Instead, many get the impression that they have been trapped by a cash machine—a physician who, while talking to you, is impatiently counting minutes and tabulating dollars so that he or she can move on to the next customer, and more dollars. After all, extra time spent with a patient is money down the drain.

Sociologist Sue Fisher (1986), who was examined for an ovarian mass, gives this account.

Speaker Sug. #4: A colleague who teaches medical ethics at a medical school in your area to discuss physician-patient relations and/or issues relating to death and dying.

CDQ 14: If you were a patient in a hospital, would you resent being referred to as "the gallbladder in Room 324?" Why does this type of practice often occur in medicine?

K.P.: Sue Fisher

Feeling trepidation about the mass . . . I started the medical process. As a new person in the community, I was without a doctor. The nurse-practitioner referred me to a gynecologist. My years of research (on the medical profession) did not prepare me for what followed. On my initial visit a nurse called me into an examination room, asked me to undress, gave me a paper gown to put on and told me the doctor would be with me soon. I was stunned. Was I not even to see the doctor before undressing? . . . How could I present myself as a competent, knowledgeable person sitting undressed on the examining table? But I had a potentially cancerous growth, so I did as I had been told.

In a few minutes the nurse returned and said, "Lie down. The doctor is coming." Again I complied. The doctor entered the examining room, nodded in my direction while reading my chart and proceeded to examine me without ever having spoken to me.

depersonalization: the practice of dealing with people as though they were objects; in the case of medical care, as though patients were merely cases and diseases, not persons

K.P.: Jack Haas and William Shaffir

Participant observation of medical students at McMaster University in Canada by sociologists Jack Haas and William Shaffir (1991) provided insight into how physicians learn to depersonalize patients. Haas and Shaffir found that students begin medical school with lay (nonprofessional) attitudes, and want to "treat the whole person." As they progress in their studies, they come under intense time pressures as endless amounts of material are thrown at them. Their feelings for patients are soon overpowered by the need to be efficient. This student's statement picks up the change.

> Somebody will say, "Listen to Mrs. Jones's heart. It's just a little thing flubbing on the table." And *you forget about the rest of her* . . . and it helps in learning in the sense that you can go in to a patient, put your stethoscope on the heart, listen to it, and walk out. . . . The advantage is that *you can go in a short time and see a patient, get the important things out of the patient, and leave* (italics added).

Another student's statement illustrates the extent to which patients truly become objects.

> You don't know the people that are under anesthesia—just practice putting the tube in, and the person wakes up with a sore throat, and well, it's just sort of a part of the procedure. . . . Someone comes in who has croaked (and you say), "Well, come on. Here is a chance to practice your intubation" (inserting a tube in the throat).

Sexism in Medicine

Sexism in medical practice takes various forms. As we saw in Chapter 11, women are less likely than men to be given heart surgery, except in the more advanced stages of heart disease; thus, women are more likely to die from the surgery. The Down-to-Earth Sociology box on page 543 illustrates a more pervasive form of sexism in medical practice.

Sue Fisher (1986), a sociologist who did participant observation in two teaching hospitals, one in the West and one in the South, details another form of medical sexism—surgery directed *against* women. Fisher listened and observed as physicians talked with patients and even made videotapes of their interactions in the examining rooms. She often heard physicians recommend total hysterectomy (the surgical removal of both the uterus and ovaries). When cancer was present, the hysterectomy was medically called for. But she noted that in many cases there was no medical reason for the surgery.

As Fisher probed this matter, she realized that many surgical operations were attributable to sexism. She found that the male doctors held a biased attitude toward the female reproductive system. After the uterus and ovaries have served their primary reproductive function, they regarded these organs as "potentially disease-producing and unnecessary." This attitude made their removal routine.

Fisher (1986) drove home the point by recounting her own experience with the physician who examined her for a mass on her ovaries (recounted on page 541). She says that after her examination,

> I went to his consulting office and was told that indeed I had a mass and that I needed to be hospitalized for tests and surgery. No other information was offered; no choices were discussed. . . . He would conduct the necessary tests one day and perform a total hysterectomy the next day. Even though I was stunned, I recovered sufficiently to ask if he thought the mass was malignant. He said "no" and then went on to explain that a woman my age *did not need her uterus or ovaries* (italics added).

CDQ 15: Do you think sexism would still exist in U.S. medicine if at least fifty percent of the physicians were women? Why or why not?

Underlying this sexism is male dominance of medicine in the United States. This is not a worldwide phenomenon. For example, while only 18 percent of American physicians are women, in the former Soviet Union three out of four physicians are women (Knaus 1981; *Statistical Abstract* 1991: Table 652). The figure of 18 percent actually represents a marked increase; in 1960 only 6 percent of American medical

DOWN-TO-EARTH SOCIOLOGY

The Doctor-Nurse Game

Leonard Stein (1988), a physician who observed nurses and doctors for many years, analyzed their interactions in terms of a game. Because physicians have higher status, nurses must try to give the impression that the doctor is always "in control." Although nurses spend more time with patients and, therefore, are often more familiar with their needs, nurses can never be perceived as giving recommendations to a doctor. Consequently, nurses disguise their recommendations. Consider the following dialogue between a nurse and a resident physician whom the nurse has called at 1:00 A.M. The rotating resident does not know the patient.

"This is Dr. Jones."

(An open and direct communication)

"Dr. Jones, this is Nurse Smith on 2W. Mrs. Brown learned today that her father died, and she is unable to fall asleep."

(This apparently direct, open communication of factual information—that the patient is unable to sleep and has learned of a death in the family—contains a hidden recommendation. The nurse has diagnosed the cause of the sleeplessness and is suggesting that a sedative be prescribed.)

The conversation continues: "What sleeping medication has been helpful to Mrs. Brown in the past?"

(This communication, supposedly a mere request for facts, is actually a request for a recommendation of what to prescribe.)

"Pentobarbital, 100 milligrams, was quite effective the night before last."

(This is a specific recommendation from the nurse to the physician, but it comes disguised in the form of factual information.)

"Pentobarbital, 100 milligrams before bedtime as needed for sleep. Got it?"

(This communication is spoken with audible authority—a little louder, a little firmer.)

"Yes, I have, and thank you very much, doctor."

The two have successfully played the doctor-nurse game. The lower-status person has made a recommendation to the higher-status person in a covert manner that requires neither of them to acknowledge what really occurred and does not threaten their relative statuses.

In an interview, Stein said that the doctor-nurse game is breaking down because of the larger number of males in nursing, the feminist movement challenging male authority, and the larger number of female physicians. As a consequence, nurses are less subservient, and physicians are less able to exert unquestioned authority.

Some version of the game will continue to be played, however, as long as status differences remain. The rules will simply be modified to meet changing circumstances.

---

degrees were earned by women. Following the changes in gender relations discussed in Chapter 11 this figure rose rapidly, and women now earn 36 percent of all American medical degrees. In the next few years women are expected to comprise 40 percent of medical school graduates (Jonas, Eitzel, and Barzansky 1991). This changing sex ratio should considerably reduce sexism in medical practice.

Medicalization of Society

As we have seen with childbirth and Fisher's research, the female organs and the reproductive process have become defined as medical matters. Sociologists use the term **medicalization** to refer to the process of turning something that was not previously considered medical into a medical matter. Examples of conditions now regarded as medical issues include balding, weight and diet, wrinkles, acne, insomnia, anxiety, depression, a sagging chin or buttocks, small breasts, and even the inability to achieve orgasm.

There is nothing inherently medical in such human conditions, yet we have become so used to medicalization that we tend to consider them somehow naturally medical concerns. Symbolic interactionists would stress that medicalization is based on arbitrary definitions, part of a cultural way of looking at life that is bound to a specific historical period. Functionalists view the medicalization of such matters as functional for the medical establishment, and for patients who have someone to listen to their problems and are sometimes helped. Conflict sociologists would argue that this process is another indication of the growing power of the medical establishment—the more physicians can medicalize human affairs, the greater their power and profits.

medicalization: the transformation of something into a matter to be treated by physicians

CDQ 16: Do you believe people have a "right to die?" Why is it now difficult to determine when an individual dies?

Essay #4

Project 6

living will: a statement people in good health sign that clearly expresses their feelings about being kept alive on artificial life-support systems

euthanasia: mercy killing

Controversy about Death

In Chapter 13, you were introduced to the sociology of death and dying. Here, we shall round out the topic by looking at how social change has led to problems in defining death and controversy about the right to die.

Defining Death.   The definition of death used to be a simple matter. A person who wasn't breathing and had no heartbeat was dead. This determination was not always right, of course; on occasion a living person who was in a deep coma was mistakenly buried.

Today, with the arrival of machines that can keep oxygen and blood circulating in the human body, determining when someone is dead has become infinitely more complex. In some cases, individuals who are unconscious and cannot breathe can survive for months and even years on artificial life-support machines. The machines insert liquid food, force in air, circulate the blood, rotate the body, and remove impurities collected in the urine.

Is such a person alive or dead? The new technology has forced a new, narrower definition of death. The term *brain dead* means that although the body is still alive, in the sense that its tissues and organs are maintained by machines, it produces no brain waves. In essence, there is no living person inside the body.

Controversy over the Right to Die.   The recent capacity for artificial life support has fueled the intriguing question of whether people have the right to die (Berger and Berger 1990). Specifically, can a hospital, the government, or your family keep you alive even though you don't want to live and you can no longer survive without being attached to machinery? If so, for how long? Do you have the right to order medical personnel to disconnect the machines? If you are unconscious, do your relatives have the right to give that order? The **living will**—a declaration that people in good health sign to make clear what they wish medical personnel to do should they become dependent on artificial life-support systems—is an attempt to deal with this issue. As medical technology grows, and with it the capacity to keep us alive long past our ordinary physical limits, this matter will grow in significance. Some take the position that physicians should practice **euthanasia,** or mercy killing, and help patients die if they request death to relieve insufferable pain or to escape from an incurable disease. This practice

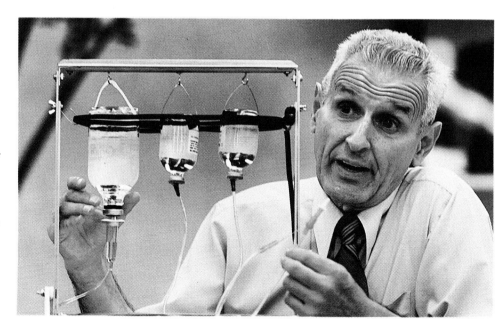

Unacknowledged, but covertly practiced, euthanasia has been a part of the practice of medicine for centuries. Retired physician Jack Kevorkian, shown here with his suicide machine, has brought euthanasia into the open and made it a matter of public debate. Using this machine, an individual self-administers poison at will. Proponents of euthanasia insist that people have the right to die, while opponents insist that it is morally wrong and also opens the door to abuse.

is also sometimes called "assisted suicide" (Humphry 1991). Other people are aghast at such proposals, while still others agree that euthanasia should be allowed in specific circumstances but are disturbed that euthanasia is too easily abused. This topic is explored in the Thinking Critically section below.

THINKING CRITICALLY ABOUT SOCIAL CONTROVERSY

Should We Legalize Euthanasia?

Proponents of euthanasia, "mercy killing," base their claim on "people's right to die." "If someone wants to be disconnected from feeding tubes," they say, "he or she should be able to die in peace. And if someone wants to commit suicide, that person should have the right to do so, even to go to a physician for help in accomplishing that desire. What right does the rest of society have to interfere?"

Framed in that way, many Americans would agree that euthanasia should be permitted. "The problem," say its opponents, "is that the vast majority of euthanasia involves other types of dying."

The best example, critics point out, is Holland, which has officially practiced euthanasia for twenty years. According to Dutch law, a physician can assist a patient in dying only if the patient makes "a free, informed, and persistent request." Euthanasia must be a "last resort," and physicians are accountable to the courts for following the letter of the law.

A Dutch government committee, however, has found that the practice is far different from the law's specifications. In 1990, more than 3 percent of deaths in Holland were from euthanasia: 2,300 cases of "voluntary" euthanasia, 400 assisted suicides, and more than 1,000 patients who did *not* request euthanasia. Another 12.6 percent of all deaths were doctor-assisted, 8,100 by administering pain-killing drugs and 8,750 by withholding or withdrawing treatment. *In not one of these 8,750 deaths did the patient consent.* Similarly, in almost 5,000 of the 8,100 cases in which drugs were administered for the purpose of euthanasia, the patients did not consent to their deaths.

Leading Dutch physicians who practice euthanasia oppose its legalization in the United States. Said one, "If euthanasia were allowed in the United States, I would not want to be a patient there. In view of the financial costs that the care of patients can impose on relatives and society under the United States health-care system, the legalization of euthanasia in America would be an open door to get rid of patients." Another added, "I wouldn't trust myself as a patient if your medical profession, with their commercial outlook, should have that power."

What do you think? (*Source:* Gomez 1991; Keown 1991.)

Health Insurance

Although the soaring costs of medical care in the United States have led to a clamor to reduce expenses, attempts to do so have been ineffective. Medical costs have risen at about twice the rate of inflation. We have already seen some of the basic reasons: advanced—and expensive—technology for diagnosis and treatment, a larger elderly population, tests performed for legal rather than medical reasons, and the approach to health care as a commodity to be sold to the highest bidder. As long as these conditions are in effect, the price of medical care will continue to soar.

Private health insurance and government-funded health care have also contributed to the cost spiral. At first, they set no upper limits on tests or treatments, leaving the physician alone to make these decisions. When it got to the point that General Motors was paying more to Blue Cross Blue Shield than to US Steel, its major supplier, people knew something had to be done (Fox and Crawford 1979). Insurance companies took four main steps to try to control prices. They introduced or increased deductibles (the

CDQ 17: Do you have health insurance? In what ways has health insurance contributed to the spiraling cost of medicine?

initial expenses a patient must cover before the insurance policy goes into effect); instituted coinsurance (requiring the patient to pay a fixed percentage of the cost of each hospital stay or medical treatment); began utilization reviews (employing medical personnel to review claims to determine whether a treatment was warranted, and refusing to pay if they decided it was not); and introduced "capping," setting the maximum amount they would pay for each procedure (one fixed price to remove a wart, another to remove an appendix, and so on).

Two more radical attempts to trim swollen medical costs are the introduction of health maintenance organizations (HMOs) and diagnostic related groups (DRGs).

Health Maintenance Organizations. In a **health maintenance organization** a company pays a predetermined fee to a group of physicians to take care of the medical needs of its employees. The employer knows its annual medical bill in advance, and since the physicians are paid a set fee for the year, to make a profit they must be efficient and avoid unnecessary procedures. Because hospitalization costs are included in the annual fee, physicians use surgery and hospitalization as a last resort. HMOs lower expenses, but patients complain about their lack of choice of physicians and hospitals. In addition, patients are sometimes rushed out of hospitals before they have recovered; in one case a woman was discharged even though she was still bleeding and running a fever (author's files).

Diagnostic Related Groups. The federal government has also taken steps to interrupt the cost spiral. In 1983, it classified all illnesses into 468 DRGs and specified the exact amount it would pay for the treatment of each. The result was that hospitals could make a profit only if they moved patients through the system quickly. If patients were discharged before the hospital had spent the allotted amount, the hospital made money. The average hospital stay immediately dropped (Easterbrook 1987).

The disadvantage of this approach, of course, is that some patients are discharged before they are fully ready to go home. Others are refused admittance because they appear to have a "worse than average" case of a particular illness, which would cost the hospital money instead of making them a profit (Easterbrook 1987; Feinglass 1987). Another negative consequence is **dumping,** sending unprofitable patients to public hospitals. The following case illustrates just how far hospitals will go.

> A young woman who was five months pregnant was taken to a hospital complaining of stomach pains. The hospital refused to admit her because she had no money or credit. As they were about to transfer her to a hospital for the poor, she gave birth. The baby was stillborn. The hospital went ahead and transferred the woman—dead baby, umbilical cord, and all (Ansberry 1988).

There is little wonder that federal legislators feel pressure for a national health insurance for Americans.

THREATS TO HEALTH

Three current major threats to health are disease, drugs, and disabling environments. Let's look at the implications of each of these for American society.

Disease

Perhaps the most pressing issue in American—and global—health today is AIDS (Acquired Immune Deficiency Syndrome). AIDS is a virus that attacks the human immune system. Although the first case of AIDS was not documented until 1981, the virus existed without being identified well before then. Frozen blood samples from Zaire taken in the early 1970s, for example, indicate the presence of the virus. Within a

CDQ 18: Do you think the practice of "dumping" by hospitals is ethical? Why or why not?

L. Obj. 10: Discuss these threats to health: disease, drugs, and disabling environments.

Essay #5

CDQ 19: How devastating do you think the AIDS virus is going to become before a cure is found?

Speaker Sug. #5: A social worker from an AIDS treatment center or hospice to discuss the "human face" of AIDS today.

health maintenance organization (HMO): a health-care organization that provides medical treatment to its members for a fixed annual cost

dumping: the practice of sending unprofitable patients to public hospitals

Because of its huge sex industry, AIDS is rapidly spreading in Asia. Shown here is a 19-year-old former prostitute who has passed the virus on to her six-month-old baby.

decade of its discovery, AIDS has become the eleventh leading cause of death in the United States.

Origin.   The origin of AIDS is unknown. The most prevalent theory is that the virus was first present in monkeys and chimpanzees in Africa and then transmitted to humans. If so, just how the transmission to humans took place remains a matter of conjecture. It may have occurred during the 1920s and 1950s when, in a peculiar test of malaria, people were experimentally inoculated with blood from monkeys and chimpanzees. This blood may unknowingly have been infected with viral ancestors of HIV (Rathus and Nevid 1993). Another possibility is that humans were bitten by infected monkeys. Finally, since monkeys are considered food in several parts of Africa, the ingestion of animal tissues that were not adequately cooked may have been responsible (Dwyer 1988:119). Although at this point scientists do not know the origin of AIDS, genetic sleuths may eventually unravel the mystery.

The Transmission of AIDS.   In the United States, AIDS first appeared in the male homosexual population. Male bisexuals provided the bridge that passed AIDS on to the heterosexual population. As a result of having sex with bisexuals and sharing needles for intravenous drugs, prostitutes quickly became a second bridge to the heterosexual population. Others were infected with AIDS through blood transfusions. Figure 19.5 illustrates the distribution of AIDS over the last decade relative to the means of transmission.

TR#51M: Distribution of AIDS by Means of Transmission, 1982–1991

A person cannot become infected with AIDS unless bodily fluids pass from one person to another. AIDS is known to be transmitted by the exchange of blood and semen, as well as by mother's milk to newborns. Since the AIDS virus is present in all bodily fluids (including sweat, tears, spittle, and urine), some people think that AIDS can also be transmitted in these forms. The United States Centers for Disease Control,

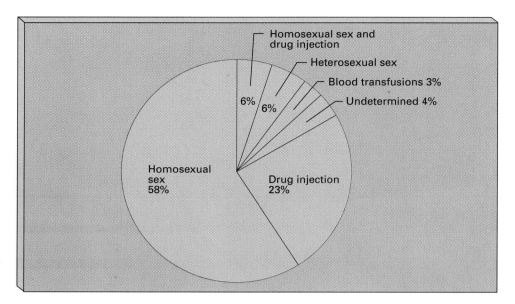

FIGURE 19.5 Distribution of AIDS by Means of Transmission, 1982–1991. (*Source:* Centers for Disease Control 1992: Table 3.)

however, say that AIDS cannot be transmitted by casual contact in which traces of these fluids would be exchanged (Jaffe and Lifson 1988; Friedland et al. 1986; Koop 1988).

Women and AIDS. Although AIDS in North America first appeared among males, in parts of Africa males and females are equally likely to have the disease. Figure 19.6 shows the increase of AIDS among American females to the extent that it is now among the top five killers of American women of childbearing age. Keep in mind that AIDS has a lengthy incubation period, and that most women diagnosed with AIDS this year were therefore infected several years ago. The Centers for Disease Control predict worldwide equality by the year 2000; in other words, they expect as many women as men to have AIDS by the end of this decade (Pearl 1990). This does not mean that the proportions will be equal in every country.

The Threat AIDS Poses to Public Health. As of April 1992, AIDS had claimed about 141,000 American lives (Centers for Disease Control 1992). AIDS has now become the leading cause of death among American men between twenty-five and

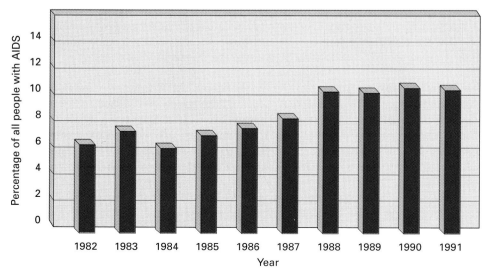

FIGURE 19.6 Women with AIDS: Percentage of All People Diagnosed with AIDS Who Are Women. (*Source: Statistical Abstract of the United States,* 1990: Table 187; Centers for Disease Control, 1992.)

Note: AIDS is sometimes misdiagnosed. An AIDS-induced death may be attributed to another disease such as pneumonia. When AIDS was first identified, the diagnosis was extremely unreliable, and for the pupose of computing a trend, the percentage for the early years should be discounted.

forty-four. Figure 19.7 portrays deaths in the United States from AIDS. These figures, however, represent only the tip of the iceberg, for somewhere between one and two million Americans are estimated to be infected by the AIDS virus. Most of these persons show no symptoms and are even unaware that they carry the deadly disease. Many thousands of them, however, have AIDS-Related Complex (ARC)—which means that they test positive for the virus and show mild symptoms of the disease, mild enough to allow them to continue their normal lives. An unknown percentage of persons with ARC will develop full-blown cases of AIDS. Some experts estimate this proportion to be 50 to 75 percent, others as high as 100 percent. In either case, we are talking about vast numbers of people.

As Figure 19.7 shows, in the United States AIDS—both deaths and new cases—declined between 1990 and 1991. The reasons for this decline are a matter of dispute. Some attribute it to the use of drugs such as AZT, others to changes in behavior, especially among homosexual men. Still others suggest that the most susceptible population has already been infected. This one-year decline does not mean that Americans should become complacent. Far from it. During the next three or four years, AIDS will claim as many Americans as it did since the disease was first detected.

AIDS is far from just an American problem; it is a global disease. Worldwide, perhaps forty million people are infected (Sorensen 1990; Waldholz 1992). The former director of the World Health Organization's AIDS project reports that the disease is underestimated. He says that AIDS "is gyrating out of control," in no country has the disease peaked, and as many as 120 million people worldwide will have AIDS by the year 2000 (Stout 1992). Due to the huge sex industry in Asia (see the Perspectives box in Chapter 9, The Patriotic Prostitute, p. 243), the majority of new cases are likely to be in Asia (Bohrer 1992).

Is There a Cure for AIDS?   Several drugs, such as AZT and DDI, have been found to slow the progress of AIDS, but no cure has yet been found for the disease (Chase 1992a). AIDS is a rapidly mutating virus and now has developed resistance to AZT. The virus's capacity to adapt to changing environments through mutation makes finding a cure especially difficult (Chase 1992b). In July 1992, several AIDS patients were identified whose strain of AIDS was not even detectable by current tests. With many strains of AIDS proliferating throughout the world, pharmaceutical companies are considering the possibility of pooling their research (Waldholz 1992).

Testing proposed vaccines raises a disturbing ethical question. If researchers think that a vaccine or drug will work, how can they place people in a control group and purposely withhold treatment from them (Waldholz and Bishop 1986)?

Kimberly Bergalis of Florida, shown here testifying before Congress in 1991, focused the nation's attention on the transmission of AIDS. A virgin and not a drug user, Kimberly contracted AIDS from her dentist, as did several of his other patients. The method of transmission has not been determined, and theories vary from the doctor accidentally puncturing himself to purposely infecting his patients while they were under anesthesia.

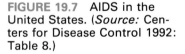

TR#44: AIDS in the United States.

FIGURE 19.7   AIDS in the United States. (*Source:* Centers for Disease Control 1992: Table 8.)

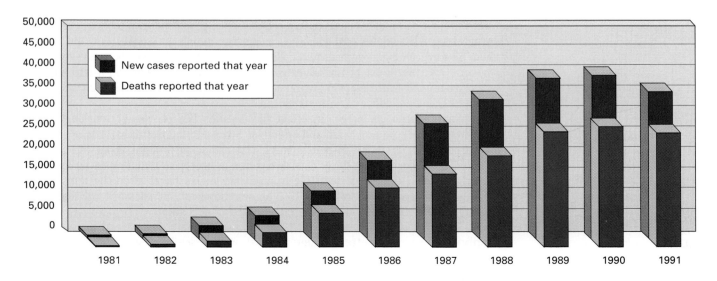

Drugs

Many drugs are popular in the United States. In this context we shall focus on nicotine and alcohol, the two most commonly used.

CDQ 20: In your opinion, why do many people keep smoking even when they know cancer and other diseases are directly related to their smoking?

Nicotine.   Tobacco presents a much less dramatic threat than the AIDS virus, but it is also deadly. The types of cancer and other diseases that result directly from cigarette smoking take years to develop, but they kill about 390,000 Americans each year (Gartner 1988). This means that *cigarette smoking accounts for one out of every six deaths in the United States*. Many of these deaths are lingering and painful, an ordeal to both the victims and their families.

Nicotine is an *addictive drug,* that is, it has the capacity to make people depend on it to get through the day. After reviewing two thousand scientific studies, C. Everett Koop, a former surgeon general of the United States, concluded that nicotine is as addictive as heroin (Tolchin 1988). Such a conclusion sounds farfetched, but consider Buerger's disease.

> In this disease, the blood vessels, especially those supplying the legs, become so constricted that circulation is impaired whenever nicotine enters the bloodstream. If a patient continues to smoke, gangrene may eventually set in. First a toe or two may have to be amputated, then the foot at the ankle, then the leg at the knee, and ultimately at the hip. . . . Patients are informed that if they will only stop smoking, it is virtually certain that the otherwise inexorable march of gangrene up the legs will be curbed. Yet surgeons report that some patients with Buerger's disease vigorously puff away in their hospital beds following a second or third amputation (Brecher et al. 1972).

Smoking, which doubles a person's risk of heart attack, also causes progressive emphysema, a disease in which breathing becomes increasingly difficult until death eventually occurs from respiratory failure. Chest specialists report that "even during the last months of their ordeal, when they must breathe oxygen intermittently instead of air, some of them go right on alternating cigarette smoke and oxygen" (Brecher et al. 1972).

K.P.: Erich Goode

Sociologist Erich Goode (1989) pointed out that smokers are three times as likely to die before reaching the age of sixty-five as nonsmokers. He added that "a nonsmoker has a better chance of reaching the age of seventy-five than a smoker has of reaching the age of sixty-five."

If a Martian were to visit the United States and learn how deadly cigarettes were, he or she would be confused to learn that over half a million acres of prime farmland are planted with tobacco, that the United States government subsidizes this crop, that 49,000 Americans work in the tobacco industry, and that tobacco companies take in $15 billion a year (*Statistical Abstract* 1991: Tables 669, 699, 1156, 1303). Our mythical Martian might be further confused to learn that each year American tobacco companies spend about $2 billion in advertising to encourage people to smoke this substance— about $9 for each man, woman, and child in the United States, or about $38 for every smoker—and that most of the advertising is designed to seduce youth into smoking by associating cigarette smoking with success, high fashion, stylishness, social acceptability, and independence (Warner 1986).

An antitobacco campaign, in effect for decades but previously working quietly behind the scenes, is now open and effective. Stressing the health hazards of smoking and of secondhand smoke to nonsmokers, this campaign brought about the smoking and nonsmoking areas that have become fixtures in American restaurants, airlines, and offices. As measured by a decrease in smoking, males have taken the antismoking message most seriously. As Table 19.2 shows, however, females are still less likely to smoke. This table also shows the significance of education.

Alcohol.   Where cigarette smoking has lost appeal, alcohol has not. It remains the standard recreational drug of Americans. The *average* American drinker consumes the

TABLE 19.2 Cigarette Smoking by Sex and Education

	1965	1975	1988
Sex			
Male	50%	43%	32%
Female	32%	31%	26%
Education			
High School	38%*	36%	33%
College	28%	28%	16%

*Note: Data for 1965 unavailable, and 1970 data is used.
Source: Statistical Abstract 1991: Tables 199, 201.

Although such an ad strikes us as strange, in the 1950s newspapers and magazines were filled with testimonials about how cigarettes were good for people's health. They were even said to "soothe the throat." The health hazards of smoking were not unknown at this time. Today's cigarette advertising may be more subtle, but it has the same effects—to seduce the young into smoking, and to assure current smokers that it is all right to continue.

equivalent of 39 gallons of alcoholic beverages per year, approximately 34 gallons of beer, 3 gallons of wine, and 2 gallons of whiskey or other distilled spirits. In fact, the average American drinks more beer than either milk, tea, coffee, soft drinks, or citrus juices (*Statistical Abstract* 1991: Table 209). Just 10 percent of drinkers drink *50* percent of all the alcohol consumed in the United States (*Sixth Special Report* 1987).

The average American spends $269 a year on alcohol, though alcohol consumption varies significantly by age, sex, race/ethnicity, and region. Southerners drink the least, Westerners the most. Younger people drink more than older people do, and consumption is highest among those aged between twenty-five and thirty-four. In every age group, males drink more than females and whites more than either African Americans or Hispanic Americans (*Statistical Abstracts* 1991: Tables 199, 204).

Alcohol is far more harmful to health than its broad social acceptability would imply. Drunken drivers are responsible for about half the 49,000 lives lost in automobile accidents each year. Pregnant women who drink are more likely than abstainers to give birth to children with birth defects. Drinkers are more likely to die violent and unnatural deaths—to be murdered, to die in accidents, or to commit suicide. They also run a higher risk than nondrinkers of developing cancer of the tongue, mouth, esophagus, larynx, stomach, liver, lung, colon, and rectum. In all, the bill for alcohol abuse in the United States totals over $11 billion a year in medical expenses alone, a cost that all Americans, abstainers and moderate drinkers alike, must share (*Statistical Abstract* 1991: Table 124; Haberman and Natarajan 1986; *Sixth Special Report* 1987; Yates et al. 1987).

CDQ 21: Have you worked in a disabling environment? What kinds of hazards were involved?

Disabling Environments

A **disabling environment** is one that is harmful to health. The health risk of some occupations is evident; mining, lumberjacking, riding bulls in a rodeo, and taming lions

disabling environment: an environment that is harmful to health

are obvious examples. In many occupations, however, the risk becomes evident only years after people have worked at what they thought was a safe occupation. For example, of the eight to eleven million laborers who worked with asbestos during and after World War II, the federal government estimates that one-quarter will eventually die of cancer from having breathed or swallowed asbestos dust (Meier 1987). It is likely that hundreds of other substances, many of which are not yet identified, cause cancer to develop twenty or thirty years after people have worked with them. Ironically, some asbestos substitutes also produce cancer (Meier 1987).

Although industrialization has increased the world's standard of living, it also now threatens to disable the basic environment of the human race, posing what may be the greatest health hazard of all time. The burning of vast amounts of carbon fuels is leading to the *greenhouse effect,* a warming of the earth that may change the globe's climate, melt its polar ice caps, and flood the earth's coastal shores. Use of fluorocarbon gases in such items as aerosol cans, refrigerators and air conditioners is threatening the *ozone shield,* the protective layer of the earth's upper stratosphere that screens out a high proportion of the sun's ultraviolet rays. High-intensity ultraviolet radiation is harmful to most forms of life. In humans, it causes skin cancer. The pollution of land, air, and water, especially through nuclear waste, pesticides, herbicides, and other chemicals, poses additional risks to life on this planet.

To identify environmental threats to world health is the first step. The second is to introduce short- and long-term policies to reduce such problems, a topic discussed in Chapter 22.

THE SEARCH FOR ALTERNATIVES

What alternatives to the United States health-care system are there? Suggestions have been made that we shift the emphasis away from the treatment of disease to prevention and holistic medicine. Health-care systems of other countries—which might contain ideas to follow, or to avoid—are compared in the Perspectives box on page 553.

CDQ 22: In regard to health, do you agree with the old statement that "an ounce of prevention is worth a pound of cure?"

L. Obj. 11: Analyze the prospects for change in medicine which might be possible through preventive and holistic medicine.

CNN: Soviet Medical Care

TR#52M: Health Status of Three Societies

Treatment or Prevention?

Most people prefer not to hear that they are largely responsible for their own health. Few people like responsibility, and that is a large one. Individuals, of course, bear no responsibility for some health problems, such as congenital defects or, as discussed, those that result from the medical establishment failing to deliver good medical care to the poor. And no one can help being exposed to germs and viruses, for work and school require being among persons who carry them.

As you have seen in this chapter, however, many of the current threats to health are preventable. Prevention implies both an individual and a group responsibility. On the individual level, doing exercises regularly, eating nutritious food, maintaining sexual monogamy, and avoiding smoking and alcohol abuse go a long way to preventing disease. Following these guidelines can add years to a person's life—and make those years healthier and more enjoyable.

On the group level, the issue is the proper role of the American health establishment. As has been noted in several contexts, sociology and the other sciences cannot answer questions about what we *should* do. These must be addressed by people who put their own value systems to work. Sociology, however, can point out alternatives and predict the consequences that may result from each.

Short of socialized medicine, which seems to go against the grain of the American ethos, one alternative is preventive medicine. What would it require to implement a national goal of "prevention, not intervention"? Money (either new money, or money

Health Care in Other Countries

No system of health care is perfect, but looking at the approaches taken by other countries can provide a broader perspective on the system in the United States. The countries chosen for comparison all view health care as a right of their citizens.

Sweden

Sweden has the most comprehensive health-care system in the world. All Swedish citizens and alien residents are covered by national health insurance financed by contributions from the state and employers. Most physicians are paid a salary by the government to treat patients, but 5 percent work full-time in private practice (Swedish Institute 1990). Except for a small consultation fee, medical and dental treatment by these government-paid doctors is free, and most of the charges of private physicians are also paid by the government. The government also reimburses travel expenses for patients, as well as for the parents of a hospitalized child. Only minimal fees are charged for prescriptions and hospitalization.

Medical treatment is just one component of Sweden's broad system of social welfare. For example, people who are sick or must stay home with sick children receive 90 percent of their salaries, Swedes are given parental leave at the birth of a child, and all Swedes are guaranteed a pension. This comprehensive system does not come cheap, running about 35 percent of each employee's salary (Cockerham 1989).

Great Britain

Under what is called the National Health Service, Great Britain also guarantees medical care to all its citizens. Physicians are paid by the government but can also accept private patients. National Health patients complain of long waits for hospitalization. Some physicians operate exclusively private practices, and Britons who can afford it patronize them. This has resulted in a two-tier system of medicine similar to that of the United States—one for the wealthy and one for the poor. The difference, however, is that everyone is guaranteed medical treatment (Doyal and Pennell 1981; Gill 1986).

The Former Soviet Union

The government owns all health-care facilities, all medical equipment, and determines how many students will attend the medical schools that it also owns and operates. The physicians, most of whom are women, are government employees, earning about the same salary as factory workers and high school teachers. Physicians are not trained well, and the health of the population has declined in the past two decades. At this point, as shown on Table 19.3, the health of ex-Soviet citizens is considerably below that of the population of either the United States or Great Britain. The only hospitals comparable with those of the United States are the hospitals reserved for the elite (Light 1992). In the rest, basic supplies and equipment are in such short supply that surgical scalpels are resharpened until they break. Sometimes razer blades are even used for surgery (Donelson 1992). Although health

TABLE 19.3 Health Status of Three Societies

Reported Cause of Death	The Former Soviet Union	Great Britain	United States
Per 1,000 births			
Maternal mortality	47.7	6.4	6.6
Infant mortality	25.1	9.0	9.7
Per 100,000 population			
Age-adjusted mortality	1160	854	827
Circulatory diseases	673	389	365
Malignant neoplasms	185	224	195
Injuries and poisonings	105	34	59
Respiratory diseases	85	16	8
Suicide	21	8	12

Source: Light 1992, based on Rowland 1991 and Rowland and Telyukov 1991, and *Statistical Abstract of the United States,* 1991: Tables 111, 113.

care is free, patients have no choice about which doctor they see or where they will be treated. Some hospitals do not even have a doctor on staff. The length of the average hospital stay is three times longer than it is in the United States. Medical care is so inefficient that the *majority* of X-rays are uninterpretable because of poor quality. Patients also complain about depersonalization (Knaus 1981). Some of the radical changes now being introduced in the former Soviet Union include employer-based health insurance (Light 1992).

Canada

In 1971, the Canadian government instituted a national health insurance program. Medical costs are shared equally between the federal and provincial governments. Unlike physicians in the Soviet Union, Great Britain, and most doctors in Sweden, Canadian physicians work in private practice and charge a fee for service. The government acts as the patient's insurer and pays the physician's bill. As in Britain, patients can choose any doctor they wish, and physicians face no restrictions in choosing a medical specialty or deciding where they will practice. If they wish, physicians can practice private medical care instead of participating in the government program, but only a handful do (Coburn et al. 1981; Grant 1984; Vayda and Deber 1984).

Canada's bill for medical care runs 8 percent of its gross national product, compared with 11.2 percent in the United States (*Statistical Abstract* 1991: Table 1443). Costs are held down in three main ways. (1) A fixed fee is established annually by the government for each medical service after negotiations with professional medical associations. In Quebec, for example, a routine examination by a general practitioner costs $12.15, an annual physical $24.20; (2) Physicians' incomes are capped. Once a general practitioner hits $39,474 in quarterly fees, the government pays only 25 percent of each bill submitted over that amount until the next quarter starts; and (3) Over-

head costs are kept low: Hospital overhead is low because hospitals run at full capacity, compared with 65 percent capacity in the United States. Fixed costs are thus spread over the greatest possible number of patients. Nor do hospitals need large accounting departments to deal with a myriad of insurance companies, for only the provincial government is billed (Goad 1991). The savings in overhead account for half the difference between the cost of health care in Canada and the United States (Walker 1991).

Although the health of Canadians is among the best in the world, access to major medical procedures is more limited than in the United States. Canada, with 10 percent of the population of the United States, has only 12 magnetic resonance imagers, the United States 1,375. In all of Canada only 11 facilities do open-heart surgery, compared with 793 in the United States (Barnes 1990). In addition, there are waiting lines for coronary bypass surgery and even for ultrasound treatment of kidney stones (Blinick 1992).

China

Like the citizens of the countries mentioned above, the Chinese have a right to medical care. A right without substance, however, has little value. Because this undeveloped nation of 1.1 billion people has a vast shortage of trained physicians, hospitals, and medicine, most Chinese see "barefoot doctors," persons who have only a rudimentary knowledge of medicine, are paid low wages, and travel from village to village. Physicians are employees of the government, and as in the former Soviet Union, the government owns all the country's medical facilities. Chinese medicine differs from that of the West, for, following their traditional culture, the Chinese stress a holistic approach to health. Westerners have scoffed at the Chinese approach, but with the success of acupuncture and some Chinese medicinal herbs, the West is reconsidering its attitude.

diverted from current medical spending) would have to be spent educating the public concerning nutrition, exercise, sexual practices, and drug use. Yet more money would need to be spent on scientific research—for a vaccine for AIDS and for ways to overcome such global threats to health as the greenhouse effect and nuclear and chemical pollution.

A policy of prevention would encounter opposition. Although few would argue that prevention is bad, preventive medicine jeopardizes vested interests. Physicians would feel threatened, for their orientation is treatment, and they do not see it as their role (or source of profits) to prevent illness and disease. For the preventive approach to succeed, its advocates must win over the medical establishment, including the private insurance industry. To do this, they would have to demonstrate that prevention is profitable. The preventive alternative would require such a change in basic orientations, however, that it would likely take decades for the medical profession to make the switch.

Holistic medicine emphasizes prevention, not treatment. Shown here is a medical practice in the East that looks far different from that of the West. Herbs are viewed as substances to prevent sickness, as well as to treat illness.

Comprehensive prevention—not simply individual efforts to improve diet and exercise, for example, but a systematic attempt to eliminate disabling environments and the use of harmful drugs—also runs into opposition. Some businesses continue to spew industrial wastes into the air and to use rivers and oceans as industrial sewers. The most effective way to bring about change is to show business that pollution control is profitable. This effort may entail a "divide and conquer" strategy. Although current polluters are unlikely to benefit financially, other parts of the American business establishment can find huge profits in the development, manufacture, sales, installation, and maintenance of pollution control equipment.

Holistic Medicine

Taking responsibility for your own health, instead of seeing yourself as a passive recipient of illness and disease, is an essential part of what is called **holistic medicine.** Holistic practitioners place emphasis on the *whole person,* making their approach stand apart from dominant medical practices. Sociologist Jan Howard (1975) described this approach to medical care as centering on the idea that a person's body, feelings, attitudes, and actions are all intertwined and cannot be segregated into discrete organ systems for the convenience of clinicians. Rather than seeing a patient as someone who has a disease or illness that has intruded the body and needs a drug to get rid of it, the holistic practitioner views the patient in terms of lifestyle and total environment. The goals are to prevent illness and disease, but to treat them when necessary, *and* to attain well-being, that is, the optimum health that comes from balanced living in a sane environment.

The obstacles to this approach are tremendous, for change as fundamental as this flies in the face of established cultural practices and threatens vested interests in the current practice of medicine. Change, if it comes, is likely to be slow. Ultimately, underlying the issues discussed is the basic ideological question of whether medical treatment should be sold as a commodity or provided as a basic right to all citizens.

Speaker Sug. #6: A holistic practitioner to discuss how their emphasis is different from those of traditional medical practitioners.

K.P.: Jan Howard

holistic medicine: an approach to medical care centering on the idea that a person's body, feelings, attitudes, and actions are all intertwined and cannot be segregated into discrete organ systems

SUMMARY

1. Health is not simply a biological matter but is intimately related to society. Health is affected by cultural beliefs, the stage of a country's development, lifestyle, and social class. People can be healthy according to some of the four dimensions of health (physical, mental, social, and spiritual) and unhealthy according to others. Cultural beliefs and practices also determine what people consider to be health and illness. The sick role excuses people from normal responsibilities but obligates them to get well in order to resume those responsibilities.

2. Patterns of disease change over time. Thus, the biggest killers of Americans today differ considerably from those of one hundred years ago. As measured by life span, Americans are healthier than they used to be, but there is no adequate way to compare the mental health of Americans today with that of their predecessors.

3. The Carnegie study and consequent effects on the funding of medical schools in the early 1900s changed the face of American health care. The study encouraged professionalization, brought control to a single group, and expanded the domain of physicians. The result was a monopoly on medicine by physicians approved by the medical establishment. As this male establishment expanded its domain, it pushed aside competing health practitioners, including midwives. Fearing the advent of socialized medicine, the medical establishment resisted Medicare and Medicaid. After these programs began, however, physicians found them to be a gold mine. Attempts by insurers

to reduce the cost spiral of medical care include the use of deductibles, coinsurance, utilization reviews, capping, HMOs, and DRGs. The medical establishment has also expanded its domain into mental problems (which some claim are a myth). Social inequality marks both the incidence of mental problems and available treatment.

4. The fundamental premise characterizing medical care in the United States is that medicine is a commodity, not a right. One consequence is a two-tier system of medical care—one level for those who can pay and another for those who cannot. Some of the main sources of the spiraling costs of medical treatment are the fee-for-service system, a larger population of older people, and the use of expensive, advanced technology. Other problems include depersonalization (learned in medical school), sexism (including the unnecessary removal of women's reproductive organs), medicalization, unsatisfactory definitions of death, the controversy over the right to die, and health insurance.

5. Major current threats to health are AIDS, smoking, alcohol abuse, and disabling environments. AIDS, transmitted by bodily fluids, has no cure. Nicotine, an addictive drug, kills 390,000 Americans a year, while alcohol abuse is another major killer. Disabling environments include risky occupations, the greenhouse effect, the depletion of the ozone shield, and pollution.

6. A fundamental issue facing American medicine is whether to change its orientation from intervention to prevention.

SUGGESTED READINGS

Albrecht, Gary L. *The Disability Business: Rehabilitation in America.* Newbury Park, Calif.: Sage, 1992. This examination of how the megabillion dollar rehabilitation industry functions focuses on how the desire for profit combines with marketing techniques to influence the quality of patient care.

Arms, Suzanne. *Immaculate Deception: A New Look at Women and Childbirth.* Westport, Conn.: Bergin & Garvey, 1984. The author, who believes that dependence on drugs and technology harms, rather than helps, mothers, lays out a blueprint for safer, simpler, and more humane methods of childbirth.

Buttino, Lou. *For the Love of Teddi: The Story Behind Camp Good Days and Special Times.* Westport, Conn.: Praeger, 1990. Twelve-year-old Teddi Mervis's fight against cancer inspired people to form an organization, Camp Good Days and Special Times, Inc., to make the brief lives of children with cancer as happy and rewarding as possible.

Cockerham, William. *Medical Sociology.* 4th ed. Englewood Cliffs, N.J.: Prentice Hall, 1989. An overview of the sociology of medicine explores in greater depth some of the issues reviewed in this chapter.

Davis, Fred. *Passage Through Crisis: Polio Victims and Their Families.* New Brunswick, N.J.: Transaction, 1990. The book focuses on communications between doctors and their patients and the meaning of physical disability in American society. The opening essay analyzes changes that have taken place in medical practice since the book was first published in 1963, including the trend toward less authoritarian relations between physicians and patients.

Fox, Renée C. *Essays in Medical Sociology: Journeys into the Field.* 2nd ed. New Brunswick, N.J.: Transaction, 1988. Based on her fieldwork, the author analyzes the process of becoming a physician and explores the evolution of medical research.

Isaac, Rael Jean, and Virginia C. Armat. *Madness in the Streets: How Psychiatry and the Law Abandoned the Mentally Ill.* New York: The Free Press, 1990. Why have so many sidewalks and parks become open-air mental wards? The authors analyze the social and political delusions that created a cultural base for justifying the abandonment of thousands of mentally ill people to the streets.

Konner, Melvin. *Becoming a Doctor: A Journey of Initiation in Medical School.* New York: Viking, 1987. A first-person account of socialization into medicine at Harvard Medical School.

Payer, Lynn. *Medicine and Culture.* New York: Holt, 1988. The author examines the extent to which people's definitions of health and illness depend on their culture.

Rosenberg, Charles E. *The Care of Strangers: The Rise of America's Hospital System.* New York: Basic Books, 1987. The author examines the way in which the development of hospitals in the United States is related to social class, ideology, philanthropy, education, and economics.

Smith, Barbara Ellen. *Digging Our Own Graves: Coal Miners and the Struggle over Black Lung Disease.* Philadelphia: Temple University Press, 1987. Smith relates the coal miners' struggle to get black lung disease recognized by the medical community.

Journals

Journal of Health and Social Behavior, Research in the Sociology of Health Care, Social Science and Medicine, and *Sociological Practice: Health Sociology* publish research articles and essays in the field of medical sociology.

CHAPTER 20

Romare Bearden, Black Manhattan, *1969*

Population and Urbanization

POPULATION

THE SPECTER OF OVERPOPULATION

Thomas Malthus: Sounding the Alarm ■ The New Malthusians ■ The Anti-Malthusians ■ Who Is Correct? ■ Why Are There Famines?

POPULATION GROWTH

Why the Poor Nations Have So Many Children ■ Implications of Different Rates of Growth ■ Estimating Population Growth: The Three Demographic Variables ■ Industrialization and the Demographic Equation ■ Problems in Forecasting Population Growth ■ *Perspectives:* **Where the United States Population Is Headed**

URBANIZATION

THE CITY IN HISTORY

MODELS OF URBAN GROWTH

The Concentric-Zone Model ■ The Sector Model ■ The Multiple-Nuclei Model ■ Critique of the Models

EXPERIENCING THE CITY

Alienation ■ *Perspectives:* **Urbanization in the Third World** ■ Community ■ Types of Urban Dwellers ■ Urban Sentiment ■ *Down-to-Earth Sociology:* **Giving Access Information—The Contrasting Perspectives of Females and Males** ■ Insiders' and Outsiders' Views: Implications for Urban Planners ■ Urban Networks ■ Urban Overload ■ Diffusion of Responsibility

THE CHANGING CITY

Urban Politics: The Transition to Minority Leadership ■ Suburbanization ■ Trends in Cities and Suburbs

SUMMARY

SUGGESTED READINGS

*T*he image still haunts me.

There stood Celia, age thirty, her distended stomach obvious proof that her thirteenth child was on its way. Her oldest was only fourteen years old! A mere boy by our standards, he had already gone as far in school as he ever would. Each morning, he joined the men to work in the fields. Each evening around twilight, we saw him return home, exhausted from hard labor in the sun.

My wife and I, who were living in a village in Colima, Mexico, had eaten dinner in Celia and Angel's home, which clearly proclaimed the family's poverty. A thatched hut consisting of only a single room served as home for all fourteen members of the family. At night, the parents and younger children crowded into a double bed, while the eldest boy slept in a hammock. As in many other homes in this village, the others slept on mats spread on the dirt floor.

The home was meagerly furnished. It had only a gas stove, a cabinet where Celia stored her cooking utensils and dishes, and a table. There being no closets, clothes were hung on pegs in the wall. There were no chairs, not even one. This really startled us. The family was so poor that they could not afford even a single chair.

Celia beamed as she told us how much she looked forward to the birth of her next child. Could she really mean it? It was hard to imagine any American woman who would want to be in her situation.

Yet Celia meant every word. She was as full of delightful anticipation as she had been with her first child—and with all the others in between.

How could Celia have wanted so many children—especially when she lived in such poverty? That question bothered me. I couldn't let go until I had the solution.

This chapter helps provide an answer. In discussing the twin themes of population and urbanization, it analyzes some of the factors that help determine people's ideas about how many children they want.

POPULATION

THE SPECTER OF OVERPOPULATION

Project 1

L. Obj. 1: Discuss the key issues in the debate between New Malthusians and Anti-Malthusians regarding the specter of overpopulation.

CDQ 1: Why are many people in the Western world so concerned about the prospects of an overcrowded world?

K.P.: Thomas Malthus

Essay #1

TR#56M: How Fast Is the World's Population Growing?

CDQ 2: Are you surprised to learn that another fifteen to twenty thousand people will be born in the time it takes you to read Chapter 20?

Celia's story takes us into the heart of **demography,** the study of the size, composition, growth, and distribution of human populations. People—at least many people in the Western world—are upset at the prospect of an overcrowded world. They fear a future world so filled with people that there remains practically no space for anybody. They imagine a planet unable to support its population, marked by chronic famine and mass starvation (Brown 1991).

Thomas Malthus: Sounding the Alarm

Thomas Malthus (1766–1834), an English economist, noticed that Europe's population had undergone a dramatic increase during the 1700s. Apparently, the potato had allowed Europe to almost double its population. When the Spanish first imported the potato from the Andes in the 1500s, the Europeans viewed it with suspicion. As it gained gradual acceptance, however, this new "miracle" vegetable became the principal food of the lower classes throughout Europe. The result of this unexpected abundance of food was to delay death and increase reproduction (Griffith 1926; McKeown 1977).

Malthus became alarmed, for he saw the rapid population increase as a sign of coming doom. In 1798, he wrote a book that became world famous, *An Essay on the Principle of Population.* In it, Malthus proposed what became known as the **Malthus theorem.** He argued that while population grows geometrically (from 2 to 4 to 8 to 16 and so forth), the food supply increases only arithmetically (from 1 to 2 to 3 to 4 and so on). This meant, he claimed, that if births went unchecked, the population of a country, or even of the world, would outstrip its food supply.

The New Malthusians

demography: the study of the size, composition, growth, and distribution of human populations

Malthus theorem: an observation by Thomas Malthus that although the food supply increases only arithmetically (from 1 to 2 to 3 to 4 and so on), population grows geometrically (from 2 to 4 to 8 to 16 and so forth)

exponential growth curve: a pattern of growth in which numbers double during approximately equal intervals, thus accelerating in the latter stages

Was Malthus right? This question has become a matter of heated debate among demographers. One group, which can be called the "New Malthusians," is convinced that today's situation is at least as grim, if not grimmer, than Malthus ever imagined. Table 20.1 shows how fast the world's population is growing. *In just the time it takes you to read this chapter, another fifteen thousand to twenty thousand people will be born!* By this time tomorrow, the earth will have an additional two hundred thousand people or so to support. This increase goes on hour after hour, day after day, without letup.

The New Malthusians point out that the world's population is following an **exponential growth curve;** in other words, if growth doubles during approximately equal

TABLE 20.1 How Fast Is the World's Population Growing?

Net gain after deaths are subtracted from births			
Each second	*Each minute*	*Each hour*	*Each day*
2.5	152	9,000	219,000
Each week	*Each month*	*Each year*	
1,538,000	7,333,000	88,000,000	

Source: Statistical Abstract of the United States, 1991: Table 1432.

intervals of time, it suddenly accelerates. To illustrate the far-reaching implications of exponential growth, sociologist William Faunce (1981) told a parable about a man who saved a rich man's life. The rich man was grateful and said that he wanted to reward the man for his heroic deed.

> The man replied he would like his reward to be spread out over a four-week period, with each day's amount being twice what he received on the preceding day. He also said he would be happy to receive only one penny on the first day. The rich man immediately handed over the penny and congratulated himself on how cheaply he had gotten by. At the end of the first week, the rich man checked to see how much he owed and was pleased to find that the total was only $1.27. By the end of the second week he owed only $163.83. On the twenty-first day, however, the rich man was surprised to find that the total had grown to $20,971.51. When the twenty-eighth day arrived the rich man was shocked to discover that he owed $1,342,177.28 for that day alone and that the total reward had jumped to $2,684,354.56!

This is precisely what alarms the New Malthusians. They claim that humanity has just entered the "fourth week" of an exponential growth curve. Figure 20.1 shows why they think the day of reckoning is just around the corner. They point out that it took thousands, some say millions, of years for the world's population to reach its first billion around 1837. It then took less than one hundred years (1927) to add the second

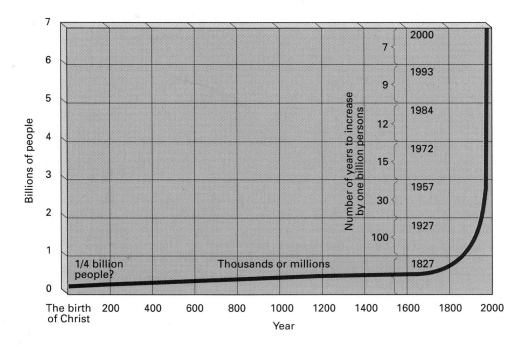

FIGURE 20.1 World Population Growth over 2,000 Years (*Source:* Modified from Piotrow 1973: 4.)

The Anti-Malthusians say that as nations industrialize they will follow the same demographic transition that occurred in Europe. When Europe's death rate dropped and its birth rate continued to climb, people became concerned that Europeans would run out of food. Now, however, as illustrated by the French couple on the left, the birth rate has dropped so greatly that the native population is not reproducing itself. The New Malthusians, however, doubt that families in the Third World, such as this Zambian husband, his two wives and their nine children, will make the demographic transition—at least not before the world's resources give out.

CDQ 3: In your opinion, are the New Malthusians or the Anti-Malthusians most accurate in their assessment of population growth?

TR#53M: World Population Growth over 2000 Years

billion. Just thirty years later (1957), the world population hit three billion. The time needed to reach the fourth billion was cut in half, to only fifteen years (1972). It then took just twelve more years (1984) for the total to hit five billion. Right now, the world population is almost six billion.

How much is a billion? Since we don't deal with such figures in our everyday lives, it is difficult to conceive of a billion of anything. A billion people is the entire population of Africa and Latin America combined (Goodwin 1987). Perhaps it will help to repeat one of the most mind-boggling statistics that demographers have come up with: *In just twenty more years, the world population will increase as much as it did from the birth of Christ to 1950* (see Reinhold 1979).

It is obvious, claim the New Malthusians, that there is going to be less and less for more and more (Brown 1992).

The Anti-Malthusians

If the New Malthusians are right, what hope can there be for such an overpopulated world? Who wants to live in a shoulder-to-shoulder world and face the constant threat of famine?

Another, much more optimistic group of demographers, whom we can call the "Anti-Malthusians," have countered by saying that such an image of the future is ridiculous. "Ever since Malthus reached his faulty conclusions," they argue, "people have been claiming that the sky is falling—that it is only a matter of time until the world is overpopulated and we all starve to death."

The facts are otherwise, add the Anti-Malthusians. Let's examine the picture that the New Malthusians have painted. They saw people as breeding like germs in a bucket, as illustrated by the following example.

> Assume there are two germs in the bottom of a bucket, and they double in number every hour. . . . If it takes one hundred hours for the bucket to be full of germs, at what point is the bucket one-half full of germs? A moment's thought will show that after ninety-nine hours the bucket is only half full. The title of this volume *[The 99th Hour]* is not intended to imply that the United States is half full of people but to emphasize that it is possible to have "plenty of space left" and still be precariously near the upper limit (Price 1967).

Anti-Malthusians, such as economist Julian Simon (1981, 1992), regard this image as dead wrong. In their view, people simply do not blindly reproduce until there is no room left. It is ridiculous just to project the world's current population growth into the indefinite future; for such a calculation fails to take into account people's intelligence and rational planning when it comes to having children. To understand human reproduction, we need to look at the historical record more closely.

The best example, according to the Anti-Malthusians, is Europe's **demographic transition,** which they believe provides a much more accurate indication of the future. This transition is diagrammed in Figure 20.2. Stage I characterized Europe during most of its history—a fairly stable population, in which high birthrates were offset by high death rates. In about 1750 came Stage II, the "population explosion" that so upset Malthus. Europe's population surged because birthrates remained high, while death rates went down. Finally, Europe made the transition to Stage III—the population stabilized as people brought their birthrates into line with their lower death rates.

This, continue the Anti-Malthusians, is precisely what will happen in the poorer countries of the world. Their current surge in growth simply indicates that they have reached the second stage of the demographic transition. The importation of hybrid seed and modern medicine from industrialized nations has cut their death rate, but their birthrate is still high. When they move into the third stage, as surely they will, we will wonder what all the fuss was about.

The Anti-Malthusians add that the demographic transition in Europe has been so successful that governments there have become concerned about their citizens *not having enough babies.* Now they are worried about **population shrinkage,** the result of not producing enough children to replace people who die (Tomlinson 1984; Bacon 1986). Already, workers from the Third World have migrated to Europe to fill this gap, which, as discussed in the Perspectives box in Chapter 12, has created another problem, a volatile mixture of ethnic groups in Germany and France.

Who Is Correct?

As you can see, both the New Malthusians and the Anti-Malthusians have projected trends into the future. The New Malthusians project world growth trends and are alarmed. The Anti-Malthusians project the demographic transition onto the nonindustrialized countries and are reassured.

Only the future will prove the accuracy of either of these projections. There is no question that the nonindustrialized countries are in Stage II of the demographic transition. The question is, will they ever enter Stage III? After World War II, modern medicine, techniques of public hygiene, hybrid seeds, herbicides, and farm machinery

TR#54M: The Demographic Transition

TR#46: Growth Rates and Doubling Times for the World, the Five Continents, and Major Countries

TR#47: Population Growth for 1750–2100: World, Less Developed Regions, and "European," More Developed Regions

demographic transition: a three-stage historical process of population growth, the first being high birthrates and high death rates, the second high birthrates and low death rates; and the third low birthrates and low death rates

population shrinkage: the process by which a country's population becomes smaller because its birthrate and immigration are too low to replace those who die and emigrate

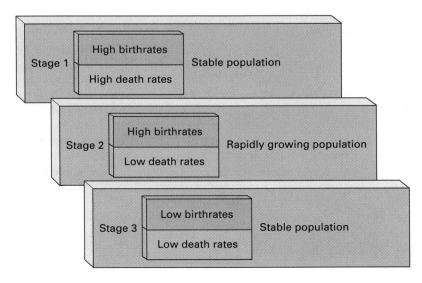

FIGURE 20.2 The Demographic Transition.

were exported around the globe. The increased food supply and improved health reduced death rates sharply. At first, almost everyone was ecstatic. Then, as these poor populations continued to reproduce as before, misgivings set in. As they tallied the mushrooming populations of the nonindustrialized countries, demographers began to predict catastrophe if something was not done to halt the world's population growth.

Conflict theorists noted that a short distance beneath the surface of the hysteria lay concern about the precarious balance of world power. Western leaders feared that their political arrangements would become unbalanced as the poorer countries, with swollen populations, pushed their way onto the scene of world power and demanded a larger share of the earth's resources. They then used the United Nations to spearhead global efforts to reduce world population growth. Those efforts first looked as though they were doomed to fail. Populations of the poorer countries continued to surge, while those of Europe fell. Then in the 1970s, demographers began to notice a change, slight at first, but increasingly visible. The birthrates in countries such as China, India, South Korea, and Sri Lanka began to fall.

As symbolic interactionists like to say, "Let's accept that as a fact. But what does it mean?" The New Malthusians say that we have only made a dent in the increase. The population of the nonindustrialized world is still growing, only not as fast as it was. A slower growth rate still spells catastrophe—it just takes a little longer to reach it. The Anti-Malthusians, of course, perceive the matter quite differently. For them, the decrease in the rate of growth signals the beginning of Stage III of the demographic transition. The death rate in the less developed countries fell first, and now their birth-rate will catch up.

Who is right? It simply is too early to tell. Like the proverbial pessimists who call the glass of water half empty, the New Malthusians continue to interpret world population growth negatively. And like the optimists, the Anti-Malthusians view the figures positively and call the same glass half full. Sometime during our lifetimes we should know the answer.

Why Are There Famines?

Pictures of starving children haunt us. They gnaw at our conscience; we live in such abundance, while these children and their parents starve before our very eyes. Why don't these children have enough food? Is it because there are too many of them, as the New Malthusians claim, or simply that the abundant food produced around the world does not reach them, as the Anti-Malthusians argue?

The basic question is this: Does the world produce enough food to feed everyone? Here, the Anti-Malthusians make a point that seems irrefutable. As Figure 20.3 shows, over the past decades *the amount of food produced for each person in the world has increased.* In spite of the world's extra billions of people, improved seeds, fertilization, and harvesting techniques have made more food available for each person on earth (Avery 1991).

Then why do people die of hunger? From Figure 20.3, we can conclude that famines do not occur in certain areas because the earth as a whole produces too little food, but because these particular places lack food—while other countries produce more food than their people can consume. In short, the cause of starvation is an imbalance between supply and demand. One of the most notable examples is that at the same time as widespread famine is ravishing West Africa, the United States government is paying American farmers to *reduce* their crops. *America's* problem is too much food, *theirs* too little.

The New Malthusians counter with the argument that the world's population continues to grow and that we do not know how long the earth will continue to produce sufficient food. It is only a matter of time, they say, until it no longer does—not "if," but "when."

The way in which governments view this matter is critical for deciding social policy. If the problem is too many people it may call for one course of action, whereas if it is

CDQ 4: Do you agree with conflict theorists that swollen populations in developing nations may cause a change in the precarious balance of world power? Why or why not?

CDQ 5: Does the world produce enough food to feed everyone? If yes, then why do people die of hunger?

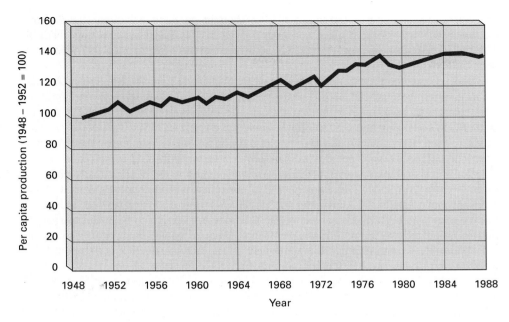

FIGURE 20.3 The World's per Capita Food Production. (*Source: U.S. Department of Agriculture,* Simon 1981: 58; *Statistical Abstract of the United States* 1988: Table 1411 recomputed to 1948–52 base.)

an imbalance of resources another solution entirely is indicated. The New Malthusians would attempt to reduce the number of people in the world, while the Anti-Malthusians would instead try to distribute food more equitably.

Meanwhile, demographers can only study trends and do their best to anticipate changes in them. Both the New Malthusians and the Anti-Malthusians have contributed significant ideas, but theories will not eliminate the problem of famines. Starving children are going to continue to peer out at us from our televisions and magazines, their tiny, shriveled bodies calling for us to do something. It is important to understand the underlying cause of such human misery, some of which could certainly be alleviated by transferring food from nations that have a surplus.

POPULATION GROWTH

Even if widespread famines are due to a maldistribution of resources rather than world overpopulation, the fact remains that the Third World is growing at *three times* the rate of the First World (1.9 percent a year compared with 0.6 percent) (*World Population Profile:* Table 1). Why do those who can least afford it have so many children?

Why the Poor Nations Have So Many Children

To move this issue out of the abstract, rather than simply asking why the population is increasing so much more rapidly in the Third World, let's figure out why Celia is so happy about having her thirteenth child. To understand the reason, it is essential to move beyond the typical Western experience. We need to apply the symbolic interactionist perspective, taking the role of the other so that we can understand the world of Celia and Angel as *they* see it. As ours does for us, their culture provides a perspective on life that governs their choices. In this case, Celia and Angel's culture tells them that twelve children are *not* enough, that they ought to have a thirteenth—as well as a fourteenth and fifteenth. How can that be? Let us consider three reasons that bearing many children plays a central role in their lives—and in the lives of millions of poor people around the world.

First is the status of parenthood. In the Third World, motherhood, the most highly exalted status a woman can achieve, provides personal and social fulfillment. The more children a woman bears, the more she is thought to have achieved the purpose for which she was born. Similarly, a man proves his manhood by fathering children. The more children he fathers, especially sons, the better—for through them his name lives on.

Second, the community supports this view. Celia and those like her live in *Gemeinschaft* communities, where people share values and closely identify with one another. This community awards or withholds status. And everyone agrees that children are a sign of God's blessing and that a couple should have many children. As people produce children, then, they achieve status in one of the primary ways held out by their community. The barren woman, not the woman with a dozen children, is to be pitied.

While the first two factors provide strong motivations for bearing many children, there is yet a third incentive. Poor people in nonindustrialized countries consider children economic assets. This attitude, too, is difficult to grasp for urbanized, industrialized people, who see children as economic liabilities, expensive to bear and to rear. In the industrialized world, potential parents are likely to consider children as luxuries and contemplate them in much the same way as any new acquisition is debated: "Can we afford one now, or shall we postpone it, and get it later?"

TR#55M: Why the Poor Need Children

How, then, can such poor people see children as economic assets? Remember that the poor in nonindustrialized countries have no Social Security or medical and unemployment insurance. As a result, they are motivated to have *more* children, not fewer, for when parents become sick or too old to work—or when no work is to be found—they rely on their families to take care of them. The more children they have, the broader their base of support. Moreover, like the eldest son of Celia and Angel, children begin contributing to the family income at a young age. See Figure 20.4.

To those of us who live in the First World, it seems irrational to have many children. And *for us it would be.* Within the framework of the Third World, however—

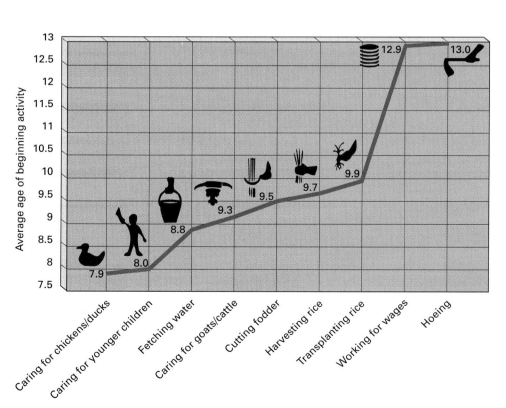

FIGURE 20.4 Why the Poor Need Children. (*Source:* U.N. Fund for Population Activities.)

Surviving children are an economic asset in the developing nations. Based on a survey in Indonesia, this figure shows that boys and girls can be net income earners for their families by the age of 9 or 10.

Most citizens of industrialized countries find it difficult to understand why people in the poorer countries have so many children. Using the symbolic interactionist principle and taking the role of the other, the vast numbers of children, as shown here in a slum in Poona, India, make sense.

the essence of the symbolic interactionist position—it makes perfect sense to have many children. For example, consider the following incident, reported by an Indian government worker.

> Thaman Singh (a very poor man, a water carrier). . . . welcomed me inside his home, gave me a cup of tea (with milk and "market" sugar, as he proudly pointed out later), and said: "You were trying to convince me in 1960 that I shouldn't have any more sons. Now, you see, I have six sons and two daughters and I sit at home in leisure. They are grown up and they bring me money. One even works outside the village as a laborer. *You told me I was a poor man and couldn't support a large family. Now, you see, because of my large family I am a rich man*" (Mamdani 1973, italics added).

Thus, our ideas of the proper number of children make sense to us—for our ideas follow our life situation. To superimpose our ideas onto people in a different culture, however, overlooks the life situation that creates their perspective. To understand the behavior of people in any group, including behavior that appears irrational to us, requires looking at life from their point of view.

Implications of Different Rates of Growth

The result of Celia and Angel's desire for many children—and of the millions of Celias and Angels like them—is that Mexico's current population will double in only twenty-eight years. In sharp contrast, Sweden's population is growing at only 0.1 percent a year, making it one of the world's slowest-growing populations. In the twenty-eight years in which Mexico's population will increase by 100 percent, Sweden's population will increase by a mere 3 percent. Demographers use **population pyramids** depicting a population by age and sex, as shown in Figure 20.5, to illustrate a country's population dynamics. Figure 20.5 contrasts Mexico, in Stage II of the demographic transition, with Sweden, in advanced Stage III.

The implications of a doubled population are mind-boggling. *Just to stay even,* within those twenty-eight years Mexico must double its jobs and all other factors thought to constitute "decent" living standards. Consider food production and factories; hospitals and schools; transportation, communication, water, gas, sewer, and electrical systems; housing, churches, civic buildings, theaters, stores, and parks. If Mexico fails to double these facilities, its already very low standard of living will drop even further.

population pyramid: a graphic representation of a population, divided into age and sex

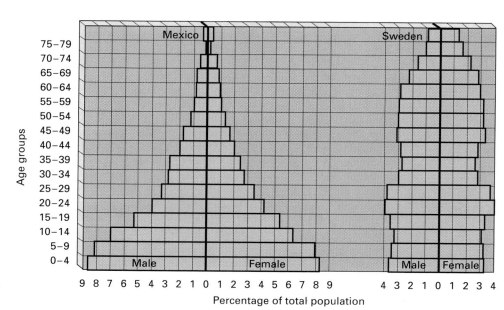

FIGURE 20.5 Population Pyramids of Mexico and Sweden. (*Source:* From "The Human Population," by Ronald Freedman and Bernard Berelson. Copyright © September 1974 by *Scientific American,* Inc. All rights reserved.)

Note: A population pyramid depicts a population's age and sex structure. It is really two bar graphs placed back-to-back. The age categories proceed from the bottom to the top. The vertical center line represents zero, and the male bars proceed leftward from it, the female bars rightward. These figures are called "pyramids" because in times past, as in Mexico today, countries had more young people than old people, making the lower bars longer than the upper ones (Yaukey 1985; Peters and Larkin 1989).

CDQ 7: Can you explain why a declining standard of living poses the danger of political instability? Could this ever occur in the United States?

Essay #2

CDQ 8: Why do you think it would be difficult to estimate population growth?

L. Obj. 3: State the three demographic variables used in estimating population growth.

L. Obj. 4: Define the following terms: fertility rate, fecundity, crude birth rate, crude death rate, mortality rate, life expectancy, life span, net migration rate, immigrants, and emigrants.

demographic variables: the factors that influence population growth: fertility, mortality, and net migration

fertility rate: the number of children that the average woman bears

fecundity: the number of children that women are theoretically *capable* of bearing

A declining standard of living poses the danger of political instability, followed by severe repression by the government to prevent it. As conflict theorists point out, this possibility is one reason that the First World is so insistent on United Nations support for worldwide birth control. Political instability in one country can spill over into others, threatening an entire region's balance of power. Consequently, to help preserve political stability, with one hand the First World gives agricultural aid, IUDs, and condoms to the masses in Third World countries—while with the other it sells arms and munitions to their elites. Both actions serve the same purpose, say conflict theorists.

Think of the worldwide attempt to achieve a higher standard of living as a race. The Third World appears destined to fall still farther behind, for not only do its countries start with less, but their swelling numbers drain the limited financial resources that might otherwise be used for industrial development. In contrast, nations such as Sweden and the United States, already highly industrialized, are far ahead and have *fewer people on whom to spend much more.*

Estimating Population Growth: The Three Demographic Variables

The ability to project the future of human populations is obviously highly significant in today's world. Educators want to know how many schools to build. Manufacturers want to anticipate changes in demand for their products. The government needs to know how many doctors, engineers, and executives to train, as well as how many people will be paying taxes and how many young people will be available to fight a war.

To project population trends, demographers use three basic **demographic variables:** fertility, mortality, and migration. Let us look at each.

Fertility.   The **fertility rate** refers to the number of children that the average woman bears. A term sometimes confused with fertility is **fecundity,** the potential number of children that women are *capable* of bearing. The fecundity of women around the world is around twenty children each. Their fertility rate, however (the actual number of children they bear) is much lower. The world's overall fertility rate is 3.6, which means that the average woman in the world can expect to bear 3.6 children during her lifetime. At 1.8, the fertility rate of American women is exactly half the world rate. The record for the world's lowest rate is held jointly by Germany, Austria, and Italy, where the average woman bears only 1.4 children. The world's highest rate is 8.5, a record shared by North Yemen and Rwanda in East Africa. This means that the average woman in North Yemen and Rwanda gives birth to *six* times as many children as the average Italian woman (Population Reference Bureau, 1988).

To compute the fertility rate of a country, demographers usually depend on a government's record of births. From these, they figure the country's **crude birthrate,** that is, the annual number of live births per 1,000 population. There may be considerable slippage here, of course, since birth records in the Third World may be haphazard. From Figure 20.5, you can see how a country's age structure affects its birthrate. If by some miracle Mexico were transformed overnight into a nation as industrialized as Sweden, its birthrate would continue to rapidly outpace Sweden's— simply because a much higher percentage of Mexican women are in their childbearing years.

Mortality. The second demographic variable, **crude death rate,** refers to the number of deaths per 1,000 population. It, too, varies around the world. Look again at Figure 20.5. If everything else were equal, because Sweden has a much higher proportion of old people than Mexico, we would expect Sweden also to have a much higher crude death rate. Life and death are not that simple, however, and not everything is equal. With inadequate diets, poor public health, and inferior medical treatment, Mexico's adults die at an earlier age than Sweden's. So do its children, and Mexico has a much higher *infant mortality rate,* the death rate of children during their first year.

As discussed in Chapter 13, the **life expectancy** of Americans, the number of years that an average newborn can expect to live, has steadily increased (see Figure 13.1, page 346). Other industrialized nations have made similar gains in life expectancy, for industrialization brings improved nutrition, public sanitation, and medical delivery systems, which in turn reduce smallpox, diphtheria, typhoid, measles, and other communicable diseases. As a consequence, mortality rates decline. As also noted in Chapter 13 (pages 343–346), the long-lived Abkhasians, who are not industrialized, illustrate factors about aging that we do not yet fully understand—indicating that perhaps patterns of work and leisure, and even a sense of integration into the community, affect life expectancy. Furthermore, life expectancy of different groups within a country can vary. On average, for example, American females live longer than males, and white Americans outlive African Americans (see Table 13.1, page 347).

Although industrialization has brought a longer life expectancy, it has not increased the human **life span,** or maximum length of life. As the years pass, the body's vital organs degenerate, determining some age beyond which humans cannot live. The longest life span in modern times was that of Shigechiyo Izumi (1865–1986) of Japan, who lived to be 120 years and 237 days (Russell 1987). Very few of us, however, celebrate even our one hundredth birthday.

Migration. The third major demographic variable is the **net migration rate,** the difference between the number of *immigrants* (people moving in) and *emigrants* (people moving out) per 1,000 population. Unlike fertility and mortality rates, this rate does not affect the global population, for people are simply shifting their residence from one location to another. The impact of migration on a particular country, however, can be enormous. One of the largest migrations in human history involved the United States. Many millions of people saw vast opportunities in this emerging nation. They uprooted themselves, made a perilous journey across a forbidding ocean, and settled a new world. As a result, the United States developed as a nation of immigrants. Migration may also be forced, as it was for the several million Africans who were brought to American shores in chains (Franklin 1969).

CDQ 9: Do you believe that industrialization has increased the life span? Why or why not?

crude birthrate: the annual number of births per 1,000 population

crude death rate: the annual number of deaths per 1,000 population

life expectancy: the number of years that an average newborn can expect to live

life span: the maximum length of life of a species

net migration rate: the difference between the number of immigrants and emigrants per 1,000 population

One of the dynamic forces in world population is immigration. With its vast wealth, opportunities, freedoms, and stable government, the United States continues to be the world's favorite destination of immigrants. The U.S. admits about 1,000,000 legal immigrants a year, with unknown numbers managing to get past customs agents, as shown in this photo of two individuals illegally crossing the Rio Grande.

CDQ 10: Should there be a limit to the number of immigrants allowed into the United States? Should individuals who are HIV-positive be allowed to enter the country? Why or why not?

TR#45: Country of Birth of Immigrants to the United States

Today, migration continues to be vast. Entrance to the United States is so coveted that each year it welcomes over one million persons from around the world. About 40 percent of them take up residence in California (*Statistical Abstract* 1991: Tables 7, 9). Table 20.2 shows these immigrants' countries of origin. The United States also experiences extensive illegal immigration, and each year an unknown number of Mexicans and Central and South Americans uproot themselves and enter the United States in the attempt to escape the poverty experienced by Celia and Angel. Although the total is unknown, it is so large that each year about a million are apprehended at the Rio Grande or at points inland and deported (Armstrong 1986). See the Perspectives box on page 572 for a summary of major changes in the United States population.

Are so many newcomers hurting the United States? Economist Julian Simon (1986) computed the cost of American immigration and concluded that the net result benefits the country. After subtracting what immigrants collect in welfare and adding what they produce in jobs and taxes, immigrants overall make a positive contribution to the economy. His analysis did not include their contributions to inventions, innovations, art, literature, and so on. To those we cannot attach a price tag; they simply enhance our quality of life.

To uproot oneself is no easy matter. It is to leave all things familiar—the childhood town, the well-known streets, friends and family. It is to leave the source of the early memories that lie at the core of one's being. Why do people make such drastic moves? The answer lies in both *push* factors, those things that people want to escape (persecution, the lack of religious freedom, or the lack of economic opportunity) and *pull* factors, those things that attract them, the opportunities and challenges they perceive. Consequently, motivated by dreams of religious freedom and a better life for themselves and their children, hundreds of thousands of Soviet Jews are migrating to Israel. Perhaps as the national borders of Europe drop, similar numbers of ex-Soviet citizens will also soon migrate there.

Industrialization and the Demographic Equation

A country's combined fertility, mortality, and migration rates constitute its *growth rate*, the net change after people have been added to and subtracted from a population.

TABLE 20.2 Country of Birth of Immigrants to the United States, 1989

Place of birth*	Total
Asia	312,149
Philippines	57,034
China	46,246
Vietnam	37,739
Korea	34,222
India	31,175
Iran	21,243
Laos	12,524
Hong Kong	9,740
Thailand	9,332
Pakistan	8,000
North America	607,398
Mexico	405,172
Domin. Rep.	26,723
Jamaica	24,523
Haiti	13,658
Canada	12,151
Cuba	10,046
Central and South America	159,960
El Salvador	57,878
Guatemala	19,049
Colombia	15,214
Guyana	10,789
Peru	10,175
Nicaragua	8,830
Europe	82,891
Poland	15,101
Great Britain	14,090
Soviet Union (former)	11,128
Africa	25,166
Total	1,090,924

Not all immigration is voluntary. As discussed in chapter 12, slavery used to be a significant cause of immigration, and many people continue to emigrate because of political persecution. Still others flee their homelands due to famine and poverty. War also causes vast numbers of people to leave their homes, as shown in this photo of a refugee camp in Amman, Jordan. Its inhabitants are poor Arabs who moved to Kuwait for work, but then had to flee after the Iraqi invasion.

*Countries of largest immigration; the total does not match that for the continent or subcontinent.

Source: Statistical Abstract of the United States 1991: Table 9.

Growth rate is summarized in what is known as the **basic demographic equation:** Growth rate = births − deaths + net migration.

As is apparent from this discussion, growth rate involves much more than biology. If a country embarks on a massive program of abortion, as has China, its rate of growth slows down. If authorities encourage childbirth through advertisements and monetary incentives, as did the Nazi regime in its attempt to build a strong "Aryan" race, its growth rate increases. Similarly, war, plagues, and famines will reduce a country's growth rate, resulting in extreme cases in a loss of population, called a "negative growth rate." The primary factor that affects the growth rate of most countries today, however, is industrialization. *In every country that industrializes, the growth rate declines.* Children become more expensive and, unlike Celia and Angel, bearing many children is no longer a source of status.

Problems in Forecasting Population Growth

Forecasting population growth should be a simple matter of just plugging the three variables of fertility, mortality, and migration into the demographic equation to make

CDQ 11: Can you explain why growth rates decline as countries industrialize?

TR#48: Progress of Depression Cohort, Baby Boom Cohort, and Baby Bust Cohort through U.S. Population. Age-Sex Pyramid: 1960–2050 (Part A)

TR#49: Progress of Depression Cohort, Baby Boom Cohort, and Baby Bust Cohort through U.S. Population. Age-Sex Pyramid: 1960–2050 (Part B)

basic demographic equation: growth rate = births − deaths + net migration

PERSPECTIVES

Cultural Diversity in U.S. Society

Where the United States Population Is Headed

During the next fifty years, the population of the United States is expected to grow by about 44 percent. To see what the population will look like in fifty years, can we simply multiply the current racial-ethnic mix by 44 percent?

The answer is a resounding no. During the next fifty years some groups will increase much more than others. The result will be a different-looking United States. Let's try to catch a glimpse of the future.

You can see momentous changes (as illustrated in the table below). First, with birthrates down, almost all the population growth will come from immigration. Second, with 80 percent of immigration to the United States now coming from Latin America and Asia, the number of Asian Americans and Hispanic Americans is expected to quintuple and triple respectively. Third, although in fifty years there will still be more non-Hispanic whites than all other groups combined, their majority will be slight (dropping from about 76 percent of the population to about 59 percent). Fourth, Hispanic Americans are expected to outnumber African Americans sometime during the first decade of the twenty-first century, when they will become the largest minority in the United States. Fifth, immigration is so vast that in fifty years about 50 million Americans will have been born outside the United States.

This population shift is one of the most significant events occurring in the United States. How do you think Americans will react? Who do you think will be threatened by this shift in racial-ethnic mix? What measures do you think American institutions should take to prepare for the future? Do you think, as some do, that "America should be for Americans" and that we should cut off immigration now? Why or why not?

Projecting the Future

Racial-Ethnic Group	Current Size	Expected Size in 50 Years	Growth Rate	Foreign Born Now	Foreign Born in 50 Years
Asian Americans	7,000,000	35,000,000	500%	67%	50%
Hispanic Americans	21,000,000	64,000,000	300%	41%	33%
African Americans	30,000,000	44,000,000	47%	5%	9%
White Americans (Non-Hispanics)	187,000,000	211,000,000	13%	3%	4%
Native Americans	2,000,000	2,000,000	0%	0%	0%
Total	247,000,000	356,000,000	44%	8.6%	14.2%

Source: Crispell 1992.

the future appear. Never, however, is life so simple, for demographers or anyone else. Because of inaccuracies in government statistics and because people unexpectedly change their behavior, to forecast population growth is to invite yourself to be wrong. Consider the following instance.

During the depression of the late 1920s and early 1930s, birthrates plunged as unemployment reached unprecedented heights. Demographers issued warnings about the dangers of depopulation almost as alarmist as some of today's forecasts of overpopulation. Because each year fewer and fewer females would enter the childbearing years, they felt that the population of countries such as Great Britain would shrink (Waddington 1978).

What actually happened? With the end of the Great Depression and the outbreak of war, the birthrate took a sharp turn upward. Then during the postwar years, it increased again. The result was a "baby boom" from 1946 to 1950 in both the United States and Great Britain.

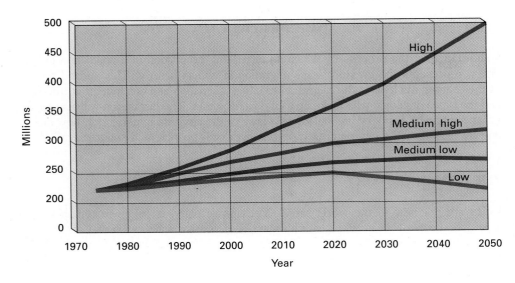

FIGURE 20.6 Population Projections for the United States. (*Source: Statistical Abstract of the United States,* 1976: 53.)

The inaccuracy of the pessimistic prophets of the 1930s should make us skeptical of demographic forecasts. Population growth depends on people's attitudes and behavior, and how can anyone know the future climate of opinion? For this reason demographers now formulate several different predictions simultaneously, each depending on different assumptions.

For example, what will the population of the United States be in the middle of the next century? Figure 20.6 shows how demographers hedge their bets on such questions. Here are some of the problems in choosing one of these four projections.

1. *Just to stay even,* to have what is called **zero population growth,** every 1,000 women must give birth to 2,100 children. The extra 100 cover the children who do not survive. (In nonindustrialized societies, this extra margin is much higher.)

2. On average, American women who are college graduates expect to have 1.8 children, high school graduates 2.1 children, and high school dropouts 2.5 children (Census Bureau 1989).

3. American women today are postponing childbirth to such an extent that 37 percent of women between the ages of eighteen and forty-four are childless. Only 10 percent expect to remain childless, but because fertility declines with age, the actual percentage is likely to be much higher (Census Bureau 1989). In addition, women on average bear about 10 percent *fewer* children than they anticipate (O'Connell and Moore 1977).

4. Trends that reduce the average number of births per woman are firmly established: more wives work for wages, more women go to college, children are more costly, and urbanization is increasing.

Based on the projected birthrate, then, the population of the United States appears destined to shrink. The demographic equation, however, also includes mortality and migration. For the immediate future, computing mortality presents few problems. Deaths are on such a regular course that we can predict within a narrow range just how many Americans of each sex in specific age groups will die next year from heart attacks, cancer, even drowning, fires, and car accidents. To peer fifty years into the future, however, presents severe problems. For example, will AIDS still be a scourge, claiming a million or more Americans a year—or will it disappear within a decade?

If only because of the extensive immigration discussed above (see Table 20.2), however, no one anticipates the United States to experience either population shrinkage or zero population growth.

CDQ 12: Were you aware of zero population growth before taking this class? Do you know of groups in the U.S. which encourage this level of growth?

zero population growth: a demographic condition in which women bear only enough children to reproduce the population

Essay #3

Project 2

L. Obj. 5: Describe the process of urbanization and outline the history of how cities came into existence.

Speaker Sug. #2: A colleague who specializes in urban sociology to discuss current research in the field.

urbanization: the process by which an increasing proportion of a population lives in cities

city: a place in which a large number of people are permanently based and do not produce their own food

URBANIZATION

Urbanization, the process by which an increasing proportion of a population live in cities, represents the greatest mass migration in human history. This second theme of the chapter will look at the migration to cities, alienation and community in the city, and the types of people who make up a city's inhabitants. The discussion will also cover urban sentiment, insiders' and outsiders' views of the city, urban networks, how males and females view the city differently, urban overload, politics, and suburbanization.

THE CITY IN HISTORY

Cities are not new to the world scene. Perhaps as early as seven to ten thousand years ago people built small cities with massive defensive walls, such as Catal Huyuk (Schwendinger and Schwendinger 1983) and biblically famous Jericho (Homblin 1973). Cities on a larger scale originated about 3500 B.C., about the same time as the invention of writing (Chandler and Fox 1974; Hawley 1981). At that time, cities appeared in several parts of the world—first in Mesopotamia (Iran) and later in the Nile, Indus, and Yellow River valleys, around the Mediterranean, in West Africa, Central America, and the Andes (Fischer 1976).

The development of more efficient agriculture holds the key to the origin of cities (Tisdale 1970; Lenski and Lenski 1987). Only when agriculture produces a surplus can people withdraw their labor from food production and gather in cities to spend time in other pursuits. A **city,** in fact, can be defined as a place in which a large number of people are permanently based and do not produce their own food. Thus more efficient agricultural techniques give impetus to urban development. When the plow was invented between five and six thousand years ago, it created widespread agricultural surplus and stimulated the development of towns and cities (Curwin and Hart 1961).

Early cities were small economic centers surrounded by walls to keep out enemies. These cities had to be fortresses, for they were constantly threatened by armed, roving tribesmen and by local leaders who raised armies to enlarge their domain and enrich their coffers by sacking neighboring cities. This fresco, by Ambrogio Lorenzetti, depicts an Italian city in 1348.

TABLE 20.3 Worldwide Urbanization

Percentage of Population Living in Cities		
Nation	1990	2000 (projected)
England, Wales, Scotland	93	94
Iceland	91	92
Venezuela	87	90
Japan	83	86
Iraq	79	83
United States	76	80
Mexico	73	77
Soviet Union (former)	71	76
Iran	58	65
Egypt	51	57
Morocco	48	55
India	27	34
Indonesia	25	32
Ethiopia	21	28

Source: Patterns of Urban and Rural Population Growth, 1980:159–162.

For a review of the sweeping historical changes that laid the organizational groundwork for the rise and expansion of cities, see Chapters 6 (pages 141–149) and 14 (pages 372–377).

During the next five thousand years, the agricultural surplus was only enough to allow a small minority of the world's population to live in cities. It took the Industrial Revolution of the 1700s and 1800s to set off the urban revolution that we are experiencing today. The Industrial Revolution provided work opportunities in central locations, stimulated the invention of mechanical means of transportation and communication, and allowed people, resources, and products to be moved efficiently—all essential factors upon which the modern city depends.

Although cities are not new to the world scene, the rapidity and extent of urbanization certainly is. Less than two hundred years ago, in 1800, 97 percent of the world population lived in rural areas. Only 3 percent lived in towns of five thousand or more people (Hauser and Schnore 1965). Now about half (47 percent) do. Each year, the world's urban population grows by about 0.5 percent, and it is expected that by the year 2020, 62 percent of the entire world population will live in cities (Palen 1986). But just as the industrialization process around the world has been uneven, so has urbanization, as Table 20.3 illustrates.

TR#57M: Worldwide Urbanization

Today's rapid urbanization not only means that more people live in cities, but also that today's cities are larger. It is unlikely that even the greatest of preindustrial cities had populations of more than a few hundred thousand (Hawley 1981). Although Chan-

TABLE 20.4 Metropolitan Statistical Areas over 1 Million

Census Year	Number of MSAs	Population (millions)	Percentage of United States Population
1950	14	45	30
1960	22	64	36
1970	31	84	41
1980	35	104	46
1990	39	125	50

Source: Census Bureau 1991: 2.

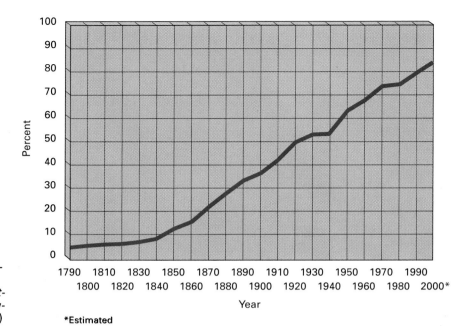

FIGURE 20.7 Urban Makeup of the United States Population, 1790–2000. (*Source: Statistical Abstract of the United States,* 1988: Table 33 and *Patterns of Urban and Rural Population Growth* 1980: 159–162.)

gan, China in 800 A.D. and Baghdad, Persia in 900 A.D. reached a population of one million for a brief period of time before they declined, two hundred years ago the only city in the world that had more than one million inhabitants was Peking, China. Yet by 1900 16 cities contained at least one million people (Chandler and Fox 1974). Today, there are about 150 such cities, and by the year 2000 this number will double to 300 (Frisbie and Kasarda 1988). Some areas are now so crowded that cities run into one another, forming a **megalopolis,** a conglomeration of overlapping cities and their suburbs.

Urbanization in the United States. The United States has both mirrored this worldwide change and, with its early industrialization, blazed a path that the Third World appears destined to follow. Early on, the United States was almost exclusively rural. Figure 20.7 illustrates the changes in the country's rural to urban ratio. Note that in 1790, only about 5 percent of Americans lived in cities. In 1920, just 130 years later, 50 percent of the American population lived in urban areas. This trend has continued without letup, and today the figure is about 80 percent. About 190 cities in the United States have more than one hundred thousand inhabitants.

The United States Census Bureau has divided the country into 283 **metropolitan statistical areas (MSAs),** each consisting of a central city and the urbanized adjacent counties that are linked to it. As Table 20.4 on page 575 shows, half of the entire United States population lives in just thirty-nine MSAs (Census Bureau 1991).

MODELS OF URBAN GROWTH

As mentioned in Chapter 1, sociologists at the University of Chicago focused on the study of urban life. One of them, Robert Park, coined the term **human ecology** to describe the way in which people adapt to their environment, such as their changing use of land (Park and Burgess 1921; Park 1936). This concept is also known as *urban ecology.* One area of interest to human ecologists is the process of urban expansion. Three main models for the growth of cities have been proposed.

The Concentric-Zone Model

As sociologists at the University of Chicago began to study cities in the 1920s, sociologist Ernest W. Burgess (1925) proposed a *concentric-zone model* to explain how cities

L. Obj. 6: Discuss the three models of urban growth and critique the models.

CDQ 13: What type of growth pattern appears to have occurred in your hometown? In the city where you are attending school?

K.P.: Robert Park

metropolitan statistical area (MSA): a central city and the urbanized counties adjacent to it

human ecology: Robert Park's term for the relationship between people and their environment (natural resources such as land)

megalopolis: a conglomeration of overlapping cities and their suburbs, forming an interconnected urban area

expand. As shown in segment 1 of Figure 20.8, the expansion of a city can be depicted as occurring outward from its center. Zone 1 is the central business district, the focus of the city's commerce and social life. Encircling the downtown area is a zone in transition (Zone 2) containing deteriorating housing and rooming houses, which, as Burgess noted, breeds poverty, disease, and vice. Zone III is the area to which thrifty workers have moved to escape the zone in transition and yet maintain easy access to their work. Zone IV contains more expensive apartments, residential hotels, single-family dwellings, and exclusive areas where the wealthy live. Still farther out, beyond the city limits, is Zone V, a commuter zone consisting of suburban areas or satellite cities that have developed around rapid transit routes.

Burgess intended this model to represent "the tendencies of any town or city to expand radially from its central business district." He noted, however, that no "city fits perfectly this ideal scheme." Some cities have physical obstacles, such as a lake, river, or railroad, which cause their expansion to depart from the model. While Burgess also noted in 1925 that businesses were deviating from the model by locating in outlying zones, he was unable to anticipate the extent of this trend—the suburban shopping malls that replaced downtown stores and now account for more than half the country's retail sales (Palen 1986).

The Sector Model

Sociologist Homer Hoyt (1939, 1971) modified Burgess's model. Hoyt noted that a city's concentric zones do not form a complete circle. As shown in segment 2 of Figure 20.8, a zone might contain a sector of working-class housing, another sector of expensive housing, a third of businesses, and so on, all competing with one another for the same land (Frisbie and Kasarda 1988). An example is the expansion of housing for the poor. When poor immigrants and rural migrants enter a city, they settle in the lowest-rent area available. As their numbers swell, they begin to encroach on adjacent areas. The middle class, for example, leave their sector as the poor move closer to them, thus expanding the sector of lower-cost housing.

TR#60M: Patterns of Urban Spatial Differentiation

K.P.: Ernest Burgess

K.P.: Homer Hoyt

Concentric zones

Sectors

Three Generalizations of the Internal Structure of Cities

District
1. Central business district
2. Wholesale light manufacturing
3. low-class residential
4. Medium-class residential
5. High-class residential
6. Heavy manufacturing
7. Outlying business district
8. Residential suburb
9. Industrial suburb
10. Commuters' zone

Multiple nuclei

FIGURE 20.8 The Nature of Cities. (*Source:* Cousins and Nagpaul, *Urban Man and Society,* 1970 McGraw-Hill, Inc.)

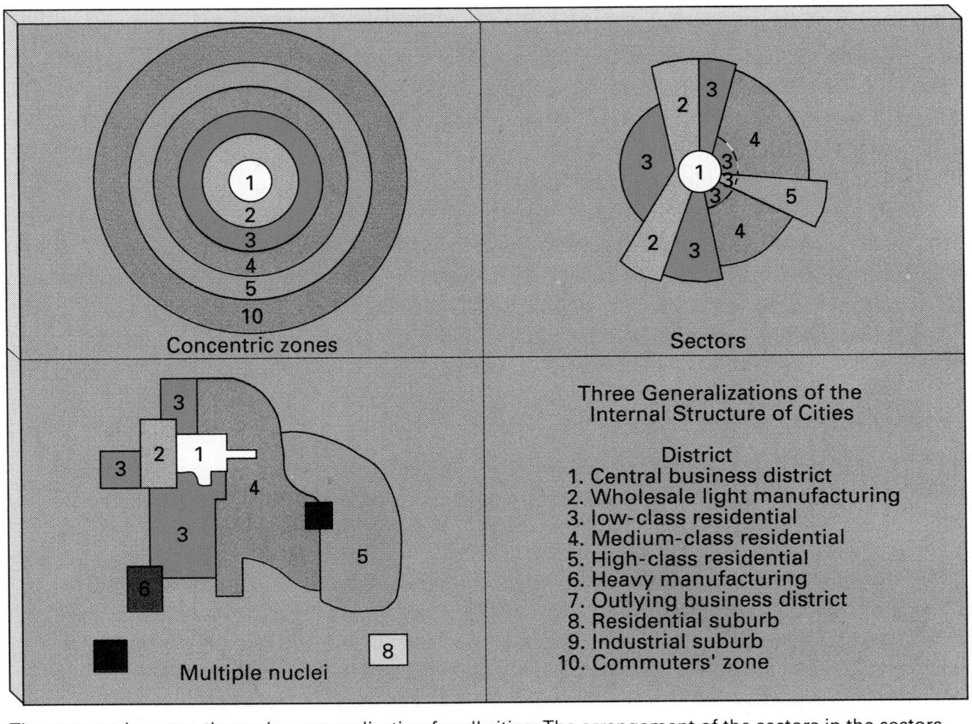

The concentric–zones theory is a generalization for all cities. The arrangement of the sectors in the sectors theory varies from city to city. The diagram for multiple nuclei represents one possible pattern among innumerable variations.

K.P.: Chauncey Harris and Edward Ullman

The Multiple-Nuclei Model

Geographers Chauncey Harris and Edward Ullman noted that in many cities land use is not based on a single center but on several centers, or nuclei (Harris and Ullman 1945; Ullman and Harris 1970). Each nucleus is the focus of a specialized activity (see Figure 20.8). Some of the most familiar examples are a clustering of restaurants in one area, banks in another, and automobile dealerships in still another. Sometimes similar activities are grouped together because they profit from cohesion; retail districts, for example, draw more customers if there are more stores. Other clustering occurs because dissimilar activities, such as factories and expensive homes, are incompatible with one another. Thus, push-pull factors separate areas by activities, and services are not evenly spread throughout an urban area.

Critique of the Models

Cities are complex, and no single model yet developed does justice to this complexity. Medieval cities looked quite different from modern cities, and cities in the Second and Third Worlds do not necessarily follow these North American models. For example, a common pattern in Latin America, striking to the North American visitor, is for the wealthy to stake a claim to the inner city, where fine restaurants and other services are readily accessible. Luxurious homes and gardens are tucked behind walls, protecting the rich from pubic scrutiny. For their part, the poor, especially rural migrants, settle unclaimed, fringe areas around the city, as discussed in the Perspectives box on page 579. Neither do the models make allowances for the extent to which elites influence the development of cities. Some individuals and groups, much more powerful than others, operate singly and in coalitions to promote policies that push a city's growth in the direction that suits them (Feagin and Parker 1990; Molotch 1976; Orum 1988).

EXPERIENCING THE CITY

CDQ 14: What type of opportunities do cities provide for you? What kinds of problems do they have?

Cities are intended to be solutions to problems. They are human endeavors to improve life collectively, to develop a way of life that transcends the limitations of farm and village. Cities hold out the hope of gaining employment, education, and other advantages. The perception of such opportunities underlies mass migration to cities throughout the world (Kasarda and Crenshaw 1991; Huth 1990; King 1991; Brueckner 1990).

Just as cities provide opportunities, however, they also create problems. Humans not only have physical needs—food, shelter, and safety—but also a need for **community,** a feeling of belonging—the sense that others care what happens to you, and that you can depend on the people around you. Some people find this sense of community in the city; others find only its opposite, *alienation,* a sense of not belonging, and a feeling that no one cares what happens to you. Still others live in isolation and fear.

Essay #4

CDQ 15: How are the experiences of people different in large cities as compared with small communities?

L. Obj. 7: Explain why many people feel a sense of alienation as a result of living in larger urban areas.

community: a place where people identify with an area and with one another, sensing that they belong and that others care what happens to them

Alienation

Twenty-eight-year-old Catherine Genovese, who was called Kitty by almost everyone in the Queens neighborhood, was returning home from work. After she had parked her car, a man grabbed her. She screamed, "Oh my God, he stabbed me! Please help me! Please help me!"

For more than half an hour, thirty-eight respectable, law-abiding citizens looked out their windows and watched as the killer stalked and stabbed Kitty in three separate attacks. Twice the sudden glow from their bedroom lights interrupted him and frightened him off. Each time he returned, sought her out, and stabbed her again. Not one person telephoned the police during the assault (The *New York Times,* March 26, 1964).

PERSPECTIVES
Cultural Diversity Around the World

Urbanization in the Third World

Images of the third world that portray simple pastoral scenes distort today's reality. In the nonindustrialized nations poor, rural people are flocking to the cities in such numbers that soon the Third World will contain the world's largest cities. Unlike the First World, where industrialization generally preceded urbanization, the Third World's vast urbanization is preceding industrialization. Mexico City is now the second-largest city in the world—its population of about 20 million making it almost equal to Tokyo-Yokohama's 22 million. By the year 2000, Mexico City is expected to have 28 million people and Tokyo-Yokohama 30 million. By then, São Paulo, Brazil will have 25 million, Seoul, South Korea 22 million, and Bombay, India 15 million. At just under 15 million, New York City will place sixth.

When rural migrants and immigrants move to American cities, they usually settle in the low-rent districts, mostly deteriorated housing located near the city's center. The wealthy reside in exclusive suburbs and in luxurious city enclaves. In contrast, Third World migrants settle in illegal squatter settlements outside the city. There, they build shacks from scrap boards, cardboard, and bits of corrugated metal. Even flattened tin cans are considered valuable building material. These squatters enjoy no city facilities—roads, transportation lines, water, sewers, or garbage pickup. After thousands of squatters settle in an area, the city acknowledges their de facto right to live there and eventually runs a water line to the area. Several hundred people then enjoy the use of one spigot. About four *million* of Mexico City's inhabitants live in such conditions.

Reflecting on conditions in Indian cities, the leading news magazine of India published the following report.

[The city is] heading for a total breakdown. The endless stream of migrants pour in, turning metropolises into giant slums. A third of the urban population lives in ramshackle huts with gunny sacks as doors and pavements for toilets. Another half of the populace is squeezed into one-room tenements or lives in monotonous rows of multi-storeyed flats (Singh 1988).

Why is this vast rush to Third World cities occurring? At its core, it represents a breakdown of the rural way of life. The countries are caught in the second leg of the demographic transition—low death rates but high birthrates—and the rural populations are multiplying. Consequently, there is no longer enough land to divide up among descendants. Recall the poor Mexican peasant preparing to migrate illegally to the United States as recounted in the Down-To-Earth Sociology Box in Chapter 12. No longer does rural life hold the key to people's well-being. In addition, as discussed in this chapter, there are the pull factors—the hopes of a better life offered by the city.

Will Third World cities satisfy the people's longing for a better life? As miserable as life for the poor is in these cities, for many it is apparently an improvement over what they left behind. If not, they would flee the city to return to pastoral pleasures. If the Anti-Malthusians are right, this second stage of the demographic transition will come to an end, the populations of the Third World will stabilize—and so will both rural and urban life. In the meantime, however, the Third World cannot catch up with its population explosion—or its urban growth.

Source: Based on Census Bureau 1989b; Huth 1990; Kasarda and Crenshaw 1991; Palen 1987; Singh 1988.

When the police interviewed them, some witnesses said, "I didn't want to get involved." Others said, "We thought it was a lovers' quarrel." Some simply said, "I don't know." People throughout the country were shocked. It was as though Americans awoke one morning to find out that the country had changed overnight. Americans took this event as a sign that people could no longer trust one another, that the city was a cold, forbidding place.

Why should the city be alienating? In a classic essay, sociologist Louis Wirth (1938) argued that the city undermines kinship and neighborhood, which are the traditional bases of social control and social solidarity. Urban dwellers live in anonymity, he pointed out, their lives marked by segmented and superficial encounters. This causes them to grow aloof from one another and indifferent to other people's problems—as did the neighbors of Kitty Genovese. In short, the very sense of personal freedom that the city provides comes at the cost of alienation.

Wirth built on some of the ideas discussed in Chapters 4 and 6. *Gemeinschaft,* the sense of community that comes from everyone knowing everyone else, is ripped apart as a country industrializes. A new society emerges, characterized by *Gesellschaft,* secondary, impersonal relationships. The end result is alienation so deep that people can sit by while someone else is being murdered. People lack identification with one another and develop the attitude, "It's simply none of *my* business." (But more is involved, as we shall see below.)

Community

K.P.: Herbert Gans

Such attitudes, however, do not do justice to the city. The city is more than a mosaic of strangers who feel disconnected and distrustful of one another. It is also made up of a series of smaller worlds, within which people do develop a sense of community (Bell and Boat 1970; Keans 1991). Some sociologists use the term *urban village* to refer to an area of the city that people know well and in which they live, work, shop, and play (Leinberger and Lockwood 1986). Even the run-down areas of a city, commonly called "slums," provide a sense of belonging in this respect. In a classic study, sociologist Herbert Gans (1962) made the following observations.

> After a few weeks of living in the West End (of Boston), my observations—and my perceptions of the area—changed drastically. The search for an apartment quickly indicated that the individual units were usually in much better condition than the outside or the hallways of the buildings. Subsequently, in wandering through the West End, and in using it as a resident, I developed a kind of selective perception, in which my eye focused only on those parts of the area that were actually being used by people. Vacant buildings and boarded-up stores were no longer so visible, and the totally deserted alleys or streets were outside the set of paths normally traversed, either by myself or by the West Enders. . . .
>
>   Since much of the area's life took place on the street, faces became familiar very quickly. I met my neighbors on the stairs and in front of my building. And, once a shopping pattern developed, I saw the same storekeepers frequently, as well as the area's "characters" who wandered through the streets every day on a fairly regular route and schedule. In short, the exotic quality of the stores and the residents also wore off as I became used to seeing them.

Living in the West End, Gans gained an insider's perspective. He found that in spite of its narrow streets, substandard buildings, and even piled-up garbage, most West Enders had chosen to live there, for to them *the West End was a low-rent district, not a slum.* Gans located a community in the West End, discovering that its residents visited back and forth with relatives and were involved in extensive networks of friendships and acquaintances. Gans therefore titled his book *The Urban Villagers* (1962). These residents were extremely upset when well-intentioned urban planners embarked on an urban renewal scheme to get rid of the "slum." And their distrust proved well founded, for the result of the gleaming new buildings was that people with more money took over the area. Its former residents were dispossessed, and their intimate patterns destroyed.

L. Obj. 8: List and briefly describe the five different types of people who live in the city as identified by sociologist Herbert Gans.

CDQ 16: Can you find examples of each of Gans' types of urban dwellers in your own city?

Types of Urban Dwellers

Whether you find alienation or community in the city largely depends on who you are, for the city offers both. Different people experience the city differently. In what has become a classic analysis, Gans (1962, 1968, 1970) identified five different types of people who live in the city. The first three types live in the city by choice, for they find a sense of community.

How people experience the city depends largely on social class, which determines their basic lifestyle. Consequently, some people find the city inherently satisfying, others terrifying. Some urban neighborhoods have tried to make the city more satisfying by holding street festivals, like this one in San Antonio, Texas. Such events are staged attempts to increase the residents' identification with the neighborhood, an attempt at producing Gemeinschaft.

The Cosmopolites.   These are the city's students, intellectuals, professionals, artists, and entertainers. They have been drawn to the city because of its conveniences and cultural benefits.

The Singles.   Young, unmarried persons come to the city seeking jobs and entertainment. Urban businesses and services such as singles bars and singles apartment complexes have sprung up to cater to their needs. Their stay in the city reflects a particular stage in their life cycle. Few put down community roots, and most will move to the suburbs after they marry.

The Ethnic Villagers.   These people live in tightly knit neighborhoods that resemble villages and small towns. United by race and social class, their neighborhoods are far from depersonalized, isolated, or disorganized. Family- and peer-oriented, the ethnic villagers try to isolate themselves from what they consider to be the harmful effects of city life.

Although an occasional individual from these first three groups is alienated, most of a city's alienated come from the next two types. Outcasts of industrial society, with little choice about where they live, they are always skirting the edge of disaster.

The Deprived.   City inhabitants in this category live in neighborhoods more like urban jungles than urban villages. Consisting of the very poor, the emotionally disturbed, and the handicapped, this group represents the bottom of society in terms of income, education, social status, and work skills. Some of them stalk their jungle in search of prey, their victims usually deprived persons like themselves. Their future holds little chance for anything better in life, either for themselves or their children.

The city dwellers whom Gans identified as ethnic villagers find community in the city. Living in tightly-knit neighborhoods, they know many other residents. Some first-generation immigrants have even come from the same village in the "old country." Here they enjoy institutions that meet their specific needs. Note in this photo a boutique, church, and bar—all catering to Latinos. Note from the political sign that the councilman and eight district leaders are all Hispanic.

The Trapped. Urban dwellers who are trapped can find no escape either. They consist of four subtypes: (1) those who could not afford to move when their neighborhood was "invaded" by another ethnic group; (2) "downwardly mobile" persons who have fallen from a higher social class; (3) elderly people who have drifted into the slums because they are not wanted elsewhere and are powerless to prevent their downward slide; and (4) alcoholics and other drug addicts. Like the deprived, the trapped also suffer high rates of assault, mugging, robbery, and rape.

Gans' typology illustrates that not all urban dwellers experience the city in the same way. Some find the city exciting and stimulating, a source of security and cultural contrasts. For others, however, the city poses a constant threat as they try to survive in what for them amounts to an urban jungle. Similarly, men and women experience the city differently, as the Down-to-Earth Sociology box on page 583 illustrates.

CDQ 17: From your own experiences, what are some ways you have created your own little world within a large-city context? Or within a large university setting?

L. Obj. 9: Describe ways in which city people create a sense of intimacy for themselves in large urban areas.

urban networks: the social networks of city dwellers

Urban Sentiment

Sociologists, especially those who have studied urban life by participant observation, have documented how people become attached to the city. They stress that *the city is divided into little worlds* that people come to know down to their smallest details. Sociologists Gregory Stone (1954) and Herbert Gans (1970) observed how city people create a sense of intimacy for themselves by *personalizing* their shopping. By frequenting the same stores, they become recognized as "regulars," and after a period of time customers and clerks greet each other by name. Particular taverns, restaurants, laundromats, and shops are more than just buildings in which to purchase items and services. They are meeting places where neighborhood residents build social relationships with one another and share informal news about the community.

Spectator sports also help urban dwellers find a familiar world in the city, one that sometimes creates high sentiment (Hudson 1991). Sociologist Gregory Stone (1981) noted that sports teams engender community identification. When the Cardinals won the World Series, for example, the entire St. Louis metropolitan area celebrated the victory of "our" team—even though less than one in seven of the area's 2.5 million people live in the city—and many of them can't even stand St. Louis. Sociologists

Giving Access Information—The Contrasting Perspectives of Females and Males

Just as urbanites try to prevent anonymity, so they also try to preserve it. Males and females are especially different in this regard. Sociologist Carol Gardner (1988) spent eighteen months in Santa Fe, New Mexico, observing men and women interacting in public places. She found that single women who meet attractive male strangers face a dilemma: They may wish to give *access information,* information that will allow them to meet in the future, yet they fear that this might lead to harassment, obscene telephone calls, or even rape. They assess the risk and give information accordingly. Interestingly, the *place* is important, for Gardner reports that women see less risk in giving access information in stores and restaurants than in bars and bar-cafes. Giving a telephone number is also seen as less dangerous than giving a name and address. But even here, women perceive the risk of harassing or obscene phone calls.

Common tactics women employ to keep men at arm's length are to give only their first name, to use a false name (sometimes an outrageous one), to give a wrong telephone number (perhaps the number for "Dial-a-Prayer" or the local rape crisis center), or to say that they are married, even though they are not. If a man in whom a woman has no interest asks her name, she may reply, "*Mrs.* Phillips," with the emphasis on the "Mrs." As some men have found to their dismay, a woman may even give another woman's name and the telephone number of *her* boyfriend.

Men, in contrast, have no such fears. They see no danger in meeting female strangers. Unlike women, who are "not supposed to" strike up acquaintances with strangers, men are given society's blessing to initiate such encounters (Gardner 1988). The man's approach is to "size up" the situation—to determine that a woman is available—and then to try to get access information from her. Apparently unable to take her perspective, men see a woman's reluctance to give access information as a sign of coyness or false modesty.

Because of their dissimilar perceptions of danger in the city, men and women live city life very differently. Seeing the same locations, times, and activities in sharply contrasting ways, they also use urban facilities differently. Men experience much more freedom in the city.

David Karp and William Yoels (1990) found out how intense such identification is; long after moving to other parts of the country, many people maintain an emotional allegiance to the sports teams of the city in which they grew up.

As sociologists Richard Wohl and Anselm Strauss (1958) pointed out, city dwellers also develop strong feelings for particular objects and locations in the city, such as trees, buildings, rivers, lakes, parks, and even street corners. In some cases objects become a type of logo that represents the city.

> We need only show persons New York's skyline, or San Francisco's Golden Gate Bridge, or New Orleans's French Quarter, and the city will be quickly identified by most. For those who live in these respective cities, such objects and places do not merely identify the city; they are also sources for personal identification *with* the city (Karp, Stone, and Yoels 1991, italics added).

Insiders' and Outsiders' Views: Implications for Urban Planners

As Karp, Stone, and Yoels pointed out, the problem of finding community in the city has serious implications for urban planning.

> Once we see that the small store acquires a new symbolic meaning in the urban context, we must be careful in our planning. . . . There is more to consider than the physical shape of a building before the decision is made to do away with it. . . . Planners going into an area should not tamper with the existing institutions because change would

Speaker Sug. #3: An urban planner from your city to talk about how long-range plans are developed.

better fit their own aesthetic conception of what the city should look like. We have to understand the crucial importance of some of the institutions [meeting places, shopping patterns] in providing a platform on which a substantial number of urban residents build their identities (1991).

They added that "the social bonds of city dwellers are as meaningfully cemented as those of small-town inhabitants," noting that "the demolition of such stores does not just eliminate a few more buildings from the community; it may also rupture the fabric of social life in that neighborhood."

CDQ 18: If you were a city planner, would you find it useful to determine how people living in an area felt about a change before proposing that the change be made?

Unfortunately, as we saw from Gans' study of the West End of Boston, city planners usually take an outsider's point of view, and let the fact that buildings are deteriorating obscure an area's vital social relationships. Sociologist Ruth Horowitz (1983) studied a "Mexican area" on 32nd Street in Chicago. Karp, Stone, and Yoels (1991) summarized her observations, showing how the insider's view contrasts with that held by outsiders, who may want to "renew" the area.

> The residents, by contrast, have a rich life of close contacts with friends and relatives. They place a high value on the "Mexicanness" of the community. Many of the things that are seen in purely physical terms as hindrances and negatives by outsiders, are redefined by residents as sources of meaning and value. Because apartments are small, people spend a great deal of time on the streets. The streets become important locales for interaction. On warm days "everyone is out on the streets from afternoon until late at night seated on kitchen and deck chairs that are scattered over the well-swept sidewalks."
>
> The density of neighborhood street contacts makes it almost impossible to walk in the community without bumping into and conversing with acquaintances. The neighborhood also has a rich social life outside street interactions. There are usually dances and weddings every weekend; "though these are usually not 'open' affairs, everyone is admitted. People often run back and forth to seek the best parties and dances."
>
> While the community generally consists of people who see themselves as the hardworking "respectable poor," several of its residents are financially able to afford homes in the suburbs, but choose instead to remain in the 32nd Street community. For such residents, "the common culture and support of kin outweighed all problems of the community."

Urban Networks

An essential element in determining whether someone finds community or alienation in the city is that person's social networks. Regardless of where they live in the city, people who are not integrated into a social network are likely to find alienation, while those who are integrated are likely to find community.

Think of the city as a series of overlapping circles. Each circle consists of one person and everyone in the city that the individual personally knows. As you draw those circles, eventually everyone in the entire city is included in several overlapping circles, with the exception of a few loners and persons who have just moved into the city. These linkages unite people into social relationships, where, ultimately, community is found in the city—not in buildings and space, but in relationships.

CDQ 19: What are some examples of the "norm of noninvolvement" and the diffusion of responsibility on campus? In this city?

L. Obj. 10: Explain why the norm of noninvolvement and the diffusion of responsibility which help urban dwellers get through everyday city life may be dysfunctional in some situations.

Urban Overload

Whether male or female, urban dwellers are careful to protect themselves from unwanted intrusions from strangers. They follow a *norm of noninvolvement* as they traverse everyday life in the city, trying to avoid encounters with people they do not know.

To do this, we sometimes use props such as newspapers to shield ourselves from others and to indicate our inaccessibility for interaction. In effect, we learn to "tune others out." In this regard, we might see the Walkman as the quintessential urban prop in that it allows us to be tuned in and tuned out at the same time. It is a device that allows us to enter our own private world and thereby effectively to close off encounters with others. The use of such devices to protect our "personal space," along with our body demeanor and facial expression (the passive "mask" or even scowl that persons adopt on subways) ensures that others will not bother us. One of the chief claims or rights that urban persons maintain in public places is the right to be left alone. In most instances people respect that right and behave mutually in a fashion to sustain it (Karp, Stone, and Yoels 1991).

Similarly, urban dwellers use a variety of filters to reduce overload. To prevent unwanted stimuli from reaching them, they use unlisted telephone numbers, telephone answering machines (to screen calls), apartment house doormen, post office boxes (to avoid revealing home addresses), as well as a series of locks—on cars, gates, houses, and mailboxes. Mace and burglar alarms can also be classified as filters.

Diffusion of Responsibility

The norm of noninvolvement helps to explain what happened to Kitty Genovese, whose story opened this section on urban life. That troubling case disturbed social psychologists Bibb Latane and John Darley (1970), who ran the series of experiments featured in the Down-to-Earth Sociology box in Chapter 6, page 157. As you may recall, they found that the *more* bystanders there are, the *less* likely people are to help. People's sense of responsibility becomes diffused, with each person assuming that *another* will do the responsible thing, "With these other people here, it is not *my* responsibility," they reason.

Allowing for the norm of noninvolvement and the diffusion of responsibility, a very different picture of the response to Kitty Genovese's murder emerges. The bystanders at her death were *not* uncaring, alienated people. They *did* care that a woman was being attacked. They were simply abiding by an urban norm—one helpful in getting them through everyday city life, but, unfortunately, dysfunctional in particular situations.

THE CHANGING CITY

American cities are subject to constant change. Of the many changes currently taking place, we shall look at urban politics, suburbanization, and trends in suburbs and cities.

Urban Politics: The Transition to Minority Leadership

One of the most significant changes in urban politics is the transition of power from white to minority leadership. Many large cities are now headed by African Americans and Hispanic Americans. Sociologist Peter Eisinger (1980), who studied this historic transition, noted that governing a city requires the cooperation of all its major groups. If whites were to withdraw their cooperation from an elected minority mayor, winning control of the formal apparatus of government would be but a hollow victory. To find out what happened in Detroit and Atlanta when African-American mayors took over, Eisinger interviewed the cities' economic, political, and social leaders. He found that the groups avoided confrontational politics and worked instead toward building coalitions.

To understand how coalitions between groups so historically opposed to one another can be formed, we need to realize that peaceful management of the city is in the

Essay #5

CDQ 20: Will your life be affected by changes now occurring in American cities? If yes, in what ways?

L. Obj. 11: Outline the major changes facing American cities regarding urban politics, suburbanization, and gentrification.

best interests of a city's elite—whether that elite be white or minority. Each elite depends on the smooth functioning of the city to maintain its position. Whether they like each other or not, a city's elites find a coalition preferable to disrupting the fragile balance of power on which the welfare of each depends.

Suburbanization

Suburbanization refers to the movement from the city to the **suburbs,** the subdivisions and sometimes urbanized areas adjacent to the political boundaries of a city. This process has had profound effects on American cities. Some of these effects will be examined in the remainder of this chapter.

CNN: A Marshall Plan for the Inner City

Suburbanization and the Inner City.   Suburbanization is not new. The dream of a place of one's own with green grass, a few trees, and kids playing in the yard was not discovered by this generation (Riesman 1970). For the past one hundred years or so, as transportation became more efficient, especially with the development of automobiles, people have moved to towns next to the cities in which they worked. What is new today is the speed and extent to which people have left the city in search of their dream (Frisbie and Kasarda 1988). In 1957, only 37 million Americans lived in the suburbs, but by 1980 this figure had swollen to 100 million (Karp et al. 1991). Currently, about as many Americans live in the suburbs as in the cities.

The city was the loser in this transition, for as its residents moved out, so did businesses and jobs, thus causing the city's tax base to shrink. The result has been a budget squeeze not only for parks, zoos, libraries, and museums but even severe problems in financing the city's basic services—its schools, streets, sewer and water systems, and police and fire departments.

This shift in population and resources left behind mainly those with no choice but to stay in the city. The movement of minorities to the suburbs, beginning around 1970, followed the same pattern as that of whites; those who could afford to move did so. Sociologist William Wilson, who has written extensively on cities, racism, and poverty, pointed out that the net result was the transformation of the inner city into a ghetto for the highly disadvantaged, filled with

> families that have experienced long-term spells of poverty and/or welfare dependency, individuals who lack training and skills and have either experienced periods of persistent unemployment or have dropped out of the labor force altogether, and individuals who are frequently involved in street criminal activity. The term ghetto . . . suggests that a fundamental social transformation has taken place . . . that groups represented by this term are collectively different from and much more socially isolated from those that lived in these communities in earlier years (quoted in Karp et al. 1991).

The Psychological Separation of City and Suburb.   Having made the move out of the city, suburbanites prefer the city to keep its problems to itself. They fight movements to share suburbia's revenues with the city and oppose measures that would allow urban and suburban governments joint control over what has become a contiguous mass of people and businesses. Suburban leadership generally see it as in their best interests to remain politically, economically, and socially separate from their nearby city. They do not mind coming into the city to work, or venturing there on weekends for the diversions it offers, but they do not want to help shoulder the city's burdens. As sociologist Kenneth Jackson (1985) pointed out, names alone tell the story. Early suburbs demonstrated their attachment to the city by calling themselves North Chicago or East Paterson. Now suburbs call themselves Park Forest or Rolling Meadows, names that reaffirm their psychological separation from the city.

It is likely that the mounting bill will ultimately come due, however, and that suburbanites will eventually have to pay for their uncaring attitude toward the urban disadvantaged. Karp, Stone, and Yoels (1991) put it this way.

suburbanization: the movement from the city to the suburbs

suburb: the communities adjacent to the political boundaries of a city

It may be that suburbs can insulate themselves from the problems of central cities, at least for the time being. In the long run, though, there will be a steep price to pay for the failure of those better off to care compassionately for those at the bottom of society.

It may be that the L.A. riots were part of that bill—perhaps just the down payment.

Trends in Cities and Suburbs

We shall close this chapter by looking at five trends in American cities and suburbs.

First, the downtown areas of many American cities are experiencing a renaissance. This resurgence is taking place alongside the loss of urban population and deterioration of huge urban areas (Sternlieb and Hughes 1983). Cities remain choice locations, and at some point the deterioration of the city, which drives down land costs, presents economic opportunity. Developers then step in, and the building cycle begins anew. As a consequence, most American cities now sport new stadiums, luxury hotels, high-rise office buildings, and luxury condominiums for the well-to-do.

A second trend, closely related to the first, is the return of many people to live in the city. Some have been drawn by the diversity the city still offers, others by economic opportunity. When housing costs soared in many suburbs, some of the middle class saw opportunity in the city's lower housing costs. In a process called **gentrification**, they bought rundown homes and restored them. One consequence was an improvement in the appearance of urban neighborhoods—freshly painted buildings, well-groomed lawns, and the absence of boarded-up windows. Another consequence, however, was not so pleasant. Residents were displaced as newcomers with more money moved in; and the process was often accompanied by intense resentment, especially when, as was often the case, one ethnic group was displacing another (Anderson 1990).

Despite the injustices of this process, some observers see gentrification as the beginning of urban revitalization. They point to Quincy Market in Boston and Waterfront Park in Baltimore, which draw millions of visitors each year (Karp et al. 1991).

Project 3

TR#59M: Megalopolis in the Year 2000

gentrification: the displacement of the poor by the relatively affluent, who renovate the former's homes

One of the fundamental changes occurring in the cities of the United States is the renaissance of downtown areas (high-rise hotels and parking garages, a stadium, restaurants, and theaters), as well as of harbor areas once relegated to warehouses and slum housing but now seen as rich real estate. South Street Seaport in New York City is one example.

At this point, it is difficult to visualize vibrant cities, sustaining a swollen tax base and providing luxurious services, on the horizon, but we shall see.

Third, American suburbs have increasing problems, just as cities do. They are aging, and thus have a deteriorating infrastructure to maintain. Their crime rate has also risen, although it is not nearly as high as that of the inner cities. In many suburbs a "taxpayers' revolt," in which voters refuse to support tax increases, has resulted in a financial pinch and reduced services.

Fourth, suburbanization nevertheless continues strong. The dream of a more tranquil life still drives many people to make extraordinary sacrifices to move to the suburbs. It is unlikely that this trend will cease, as it is continually fed by the decentralization of industry, improved transportation and communication, and—increasingly—fear of the inner city (Patterson 1991).

Finally, a new development is "edge cities" (Gans 1991; Rybczynski 1991; Walker 1991). Edge cities are not synonymous with any city's political boundaries but consist of a clustering of shopping malls, hotels, office parks, and residential areas near the intersection of major highways (Garreau 1991a, b). This clustering of services, which overlaps political boundaries and includes parts of several cities or towns, provides a sense of place to those who live there. Edge cities are growth areas in which many of the nation's new jobs are developing. The term "edge city" has so far only been used tentatively to identify this new urban phenomenon, and it may well eventually be replaced by another term (Lagerfeld 1991).

SUMMARY

1. Many demographers are convinced that the world is on a collision course with its food supply. Thomas Malthus was the first to make this observation. Those who hold this view today, called New Malthusians, fear that we are in the latter stages of an exponential growth curve. Anti-Malthusians, in contrast, point to the demographic transition of Europe as the future for the world. Anti-Malthusians stress that the earth now produces more food for each person than it did a generation ago, when there were far fewer people. The New Malthusians fear that this growth in food production will not continue. The basic cause of famines today is the maldistribution of food.

2. The basic reason that people in the Third World have so many more children than people in the First or Second World is that children play a very different role in Third World cultures, and, not insignificantly, in their economy. Although they are poor, it is as rational for them to have many children as it is for people in the First World to have few. Mexico's population growth rate is so great that it will double its population in just twenty-eight years. Just to stay even, therefore, it must double all its facilities and services within the same length of time.

3. To estimate population growth, demographers use the following demographic equation: Growth rate = births − deaths + net migration. Because of inaccuracies in government statistics and because people unexpectedly change their behavior, however, demographers must include many estimates in the demographic equation. This leads to distortions. Consequently, demographers make several projections of growth for the same group.

4. Although the beginning of urbanization can be traced back to 3,500 B.C., the process did not begin in earnest until the Industrial Revolution centralized production. About half of the entire world population now lives in cities; in the United States, the figure is about 80 percent. Three major models have been proposed to explain how cities expand: the concentric-zone, sector, and multiple-nuclei models.

5. An earlier generation of sociologists assumed that the city was inherently alienating. Using participant observation, however, contemporary researchers have identified different types of urban dwellers, who experience the city differently. Five types of urbanites have been identified, three of whom find community in the city, and two of whom find alienation.

6. To develop community in the city, people personalize their shopping, identify with sports teams, and even become sentimental about objects in the city. The destruction of buildings by urban planners, who often fail to see how people use the city to build social bonds, disrupts social relationships.

7. Urban networks are central to the development of community in the city. Women are more fearful of the city and more protective about giving access information. Men's experience of the city is so different that they have a difficult time taking the woman's point of view. Urban dwellers use a variety of mechanisms to filter out unwanted interaction with strangers. The norm of noninvolvement is generally functional for urbanites, but it impedes giving help in emergencies.

8. American cities are undergoing extensive change. The transition is being made from white to minority leadership. When the middle class fled the city for the suburbs, a group of chronically poor people was left behind. The loss of jobs and businesses has reduced the city's tax base, leading to severe problems in maintaining basic services. Some developments, such as gentrification and the renaissance of downtown areas, may point to the revitalization of American cities. Suburbs are aging and experiencing problems similar to those of the city. The latest stage in urban development has been termed "edge cities."

SUGGESTED READINGS

Anderson, Elijah. *StreetWise: Race, Class, and Change in an Urban Community.* Chicago: University of Chicago Press, 1990. A participant observation study that explores the relationships between those who are gentrifying an inner city area and those who are being displaced.

Department of Agriculture. *Yearbook of Agriculture.* Washington, D.C.: Department of Agriculture, published annually. The yearbook focuses on specific aspects of American agribusiness, especially international economies and trade.

Feagin, Joe R,. and Robert Parker. *Building American Cities: The Urban Real Estate Game.* 2nd ed. Englewood Cliffs, N.J.: Prentice Hall, 1990. Analyzes how the movement of capital underlies the growth and decline of American cities; includes urban renewal, gentrification, corporate relocations.

Gans, Herbert J. *The Urban Villagers.* New York: Free Press, 1962. This participant observation study of the West End of Boston provides insight into and understanding of white lower-class urban life.

Garreau, Joel. *Edge City: Life on the New Frontier.* New York: Doubleday, 1991. Garreau gives the first overview of "edge cities," discussed in this chapter.

Karp, David A., Gregory P. Stone, and William C. Yoels. *Being Urban: A Sociology of City Life.* 2nd ed. New York: Praeger, 1991. This overview of urban life stresses the everyday lives of city dwellers—what people *do* in cities, how they adjust and get along.

Liebow, Elliot. *Tally's Corner: A Study of Negro Streetcorner Men.* Boston: Little, Brown, 1967. This participant observation study of black streetcorner men and their families in Washington, D.C., has become a classic in sociology.

Nyden, Philip, and Wim Wlewel, eds. *An Urban Agenda for the 1990s: Research and Action.* New Brunswick, N.J.: Rutger's University Press, 1991. The authors of these articles propose social policies for dealing with consequences of gentrification and the replacement of blue-collar workers by white-collar workers.

Simon, Julian L. *The Ultimate Resource.* Princeton, N.J.: Princeton University Press, 1981. This controversial, path-breaking book presents the Anti-Malthusian position and defends population growth, indicating that the problem is political arrangements, not too many people or too few resources.

Whitaker, Jennifer Seymour. *How Can Africa Survive?* New York: Harper & Row, 1988. A broad overview of population and food problems in Africa; emphasizes social policy from a capitalist perspective, stressing the political and cultural implications of social policy.

Whyte, William Foote. *Street Corner Society: The Social Structure of an Italian Slum.* Chicago: University of Chicago Press, 1943. Rev. ed. 1955. Still quoted and reprinted, this classic participant observation study provides insight into the social organization of an area of an American city that, from an outsider's perspective, appeared socially disorganized.

CHAPTER 21

Orlando Agudelo-Botero, Dialogo de los Sordos, *1990*

Collective Behavior and Social Movements

COLLECTIVE BEHAVIOR

EARLY EXPLANATIONS: THE TRANSFORMATION
OF THE INDIVIDUAL
   Charles Mackay: "The Herd Mentality" ■ Gustave
   LeBon: How the Crowd Transforms the
   Individual ■ Robert Park: Social Unrest and Circular
   Reaction ■ Herbert Blumer: The Acting
   Crowd ■ Comparing LeBon and Blumer

THE CONTEMPORARY VIEW: THE RATIONALITY
OF THE CROWD
   Critique of LeBon and Blumer: More Than a Creature
   of the Crowd ■ Ralph Turner and Lewis Killian:
   Emergent Norms ■ Richard Berk: Minimax
   Strategy ■ Can Collective Behavior Really Be
   Rational? The Anatomy of a Lynching

OTHER FORMS OF COLLECTIVE BEHAVIOR
   Riots ■ Panics ■ Rumors ■ Fads and
   Fashions ■ Urban Legends

SOCIAL MOVEMENTS

UNDERSTANDING SOCIAL MOVEMENTS:
THE CASE OF THE NAZIS
   Why Social Movements Exist ■ Dehumanization:

Why Normal People Do Evil Things ■ Propaganda
and Advertising: Manufacturing and Selling Ideas

BREADTH, TYPES, AND TACTICS OF SOCIAL
MOVEMENTS
   Breadth of Social Movements ■ *Down-to-Earth
   Sociology: "Tricks of the Trade"—The Fine Art
   of Propaganda* ■ New Social Movements ■
   Types of Social Movements ■ Tactics of Social
   Movements ■ The Life Course of Social
   Movements ■ *Thinking Critically about Social
   Controversy: Which Side of the Barricades? Abortion
   as a Social Movement*

WHY PEOPLE JOIN SOCIAL MOVEMENTS
   Deprivation Theory ■ Mass Society Theory

ON THE SUCCESS AND FAILURE OF SOCIAL
MOVEMENTS
   Resource Mobilization

SUMMARY

SUGGESTED READINGS

 he news spread like wildfire. A police officer had been killed. In just twenty minutes, the white population was armed and heading for the cabin. Men and mere boys, some not more than twelve years old, carried rifles, shotguns, and pistols.

The mob, now about four hundred, surrounded the log cabin. Tying a rope around the man's neck, they dragged him to the center of town. While the men argued about the best way to kill him, the women and children looked on. Some yelled to hang him, others to burn him alive.

Someone pulled a large wooden box out of a store and placed it in the center of the street. Others filled it with straw. Then they lifted the man, the rope still around his neck, and shoved him head first into the box. One of the men poured oil over him. Another lit a match.

As the flames shot upward, the man managed to lift himself out of the box, his body a mass of flames. Trying to shield his face and eyes from the fire, he ran the length of the rope, about twenty feet, when someone yelled, "Shoot!" In an instant, several hundred shots rang out. Men and boys walked to the lifeless body and emptied their guns into it.

They dragged the man's body back to the burning box, then piled on more boxes from the stores, and poured oil over them. Each time someone threw more oil onto the flames, the crowd would break out into shouts.

Standing about seventy-five feet away, I could smell the poor man's burning flesh. No one tried to hide their identity. I could clearly see town officials help in the burning. The inquest, dutifully held by the coroner, concluded that the man met death "at the hands of an enraged mob unknown to the jury." What else could he conclude? Any jury from this town would include men who had participated in the man's death.

They dug a little hole at the edge of the street, and dumped in it the man's ashes and what was left of his body.

The man's name was Sam Pettie, known by everybody to be quiet and unoffensive. I can't mention my name. If I did, I would be committing suicide. (Based on a May 1914 letter to *The Crisis*.)

COLLECTIVE BEHAVIOR

Why did the people in this little town "go mad"? These men—and the women who watched in agreement—were ordinary, law-abiding citizens. Even some of the "pillars of the community" joined in the vicious killing of Sam Pettie, who may have been innocent.

collective behavior: extraordinary activities carried out by groups of people; includes lynchings, rumors, panics, urban legends, and fads and fashions

Lynching is an instance of **collective behavior,** characterized by large numbers of people becoming emotionally aroused and engaging in extraordinary behavior, in which the usual norms do not apply (Lofland 1985, 1990). Collective behavior is a very broad term, for it includes not only such violent acts as lynching, but also phenomena

Contemporary sociologists analyze collective behavior as rational behavior; that is, the group is seen as utilizing accessible means to reach a goal, even though that goal may be barbaric, as in this photo of a lynching in Rayston, Georgia, on April 28, 1936. Earlier in the day, the 40-year-old victim, Lint Shaw, accused of attacking a white girl, had been rescued from a mob by National Guardsmen. After the National Guard left, the mob forced their way into the jail.

as diverse as rumors, panics, fads, and fashions. The sociological findings on collective behavior place the actions of this lynch mob in a different light. As you will see, these people were far from "mad."

EARLY EXPLANATIONS: THE TRANSFORMATION OF THE INDIVIDUAL

When people can't figure something out, they often resort to some form of "madness" as the explanation. People are apt to say, "She went 'off her rocker,' that's why she drove her car off the bridge." "He must have 'gone nuts,' or he wouldn't have shot into the crowd." Early explanations of mobs and crowds were not far from such assumptions of madness. The behavior seemed so bizarre that it could be accounted for only by extraordinary explanations. Let's look at how these ideas developed.

Charles Mackay: The "Herd Mentality"

In 1852, Charles Mackay came up with an idea that was destined to have an extraordinary impact on what later became the study of collective behavior. Mackay was perplexed by the behavior of "country folks." He observed that they worked hard on their land and were reasonable people. But when in crowds, they sometimes "went mad" and did "disgraceful and violent things." Mackay concluded that just as a herd of cows will go into a stampede, so people can come under the control of a "herd mentality."

Gustave LeBon: How the Crowd Transforms the Individual

In 1895, Gustave LeBon (1841–1931) used Mackay's idea in *The Psychology of the Crowd,* a book destined to influence generations of scholars. LeBon's central thesis was that the individual is transformed by the crowd.

> Whoever be the individuals that compose it, however like or unlike be their mode of life, their occupations, their character, or their intelligence, the fact that they have been *transformed* into a crowd puts them in possession of a sort of *collective mind* which makes them feel, think, and act in a manner quite different from that in which each individual of them would feel, think, and act were he in a state of isolation (in McPhail 1991, italics added).

LeBon then explained how a crowd transforms people so that they will do unusual things. In a crowd, he argued, people feel anonymous, as though they are *not accountable* for what they do. They develop feelings of *invincibility,* believing that together they can accomplish almost anything. Their capacity for critical thought is swept away as they are caught up in the crowd's **collective mind,** making them highly suggestible. This paves the way for *contagion* (something like collective hypnosis), which in turn releases the destructive instincts that society has so carefully repressed.

LeBon's analysis of how the crowd overwhelms the individual was so convincing that *The Psychology of the Crowd* became one of the most influential books in the social sciences. Reprinted through forty-seven editions in France and translated into sixteen languages, this book set the framework for sociological thinking on the subject around the world (McPhail 1991).

Robert Park: Social Unrest and Circular Reaction

Robert Park (1864–1944) was one of the sociologists greatly influenced by LeBon. After studying in Germany, where in 1904 he wrote a doctoral thesis on the crowd, Park became a professor at the University of Chicago (McPhail 1991). To LeBon's analysis, Park added the idea of *social unrest.*

Essay #1

L. Obj. 1: Discuss early explanations of collective behavior and note how these explanations focused on the transformation of the individual.

CDQ 2: Why do people often use "madness" or mental illness as an explanation for the behavior of others?

K.P.: Charles Mackay

K.P.: Gustave LeBon

CDQ 3: Have you ever been in a crowd which was transformed so that it did something its members normally would not do as individuals?

K.P.: Robert Park

collective mind: Gustave LeBon's term for the tendency of people in a crowd to feel, think, and act in extraordinary ways

Social unrest . . . is transmitted from one individual to another . . . so that the manifestations of discontent in A (are) communicated to B, and from B reflected back to A . . . (Park and Burgess 1921).

Park used the term **circular reaction** to refer to this back-and-forth communication. Circular reaction, he said, creates a "collective impulse" that comes to "dominate all members of the crowd." If "collective impulse" sounds just like LeBon's "collective mind," that's because it really is. As noted, Park was heavily influenced by LeBon, and his slightly different term did not change the basic idea at all.

K.P.: Herbert Blumer

Herbert Blumer: The Acting Crowd

Herbert Blumer (1900–1987), one of Park's graduate students, became influential in symbolic interaction theory. Blumer enjoyed a long, productive career, culminating in the 1980s in his chairing of the Department of Sociology at the University of California at Berkeley. Blumer's analysis synthesized both LeBon's and Park's ideas. As you can see from Figure 21.1, Blumer (1939) identified five stages of collective behavior. As we examine his model, let's apply it to the lynching of Sam Pettie.

1. Collective behavior requires a background condition of *social unrest.* This condition occurs either when people's routine activities are thwarted or when they develop new needs that go unsatisfied. In either case the results are restlessness, apprehension about the future, and vulnerability to rumors and suggestions.

The lynching of Sam Pettie took place during the early 1900s, a period of immense social change. The United States was undergoing industrialization on a vast scale. Millions of Americans were moving to where the jobs were, from farm to city and from South to North. Left behind in stagnating country towns, many southerners faced a bleak future. Moreover, their customary way of life was threatened as African Americans more actively questioned the legitimacy of their deprivation.

2. An *exciting event* occurs, one so startling that people become preoccupied with it. In this instance, that event was the killing of a police officer.

3. Next people engage in **milling,** the act of standing or walking around. As they talk about the exciting event, circular reaction sets in. That is, by words and gestures people communicate ideas and attitudes. Each person who picks up these cues to the

> **circular reaction:** Robert Park's term for a back-and-forth communication between the members of a crowd whereby a "collective impulse" is transmitted
>
> **milling:** a crowd standing or walking around as they talk excitedly about some event

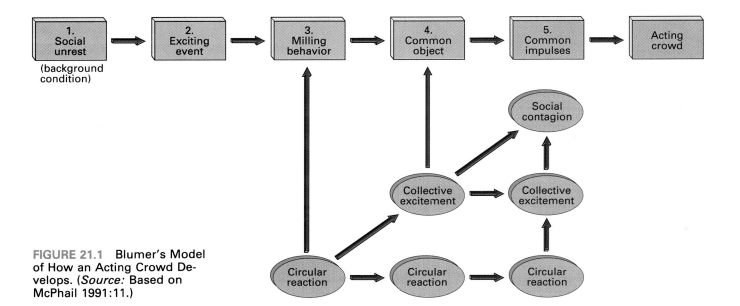

FIGURE 21.1 Blumer's Model of How an Acting Crowd Develops. (*Source:* Based on McPhail 1991:11.)

"right" way of thinking and feeling reinforces them in others. During the short period in which Sam Pettie's lynch mob milled, the inhabitants of this small town became increasingly agitated as they discussed the officer's death.

4. In this stage, a *common object of attention* emerges. That is, people's attention becomes riveted on some aspect of the exciting event. Normal reasoning goes out the window as people get caught up in the collective excitement.

In this case, the lynch mob's attention turned to the African American who lived in the little cabin on the outskirts of town. Someone may have said that he had been talking to the officer or that they had been arguing. As the crowd's attention riveted on Sam Pettie, people were caught up in the collective excitement. The killing of a police officer could not go unpunished. *Something* had to be done!

5. The fifth stage is the *stimulation of common impulses*. As people's attention becomes fixed on certain ideas, they attain a sense of collective agreement about what they should do. The mechanism that stimulates these common impulses, said Blumer, is *social contagion,* another term for collective excitement passed from one person to another.

This particular lynch mob concluded that the killer had to be punished, and that only an immediate, public death would be adequate vengeance—as well as a powerful warning for any other African American who might even think about getting "out of line."

The end result of this process is what Blumer termed an **acting crowd,** an excited group that collectively moves toward a goal. The goal can be constructive or, as in Sam Pettie's case, destructive. Acting crowds include not only lynch mobs but also people engaged in riots—whether at rock concerts or in the inner city—food fights, mutinies, picketing, and sit-ins.

Comparing LeBon and Blumer

Like LeBon, Blumer saw the crowd as transforming the individual and causing people to get so caught up in events that they no longer think, at least not in the usual sense of self-conscious interpretation. Instead, he believed, collective excitement and social contagion make people vulnerable to suggestions and release their basest impulses.

Blumer's analysis, like that of LeBon's before him, also became highly influential. Even today, over fifty years since its appearance, Blumer's analysis continues to dominate police manuals on crowd behavior (McPhail 1989).

THE CONTEMPORARY VIEW: THE RATIONALITY OF THE CROWD

Critique of LeBon and Blumer: More Than a Creature of the Crowd

Contemporary analysts find the view that people can be transformed by the crowd into nonthinking beings unacceptable. In the past several decades, as sociologists have studied natural disasters—fires, hurricanes, floods, tornados, explosions—they have found that people who experience such severe disruptions to their lives nevertheless remain in control of their wits and their behaviors (McPhail 1991).

Consequently, sociologists today stress that we need to view people who commit even "cruel and destructive" acts as thinking people. Members of an acting crowd are in agreement that the present circumstances are unusual. Some agree that the event permits behaviors that ordinary circumstances would not allow. Since acting crowds do not walk aimlessly about, but move toward a goal, cooperation is essential. As sociologist Clark McPhail (1991) pointed out, even a lynch mob must find a strong enough tree, obtain a rope, tie a knot, and hoist the body. Such acts require rational thought and cooperative actions—a far cry from people who have "gone mad."

Essay #2

L. Obj. 2: Contrast early explanations with contemporary theories about collective behavior.

Speaker Sug. #1: University or city police officers who are responsible for crowd control to discuss their methods.

CDQ 4: In your opinion, are people who engage in crowd behavior acting rationally or irrationally?

acting crowd: Herbert Blumer's term for an excited group that collectively moves toward a goal

The rationality of the crowd becomes more visible when *cultural options* are factored into Blumer's analysis. When a crowd grows ugly and concludes that something must be done, is it simply carried away, doing whatever anyone suggests? Doesn't it, rather, choose from options that it deems appropriate? Simply put, lynching is not a cultural option in contemporary American society, as it was in the frontier West for dealing with cattle rustlers and horse thieves. It was, however, a cultural option in the South, where about three thousand African Americans were lynched between 1860 and 1930 (Beck and Tolnay 1990). One of the last persons to be put to death in this way in Mississippi was Emmett Till, whose offense was whistling at a white woman (Ploski and Marr 1976).

In other words, when lynching was an acceptable act and the conditions that Blumer specifies existed, crowds chose to lynch. Today's elected officials, police, and general citizenry hold a different attitude toward lynching, more akin to the horror felt by the anonymous author of the opening vignette. Consequently, with lynching no longer a cultural option, mobs do not "go mad" and lynch people.

Ralph Turner and Lewis Killian: Emergent Norms

K.P.: Ralph Turner and Lewis Killian

L. Obj. 3: Explain the emergent norm theory of Turner and Killian and the minimax strategy of Berk.

If we were to witness a lynching—or screaming mobs in a ghetto or prison riot—most of us would probably feel that some sort of "madness" had swept over the crowd. How, then, can we reconcile a highly emotional crowd with the idea of rationality?

Sociologists Ralph Turner and Lewis Killian (1957) found a way to tie rational thought and high emotion together. Human behavior, they pointed out, is regulated by the **normative order,** the socially approved ways of doing things that make up our everyday lives. Most of life goes on much as we expect, and our norms are adequate. When an extraordinary event occurs that disrupts the usual ways of doing things, however, these norms do not cover the new situation. People then develop *new* norms to deal with the problem, sometimes even producing new definitions of right and wrong to justify actions that would otherwise be considered immoral.

Turner and Killian (1972) used the term **emergent norms** to describe this change. To understand why new norms emerge, we must first note that not everyone in a crowd is equally involved, for a crowd is made up of people who have different degrees of commitment to the collective activities (Zurcher and Snow 1990). Turner and Killian identified five kinds of crowd participants.

1. The *ego-involved* are those who feel a high personal stake in the extraordinary event. Both lynchers and the victim are examples of ego-involved participants.
2. The *concerned* have a personal interest in the event, but less so than the ego-involved.
3. The *insecure* have little concern about the issue. They have sought out the crowd because it gives them a sense of power and security.
4. The *curious spectators* are present simply because they are inquisitive about what is going on. Although they do not care about the issue, they may cheer the crowd on.
5. The *exploiters,* who also do not care about the event personally, use it for their own purposes, such as hawking food or T-shirts.

These five types of participants play different roles in the emergence of norms. The most significant role goes to the "ego-involved," who make suggestions about what should be done. By acting on these suggestions, the "concerned" help to set the crowd on a particular course of action. The "insecure" join in, and even the "curious spectators" may take part. Because the "exploiters" are concerned with other matters, they are unlikely to interfere with whatever the crowd does, thus lending the crowd passive support. At this point, a common mood may develop, and new norms emerge. The particular activity—whether "mooning" the cops or cursing the college dean—is now "OK." As more and more people participate in the crowd's activities, the rest find it increasingly difficult to cling to their old norms.

normative order: the socially approved ways of doing things that make up our everyday lives

emergent norms: Ralph Turner and Lewis Killian's term for the development of new norms to cope with a new situation, especially among crowds

The significance of Turner and Killian's concept of emerging norms is that it points to a *rational* process as the essential component of collective behavior. Turner and Killian noted, for example, that the crowd does not consider all suggestions made by the ego-involved to be equal: To be acceptable, a suggestion must match predispositions or tendencies that the crowd already has. This analysis is a far cry from earlier interpretations, according to which people went out of their minds as they were transformed by a crowd.

Richard Berk: Minimax Strategy

K.P.: Richard Berk

Sociologist Richard Berk (1974) went a step farther in stressing the rationality of crowds. Berk pointed out that whether they are in small groups or in crowds, people use a **minimax strategy;** that is, they try to minimize their costs and maximize their rewards. Following sociologist Erving Goffman (1959) and others, he stressed that whenever people come into the presence of others they try to get information about them. They then use that information to estimate the course of action that best fits the minimax strategy.

Crowds are no exception to this principle, said Berk. People in crowds still guide their behavior by evaluating costs and rewards. The fewer costs and the more rewards that people anticipate, the more likely they are to carry out a particular act. The belief that others will approve a deed, for example, increases the likelihood that someone will do it. What that act is makes no difference. It can be yelling for the referee's blood at a bad call in football, or shouting for real blood as a member of a lynch mob. The particulars do not change the principles underlying the behavior.

CDQ 5: In what way is yelling for a referee's blood at a football game similar to shouting for real blood as a member of a lynch mob?

Can Collective Behavior Really Be Rational?
The Anatomy of a Lynching

L. Obj. 4: Discuss the question, "Can collective behavior really be rational?"

To better uncover the rationality of collective behavior, let us look at another lynch mob, this time in Jackson County, Florida. First we need to note the broad context of social unrest that provided the "background motive" for this lynching (McPhail 1991). Whites in this county feared physical attacks by African American males in general, and sexual attacks on white females in particular. The lynching took place in 1933, in the midst of the Great Depression. African Americans were working for less money than whites, and whites were feeling severe pressure from this economic competition.

> The murder victim was a young white female, the suspect a young black male who lived on the farm across the road. They had known one another since childhood. Members of the local black community believed that the two had been sexually intimate for some time and that when she threatened to "tell some white men" about their relationship, her frightened lover killed her and hid the body. When the body was discovered the following day, the young man was arrested and charged with rape and murder. The accused "confessed," although the confession was probably coerced by the police.
>
> Accounts of the murder, arrest, and confession spread rapidly. A mob seized the accused from his jailers, and somewhere between three thousand and seven thousand people then converged on the farm. At another location, a smaller mob tortured the man for several hours. He was castrated, and red hot irons were plunged into his body. Several times he was promised a swift death. Each time, they simulated a hanging, almost choking the life out of him, only to cut him down and torture him some more. They sliced his belly and sides with knives and cut off his fingers and toes. Finally, he was "just killed."
>
> They tied his lifeless body behind a car and dragged it to the farm where a larger crowd was waiting. Roaring approval when the car pulled up, the mob lunged toward the body. A woman drove a butcher's knife into the dead man's heart. Some kicked the body; others drove sharpened sticks into it. The mob then burned down the house of the accused's mother, which was just across the road. They then hung the man's body to a tree. (McPhail 1991)

minimax strategy: Richard Berk's term for the effort people make to minimize their costs and maximize their rewards

This account certainly sounds as though those who made up the mob had gone "out of their minds," driven "mad" by rage and the desire for vengeance. "Quite the contrary," argued sociologist Clark McPhail (1991). After analyzing this lynching in detail, he found no mob out of control, much less people "out of their minds," but rather participants who knew precisely what they were doing. Why did he draw this conclusion?

First, the kidnapping of the accused from the hands of the police did not "just happen." It was a well-planned event. Fearing for his safety, the authorities had moved the young man to a jail in Alabama. Men from three or more communities in Jackson County made the round trip of 400 miles in five or six cars. When they arrived at Brewton, Alabama, one group proceeded to the courthouse, where some identified themselves as Florida State Police officers. When the Alabama authorities didn't buy their story, the men pulled out shotguns. The sheriff, who had hidden the accused inside the building, took them on a tour of the jail to show them that the accused was not there. Apparently satisfied, the men drove away.

This was a ruse, however, for as the sheriff followed them out of town, the other Floridians arrived at the jail. When they threatened to dynamite the jail unless the man was handed over, the jailer complied. Four hours later, the accused was back in Jackson County.

Second, this was an "invitational lynching." The telephones of northwest Florida buzzed with news of the jail seizure, and people throughout the area set out to rendezvous at the farm. Amazingly, the raiders notified the local media where and when the lynching would occur, and a newspaper even printed directions to the lynching in a special early afternoon edition. A local radio station broadcast the directions throughout the afternoon, saying that there was "a lynching party to which all white people are invited." When contacted by state authorities, the sheriff claimed that he could find no trace of the abducted man.

Although this case has unusual elements, especially its "invitational" aspect, it makes clear that beneath the surface of collective behavior are people engaged in coordinated activities. People in crowds certainly do things that they ordinarily would not do—for they are encouraged by the support of like-minded people—but their activities are rationally coordinated in the attempt to reach whatever goals they set.

Although it was the bloodiest riot in U.S. history, the Los Angeles riot of 1992 followed the pattern of other riots in being set off by a precipitating event against a background of mounting frustrations. This aerial photo of Venice Boulevard and Western Avenue was taken during the second day of the riots.

Again, although collective behavior may be unusual, the principles are the same as they are for any other social behavior.

Contemporary analysts, then, have come a long way from the original idea of the individual as a creature of the crowd, driven mad by some sort of crowd mentality. Sociologists today emphasize rationality, seeing the individual as squarely in control of his or her own behavior.

OTHER FORMS OF COLLECTIVE BEHAVIOR

Now that we have examined lynchings in detail, to clarify the basic principles of collective behavior let's look at other forms of collective behavior: riots, panics, rumors, fads, fashions, and urban legends.

Riots

The nation watched in horror. White Los Angeles police officers had been caught on videotape beating an African-American traffic violator with their nightsticks. The videotape clearly showed the officers savagely bringing their nightsticks down on a man prostrate at their feet. Television stations around the United States—and the world— broadcast the pictures to stunned audiences.

When the officers went on trial fourteen months later for the beating of the man identified as Rodney King, no one who had seen that videotape had any doubt that the men would be found guilty. With evidence so vivid and irrefutable, how could the verdict be anything but guilty? Yet in May 1992, a jury consisting of eleven whites and one Asian American found the officers innocent of using excessive force. The trial had been moved to Ventura County, California, because the defense attorneys claimed the accused could not get a fair trial in Los Angeles.

The result was a **riot**—violent crowd behavior aimed against people and property. Within minutes of the verdict, angry crowds began to gather in Los Angeles. That night, mobs set fire to businesses in South-Central Los Angeles, and looting and arson began in earnest. The rioting spread to other cities, including Atlanta, Georgia, Tampa, Florida, and even Madison, Wisconsin, and Las Vegas, Nevada. Whites and Koreans were favorite targets of violence.

L. Obj. 5: Describe other forms of collective behavior, including riots, panics, rumors, fads and fashions, and urban legends.

CNN: Los Angeles Riots

Essay #3

Speaker Sug. #2: A colleague who has conducted research on riots, such as the Los Angeles riot of 1992.

CDQ 6: Do you think riots can be caused by media coverage of certain events? Why or why not?

riot: violent crowd behavior aimed against people and property

One consequence of the L.A. riots was the mass destruction of businesses that served the rioters and looters. Pictured here is one of those businesses. Attached to the burned-out hulk of one of the cars being serviced at this business is an individual's plea for the violence to end.

Again Americans sat transfixed before their television sets as they saw large parts of Los Angeles go up in flames and looters carrying television sets and lugging sofas in full view of the Los Angeles Police department, which took no steps to stop them. But most memorably seared into the American public's collective consciousness was the sight of Reginald Denny, a thirty-six-year-old white truck driver who was pulled from his truck in South Los Angeles. As he sat injured in the street, one man hit him over the head with a hammer; then another man, laughing, knocked him senseless with a brick.

On the third night, after four thousand fires had been set and more than thirty lives had been lost, President George Bush, made a speech on national television. He announced that the United States Justice Department had appointed special prosecutors to investigate possible federal charges against the police officers for violating the civil rights of Rodney King. He then stated that he had ordered the Seventh Infantry, SWAT teams, and the FBI into Los Angeles. The president also federalized the California National Guard and placed it under the command of General Colin Powell, the African-American chairman of the Joint Chiefs of Staff. Even Rodney King went on television and tearfully pleaded for peace.

The Los Angeles riot was the bloodiest in United States history. Before it was over, sixty people lost their lives, 2,300 people were injured, thousands of small businesses were burned, and about $750 million of property was destroyed. (*Associated Press* April 30, 1992; May 1, 1992; May 2, 1992; Rose 1992; Stevens and Lubman 1992.)

CDQ 7: What factors do you feel contribute to urban riots in the United States?

CDQ 8: Why is it illegal to shout "Fire!" in a public building if no such danger exists?

Urban riots are usually caused by frustration and anger at deprivation. Frustrated at being kept out of mainstream society—limited to a meager education, denied jobs and justice, and kept out of good neighborhoods—frustration builds to such a boiling point that it takes only a precipitating event to erupt in collective violence. As in the Los Angeles riot, this was the case.

It is not only the deprived who participate in riots, for studies establish widespread participation in riots (Porter and Dunn 1984). After the assassination of Dr. Martin Luther King, Jr., in 1968, many American cities also erupted in riots. Researchers who systematically compared riot and nonriot cities found that cities in which riots occurred were no more deprived than those that did not have riots. They also compared participants and nonparticipants. Again, the one was neither more deprived nor more frustrated than the other (McPhail 1991).

In fact, the event that precipitates a riot is much less important than the riot's general context. The precipitating event is only the match that lights the fuel. The fuel is the area's background of unrest—a perceived sense of injustice that is being ignored or even condoned and encouraged by officials. It is this seething rage just underneath the surface that erupts following incidents such as the Rodney King verdict. Because

The Palestinian youths shown here throwing stones at Israeli soldiers know that their stones will not drive away the Israelis. The stone-throwing is a tactic designed to elicit reaction from publics. If the soldiers are provoked into firing, others may be recruited to the cause and newspapers will carry photos of the victims that may provoke worldwide sympathy.

this rage is felt by the poor and the unemployed and by those who are materially better off, both groups participate. Finally, there are opportunists—individuals who participate not out of rage, or even because they are particularly concerned about the precipitating event, but because the riot provides an opportunity for looting.

Panics

> In 1938, on the night before Halloween, a radio program of dance music was interrupted with a report that explosions had been observed on the surface of Mars. The announcer breathlessly added that a cylinder of unknown origin had been discovered embedded in the ground on a farm in New Jersey. The radio station then switched to the farm, where an alarmed reporter gave details of horrible-looking Martians coming out of the cylinder. Their death-ray weapons had destructive powers unknown to humans. An interview with an astronomer confirmed that Martians had invaded the Earth.

Perhaps six million Americans heard this broadcast. About one million were frightened, and thousands panicked. Unknown numbers simply burst into tears, while thousands more grabbed weapons and hid in their basements or ran into the streets. Hundreds of others bundled up their families and jumped into their cars, jamming the roads as they headed to who knows where.

Of course, there was no invasion. This was simply a dramatization of H. G. Wells's *War of the Worlds,* starring Orson Welles. Although there had been an announcement at the beginning of the program and somewhere in the middle that the account was fictional, apparently many people missed it. Although the panic reactions to this radio play may appear humorous to us, to anyone who is in a panic the situation is far from humorous. **Panic** is a behavior that results when people become so fearful that they cannot function normally, and may even flee.

Why did people panic? Psychologist Hadley Cantril (1941) attributed the result to widespread anxiety about world conditions. The Nazis were marching in Europe, and millions of Americans (correctly, as it turned out) were afraid that the United States would get involved. War jitters, he said, created fertile ground for the broadcast to touch off a panic.

Pictured here is Orson Welles, who starred in the radio dramatization of H. G. Wells's War of the Worlds. *The broadcast set off a panic, as described in the text. Or was the panic really the fabrication of news-hungry reporters?*

Contemporary analysts, however, have questioned whether there even was a panic. Sociologist William Bainbridge (1989) acknowledged that some people did become frightened, and that a few actually did get in their cars and drive like maniacs. However, most of this famous panic was actually blown out of proportion by the news media, who found a good story and milked it, exaggerating as they went along.

Quite possibly there was no panic, at least not on the large scale reported, for as Bainbridge pointed out, a similar thing happened in Sweden in 1973. To dramatize the dangers of atomic power, Swedish Radio broadcast a play about an accident at a nuclear power plant. Knowing about the 1938 broadcast in the United States, Swedish sociologists were waiting to see what would happen. Might some people fail to realize that it was a dramatization and panic at the threat of ruptured reactors spewing out radioactivity? The expectant sociologists found no panic, although a few people did become frightened, some telephoned family members and the police, and others simply shut windows to keep out the radioactivity—all rather reasonable responses, considering what they thought had occurred.

The Swedish media, however, reported a panic! Apparently, a reporter had telephoned two police departments and learned that each had received calls from concerned citizens. With a deadline hanging over his head, the reporter decided to gamble. He reported that police and fire stations were jammed with citizens, that people were flocking to the shelters, and that others were fleeing south (Bainbridge 1989).

Panics do occur, of course—which is why nobody has the right to shout "Fire!" in a public building when no such danger exists—for if people fear immediate death, they will lunge toward the nearest exit in a frantic effort to escape. Such a panic occurred on Memorial Day weekend in 1977 at the Beverly Hills Supper Club, a popular

panic: a behavior that results when people become so fearful that they cannot function normally, and may even flee

nightspot in Southgate, Kentucky, just a few minutes drive from Cincinnati, Ohio. About half the 2,500 patrons were crowded into the Cabaret Room, awaiting the appearance of singer John Davidson. The fire, which began in the Zebra Room, a small banquet room near the front of the building, burned undetected until it was beyond control. When employees discovered the fire, they warned patrons and ushered them out of the building. Patrons in the Cabaret Room were the last to be notified. Because of the size of the crowd and the few available exits, they were also the least able to exit quickly.

The result was sheer panic. Patrons trampled one another in a furious attempt to reach the exits, which were immediately blocked by the masses of screaming people simultaneously trying to push their way through. The writhing bodies at the exits created further panic among the remainder, who pushed even harder to force their way through the bottlenecks. One hundred sixty-five people died, all but two within thirty feet of two exits of the Cabaret Room.

Sociologists who studied this panic found what other researchers have discovered in analyzing other disasters. *Not everyone panics.* Many people continue to perform their roles, concentrating on how they can help others. Sociologists Drue Johnston and Norris Johnson (1989) found that only 29 percent of the employees of the Beverly Hills Supper Club left when they learned of the fire. As noted on Table 21.1, 41 percent helped customers, 17 percent reported or fought the fire, 7 percent simply went about their routines, and 5 percent did such things as search for friends and relatives.

Sociologists use the term **role extension** to describe the actions of most of the employees. In other words, the employees incorporated other activities into their occupational roles. For example, servers extended their role to include helping people to safety. How do we know that giving help was an extension of the occupational role, not simply helping in general? Johnston and Johnson found that servers who were away from their assigned stations returned to them in order to help *their* customers.

Rumors

CDQ 9: How frequently do you hear rumors? Why are most rumors short-lived?

"Did you hear about . . . ?" can be the introduction to a joke or to a rumor. **Rumors,** consisting of information for which there is no discernible source and which is usually unfounded, are part of everyday life. Every work setting has them—especially when times are uncertain. The function of rumors is to fill in missing information (Shibutani 1966). People want to know about conditions that will have an impact on them, so when hard information is lacking, the void provides fertile ground for rumors, as people jump at cues and read into them what they are searching for.

The key to understanding rumors is *uncertainty,* some ambiguous situation that the rumor solves. During a period of economic downturn, for example, large work

role extension: the incorporation of additional activities into a role

rumors: unfounded information spread among people

TABLE 21.1 Employees' First Action after Learning of the Fire

Action	Percentage
Left	29%
Helped others to leave	41%
Fought or reported the fire	17%
Continued routine activities	7%
Other (e.g., looked for a friend or relative)	5%

Note: These figures are based on interviews with 95 of the 160 employees present at the time of the fire: forty-eight males and forty-seven females, ranging in age from fifteen to fifty-nine.

Source: Based on Johnston and Johnson 1989.

settings are filled with rumors concerning impending layoffs, mass firings, and what is now called "downsizing." Smaller work settings apparently do not provide the same fertile ground for rumors, because individuals there have more direct access to the sources of information. In smaller settings, however, **gossip** apparently serves the same purpose: False, distorted, or blatantly untrue information of a more personal nature is passed from one person to another to fill in missing "gaps" about people's lives.

Most rumors are short-lived. They arise in a situation of ambiguity, only to dissipate when they are replaced either by another rumor or by factual information. Occasionally, however, rumors have a long life. For example, a dozen years ago a rumor began in France that Coca-Cola, Schweppes, Martini, and other products were contaminated with toxic substances. Despite denials from the companies, the rumor of mass poisoning not only persisted in France but spread to Germany, Italy, Great Britain, and even to Africa and the Middle East (Kapferer 1989). This rumor was transmitted not only by word of mouth, but also by leaflet. Various versions of the leaflet listed the code names for seventeen "toxic and carcinogenic" substances that supposedly had been added to these products, all verified by "a hospital in Paris." The substance identified as the "most dangerous" of the seventeen turned out to be citric acid, found in citrus fruits. Apparently this rumor persisted because it hit a responsive chord—mass confusion about what is safe or unsafe in our contaminated environment.

Why do people believe rumors? Three main factors have been identified. First, rumors deal with a subject that is important to an individual. Second, they replace ambiguity with some form of certainty. Third, they are attributed to a creditable source. An office rumor may be preceded by, "Jane has it on good authority that . . . ," or "Bill overheard the boss say that. . . ." The rumor of mass poisoning in Europe was supposedly based on a report from a "hospital in Paris."

Procter and Gamble, the maker of numerous household products such as Tide, Crest, Head and Shoulders, Pampers, Folgers, and Ivory soap, has also been the victim of a persistent rumor, this one, too, disseminated by leaflet. According to the rumor, the company logo—the man in the moon and 13 stars—represented witchcraft. (See Figure 21.2.) The rumor also reported that the president of the company gave a percentage of his earnings to satanic causes (Brunvand 1984). At the height of the rumor, when the company received fifteen thousand calls a month on the subject, Procter and Gamble employed fifteen persons simply to deny the rumor.

Ambiguity or uncertainty also underlay this rumor. Many Americans were upset about satanic activity: self-proclaimed witches granting media interviews, satanic graffiti

gossip: false, distorted, or blatantly untrue information of a more personal nature than a rumor

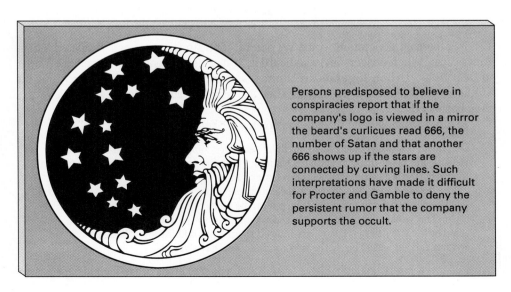

Persons predisposed to believe in conspiracies report that if the company's logo is viewed in a mirror the beard's curlicues read 666, the number of Satan and that another 666 shows up if the stars are connected by curving lines. Such interpretations have made it difficult for Procter and Gamble to deny the persistent rumor that the company supports the occult.

FIGURE 21.2 Procter and Gamble's Logo.

in public places, and satanic churches such as the one led by Anton LaVey in San Francisco. Although Procter and Gamble had used the logo since 1851, in the face of this persistent rumor, in 1985 the company began to remove the logo from its products.

Fads and Fashions

A **fad** is a temporary pattern of behavior that catches people's attention, while a **fashion** is a more enduring version of the same. Sociologist John Lofland (1985) identified four types of fads. First are object fads, such as the hula hoop of the 1950s, pet rocks of the 1970s, and baseball cards of the 1980s and 1990s. Second are activity fads, such as eating goldfish in the 1920s and playing Trivial Pursuit during the 1980s. Third are idea fads, such as astrology. Fourth are personality fads, such as Elvis Presley, Vanna White, and Michael Jordan. Some fads are extremely short-lived, such as "streaking" (running naked in a public place), which lasted only a couple of months in 1974. Others last much longer. Some fads spread rapidly, involve millions of people, and then die just as quickly as they appeared. For example, in the 1950s the Hula Hoop sold so quickly that stores couldn't keep them in stock. Children cried and pleaded for these brightly colored plastic hoops. Across the nation, children, and some adults, gyrated with this object encircling their waists. Hula Hoop contests were held to see who could keep the hoops up the longest or who could rotate the most hoops at one time. Then, in a matter of months it was over, and parents wondered what to do with the abandoned items, now useless for any other purpose.

When we think of fashion, which lasts somewhat longer, we tend to think of clothing. Clothing fashions are usually the result of a coordinated international marketing system that ranges from designers and manufacturers to advertisers and retailers. Billions of dollars worth of clothing are sold by manipulating the tastes of the public. Fashion, however, also refers to hairstyles, home decorating, even the design and colors of buildings. Sociologist John Lofland (1985) pointed out that fashion even applies to language, as demonstrated by these roughly comparable terms: "Neat!" in the 1950s; "Right on!" in the 1960s, "Really!" in the 1970s, "Awesome!" in the 1980s, and "Bad!" in the early 1990s.

Urban Legends

> Did you hear about Nancy and Bill? They were parked at Downer's Landing. They were listening to the car radio, and the music was interrupted by an announcement that a rapist-killer had escaped from prison. Instead of a right hand, he had a hook. Nancy said they should leave, but Bill laughed and said there wasn't any reason to go. When they heard a strange noise, Bill agreed to take her home. When Nancy opened the door, she heard something clink. It was a hook hanging on the door handle!

For the past generation, some version of "The Hook" story has circulated among Americans. As a teenager, my wife heard it. It has also appeared as a "genuine" letter in Dear Abby. **Urban legends** are stories with an ironic twist that sound realistic but are false. Although they are untrue, they are usually told by people who believe that they happened.

Another urban legend making the rounds is the "Kentucky Fried Rat".

> One night, a woman didn't have anything ready for supper, so she and her husband went to the drive-through line at Kentucky Fried Chicken. While they were eating in their car, the wife said, "My chicken tastes funny."
> Her husband said, "You're always complaining about something." When she insisted that the chicken didn't taste right, he put on the light. She was holding fried rat—crispy style. The woman went into shock and was rushed to the hospital.
> A lawyer from the company has offered them $100,000 if they will sign a release and not tell anyone. This is the second case they have had.

Folklorist Jan Brunvand (1981, 1984, 1986) reported that urban legends are passed on by people who think that the event happened just one or two people down the line

---

Project 2

CDQ 10: What examples can you give of current fads and fashions? How long do you think they will last?

CDQ 11: Are you aware of urban legends in your hometown? On campus?

fad: a temporary pattern of behavior that catches people's attention

fashion: a pattern of behavior that catches people's attention, which lasts longer than a fad

urban legend: a story with an ironic twist that sounds realistic but is false

of transmission, often to a "friend of a friend." The story has strong appeal and gains credibility from naming specific people or local places. Brunvand views urban legends as "modern morality stories," with each teaching a moral lesson about life.

If we apply Brunvand's analysis to these two urban legends, three major points emerge. First, their moral serves as a warning. "The Hook" warns young people that they should be careful about where they go, who they go with, and what they do. The world is an unsafe place, and "messing around" is risky. "The Kentucky Fried Rat" contains a different moral: Do you *really* know what you are eating when you buy food from a fast-food outlet? Wouldn't it be better to eat at home, where you know what you are getting?

Second, each story is related to social change; "The Hook" to changing morality, especially the privacy from parents provided by the automobile; the "Kentucky Fried Rat" to changing male-female relationships, especially to changing sex roles at home. Third, each is calculated to instill guilt and fear: guilt—the wife failed in her traditional role, and she gets punished—and fear, the dangerous unknown, whether the dark countryside or fast food. The ultimate moral of these stories is that we should not abandon traditional roles or the safety of the home.

These principles can equally be applied to an urban legend that made the rounds in the late 1980s. I heard several versions of this one, each narrator swearing that it had happened to a friend of a friend.

> Jerry (or whoever) went to a night club last weekend. He met an attractive woman, and they hit it off. They spent the night in a motel, and when he awoke the next morning, the young woman was gone. When he went into the bathroom, he saw a message scrawled on the mirror in lipstick: "Welcome to the wonderful world of AIDS."

SOCIAL MOVEMENTS

UNDERSTANDING SOCIAL MOVEMENTS: THE CASE OF THE NAZIS

When the Nazis, a small group of malcontents in Bavaria, first appeared on the scene in the 1920s, their ideas appeared laughable to the world. They believed that the Germans were a race of supermen (*Übermenschen*), who would launch a Third Reich (kingdom) that would control the world for a thousand years. Their race destined them for greatness, lesser races to their service and exploitation.

From a little band of comic characters who looked as though they had stepped out of a cheap movie, the Nazis rose to threaten the existence of Western civilization. How could a little man with a grotesque moustache, surrounded by a few sycophants in brown shirts, ever come to threaten the world? Such things happen only in novels or in movies, the deranged nightmare of some imaginative author. Not in real life. Only this was real life, and the Nazis were more than real, their appearance on the human scene causing the deaths of millions of people and changing the course of civilization itself.

To see how this happened, we need to understand social movements, the second major topic of this chapter. **Social movements,** which also involve unusual behavior, are sometimes difficult to distinguish from collective behavior, but they usually involve more people, are more prolonged, are more organized, and focus on social change.

Why Social Movements Exist

Protest marches and demonstrations are not only fascinating to watch—and to be a part of—they also are a regular feature of modern society. To understand why, we first need to know their six chief characteristics. Let's summarize these features and then apply them to the rise of the Nazis.

■ Social unrest provides fertile ground for social movements.

Project 3

Speaker Sug. #3: A spokesperson for a social movement on your campus or in your community.

Essay #4

CDQ 12: Have you participated in a social movement? Why do social movements exist?

L. Obj. 6: State the major reasons why social movements exist.

social movement: unusual behavior that, compared with other forms of collective behavior, usually involves more people, is more prolonged, is more organized, and focuses on social change

- Social movements express dissatisfaction with current conditions and promise something better.
- Social movements are highly organized.
- Social movements attract committed followers, including a core of "true believers."
- Social movements attempt to change social conditions.
- Social movements potentially lead to extensive social change, even the transformation of society.

The Background of Social Unrest.   First, we need to note that Germany was in chaos after suffering a humiliating defeat in World War I. The 1919 peace treaty, signed at Versailles, proclaimed Germany the party responsible for starting the war. It also forced Germany to give up extensive territory and set up a schedule for Germany to pay $1 trillion to the victors (Bridgwater 1953). Those payments, known as reparations, crippled the German economy. The government began to print more and more money to make its payments, but as noted in Chapter 14, money not backed up by gold or productivity leads to inflation. In 1921, it took 75 German marks to equal one U.S. dollar (Schirer 1960). By the beginning of 1923, it took 7,000. By August it took 1 million! By the end of the year, it took several trillion.

This hyperinflation wiped out the life savings of the middle class overnight. It disrupted the economy, for how could industrialists make plans to manufacture anything if they did not know what they would pay for raw materials or wages or what price they would get for their products? The result was breadlines, as millions were thrown out of work. In those breadlines stood people who had worked proudly all of their lives and saved money for the future—only now they had no work, no savings, and no future.

During that same year, 1923, when Germany was unable to make payments with money that was worth anything, France took matters into its own hands and invaded the Ruhr, Germany's heartland of industrialization. Germany was in despair, sick over its humiliating loss in the war, and now even sicker at being able to do nothing about the invasion of its territory. Germany could not defend itself, much less keep its people employed and fed.

Dissatisfaction and the Promise of Something Better: The Emergence of a Leader.   Into this chaos stepped a man who promised to bring back prosperity and pride. His party, the *Nationalsozialistische Deutsche Arbeiter Partei* (the National Socialist German Workers' Party), promised solutions to the nation's problems. The Nazis could regain the nation's stature on the world stage and put Germans back to work. Never again would Germany suffer the humiliation of France taking its territory with impunity.

The poor listened to Hitler, for he promised to put them to work; so did the wealthy industrialists, for he also promised to end the hyperinflation that made their plans impossible. The army listened too, for Hitler promised to restore national strength. And everyone was enchanted by the prospect of regaining national pride, thus removing the disgrace that hung like an albatross around Germany's neck.

Hitler also crafted a message that pointed to "enemies within," wealthy Jewish industrialists whom he accused of betraying the nation by selling out to foreign powers. He had spelled out his racist ideas in *Mein Kampf,* but few paid attention. To Hitler, ideology was all-important. As far as the German people were concerned, he offered jobs and social stability.

Effective Organization: Gaining Power.   Only gradually, however, did Hitler win at the ballot box. According to the European system of democracy described in Chapter 15, in which parties gain seats in the legislature according to the proportion of votes they receive, the Nazis were unable to win more than 20 percent of the seats in the *Reichstag* (German parliament). Then in 1929 the American stock market crashed, precipitating a world depression. The situation in Germany grew even more desperate, and in 1933 the Nazis won about 45 percent of the vote.

Prior to Hitler's rise to the chancellorship, the Nazis had developed a tightly knit organization throughout Germany. At the top was Adolf Hitler, who was known as *der Führer* (the leader). Throughout the country were district leaders, called *Gauleiters*. Below each Gauleiter were subleaders. When the Nazis achieved national power with the resignation of Chancellor Hindenburg in 1933, they were able to use this "state within a state" to move against their opponents. They brutally suppressed dissent and canceled future elections.

Committed Followers and the Inner Core of "True Believers": The SS.   Although few people had taken Hitler's racist ideas seriously, he had meant them. To assure that they would be carried out, Hitler had formed a secret organization within the Nazi party, the *Schutzstaffel,* the dreaded SS (Hughes 1993). All SS candidates had to have their lineage checked for any sign of racial impurity, such as intermarriage with a non-Aryan. An ancestor's intermarriage with a Jew, Gypsy, or Slav disqualified the individual from membership. To this inner core of "true believers" went the assignment of carrying out Hitler's dream of a pure Aryan nation.

Attempts to Change Social Conditions.   Hitler took many steps to change the existing order. Although it was illegal to do so under the terms of the Treaty of Versailles, he built up an army and extensive munitions. He brought inflation under control and ended the breadlines. The beginning of prosperity pleased the Germans.

The steps that Hitler took that most interest us, however, are those concerning race. Laws were passed that made it illegal for Aryans and Jews to intermarry. Jews were forced to resign government positions. Jewish professors could no longer teach. Jewish physicians could not treat Aryan patients; for a Jew even to touch an Aryan was contamination. Mobs were encouraged by the police to ransack stores run by Jews. Jews were moved out of Aryan neighborhoods and forced to live in ghettos. To identify themselves in public, Jews were required to wear a yellow Star of David.

With the machinery in place and Nazi political power secure, the SS began its campaign of mass killing in the name of racial purity. They first constructed gas chambers at state hospitals, where they gassed children who were physically disabled and mental patients whom physicians reported as unlikely to be cured. Being deemed Aryan was not enough to prevent their deaths, for their disabilities were viewed as signs of racial inferiority in the Aryan stock. The Nazis then turned to Jews, rounding them up and sending them to "rehabilitation" camps, the infamous concentration camps from which few ever returned. After deciding that individual killing of Jews in the captured nations was inefficient, Jews there were also deported to these camps. So were Gypsies and Slavs.

Social Change Accomplished.   Few social movements in history have had as much impact as the Nazis did. They transformed Germany into a police state, with a system of surveillance so extensive that even moviegoers whose facial expressions during newsreels were "inappropriate" were reported to the authorities (Moyers 1989). The country became a war machine to do Hitler's bidding. The social change ushered in by the Nazis was not limited to Germany, of course, as the Nazis plunged the world into the most far-reaching war it has ever known. No industrialized society remained untouched.

The human destruction perpetrated by the Nazis is mind-boggling. The total number killed in concentration camps is somewhere around six million. Battle deaths during World War II ran another 15 million or so (Finsterbusch and Greisman 1975).

In Sum.   When people are dissatisfied with social conditions, their search for solutions provides fertile ground for social movements. Groups that promise to change conditions

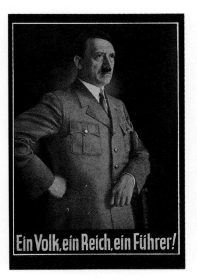

Adolf Hitler posed for this official portrait in 1938. Pleased with the results, he had it circulated throughout Germany. The title at the bottom reads, "One People, One Nation, One Leader." Explicit in this slogan is Hitler as the unifying force of Germany. Implicit is the idea that only "Aryans" are part of "one people."

CDQ 13: Would you predict an increase in the number of social movements in the United States in the future? Why or why not?

are able to tap into these dissatisfactions and encourage people to organize to solve the problems that bother them. At the core of a social movement lies a cluster of "true believers," individuals more committed than the others.

Not all social movements, however, share these characteristics equally. Except for extreme political movements such as nazism and communism, few ever organize so tightly that they form a "state within a state." And though few do so, social movements nevertheless have the potential to transform society—for good or for evil.

CDQ 14: Can you explain how the Nazis were successful in their takeover of Germany in spite of the fact that their actions seem so reprehensible today?

L. Obj. 7: Identify the functions of dehumanization and propaganda in social movements

Dehumanization: Why Normal People Do Evil Things

The Nazis provide an unusual case in that their social movement was organized for evil. The question arises how the Nazis could have slaughtered so many people. How could people bash in the heads of children, or shoot men and women lined up at the edge of trenches dug to receive their lifeless corpses, on a daily basis, as part of a "job"? What happened to their consciences? As noted in Chapter 15 (pages 424–425), the concept of dehumanization helps to explain such acts. *Dehumanization* is the process of reducing people to objects not deserving the treatment accorded humans. Dehumanization involves four main characteristics: increased emotional distance from others, an emphasis on following orders, inability to resist pressures, and a diminished sense of responsibility (Bernard, Ottenberg, and Redl 1971).

The Nazis were not remarkable for this process, which is found among many groups, but rather for the extent to which they employed it so that ordinary citizens could participate in inhumane acts with a good conscience.

Symbolic interactionists stress that at the essence of dehumanization is a label classifying people as less than human. The Nazis' use of labels was extremely effective, transforming killing from an unusual act to a normal part of work. This process is chillingly illustrated by letters written home by prison guards. They were far more disturbed by delayed vacation leave or by shortages of small luxuries than by the executions they carried out daily, which they also note briefly and without comment. As the camp guards became more efficient in their killing, they found more time to gather informally, where they played musical instruments, drank, and laughed together—all after a hard day's "work" (Klee, Dressen, and Riess 1991).

As difficult as it is for us to grasp, these were "normal" people, not monsters, who through a process of dehumanization had neutralized their morality to participate in acts that they, too, would otherwise condemn. The process is alive today; war continues to exalt treachery, bribery, and killing, and to award medals to soldiers specifically glorifying actions for which they would in all other contexts be imprisoned.

Essay #5

Propaganda and Advertising: Manufacturing and Selling Ideas

Another key to understanding the successful takeover of Germany by the Nazis is propaganda. Although the word generally evokes negative images, **propaganda** is actually a neutral term, meaning simply the presentation of information in the attempt to influence people. Its original connotation was positive, for propaganda referred to a committee of cardinals of the Roman Catholic Church whose assignment was the care of foreign missions. (They were to *propagate* the faith.) The term has traveled a long way since then, however, and today it is usually used in the much narrower sense of a one-sided presentation of information that distorts reality.

Propaganda is used to influence **public opinion,** how people think about some issue. Although we often use "public" to refer to everyone in the country, the term actually refers to any group of people who have a particular interest in some topic. For example, the "public" for state elections is not the same as the "public" for national elections. Propaganda, then, in the sense of organized attempts to manipulate public opinion, is a regular part of modern life.

propaganda: in its broad sense, the presentation of information in the attempt to influence people; in its narrow sense, one-sided information used to try to influence people

public opinion: how people think about some issue

Note that advertising fits both the broad and the narrow definition of propaganda perfectly; for advertising is not only an organized attempt to manipulate public opinion but also a one-sided presentation of information that distorts reality. Advertisers, for example, hawk "beauty" soap. While the term for this product is certainly ridiculous, its advertising is so effective that many millions of women take the name seriously. The advertisers do not mention that their soap contains chemical additives harmful to the skin, or that when flushed down the toilet its harmful components enter the food chain and end up back in our own bodies! Would as many consumers buy their products if manufacturers presented both sides of the issue?

The Nazis were extremely skillful in the art of propaganda. Much as advertisers today sell beauty soap, they sold the various publics on their ideas. Their success was not due only to propaganda; terror also played its part. If the Nazis couldn't convince someone to buy their ideas, they could convince them to remain silent—or the Gestapo would make a midnight call. Most Germans apparently bought their viewpoints, however, just as Americans buy heavily advertised products. In fact, a cynic might conclude that advertisers honed their skills on the Nazi experience!

Dr. Paul Joseph Goebbels (1897–1945) headed the Nazi propaganda machine. His work was considered as important as the manufacture of tanks and ammunition, for then, as now, the manufacture of opinion was essential to waging war. Goebbels's philosophy of propaganda was simple. "It is just as easy to tell a big lie as a small one. If you repeat it often enough, most people will believe it." Underlying Goebbels's campaign of unifying the German people for the war effort and destroying "inferior" racial stock were two basic principles. The first was to simplify, to break a complex issue into simple parts. The second, Goebbels said, was to repeat, to continue to recite the simplified version of reality over and over again. The way that Goebbels (Moyers 1989) put the matter drives home the point. "Simplify! Simplify! Simplify! Then, Repeat! Repeat! Repeat!"

As these events occurred, sociologists Alfred and Elizabeth Lee (1939) analyzed propaganda to determine its essential techniques. Their findings, which shed light on both advertising and politics, are summarized in the Down-to-Earth Sociology box on page 610. Perhaps by understanding these techniques, you will be better able to resist one-sided appeals—whether they come from hawkers of products or from people trying to convince you to vote them into office.

BREADTH, TYPES, AND TACTICS OF SOCIAL MOVEMENTS

Breadth of Social Movements

Not many social movements are evil. The Nazis merely provide an outstanding example, for they played out on the world stage one of the most significant of social movements humanity has experienced. Social movements include such diverse activities as **millenarian movements** (based on the prophecy of coming social upheaval), the American civil rights movement of the 1960s, the worldwide charismatic movement among Christians, starting around the turn of the century and apparently peaking in the 1980s, and even the development of space flight (Bainbridge 1989).

Cargo cults are among the more interesting examples of social movements. About one hundred years ago, Europeans colonized the Melanesian Islands of the South Pacific. From the home countries of the colonizers arrived ship after ship, each loaded with strange cargo. As the Melanesians watched the items being unloaded, they noted that the cargo always went to the Europeans. They waited, but none ever arrived for them. Melanesian prophets then revealed the secret of this exotic merchandise: Their own ancestors were manufacturing and sending the cargoes to them. The colonists, however, were intercepting the merchandise. Since the colonists were too strong for them to fight, and too selfish to share the cargo, there was little the Melanesians could do. However, their initial prophecies were followed by further prophecies revealing

L. Obj. 8: List the four types of social movements, the three levels of membership found in such movements, and the three publics which each movement has.

millenarian movement: a social movement based on the prophecy of coming social upheaval

cargo cult: a social movement in which South Pacific islanders destroyed their possessions in the anticipation that their ancestors would send items by ship

the solution to the problem. If they would destroy their crops and food and build harbors, their ancestors would see their sincerity and send the cargo directly to them. The Melanesians did so.

Interestingly, these prophecies came true. Colonial administrators of the islands informed the home government of the problem. The prospect of thousands of natives sitting in the hills starving to death as they awaited cargo from their ancestors was too horrifying to allow. The government sent ships to the islands with cargo earmarked for the natives (Worsley 1957).

DOWN-TO-EARTH SOCIOLOGY

"Tricks of the Trade"—The Fine Art of Propaganda

Sociologists Alfred and Elizabeth Lee (1939) found that propaganda relies on seven basic techniques, which they termed "tricks of the trade." To be effective, the techniques should be subtle, with the audience remaining unaware just which part of their mind or emotions is being manipulated. If propaganda is effective, people will not know *why* they support something, only that they do—as they fervently defend it.

1. *Name calling*   This technique aims to arouse opposition to the competing product, candidate, or policy by associating it with a negative image. By comparison, one's own product, candidate, or policy appears attractive. Political candidates who call an opponent a communist or "pinko" are using this technique. The "more refined" version is to call the opponent "soft" (on communism, crime, defense, and so on).

2. *Glittering generality*   Essentially the opposite of the first, this technique surrounds the product, candidate, or policy with "virtue words," phrases that arouse positive feelings. "She's a *real* Democrat" has little meaning, but it makes the audience feel that something important has been said. "He stands for individualism" is so general that it is meaningless, yet the audience thinks that it has heard a specific message about the candidate.

3. *Transfer*   In its positive form, this technique associates the product, candidate, or policy with something that the public respects; in its negative form, with something of which it disapproves. Let's look at the positive form: You might not be able to get by with saying, "Busch beer is patriotic," but surround a beer with the American flag, and beer drinkers will somehow get the idea that it is more patriotic to drink this brand of beer than another. It is no accident that attractive, skimpily dressed, young, slender females open car doors in automobile commercials. This technique is even more effective when the camera is located inside the automobile as the model bends over to peer inside, and a generous amount of cleavage shows. All in good taste, of course. Advertisers in some European countries use nude females; a Spanish television commercial for chocolate syrup contains a close-up of the syrup slowly being poured onto the stomach of a nude stretched out on the floor.

4. *Testimonials*   Famous and admired individuals are frequently used to endorse a product, candidate, or policy. Movie stars hawk skin cream, coffee, or perhaps extol the relief offered by a particular brand of hemorrhoid ointment. Although testimonials have always been part of American politics, in recent years they have taken on a different flavor as candidates for political office solicit the endorsement of movie stars—who may know next to nothing about the candidate, or even about politics itself. In the negative form of this technique, a hated person is associated with the competing product. If propagandists could manage it, they would show Saddam Hussein drinking a competing beer or announcing support for an opposing candidate.

5. *Plain folks*   Sometimes it pays to take a contrasting approach to that of testimonials by the rich and famous, instead associating the product, candidate, or policy with "just plain folks." "If Mary or John Q. Public like it, you will, too." A political candidate who kisses babies, gets out into the crowd and shakes hands, dons a hard hat, has lunch at McDonald's—and makes certain that photographers "catch him or her in the act"—is using the "plain folks" strategy. "I'm just a regular person," is the message of the presidential candidate posing for the photographers in jeans and work shirt—while making certain that the Mercedes and yacht do not show up in the photograph.

6. *Card stacking*   The aim of this technique is to present only positive information about what you support, only negative information about what you oppose. Make it sound as though there is only one conclusion that a rational person can draw. Use falsehoods, distortions, and illogical statements if you must.

7. *Bandwagon*   "Everyone is doing it" is the idea behind this technique. After all, "20 million Frenchmen can't be wrong," can they? Emphasizing how many others buy the product or support the candidate or policy conveys the message that anyone who doesn't join in is on the wrong track.

The Lees (1939) added, "Once we know that a speaker or writer is using one of these propaganda devices in an attempt to convince us of an idea, we can separate the device from the idea and see what the idea amounts to on its own merits."

New Social Movements

Many recent social movements are huge in scale and focus on broad concerns. Some even deal with global matters and spill across national borders. Two main reasons can be identified for these new social movements: emerging values and attempts to regain control by countering exploitive profits and the immense size of current government (cf. McAdam, McCarthy, and Zald 1988; Melucci 1980, 1981; Klandermans 1986).

Emerging Values: Animal Rights.   The animal-rights movement is still in an early stage of development. Its adherents represent what sociologist James Jasper (1991) called a moral social movement. Its members are motivated not by personal gain but by concern for the welfare of animals and the desire to produce a more moral society. At this point their following is weak, but members are highly committed and see themselves as moral crusaders out to change society. They are fond of quoting John Stuart Mill, who said, "Every great movement must experience three stages: ridicule, discussion, adoption." They take pride in being part of a movement ahead of its time, at the stage of ridicule, feel certain that history will vindicate their views, and are confident that their movement will attain the other stages (Jasper 1991, 1993).

Regaining Control: The Environmental Movement.   The environmental movement is an attempt to reclaim the people's right to a healthy, clean environment in the face of profits gained from polluting it. This new social movement that draws highly committed adherents throughout the Western world centers on the goal of improving the earth's air, water, and land. As with other organized social movements, subgroups focus on various specific issues relating to the movement's broader concerns. Perhaps the best known activity is that directed against nuclear power plants and weapons (Jasper 1991). Chapter 22 examines environmental concerns in some detail.

Types of Social Movements

With such variety—from Nazis to cargo cults—what framework can be used to classify social movements? Figure 21.3 on page 612 shows a typology provided by sociologist

L. Obj. 9: Describe the characteristics of recent social movements and identify some of their major concerns.

CDQ 15: How successful do you think animal rights and environmental activist groups will be?

Essay #6

Still in its infancy, but picking up steam, is the social movement known as animal rights. Like other social movements, this one also has a core of dedicated, true believers, who are convinced that their picture of the world is correct and that its opposition is unenlightened, deluded, or both. Represented here by the World Laboratory Animal Liberation Week held at the Berkeley campus of the University of California—this social movement may represent the wave of the future. If unable to mobilize sufficient resources, however, it may disappear.

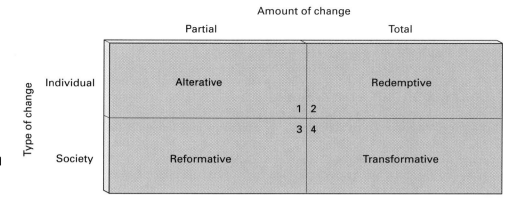

FIGURE 21.3 Types of Social Movements. (*Source:* Aberle 1966.)

David Aberle (1966). He classified social movements according to the type and amount of social change they seek. By *type* of social change, Aberle referred to whether the goal is to change people or society. By *amount,* he meant whether the change is to be partial or total.

Let's look at Aberle's classification. The first two seek to change *people.*

Alterative social movements seek to alter only particular aspects of people. The Women's Christian Temperance Union, active in the earlier part of this century, is an example. This group intended to change only people's consumption of alcoholic beverages, while leaving everything else in society alone. Its members were convinced that if people did not drink, such problems as poverty, spouse abuse, and neglect of families would decline.

Redemptive social movements also seek to change people, but they aim for total change. An example is a religious social movement that stresses conversion. In fundamentalist Christianity, for example, when someone converts to Christ, the entire person is supposed to change. Selfish and self-destructive behaviors are to recede as the convert becomes in their terms, a "new creation."

The next two types of social movements seek to change *society.*

Reformative social movements seek to reform only one part of society. Examples are the new social movements centering on animal rights, the environment, and nuclear power and weapons. Members of reformative social movements see most aspects of society as satisfactory and wish to change only the part they find intolerable.

Transformative social movements also focus on society. Their goal, however, is to change the social order itself and to replace it with their own version of the ideal society. The revolutions in the American colonies, France, Russia, and Cuba are examples of transformative social movements. The Nazis are another example.

Tactics of Social Movements

The tactics of a social movement can best be understood by examining its levels of membership, the publics it addresses, and its relationship to authorities.

Figure 21.4 shows the composition of social movements. First, there are three levels of membership. As demonstrated by the Nazis, a social movement has an inner core consisting of those persons who are most committed to the movement. The inner core is the leadership that sets goals, timetables, strategies, and inspires the other members. The second level consists of people who are committed to the goals of the social movement, but not to the same degree as members of the inner core. They can, however, be counted on to run mimeograph machines, to make telephone calls, and to show up for demonstrations. The third level of membership consists of a wider circle of people who are neither as committed nor as dependable. Their participation is primarily a matter of convenience. If an activity does not interfere with something else they want to do, they will participate.

alterative social movement: a social movement that seeks to alter only particular aspects of people

redemptive social movement: a social movement that seeks to change people totally

reformative social movement: a social movement that seeks to change only particular aspects of society

transformative social movement: a social movement that seeks to change society totally

As also shown in Figure 21.4, social movements have three types of publics. The sympathetic public is not too unlike the group's own wider circle of members, but it has no commitment to the social movement. Its sympathy with the goals of the movement, however, makes this public a fertile ground for recruiting new members. The second public is hostile. It is keenly aware of the group's goals and does not like them. This public wants the social movement stopped, for the movement's values are antithetical to its own. The third public consists of persons who are unaware of the social movement, or if aware, are indifferent to it.

In determining tactics, the leadership pays attention to which public it is addressing. The sympathetic public is often the target of a group's tactics, for it is the source of new members and support at the ballot box. The goal of a demonstration, for example, may be to elicit greater sympathy from this group. Sometimes the leadership even uses the hostile public to force a confrontation, trying to make itself appear a victim, a group whose rights are being trampled on. Tactics directed toward the unaware or indifferent public are designed to neutralize their indifference and increase their awareness. Because the indifferent and unaware are usually the largest of the publics, their arousal can swell the ranks of either the sympathetic or the hostile.

The movement's relationship to the authorities is also significant in determining tactics. First, if authorities are hostile to a social movement, aggressive or even violent tactics are likely. For example, since the goal of a transformative (revolutionary) social movement is to replace the government, the movement and the government are clearly on a collision course. Second, if the authorities are sympathetic to a social movement, violence is not likely. For example, reformative social movements that receive either a positive or indifferent reception by authorities have a low likelihood of causing violence. Third, if a social movement is *institutionalized*, accepted by the authorities and given access to resources they control, the likelihood of violence is very low. Even though dissatisfied, the group simply has too much to risk by adopting violence.

That these are only rough principles can be seen from the case of the Nazis. The Nazis were institutionalized—indeed, they *became* the government—yet violence was at the center of their tactics, both within their own country and outside it. Much research is still needed to refine these basic ideas.

The Life Course of Social Movements

Social movements have a life course; that is, they go through different stages as they grow and mature. Although sociologists do not agree on just what those stages are (Jasper 1991), works by a number of sociologists—Charles Tilly (1978), Kurt and

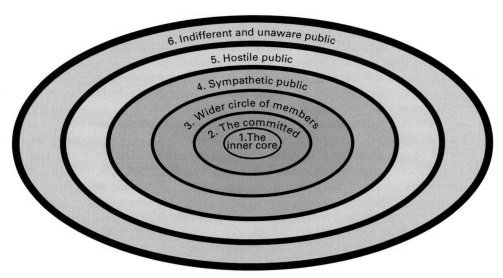

FIGURE 21.4 The Memberships and Publics of Social Movements.

Gladys Lang (1961), Armand Mauss (1975), Malcolm Spector and John Kitsuse (1977)—have identified five stages of social movements.

The first is a period of *initial unrest and agitation,* during which people are upset about some condition of society and want it changed. During this stage, leaders emerge who are able to verbalize people's feelings and to crystallize issues. Most incipient social movements fail at this stage. They simply cannot gain enough support, and after a brief flurry of activity they quietly die.

The second is *mobilization,* which occurs when a relatively large number of people are disturbed by the problem and demand that something be done about it. Leaders arise, and the movement is likely to take shape around a charismatic leader. The movement's leaders may become celebrities, guests on national talk shows, and the topic of news stories.

The next stage is *organization.* A division of labor is set up, with a leadership that makes policy decisions and a rank and file that actively supports the movement. There is still much collective excitement about the issue, the movement's focal point of concern.

Institutionalization is the fourth stage. The movement becomes a bureaucracy, developing the type of formal hierarchy described in Chapter 7. Leadership passes to career officials, who may care more about their own position in the organization than the movement for which the organization's initial leaders made sacrifices.

The final stage is *organizational decline and possible resurgence.* Day-to-day affairs of the organization may come to dominate the leadership, diverting attention away from the issues around which the movement originated. No longer a collection of persons who share a common cause, the movement may decline at this point.

Decline is not certain, however. Emerging groups committed to the same goal led by more idealistic and committed leaders may step to the forefront and reinvigorate the movement with new strength. Or, as in the case of abortion, social movements in conflict with each other may fight on opposite sides of the issue, each continuously invigorating the other and preventing its decline. The Thinking Critically section below contrasts the two opposing groups in regard to abortion.

THINKING CRITICALLY ABOUT SOCIAL CONTROVERSY

Which Side of the Barricades? Abortion as a Social Movement

No issue so divides Americans as abortion does. Polls show that in regard to abortion in the first trimester (the first three months) of pregnancy, opinion is evenly divided. While 45 percent oppose a woman's right to obtain an abortion during this time, 45 percent favor it. This polarization constantly invigorates life into the movement.

When the United States Supreme Court determined in its 1973 decision, *Roe* v. *Wade,* that states could not restrict abortion, the pro-choice side relaxed. Victory was theirs, and they thought their opponents would quietly disappear. Instead, large numbers of Americans were disturbed by what they saw as gross immorality. For them, the legal right to abortion amounted to the right to murder unborn children.

The two sides see matters in totally incompatible ways. On the one hand, those in favor of choice view the 1.5 million abortions performed annually in the United States as examples of women exercising their basic reproductive rights. On the other, anti-abortionists see them as legalized murder. To the pro-choice side, those who oppose abortion stand in the way of women's rights, setting basic gender relations on their head by forcing women to continue pregnancies they desire to terminate. To the pro-life forces, those who favor abortion are seen as condoning the wholesale slaughter of children, of putting their own desires for school, career, or convenience ahead of the lives of the unborn.

There is no way to reconcile such opposing views. Each sees the other as unreasonable and extremist. And each focuses on worst-case scenarios: pro-choice images of young women, raped at gunpoint, forced to bear the children of rapists; or pro-life images of women who are eight months pregnant killing their children instead of nurturing them.

Since these views are in permanent conflict, each side, fighting for what it considers basic rights, reinvigorates the other. When in 1989 the United States Supreme Court decided in *Webster* v. *Reproductive Services* that states could restrict abortion, one side hailed it as a defeat, the other as a victory. Seeing the political battle going against them, the pro-choice side regrouped for a determined struggle. The pro-life side, sensing judicial victory within its grasp, gathered forces for a push to complete the overthrow of *Roe* v. *Wade*.

This goal of the pro-life side came close to becoming reality in *Casey* v. *Planned Parenthood*. On June 30, 1992, in a 6 to 3 decision the Supreme Court upheld a Pennsylvania law that requires a woman to wait 24 hours between the confirmation of pregnancy and abortion, girls under 18 to obtain the consent of one parent to have an abortion, and women to be informed about options to abortion and to be given materials that describe the fetus. In the same case, by a 5 to 4 decision, the Court ruled that a wife does not have to inform her husband if she intends to have an abortion.

Because the two sides see reality in entirely contrasting ways, this social movement cannot end unless the vast majority of Americans commit to one side or the other. Otherwise, all legislative and judicial outcomes—whether the overthrow of *Roe* v. *Wade* or such extremes as a constitutional amendment declaring abortion either murder or a woman's right—are victories to one and defeats to the other. Nothing, then, is ever complete, but each action is only a way station in a moral struggle.

Typically, the last stage of a social movement is decline. Why does this last stage not apply to this social movement? What is different about it? Do you see this continuing back-and-forth struggle as temporary? Under what conditions other than those listed above will this social movement decline?

Activists in social movements become committed to "the cause." The social movement around abortion, currently one of the most dynamic in the United States, has split Americans, is highly visible, and has articulate spokespeople on both sides. Each side is convinced that it represents true morality. One of the more controversial strategies followed by some segments of the pro-life side (but disapproved by many on the pro-life side) is Operation Rescue, in which activists attempt to shut down abortion clinics. Shown here is Operation Rescue in Buffalo, New York, and a counterdemonstration by pro-choice activists just as determined to keep the abortion clinic open.

As stated above, the abortion issue has produced the most polarizing of all social movements. Americans are less than evenly divided, however, when it comes to abortions after the first trimester of pregnancy. The longer the pregnancy, the smaller the proportion of Americans who approve abortion. What is your opinion about abortion? Does it change depending on the length of pregnancy? For example, how do you feel about abortion during the second month versus the eighth month? What do you think about abortion in cases of rape and incest? Finally, can you identify some of the *social* reasons that underlie your opinions? (*Source:* Henslin 1990; Jasper 1991; Luker 1984; Neikirk and Elsasser 1992; Rosenblatt 1992; Rothenberg 1992.)

WHY PEOPLE JOIN SOCIAL MOVEMENTS

Deprivation Theory

One explanation to account for why people join social movements is *deprivation theory*. According to this theory, people who are deprived of things deemed valuable in society—whether money, justice, status, or privilege—join social movements with the hope of redressing their grievances. This theory may seem so obvious as to need no evidence. Aren't the thousands of African Americans who participated in the civil rights movement of the 1950s (discussed in Chapter 12), the mass protests of South African blacks against apartheid, the tractor caravans driven by dispossessed farmers in the 1980s, and the World War I soldiers who marched on Washington after Congress refused to pay their promised bonuses ample evidence that the theory is true?

Deprivation theory does provide a beginning point. But there is more to the matter than this. We must also pay attention to what Alexis de Tocqueville (1856, 1955) noted almost 150 years ago. The peasants of Germany were worse off than the peasants of France, and from deprivation theory we would expect the Germans to have rebelled and to have overthrown their king. Revolution, however, occurred in France, not Germany. The reason, said de Tocqueville, is *relative* deprivation. French peasants had experienced improved living conditions, and could imagine even better conditions, while German peasants, having never experienced anything but depressed conditions, had no comparative basis for feeling deprived.

According to **relative deprivation theory,** then, it is not people's actual negative conditions (their *absolute* deprivation) that matters. Rather, the key to participation is *relative* deprivation—that is, what people *think* they should have relative to what others have, or even compared with their own past or perceived future. This theory, which has provided excellent insight into revolutions, also holds a surprise. As sociologist James Davies (1962) says, improved conditions fuel human desires for even better conditions; in some instances, then, *improved* conditions can spark revolutions.

Finally, we can note that many who risked their lives for the civil rights movement in southern demonstrations were white, middle-class northerners (McAdam 1988). From this example it is clear that people whose own personal welfare is not at stake may become active in a social movement for *moral* reasons, in this instance to combat injustice (Jasper 1991).

Mass Society Theory

A second theory explaining who joins social movements was proposed by sociologist William Kornhauser (1959). In what is called **mass-society theory,** Kornhauser argued that **mass society**—an industrialized, highly bureaucratized, impersonal society—makes many people feel isolated. These people are attracted to social movements because they offer a sense of belonging. In geographical areas where social ties are supposedly weaker, such as the western United States, one would then expect to find

---

CDQ 16: Why do you think peo ple join social movements?

L. Obj. 10: Compare deprivation theory and mass society theory as explanations of why people join social movements.

K.P.: William Kornhauser

relative deprivation theory: the belief that people join social movements based on their evaluations of what they think they should have compared with what others have

mass-society theory: an explanation for participation in social movements based on the assumption that such movements offer a sense of belonging to people who have weak social ties

mass society: industrialized, highly bureaucratized, impersonal society

more social movements than in areas where traditional ties are supposedly stronger, such as in the Midwest and South.

This theory seems to match commonsense observations. Certainly, social movements seem to proliferate on the West Coast. But sociologist Doug McAdam (1988), who interviewed people who had risked their lives in the civil rights movement, found that these people were firmly rooted in families and communities. It was their strong desire to right wrongs and to overcome injustices, not their isolation, that motivated their participation. Even the Nazis attracted many people firmly rooted in their communities (Oberschall 1973). Finally, those most isolated of all, the homeless, generally do not join anything—except food lines.

In Sum. No current theory adequately accounts for who joins social movements. Motivations for all human activities are complicated, and theories that focus on a single motivation can never provide more than partial explanations. Both deprivation and relative deprivation help to explain participation in social movements, but as sociologist James Jasper (1991) stressed, even a sense of moral outrage can be the basic motivation for joining a social movement. It is also significant to note that participants in social movements, as in the case of other forms of collective behavior, differ in their level of commitment, their interest, and even their understanding of the issues. An overarching theory that satisfactorily explains why people join social movements has yet to be developed.

ON THE SUCCESS AND FAILURE OF SOCIAL MOVEMENTS

L. Obj. 11: State the key ingredients which contribute to the success or failure of social movements.

Why do some social movements succeed, while others wither away? As we have seen, social movements arise in response to pressing needs felt by large numbers of people. A leadership draws attention to the problem by agitating on behalf of "the cause." Some social movements fail to gain broad support, however, and die before they have a chance to mature. Why?

Resource Mobilization

Some sociologists have determined that the critical factor that enables social movements to make it past the first stage of agitation is **resource mobilization.** By this term they mean the mobilization of resources such as time, money, and people's skills. As sociologists John McCarthy and Mayer Zald (1973, 1977) pointed out, even though large numbers of people may be upset over some condition of society, without resource mobilization they are only upset people, perhaps even agitators, but not a social movement.

CDQ 17: Do you think social movements actually solve problems? Why or why not?

In some groups an indigenous leadership arises to mobilize available resources. Other groups, having no capable leadership of their own, turn to outsiders for help. The outsiders, sympathetic to the group's plight or simply "specialists for hire," mobilize resources for the group. In either case, without such mobilization there can be no social movement.

Seldom do social movements actually solve problems, primarily because they find it necessary to appeal to a broad constituency. To tap broad discontent on a large scale, the group must focus on large-scale issues, which are deeply embedded in society. For example, the fact that workers at one particular plant earn low wages is not adequate to recruit the broad support necessary for a social movement. At best, it will result in local agitation. The low wages and unsafe working conditions of millions of workers, however, have a chance of becoming the focal point of a social movement.

Such broad problems, however, do not lend themselves to easy or quick solutions. They require much more than merely tinkering with some small part of society. Just

resource mobilization: a theory that social movements succeed or fail based on their ability to mobilize resources such as time, money, and people's skills

as the problem touches many interrelated components of society, so the solutions require changes in those many parts. In these circumstances the social movement must last long enough to play off one interest group against another. But longevity brings its own danger of failure, mentioned above, of turning inward and concentrating on its own bureaucracy.

Many social movements, however, make valuable contributions to solving social problems, for they highlight areas of society to be changed—if the society has the desire to make the changes and is willing to mobilize the resources necessary to do so.

SUMMARY

1. Collective behavior involves groups of people doing things that are out of the ordinary. Collective behavior is a broad term; it includes lynchings, riots, rumors, panics, urban legends, fads, even fashion. Lynching is a particularly powerful example.

2. Early explanations of collective behavior centered on some form of "madness." Charles Mackay wrote of the "herd mentality," Gustave LeBon of the transformation of the individual by a "collective mind," and Robert Park of social unrest and circular reaction. Herbert Blumer noted that acting crowds are characterized by social unrest, an exciting event, milling, a common object of attention (collective sentiment), and the stimulation of common impulses through social contagion. All of these explanations view the individual as transformed by the crowd.

3. Contemporary explanations emphasize the rationality of the crowd and see collective behavior as directed toward a goal, even though that goal may be cruel and destructive. Ralph Turner and Lewis Killian analyzed how new norms emerge in a crowd. They also identified five kinds of participants in crowds: ego-involved, concerned, insecure, curious spectators, and exploiters. Richard Berk stressed that people in crowds use a minimax strategy, weighing costs and rewards as they decide whether or not to participate in a crowd's activities. A 1933 lynching in Florida illustrates his argument.

4. Urban riots are usually explained as being precipitated by a particular event in a context of general social resentment and deprivation. While many rioters come from deprived backgrounds, others do not; consequently, a rationality approach is also useful in these cases. Panics, rumors, fads, fashion, and urban legends are also examples of different types of collective behavior.

5. Social movements are characterized by unusual behavior involving more people, are more prolonged and more organized, and focus on social change. Social movements exhibit the following six features. They arise during social unrest; express dissatisfaction with current conditions and promise something better; are highly organized; attract committed followers, including a core of "true believers"; attempt to change social conditions; and have the potential of leading to extensive social change. The Nazis

are an example of one of the most powerful social movements in history.

6. Symbolic interactionists use the concept of dehumanization to explain how normal people are turned into killing machines whose conscience allows them to commit inhumane acts. Propaganda is one-sided information manipulated in an attempt to influence others. Seven propaganda techniques are name calling, glittering generality, transfer, testimonials, plain folks, card stacking, and the bandwagon.

7. Social movements can be classified into four types: alterative, redemptive, reformative, and transformative. Their classification depends on whether they are directed to changing the individual or society and on the degree of intended change. Social movements have three levels of membership: an inner core, the committed, and a wider circle. They also have three publics: the sympathetic, the hostile, and the indifferent or unaware. The tactics of a social movement depend on which public is being addressed, as well as on the movement's relationship to the authorities. If authorities are hostile, tactics of violence are more likely to be used.

8. Recent social movements are huge in scale and focus on broad concerns. Termed "new social movements," some even deal with global matters and spill across national borders. Social movements have a life course, typically initial unrest and agitation, mobilization, organization, institutionalization, and decline. Instead of decline, however, a movement may experience resurgence, as in the case of the abortion movement today.

9. Relative deprivation theory explains why revolutions may occur in countries with better conditions and bypass those with worse conditions. Although mass-society theory attributes involvement in social movements to weak social ties, many participants have strong ties to family and community.

10. Resource mobilization theory accounts for why some social movements never get off the ground, while others enjoy great success. Social movements seldom solve social problems. To gain adequate support they must appeal to a broad constituency. Consequently, they must focus on broad social problems, deeply embedded in society, which do not lend themselves to easy solutions.

SUGGESTED READINGS

Brunvand, Jan Harold. *The Vanishing Hitchhiker: American Urban Legends and Their Meanings.* New York: Norton, 1981. This humorous analysis of urban legends helps us better understand how people adapt to social change. If you enjoy this book, you might try its 1984 sequel by the same author and publisher: *The Choking Doberman and Other "New" Urban Legends.*

Gitlin, Tod. *The Sixties: Years of Hope, Days of Rage.* New York: Bantam, 1987. The author, now a sociologist, was a leader in the peace movement that arose during the social unrest of the 1960s. He combines personal experience with a sociological perspective.

Hall, John R. *Gone from the Promised Land: Jonestown in American Cultural History.* New Brunswick, New Jersey: Transaction, 1987. The account of a sect called People's Temple, which came to an alarming end with the mass suicide or murder of nine hundred members in Jonestown, Guyana.

Klee, Ernst, Willi Dressen, and Volker Riess. *"The Good Old Days": The Holocaust as Seen by Its Perpetrators and Bystanders.* Trans. Deborah Burnstone. New York: Free Press, 1991. This chilling account of massacres by the SS is based on the photographs they took of their "work," their letters home, and their scrapbooks.

Koenig, Frederick. *Rumor in the Marketplace: The Social Psychology of Commercial Hearsay.* Dover, Mass.: Auburn House, 1985. The author analyzes rumors about American corporations and discusses how the corporations have fought back. Examples include the rumor covered in this chapter concerning the Procter and Gamble logo, as well as the one about worms in McDonald's hamburgers.

McPhail, Clark. *The Myth of the Madding Crowd.* New York: Aldine de Gruyter, 1991. McPhail provides a thorough overview of the history of research and theorizing about collective behavior, on which much of the materials on collective behavior in this chapter is based.

Morris, Aldon. *The Origins of the Civil Rights Movement: Black Communities Organizing for Change.* New York: Free Press, 1984. This account of the civil rights movement in the United States shows how social discontent underlies social movements.

Speer, Albert. *Inside the Third Reich.* Trans. Richard and Clara Winston. New York: Avon, 1970. Written by one of Hitler's intimates, the author provides a close-up view of Hitler and his times.

Timothy, Garton Ash. *The Polish Revolution: Solidarity.* New York: Charles Scribner's Sons, 1983. Timothy recounts the rise of Solidarity, the worker-based political party that successfully challenged the Communist government.

Turner, Ralph H., and Lewis M. Killian. *Collective Behavior.* 3rd ed. Englewood Cliffs, N.J.: Prentice Hall, 1987. This overview of collective behavior and social movements contains fascinating materials from real-life cases.

Yuan, Gao. *Born Red: A Chronicle of the Cultural Revolution.* Stanford, Calif.: Stanford University Press, 1987. A first-person account chronicles the cultural revolution in China during the late 1960s.

CHAPTER 22

Romare Bearden, Calypso's Sacred Grove, *1977*

Social Change, Technology, and the Environment

SOCIAL CHANGE: A REVIEW
The Four Social Revolutions ■ From *Gemeinschaft* to *Gesellschaft* ■ The Transformation of Society through Capitalism ■ Effects of Industrialization on the Third World ■ Globalization and Dependency ■ Shifts in International Stratification ■ Changes in the Social Institutions of the United States

THEORIES OF SOCIAL CHANGE
Evolutionary Theories ■ Cyclical Theories ■ Conflict Theory ■ Modernization

SOCIAL CHANGE AND TECHNOLOGY
Ogburn's Processes of Cultural Innovation ■ Types of Technology ■ How Technology Transforms Society ■ An Extended Example: Effects of the Automobile ■ An Extended Example: Effects of the Computer ■ Concerns about Computers ■ Telecommunications and Global Social Change ■ *Perspectives:* **Lost Tribes, Lost Knowledge**

SOCIAL CHANGE AND THE NATURAL ENVIRONMENT
Environmental Degradation in the Past ■ The Environmental Problem Today ■ Environmental Problems in the Second World ■ Environmental Problems in the Third World ■ The Environmental Movement ■ *Thinking Critically about Social Controversy:* **Ecosabotage** ■ Environmental Sociology ■ The Goal of Harmony between Technology and the Environment

SUMMARY

SUGGESTED READINGS

The morning of January 28, 1986, dawned clear but near freezing, strange weather for subtropical Florida. At the Kennedy Space Center, launch pad 39B was lined with three inches of ice. Icicles six to twelve inches long hung like stalactites from the pad's service structure.

Shortly after 8 A.M., the crew took the elevator to the white room, where they entered the crew module. By 8:36 A.M., the seven members of the crew were strapped in their seats. They were understandably disappointed when liftoff, scheduled for 9:38 A.M., was delayed because of the ice.

After a strong public relations campaign, public interest in the flight ran high. Attention focused on Christa McAuliffe, a thirty-seven-year-old high school teacher from Concord, New Hampshire, the first private citizen to fly aboard a space shuttle. Across the nation, schoolchildren watched with great anticipation, for Mrs. McAuliffe, selected from thousands of applicants, was to give two televised lessons during the flight. The first was to describe life aboard a spacecraft in orbit, the second to discuss the prospects of using space's microgravity to manufacture new products.

From the internal combustion engine to the telephone and the computer, technology lies at the center of our lives. The Challenger *represents both the success and failure of technology: the general success of space exploration, but the stunning failure of this particular endeavor.*

At the viewing site, thousands of spectators had joined the families and friends of the crew eagerly awaiting the launch. They were delighted to see *Challenger's* two solid-fuel boosters ignite and broke into cheers as the *Challenger,* amidst billows of white smoke, lifted into the air. This product of technical innovation thundered majestically into space.

The time was 11:38 A.M. Seventy-three seconds later, the *Challenger,* racing skyward at 2,900 feet per second, had reached an altitude of fifty thousand feet and was seven miles from the launch site. Suddenly, a brilliant glow appeared on one side of the external tank. In seconds, the glow blossomed into a gigantic fireball. Screams of horror arose from the crowd as the *Challenger,* now nineteen miles away, exploded, and bits of debris began to descend from the sky.

In classrooms across the country, children burst into tears. Adult Americans stared at their televisions in stunned disbelief. (Based on Broad 1986; Lewis 1988; Magnuson 1986; Malone 1988; Nelson 1988; Sanders 1988.)

Although technology seldom fails as dramatically as in the case of the *Challenger* disaster, it is only because of thousands of years of technological change that humans have been able to begin fulfilling the millennia-old dream of space travel. This chapter will examine the effects of technology on society by focusing on social change.

SOCIAL CHANGE: A REVIEW

Social change, the alteration of culture and society over time, is such a vital part of social life that it has been a theme throughout this book. Let's begin this theme by first reviewing the discussions on social change in preceding chapters.

The Four Social Revolutions

The rapid social change that the world is currently experiencing is not a random event but the end result of fundamental forces unleashed upon the world millennia ago. Chapters 6 and 14 described how major inventions and developments stimulated evolutionary changes in human societies themselves (Bell 1973; Boulding 1976; Lee 1979;

CDQ 1: Have you had specific times when you found yourself hoping that technology "really works?" For example, when you are boarding an airplane or entering a hospital for surgery?

CDQ 2: Do you have a better grasp of how social change occurs in society as a result of taking this course?

Speaker Sug. #1: A colleague whose research has involved social change in various types of societies.

Essay #1

L. Obj. 1: Describe the four major social revolutions which have occurred.

Lipset 1979; Sahlins 1972; Zuboff 1991). They reviewed Gerhard and Jean Lenski's (1987) analysis of four social revolutions that transformed the face of humanity. These chapters traced the historical development of technological change: the cultivation of plants and the taming of animals that transformed human societies from simple hunting and gathering bands to pastoral and horticultural societies; the invention of the plow that led to agricultural societies; and later the Industrial Revolution that created industrialized societies. Finally, Chapter 14 examined how the computer chip is now transforming society once again, into a social form called postindustrial society, which is likely to transform almost every aspect of our lives.

From *Gemeinschaft* to *Gesellschaft*

These social revolutions ushered in changes so extensive that they transformed even fundamental social relationships—from social inequality and gender relations to the size and scope of government. Chapters 4 and 6 examined how industrialization transformed *Gemeinschaft* society—in which people know one another and daily life centers on intimate and personal relationships—to *Gesellschaft* society—in which people are immersed in fleeting, impersonal relationships (Tönnies 1887, 1988).

The Transformation of Society through Capitalism

Karl Marx.   As noted in Chapters 1 and 7, Karl Marx (1844, 1964; Marx and Engels 1848, 1967) identified capitalism as the basic reason behind the change in traditional societies. He analyzed how the breakup of feudal society created a surplus of labor as masses of people who were thrown off the land moved to the cities. Marx focused his analysis on the means of production (factories, machinery, tools): Those who owned them dictated the conditions under which workers could work—and live (Chambliss 1964; Michalowski 1985).

Max Weber.   But why did capitalism come into being? As noted in Chapters 1 and 7, Max Weber (1904–1905, 1958) saw religion as the core reason for this development. The Reformation, he said, removed from Protestants the assurance that they were saved simply by virtue of church membership. Their resulting agonizing over heaven and hell led them to conclude that God would show visible favor to the elect. This belief encouraged Protestants to work hard and be thrifty. The unexpected consequence of the Reformation, then, was an economic surplus, which in turn stimulated industrialization.

Effects of Industrialization on the Third World

Regardless of their causes, capitalism and industrialization have transformed humanity. As explained in Chapter 19, the technological changes that resulted have led to new understandings of disease and the export of Western medicine to Third World nations. This development has brought the Third World to the second stage of the demographic transition: reduced death rates but continuing high birthrates. The Third World's rapidly increasing population has put pressure on its resources, led to widespread hunger and starvation, and made traditional land inheritance patterns difficult to maintain. Consequently, as discussed in Chapter 20, masses of peasants around the world are fleeing to urban areas in the hope of finding a better way of life. With urbanization now a worldwide phenomenon, almost half of the world's population live in urban areas—most in squalor.

Globalization and Dependency

As noted in Chapter 9, Immanuel Wallerstein (1974, 1979, 1984) observed that a *world system* had already begun to emerge during the sixteenth century. During the eighteenth and nineteenth centuries, capitalism and industrialization extended the economic

social change: the alteration of culture and societies over time

and political ties among the world's nations and speeded up the process by which these ties develop. Today, these ties are global, yielding a form of international stratification in which the industrialized countries of the First World dominate all the others. According to dependency theory, because the Third World countries have become dependent on the First World, they are unable to develop their own resources (Anderson 1974; Cardoso 1972; Furtado 1984).

Shifts in International Stratification

Chapter 14 described how alignments between nations must shift to accommodate changing realities, specifically, the way in which Japan's growing economic dominance is forcing adjustments in international stratification. The chapter focused especially on how this challenge to the economic preeminence of the United States is transforming the American workplace.

The Coming of a New World Order.   As noted in Chapter 15, an attempt is now under way to create a new world order. The world's industrial giants—the United States, Canada, Great Britain, France, Germany, Italy, and Japan, collectively known as G-7—foresee that the new order will build on the current system of international stratification. Apparently, these nations are intent on deciding how they will share the world's markets, and on regulating global economic and industrial policy. They intend to guarantee their own global dominance, including continued access to cheap raw materials from the Second and Third Worlds. These industrial giants, however, are also feeling pressure to promote economic growth in the Third World (Cleveland 1990). The breakup of the Soviet Union is a central consideration in the emerging order, and events there will help determine the shape of future alliances.

Changes in the Social Institutions of the United States

Although even preliterate societies gradually alter their way of life, the change that occurs is usually so gradual that even a hundred-year interval produces little noticeable difference. In contrast, industrialized societies change so fast that life today bears few similarities to life one hundred years ago. Chapters 14–19 discussed the six major social institutions of the United States and examined how social change had transformed their character. Chapters 1 and 16 considered why the American family has grown more fragile, Chapter 19 why modern medicine and hospitals have changed so radically, and Chapter 18 why new religions arise and old ones splinter. Chapters 11, 12, and 13 also examined fundamental changes in gender relations, in racial and ethnic relations, and in attitudes toward the elderly.

CDQ 3: Does social change usually produce progress in societies?

Essay #2

L. Obj. 2: Explain evolutionary and cyclical theories of social change, and note why these theories generally are not considered to be useful today.

THEORIES OF SOCIAL CHANGE

Social theorists have proposed various explanations of why societies change. Let's first consider two major types of theories—evolutionary and cyclical—and then look at conflict theory and modernization.

Evolutionary Theories

Unilinear Evolution.   *Unilinear* evolutionary theories assume that all societies follow the same path, evolving from the simple to the complex through uniform sequences (Barnes 1935). Lewis Henry Morgan (1877), for example, proposed that societies go through three stages: savagery, barbarism, and civilization. In his eyes English society served as the epitome of civilization, which all others were destined to follow. Sociolo-

The dominating assumption during the 1800s and in the earlier part of this century was that European and European-derived cultures represented the pinnacle of human development. Consequently, other groups represented a lesser stage of development. When they evolved, they, too, would become like the Europeans. Such an assumption underlies this 1828 portrait of Hoowaunneka, a Native American of the Winnebago tribe. Note that this assumption went so far that the painter, C. B. King, even (inadvertently) gave Hoowaunneka European features.

gists Herbert Spencer (1884) and Robert MacIver (1937) also held evolutionary views of social change. Since the basic assumption that all preliterate groups have the same form of social organization has been found to be untrue, views of unilinear evolution have been discredited. In addition, seeing one's own society as the top of the evolutionary ladder is now considered unacceptably ethnocentric.

Multilinear Evolution. *Multilinear* views of evolution have now replaced unilinear theories. The assumption remains that societies evolve from smaller to larger, more complex forms as they adapt to their environments. Instead of assuming that all societies follow the same invariant path, however, multilinear theories presuppose that different routes can lead to a similar stage of development. Thus, societies need not pass through the same sequence of stages to become industrialized (Sahlins and Service 1960; Lenski and Lenski 1987).

Central to both unilinear and multilinear theories is the idea of *progress*, that societies evolve toward a higher state. Greater appreciation of the rich diversity of traditional cultures, however, has brought this idea under attack. Now that Western culture is in crisis (continued poverty, racism, discrimination, war, alienation, crime) and no longer regarded as holding all the answers to human happiness, the assumption of progress has been cast aside and evolutionary theories have been rejected (Eder 1990; Smart 1990).

Cyclical Theories

Cyclical theories attempt to account for the rise of great civilizations, not a particular society. Why, for example, did Egyptian, Greek, and Roman civilizations rise to a peak of dominance and then disappear? Cyclical theories assume that civilizations are like organisms: They are born, see an exuberant youth, come to maturity, decline as they reach old age, and finally die (Hughes 1962).

K.P.: Pitirim Sorokin

K.P.: Oswald Spengler

Historian Arnold Toynbee (1946), who undertook a survey of world civilizations, proposed what he called the life course of civilizations. His model is very detailed (for example, it has three stages of disintegration preceding the breakup of a civilization). At the crux of Toynbee's theory is the notion that while societies grow as they successfully meet challenges, each success sets up oppositional forces that must again be overcome. At its peak, when a civilization has become an empire, the ruling elite (which Toynbee calls the "leading minority") loses its capacity to keep the masses in line "by charm rather than by force." The fabric of society is then ripped apart. Although force may hold the empire together for hundreds of years, the civilization is doomed.

Pitirim Sorokin (1937–1941, 1941), a Russian sociologist, took a somewhat different approach. He proposed that the distinguishing mark of a civilization is how it defines the nature of reality. As Sorokin saw it, there are two paths to reality (Cuzzort and King 1980). The first, which he called *ideational culture,* stresses faith and spirituality. In the second, *sensate culture,* reality is presumed to be located in "things" that are apparent to the mind. Sensate culture, such as that of the Western world today, is characterized by logic, sensory gratification, and relativistic morals. Societies alternate between these two forms of knowing.

In a book that provoked widespread controversy, *The Decline of the West* (1926–1928), Oswald Spengler, a German teacher and social critic, proposed that Western civilization was on the wane. Although critics have rejected Spengler's arguments, stressing that the West succeeded in overcoming the crises provoked by Hitler and Mussolini that so disturbed him, civilizations do not necessarily end in a sudden and total collapse. As Toynbee noted, the decline can last for hundreds of years. Some analysts think that the crisis in Western civilization mentioned above (poverty, crime, etc.) may indicate that Spengler was right.

Conflict Theory

L. Obj. 3: State the major assumptions of conflict and modernization theories regarding social change.

K.P.: Karl Marx

As noted earlier (see also pp. 10–11, 23, 228–229), Marx proposed a conflict view of social change (1844, 1964; Marx and Engels 1848, 1967). Like Toynbee, Marx took a sweeping view of human history. He viewed social change as a *dialectical process,* in which a *thesis* (the status quo) contains within it its own *antithesis,* or opposition. The resulting struggle between the thesis and its antithesis leads to a new state, or *synthesis.* This new social order in turn becomes a thesis that will be challenged by its own antithesis, and so on.

In short, Marx saw the history of a society as a series of confrontations in which each ruling group sows the seeds of its own destruction. Capitalism, for example, sets workers and capitalists on a collision course. Capitalism is the thesis, the misery of workers the antithesis, and a classless state the synthesis. The dialectical process will not stop until workers establish this classless state.

Modernization

K.P.: Max Weber

TR#50: A Typology of Traditional and Modern Societies

Chapters 6 and 14 (pp. 141–149, 372–375) discussed *modernization,* the change from agricultural to industrial societies. The major theoretical problem examined was the one with which both Marx and Weber struggled: how rigid, traditional societies broke through the restraints of their centuries-old, established way of life. Table 22.1 reviews the sweeping changes ushered in by modernization, already described in earlier chapters. This table is an ideal type, in Weber's sense of the term, for no society comprises all the traits listed to the maximum degree. For example, as noted in Chapter 14, although most Americans now work in the tertiary sector of the economy, many millions still work in the primary and secondary sectors. Accordingly, all characteristics shown in Table 22.1 should be interpreted as "more" or "less," rather than "either or."

This table shows how extensively industrialization has changed human life. Compared with traditional societies, modern societies are larger, more urbanized, and

TABLE 22.1   A Typology of Traditional and Modern Societies

Characteristics	Traditional Societies	Modern Societies
General Characteristics		
Social Change	Very slow	Rapid
Size of Group	Small	Large
Religious Orientation	More	Less
Formal Education	No	Yes
Place of Residence	Rural	Urban
Demographic Transition	First Stage	Third Stage
Family Size	Larger	Smaller
Infant Mortality	High	Low
Life Expectancy	Low	High
Health Care	Home	Hospital
Temporal Orientation	Past	Future
Material Relations		
Industrialized	No	Yes
Technology	Simple	Complex
Division of Labor	Simple	Complex
Economic Sector	Primary	Tertiary
Income	Low	High
Material Possessions	Few	Many
Social Relationships		
Basic Organization	*Gemeinschaft*	*Gesellschaft*
Families	Extended	Nuclear
Respect for Elders	More	Less
Social Stratification	Rigid	More Open
Statuses	More Ascribed	More Achieved
Gender Equality	Less	More
Norms		
View of Reality, Life, and Morals	Absolute	Relativistic
Social Control	Informal	Formal
Tolerance of Differences	Less	More

subject to faster change. They stress formal education and the future and are less religiously oriented. In the third stage of the demographic transition, they have smaller families, lower rates of infant mortality, and higher life expectancy. Serious illnesses are treated in hospitals rather than at home. Material relations in modern societies are based on industrialization, a highly developed technology, and a complex division of labor. People in modern societies also have higher incomes and more material possessions. In traditional societies—based on extended families, greater respect for elders, rigid social stratification, more ascribed statuses, and greater inequality between the sexes—social relationships are based on *Gemeinschaft*. Traditional societies tend to view life and morals in absolute terms, tolerate few differences, and depend on more informal social control.

As indicated in other chapters, the transition to the postindustrial era seems to be bringing with it a new type of society, one that rejects much of what modern society takes for granted. Perhaps, then, Table 22.1 should have a last column headed "Postmodern Societies." The contours of postmodern society, however, if, indeed, one is emerging, are not yet clear enough to define (Smart 1990; Eder 1990).

The question of how societies break through their traditional ways and modernize has been at the center of much sociological theory. Shown here is an example of the transition some societies are now caught up in. Although this woman in New Delhi, India, is working at a company that manufactures postindustrial equipment, her own society has not yet entered the industrial era. The contrast between her work and traditional dress—indicating centuries-old social relationships—is startling.

CDQ 4: How do you think technology will change society in the future?

Project 1

Essay #3

CDQ 5: Can you give examples of recent inventions, discoveries, and diffusion in the United States?

L. Obj. 4: Identify and define Ogburn's three processes of social change, and explain what is meant by "cultural lag."

K.P.: William Ogburn

technology: often defined as the applications of science, but can be conceptualized as tools, items used to accomplish tasks

SOCIAL CHANGE AND TECHNOLOGY

As discussed in Chapter 6, technology is a driving force in social change. A simple and useful definition of **technology** is *tools*, items used to accomplish tasks. In this sense, technology refers both to a club used to kill animals and to telephones and spacecraft. The explosion of the *Challenger*, described in the opening vignette, is a stunning example both of the failure of technology and of how far technology has advanced. A design flaw, troublesome in previous flights, proved fatal in this one. A simple gasket, an O-ring found in cars and many household appliances, did not fit properly. During the thirty-seven days that the *Challenger* stood on the launch pad, seven inches of rain had fallen. Apparently some rain had bypassed the ill-fitting O-ring, lodged in a joint, and frozen during the inclement weather. Inadequate sealing caused the combustion gases to leak—and ignite.

At the root of the design failure lay human error, complicated by political pressure. NASA needed a striking success to show Congress what it was getting for the huge sums of money pumped into the nation's space program. A highly publicized success by *Challenger* would pave the way for approval of the billions of dollars it would take to build a base on the moon and to send astronauts to Mars. Facing this pressure, NASA officials made the fateful decision to overlook certain flaws.

In spite of glaring failures like the *Challenger*, modern technology is so advanced that experts are able to build space platforms and send people to the moon. We can pick up a telephone at home and call any city in the world. In just seconds, we can fax copies of documents overseas. While the devices that allow such feats are fascinating, technology is much more than the apparatus. Technology changes society. Without automobiles, telephones, televisions, printing presses, and so on, our entire way of life would be strikingly different. Let's first look at how technology spreads, then at how technology affects the way people live, and, finally, at its impact on the natural environment.

Ogburn's Processes of Cultural Innovation

Sociologist William Ogburn (1922, 1938, 1961, 1964) identified three processes of social change. Technology, he said, can lead to social change through invention, discovery, and diffusion.

Invention.   Ogburn defined **invention** as the combination of existing elements and materials to form new ones. While we think of inventions as being only material, such as computers, there are also social inventions, such as capitalism and the corporation, examined in Chapter 14.

Inventions, whether material or social, can have far-reaching consequences for a society. Later on, this chapter will explore ways in which the automobile and the computer have transformed society, affecting not just some small part of social life but having ramifications for almost everything we do.

Discovery.   **Discovery,** Ogburn's second process of change, is a new way of seeing reality. The reality is already present, but is now seen for the first time. Space travel and telecommunications have brought exciting new discoveries. For example, in 1992 the Cosmic Background Explorer (COBE), a satellite located 560 miles above the earth, provided data for the discovery of "ripples" in space. These ripples, 50 billion trillion miles across, are supposedly left over from density fluctuations in the afterglow of radiation from the birth of the cosmos. They are, presumably, the seeds that gave rise to the stars and planets three-hundred-thousand years after the "Big Bang" (Begley and Glick 1992; Wilford 1992).

Some discoveries, such as this one, may have little or no impact on a society. The discovery will funnel grants to certain scientists, of course, but that result represents only personal, not social change. Other discoveries, however, can produce such large-scale effects that they alter the course of history. Columbus's "discovery" of North America is an example; and it also illustrates another principle. A discovery brings extensive change only when it comes at the right time. Other groups, such as the Vikings, had already "discovered" America in the sense of learning that a new land existed (the land, of course, was no discovery to the Native Americans already living in it). Viking settlements disappeared into history, however, and Norse culture was untouched by the discovery.

invention: the combination of existing elements and materials to form new ones; identified by William Ogburn as the first of three processes of social change

discovery: a new way of seeing reality; identified by William Ogburn as the second of three processes of social change

As Ogburn analyzed social change, invention and discovery underlie diffusion, which creates cultural lag. Shown here is an individual using virtual reality, an invention based on the microchip that makes the world inside the mask seem as real as the ordinary world outside it. The viewer's angle of vision changes in response to head movements. The impact of this particular form of post-industrial technology on human relationships is not yet known.

Diffusion. **Diffusion,** said Ogburn, is the spread of an invention or discovery from one area to another. The usual reasons for diffusion are travel, trade, and conquest. As people migrate or visit an area, trade with one another, or one group conquers another, change occurs both in material objects and in human thought. Each can extensively affect social life. On the material level, steel implements may replace stone items, or one group may learn the secrets of silkworm farming. As a consequence, the economy may be transformed. On the intellectual level, one idea may replace another. As it diffused among groups, it changed people's way of thinking about their relationship to government and to one another. Eventually, it also changed their political structure, for no longer was the monarch an unquestioned source of power and authority. Today, the diffusion of telecommunications is most likely to be the source of social change (cf. Ausubel 1991; Bell 1989), a topic we shall examine later in this chapter.

Cultural Lag. Ogburn coined the term **cultural lag** to describe the situation in which some elements of a culture adapt to an invention or discovery more rapidly than others. Technology, he suggested, usually changes first, followed by culture. People often resist changes, adapting only slowly to new technology. The nine-month school year is an example. In the nineteenth century, the school year matched the technology of the time, which required that children work with their parents at the critical times of planting and harvesting. Current technology has eliminated the need for the school year to be so short, but the cultural form has lagged severely behind technology.

Types of Technology

There are three types of technology. The first is **primitive technology,** natural items that people have adapted for their use. Primitive technology includes spears, clubs, animal skins, and swords. Both hunting and gathering societies and pastoral and horticultural societies are based on primitive technology. Most technology of agricultural societies is also primitive, for it centers on harnessing animals to do work. The second type, **industrial technology,** corresponds roughly to industrial society. Industrial technology marks a giant step forward, for it uses machines powered by fuels instead of natural forces such as winds and rivers. The third type, **postindustrial technology,** centers on information, transportation, and communication. At the core of postindustrial technology is the microchip.

A fourth type, which we might call the **new technology,** has yet to make its appearance on the human scene. When it does, it will be such a leap forward that we will not want to classify it as part of postindustrial technology. For example, should the transporters of *Star Trek* ever become reality, they would be part of the "new technology."

How Technology Transforms Society

When a technology is introduced into a society, it forces other parts of society to give way. In fact, *technology can shape an entire society,* changing its existing technology, social organization, ideology, values, and social relationships. Let's look at these five ways that technology changes society.

Transformation of Existing Technologies. The first impact is felt by the technology that is being displaced. Currently, for example, the rotary dial telephone is a living dinosaur. Some of us still use one, but these machines are clearly doomed to extinction in the wake of newer, more efficient touchtone telephones, and, eventually, devices into which we will simply speak the number we desire. Similarly, IBM electric typewriters, "state of the art" equipment just a few years ago, have been rendered practically useless by the desktop computer.

CDQ 6: Do you think cultural lag is a major problem in the United States? Why or why not?

CDQ 7: Using television as an example, can you explain how technology has had a great impact on social life?

Project 2

L. Obj. 5: Using the automobile or the computer as an example, explain how technology transforms society.

diffusion: the spread of invention or discovery from one area to another; identified by William Ogburn as the final of three processes of social change

cultural lag: Ogburn's term for human behavior lagging behind technological innovations

primitive technology: the adaptation of natural items for human use

industrial technology: technology centered on machines powered by fuels instead of natural forces such as wind and rivers

postindustrial technology: technology centering on information, transportation, and communication

new technology: technology constituting such a leap forward that it cannot be classified as part of current technology

Changes in Social Organization.   Technology also changes social organization. As discussed in Chapter 6, for example, machine technology gave birth to the factory. Prior to machine technology, most workers labored at home, but the advent of power-driven machinery made it more efficient for people to gather in one place to do their work. Then it was discovered that workers could produce more items if they did specialized tasks. Instead of each worker making an entire item, as had been the practice, each individual worked on only part of an item. One worker would do so much hammering on a single part, or turn so many bolts, and then someone else would take the item and do some other repetitive task before a third person took over, and so on. Henry Ford then built on this improvement by developing the assembly line: Instead of workers moving to the parts, a machine moved the parts to the workers. In addition, the parts were made interchangeable and easy to attach (Womack et al. 1990).

Changes in Ideology.   Technology also spurs ideology. Karl Marx saw the change-over to the factory system as a source of **alienation.** He noted that workers who were assigned repetitive tasks on just a small part of a product no longer felt connected to the finished product and could therefore no longer take pride in it. In Marx's terms, they became alienated from the product of their labor. Such alienation, he added, bred dissatisfaction and unrest.

The factory system, said Marx, was set up so that the owners of the factories could exploit workers. Before factories came on the scene, workers owned their tools and were essentially independent. If workers did not like their work situation, they could pack up their hammers, saws, and chisels and leave. Because their work and tools were needed, others would hire them to build a wagon, make a harness, and so on. In the factory, however, because the capitalists owned the tools and machinery, they were able to dictate terms to the workers. The workers had to knuckle under, for even if they left the tools stayed, and other workers simply took their place. Because capitalists take advantage of their power to extract every ounce of sweat and blood they can, claimed Marx, only a workers' revolution will change this exploitation. When the workers realize the common basis of their exploitation and the immense power that comes from being united, they will forcibly take over the means of production and establish a workers' state.

In short, the new technology that led both to the factory and the accompanying exploitation of workers for profits stimulated new ideologies. On the one hand, some social analysts fervently defended the principle of maximizing profits. As ardent capitalists, they developed an ideology to support the new social arrangements. On the other hand, followers of Marx believed his message and built theories of socialism on it. As noted in Chapter 1, however, the dictatorships of the Communist nations are a gross perversion of Marx's social analysis. Finally, just as changes in technology stimulated the development of communism, as discussed in the section on telecommunications below, changes in technology are also bringing about its end.

Transformation of Values.   Technology also changes people's values. If technology is limited to clubbing animals, then strength and cunning are valued. So are animal skins. No doubt some primitive man and woman walked with heads held high as they wore the skins of some especially unusual or dangerous animal—while their neighbors looked on in envy as they trudged along wearing only the same old sheepskins. Today's technology produces an abundance of synthetic fabrics for clothing, which, together with a changing awareness of other species, leads to quite different values (Eder 1990; Bryant 1993). In contrast to this primitive couple, Americans today brag about hot tubs and jacuzzis and make certain that their jeans have the right labels prominently displayed. In short, while jealousy, envy, and pride may be basic to human nature, the particular emphasis on materialism depends on the state of technology.

alienation: Marx's term for workers' lack of connection to the product of their labor caused by their being assigned repetitive tasks on a small part of a product

Transformation of Social Relationships.   Technology changes social relationships. As men were drawn out of their homes to work in factories, family relationships changed. No longer present in the home on a daily basis, the husband-father became isolated from many of the day-to-day affairs of the family. One consequence of husbands becoming strangers to their wives and children was a higher divorce rate, which, as discussed in Chapter 1, is also attributable to many other changes in society. As current technology draws more and more women from the home to offices and factories, the consequences will be similar—greater isolation from husband and children, and one more impetus toward a higher divorce rate.

An Extended Example: Effects of the Automobile

If we try to pick the single item that has had the greatest impact on social life in this century, among the many candidates the automobile and the microchip stand out, though it is still early to judge the full effects of the latter technology. Let us first look at some of the ways in which the automobile changed American society.

Displacement of Existing Technology.   The automobile gradually pushed aside the old technology, a replacement that began in earnest when Henry Ford began to mass-produce the Model T in 1908. People immediately found automobiles attractive (Flink 1988). They considered them cleaner, safer, more reliable, and more economical than horses. Cars also offered the appealing prospect of lower taxes, for no longer would the public have to pay to clean up the tons of horse manure that accumulated on the city streets each day. Humorous as it sounds now, it was even thought that automobiles would eliminate the cities' parking problems, for an automobile took up only half as much space as a horse and buggy.

The automobile also replaced a second technology. During the early part of this century, the United States had developed a vast system of urban transit. Electric streetcar lines radiated outward from the center of our cities. As the automobile became affordable and more dependable, Americans demonstrated a clear preference for the greater convenience of private transportation. Instead of walking to a streetcar and then having to wait in the cold and rain, people were able to travel directly from home on their own schedule.

Speaker Sug. #2: An expert from the computer science department or from a local high tech industry.

CDQ 8: Do you think computers ultimately will make our lives easier or more complicated? Why?

This 1879 engraving of Third Avenue in New York City shows the city prior to the automobile. Other than walking and the steam engine, shown here powering an elevated train, horses were the primary means of transportation. Note that horses were even used to pull streetcars. The automobile transformed not only transportation, but, as analyzed in the text, even the shape of cities and basic social relationships.

Effects on Cities.   The decline in the use of streetcars actually changed the shape of American cities. Before the automobile, American cities were web-shaped, for residences and businesses were located along the streetcar lines. Freed from having to live so close to the tracks, people filled in the areas between the "webs."

The automobile also stimulated America's mass suburbanization. Already in the 1920s, residents began to leave the city, for they found that they could commute to work in the city from outlying areas where they benefited from more room and fewer taxes (Preston 1979). Their departure significantly reduced the cities' tax base, thus contributing, as discussed in Chapter 20, to many of the problems that American cities experience today.

Effects on Farm Life and Villages.   The automobile also had a fundamental impact on farmers. Prior to the 1920s, most farmers were isolated from the city. Because using horses for a trip to town was slow and cumbersome, they made such trips infrequently. By the 1920s, however, the popularity and low price of the Model T made the "Saturday trip to town" a standard event. There, farmers would market products, shop, and visit with friends. As a consequence, many aspects of farm life were altered; for example, mail order catalogs stopped being the primary source of shopping, and access to better medical care and education improved (Flink 1988).

The automobile also enabled farmers to travel to bigger towns, where they found an even greater variety of goods. Farmers then began to use the nearby villages only for immediate needs; and these flourishing centers of social and commercial life dried up as businesses followed the farmers to the regional shopping areas.

Changes in Architecture.   The automobile's effects on commercial architecture are clear—from the huge parking lots that decorate malls like necklaces to the drive-up windows of banks, restaurants, photo developers, and so forth. But the automobile also fundamentally altered the architecture of American homes (Flink 1988). Before the advent of the car, each home had a stable in the back where the family kept its buggy and horses. The stable was the logical place to shelter the family's first car, and it required no change in architecture. The change occurred in three steps. First, new homes were built with a detached garage located like the stable, at the back of the home. Second, as the automobile became a more essential part of the American family, the garage was incorporated into the home by moving it from the back to the front of the house, and connecting it by a breezeway. In the final step the breezeway was removed, and the garage integrated into the home so that Americans could enter their automobiles without even going outside.

Changed Courtship Customs and Sexual Norms.   By the 1920s, the automobile was becoming essential for dating, thereby removing children from the watchful eye of worried parents and undermining parental authority. The police even began to receive complaints about "night riders" who parked their cars along country lanes, "doused their lights, and indulged in orgies" (Brilliant 1964). Automobiles became so popular for courtship that by the 1960s about 40 percent of marriage proposals took place in them (Flink 1988).

In 1925 Jewett introduced cars with a foldout bed, as did Nash in 1937. The Nash version became known as "the young man's model" (Flink 1988). Since the 1970s, mobile lovemaking has declined, partly because urban sprawl (itself due to the automobile) left fewer safe trysting spots, and partly because changed sexual norms made beds more accessible.

Effects on Women's Roles.   The automobile may also lie at the heart of the changed role of women in American society. To see how, we first need to see what a woman's life was like before the automobile. Historian James Flink (1988) described it this way.

Until the automobile revolution, in upper-middle-class households groceries were either ordered by phone and delivered to the door or picked up by domestic servants or the husband on his way home from work. Iceboxes provided only very limited space for the storage of perishable foods, so shopping at markets within walking distance of the home was a daily chore. The garden provided vegetables and fruits in season, which were home-canned for winter consumption. Bread, cakes, cookies, and pies were home-baked. Wardrobes contained many home-sewn garments. Mother supervised the household help and worked alongside them preparing meals, washing and ironing, and house cleaning. In her spare time she mended clothes, did decorative needlework, puttered in her flower garden, and pampered a brood of children. Generally, she made few family decisions and few forays alone outside the yard. She had little knowledge of family finances and the family budget. The role of the lower-middle-class housewife differed primarily in that far less of the household work was done by hired help, so that she was less a manager of other people's work, more herself a maid-of-all-work around the house.

Because automobiles required skill rather than strength, women were able to drive as well as men. This new mobility freed women physically from the narrow confines of the home. As Flink (1988) observed, the automobile changed women "from producers of food and clothing into consumers of national-brand canned goods, prepared foods, and ready-made clothes. The automobile permitted shopping at self-serve supermarkets outside the neighborhood and in combination with the electric refrigerator made buying food a weekly rather than a daily activity." When women began to do the shopping, they gained greater control over the family budget and as their horizons extended beyond the confines of the home, they also gained different views of life.

In short, the automobile changed women's roles at home, including their relationship with their husbands, altered their attitudes, transformed their opportunities, and stimulated them to participate in areas of social life not connected with the home.

In Sum. With changes this extensive, it would not be inaccurate to say that the automobile also shifted basic values and changed the way we look at life. No longer isolated, women, teenagers, and farmers began to see the world differently. So did husbands and wives, whose marital relationship had also been altered. The automobile even transformed views of courtship, sexuality, and gender relations.

No one attributes such fundamental changes solely to the automobile, of course, for many other technological changes, as well as historical events, occurred during this same period, each of which has made its own contributions to social change. Even this brief overview of the social effects of the automobile, however, illustrates that technology is not merely an isolated tool but exerts a profound influence on social life.

Let us now consider the computer, that technological marvel that, in its turn, is transforming society.

An Extended Example: Effects of the Computer

The ominous wail seemed too close for comfort. Sally looked in her rearview mirror and realized that the flashing red lights and the screaming siren might be for her. She felt confused. "I'm just on my way to Soc class," she thought. "I'm not speeding or anything." After she pulled over, an angry voice over a loudspeaker ordered her out of the car.

As she got out, someone barked the command, "Back up with your hands in the air!" Bewildered, Sally stood frozen for a moment. "Put 'em up now! Right now!" She did as she was told.

The officer crouched behind his open car door, his gun drawn. When Sally reached the car—still backing up—the officer grabbed her, threw her to the ground, and handcuffed her behind her back. She heard words she would never forget, "You are under arrest for murder. You have the right to remain silent. Anything you say can and will be used against you in a court of law. You have the right to an attorney. If you cannot afford one, one will be provided for you."

Traces of alarm still flicker across Sally's face when she recalls her arrest. She had never even been issued a traffic ticket, much less been arrested for anything. The nightmare that Sally experienced happened because of a "computer error." With the inversion of two numbers, her car's license number had been entered instead of that of a woman wanted for a brutal killing earlier that day.

The police later apologized. "These things happen," they said, "but not very often. We're sorry, but I'm sure you understand."

None of us is untouched by the computer, but it is unlikely that many of us have felt its power as directly and dramatically as Sally did. For most of us, the computer's control lies quietly behind the scenes. Although the computer has intruded into our daily lives, most of us never think about it. Our grades are computerized, and probably our paycheck as well. When we buy groceries, a computer scans our purchases and presents a printout of the name, price, and quantity of each item. Essentially, the computer's novelty has given way to everyday routine; it is simply another tool.

Many people rejoice over the computer's capacity to improve their quality of life. They are pleased with the quality control of manufactured goods and the ease with which they can keep detailed records. Computers have also reduced the drudgery of many jobs. A typist can now type just one letter and let the computer print and address it to ten individuals—or one thousand or ten thousand. Architects use software programs that show buildings in three dimensions. Using a technology called "virtual reality," people can view their dream house from any angle and even "enter" the building and open and close cabinet doors (Carroll 1992; Yamada 1992).

Some individuals, however, worry about errors that can creep into computerized records, aware that something like Sally's misfortune may happen to them. Others fear that confidentiality of computer data will be abused, in the way that Orwell's Big Brother used information to achieve total control. Let us first look at some of the effects of the computer on education, medicine, the military, and the workplace, then consider the concerns it has raised about the invasion of privacy.

Education.   Record keeping has certainly become much simpler since the arrival of the computer. Computers allow college administrators to keep track of thousands of students at once—their courses, grades, and progress in meeting graduation requirements. Faculty members can call a central office and receive academic information on any student. But computerized academic records represent only a small part of how the computer is transforming education.

Almost every grade school in the United States now introduces its students to the computer. Children learn how to type, or "key," on it, as well as how to use mathematics software. High school students learn word processing, and college students routinely use computers to prepare term papers. Successful educational computer programs use a gamelike, challenging format that makes students forget that they are "studying."

The computer has made a visit to university libraries a different experience. Although card catalogs still stand in neat rows, the computer terminal is where the action is. By keying in a single word, the user can instruct the computer to search its huge memory and list every item that contains that word. If the user types in two words connected by "and," the computer will reproduce only references that contain both topics. Another command can make the computer print an abstract of the reference. Some programs even print the entire article.

Will computers lead to "teacherless" classrooms, as some have envisioned? With the computer's capacity to store huge amounts of knowledge and to retrieve information on demand, some analysts foresee the day when computers will replace "flesh and blood" teachers. They visualize rows of students hunched over computers, each student following his or her own pace in individualized courses, the computer giving the tests and scoring the results. In effect, the computer would be a personal tutor for each student. A "flesh and blood" teacher would still serve as a guide to the technology and the information, but no longer as a "custodian of knowledge" (Johnston and Packer 1987).

The "teacherless" classroom does not seem to be the wave of the future, however. It is likely that the computer's capacity to enhance teaching and learning will be tapped much more extensively in the years to come, but that teachers will remain essential to the educational process. There is a qualitative difference between the solitary learning envisaged by futurists and the dynamics of classroom teaching—lectures, discussions with peers, and the opportunity to question an expert who uses his or her experience in an academic discipline to challenge students' thinking and attitudes. In short, there is much more to teaching than merely transmitting knowledge.

If computers become truly "interactive," that is, gain the capacity to "converse" creatively with students, many courses will be entirely computerized, and students will be able to work at their own speed. Such a scenario requires "artificial intelligence" for the machine, however, a technology still in its infancy.

Medicine.   Computer technology has transformed medicine in the United States. Computers allow medical personnel to "image" the body, to peer within the body's hidden recesses to determine how its parts are functioning or to see if surgery is necessary. Computers also allow surgeons to operate on unborn babies and on previously inaccessible parts of the brain. Computers provide the answer to complicated tests in minutes instead of days. Physicians can feed vital information into a computer—sex, age, race, family medical history, symptoms, and test results—and find out what the chances are that a patient has cancer or some other disease.

Will the computer lead to "doctorless" medical offices? Will we perhaps one day feed vital information about ourselves into a computer and receive a printout of what is wrong with us—and, of course, a prescription? (Somehow, "Take two aspirins and key in in the morning" doesn't sound comforting.) Such an office is likely to remain only a concept in some futurist's fanciful imagination, however, for physicians would repel such an onslaught on their expertise, even if computers do outperform physicians in diagnostics (Waldholz 1991). Patients, similarly, would miss the interaction with their doctors, especially the assurances and other psychological support that good physicians provide. It appears safe to say that the computer will continue to be a diagnostic tool for physicians, not a replacement for them.

The Military and War.   The military has also been profoundly affected by the computer. This point was dramatically driven home to the American public—and the world—during the Persian Gulf War by televised footage of "smart" weapons honing in on targets. Most impressive were pictures videotaped from the nose of a ballistic missile as it hit a designated air shaft in Iraq's military headquarters in the heart of Baghdad.

The computer apparently allowed pinpoint accuracy, and television brought the war into the world's living rooms. But on another level these machines also made the war less real. The only pictures that were shown were of exploding buildings, looking for all the world like computerized targets on a video game. The literal blood and guts were strangely absent. No suffering was visible, no screams of agony were heard. Indeed they were there, but not on the screen.

During the months in which the West's soldiers trained in the desert before the attack against Saddam Hussein's army, one sociology student, like thousands of other civilians, wrote a letter "to any soldier in Desert Shield." Her military pen pal sent her unauthorized photos of the slaughter of Iraqi troops as they fled Kuwait City. They showed the charred remains of young soldiers, bodies clutched in agony. When the soldier's commander discovered that he had disclosed his "photo album of the war," the student had to return it immediately, or her pen pal's military career would have been over (author's files).

The Workplace.   The computer is also transforming the workplace. Local insurance agencies use computerized record keeping, their clerks sitting behind terminals as they key in information on clients and policies. The computer even bills the clients on the correct due date. In larger work settings, people who have never met one another "talk" via computer. After one person keys in a message, a computer determines which employee in which building handles that topic and routes the message to that person, who in turn responds via computer. Similarly, a supervisor on this side of the Atlantic or Pacific can communicate via computer with workers thousands of miles away. The result is a marked decrease in errors and an increase in efficiency.

Project 3

K.P.: Shoshana Zuboff

Control and Depersonalized Relationships.   Social psychologist Shoshana Zuboff (1991) reported that a major problem with computerizing the workplace is that personal relationships become less important. Managers are able to increase surveillance without depending on face-to-face supervision. Consider the electronic time card.

> The employee picks [it] up on arriving at work and uses [it] to keep a detailed record of his or her activities throughout the day. At day's end, the information contained in the device is fed into a computer that creates a report on the worker's activities for the day, week, and month (Hodson and Parker 1988).

Computers can report the number of strokes a word processor makes each minute or hour, or inform supervisors how long each telephone operator takes per call. Operators who are "underperforming" can then be singled out for discipline. It does not matter that the slower operators may be more polite or more helpful to customers, just that the computer reports slower performance.

Job "Multiskilling" and "Deskilling."   The terms "multiskilling" and "deskilling" sound like computer jargon—and they are. As computer technology advances, the skills of workers must keep pace. Adding skills to those a worker already possesses is termed **job multiskilling.** Typists, for example, must learn to use a keyboard and monitor instead of a typewriter and paper. Computers cut both ways, however, and they also have the interesting consequence of **job deskilling,** that is, reducing the skills necessary to do a job. Job deskilling comes about when machines tell workers what to do. In a biscuit factory, for example, a master baker used to oversee the correct mixing of the dough, but now a computer "supervises" the mixing process. The master baker has been replaced by an unskilled employee who needs only press a button to start the mixing process (Hodson and Parker 1988).

job multiskilling: adding skills to those a worker already possesses

job deskilling: reducing the amount of skills that a job requires

Shoshana Zuboff (1991) noted deskilling in her study of the collection department of a large business. Before computerization, collectors had to be very skilled, relying

Although computers increase production, and have made such products as the automobile superior to what they were just a few years ago, their transformation of industry also puts people out of work and causes job deskilling. The worker in this photo, for example, now simply checks specifications while computer-driven robots perform the welding.

on their past experience to make individual decisions at each stage in the collection procedure. Now rules have been written into the computer program, and much less skilled workers simply do what the machine tells them. One collection manager described the change this way.

> It gives us a tighter lock on the collector, and we can hire less skilled people. But there's a real loss to the job of skills and knowledge. You are being told what to do by the machine (Zuboff 1991).

Depending on the industry and the specific job within that industry, then, computerization has caused both multiskilling and deskilling. Whether the *net* effect of computers is to increase or to decrease skills required remains a matter of debate among sociologists (Hodson and Parker 1988).

Depersonalization and the "Workerless" Office.   Computers hold out the interesting possibility of the "workerless" office, inhabited only by computers and linked to workers at home terminals, doing what they formerly did in the office. Some workers, or *telecommuters,* like to work at home, for it eliminates commuting time and provides a high degree of flexibility—they can take a break when they want to or take a morning off and work into the evening instead. Others, however, miss the office interaction—the latest gossip, the approval and sympathy from fellow workers, and so on. Working at home, they say, is too impersonal; moreover, it isolates them from the office network—the personal relationships on which raises and promotions often depend.

The future will undoubtedly bring an increase in the number of persons who work at home, but the "workerless" office, like the much-touted "paperless" office the computer was supposed to usher in, will probably not come about. Personal interaction will remain vital for most work situations, for "reading the look" on a customer's face—or on the boss's—simply cannot be done from a computer terminal.

L. Obj. 6: State the major concerns about computers.

Concerns about Computers

Every new technology has its critics. The first to make their displeasure known are usually those who are directly threatened by it. When the automobile first appeared, the makers of buggies laughed at their feebleness. When automobiles became popular, they stopped laughing and started complaining. When the computer came on the scene, typists felt threatened as some of their skills became outmoded. They made the adjustment, however, and many, if not most, became word processors. Others fear the computer's capacity to destroy jobs. Another concern centers on potential abuse of computers, especially in relation to privacy. Let us look at these two concerns.

Loss of Jobs.   A common concern is that computers will take away people's jobs. After all, a letter typed by a computer is typed fast, and without mistakes; an automobile part welded through computerized robots is welded at the precise spot for the specified number of seconds. For some jobs, then, computers are better than people.

But while computers do replace workers, they also create jobs. Computers underlie the expansion of health care, both in the diagnosis and treatment of disease as well as in the burgeoning area of medical insurance. Computers have even created new "employment frontiers," careers in the information industry, robotics, the ocean, and space (Feingold 1984). Many of these new jobs are becoming standard in industrialized societies. "Computer programmer," for example, sounded exotic a few years back; now it is just another job title.

Whether the *net* effect of computers has been to increase or decrease the number of workers has not yet been determined (Hodson and Parker 1988). Part of the problem is how to count the number of jobs that computers create indirectly. For example, if robots increase productivity and lower prices, the resulting increase in demand will create new jobs in unrelated areas of the economy.

Even if the net effect of computerization is to increase jobs, however, it does not detract from the pain of those who are displaced by a computer. It is difficult to learn new skills and to adapt to new work. The adjustment to the new society can be extremely difficult, and the problem is not evenly distributed throughout society.

The Invasion of Privacy.   Americans value privacy. They retreat into single-family homes and then build fences around their backyards. They commute to work and school alone in their cars. Their privacy, however, is threatened by the vast amounts of personal information stored in computers. A driver's license number enables a police officer's dashboard-mounted computer to display almost instantly the owner's vital statistics—address, sex, race, age, height, weight, and color of eyes. When the Internal Revenue Service enters a Social Security number, its owner's tax history—earnings, deductions, dependents, and business relationships—is revealed. If you apply for a credit card or buy an item on credit, computers somewhere spin momentarily as that particular bit of information is embedded into their memories.

Concerns center on access to this information. How is the information protected from getting into the wrong hands? If misinformation is entered into an agency's computer, how can it be corrected? Some fear that misinformation will deny people credit, others that the government will use computers to keep such close tabs on citizens that they will have hardly any freedom left.

Sally, who was featured in the opening vignette, can tell you about the consequences of wrong information being entered into a computer. Others can recount how their lives were complicated when misinformation denied them a loan to buy a house or car, and how that misinformation spread from one credit agency to another. A computer cannot tell the difference between truth and falsehood, or between objective information and slander from a malicious neighbor given during a credit check.

Guardians and Power.   At this point, most concerns about the negative consequences of computers appear unfounded. There are individual cases of misinformation, such as Sally's, and of gross abuse of computers, such as Richard Nixon's order to the IRS to track down the personal political enemies on his "hit" list. The United States government, however, has not so far turned into Big Brother, and it uses its computerized records for legitimate purposes—to catch tax cheats, to locate spouses who renege on child support payments, and so on. Alive to the possibility of abuse, legislators have even intervened on behalf of citizens by passing laws limiting access to information and establishing procedures by which an individual can make corrections in his or her computerized records.

The computer is such a powerful information machine, however, that a government could easily turn it against its citizens. If we apply to computers the saying, "The price of liberty is eternal vigilance," we can conclude that only if we are vigilant can we be sure that the computer will be used for our benefit, not for our exploitation. As conflict theorists point out, however, the basic issue is not the occasional abuse of computers, nor invasion of privacy, but rather the fact that computers enhance the power of those who are already powerful (Hourani 1987).

Of course, it is not the computer itself that is dangerous. The computer has no mind, no power to plot against human freedom, no desire to detract from human dignity. The computer is simply a tool, albeit a powerful one. The people whom we need to be on guard against are, as always, those who wish to control or hurt us and can use this powerful instrument for their own ends. Ultimately, that is the risk posed by computers. The fundamental question, of course, is this: Who will be the guardians?

Telecommunications and Global Social Change

Computers have improved so rapidly that today's desktop microcomputers are more powerful than the machines that guided the Apollo rocket and its astronauts to the moon in 1969! Today's memory chips that store a million bits of information will be replaced by chips with up to one hundred times more storage capacity. We can expect

L. Obj. 7: Describe ways in which telecommunications has created global social change.

"silicon secretaries" that can take dictation and edit letters, reservation clerks that can understand any language.

Satellite relays and fiber optics will blanket the globe with a telecommunications network offering instantaneous access to almost all homes and businesses in the First World. Most citizens of the First World will have a terminal at home to tap into a global store of information. They will do their shopping and banking at home, print out the latest news bulletins on any subject they select, as well as play the latest video games—perhaps with partners in another nation. Access to the most recent catalog of any college in the world will be only a few keystrokes away.

The world, indeed, is shrinking—in both space and time. The impact of telecommunications on social change is already clear (Smart 1990). National boundaries mean nothing to telecommunications. Much to the dismay of dictators who want to keep their people ignorant and thereby more easily controlled, information can no longer be contained. Even during the Tiananmen Square massacre in Beijing, Chinese students faxed reports to Americans (Cleveland 1990). Telecommunications was one of the many factors that contributed to the collapse of the Soviet empire. No matter what the ruling elite told the people, they were acutely aware through telecommunications (from television to fax) that the citizens of the capitalist countries enjoyed a much higher standard of living.

The Kayapo Indians of Brazil illustrate the impact telecommunications have had even on preliterate peoples (Simons 1989). With no written language, these traditional people used to spend their evenings gathered around the camp fire, the children listening attentively as the elders told stories. The stories were not mere entertainment, but a primary means of imparting the tribe's history and culture to the children. They integrated the people through shared beliefs, values, and life goals.

And now? Television has come to the Amazon. After selling gold and mahogany trees, the Kayapo installed a satellite dish. Now at night the children sit transfixed before colored images of a culture utterly foreign to them. The elders lament their loss of audience, wondering if they should destroy what they call the "Big Ghost" before it destroys their culture. This topic is explored further in the Perspectives box on page 641.

SOCIAL CHANGE AND THE NATURAL ENVIRONMENT

CDQ 9: Is today's concern with the environment a passing fad or will this issue become a focal point in the twenty-first century? Why?

Essay #4

L. Obj. 8: Discuss the environmental degradation which has occurred in the past and note the extent of environmental problems today.

Of all the changes in which societies today are immersed, perhaps those affecting the natural environment hold the most serious implications from human life. Industrialization and technology have brought such changes to the earth's air, water, soil, and atmosphere that some experts believe human existence itself on this planet is threatened.

Environmental Degradation in the Past

Environmental degradation did not begin with industrialization, and the image of primitive humans living in harmony with their physical environment is a myth. Some early civilizations actually destroyed themselves by ignorant treatment of the environment. One of the best examples of such destruction is the Mesopotamian civilization, which flourished between the Tigris and Euphrates rivers in what is today Iraq four thousand years ago. The Mesopotamians built extensive canals that provided food in abundance. The irrigation system had no drainage, however, and constant evaporation left the water salty. Over the centuries, the water table rose as more and more salty water seeped into the ground. When the land became too salty to grow crops, the civilization collapsed (Jacobsen and Adams 1958). Perhaps environmental degradation also caused the fall of the great Mayan civilization of Central America. It is theorized that as their population grew, the Mayans cleared the land of trees. As rain subsequently washed

Lost Tribes, Lost Knowledge

Since 1900, 90 of Brazil's 270 Indian tribes have disappeared. As settlers have taken over their lands, many other tribes have abandoned their traditional lands and settled in villages. Here as elsewhere in the world, with village life comes a loss of the tribe's knowledge. The Penans, for example, a hunting and gathering tribe that used to wander the woodlands of Borneo, now live in villages. The villagers know that their elders used to watch for the appearance of a certain butterfly, which heralded good hunting. Now, few can remember which butterfly to look for.

What difference does this make? Concerning the loss of memory about the butterfly, very little. But concerning the loss of memory about many other tribal activities, it makes a great deal of difference. Tribal groups are not just people who are living "wild," barely surviving because of their ignorance. On the contrary, they possess intricate forms of social organization and knowledge accumulated over thousands of years. The 2,500 Kayapo Indians, for example, belong to one of the Amazon's endangered Indian tribes. The Kayapo make use of 250 types of wild fruit and hundreds of nut and tuber species. They cultivate thirteen distinct bananas, eleven kinds of manioc (cassava), sixteen sweet potato strains, and seventeen different yams. Many of these varieties are unknown to non-Indians. The Kayapo also use thousands of medicinal plants, one of which contains a drug effective against intestinal parasites.

Until recently, Western scientists dismissed tribal knowledge as superstitious and worthless. Now, however, the West is coming to realize that to lose tribes is to lose knowledge. In the Central African Republic, a man whose chest was being eaten away by a subcutaneous amoeboid infection lay dying because he did not respond to drugs. Out of desperation, the Catholic nuns who were treating him sought the advice of a native doctor, who applied washed and crushed soldier termites to the open wounds. The "dying" man made a remarkable recovery.

Along with the disappearance of a language goes a tribe's collective knowledge—and about half of the world's six thousand languages are doomed because no children speak them. And the disappearance of the forests destroys many species yet unknown that may hold healing properties. Of the earth's 265,000 species of plants, only 1,100 have been thoroughly studied by Western scientists. Yet 40,000 may possess medicinal or undiscovered nutritional value for humans. For example, scientists have recently discovered that the leaves of Taxus baccata, a Himalayan tree found in mountainous parts of India, contain taxol, a drug effective against ovarian cancer.

On average, one tribe of Amazonian Indians has been lost each year of this century—due to violence, greed for their native lands, and exposure to infectious diseases against which they have little resistance. Ethnocentrism underlies much of this assault. Perhaps the extreme is represented by the cattle ranchers in Colombia who killed eighteen Cueva Indians. The cattle ranchers were perplexed when they were put on trial for murder. They asked why they should be charged with a crime, since everyone knew that the Cuevas were animals, not people. They pointed out that there was even a verb in Colombian Spanish, *cuevar,* which means "to hunt Cueva Indians." So what was their crime, they asked? The jury found them innocent because of "cultural ignorance."

Sources: Durning 1990; Gorman 1991; Linden 1991; Simons 1989; Stipp 1992.

away their topsoil, it took with it the productivity on which their civilization depended (Deevey et al. 1979).

The Environmental Problem Today

Speaker Sug. #3: An environmental specialist such as a person with the E.P.A. or O.S.H.A.

Ordinarily, however, primitive technology produced minimal pollution, and the frontal assault on the natural environment did not begin in earnest until the advent of industrialization. Today, Los Angeles and Mexico City announce "smog days" on radio and television, warning people to stay indoors and keeping schoolchildren inside during recess. The depletion of the ozone layer, which may represent a folly that will harm all of humanity, is being debated by scientists (Gliedman 1989; Tolba 1989). Pollution is so extensive that even the reindeer herded by the Laplanders in the Arctic Circle in northern Sweden, Norway, and Finland have been contaminated by the nuclear radiation released following the disaster at the nuclear reactor in Chernobyl (Clines 1986).

Extensive burning of fossil fuels to power factories, motorized vehicles, and power plants has been especially harmful. Fish can no longer survive in some lakes in Canada and the northeastern United States because of **acid rain**—the burning fossil fuels release sulfur dioxide and nitrogen oxide, which react with moisture in the air to become sulfuric and nitric acid (Luoma 1989). An invisible but infinitely more serious consequence is the **greenhouse effect.** Like the glass of a greenhouse, the gases emitted from burning fossil fuels allow sunlight to enter the earth's atmosphere freely, but inhibit the release of heat. It is as though the gases have closed the atmospheric window through which our planet breathes. Some scientists say that the resulting **global warming** may melt the polar ice caps and inundate the world's shorelines, cause the climate boundaries to move about four hundred miles north, and make many animal and plant species extinct (Smith and Tirpak 1988; Thomas 1988; Weisskopf 1992). Not all scientists agree with this scenario, however; some even doubt that a greenhouse effect exists (Balling 1992; Davis 1992).

One problem that has unknown consequences for the future of humanity is that numerous plant and animal species are becoming extinct as the tropical rain forests are relentlessly cleared for lumber, farms, and pastures. Although the rain forests cover just 7 percent of the planet's land area, they are home to half of all its plant species. It is estimated that ten thousand species are becoming extinct each year—about one per hour (Durning 1990). Finally, the threat of nuclear pollution through accidents at nuclear power plants, leakage during testing of nuclear weapons, and nuclear explosions in war hangs over the world like a shroud (Fialka 1992).

Environmental Problems in the Second World

Environmental degradation is not only a First World problem. With the dissolution of the Soviet Union came revelations of extensive pollution throughout its territory (Feshbach 1992). Strangely, pollution had been treated as a state secret. Scientists and journalists could not mention pollution in public, and even a peaceful demonstration to call attention to pollution could net its participants a two-year prison sentence. With protest stifled, no environmental protection laws to inhibit pollution, and production quotas to be met, environmental pollution was rampant. In Poland, for example, more than three-quarters of the sources of drinking water are contaminated. Warsaw does not even treat its sewage. The level of pollution in Budapest makes a one-hour walk there as damaging to the lungs as smoking a pack of cigarettes (Diehl 1992; Okie 1992).

The dissolution of the Soviet Union brought new freedoms, including the right to environmental protest. For the most part, however, the protests have fallen on deaf ears, and the pollution continues. Considering the Second World's rush to compete industrially with the West, the desire to improve a low standard of living, and the lack

L. Obj. 9: Describe the environmental problems of the Second and Third World countries. State ways in which First World countries may have contributed to these problems.

acid rain: rain containing sulfuric and nitric acid, produced by the reaction of sulfur dioxide and nitrogen oxide with moisture when released into the air with the burning of fossil fuels

greenhouse effect: the buildup of carbon dioxide in the earth's atmosphere that allows light to enter but inhibits the release of heat; believed to cause global warming

global warming: an increase in the earth's temperature due to the greenhouse effect

On a scale of pollution infamy, if it does not take first place Poland certainly ranks near the top. Devastated environmentally by an inept communist regime, it is one of the most polluted countries in the world. Its current extensive pollution, however, may be only the tip of the iceberg, for its nuclear power stations, such as those shown here at Katowice, Poland, were designed by the same group that brought about the Chernobyl disaster.

As Third World nations feel the intense pressure of rapid population growth (reviewed in Chapter 20) and global economic competition (reviewed in Chapter 14), they are exploiting their resources to keep up in this global race. Shown here is a paper mill in Brazil's rain forest. The short-term gain is employment and increased production, but the long-term loss for the world in extinct plant and animal species and on the earth's atmosphere is incalculable.

of funds to purchase expensive pollution controls, it seems doubtful that the curtain will be pulled back on pollution for many years. Indeed, it is likely that pollution levels will increase.

Environmental Problems in the Third World

With its greater poverty and swelling population, the Third World has an even greater incentive to industrialize at any cost. The world population increases by a quarter of a million people every day, and as noted in Chapter 20, most of this increase occurs in the Third World. The combined pressures of population growth and almost nonexistent environmental regulations destine the Third World to become the earth's major source of pollution. The Third World's lack of environmental protection laws has not gone unnoticed by opportunists in the First World, who have begun to use those countries as a garbage dump for hazardous wastes and for producing chemicals that their own will no longer tolerate (La Dou 1991). Alarmed at the implications of increasing environmental destruction, the World Bank, a monetary arm of First World nations, has placed pressure on Third World nations to reduce pollution and soil erosion (Lachica 1992). Understandably, the basic concern of the people of the Third World is to produce food and housing first, and to worry about environmental matters later.

The Environmental Movement

Concern about the world's severe environmental problems has produced a worldwide social movement. Sociologist Celene Krauss (1989, 1991) found an unanticipated consequence of the quest for a healthy environment: the political radicalization of many of its participants. In one instance, a dump leaking chemicals into local wells and making families sick caused working-class people, who placed high trust in their government, to assume, naively, that officials would be happy to solve the problem when they learned of it. Instead, they were told that it wasn't the government's business, or that it was the cost they had to pay for a "better" life! Frustrated, they pursued the matter on their own, but in the courts were shocked and disillusioned to find that deep pockets make a difference in justice. The small groups of protesters could not afford lawyers to deal with the endless barrage of legal motions filed by the polluters. Many underwent

With the continued degradation of the environment, some groups choose dramatic ways to drive home their belief that to continue doing business as usual will result in the destruction of the earth. Shown here is a demonstration by Greenpeace at NATO in Brussels, Belgium. Activities by this and other groups with similar goals are featured in the box on ecosabotage.

a political awakening as a result, having lost their trust in government, and gaining a disturbing insight into the relationship between wealth and political power.

In some countries, the environment has become a major issue in local and national elections. In Germany, for example, concern about the environment created the impetus for a political party, the Green party, which has won seats in the national legislature (Kiefer 1991). Green parties have also arisen in Great Britain (Rootes 1990), Switzerland (Hug 1990), and even Mexico (Golden 1991). In the United States, a Green party tried to field a candidate in the 1992 presidential election but managed to get on the ballot in only two or three states.

The environmental movement, which often transcends social class, gender, and race (Bullard and Wright 1987, 1990; Bullard 1990; Krauss 1991), generally sees solutions in education, legislation, and political activism. Some activists, however, seeing that pollution continues, that forests are still being clear-cut, and that species are still becoming extinct, have become convinced that the planet is doomed if immediate steps are not taken and have chosen a more radical course. Using extreme tactics to confront those who abuse the environment, they try to arouse indignation among the public and thus force the government to act. Convinced that they stand for true morality, many in this extreme segment of the environmental movement are willing to break the law and go to jail for their actions. These activists are featured in the Thinking Critically section below.

THINKING CRITICALLY ABOUT SOCIAL CONTROVERSY

Ecosabotage

CNN: Earth First!

Blocking a logging road by standing in front of a truck; climbing atop a giant Douglas fir slated for cutting; pouring sand down the gas tank of a bulldozer; tearing down power lines and ripping up survey stakes; driving spikes into redwood trees and sinking whaling vessels—are these the acts of dangerous punks, intent on vandalism and with little understanding of the needs of modern society or of brave men and women willing to put their freedom, and even their lives, on the line on behalf of the earth itself?

To get some idea of why ecosabotage is taking place, consider the Medicine Tree, a three-thousand-year-old redwood in the Sally Bell Grove near the northern California coast. Georgia Pacific, a lumbering company, was determined to cut down the Medicine Tree, the oldest and largest of the region's redwoods, which rests upon an ancient sacred site of the Sinkyone Indians. Members of Earth First!, an organization founded by Dave Foreman, chained themselves to the tree. After they were arrested, the sawing began. Other protesters jumped over the police-lined barricade and planted themselves in front of the axes and chain saws. A logger swung an axe and missed a demonstrator. At that moment, the sheriff received a restraining order, and the cutting stopped.

How many three-thousand-year-old trees remain on this planet? Do picnic tables and fences for backyard barbecues justify cutting them down? It is questions like these, as well as the slaughter of baby seals, the destruction of the rain forests, the drowning of dolphins in mile-long drift nets, and a host of other concerns, that have spawned Earth First! and other organizations, such as Greenpeace and Sea Shepherds, which are devoted to preserving the environment at any cost.

"We feel like there are insane people who are consciously destroying our environment, and we are compelled to fight back," explains a member of one of the militant groups. "No compromise in defense of Mother Earth!" says another. "With famine and death approaching, we're in the early stages of World War III," adds another.

The dedication of some of these activists has brought them close to martyrdom. When Paul Watson, founder of the Sea Shepherds, sprayed seals with green dye, which destroys the value of their pelts but doesn't hurt the animals, hunters hogtied him, dragged him across the ice, and threatened to toss him into the sea. "It's no big deal," says Watson, "when you consider that one hundred million people in this century have died in wars over real estate."

Radical environmentalists represent a broad range of activities and purposes. They are united neither on tactics nor goals. Some want to stop a specific action, such as the killing of whales, or to destroy all nuclear weapons and dismantle nuclear power plants. Others want everyone to become vegetarians. Still others want the earth's population to be reduced to one billion, roughly what it was in 1800. Some even want humans to return to hunting and gathering bands. Most espouse a simpler lifestyle that will consume less energy and thereby place less pressure on the earth's resources. These groups are so splintered that the founder of Earth First!, Dave Foreman, quit his own organization when it became too confrontational for his tastes.

Among their successes, the radical groups count a halt to the killing of dolphins off Japan's Iki Island, a ban on whaling, trash recycling in many communities, hundreds of thousands of acres of uncut trees, and, of course, the Medicine Tree.

Who then, are these people? Should we applaud them or jail them? As symbolic interactionists stress, it all depends on your definition. And as conflict theorists emphasize, your definition will depend on your location in the economic structure. That is, if you are the owner of a lumbering firm you will see ecosaboteurs differently than if you are a hiking and camping enthusiast. What is your own view of ecosaboteurs, and how does your view depend on your life situation?

When social movements first begin, radical groups serve to call attention to issues. When a movement gains public acceptance and becomes mainstream, as environmentalism has, do you think radical acts do more harm than good? Do they alienate people who support the movement, rather than unite them?

Finally, what effective alternatives to ecosabotage are there for people who are convinced that modernization is destroying the very life-support system of the planet itself? (*Source:* Borrelli 1988; Carpenter 1990; Eder 1990; Foote 1990; Guha 1989; Keyser 1991; Martin 1990; Parfit 1990; Reed and Benet 1990; Rhyne 1987; Russell 1987.) ■

L. Obj. 11: List the assumptions of environmental sociology.

Speaker Sug. #5: A colleague whose area of specialization is environmental sociology.

Environmental Sociology

Environmental sociology, which examines the relationship between human societies and the environment, emerged as a subdiscipline of sociology about 1970 (Albrecht and Murdock 1986; Buttel 1987; Dunlap and Catton 1979, 1983; Freudenburg and Gramling 1989). Its main assumptions are listed below.

1. The physical environment is a significant variable in sociological investigation.
2. Human beings are but one species among many that are dependent on the natural environment.

environmental sociology: a subdiscipline of sociology that examines how human activities affect the physical environment and how the physical environment affects human activities

3. Because of intricate feedbacks to nature, human actions have many unintended consequences.
4. The world is finite, so there are potential physical limits to economic growth.
5. Economic expansion requires increased extraction of resources from the environment.
6. Increased extraction of resources leads to ecological problems.
7. These ecological problems place restrictions on economic expansion.
8. The state creates environmental problems by trying to create conditions for the profitable accumulation of capital.

As you can see, the goal of environmental sociology is not to stop pollution or nuclear power, but rather to study the ways in which human cultures, values, and behavior affect the physical environment and the ways in which the physical environment affects human activities. Environmental sociologists, however, are generally also environmental activists, and the Section on Environment and Technology of the American Sociological Association tries to influence governmental policies (American Sociological Association, n.d.).

The Goal of Harmony between Technology and the Environment

It is inevitable that humans will continue to develop new technologies. But the extensive abuse of those technologies is not inevitable. Neither is the destruction of the planet. That is simply an unwise choice.

If we are to have a world that is worth passing on to the coming generations, we must seek harmony between technology and the natural environment (Stead and Stead 1991). This will not be easy. At one extreme are persons who claim that to protect the environment we must eliminate industrialization and go back to some sort of preindustrialized way of life. At the other extreme are persons unable to see the harm that industrialization does to the natural environment, who want the entire world to continue industrializing at full speed. Somewhere, there must be a middle ground, one that recognizes that industrialization is here to stay but that we *can* control it, for it is our creation. Industrialization, controlled, can enhance our quality of life, not destroy us.

As a parallel to the development of technologies, then, we must develop a greater awareness of their harmful effects on the planet, systems of control that give more weight to reducing technologies' harm to the environment than to lowering monetary costs, and mechanisms to enforce rules for the production, use, and disposal of technology. The question, of course, is whether we have the resolve to do these things.

Will we use technology for exploitation, to make short-term gains regardless of long-term consequences? Or will we apply technology not just to enhance our quality of life but also to preserve the environment for future generations? These are issues that this generation must decide. The stakes—no less than the welfare of the entire planet—are surely high enough to motivate us to make the correct choices.

L. Obj. 12: Describe some of the actions which would be necessary to reach the goal of harmony between technology and the environment.

CDQ 10: In your opinion, is it possible for there to be harmony between technology and the environment? Why or why not?

SUMMARY

1. Social change, the alteration of culture and society over time, is such a vital part of social life that it has been a theme throughout this book. Its major landmarks include the four social revolutions, the change from *Gemeinschaft* to *Gesellschaft* society, and the transformation of society by capitalism. Industrialization has affected the Third World, causing globalization and dependency, and shifts in international stratification. The social institutions of the United States have changed significantly as a result of industrialization.

2. There are several theories of social change. Evolutionary theories of social change assume that societies evolve from the simple to the complex. Unilinear theories assume that all societies go through uniform sequences, while multilinear theories assume several paths to the same stage of development. Cyclical theories attempt to account for the rise and fall of great civilizations. They presume that societies are like organisms: they are born, reach adolescence, get old, and die. Marx's conflict theory is based on the presupposition of thesis, antithesis, and synthesis.

3. Technology stimulates social change, as illustrated in Ogburn's three processes of social change: invention, discovery, and diffusion. There are four types of technology: primitive, industrial, postindustrial, and a new technology still to emerge. Technology is a driving force in social change, for when a technology is introduced it forces other parts of society to give way. Technology can shape an entire society by changing existing technology, social organization, ideology, values, and social relationships.

4. The introduction of the automobile in American society provides an extended example of how technology brings vast, and sometimes unexpected, change. The automobile replaced existing technology, integrated farmers into regional life, and influenced developments ranging from the shape of cities, and the architecture of businesses and homes to courtship customs, sexual norms, and women's roles. The transformation of society by the computer is still under way. Its effects extend to education, medicine, the military and war, and the workplace. The computer has also caused both the multiskilling and deskilling of workers. Major concerns about the computer center on the potential for its abuse—for invasion of privacy, the integration of misinformation into computerized records, and as an instrument for social control.

5. In regard to the relationship between technology and the natural environment, human pollution is not new; it even caused the fall of earlier civilizations. Today's environmental problems, such as the greenhouse effect, acid rain, the clearing of the rain forests, and the extinction of multiple species, have come about because of technology. Environmental degradation in the Second and Third worlds is widespread and also related to technology. Environmental sociology is based on eight main assumptions. The environmental movement is growing and contains extreme activists who engage in ecosabotage. As a legacy for future generations we need to seek harmony between technology and the natural environment.

SUGGESTED READINGS

Brown, Lester R., ed. *State of the World.* New York: W. W. Norton, published annually. Experts on environmental issues analyze environmental problems throughout the world.

Council on Environmental Quality. *Environmental Quality.* Washington, D.C.: U.S. Government Printing Office, published annually. Each report evaluates the condition of some aspect of the environment.

Edelstein, Michael R. *Contaminated Communities: The Social and Psychological Impacts of Residential Toxic Exposure.* Boulder, Colo.: Westview Press, 1988. Edelstein examines the social dynamics of exposure to toxic chemicals, including effects on lifestyle and changes in perceptions of the self, family, community, and environment.

Feshbach, Murray, and Alfred Friendly. *Ecocide in the USSR.* New York: Basic Books, 1992. The authors analyze the political repression of environmentalists and the government's willing sacrifice of the environment for the sake of "building a brighter, industrial future."

Flink, James J. *The Automobile Age.* Cambridge, Mass.: MIT Press, 1988. This wide-ranging overview of the United States automobile industry also discusses the automobile's effects on society.

Hafner, Katie, and John Markoff. *Cyberpunk: Outlaws and Hackers on the Computer Frontier.* New York: Simon & Schuster, 1991. The stories of three of the most famous computer hackers—their crimes and their downfall—are revealed.

Mokyr, Joel. *The Lever of Riches: Technological Creativity and Economic Progress.* New York: Oxford University Press, 1991. Using a broad historical and cross-cultural sweep to analyze how advances in technology raise productivity, spur economic growth, and increase wealth, the author probes why some societies are more technologically creative than others.

Stead, W. Edward, and Jean Garner Stead. *Management for a Small Planet.* Newbury Park, Calif.: Sage, 1992. The authors examine how we can reconcile our need for economic production with our need to protect the earth's ecosystem.

Womack, James P., Daniel T. Jones, and Daniel Roos. *The Machine That Changed the World.* New York: Macmillan, 1990. This overview of automobile manufacturing emphasizes the lean production techniques developed by Toyota and shows how they can be applied to other industries.

World Commission on Environment and Development. *Our Common Future.* Oxford: Oxford University Press, 1987. Exploring the relationship between industrial development and the natural environment, the book stresses that a global agenda is needed to preserve the environment and resources of the earth for future generations.

References

Aberle, David. *The Peyote Religion Among the Navaho.* Chicago: Aldine, 1966.

Aberle, David F., A. K. Cohen, A. K. David, M. J. Leng, Jr., and F. N. Sutton. "The Functional Prerequisites of a Society." *Ethics, 60,* January 1950:100–111.

Abramson, Jill. "How Outsider Clinton built a Potent Network of Insider Contacts." *Wall Street Journal,* March 12, 1992:A1, A4.

Abramson, Jill, and David Rogers. "The Keating 535." *Wall Street Journal,* January 10, 1991:A1, A8.

Achenbaum, W. Andrew. *Old Age in the New Land: The American Experience Since 1870.* Baltimore: Johns Hopkins University Press, 1978.

Acker, Joan. "Class, Gender, and the Relations of Distribution." *Signs: Journal of Women in Culture and Society, 13* (3), 1988:473–497.

Adler, Freda. *Sisters in Crime.* New York: McGraw Hill, 1975.

Adler, Stephen J. "Lawyers Advise Concerns to Provide Precise Written Policy to Employees." *Wall Street Journal,* October 9, 1991:B1, B4.

Adorno, Theodor W., Else Frenkel-Brunwick, D. J. Levinson, and R. N. Sanford. *The Authoritarian Personality.* New York: Harper and Row, 1950.

Albert, Ethel M. "Women of Burundi: A Study of Social Values." In *Women of Tropical Africa,* Denise Paulme (ed.). Berkeley, California: University of California Press, 1963:179–215.

Albrecht, Donald E., and Steven H. Murdoch. "Natural Resource Availability and Social Change." *Sociological Inquiry, 56,* 3, Summer 1986:381–400.

Aldrich, Nelson W., Jr. *Old Money: The Mythology of America's Upper Class.* New York: Vintage Books, 1989.

Allport, Floyd. *Social Psychology.* Boston: Houghton Mifflin, 1954.

Alpert, Harry. *Emile Durkheim and His Sociology.* New York: Columbia University Press, 1939.

American Sociological Association. "Section on Environment and Technology." Pamphlet, no date.

American Sociological Association. "Code of Ethics." Washington, D.C.: American Sociological Association, August 14, 1989.

Amott, Teresa, and Julie Matthaei. *Race, Gender, and Work: A Multicultural Economic History of Women in the United States.* Boston: South End Press, 1991.

Andersen, Margaret L. *Thinking About Women: Sociological Perspectives on Sex and Gender.* New York: Macmillan, 1988.

Anderson, Charles H. *The Political Economy of Social Class.* Englewood Cliffs, New Jersey: Prentice Hall, 1974.

Anderson, Chris. "NORC Study Describes Homeless." *Chronicle,* 1986:5, 9.

Anderson, Elijah. *A Place on the Corner.* Chicago: University of Chicago Press, 1978.

Anderson, Elijah. *Streetwise.* Chicago; University of Chicago Press, 1990.

Anderson, Nels. *Desert Saints: The Mormon Frontier in Utah.* Chicago: University of Chicago Press, 1966. First published in 1942.

Anderson, Teresa A. "The Best Years of Their Lives." *Newsweek,* January 7, 1985:6.

Angell, Robert C. "The Sociology of Human Conflict." In *The Nature of Human Conflict,* Elton B. McNeil, ed. Englewood Cliffs, New Jersey: Prentice Hall, 1965.

Ansberry, Clare. "Despite Federal Law, Hospitals Still Reject Sick Who Can't Pay." *Wall Street Journal,* November 29, 1988:A1, A4.

Apple, Michael W. *Education and Power: Reproduction and Contradiction in Education.* London: Routledge and Kegan Paul, 1982.

Applefrome, Peter. "Judge Cuts Bakker's Prison Term, Making Parole Possible in 4 Years." *New York Times,* August 24, 1991:A10.

Ariés, Philippe. *Centuries of Childhood.* R. Baldick (trans.). New York: Vintage Books, 1965.

Ariés, Philippe. *Centuries of Childhood: A Social History of Family Life.* Robert Baldick (trans.) New York: Vintage, 1962.

Arlacchi, P. *Peasants and Great Estates: Society in Traditional Calabria.* Cambridge: Cambridge University Press, 1980.

Armitage, Richard L. "Red Army Retreat Doesn't Signal End of U.S. Obligation." *Wall Street Journal,* February 7, 1989:A20.

Armstrong, Scott. "Violence Surges with Alien Influx." *Christian Science Monitor,* March 12, 1986:1, 36.

Arndt, William F., and F. Wilbur Gingrich. *A Greek-English Lexicon of the New Testament and Other Early Christian Literature.* Chicago: University of Chicago Press, 1957.

Asch, Solomon. "Effects of Group Pressure Upon the Modification and Distortion of Judgments." In *Readings in Social Psychology,* Guy Swanson, Theodore M. Newcomb, and Eugene L. Hartley, eds. New York: Holt, Rinehart and Winston, 1952.

Ash, Arthur. "A Zero-Sum Game That Hurts Blacks." *Wall Street Journal,* February 27, 1992:A10.

Ashley, Richard. *Cocaine: Its History, Uses, and Effects.* New York: St. Martin's, 1975.

Atchley, Robert C. "Dimensions of Widowhood in Later Life." *The Gerontologist, 15,* April 1975:176–178.

Athens, Lonnie H. *Violent Criminal Acts and Actors: A Symbolic Interactionist Study.* Boston: Routledge, 1980.

Auerbach, Judith D. "Employer-Supported Child Care as a Women-Responsive Policy." *Journal of Family Issues, 11,* 4, December 1990:384–400.

Ausubel, Jesse H. "Rat-Race Dynamics and Crazy Companies: The Diffusion of Technologies and Social Behavior." *Technological Forecasting and Social Change, 39,* 1991:11–22.

Avery, Dennis T. "Mother Earth Can Feed Billions More." *Wall Street Journal,* September 19, 1991:A14.

Bacon, Kenneth H. "The 'Birth Dearth' and Immigration." *Wall Street Journal,* October 13, 1986:1.

Bagne, Paul. "High-Tech Breeding." In *Marriage and Family in a Chang-*

ing Society, Fourth edition. James M. Henslin, ed. New York: Free Press, 1989:226–234.

Bahr, Howard M. *Skid Row: An Introduction to Disaffiliation.* New York: Oxford University Press, 1973.

Bahr, Stephen. "Effects of Power and Division of Labor in the Family." In *Working Mothers,* Lois W. Hoffman and F. Ivan Nye (eds.). San Francisco: Jossey-Bass, 1974:167–185.

Bainbridge, William Sims. "Collective Behavior and Social Movements." In *Sociology,* Rodney Stark. Belmont, California: Wadsworth, 1989:608–640.

Bales, Robert F. "The Equilibrium Problem in Small Groups." In *Working Papers in the Theory of Action,* Talcott Parsons, et al, eds. New York: Free Press, 1953:111–115.

Bales, Robert F. *Interaction Process Analysis.* Reading, Massachusetts: Addison-Wesley, 1950.

Ballentine, Jeanne H. *The Sociology of Education: A Systematic Analysis.* Englewood Cliffs, New Jersey: Prentice Hall, 1983.

Balling, Robert C. "A Climate of Doubt About Global Warming." *Wall Street Journal,* April 22, 1992:A18.

Baltes, P. B. "Life-Span Developmental Psychology: Some Converging Observations on History and Theory." In *Life-Span Development and Behavior,* Vol. 2, P. B. Baltes and O. G. Brim, Jr., eds. New York: Academic Press, 1979:255–279.

Baltzell, E. Digby. *The Protestant Establishment: Aristocracy and Caste in America.* New York: Vintage, 1964.

Baltzell, E. Digby. *Puritan Boston and Quaker Philadelphia.* New York: Free Press, 1979.

Banfield, Edward C. *The Unheavenly City Revisited.* Boston: Massachusetts: Little, Brown, 1974.

Barbeau, Clayton. "The Man-Woman Crisis." In *Marriage and Family in a Changing Society,* James M. Henslin, ed. Fourth edition. New York: Free Press, 1992:193–199.

Barber, Bernard. "The Sociology of Science." In *Sociology Today: Problems and Prospects.* New York: Basic Books, 1959:215–228.

Bardwick, Judith M. *Psychology of Women: A Study of Bio-Cultural Conflicts.* New York: Harper & Row, 1971.

Barnes, Harry Elmer. *The History of Western Civilization,* volume 1. New York: Harcourt, Brace, and Company, 1935.

Barnes, John A. "Canadians Cross Border to Save Their Lives." *Wall Street Journal,* December 12, 1990:A14.

Baron, Robert and Gerald Greenberg. *Behavior in Organizations,* Boston, Massachusetts: Allyn and Bacon, 1990.

Barry, Kathleen. *Susan B. Anthony: A Life or the Love of Women.* New York: Free Press, 1986.

Beals, Ralph L., and Harry Hoijer. *An Introduction to Anthropology,* Third edition. New York: Macmillan, 1965.

Beals, Ralph L., Harry Hoijer, and Alan R. Beals. *An Introduction to Anthropology,* Fifth edition. New York: Macmillan, 1977.

Beardsley, Tim. "Getting Warmer?" *Scientific American,* July 1988:32.

Beck, Allen J., Susan A. Kline, and Lawrence A. Greenfield. "Survey of Youth in Custody, 1987." Washington, D.C.: U.S. Department of Justice, September 1988.

Beck, E. M., and Stewart E. Tolnay. "The Killing Fields of the Deep South: The Market for Cotton and the Lynching of Blacks, 1882–1930." *American Sociological Review, 55,* August 1990:526–539.

Becker, Howard S. *Outsiders: Studies in the Sociology of Deviance.* New York: Free Press, 1966.

Begley, Sharon. "Twins: Nazi and Jew." *Newsweek, 94,* December 3, 1979:139.

Begley, Sharon, and Daniel Glick. "The Handwriting of God." *Newsweek,* May 4, 1992:76.

Beirne, Piers, and Richard Quinney (eds.). *Marxism and Law.* New York: Wiley, 1982.

Belknap, Joanne. "Racism on Campus: Prejudice Plus Power." *Vital Speeches, 57,* 10, March 1, 1991:308–312.

Bell, Daniel. *The Coming of Post-Industrial Society: A Venture in Social Forecasting.* New York: Basic Books, 1973.

Bell, Daniel. "The Third Technological Revolution and Its Possible Socio-economic Consequences." *Dissent,* Spring 1989:164–176.

Bell, David A. "An American Success Story: The Triumph of Asian-Americans." In *Sociological Footprints: Introductory Readings in Sociology,* Leonard Cargan and Jeanne H. Ballantine, eds. Fifth edition. Belmont, California: Wadsworth, 1991:308–316.

Bell, Inge Powell. "The Double Standard." In *Growing Old in America,* Beth B. Hess, ed. New Brunswick, New Jersey: Transaction Books, 1976:150–162.

Bell, Wendell. "Anomie, Social Isolation, and the Class Structure." *Sociometry, 20,* 1957:105–116.

Bell, Wendell, and Marion D. Boat. "Urban Neighborhoods and Informal Social Relations." In *Urban Man and Society: A Reader in Urban Ecology,* Albert N. Cousins and Hans Nagpaul, eds. New York: Knopf, 1970:211–220.

Bellaby, Paul. "What is Genuine Sickness? The Relation Between Work-discipline and the Sick Role in a Pottery Factory." *Sociology of Health and Illness, 12,* 1, 1990:47–68.

Bellah, Robert N. *Beyond Belief.* New York: Harper and Row, 1970.

Bellah, Robert N. *Tokagawa Religion: The Values of Pre-Industrial Japan.* Glencoe, Illinois: Free Press, 1957.

Bellah, Robert N., Richard Madsen, William M. Sullivan, Ann Swidler, and Steven M. Tipton. *Habits of the Heart: Individualism and Commitment in American Life.* Berkeley, California: University of California Press, 1985.

Benales, Carlos. "70 Days Battling Starvation and Freezing in the Andes: A Chronical of Man's Unwillingness to Die." *New York Times,* January 1, 1973:3.

Bender, Sue, "Everyday Sacred: A Journey to the Amish." *Utne Reader,* September–October 1990:91–97.

Benet, Sula. "Why They Live to Be 100, or Even Older, in Abkhasia." *New York Times Magazine, 26,* December 1971.

Bennett, Neil G., Ann Klimas Blanc, and David E. Bloo. "Commitment and the Modern Union: Assessing the Link Between Premarital Cohabitation and Subsequent Marital Stability." *American Sociological Review, 53,* 1988:127–138.

Benokraitis, Nijole V., and Joe R. Feagin. "Sex Discrimination: Subtle and Covert." In *Down to Earth Sociology: Introductory Readings,* Seventh edition. James M. Henslin, ed. New York: Free Press, 1993.

Benokraitis, Nijole V., and Joe R. Feagin. *Modern Sexism.* Englewood Cliffs: Prentice-Hall, 1986.

Benson, Ian, and John Lloyd. *New Technology and Industrial Change: The Impact of the Scientific-Technical Revolution on Labour and Industry.* New York: Nichols Publishing, 1983.

Berger, Arthur S., and Joyce Berger, eds. *To Die or Not to Die: Cross-Disciplinary, Cultural, and Legal Perspectives on the Right to Choose Death.* Westport, Connecticut: Praeger, 1990.

Berger, Peter L. *Invitation to Sociology: A Humanistic Perspective.* New York: Doubleday, 1963.

Berger, Peter L. "Invitation to Sociology." In *Down to Earth Sociology: Introductory Readings,* Seventh edition, James M. Henslin, ed. New York: The Free Press, 1993.

Berger, Peter L. *The Sacred Canopy: Elements of a Sociological Theory of Religion.* Garden City, New York: Doubleday, 1967.

Berger, Peter L., and Hansfried Kellner. "Marriage and the Construction of Reality." In *Marriage and Family in a Changing Society* (fourth edition). New York: Free Press, 1992:165–174.

Berger, Peter L., and Thomas Luckmann. *The Social Construction of Reality: A Treatise in the Sociology of Knowledge.* Garden City, New York: Anchor Books, 1967.

Berk, Richard A. *Collective Behavior.* Dubuque, Iowa: William C. Brown, 1974.

Berkeley, Arthur Eliot. "Job Interviewers' Dirty Little Secret." *Wall Street Journal,* March 20, 1989:A14.

Berle, Adolf, Jr., and Gardiner C. Means. *The Modern Corporation and Private Property.* New York: Harcourt, Brace and World, 1932. As cited in Useem 1980:44.

Bernard, Jessie. *The Future of Marriage.* New York: Bantam, 1972.

Bernard, Jessie. "The Good-Provider Role." In *Marriage and Family in a Changing Society,* fourth edition, James M. Henslin, ed. New York: Free Press, 1992:275–285.

Bernard, Viola W., Perry Ottenberg, and Fritz Redl. "Dehumanization: A Composite Psychological Defense in Relation to Modern War." In *The Triple Revolution Emerging: Social Problems in Depth,* Robert Perucci and Marc Pilisuk (eds.). Boston: Little Brown, 1971:17–34.

Berrueta-Clement, J. R., C. J. Schweinhart, W. S. Barnett, A. S. Epstein, and D. P. Weikart. "Changed Lives: The Effects of the Perry Preschool Program on Youths Through Age 19." *Monographs of the High/Scope Educational Research Foundation, 8,* 1984.

Bettelheim, Bruno. "Difficulties between Parents and Children: Their Causes and How to Prevent Them." In *Family Strengths 4: Positive Support Systems,* Nick Stinnett, John DeFrain, Kay King, Herbert Lingren, George Row, Sally Van Zandt, and Roseanne Williams, eds. Lincoln: University of Nebraska Press, 1982:5–14.

Billingsley, Andrew. *Black Families in White America.* Englewood Cliffs, New Jersey: Prentice Hall, 1968.

Bishop, Jerry E. "Study Finds Doctors Tend to Postpone Heart Surgery for Women, Raising Risk." *Wall Street Journal,* April 16, 1990:B4.

Blackwood, Roy E. "The Content of News Photos: Roles Portrayed by Men and Women." *Journalism Quarterly, 60,* 1983:710–714.

Blau, Peter M. *Exchange and Power in Social Life.* New York: Wiley, 1964.

Blau, Peter M., and Otis Dudley Duncan. *The American Occupational Structure.* New York: John Wiley, 1967.

Blauner, Robert. "Death and Social Structure." *Psychiatry, 29,* 1966:378–394.

Blauner, Robert. *Racial Oppression in America.* New York: Harper and Row, 1972.

Blinick, Abraham. "Socialized Medicine Is No Cure-All." *Wall Street Journal,* January 17, 1992:A11.

Blood, Robert O., Jr., and Donald M. Wolfe. *Husbands and Wives.* New York: Free Press, 1960.

Blumer, Herbert George. "Collective Behavior." In *Principles of Sociology,* Robert E. Park, ed. New York: Barnes and Noble, 1939: 219–288.

Blumer, Herbert. "Sociological Implications of the Thought of George Herbert Mead." *American Journal of Sociology, 71,* 1966:535–544.

Blumstein, Alfred, and Jacqueline Cohen. "Characterizing Criminal Careers." *Science, 237,* August 1987:985–991.

Blumstein, Philip, and Pepper Schwartz. *American Couples: Money, Work, Sex.* New York: Pocket Books, 1985.

Bobo, Lawrence, and James R. Kluegel. "Modern American Prejudice: Stereotypes, Social Distance, and Perceptions of Discrimination toward Blacks, Hispanics, and Asians." Paper presented at the 1991 annual meeting of the American Sociological Association.

Boden, Deirdre, Anthony Giddens, and Harvey L. Molotch. "Sociology's Role in Addressing Society's Problems Is Undervalued and Misunderstood in Academe." *Chronicle of Higher Education,* February 21, 1990: B1, B3.

Bodenheimer, Thomas. "Should We Abolish the Private Health Insurance Industry?" *International Journal of Health Services, 20,* 2, 1990: 199–220.

Bogue, Donald J. *Skid Row in American Cities.* Chicago: University of Chicago Press, 1963.

Bohrer, Linda. "AIDS Impact Grows in Asia." *Wall Street Journal,* April 13, 1992:A11.

Borrelli, Peter. "The Ecophilosophers." *The Amicus Journal,* Spring 1988:30–39.

Boulard, Gerry. "Student Staffers May Lose Control of Campus Paper." *Editor and Publisher, 124,* 41, October 12, 1991:20, 40.

Boulding, Elise. *The Underside of History.* Boulder, Colorado: Westview Press, 1976.

Bowen, Crosswell. "Donora, Pennsylvania. In *Society and Environment: The Coming Collision,* Rex R. Campbell and Jerry L. Wade, eds. Boston: Allyn and Bacon, 1972:163–168.

Bowles, Samuel. "Unequal Education and the Reproduction of the Social Division of Labor." In *Power and Ideology in Education,* J. Karabel and A. H. Halsey, eds. New York: Oxford University Press, 1977:

Bowles, Samuel, and Herbert Gintis. *Schooling in Capitalist America.* New York: Basic Books, 1976.

Brajuha, Mario, and Lyle Hallowell. "Legal Intrusion and the Politics of Fieldwork: The Impact of the Brajuha Case." *Urban Life, 14* (4), January 1986:454–478.

Brecher, Edward M., and the Editors of Consumer Reports. *Licit and Illicit Drugs.* Boston: Little Brown, 1972.

Bridgwater, William, ed. *The Columbia Viking Desk Encyclopedia.* New York: Viking Press, 1953.

Brilliant, Ashleigh E. *Social Effects of the Automobile in Southern California During the 1920s.* Berkeley: Unpublished Ph.D. dissertation, University of California, 1964. Cited in Flink 1988.

Brinton, Mary C. "Gender Stratification in Contemporary Urban Japan." *American Sociological Review, 54,* August 1989:549–564.

Broad, William J. "The Shuttle Explodes." *New York Times,* January 29, 1986, A1, A5.

Brodie, H. Keith H. "We Must Engage Intolerance and Inhumanity Openly and Publicly, as a Community, at Every Opportunity." *Chronicle of Higher Education, 36,* 4, September 27, 1989:B3.

Bronfenbrenner, Urie. "Principles for the Healthy Growth and Development of Children." In *Marriage and Family in a Changing Society,* Fourth edition, James M. Henslin, ed. New York: The Free Press, 1992:243–249.

Brooks, Geraldine. "Saudi Duty Brings Novel Challenges." *Wall Street Journal,* August 16, 1990:A8.

Brooks, Virginia R. "Sex Differences in Student Dominance Behavior in Female and Male Professors' Classrooms." *Sex Roles, 8,* 7, 1982: 683–690.

Brown, Diane Robinson, and Lawrence E. Gary. "Unemployment and Psychological Distress Among Black American Women." *Sociological Focus, 21,* 1988:209–221.

Brown, Lester R. "The New World Order." In *Taking Sides: Clashing Views on Controversial Social Issues,* Kurt Finsterbusch and George McKenna, eds. Guilford, Connecticut: Dushkin, 1992:338–346.

Brown, Lester R. *State of the World 1991.* New York: W. W. Norton, 1991.

Browne, A., and K. Williams. "Exploring the Effect of Resource Availability on the Likelihood of Female-Perpetrated Homicides." *Law and Society Review, 23,* 1989:75–94.

Brueckner, Jan K. "Analyzing Third World Urbanization: A Model with Empirical Evidence." *Economic Development and Cultural Change, 38,* 3, April 1990:587–610.

Brunvand, Jan Harold. *The Choking Doberman and Other "New" Urban Legends.* New York: Norton, 1984.

Brunvand, Jan Harold. *The Study of American Folklore.* New York, Norton, 1986.

Brunvand, Jan Harold. *The Vanishing Hitchhiker: American Urban Legends and Their Meanings.* New York: Norton, 1981.

Bryant, Clifton D. "Cockfighting: America's Invisible Sport." In *Down to Earth Sociology: Introductory Readings.* Seventh edition. James M. Henslin, ed. New York: The Free Press, 1993.

Buckley, Stephen. *The Washington Post,* "Shrugging Off the Burden of a Brainy Image." June 17, 1991:D1.

Bullard, Robert D. *Dumping in Dixie: Race, Class, and Environmental Quality.* Boulder, Colorado: Westview Press, 1990.

Bullard, Robert, and Beverly Hendrix Wright. "Environmentalism and the Politics of Equity: Emergent Trends in the Black Community." *Mid-American Review of Sociology, 12,* 2, 1987:21–38.

Bullard, Robert, and Beverly Hendrix Wright. "The Quest for Environmental Equality: Mobilizing the African-American Community for Social Change." *Society and Natural Resources, 3,* 1990:301–311.

Bumiller, Elisabeth. "First Comes Marriage—Then, Maybe, Love." In *Marriage and Family in a Changing Society,* James M. Henslin, ed. Fourth edition. New York: The Free Press, 1992:120–125.

Bumpass, Larry L., James A. Sweet, and Andrew Cherlin. "The Role of Cohabitation in Declining Rates of Marriage." *Journal of Marriage and the Family, 53,* November 1991:913–927.

Bureau of the Census. *Current Population Reports: Consumer Income.* Series P-60, No. 157. "Money Income and Poverty Status of Families and Persons in the United States, 1986." Washington, D.C.: U.S. Government Printing Office, 1987.

Bureau of the Census. *Statistical Abstract of the United States.* Washington, D.C.: United States Government Printing Office, 1989.

Burgess, Ernest W. "The Growth of the City: An Introduction to a Research Project." In *The City,* Robert E. Park, Ernest W. Burgess, and Roderick D. McKenzie, eds. Chicago: University of Chicago Press, 1925:47–62.

Burgess, Ernest W., and Harvey J. Locke. *The Family: From Institution to Companionship.* New York: American Book, 1945.

Burke, Anna Celeste, and Jane A. Rafferty. "The Transformation of the European Community (EC): A Study in Competing Political and Economic Structures in the Global Arena." Presented at the annual meetings of the American Sociological Association, 1991.

Burnham, Walter Dean. *Democracy in the Making: American Government and Politics.* Englewood Cliffs, New Jersey: Prentice Hall, 1983.

Burton, Thomas M. "How Industrial Foam Came to Be Employed in Breast Implants." *Wall Street Journal,* March 25, 1992:A1, A4.

Burton, Thomas M., Bruce Ingersoll, and Joan E. Rigdon. "Dow Corning Makes Changes in Top Posts." *Wall Street Journal,* February 11, 1992:A3, A4.

Burton, Thomas M., and Scott McMurray. "Dow Corning Still Keeps Implant Data From Public, Despite Vow of Openness." *Wall Street Journal,* February 18, 1992:B8.

Bush, Diane Mitsch, and Roberta G. Simmons. "Socialization Processes Over the Life Course." In *Social Psychology: Sociological Perspectives,* Morris Rosenberg and Ralph H. Turner, eds. New Brunswick, New Jersey, Transaction, 1990:133–164.

Butler, Robert N. "Ageism: Another Form of Bigotry." *Gerontologist, 9,* Winter 1980:243–246.

Butler, Robert N. *Why Survive? Being Old in America.* New York: Harper and Row, 1975.

Buttel, Frederick H. "New Directions in Environmental Sociology." *Annual Review of Sociology, 13,* W. Richard Scott and James F. Short, Jr., eds. Palo Alto, California: Annual Reviews, 1987:465–488.

Buttel, Frederick H. "Sociology and the Environment: The Winding Road Toward Human Ecology." *International Social Science Journal, 38,* 1986:337–356.

Butterworth, Katharine M. "The Story of a Nursing Home Refugee." In *Social Problems 92/93,* LeRoy W. Barnes, ed. Guilford, Connecticut: Dushkin, 1992:90–93.

Cain, L. D. "Adding Spice to Middle Age." *Contemporary Sociology, 8,* 1979:547–550.

Callahn, Daniel. *Setting Limits: Medical Goals in an Aging Society.* New York: Simon and Schuster, 1987.

Calloway, Michael, and Donald Tomaskovic-Devey. "Does Class Matter? The Relationship between Class Position and Political Ideology." *Journal of Political and Military Sociology, 17,* 2, Winter 1989:241–262.

Camp, Roderick A., and James D. Riley. "Mexico." In *World Book Encyclopedia.* Chicago: World Book, Inc., 1990:448–475.

Cantril, Hadley. *The Psychology of Social Movements.* New York: John Wiley, 1941.

Caplin, Mortimer M. "A History of the Internal Revenue Service, 1862–1962." Washington, D.C.: U.S. Government Printing Office, November 1962.

Caplow, Theodore. "The American Way of Celebrating Christmas." In *Down to Earth Sociology: Introductory Readings,* Sixth Edition. New York: Free Press, 1991:88–97.

Cardoso, Fernando Henrique. "Dependent Capitalist Development in Latin America." *New Left Review, 74,* July/August 1972:83–95.

Carlson, Lewis H., and George A. Colburn. *In Their Place: White America Defines Her Minorities, 1850–1950.* New York: Wiley, 1972.

Carlton, Jim, and Neil Barsky. "Japanese Purchases of U.S. Real Estate Fall on Hard Times." *Wall Street Journal,* March 4, 1992:A2.

Carpenter, Betsy. "Redwood Radicals." *U.S. News & World Report, 109,* 11, September 17, 1990:50–51.

Carr, Donald E. "The Disasters." In *Society and Environment: The Coming Collision,* Rex R. Campbell and Jerry L. Wade, eds. Boston: Allyn and Bacon, 1972:129–134.

Carroll, Paul B. "Let the Games Begin." *Wall Street Journal,* April 6, 1992:R10.

Carroll, Peter N., and David W. Noble. *The Free and the Unfree: A New History of the United States.* New York: Penguin, 1977.

Carter, Timothy J., and Donald Cleland. "A Neo-Marxian Critique, Formulation and Test of Juvenile Dispositions as a Function of Social Class." *Social Problems, 27,* October 1979:96–108.

Cartwright, Dorwin, and Alvin Zander, eds. *Group Dynamics,* Third edition. Evanston, Illinois: Peterson, 1968.

Census Bureau. "Census and You: April 1991." Washington, D.C.: U.S. Government Printing Office, 1991.

Census Bureau. *World Population Profile: 1985.* Washington, D.C.: U.S. Government Printing Office, October 1986.

Census Bureau. *World Population Profile: 1989.* Washington, D.C.: U.S. Government Printing Office, October 1989b.

Census Bureau. *Population Profile of the United States: 1989.* Washington, D.C.: U.S. Government Printing Office, 1989.

Centers for Disease Control. *HIV/AIDS Surveillance Report,* January 1992.

Cerhan, Jane Ugland. "The Hmong in the United States: An Overview for Mental Health Professionals." *Journal of Counseling and Development, 69,* 1, September–October 1990:88–92.

Chafetz, Janet Saltzman. *Sex and Advantage: A Comparative Macro-Structural Theory of Sex Stratification.* Totowa, New Jersey: Rowman and Allenheld, 1984.

Chagnon, Napoleon A. *Yanomamo: The Fierce People,* Second edition. New York: Holt, Rinehart and Winston, 1977.

Chalfant, H. Paul, Robert E. Beckley, and C. Eddie Palmer. *Religion in Contemporary Society,* Second edition. Palo Alto, California: Mayfield Publishing Company, 1987.

Chamberlain, John. "Should We Auction Immigration Visas?" *St. Louis Post-Dispatch,* September 11, 1986:3E.

Chambliss, William J. "The Saints and the Roughnecks." *Society, 11,* November–December 1973:24–31.

Chambliss, William J. "The Saints and the Roughnecks." In *Down to Earth Sociology: Introductory Readings.* Seventh edition, James M. Henslin, ed. New York: The Free Press, 1993.

Chambliss. William J. "A Sociological Analysis of the Law of Vagrancy." *Social Problems, 12,* Summer 1964:67–77.

Chandler, Tertius, and Gerald Fox. *3000 Years of Urban Growth.* New York: Academic Press, 1974.

Charon, Joel M. *Ten Questions: A Sociological Perspective.* Belmont, California: Wadsworth, 1992.

Chase, Marilyn. "Bristol-Myers AIDS Drug, DDI, Equals or Tops Wellcome's AZT, Study Shows." *Wall Street Journal,* April 14, 1992a:B5.

Chase, Marilyn. "Multiple Mutating HIV Strains Stymie Researchers Seeking a Vaccine for AIDS." *Wall Street Journal,* May 26, 1992:B1, B6.

Chavez, Linda. "Rainbow Collision." *New Republic,* November 19, 1990:14–16.

Chen, Edwin. "Twins Reared Apart: A Living Lab." *New York Times Magazine.* December 9, 1979:112.

Cherlin, Andrew. "Remarriage as an Incomplete Institution." In *Marriage and Family in a Changing Society,* Third edition. James M. Henslin, ed. New York: Free Press, 1989:492–501.

Cherlin, Andrew, and Frank F. Furstenberg, Jr. "The American Family in the Year 2000." In *Down to Earth Sociology,* Fifth edition. James M. Henslin, ed. New York: Free Press, 1988:325–331.

Chodorow, Nancy J. "What is the Relation between Psychoanalytic Feminism and the Psychoanalytic Psychology of Women?" In *Theoretical Perspectives on Sexual Difference,* Deborah L. Rhode, ed. New Haven, Connecticut: Yale University Press, 1990:114–130.

Christensen, Harold T., and Kathryn P. Johnsen. In *Marriage and Family in a Changing Society,* Third edition. James M. Henslin, ed. New York: Free Press, 1989:15–26.

Cicerelli, Victor G., J. W. Evans, and J. S. Schiller. *The Impact of Head Start: An Evaluation of the Effects of Head Start on Children's Cognitive and Affective Development,* two volumes. Athens, Ohio: Ohio University, 1969.

Clark, Burton R. "The 'Cooling-Out' Function in Higher Education." In *Social Problems Today: Coping with the Challenges of a Changing Society,* James M. Henslin, ed. Englewood Cliffs, New Jersey: Prentice Hall, 1990:309–316.

Clark, Candace. "Sympathy in Everyday Life." In *Down to Earth Sociology: Introductory Readings,* Sixth edition, James M. Henslin, ed. New York: Free Press, 1991:193–203.

Clark, Curtis B. "Geriatric Abuse: Out of the Closet." In *The Tragedy of Elder Abuse: The Problem and the Response.* Hearings before the Select Committee on Aging, House of Representatives. Washington, D.C.: U.S. Government Printing Office, July 1, 1986:49–50.

Clausen, J. A. "The Life Course of Individuals." In *Aging and Society,* Matilda White Riley, ed. 1973.

Clay, Jason W. "What's A Nation?" *Mother Jones,* November–December 1990:28, 30.

Cleveland, Harlan. "The Age of Spreading Knowledge." *The Futurist,* 24, 2, March–April 1990:35–39.

Clinard, Marshall B., Peter C. Yeager, Jeanne Brisette, David Petrashek, and Elizabeth Harries. *Illegal Corporate Behavior.* Washington, D.C.: U.S. Department of Justice, 1979.

Clines, Francis X. "Chernobyl Shakes Reindeer Culture of Lapps." *New York Times,* September 14, 1986:1, 20.

Clingempeel, W. Glenn, and N. Dickon Repucci. "Joint Custody after Divorce: Major Issues and Goals for Research." *Psychological Bulletin,* 9, 1982:102–127.

Cloward, Richard A., and Lloyd E. Ohlin. *Delinquency and Opportunity: A Theory of Delinquent Gangs.* New York: Free Press, 1960.

Coburn, David, Carl D'Arcy, Peter New, and George Torrance. *Health and Canadian Society.* Toronto: Fitzhenry and Whiteside, 1981.

Cockerham, William. *Medical Sociology.* Fourth edition. Englewood Cliffs, New Jersey: Prentice Hall, 1989.

Cohen, Deborah L. "Inordinate Share of Poverty Said to Rest on Children." *Education Week, 11,* 6, October 9, 1991:4.

Cohen, Erik. "Lovelorn Farangs: The Correspondence Between Foreign Men and Thai Girls." *Anthropological Quarterly, 59,* 3, July 1986: 115–127.

Cohen, Laurie P., William Power, and Michael Siconolfi. "Financial Firms Act to Curb Office Sexism, With Mixed Results." *Wall Street Journal,* November 5, 1991:A1, A6.

Cohen, Morris R. "Moral Aspects of the Criminal Law." *Yale Law Journal, 49,* April 1940:1009–1026.

Cohen, Murray, Theoharis Seghorn, and Wilfred Calamas. "Sociometric Study of the Sex Offender." *Journal of Abormal Psychology, 74,* April 1969:249–255.

Cohen, Ronald. "Brittle Marriage as a Stable System: The Kanuri Case." In *Divorce and After: An Analysis of the Emotional and Social Problems of Divorce,* Paul Bohannan, ed. New York: Doubleday, 1971:205–239.

Coleman, James S. *Public and Private High Schools: The Impact of Communities.* New York: Basic Books, 1987.

Coleman, James S. "Racial Segregation in the Schools: New Research with New Policy Implications." *Phi Delta Kappan, 57,* 1975:75–78.

Coleman, James S., Ernest Q. Campbell, Carol J. Hobson, James McPartland, Alexander M. Mood, Frederic D. Weinfeld, and Robert L. York. *Equality of Educational Opportunity.* Washington, D.C.: U.S. Government Printing Office, 1966.

Coleman, James S., Thomas Hoffer, and Sally Kilgore. *High School Achievement: Public, Catholic, and Private Schools Compared.* New York: Basic Books, 1982.

Coleman, James S., Thomas Hoffer, and Sally Kilgore. *Trends in School Desegregation, 1968–73.* Washington, D.C.: Urban Institute, 1975.

Coleman, James William. *The Criminal Elite: The Sociology of White Collar Crime.* New York: St. Martin's Press, 1989.

Collins, Patricia Hill. "Learning from the Outsider Within: The Sociological Significance of Black Feminist Thought." *Social Problems, 33,* 6, December 1986:514–532.

Collins, Randall. *Conflict Sociology: Toward an Explanatory Science.* New York: Academic Press, 1974.

Collins, Randall. *The Credential Society: An Historical Sociology of Education.* New York: Academic Press, 1979.

Collins, Randall. "Love and Property." In *Marriage and Family in a Changing Society,* Fourth edition. James M. Henslin, ed. New York: The Free Press, 1992:126–134.

Congressional Quarterly Researcher, 1, 13, August 9, 1991: Special Issue on sexual harassment.

Cookson, Peter W., Jr., and Caroline Hodges Persell. *Preparing for Power: America's Elite Boarding Schools.* New York: Basic Books, 1985.

Cooley, Charles Horton. *Human Nature and the Social Order.* New York: Scribner's, 1902.

Cooley, Charles Horton. *Social Organization.* New York: Charles Scribner, 1909.

Cooley, Charles Horton. *Social Organization.* New York: Schocken, 1962.

Cooper, Kenneth J. "National Test for High School Seniors Gains Backing." In *Ourselves and Others: The Washington Post Sociology Companion.* Boston: Allyn Bacon, 1992:245–246.

Cooper, Kenneth J. "New Focus Sought in National High School Exams: NEH Backs Approach Used in Europe and Japan to Assess Knowledge Rather Than Aptitude." *Washington Post,* May 20, 1991:A7.

Corchado, Alfredo. "Hispanic Supermarkets Are Blossoming." *Wall Street Journal,* January 23, 1989:B1.

Corcoran, Mary, Greg J. Duncan, Gerald Gurin, and Patricia Gurin. "Myth and Reality: The Causes and Persistence of Poverty." *Journal of Policy Analysis and Management, 4,* (4), 1985:516–536.

Coser, Lewis A. *Masters of Sociological Thought: Ideas in Historical and Social Context* (second edition). New York: Harcourt Brace Jovanovich, 1977.

Cottin, Lou. *Elders in Rebellion: A Guide to Senior Activism.* Garden City, N.Y.: Anchor Doubleday, 1979.

Couch, Carl J. *Social Processes and Relationships: A Formal Approach.* Dix Hills, New York: General Hall, 1989.

Coughlin, Ellen K. "Studying Homelessness: The Difficulty of Tracking a Transient Population." *The Chronicle of Higher Education,* October 19, 1988:A6–A12.

Cowen, Emory L., Judah Landes, and Donald E. Schaet. "The Effects of Mild Frustration on the Expression of Prejudiced Attitudes." *Journal of Abnormal and Social Psychology.* January 1959:33–38.

Cowgill, Donald. "The Aging of Populations and Societies." *Annals of the American Academy of Political and Social Science, 415,* 1974:1–18.

Cowley, Joyce. *Pioneers of Women's Liberation.* New York: Merit, 1969.

Cox, Meg. "Clearer Connections." *Wall Street Journal,* March 24, 1986:200.

Cressey, Donald R. *Other People's Money.* New York: Free Press, 1953.

Crispell, Diane, "People Patterns." *Wall Street Journal,* March 16, 1992:B1.

Crosbie, Paul V., ed. *Interaction in Small Groups.* New York: Macmillan, 1975.

Crossen, Cynthia. *Wall Street Journal,* November 14, 1991:A1, A7.

Cumming, Elaine. "Further Thoughts on the Theory of Disengagement." In *Aging in America: Readings in Social Gerontology,* Cary S. Kart and Barbara B. Manard, eds. Sherman Oaks, California: Alfred Publishing, 1976:19–41.

Cumming, Elaine, and William E. Henry. *Growing Old: The Process of Disengagement.* New York: Basic Books, 1961.

Curtin, Sharon. "Nobody Ever Died of Old Age: In Praise of Old People." In *Growing Old in America,* Beth Hess (ed.). New Brunswick, N.J.: Transaction, 1976:273–284.

Curwin, E. Cecil, and Gudmond Hart. *Plough and Pasture.* New York: Collier Books, 1961.

Cuzzort, R. P. *Using Social Thought: The Nuclear Issue and Other Concerns.* Mountain View, California: Mayfield, 1989.

Cuzzort, Ray P., and Edith W. King. *20th Century Thought,* Third edition. New York: Holt, Rinehart and Winston, 1980.

Dahl, Robert A. *Dilemmas of Pluralist Democracy: Autonomy vs. Control.* New Haven, Connecticut: Yale University Press, 1982.

Dahl, Robert A. *Who Governs?* New Haven, Connecticut: Yale University Press, 1961.

Dahrendorf, Ralf. *Class and Class Conflict in Industrial Society.* Palo Alto, California: Stanford University Press, 1959.

Daly, Martin, and Margo Wilson. *Homicide.* New York: Aldine de Gruyter, 1988.

Daniels, Roger. *The Decision to Relocate the Japanese Americans.* Philadelphia: Lippincott, 1975.

Dannefer, Dale. "Adult Development and Social Theory: A Reappraisal." *American Sociological Review,* 49 (1), February 1984:100–116.

Danzi, Angela D. "Savaria, The Midwife: Childbirth and Change in the Immigrant Community." In *Contemporary Readings in Sociology,* Judith N. DeSena, ed. Dubuque, Iowa: Kendall/Hunt, 1989:47–56.

Darley, John M., and Bibb Latane. "Bystander Intervention in Emergencies: Diffusion of Responsibility." *Journal of Personality and Social Psychology,* 8, (4), 1968:377–383.

Darwin, Charles. *The Origin of Species.* Chicago: W. B. Conley, 1859.

Davidson, Joe. "Differing Social Programs for Young, Old Result In Contrasting Poverty Levels for Two Groups." *Wall Street Journal,* June 27, 1985:56.

Davies, James C. "Toward a Theory of Revolution." *American Sociological Review,* 27, 1, February 1962:5–19.

Davis, Allison, Burleigh B. Gardner, and Mary R. Gardner. *Deep South: A Social-Anthropological Study of Caste and Class.* Chicago: University of Chicago Press, 1941.

Davis, Bob. "In Rio, They're Eyeing Greenhouse Two-Step." *Wall Street Journal,* April 21, 1992:A1.

Davis, Fred. "The Cabdriver and His Fare: Facets of a Fleeting Relationship." *American Journal of Sociology,* 65, September 1959:158–165.

Davis, James. "Up and Down Opportunity's Ladder." *Public Opinion,* 5, June–July, 1982:11–15, 48–51.

Davis, Junetta. "Sexist Bias in Eight Newspapers." *Journalism Quarterly,* 59, 1982:456–460.

Davis, Kingsley. "Extreme Isolation." In *Down to Earth Sociology: Introductory Readings,* Seventh edition. James M. Henslin, ed. New York: The Free Press, 1993.

Davis, Kingsley, and Wilbert E. Moore. "Reply to Tumin." *American Sociological Review,* 18, 1953:394–396.

Davis, Kingsley, and Wilbert E. Moore. "Some Principles of Stratification." *American Sociological Review,* 10, 1945:242–249.

Davis, Nanette J. "The Prostitute: Developing a Deviant Identity." In *Studies in the Sociology of Sex,* James M. Henslin, ed. New York: Appleton Century Crofts, 1971:297–322.

Davis, Nanette J. "Prostitution: Identity, Career, and Legal-Economic Enterprise." In *The Sociology of Sex: An Introductory Reader,* Revised edition, James M. Henslin and Edward Sagarin, eds. New York: Schocken Books, 1978:195–222.

Day, Charles R., Jr. "Tear Up the Tracks." *Industry Week, 239,* 5, March 5, 1990:5.

de Beauvoir, Simone. *The Second Sex.* New York: Alfred A. Knopf, 1953.

de Cordoba, Jose. "One Newspaper Finds Way top Lure Readers: Publish in Spanish." *Wall Street Journal,* April 23, 1992:A1, A8.

De George, Richard T. *The New Marxism: Soviet and East European Marxism Since 1956.* New York: Pegasus 1968.

De Witt, Karen. "Verbal Scores Hit New Low in Scholastic Aptitude Test." *New York Times,* August 27, 1991:A1, A20.

Deevey, E. S., Don S. Rice, Prudence M. Rice, H. H. Vaughan, Mark Brenner, and M. S. Flannery. "Mayan Urbanism: Impact on a Tropical Karst Environment." *Science,* October 19, 1979:298–306.

DeMause, Lloyd. "Our Forebears Made Childhood a Nightmare." *Psychology Today 8* (11): April 1975:85–88.

Demos, John. "The American Family of Past Time." In *Family in Transition,* Second edition. Arlene S. Skolnick and Jerome H. Skolnick, eds. Boston: Little Brown, 1977:59–77. (As quoted in Zinn and Eitzen 1990.)

Dentzler, Susan. "The Vanishing Dream." *U.S. News and World Report,* April 22, 1991:39–43.

Derber, Charles, and William Schwartz. "Toward a Theory of Worker Participation." In *The Transformation of Industrial Organization: Management, Labor, and Society in the United States,* Frank Hearn, ed. Belmont, California: Wadsworth, 1988:217–229.

Deutsch, Claudia H. "Saying No to the 'Mommy Track.'" *New York Times,* January 28, 1990:29.

Di Leonardo, Micaela. "The Female World of Cards and Holidays: Women, Families, and the Work of Kinship." *Signs, 12,* Spring 1987:40–53.

Diamond, Milton. "Sexual Identity: Monozygotic Twins Reared in Discordant Sex Roles and a BBC Follow-Up." *Archives of Sexual Behavior, 11* (2), 1982:181–186.

Dickson, Tony, and Hugh V. McLachlan. "In Search of 'The Spirit of Capitalism': Weber's Misinterpretation of Franklin." *Sociology, 23,* 1, 1989:81–89.

Diehl, Jackson. "New Breeze in Eastern Europe Is Fouled by Pollution: Large Areas May Become Uninhabitable." In *Ourselves and Others: The Washington Post Sociology Companion.* The Washington Post Writers Group, eds. Boston: Allyn and Bacon, 1992:290–296.

DiGiulio, Robert C. "Beyond Widowhood." In *Marriage and Family in a Changing Society,* Fourth edition. James M. Henslin, ed. New York: Free Press, 1992:457–469.

Dobash, Russell P., and R. Emerson Dobash. "Community Response to Violence Against Wives: Charivari, Abstract Justice and Patriarchy." *Social Problems, 28,* June 1981:563–581.

Dobash, Russell P., and R. Emerson Dobash, Margo Wilson, and Martin Daly. "The Myth of Sexual Symmetry in Marital Violence." *Social Problems, 39,* 1, February 1992:71–91.

Dobriner, William M. "The Football Team as Social Structure and Social System." In *Social Structures and Systems: A Sociological Overview.* Pacific Palisades, California: Goodyear, 1969:116–120.

Dobriner, William M. *Social Structures and Systems.* Pacific Palisades, California: Goodyear, 1969.

Dobson, Richard B. "Mobility and Stratification in the Soviet Union." *Annual Review of Sociology.* Palo Alto, California: Annual Reviews, 1977.

Dobyns, Henry F. *Their Numbers Became Thinned: Native American Population Dynamics in Eastern North America.* Knoxville: University of Tennessee Press, 1983.

Dollard, John, et. al. *Frustration and Aggression.* New Haven, Connecticut: Yale University Press, 1939.

Domhoff, G. William. "The Bohemian Grove and Other Retreats." In

Down to Earth Sociology: Introductory Readings. Seventh edition. James M. Henslin, ed. New York: The Free Press, 1993.

Domhoff, G. William. *The Higher Circles: The Governing Class in America.* New York: Random House, 1970.

Domhoff, G. William. *The Power Elite and the State: How Policy is Made in America.* New York: Aldine de Gruyter, 1990.

Domhoff, G. William. *The Powers that Be.* New York: Random House, 1979.

Domhoff, G. William. *Who Really Rules? New Haven and Community Power Reexamined.* New Brunswick, New Jersey: Transaction, 1978.

Domhoff, G. William. *Who Rules America?* Englewood Cliffs, New Jersey: Prentice Hall, 1967.

Domhoff, G. William. *Who Rules America Now? A View for the 80s.* Englewood Cliffs, New Jersey: Prentice Hall, 1983.

Donelson, Samuel. "World News Tonight." May 25, 1992.

Dornbusch, Sanford H., J. Merrill Carlsmith, Steven J. Bushwall, Philiip L. Ritter, Herbert Leiderman, Albert H. Hastorf, and Ruth T. Gross. "Single Parents, Extended Households, and the Control of Adolescents." *Child Development, 56,* 1985:326–341.

Doudna, Christine. "American Couples: Surprising New Findings about Sex, Money, and Work." *Ms., 12,* November 1983:116, 119.

Douglass, Richard L. "Domestic Neglect and Abuse of the Elderly: Implications for Research and Service." *Family Relations, 32,* July 1983:395–402.

Dove, Adrian. "Soul Folk 'Chitling' Test or the Dove Counterbalance Intelligence Test." n.d. (mimeo).

Dowie, Mark. "The Corporate Crime of the Century." *Mother Jones, 2,* September–October, 1977:18–32.

Doyal, Lesley, and Imogen Pennell. *The Political Economy of Health.* London: Pluto Press, 1981.

Doyle, Denis P., Bruce S. Cooper, and Roberta Trachtman. *Taking Charge: State Action on School Reform in the 1980s.* New York: Hudson Institute, 1991.

Draper, R. "The History of Advertising in America." *New York Review of Books 33,* June 26, 1986:14–18.

Drucker, Peter F. "The Rise and Fall of the Blue-Collar Worker." *Wall Street Journal,* April 22, 1987:36.

Drucker, Peter F. "There's More Than One Kind of Team." *Wall Street Journal,* February 11, 1992:A16.

Duncan, Greg J., and James N. Morgan, eds. *Five Thousand American Families: Patterns of Economic Progress.* Ann Arbor, Michigan: Institute for Social Research, 1979.

Duncan, Greg J., and Willard Rodgers. "Has Children's Poverty Become More Persistent?" *American Sociological Review, 56,* August 1991:538–550.

Dunlap, Riley E., and William R. Catton, Jr. "Environmental Sociology." *Annual Review of Sociology, 5,* 1979:243–273.

Dunlap, Riley E., and William R. Catton, Jr. "What Environmental Sociologists Have in Common Whether Concerned with 'Built' or 'Natural' Environments." *Sociological Inquiry, 53,* 2/3, 1983:113–135.

Durkheim, Emile. *The Division of Labor in Society.* Translated by George Simpson. New York: The Free Press, 1933. Originally published in 1893.

Durkheim, Emile. *The Elementary Forms of the Religious Life.* New York: Free Press, 1965. Originally published in 1912.

Durkheim, Emile. *The Rules of Sociological Method,* Sarah A. Solovay and John H. Mueller, translators. Glencoe, Illinois: Free Press, 1958.

Durkheim, Emile. *The Rules of Sociological Method.* New York: Free Press, 1964. Originally published in 1893.

Durkheim, Emile. *Suicide: A Study in Sociology.* Translated by John A. Spaulding and George Simpson. New York: The Free Press, 1966. Originally published in 1897.

Durning, Alan. "Cradles of Life." In *Social Problems 90/91,* LeRoy W. Barnes, ed. Guilford, Connecticut: Dushkin, 1990:231–241.

Dwyer, John M. *The Body at War: The Miracle of the Immune System.* New York: New American Library, 1989:119.

Easterbrook, Gregg. "The Revolution in Modern Medicine." *Newsweek,* *109,* January 26, 1987:40, 42–44, 49–54, 56–59, 61–64, 67–68, 70–74.

Easterbrooks, M. Ann, and Wendy A. Goldberg. "Toddler Development in the Family: Impact of Father Involvement and Parenting Characteristics." *Child Development, 55,* 1984:740–752.

Eckholm, Erik. "Pygmy Chimp Readily Learns Language Skill." *New York Times,* June 24, 1985:A1, B7.

Eder, Klaus. "The Rise of Counter-culture Movements Against Modernity: Nature as a New Field of Class Struggle." *Theory, Culture & Society, 7,* 1990:21–47.

Edgerton, Robert B. *Deviance: A Cross-Cultural Perspective.* Menlo Park, California: Benjamin Cummings, 1976.

Edwards, Richard. *Contested Terrain: The Transformation of the Workplace in the Twentieth Century.* New York: Basic Books, 1979.

Ehrenreich, Barbara, and Deidre English. *Witches, Midwives, and Nurses: A History of Women Healers.* Old Westbury, New York: Feminist Press, 1973.

Ehrensaft, Diane. *Parenting Together: Men and Women Sharing the Care of Their Children.* New York: Free Press, 1987.

Ehrensaft, Diane. "Shared Parenting." In *Marriage and Family in a Changing Society,* Third edition. James M. Henslin, ed. New York: The Free Press, 1989:242–247.

Ehrlich, Elizabeth. "The Mommy Track." *Business Week, 3096,* March 20, 1989:126–134.

Eibl-Eibesfeldt, Irrenäus. *Ethology: The Biology of Behavior.* New York: Holt, Rinehart, and Winston, 1970.

Eisenhart, R. Wayne. "You Can't Hack It, Little Girl: A Discussion of the Covert Psychological Agenda of Modern Combat Training." *Journal of Social Issues, 31,* Fall 1975:13–23.

Eisinger, Peter K. *The Politics of Displacement: Racial and Ethnic Transition in Three-American Cities.* Campbell, California: Academic Press, 1980.

Ekman, Paul, Wallace V. Friesen, and John Bear. "The International Language of Gestures." *Psychology Today,* May 1984:64.

Elder, Glen H., Jr. "Age Differentiation and Life Course." *Annual Review of Sociology, 1,* 1975:165–190. (As quoted in Bush and Simmons 1990)

Elkind, David. *The Hurried Child: Growing Up Too Fast Too Soon.* Reading, Massachusetts: Addison-Wesley, 1981.

Elkins, Stanley M. *Slavery: A Problem in American Institutional and Intellectual Life,* Second edition. Chicago: University of Chicago Press, 1968.

Engardio, Pete. "Fast Times on *Avenida Madison.*" *Business Week,* June 6, 1988:62–64, 67.

Engels, Friedrich. *The Origin of the Family, Private Property, and the State.* New York: International Publishing, 1942. Originally published in 1884.

Epstein, Cynthia Fuchs. *Deceptive Distinctions: Sex, Gender, and the Social Order.* New Haven, Connecticut: Yale University Press, 1988.

Epstein, Cynthia Fuchs. Letter to the author, January 26, 1989.

Epstein, Cynthia Fuchs. "Inevitabilities of Prejudice." *Society,* September–October 1986:7–15.

Erikson, Erik H. *Childhood and Society.* New York: Norton, 1950.

Erikson, Robert S., Norman R. Luttberg, and Kent L. Tedin. *American Public Opinion: Its Origins, Content, and Impact.* Second edition. New York: John Wiley, 1980.

Ernst, Eldon G. "The Baptists." In *Encyclopedia of the American Religious Experience: Studies of Traditions and Movements,* Volume 1, Charles H, Lippy and Peter W. Williams, eds. New York: Charles Scribners Sons, 1988:555–577.

Eron, Leonard D. "Parent-Child Interaction, Television Violence, and Aggression of Children. *American Psychologist, 37* (2), February 1982:197–211.

Etzioni, Amitai. *An Immodest Agenda: Rebuilding America Before the Twenty-First Century.* New York: McGraw-Hill, 1982.

Etzioni, Amitai, ed. *The Semi-Professions and Their Organization.* New York: Free Press, 1969.

Evanier, David. "Invisible Man." *New Republic,* October 14, 1991:21–25.

Farber, Susan I. *Identical Twins Raised Apart.* New York: Basic Books, 1981.

Faris, Robert E. L., and Warren Dunham. *Mental Disorders in Urban Areas.* Chicago: University of Chicago Press, 1939.

Farkas, George, Daniel Sheehan, and Robert P. Grobe. "Coursework Mastery and School Success: Gender, Ethnicity, and Poverty Groups Within an Urban School District." *American Educational Research Journal, 27* (4), Winter 1990b:807–827.

Farkas, George, Robert P. Grobe, Daniel Sheehan, and Yuan Shuan. "Cultural Resources and School Success: Gender, Ethnicity, and Poverty Groups Within an Urban School District." *American Sociological Review, 55,* February 1990a:127–142.

Farley, John E. *Sociology.* Englewood Cliffs, New Jersey: Prentice Hall, 1990.

Farley, Reynolds, and Walter R. Allen. *The Color Line and the Quality of Life in America.* New York: Russell Sage, 1987.

Farrell, Walter C., Jr., and Cloyzelle K. Jones. "Recent Racial Incidents in Higher Education: A Preliminary Survey." *Urban Review, 20,* 3, 1988:211–226.

Faunce, William A. *Problems of an Industrial Society,* Second edition. New York: McGraw-Hill, 1981.

FBI Uniform Crime Reports. Washington, D.C.: U.S. Government Printing Office, 1990.

Feagin, Joe R. "The Continuing Significance of Race: Antiblack Discrimination in Public Places." *American Sociological Review, 56,* February 1991:101–116.

Feagin, Joe R., and Clairece Booher Feagin. *Discrimination American Style,* revised edition. Melbourne, Florida: Krieger Publishing, 1986.

Feagin, Joe R., and Robert Parker. *Building American Cities: The Urban Real Estate Game.* Second edition. Englewood Cliffs, New Jersey: Prentice Hall, 1990.

Featherman, David L. "Opportunities are Expanding." *Society, 13,* 1979:4–11.

Featherman, David L., and Robert M. Hauser. *Opportunity and Change.* New York: Academic Press, 1978.

Feiler, Bruce S. "Cliff Notes." *The New Republic,* March 23, 1992:8–10.

Feinglass, Joe. "Next, the McDRG." *The Progressive, 51,* January 1987:28.

Ferguson, Trudi, and Joan S. Dunphy. *Answers to the Mommy Track: How Wives and Mothers in Business Reach the Top and Balance Their Lives.* New York: New Horizon Press, 1991.

Feshbach, Murray. "Russia's Farms, Too Poisoned for the Plow." *Wall Street Journal,* May 14, 1992:A14.

Feshbach, Murray. "Soviet Health Problems." *Society,* March/April, 1984:79–89.

Feshbach, Murray, and Alfred Friendly, Jr. *Ecocide in the USSR: Health and Nature Under Siege:* New York, Basic Books, 1992.

Fialka, John J. "Russian Scientists Change Their Work, Not Always Along Lines the U.S. Likes." *Wall Street Journal,* May 5, 1992:A12.

Fichter, Joseph H., and William L. Kolb. "Ethical Limitations on Sociological Reporting." *Sociological Practice, 7,* 1989:148–157.

Fields, George. "Racism Is Accepted Practice in Japan." *Wall Street Journal,* November 10, 1986:19.

Fierman, Jaclyn. "Shaking the Blue-Collar Blues." *Fortune,* April 22, 1991:209–218.

Finkelhor, David. "Common Features of Family Abuse." In *Marriage and Family in a Changinig Society,* Third edition, James M. Henslin, ed. New York: Free Press, 1989:403–410.

Finkelhor, David. "Long-Term Effects of Childhood Sexual Victimization in a Non-Clinical Sample." Unpublished paper, October 2, 1980.

Finkelhor, David. *Sexually Victimized Children.* New York: Free Press, 1979.

Finkelhor, David, and Kersti Yllo. *License to Rape: Sexual Abuse of Wives.* New York: Henry Holt, 1985.

Finkelhor, David, and Kersti Yllo. "Marital Rape: The Myth Versus the Reality." In *Marriage and Family in a Changing Society,* Third edition. James M. Henslin, ed. New York: Free Press, 1989:382–391.

Finn, Chester E. "Fear of Standards Threatens Education Reform." *Wall Street Journal,* March 23, 1992:A10.

Finsterbusch, Kurt, and H. C. Greisman. "The Unprofitability of Warfare in the Twentieth Century." *Social Problems, 22,* February 1975:450–463.

Firestone, Shulamith. *The Dialectic of Sex: The Case for Feminist Revolution.* New York: Morrow, 1970.

Fischer, Claude S. *The Urban Experience.* New York: Harcourt, 1976.

Fischer, David Hackett. *Growing Old in America: The Bland-Lee Lectures Delivered at Clark University.* New York: Oxford University Press, 1977.

Fischer, Michael M. J. *Iran: From Religious Dispute to Revolution.* Cambridge, Massachusetts: Harvard University Press, 1980.

Fisher, Sue. *In the Patient's Best Interest: Women and the Politics of Medical Decisions.* New Brunswick, New Jersey: Rutgers University Press, 1986.

Fitzgerald, Mark. "Other Michigan College Papers Embroiled in Controversies." *Editor and Publisher, 122,* 16, April 22, 1989:55.

Flavell, J. H., et al. *The Development of Role-Taking and Communication Skills in Children.* New York: John Wiley, 1968.

Fleming, Joyce Dudney. "The State of the Apes." *Psychology Today, 7,* 1974:31–38.

Flexner, Abraham, *Medical Education in the United States and Canada: A Report to the Carnegie Foundation for the Advancement of Teaching.* Bulletin No. 4. Boston: Merrymount Press, 1910.

Flink, James J. *The Automobile Age.* Cambridge, Massachusetts: MIT Press, 1988.

Foley, Douglas E. "The Great American Football Ritual: Reproducing Race, Class, and Gender Inequality." *Sociology of Sport Journal, 7,* 1990:111–135.

Foote, Jennifer. "Trying to Take Back the Planet." *Newsweek, 115,* 6, February 5, 1990:24–25.

Forer, Lucille K. *The Birth Order Factor: How Your Personality Is Influenced by Your Place in the Family.* New York: David McKay, 1976.

Form, William. "Comparative Industrial Sociology and the Convergence Hypothesis." In *Annual Review of Sociology, 5* (1), Alex Forman, Craig, and Tim Carrington, eds.

Forrest, Jacqueline Darroch, and Susheela Singh. "The Sexual and Reproductive Behavior of American Women, 1982–1988." *Family Planning Perspectives, 22,* 5, September–October 1990:206–214.

Fox, Daniel M., and Robert Crawford. "Health Politics in the United States." In *Handbook of Medical Sociology,* Third edition. Freeman, Howard E., Sol Levine, and Leo G. Reeder, eds. Englewood Cliffs, New Jersey: Prentice Hall, 1979:392–411. As cited in Farley 1990.

Fox, Renee C. *The Sociology of Medicine: A Participant Observer's View.* Englewood Cliffs, New Jersey: Prentice Hall, 1989.

Fox, Elaine, and George E. Arquitt. "The VFW and the 'Iron Law of Oligarchy.' " In *Down to Earth Sociology,* Fourth edition. James M. Henslin, ed. New York: Free Press, 1985:147–155.

Frank, Anthony. "Through the Open Door: What Is It Like to Be an Immigrant in America?" *Wall Street Journal,* July 3, 1990:A8.

Franklin, John Hope. *From Slavery to Freedom: A History of Negro Americans.* Third edition. New York: Vintage Books, 1969.

Freedman, Alix M. "Amid Ghetto Hunger, Many More Suffer Eating Wrong Foods." *Wall Street Journal,* December 18, 1990:A1, A8.

Freidson, Eliot. *Profession of Medicine: A Study of the Sociology of Applied Knowledge.* Chicago: University of Chicago Press, 1988.

Freudenburg, William R., and Robert Gramling. "The Emergence of Environmental Sociology: Contributions of Riley E. Dunlap and William R. Catton, Jr." *Sociological Inquiry, 59,* 4, November 1989:439–452.

Friedl, Ernestine. "Society and Sex Roles." In *Conformity and Conflict: Readings in Cultural Anthropology.* James P. Spradley and David W. McCurdy, eds. Glenview, Illinois: Scott, Foresman, 1990:229–238.

Friedland, Gerald H., Brian R. Saltzman, Martha F. Rogers, Patricia A. Kahl, Martin L. Lesser, Marguerite M. Mayers, and Robert S. Klein. "Lack of Transmission of HTLV-III/LAV Infection to Household Contacts of Patients with AIDS or AIDS-Related Complex with Oral Candidiasis." *New England Journal of Medicine, 314,* February 6, 1986:344–349.

Frisbie, W. Parker, and John D. Kasarda. "Spatial Processes." In *Handbook of Sociology,* Neil J. Smelser, ed. Newbury Park, California: Sage, 1988:629–666.

Fritz, Jan M. "The History of Clinical Sociology." *Sociological Practice, 7,* 1989:72–95.

Frumkin, Robert M. "Early English and American Sex Customs." In *Encyclopedia of Sexual Behavior,* Volume 1. New York: Hawthorne Books, 1967.

Fuchs, Janet A., Richard M. Levinson, Ronald R. Stoddard, Maurice E. Mullet, and Diana H. Jones. "Health Risk Factors among the Amish: Results of a Survey." *Health Education Quarterly, 17,* 2, Summer 1990:197–211.

Fuchs, Victor R. "A Tale of Two States." In *The Sociology of Health and Illness: Critical Perspectives,* Peter Conrad and Rochelle Kern, eds. New York: St. Martin's Press, 1981:67–70.

Fuchsberg, Gilbert. "Well, at Least 'Terminated With Extreme Prejudice' Wasn't Cited." *Wall Street Journal,* December 7, 1990:B1.

Fuller, Rex, and Richard Schoenberger. "The Gender Salary Gap: Do Academic Achievement, Internship Experience, and College Major Make a Difference?" *Social Science Quarterly, 72,* 4, December 1991:715–726.

Furtado, Celso. *The Economic Growth of Brazil: A Survey from Colonial to Modern Times.* Westport, Connecticut: Greenwood Press, 1984.

Galagan, Patricia A., and Ernest Savoie. "Tapping the Power of a Diverse Work Force." *Training and Development Journal, 45,* 3, March 1991:38–44.

Galanter, Marc. *Cults: Faith, Healing, and Coercion.* New York: Oxford University Press, 1989.

Galbraith, John Kenneth. *The Nature of Mass Poverty.* Cambridge: Harvard University Press, 1979.

Galinsky, Ellen, and Peter J. Stein. "The Impact of Human Resource Policies on Employees: Balancing Work/Family Life." *Journal of Family Issues, 11,* 4, December 1990:368–383.

Gallese, Liz Roman. "Blue-Collar Women." *Wall Street Journal,* July 28, 1980.

Galliher, John F. *Deviant Behavior and Human Rights.* Englewood Cliffs, New Jersey: Prentice Hall, 1991.

Gallup, George, Jr. *The Gallup Poll: Public Opinion 1989.* Willmington, Delaware: Scholarly Resources, 1990.

Gallup Opinion Index. *Religion in America, 1987.* Report 259, April 1987.

Galuszka, Peter, Brian Bremner, and Rose Brady. "Will Bush's Inaction Doom Yeltsin—and the New World Order?" *Business Week,* March 23, 1992:53.

Gans, Herbert J. *People and Plans: Essays on Urban Problems and Solutions.* New York: Basic, 1968.

Gans, Herbert J. *The Urban Villagers.* New York: Free Press, 1962.

Gans, Herbert J. "Urbanism and Suburbanism." In *Urban Man and Society: A Reader in Urban Ecology,* Albert N. Cousins and Hans Nagpaul, eds. New York: Knopf, 1970:157–164.

Gans, Herbert J. "The Way We'll Live Soon." *Washington Post,* September 1, 1991:BW3.

Garbarino, Merwin S. *American Indian Heritage.* Boston: Little Brown, 1976.

Gardner, Carol Brooks. "Access Information: Public Lies and Private Peril." *Social Problems, 35* (4), October 1988:384–397.

Gardner, R. Allen, and Beatrice T. Gardner. "Teaching Sign Language to a Chimpanzee." *Science, 165,* 1969:664–672.

Garfinkel, Harold. "Conditions of Successful Degradation Ceremonies." *American Journal of Sociology, 61* (2), March 1956:420–424.

Garfinkel, Harold. *Studies in Ethnomethodology.* Englewood Cliffs, New Jersey: Prentice-Hall, 1967.

Garreau, Joel. *Edge City: Life on the New Frontier.* New York: Doubleday, 1991a.

Garreau, Joel. "Life on the Edge." *Washington Post,* September 8, 1991b:C1.

Gartner, Michael. "Legal 'Killer' Under Attack With the Wrong Weapons." *Wall Street Journal,* January 12, 1988:A11.

Gatewood, Willard B. *Aristocrats of Color: The Black Elite, 1880–1920.* Bloomington, Indiana: Indiana University Press, 1990.

Gay, Jill. "The Patriotic Prostitute." *The Progressive,* February 1985:34–36.

Gecas, Viktor. "Contexts of Socialization." In *Social Psychology: Sociological Perspectives,* Morris Rosenberg and Ralph H. Turner, eds. New Brunswick, New Jersey, Transaction, 1990:165–199.

Gelles, Richard J. "The Myth of Battered Husbands and New Facts about Family Violence." In *Social Problems 80–81,* Robert L. David (ed.). Guilford, Conn.: Dushkin, 1980.

Gellhorn, Martha. *The Face of War.* New York: Simon and Schuster, 1959.

Gelman, David. "Who's Taking Care of Our Parents?" *Newsweek.* May 6, 1985:61–64, 67–68.

Gerson, Kathleen. "Hard Choices." In *Marriage and Family in a Changing Society,* Fourth edition, James M. Henslin, ed. New York: Free Press, 1992:286–296.

Gerson, Kathleen. *Hard Choices: How Women Decide about Work, Career, and Motherhood.* Berkeley: University of California Press, 1985.

Gerth, H. H., and C. Wright Mills. *From Max Weber: Essays in Sociology.* New York: Galaxy, 1958.

Gest, Ted, and Patricia M. Scherschel. "Stealing $200 Billion 'The Respectable Way.'" *U.S. News & World Report,* May 20, 1985:83–85.

Giele, Janet Zollinger. *Women and the Future: Changing Sex Roles in Modern America.* New York: Free Press, 1978.

Gilbert, Dennis, and Joseph A. Kahl. *The American Class Structure: A New Synthesis.* Homedwood, Illinois: Dorsey Press, 1982.

Gilbert, Dennis, and Joseph A. Kahl. *The American Class Structure: A New Synthesis.* Third edition. Homewood, Illinois: Dorsey Press, 1987.

Gilham, Steven A. "The Marines Build Men: Resocialization in Recruit Training." In *The Sociological Outlook: A Text with Readings,* Reid Luhman, ed. Second edition. San Diego, California: Collegiate Press, 1989:232–244.

Gill, Derek. "A National Health Service: Principles and Practice." In *The Sociology of Health and Illness,* Peter Conrad and Rochelle Kern, eds. Second edition. New York: St. Martin's Press, 1986:454–467.

Gilmore, David D. *Manhood in the Making: Cultural Concepts of Masculinity.* New Haven, Connecticut: Yale University Press, 1990.

Gimenez, Martha E. "The Feminization of Poverty: Myth or Reality?" *Social Justice, 17,* 3, 1990:43–69.

Githens, Marianne, and Jewel L. Prestage. *A Portrait of Marginality: The Political Behavior of the American Woman.* New York: David McKay, 1977.

Glazer, Nathan. "In Defense of Multiculturalism." *New Republic,* September 2, 1991:18–22.

Glick, Paul C., and S. Lin. "More Young Adults are Living with Their Parents: Who Are They?" *Journal of Marriage and Family, 48,* 1986:107–112.

Glik, Deborah C., and Jennie J. Kronenfeld. "Well Roles: An Approach to Reincorporate Role Theory into Medical Sociology." *Research in the Sociology of Health Care, 8,* 1989:289–309.

Gliedman, John. "The Ozone Follies: Is the Pact Too Little, Too Late?" In *Taking Sides: Clashing Views on Controversial Environmental Issues,* Third edition, Theodore D. Goldfarb, ed. Guilford, Connecticut: Dushkin, 1989:317–323.

Glock, Charles Y., and Rodney Stark. *Religion and Society in Tension.* Chicago: Rand McNally, 1965.

Glotz, Peter. "Forward to Europe." *Dissent, 33* (3), Summer 1986:327–339. (As quoted in Harrison and Bluestone 1988)

Glueck, Sheldon, and Eleanor Glueck. *Physique and Delinquency.* New York: Harper and Row, 1956.

Goad, G. Pierre. "Canada Seems Satisfied With a Medical System That Covers Everyone." *Wall Street Journal,* December 3, 1991:A1, A10.

Goffman, Erving. *Asylums: Essays on the Social Situation of Mental Patients and Other Inmates.* Chicago: Aldine, 1961.

Goffman, Erving. *The Presentation of Self in Everyday Life*. New York: Doubleday, 1959.

Gold, Ray. "Janitors Versus Tenants: A Status-Income Dilemma." *American Journal of Sociology, 58*, 1952:486–493.

Goldberg, Steven. "Reaffirming the Obvious." *Society*, September–October 1986:4–7.

Goldberg, Steven. *The Inevitability of Patriarchy* (revised edition). New York: William Morrow, 1974.

Goldberg, Steven. Letter to the author, January 18, 1989.

Goldberg, Susan, and Michael Lewis. "Play Behavior in the Year-Old Infant: Early Sex Differences." *Child Development, 40*, March 1969:21–31.

Golden, Tim. "For Mexico's Green Party, It's a Very Grey World." *New York Times*, August 14, 1991:A3.

Goldner, Fred H. "Pronoia." In *Down to Earth Sociology: Introductory Readings*, Fourth edition, James M. Henslin, ed. New York: The Free Press, 1985:205–214.

Goleman, Daniel. "Spacing of Siblings Strongly Linked to Success in Life." *New York Times*, May 28, 1985:C1, C4.

Goleman, Daniel. "Girls and Math: Is Biology Really Destiny?" *New York Times*, August 2, 1987:42–44, 46.

Gomez. Carlos F. *Regulating Death: Euthanasia and the Case of the Netherlands*. New York: Free Press, 1991.

Goode, William J. "Encroachment, Charlatanism, and the Emerging Profession: Psychology, Sociology, and Medicine." *American Sociological Review, 25* (6), December 1960:902–914.

Goode, William J. "Why Men Resist." In *Rethinking the Family*, Barrie Thorne and Marilyn Yalom, eds. New York: Longman, 1982:131–150.

Goodwin, Glenn A., Irving Louis Horowitz, and Peter M. Nardi. *Sociological Inquiry, 61* (2), May 1991:139–147.

Goodwin, Tom. "What is the Limit?" Washington, D.C.: National Audobon Society, 1987. (A video)

Gordon, C. "Role and Value Development Across the Life Cycle." In *Role*, J. A. Jackson, ed. London: Cambridge University Press: 65–105.

Gordon, David M. "Class and the Economics of Crime." *The Review of Radical Political Economics, 3*, Summer 1971:51–57.

Gordon, Milton M. "The Concept of Sub-Culture and its Application." *Social Forces, 26*, 1947:40–42.

Gordon, Robert J. *Macroeconomics* (fourth edition). Boston: Little Brown, 1987.

Gorman, Peter. "A People at Risk: Vanishing Tribes of South America." *The World & I*. December 1991:678–689.

Gortmaker, Steven L. "Poverty and Infant Mortality in the United States." *American Journal of Sociology, 44*, (2), April 1979:280–297.

Gould, R. M. "The Phases of Adult Life: A Study in Developmental Psychology." *American Journal of Sociology 129*, 1972:521–531.

Gracey, Harry L. "Kindergarten as Boot Camp." In *Down to Earth Sociology*, Seventh edition. James M. Henslin, ed. New York: Free Press, 1993.

Graham, Ellen. "Christian Bikers are Holy Rollers of a Different Kind." *Wall Street Journal*, September 19, 1990:A1, A6.

Grant, Karen R. "The Inverse Care Law in the Context of Universal Free Health Insurance in Canada: Toward Meeting Health Needs Through Social Policy." *Sociological Focus, 17* (2), April 1984:137–155.

Grant, Nigel. *Soviet Education*. New York: Pelican Books, 1979.

Graven, Kathryn. "Sex Harassment at the Office Stirs Up Japan." *Wall Street Journal*, March 21, 1990:B1, B7.

Greeley, Andrew M. "The Protestant Ethic: Time for a Moratorium." *Sociological Analysis, 25*, Spring 1964:20–33.

Greene, Elizabeth. "Minority-Affairs Officials, Picked to Help Campuses Improve Racial Climate, Report Some Progress." *Chronicle of Higher Education, 35*, 28, March 22, 1989:A32–A34.

Greenwood, Ernest. "Attributes of a Profession." In *Man, Work, and Society: A Reader in the Sociology of Occupations*, Sigmund Nosow and William H. Form, eds. New York: Basic Books, 1962:206–218.

Greer, Germaine. *The Female Eunuch*. New York: Bantam Books, 1972.

Greif, Geoffrey L. *Single Fathers*. Lexington, Massachusetts: Lexington Books, 1985.

Grella, Christine E. "Irreconcilable Differences: Women Defining Class after Divorce and Downward Mobility." *Gender and Society, 4*, 1, March 1990:41–55.

Grossman, Laurie M., and Michael J. McCarthy. "Hollilngs Invokes Hiroshima as Reply to Japanese Critic." *Wall Street Journal*, March 4, 1992:A2.

Grunebaum, Henry, Leonard Solomon, Simon H. Budman, John J. O'Hearne, and Myron F. Weiner. *International Journal of Group Psychotherapy, 37*, 4, October 1987:475–513.

Guha, Ramachandra. "Radical American Environmentalism and Wilderness Preservation: A Third World Critique." *Environmental Ethics, 11*, 1, Spring 1989:71–83.

Gumbel, Peter. "France First! Election Gives Voice to Far-Right Party." *Wall Street Journal*, March 23, 1992:A1, A6.

Gupta, Giri Raj. "Love, Arranged Marriage, and the Indian Social Structure." In *Cross-Cultural Perspectives of Mate Selection and Marriage*, George Kurian, ed. Westport, Connecticut: Greenwood Press, 1979:

Gwartney-Gibbs, Patricia A. "The Institutionalization of Premarital Cohabitation: Estimates from Marriage License Applications, 1970 and 1980." *Journal of Marriage and Family, 48* (2), May 1986:423–434.

Haas, Jack. "Binging: Educational Control among High-Steel Iron Workers." *American Behavioral Scientist, 16*, 1972:27–34.

Haas, Jack, and William Shaffir. "The Cloak of Competence." In *Down to Earth Sociology: Introductory Readings*, Seventh edition. James M. Henslin, ed. New York: The Free Press, 1993.

Haberman, Paul W., and Geetha Natarajan. "Trends in Alcoholism and Narcotics Abuse from Medical Examiner Data." *Journal of Studies on Alcohol, 47* (4), 1986:316–321.

Hacker, Helen. Mayer. "Women as a Minority Group." *Social Forces, 30*, October 1951:60–69.

Hagan, John. "The Gender Stratification of Income Inequality Among Lawyers." *Social Forces, 68*, 3, March 1990:835–855.

Hagerty, Bob. "The Squeamish Had Better Close Their Eyes and Not Take a Gander." *Wall Street Journal*, April 11, 1990:B1.

Hall, Douglas T. "Promoting Work/Family Balance: An Organizational-Change Approach." *Organizational Dynamics, 18*, 3, Winter 1990:5–18.

Hall, Edward T. *The Hidden Dimension*. Garden City, New York: Anchor Books, 1969.

Hall, Edward T. *The Silent Language*. Greenwich, Connecticut, 1959.

Hall, G. Stanley. *Adolescence: Its Psychology and Its Relations to Physiology, Anthropology, Sociology, Sex, Crime, Religion, and Education*. New York: D. Appleton and Company, 1904.

Hall, J. A. *Nonverbal Sex Differences: Communication Accuracy and Expressive Style*. Baltimore: Johns Hopkins University Press, 1984.

Hall, Jerome. *Theft, Law, and Society*. Second edition. Indianapolis: Bobbs-Merrill, 1952.

Hall, Peter M. "Interactionism and the Study of Social Organization." *Sociological Quarterly, 28*, November 1987:1–22.

Hall, Richard H. "The Concept of Bureaucracy: An Empirical Assessment." *American Journal of Sociology, 69*, July 1963:32–40.

Hallinan, Maureen T., and Richard A. Williams. *Sociology of Education, 63*, 2, April 1990:122–132.

Hamilton, Richard F. "Work and Leisure: On the Reporting of Poll Results." *Public Opinion Quarterly, 55*, 1991:347–356.

Hammes, Sara, and Richard S. Teitelbaum. "The Global 500: How They Performed." *Fortune*, July 29, 1991:238–273.

Hardy, Dorcas. *Social Insecurity: The Crisis in America's Social Security and How to Plan Now for Your Own Financial Survival*. New York: Villard Books, 1991.

Harlow, Harry F., and Margaret K. Harlow. "The Affectional Systems." In *Behavior of Nonhuman Primates: Modern Research Trends*, Volume 2, Allan M. Schrier, Harry F. Harlow, and Fred Stollnitz (eds.). New York: Academic Press, 1965:287–334.

Harlow, Harry F., and Margaret Kuenne Harlow. "Social Deprivation in Monkeys." *Scientific American, 207*, 1962:137–147.

Harrington, Michael. *The Other America: Poverty in the United States.* New York: Macmillan, 1962.

Harrington, Michael. *The Vast Majority: A Journey to the World's Poor.* New York: Simon and Schuster, 1977.

Harrington, Michael, and Mark Levinson. "The Perils of a Dual Economy." In *The Transformation of Industrial Organization: Management, Labor, and Society in the United States,* Frank Hearn, ed. Belmont, California: Wadsworth, 1988:333–341.

Harris, Chauncey, and Edward Ullman. "The Nature of Cities." *Annals of the American Academy of Political and Social Science, 242,* 1945:7–17.

Harris, Diana K. *The Sociology of Aging* New York: Harper, 1990.

Harris, Louis, and Associates. *A Study of Attitudes Toward Racial and Religious Minorities and Toward Women.* New York: National Conference of Christians and Jews, November 1978.

Harris, Marvin. *Cows, Pigs, Wars, and Witches: The Riddles of Culture.* New York: Vintage Books, 1974.

Harris, Marvin. "Why Men Dominate Women." *New York Times Magazine,* November 13, 1977:46, 115, 117–123.

Harrison, Bennett, and Barry Bluestone. *The Great U-Turn: Corporate Restructuring and the Polarizing of America.* New York: Basic Books: 1988.

Harry, Joseph. *Gay Couples.* New York: Praeger, 1984.

Hart, Charles W. M., and Arnold R. Pilling. *The Tiwi of North Australia.* New York: Holt, Rinehart, and Winston, 1960.

Hart, Hornell. "Acceleration in Social Change." In *Technology and Social Change,* Francis R. Allen, Hornell Hart, Delbert C. Miller, William F. Ogburn, and Meyer F. Nimkoff. New York: Appleton, 1957:27–55.

Hartig, Karl. "Snapshot of the Seven: A Statistical Portrait of the Summit Countries." *Wall Street Journal,* July 9, 1990:R16–R17.

Hartley, Eugene. *Problems in Prejudice.* New York: King's Crown Press, 1946.

Hartmann, Heidi I. "The Family as the Locus of Gender, Class, and Political Struggle: The Example of Housework." *Signs, 6* (3), 1981:366–394.

Haslick, Leonard. *The Gerontologist, 14,* 1974:37–45.

Hauser, Philip, and Leo Schnore (eds). *The Study of Urbanization.* New York: Wiley, 1965.

Hawley, Amos H. *Urban Society: An Ecological Approach.* New York, John Wiley, 1981.

Hayes, Arthur S. "How the Courts Define Harassment." *Wall Street Journal,* October 11, 1991:B1, B3.

Hearn, Frank, ed. *The Transformation of Industrial Organization: Management, Labor, and Society in the United States.* Belmont, California: Wadsworth, 1988.

Hechinger, Fred M. "Toward Educating the Homeless." *New York Times,* February 2, 1988:24.

Heider, Karl G. *The Dugum Dani: A Papuan Culture in the Highlands of West New Guinea.* Chicago: Aldine, 1970.

Heilbrun, Alfred B. "Differentiation of Death-Row Murderers and Life-Sentence Murderers by Antisociality and Intelligence Measures." *Journal of Personality Assessment, 64,* 1990:617–627.

Heller, Celia Stopnicka. Letter to the author. May 7, 1991.

Heller, Celia Stopnicka. "Social Stratification of the Jewish Community in a Small Polish Town." *American Journal of Sociology, 59* (1), July 1953:

Hellinger, Daniel, and Dennis R. Judd. *The Democratic Facade.* Pacific Grove, California: Brooks/Cole, 1991.

Hemp, Paul. "Houghton Mifflin's Textbook Troubles." *Boston Globe,* June 25, 1991:37, 46.

Henley, Nancy, Mykol Hamilton, and Barrie Thorne. "Womanspeak and Manspeak." In *Beyond Sex Roles,* Alice G. Sargent, ed. St. Paul, Minnesota: West, 1985.

Henry, William A., III. "Beyond the Melting Pot." *Time,* April 9, 1990: 28–31.

Henslin, James M. "Centuries of Childhood." In *Marriage and Family in a Changing Society,* Fourth edition, James M. Henslin, ed. New York: The Free Press, 1992:214–225.

Henslin, James M. "Cohabitation: Its Context and Meaning." In *Marriage and Family in A Changing Society,* Third edition, James M. Henslin, ed. New York: The Free Press, 1980:101–115.

Henslin, James M. "Craps and Magic." *American Journal of Sociology, 73,* 3, November 1967:316–330.

Henslin, James M. *Introducing Sociology: Toward Understanding Life in Society.* New York: Free Press, 1975.

Henslin, James M. "It's Not a Lovely Place to Visit, and I Wouldn't Want to Live There." In *Studies in Qualitative Methodology: Reflections on Field Experience,* Volume II. Robert G. Burgess, ed. Greenwich, Connecticut: JAI Press, 1990:51–76.

Henslin, James M., ed. *Marriage and Family in a Changing Society,* Fourth edition, New York: Free Press, 1992.

Henslin, James M. "On Becoming Male: Reflections of a Sociologist on Childhood and Early Socialization." In *Down to Earth Sociology,* Seventh edition, James M. Henslin, ed. New York: Free Press, 1993.

Henslin, James M. *Social Problems,* Second edition. Englewood Cliffs, N.J.: Prentice-Hall, 1990.

Henslin, James M. "Sociology and the Social Sciences." In *Down to Earth Sociology: Introductory Readings,* Seventh edition, James M. Henslin, ed. New York: The Free Press, 1993.

Henslin, James M. "Trust and Cabbies." In *Down to Earth Sociology: Introductory Readings,* Seventh edition, James M. Henslin, ed. New York: Free Press, 1993.

Henslin, James M. "When Life Seems Hopeless: Suicide in American Society." In *Social Problems Today: Coping with the Challenges of a Changing Society.* Englewood Cliffs, New Jersey: Prentice Hall, 1990b:99–107.

Henslin, James M., Linda K. Henslin, and Steven D. Keiser. "Schooling for Social Stability: Education in the Corporate Society." In *Social Problems in American Society,* Second edition, James M. Henslin and Larry T. Reynolds, eds. Boston: Holbrook, 1976.

Henslin, James M., and Mae A. Biggs. "The Sociology of the Vaginal Examination." In *Down to Earth Sociology: Introductory Readings,* Seventh edition, James M. Henslin, ed. New York: The Free Press, 1993.

Herring, George C. "Vietnam War." *World Book Encyclopedia, 20.* Chicago: World Book, 1989:389–393.

Hershey, Robert D., Jr. "Underground Economy is Not Rising to the Bait." *New York Times,* January 24, 1988:E5.

Hertzler, Joyce O. *A Sociology of Language.* New York: Random House, 1965.

Hevesi, Dennis. "Rooted in Slavery, Pogrom and Stereotypes, Crown Heights Is No Blend." *New York Times,* August 21, 1991:B1, B3.

Hibbert, Christopher. *The Roots of Evil: A Social History of Crime and Punishment.* New York: Minerva, 1963.

Hills, Stuart L. *Demystifying Social Deviance.* New York: McGraw-Hill, 1980.

Hilts, Philip J. "Forecast of AIDS Cases is Cut by 10%." *New York Times,* January 4, 1990:Y11.

Hiltz, Starr Roxanne. "Widowhood." In *Marriage and Family in a Changing Society,* James M. Henslin, ed. Third edition. New York: The Free Press, 1989:521–531.

Hipler, Fritz. Interview in a television documentary with Bill Moyers in *Propaganda,* part of a series on "Walk Through the 20th Century," 1987.

Hirschi, Travis. *Causes of Delinquency.* Berkeley: University of California Press, 1969.

Hobson, John A. *Imperialism: A Study,* revised edition. London: G. Allen, 1939. First published in 1902.

Hochschild, Arlie. "Note to the Author." 1991.

Hochschild, Arlie. *The Second Shift: Working Parents and the Revolution at Home.* New York: Viking 1989.

Hochschild, Arlie Russell. "The Sociology of Feeling and Emotion: Selected Possibilities." In *Another Voice: Feminist Perspectives on Social Life and Social Science,* Marcia Millman and Rosabeth Moss Kanter (eds.). Garden City, New York: Anchor Books, 1975.

Hodson, Randy, and Robert E. Parker. "Work in High-Technology Settings: A Review of the Empirical Literature." *Research in the Sociology of Work, 4,* 1988:1–29.

Holden, Constance. "Female Math Anxiety on the Wane." *Science, 236* (4802), May 8, 1987:660–661.

Holden, Constance. "Twins Reunited." *Science, 80,* 1980:1, 55–59.

Holder, Wayne M., ed. *Sexual Abuse of Children: Implications for Treatment.* Englewood, Colorado: American Humane Association, 1980.

Holtzman, Abraham. *The Townsend Movement: A Political Study.* New York: Bookman, 1963.

Homans, George Caspar. *Social Behavior: Its Elementary Forms.* New York: Harcourt, Brace & World, 1961.

Homans, George Caspar. "Social Behavior as Exchange." *American Journal of Sociology, 62,* May 1958:597–605.

Homblin, Dora Jane. *The First Cities.* Boston: Little Brown, Time-Life Books, 1973.

Hong, Lawrence K., and Marion V. Dearman. "The Streetcorner Preacher." In *Down to Earth Sociology,* Seventh edition, James M. Henslin, ed. New York: Free Press, 1993.

Honig, Alice Sterling. "The Gifts of Families: Caring, Courage, and Competence." In *Family Strengths 4: Positive Support Systems,* Nick Stinnett, John DeFrain, Kay King, Herbert Lingren, George Rowe, Sally Van Zandt, and Roseanne Williams, eds. Lincoln: University of Nebraska Press, 1982:331–349.

Hope, Christine A., and Ronald G. Stover. "Gender Status, Monotheism, and Social Complexity." *Social Forces, 65,* 1987:1132–1138.

Horowitz, Irving Louis. "Socialist Utopias and Scientific Socialists: Primary Fanaticisms and Secondary Contradictions." *Sociological Forum, 4,* 1989:107–113.

Horowitz, Irving Louis. *Three Worlds of Development: The Theory and Practice of International Stratification.* New York: Oxford University Press, 1966.

Horowitz, Ruth. "Community Tolerance of Gang Violence." *Social Problems, 34,* 5, December 1987:437–450.

Horowitz, Ruth. *Honor and the American Dream: Culture and Identity in a Chicano Community.* New Brunswick: Rutgers University Press, 1983.

Horwitz, Tony. "Toughing It Out In Kuwait Tested the 'Sultan' Family." *Wall Street Journal,* March 4, 1991:A1, A6.

Horwitz, Tony, and Craig Forman. "Immigrants to Europe from the Third World Face Racial Animosity." *Wall Street Journal,* August 14, 1990:A1, A9.

Hostetler, John A. *Amish Society,* Third edition. Baltimore: Johns Hopkins University Press, 1980.

Hotchkiss, Sandy. "The Realities of Rape." *Human Behavior, 12,* December 1978:18–23.

Hourani, Benjamin T. "Toward the 21st Century: The Organization of Power in Post-Industrial Society." *Science and Public Policy, 14* (4), August 1987:217–229.

House, Karen Elliott. "Iraqi President Hussein Sees New Mideast War Unless America Acts." *Wall Street Journal,* June 28, 1990:A1, A11.

Houseknecht, Sharon K., and Graham B. Spanier. "Marital Disruption and Higher Education in the United States." *Sociological Quarterly, 21,* 3, 1980:375–389.

Houseknecht, Sharon K., Suzanne Vaughan, and Anne S. Macke. "Marital Disruption Among Professional Women: The Timing of Career and Family Events." *Social Problems, 31,* 3, February 1984:273–284.

Hout, Michael, and Andrew Greeley. "The Center Doesn't Hold: Church Attendance in the United States, 1940–1984." *American Sociological Review, 52,* 1987:324–345.

Howells, Lloyd T., and Selwyn W. Becker. "Seating Arrangement and Leadership Emergence." *Journal of Abnormal and Social Psychology, 64,* February 1962:148–150.

Hoyt, Homer. "Recent Distortions of the Classical Models of Urban Structure." In *Internal Structure of the City: Readings on Space and Environment,* Larry S. Bourne, ed. New York: Oxford University Press, 1971:84–96.

Hoyt, Homer. *The Structure and Growth of Residential Neighborhoods in American Cities.* Washington, D.C.: Federal Housing Administration, 1939.

Hsu, Francis L. K. *The Challenge of the American Dream: The Chinese in the United States.* Belmont, Calif.: Wadsworth, 1971.

Huang, Chien Ju, and James G. Anderson. "Anomie and Deviancy: Reassessing Racial and Social Status Differences." Paper presented at the annual meetings of the American Sociological Association, 1991.

Hubbard, Ruth. "The Political Nature of 'Human Nature.' " In *Theoretical Perspectives on Sexual Difference,* Deborah L. Rhode, ed. New Haven: Yale University Press, 1990:63–73.

Huber, Joan. "From Sugar and Spice to Professor." In *Down to Earth Sociology,* fifth edition, James M. Henslin, ed. New York: The Free Press, 1988:92–101.

Huber, Joan. "Micro-Macro Links in Gender Stratification." *American Sociological Review, 55,* February 1990:1–10.

Huber, Joan. "Trends in Gender Stratification, 1970–1985." *Sociological Forum, 1,* 1986:476–495.

Huber, Joan, and William H. Form. *Income and Ideology.* New York: Free Press, 1973.

Hudson, James R. "Professional Sports Franchise Locations and City, Metropolitan and Regional Identities." Paper presented at the 1991 meetings of the American Sociological Association.

Hudson, Robert B. "The 'Graying' of the Federal Budget and Its Consequences for Old-Age Policy." *The Gerontologist, 18,* October 1978: 428–440.

Huff-Corzine, Lin, Jay Corzine, and David C. Moore. "Southern Exposure: Deciphering the South's Influence on Homicide Rates." *Social Forces, 64,* 1986:906–924.

Hug, Simon. "The Emergence of the Swiss Ecological Party: A Dynamic Model." *European Journal of Political Research, 18,* 6, November 1990:645–670.

Hughes, Everett C. "Good People and Dirty Work." In *Down to Earth Sociology,* Seventh edition. James M. Henslin, ed. New York: The Free Press, 1993.

Hughes, H. Stuart. *Oswald Spengler: A Critical Estimate.* Revised edition. New York: Charles Scribner's Sons, 1962.

Hughes, Kathleen A. "Even Tiki Torches Don't Guarantee a Perfect Wedding." *Wall Street Journal,* February 20, 1990:A1, A16.

Humphreys, Laud. "Impersonal Sex and Perceived Satisfaction." In *Studies in the Sociology of Sex,* James M. Henslin, ed. New York: Appleton-Century-Crofts, 1971:351–374.

Humphreys, Laud. *Tearoom Trade: Impersonal Sex in Public Places.* Chicago: Aldine, 1970.

Humphreys, Laud. *Tearoom Trade: Impersonal Sex in Public Places* (enlarged edition). Chicago: Aldine, 1975.

Humphry, Derek. *Final Exit: The Practicalities of Self-Deliverance and Assisted Suicide for the Dying.* Eugene, Oregon: The Hemlock Society, 1991.

Hurn, Christopher J. *The Limits and Possibilities of Schooling,* Second edition. Boston: Allyn and Bacon, 1985.

Huth, Mary Jo. "China's Urbanization under Communist Rule, 1949–1982." *International Journal of Sociology and Social Policy, 10,* 7, 1990:17–57.

Ingersoll, Bruce. "Dow Corning Corp. Agrees to the Release of More Data on Breast-Implant Safety." *Wall Street Journal,* February 10, 1992:A8.

Inkeles, James Coleman, and Ralph H. Turner, eds. Palo Alto, California, Annual Reviews, 1979.

Iori, Ron. "The Good, the Bad and the Useless." *Wall Street Journal,* June 10, 1988:18R.

Itard, Jean Marc Gospard. *The Wild Boy of Aveyron.* Translated by George and Muriel Humphrey. New York: Appleton-Century-Crofts, 1962.

Jackall, Robert. "Moral Mazes: Bureaucracy and Managerial Work." *Harvard Business Review, 61,* 5, September–October, 1983:118–130.

Jackson, Kenneth. *Crabgrass Frontier: The Suburbanization of the United States.* New York: Oxford University Press, 1985. (In Karp, Stone, and Yoels, 1991.)

Jackson, Phillip W. *Life in Classrooms.* New York: Holt, Rinehart, and Winston, 1968.

Jacobs, David. "Inequality and the Legal Order: An Ecological Test of the Conflict Model." *Social Problems, 25,* June 1978:515–525.

Jacobsen, Thorkild, and Robert M. Adams. "Salt and Silt in Ancient Mesopotamian Agriculture." *Science,* November 21, 1958:1251–1258.

Jaffe, Harold W., and Alan R. Lifson. "Acquisition and Transmission of HIV." *Infectious Disease Clinics of North America, 2,* 2, June 1988: 299–306.

Jaggar, Alison M. "Sexual Difference and Sexual Equality." In *Theoretical Perspectives on Sexual Difference,* Deborah L. Rhode, ed. New Haven: Yale University Press, 1990:239–254.

James, Selma. "The American Family: Decay and Rebirth." In *From Feminism to Liberation,* Edith Hoshino Altbach (ed.). Cambridge, Mass: Schenkman, 1971.

Janis, Irving. *Victims of Groupthink.* Boston, Massachusetts: Houghton Mifflin, 1972.

Jaspar, James M. "Moral Dimensions of Social Movements." Paper presented at the 1991 meetings of the American Sociological Association.

Jaspar, James M., and Dorothy Nelkin. *Animal Crusades.* New York: Free Press, 1993.

Jencks, Christopher, Lauri Perman, and Lee Rainwater. "What is a Good Job? A New Measure of Labor-Market Success." *American Journal of Sociology, 93,* 1988:1322–1357.

Jenness, Valerie. "From Sex as Sin to Sex as Work: COYOTE and the Reorganization of Prostitution as a Social Problem." *Social Problems, 37,* 3, August 1990:103–120.

Johnson, Benton. "On Church and Sect." *American Sociological Review, 28,* 1963:539–549.

Johnson, Dirk. "Murder Charges Are Met by Cries of Compassion." *New York Times,* August 8, 1988:A14.

Johnston, Drue M., and Norris R. Johnson. "Role Extension in Disaster: Employee Behavior at the Beverly Hills Supper Club Fire." *Sociological Focus, 22* (1), February 1989:39–51.

Johnston, William B., and Arnold E. Packer. *Workforce 2000: Work and Workers for the Twenty-first Century.* Indianapolis, Indiana: Hudson Institute, 1987.

Jonas, Harry S., Sylvia I. Etzel, and Barbara Barzansky. "Educational Programs in US Medical Schools." *Journal of the American Medical Association, 266,* 7, August 21, 1991:913–920.

Jones, Timothy K. "American Anabaptists: Where They Are Going." *Christianity Today,* October 22, 1990:34–36.

Jones, Woodrow, Jr., and Paul Strand. "Adaptation and Adjustment Problems Among Indochinese Refugees." *Sociology and Social Research, 71,* 1, October 1986:42–46.

Josephson, Matthew. "The Robber Barons." In *John D. Rockefeller: Robber Baron or Industrial Statesman?* Earl Latham, ed. Boston: D. C. Heath, 1949:34–48.

Josephy, Alvin M., Jr. "Indians in History." *Atlantic Monthly, 225,* June 1970:67–72.

Judis, John B. "The Japanese Megaphone." *New Republic, 202* (4), January 22, 1990:20–25.

Jurik, Nancy C., and Russ Winn. "Gender and Homicide: A Comparison of Men and Women Who Kill." *Violence and Victims, 5,* (4), 1990: 227–242.

Kagan, Jerome. "The Idea of Emotions in Human Development." In *Emotions, Cognition, and Behavior,* Carroll E. Izard, Jerome Kagan, and Robert B. Zajonc, eds. New York: Cambridge University Press, 1984:38–72.

Kahn, Joan R., and Kathryn A. London. "Premarital Sex and the Risk of Divorce." *Journal of Marriage and the Family, 53,* November 1991:845–855.

Kain, Edward L. *The Myth of Family Decline.* New York: Lexington Books, 1990.

Kalichman, Seth C. "MMPI Profiles of Women and Men Convicted of Domestic Homicide." *Journal of Clinical Psychology, 44,* 6, November 1988:847–853.

Kalish, Richard A. *Late Adulthood: Perspectives on Human Development,* Second edition. Monterey, California: Brooks/Cole, 1982.

Kamin, Leon J. "Is Crime in the Genes? The Answer May Depend on Who Chooses What Evidence." *Scientific American,* February 1986:22–27.

Kamin, Leon J. *The Science and Politics of I.Q.* Hillsdale, New Jersey: Erlbaum, 1975.

Kanter, Rosabeth Moss. *The Change Masters: Innovation and Entrepreneurship in the American Corporation.* New York: Simon and Schuster, 1983.

Kanter, Rosabeth Moss. *Men and Women of the Corporation.* New York: Basic Books, 1977.

Kanter, Rosabeth Moss, and Barry A. Stein. "The Gender Pioneers: Women in an Industrial Sales Force." In *Life in Organizations,* Rosabeth Moss Kanter and Barry A. Stein, eds. New York: Basic Books, 1979:134–160.

Kantrowitz, Barbara. "Sociology's Lonely Crowd." *Newsweek,* February 3, 1992:55.

Kapferer, J. N. "A Mass Poisoning Rumor in Europe." *Public Opinion Quarterly. 53,* 1989:467–481.

Kaplan, H. Roy. "Lottery Winners and Work Commitment." *Journal of the Institute for Socioeconomic Studies, 10* (2), 1985:82–94.

Karp, David A., Gregory P. Stone, and William C. Yoels. *Being Urban: A Sociology of City Life.* Second edition. New York: Praeger, 1991.

Karp, David A., and William C. Yoels. "Sport and Urban Life." *Journal of Sport and Social Issues, 14* (2), 1990:77–102.

Kasarda, John D., and Edward M. Crenshaw. "Third World Urbanization: Dimensions, Theories, and Determinants." *Annual Review of Sociology, 17,* 1991:467–501.

Katz, Michael B. *The Undeserving Poor: From the War on Poverty to the War on Welfare.* New York: Pantheon, 1989.

Keans, Carl. "Socioenvironmental Determinants of Community Formation." *Environment and Behavior, 23,* 1, January 1991:27–46.

Keith, Jennie. *Old People, New Lives: Community Creation in a Retirement Residence,* Second edition. Chicago: University of Chicago Press, 1982.

Keith, Verna M., and Cedric Herring. "Skin Tone and Stratification in the Black Community." *American Journal of Sociology, 97,* 3, November 1991:760–778.

Kellogg, W. N., and L. A. Kellogg. *The Ape and the Child: A Study of Environmental Influence upon Early Behavior.* New York: Whittlesey House, 1933.

Kelly, Joan B. "How Adults React to Divorce." In *Marriage and Family in a Changing Society,* Fourth edition, James M. Henslin, ed. New York: Free Press, 1992:410–423.

Kemp, Alice Abel. "Estimating Sex Discrimination in Professional Occupations with the *Dictionary of Occupational Titles.*" *Sociological Spectrum, 10,* 3, 1990:387–411.

Keniston, Kenneth. *Youth and Dissent: The Rise of a New Opposition.* New York: Harcourt, Brace, Jovanovich, 1971.

Kephart, William M. *Extraordinary Groups: An Examination of Unconventional Life-Styles,* Third edition. New York: St. Martin's Press, 1987.

Kerr, Clark. *The Future of Industrialized Societies.* Cambridge, Massachusetts: Harvard University Press, 1983.

Kerr, Clark, et al. *Industrialism and Industrial Man: The Problems of Labor and Management in Economic Growth.* Cambridge, Massachusetts: Harvard University Press, 1960.

Kettl, Donald F. "The Savings-And-Loan Bailout: The Mismatch Between the Headlines and the Issues." *PS, 24,* 3, September 1991:441–447.

Keyser, Christine. "Compromise in Defense of Earth First!" *Sierra, 76,* 6, November 1991:45–47.

Kiefer, Francine S. "Radical Left Exits German Green Party After Sharp Dispute." *Christian Science Monitor,* April 29, 1991:4.

Killian, Lewis M., and Charles M. Grigg. "Urbanism, Race, and Anomie." *American Journal of Sociology, 67,* 1962:661–665.

Kimball, M. M. "Television and Sex-Role Attitudes." In *The Impact of Television: A Natural Experiment in Three Communities,* T. M. Williams, ed. Orlando, Florida: Academic Press, 1986.

King, David. "Contradictions in Policy Making for Urbanization and Economic Development." *Cities, 8,* 1, February 1991:11–53.

King, Martin Luther, Jr. *Stride Toward Freedom: The Montgomery Story.* New York: Harper and Brothers, 1958.

Kitano, Harry H. L. *Race Relations.* Englewood Cliffs N.J.: Prentice-Hall, 1974.

Kitsuse, John I. "Coming Out All Over: Deviants and the Politics of Social Problems." *Social Problems, 28* (1), October 1980:1–13.

Klandermans, Bert. "Mobilization and Participation: Social-Psychological Expansions of Resource Mobilization Theory." *American Sociological Review, 49,* October 1984:583–600.

Klandermans, Bert. "New Social Movements and Resource Mobilization: The European and the American Approach." *Journal of Mass Emergencies and Disasters, 4,* 1986:13–37.

Klee, Ernst, Willi Dressen, and Volker Riess. *"The Good Old Days": The Holocaust as Seen by Its Perpetrators and Bystanders.* (Deborah Burnstone, translator) New York: Free Press, 1991.

Kletzer, Lori G. "Job Displacement, 1979–86: How Blacks Fared Relative to Whites." *Monthly Labor Review,* July 1991:17–24.

Kluegel, James R., and Eliot R. Smith. *Beliefs About Inequality: America's Views of What Is and What Ought to Be.* Hawthorne, New York: Aldine de Gruyter, 1986.

Knaus, William A. *Inside Russian Medicine: An American Doctor's First-Hand Report.* New York: Everest House, 1981.

Koenig, Frederick. *Rumor in the Market Place: The Social Psychology of Commercial Hearsay.* Dover, Massachusetts: Auburn House, 1985.

Kohfeld, Carol W., and Leslie A. Leip. "Bans on Concurrent Sale of Beer and Gas: A California Case Study." *Sociological Practice Review, 2* (2), April 1991:104–115.

Kohlberg, Lawrence, and Carol Gilligan. "The Adolescent as a Philosopher: The Discovery of the Self in a Postconventional World." *Daedalus, 100,* 1971:1051–1086.

Kohn, Alfie. "Make Love, Not War." *Psychology Today,* June 1988:35–38.

Kohn, Melvin L. *Class and Conformity: A Study in Values,* Second edition. Homewood, Illinois: Dorsey Press, 1977.

Kohn, Melvin L. "Occupational Structure and Alienation." *American Journal of Sociology, 82,* 1976:111–130.

Kohn, Melvin L. "Social Class and Parent-Child Relationships: An Interpretation." *American Journal of Sociology, 68,* 1963:471–480.

Kohn, Melvin L. "Social Class and Parental Values." *American Journal of Sociology, 64,* 1959:337–351.

Kohn, Melvin L., Atsushi Naoi, Carrie Schoenbach, Carmi Schooler, and Kazimierz M. Slomczynski. "Position in the Class Structure and Psychological Functioning in the United States, Japan, and Poland." *American Journal of Sociology, 95,* 1990:964–1008.

Kohn, Melvin L., and Carmi Schooler. "Class, Occupation, and Orientation." *American Sociological Review, 34,* 1969:659–678.

Kohn, Melvin L., and Carmi Schooler. *Work and Personality: An Inquiry into the Impact of Social Stratification.* New York: Ablex Press, 1983.

Komarovsky, Mirra, and S. S. Sargent. "Research into Subcultural Influences Upon Personality. In *Culture and Personalities,* S. S. Sargent and M. W. Smith (eds.). New York: The Viking Fund, 1949:143–159.

Komisar, Lucy. "The Image of Woman in Advertising." In *Woman in Sexist Society: Studies in Power and Powerlessness,* Vivian Gornick and Barbara K. Moran (eds.). New York: Basic Books, 1971:207–217.

Komter, Aafke. "Hidden Power in Marriage." *Gender and Society, 3,* 2, June 1989:187–216.

Koop, C. Everett. "Understanding AIDS." Rockville, Maryland: Centers for Disease Control, 1988.

Korda, Michael. *Male Chauvinism: How It Works.* New York: Random House, 1973.

Kornhauser, William. *The Politics of Mass Society.* New York: Free Press, 1959.

Kotlowitz, Alex. "A Businessman Turns His Skills to Aiding Inner-City Schools." *Wall Street Journal,* February 25, 1992:A1, A6.

Krauss, Celene. "Community Struggle and the Shaping of Democratic Consciousness." *Sociological Forum, 4,* 2, 1989:227–239.

Krauss, Celene. "Blue-collar Women and Toxic Waste Protests: The Process of Politicization." Proceedings of the Second Annual Conference of the Institute for Women's Policy Research, 1991.

Kraybill, Donald B. *The Riddle of Amish Culture.* Baltimore: Johns Hopkins University Press, 1989.

Kretschmer, Ernst. *Physique and Character.* New York: Harcourt Brace, 1925.

Krich, John. "Here Come the Brides: The Blossoming Business of Imported Love." In *Men's Lives,* Michael S. Kimmel and Michael A. Messner, eds. New York: Macmillan, 1989:382–392.

Krieger, Nancy. "Racial and Gender Discrimination: Risk Factors for High Blood Pressure." *Social Science and Medicine, 30,* 12, 1990: 1273–1281.

Kübler-Ross, Elisabeth. *Death: The Final Stage of Growth.* Englewood Cliffs, New Jersey: Prentice Hall, 1989.

Kübler-Ross, Elisabeth. *Living with Death and Dying.* New York: Macmillan, 1981.

Kübler-Ross, Elisabeth. *On Death and Dying.* New York: Macmillan, 1969.

Kuhn, Margaret E. "The Gray Panthers." In *Social Problems,* James M. Henslin. Englewood Cliffs, New Jersey: 1990:56–57.

Kuttner, Bob. "Jobs." In *The Transformation of Industrial Organization: Management, Labor, and Society in the United States,* Frank Hearn, ed. Belmont, California: Wadsworth, 1988:355–366.

La Barre, Weston. *The Human Animal.* Chicago: University of Chicago Press, 1954.

Lachica, Eduardo. "Third World Told to Spend More on Environment." *Wall Street Journal,* May 18, 1992:A2.

Ladner, Joyce A. "Teenage Pregnancy: The Implications for Black Americans." In *The State of Black America,* James D. Williams, ed. New York: National Urban League, 1986:65–84.

LaDou, Joseph. "Deadly Migration: Hazardous Industries' Flight to the Third World." *Technology Review, 94,* 5, July 1991:46–53.

Lagerfeld, Steven. "A Look at the Urban Future." *Wall Street Journal,* October 2, 1991:A10.

Lamb, Michael E. "The Effect of Divorce on Children's Personality Development." *Journal of Divorce, 1,* Winter, 1977:163–174.

Landry, Bart. *The New Black Middle Class.* Berkeley: University of California Press, 1987.

Landtman, Gunnar. *The Origin of the Inequality of the Social Classes.* New York: Greenwood Press, 1968. Originally published in 1938.

Lang, Kurt, and Gladys E. Lang. *Collective Dynamics.* New York: Crowell, 1961.

Lang, Susan S. *Women Without Children: The Reasons, the Rewards, the Regrets.* New York: Pharos Books, 1991.

Langan, Patrick A., and Mark A. Cunniff. "Recidivism of Felons on Probation, 1986–89." Washington, D.C.: U.S. Department of Justice, February 1992.

Lannoy, Richard. *The Speaking Tree: A Study of Indian Culture and Society.* New York: Oxford University Press, 1975.

LaPiere, Richard T. "Attitudes Versus Action." *Social Forces, 13,* December 1934:230–237.

Larson, Jeffry H. "The Marriage Quiz: College Students' Beliefs in Selected Myths About Marriage." *Family Relations,* January 1988:3–11.

Lasch, Christopher. *Haven in a Heartless World: The Family Besieged.* New York: Basic, 1977.

Laslett, Peter. *The World We Have Lost: England Before the Industrial Age* (third edition). New York: Charles Scribner's Sons, 1984.

Lauer, Jeanette, and Robert Lauer. "Marriages Made to Last." In *Mar-*

riage and Family in a Changing Society, Fourth edition, James M. Henslin, ed. New York: Free Press, 1992:481–486.

Lawton, Millicent. "Poverty Rate Seen Rising Fastest for Latino Children." *Education Week,* September 11, 1991:10.

Lazar, Irving, R. Darlington, H. Murray, J. Royce, and A. Snipper. "Lasting Effects of Early Childhood Education." *Monographs of the Society for Research in Child Development, 47* (1, 2 Serial No. 194), 1982.

Lazar, Irving, V. R. Hubbel, H. Murray, M. Rosche, and J. Royce. *The Persistence of Pre-School Effects: A Long-Term Follow-Up of Fourteen Infant and Pre-School Experiments.* Washington, D.C.: U.S. Government Printing Office, 1977.

Lazarsfeld, Paul F., and Jeffrey G. Reitz. "History of Applied Sociology." *Sociological Practice, 7,* 1989:43–52.

Leacock, Eleanor. *Teaching and Learning in City Schools.* New York: Basic Books, 1969.

LeBon, Gustave. *Psychologie des Foules (The Psychology of the Crowd).* Paris: Alcan, 1895. Various editions in English.

Lee, Alfred McClung, and Elizabeth Briant Lee. *The Fine Art of Propaganda: A Study of Father Coughlin's Speeches.* New York: Harcourt Brace, 1939.

Lee, Felicia R., and Ari L. Goldman. "The Bitterness Flows in 2 Directions." *New York Times,* August 21, 1991:B1, B3.

Lee, Marcia M. "Toward Understanding Why Few Women Hold Public Office: Factors Affecting the Participation of Women in Local Politics." In *A Portrait of Marginality: The Political Behavior of the American Woman,* Marianne Githens and Jewel L. Prestage (eds.). New York: David McKay, 1977:118–138.

Lee, Richard B. *The !Kung San: Men, Women, and Work in a Foraging Society.* New York: Cambridge University Press, 1979.

Leinberger, Christopher B., and Charles Lockwood. "How Business is Reshaping America." *Atlantic Monthly, 10,* October 1986:43–52.

Lekachman, Robert. "The Specter of Full Employment. In *Crisis in American Institutions,* Jerome H. Skolnick and Elliott Curie, eds. Fifth edition. Glenview, Illinois: Scott Foresman, 1982:68–74.

Lemert, Edwin M. *Human Deviance, Social Problems, and Social Control.* Second edition. Englewood Cliffs, New Jersey: Prentice Hall, 1972.

Lengermann, Patricia Madoo, and Ruth A. Wallace. *Gender in America: Social Control and Social Change.* Englewood Cliffs, New Jersey: Prentice Hall, 1985.

Lenski, Gerhard. *Power and Privilege: A Theory of Social Stratification.* New York: McGraw-Hill, 1966.

Lenski, Gerhard. "Status Crysallization: A Nonvertical Dimension of Social Status." *American Sociological Review, 19,* 1954:405–413.

Lenski, Gerhard, and Jean Lenski. *Human Societies: An Introduction to Macrosociology.* Fifth edition. New York: McGraw-Hill, 1987.

Lerner, Gerda. *Black Women in White America: A Documentary History.* New York: Pantheon Books, 1972.

Lerner, Gerda. *The Creation of Patriarchy.* New York: Oxford, 1986.

Lesser, Alexander. "War and the State." In *War: The Anthropology of Armed Conflict and Aggression,* Morton Fried, Marvin Harris, and Robert Murphy (eds.). Garden City, N.Y.: Natural History, 1968:92–96.

Levi-Strauss, Claude. "The Family." In *Man, Culture, and Society,* Harry L. Shapiro, ed. New York: Oxford University Press, 1956:261–285.

Levinson, D. J. *The Seasons of a Man's Life.* New York: Knopf, 1978.

Lewin, Tamar. "Hospitals Pitch Harder for Patients." *New York Times,* May 10, 1987:F1, F27–28.

Lewis, Bernard. "The Roots of Muslim Rage." *The Atlantic,* September 1990:47–54, 56, 59–60.

Lewis, David L. "Sex and the Automobile: From Rumble Seats to Rockin' Vans. In *The Automobile and American Culture,* David L. Lewis and Lawrence Goldstein, eds. Ann Arbor: University of Michigan Press, 1983. Quoted in Flink 1988.

Lewis, Dorothy Otnow, ed. *Vulnerabilities to Delinquency.* New York: Spectrum Medical and Scientific Books, 1981.

Lewis, Oscar. "The Culture of Poverty." *Scientific American, 115,* October 1966:19–25.

Lewis, Oscar. *La Vida.* New York: Random House, 1966.

Lewis, Richard S. *Challenger: The Final Voyage.* New York: Columbia University Press, 1988.

Lewontin, R. C., Steven Rose, and Leon J. Kamin. *Not in Our Genes: Biology, Ideology, and Human Nature.* New York: Pantheon, 1984.

Liebow, Elliot. *Tally's Corner: A Study of Negro Streetcorner Men.* Boston: Little Brown, 1967.

Light, Donald W. "Perestroika for Russian Health Care?" *Footnotes, 20,* 3, March 1992:7, 9.

Lin, Nan, Walter M. Ensel, and John C. Vaughn. "Social Resources and Strength of Ties: Structural Factors in Occupational Status Attainment." *American Sociological Review, 46* (4), August 1981:393–405.

Linden, Eugene. "Lost Tribes, Lost Knowledge." *Time,* September 23, 1991:46, 48, 50, 52, 54, 56.

Linton, Ralph. *The Study of Man.* New York: Appleton-Century-Crofts, 1936.

Lippitt, Ronald, and Ralph K. White. "An Experimental Study of Leadership and Group Life." In *Readings in Social Psychology,* Third edition, Eleanor E. Maccoby, Theodore M. Newcomb, and Eugene L. Hartley, eds. New York: Holt, Rinehart and Wintson, 1958:340–365. (as summarized in Olmsted and Hare 1978:28–31.)

Lipset, Seymour Martin. *The First New Nation.* New York: Basic Books, 1963.

Lipset, Seymour Martin, ed. *The Third Century: America as a Post-Industrial Society.* Stanford, California: Hoover Institution Press, 1979.

Lipset, Seymour Martin, and Reinhard Bendix. *Social Mobility in Industrial Society.* Berkeley: University of California Press, 1959.

Lipton, Michael. *Why Poor People Stay Poor: Urban Bias in World Development.* Cambridge: Harvard University Press, 1979.

Lochhead, Carol. "Nowhere to Go, Always in Sight." *Insight On the News, 4,* 20, May 16, 1988:8–11.

Lofland, John F. "Collective Behavior: The Elementary Forms." In *Social Psychology: Sociological Perspectives,* Morris Rosenberg and Ralph H. Turner, eds. New Brunswick, New Jersey: Transaction Books, 1990:411–446.

Lofland, John F. *Protest: Studies of Collective Behavior and Social Movements.* New Brunswick, New Jersey: Transaction Books, 1985.

Logan, John R., and Harvey L. Molotch. *Urban Fortunes: The Political Economy of Place.* Berkeley: University of California Press, 1987.

Lombroso, Cesare. *Crime: Its Causes and Remedies.* H. P. Horton, translator. Boston: Little Brown, 1911.

London, Kathryn A., and Barbara Foley Wilson. "Divorce." *American Demographics, 10,* 10, 1988:23–26.

Loomis, Charles P., and Zona K. Loomis. *Modern Social Theories.* Princeton, New Jersey: Van Nostrand, 1965.

Lopez, Julie Amparano. "Study Says Women Face Glass Walls as Well as Ceilings." *Wall Street Journal,* March 3, 1992:B1, B8.

Lublin, Joann S. "Sexual Harassment Is Topping Agenda in Many Executive Education Programs." *Wall Street Journal,* December 2, 1991b:B1, B5.

Lublin, Joann S. "Trying to Increase Worker Productivity, More Employers Alter Management Style." *Wall Street Journal,* February 13, 1991:B1, B7.

Luebke, Barbara F. "Out of Focus: Images of Women and Men in Newspaper Photographs." *Sex Roles, 20* (3/4), 1989:121–133.

Luke, Timothy W. *Ideology and Soviet Industrialism.* Westport, Connecticut: Greenwood Press, 1985.

Luker, Kristin. *Abortion and the Politics of Motherhood.* Berkeley: University of California Press, 1984.

Luoma, Jon R. "Acid Murder No Longer a Mystery." In *Taking Sides: Clashing Views on Clashing Environmental Issues,* Third edition, Theodore D. Goldfarb, ed. Guilford, Connecticut, Dushkin, 1989: 186–192.

Lynd, Robert S., and Helen Merell Lynd. *Middletown: A Study in American Culture.* New York: Harcourt, Brace, 1929.

Lynd, Robert S., and Helen Merell Lynd. *Middletown in Transition: A Study in Cultural Conflicts.* New York: Harcourt, Brace, 1937.

Lynn, Naomi, and Cornelia Butler Flora. "Societal Punishment and Aspects of Female Political Participation: 1972 National Convention Delegates." In *A Portrait of Marginality: The Political Behavior of the American Woman*, Marianne Githens and Jewel L. Prestage (eds.). New York: David McKay, 1977:139–149.

Maccoby, Eleanor E. "Current Changes in the Family and Their Impact upon the Socialization of Children." In *Major Social Issues*, J. M. Yinger and S. J. Cutler, eds. New York: Free Press, 1978.

Mace, Roland L. *Hellrats and Headbangers: An Analysis of Heavy Metal.* M.A. Thesis, Southern Illinois University, Edwardsville. March 31, 1986.

MacIver, Robert M. *Society.* New York: Holt, Rinehart and Winston, 1937.

Mack, Raymond W., and Calvin P. Bradford. *Transforming America: Patterns of Social Change* (second edition). New York: Random House, 1979.

Mackay, Charles. *Extraordinary Popular Delusions and the Madness of Crowds.* London: Office of the National Illustrated Library, 1852.

MacKinnon, Catharine A. *Sexual Harassment of Working Women: A Case of Sex Discrimination.* New Haven, Conn.: Yale University Press, 1979.

Maeda, Daisaku. "Japan." In *International Handbook on Aging: Contemporary Developments and Research.* Westport, Connecticut: Greenwood Press, 1980:253–270.

Magnuson, E. "A Cold Soak, a Plume, a Fireball." *Time,* February 17, 1986:25.

Mahard, Rita E., and Robert L. Crain. "Research on Minority Achievement in Desegregated Schools." In *The Consequences of School Desegregation,* Christine H. Russell and Willis D. Hawley, eds. Philadelphia: Temple University Press, 1983:103–125.

Main, Jackson Turner. *The Social Structure of Revolutionary America.* Princeton, New Jersey: Princeton University Press, 1965.

Mainardi, Pat. "The Politics of Housework." In *Social Problems in American Society,* Third edition. James M. Henslin and Larry T. Reynolds, eds. Boston: Holbrook Press, 1979:174–177.

Malinowski, Bronislaw. *The Dynamics of Culture Change.* New Haven: Yale University Press, 1945.

Malinowski, Bronislaw. *Sex and Repression in Savage Society.* Cleveland, Ohio: World, 1927.

Malson, Lucien. *Wolf Children and the Problem of Human Nature.* New York: Monthly Review Press, 1972.

Mamdani, Mahmood. "The Myth of Population Control: Family, Caste, and Class in an Urban Village." New York: Monthly Review Press, 1973.

Mann, Arthur. "When Tammy was Supreme." In William L. Riordin. *Plunkitt of Tammany Hall.* New York: E. P. Dutton, 1963:vii–xxii.

Marger, Martin N. *Elites and Masses: An Introduction to Political Sociology,* Second edition. Belmont, California: Wadsworth, 1987.

Marshall, Gordon. *In Search of the Spirit of Capitalism: An Essay on Max Weber's Protestant Ethic Thesis.* New York: Columbia University Press, 1982.

Martin, Michael. "Ecosabotage and Civil Disobedience." *Environmental Ethics, 12,* 4, Winter 1990:291–310.

Martin, Teresa Castro, and Larry Bumpass. "Recent Trends in Marital Disruption." *Demography, 26,* 1989:37–51.

Marx, Gary T. *Protest and Prejudice.* New York: Harper and Row, 1967.

Marx, Karl. "Contribution to the Critique of Hegel's Philosophy of Right." In *Karl Marx: Early Writings,* T. B. Bottomore, ed. New York: McGraw-Hill, 1964:45. Originally published in 1844.

Marx, Karl, and Friedrich Engels. *Communist Manifesto.* New York: Pantheon, 1967. Originally published in 1848.

Masheter, Carol. "Postdivorce Relationships between Ex-spouses: The Role of Attachment and Interpersonal Conflict." *Journal of Marriage and the Family, 53,* February 1991:103–110.

Massey, Douglas, and Mitchell L. Eggers. "The Ecology of Inequality: Minorities and the Concentration of Poverty, 1970–1980." *American Journal of Sociology, 95,* March 1990:1153–1188.

Matthews, Marvyn. "Long Term Trends in Soviet Education." In *Soviet Education in the 1980s,* J. J. Tomiak, ed. London: Croom Helm, 1983:1–23.

Mauldin, Teresa A. "Economic Consequences of Divorce or Separation Among Women in Poverty." *Journal of Divorce and Remarriage, 14,* 3–4, 1991:163–177.

Mauss, Armand. *Social Problems as Social Movements.* Philadelphia, Pennsylvania: Lippincott, 1975.

Mayo, Elton. *Human Problems of an Industrial Civilization.* New York: Viking, 1966.

McAdam, Doug. *Freedom Summer.* New York: Oxford University Press, 1988.

McAdam, Doug, John D. McCarthy, and Mayer N. Zald. "Social Movements." In *Handbook of Sociology,* Neil J. Smelser, ed. Newbury Park, California: Sage, 1988:695–737.

McAlexander, James H., and John W. Schouten. "Hair Style Changes as Transition Markers." *Sociology and Social Research, 74* (91), October 1989:58–62.

McCabe, J. Terrence, and James E. Ellis. "Pastoralism: Beating the Odds in Arid Africa." In *Conformity and Conflict: Readings in Cultural Anthropology.* James P. Spradley and David W. McCurdy, eds. Glenview, Illinois: Scott, Foresman, 1990:150–156.

McCall, Michal. "Who and Where Are the Artists?" In *Fieldwork Experience: Qualitative Approaches to Social Research,* William B. Shaffir, Robert A. Stebbins, and Allan Turowetz, eds. New York: St. Martin's, 1980:145–158.

McCarthy, John D., and Mayer N. Zald. "Resource Mobilization and Social Movements: A Partial Theory." *American Journal of Sociology, 82* (6), 1977:1212–1241.

McCarthy, John D., and Mayer N. Zald. *The Trend of Social Movements in America: Professionalization and Resource Mobilization.* Morristown, New Jersey: General Learning Press, 1973.

McCasland, S. Veron, Grace E. Cairns, and David C. Yu. *Religions of the World.* New York: Random House, 1969.

McCoy, Elin. "Childhood Through the Ages." In *Marriage and Family in a Changing Society,* Second edition. James M. Henslin, ed. New York: The Free Press, 1985:386–394.

McGregor, James. "China's Aging Leader Seems Set to Carve Reformist Idea in Stone." *Wall Street Journal,* March 20, 1992:A9.

McKeown, Thomas. *The Modern Rise of Population.* New York: Academic Press, 1977.

McLanahan, Sara. "Family Structure and the Reproduction of Poverty." *American Journal of Sociology, 90* (4), January 1985:873–901.

McMurray, Scott. "Studies of Women With Breast Implants Show Risk of Human Immune Diseases." *Wall Street Journal,* February 19, 1992:A3.

McPhail, Clark. "Blumer's Theory of Collective Behavior: The Development of a Non-Symbolic Interaction Explanation." *Sociological Quarterly, 30,* 3, 1989:401–423.

McPhail, Clark. *The Myth of the Madding Crowd.* New York: Aldine de Gruyter, 1991.

McPherson, J. Miller, and Lynn Smith-Lovin. "Sex Segregation in Voluntary Associations." *American Sociological Review, 51,* February 1986:61–79.

McPherson, J. Miller, and Lynn Smith-Lovin. "Women and Weak Ties: Differences by Sex in the Size of Voluntary Organizations." *American Journal of Sociology, 87,* January 1982:883–904.

Mead, George Herbert. *Mind, Self and Society.* Chicago: University of Chicago Press, 1934.

Mead, Margaret. *Sex and Temperament in Three Primitive Societies.* New York: The New American Library, 1950.

Mead, Margaret. *Sex and Temperament in Three Primitive Societies.* New York: William and Morrow, 1935.

Meier, Barry. "Health Studies Suggest Asbestos Substitutes Also Pose Cancer Risk." *Wall Street Journal,* May 12, 1987:1, 21.

Melbin, Murray. "Night As Frontier." In *Down to Earth Sociology: Introductory Readings,* Fifth edition, James M. Henslin, ed. New York: Free Press, 1988:397–403.

Melloan, George. "Breaking the Cycle of Failure." In *Social Problems*

Today: Coping with the Challenges of a Changing Society, James M. Henslin, ed. Englewood Cliffs, New Jersey: Prentice Hall, 1990: 302–304.

Meltzer, Bernard N., John W. Petras, and Larry T. Reynolds. *Symbolic Interactionism: Genesis, Varieties, and Criticism.* London: Routledge & Kegan Paul, 1975.

Melucci, Alberto. "The New Social Movements: A Theoretical Approach." *Social Science Information, 19,* 1980:199–226.

Melucci, Alberto. "The Symbolic Challenge of Contemporary Movements." *Social Research, 52,* 4, 1985:789–816.

Melucci, Alberto. "Ten Hypotheses for the Analysis of New Movements." In *Contemporary Italian Sociology,* D. Pinto, ed. Cambridge, Massachusetts: Cambridge University Press, 1981:173–194.

Meredith, William H. "Level and Correlates of Perceived Quality of Life for Lao Hmong Refugees in Nebraska." *Social Indicators Research, 14,* January 1984:83–97.

Merit Systems Protection Board. *Sexual Harassment in the Federal Workplace: Is It a Problem?* Washington, D.C.: Office of Merit Systems Review and Studies, 1981.

Merton, Robert K. "Discrimination and the American Creed." In *Discrimination and National Welfare,* R. M. MacIver, ed. New York: Harper and Brothers, 1948:99–126.

Merton, Robert K. "Discrimination and the American Creed." In *Sociological Ambivalence and Other Essays.* New York: Free Press, 1976:189–216.

Merton, Robert King. "Intermarriage and the Social Structure." In *Sociological Ambivalence and Other Essays.* New York: Free Press, 1976:217–250.

Merton, Robert K. *Social Theory and Social Structure.* Glencoe, Illinois: The Free Press, 1949.

Merton, Robert K. *Social Theory and Social Structure* (enlarged edition). New York: Free Press, 1968.

Merton, Robert K. "The Social-Cultural Environment and *Anomie."* In *New Perspectives for Research on Juvenile Delinquency,* Helen L. Witmer and Ruth Kotinsky, eds. Washington, D.C.: U.S. Department of Health, Education, and Welfare, 1956:24–50.

Messner, Steven F. "Television Violence and Violent Crime: An Aggregate Analysis." *Social Problems, 33* (3), February 1986:218–234.

Meyerson, Per-Martin. "Where Is Sweden Heading?" New York: Swedish Information Service, January 1992.

Meyrowitz, Joshua. "The Adultlike Child and the Childlike Adult: Socialization in an Electronic Age." *Daedalus, 113,* 1984:19–48.

Miall, Charlene E. "The Stigma of Involuntary Childlessness." *Social Problems, 33* (4), April 1986:268–282.

Michalowski, Raymond J. *Order, Law, and Crime: An Introduction to Criminology.* New York: Random House, 1985.

Michels, Robert. *Political Parties.* Glencoe, Illinois: Free Press, 1949. Originally published in 1911.

Miles, Rufus E., Jr. "The Population Challenge of the 70's: Achieving a Stationery Population." In *The Crisis of Survival,* editors of *The Progressive* (eds.). Glenview, Ill.: Scott Foresman, 1970:122–140.

Milgram, Stanley. "Behavioral Study of Obedience." *Journal of Abnormal and Social Psychology, 67,* (4), 1963:371–378.

Milgram, Stanley. "The Experience of Living in Cities." *Science, 67,* March 1970:1461–68.

Milgram, Stanley. "The Small World Problem." *Psychology Today, 1,* 1967:61–67.

Milgram, Stanley. "Some Conditions of Obedience and Disobedience to Authority." *Human Relations, 18,* February 1965:57–76.

Miller, Brent C., and Donna L. Sollie. "The Transition to Parenthood." In *Marriage and Family in a changing Society* (second edition). New York: Free Press, 1985:395–400.

Miller, Dan E. "Milgram Redux: Obedience and Disobedience in Authority Relations." In *Studies in Symbolic Interaction,* Norman K. Denzin, ed. Greenwich, Connecticut: JAI Press, 1986:77–106.

Miller, Walter B. "Lower Class Culture as a Generating Milieu of Gang Delinquency." *Journal of Social Issues, 14,* 3, 1958:5–19.

Mills, C. Wright. *The Power Elite.* New York: Oxford University Press, 1956.

Mills, C. Wright. *The Sociological Imagination.* New York: Oxford University Press, 1959.

Mills, Karen M., and Thomas J. Palumbo. *A Statistical Portrait of Women in the United States: 1978,* U.S. Bureau of the Census, *Current Population Reports,* Ser. P-23, no. 100, 1980.

Miner, Horace. "Body Ritual among the Nacirema." In *Down to Earth Sociology: Introductory Readings,* Seventh edition, James M. Henslin, ed. New York: Free Press, 1993.

Mintz, Beth A., and Michael Schwartz. *The Power Structure of American Business.* Chicago: University of Chicago Press, 1985.

Mintz, John, and Peter Pae. "The High Price of Success: Immigrants Suffer Alienation, Loneliness." *Washington Post,* September 7, 1988:A1.

Mirande, Alfredo. "Chicano Families." In *Marriage and Family in a Changing Society,* Third edition. James M. Henslin, ed. New York: The Free Press, 1989:56–61.

Mitchell, Roger, Touly Xiong, Charles Vue, Moua Xiong, and Leanne Martin. "The Eau Claire Hmong Community: A Cooperative Study." *Wisconsin Sociologist, 26,* 1, Winter 1989:33–37.

Modell, John, and Tamara K. Hareven. "Urbanization and the Malleable Household: An Examination of Boarding and Lodging in American Families." In *Family and Kin in Urban Communities, 1700–1930.* New York: New Viewpoints, 1977:167–186.

Molotch, Harvey L. "The City as a Growth Machine." *American Journal of Sociology, 82,* 2, September 1976:309–333.

Money, John, and Anke A. Ehrhardt. *Man and Woman, Boy and Girl.* Baltimore: Johns Hopkins University Press, 1972.

Montagu, M. F. Ashley. *The Concept of Race.* New York: Free Press, 1964.

Montagu, M. F. Ashley. *Introduction to Physical Anthropology* (third edition). Springfield, Ill.: C. C. Thomas, 1960.

Montero, Darrel M. "Japanese Americans: Changing Patterns of Assimilation over Three Generations." *American Sociological Review, 46,* December 1981:829–839.

Montero, Darrel M. *Japanese Americans: Changing Patterns of Ethnic Affiliation over Three Generations.* Boulder, Colo.: Westview, 1980.

Montero, Darrel M. *Vietnamese Americans: Patterns of Resettlement and Socioeconomic Adaptation in the United States.* Boulder, Colo.: Westview, 1979.

Montero, Darrel M., and Ismael Dieppa. "Resettling Vietnamese Refugees: The Service Agency's Role." *Social Work, 27,* January 1982:74–81.

Moore, Elizabeth, and Michael Mills. "The Neglected Victims and Unexamined Costs of White-Collar Crime." *Crime and Delinquency, 36,* 3, July 1990:408–418.

Moore, Wilbert E. "Occupational Socialization." In *Handbook on Socialization: Theory and Research,* David A. Goslin (ed.). Chicago: Rand McNally, 1968:861–883.

Morgan, Lewis Henry. *Ancient Society.* 1877.

Morgan, M. "Television and Adolescents' Sex-Role Stereotypes: A Longitudinal Study." *Journal of Personality and Social Psychology, 43,* 1982:947–955.

Morgan, M. "Television, Sex-Role Attitudes, and Sex-Role Behavior." *The Journal of Early Adolescence, 7,* 3, 1987:269–282.

Morris, Aldon. *The Origins of the Civil Rights Movement: Black Communities Organizing for Change.* New York: The Free Press, 1984.

Mortimer, Jeylan T., and Jon Lorence. "Satisfaction and Involvement: Disentangling a Deceptively Simple Relationship." *Social Psychology Quarterly, 52,* 1989:249–265.

Mosca, Gaetano. *The Ruling Class.* New York: McGraw-Hill, 1939. First published in 1896.

Mosher, Steven W. "Why Are Baby Girls Being Killed in China?" *Wall Street Journal,* July 25, 1983:9.

Moyers, Bill. "Propaganda." Part of the series on "A Walk Through the 20th Century." 1989. (A Video)

Moynihan, Daniel Patrick. *The Negro Family: The Case for National Action*. Washington, D.C.: U.S. Department of Labor, U.S. Government Printing Office, 1965.

Moynihan, Daniel Patrick. "Social Justice in the *Next* Century." *America*, September 14, 1991:132–137.

Muehlenhard, Charlene L., and Melaney A. Linton. "Date Rape and Sexual Aggression in Dating Situations: Incidence and Risk Factors." *Journal of Counseling Psychology, 34, 2*, 1987:186–196.

Murdock, George Peter. "The Common Denominator of Cultures." In *The Science of Man and the World Crisis*, Ralph Linton (ed.). New York: Columbia University Press, 1945.

Murdock, George Peter. "Comparative Data on the Division of Labor by Sex." *Social Forces, 15, 4*, May 1937:551–553.

Murdock, George Peter. *Social Structure*. New York: Macmillan, 1949.

Murray, Charles, and R. J. Herrnstein. "What's Really Behind the SAT-score Decline?" *The Public Interest, 106*, Winter 1992:32–56.

Murray, G. W. *Sons of Ishmael*. London: George Routledge and Sons, 1935.

Myerts, Henry F. "Look for Jobless Rate to Stay High in '90s." *Wall Street Journal*, March 2, 1992:1.

Nakao, Keiko, and Judith Treas. "Occupational Prestige in the United States Revisited: Twenty-Five Years of Stability and Change." Paper presented at the annual meeting of the American Sociological Association, 1990. (As referenced in Kerbo, Harold R. *Social Stratification and Inequality: Class Conflict in Historical and Comparative Perspective*. Second Edition. New York: McGraw-Hill, 1991:181.)

National Center for Education Statistics. *Digest of Education Statistics*. Washington, D.C.: U.S. Government Printing Office, 1989.

National Center for Education Statistics. *Digest of Education Statistics*. Washington, D.C.: U.S. Government Printing Office, 1991.

Navarro, Mireya. "AIDS and Hispanic People: A Threat Ignored." *New York Times*, December 29, 1989:1, 15.

Neikirk, William, and Glen Elsasser. "Ruling Weakens Abortion Right." *Chicago Tribune*, June 30, 1992:1, 8.

Neugarten, Bernice L. "Grow Old with Me. The Best Is Yet to Be." *Psychology Today, 5*, December 1971:45–48, 79, 81.

Neugarten, Bernice L. "Middle Age and Aging." In *Growing Old in America*, Beth B. Hess, ed. New Brunswick, New Jersey: Transaction Books, 1976:180–197.

Neugarten, Bernice L. "Personality and Aging." In *Handbook of the Psychology of Aging*, James E. Birren and K. Warren Schaie, eds. New York: Van Nostrand Reinhold, 1977:626–649.

Newdorf, David. "Bailout Agencies Like to Do It in Secret." *Washington Journalism Review, 13, 4*, May 1991:15–16.

Newman, Barry. "Amid Soviet Disarray, Some Farmers Refuse to Ship Food to Cities." *Wall Street Journal*, November 12, 1991:A1, A10.

Newman, Katherine S. *Falling from Grace: The Experience of Downward Mobility in the American Middle Class*. New York: Free Press, 1988.

Niebuhr, H. Richard. *The Social Sources of Denominationalism*. New York: Henry Holt, 1929.

Niebuhr, R. Gustav. "Catholic Church Faces Crisis as Priests Quit and Recruiting Fails." *Wall Street Journal*, November 13, 1990:A1, A13.

Niggle, Christopher J. "Monetary Policy and Changes in Income Distribution." *Journal of Economic Issues, 23, 3*, September 1989:809–822.

Nilsson, Nic. "Children and the Commercial Exploitation of Violence in Sweden" *Current Sweden, 384*, October 1991:1–8.

Nussbaum, Bruce, Ann Therese Palmer, Alice Z. Cuneo, and Barbara Carlson. "Downward Mobility." *Business Week*, March 23, 1992: 56–60. 62–63.

O'Connell, Martin, and Amara Bachu. *Who's Minding the Kids? Child Care Arrangements, Winter, 1986–87*. Series P-70, No. 20. Washington: Bureau of the Census, July 1990.

O'Connell, Martin, and Maurice J. Moore. "New Evidence on the Value of Birth Expectations." *Demography, 14*, August 1977:255–264.

O'Dea, Thomas F., and Janet O'Dea Aviad. *The Sociology of Religion*, Second edition. Englewood Cliffs, New Jersey: Prentice Hall, 1983.

O'Hare, William. "The Working Poor." *Population Today*, February 1988:6.

O'Hare, William P., and Judy C. Felt. "Asian Americans: America's Fastest Growing Minority Group." Washington, D.C.: Population Reference Bureau, February 1991.

O'Hare, William P., Kelvin M. Pollard, Taynia L. Mann, and Mary M. Kent. "African Americans in the 1990s." *Population Bulletin, 46* (1). Washington, D.C.: Population Reference Bureau, July 1991.

O'Malley, Jeff. "Sex Tourism and Women's Status in Thailand." *Society and Leisure, 11, 1*, Spring 1988:99–114.

O'Reilly, Jane "In Massachusetts: 'Divorced Kids' " *Time*, June 11, 1979, pp. 6–7.

Oberschall, Anthony. *Social Conflict and Social Movements*. Englewood Cliffs, New Jersey, 1973.

Offen, Karen. "Feminism and Sexual Difference in Historical Perspective." In *Theoretical Perspectives on Sexual Difference*, Deborah L. Rhode, ed. New Haven: Yale University Press, 1990:13–20.

Ogburn, William F. *On Culture and Social Change: Selected Papers*, Otis Dudley Duncan, ed. Chicago: University of Chicago Press, 1964.

Ogburn, William F. "The Family and Its Functions." In *Recent Social Trends in the United States, Report of the President's Research Committee on Social Trends*. New York: McGraw-Hill, 1933:661–708.

Ogburn, William F. "The Hypothesis of Cultural Lag." In *Theories of Society: Foundations of Modern Sociological Theory*, Volume II, Talcott Parsons, Edward Shils, Kaspar D. Naegele, and Jesse R. Pitts, eds. New York: Free Press, 1961:1270–1273.

Ogburn, William F. *Social Change, With Respect to Culture and Original Nature*, New York: Viking Press, 1938. Originally published in 1922.

Okie, Susan. "Developing World's Role in Global Warming Grows: Population Rise, Technology Spread Cited." In *Ourselves and Others: The Washington Post Sociology Companion*. The Washington Post Writers Group, eds. Boston: Allyn and Bacon, 1992:288–289.

Oliver, Melvin L., and Mark A. Glick. "An Analysis of the New Orthodoxy on Black Mobility." *Social Problems, 29* (5), June 1982:511–523.

Olmsted, Michael S., and A. Paul Hare. *The Small Group*, Second edition. New York: Random House, 1978.

Olneck, Michael R., and David B. Bills. "What Makes Sammy Run? An Empirical Assessment of the Bowles-Gintis Correspondence Theory." *American Journal of Education, 89*, 1980:27–61.

Olsen, Marvin E. "The Affluent Prosper While Everyone Else Struggles." *Sociological Focus, 23, 2*, May 1990:73–87.

Olson, Mancur. *The Logic of Collective Action*. Cambridge, Massachusetts: Harvard University Press, 1965.

Orum, Anthony M. "Political Sociology." In *Handbook of Sociology*, Neil J. Smelser, ed. Newbury Park, California: Sage, 1988:393–423.

Orwell, George. *1984*. New York: Harcourt Brace, 1949.

Otten, Alan L. "Ethicist Draws Fire with Proposal for Limiting Health Care to Aged." *Wall Street Journal*, January 22, 1988:22.

Ouchi, William. "Decision-Making in Japanese Organizations." In *Down to Earth Sociology*, Seventh edition, James M. Henslin, ed. New York: Free Press, 1993.

Ouchi, William. *Theory Z: How American Business Can Meet the Japanese Challenge*. Reading, Massachusetts: Addison-Wesley, 1981.

Owen, David. *None of the Above: Behind the Myth of Scholastic Aptitude*. Boston: Houghton Mifflin, 1985.

Palen, John J. *The Urban World*, Third edition. New York: McGraw Hill, 1987.

Palmore, Erdman. *The Honorable Elders Revisited*. Durham, North Carolina: Duke University Press, 1985.

Palmore, Erdman. "What the USA Can Learn from Japan about Aging." *Gerontologist, 15*, February 1975:64–67.

Parfit, Michael. "Earth First!ers Wield a Mean Monkey Wrench." *Smithsonian, 21, 1*, April 1990:184–204.

Park, Robert Ezra. "Human Ecology." *American Journal of Sociology, 42, 1*, July 1936:1–15.

Park, Robert E., and Ernest W. Burgess. *Human Ecology*. Chicago: University of Chicago Press, 1921.

Park, Robert E., and Ernest W. Burgess. *Introduction to the Science of Sociology.* Chicago: University of Chicago Press, 1921. (As quoted in McPhail 1991:6)

Parkinson, C. Northcote. *Parkinson's Law and Other Studies in Administration.* New York: Ballantine Books, 1957.

Parsons, Talcott. "An Analytic Approach to the Theory of Social Stratification." *American Journal of Sociology, 45,* 1940:841–862.

Parsons, Talcott. "Illness and the Role of the Physician: A Sociological Perspective." In *Personality in Nature, Society, and Culture,* Second edition, Clyde Kluckhohn and Henry A. Murray, eds. New York: Alfred A. Knopf, 1953:609–617.

Parsons, Talcott. "The Professions and Social Structure." In *Essays in Sociological Theory* (revised edition), Talcott Parsons, ed. New York: The Free Press, 1954:34–49.

Parsons, Talcott. "The Sick Role and the Role of the Physician Reconsidered." *Milbank Memorial Fund Quarterly/Health and Society, 53,* 3, Summer 1975:257–278.

Parsons, Talcott. *The Social System.* New York: Free Press, 1951.

Patterns of Urban and Rural Population Growth. Population Study no. 68. New York: United Nations Department of International Economic and Social Affairs, 1980.

Patterson, Gregory A. "Black Middle Class Debates Merits of Cities and Suburbs." *Wall Street Journal,* August 6, 1991:B1, B8.

Pearl, Daniel. "AIDS Spreads More Rapidly Among Women." *Wall Street Journal,* November 30, 1990:B1, B2.

Pearlin, L. I., and M. A. Lieberman. "Social Sources of Emotional Distress." In *Research in Community and Mental Health,* Vol. 1., R. G. Simmons, ed. Greenwich, Connecticut: JAI Press, 1979:217–248.

Pearlin, L. I., and Melvin L. Kohn. "Social Class, Occupation, and Parental Values: A Cross-National Study." *American Sociological Review, 31,* 1966:466–479.

Pebley, Anne R., and David E. Bloom. "Childless Americans." *American Demographics, 4,* January 1982:18–21.

Pepinsky, Harold E. "A Sociologist on Police Patrol." In *Fieldwork Experience: Qualitative Approaches to Social Research,* William B. Shaffir, Robert A. Stebbins, and Allan Turowetz, eds. New York: St. Martin's, 1980:223–234.

Perry, James M. "Virginia's Wilder to Base Run for White House on Blend of Fiscal Conservatism and Compassion." *Wall Street Journal,* December 19, 1990:A18.

Persell, Caroline Hodges, and Peter W. Cookson, Jr. "Where the Power Starts." *Signature,* August 1986:51–57.

Persell, Caroline Hodges, Sophia Catsambis, and Peter W. Cookson, Jr. "Family Background, School Type, and College Attendance: A Conjoint System of Cultural Capital Transmission." *Journal of Research on Adolescence, 2* (1), 1992:1–23.

Persell, Caroline Hodges, and Peter W. Cookson, Jr. "Chartering and Bartering: Elite Education and Social Reproduction." *Social Problems, 33* (2), December 1985:114–129.

Persell, C. H. *Education and Inequality: The Roots and Results of Stratification in America's Schools.* New York: Free Press, 1977.

Peter, Laurence J., and Raymond Hull. *The Peter Principle: Why Things Always Go Wrong.* New York: William Morrow, 1969.

Peters, Gary L., and Robert P. Larkin. *Population Geography: Problems, Concepts, and Prospects.* Dubuque, Iowa: Kendall/Hunt, 1989.

Peterson, James L., and Nicholas Zill. "Marital Disruption, Parent-Child Relationships, and Behavior Problems in Children." *Journal of Marriage and the Family, 48,* 1986:295–307.

Petrini, Cathy. "How Do You Manage a Diverse Workforce?" *Training and Development Journal,* February 1989:13–21.

Pettigrew, Thomas. "How the People Really Feel." *The Center Magazine, 9,* January–February 1976:35.

Phillips, John L., Jr. *The Origins of Intellect: Piaget's Theory.* San Francisco: W. H. Freeman, 1969.

Piaget, Jean. *The Construction of Reality in the Child.* New York: Basic Books, 1954.

Piaget, Jean. *The Psychology of Intelligence.* London: Routledge and Kegan Paul, 1950.

Pillemer, Karl. "Dangers of Dependency: New Findings on Domestic Violence against the Elderly." *Social Problems, 33,* December 1985:146–158.

Pillemer, Karl, and Rosalie S. Wolf. *Elder Abuse: Conflict in the Family.* Dover, Massachusetts: Auburn House, 1987.

Pilling, D., and M. Kellmer Pringle. *Controversial Issues in Child Development.* London: Paul Elek, 1978.

Pines, Maya. "The Civilizing of Genie." *Psychology Today, 15,* September 1981:28–34.

Piotrow, Phylis Tilson. *World Population Crisis: The United States' Response.* New York: Praeger, 1973.

Piturro, Marlene. "Managing Diversity." *Executive Female,* May/June 1991:45–46, 48.

Piven, Frances Fox, and Richard A. Cloward. *Why Americans Don't Vote.* New York: Pantheon Books, 1988.

Platt, Tony. "'Street' Crime—A View from the Left." *Crime and Social Justice: Issues in Criminology.* (9), 1978:26–34.

Pleck, Elizabeth. "The Unfulfilled Promise: Women and Academe." *Sociological Forum, 5,* 3, September 1990:517–524.

Ploski, Harry A., and Warren Marr, II, eds. *The Afro Americans.* New York: Bellwether, 1976.

Polenberg, Richard. *One Nation Divisible: Class, Race, and Ethnicity in the United States Since 1938.* New York: Penguin, 1980.

Pollak, Lauren Harte, and Peggy A. Thoits. "Processes in Emotional Socialization." *Social Psychological Quarterly, 52,* 1, 1989:22–34.

Polsby, Nelson W. "Three Problems in the Analysis of Community Power." *American Sociological Review, 24,* 6, December 1959: 796–803.

Polsky, Ned. *Hustlers, Beats, and Others.* Chicago: Aldine, 1967.

Pope, Liston. *Millhands and Preachers: A Study of Gastonia.* New Haven, Connecticut: Yale University Press, 1942.

Population Reference Bureau. *1988 World Population Data Sheet.* Washington, D.C.: Population Reference Bureau, 1988.

Porter, Bruce, and Marvin Dunn. *The Miami Riot of 1980: Crossing the Bounds.* Lexington, Massachusetts, Lexington Books, 1984.

Portes, Alejandro, and Ruben G. Rumbaut. *Immigrant America.* Berkeley, California: University of California Press, 1990.

Powell, Brian, and Lala Carr Steelman. "Variations in State SAT Performance: Meaningful or Misleading?" *Harvard Educational Review, 54* (4), November 1984:389–412.

Prakasa, V. V., and V. Nandini Rao. "Arranged Marriages: An Assessment of the Attitudes of the College Students in India." In *Cross-Cultural Perspectives of Mate Selection and Marriage,* George Kurian, ed. Westport, Connecticut: Greenwood Press, 1979:

Preston, Howard L. *Automobile Age Atlanta: The Making of a Southern Metropolis, 1900–1935.* Athens: University of Georgia Press, 1979.

Price, Daniel O. (ed.). *The 99th Hour.* Chapel Hill: University of North Carolina Press, 1967 (as contained in Simon 1981b).

Prosser, William R. "The Underclass: Assessing What We Have Learned." *Focus, 13,* 2, 1991:1–5, 9–18.

Prud'Homme, Alex. "Getting a Grip on Power." *Time,* July 29, 1991:15–16.

Prus, Robert. "Sociologist as Hustler: The Dynamics of Acquiring Information." In *Fieldwork Experience: Qualitative Approaches to Social Research,* William B. Shaffir, Robert A. Stebbins, and Allan Turowetz, eds. New York: St. Martin's, 1980:132–145.

Querlin, Maurise. *Women Without Men.* London: Mayflower Books, 1965.

Rathus, Spencer, and Jeffrey Nevid. *Human Sexuality in a World of Diversity.* Boston: Allyn and Bacon, 1993.

Raymond, Chris. "New Studies by Anthropologists Indicate Amish Communities Are Much More Dynamic and Diverse Than Many Believed." *Chronicle of Higher Education,* December 19, 1990:A1, A9.

Read, Piers Paul. *Alive. The Story of the Andes Survivors.* Philadelphia: J. B. Lippincott, 1974.

Reckless, Walter C. *The Crime Problem* (fifth edition). New York: Appleton, 1973.

Reed, Susan, and Lorenzo Benet. "Ecowarrior Dave Foreman Will Do Whatever It Takes in His Fight to Save Mother Earth." *People Weekly, 33,* 15, April 16, 1990:113–116.

Reich, Michael. "The Economic Impact in the Postwar Period." In *Impacts of Racism on White Americans,* Benjamin P. Bowser and Raymond G. Hunt (eds.). Beverly Hills, Calif.: Sage, 1981:165–176.

Reich, Michael. "The Economics of Racism." In *The Capitalist System,* Richard C. Edwards, Michael Reich, and Thomas E. Weiskopf (eds.). Englewood Cliffs, N.J.: Prentice-Hall, 1972:313–321.

Reiman, Jeffrey H. "A Crime By Any Other Name." In *Taking Sides: Clashing Views on Controversial Social Issues,* (seventh edition), Kurt Finsterbusch and George McKenna, eds. Guilford, Connecticut: Dushkin, 1992:288–295.

Reimers, Cordelia W. "Sources of the Family Income Differentials Among Hispanics, Blacks, and White Non-Hispanics." *American Journal of Sociology, 89* (4), January 1984:889–903.

Reinhold, Robert. "50% Rise in World Population Forecast by Year 2000." *New York Times,* February 25, 1979:1.

Renzetti, Claire M., and Daniel J. Curran. *Women, Men, and Society,* Second edition. Boston: Allyn and Bacon, 1992.

Resnick, Melvyn C. "Beyond the Ethnic Community: Spanish Language Roles and Maintenance in Miami" *International Journal of the Sociology of Language, 69,* 1988:89–104.

Revzin, Philip. "France and Germany Present Proposal for a Future Political Union of Europe." *Wall Street Journal,* December 10, 1990:A8.

Rhode, Deborah L., ed. *Theoretical Perspectives on Sexual Difference.* New Haven, Connecticut: Yale University Press, 1990.

Rhyne, Edwin H. "Making Environmental Sociology Sociological." *Sociological Spectrum, 7,* 4, 1987:335–346.

Rich, Spencer. "Number of Elected Hispanic Officials Doubled in a Decade, Study Shows." *Washington Post,* September 19, 1986:A6.

Richards, Bill. "Home on the Range Means Saki, Slippers for Some Cowboys." *Wall Street Journal,* July 16, 1990:A1, A7.

Richardson, Lewis F. *Statistics of Deadly Quarrels.* Chicago: Quadrangle, 1960.

Ricketts, Erol R., and Isabel V. Sawhill. "Defining and Measuring the Underclass." *Journal of Policy Analysis and Management, 7,* 2, 1988:316–325.

Rieder, Jonathan. "Crown of Thorns." *New Republic,* October 14, 1991:26–31.

Riesman, David. *The Lonely Crowd.* New Haven, Connecticut: Yale University Press, 1950.

Riesman, David. "The Suburban Dislocation." In *Urban Man and Society: A Reader in Urban Ecology,* Albert N. Cousins and Hans Nagpaul, eds. New York: Knopf, 1970:172–184.

Rigdon, Joan E., and Alecia Swasy. "Distractions of Modern Life at Key Ages Are Cited for Drop in Student Literacy." *Wall Street Journal,* October 1, 1990:B1, B3.

Riger, Stephanie, Margaret T. Gordon, and Robert LeBailly. "Women's Fear of Crime." *Victimology, 3,* 1978:274–284.

Rist, Ray C. "Student Social Class and Teacher Expectations: The Self-Fulfilling Prophecy in Ghetto Education." *Harvard Educational Review, 40* (3), August 1970:411–451.

Roache, Joel. "Confessions of a Househusband." In *Marriage and Family in a Changing Society,* Fourth edition, James M. Henslin, ed. New York: Free Press, 1992:305–310.

Robert Wood Johnson Foundation. *Special Report: Updated Report on Access to Health Care for the American People.* Princeton, New Jersey: Robert Wood Johnson Foundation, 1983.

Robertson, Ian. "Social Stratification." In *The Study of Anthropology,* David E. Hunter and Phillip Whitten, eds. New York: Harper and Row, 1976.

Robertson, Ian. *Sociology* (third edition). New York: Worth, 1987.

Robinson, John P. "I Love My TV." *American Demographics, 12,* 9, September 1990:24–27.

Rodash, Mary Flannery. *The College of Midwifery: A Sociological Study of the Decline of a Profession.* Southern Illinois University at Carbondale, Ph.D. Dissertation, 1982.

Rodriguez, Richard. "The Late Victorians: San Francisco, AIDS, and the Homosexual Stereotype." *Harper's Magazine,* October 1990:57–66.

Rodriguez, Richard. *Mexico's American Children. Harper's Magazine, 273,* July 1986:12–14.

Rodriguez, Richard. "Mixed Blood." *Harper's Magazine, 283,* November 1991:47–56.

Rodriguez, Richard. "The Education of Richard Rodriguez." *Saturday Review,* February 8, 1975:147–149.

Rodriguez, Richard. "The Fear of Losing a Culture." *Time, 132,* July 11, 1988:84.

Rodriguez, Richard. *Hunger of Memory: The Education of Richard Rodriguez.* Boston: David R. Godine, 1982.

Roethlisberger, Fritz J., and William J. Dickson. *Management and the Worker.* Cambridge: Harvard University Press, 1939.

Rogers, Joseph W. *Why Are You Not a Criminal?* Englewood Cliffs, N.J.: Prentice-Hall, 1977.

Rohen, Thomas P. *Japan's High Schools.* Berkeley: University of California Press, 1983.

Rohner, Sharon W. "Fetal Alcohol Effects Linked to Moderate Drinking Levels." In *Formation and Feature Service of the National Clearinghouse for Alcohol Information of the National Institute of Alcohol Abuse and Alcoholism, 72,* June 1980:4.

Rootes, Chris A. "The Future of the 'New Politics': A European Perspective." *Social Alternatives, 8,* 4, January 1990:7–12.

Rosaldo, Michelle Zimbalist. "Women, Culture and Society: A Theoretical Overview." In *Women, Culture, and Society,* Michelle Zimbalist Rosaldo and Louise Lamphere (eds.). Stanford: Stanford University Press, 1974.

Rose, Frederick. "Los Angeles Tallies Losses; Curfew is Lifted." *Wall Street Journal,* May 5, 1992:A3, A18.

Rose, Steven. "Stalking the Criminal Chromosome." *The Nation 242* (20), 1986:732–736.

Rosenberg, Charles E. *The Care of Strangers: The Rise of America's Hospital System.* New York: Basic Books, 1987.

Rosenblatt, Roger. *Life Itself: Abortion in the American Mind.* New York: Random House, 1992.

Rosenfeld, Rachel A., and Arne L. Kalleberg. "A Cross-National Comparison of the Gender Gap in Income." *American Journal of Sociology, 96,* 1, July 1990:69–106.

Rosenthal, Robert, and Lenore Jacobson. *Pygmalion in the Classroom: Teacher Expectation and Pupils' Intellectual Development.* New York: Holt, Rinehart, and Winston, 1968.

Ross, Catherine E. "The Division of Labor at Home" *Social Forces, 65,* 1987:816–833.

Rossi, Alice S. "A Biosocial Perspective on Parenting." *Daedalus, 106,* 1977:1–31.

Rossi, Alice S. *The Feminist Papers: From Adams to de Beauvoir.* New York: Bantam, 1974.

Rossi, Alice S. "Gender and Parenthood." *American Sociological Review, 49,* 1984:1–18.

Rossi, Peter H. *Down and Out in America: The Origins of Homelessness.* Chicago: University of Chicago Press, 1989.

Rossi, Peter H., Gene A. Fisher, and Georgianna Willis. *The Condition of the Homeless of Chicago.* Amherst: University of Massachusetts, September 1986.

Rossi, Peter H., and James D. Wright. "The Urban Homeless: A Portrait of Urban Dislocation." *Annals of the American Academy of Political and Social Sciences,* January 1989:132–142.

Rossi, Peter H., James D. Wright, Gene A. Fisher, and Georgianna Willis. "The Urban Homeless: Estimating Composition and Size." *Science, 235,* March 13, 1987:1136–1140.

Rothenberg, Paula. "The Construction, Deconstruction, and Reconstruction of Difference." *Hypatia, 5,* Spring 1990:42–57.

Rothenberg, Stuart. "Abortion's New Battlefield is Congress." *Wall Street Journal,* April 27, 1992:A16.

Rothschild, Joyce, and J. Allen Whitt. *The Cooperative Workplace: Potentials and Dilemmas of Organizational Democracy and Participation.* Cambridge: Cambridge University Press, 1986.

Rothschild, N. "Small Group Affiliation as a Mediating Factor in the Cultivation Process." In *Cultural Indicators: An International Symposium,* G. Melischek, K. E. Rosengren, and J. Strappers, eds. Vienna: Osterreichischen Akademie der Wissenschaften, 1984.

Rubenstein, Carin. "Is There Sex After Baby?" In *Marriage and Family in a Changing Society,* Fourth edition. James M. Henslin, ed. New York: Free Press, 1992:235–242.

Rubenstein, Richard L. "The Modernization of Slavery." In *Structured Social Inequality: A Reader in Comparative Social Stratification,* Celia S. Heller, ed. New York: Macmillan, 1987:74–81.

Rubin, Lillian Breslow. "The Empty Nest." In *Marriage and Family in a Changing Society,* Fourth edition, James M. Henslin, ed. New York: Free Press, 1992:261–270.

Rubin, Lillian Breslow. "Worlds of Pain." In *Marriage and Family in a Changing Society,* Fourth edition. James M. Henslin, ed. New York: Free Press, 1992:44–50.

Rubin, Lillian Breslow. *Worlds of Pain: Life in the Working-Class Family.* New York: Basic Books, 1976.

Rubinson, Richard. "Class Formation, Politics, and Institutions: Schooling in the United States." *American Journal of Sociology, 92* (3), November 1986:519–48.

Ruesch, Hans. *Top of the World.* New York: Permabooks, 1959.

Ruffenbach, Glenn. "Nursing-Home Care as a Work Benefit." *Wall Street Journal,* June 30, 1988:23.

Ruffins, Paul. "How to Survive Campus Bigotry." *Washington Post,* June 16, 1991:B2.

Ruggles, Patricia. *Drawing the Line: Alternative Poverty Measures and Their Implication for Public Policy.* Washington, D.C.: Urban Institute, 1990.

Ruggles, Patricia. "Short and Long Term Poverty in the United States: Measuring the American 'Underclass' ". Washington, D.C.: Urban Institute, June 1989.

Rummel, R. J. *Lethal Politics: Soviet Genocide and Mass Murder Since 1917.* New Brunswick, New Jersey: Transaction Books, 1990.

Russell, Alan. *Guiness Book of World Records.* New York: Bantam Books, 1987.

Russell, Diana E. H. *The Politics of Rape: The Victim's Perspective.* New York: Scarborough, 1979.

Russell, Diana E. H. "Preliminary Report on Some Findings Relating to the Trauma and Long-Term Effects of Intrafamily Childhood Sexual Abuse." Unpublished paper, n.d.

Russell, Diana E. H. "Rape in Marriage: A Case Against Legalized Crime." Paper presented at the annual meeting of the American Society of Criminology, 1980.

Russell, Diana E. H. *The Secret Trauma: Incest in the Lives of Girls and Women.* New York: Basic Books, 1986.

Russell, Diana E. H. *Sexual Exploitation: Rape, Child Sexual Abuse, and Workplace Harassment.* Beverly Hills, Calif: Sage, 1984.

Russell, Dick. "The Monkeywrenchers." *The Amicus Journal,* Fall 1987:28–42.

Ruth, John L. "American Anabaptists: Who They Are." *Christianity Today,* October 22, 1990:25–29.

Rutter, Michael, Barbara Maughan, Peter Mortimore, Janet Ouston, and Alan Smith. *Fifteen Thousand Hours.* Cambridge, Massachusetts: Harvard University Press, 1979.

Rybczynski, Withold. " 'Edge Cities': The People's Answer to Planners." *New York Times,* November 17, 1991:36.

Sahlins, Marshall D. *Stone Age Economics.* Chicago: Aldine. 1972.

Sahlins, Marshall D., and Elman R. Service. *Evolution and Culture.* Ann Arbor, Michigan: University of Michigan Press, 1960.

Sakharov, Andrei D. *Sakharov Speaks.* Harrison E. Salisbury, ed. New York: Vintage, 1974.

Sales, E. "Women's Adult Development." In *Women and Sex Roles: A Social Psychological Perspective,* I. H. Frieze, J. E. Parsons, P. B. Johnson, D. N. Ruble, and G. L. Zellman, eds. New York: Norton, 1978:157–190.

Salholz, Eloise. "The Push for Power." *Newsweek,* April 9, 1990:19–20.

Samuelson, Paul A., and William D. Nordhaus. *Economics.* Thirteenth edition. New York: McGraw-Hill, 1989.

Samuelson, Robert J. "The Elderly Aren't Needy." *Newsweek,* March 21, 1988:68.

Sarnoff, Irving, and Suzanne Sarnoff. "Love-Centered Marriage." In *Marriage and Family in a Changing Society,* Fourth edition. James M. Henslin, ed. New York: Free Press, 1992:158–164.

Sawhill, Isabel V. "Poverty in the U.S.: Why Is It So Persistent?" *Journal of Economic Literature, 26* (3), September 1988:1073–1119.

Sayres, William. "What Is a Family Anyway?" In *Marriage and Family in a Changing Society,* Fourth edition. James M. Henslin, ed. New York: Free Press, 1992:23–30.

Scanzoni, John. *Opportunity and the Family.* New York: Free Press, 1970.

Schachter, Stanley, and Jerome Singer. "Cognitive, Social, and Physiological Determinants of Emotional State." *Psychological Review, 69,* 1962:379–399.

Schaefer, Richard T. *Racial and Ethnic Groups.* Boston: Little Brown, 1979.

Schaeffer, Richard T. *Sociology,* Third edition. New York: McGraw-Hill, 1989.

Schoen, Robert, and John Wooldredge. "Marriage Choices in North Carolina and Virginia, 1969–71 and 1979–81." *Journal of Marriage and the Family, 51,* 1989:465–481.

Schoen, Robert, John Wooldredge, and Barbara Thomas. "Ethnic and Educational Effects on Marriage Choice." *Social Science Quarterly, 70,* 3, September 1989:617–629.

Schoenherr, Richard A., Lawrence A. Young, and Jose Perez Vilarino. "Demographic Transitions in Religious Organizations: A Comparative Study of Priest Decline in Roman Catholic Dioceses." *Journal for the Scientific Study of Religion, 27,* 4, December 1988:499–523.

Schor, Juliet B. "Americans Work Too Hard." *New York Times,* July 25, 1991:A21.

Schottland, Charles I. *The Social Security Plan in the U.S.* New York: Appleton, 1963.

Schrieke, Bertram J. *Alien Americans.* New York: Viking, 1936.

Schur, Edwin M. *The Awareness Trap: Self Absorption Instead of Social Change.* New York: Quadrangle, 1976.

Schur, Edwin M. *Labeling Women Deviant: Gender, Stigma, and Social Control.* New York: Random House, 1984.

Schwartz, Barry. "Waiting, Exchange, and Power: The Distribution of Time in Social Systems." In *Down to Earth Sociology: Introductory Readings,* Sixth Edition. New York: Free Press, 1991:217–224.

Schwartz, Felice N. "Management Women and the New Facts of Life." *Harvard Business Review, 89,* 1, January–February 1989:65–76.

Schwartz, Mildred A. *A Sociological Perspective on Politics.* Englewood Cliffs, New Jersey: Prentice Hall, 1990.

Schwendinger, Julia R., and Herman Schwendinger. *Rape and Inequality.* Beverly Hills, Calif.: Sage, 1983.

Scott, Richard R. "Indirect Effects of Desegregation." In *Redefining Social Problems,* Edward Seidman and Julian Rappaport (eds.). New York: Plenum Press, 1988:275–287.

Scully, Diana. *Understanding Sexual Violence: A Study of Convicted Rapists.* Boston: Unwin Hyman, 1990.

Scully, Diana, and Joseph Marolla. " 'Riding the Bull at Gilley's': Convicted Rapists Describe the Rewards of Rape." *Social Problems, 32* (3), February 1985:251–263.

Seaver, W. J. "Effects of Naturally Induced Teacher Expectancies." *Journal of Personality and Social Psychology, 28,* 1973:333–342.

Segal, Elizabeth A. "The Juvenilization of Poverty in the 1980s." *Social Work, 36,* 5, September 1991:454–457.

Sennett, Richard, and Jonathan Cobb. "Some Hidden Injuries of Class."

In *Down to Earth Sociology*. Fifth edition. James M. Henslin, ed. New York: The Free Press, 1988:278–288.

Sewell, William H., Robert M. Hauser, and Wendy C. Wolf. "Sex, Schooling, and Occupational Status." *American Journal of Sociology, 86,* 1980:551–583.

Sewell, William H., and Vimal P. Shah. "Parents' Education and Children's Educational Aspirations and Achievements." *American Sociological Review, 33* (2), April 1968:191–209.

Shanas, Ethel. "The Family as a Social Support System in Old Age." *The Gerontologist, 19,* April 1979:169–174.

Shannon, William H. "Are There Any More Priests Out There?" *America, 165,* 10, October 12, 1991:240–242.

Sharp, Deborah. "Miami's Language Gap Widens." *USA Today,* April 3, 1992:A3.

Shaw, Sue. "Wretched of the Earth." *New Statesman, 20,* March 1987:19–20.

Sheldon, William. *Varieties of Delinquent Youth: An Introduction to Constitutional Psychiatry.* New York: Harper, 1949.

Shepelak, Norma J. "Ideological Stratification: American Beliefs about Economic Justice." *Social Justice Research, 3,* 3, September 1989: 217–231.

Sherif, Muzafer, and Carolyn Sherif. *Groups in Harmony and Tension.* New York: Harper & Row, 1953.

Sherkat, Darren E., and John Wilson. "Status, Denomination, and Socialization: Effects on Religious Switching and Apostasy." Presented at the 1991 meetings of the American Sociological Association.

Sherman, Spencer. "The Hmong in America." *National Geographic,* October 1988:586–610.

Shibutani, Tamotsu. *Improvised News: A Sociological Study of Rumor.* Indianapolis, Indiana: Bobbs-Merrill, 1966.

Shibutani, Tamotsu. "On the Personification of Adversaries." In *Human Nature and Collective Behavior,* Tamotsu Shibutani (ed.). Englewood Cliffs, N.J.: Prentice-Hall, 1970.

Shim, Kelly H., and Marshall DeBerry. *Criminal Victimization in the United States, 1986.* Washington, D.C.: U.S. Department of Justice, Bureau of Justice Statistics, August 1988.

Shingles, Richard D. "Class, Status, and Support for Government Aid to Disadvantaged Groups." *Journal of Politics, 51,* 4, November 1989:933–962.

Shipler, David K. *Russia: Broken Idols, Solemn Dreams.* New York: Times Books, 1982.

Shirer, William L. *The Rise and Fall of the Third Reich.* Greenwich, Connecticut: Fawcett, 1960.

Shively, JoEllen. "Cultural Compensation: The Popularity of Westerns among American Indians." Paper presented at the annual meetings of the American Sociological Association, 1991.

Shlaes, Amity. "Germany 'Manages' Away an Asset." *Wall Street Journal,* January 23, 1992:A18.

Shreve, Herbie. "Personal Communication." 1991.

Sibbison, Jim. "Death at Work." *The New Physician,* May 1979:18–21.

Signorielli, Nancy. "Children, Television, and Gender Roles: Messages and Impact." *Journal of Adolescent Heath Care, 11,* 1990:50–58.

Signorielli, Nancy, "The Demography of the Television World." In *Proceedings from the Tenth Annual Telecommunications Policy Research Conference,* O. H. Gandy, P. Espinosa, and J. A. Ordover, eds. Norwood, New Jersey: Ablex, 1983.

Signorielli, Nancy. "Television and Conceptions About Sex Roles: Maintaining Conventionality and the Status Quo." *Sex Roles, 21,* 5/6, 1989:341–360.

Silberman, Charles E. *Criminal Violence, Criminal Justice.* New York: Random House, 1978.

Sills, David L. "Voluntary Associations: Sociological Aspects." In *International Encyclopedia of the Social Sciences, 16,* David L. Sills, ed. New York: Macmillan, 1968:362–379.

Sills, David L. *The Volunteers.* Glencoe, Illinois: Free Press, 1957.

Silver, Isidore. "Crime and Conventional Wisdom." *Society, 14,* March–April, 1977:9, 15–19.

Silverman, Deidre. "Sexual Harassment: The Working Women's Dilemma." *Building Feminist Theory: Essays From Quest.* New York: Longman, 1981.

Simmel, Georg, *The Sociology of Georg Simmel,* Kurt H. Wolff, ed. and trans. Glencoe, Illinois: Free Press, 1950. Originally published between 1902 and 1917.

Simmons, R. G., D. A. Blyth, E. F. Van Cleave, and D. M. Bush. "Entry Into Early Adolescence." *American Sociological Review, 44,* 1979:948–967.

Simon, Carl P., and Ann D. Witte. *Beating the System: The Underground Economy.* Boston, Massachusetts: Auburn House, 1982.

Simon, David R. "The Political Economy of Crime." In *Political Economy: A Critique of American Society,* Scott G. McNall (ed.). Glenview, Ill.: Scott Foresman, 1981:347–366.

Simon, David R., and D. Stanley Eitzen. *Elite Deviance.* Second edition. Boston: Massachusetts: Allyn and Bacon, 1986.

Simon, Julian L. "Population Growth is Not Bad for Humanity." In *Taking Sides: Clashing Views on Controversial Social Issues,* Kurt Finsterbusch and George McKenna, eds. Guilford, Connecticut: Dushkin, 1992: 347–352.

Simon, Julian L. *Theory of Population and Economic Growth.* New York: Basil Blackwell, 1986.

Simon, Julian L. *The Ultimate Resource.* Princeton, New Jersey: Princeton University Press, 1981b.

Simon, Rita J. *The Contemporary Woman and Crime.* Washington, D.C.: National Institutes of Mental Health, 1975.

Simons, Marlise. "The Amazon's Savvy Indians." *New York Times Magazine,* February 26, 1989:36–37, 48–52.

Simpson, George Eaton, and J. Milton Yinger. *Racial and Cultural Minorities: An Analysis of Prejudice and Discrimination* (fourth edition). New York: Harper & Row, 1972.

Singer, Dorothy G. "A Time to Reexamine the Role of Television in Our Lives." *American Psychologist, 38* (7), July 1983:815–816.

Singer, Jerome L., and Dorothy G. Singer. "Psychologists Look at Television: Cognitive, Developmental, Personality, and Social Policy Implications." *American Psychologist, 38* (1), July 1983:826–834.

Singh, Ajit. "Urbanism, Poverty, and Employment: The Large Metropolis in the Third World." Unpublished monograph. Cambridge University, 1988. As quoted in Giddens, Anthony. *Introduction to Sociology.* New York: W. W. Norton, 1991:690.

Sixth Special Report to the U.S. Congress on Alcohol and Health. Washington, D.C.: U.S. Department of Health and Human Services, 1987.

Skeels, H. M. *Adult Status of Children with Contrasting Early Life Experiences: A Follow-up Study.* Monograph of the Society for Research in Child Development, *31* (3), 1966.

Skeels, H. M., and H. B. Dye. "A Study of the Effects of Differential Stimulation on Mentally Retarded Children." *Proceedings and Addresses of the American Association on Mental Deficiency, 44,* 1939: 114–136.

Skerry, Peter, and Michael Hartman. "Latin Mass." *New Republic,* June 10, 1991:18–20.

Small, Albion W. *General Sociology.* Chicago: University of Chicago Press, 1905. As cited in Olmsted and Hare 1978:10.

Smart, Barry. "On the Disorder of Things: Sociology, Postmodernity and the 'End of the Social.'" *Sociology, 24,* 3, August 1990:397–416.

Smith, Clark. "Oral History as 'Therapy': Combatants' Accounts of Vietnam War." In *Strangers at Home: Vietnam Veterans Since the War,* Charles R. Figley and Seymore Leventman (eds.). New York: Praeger, 1980:9–34.

Smith, Daniel Scott, and Michael Hindus. "Premarital Pregnancy in America, 1640–1971: An Overview and Interpretation." *Journal of Interdisciplinary History, 4,* Spring 1975:537–570.

Smith, Harold. "A Colossal Cover-Up." *Christianity Today,* December 12, 1986:16–17.

Smith, James P., and Finis R. Welch. *Closing the Gap: Forty Years of Economic Progress for Blacks,* Santa Monica, CA.: Rand, 1986.

Smith, Joel B., and Dennis A. Tirpak. *The Potential Effects of Global*

Climate Change on the United States. Washington, D.C.: United States Environmental Problems Agency, October 1988.

Smith, Kristen F., and Vern L. Bengston. "Positive Consequences of Institutionalization: Solidarity Between Elderly Parents and Their Middle-Aged Children." *The Gerontologist, 19,* October 1979:438–447.

Smith, Lee. "The War Between the Generations." *Fortune,* July 20, 1987:78–82.

Smith-Lovin, Lynn, and Charles Brody. "Interruptions in Group Discussions: The Effects of Gender and Group Composition." *American Sociological Review, 54,* 1989:424–435.

Snider, William. "Fresno Schools, Hmong Refugees Seek Common Ground." *Education Week, 10,* 14, December 5, 1990:1, 12–13.

Snipp, C. Matthew, and Alan L. Sorkin. "American Indian Housing: An Overview of Conditions and Public Policy." In *Race, Ethnicity, and Minority Housing in the United States,* Jamshid A. Momeni (ed.). New York: Greenwood Press, 1986:147–175.

Snow, Margaret E., Carol Nagy Jacklin, and Eleanor E. Maccoby. "Birth-Order Differences in Peer Sociability at Thirty-Three Months." *Child Development, 52,* 1981:589–595.

Snyder, Mark. "Self-Fulfilling Stereotypes." In *Down to Earth Sociology,* Seventh edition. James M. Henslin, ed. New York: Free Press, 1993.

Snyder, Thomas D., and Charlene M. Hoffman. *Digest of Education Statistics, 1990.* Washington, D.C.: National Center for Education Statistics, February 1991.

Sorensen, Andrew. "AIDS: What Should We Do? *Johns Hokpkins Magazine,* August 1990:38–41.

Sorensen, Jesper B. "Perceptions of Women's Opportunity in Five Industrialized Nations." *European Sociological Review, 6,* 2, September 1990:151–164.

Sorokin, Pitirim A. *The Crisis of Our Age.* New York: E. P. Dutton, 1941.

Sorokin, Pitirim A. *Social and Cultural Dynamics.* 4 volumes. New York: American Book Company, 1937–1941.

Sorrentino, Constance. "The Changing Family in International Perspective." *Monthly Labor Review,* March 1990:41–55.

South, Scott J. "Sociodemographic Differentials in Mate Selection Preferences." *Journal of Marriage and the Family, 53,* November 1991:928–940.

Spector, Malcolm, and John Kitsuse. *Constructing Social Problems.* Menlo Park, California: Cummings, 1977.

Speizer, Jeanne J. "Education." In *The Women's Annual, 1982–1983,* Barbara Haber, ed. Boston: G. K. Hall, 1983:29–54.

Spencer, Herbert. *Principles of Sociology.* New York: Appleton, 1884. Three volumes.

Spengler, Oswald. *The Decline of the West,* 2 vols. Translated by Charles F. Atkinson. New York: Alfred A. Knopf, 1926–1928. (Originally published in 1919–1922.)

Sperber, Irwin. "The Marketplace Personality: On Capitalism, Male Chauvinism, and Romantic Love." In *Social Problems in American Society,* James M. Henslin and Larry T. Reynolds, eds. Boston: Holbrook Press, 1973:131–139.

Spitz, Renee. "Hospitalism." *Psychoanalytic Study of the Child, 1,* 1945:53–72.

Spitzer, Steven. "Toward a Marxian Theory of Deviance." *Social Problems, 22,* June 1975:608–619.

Spivak, Jonathan. "Israel's Discrimination Problem." *Wall Street Journal,* December 3, 1980.

Spurr, Stephen J. "Sex Discrimination in the Legal Profession: A Study of Promotion." *Industrial and Labor Relations Review, 43,* 4, April 1990:406–417.

Srisang, Koson. "The Ecumenical Coalition on Third World Tourism." *Annals of Tourism Research, 16,* 1, 1989:119–121.

Srole, Leo, et al. *Mental Health in the Metropolis: The Midtown Manhattan Study.* New York: New York University Press, 1978.

Stack, Carol B. *All Our Kin: Strategies for Survival in a Black Community.* New York: Harper, 1974.

Stack, Steven. "The Effect of Religious Commitment on Suicide: A Cross-national Analysis." *Journal of Health and Social Behavior, 24,* 1983:362–374.

Stafford, Linda, Sonya R. Kennedy, Joanne E. Lehman, and Gail Arnold. "Wealth in America." *ISR Newsletter,* Winter 1986–87.

Stampp, Kenneth M. *The Peculiar Institution: Slavery in the Ante-Bellum South.* New York: Vintage Books, 1956.

Stanley, Julian C., ed. *Compensatory Education for Children Ages 2 to 8: Recent Studies of Environmental Intervention.* Baltimore: Johns Hopkins University Press, 1973.

Stanley, Kay O. "Homeless Data Debate." *Black Enterprise, 1,* 15, November 1984:28.

Stark, Elizabeth. "Friends Through It All." In *Marriage and Family in a Changing Society,* Third edition. James M. Henslin, ed. New York: Free Press, 1989:441–449.

Stark, Rodney. *Sociology* (third edition). Belmont, California: Wadsworth, 1989.

Starna, William A., and Ralph Watkins. "Northern Iroquoian Slavery." *Ethnohistory, 38,* 1, Winter 1991:34–57.

Starr, Paul. *The Social Transformation of American Medicine.* New York: Basic Books, 1982.

Statham, Anne, Eleanor M. Miller, and Hans O. Mauksch. "The Integration Work: A Second-order Analysis of Qualitative Research." In *The Worth of Women's Work: A Qualitative Synthesis,* Statham, Anne, Eleanor M. Miller, and Hans O. Mauksch, eds. Albany: State University of New York Press, 1988:11–35.

Stein, Leonard I. "The Doctor-Nurse Game." In *Down to Earth Sociology: Introductory Readings.* Fifth edition. James M. Henslin, ed. New York: The Free Press, 1988:102–109.

Sterba, James P. "India's Kashmir Stands as a Violent Reminder of Hindu-Moslem Rift." *Wall Street Journal,* November 9, 1990:A1, A8.

Sternlieb, George, and James W. Hughes. "The Uncertain Future of the Central City." *Urban Affairs Quarterly, 18,* 1983:455–472.

Stevens, Amy, and Sarah Lubman. "Deciding Moment of the Trial May Have Been Five Months Ago." *Wall Street Journal,* May 1, 1992:A6.

Stevens, Charles, W. "Integration Is Elusive Despite Recent Gains; Social Barriers Remain." *Wall Street Journal,* September 29, 1980.

Stinnett, Nicholas. "Strong Families." In *Marriage and Family in a Changing Society,* Fourth edition. James M. Henslin, ed. New York: Free Press, 1992:496–507.

Stipp, David. "Einstein Bird Has Scientists Atwitter Over Mental Feats." *Wall Street Journal,* May 9, 1990: A1, A4.

Stipp, David. "Himalayan Tree Could Serve as Source of Anti-cancer Drug Taxol, Team Says." *Wall Street Journal,* April 20, 1992:B4.

Stockard, Jean, and Miriam M. Johnson. *Sex Roles: Sex Inequality and Sex Role Development.* Englewood Cliffs, N.J.: Prentice-Hall, 1980.

Stockwell, John. "The Dark Side of U.S. Foreign Policy." *Zeta Magazine,* February 1989:36–48.

Stodgill, Ralph M. *Handbook of Leadership: A Survey of Theory and Research.* New York: Free Press, 1974.

Stone, Gregory P. "City Shoppers and Urban Identification: Observations on the Social Psychology of City Life." *American Journal of Sociology, 60,* November 1954:276–284.

Stone, Gregory P. "Sport as a Community Representation." In *Handbook of Social Science and Sport,* Gunther Luschen and George H. Sage, eds. Champaign, Illinois: Stipes, 1981:214–245.

Stone, Michael H. "Murder." *Psychiatric Clinics of North America, 12,* 3, September 1989:643–651.

Stouffer, Samuel A., Arthur A. Lumsdaine, Marion Harper Lumsdaine, Robin M. Williams Jr., M. Brewster Smith, Irving L. Janis, Shirley A. Star, and Leonard S. Cottrell, Jr. *The American Soldier: Combat and Its Aftermath,* vol. 2. New York: Wiley: 1949.

Stout, Hilary. "Determined Principal and Faculty Use Discipline and Peer Pressure to Make a School 'Drug Free.' " *Wall Street Journal,* October 1, 1991:A20.

Stout, Hillary. "Harvard Team Says That AIDS Is Accelerating." *Wall Street Journal*, June 4, 1992:B10.

Straus, Murray A. "Explaining Family Violence." In *Marriage and Family in a Changing Society*. Fourth edition, James M. Henslin, ed. New York: Free Press, 1992:344–356.

Straus, Murray A. "Victims and Aggressors in Marital Violence." *American Behavioral Scientist, 23*, May–June 1980:681–704.

Straus, Murray A., and Richard J. Gelles. "Violence in American Families: How Much Is There and Why Does It Occur?" In *Troubled Relationships*, Elam W. Nunnally, Catherine S. Chilman, and Fred M. Cox (eds.). Newbury Park: Sage, 1988:141–162.

Straus, Murray A., Richard J. Gelles, and Suzanne K. Steinmetz. *Behind Closed Doors: Violence in the American Family*. New York: Anchor/Doubleday, 1980.

Stryker, Sheldon. "Symbolic Interactionism: Themes and Variations." In *Social Psychology: Sociological Perspectives*, Morris Rosenberg and Ralph H. Turner, eds. New Brunswick, New Jersey: Transaction, 1990.

Sue, Stanley, and Nathaniel N. Wagner, eds. *Asian-Americans: Psychological Perspectives*. Palo Alto, California: Science and Behavior Books, 1973.

Sullivan, Mercer L. *"Getting Paid:" Youth Crime and Work in the Inner City*. Ithaca, New York: Cornell University Press, 1989.

Sutherland, Edwin H. *The Professional Thief*. Chicago: University of Chicago Press, 1937.

Sutherland, Edwin H. *White Collar Crime*. New York: Dryden Press, 1949.

Sutherland, Edwin H. *Principles of Criminology* (fourth edition). Philadelphia: Lippincott, 1947.

Sutherland, Edwin H., and Donald Cressey. *Criminology*, Ninth edition. Philadelphia: Lippincott, 1974.

Suzuki, Bob H. "Asian-American Families." In *Marriage and Family in a Changing Society*, James M. Henslin, ed. Second edition. New York: The Free Press, 1985:104–119.

Swafford, Michael. *Perceptions of Social Status in the USSR*. Champaign, Illinois: Soviet Interview Project, 1986.

Swedish Institute, The. "Health and Medical Care in Sweden." July 1990:1–4.

Sweet, Stuart J. "A Looming Federal Surplus." *Wall Street Journal*, March 28, 1984:28.

Sykes, Gresham M., and David Matza. "Techniques of Neutralization." In *Down to Earth Sociology*, Fifth edition, James M. Henslin, ed. New York: The Free Press, 1988:225–231.

Szymanski, Albert. *The Logic of Imperialism*. New York: Praeger, 1981.

Szasz, Thomas. *Ceremonial Chemistry: The Ritual Persecution of Drugs, Addicts, and Pushers*. Garden City, N.Y.: Anchor/Doubleday, 1975.

Szasz, Thomas S. "Law and Psychiatry: The Problems that Will Not Go Away." *Journal of Mind and Behavior. 11*, 3–4, 1990:557–563.

Szasz, Thomas S. *The Manufacture of Madness: A Comparative Study of the Inquisition and the Mental Health Movement*. New York: Harper and Row, 1970.

Szasz, Thomas S. *The Myth of Mental Illness*. Revised edition. New York: Harper and Row, 1986.

Szasz, Thomas S. "Psychiatric Injustice." *British Journal of Psychiatry, 154*, June 1989:864–869.

Szelenyi, Szonja. "Social Inequality and Party Membership: Patterns of Recruitment in the Hungarian Socialist Workers' Party." *American Sociological Review, 52*, 1987:559–573.

Szymanski, Albert. "Racial Discrimination and White Gain." *American Sociological Review, 41*, June 1976:403–414.

Tannen, Deborah. *You Just Don't Understand: Women and Men in Conversation*. New York: William Morrow, 1990.

Thomas, Paulette. "U.S. Examiners Will Scrutinize Banks with Poor Minority-Lending Histories." *Wall Street Journal*, October 22, 1991:A2.

Thomas, Paulette. "EPA Predicts Global Impact From Warming." *Wall Street Journal*, October 21, 1988:B5.

Thomas, R. Roosevelt, Jr. "From Affirmative Action to Affirming Diversity." *Harvard Business Review, 90*, 2, March–April, 1990:107–117.

Thomas, William I., and Florian Znaniecki. *The Polish Peasant in Europe and America*. Chicago: University of Chicago Press. 1918.

Thompson, William E. "Hanging Tongues: A Sociological Encounter with the Assembly Line." In *Down to Earth Sociology: Introductory Readings*, Seventh Edition. James M. Henslin, ed. New York: Free Press, 1993.

Thorne, Barrie. "Children and Gender: Constructions of Difference." In *Theoretical Perspectives on Sexual Difference*, Deborah L. Rhode, ed. New Haven, Connecticut: Yale University Press, 1990:100–113.

Thorne, Barrie, and Zella Luria. "Sexuality and Gender in Children's Daily Worlds." In *Down to Earth Sociology*, Seventh edition. James M. Henslin, ed. New York: Free Press, 1993.

Tiffany, Paul. "The Rise of Japanese Lobbying in America." *Chief Executive, 55* (1), January/February 1990:62–65.

Tilly, Charles. *From Mobilization to Revolution*. Reading, Massachusetts: Addison-Wesley, 1978.

Timasheff, Nicholas S. *War and Revolution*. Joseph F. Scheuer (ed.). New York: Sheed & Ward, 1965.

Timerman, Jacobo. *Prisoner Without a Name, Cell Without a Number*. New York: Knopf, 1981.

Tiryakian, Edward A., ed. *The Phenomenon of Sociology: A Reader in the Sociology of Sociology*. New York: Appleton Century Crofts, 1971.

Tisdale, Hope. "The Process of Urbanization." In *Urban Man and Society: A Reader in Urban Ecology*, Albert N. Cousins and Hans Nagpaul, eds. New York: Knopf, 1970:101–109.

Tittle, Charles R., and Michael R. Welch. "Religiosity and Deviance: Toward a Contingency Theory of Constraining Effects." *Social Forces, 61*, 1983:653–682.

Toby, Jackson. "To Get Rid of Guns in Schools, Get Rid of Some Students." *Wall Street Journal*, March 23, 1992:A12.

Tocqueville, Alexis de. *Democracy in America*, J. P. Mayer and Max Lerner, eds. New York: Harper and Row, 1966. First published in 1835.

Tocqueville, Alexis de. *The Old Regime and the French Revolution*. Stuart Gilbert, translator. Garden City, New York: Doubleday Anchor, 1955. Originally published in 1856.

Toennies, Ferdinand. *Community and Society (Gemeinschaft und Gesellschaft)*, with a new introduction by John Samples. New Brunswick, New Jersey: Transaction Publishers, 1988. Originally published in 1887.

Toffler, Alvin. *The Third Wave*. New York: William Morrow, 1980.

Tolba, Mostafa K. "The Ozone Agreement—And Beyond." In *Taking Sides: Clashing Views on Controversial Environmental Issues*, Third edition, Theodore D. Goldfarb, ed. Guilford, Connecticut, Dushkin, 1989:310–316.

Tolchin, Martin. "Mildest Possible Penalty Is Imposed on Neil Bush." *New York Times*, April 19, 1991:D2.

Tolchin, Martin. "Surgeon General Asserts Smoking Is an Addiction." *New York Times*, May 17, 1988:A1, C4.

Tomlinson, Richard. "Where Population Control Cuts a Different Way." *Wall Street Journal*, June 20, 1984:23.

Toynbee, Arnold. *A Study of History*. Abridged and edited by D. C. Somervell. New York: Oxford University Press, 1946.

Treen, Joe, Bonnie Bell, and John McGuire. "Die, My Daughter, Die!" *People*, January 20, 1992:71–72, 75.

Treiman, Donald J. *Occupational Prestige in Comparative Perspective*. New York: Academic Press, 1977.

Troeltsch, Ernst. *The Social Teachings of the Christian Churches*, New York: Macmillan, 1931.

Trost, Cathy. "Labor Letter." *Wall Street Journal*, March 24, 1992:A1.

Trueba, Henry T., Lila Jacobs, and Elizabeth Kirton. *Cultural Conflict and Adaptation: The Case of Hmong Children in American Society*. Bristol, Pennsylvania: Falmer Press, 1990.

Tucker, Belinda M., and Claudia Mitchell-Kernan. "New Trends in Black

American Interracial Marriage: The Social Structural Context." *Journal of Marriage and the Family, 52,* 1990:209–218.

Tumin, Melvin M., and Roy C. Collins. "Status Mobility and Anomie: A Study in Readiness for Desegregation." *British Journal of Sociology, 10,* 1959:253–267.

Turner, Bryan S. "Outline of a Theory of Citizenship." *Sociology, 24,* 2, May 1990:189–217.

Turner, Jonathan H. *American Society: Problems of Structure.* New York: Harper and Row, 1972.

Turner, Jonathan H. *The Structure of Sociological Theory.* Homewood, Illinois: Dorsey, 1978.

Turner, Ralph, and Lewis Killian. *Collective Behavior.* Englewood Cliffs, New Jersey: Prentice Hall, 1957.

Turner, Ralph, and Lewis Killian. *Collective Behavior* (second edition). Englewood Cliffs, New Jersey: Prentice Hall, 1972.

Udy, Stanley H., Jr. "Bureaucracy and Rationality in Weber's Organizational Theory: An Empirical Study." *American Sociological Review, 24,* December 1959:791–795.

Ullman, Edward, and Chauncey Harris. "The Nature of Cities." In *Urban Man and Society: A Reader in Urban Ecology,* Albert N. Cousins and Hans Nagpaul, eds. New York: Knopf, 1970:91–100.

Ulrich, Patricia M., George J. Warheit, and Rick S. Zimmerman. "Race, Socioeconomic Status, and Psychological Distress: An Examination of Differential Vulnerability." *Journal of Health and Social Behavior, 30,* 1989:131–146.

Usdansky, Margaret L., "English a Problem for Half of Miami." *USA Today.*

Useem, Michael. "Corporations and the Corporate Elite." In *Annual Review of Sociology, 6,* Alex Inkeles, Neil J. Smelser, and Ralph H. Turner, eds. Palo Alto, California: Annual Reviews, 1980:41–77.

Useem, Michael. *The Inner Circle: Large Corporations and the Rise of Business Political Activity in the U.S. and U.K.* New York: Oxford University Press, 1984.

van den Haag, Ernest. *Punishing Criminals: Concerning a Very Old and Painful Question.* New York: Basic Books, 1975.

Van Lawick-Goodall, Jane. *In the Shadow of Man.* Boston: Houghton Mifflin, 1971.

Vanneman, Reeve, and Lynn Weber Cannon. *The American Perception of Class.* Philadelphia: Temple University Press, 1987.

Vaughan, Diane. "Uncoupling: The Social Construction of Divorce." In *Marriage and Family in a Changing Society,* Second edition. James M. Henslin, ed. New York: The Free Press, 1985:429–439.

Vayda, Eugene, and Ralsa B. Deber. "The Canadian Health Care System: An Overview." *Social Science and Medicine, 18,* 1984:191–197.

Veblen, Thorstein. *The Theory of the Leisure Class.* New York: Macmillan, 1912.

Veevers, Jean E. *Childless by Choice.* Toronto: Butterworths, 1980.

Veevers, Jean E. "Voluntarily Childless Wives." *Sociology and Social Research, 57,* April 1973:356–366.

Vega, William A. "Hispanic Families in the 1980s: A Decade of Research." *Journal of Marriage and the Family, 52,* November 1990:1015–1024.

Vincent, Richard C., Dennis K. Davis, and Lilly Ann Boruszkowski. "Sexism on MTV: The Portrayal of Women in Rock Videos." *Journalism Quarterly 64* (4), Winter 1987:750–755, 941–942.

Vinokur, Aaron, and Gur Ofer. *Inequality of Earnings, Household Income and Wealth in the Soviet Union in the 70s.* Champaign, Illinois: Soviet Interview Project, 1986.

Violas, P. C. *The Training of the Urban Working Class: A History of Twentieth Century American Education.* Chicago: Rand McNally, 1978.

Von Hoffman, Nicholas. "Sociological Snoopers." *Transaction 7,* May 1970:4, 6.

Voslensky, Michael. *Nomenklatura: The Soviet Ruling Class.* New York: Doubleday, 1984.

Waddington, Conrad H. *The Man-Made Future.* New York: St. Martin's, 1978.

Wagley, Charles, and Marvin Harris. *Minorities in the New World.* New York: Columbia University Press, 1958.

Waldholz, Michael. "Computer Brain' Outperforms Doctors In Diagnosing Heart Attack Patients." *Wall Street Journal,* December 2, 1991:7B.

Waldholz, Michael. "New Discoveries Dim Drug Makers' Hopes For Quick AIDS Cure." *Wall Street Journal,* May 26, 1992:A1, A6.

Waldholz, Michael, and Jerry E. Bishop. "Testing an AIDS Vaccine in People May be Tougher Than Creating It." *Wall Street Journal,* April 14, 1986:26.

Waldman, Peter. "Iran Votes Mainly Moderate Reformers to First Post-Revolutionary Parliament." *Wall Street Journal,* April 13, 1992:A11.

Walker, Michael. "Canadian Health Care Is a Model for Disaster." *Wall Street Journal,* October 18, 1991:A15.

Walker, Tom. " 'Edge Cities' Represent a Quiet Social Revolution." *Atlanta Journal,* September 29, 1991:C1.

Wallace, Anthony F. C. *Religion: An Anthropological View.* New York: Random House, 1966.

Wallerstein, Immanuel. *The Capitalist World-Economy.* New York: Cambridge University Press, 1979.

Wallerstein, Immanuel. *The Modern World System: Capitalist Agriculture and the Origins of the European World-Economy in the Sixteenth Century.* New York: Academic Press, 1974.

Wallerstein, Immanuel. *The Politics of the World-Economy: The States, the Movements, and the Civilizations.* Cambridge; Cambridge University Press, 1984.

Wallerstein, Judith S., and Joan B. Kelly. "How Children React to Parental Divorce." In *Marriage and Family in a Changing Society,* Fourth edition. James M. Henslin, ed. New York: Free Press, 1992:397–409.

Walters, Jonathan. "Chimps in the Mist." *USA Weekend,* May 18–20, 1990:24.

Ward, D. A., M. Jackson, and R. E. Ward. "Crimes of Violence by Women." In *Crimes of Violence,* Donald Mulvihill, ed. Washington, D.C.: U.S. Government Printing Office, 1969:864–889.

Warner, Kenneth E. *Selling Smoke: Cigarette Advertising and Public Health.* Washington, D. C.: American Public Health Association, 1986.

Warner, W. Lloyd, and Paul S. Hunt. *The Social Life of a Modern Community.* New Haven, Connecticut: Yale University Press, 1941.

Warner, W. Lloyd, Paul S. Hunt, Marchia Meekr, and Kenneth Eels. *Social Class in America.* New York: Harper, 1949.

Watson, J. Mark. "Outlaw Motorcyclists." In *Down to Earth Sociology: Introductory Readings,* Fifth edition, James M. Henslin, ed. New York: The Free Press, 1988:203–213.

Webb, Eugene J., Donald T. Campbell, Richard D. Schwartz, and Lee Sechrest. *Ubobtrusive Measures: Nonreactive Research in the Social Sciences.* Chicago: Rand McNally, 1966.

Weber, Max. *Economy and Society.* New York: Bedminster Press, 1968. Translated by Ephraim Fischoff. First published in 1922.

Weber, Max. *Economy and Society,* G. Roth and C. Wittich, eds. Berkeley, California: University of California Press, 1978.

Weber, Max. *From Max Weber: Essays in Sociology.* Hans Gerth and C. Wright Mills, translators and editors. New York: Oxford University Press, 1946.

Weber, Max. "Politics as a Vocation." In *From Max Weber: Essays in Sociology,* Hans Gerth and C. Wright Mills, eds. New York: Oxford University Press, 1946:77–128.

Weber, Max. *The Protestant Ethic and the Spirit of Capitalism.* New York: Charles Scribner's Sons, 1958. Originally published 1904–1905.

Weber, Max. *The Theory of Social and Economic Organization,* A. M. Henderson and Talcott Parsons, translators. Talcott Parsons, ed. Glencoe, Illinois: Free Press, 1947. Originally published in 1913.

Weinstein, Deena. *Heavy Metal: A Cultural Sociology.* New York: Lexington Books, 1991.

Weintraub, Richard M. "A Bride in India." *The Washington Post,* February 28, 1988.

Weisburd, David, Stanton Wheeler, and Elin Waring. *Crimes of the Middle Classes: White-Collar Offenders in the Federal Courts.* New Haven, Connecticut: Yale University Press, 1991.

Weisner, Thomas S., and Bernice T. Eiduson. "The Children of the 60s as Parents." *Psychology Today,* January 1986:60–66.

Weisskopf, Michael. "Scientist Says Greenhouse Effect Is Setting In." In *Ourselves and Others: The Washington Post Sociology Companion.* The Washington Post Writers Group, eds. Boston: Allyn and Bacon, 1992:297–298.

Weitz, Rose. "From Accommodation to Rebellion: Tertiary Deviance and the Radical Redefinition of Lesbianism." In *Studies in the Sociology of Social Problems,* Joseph W. Schneider and John I. Kitsuse, eds. Norwood, New Jersey: Ablex, 1984:140–161.

Weitzman, Lenore J. *The Divorce Revolution.* New York: Free Press, 1985.

Weitzman, Lenore J. "Sex-Role Socialization: A Focus on Women." In *Women: A Feminist Perspective,* Third edition, Jo Freeman, ed. Palo Alto, California: Mayfield, 1984:157–237.

Weitzman, Lenore J., Deborah Eifler, Elizabeth Hokada, and Catherine Ross. "Sex Role Socialization in Picture Books for Pre-School Children." *American Journal of Sociology, 77,* May 1972:1125–1150.

Wellman, Barry. "Domestic Work, Paid Work, and Net Work." In *Understanding Personal Relationships,* Steve Duck and Daniel Perlman, eds. London: Sage, 1985.

Wenneker, Mark B., and Arnold M. Epstein. "Racial Inequalities in the Use of Procedures for Patients with Ischemic Heart Disease in Massachusetts." *Journal of the American Medical Association, 261* (2), January 13, 1989:253–257.

Werner, Dennis. "Gerontocracy Among the Mekranoti of Central Brazil." *Anthropological Quarterly, 54,* 1, January 1981:15–27.

Werthman, Carl, and Irving Piliavin. "The Police Perspective on Delinquency." In *Deviance: The Interactionist Perspective.* Fourth edition, Earl Rubington and Martin S. Weinberg, eds. New York: Macmillan, 1981:162–168.

Wertz, Richard W., and Dorothy C. Wertz. "Notes on the Decline of Midwives and the Rise of Medical Obstetricians." In *The Sociology of Health and Illness: Critical Perspectives,* Peter Conrad and Rochelle Kern, eds. New York: St. Martin's Press, 1981:165–183.

West, Candace, and Angela Garcia. "Conversational Shift Work: A Study of Topical Transitions Between Women and Men." *Social Problems, 35,* 1988:551–575.

Westergaard, John, and Henrietta Resler. *Class in a Capitalist Society: A Study of Contemporary Britain.* New York: Basic Books, 1975.

Westley, William A. "Violence and the Police." *American Journal of Sociology, 59,* July 1953:34–41.

White, Burton L., Barbara T. Kaban, and Jane S. Attanucci. *The Origins of Human Competence.* Lexington, Massachusetts: D. C. Heath, 1979.

White, James A. "When Employees Own Big Stake, It's a Buy Signal for Investors." *Wall Street Journal,* February 13, 1991:C1, C19.

White, Joseph B., and Melinda Grenier Guiles. "GM's Plan for Saturn, To Beat Small Imports, Trails Original Goals." *Wall Street Journal,* July 9, 1990:A1, A4.

White, Lynn K., and Alan Booth. "The Quality and Stability of Remarriages: The Role of Stepchildren." *American Sociological Review, 50,* 1985:689–698.

Whitman, David. "For Latinos, A Growing Divide." *U.S. News & World Report,* August 10, 1987:47–49.

Whyte, Martin King. "Choosing Mates—The American Way." *Society,* March–April 1992:71–77.

Whyte, Martin King. *Dating, Mating, and Marriage.* New York: Aldine de Gruyter, 1990.

Whyte, Merry. *The Japanese Educational Challenge: A Commitment to Children.* New York: Free Press, 1987.

Whyte, William H. *The City: Rediscovering the Center.* New York: Doubleday, 1989.

Whyte, William H. "Street People." In *Down to Earth Sociology: Introductory Readings,* Sixth Edition. New York: Free Press, 1991:165–178.

Wilbanks, W. "The Female Homicide Offender in Dade County, Florida." *Criminal Justice Review, 8,* 1983:9–14.

Wilford, John Noble. "In the Glow of Discovery: Scientist Ponders Fame." *New York Times,* May 5, 1992:B5.

Willhelm, Sidney M. "Can Marxism Explain America's Racism?" *Social Problems, 28,* December 1980:98–112.

Williams, J. Allen, JoEtta A. Vernon, Martha C. Williams, and Karen Malecha. "Sex Role Socialization in Picture Books: An Update." *Social Science Quarterly, 68* (1), March 1987:148–156.

Williams, Robin M., Jr. *American Society: A Sociological Interpretation* (third edition). New York: Alfred A. Knopf, 1970.

Wilson, Edward O. *Sociobiology: The New Synthesis.* Cambridge, Massachusetts: Harvard University Press, 1975.

Wilson, James Q. "Is Incapacitation the Answer to the Crime Problem?" In *Taking Sides: Clashing Views on Controversial Social Issues,* (seventh edition), Kurt Finsterbusch and George McKenna, eds. Guilford, Connecticut: Dushkin, 1992:318–324.

Wilson, James Q. "Lock 'Em Up and Other Thoughts on Crime." *New York Times Magazine,* March 9, 1975:11, 44–48.

Wilson, James Q. "Police Work in Two Cities." In *Deviance: The Interactionist Perspective.* Fourth edition, Earl Rubington and Martin S. Weinberg, eds. New York: Macmillan, 1981:169–177.

Wilson, James Q., and Richard J. Hernstein. *Crime and Human Nature.* New York: Simon and Schuster, 1985.

Wilson, William Julius. "The Black Underclass." *The Wilson Quarterly, 8,* Spring 1984:88–99.

Wilson, William Julius. *The Declining Significance of Race: Blacks and Changing American Institutions.* Chicago: University of Chicago Press, 1978.

Wilson, William Julius. "Race, Class, and Public Policy." *American Sociologist, 16,* 1981:125–134.

Wilson, William Julius. *The Truly Disadvantaged: The Inner City, the Underclass, and Public Policy.* Chicago: University of Chicago Press, 1987.

Winslow, Ron. "Study Finds Blacks Get Fewer Bypasses." *Wall Street Journal,* March 18, 1992:B1.

Wirth, Louis. "The Problem of Minority Groups." In *The Science of Man in the World Crisis,* Ralph Linton (ed.). New York: Columbia University Press, 1945.

Wirth, Louis. "Urbanism as a Way of Life." *American Journal of Sociology, 44,* July 1938:1–24.

Wohl, R. Richard, and Anselm Strauss. "Symbolic Representation and the Urban Milieu." *American Journal of Sociology, 63,* March 1958:523–532.

Wolfgang, Marvin E. *Patterns in Criminal Homicide.* Philadelphia; University of Pennsylvania, 1958.

Wolfgang, Marvin E., and Franco Ferracuti. *The Subculture of Violence: Toward an Integrated Theory in Criminology.* London: Tavistock, 1967.

Wolfinger, Raymond E., and Steven J. Rosenstone. *Who Votes?* New Haven, Connecticut: Yale University Press, 1980.

Woods, John E., and Phillip G. Arnold. "Fiction Obscures the Facts of Breast Implants." *Wall Street Journal,* April 7, 1992:A16.

Woodward, C. Vann. "Equal But Separate." *New Republic,* July 15 & 22, 1991:41–43.

Woodward, Kenneth L. "Heaven." *Newsweek, 113* (13), March 27, 1989:52–55.

Woon, Yuen-Fong. "Growing Old in a Modernizing China." *Journal of Comparative Family Studies, 12,* 2, Spring 1981:245–257.

World Population Profile: 1985. Washington, D.C.: Bureau of the Census, U.S. Department of Commerce, 1986.

World Population Profile: 1986. Washington, D.C.: Bureau of the Census, U.S. Department of Commerce, 1987.

World Health Organization. *Constitution of the World Health Organization.* New York: World Health Organization Interim Commission, 1946.

Worsley, Peter. *The Trumpet Shall Sound.* London: MacGibbon and Kee, 1957.

Wright, Erik Olin. *Class.* London: Verso, 1985.

Wright, Erik Olin. *Class, Crisis, and the State.* London: Verso, 1979.

Wright, Erik Olin. *Class Structure and Income Determination.* New York: Academic Press, 1979.

Wrong, Dennis H. "The Over-Socialized Conception of Man in Modern Sociology." *American Sociological Review, 26,* April 1961:185–193.

Yamada, Ken. "Almost Like Being There." *Wall Street Journal,* April 6, 1992:R10.

Yates, William R., Russell Noyes, Jr., Frederick Petty, Keith Brown, and Thomas O'Gorman. "Factors Associated with Motor Vehicle Accidents among Male Alcoholics." *Journal of Studies on Alcohol, 48* (6), 1987:586–590.

Yaukey, David. *Demography: The Study of Human Population.* New York: St. Martin's, 1985.

Yinger, J. Milton. *The Scientific Study of Religion.* New York: Macmillan, 1970.

Yinger, J. Milton. *Toward a Field Theory of Behavior: Personality and Social Structure.* New York: McGraw-Hill, 1965.

Young, Robert J. "What Kinds of Immigrants Have Come to the Philadelphia Area, Where Did They Settle, and How Are They Doing? In *The Family Experience: A Reader in Cultural Diversity,* Mark Hutter, ed. New York: Macmillan, 1991:178–191.

Yuan, D. Y. "Voluntary Segregation: A Study of New York Chinatown." *Phylon, 24,* Fall 1963:255–265.

Zakuta, Leo. "Equality in North American Marriages." In *Marriage and Family in a Changing Society* (3rd edition). New York: Free Press, 1989:105–114.

Zawitz, Marianne W. *Report to the Nation on Crime and Justice.* Second edition. Washington, D.C.: U.S. Department of Justice, Bureau of Justice Statistics, July 1988.

Ziegenhals, Gretchen E. "Confessions of an Amish Watcher." *Christian Century,* August 21–28, 1991:764–765.

Zinn, Maxine Baca, and D. Stanley Eitzen. *Diversity in Families* (second edition). New York: HarperCollins, 1990.

Zipp, John F. "Perceived Representativeness and Voting: An Assessment of the Impact of 'Choices' vs. 'Echoes.'" *American Political Science Review, 79,* 1, March 1985:50–61.

Zola, Irving K. *Socio-Medical Inquiries.* Philadelphia: Temple University Press, 1983. (Referenced in Richard T. Schaefer, *Sociology,* Third edition, New York: McGraw-Hill, 1989:472.)

Zuboff, Shoshana. *In the Age of the Smart Machine: The Future of Work and Power.* New York: Basic Books, 1984.

Zuboff, Shoshana. "New Worlds of Computer-Mediated Work." In *Down to Earth Sociology: Introductory Readings,* Sixth edition. James M. Henslin, ed. New York: The Free Press, 1991:476–485.

Zuckerman, Harriet, Jonathan R. Cole, and John T. Bruer. *The Outer Circle: Women in the Scientific Community.* New York: Norton, 1991.

Zurcher, Louis A., and David A. Snow. "Collective Behavior: Social Movements." In *Social Psychology: Sociological Perspectives,* Morris Rosenberg and Ralph H. Turner, eds. New Brunswick, New Jersey: Transaction Books, 1990:447–482.

——. "The Boss's Pay," *Wall Street Journal,* April 18, 1990:R13–R20.

——. "Europe's Economies Are Dragging Along Despite Hopes for 1992." *Wall Street Journal,* November 26, 1991:A1, A11.

——. "The New Alchemy: How Science is Molding Molecules into Miracle Materials." *Business Weekly,* July 29, 1991:48–55.

——. "New Government in Sweden Unveils Plans for Sale of State-Run Industries." *Wall Street Journal,* November 12, 1991:A13.

——. *Special Report: On Family,* Knoxville, Tennessee: Whittle Communications, 1989.

——. "Terror and Death at Home Are Caught in F.B.I. Tape." *New York Times,* October 28, 1991:A14.

——. "U.S. Arrests Boy, 5 Others in Computer Hacker Case." *Wall Street Journal,* August 17, 1990:B2.

——. "Working Toward Self-Sufficiency." *ISR Newsletter,* Spring-Summer 1985:4–5, 7.

——. "The World's Wars." *The Economist,* March 12, 1988:19–22.

Glossary

ablution: a washing ritual designed to restore ritual purity

acculturation: the transmission of culture from one generation to the next

achieved statuses: positions that are earned, accomplished, or involve at least some effort or activity on the individual's part

acid rain: rain containing sulfuric and nitric acid, produced by the reaction of sulfur dioxide and nitrogen oxide with moisture when released into the air with the burning of fossil fuels

acting crowd: Herbert Blumer's term for an excited group that collectively moves toward a goal

activity theory: the belief that satisfaction during old age is related to a person's level and quality of activity

age cohort: people born at roughly the same time who pass through the life course together

ageism: prejudice, discrimination, and hostility directed against people because of their age; can be directed against any age group

aggregate: people who have similar characteristics

agricultural revolution: the second social revolution, based on the invention of the plow, which led to agricultural societies

agricultural society: a society based on large-scale agriculture, dependent on plows drawn by animals

alienation: a feeling of powerlessness and normlessness; the experience of being cut off from the product of one's labor [1]Marx's term for workers' lack of connection to the product of their labor caused by their being assigned repetitive tasks on a small part of a product

alterative social movement: a social movement that seeks to alter only particular aspects of people

anarchy: a state of lawlessness or political disorder caused by the absence or collapse of governmental authority

Anglo-conformity: the expectation that immigrants to the United States would adopt the English language and other Anglo-Saxon ways of life

animal culture: learned, shared behavior among animals

animism: the belief that all objects in the world have spirits, many of which are dangerous and must be outwitted

anomie: Emile Durkheim's term for lack of social integration—a feeling of being out of place, of not belonging, of having lost a sense of direction or purpose in life [1]feelings of not belonging, of being detached or uprooted

antisemitism: prejudice, discrimination, and persecution directed against Jews

apartheid: the separation of races as was practiced in South Africa

appearance: how an individual looks when playing a role

applied sociology: the use of sociology to solve problems—from the micro level of family relationships to the macro level of crime and pollution

ascribed statuses: positions an individual either inherits at birth or receives involuntarily later in life

assimilation: the process of being absorbed into the mainstream culture

authoritarian leader: a leader who leads by giving orders

authoritarian personality: Theodor Adorno's term for people who are prejudiced and rank high on scales of conformity, intolerance, insecurity, excessive respect for authority, and submissiveness to superiors

authority: power that people accept as rightly exercised over them; also called legitimate power [1]power that people consider legitimate

back stage: where people rest from their performances, discuss their presentations, and plan future performances

background assumptions: deeply embedded common understandings, or basic rules, concerning our view of the world and of how people ought to act

barter: the direct exchange of one item for another

basic demographic equation: growth rate = births − deaths + net migration

bilateral: (system of descent) a system of reckoning descent that counts both the mother's and the father's side

blended family: a family whose members were once part of other families

born again: a term describing Christians who have undergone a life-transforming religious experience so radical that they feel they have become new persons

bourgeoisie: Karl Marx's term for capitalists, those who own the means to produce wealth [1]Karl Marx's term for the people who own the means of production

bureaucracy: a formal organization with a hierarchy of authority; a clear division of labor; emphasis on written rules, communications, and records; and impersonality of positions

bureaucratic engorgement: the tendency for bureaucracies to keep on growing

capitalism: the investment of capital in the hope of producing profits [1]an economic system characterized by the private ownership of the means of production, the pursuit of profit, and market competition

capitalist class: the wealthy who own the means of production and buy the labor of the working class

capitalist world economy: the dominance of capitalism in the world along with the international interdependence that capitalism has created

cargo cult: a social movement in which South Pacific islanders destroyed their possessions in the anticipation that their ancestors would send items by ship

caste system: a form of social stratification in which individual status is determined by birth and is lifelong

centrist party: a political party that represents the center of political opinion

charisma: literally, an extraordinary gift from God; more commonly, outstanding "magnetic" attraction

charismatic authority: authority based on an individual's outstanding traits, which attract followers

charismatic leader: literally, someone to whom God has given a gift; more commonly, someone who exerts extraordinary appeal to a group of followers

checks and balances: the separation of powers among the three branches of U.S. government—legislative, executive, and judicial—so that one is able to nullify the actions of the other two, thus preventing the domination of any single branch

Chicanos: Hispanic Americans whose country of origin is Mexico

circular reaction: Robert Park's term for a back-and-forth communication between the members of a crowd whereby a "collective impulse" is transmitted

citizenship: the concept that birth (and residence) in a country impart basic rights

city: a place in which a large number of people are permanently based and do not produce their own food

city-state: an independent city whose power radiates outward, bringing the adjacent area under its rule

church: a large, highly organized religious group with little emphasis on personal conversion and formal, sedate worship services

civil disobedience: the act of deliberately but peacefully disobeying laws considered unjust

civil religion: Robert Bellah's term for the development of religion into such an established feature of a country's life that its history and social institutions become sanctified by being associated with God

clan system: a form of social stratification in which individuals receive their social standing through belonging to an extended network of relatives

class conflict: Marx's term for the struggle between the proletariat and the bourgeoisie

class consciousness: Karl Marx's term for awareness of a common identity based on one's position in the means of production

class system: a form of social stratification based primarily on the possession of money or material possessions

clinical sociology: the direct involvement of sociologists in bringing about social change

closed-ended questions: questions followed by a list of possible answers to be selected by the respondent

coalition: the alignment of some members of a group against others

coalition government: a government in which a country's largest party aligns itself with one or more smaller parties

coding: categorizing data

coercion: power that people do not accept as rightly exercised over them; also called illegitimate power

cohabitation: the condition of living together as an unmarried couple

collective behavior: extraordinary activities carried out by groups of people; includes lynchings, rumors, panics, urban legends, and fads and fashions

collective mind: Gustave LeBon's term for the tendency of people in a crowd to feel, think, and act in extraordinary ways

colonization: the process in which one nation takes over another nation, usually for the purpose of exploiting its labor and natural resources

common sense: those things that "everyone knows" are true

community: a place where people identify with an area and with one another, sensing that they belong and that others care what happens to them

compartmentalize: to separate acts from feelings or attitudes

compensatory education: educational programs designed to fill a gap in the background of lower-class children

conflict theory: a theoretical framework in which society is viewed as composed of groups competing for scarce resources

conspicuous consumption: Thorstein Veblen's term for a change from the Protestant ethic to an eagerness to show off wealth by the elaborate consumption of goods

content analysis: the examination of a source, such as a magazine article, a television program, or even a diary, to identify its themes

contradictory class location: Erik Wright's term for a position in the class structure that generates contradictory interests

control group: the group of subjects not exposed to the independent variable in a study

control theory: the idea that two control systems—inner controls and outer controls—work against our pushes and pulls toward deviance

convergence theory: the view that as capitalist and socialist economic systems each adopt features

of the other, a hybrid (or mixed) economic system may emerge

corporate capitalism: the domination of the economic system by giant corporations

corporate culture: the orientations that characterize corporate work settings

corporation: the joint ownership of a business enterprise, whose liabilities and obligations are separate from those of its owners

correlation: the simultaneous occurrence of two or more variables

correspondence principle: the sociological principle that schools correspond to (or reflect) the social structure of society

cosmology: teachings or ideas that provide a unified picture of the world

counterculture: a group whose values place its members in opposition to the values of the broader culture

credential society: the use of diplomas and degrees to determine who is eligible for jobs, even though the diploma or degree may be irrelevant to the actual work

credit card: a device that allows its owner to purchase goods but to be billed later

crime: the violation of norms that are written into law

criminal justice system: the system of police, courts, and prisons set up to deal with people who are accused of having committed a crime

crude birthrate: the annual number of births per 1,000 population

crude death rate: the annual number of deaths per 1,000 population

cult: a new religion with few followers, whose teachings and practices put it at odds with the dominant culture and religion

cultural diffusion: the spread of items from one culture to another [1]the spread of cultural characteristics from one group to another

cultural goals: the legitimate objectives held out to the members of a society

cultural lag: William F. Ogburn's term for the situation in which nonmaterial culture lags behind changes in material culture [1]Ogburn's term for human behavior lagging behind technological innovations.

cultural leveling: the process by which cultures become similar to one another, and especially by which Western industrial culture is imported and diffused into developing nations

cultural relativism: understanding a people in the framework of its own culture

cultural transmission: in reference to education, the way in which schools transmit a society's culture, especially its core values

cultural universal: a value, norm, or other cultural trait that is found in every group

culture: the language, beliefs, values, norms, behaviors, and even material objects that are passed from one generation to the next

culture contact: encounter between people from different cultures, or contact with some parts of a different culture

culture of poverty: a culture that perpetuates poverty from one generation to the next [1]the assumption that the values and behaviors of the poor make them fundamentally different from other people and that these factors are largely responsible for their poverty

culture shock: the disorientation that people experience when they come in contact with a fundamentally different culture and can no longer depend on their taken-for-granted assumptions about life

currency: paper money

debit card: a device that allows its owner to charge purchases against his or her bank account

deferred gratification: forgoing something in the present in the hope of achieving greater gains in the future

degradation ceremony: a term coined by Harold Garfinkel to describe an attempt to remake the self by stripping away an individual's self-identity and stamping a new identity in its place [1]ritual designed to strip an individual of his or her identity as a group member; for example, a court martial or the defrocking of a priest

dehumanization: the act or process of reducing people to objects that do not deserve the treatment accorded humans

deinstitutionalization: the release of mental patients from institutions into the community pending treatment by a network of outpatient services

democracy: a system of government in which authority derives from the people, derived from two Greek words that translate literally as "power to the people"

democratic leader: a leader who leads by trying to reach a consensus

democratic socialism: a hybrid economic system in which capitalism is mixed with state ownership

demographic transition: a three-stage historical process of population growth, the first being high birthrates and high death rates, the second high birthrates and low death rates; and the third low birthrates and low death rates

demographic variables: the factors that influence population growth: fertility, mortality, and net migration

demography: the study of the size, composition, growth, and distribution of human populations

denomination: a "brand name" within a major religion, for example, Methodist or Baptist

dependency ratio: the number of workers required to support one person on Social Security

dependency theory: the belief that lack of industrial development in Third World nations is caused by the industrialized nations dominating the world economy

dependent variable: a factor that is changed by an independent variable

depersonalization: the practice of dealing with people as though they were objects; in the case of medical care, as though patients were merely cases and diseases, not persons

deposit receipts: a receipt stating that a certain amount of goods is on deposit in a warehouse or bank; the receipt is used as a form of money

deterrence: creating fear so people will refrain from breaking the law

deviance: the violation of rules or norms

deviants: people who violate rules, as a result of which others react negatively to them

dictatorship: a form of government in which power is seized and held by an individual or small clique

differential association: Edwin Sutherland's term for the ways in which association with some groups results in learning an "excess of definitions" of deviance, and, by extension, in a greater likelihood that their members will become deviant

diffusion: the spread of invention or discovery from one area to another; identified by William Ogburn as the final of three processes of social change

direct democracy: a form of democracy in which the eligible voters meet together to discuss issues and make their decisions

disabling environment: an environment that is harmful to health

discovery: a new way of seeing reality; identified by William Ogburn as the second of three processes of social change

discrimination: an *act* of unfair treatment directed against an individual or a group

disengagement theory: the belief that society prevents disruption by having the elderly vacate (or disengage from) their positions of responsibility

divest: to sell off

divine right of kings: the idea that the king's authority comes directly from God

division of labor: Emile Durkheim's term for the allocation of people into occupational specialties ¹the splitting of society's tasks into specialties

documents: written sources

domestication revolution: the first social revolution, based on the domestication of plants and animals, which led to pastoral and horticultural societies

dominant group: the group with the most power, greatest privileges, and highest social status

downward social mobility: movement down the social class ladder

dramaturgy: an approach, pioneered by Erving Goffman, analyzing social life in terms of drama or the stage; also called dramaturgical analysis

dumping: the practice of sending unprofitable patients to public hospitals

dyad: the smallest possible group, consisting of two persons

ecclesia: a religious group so integrated into the dominant culture that it is difficult to tell where the one begins and the other leaves off; also called a state religion

economic cycle: periods of economic "booms" (expansion) followed by periods of "busts" (contraction)

economy: a system of distribution of goods and services

education: a formal system of teaching knowledge, values, and skills

ego: Freud's term for a balancing force between the id and the demands of society

embarrassment: in dramaturgical terms, the feelings that result when a performance fails

emergent norms: Ralph Turner and Lewis Killian's term for the development of new norms to cope with a new situation, especially among crowds

empty nest: a married couple's domestic situation after the last child has left home

endogamy: the practice of marrying within one's own group ¹marriage within one's own group

environmental sociology: a subdiscipline of sociology that examines how human activities affect the physical environment and how the physical environment affects human activities

epidemiology: the study of disease and disability patterns in a population

erotic property: persons about whom one feels jealous

ethnic (and ethnicity): having distinctive cultural characteristics

ethnocentrism: the use of one's own culture as a yardstick for judging the ways of other individuals or societies, generally leading to a negative evaluation of their values, norms, and behaviors

ethnomethodology: the study of how people use background assumptions to make sense of life

euthanasia: mercy killing

exchange mobility: about the same numbers of people moving up and down the social class ladder, such that, on balance, the social class system shows little change

exogamy: the practice of marrying outside one's group

experiment: the use of control groups and experimental groups and dependent and independent variables to test causation

experimental group: the group of subjects exposed to the independent variable in a study

exponential growth curve: a pattern of growth in which numbers double during approximately equal intervals, thus accelerating in the latter stages

expressive leader: an individual who increases harmony and minimizes conflict in a group; also known as a socioemotional leader

extended family: a nuclear family plus other relatives, such as grandparents, uncles and aunts, who live together

face-saving behavior: techniques used to salvage a performance that is going sour

fad: a temporary pattern of behavior that catches people's attention

false consciousness: Karl Marx's term for the mistaken identification of workers with the interests of capitalists

family: a group of people who consider themselves related by blood, marriage, or adoption; they usually live together

family of orientation: the family in which a person grows up

family of procreation: the family formed when a couple's first child is born

fashion: a pattern of behavior that catches people's attention, which lasts longer than a fad

fecundity: the number of children that women are theoretically *capable* of bearing

fee for service: payment by a patient to a physician to diagnose and treat the patient's medical problems

feminization of poverty: a trend in American poverty whereby most poor families are headed by women

feral children: children assumed to have been raised by animals, in the wilderness isolated from other humans

fertility rate: the number of children that the average woman bears

fiat money: currency issued by a government that is not backed by stored value

folkways: norms which are not strictly enforced

formal organization: a secondary group designed to achieve explicit objectives

front stage: where performances are given

functional analysis: a theoretical framework in which society is viewed as composed of various parts, each with a function that, when fulfilled, contributes to society's equilibrium; also known as functionalism and structural functionalism

functional equivalent: in this context, a substitute that serves the same functions (or meets the same needs) as religion, for example, psychotherapy

functional illiterate: a high school graduate who has difficulty with basic reading and math

functional requisites: the major tasks that a society must fulfill if it is to survive

fundamentalism: the belief that true religion is threatened by modernism and that the faith as it was originally practiced should be restored

gatekeeping: the process by which education opens and closes doors of opportunity; another term for the social placement function of education

Gemeinschaft: a type of society in which life is intimate; a community in which everyone knows everyone else and people share a sense of togetherness

gender: the social characteristics that a society considers proper for its males and females; masculinity or femininity

gender socialization: the ways in which society sets children onto different courses in life purely *because* they are male or female

gender stratification: men's and women's unequal access to power, prestige, and property on the basis of their sex

generalizability: the extent to which the findings from one group (or sample) can be generalized or applied to other groups (or populations)

generalization: a statement that goes beyond the individual case and is applied to a broader group or situation

generalized other: taking the role of a large number of people

genetic predispositions: inborn tendencies, in this context, to commit deviant acts

genocide: the systematic annihilation or attempted annihilation of a race or ethnic group

gentrification: the displacement of the poor by the relatively affluent, who renovate the former's homes

gerontocracy: a society (or other group) run by the old

Gesellschaft: a type of society dominated by impersonal relationships, individual accomplishments, and self-interest

gestures: the ways in which people use their bodies to communicate with one another

globalization: the extensive interconnections among world nations resulting from the expansion of capitalism

global warming: an increase in the earth's temperature due to the greenhouse effect

goal conflict: goals that conflict with one another, in this context, those of a unit in a formal organization and those of the organization as a whole

goal displacement: a goal displaced by another, in this context, the adoption of new goals by an organization; also known as *goal replacement*

gold standard: paper money backed by gold

gossip: false, distorted, or blatantly untrue information of a more personal nature than a rumor

graying of America: the process by which older persons make up an increasing proportion of the United States population

greenhouse effect: the buildup of carbon dioxide in the earth's atmosphere that allows light to enter but inhibits the release of heat; believed to cause global warming

gross national product: the amount of goods and services produced by a nation

group: people who regularly and consciously interact with one another [1] in a general sense, people who have something in common and who believe that what they have in common is significant; also called a social group

group dynamics: the ways in which individuals affect groups and the ways in which groups affect individuals

groupthink: Irving Janis's term for a narrowing of thought by a group of people, leading to the perception that there is only one correct answer, in which the suggestion of alternatives becomes a sign of disloyalty

halfway house: community support facilities where ex-prisoners supervise many aspects of their own lives, such as household tasks, but continue to report to authorities

health: a human condition measured by four components: physical, mental, social, and spiritual

health maintenance organization (HMO): a health-care organization that provides medical treatment to its members for a fixed annual cost

hidden curriculum: the set of unwritten rules of behavior and attitudes, such as obedience to authority and conformity to cultural norms, which are taught in schools in addition to the formal curriculum

holistic medicine: an approach to medical care centering on the idea that a person's body, feelings, attitudes, and actions are all intertwined and cannot be segregated into discrete organ systems

homogamy: the tendency of people with similar characteristics to marry one another

horticultural society: a society based on the cultivation of plants by the use of hand tools

hospice: a place, or services brought into someone's home, for the purpose of bringing comfort and dignity to a dying person

human ecology: Robert Park's term for the relationship between people and their environment (natural resources such as land)

humanizing a work setting: organizing a workplace in such a way that it develops rather than impedes human potential

hunting and gathering society: a society dependent on hunting and gathering for survival

hypothesis: a statement of the expected relationship between variables according to predictions from a theory

id: Freud's term for the individual's inborn basic drives

ideal culture: the ideal values and norms of a people, the goals held out for them

ideal type: composite of characteristics based on many specific examples ("ideal" in this case means an objective description of the abstracted characteristics)

ideology: beliefs about human life or culture that justify social arrangements

illegitimate opportunity structures: opportunities for remunerative crimes woven into the texture of life

imperialism: a nation's pursuit of unlimited geographical expansion

impression management: the term used by Erving Goffman to describe people's efforts to control the impressions that others receive of them

incapacitation: the removal of offenders from "normal" society; taking them "off the streets"

incest: sexual relations between specified relatives, such as brothers and sisters or parents and children

incest taboo: rules specifying the degrees of kinship that prohibit sex or marriage

indentured service: a contractual system in which someone sells his or her body (services) for a specified period of time in an arrangement very close to slavery, except that it is voluntarily entered into

independent variable: a factor that causes a change in another variable, called the dependent variable

individual discrimination: the negative treatment of one person by another on the basis of that person's characteristics

industrial revolution: the third social revolution, occurring when machines powered by fuels replaced most animal and human power

industrial society: a society based on the harnessing of machines powered by fuels

industrial technology: technology centered on machines powered by fuels instead of natural forces such as wind and rivers

inflation: an increase in prices

information revolution: the fourth social revolution, based on technology that processes information

in-groups: groups toward which one feels loyalty

institutional discrimination: negative treatment of a minority group that is built into a society's institutions

institutionalized means: approved ways of reaching cultural goals

instrumental leader: an individual who tries to keep the group moving toward its goals; also known as a task-oriented leader

intergenerational mobility: the change that family members make in social class from one generation to the next

interlocking directorates: the phenomenon of one person holding directorships in several companies

internal colonialism: the economic exploitation of a minority group

interview: direct questioning of respondents

interview bias: effects that interviewers have on respondents that lead to biased answers

invention: the combination of existing elements and materials to form new ones; identified by William Ogburn as the first of three processes of social change

involuntary memberships: (or involuntary associations) groups in which people are assigned membership rather than choosing to join

the iron law of oligarchy: Robert Michels's phrase for the tendency of formal organizations to be dominated by a small, self-perpetuating elite

job deskilling: reducing the amount of skills that a job requires

job multiskilling: adding skills to those a worker already possesses

labeling theory: the view, developed by symbolic interactionists, that the labels people are given affect their own and others' perceptions of them, thus channeling their behavior either into deviance or into conformity

labor force participation rate: the proportion of the population or of some group sixteen years and older in the work force

laissez-faire capitalism: unrestrained manufacture and trade (literally, "hands off" capitalism)

laissez-faire leader: an individual who leads by being highly permissive

language: a system of symbols that can be combined in an infinite number of ways and can represent not only objects but also abstract thought

latent functions: unintended consequences of people's actions [1] the unintended consequences of people's actions that keep a social system in equilibrium

leader: someone who influences the behaviors of others

leadership styles: ways in which people express their leadership

leisure: time not taken up by work or required activities such as eating and sleeping

life chances: the probabilities concerning the fate an individual may expect in life

life expectancy: the number of years that an average newborn can expect to live

life span: the maximum length of life of a species

living will: a statement people in good health sign that clearly expresses their feelings about being kept alive on artificial life-support systems

lobbyists: people paid to influence legislation on behalf of their clients

looking-glass self: a term coined by Charles Horton Cooley to refer to the process by which our self develops through internalizing others' reactions to us

lumpenproletariat: Karl Marx's term for marginal people such as migrant workers, beggars, vagrants, and criminals

machismo: an emphasis on male strength and dominance

macro-level analysis: an examination of large-scale patterns of society

macropolitics: the exercise of large-scale power, the government being the most common example

macrosociology: analysis of social life focusing on broad features of social structure, such as social class and the relationships of groups to one another; an approach usually used by functionalist and conflict theorists

Malthus theorem: an observation by Thomas Malthus that although the food supply increases only arithmetically (from 1 to 2 to 3 to 4 and so on), population grows geometrically (from 2 to 4 to 8 to 16 and so forth)

mandatory education laws: laws that require all children to attend school until a specified age or until they complete a minimum grade in school

manifest function: the intended consequences of people's actions designed to help some part of a social system [1] intended consequences of people's actions

manner: the attitudes that people show as they play their roles

marginality: the condition of belonging to two groups whose values are incompatible with each other and not feeling fully accepted and comfortable in either

marginal working class: the most desperate members of the working class, who have few skills, little job security, and are often unemployed

market: any process of buying and selling; on a more formal level, the mechanism that establishes values for the exchange of goods and services

market competition: the exchange of items between willing buyers and sellers

market forces: the law of supply and demand

market restraints: laws and regulations that limit the capacity to manufacture and sell products

marriage: a group's approved mating arrangements, usually marked by a ritual of some sort

mass media: forms of communication directed to huge audiences

mass society: industrialized, highly bureaucratized, impersonal society

mass-society theory: an explanation for participation in social movements based on the assumption that such movements offer a sense of belonging to people who have weak social ties

master status: a status that cuts across the other statuses that an individual occupies

material culture: the material objects that distinguish a group of people, such as their art, buildings, weapons, utensils, machines, hairstyles, clothing, and jewelry

matriarchy: a society in which women dominate men [1]female control of a society or group

matrilineal (system of descent): a system of reckoning descent that counts only the mother's side

means of production: the tools, factories, land, and investment capital used to produce wealth

mechanical solidarity: a collective consciousness that people experience as a result of performing the same or similar tasks [1]Durkheim's term for the unity that comes from being involved in similar occupations or activities

medicalization: the transformation of something into a matter to be treated by physicians

medicalization of deviance: the view of deviance as a medical matter, a symptom of some underlying illness that needs to be treated by physicians

medium of exchange: the means by which people value goods and services in order to make an exchange, for example, currency, gold, and silver

megalopolis: a conglomeration of overlapping cities and their suburbs, forming an interconnected urban area

meritocracy: a form of social stratification in which all positions are awarded on the basis of merit

metropolitan statistical area (MSA): a central city and the urbanized counties adjacent to it

micro-level analysis: an examination of small-scale patterns of society

micropolitics: the exercise of power in everyday life, such as deciding who is going to do the housework

microsociology: analysis of social life focusing on social interaction; an approach usually used by symbolic interactionists

middle-range theories: explanations of human behavior that go beyond a particular observation or research but avoid sweeping generalizations that attempt to account for everything

millenarian movement: a social movement based on the prophecy of coming social upheaval

milling: a crowd standing or walking around as they talk excitedly about some event

minimax strategy: Richard Berk's term for the effort people make to minimize their costs and maximize their rewards

minimum competency tests: national tests on which students must attain some minimum score

minority group: a group that is discriminated against on the basis of its members' physical characteristics [1]people who are singled out for unequal treatment, and who regard themselves as objects of collective discrimination

modernization: the transformation of traditional societies into industrial societies

monarchy: a form of government headed by a king or queen

money: a general term for a medium of exchange, currency being the most common form in our society

monopoly: the control of an entire industry by a single company

monotheism: the belief that there is only one God

mores: (MORE-rays) norms that are strictly enforced because they are thought essential to core values

multinational corporations: companies that operate across many national boundaries

natural sciences: the intellectual and academic disciplines designed to comprehend, explain, and predict events in our natural environment

negative sanction: an expression of disapproval for breaking a norm, ranging from a mild, informal reaction such as a frown to a formal prison sentence [1]punishment or negative reaction to deviance

neocolonialism: the economic and political dominance of Third World nations by First World nations

net migration rate: the difference between the number of immigrants and emigrants per 1,000 population

networking: the process of consciously using or cultivating networks for some gain

new technology: technology constituting such a leap forward that it cannot be classified as part of current technology

noncentrist party: a political party that represents marginal ideas

nonmaterial culture: a group's ways of thinking (including its beliefs, values, and other assumptions about the world) and doing (its common patterns of behavior, including language and other forms of interaction)

nonverbal interaction: communication without words through gestures, space, silence, and so on

normative order: the socially approved ways of doing things that make up our everyday lives

norms: the expectations, or rules of behavior, that develop out of values

nuclear family: a family consisting of a husband, wife, and child(ren)

objective method: (of measuring social class) a system in which people are ranked according to objective criteria such as wealth, power, and prestige

objectivity: total neutrality

object permanence: Piaget's term for children's ability to realize that objects continue to exist even when they are not visible

official deviance: a society's statistics on lawbreaking; its measures of victims, lawbreakers, and the outcomes of criminal investigations and sentencing

oligarchy: power held by a small group of individuals; the rule of the many by the few

oligopoly: the control of an entire industry by several large companies

open-ended questions: questions that a respondent is able to answer in his or her own words

operational: Piaget's term for abstract reasoning skills

operational definitions: the ways in which the variables in a hypothesis are measured

organic solidarity: a collective consciousness based on the interdependence brought about by the division of labor [1]the interdependence that results from people's mutual need that each fulfill his or her job

out-groups: groups toward which one feels antagonisms

panic: a behavior that results when people become so fearful that they cannot function normally, and may even flee

pan-Indianism: the emphasis of common elements in Native American culture in order to develop a mutual self-identification and to work toward the welfare of all Native Americans

participant observation: (or fieldwork) research in which the researcher *participates* in a research setting while observing what is happening in that setting

pastoral society: a society based on the pasturing of animals

patriarchy: a society in which men dominate women [1]male control of a society or group

patrilineal: (system of descent) a system of reckoning descent that counts only the father's side

patterns: recurring characteristics or events

peer group: a group of individuals roughly the same age linked by common interests

personal identity kit: items people use to decorate their bodies

personality disorders: the view that a personality disturbance of some sort causes an individual to violate social norms

Peter Principle: a bureaucratic law, according to which the members of an organization are promoted for good work until they reach their level of incompetence, the level at which they can no longer do good work

pluralism: a philosophy that permits or encourages ethnic variation [1]the diffusion of power among many interest groups, preventing any single group from gaining control of the government

pluralistic society: a society made up of many different groups

pluralistic theory of social control: the view that society is made up of many competing groups, whose interests manage to become balanced

police discretion: routine judgments by the police concerning whether to arrest someone or to ignore a matter

political action committee: (PAC) an organization formed by one or more special-interest groups to solicit and spend funds for the purpose of influencing legislation

polyandry: a marriage in which a woman has more than one husband

polygyny: a marriage in which a man has more than one wife

polytheism: the belief that there are many gods

population: the target group to be studied

population pyramid: a graphic representation of a population, divided into age and sex

population shrinkage: the process by which a country's population becomes smaller because its birthrate and immigration are too low to replace those who die and emigrate

population transfer: involuntary movement of a minority group

positive sanction: a reward given for following norms, ranging from a smile to a prize [1] device for rewarding desired behavior

positivism: the application of the scientific approach to the social world

postindustrial society: a society based on information, services, and high technology, rather than on raw materials and manufacturing

postindustrial technology: technology centering on information, transportation, and communication

poverty line: the official measure of poverty calculated to include those whose incomes are less than three times a low-cost food budget

power: the possession of enough authority to carry out one's will, even over the resistance of others

power elite: C. Wright Mills's term for those who rule America: the top people in the leading corporations, the most powerful generals and admirals of the armed forces, and certain elite politicians

prejudice: an *attitude* or prejudging, usually in a negative way

prestige: respect or regard

primary deviance: Edwin Lemert's term for acts of deviance that have little effect on the self-concept

primary group: a group characterized by intimate, long-term, face-to-face association and cooperation

primary sector: that part of the economy that extracts raw materials from the environment

primitive technology: the adaptation of natural items for human use

private ownership of the means of production: the possession of machines and factories by individuals, who decide what shall be produced

privatization: the selling of a nation's state-run industries to the private sector

profane (the): Durkheim's term for mundane elements of everyday life

profession: an occupation characterized by rigorous education, a theoretical perspective, self-regulation, authority, and service (as opposed to a job)

professionalization of medicine: the development of medicine into a field in which education becomes rigorous, and in which physicians claim a theoretical understanding of illness, regulate themselves, claim to be doing a service to society (rather than just following self-interest), and take authority over clients

profit: the amount gained from selling something for more than it cost

proletariat: Marx's term for the exploited class, the mass of workers who do not own the means of production [1] Karl Marx's term for the people who work for those who own the means of production

propaganda: in its broad sense, the presentation of information in the attempt to influence people; in its narrow sense, one-sided information used to try to influence people

property: the rights, by law or custom, to act toward something in certain ways

propinquity: spatial nearness

proportional representation: an electoral system in which seats in a legislature are divided according to the proportion of votes each political party receives

props: personal items used to communicate messages about the self

Protestant ethic (the): Weber's term to describe the ideal of a highly moral life, hard work, industriousness, and frugality

public opinion: how people think about some issue

pure or basic sociology: sociological research whose only purpose is to make discoveries about life in human groups, not to make changes in those groups

qualitative techniques: research in which the emphasis is placed on describing and interpreting people's behavior

quantitative techniques: research in which the emphasis is placed on precise measurement, the use of statistics and numbers

questionnaires: a list of questions to be asked

quiet revolution (the): the fundamental changes in society that follow the movement of vast numbers of women from the home to the work force

race: inherited physical characteristics that distinguish one group from another

racism: prejudice and discrimination on the basis of race

random sample: a sample in which everyone in the target population has the same chance of being included in the study

rapport: a feeling of trust between researchers and subjects

rational-legal authority: authority based on law or written rules and regulations; also called bureaucratic authority

rationality: the acceptance of rules, efficiency, and practical results as the right way to approach human affairs

rationalization of society: a widespread acceptance of rationality and a social organization largely built around this idea

real culture: the norms and values that people actually follow

recidivism rate: the proportion of persons who are rearrested

redemptive social movement: a social movement that seeks to change people totally

reference group: Herbert Hyman's term for the groups we use as standards to evaluate ourselves

rehabilitation: the resocialization of offenders so that they can become conforming citizens

reformative social movement: a social movement that seeks to change only particular aspects of society

reincarnation: in Hinduism and Buddhism, the return of the soul after death in a different form

relative deprivation theory: the belief that people join social movements based on their evaluations of what they think they should have compared with what others have

reliability: the extent to which data produce consistent results

religion: according to Durkheim, beliefs and practices that separate the profane from the sacred and unite its adherents into a moral community

religious experience: a sudden awareness of the supernatural or a feeling of coming in contact with God

replication: the repetition of research in order to test its findings

representative democracy: a form of democracy in which voters elect representatives to govern and make decisions on their behalf

reputational method: (of measuring social class) a system in which people who are familiar with the reputations of others are asked to judge their social class

research method: (or research design) one of six strategies or procedures sociologists use to collect data: surveys, documents, secondary analysis, participant observation, experiments, and unobtrusive measures

reserve labor force: the term used by conflict theorists for the unemployed, who can be put to work during times of high production and then discarded when no longer needed [1] conflict theorists' term for the unemployed

resocialization: the process of learning new norms, values, attitudes, and behaviors

resource mobilization: a theory that social movements succeed or fail based on their ability to mobilize resources such as time, money, and people's skills

respondents: people who respond to a survey, either in interviews or in self-administered questionnaires

retribution: the punishment of offenders in order to restore the moral balance upset by the offense

revolution: armed resistance designed to overthrow a government

riot: violent crowd behavior aimed against people and property

rising expectations: the sense that better conditions are soon to follow, which, if unfulfilled, creates mounting frustration

rituals: ceremonies or repetitive practices; in this context, religious observances or rites

role: a social position available in a society [1] the behaviors, obligations, and privileges attached to a status

role conflict: conflicts that someone feels *between* roles because the expectations attached to one role are incompatible with the expectations of another role.

role extension: the incorporation of additional activities into a role

role performance: how people play a role [1] the way in which an individual actually performs a role within the limits that it provides; showing a particular "style" or "personality"

role strain: conflicts that someone feels *within* a role

routinization of charisma: the transfer of authority from a charismatic figure to either a traditional or a rational-legal form of authority

rumors: unfounded information spread among people

sacred (the): Durkheim's term for things set apart or forbidden, which inspire fear, awe, reverence, or deep respect

sample: the individuals intended to represent the population to be studied

sanction: an expression of approval or disapproval given to people for upholding or violating norms

Sapir-Whorf hypothesis: Edward Sapir and Benjamin Whorf's hypothesis that language itself creates a particular way of thinking and perceiving

scapegoat: an individual or group unfairly blamed for someone else's troubles

scenery: the furnishings of a social setting that people use to communicate messages about the self

science: the application of systematic methods to obtain knowledge and the knowledge obtained by those methods

secondary analysis: the analysis of data already collected by other researchers

secondary deviance: Edwin Lemert's term for acts of deviance incorporated into the self-concept, around which an individual orients his or her behavior

secondary group: compared with a primary group, a larger, relatively temporary, more anonymous, formal, and impersonal group based on some interest or activity, whose members are likely to interact on the basis of specific roles

secondary sector: that part of the economy in which raw materials are turned into manufactured goods

sect: a group larger than a cult that still feels substantial hostility from and toward society

secular: belonging to the world and its affairs

secularization of culture: the process by which a culture becomes less influenced by religion

secularization of religion: the replacement of a religion's "otherworldly" concerns with concerns about "this world"

segregation: the policy of keeping racial or ethnic groups apart

selective perception: the ability to see certain points but remain blind to others

self: the concept, unique to humans, of being able to see ourselves "from the outside"; to gain a picture of how others see us

self-administered questionnaires: questionnaires filled out by respondents

self-fulfilling prophecy: Robert Merton's term for an originally false assertion that becomes true simply because it was predicted

sex: biological characteristics that distinguish females and males, consisting of primary and secondary sex characteristics

sex-typed: the association of behaviors with one sex or the other

sexual harassment: the use of a person's position to force unwanted sexual demands on someone

shaman: a priest in a preliterate society [1]the healing specialist of a preliterate tribe who attempts to control the spirits thought to cause a disease or injury; commonly called a witch doctor

sick role: a social role that excuses people from normal obligations because they are sick or injured, while at the same time expecting them to seek competent help and cooperate in getting well

significant other: an individual who significantly influences someone else's life

sign-vehicles: the term used by Goffman to describe the ways in which a person communicates information about the self: social setting, appearance, and manner

slavery: a form of social stratification in which some people own other people

small group: a group small enough for everyone to interact directly with all the other members

social change: the alteration of culture and societies over time

social class: a large number of people with similar amounts of income and education who work at jobs that are roughly comparable in prestige [1]according to Weber, a large group of people who rank close to one another in wealth, power, and prestige; according to Marx, one of two groups: capitalists who own the means of production and workers who sell their labor

social cohesion: the degree to which members of a group or society feel united by shared values and other social bonds

the social construction of reality: what people define as real because of their background assumptions and life experiences

social control: formal and informal means of enforcing norms

social devaluation: a reduction in the value or social worth placed on something or someone

social environment: the entire human environment, including direct contact with others

social facts: Durkheim's term for the patterns of behavior that characterize a social group

social inequality: a state in which privileges and obligations are given to some but denied to others

social institutions: the standard means by which society meets its basic needs

social integration: the degree to which people feel a part of social groups

social interaction: what people do when they are in one another's presence [1]what people do when they come together

social location: people's group memberships because of their location in history and society

social mobility: movement up or down the social class ladder

social movement: unusual behavior that, compared with other forms of collective behavior, usually involves more people, is more prolonged, is more organized, and focuses on social change

social networks: the social ties radiating outward from the self, that link people together

social order: a group's usual and customary social arrangements, on which its members depend and on which they base their lives

social placement: a function of education that funnels people into a society's various positions

social promotion: the practice of passing students from one grade to the next even though they have not mastered basic materials

social psychology: an academic discipline that attempts to blend parts of psychology and sociology

social sciences: the intellectual and academic disciplines designed to understand the social world objectively by means of controlled and repeated observations

social setting: the place where the action of everyday life unfolds

social stratification: the division into layers of nations or of people according to their relative power, property, and prestige

social structure: the relationship of people and groups to one another; the characteristics of groups—all of which give direction to and set limits on behavior

socialism: an economic system characterized by the public ownership of the means of production, central planning, and the distribution of goods without a profit motive

socialization: the process by which people learn the characteristics of their group—the attitudes, values, and actions thought appropriate for them

society: people who share a culture and a territory

sociobiology: a framework of thought that views human behavior as the result of natural selection and considers biological characteristics to be the fundamental cause of human behavior

sociological perspective: an approach to understanding human behavior by placing it within its broader social context

sociology: the scientific study of society and human behavior

special-interest group: a group of people who have a particular issue in common and can be mobilized for political action

spirit of capitalism (the): Weber's term for the desire to accumulate capital as a duty—not to spend it, but as an end in itself

split-labor market: a term used by conflict theorists for the capitalist practice of weakening the bargaining power of workers by splitting them along racial, ethnic, sex, age, or any other lines

spurious correlation: the correlation of two variables actually caused by a third variable; there is no cause-effect relationship

state: synonymous with government; the source of legitimate violence in society

state religion: a government-sponsored religion

status: the position that someone occupies in society or a social group [1]social ranking

status inconsistency: a contradiction or mismatch between statuses [1]a condition in which a person ranks high on some dimensions of social class and low on others

status set: all the statuses or positions that an individual occupies

status symbols: items used to identify a status

stigma: "blemishes" that discredit a person's claim to a "normal" identity

stockholders' revolt: the refusal of a corporation's stockholders to rubber-stamp decisions made by its managers

stored value: the backing of a currency by goods that have been stored

strain theory: Robert Merton's term for the strain engendered when a society socializes large numbers of people to desire a cultural goal (such as success) but withholds from many the approved means to reach that goal; one adaptation to the strain is crime, the choice of an innovative means (one outside the approved system) to attain the cultural goal

stratified random sample: a sample of specific subgroups of the target population in which everyone in the subgroups has an equal chance of being included in the study

street crime: crimes such as mugging, rape, and burglary

structural mobility: movement up or down the social class ladder that is attributable to changes in the structure of society, not to individual efforts

structured interviews: a form of interview that uses closed-ended questions

studied nonobservance: a face-saving technique in which people give the impression that they are unaware of a flaw in someone's performance

subculture: the values and related behaviors of a group that distinguish its members from the larger culture; a world within a world

subjective meanings: the meanings that people attach to their own behavior

subjective method: (of measuring social class) a system in which people are asked to define their own social class

subsistence economy: the type of economy in which human groups live off the land with little or no surplus

suburb: the communities adjacent to the political boundaries of a city

suburbanization: the movement from the city to the suburbs

superego: Freud's term for the conscience, the internalized norms and values of our social groups

survey: the collection of data by having people answer a series of questions

symbol: something to which people attach meaning and then use to communicate with others

symbolic culture: another term for nonmaterial culture

symbolic interactionism: a theoretical perspective in which society is viewed as composed of symbols that people use to establish meaning, develop their views of the world, and communicate with one another

taboo: a norm so strong that it brings revulsion if it is violated

tact: in dramaturgical terms, ignoring a flaw in someone's performance

taking the role of the other: putting oneself in someone else's shoes; understanding how someone else feels and thinks and thus anticipating how that person will act

teamwork: the collaboration of two or more persons interested in the success of a performance to manage impressions jointly

techniques of neutralization: ways of thinking or rationalizing that help people deflect society's norms

technology: often defined as the applications of science, but can be conceptualized as tools, items used to accomplish tasks

tertiary deviance: the "normalization" of acts considered deviant by mainstream society; relabeling the acts as nondeviant

tertiary sector: that part of the economy that consists of service-oriented occupations

theory: a general statement about how some parts of the world fit together and how they work; an explanation of how two or more facts are related to one another

Thomas theorem: an interpretation of the social construction of reality summarized in William I. Thomas's statement: "If people define situations as real, they are real in their consequences."

tool: an object that is modified for a specific purpose

total institution: a place in which people are cut off from the rest of society and are almost totally controlled by the officials who run the place

totalitarianism: a form of government that exerts almost total control over the people

tracking: the sorting of students into different educational programs on the basis of real or perceived abilities

traditional authority: authority based on custom

traditional orientation: the idea, characteristic of feudal society, that the past is the best guide for the present

trained incapacity: a bureaucrat's inability to see the goals of the organization and to function as a cooperative, integrated part of the whole, caused by the highly specific nature of the tasks he or she performs

transformative social movement: a social movement that seeks to change society totally

triad: a group of three persons

underclass: a small group of people for whom poverty persists year after year and across generations

underemployment: the condition of having to work at a job beneath one's level of training and abilities, or of being able to find only part-time work

underground economy: an exchange of goods and services that is not reported to the government

universal citizenship: the idea that everyone has the same basic rights by virtue of being born in a country (or by immigrating and becoming a naturalized citizen)

unobtrusive measures: the observation of people who do not know they are being studied

unstructured interviews: a form of interview that uses open-ended questions

upward social mobility: movement up the social class ladder

urban legend: a story with an ironic twist that sounds realistic but is false

urban networks: the social networks of city dwellers

urbanization: the process by which an increasing proportion of a population lives in cities

validity: the extent to which operational definitions measure what was intended

value contradictions: values that conflict with one another; to follow the one means to come into conflict with the other

value clusters: a series of interrelated values that together form a larger whole

value free: the view that a sociologist's personal values or biases should not influence social research

values: ideas about what is good or worthwhile in life; attitudes about the way the world ought to be [1]the standards by which people define what is desirable or undesirable, good or bad, beautiful or ugly

variable: a factor or concept thought to be significant for human behavior, which varies from one case to another

Verstehen: a German word used by Weber that is perhaps best understood as "to have insight into someone's situation"

voluntary association: a group made up of volunteers who have organized on the basis of some mutual interest

voluntary memberships: (or voluntary associations) groups to which people belong

voter apathy: indifference and inaction on the part of individuals or groups with respect to the political process

war: armed conflict between nations or politically distinct groups

WASP: a white Anglo-Saxon Protestant; narrowly, an American of English descent; broadly, an American of western European ancestry

wealth: property and income

white-collar crime: Edwin Sutherland's term for crimes committed by people of respectable and high social status in the course of their occupations; for example, bribery of public officials, securities violations, embezzlement, false advertising, and price fixing

white ethnics: white immigrants to the United States whose culture differs from that of WASPs

working class: those who sell their labor to the capitalist class

world system: the way in which the world's countries are tied together by economic and political connections

zero population growth: a demographic condition in which women bear only enough children to reproduce the population

Name Index

Aberle, David, 95, 611
Abraham, 506, 507, 508
Abramson, Jill, 154, 418
Achenbaum, Andrew, 353
Achenbaum, W., 83
Adams, Robert M., 640
Adler, Freda, 302
Adler, Stephen J., 300
Adorno, Theodor, 317
Albert, Ethel M., 47
Albrecht, Donald E., 645
Aldrich, Nelson W., Jr., 259, 266
Alger, Horatio, 271
Allen, Walter R., 328
Allende, Salvador, 385
Allport, Gordon, 319, 339
Alpert, Harry, 497
American Sociological Association, 131, 646
Amott, Teresa, 334, 430
Andersen, Margaret L., 290, 298
Anderson, Charles H., 228, 624
Anderson, Chris, 131
Anderson, Elijah, 88, 203, 587
Anderson, James, 202
Anderson, Nels, 45
Anderson, Teresa, 357
Angell, Robert C., 23
Ansberry, Clare, 546
Apple, Michael W., 483
Applefrome, Peter, 521
Ariés, Philippe, 18, 81
Armitage, Richard L., 423
Armstrong, Scott, 330, 570
Arndt, William F., 406
Arnold, Phillip G., 204
Aron, Arthur, 440
Arquitt, George, 177
Asch, Solomon, 159, 160, 161, 162
Ashe, Arthur, 194, 480
Ashley, Richard, 379
Associated Press, 519
Atchley, Robert, 446
Athens, Lonnie H., 135, 302
Attanucci, Jane S., 445
Auerbach, Judith D., 300
Ausubel, Jesse H., 630
Avery, Dennis T., 564
Aviad, Janet O'Dea, 497

Bachu, Amara, 454
Bacon, Kenneth H., 563
Bainbridge, William, 601
Bainbridge, William Sims, 609, 610
Bakker, Jim, 521
Bales, Robert F., 156
Ballentine, Jean H., 470

Balling, Robert C., 642
Baltes, P. B., 81
Baltzell, E. Digby, 266, 325
Banfield, Edward, 275
Barbeau, Clayton, 439
Barber, Bernard, 145
Bardwick, Judith M., 285
Barnes, Harry Elmer, 624
Barnes, John A., 554
Barry, Kathleen, 289
Barsky, Neil, 187
Barzansky, Barbara, 543
Beals, Alan R., 435
Beals, Ralph L., 47, 435
Beck, Allen, 197
Beck, E. M., 596
Becker, Howard S., 192, 193
Becker, Selwyn, 159
Beckley, Robert E., 497
Begley, Sharon, 59, 629
Beirne, Piers, 205
Belknap, Joanne, 317
Bell, Alexander Graham, 419
Bell, Bonnie, 198
Bell, Daniel, 148, 374, 470, 622, 630
Bell, David A., 335
Bell, Inge, 350
Bell, Wendell, 202, 580
Bellaby, Paul, 532
Bellah, Robert N., 47, 498, 505
Benales, Carlos, 41
Bender, Sue, 100
Bendix, Reinhard, 237
Benet, Lorenzo, 645
Benet, Sula, 343, 344
Bengston, Vern L., 361, 362
Bennett, Neil G., 453, 460
Benokraitis, Nijole V., 72, 179
Benson, Ian, 243
Berger, Arthur S., 544
Berger, Joyce, 544
Berger, Peter L., 3, 6, 109, 133, 225, 382, 403, 404, 439, 517
Berk, Richard, 597
Berkeley, Arthur Eliot, 296
Berle, Adolph, Jr., 384
Bernard, Jessie, 24, 439
Bernard, Viola W., 323, 424, 608
Berrueta-Clement, J. R., 487
Bettelheim, Bruno, 466
Biggs, Mae E., 108
Bills, David B., 477, 481
Bishop, Jerry E., 291, 549
Blackwood, Roy E., 73
Blanc, Ann, 453
Blanc, Ann Klimas, 460

Blau, Peter M., 268
Blauner, Robert, 324, 365
Blinick, Abraham, 554
Bloo, David E., 453, 460
Bluestone, Barry, 384, 397
Blumer, Herbert, 38, 594, 595
Blumstein, Alfred, 208
Blumstein, Philip, 436, 451
Boat, Marion D., 580
Bobo, Lawrence, 315, 317
Boden, Deirdre, 26
Bohrer, Linda, 549
Booth, Alan, 458
Borrelli, Peter, 645
Boulard, Gerry, 317
Boulding, Elise, 145, 622
Bowles, Samuel, 477, 480, 481, 483
Bradford, Calvin P., 95
Brady, Rose, 414
Brahma, 508
Brajuha, Mario, 131
Bremner, Brian, 414
Brecher, Edward M., 550
Bridgwater, William, 168, 406, 499, 507, 508, 509, 510, 513, 515, 606
Brilliant, Ashleigh E., 633
Brinton, Mary C., 187, 297
Broad, William J., 622
Brodie, H. Keith H., 317
Brody, Charles, 294
Bronfenbrenner, Urie, 63
Brooks, Virginia R., 294
Brown, Diane Robinson, 263
Brown, Jerry, 451
Brown, Lester R., 560, 562
Browne, A., 302
Brueckner, Jan K., 578
Bruer, John T., 296
Brunvand, Jan Harold, 603, 604
Bryant, Clifton D., 631
Buckley, Stephen, 486
Bullard, Robert, 644
Bumiller, Elisabeth, 18, 441
Bumpass, Larry L., 453, 456
Bureau of the Census, 272, 573, 576, 579
Burgess, Ernest W., 15, 16, 18, 576, 577, 594
Burke, Ann Celeste, 375
Burnham, Walter Dean, 412
Burns, Lucy, 290
Burton, Thomas M., 204
Bush, Diane Mitsch, 68, 79
Bush, George, 490, 600
Bush, Neil, 204
Butler, Robert N., 352
Buttel, Frederick H., 645
Butterworth, Katherine M., 361

Caesar, 507
Cain, L. D., 84
Cairns, Grace E., 518
Callahan, Daniel, 357
Calloway, Michael, 266
Calmas, Wilfred, 135
Calvin, John, 167
Camp, Roderick A., 386
Cannon, Lynn Weber, 248
Cantril, Hadley, 601
Caplin, Mortimer M., 389
Caplow, Theodore, 45, 114
Cardoso, Fernando Henrique, 241, 624
Carlson, Lewis H., 334
Carlton, Jim, 187
Carpenter, Betsy, 645
Carroll, Paul B., 635
Carroll, Peter N., 327
Carter, Timothy J., 205
Cartwright, Corwin, 156
Castro, Fidel, 39, 333
Catsambis, Sophia, 481
Catton, William R., Jr., 645
Census Bureau. See Bureau of the Census
Centers for Disease Control, 548
Cerhan, Jane Ugland, 147
Chafetz, Janet Saltzman, 305
Chagnon, Napoleon, 192, 193
Chalfant, H. Paul, 497
Chambliss, William J., 109, 110, 146, 206, 207, 623
Chandler, Tertius, 574, 576
Charles VII, King of England, 406
Charon, Joel M., 68
Chase, Marilyn, 549
Chavez, Cesar, 331
Chavez, Linda, 330, 333
Chen, Edwin, 59
Cherlin, Andrew, 453, 458, 460
Chodorow, Nancy J., 68
Christensen, Harold T., 435
Cicerelli, Victor G., 487
Clark, Burton, 483
Clark, Candace, 69
Clark, Curtis B., 362
Clarke, Edward, 290
Clausen, J. A., 81
Clay, Jason W., 426
Clelland, Donald, 205
Cleveland, Harlan, 624, 640
Clinard, Marshall B., 203
Clines, Francis X., 642
Clingempeel, W. Glenn, 457
Cloward, Richard W., 114, 201, 203
Cobb, Jonathan, 268
Coburn, David, 554
Cockerham, William, 553
Cohen, Deborah L., 273
Cohen, Erik, 243
Cohen, Jacqueline, 208
Cohen, Laurie P., 301
Cohen, Morris R., 209
Cohen, Murray, 135
Cohen, Ronald, 433
Colburn, George A., 334
Cole, Jonathan R., 296
Coleman, James, 487, 488
Coleman, James William, 205
Collins, Patricia Hill, 324
Collins, Randall, 233, 442, 466, 483
Collins, Roy C., 202
Columbus, Christopher, 409, 629
Comte, Auguste, 9, 10, 11
Confucius, 467, 510

Congressional Quarterly Researcher, 300
Consumer Reports, 539
Cookson, Peter W., Jr., 260, 481
Cooley, Charles Horton, 17, 63, 64, 65, 68, 149, 150, 441
Cooper, Bruce S., 466
Cooper, Kenneth J., 469, 490
Corchado, Alfredo, 330
Corcoran, Mary, 274
Coser, Lewis, A., 11, 23
Cottin, Lou, 353
Couch, Carl J., 84
Coughlin, Ellen K., 131
Cowen, Emory, 317
Cowgill, Donald, 353
Cowley, Joyce, 290
Cox, Meg, 299
Crawford, Robert, 545
Crenshaw, Edward M., 578, 579
Cressey, Donald R., 203
Crispell, Diane, 572
Crosbie, Paul V., 159
Crossen, Cynthia, 121
Cumming, Elaine, 354, 355
Cunniff, Mark A., 208
Curran, Daniel J., 284
Curtin, Sharon, 361
Curwin, E. Cecil, 574
Custer, George, 336, 337
Cuzzort, Ray P., 114, 626

Dahl, Robert A., 419, 420
Dahrendorf, Ralf, 23, 233
Daly, Martin, 302
Daniels, Roger, 334
Dannefer, Dale, 82
Darley, John, 157, 585
Darwin, Charles, 10, 48
Davies, James, 616
Davis, Allison, 249
Davis, Bob, 642
Davis, Fred, 41
Davis, Junetta, 73, 268
Davis, Kingsley, 58, 59, 230–231, 475
Davis, Nanette J., 42, 210
Day, Charles R., Jr., 299
Dearman, Marion V., 520
Deber, Ralsa B., 554
DeBerry, Marshall, 123
Deevey, E. S., 641
De George, Richard T., 523
DeMause, Lloyd, 81
Demos, John, 436
Dentzler, Susan, 271
Derber, Charles, 183
Deutsch, Claudia H., 300
Dewey, John, 17
Diamond, Milton, 284
Diamond, Timothy, 362
Dickson, Tony, 12
Dickson, William J., 128
Diehl, Jackson, 642
Dieppa, Ismael, 335
DiGiulio, Robert C., 435, 446
Dirkson, Everett, 204
Dobash, R. Emerson, 24
Dobash, Russell P., 24, 459
Dobriner, William M., 10, 90
Dobyns, Henry F., 323, 336
Dollard, John, 317
Domhoff, William, 96, 195, 232, 236, 254, 260, 385, 413, 420, 421, 425
Donelson, Samuel, 553
Dornbusch, Sanford H., 450

Doudna, Christine, 436
Douglass, Richard L., 363
Dove, Adrian, 480
Dowie, Mark, 203
Doyal, Lesley, 553
Doyle, Denis P., 466
Dressen, Willi, 608
Drucker, Peter F., 183, 387
Du Bois, W. E. B., 15
Duncan, Greg J., 8, 273
Duncan, Otis Dudley, 268
Dunham, Warren, 263
Dunlap, Riley E., 645
Dunn, Marvin, 600
Dunphy, Joan S., 300
Durkheim, Emile, 11, 12, 14, 20, 97, 99, 149, 200, 215, 364, 366, 496, 497
Durning, Alan, 641, 642
Dutton, Donald, 440
Dwyer, John M., 547
Dye, H. A., 60, 61

Easterbrook, Gregg, 546
Easterbrooks, M. Ann, 445
Eckholm, Erik, 52–53
Eder, Klaus, 625, 627, 631, 645
Edgerton, Robert, 193
Edwards, Richard, 183
Eggers, Mitchell, 329
Ehrenreich, Barbara, 286, 536
Ehrensaft, Diane, 444
Ehrhardt, Anke A., 284
Ehrlich, Elizabeth, 299
Eibl-Eibesfeldt, Irenius, 40, 50
Eiduson, Bernice T., 450
Einstein, Albert, 10
Eisenhart, R. Wayne, 294
Eisinger, Peter, 585
Eitzen, E. Stanley, 204, 387, 436, 442, 447
Ekman, Paul, 40
Elder, Glen, 84
Elkind, David, 445
Elkins, Stanley M., 222
Ellis, James E., 3
Elsasser, Glen, 616
Ely, Ezra Stiles, 536–537
Engardio, Pete, 330
Engels, Friederick, 10, 228, 288, 499, 623, 626
English, Deidre, 286, 536
Ensel, Walter M., 154
Epstein, Arnold, 320
Epstein, Cynthia Fuchs, 68, 74, 83, 281, 282, 283
Erikson, Erik H., 81
Erikson, Robert S., 266
Ernst, Eldon G., 504, 514
Eron, Leonard D., 79
Etzel, Sylvia I., 543
Etzioni, Amitai, 47, 394
Evans, J. W., 487

Faris, Robert E. L., 263
Farkas, George, 486
Farley, Reynolds, 328
Farrell, Walter C., Jr., 315, 317
Faunce, William, 561
FBI Uniform Crime Reports, 204
Feagin, Clairece Booher, 329
Feagin, Joe R., 72, 179, 315, 317, 329, 578
Featherman, David L., 268
Feinglass, Joe, 546
Felt, Judy C., 335
Ferdinand, King of Spain, 324, 409
Ferguson, Trudi, 300

Ferracuti, Franco, 199, 302
Feshbach, Murray, 642
Fialka, John J., 642
Fichter, Joseph H., 131
Fields, George, 313
Fierman, Jaclyn, 271
Finkelhor, David, 135, 459, 460
Finn, Chester E., 490
Finsterbusch, Kurt, 607
Firestone, Shulamith, 24
Fischer, Claude S., 409, 574
Fischer, David, 353
Fischer, Michael M. J., 518
Fisher, Ann, 300
Fisher, Gene A., 131, 395
Fisher, Sue, 541, 542
Fitzgerald, Mark, 317
Flavel, J., 65
Fleming, Joyce Dudney, 51, 52
Flexner, Abraham, 535
Flink, James J., 632, 633, 634
Foley, Douglas E., 291, 294
Foote, Jennifer, 645
Ford, Henry, 631, 632
Foreman, Dave, 644
Forer, Lucille K., 445
Form, William H., 383, 419
Forman, Craig, 313
Forrest, Jacqueline Darroch, 21
Fouts, Roger, 51–52
Fox, Daniel M., 545
Fox, Elaine, 177
Fox, Gerald, 574, 576
Fox, Renee C., 540
Frank, Anthony, 170
Franklin, John Hope, 569
Freidson, Eliot, 532
Freud, Sigmund, 10, 67–68, 213
Freudenburg, William R., 645
Friedl, Ernestine, 287
Friedland, Gerald H., 548
Frisbie, W. Parker, 576, 586
Fritz, Jan M., 26
Frumkin, Robert M., 519
Fuchs, Victor R., 529
Fuller, Rex, 297
Furstenberg, Frank F., 460
Furtado, Celso, 241, 624

Galagan, Patricia A., 181
Galanter, Marc, 497
Galbraith, John Kenneth, 242
Galinsky, Ellen, 300
Gallese, Liz Roman, 285
Galliher, John, 13
Gallup, George, Jr., 519
Gallup Poll, 305
Galuszka, Peter, 414
Gans, Herbert, 580, 582, 584, 588
Garbarino, Merwin S., 323
Garcia, Angela, 294
Gardner, Allen, 51
Gardner, Beatrice, 51
Gardner, Burleigh, 249
Gardner, Carol, 583
Gardner, Mary, 249
Garfinkel, Harold, 80, 106, 107, 208
Garreau, Joel, 588
Gartner, Michael, 550
Gary, Lawrence E., 263
Gatewood, Willard B., 275, 447
Gautama, Siddhartha, 509, 510
Gavrielides, Nocolas, 198
Gay, Jill, 243

Gecas, Viktor, 73, 84
Gelles, Richard, 458, 459
Gellhorn, Martha, 425
Gelman, David, 363
Genovese, Kitty, 578, 580, 585
Gerson, Kathleen, 450
Gerth, H. H., 229
Gest, Ted, 204
Giddens, Anthony, 26
Giele, Janet, 305
Gilbert, Dennis, 220, 259–262, 260, 262, 266
Gilham, Steven A., 294
Gill, Derek, 553
Gilligan, Carol, 67, 68
Gilmore, David D., 74, 82
Gimenez, Martha E., 272
Gingrich, F. William, 406
Gintis, Herbert, 477, 480, 483
Githens, Marianne, 304–305
Glazer, Nathan, 338
Glick, Daniel, 629
Glick, Deborah C., 531
Glick, Mark A., 329
Glick, Paul C., 458
Gliedman, John, 641
Glock, Charles Y., 497
Glotz, Peter, 397
Glueck, Eleanor, 196
Glueck, Sheldon, 196
Goad, G. Pierre, 554
Goebbels, Paul Joseph, 609
Goffman, Erving, 18, 79, 103, 104, 105, 194, 597
Gold, Ray, 258
Goldberg, Steven, 283
Goldberg, Susan, 71
Goldberg, Wendy A., 445
Golden, Tim, 644
Goldfarb, William, 61
Goldner, Fred, 64
Goleman, Daniel, 285, 445
Gomez, Carlos F., 545
Goodall, Jane, 49
Goode, Erich, 550
Goode, William J., 305, 394, 535
Goodwin, Glenn A., 132
Gorbachev, Mikhail, 26
Gordon, C., 81
Gordon, David M., 205
Gordon, Milton M., 42
Gordon, Robert J., 356
Gorman, Peter, 641
Gortmaker, Steven L., 263
Gould, R. M., 81
Gracey, Harry, 478
Graham, Ellen, 517
Gramling, Robert, 645
Grant, Karen R., 554
Grant, Nigel, 470
Graven, Katherine, 298
Greeley, Andrew M., 505, 520
Greene, Elizabeth, 317
Greenfeld, Lawrence, 197
Greenwood, Ernest, 394, 396
Greer, Germaine, 24
Greif, Geoffrey L., 444
Greisman, H. C., 607
Grella, Christine, 457
Grigg, Charles M., 202
Grossman, Laurie M., 187
Grunebaum, Henry, 491
Guevara, Che, 499
Guha, Ramachandra, 645
Guiles, Melinda Grenier, 187

Gumbel, Peter, 313
Gupta, Giri Raj, 441
Gwartney-Gibbs, Patricia A., 453

Haas, Jack, 42, 105, 106, 542
Haberman, Paul W., 551
Hacker, Helen, 285
Hall, Douglas T., 300
Hall, Edward, 102
Hall, G. Stanley, 82
Hall, J. A., 294
Hall, Jerome, 195
Hall, Peter, 154
Hall, Richard H., 170
Hallinan, Maureen T., 491
Hallowell, Lyle, 131
Hamilton, Mykol, 8
Hamilton, Richard F., 45
Hardy, Dorcas, 359
Hare, A. Paul, 140, 157
Harlow, Harry, 62–63
Harlow, Margaret, 62–63
Harrington, Michael, 242, 244, 274, 397
Harris, Chauncey, 578
Harris, Diana K., 343
Harris, Louis, 339
Harris, Marvin, 288, 312, 514
Harrison, Bennett, 384, 397
Harry, Joseph, 451
Hart, Charles W. M., 350, 432
Hart, Gudmond, 574
Hart, Hornell, 423
Hartig, Karl, 187
Hartley, Eugene, 315, 317
Hartman, Michael, 333
Hartmann, Heidi I., 435
Haslick, Leonard, 343
Hauser, Philip, 575
Hauser, Robert M., 268
Hawley, Amos H., 574, 575
Hawthorne, Nathaniel, 208
Hayes, Arthur S., 300
Hechinger, Fred M., 131
Heider, Karl G., 432
Heilbrun, Alfred B., 197
Heller, Celia, 226
Hellinger, Daniel, 254, 410, 420, 423, 471, 472, 474
Hemp, Paul, 338
Henley, Nancy, 8
Henry, William, 354, 355
Henry, William A., III, 331, 332
Henslin, 616
Henslin, James M., 36, 41, 44, 107, 108, 125, 135, 203, 248, 267, 331, 435
Henslin, Linda K., 203, 267
Hering, Cedric, 329
Hernstein, Richard J., 196
Herod, 507
Herring, George C., 423
Herrnstein, R. J., 489
Hershey, Robert D., Jr., 390
Hertzler, Joyce O., 36, 38
Hibbert, Christopher, 210
Hills, Stuart L., 135
Hiltz, Starr, 446
Hindus, Michael, 21
Hippler, Fritz, 318, 411
Hirschi, Travis, 200
Hitler, Adolf, 226, 317, 322, 407–408, 425, 506, 606, 607
Hobson, John, 240
Hochschild, Arlie, 68, 436, 437, 438, 439
Hodson, Randy, 637, 638

Hoffer, Thomas, 488
Hoijer, Harry, 47, 435
Holden, Constance, 285
Holder, Wayne M., 460
Holtzman, Abraham, 356
Homans, George, 89
Homblin, Dora Jane, 574
Hong, Lawrence K., 520
Hoover, Herbert, 417
Hoover, J. Edgar, 229
Hope, Christine A., 287
Horowitz, Irving Louis, 132, 232, 380
Horowitz, Ruth, 199, 584
Horwitz, Tony, 227, 313
Hostetler, John A., 100, 502
Hotchkiss, Sandy, 135
Hourani, Benjamin T., 420, 639
Houseknecht, Sharon, 456
Hout, Michael, 520
Howard, Jan, 555
Howells, Lloyd, 159
Hoyt, Homer, 577
Hsu, Francis L. K., 334
Huang, Chien, 202
Hubbard, Ruth, 306
Huber, Joan, 228, 232, 280, 287, 305, 419
Hudson, James R., 582
Hudson, Robert B., 356, 363
Huff-Corzine, Lin, 302
Hug, Simon, 644
Hughes, Everett C., 161, 323, 607
Hughes, H. Stuart, 625
Hughes, James W., 587
Hughes, Kathleen A., 103, 310
Hull, Raymond, 174
Humphreys, Laud, 131–133
Humphry, Derek, 545
Hurn, Christopher J., 483
Hussein, Saddam, 411, 636
Huth, Mary Jo, 578, 579

Ingersoll, Bruce, 204
Iori, Ron, 36
Isaac, 506
Isabella, Queen of Spain, 324, 409
Ishmael, 507
Itard, Jean Marc Gaspard, 58
Izumi, Shigechiyo, 569

Jacklin, Carol Nagy, 445
Jackson, Jesse, 328
Jackson, Kenneth, 586
Jackson, M., 302
Jacob, 506
Jacobs, David, 205
Jacobs, Lila, 147
Jacobsen, Thorkild, 640
Jacobson, Lenore, 101, 485
Jaffe, Harold W., 548
Jagger, Alison, 306
James, Selma, 24
James, William, 17
Janis, Irving, 161
Jasper, James, 611, 613, 616, 617
Jefferson, Thomas, 410, 471
Jencks, Christopher, 397
Jenness, Valerie, 211
Jesus, 500, 506, 507, 508
Joan of Arc, 406, 408
Johnsen, Kathryn P., 435
Johnson, Benton, 511
Johnson, Lyndon B., 162, 229, 252, 358
Johnson, Magic, 194
Johnson, Miriam M., 72, 294
Johnson, Norris, 602

Johnston, Drue, 602
Johnston, William B., 636
Jonas, Harry S., 543
Jones, Cloyzelle K., 315, 317
Jones, Timothy K., 100
Jones, Woodrow, Jr., 147
Joseph, 506
Josephson, Matthew, 379
Josephy, Alvin M., Jr., 337
Judd, Dennis R., 254, 410, 420, 423, 471, 472,
    474
Judis, John B., 419
Jurik, Nancy, 302–303

Kaban, Barbara T., 445
Kagan, Jerome, 67, 68, 70
Kahl, Joseph A., 220, 259–262, 260, 261, 262,
    266
Kalichman, Seth C., 197
Kalish, Richard A., 445
Kalleberg, Arne L., 297
Kamin, Leon J., 196
Kanter, Rosabeth Moss, 27, 178, 179, 180,
    182
Kapferer, J. N., 603
Karp, David, 583, 584, 585, 586, 587
Kasarda, John D., 576, 577, 578, 579, 586
Katz, Michael, 271
Keans, Carl, 580
Keiser, Steven D., 267
Keith, Jennie, 355
Keith, Verna M., 329
Kellner, Hansfried, 439
Kellogg, L. A., 51
Kellogg, W. N., 51
Kelly, Joan B., 456, 457
Kemp, Alice Abel, 297
Keniston, Kenneth, 18
Kennedy, John F., 162, 219, 220, 225, 229,
    231, 236, 253, 408
Kennedy, Robert F., 220
Kennedy, Ted, 220, 253
Kephart, William M., 100
Kerr, Clark, 383
Kettl, Donald F., 204
Keyser, Christine, 645
Khomeini, Ayatollah, 408, 518
Kiefer, Francine S., 644
Kilgore, Sally, 488
Killian, Lewis M., 202, 596
Kimball, M. M., 72
King, David, 578
King, Edith W., 626
King, Martin Luther, Jr., 327, 328, 499, 600
King, Rodney, 599, 600
Kirton, Elizabeth, 147
Kitano, Henry H. L., 323, 337
Kitsuse, John, 193
Kitsuse, John I., 211, 614
Klandermans, Bert, 611
Klee, Ernst, 608
Kletzer, Lori G., 271
Kline, Susan, 197
Kluegel, James R., 271, 315, 317
Knaus, William A., 542, 553
Kohfeld, Carol W., 8
Kohlberg, Lawrence, 67
Kohn, Alfie, 423
Kohn, Melvin L., 73–74, 265, 397, 444
Kolb, William L., 131
Komarovsky, Mirra, 42
Komter, Aafke, 436, 439
Koop, C. Everett, 548, 550
Korda, Michael, 293
Kornhauser, William, 616

Kotlowitz, Alex, 489
Krauss, Celene, 643, 644
Kraybill, Donald B., 100
Kretschmer, Ernst, 196
Krieger, Nancy, 321
Kronenfied, Jennie R., 531
Kübler-Ross, Elisabeth, 366, 367
Kuhn, Margaret, 360
Kuttner, Bob, 397

La Barre, Weston, 47, 431
Lachica, Eduardo, 643
LaDou, Joseph, 242
La Dou, Joseph, 643
Lagerfeld, Steven, 588
Lamb, Michael E., 457
Landes, Judah, 317
Landry, Bart, 329
Landtman, Gunnar, 221, 222, 227
Lang, Gladys, 614
Lang, Kurt, 613–614
Lang, Susan S., 451
Langan, Patrick A., 208
Lannoy, Richard, 224
LaPiere Richard, 314
Larson, Jeffry H., 8
Lasch, Christopher, 18
Laslett, Peter, 8
Latane, Bibb, 157, 585
Lauer, Jeanette, 460
Lauer, Robert, 107, 460
LaVey, Anton, 604
Lawrence, David, Jr., 39
Lawton, Millicent, 273
Lazar, Irving, 487
Leacock, Eleanor, 486
Leakey, Louis, 49
LeBon, Gustave, 593, 594, 595
Lee, Alfred, 609, 610
Lee, Elizabeth, 609, 610
Lee, Lois, 215, 216
Lee, Marcia, 304
Lee, Richard B., 143, 622
Leinberger, Christopher B., 580
Leip, Leslie A., 8
Lekachman, Robert, 394
Lemert, Edwin, 210
Lengermann, Patricia Madoo, 285
Lenin, Vladimir Ilyich, 234, 499, 523
Lenski, Gerhard, 143, 233, 258, 373, 574, 623,
    625
Lenski, Jean, 143, 373, 574, 623, 625
Lerner, Gerda, 221, 286, 287, 288, 447
Lesser, Alexander, 422
Le Vine, Victor, 198
Levinson, D. J., 81
Levinson, Mark, 397
Levi-Strauss, Claude, 431, 432
Levitan, Sar, 391
Lewin, Tamar, 536
Lewis, David L., 622
Lewis, Dorothy, 196
Lewis, Michael, 71
Lewis, Oscar, 242, 274
Lewontin, R. C., 48
Lieberman, M. A., 81
Liebow, Elliot, 88, 203, 275
Lifson, Alan R., 548
Light, Donald W., 553, 554
Lin, Nan, 154
Lin, S., 458
Lincoln, Abraham, 520
Linden, Eugene, 641
Linton, Melaney A., 135
Linton, Ralph, 33, 93, 286

Lippitt, Ronald, 158
Lipset, Seymour Martin, 148, 237, 413, 623
Lipton, Michael, 244
Lloyd, John, 243
Lochhead, Carol, 131
Locke, Harvey, 18
Lockwood, Charles, 580
Lofland, John F., 592, 604
Logan, John R., 114
Lombroso, Cesare, 196
London, Kathryn A., 458
Loomis, Charles P., 441
Loomis, Zona K., 441
Lopez, Julie Amparano, 298
Lorence, Jon, 397
Lublin, Joann S., 183, 300
Lubman, Sarah, 600
Luckmann, Thomas, 109
Luebke, Barbara, 73
Luke, Timothy W., 499
Luker, Kristin, 616
Luoma, Jon R., 642
Luria, Zella, 474
Luther, Martin, 507
Luttberg, Norman R., 266

McAdam, Doug, 611, 616, 617
McAlexander, James H., 82
McAuliffe, Christa, 621
McCabe, J. Terrence, 3
McCall, Michal, 41
McCarthy, John D., 611, 617
McCarthy, Michael J., 187
McCasland, S. Vernon, 518
Maccoby, Eleanor E., 445
McCoy, Elin, 81
Mace, Roland L., 42
McGregor, James, 383
McGuire, John, 198
MacIver, Robert, 625
Mack, Raymond W., 95
Mackay, Charles, 593
Macke, Anne, 456
McKeown, Thomas, 560
MacKinnon, Catherine A., 300
McLachlan, Hugh V., 12
McLanahan, Sara, 450
McMurray, Scott, 204
McPhail, Clark, 593, 595, 597, 598, 600
McPherson, J. Miller, 154
Maeda, Daisaku, 350
Magnuson, E., 622
Main, Jackson Turner, 222
Malinowski, Bronislaw, 38, 431
Malson, Lucien, 58
Malthus, Thomas, 560, 562, 563
Mamdani, Mahmood, 567
Mann, Horace, 472
Marger, Martin N., 76, 232, 254, 420
Marolla, Joseph, 134, 135, 136
Marr, Warren, III, 596
Marshall, Gordon, 505
Martin, Michael, 645
Martin, Teresa, 456
Marx, Gary, 258
Marx, Karl, 10–11, 12, 23, 24, 167, 171, 172, 228, 229, 230, 232, 233, 234, 254, 258–259, 499, 502, 503, 523, 623, 626, 631
Masheter, Carol, 457
Massey, Douglas, 39, 329
Matthaie, Julie, 334, 430
Matthews, Marvyn, 470
Matza, David, 211
Mauksch, Hans O., 153, 389

Mauldin, Teresa A., 457
Mauss, Armand, 614
Mayo, Elton, 128
Mead, George Herbert, 15, 17, 64–65, 68
Mead, Margaret, 47
Means, Gardiner C., 384
Meier, Barry, 552
Melbin, Murray, 8
Meltzer, Bernard N., 84
Melucci, Alberto, 611
Merit Systems Protection Board, 300
Merton, Robert K., 16, 20, 152, 172, 201, 202, 213, 314, 441, 485
Messner, Steven F., 79
Meyerson, Per-Martin, 383
Meyrowitz, Joshua, 78
Miall, Charlene, 450
Michalowski, Raymond J., 146, 623
Michels, Robert, 178
Milgram, Stanley, 160, 161, 162
Mill, John Stuart, 611
Miller, Brent, 444
Miller, Dan E., 161
Miller, Eleanor M., 153, 389
Miller, Walter B., 199
Mills, C. Wright, 3, 16, 84, 133, 229, 232, 233, 254, 420, 421
Mills, Michael, 204
Miner, Horace, 535
Mintz, Beth A., 385
Mintz, John, 450
Mirande, Alfredo, 448
Mitchell, Roger, 147
Mitchell-Kerman, Claudia, 442
Mohammad Reza Shah Pahlavi, 518
Molotch, Harvey L., 26, 114, 578
Money, John, 284
Montagu, Ashley, 311
Montero, Darrel M., 335
Moore, Elizatbeth, 204
Moore, Maurice J., 573
Moore, Wilbert, 79, 230–231, 475
Morgan, James M., 8
Morgan, Lewis Henry, 624
Morgan, M., 72
Morris, Aldon, 499
Mortimer, Jeylan T., 397
Mosca, Gaetano, 232
Moses, 506, 508
Mosher, Steven W., 382
Moyers, Bill, 607
Moynihan, Daniel, 273
Muehlenhard, Charlene L., 135
Muhammad (prophet), 507, 508, 512
Murdock, George, 47, 285–286
Murdock, George Peter, 430, 442
Murdock, Steven H., 645
Murray, Charles, 489
Murray, G. W., 3
Myers, Henry F., 10, 395

Nardi, Peter M., 132
Natarajan, Geetha, 551
Navarro, Mireya, 36
Neikirk, William, 616
Neugarten, Bernice L., 83, 354, 355
Nevid, Jeffrey, 547
Newdorf, David, 204
Newman, Barry, 382
Newman, Katherine S., 271, 275
New York Times, The, 198, 578
Niebuhr, Richard, 516
Niggle, Christopher J., 252
Nilsson, Nic, 405

Nixon, Richard M., 162, 639
Noble, David W., 327
Nordhaus, William D., 251
North, Gary, 359
Nussbaum, Bruce, 271

Oberschall, Anthony, 617
O'Connell, Martin, 454, 573
O'Connor, Sandra Day, 300
O'Dea, Thomas F., 497
Offen, Karen, 289, 306
Ogburn, William F., 18, 145, 628
O'Hare, William P., 271, 329, 335
Ohlin, Lloyd, 201, 203
Okie, Susan, 642
Oliver, Melvin L., 329
Olmsted, Michael S., 140, 157
Olneck, Michael R., 477, 481
Olsen, Marvin E., 271
O'Malley, Jeff, 243
O'Reilly, Jane, 430
Orum, Anthony M., 578
Orwell, George, 402
Otten, Alan L., 360
Ottenberg, Perry, 323, 424, 608
Ouchi, William, 184, 186, 469
Owen, David, 489

Packer, Arnold E., 636
Pae, Peter, 450
Pahlavi. *See* Mohammad Reza Shah Pahlavi
Palen, John J., 575, 577, 579
Palmer, C. Eddie, 497
Palmer, Jessica, 301
Palmore, Erdman, 350, 353
Parfit, Michael, 645
Park, Robert E., 15, 16, 576, 593, 594
Parker, Robert E., 578, 637, 638
Parkinson, C. Northcote, 174
Parks, Rosa, 327
Parsons, Talcott, 16, 394, 475, 531
Patterson, Gregory A., 588
Paul, Alice, 290
Pearl, Daniel, 548
Pearlin, L. I., 75, 81
Pennell, Imogen, 553
Pepinsky, Harold E., 42
Pepperberg, Irene, 53
Perman, Lauri, 397
Perry, James M., 328
Persell, Caroline, 481
Persell, Caroline Hodges, 84, 260, 261
Peter, Laurence J., 174
Peterson, James L., 457
Petras, John W., 84
Petrini, Cathy, 181
Pettie, Sam, 592, 594, 595
Pettigrew, Thomas, 339
Phillips, John L., Jr., 66
Piaget, Jean, 65–66
Piliavin, Irving, 207, 208
Pillemer, Karl, 362, 363
Pilling, Arnold R., 350, 432
Pilling, D., 486
Pines, Maya, 61
Piven, Frances Fox, 114
Platt, Tony, 205
Ploski, Harry A., 596
Polenberg, Richard, 327
Pollak, Lauren Harte, 68
Polsby, Nelson W., 419
Polsky, Ned, 41
Pope, Liston, 511
Population Reference Bureau, 569
Porter, Bruce, 600

Portes, Alejandro, 416
Powell, Brian, 489
Powell, Colin, 600
Power, William, 301
Prakasa, V. V., 441
Prestage, Jewel E., 304–305
Preston, Howard L., 633
Price, Daniel O., 562
Pringle, M. Kellmer, 486
Prosser, William R., 261
Prud'Homme, Alex, 416
Prus, Robert, 42

Querlin, Maurise, 431
Quinney, Richard, 205

Rafferty, Jane A., 375
Rainwater, Lee, 397
Rao, V. Nandini, 441
Rathus, Spencer, 547
Raymond, Chris, 100
Read, Pers Paul, 41
Reagan, Ronald, 162, 252
Reckless, Walter C., 199
Redl, Fritz, 323, 424, 608
Reed, Susan, 645
Reich, Michael, 319
Reimers, Cordelia W., 449
Reinhold, Robert, 562
Reitz, Jeffrey, 25
Renzetti, Claire M., 284
Reppucci, N. Dickon, 457
Resler, Henrietta, 233
Revzin, Phillip, 375
Reynolds, Larry T., 84
Rhode, Deborah L., 74
Rhyne, Edwin H., 645
Rich, Spencer, 328
Richards, Bill, 187
Ricketts, Erol R., 261
Ridgon, Joan E., 489
Riesman, David, 195, 586
Riess, Volker, 608
Rigdon, Joan E., 204
Riley, James D., 386
Rist, Ray, 484, 485, 486
Roache, Joel, 24
Robertson, Ian, 41, 225, 234, 499
Robertson, Pat, 521
Robert Wood Johnson Foundation, 541
Robinson, John P., 78
Rockefeller, John D., 379
Rodash, Mary Flannery, 535, 536
Rodgers, Willard, 273
Rodriguez, Richard, 77
Roethlisberger, Fritz J., 128
Rogers, David, 418
Rogers, Joseph W., 200
Rohen, Thomas P., 470
Roosevelt, Franklin D., 162, 219, 334, 356, 417
Rootes, Chris A., 644
Rosaldo, Michelle Zimbalist, 286
Rose, Frederick, 600
Rose, Steven, 196
Rosenberg, Charles E., 534, 538
Rosenblatt, Roger, 616
Rosenfeld, Rachel, 297
Rosenstone, Steven J., 266
Rosenthal, Robert, 101, 485
Rossi, Alice, 83–84, 284
Rossi, Peter H., 129, 130, 131, 395
Rothenberg, Paula, 311
Rothenberg, Stuart, 616
Rothschild, Joyce, 181, 184

Rothschild, N., 72
Rubenstein, Carin, 155, 443
Rubenstein, Richard L., 310
Rubin, Lillian, 443, 445
Rubinson, Richard, 472
Ruesch, Hans, 432
Ruffenbach, Glenn, 361
Ruffins, Paul, 317
Ruggles, Patricia, 8, 271, 274
Rumbaugh, Duane, 52
Rumbaut, Ruben G., 416
Russell, Alan, 645
Russell, Diana, 459, 460
Russell, Diane E. H., 182
Russell, Dick, 569
Ruth, John L., 100
Rutter, Michael, 490
Rybczynski, Withold, 588

Sahlins, Marshall D., 143, 623, 625
Sakharov, Andrei D., 384
Sales, E., 84
Salholz, Eloise, 416
Samuelson, Paul A., 251
Samuelson, Robert, 357
Sapir, Edward, 37
Sargent, S. S., 42
Savage-Rumbaugh, Sue, 52, 53
Savoie, Ernest, 181
Sawhill, Isabel V., 261, 274
Sayres, William, 430
Schachter, Stanley, 69
Schaefer, Richard T., 305, 323, 334, 338
Schaet, Donald, 317
Scherschel, Patricia M., 204
Schiller, J. S., 487
Schnore, Leo, 575
Schoen, Robert, 442
Schoenberger, Richard, 297
Schoenherr, Richard A., 513
Schooler, Carmi, 75
Schor, Juliet, 391
Schottland, Charles I., 356
Schouten, John W., 82
Schrieke, Bertram J., 334
Schuler, Robert, 521
Schur, Edwin M., 47, 293
Schwartz, Barry, 114, 257
Schwartz, Felice N., 298, 299
Schwartz, Michael, 385
Schwartz, Mildred A., 402, 405
Schwartz, Pepper, 436, 451
Schwartz, William, 183
Schwendinger, Herman, 135, 574
Schwendinger, Julia R., 135, 574
Scott, Richard R., 328
Scully, Diana, 134, 135, 136
Seaver, W. J., 486
Segal, Elizabeth A., 273
Seghorn, Theoharis, 135
Sennett, Richard, 268
Service, Elman R., 625
Sewell, William H., 268
Shaffir, William, 105, 106, 542
Shakespeare, William, 93, 94
Shanas, Ethel, 361
Shannon, William H., 513
Shaw, Sue, 243
Sheldon, William, 196
Shepelak, Norma J., 275
Sherif, Carolyn, 318
Sherif, Muzafer, 318
Sherkat, Darren E., 522
Sherman, Spencer, 198
Shibutani, Tamotsu, 424, 602

Shim, Kelly H., 123
Shingles, Richard D., 266
Shively, JoEllen, 44
Shlaes, Amity, 313
Shreve, Herbie, 517
Siconolfi, Michael, 301
Signorielli, Nancy, 72
Silberman, Charles E., 202
Sills, David L., 173, 177
Silver, Isidore, 205
Simmel, Georg, 155
Simmons, Robert G., 68, 79, 84
Simon, Carl P., 390
Simon, David R., 204
Simon, Julian, 562, 570
Simon, Rita J., 302
Simons, Marlise, 640, 641
Simpson, George, 319
Simpson, George Eaton, 324, 325, 337
Singer, Dorothy G., 78–79
Singer, Jerome L., 69, 78–79
Singh, Ajit, 579
Singh, Susheela, 21
Sinnett, Nicholas, 460
Sixth Special Report, 551
Skeels, H. M., 60, 61
Skerry, Peter, 333
Small, Albion, 15, 25, 140
Smart, Barry, 625, 627, 640
Smith, Clark, 425
Smith, Daniel Scott, 21
Smith, Eliot R., 271
Smith, Harold, 359
Smith, James P., 329
Smith, Joel B., 642
Smith, Joseph, 515
Smith, Kristen F., 361, 362
Smith, Lee, 359
Smith-Lovin, Lynn, 154, 294
Snider, William, 147
Snipp, C. Matthew, 338
Snow, David A., 596
Snow, Margaret E., 445
Snyder, Mark, 99, 101, 486
Sociological Abstract, 291, 292
Sollie, Donna, 444
Sorensen, Andrew, 297
Sorensen, Jesper B., 549
Sorkin, Alan L., 338
Sorokin, Pitirim, 423, 626
Sorrentino, Constance, 430, 453, 456
South, Scott J., 442, 447
Spanier, Graham B., 456
Spector, Malcolm, 193, 614
Speizer, Jeanne J., 154
Spencer, Herbert, 10, 11, 20, 625
Spengler, Oswald, 626
Spitz, Renee, 60
Spitzer, Steven, 205
Spivak, Jonathan, 313
Spurr, Stephen J., 296
Srisang, Koson, 243
Srole, Leo, 263, 538
Stack, Steven, 497
Stafford, Linda, 250, 251, 254
Stampp, Kenneth M., 222
Stanley, Julian C., 487
Stanley, Kay O., 131
Stark, Elizabeth, 15, 50, 457, 511
Stark, Rodney, 497
Starna, William A., 221
Starr, Paul, 534
Statham, Anne, 153, 389
Statistical Abstract, 15, 75, 235, 250, 252, 266, 272, 273, 285, 293, 297, 303, 328, 346,

347, 359, 361, 384, 388, 416, 417, 418, 449, 455, 456, 472, 473, 519, 520, 529, 530, 539, 542, 550, 551, 554, 570
Steelman, Lala Carr, 489
Stein, Barry A., 179
Stein, Leonard, 543
Stein, Peter J., 300
Steinmetz, Susan, 458, 459
Sterba, James P., 514
Sternlieb, George, 587
Stevens, Amy, 600
Stevens, Charles W., 328
Stinnett, Nicholas, 461
Stipp, David, 53, 641
Stockard, Jean, 72, 294
Stockwell, John, 425
Stodgdill, Ralph M., 159
Stone, Gregory P., 582, 583, 584, 585, 586
Stone, Michael H., 197
Stouffer, Samuel, 293
Stout, Hilary, 491
Stout, Hillary, 549
Stover, Ronald G., 287
Strand, Paul, 147
Straus, Murray, 458, 459
Strauss, Anselm, 583
Stryker, Sheldon, 17
Sue, Stanley, 450
Sullivan, Mercer L., 203
Sutherland, Edwin H., 42, 197, 203
Suzuki, Bob H., 335, 448, 450
Swaggert, Jim, 521
Swasy, Alecia, 489
Swedish Institute, 553
Sweet, James A., 453
Sykes, Gresham, 211
Syzmanski, Albert, 266
Szasz, Thomas, 213, 214, 538
Szelenyi, Szonja, 382
Szymanski, Albert, 319

Tannen, Deborah, 294
Tedin, Kent L., 266
Teresa, Mother, 256
Terrace, Herbert S., 53
Thoits, Peggy A., 68
Thomas, Clarence, 300–301, 328
Thomas, Paulette, 642
Thomas, R. Roosevelt, Jr., 181
Thomas, William I., 17, 107, 450
Thompson, Willliam E., 114
Thorne, Barrie, 8, 71, 474
Thornton, Russell, 323, 336, 337, 338, 339
Tiffany, Paul, 419
Till, Emmett, 596
Tilly, Charles, 613
Timasheff, Nicholas S., 422
Timerman, Jacobo, 236
Tirpak, Dennis A., 642
Tiryakian, Edward A., 42
Tisdale, Hope, 574
Tittle, Charles R., 497
Toby, Jackson, 491
Tocqueville, Alexis de, 175, 616
Toffler, Alvin, 148
Tolba, Mostafa K., 641
Tolchin, Martin, 204, 550
Tolnay, Stewart E., 596
Tomaskovic, Donald, 266
Tomlinson, Richard, 563
Tönnies, Ferdinand, 99, 100, 623
Townsend, Robert C., 356
Toynbee, Arnold, 626
Trachtman, Roberta, 466
Treen, Joe, 198

Troeltsch, Ernst, 511
Trost, Cathy, 391
Trotsky, Leon, 234
Trudeau, Gary, 439
Trueba, Henry T., 147
Truman, Harry S, 257
Tucker, Belinda M., 442
Tumin, Melvin M., 202, 231–232
Turner, Bryan S., 410
Turner, Jonathan H., 20, 23, 480
Turner, Ralph, 596

Udy, Stanley H., Jr., 170
Ullman, Edward, 578
Ulrich, Patricia M., 263
USA Today, 39
Useem, Michael, 96, 384, 385

van den Haag, Ernest, 209
Van Lawick-Goodhall, Jane, 49
Vanneman, Reeve, 248
Vaughan, Diane, 457
Vaughan, Suzanne, 456
Vaughn, John C., 154
Vayda, Eugene, 554
Veblen, Thorstein, 374
Vega, William W., 330, 448
Vilarino, Jose Perez, 513
Vincent, Richard C., 72
Violas, P. C., 474
Von Hoffman, Nicholas, 132

Waddington, Conrad H., 572
Wagley, Charles, 312
Wagner, Nathaniel N., 450
Waldholz, Michael, 549, 636
Waldman, Peter, 519
Walker, Michael, 554
Walker, Tom, 588
Wallace, Anthony, 523
Wallace, Ruth A., 285
Wallerstein, Immanuel, 237, 240, 241, 623
Wallerstein, Judith S., 456, 457
Wall Street Journal, 264, 298, 380, 383, 454
Walters, Jonathan, 50
Ward, D. A., 302
Ward, R. E., 302
Waring, Elin, 203
Warner, Kenneth E., 550
Warner, W. Lloyd, 248
Washington, George, 474
Watkins, Ralph, 221
Watson, J. Mark, 42
Watson, Mark, 212
Watson, Paul, 645
Webb, Eugene J., 128
Weber, Max, 12, 13, 14, 166–167, 168, 169, 170, 180, 229–230, 259, 391, 402, 404, 405, 504, 505, 623
Webster, Noah, 471
Weintraub, Richard M., 441
Weisburd, David, 203
Weisner, Thomas S., 450
Weisskopf, Michael, 642
Weitz, Rose, 211
Weitzman, Lenore J., 71, 291, 457
Welch, Michael R., 497
Welch, Phinis R., 329
Welles, Orson, 601
Wells, H. G., 601
Wenneker, Mark, 320
Werthman, Carl, 207, 208
Wertz, Dorothy C., 536
Wertz, Richard W., 536
West, Candace, 294

Westergaard, John, 233
Westley, William A., 207
Wheeler, Stanton, 203
White, Burton L., 445
White, Joseph B., 187
White, Lynn K., 458
White, Ralph, 158
Whitehurst, Carol, 291
Whitman, David, 331, 332
Whitt, Allen, 184
Whitt, J. Allen, 181
Whorf, Benjamin, 37
Whyte, Martin, 441, 443, 445, 450, 453, 460, 461
Whyte, William H., 8, 114
Wilbanks, W., 302
Wilder, L. Douglas, 328
Wilford, John Noble, 629
Willhelm, Sydney M., 319
Williams, J. Allen, 72
Williams, K., 302
Williams, Richard A., 491
Williams, Robin M., Jr., 40, 43
Willis, Georgianna, 131, 395
Wilson, Barbara Foley, 458
Wilson, Edward O., 48
Wilson, James Q., 196, 208, 210, 329
Wilson, John, 522
Wilson, Margo, 302
Wilson, William J., 114, 261, 267, 319, 329, 586
Winn, Russ, 302–303
Winslow, Ron, 320
Wirth, Louis, 312, 579
Witte, Ann D., 390
Wohl, Richard, 583
Wolf, Rosalie S., 362
Wolf, Wendy C., 268
Wolfgang, Marvin E., 199, 302
Wolfinger, Raymond E., 266
Woods, John E., 204
Woodward, C. Vann, 338
Woodward, Kenneth L., 519
Wooldredge, John, 442
World Health Organization, 528
World Population Profile, 565
Worsley, Peter, 610
Wright, Beverly Hendrix, 644
Wright, Eric, 258–259
Wright, Erik Olin, 319
Wright, James D., 131, 395
Wrong, Dennis H., 84

Yamada, Ken, 635
Yinger, J. Milton, 318, 319, 324, 325, 337, 505
Yllo, Kersti, 135, 459
Yoels, William, 583, 584, 585, 586
Young, Lawrence A., 513
Young, Robert J., 450
Yu, David C., 518

Zakuta, Leo, 18, 435
Zald, Mayer N., 611, 617
Zander, Alvin, 156
Zawitz, Marianne, 208
Ziegenhals, Gretchen E., 100
Zill, Nicholas, 457
Zinn, Maxine Baca, 387, 436, 442, 447
Zipp, John F., 416
Znaniecki, Florian, 450
Zola, Irving K., 528
Zuboff, Shoshana, 149, 390, 623, 637, 638
Zuckerman, Harriet, 296
Zurcher, Louis A., 596

Subject Index

Abkhasians, 343–346, 350, 354
Ablution, 224
Aborigines, 143
Abortion, social movement of, 614–615
Absenteeism, 183
Abstract reasoning, 67
Abuse
  of the elderly, 361, 362–363
  family, 458–460
  types of, 458–459
Access information, 583
Accountability
  in collective behavior, 593
  position and, 231
Acculturation, 467
Achieved statuses, 92, 146
Acid rain, 642
Activism, 181
Activity theory, 355
Adaptation, religion and, 497
Adolescence
  deviance in, 212
  historical perspective, 82
  peer group influence in, 77
  socialization in, 82
Adultery
  cross-cultural perspective of, 193
Adulthood, 82
Advertising, 608–609
  power of, 381
Affirmative action, 179, 181
Afghanistan War, 423
AFL-CIO, 331
African Americans, 36, 327–329
  discrimination against, 327, 329
  families of, 446–447
  gains of, 328–329
  King's leadership and, 327–328
  poverty of, 275, 328–329
  relations with other minorities, 322–325, 332
  segregation and, 324
  social mobility and, 270
  status of, 329
Age cohort, 354
Ageism, 352–353
  mass media and, 353–354
Aggregates, 149
Aging
  among the Abkhasians, 343–346
  conflict perspective, 356–360
  cross-cultural comparisons, 350–352
  functionalist perspective, 354–355
  historical perspective, 353

in industrialized nations, 346–348
  social factors in, 344–348
  stereotypes, 352–353
  symbolic interactionist perspective, 348–354
  worldwide trends, 347–348
  see also Elderly; Old age
Agricultural economies, 373–374, 391
  medium of exchange in, 376
Agricultural revolution, 144
Agricultural societies, 144–145, 344
Agta, 282
AIDS, 36, 132, 533, 546–549, 605
  stigma of, 194
  transmission of, 547–548
Alcohol, 550–551
Alienation
  bureaucratic, 170–172
  in the cities, 578–580
  factory system as a source of, 631
Alien Land Act, 334
Alternative social movements, 612
Altruistic suicide, 11
Amazonian Indians, 641
America 2000, 490
American Association of Retired Persons
    (AARP), 357, 360
American Journal of Sociology, 15
American Medical Association (AMA),
    534–535
American Revolution, 8
American society. *See* United States
American Sociological Association, 26
American Soldier, The (Stouffer), 293
Amish, 100, 153, 502, 514, 515, 529
Analects, 510
Analysis
  content, 117
  of research results, 117, 121
  secondary, 135, 123
Anarchy, 419
Andaman Islanders, 422
Anglo-conformity, 325
Animal rights movement, 611
Animals
  culture of, 49–53
  deprived, 61–63
  domestication of, 143–144
  instincts of, 49
  language of, 51–53
  mating behavior in, 50
Animism, 506
Anomie, 11–12, 149
  adaptation to, 201
  social class and, 202

Anorexia nervosa, 529
Anthropology, 4, 5
  cultural and physical, 4
Anticipatory socialization, 79
Antisemitism, 506
Apartheid, 225, 324, 504
Appearance, in role playing, 104–105
Applied sociology, 25–27
Apprenticeship, 81
Arab Brotherhood, 152
Arab countries, social stratification in, 227
Armenians, 325
Arunta, 422
Aryans, 310–311, 607
Asch experiment, 159–160
Ascribed statuses, 92, 146
Asian Americans, 330, 332, 334–336, 572
  cultural and ethnic diversity of, 335
  discrimination against, 334
  families of, 448–449
  intergroup rivalries, 334
  most recent immigrants, 335–336
Assimilation, 181
  cultural, 325
  forced and permissable, 325
  of immigrants, 326–327, 416
Atlanta University, 15
Attachments, 200
Attitude, and prejudice, 314–315
Auschwitz, 310
Authoritarian leader, 158
Authoritarian personality, 317–318
Authority, 23
  bureaucratic, 170, 405
  charismatic, 406–407, 408–409
  coercion and, 402–409
  collapse of, 404–405
  as ideal type, 407–408
  legitimate violence and, 403–405
  obedience to, 160–161
  parental, 405
  patterns of, in families, 434
  rational-legal, 405–406, 408
  social movements and, 613
  traditional, 405, 408
  transfer of, 408–409
Automobile, effects of, 632–634
Automobile industry, social class in, 262–263
Average, 120

Background assumptions, 106–107
Back stages, 103
Bandwagon, 610
Barter, 376

Basic demographic equation, 571
Battering, 458–459
Beliefs, 496
Berlin Wall, 382
Beverly Hills Supper Club fire, 601–602
Bias
    cultural, in intelligence testing, 480
    gender, 291 (*see also* Sexism; Sexual
        harassment)
    interview, 122
    of male physicians, 542
    in research, 120, 121
    in samples, 121
Bible, 506
Bible Belt, 517
Bigotry, 314, 334
Bilateral system of descent, 433
Bilingualism, 39
    and loss of culture, 77
Biology
    and aging, 350
    and deviance, 196
    and gender behavior, 281–285
Biomedicine, 148
Birds, culture of, 50
Birth order, 445
Birth rate, 572
    crude, 569
Black Panthers, 360
Blended families, 451
Books, children's, gender stereotypes in,
    71–72
"Boom," economic, 393
Boot camp, 80
Born again, 501, 507
Boston Tea Party, 389
Bourgeoisie, 10, 23, 228
    petty, 259
Brajuha research, 131
Brazilians, 325
Buddhism, 496, 509
Buerger's disease, 550
Bureaucracies
    alienation in, 170–172
    careers in, 178–180
    college, 171
    dysfunctions of, 170–175
    essential characteristics of, 169–170
    humane, 181–182
    ideal and real types, 170
Bureaucratic alienation, 170–172
Bureaucratic authority, 405
Bureaucratic engorgement, 174
Bureaucratic incompetence, 174–175
Bureaucrats, alienated, 172
Burundi, 47
Business, women in, 179
Busing, 488–489

Caldecott Award, 71, 72
California Foreign Miners' Act, 334
Calvinism, and capitalism, 167
Canada, health care in, 553
Capitalism, 23, 167, 378–380, 626
    compared to socialism, 381, 382–383
    corporate, 384–385
    criticisms of, 381–382
    ideology of, 381, 382–383
    laissez-faire, 378–380
    Marx on, 167–168
    multinational corporations, 386
    and Protestantism, 12
    and rationalization, 167

and religion, 167, 504–505
    and social class, 259
    transformation of society through, 623
    welfare (or state), 378–380
Capitalist class, 205, 259–260, 262, 420
Capitalist world economy, 241
Card stacking, 610
Career choice, 79
Careers, in bureaucracies, 178–180
Cargo cults, 609
Casey v. *Planned Parenthood,* 615
Caste system, 227
    in India, 223–225, 441, 504
    in South Africa, 223, 225
Catholicism. *See* Roman Catholic Church
Centers for Disease Control, 547–548
Centrist parties, 413
Ceremony, degradation, 80, 208
Challenger, 622, 628
Change, 8
Charisma, 406, 511
    routinization of, 408–409
Charismatic authority, 406–407, 408–409
    threat posed by, 406–407
Charismatic leader, 511
Checking accounts, 377
Checks and balances, 419
Cherokee Indians, 336
Chicanos, 330, 331, 333
Chief executive officers (CEOs)
    income of, 252–253, 298
    power of, 385
Childbirth, 443–444
    midwifery and, 536
    postponing, 572
    and social experiences, 287
Child care, 454–455
Childhood
    historical perspective, 81
    perception of, 18
    socialization in, 81–82
Child rearing
    birth order and, 445
    cross-cultural perspective on, 432
    gender styles in, 444–445
    sex typing and, 71
    social class and, 74–75, 265–266, 444–445
Children of the night, 215, 216
Chile, 385
Chimpanzees
    Goodall's research on, 49
    language research of, 51–53
    see also Monkeys
China
    aging in, 351–352
    economy of, 382–383
    health care in, 553
    life expectancy in, 348
Chinese Americans, 334
    families of, 448
    prejudice against, 314
Chinese Exclusion Act, 334
Chippewa Indians, 44
Christianity, 501, 506–507
Christian Motorcyclists Association (CMA),
    517
Chrysler plant, 183
Church, 496, 512
Church of England, 513
CIA, 385
Circular reaction, 593–594
Cities
    constant change of, 585–588

edge, 588
    historical perspective, 574–576
    opportunities and problems of, 578–585
    psychological separation from suburbs, 586
    trends in, 587–588
    see also Urbanization
Citizenship, 409–410, 410
    universal, 410–411
City-states, 409
Civil disobedience, 327–328
Civilizations, life course of, 626
Civil Rights Act of 1964, 328
    Title VII of, 181
Civil Rights Act of 1968, 328
Civil rights movement, 181
Clan system, 226–227
Class, 225. *See also* Social class
Class conflict, 10–11, 232
Class consciousness, 228, 232–234
Class system, 225. *See also* Social class
Clinical sociology, 25–27
Close-ended questions, 122
Clothing fads and fashions, 604
Coalition government, 413
Coalitions, 155
Cocaine, 126
Coercion, 402
Cognitive development, Piaget's theory of,
    66–67
Cohabitation, versus marriage, 453–454
Cold war, 424
Coleman report, 487
Collective behavior, 592–593
    anatomy of a lynching, 597–599
    emergent norms, 596–597
    fads and fashions, 604
    "herd mentality," 593
    minimax strategy in, 597
    panics, 601–602
    rationality of the crowd, 595–599
    rational process as a component of, 597
    riots, 599–601
    rumors, 602–604
    social unrest and circular reaction, 593–594
    stages of, 594–595
    transformation of the individual, 593
    urban legends, 604–605
    see also Social movements
Collective decision making, in Japan, 185–186
Collective impulse, 594
Collective mind, 593
College campuses, racism on, 316
Colonialism, 240
    internal, 324
Commitment
    career, 79
    company, 185
    inner control and, 200
    religious, 520
Common sense, 6, 7, 114
Communication
    cultural differences in, 36
    and cultural leveling, 53–54
    in dramaturgy, 103–106
    gestures and, 38–40
    language and, 39
    in marriage, 439–440
Communism
    compared to Marxism, 10
    as religion, 499
Community
    moral, 496, 501–502
    sense of, 578, 580

Compartmentalize, 323
Compensatory education, 487
Competition
  in American society, 186
  capitalist, 379
  in educational system, 473–474
  market, 378
  in religion, 520
  for scarce resources, 232
  socialist, 380
Computer chip, 148, 623
Computers
  abuse of, 639
  for analysis of research, 122
  concerns about, 638–639
  and depersonalized relationships, 637
  and education, 635–636
  effects of, 634–638
  and job multiskilling and deskilling, 637–638
  and medicine, 636
  and war and the military, 636
Concentric-zone model, 576–577
Concrete operational stage, in Piaget's theory, 66–67
Conflict perspective
  on aging, 356–360
  on the American political system, 420–421
  on corporate culture, 183
  on deviance, 204–205
  on education, 477–484
  on family, 435–436
  managing diversity, 181
  on the power elite and ruling class, 420–421
  on prejudice, 318
  on religion, 502–504
  and school socialization, 76
  on social control, 195
  on social institutions, 96–97
  on social stratification, 232–233
  on work, 394
Conflict theory, 17, 23–24, 88
Conformity
  cultural framework of, 192–193
  to cultural goals, 201–202
  norms and, 194
  to peer pressure, 159–160
  social class and, 73–74
  to stereotypes, 101
Confucianism, 496, 510, 513
Conspicuous consumption, 374
Constitution, U. S., 419, 519
Contagion, 593, 595
Content analysis, 117
Contradictory class locations, 259
Control theory, 199–200
Convergence theory, 383–384
Cooperatives, 184
Core nations, 241
Corporate capitalism, 384–385
Corporate culture
  hidden values in, 178–180
  humanizing the, 180–183
Corporate elite, 179–180
Corporations, 384
  in Japan, 184–187
  multinational, 243–244, 386–387
  political power of, 420–421
  separation of ownership and management in, 384
  top twenty-five, 386
  values in, 178–180
  women career paths in, 299
Correlation coefficient, 126
Correlations, 125

covariance, 126
  perfect negative, 126
  perfect positive, 126
  spurious, 125–127
Correspondence principle, 480–481
Cosmic Background Explorer (COBE), 629
Cosmology, 501
Cost of living, divorce and, 457
Counterculture, 42
Courtship, 440, 633
Covary, 126
Cowboys, 44, 187
COYOTE (Call Off Your Old Tired Ethics), 211
Credential society, 466–467
Credit card, 377
Crime, 197
  adult, by juveniles, 210
  cost of, 204
  national surveys on, 123
  official statistics, 207–208
  public fear of, 210
  social values and, 201, 202–205
  street, 196
  white-collar, 203–204
Criminal justice system
  inconsistency in, 205
  social class and, 204–205, 207–208, 267
Crowd behavior. See Collective behavior
Crude birthrate, 569
Crude death rate, 569
Cuban Americans, 330
Cubans, 448
Cueva Indians, 641
Cults, 511–512, 514–515
  cargo, 609
Cultural assimilation. See Assimilation
Cultural beliefs, and health, 529
Cultural bias, in intelligence testing, 480
Cultural diffusion, 53–54, 144
Cultural goals, 201
Cultural lag, 145, 630
Cultural leveling, 53–54
Cultural options, 596
Cultural relativism, practicing, 35
Cultural transmission, 473–474
Cultural universals, 47–49
Culture, 5
  American work, 186
  animal, 49–53
  clashing, 198, 313, 448–449, 450
  components of, 5, 35
  concept of, 32–35, 91
  content of, 67
  dominant, 42
  and gender behavior, 281–285
  ideal and real, 47, 193
  ideational, 626
  language and, 59
  loss of, through socialization, 77
  material, 33, 145
  nonmaterial, 33, 145
  peer, 474
  of poverty, 242, 274
  secularization of, 518–519
  sensate, 626
  symbolic, 35
  and taken-for-granted orientations to life, 33
  within us, 34, 67
  see also Corporate culture
Culture contact, 36
Culture shock, 34
Currencies, 375, 376
Custody, child, 457

Customs, 47, 405. See also Culture
Cyclical theories, 625–626

Dani, 432
Dark Ages, 467
Data
  analysis of, 121
  collecting, 116
Day care, 454–455
Death, 83, 364–368
  coming to terms with, 366
  controversy about, 544–545
  defining, 544
  family role in, 22–23
  language of, 365
  leading causes of, 532–533
  see also Dying
Death rate. See also Mortality rate
Death rate, crude, 569
Debit card, 377
Decision making
  bottom-up, 186
  collective, in Japan, 185–186
  groupthink, 161–162
Declaration of Independence, 519
Decline of the West, The (Spengler), 626
Deferred gratification, 275
Definitions, operational, 116, 117
Degradation ceremonies, 80, 208
Dehumanization
  characteristics of, 608
  Nazis and, 608
  nursing homes and, 361–362
  war and, 424
Deinstitutionalization, 214, 216, 538
Delinquency, 206
Democracy, 409–410
  direct, 410
  in Europe, 413–414
  representative, 410
  value of, 43
Democracy in America (Tocqueville), 175
Democratic leader, 158
Democratic party, 266, 412–413
Democratic socialism, 380, 383, 384
Demographic equation, 570–571
Demographic transition, 563
Demographic variables, 568–570
Demography, 560
Demonstrations. See Collective behavior;
  Social movements
Denomination, 514
Dependency, in old age, 360–364
Dependency ratio, 357
Dependency theory, 241–242
Dependent variables, 125
Depersonalization
  computers and, 637
  in medicine, 541–542
Deposit receipts, 376
Deprivation, animal, 61–63
Deprivation theory, 616
  relative, 616
Descent, patterns of, 433
Desexualization, 108–109
Deterrence, 209–210
Deviance, 192–197
  biological, psychological, and sociological explanations of, 196–197
  conflict perspective, 204–205
  cross-cultural perspective, 193, 198
  cultural framework of, 192–193
  embracing, 212–213
  as functional for society, 200

functionalist perspective, 200
humane approach to, 215–216
labeling, 206–207, 208
medicalization of, 213–215
as mental illness, 213–215
neutralizing, 211
official, 195
primary, secondary, and tertiary, 210–211
reactions to, 205–210
relativity of, 192–194, 199
sanctioning, 206
sexual, 210–211
and social class, 207
social control and, 194–195
sociological perspective, 192, 196, 197
symbolic interactionist perspective, 193, 197–200
see also Norms
Dialectical process, 626
Dictatorships, 411
Diet, and aging, 344–345
Differential association theory, 197–199
Diffusion, 630
Diffusion of responsibility, 157, 585
Direct democracy, 410
Disabled, as master status, 93
Disabling environments, 551–552
Discovery, 629
Discrimination
dominant group and, 312
educational, 481, 482
in employment, 181
in hiring, 296
individual, 320–322
institutional, 320–322, 339
by IQ, 479–480
prejudice and, 313–316
racial, 320, 327, 334
religious, 313
self-fulfilling prophecy and, 319–320
stereotypes and, 319–320
against women, 283, 296–299
in the workplace, 296–299
Diseases
causes of, 537
and life expectancy, 569
threats to health, 546–549
Disengagement theory, 354–355
Distance zones, 102–103
Diversity, managing, in the workplace, 181
Divest, 380
Divine right of kings, 236, 504
Division of labor, 11, 98, 142, 144
in bureaucracies, 169
in industrialized societies, 383
Divorce
changes in the laws of, 19
children of, 456–457
conflict theory perspective, 24
cross-cultural perspective, 433
custody and, 457
ex-spouses and, 457
functionalist perspective, 21
meaning of, 19
and remarriage, 455–456
statistics, 455–456
symbolic interactionist perspective, 18–19
Documents, in research, 123–124
Domestication revolution, 143–144
Dominant group, 312
Downward social mobility, 268, 270
Dramaturgy, 103–106
Drug dealing, 389
Drug problem, 491

Drugs
threats to health, 550–551
use of, 126
Dumping, 546
Dyads, 155, 443
Dying, 364–368
effects of industrialization on, 365–366
hospices and, 367–368
Kübler-Ross's stages of, 366
process of, 365–366
see also Death
Dysfunctions, 20
latent, 20

Early adulthood, 82
Earth First!, 644, 645
Ecclesia, 513
Economic cycles, 394
Economics, 4, 5
micro- and macro-, 4
Economic sectors, 387–388
Economic systems
historical perspective, 372–375
medium of exchange, 376–377
world, 378–384
see also Capitalism; Socialism
Economists, 5
Economy(s)
agricultural, 373–374, 391
defined, 373
global, 270
horticultural, 373
hunting and gathering, 373, 391
industrial, 373
mixed, 384
pastoral, 373
postindustrial, 374–375, 377
role of government in, 417
subsistence, 373
underground, 389–390
of the U. S., 397–398
Ecosabotage, 644–645
Education
busing and, 488–489
compensatory, 487
compulsory, 467
computer's effect on, 635–636
conflict perspective, 477–484
credential society and, 466–467
cross-cultural perspective, 468–471
development of modern, 467–468
formal, 467
in the former Soviet Union, 470–471
functionalist perspective, 472–476
funding for, 477–479
funneling effect of, 481, 482
gatekeeping function in, 475
gender inequality in, 290–292
in Great Britain, 468–469
higher, "cooling out" function of, 483
how we can improve schools, 487–492
intelligence testing and, 479–480
in Japan, 469–470
mandatory laws on, 467
national report card, 489–490
and patriotism, 474
public, 472
sex, 476
sex-linked aspirations, 290
and social change, 475–476
social class and, 267
as a social institution, 95
social integration and, 474–475
social mobility and, 268, 270

symbolic interactionist perspective, 484–487
teacher expectations and, 484–487
in the Third World, 467
tracking and, 475, 484–485
universal, 471–472
in the U. S., 471–472, 481–482
value of, 44
Elderly
abuse of, 361, 362–363
care of, 21
changing sentiment about, 357
dependency of, 360–364
independence of, 361
medical care for, 357, 359–360
poverty of, 363–364
social devaluation and, 83
stereotypes of, 83, 357, 360
suicide and, 364, 366–367
in the U. S., 346
see also Aging; Old age
Elections, 412–413, 414
cost of, 418–419
Electronic church, 521
Elementary Forms of the Religious Life, The (Durkheim), 496
Embarassment, 105
Emergent norms, 596–597
Emigrants, demographics, 569
Emotions
cultural differences in expression of, 69
development of, 68–69
environmental influences on, 69
norms of, 69
as social constraints, 70
socialization and, 68–70
Emphysema, 550
Employee stock ownership, 182
Empty nest, myth of, 445
Endogamy, 224, 433
"English First" movement, 330, 332
Entrepreneurial immigrants, 416
Environment
concern for, 46
disabling, 551–552
industialization and, 552
technology and, 646
see also Nature versus nuture; Social environment
Environmental degradation, 640–641
Environmental movement, 611, 643–644
Environmental problems
in the Second World, 641–643
in the Third World, 643
today, 641–642
Environmental sociology, 645–646
Epidemiology, 532
Equal Employment Opportunity Commission, 300
Equality
greater to lesser, 144
value of, 43
Erotic property, 442
Eskimos, 37–38, 351, 352, 422, 432
Essay on the Principle of Population, An (Malthus), 560
Ethics, research, 127, 128, 131–133, 161
Ethnic, 311
Ethnic groups, 311–312
social class divisions within, 333
see also Minority groups
Ethnicity, 311
health and, 321
and political participation, 416
and religion, 523

Ethnic relations
    basic concepts in, 310–312
    principles for improving, 339
    in the U. S., 325–339
Ethnocentrism, 35
Ethnomethodology, 106–107
Europe
    democracy in, 413–414
    economies in, 375, 383
    history of wars in, 423
    Industrial Revolution in, 8
    population growth in, 560, 563
European Community (EC), nations of, 375
European Free Trade Association (EFTA),
    nations of, 375
Euthanasia, 544–545
Evolutionary theories, 624–625
Exchange mobility, 268
Exchange theory, 89
Executive Order 9066, 334
Exogamy, 433
Experimental group, 127
Experiments, 125–128
Exploiters, 596
Exponential growth curve, 560–561
Expressive leader, 157
Extended family, 432, 435
Extinction, of plant and animal species, 641,
    642

Face-saving behavior, 105
Factory system, 631
Fads, 604
False consciousness, 229, 233
Families
    abuse in, 458–460
    African-American, 446–447
    Asian-American, 448–449
    blended, 451
    conflict perspective on, 435–436
    cross-cultural perspective, 430–434
    defining, 430–432
    dysfunctions of, 435
    essential functions of, 434–435
    extended, 432, 435
    functionalist perspective, 434–435
    future of, 461–462
    gender roles in, 71, 435–436
    Hispanic-American, 447–448
    homosexual, 451
    incest in, 435, 460
    industrialism and, 21
    Korean-American, 450
    in later life, 445
    life cycle of, 440–446
    nuclear, 432
    one-parent, 449–450
    of orientation, 432
    as primary group, 150
    of procreation, 432
    in the 1800s, 21–22
    shifting foundations of, 435
    and social class, 73–74, 265
    as a social institution, 95
    socialization and, 73–74
    symbolic interaction perspective, 439–440
    that work, 460–461
    trends in American, 451–455
    two-paycheck, 436–438
    without children, 450–451
    working women and, 299
    see also Child rearing; Marriage
Famine, 426, 564–565
FBI, 229

Fecundity, 568
Federal debt, 358–359
Federal Reserve Board, 393
Fee-for-service, 535
Femininity, 283, 293
Feminism
    and Freudian theory, 68
    and gender stereotypes in books, 72
    rise of, 289, 290
Feminization of poverty, 272
Feral children, 58
Fertility, 568–569
Fertility rate, 568–569
Fiat money, 377
Fieldwork, 124–125
Filipinos, 335
First social revolution, 143–144
First World, 237
    health issues, 529
    industrialization and urbanization in, 579
Flexner Report, 535
Folkways, 41
Food, and famine, 564–565
Formal operational stage, in Piaget's theory, 67
Formal organizations, 168
"Fortune 500," 384
Foster homes, 61
Founding Fathers, 519
Freedom, value of, 43
French Revolution, 8, 9
Freud's theory, 67–68
Front stages, 103
Functional analysis, 20, 21
Functional illiterates, 489
Functionalism, 17, 20, 88
    structural, 20
Functionalist perspective
    on aging, 354–355
    on the American political system, 419–420
    on deviance, 200–204
    on education, 472–476
    on family, 434–435
    managing diversity, 181
    on pluralism, 419–420
    on prejudice, 318
    on religion, 497–499
    and social control, 194–195
    on social institutions, 95–96
    on social stratification, 230–231
    on work, 392–393
Functional requisites, 95–96
Functions, 20
    latent, 20
    manifest, 20
Fundamentalism, 507
Fundamentalist revival, 521

Games, and development of self, 65
Gatekeeping, 475
Gemeinschaft, 98–99, 146, 517, 566, 580, 623,
    627
Gender
    as master status, 92
    versus sex, 280–281
    and social stratification, 227–228
    see also Sex
Gender bias. See also Sexism
Gender bias, in medicine, 291, 542–543
Gender inequality
    in conversation, 294
    cross-cultural, 285–286
    in education, 290–292
    in everyday life, 292–294
    and prestige of work, 286

    roots of, 286–288
    sex-typing of work, 285–286
    in the U. S., 289–294
    and violence, 302
    in the workplace, 294–301
Gender relations, changes in, 305–306
Gender roles, 71
    effect of the automobile on, 633–634
    in the family, 435–438
    in marriage, 265
    social class and, 265
Gender socialization, 70–73
Gender stereotypes
    in children's books, 71–72
    and socialization, 74
Gender stratification, 280
    biology or culture, 281–285
    male and female differences, 280–285
Generalizability, 125
Generalizations, 5–6
Generalized others, 65
Genetic predisposition, 196
Genetics, 48. See also Heredity
Genocide, 322–323
    of Jews, 322–325
    of Native Americans, 323, 336–337
Gentrification, 587
Germany
    environmental problems in, 644
    social change in, 607
    see also Nazis
Gerontocracy, 351
Gesellschaft, 98–99, 100, 517, 566, 580, 623
Gestapo, 411
Gestures, 38–40
    cultural differences in, 38
    universal, 40
"Glass ceiling," 298
"Glass walls," 298
Glittering generality, 610
Global economy, 270
Globalization, 241
Global stratification, 237–239
    historical perspective, 240–242
    maintaining, 242–244
Global warming, 642
Goal conflicts, 173
Goal displacement, 173
Gold standard, 376–377
Gossip, 603
Government, 4
    coalition, 413
    groupthink in, 162
    historical perspective, 409
    types of, 409–411
    see also Political power
Gramm-Rudman provisions, 358
Gratification, deferred and immediate, 275
Graying of America, 346
Gray Panthers, 360, 363
Great Britain
    education in, 468–469
    health care in, 553
    social stratification in, 233–234
Great Depression, 356, 417, 572
Great U-turn of American society, 397
Greek Orthodox Church, 507
Greeks, 7, 221
Greenhouse effect, 642
Green parties, 644
Gross national product, 377
Group dynamics, 154–162
    conformity, 159–160
    decision making, 161–162

leadership, 156–159
obedience, 160–161
size, 155–156
see also Groups
Group hiring, 187
Group promotions, 187
Groups, 94–95, 140–141
and aggregates, 149
control, 127
defined, 140
experimental, 127
extremist, 177
in- and out-, 151–152
involuntary and voluntary memberships in, 94
labeling, 206–207
political power in, 402
primary, 149–150
reference, 152–153
secondary, 150–151, 168
small, 155
within society, 149–154
work, 182–183
see also Group dynamics; Societies
Group size, 155–156
and willingness to help strangers, 157
Groupthink, 161–162
Guilds, 168
Gypsies, 323, 607

Halfway houses, 210
Hara-kiri, 193
Hartijans, 224
Hawthorne effect, 128
Hawthorne experiments, 128
Head Start, 487
Health
cultural beliefs and, 529
defining, 528
effects of social class on, 529
historical patterns of, 532–534
issues in, 539–546
mental, 533–534
physical, 532–533
public, 548–549
subcultural patterns and lifestyle and, 529
symbolic interactionist perspective, 528
threats to, 546–552
treatment or prevention, 552–555
see also Medecine; Mental health
Health care
adequacy issue, 541
as a commodity, 539–540
costs of, 539–540
depersonalization and, 541–542
for the elderly, 357, 359–360
inequality in distribution, 541
international stratification in, 529–531
issues in, 539–546
in other countries, 553–554
search for alternatives, 552–555
Health insurance, 545–546
Health maintenance organizations (HMOs), 546
Heredity, versus environment, 59
Hidden curriculum, 76, 477–484
Hinduism, 496, 504, 508, 514
Hiring
discrimination in, 296
group, 187
in Japan, 184
Hispanic Americans, 36, 39, 330–333, 572
education and, 77
families of, 447–448
politics of, 331–333

population of, 181, 330, 332
poverty of, 271, 273, 321, 364
see also Mexican Americans
History, issue of perspective in teaching, 337–338
Hmong, 146, 147, 198, 200
Holistic medicine, 555
Holocaust, 323, 607
Homeless, 1–2, 14, 264
counting the, 129–131
mental illness and, 214
perspectives on, 25
Homogamy, 442
Homosexual families, 451
Homosexual marriage, 431
Honor, concept of, 199
Hopelessness, 14
Hopi Indians, 37
Horticultural economies, 373
Horticultural societies, 143–144
Hospices, 367–368
Hospital care, cost of, 538
Hospitals, 367–368
average stay, 546
historical perspective, 537
and professionalization of medicine, 536–537
Hottentots, 323
Humanitarianism, value of, 43
Humanizing a work setting, 181
Human nature, 58–60
Humanness, 63
Humphreys research, 131–133
Hunting and gathering economies, 373, 391
Hunting and gathering societies, 142–143, 373, 409
"Hurried" child, 445
Hypothesis, 116, 117, 127

Ideal culture, 47
Ideal type, 170
Ideational culture, 626
Identical twins, nature versus nuture and, 59
Identity, deviant, 212
Ideology, 222
how technology changes, 631
Ifaluk, 70
Illegal immigrants, 330, 570
Illegitimate opportunity structures, 203
Illegitimate opportunity theory, 202–204
Illness
causes of, 537
classification of, 546
leading causes of death, 532–533
sick role, 531–532
sociological perspective, 528
see also Mental illness
Imitation, 65
Immigrants
assimilation of, 326–327, 416
clashing cultures of, 448–449, 450
demographics, 569
discrimination against, 334
entrepreneurial, 416
European, 416
most recent, 416
political participation of, 416
stereotypes of, 326–327
Imperialism, 240
Impression management, 104
Imprisonment, 208–210
reasons for, 208–210
recidivism rate, 208, 210
Incapacitation, 210
Incest, cultural definitions, 47

Incest taboo, 435
Income
distribution of, 251–253
equality of, under socialism, 380
gender discrimination in, 296–299
illegal, 389
racial and ethnic inequalities, 375
in the U. S., 397
wealth versus, 249–250
Income inequality, around the world, 238
Incompetence, level of, 174–175
Indentured service, 222
Independent variable, 125, 127–128
India
arranged marriage in, 441
caste system in, 223–225, 441, 504
population growth in, 579
religion and culture in, 514
Individual discrimination, 320–322
Individualism
in American society, 186
in educational system, 473
value of, 47
Industrial economies, 374
medium of exchange in, 376–377
Industrialization, 374
and the environment, 552
and the family, 21
formal organizations and, 168
and Gesellschaft, 98
and population growth, 570–571
social change following, 145–146
stages of, 236–237
and the Third World, 623
Industrial Revolution, 7, 8, 82, 145, 575
Industrial societies, 141, 145–146, 148, 194
aging in, 346–348
social class in, 258–264
Industrial technology, 630
Inflation, 377
Information age, 374–375. *See also* Communications
Information revolution, 148–149
In-groups, 151–152, 176
Inheritance, patterns of, 433
Inner circle, 385
Inner control, 199–200
Innovation, 202
Instincts, animal, 49
Institutional discrimination, 320–322, 339
Institutionalization, in social movements, 613, 614
Institutionalized chidren, 60–61
Institutionalized means, 201
Institutions
total, 79–80
see also Social institutions
Instrumental leaders, 156
Insurance, health, 545–546
Intelligence quotient (IQ), 479–480
Intelligence testing, 479–480, 487
cultural bias in, 480
institutionalized children and, 61
national report card on, 489–490
performance of children and, 66
Interaction, styles of, 207
Intergenerational mobility, 267–268
Intergroup relations, 322–325, 332
Interlocking directorates, 385
Internal colonialism, 324
Internal Revenue Service (IRS), 389–390
International stratification, shifts in, 624
International Telephone and Telegraph Company (ITT), 385

Interviews, 122
  bias in, 122
    structured, 122
    unstructured, 122
Intimacy, in groups, 155
Intimate distance, 102
Inventions, 145, 574, 629
Involuntary memberships, 94
IQ tests. *See* Intelligence testing
Iran, religion in, 518–519
Iran-Contra scandal, 162
Iran-Iraq war, 423–424
Iron law of oligarchy, 178, 179
Islam, 507–508, 512
Isolation
    children and, 58–59
    monkeys and, 62–63
Italy, gestures in, 40

Japan
    aging in, 350
    changing culture of, 54
    corporate model in, 184–187
    education in, 469–470
    sexual harassment in, 298
    suicide in, 193
    women in, 36
Japanese Americans, 334
    families of, 448
    success of, 335
Jealousy, sociological base of, 442
Jews
    Hitler and, 318, 322–323, 506, 607
    social stratification among, 226
Job, versus profession, 394–397
Job deskilling, 637
Job multiskilling, 637
Jobs, loss of, 638
Job satisfaction, 397
Job security
    in Japan, 184–185
    in the U. S., 184–185
Job skills, 466
Judaism, 500, 505–506
Juveniles, adult crimes by, 210

Kaiapo Indians, 640
Kamasutra, 441
Kamikaze pilots, 11, 193
Kanuri, 433
Karma, 508
Kayapo Indians, 641
Kindergarten, 478
Kiwi Papuans, 227–228
Koran, 507
Korean Americans, families of, 450
Kurds, 426

Labeling
    deviance, 200, 206–207, 208
    re-, 211
    self-, 211
Labels
    ethnic, 322–323
    Nazis' use of, 608
    racial and ethnic, 319
    and selective perception, 319
    that create prejudice, 319
    see also Stereotypes
Labor, division of. *See* Division of labor
Laissez-faire capitalism, 378–380
Laissez-faire leader, 158
Language, 35–38
    in animals, 51–53

as a communal tie, 100
    and communication, 36–37, 39
    and cultural change, 39
    and culture, 59
    and perception, 37–38
Latchkey children, 454–455
Latent functions, 20, 75–76, 472–473
Later adulthood, 83
Latinos. *See* Hispanic Americans
Laws
    of divorce, 19
    on market restraints, 379
    retirement, 356
    as a social institution, 95
    see also Supreme Court decisions
Leaders, 156
    authoritarian, 158
    democratic, 158
    expressive, 157
    instrumental, 156
    laisse-faire, 158
Leadership, 156–159
Leadership styles, 158
Leisure, 391
    patterns of, 390–393
    value of, 45
Life chances, 263
Life course, 81–84
    distinctive patterns, 83–84
    socialization through the, 80–84
Life expectancy, 346
    gender and, 347
    racial or ethnic inequalities and, 347
    statistics, 347
Lifespan, 569
    longer, 83
    see also Aging; Life expectancy
Lifestyle, and health, 529
Life support, 544–545
Living will, 544–545
Lobbyists, 417–418
    criticism of, 419
Longevity. *See* Aging
Looking-glass self, 63–64
Los Angeles riots, 599–600
Love
    and courtship, 440
    romantic, 440
    social channels of, 442
Love symbol, 18
Lower-middle class, 261, 262
Loyalties, appeal to higher, 212
Lumpenproletariat, 228
Lutheran Church, 498, 513
Lynching, 592, 594, 595, 596, 597–599

Machines, 145, 374, 631
Machismo, 448
Macro-level analysis, 25
Macropolitics, 402. *See also* Political power
Macrosociology, 88–95, 109–110
Malaysia, 74
Malpractice suits, 540–541
Malthus theorem, 560–563
Management
    corporate, 385
    and diversity, 181
Mandatory education laws, 467
Manhood, 74, 199
Manifest functions, 20, 75, 472–473
Manner, 104–105
Marginality, 304
Marginal working class, 205
Marijuana smoking, 126

Marital communication, 439–440
Marital relationship, 438
Marital roles, 19, 436–438
Market, 372–373
Market competition, 378
Market forces, 380
Market restraints, 379
Marriage
    abuse in, 459–460
    age at, 432
    arranged, 441
    and child care, 454–455
    with children, 443–444
    without children, 450–451
    versus cohabitation, 453–454
    communication in, 439–440
    conflict in, 24
    conflict theory of, 24
    courtship and, 440
    cross-cultural perspective, 430–434, 442,450
    defining, 432
    and divorce, 433, 455–458
    emotional satisfaction in, 18
    expectations of, 18–19
    future of, 461–462
    gender roles in, 265, 435–438
    homosexual, 431
    jealousy in, 442
    love and, 44, 440
    patterns of mate selection, 433
    postponing, 452–453
    power relationships in, 24, 436–438
    rape in, 459–460
    sexual differences in the experience of, 24
    sexual relations in, 432, 439, 443
    social channels of, 442
    successful, 460–461
    in the U. S., 441–442
    see also Child rearing; Family
Martyrs, 407
Marxism, compared to communism, 10
Masculinity, 283, 293
    cultural differences in, 74
Mass media
    ageism and, 353–354
    gender images in, 71–73
    socialization and, 78–79
Mass society, 616
Mass-society theory, 616–617
Master statuses, 92–93
Material culture, 33, 145
Materialism, value of, 43
Mate selection, 433
Mating behavior, in animals, 50
Matriarchies, 283
Matrilineal system of descent, 433
Mayans, 640–641
Mbuti, 282
Mean, 120
Means of production, 228–229
    private ownership of the, 378
Mechanical solidarity, 97–99
Media. *See* Mass media; Television
Median, 120
Medicaid, 359, 535, 541
Medical care. *See* Health care
Medicalization
    of deviance, 213–215
    of society, 543
Medical profession. *See* Medicine
Medicare, 320, 357, 359, 535, 541
Medicine
    as a commodity, 539–540
    computer's effect on, 636

defensive, 540–541
dehumanization and, 425
depersonalization and, 541–542
holistic, 555
male dominance of, 542–543
malpractice, 540–541
medicalization and, 543
monopoly of, 535–538
preventive, 552
professionalization of, 534–535
racial discrimination in, 320
sexism in, 291, 542–543
as a social institution, 95
in the U. S., 534–538
see also Health; Health care
Medium of exchange, 376–377
in agricultural economies, 376
historical perspective, 376–377
in industrial economies, 376–377
in postindustrial economies, 377
Mein Kampf, 606
Melanesians, 609
Mental health, 533–534
social class and, 263
Mental illness
causes of, 213
deviance as, 213–215
homeless, 214
myths about, 213–214
and social inequality, 538
Mental retardation, institutionalization and, 60
Mentawei, 430
Meritocracy, 231
Mesopotamians, 640
Metropolitan statistical areas (MSAs), 576
Mexican Americans. *See* Hispanic Americans
Mexico
gestures in, 38
markets in, 372
oil industry, 386
population growth in, 567, 579
Mexico City, 579
Miami, changing culture of, 39, 330
Miami Herald, 39
Micro-level analysis, 25
Micronesia, 70
Micropolitics, 402. *See also* Political power;
Politics; Power
Microsociological perspective, 99–109
Microsociology, 88–89, 109–110
Middle adulthood, 82
Middle Ages, childhood in, 81
Middle class, 260–261
Middle-range theories, 16
Mid-life crisis, 83
Midwifery, physicians versus, 536
Migrant workers, 330, 331, 579
Migration, 569–570
Milgram experiment, 160–161
Military, 168
computer's effect on, 636
as a social institution, 95
Millenarian movements, 609
Milling, 594–595
Minimum competency tests, 490
Minimum wage, 383
Minority groups
assimilation of (*see* Assimilation)
emergence of, 312
intergroup relations, 322–325
populations of, 330, 332
shared characteristics, 312
women as, 285–288
see also Ethnic groups

Minority leadership, 585–586
Mission Indians, 422
Mobilization
resource, 617–618
in social movements, 614
Mode, 120
Modernization, 504–505, 626–627
"Mommy track," 299–300
Monarchy, 409
Money, 376
Monkeys, deprivation studies, 62. *See also*
Chimpanzees
Monogamy, value of, 44
Monopoly, 379
Monotheism, 506
Moral boundaries, 200
Moral community, 496, 501–502
Morality, and war, 425
Mores, 41
Mormons, 44, 515, 529
Mortality rates, 533, 569
Motherhood, unwed, 449
Motorcycle gangs, 212–213
Multilinear evolution, 625
Multinational corporations, 243–244, 386–387
Multiple-nuclei model, 578
Mundugumors, 47
Murder, gender styles in, 302
Music, gender stereotypes in, 72
Muslims, 198, 325, 500, 507–508, 518

Name calling, 610
National Aeronautics and Space Administration
(NASA), 628
National Association for the Advancement of
Colored People (NAACP), 15, 177
National Commission on Excellence in Educa-
tion, 489
National Foundation for the March of Dimes,
173
National health care, 384
National Opinion Research Center, 129
National report card, 489–490
National Women's Party, 290
Nation At Risk, A, 489
Nations, versus states, 425–426
Native Americans
customs of, 430
genocide of, 323, 336–337
and the government, 336, 339
liking of Westerns, 44
reservations of, 338
stereotypes of, 337
Natural sciences, 4
Natural selection, 48–49
Nature versus nurture, 58, 284
and identical twins, 59
Nayar of Malabar, 431, 432
Nazis, 195, 318, 470, 605–609
Negative sanctions, 41, 206
Neocolonialism, 242–243
Net migration rate, 569
Networking, 476
social, 153–154, 584
urban, 582, 584
Neutralization, techniques of, 211
New money, 260
Newspapers, gender stereotypes in, 73
New technology, 630
New world order, 624
Nicotine, 550
1984, 402
Nirvana, 508
Noncentrist parties, 413

Nonmaterial culture, 33, 145
Nonverbal interactions, 25
Norms, 40–41
and conformity, 194
deviance as affirming, 200
emergent, 596–597
of emotion, 69
historical, 81
moral component of, 67–68
of noninvolvement, 584–585
official versus covert, 193
sexual, 633
and social order, 195–196
and status, 93
total institutions and, 80
violation of, 192
see also Deviance
Nuclear family, 432
Nurses, and physicians, 543
Nursing homes, 361–362
dehumanization in, 361–362

Obedience, to authority, 160–161
Objective method, 249
Objectivity, 12
Object permanence, 66
Observation, participant, 129
Occupations
and prestige, 255–257
of risk, 552
as subcultures, 41
Official deviance, 195
Old age, 83
benefits, 356
dependency in, 360–364
and poverty, 272
satisfaction in, 355
self-labeling, 349
see also Aging; Elderly
"Old boy" network, 154, 298
Old money, 259–260
Olduvai Gorge, 49
Oligarchy, 411
iron law of, 178, 179
problem of, 177–178
Oligopolies, 385
One-parent families, 449–450
Open-ended questions, 122
Operational definitions, 116, 117
Operational stage, in Piaget's theory, 66
Organic solidarity, 97–99
Organization, of social movements, 614
Oromos, 426
Orphanages, 60
Outer control, 200
Out-groups, 151–152
Overpopulation, 560–565
Malthus' theorem and, 560–563
see also Population growth
Ozone layer, 641

PACs. *See* Political action committees
Palestinians, 426
Panics, 601–602
Pan-Indianism, 338
Parenthood
meaning of, 18
status of, 565
Parenting. *See* Child rearing
Parkinson's Law, 174
Participant observation (fieldwork), 124–125,
129
Pastoral economies, 373
Pastoral societies, 143–144

Patriarchy, 286, 288
Patrilineal system of descent, 433
Patriotism, education and, 474
Patterns, 6
Peace Corps, 408
Peer culture, 474
Peer groups
   power of, 76
   socialization and, 76–78
Peer pressure
   conformity to, 159–160
   and drugs, 491
Penan people, 426, 641
Perestroika, 26
Perfect negative correlation, 126
Perfect positive correlation, 126
Persian Gulf War, 636
Personal distance, 102
Personal identity kit, 80
Personality, Freud's theory of, 67
Personality disorders, 197
Personal space, 101–103, 585
   cultural differences in, 102
   distance zones, 102–103
Peter Principle, 174–175
Petty bourgeoisie, 259
Pharaohs, 504
Physical attractiveness, stereotypes of, 99
Physical fitness, value of, 45
Physicians
   midwives and, 536
   nurses and, 543
   sexism of, 542
   see also Medicine
Piaget's theory, 65–67
Pilgrims, 519
Plain folks, 610
Plants, domestication of, 143–144
Play, and development of self, 64, 65
Plow, 574
Pluralism, 325, 419–420, 520
   religious, 325
Pluralistic society, 42
Pluralistic theory of social control, 195
Pokot people, 193
Police discretion, 208
Police reports, 123
Polio, 173
Political action committees (PACs), 418–419
Political instability, in the Third World, 568
Political involvement, social class and, 266
Political parties, 412–413
   in Europe, 413
Political power
   American political system, 411–419
   authority and coercion, 402–409 (see also
     Authority)
   conflict perspective, 420–421
   elections and, 412–413, 414, 418–419
   functionalist perspective, 419–420
   implications for a new world order, 426
   lobbyists, 417–418
   PACs, 418–419
   political parties, 412–413
   politics and power, 402
   special-interest groups, 417–418
   types of governments and, 409–411
   violence and, 403–405
   war as, 422–425
   see also Politics
Political science, 4–5
Politics, 4
   African Americans in, 328
   minorities in, 585–586

as a social institution, 95
   urban, 585–586
   women in, 303–305
   see also Political power
Pollution, 642, 643
Polyandry, 430
Polygyny, 430, 508
Polytheism, 506, 508
Poor
   defining, 271–273
   working, 261
Population, 560
   in surveys, 119
   see also Overpopulation
Population growth, 565–573
   estimating, 568–570
   in Europe, 560, 563
   forecasting, 571–573
   industrialization and, 570–571
   rates of, and implications, 567–568
   in the Third World, 565–567
   in the U. S., 572, 573
   zero, 572
   see also Overpopulation
Population pyramids, 567
Population shift, 572
Population shrinkage, 563
Population transfer, 323–324, 336
   indirect and direct, 323–324
Pornography, 125
Positive sanctions, 41, 206
Positivism, 9
Postindustrial economies, 374
   medium of exchange in, 377
Postindustrial societies, 146–149, 623
   basic component of, 148
   tribal cultures in, 147
Postindustrial technology, 630
Poverty
   children of, 273
   culture of, 242, 274
   defining, 271–273
   of the elderly, 363–364
   feminization of, 272
   and health care, 538
   individual versus structural explanations of,
     274–275
   and mental illness, 538
   short-term and long-term, 274
   in the Third World, 239
   in the U. S., 271–275
Poverty line, 271
Power, 402
   concentration in hands of the few, 254
   exercise of, 402
   legitimate and illegitimate, 402–409
   in marriage, 436–438
   seizure of, 411
   wealth and, 253–254
   see also Political power
Power, and social class, 229
Power elite, 420–421
Prediction, as a goal, 6
Prejudice
   and discrimination, 313–316
   extent of, 315–316
   labels that create, 319
   personality as a cause of, 317
   sociological perspectives, 318
   theories of, 316–320
Preliterate societies, 405, 624
Preoperational stage, in Piaget's theory, 66
Prestige, 91, 255–257
   displaying, 256–257

occupations and, 255–257
   and social class, 229
   of work, 286
   see also Status
Preventive medicine, 552–553
Priests, loss of, 513
Primary deviance, 210–211
Primary groups, 149–150
   family as, 150
   that fail, 150
Primary sector, 387
Primitive technology, 630
Prisoners, characteristics of, 209
Prisons, 80, 216
   populations in, 208
Privacy, computers and, 639
Private ownership of the means of production, 378
Privatization, 383
Privilege. See Social stratification
Problem behaviors, 213
Pro-choice, 614–615
Productivity, 183
Profane, 496
Profession, versus job, 394–397
Professionalization of medicine, 535
Profit, 378
   socialist, 381, 383
Progress
   idea of, 625
   value of, 43
Proletariat, 10, 23, 228
Pro-life, 614–615
Promotion
   group, 187
   in Japan, 184
Propaganda, 608–609
   Nazi, 609
   seven basic techniques of, 610
Property, 442
   erotic, 442
   versus income and wealth, 249–250
   and social class, 229
   U.S. statistics on, 250–251
Propinquity, 442
Proportional representation, 413
Prostitution, 210–211, 215
   Third World, 243
Protestant ethic, 504, 505
Protestant Ethic and the Spirit of Capitalism,
   The (Weber), 166–167, 504
Protestantism, 623
   and capitalism, 167
   and social change, 12
   and suicide, 11
Protest marches. See Collective behavior;
   Social movements
Psychology, 4, 5, 125
   and deviance, 196
   and prejudice, 317–318
Psychology of the Crowd, The (LeBon), 593
Public distance, 103
Public education, 472
Public health, 346, 548–549
Public opinion, 608
Public ownership, 380
Puerto Ricans, 330, 333, 448
Punishment
   corporal, 81
   crime and, 208–210
   Milgram experiment, 160–161
Pure Food and Drug Act, 379
Pure or basic sociology, 26
Push and pull factors, 570
Pygmies, 143, 283

Qualitative techniques, 129
Quality circles, 182
Quantitative techniques, 129
Questionnaires, 120–122
　self-administered, 122
Questions
　biased, 121
　closed-ended, 122
　open-ended, 122
　in surveys, 120
Quiet revolution, 389

Race, 312
　and health, 321
　myth and reality, 310–311
　and poverty, 271
　and religion, 523
　versus social class, 329
Race relations
　basic concepts in, 310–312
　in the U. S., 325–339
Racial caste system, 225
Racial groups, classification of, 311
Racial superiority, 310–311
Racism, 313, 606
　on college campuses, 316
　core values and, 43
Railroads, 334
Ranching, Japanese style, 187
Random sample, 119–120, 133
　stratified, 120, 130
Rape
　marital, 459–460
　motivations underlying, 135
　sociological research on, 113–136
Rape crisis centers, 123, 124
Rape victims, 122–124
Rapists, 115, 127, 133–136
Rapport, 122–123
Rationality, 166
Rationalization
　Marx on, 167–168
　of society, 166–168
　Weber on, 166–167
Rational-legal authority, 405–406, 408
Real culture, 47
Reality
　defining our own, 107
　objective and subjective, 108
　social construction of, 107–109
Reasoning
　abstract, 67
　concrete, 66
　content of, 67
　cultural differences in, 67
Rebellion, 202
Recessions, 393, 394
Recidivism rate, 208, 210
Records, in bureaucracies, 169
Redemptive social movements, 612
Redwoods, cutting of, 644
Reference groups, 152–153
　conflicting, 153
Reformation, 623
Reformative social movements, 612
Refugees, 147
Rehabilitation, 210
Relative deprivation theory, 616
Reliability, 117
Religion
　in American society, 75
　and authority, 407, 408
　and capitalism, 167, 504–505
　characteristics of members in, 521–523

conflict perspective, 502–504
defined, 496
dysfunctions of, 499
elements of, 496
freedom of, 325
functional equivalents of, 499
functionalist perspective, 497–499
future of, 523–524
and government, 519
as opium of the people, 502–504
and science, 519, 523–524
secularization of, 515–517
and social change, 12, 498–499
and social class, 266–267, 522
as a social institution, 95
socialization and, 75
state, 513
as support for the government, 498
symbolic interactionist perspective, 499–502
universality of, 497
in the U. S., 519–523
world's major, 505–510
Religiosity, value of, 44
Religious experience, 501
Religious organizations, 510–515
　churches, 512
　cults, 511–512, 514–515
　ecclesia, 513
　sects, 512, 514–515
　variations in patterns, 513–514
Religious persecution, 499
Religious rituals, 501, 508
Religious symbols, 500–501
Religious toleration, 521
Relocation camps, 334
Remarriage, 455–456, 458
Replication, 13, 119
Representation, proportional, 413
Representative democracy, 410
Republican Party, 266, 412–413
Reputational method, 248
Research
　basic steps involved in, 115
　bias in, 120, 121
　common sense and the need for, 114–115
　controversial, 129–131
　ethics in, 127, 128, 131, 161
　methods (see Research methods)
　model, 115–119
　social, 12, 13
　and theory, 133–136
　valid topics for, 114, 115
Researchers
　misrepresentation of, 131–133
　personal characteristics of, 124–125
Research methods, 119–131
　choice of method, 116, 129–131
　documents, 123–124
　experiments, 125–128
　participant observation (fieldwork), 124–125
　secondary analysis, 123
　surveys, 119–123
　unobtrusive measures, 128
Reservations, Indian, 338
Reserve labor force, 319
Resocialization, 79–80, 210
　involuntary, 79–80
　voluntary, 80
Resource mobilization, 617–618
Respondents, to surveys, 120
Responsibility, diffusion of, 157, 585
Retirement, 445–446

Retirement benefits, 356
Retreatism, 202
Retribution, 209
Revolution, 404
Right to die, 544–545
Riots, 599–601
Rising expectations, 328
Rist research, 484–485
Ritualism, 202
Ritual pollution, 224
Rituals, 496, 499, 501
　ancient, 508
　religious, 501, 508
Roe v. *Wade*, 614, 615
Role conflict, 103
Role extension, 602
Role performance, 90, 103
Roles, 90
　according to status, 93–94
Role strain, 103
Role taking, 64–65
Roman Catholic Church, 507, 513, 521
　charismatic authority and, 407
　and social change, 12
　traditional orientation of, 167
Romans, 7, 221, 515
Rosenthal/Jacobson experiment, 485–486
Routinization of charisma, 408–409
Rules
　in bureaucracies, 169
　written, 405
Ruling class, 318, 319, 420–421
Ruling Class, The (Mosca), 232
Rumors, 602–604
Rural Electrification Association (REA), 417
Russians, 325
Rutter report, 490

Sacred, 496
Samples, 119
　bias in, 121
　random, 119–120, 133
San, 143
Sanctions, 40–41, 206
　negative, 41, 206
　positive, 41, 206
Sapir-Whorf hypothesis, 37–38
Satanic activity, 603
Scapegoats, 317
Scarce resources, competition for, 232
Scenery, 104
Scholastic Aptitude Test (SAT), 469, 489
Schools
　how we can improve, 487–492
　segregation in, 488
　socialization and, 75–76
Schutzstaffel, 310
Science
　goals of, 5–6
　and religion, 519, 523–524
　as a social institution, 95
　sociology and, 4–6
　theories in, 7
Scientific method, 9
Secondary analysis, 123, 135
Secondary deviance, 210–211
Secondary groups, 150–151, 168
Secondary sector, 387
Second social revolution, 144
Second World, 237–238
　environmental problems in, 642–643
Sector model, 577
Sects, 512, 516
Secular, 515

Secularization, 515–520
of culture, 518–519
of religion, 515–517
of a sect, 516
Segregation, 327
school, 488
in the South, 324
Supreme Court decisions on, 328
Selective perception, 319
Self
development of, 63–65
looking-glass, 63–64
sense of, 68
and social constraint, 70
and socialization, 84
Self-administered questionnaires, 122
Self-concept, 64
Self-fulfilling prophecy
and discrimination, 319–320
in teaching, 484–487
Self-fulfillment, value of, 45
Self-gratification, 67
Self-management teams, 183
Semai, 74
Sensate culture, 626
Sensorimotor stage, in Piaget's theory, 66
Sex
versus gender, 280–281
and poverty, 272
and superiority, 285
see also Gender
Sex characteristics, primary and secondary, 280
Sex education, 476
Sexism
in medicine, 291, 542–543
in the workplace, 301
Sex roles. *See* Gender roles
Sex stereotypes. *See* Gender stereotypes
Sex-typing, 285
of work, 285–286
see also Gender stereotypes
Sexual attraction, 440
Sexual behavior
cultural differences in, 47
in Hispanic culture, 36
in marriage, 432, 443
Sexual control, 21
Sexual fidelity, 432
Sexual harassment, 328
in Japan, 298
male and female, 300–301
on Wall Street, 301
Sexuality
cross-cultural perspective, 193
norms of, 193
Sexual norms, 633
Sexual revolution, 21
Shaman, 142, 528
Shi'ite Muslims, 507
Shunning, 502
Sick role, 531–532
Significant others, 65
Sign-vehicles, 104
Silicone breast implants, 204
Sin, 506
Single-parent families, 449–450
Sinkyone Indians, 644
Slavery, 221–223, 327
common characteristics of, 223
inheritable, 222
in the New World, 222
types, causes, and conditions of, 221–222
Slavs, 323, 607

Small groups, 155
Social activism, 16
Social change, 26, 201, 622–624
conflict theory and, 626
cyclical theories and, 625–626
defined, 622, 624
education and, 475–476
evolutionary theories and, 624–625
modernization and, 626–627
and the natural environment, 640–646
in Nazi Germany, 607
religion and, 498–499
technology and, 628–640
telecommunications and, 639–640
value clusters and, 45
Social class, 197, 220, 248–249
in the automobile industry, 262–263
capitalist, 259–260
child rearing and, 74–75, 444–445
as a component of social structure, 91
consequences of, 265–267
crime and, 202–204
criminal justice system and, 267
deviance and, 207
education and, 267
family and, 73–74, 265
goals and, 110
health and, 529
in industrial society, 258–264
life chances and, 263
Marx on, 228–229, 258–259
objective measures of, 249
political involvement and, 266
political participation and, 416
power and, 253–254
prestige and, 255–257
versus race, 329
religion and, 266–267, 522
reputational measures of, 248–249
self-identification of, 248
subjective measures of, 248–249
values and attitudes and, 266
wealth and, 249–253
Weber on, 229, 259–262
what determines, 228–230
see also Social stratification
Social cohesion, 97–98
Social constraints, self and emotions as, 70
Social construction of reality, 107–109
Social control
conflict perspective, 195
deviance and, 194–195
functionalist perspective, 194–195
industrialized societies and, 194
pluralistic theory of, 195
religion and, 497
Social Darwinism, 10
Social devaluation, 83
Social distance, 102
Social dynamics, 9
Social environment, 58
Social experiences, 3
and abstract reasoning, 67
and life course, 84
Social facts, and verstehen, 13–15
Social groups. *See* Groups
Social inequality, 73
growth of, 144, 145
maintaining, 477–484
mental illness and, 538
perpetuation of, 154
religion as reflection of, 503–504
Social institutions, 95–99, 146
changes in the U. S., 624

conflict perspective, 96–97
functionalist perspective, 95–96
Social integration, 11
and education, 474–475
Social interaction, 25, 88–89
in everday life, 99–109
Socialism, 380
compared to capitalism, 381, 382–383
criticisms of, 381–382
democratic, 380, 383, 384
ideology of, 381, 382–383
Socialization, 21, 63–70
anticipatory, 79
career, 79
deviance and, 197
emotions and, 68–70
family and, 73–74
gender, 70–73
gender behavior and, 282–283
mass media and, 78–79
peer groups and, 76–78
religion and, 75
schools and, 75–76
self and, 84
social constraints and, 70
through the life course, 80–84
workplace and, 79
Social location, 2
Social mobility, 225, 267–271
costs of, 268–271
downward, 268, 270
education and, 268, 270
exchange, 268
intergenerational, 267–268
structural, 268
upward, 267–268, 269
in the U. S., 268
Social movements, 605
alternative, 612
breadth of, 609–610
case of the Nazis, 605–609
five stages of, 614
life course of, 613–616
new, 611, 614
redemptive, 612
reformative, 612
success and failure of, 617–618
tactics of, 612–613
transformative, 612
types of, 611–612
why people join, 616–617
Social networks, 153–154, 236, 476, 584
Social order
norms and, 195–196
preservation of, 97
Social organization, how technology changes, 631
Social placement, 475
Social promotion, 489
Social psychology, 125
Social reform, 10, 15–16
Social relationships
and technology, 632
Social research
purposes and uses of, 13
role of values in, 12–13
Social revolutions, 622–623
Social sciences, 4, 125
Social Security
costs of, 356–357, 360
legislation, 356
system, 100, 358–359, 383
taxes, 356–357, 358, 359, 379
Social setting, 104

Social statics, 9
Social status. *See* Status
Social stratification, 220–221
 among Polish Jews, 226
 comparative, 233–235
 conflict perspective, 232–233
 functionalist perspective, 230–231
 gender and, 227–228
 global, 237–239
 in Great Britain, 233–234
 national, maintaining, 235–237
 in Soviet Union, 234–235
 systems of, 221–227
 universal nature of, 230–233
Social structure, 90
 changes in, 97
 college football as, 90
 macrosociological perspective, 88, 89–95,
  109–110
 major components of, 91
 microsociological perspective, 88, 99–109,
  109–110
Social unity, 200
Social unrest, 593–594, 605–606
Social years, 350
Societies, 140–141
 agricultural, 144–145, 344
 American (*see* United States)
 defining, 97
 groups within, 149–154
 historical perspective on, 141–149
 horticultural, 143–144
 how technology transforms, 630–632
 hunting and gathering, 142–143, 373, 409
 industrial, 141, 145–146, 148
 pastoral, 143–144
 postindustrial, 146–149, 623
 preliterate, 405, 624
 traditional, 405, 626–627
 within us, 3
Society of Mayflower Descendants, 325
Sociobiology, 48–49
 and deviance, 196
Sociological analysis, levels of, 88–89
Sociological perspective, 2–3
 and broader social context, 2–3
Sociological research. *See* Research; Research
 methods
Sociology, 9
 applications of, 16–25
 applied, 25–27
 clinical, 25–27
 development of, 7–12
 educational movement in, 15–16
 future of, 27
 and other sciences, 4–6
 pure or basic, 26
Sociology departments, 15, 16
South Africa
 apartheid in, 223, 225, 324
 genocide in, 323
Southeast Asians, 147
Soviet Union, former
 breakup of, 624
 economy of, 382
 education in, 470–471
 groups in, 140–141
 health care in, 553
 social stratification in, 234
Spanish language, 331
Special-interest groups, 417–418
Spectator sports, 582
Spirit of capitalism, 504–505
Split-labor market, 319

Spurious correlation, 125–127
Sputnik, 471
SS, 607
Standard of living
 divorce and, 457
 and politial instability, 568
State capitalism. *See* Welfare capitalism
States, 404
 nations versus, 425–426
 see also Government
Statistics
 trouble with official, 207–208
Status, 90, 91–93, 226
 achieved, 92, 146
 ascribed, 92, 146
 as guidelines to behavior, 92
 inconsistency, 93, 257–258
 master, 92–93
 norms and, 93
 of parenthood and motherhood, 565
 of women, 282, 286–288
Status set, 91
Status symbols, 92, 266
 negative, 92
 work, 394–397
Stereotypes
 conforming to, 101
 and discrimination, 319–320
 elderly, 83, 352–353, 357, 360–361
 ethnic, 319, 322–323
 in everyday life, 99–101
 gender, 71–72
 immigrant, 326–327
 Native American, 337
 of physical attractiveness, 99
 racial, 319
 self-fulfilling, 101
 see also Labels
Stigma, 194
Stock exchanges, 375
Stockholders' revolt, 385
Stored value, 376–377
Strain theory, 201
Stratified random sample, 120, 130
Street crime, 196
Structural mobility, 268
Structured interviews, 122
Studied nonobservance, 105
Subconscious, Freud's theory of, 67–68
Subcultures, 41–41, 126
Subjective meanings, 14
Subjective method, 248
Subsidized housing, 383
Subsistence economy, 373
Suburbanization, 586
Suburbs, 586
 increasing problems in, 588
 psychological separation from cities, 586
 trends in, 587–588
Success, value of, 43, 92
Succession, rules of, 408
Suicide
 altruistic, 11
 cross-cultural perspective, 193
 elderly and, 364, 366–367
 religion and, 11
 social factors underlying, 11
Sunni Muslims, 507
Supreme Court decisions
 on abortion, 614–615
 against Asian Americans, 334
 on segregation, 328
Surgery, sexism in, 542
Surplus, 373

Surveys, 119–123
 misrepresentation in, 121
Survival of the fittest, 10
Sweden, 383, 405, 601
 health care in, 553
 population growth in, 567
Swiss, 325
Symbolic culture, 35
Symbolic interactionism, 17–20, 89, 99
 application of, 18–19
 and dramaturgy, 103–106
 and ethnomethodology, 106–107
 and personal space, 101–103
 and prejudice, 319
 and social construction of reality, 107–109
 and stereotypes, 99–101
Symbolic interactionist perspective, 15
 on aging, 348–354
 of deviance, 193, 197–200
 on education, 484–487
 on family, 439–440
 on health, 528
 on managing diversity, 181
 on religion, 499–502
 on work, 394–397
Symbols, 35
 children's ability to use, 66
 male and female, 73
 status, 92, 266, 394–397

Tables, learning to read, 118
Taboos, 41, 47
 incest, 435
Tact, 105
Tahitians, 74
Taking the role of the other, 64. *See also* Role
 taking
Tamil society, 281
Taxes
 and the economy, 389–390
 Social Security, 356–357, 358, 359, 379
Teacher expectations, 484–487
Teachers, role of, 490–491, 492
Teaching, 467
Teamwork, in performance, 105
Technology
 agricultural, 144
 and changes in ideology, 631
 and changes in social organization, 631
 defined, 628
 effects of the automobile, 632–634
 effects of the computer, 634–638
 and the environment, 646
 failure of, 622, 628
 and the Industrial Revolution, 145
 Ogburn's processes of cultural innovation,
  628–630
 social change and, 628–640
 telecommunications and, 639–640
 transformation of existing, 630
 and transformation of social relationships, 632
 transformation of society by, 630–632
 and transformation of values, 631
 types of, 630
Telecommunications
 diffusion of, 630
 and global social change, 639–640
Telecommuters, 638
Television
 advertisements on, 381
 ageism and, 353–354
 gender stereotypes on, 72
 socialization and, 78–79
 violence on, 78–79

Tertiary deviance, 210–211
Tertiary sector, 387, 387
Testimonials, 610
Thai women, 243
Theory, 7, 16
  middle-range, 16
  and research, 133–136
Thinking
  abstract, 67
  development of, 65–67
Third revolution, 145
Third World, 239, 240
  aid to, 426
  debt, 426
  dependency of, 623–624
  education in, 467
  effects of industrialization on, 623
  environmental problems in, 643
  exploitation of, 243
  health issues, 530
  political instability in, 568
  population growth in, 565–567, 623
  urbanization in, 579
Thomas theorem, 107
Tiananmen Square massacre, 382, 640
Tiwi, 350–351, 352, 432
Tobacco, 550
Tools, 50, 143
Torah, 506
Total institutions, 79–80
Totalitarianism, 411
Townsend Plan, 356
Tracking, 475, 484–485
Trade, growth of, 373–374
Tradition, 8
Traditional authority, 405, 408
Traditional orientation, 166
  religion and, 167
Traditional societies, 405, 626–627
Trail of Tears, 336
Trained incapacity, 172–173
Transfer, 610
Transformative social movements, 612
Treasury bonds, 358
Triads, 155, 443
Tribal groups, 641
Tribal societies, 312
Trobriand Islanders, 431, 432
"Two-thirds society," 397

Underclass, 261–262, 263
Underemployment, 382
Underground economy, 389–390
Unemployment, 319, 395
Unemployment compensation, 383
Unilinear evolutionary theories, 624–625
Unions, 187
United Nations, 425
United States
  economy of, 397–398
  education in, 471–472, 481–482
  elderly in, 352–353
  family trends in, 451–455
  gender inequality in, 289–294
  marriage in, 441–442
  medicine in, 534–538
  political system in, 411–419
  population growth in, 572, 573
  poverty in, 271–275
  race and ethnic relations in, 325–339
  religion in, 75, 519–523
  social mobility in, 268
  urbanization in, 576
  values in, 42–47
  work in, 387–397

Universal citizenship, 410–411
University of Chicago, 15, 16
Unmarried persons, suicide and, 11
Unobtrusive measures, 128
Unstructured interviews, 122
Untouchables, 224
Unwed mothers, 449
Upper-middle class, 260–261, 262
Upward social mobility, 267–268
  vanishing dream of, 269
Urban dwellers, 580–585
Urban ecology, 576
Urban growth, models of, 576–578
Urbanization, 574–576
  in the Third World, 579
  in the U. S., 576
  worldwide, 575
  see also Cities
Urban legends, 604–605
Urban networks, 582–584
Urban overload, 584–585
Urban planners, 583–584
Urban sentiment, 582–583
Urban village, 580
Urban Villagers, The (Gans), 580

Validity, 116–117
Value clusters, 45
Value contradictions, and social change, 45
Value free, 12
Values, 40–41
  in American society, 42–47
  change in, 145
  core, 43, 44, 45–47
  cultural transmission of, 473–474
  emergent, 45–46
  hidden, in corporations, 178–180
  middle-class, 202
  role of, in research, 12–13
  social class and, 73, 266
  transformation of, by technology, 631
Variables, 116, 124–125
  dependent, 125
  independent, 125, 127–128
  underlying, 127
Verstehen, 13–15
Veterans of Foreign Wars (VFW), 177–178
Vietnamese Americans, 335–336
Vietnam War, 16, 423
  cost of, 358
  groupthink and, 162
Violence
  gender inequality and, 302
  legitimate, authority and, 403–405
  marital, 458–460
  on television, 78–79
Voluntary associations, 175–178
  functions of, 176–177
Voluntary memberships, 94
Voter apathy, 415–416
Voting patterns, 414–416
Voting rights, 411
Voting Rights Act, 328

Wall Street, sexual harassment on, 301
War
  cold, 424
  computer's effect on, 636
  costs of, 423–424
  and dehumanization, 424–425
  in European history, 423
  glorification of, 422–423
  as a means to objectives, 422–425
  and religion, 499
Warfare, patriarchy and, 288

War of the Worlds (Wells), 601
WASP (White Anglo-Saxon Protestant), 325, 326
Watts riots, 328
Wealth
  concentration in hands of the few, 254
  distribution of, 250
  versus income, 249–250
  and power, 253–254
  and social class, 249–253
Webster v. Reproductive Services, 615
Welfare, 383
Welfare (or state) capitalism, 378–380
White-collar crime, 203–204
White ethnics, 326–327
Widowhood, 446
  in Spain and Portugal, 405
Witchcraft, 603
Women
  in business, 179
  career paths, 299
  discrimination against, 283, 296–299
  early status of, 145
  historical role of, 24
  in the labor force, 389
  as a minority group, 285–288
  networking by, 154
  in politics, 303–305
  in religious organizations, 503
  self-concept of, 438
  single, 388–389, 583
  status of, 282, 286–288
  in the work force, 294–295, 305–306
  working, 388–389, 436, 454
  see also Gender roles
Women's movement, 181
Work
  and aging, 344
  in American society, 387–397
  conflict perspective on, 394
  functionalist perspective on, 392–393
  patterns of, 390–393
  symbolic interactionist perspective on, 394–397
  women and, 388–389
Worker productivity, 128
Workers, exploitation of, 394
Work ethic, 43, 147
Work force
  pay gap, 296–299
  women in the, 294–295, 305–306
Working class, 205, 261
Working poor, 261, 263
Workplace
  computer's effect on, 637, 638
  gender inequality in, 294–301
  managing diversity in, 181
  sexism in, 301
  socialization and, 79
Work satisfaction, 397
Works Progress Administration (WPA), 417
Work week, 391
World Health Organization (WHO), 549
World system theory, 240, 623–624
World War I, 423
World War II, 423, 470

Xenophobia, American, 187
XYY theory, 196

Yanomamo tribe, 67, 192, 193, 194
Youth to Youth, 491

Zapotec Indians, 193
Zero population growth, 572